Bө and Bön

Bɵ and Bön

Ancient Shamanic Traditions of Siberia and Tibet
in their Relation to the Teachings of
a Central Asian Buddha

Dmitry Ermakov

Vajra Publications
Kathmandu, Nepal

Published by
Vajra Publications
Jyatha, Thamel
P.O. Box 21779, Kathmandu, Nepal
Tel.: 977-1-4220562, Fax: 977-1-4246536
e-mail: bidur_la@mos.com.np
www.vajrabooks.com.np

Distributor
Vajra Book Shop
Kathmandu, Nepal

ISBN 978-9937-506-11-3

Printed in Nepal

Homage to Chase Kengtse whose Wisdom knows no limits!

[illegible]

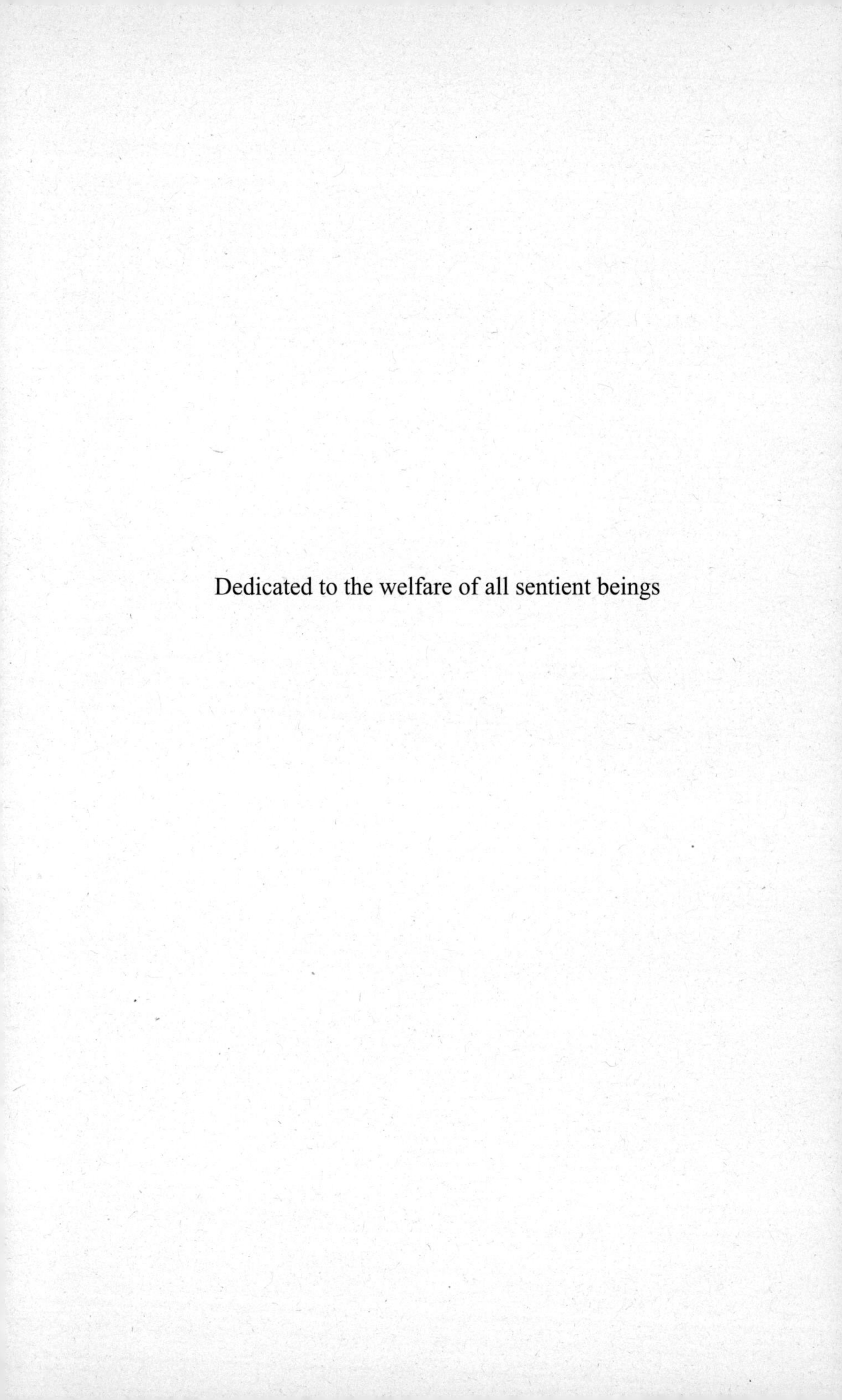

Dedicated to the welfare of all sentient beings

…If one administers the world according to DAO
then the ancestors do not swarm about as spirits.
Not that the ancestors are not spirits,
but their spirits do not harm men.
Not only do the spirits not harm men,
the Man of Calling, too, does not harm them.
If then, these two powers do not harm one another,
then their Life-Forces are united in their effect.

Lao Tzu, Tao Te Ching[1]

---

1 Lao Tzu, *Tao Te Ching*, The Richard Wilhelm Edition, Penguin, Arkana, 1989, st. 60, p. 54.

Acknowledgements

This book would not have come about without the help, support, teachings, encouragement and generosity of many people over the eleven years it took shape. I would particularly like to express my heartfelt gratitude to my kind lamas: to Yongdzin Lopön Tenzin Namdak Rinpoche for showing me in a direct, powerful and lucid way how to enter into and continue the practice of Dzogchen and Tantra, for tirelessly answering countless questions clarifying difficult points of the Teachings as well as providing invaluable and unique information on various aspects of Bönpo rituals, culture and history which proved absolutely invaluable for this research; to Chögyal Namkhai Norbu for introducing me to the Nature of Mind and stirring a deep interest in Bön; to Khenpo Tenpa Yungdrung for his unflagging interest, encouragement and patient answers; to Geshe Geleg Jinpa for his teachings and lively support in many aspects of my research, and to many senior monks from Triten Norbutse Monastery, particularly Drubdra Khenpo Tsultrim Tenzin, Geshe Samten Tsugphü, Geshe Tenzin Yangton and Geshe Lungrig Nyima.

Thanks also go to my friend Utgan Vera Naguslaeva with whom I shared travels to sacred power places of Buryatia, who was instrumental in introducing me to Bө and Utgan, and who helped me in so many ways. I must also thank Bө Doogar Ochirov, 'Uncle' Sasha Andreyev, Sodnom Gomboev, Utgan Nadezhda Stepanova, and many other Bө and Utgan who shared their experiences and knowledge with me, especially Boris Bazarov who provided invaluable information on the origin of *hii moriin*. I would also like to thank the Doogarov family, in particular the late Batodalai Doogarov, who introduced me to Bө and Utgan, and Dorjo Doogarov who drew my attention to and provided me with many materials pertinent to my reasearch, including the Kudarinskiy version of the Bө Murgel creation myth which he kindly translated for me.

I would also like to acknowledge Jean-Luc Archard's role in encouraging me years ago to publish my research, as well as Alejandro Chaul for sending me his dissertation on Bönpo *Chöd,* Charles Ramble for his valuable help in adding the finishing touches, and John Reynolds for his sound advice on publishing. I am also grateful to my good friend Richard Williamson for his continued support over the years, and for his superb artwork. Thanks also go to the many people who generously provided photographs or pictures: Khenpo Tenpa Yungdrung; Takahiko Wakishima; Shang Shung Institude; St. Petersburg Hermitage State Museum; Nigel Wellings; Robert Beer; Fabio Tomassoni; Molly Thoron-Duran, Christophe Moulin; Rosa-Maria Mendez; Ans Swart, Martino Nicoletti; Alessandra Campoli; Charles Ramble and Juliette Hanson, as well as Benoît Pinchera for cartographic computer graphics.

My in-laws, Rev. Alan and Pearl Stears, deserve a special mention as without their loving moral and financial support this book would simply not have been completed. Their input on Biblical references was also much appreciated. I am also grateful to Marian and the late Ken Hamilton for their generous life-saving help in difficult moments.

I would like to thank Bidur Dangol of Vajra Publications as well as Ram Krishna and Nabindra Dongol of Dongol Printers for their professionalism and good humour.

Last but not least, my deep thanks go to my wife, Carol, for her painstaking editing of this book, unwavering support and help during the years, without which this project would not have come to fruition.

The Bө and Utgan who shared information and experiences with me:

Vera Grigoryevna Naguslaeva – clan Hengelder, tribe Ehirit, Korsakovo/ Ulaan-Ude.
Вера Григорьевна Нагуслаева – Һэнгэлдэр, Эхирит, Корсаково/ Улаан-Удэ.

Doogar Dorzhievich Ochirov – clan Hengelder, tribe Ehirit, Kurumkan/ Ulaan-Ude.
Дугар Доржиевич Очиров – Һэнгэлдэр, Эхирит, Курумкан/Улаан-Удэ.

Nadezhda Ananyevna Stepanova – clan Galzuud, tribe Horëodoi, Kabansk - Ulaan-Ude.
Надежда Ананьевна Степанова – Галзууд, Хорёодой, Кабанск/Улан-Удэ.

Aleksandr Vladimirovich Andreev, 'Uncle Sasha' – clan Hengelder, tribe Ehirit, Korsakovo.
Александр Владимирович Андреев, «Дядя Саша» – Һэнгэлдэр, Эхирит, Корсаково.

Sodnom Dorzhievich Gomboev – clan Bodongut, tribe Horёodoi, Aga/Ulaan-Ude.
Содном Доржиевич Гомбоев – Бодонгут, Хорёодой, Ага/Улан-Удэ.

Boris Doogarovich Bazarov – clan Hengelder, tribe Ehirit, Kurumkan/Ulaan-Ude.
Борис Дугарович Базаров – Һэнгэлдэр, Эхирит, Курумкан/Улаан-Удэ.

Margarita Gonchikovna Danchinova – clan Hal'ban, Horёodoi, Hezhenge/Kurumkan.
Маргарита Гончиковна Данчинова – Хальбан, Хорёодой, Хэжэнгэ/Курумкан.

Nadagurova Roza Zhamyanovna – clan Bayande, tribe Ehirit.
Надагурова Роза Жамьяновна – Баяндэ, Эхирит.

Bayan-Dalai – Baraghan.
Баяндалай – Баргхан.

Badmazhab tөөde – clan Hengelder, Ehirit, Baraghan.
Бадмажаб төөдэ – Һэнгэлдэр, Эхирит, Баргхан.

Dulma tөөde – clan Shono, tribe Ehirit, Baraghan.
Дулма төөдэ – Шоно, Эхирит, Баргхан.

Natalya Doogarovna Hengelova – clan Terte, tribe Hongo'odor, Zhemchug, Tunka.
Наталья Дугаровна Хенегелова – Тэртэ, Хонгоодор, Жемчуг, Тункинская долина.

Vladimir Ukoev – clan Shono, tribe Ehirit, Tunka.
Владимир Укоев – Шоно, Эхирит, Тунка.

Bair – Zhemchug.
Баир – Жемчуг, Тункинская долина.

Lyubov' Zhembievna Sangadieva – Tunka.
Любовь Жембиевна Сангадиева – Тунка.

Tatyana Nimaevna Sholohova – clan Shono, tribe Ehirit, Orlik.
Татьяна Нимаевна Шолохова – Шоно, Эхирит, Орлик – Улан-Удэ.

Galina Dorzhievna Dabaeva – clan Hubuud, tribe Horëodoi, Muhor-Shibir'.
Галина Доржиевна Дабаева – Хубууд, Хорёодой, Мухор-Шибирь.

Lama-Bɵ Zundy – clan Galzuud, tribe Horëodoi, Hezhenge.
Лама-бөө Зуунды – Галзууд, Хорёодой, Хэжэнгэ.

Vera – clan Galzuud, tribe Horëodoi, Hezhenge.
Вера – Галзууд, Хорёодой, Хэжэнэгэ.

Bairma – clan Galzuud, tribe Horëodoi, Hezhenge.
Баирма – Галзууд, Хорёодой , Хэжэнэгэ.

Contents

Foreword

The word 'bön' is an ancient Tibetan word with a wide semantic field. In the language of Zhang Zhung, it is equivalent to the Zhang Zhung word 'gyer', and these two are quite often used interchangeably in Bön texts, including both classical teachings texts as well as ritual texts. The word 'bön' can be used as a verb and also as a noun. As a verb it means 'to express', 'to recite' or 'to preach' while as a noun, it has several meanings; it can be used to denote phenomena or existence in general, and its meaning fluctuates according to different contexts. However, the most popular meaning of 'bön' is 'teaching' or 'doctrine', and in this way it is used as the name for a religion, the ancient religion of Tibet. Due to the complexity of its semantic range, nowadays scholars have come up with different interpretations for this word. However, if we go according to classical Bön teachings and historical accounts, we may come to classify the word 'bön' in two main semantic pools. Broadly speaking, the first is the teaching or doctrine while the second is the meaning or content of the teaching. That is why this word is nowadays mostly understood in the sense of religion or practice. Because of this, in ancient times 'bön' was used as a general term for religion, not to refer to one specific belief system. In fact, we can say there are two main types of Bön – one is a primitive religion, the other is Yungdrung Bön. Primitive Bön refers to a belief system centring on the worship of different mighty, supernatural beings and certain elements. Since time immemorial, humans have possessed knowledge of how to deal with the elements and such powerful spirits in order to meet the needs of their spiritual and temporal life. In the ancient kingdoms of Zhang Zhung and Tibet, there was already a strong tradition of this system of spiritual practice which eventually became the cultural basis for the spread of the Yungdrung Bön tradition which was preached by Buddha Tonpa Shenrab.

Yungdrung Bön is a religious tradition which contains methods and wisdom to bring benefit to individuals on all levels of their life, according to each person's constituent capacity. All the teachings of Yungdrung Bön are classified into nine successive ways, known as *Bon theg pa rim dgu*, the Nine Successive Ways of Bön, to suite the nine different mental dispositions of its followers. These Ways contain wisdom and practical methods spanning situations relating to one's day to day life right up to the pure and perfect state of Buddha, known in Tibetan as *Yang dag rdzogs p'i sangs rgyas*. Eventually, Yungdrung Bön became the predominant religion of the kingdom of Zhang Zhung and many parts of Central Asia, and also remained the predominant religion of Great Tibet until the eighth century. This ancient tradition is still alive in Tibet, Nepal, India, China and elsewhere, with its long, unbroken lineage and history.

Running parallel to this, the Primitive Bön system of spiritual practice which existed before the advent of Yungdrung Bön is also alive in different corners and fringes of Tibet, Nepal, India, Bhutan, Mongolia, Southern Siberia and so on, where it takes different shapes and forms, benefitting many through its own spiritual methods and system. Some of these traditions apparently combined with the methods of Yungdrung Bön's Causal Ways forming, various hybrids and blurring the lines between Primitive Bön and Yungdrung Bön.

Due to changes in Tibet's political climate in the early Middle Ages, from the mid-eighth century up until now, a number of Tibetan scholars – and later Western scholars whose research relies on these earlier Tibetan sources – have maintained a different point of view and interpretation regarding the Bön religion and its history. Many defined Bön as a shamanistic tradition, or a strand of shamanism, while others think of Yungdrung Bön as an organized Bön tradition which comingled with Indian Buddhism before or after the eighth century. The traditional Yungdrung Bön historical accounts, however, make it clear that Yungdrung Bön has its own independent spiritual and historical source along with its own canonical texts, including treaties on Sutra, Tantra and Dzogchen which have been preserved and studied up until now. In particular, Dzogchen is considered to be the highest and most essential practice of Yungdrung Bön with an ancient, uninterrupted spiritual lineage of transmission which has remained intact to this day.

At the same time, Yungdrung Bön also contains a great wealth of practices and rituals relating to matters such as healing and astrology which address the temporal welfare of beings, and these, too, have been used since ancient times up until today. In fact, one could find that most Tibetan spiritual ritual systems – whether Buddhist or Bönpo – are based on traditions pertaining to Yungdrung Bön. Since these aspects are very much related to obtaining tangible benefits in this life, they have become an integral part of the Tibetan spiritual and social way of life, and this system has been upheld by Tibetan Bönpos – and later Buddhists – of all levels of society; some of these methods even mingled with the ancient Primitive Bön. This may be the core reason why scholars compare

Yungdrung Bön with shamanism; nevertheless, I would suggest that this alone is not a strong or valid reason to equate the two belief systems, all the more so as the exact meaning of 'shamanism' still remains unclear to many, as does the exact meaning of 'Bön'. In order to define one thing as another, one must be clear about the precise meaning of both parties. This book, *Bɵ and Bön: Ancient Shamanic Traditions of Siberia and Tibet in their Relation to the Teachings of a Central Asian Buddha* by Dmitry Ermakov, sets out to clarify the differences and relationships between Bön and the shamanism of Tibet, Mongolia and Siberia by looking through quite a wide and complex range of subjects. Mr. Ermakov has studied and practised Bɵ Murgel since 1990 and has travelled with shamans, visiting their sacred places and participating in many of their rituals. He first met the Bön tradition and its teachers in 1995, and has practised Yungdrung Bön for thirteen years. Thanks to his intimate knowledge of both traditions, his book could be of great benefit, helping the reader to gain a clear understanding of the similarities, differences and relationships between Yungdrung Bön and shamanic traditions. By studying *Bɵ and Bön*, even though many parallels may be apparent, one will be able to clearly distinguish the fundamental differences in the origin, practices and goals of these ancient religions. Therefore this book can be equally useful for practitioners and scholars of Bön, Tibetan Buddhism and shamanism.

I would like to congratulate Dmitry on the completion of this book which he has been working on for many years, and I hope it will be of great benefit to many.

Khenpo Tenpa Yungdrung
10th day of the first month,
Earth Mouse year (16th February, 2008)

Events that led to the writing of this book

Before I can start talking about my main subject I feel I need to give a little background and history to the events which led me to write this book.

I have been fascinated by ancient cultures and religions from childhood thanks to my mother, who introduced me to the myths and legends of ancient Greece. My paternal auntie, Galina Mezentseva, Professor of Archaeology at the University of Kiev, also played a role in this as, although I was born and bred in St. Petersburg (then Leningrad) and studied in a privileged music college, at the age of eight – and for many subsequent summers – my father and I took part in the archaeological digs she led in the fortress of Belgorod-Dnestrovskiy near Odessa on the Black Sea coast. It was an ideal solution for my family as we could combine holidays and study. I was able to participate in fieldwork and also joined my auntie's afternoon classes with the university students. During term time, I attended after school classes on History and Art at the Hermitage State Museum where, among other teachers, we were taught Archaeology by Professor Boris Piotrovskiy who discovered the ancient state of Urartu.

At the age of ten I read a book entitled *Gods of the Lotus*, a richly illustrated diary of the author Parfyonov's expedition in the Himalayas. That book struck a deep chord within me and since then my interest in the religions, cultures and history of that region has never faded.

My first trip to Siberia came in 1986 when I joined a team from Leningrad University's Faculty of Archaeology on an archaeological dig in Khakassia. We were unearthing Scythian *kurgans*[1] near the village of Askiz 150 kilometres from the city of Abakan. While there I had several strange experiences which in many ways triggered rapid changes in my life and perceptions. On two occasions our entire group saw a UFO, once at night and once during the day, and also one night I was woken by the feeling of a sudden opening up of the crown of my head accompanied by

[1] *Kurgan* is a Scythian burial mound.

an internal sound like a sable being drawn from its scabbard. I became quite frightened as the sensation that there was no boundary between the top of my head and the boundless universe grew stronger, and an unfamiliar breeze of cool energy descended from above.

Back in St. Petersburg I began practising martial arts and studying their background in the Taoist and Chan'/Zen philosophy. Later I met a Qi-gong master from Nankin, China, and started practising Qi-gong. This affected me profoundly and it is that work with energy that led me to several healers, shamans, Bɵ[2] and Utgan.[3]

It was in 1989 while reading the *samizdat*[4] underground translation of *Crystal and the Way of Light* by Chögyal Namkhai Norbu that I came across information about Bön and Yungdrung Bön for the first time, and a very profound interest awoke in me. I felt a deep connection to the Tibetan tradition and had several lucid dreams as a result of which, in the summer of 1990, I decided to go to Buryatia, the only place in the Soviet Union where I could find a functioning Buddhist monastery (albeit still full of KGB spies) and where, in fact, Bɵ and Utgan were still practising. I didn't know these names then as adepts of the native Buryatian religion were always referred to in Russia as simply 'shamans'.

My original plan was to go to the *datsan*[5] near Ulaan-Ude first and then go on to the Altai and roam around Mount Belukha, a beautiful mountain considered holy by the *kams*,[6] Buddhists and Christians alike. But things turned out differently and I stayed in Buryatia for the whole length of my trip.

There was a lot happening at that time. It was the early days of Perestroika and a policy of liberalization towards religions was cautiously being introduced. People began rebuilding the monasteries and temples

---

2 Bur. бөө – priest of Bɵ Murgel.

3 Bur. утган, удган, одёгон, одигон – priestess of Bɵ Murgel.

4 Rus. самиздат – literally 'self-published'. This term from the Soviet epoch refers to all sorts of underground literature such as the writings of dissidents, novels, poetry, plays, religious literature and so on which were not sanctioned by or forbidden by the Communist censorship. *Samizdat* also included reel-to-reel albums of Soviet underground rock bands. Authors, producers and distributors of *samizdat* were tracked by KGB and persecuted. Punishment included compulsory redundancy from work; arrests which often ended in prison sentences, beatings and even executions. Those caught reading *samizdat* literature also faced prison sentences. By the end of 1980s the policy of persecution of *samizdat* gradually eased.

5 Bur. дацан, a Mongolian word for a Buddhist monastery or temple.

6 Rus. кам – a type of priest in the native religion of Altai.

which had been destroyed by the Communists after the 1917 Revolution. Nature was reacting strongly to these changes; there were continuous thunder storms and downpours for the whole of June. The old people said it was very unusual weather indeed for this time of year and that similar phenomena occurred when the Communists destroyed the monasteries and killed the lamas in the late thirties.

During that first visit I initially spent some time around the Ivolginskiy Datsan[7] near Ulaan-Ude with my then girlfriend in the run-up to the big celebration of Maidari Huural.[8]

Fig. 1. *Ivolginskiy Datsan* 1993.

Many people gathered from all around Buryatia and other Republics. The air was buzzing with energy and things happened very quickly. I met someone who had just came from the east of Buryatia and told me about powerful places near the village of Hezhenge[9], and about Buddhist Tantric practitioners living there. While he was talking I felt it was there that I needed to go, not to the Altai. I asked a lama in the monastery to do a divination for me as I wanted to be completely sure of doing the right thing, of not wasting this opportunity. The oracle was quite definite about going to Hezhenge and so a group of us set off together as the chap who

---

7 Rus. Иволгинский дацан.

8 Bur. Майдари хуурал – the Maitreya festival

9 Bur. Хэжэнгэ; Rus. Кижинга.

had first fired my enthusiasm was interested in finding a *shamanka*,[10] an Utgan who lived in that region.

While waiting for the train at the railway station my new friend met a herbalist and Tantric practitioner with a group of followers who were on their way to the Altai to gather herbs. He decided to join them and they tried to persuade me to go along, too, but I was bent on going to Hezhenge. So it was as though we exchanged directions – I went to Hezhenge instead of the Altai, he went to the Altai instead of to Hezhenge! While camping near the Hezhenge Datsan I was befriended by an old man, Dasha Dorje. He asked me to find a translator in St. Petersburg who could translate a text by the Fifth Dalai Lama on Dzogchen,[11] which he had in his possession, from Old Mongolian into Russian. It was through him that I met the Doogarov family and their friends who were very interested in the teachings of Chögyal Namkhai Norbu and who later invited him to Buryatia in 1992.

While staying with the Doogarovs I gained their trust by correctly diagnosing some of their health problems and because of my keen interest in Buryatian culture and Buddhism, so they invited me to visit them again in September. In the meantime, back in St. Petersburg, I met a Buryatian Utgan, Natasha Hengelova, who introduced me to some aspects of Buryatian Bө Murgel.[12]

It was not until late October that year that I managed to return to Buryatia. This time I stayed mainly at the Doogarovs' house in Hezhenge where I was giving healing sessions to Batodalai, the head of the family. The old man, Dasha Dorje, wasn't very much respected by the Doogarovs as they thought he had been a KGB informant in the past involved in spying on their Tantric master Dandaron while working for him as a driver. Dandaron was later arrested and died or was killed in prison. All that happened in Brezhnev's era of Stagnation. What the Doogarovs were saying didn't correspond with what Dasha Dorje had told me earlier. He said that he himself was a student of Dandaron's mother, the *yogini* Sodnom Balzhenemai. Whatever the real story was, I didn't want to take sides so I visited the old man anyway. He lived on the far side of the village and I went round and took him some presents. We drank tea with biscuits,

---

10 Rus. шаманка – a Russian word for a female shaman.

11 Tib. rdzogs chen – Great Perfection, the nature of mind. This term refers to both the state of liberation and the teachings which show the way of obtaining it. Dzogchen teachings are the pinnacle of all the teachings of Yungdrung Bön and Buddhism and are contained in the Ninth Way of Yungdrung Bön and the Ninth Vehicle of the Nyingma School of Tibetan Buddhism.

12 Bur. Бөө Мүргэл.

as is the custom in Buryatia before any conversation can begin, and then he opened a cupboard which was in fact a hidden altar. Together with images of the Buddhas and Protectors I was amazed to see a photograph of Lev Tolstoy! When I asked him why he kept Tolstoy on his altar he replied that it was because Tolstoy preached non-violence. Then I told him I had found a translator for his text. To my surprise he pretended not to know what I was talking about. I tried to remind him about our last conversation, but he said he didn't know anything about the text. Then I said it was probably better for me not to come and visit him again because of the Doogarovs viewing him as a traitor. He smiled softly and agreed. So, I didn't see him after that. But after some time I was surprised once again when a Dzogchen text by the Fifth Dalai Lama was 'found' in the *datsan* near the village. Soon after that, the *datsan* was destroyed by a fire which started at night. While staying with the Doogarovs I visited several important power places in the area with Batodalai and entered into contact with the local gods and spirits. Despite being a Yamantaka Tantric practitioner and a very good *thangka*[13] painter, Batodalai had a keen interest in the Buryatian Bɵ Murgel culture as well and it was he who first introduced me to Buryatian 'shamans' – Bɵ and Utgan.

I returned to western Russia sometime around New Year 1991. On the way back I had a nasty run-in with a couple of drunk Buryatian hunters who assaulted me in a friend's flat in Ulaan-Ude while my girlfriend and I were staying there for a couple of days waiting for our flight back. The only thing I could do was to pray to my Protectors – the invisible powers intervened and a drunk hunter was stopped short with his hand in midair, just about to smash a bottle of champagne over my head.

Back in St. Petersburg, I continued my healing practice and developed further contacts with various psychics, *koldus*[14] and shamans living in the city. Gradually I grew disillusioned with the many people I met and began questioning their methods and motivations, as well as my own. At the same time my interest in Buddhist teachings was deepening. In December 1991 I went to Moscow to meet Nyingmapa lamas Khenchen Palden Sherab and Khenpo Tsewang Dongyal who were giving a Direct Introduction into the Nature of Mind and the Preliminaries from the Dzogchen cycle of *Longchen Nyingthig.*[15] It is then that I realized that the applications of any kind of magic are secondary to real spiritual insight into

---

13 *Thangkas* are Bönpo or Buddhist icons painted on cloth.

14 Rus. колдун (sing.), колдуны (pl.) – Russian wizards with healing, magical and clairvoyant abilities. They can be white, black or both.

15 Tib. Klong chen snying thig.

the Nature of Mind and also that without a clear, correct understanding of the law of karma[16] there is a danger that many healing methods and magic practices could actually bring harm to both the magician and the client in the long term. On seeing that I decided to put the teachings I had received from the Khenpos into practice. I spoke about my insight and intention with my friends from the psychic circles in St. Petersburg but my ideas didn't go down well with many of them. Undaunted, I went into retreat in a *datcha*[17] on the coast of the Gulf of Finland. My new experiences with Tibetan Buddhism meant I started drifting away from one particular group of psychics with whom I had previously worked very closely. They didn't like this and unleashed a magic attack against me. It was probably because of that – and maybe also partly due to the purification of my negative karma brought about by practising the Preliminaries[18] – that I became seriously ill for several months and reached the brink of death. I managed to pull through somehow and it was my good luck that I was able to go to Riga in the spring of 1992 to meet Chögyal Namkhai Norbu who from then on became my main Buddhist lama.[19] That year I followed him through to St. Petersburg and Moscow. Entering his *mandala*, receiving his teachings, and putting them into practice, I felt better and better.

With a group of Chögyal Namkhai Norbu's western students, I took the Trans-Siberian Railway to Ulaan-Ude from Moscow as Rinpoche was to give a retreat at the Kotokel[20] Lake near Lake Baikal.[21] That was the summer of 1992. Batodalai Doogarov was one of the principal organizers and introduced me to a group of Bɵ and Utgan who had come to listen to the teachings. We quickly became friends and I was asked to translate when they had an interview with Chögyal Namkhai Norbu. He was curious about their rituals and customs and asked them about their views in detail, probably for his research on Bön.

I returned to Buryatia in the summer of 1993, this time with Carol, my future wife and companion in practice, and two friends, a Buryatian Utgan Natasha and her American husband Geoff. Together we visited the

---

16 Tib. las.

17 Rus. дача – a simple Russian country house used mainly in summer.

18 Tib. sngon 'gro.

19 Tib. bla ma – literally 'mother of the *la*' (Tib. bla – a complex Bönpo concept tentatively translated as 'soul', see ch. XIII). Lama is the spiritual guide in Yungdrung Bön and Tibetan Buddhism, equivalent to Sans. *guru*.

20 Rus. Котокель.

21 Bur. Байгал; Rus. Байкал.

Tunka[22] region to the west of Lake Baikal, an area where some ancient Bɵ Murgel traditions are still preserved to this day. Before setting off we visited Batodalai Doogarov and found that he, too, was going to Tunka, to take part in a trip with some Bɵ. They were going to perform *tailgans*[23] there and in particular to make offerings to the deity Buha Noyon Baabai,[24] who is also a Protector of Buddhists and known to them as Rinchin Khaan.[25] Batodalai was going to perform a Buddhist ritual equivalent to the *tailgan*. While we were talking to him two Utgan, Vera Grigoryevna Naguslaeva and Nadezhda Ananyevna Stepanova, came to visit him. Although we had met a year earlier, on this occasion we established a good connection, but even though we were all going to Tunka, we couldn't join them for the *tailgan* as we had our own program. In fact, our friends had some personal problems so were seeking advice and assistance from Bɵ, as a result of which we met several local Bɵ and

Fig. 2. Soviet monument and Buddhist Datsan in the Village of Zhemchug, 1993.

[22] Rus. Тунка.

[23] Bur. тайлган. A communal sacrifice and celebration usually held at special power places once a year, although this varies depending on tradition. Usually representatives of several clans, led by the Bɵ, come together to pray and offer sacrifices to the Tengeri, *Ezhen* and various local spirits and guardians in order to harmonize people with all different levels of existence thus resulting in prosperity and the fulfillment of wishes and prayers.

[24] Bur. Буха Ноён баабай.

[25] Bur. Ринчин хаан.

Utgan and participated in various rituals in Arshan,[26] Zhemchug[27] and Tunka.

In May the following year, my wife Carol and I travelled east again, this time to Ulaan-Baatar in Mongolia for a retreat with Chögyal Namkhai Norbu. After our attempts to trace the Mongolian Consulate in St. Petersburg failed, we went to Moscow to obtain a visa for Carol and took a plane to Irkutsk, and from there continued our journey by train – a crazy thing to do in those times as crossing the Russian-Mongol border was fraught with danger due to frequent knife fights on the train. We did all right and once in Mongolia were welcomed to stay in the yurt in the monastery's courtyard; the retreat was to be held in the only Nyingma[28] monastery in Ulaan-Baatar. The head lama of the monastery, Purevsuren, the head of the Mongolian Nyingma School and the Head of the Union of Astrologers of Mongolia, was very kind to us and we had a good rapport with the monks and local practitioners.

From Ulaan-Baatar we followed Chögyal Namkhai Norbu to Buryatia where he gave further teachings. Batodalai Doogarov kindly arranged a place for us to stay and it turned out to be crucial for my further involvement with the Bө and Utgan as our host was Vera Naguslaeva, the lady I had met at Batodalai's a couple of years earlier. An Utgan from a blacksmith clan, she is held in high esteem in Buryatian society in general as well as among the Bө and Utgan. For forty years she worked in a medical clinic where alongside conventional treatment methods, she secretly used her psychic abilities to help patients who asked her to. By doing so she ran the risk of being arrested and losing her job as such alternative medicine was deemed 'antisocial' by the Soviet authorities.

On the evening of our arrival we were chatting in the living room when my perception suddenly changed and I saw two figures flanking Vera on both sides. I described them to her. She looked at me, somewhat surprised, and then said that they were Protectors of her clan. She warmed to us and said that she remembered a dream in which she was shown a young lad and was told that he would help her; she reckoned it was me. On another occasion her relative 'Uncle' Sasha came to visit. He was from Vera's village of Korsakovo[29] on the shore of Lake Baikal, and about her same age. We drank some tea and chatted about this and that. Then they

---

26 Bur. Аршан.

27 Rus. Жемчуг.

28 Tib. rNying ma; rNying ma pa – 'Ancient' School which contains the teachings of Indian Buddhism brought to Tibet in the 8th century A.D.

29 Rus. Корсаково.

went to another room to 'sprinkle' – offer *serzhim*[30] with vodka – and invited me to join them. Once we had finished I described what I had seen – a deity mounted on a white horse riding in the sky. Then we spread out a map of Buryatia and I pointed out a place where I thought the deity was residing. It was correct. Uncle Sasha was a bit surprised but then changed the subject and started to talk about the problems of their village which was on the edge of the 'Downfall', a landslide into the lake, and risked going under water, a fate which had already befallen several villages some years earlier. They were quite worried because inauspicious signs had appeared recently indicating possible disaster. The Bө believed that the landslide was caused by Lusuut Khaan,[31] a king of water-spirits, who resides in the waters near the village and who had become displeased. They were planning to make a long succession of rituals and ask the deities for support. Then they were planning to invite Lusuut Khaan to leave his present residence and move to a new one on the opposite side of the lake. The whole procedure was quite complicated as it was necessary to reach an agreement with many gods and spirits of the region. They asked me what I thought about it. I replied that I was quite young and inexperienced, but due to a state of changed perception, I pointed out several places on the map and described a man who I could see at that moment. He was given a fur hat by a group of Bө. I pointed to the place where it was going to happen. Now I was the one to be surprised, as that was what the Bө were planning and man I described was called Doogar Dorzhievich Ochirov. He was to lead the party, become initiated and be given the hat on the very spot I had pointed to on the map. I actually saw a second man with him, less tall and plumper, but I saw an obstacle for him. He was Doogar Ochirov's cousin who was also meant to go, but later some things arose at his workplace, so he remained in Ulaan-Ude.

The next day, 'Uncle Sasha' brought Doogar Ochirov with him and introduced us to each other. Doogar Ochirov showed me his Bө-stick which he had recently been given and as I looked at it, I saw rainbow waves coming out of it and spreading like ripples in water. We sprinkled together and then the Bө invited me to join them in the round of *tailgans* to be performed in the Barguzin[32] area and around Lake Baikal that June. I thanked them, saying it was a possibility, but I should see how things turned out. Towards the end of the retreat Chögyal Namkhai Norbu was

---

30 Bur. сэржим, сэржэм; equivalent to Tib. gser skyems; ritual 'sprinkling' of tea, milk, Buryatian *arkhi* or Russian grain vodka to the gods and spirits.

31 Bur. Лусуут (Лусуун) Хаан.

32 Bur. Баргузин.

asked to perform an offering ritual to the local gods at Baisa[33] in the Zaigraevo[34] region of Buryatia. A few Bө and Utgan, including my new friends Vera Naguslaeva and 'Uncle' Sasha, also went along and together the three of us made offerings to the local gods there afterwards according to the Bө Murgel tradition.

Fig. 3. 'Uncle' Sasha, Vera Naguslaeva and the author making offerings to the gods and spirits at Baisa.

We had several other meetings, then the retreat was over and Carol and I went to Moscow. From there she flew to London to sit university exams while I stayed on for the retreat with Chögyal Namkhai Norbu.

While I was at the retreat my step-father had a stroke but for some mysterious reason the telegram with the news never reached me. If it had, I would have gone to St. Petersburg and my pilgrimage with the Bө and Utgan would never have happened.

When the retreat was over I went back to Ulaan-Ude but on my way I found myself in a predicament. I was checking in for the flight and my luggage had gone through the ex-ray machine, but just as I was preparing to go to the boarding gate a young customs officer came to me and asked me to follow him with my luggage. It felt like trouble. In the detention box

---

33 Bur. Байса.

34 Bur. Заиграевский район.

I was made to unpack my rucksack until I took out the *phurba*[35] which I was carrying with me. There were two officers in the box. They got very agitated and grabbed it from my hand. "You're looking for five years in prison for that, son", said the older officer with sweetly-sadistic overtones in his voice. "This is a silent weapon." I tried to explain that I was a Buddhist and it was a Buddhist ritual object which I had brought with me from the UK and that it was on my customs declaration. They would have none of that and continued chuntering, "It's a murder weapon." The situation was becoming bad so I mentally invoked the Protectors. The young policeman suddenly remembered he had an acquaintance who was a Buddhist and a very nice guy. He softened towards me, telling his colleague, "Let's let him go. Those Buddhists are OK, you know." The older guy was tossing the *phurba* in his hand for a while and then asked me, "Got any alcohol on you?" I said, "No." He laughed and said, "Next time you should bring a bottle of cognac with you, but this time we'll let you off!" and they set me free. I couldn't believe it! I boarded the plane and flew to Ulaan-Ude to join the Bө and Utgan.

Religious liberalization was becoming a reality in Russia and the early stages of a Bө Murgel revival were stirring in Buryatia. The Bө-priests were undertaking pilgrimages around Lake Baikal and other powerful regions such as Tunka and Barguzin. Led by groups of Bө from different clans and places, these were kind of 'ecumenical' events; Bө travelled to different power spots and performed *tailgans* there together. The aim of such pilgrimages was to unify the energies of the Bө and the people with those of the protective deities of the clans, local spirits and Tengeri thereby speeding up the process of spiritual and environmental healing and harmonization which was much needed after the many years of repressions and pollution under the Communist regime. The pilgrimage in which I was invited to participate was one in a series of such events.

While on the pilgrimage I visited many power places around Lake Baikal and in the Barguzin Valley and Mountains, participated in many offering and healing rituals, shared magic activities, had contacts with local spirits, gods and Tengeri Sky-dwellers, and witnessed several strange phenomena. I had many conversations with the Bө and Utgan in which they explained various practical and theoretical aspects of their tradition. I kept a diary and took some photos, both of which came handy when I started writing this book. Towards the end of the pilgrimage the Bө and Utgan in our group recognized me as a Bө and suggested that

---

[35] Tib. phur ba, phur bu – a ritual dagger used in both Yungdrung Bön and Buddhist Tantra.

I take an initiation; I had to decline because the initiation rite involves sacrificing an animal.

When we came back to Ulaan-Ude a telegram with the news of my step-father's death was waiting for me – I had to leave immediately. Nadezhda Ananyevna Stepanova called someone in the airport and they fixed me up on the next plane. We left for the airport in a hurry but got stuck in a traffic jam which was uncharacteristic of Ulaan-Ude in those days. I was upset because it meant I missed the plane. When we finally arrived at the airport we discovered the plane on which I was supposed to fly had caught fire in one engine immediately after take-off. It had been limping above the airport in circles on one engine for about twenty minutes before managing to land so the lounge was filled with scared passengers. After an hour we all were put onto another flight and I flew back west not knowing that it would be nine years before I would manage to return to Buryatia.

The following year, 1995, I met my main Bönpo lama, Yongdzin Lopön Tenzin Namdak, in Amsterdam. From then on I have attended many of his retreats in different countries and immersed myself in the practice and study of various aspects of the Yungdrung Bön tradition, especially Dzogchen, Tantra and Bönpo culture in general. In February 1996, Carol and I went to Yongdzin Rinopche's monastery in Kathmandu, Nepal, where we stayed for three months. Yongdzin Rinpoche was very kind to give us several teachings, instructions and explanations on various topics including Bön history, culture and rituals.

Fig. 4. Triten Norbutse monastery in 1996.

The mid and late nineties were not easy years for us; we had many difficulties and I became seriously ill in the spring of 1998. Virtually bed-ridden for a year, I was unable to do anything of an active or physical nature: at times I couldn't even read. I used my time for practice and study as much as my health allowed. It is then that I started writing this book, putting my diaries and notes from the trips in Siberia and elsewhere in order. Some Bɵ had suggested I publish them together with my photos from the 1994 pilgrimage but I realized they were not suitable for publication in the present form.

Looking into those materials again, I decided to write down some of my observations and codify the knowledge I had gathered over the years when I was exposed to and participated in the life and practices of Buryatian Bɵ Murgel. At the same time I started pinning that information against my newly acquired and growing knowledge of the Bön tradition. It was a discovery for me as many aspects of the more archaic levels of Bön had features which were parallel or identical to practices and rituals of Buryatian Bɵ Murgel: I was looking at two traditions which had a common root or source in the remote past!

I started digging deeper, consulting all the materials available to me on these two subjects and examining them from the angle of my own knowledge and experience. As the body of materials and observations grew I decided to put it in the form of an article just for the sake of making things clearer for myself. But as I continued my research this 'article' grew and grew.

In 1999 my wife and I moved to Italy. I gradually grew stronger and continued reworking my research as my health improved. We moved to Perugia, and made good friends with the local Dzogchen Community, often meeting for communal practices, rambles in the uplifting Umbrian countryside, and lively discussions. Every summer Carol and I travelled to attend a retreat led by Yongdzin Lopön Tenzin Namdak somewhere in Europe and he always made time to answer the questions my research and practice had sparked since our last meeting.

In 2002 life took another unexpected turn and we found ourselves living in Moscow. Having originally only planned a three-month visit for me to undergo a new health treatment, we ended up staying for nearly two years. This unexpectedly gave me access to many Russian books both old and new which were freely available under the new liberalism, and I gleaned much important information from these sources. More importantly, in the autumn of 2003, I was once again able to visit Buryatia. I stayed with Utgan Vera Grigoryevna Naguslaeva at her apartment in Ulaan-Ude and also at her *datcha* on Lake Baikal. It was a wonderful opportunity to catch up with old friends and quiz the Bө and Utgan on many points so I managed to clarify many things on that trip. It was during this time in Russia that my work began to take on its present form. On several occasions I had discussed my observations and ideas contained in this growing article with people from academic circles as well as with lamas and practitioners from various countries, and was advised by some of them to consider a publication.

On leaving Moscow Carol and I were fortunate enough to be able to spend another month with Yongdzin Lopön Tenzin Namdak at his Triten Norbutse[36] monastery in Kathmandu. Once again, he and the Abbot, Khenpo Tenpa Yungdrung, were extremely generous with their time and painstakingly answered my many questions. We were also able to observe and record the monks performing rituals.

We returned to Britain in 2004 but, contrary to our original plans, did not stay much over a year. In 2005 the Bönpo community in the West secured a permanent base in Europe, Shenten Dargye Ling,[37] in France. With growing political unrest in Nepal, Yongdzin Lopön Tenzin Namdak and Khenpo Tenpa Yungdrung were concerned about the destabilizing effect this could have on the social fabric of the country. To ensure the preservation of precious Yungdrung Bön texts, the whole of the Bönpo *Kanjur*[38] and *Katen*[39] were soon installed in the newly converted library, along with many other precious books. Carol and I spent that summer cleaning, gardening, doing DIY and being in Yongdzin Rinpoche's presence along with a handful of other western Bönpo from all over Europe and beyond. At the end of the summer Khenpo Tenpa Yungdrung unexpectedly asked us to stay on and become the first caretakers of this new centre. We hesitated, knowing it would cause us no little upheaval in our 'worldly life', but knew in our hearts that this was our path. Yongdzin Rinpoche confirmed this, so, leaving our few belongings in Carol's parents' garage, we headed back to France. Apart from welcoming visitors and keeping an eye on the rambling château and grounds, our main task was to transcribe and edit the teachings Yongdzin Lopön Tenzin Namdak had given in France and the rest of Europe over the years. This was an immense but rewarding task and we were stretched to our limits; we have so far produced around 30 books and a considerable body of Yongdzin

---

36 Tib. Khri brten Norb bu rtse.

37 Tib. gShen bstan Dar rgyas gLing.

38 Tib. bka' 'jyur.

39 Tib. bka' brten.

Rinpoche's commentaries on Bön Dzogchen texts is now preserved in English. I had hoped to devote one day a week to my writing, but it very soon became apparent that our responsibilities in Shenten consumed all our time and energy, so while I was able to benefit greatly from the materials we were transcribing, all writing as such came to a complete standstill.

After a couple of months of solitude in this new centre, we were joined by Geshe Gelek Jinpa whose joviality and energy was a source of constant inspiration. We spent considerable amounts of time together doing practice, preparing study and practice materials, shared many jokes and also learnt a lot from this knowledgeable and generous Geshe. The other resident Geshe, Samten Tsugphü, although much quieter by nature, also helped us considerably, especially regarding some aspects of Tantric ritual liturgy.

The political scene in Nepal did indeed worsen and Yongdzin Lopön Tenzin Namdak was flown out of Kathmandu in April 2005, arriving in Shenten almost as a refugee. However, for us it was a marvellous time as he generously offered to teach a series of weekend seminars on the Nine Ways of Bön, material never before made available to western students in such detail. We also had many private conversations with Yongdzin Rinpoche and he gave several spontaneous teachings to us during this time. The information I gained during my stay in Shenten has proven invaluable for this research and I am indebted to my teachers for their help and encouragement.

We finally left Shenten in September 2006, collected our belongings from Carol's parents and set up home in a little rented cottage in the North Pennines. I settled down to writing in earnest. What had once been my own personal jottings has over the years been rearranged and rewritten several times, more material has been added in order to better support and strengthen the arguments and conclusions presented, so finally this has grown into a fully-fledged book.

Author's Preface

In this study, I take an approach which may be somewhat unorthodox for research into comparative religions, namely that of an 'insider'. That means that, while reference is made to other sources, the main core of presentations on Yungdrung Bön and Bɵ Murgel is based on traditional texts and information given by adherents to these traditions. This includes matters relating to the origin of the teachings, their history, mythology and so on. Although I am aware that some of the traditional dates – especially as regards Bön – are disputed by some Western and Buddhist scholars, I have chosen to follow the traditional reckoning, following the premise of 'innocent until proven guilty': although there is insufficient hard proof to support these ancient dates at present, they cannot be simply discarded outright as there is equally insufficient evidence to disprove traditional chronology. In Chapter XV in particular, I put forward some arguments based on scientific findings and theories which may support the antiquity of the founder of Yungdrung Bön, Tonpa Shenrab Miwo, and his teachings. As regards the study of rituals, in many instances I draw upon my own experiences and observations in both Yungdrung Bön and Bɵ Murgel which are pinned against materials contained in works of prominent scholars in the fields of Bön and Siberian Shamanism. I have been privileged to work closely with Yongdzin Lopön Tenzin Namdak Rinpoche and with his kind permission have included some lengthy excerpts from edited transcripts of his teachings, as well as interviews and presentations given for the purpose of this publication.

Although I have consulted many knowledgeable scholars and practitioners of both Yungdrung Bön and Bɵ Murgel in the course of my research, I must point out that the ideas presented in this book and the conclusions I have drawn are my own and do not represent the views of the individual practitioners or informants from Yungdrung Bön, Tibetan Buddhism or Bɵ Murgel unless otherwise stated. The nature of the field of this research allows for different interpretations depending on the angle from which a topic is observed and which aspects are emphasized. Research is in a state of constant flux and as new facts come to light, assumptions based on outdated information are naturally challenged. I invite readers to keep an open mind and make their own judgment on the materials and views presented here.

Transliteration

In the main body of the text I use a free transliteration system for all languages based on pronunciation for ease of reading. In the case of Russian, Mongolian, Buryatian and some other languages, I give the original in a footnote at first mention while the transliteration according to the Wylie system is given for Tibetan names and terms. In the bibliography, Russian titles are given according to the British Standards transliteration system.

Throughout the book I use the spelling 'Tyurk' to distinguish the original Tyurkyut and Tyurks from the modern Turks. Wherever possible and appropriate, I give alternative spellings for other tribes and states.

Dates

Dates relating to Yungdrung Bön are mainly given according to the Bönpo chronology of *bsTan rtsis* composed in 1842 by Menri Khenchen Nyima Tenzin (Tib. sMan ri mKhan chen Nyi ma bsTan 'dzin), the Abbot of Menri Monastery, and in *Introduction of Bon which opens the mind*, (Tib. *Bon gyi ngo sprod blo gsar sgo 'byed*) by Geshe Tenzin Drugdrag (Tib. dGe bShes bsTan 'zin 'Brug Grags). The abbreviation AD is used to denote dates up to the first millennium, but not afterwards.

Maps

I have included several maps to facilitate the reader's understanding of the material presented. However, it should be pointed out that many of these maps are best approximations and I in no way claim they are definite representations of historical or geographical boundaries as these cannot be established with certainty.

A word of warning

I must point out that all accounts and descriptions in this book are provided solely for the purposes of information and comparative study. All the methods and rituals of both Bө Murgel and Bön have been transmitted from generation to generation in keeping with strict lineages and commitments. The integrity of these methods and practices is guarded by powerful spiritual beings who ensure they are not misused or used without *bona fide* authorization and permission. Those who attempt to use any of these methods without proper transmission and authorization, especially with the intent of causing harm, will bring upon themselves the wrath of the protective deities of both Bө Murgel and Bön.

Introduction

Brief presentation on Bön

Although this issue will be dealt with thoroughly in the following pages, for the sake of clarity I should briefly outline here the different types of Bön forming the basis of this study. The Bön we shall study here can be divided into four major categories:

Prehistoric Bön
Yungdrung Bön[1]
Bön Sarma[2]
Mixed Bön.

Prehistoric Bön

I divide Prehistoric Bön itself into two broad categories:

Prehistoric Bön of Zhang Zhung[3] and Tibet, known in Tibetan as Dömai Bön;[4]

Prehistoric Bön of Eurasia, a term I have coined to cover a much larger phenomenon, namely the many spiritual and ritualistic streams practised by the various nations and tribes of different racial types who roamed Eurasia in remote prehistory. Part of the scope of this book is to establish a loose commonality between these ancient traditions, thereby justifying the epithet 'Eurasia'. As for bringing all these traditions under the umbrella of Bön, the reasons for this will become apparent as the reader progresses through this book; here, suffice to say that in Tibetan the term *bön* is not limited to a restrictive meaning linked to only one religion, and several streams of Bön may have come to the Tibet-Qinghai Plateau from other parts of Eurasia. Moreover, the Bɵ Murgel belief system of Mongolia and Buryatia – thousands of miles from Tibet – has many features in common with Tibetan Bön, not least of which is its name, Bɵ (pronounced like 'boar' with a double 'oar' sound).

---

1 Tib. g.yung drung bon.
2 Tib. bon gsar ma.
3 Tib. Zhang zhung.
4 Tib. gdod ma'i bon.

Yungdrung Bön

According to traditional sources, Yungdrung Bön is the teaching of the Central Asian Buddha, Tonpa Shenrab Miwoche, who lived and preached in the heart of Tagzig,[5] an ancient country located somewhere in the Pamir Mountains, possibly in modern-day Tajikistan and/or the surrounding Central Asian republics. The teachings of this Buddha were brought into and flourished in the land of Zhang Zhung, an empire or tribal confederation centred in western Tibet around Tise (Mount Kailash). It is from this heartland that Yungdrung Bön reached Tibet, initially a small vassal-state of Zhang Zhung which eventually overthrew its overlord in the sixth-eighth centuries AD.

Yungdrung Bön is divided into two major parts, Causal and Fruitional. In a nutshell, Causal Bön is comprised of a vast body of rituals designed to improve worldly conditions and lessen hardships in this life and gradually guide the practitioner towards the higher teachings of Fruitional Bön which ultimately lead to Buddhahood.

Bön Sarma

Often referred to as New Bön, this is an eclectic tradition combining elements of Indian Buddhism and Yungdrung Bön which appeared in the eighth century AD and is still very popular in eastern Tibet, particularly in Kham.

Mixed Bön

This refers to the wide range of tribal traditions practised in the borderlands surrounding Tibet and the Himalayas in which Prehistoric Bön, Yungdrung Bön and various other elements mingle in various proportions.

Scope of this book

One of the main aims of this book is to dispel the misconceptions and disinformation that Yungdrung Bön is a kind of Tibetan shamanism using blood sacrifices and black magic which later took on some aspects of Indian Buddhism in a deliberate attempt to appear more 'Buddhist'. We dismantle this myth from many sides: firstly, by looking into the history and doctrines of Yungdrung Bön itself, which are the teachings of Tonpa Shenrab Miwo, the Central Asian Buddha who – according to traditional

---

5 Tib. sTag zig, rTag gzigs.

Bönpo reckoning – predates the later Indian Buddha Shakyamuni by many thousands of years; secondly, by detailing the differences and similarities between the multiple aspects of various types of Tibetan Bön; thirdly, by methodically comparing Yungdrung Bön's base, view, path, myths, beliefs, rituals and deities with those of Tibetan Buddhism, Prehistoric Bön in general and Buryatian Bө Murgel in particular. It is my hope that the materials presented here will aid the reader in gaining a better understanding of the true relationship between Yungdrung Bön and Buddhism and thereby contribute to overcoming sectarianism, a serious obstacle for practice and study both among Tibetans and in the West.

The other tradition we shall examine in detail is Bө Murgel of Buryatia. We shall demonstrate that Bө Murgel, sometimes called Tengrism by Russian scholars, is in reality a syncretic tradition embracing several kinds of Prehistoric Bön akin to Tibetan Lha Bön[6] and Düd Bön[7] which, possibly, includes fragments of Yungdrung Bön along with methods from other Siberian spiritual and cultural streams. Because of this rich diversity and the many layers contained within it, and because it is a living tradition related to Tibetan Bön which can still be studied from 'within', Buryatian Bө Murgel can play a unique and important role in shedding light on the origins and culture of Bön. Through the comparative study of the views, myths and practical methods of Bө Murgel and what we know about the Prehistoric Bön of Tibet, poorly understood aspects of both belief systems can be further illuminated.

Our examination of living traditions and historical sources will also demonstrate that a prehistoric form, or forms, of Bön was most likely practised by many peoples over many eons in many diverse locations in Eurasia and elsewhere with considerable impact on the development of subsequent belief systems.

As for so-called 'shamanism', it is my hope that the detailed exposition covering the initiation process, lives and techniques of Buryatian Bө and Utgan found in this book will help to lift the veil of ignorance surrounding the indispensable qualities needed to become a shaman and the tremendous challenges, responsibilities and suffering this calling entails.

Finally, by making available hitherto unpublished materials and pictures pertaining to both Yungdrung Bön and Bө Murgel, I hope the reader will gain a wider understanding and appreciation of these little-known traditions which are in fact an important part of our common world heritage.

---

6 Tib. lha bon – Bön of the Deities.

7 Tib. bdud bon – Bön of the Demons.

A word on terminology

I use the term 'Prehistoric Bön' to denote all pre-Yungdrung Bön traditions of Tagzig, Zhang Zhung, Tibet and its borderlands while the term 'Prehistoric Bön of Eurasia' refers to the array of ancient magical traditions once found in Eurasia. These include: the so-called 'folk religion' of China or pre-Taoism; ancient traditions of the Aryan tribes; Siberian 'shamanic' traditions; the traditions of ancient peoples of the Great Steppe such as Hunnu (Xiyụng-nu), Syanbi (Xianbei), Zhu-Zhang; and even some Native American traditions which came to the Americas from the Eurasian continent via Beringia. To a greater or lesser extent, these traditions all bear resemblance to one another, like cousins or close relatives, and while some of these similarities can be put down to borrowings, on closer examination the archaic layers of the ancient religions practised by those nations show common characteristics and elements which must have sprung from a common cultural and religious field or source – the Prehistoric Bön of Eurasia. 'Folk religions' of Eurasia, it would seem, have a common ancestor, a common source which cannot be traced through written records because it is so old, and as such are the remnants of an ancient yet spiritually and culturally advanced religion – or number of religions – which was at one time practised over vast stretches of our planet. This hypothesis becomes more and more tenable as new archaeological finds and intensive research into different cultures (such as the Uighur archaeologist Dolkun Kamberi's discovery of a 500,000 year-old piece of human skull in Xinjiang; modern archaeological research and DNA analysis of the Xinjiang mummies carried out by Victor Mair and associates; the discovery of the famous Ice Man in the Italian Alps in 1991; the Indian oceanographers' accidental discovery of the submerged remains of a pre-Harappa city off the Bay of Cambay, Gujrat, in 2001)[8] push the dawn of humanity and the development of human culture back to progressively earlier dates.

As we can see from the myths and rituals which have been handed down to us over the millennia, and as the powers of some priests of surviving streams – such as Bө Murgel – attest, the Prehistoric Bön of Eurasia contained very deep knowledge of the unseen energy dimension and the ways of manipulating this to the advantage of the priest and the 'congregation'; knowledge on how to appease, subdue, befriend, attract, control and repel human and non-human beings and energies of different dimensions and dispositions; knowledge of how to harmonize the human

---

[8] See ch. XV.

dimension with that of other beings; knowledge of the human energy system of channels, chakras and subtle winds and its interaction with the immediate environment and the cosmos at large; extensive knowledge of herbal and mineral substances for medicine, poison and magic; knowledge of our planet's geomantic energy currents – and the list goes on. The fruits of possessing such vast and deep knowledge cannot be imagined nowadays but echoes of this mighty religion can be heard in the numerous myths and legends of hero-wizards found in any culture on Earth. They may sometimes be weak signals, sometimes distorted and confused or sometimes incredibly accurate and precise, but they all belie the great wealth of this Ur-religion, the Prehistoric Bön of Eurasia.

It is very difficult to say exactly where and when the Prehistoric Bön of Eurasia originated and who its prophets or teachers were, or indeed what its main core or doctrine was. Technically speaking the origin of this cultural and religious phenomenon is in the dimension of the Sky, home of principal gods and demons. According to the majority of archaic religions, it was the sky-gods and sky-demons[9] who gave all sorts of magical knowledge both 'white' and 'black' to humanity and taught the emerging human race many skills necessary to survive and prosper in the world. As far as geographical location is concerned, it is my opinion that Prehistoric Bön originated in the Northern Hemisphere in the circumpolar regions of Eurasia and spread from there all over the world; it is this supposition which led me to coin the term 'Prehistoric Bön of Eurasia'. It was mostly focused on acquiring worldly benefits and ordinary magical powers (common *siddhi*[10] in Yungdrung Bön and Buddhist terms) or did it in fact incorporate profound teachings by which one could realize the Base of the Universe? There are no ready answers. We only can see fragments reflected in different so-called 'primitive' traditions but it is impossible to reconstruct a real picture of the source religion(s) because they have undergone thousands and thousands of years of transformations, adapting themselves to new environments and changes, destruction, loss of the essential teachings, later additions and cross-pollination.

---

9 Although in some traditions some material skills are said to have been given by the gods of the Underworld, these gods are themselves either fallen sky-gods or were assigned their posts in the lower realms by the sky-gods.

10 Tib. dngos grub; spiritual attainments. Ordinary *siddhi* are various kinds of magic powers together with wealth, prosperity, long-life etc. while supreme *siddhi* is the realization of the state of Buddha.

Dubious legacy of the term 'Shamanism'

These uncharted belief systems are often referred to as Shamanism, a word which nowadays covers a multitude of sins. For some, 'Shamanism' is defined as an ancient technique of ecstasy - i.e. all sorts of possession and mediumistic techniques; others apply it indiscriminately to a great variety of spiritual paths belonging to very different cultures all over the globe including those which make little or no use of possession techniques. On top of that we now have the so-called 'New Age shamans' who just believe in what they like, following a mixture of their own making with all but no idea about the choosing, obligations and work of a real shaman. In Siberian shamanic traditions, as in Bön and Buddhism, all techniques and teachings have their own precise source and are passed down through a line of authentic masters. Thus the principle of lineage is of great importance and has mechanisms safeguarding the purity of its transmission against external interference or corruption from within. It is precisely thanks to this principle of lineage that these traditions have come down to us today in good working order. Furthermore there is confusion between 'Shamanism' and 'Paganism', names which are often used interchangeably. In view of this I have tried to avoid the term wherever possible.

In fact, the word 'shaman' has a very precise meaning; it is a Russian corruption of the Tungus-Evenki word *šaman*, an adjective used to designate the priest of their religion. Many scholars have tried to lend the Tungus word *šaman* additional meanings such as 'one who is excited, moved or raised', 'inner heat'[11] or to trace it to other languages saying that it is derived from Chinese *sha men* (沙弥), Pali *śamana* or Sanskrit *śramana*, meaning 'listener' and used to designate a Buddhist monk or wandering Buddhist preacher. These suggestions find no support in Tungus language or culture, and the last one is obviously completely off the mark as Tungus shamans have nothing whatsoever to do with practices and teachings of Buddhism. To clarify all this confusion I contacted the Russian scholar and Doctor of Philology, the leading specialist in Tungus language and culture at the Institute of Linguistic Research, Russian Academy of Sciences,[12] St. Petersburg, A.A. Burykin, who kindly sent me the following reply:

---

[11] Stanley Krippner, 'The Epistemology and Technologies of Shamanic States of Consciousness', *Journal of Consciousness Studies*, <www.imprint-academic.com/jcs> accessed 24.06.07.

[12] Институт лингвистических исследований РАН, Санкт-Петербург, 199053, Тучков пер. д. 9.

> The word *šaman* 'shaman' has only one meaning in the Tungus language group: it just means 'shaman', the priest. Some trace it to the verb sa-, 'to know' but this is highly unlikely because this verb has a long vowel while *šaman* has a short one [...] As for me, this Tungus word should be compared with the Nenets word *sambana*, a designation of one category of Nenets shamans. These *sambana* shamans shamanize to the Underworld in a similar way to the shamans of Tungus who, basically do mainly that.

At the beginning of the twentieth century, the absolute majority of western scholars who studied the native Siberian spiritual traditions insisted that the term 'Shamanism' should be applied only to the traditions of the peoples of North Asia and some small locations in Europe such as southern regions of Russia where Kalmyk Mongols settled. Scholars such as D. Klemenz, M.N. Hangalov, W. Radloff, R.Maack, L. von Shrenck, V. Bogoraz, V. Jochelson and many others unreservedly stood by the understanding that Shamanism as a religious and cultural phenomenon is limited to these territories and nations who traditionally inhabited them before the conquest of Siberia by the Russians.[13] However, later researchers gradually departed from this clear definition and the term began losing its precise meaning and value. With the onset of the New Age movement, which makes an indigestible and confusing mixture of everything, this term came to be applied to any kind of traditional or questionable, to say the least, New Age psychic techniques regardless of whether they have anything to do with Native Siberian traditions or the methods of Siberian shamans or not, thereby rendering this term completely meaningless and unsuitable for use in serious research. Some teachers adhering to religions devoid of the figure of a shaman nevertheless try to re-invent themselves as 'shamans' and their teachings as 'shamanic' in order to better sell themselves and their beliefs to the audience. In fact, they only damage their own tradition and further degrade the meaning of the word 'shaman'. The term 'Shamanism' is not bad in itself; although it suffers from the problem faced by all 'isms' – undue generalization – it can still be employed positively in the future if, by some caprice of fate, its use returns to its original definition and to the cultural and religious phenomenon it once represented.

---

13 See L. Krader, 'Shamanism; Theory and History in Buryat Society', in V.Diósziegy and M. Hoppál (ed), *Shamanism in Siberia*, p. 231.

Buryatian Bɵ Murgel as a key to understanding the secrets of Prehistoric Bön of Eurasia

Buryatian 'shamans' call their religion Bɵ Murgel or Bɵ Shazhan[14] with *murgel* and *shazhan* both meaning 'religion' in general and *bɵ*[15] being the main name. They call male priests 'Bɵ' and female priests 'Utgan'. The Bɵ Murgel religion is not peculiar to Buryats alone but is found in various forms among various Mongol tribes and also in Tuva. In this book we will focus on the Buryatian version as it is this strand which I have studied and, to some extent, practised.

Despite the fact that the various native Siberian spiritual traditions have many cults and concepts in common due largely to their similar cultural, religious and geographical environment, the differences between them are comparable to those between major world religions. One of the most important aspects found in all Siberian religions is Polytheism and indeed this is very developed in modern-day Buryatian Bɵ Murgel which probably has the biggest and most complex pantheon among all the native Siberian religions. The main distinctive feature of Bɵ Murgel, however, is its cults of Huhe Münhe Tengeri[16] (Eternal Blue Sky) and Tengeri[17] (Sky-Dwelling Gods), so we pay special attention to these in this book. In my opinion it is these cults which are central to Bɵ Murgel and define the Bɵ's distinct techniques and approach, although their real meaning and significance can be easily overlooked or misinterpreted.

Any religion has several stages: appearance, development and evolution, decline and degradation and finally, disappearance – that is the natural law of all things in the universe. Religions are used by people and people in general have many shortcomings and limitations so things can go amiss in the later stages of development. Although all spiritual traditions have ways of safeguarding the purity of their teachings, the

---

14 Bur. Бөө Шажан is an alternative spelling of Bɵ Murgel. There is no real semantic difference between *murgel* and *shazhan* and their use is similar to Tib. bon and Tib. chos. *Murgel* remained closely tied to the Bɵ religion while *shazhan* is nowadays mostly used to designate the Buryatian adaptation of Tibetan Buddhism.

15 Modern Cyrillic spelling is Bur. бөө, as given above. Other spellings are Bur. бөөгe, бөөги and in Old Mongol script it is spelt as BJHt.

16 Bur. Хүхэ Мүнхэ Тэнгэри.

17 Bur. Тэнгэриин – literally 'Sky-dwellers' are the long-living Sky-gods who dwell in the dimension of the Eternal Blue Sky. Actually, the plural of Tengeri is Tengeriin but in this book I use Tengeri for both singular and plural to simplify matters.

success rate varies thus some very enlightened and beneficial teachings can be transformed into just the opposite or the central message can be severely distorted. Many aspects of this process of degradation are found among all so-called 'advanced' modern world religions, so one should be wary of using the term 'primitive religion' as a label for the ancient traditions which preceded them.

Since the ritual traditions of the Prehistoric Bön of Eurasia were entirely oral and exist today as scattered fragments, we can understand the way they worked only indirectly via the medium of folk culture; through studying Buryatian Bɵ and Utgan, Tibetan *lhapa*[18] and *lhamo*[19] mediums or their equivalents in other cultures; by studying spiritual traditions of the Nakhi (Naxi), Moso and Lolo peoples where Prehistoric Bön is mixed with Yungdrung Bön; by studying the archaic methods adapted and transformed by Tonpa Shenrab Miwoche[20] and now found in the Causal Bön[21] teachings of his Yungdrung Bön tradition, and through comparing all kinds of Tibetan Bön with Buryatian Bɵ Murgel not just in a scholarly manner but also experientially. In my view this is a very valuable method of research because Bɵ Murgel is a living tradition in which many archaic notions and rituals identical or parallel to those of the Prehistoric Bön of Tibet and of Eurasia in general are kept alive and practised to this day.

Difficulties facing the researcher of Bɵ and shamans

Studying and comparing spiritual traditions is not an easy task and is often done on the basis of external similarities observed in rituals or textual/oral materials dealing with the exposition of dogma and related matters. While this is, no doubt, an important part of research, what is mostly missed is the actual living experience of the tradition which can only be obtained through practising it. Without this experience it is impossible to understand the real meaning of texts, rituals and meditations. In Buryatian Bɵ Murgel, Yungdrung Bön and Tibetan Buddhism alike, receiving a transmission of spiritual power is considered indispensable in order to truly understand and practise these spiritual paths.[22] Without such a transmission one is unable to achieve the result

---

18 Tib. lha pa.

19 Tib. lha mo.

20 Tib. sTon pa gShen rab Mi bo che – Buddha of Yungdrung Bön.

21 Tib. rgyu'i bon.

22 There are different levels of such empowerments in both Yungdrung Bön and

of a given path and will most probably go astray. Sadly, this important point is not given much weight in scientific research and consequently numerous misinterpretations arise. To give but one example, there is the widely held but wholly mistaken idea that the practice of *Chöd* has its roots in shamanic traditions and is comparable to the Siberian 'shamanic illness', a suggestion found, for example, in Tsultrim Allione's 'Women of Wisdom'.[23] By its very nature, the sphere of spiritual experience lies beyond the reach of science as scientific methods have nothing to grasp at – there is no matter. This goes against the mainstream view of science which by its definition is a materialistic worldview denying spiritual phenomena any actual existence in their own terms but looking at them as a manifestation of human creativity in the face of the complex struggle for survival and the search for the meaning of life. However, a growing awareness of the limitations of the scientific methods in the field of human studies is springing from the within the scientific community itself. For example, Simon Blackburn, a professor of philosophy at the University of Cambridge writes:

> How far can science go in the pursuit of truth? There are limits: science only works where there are constancies, such as the physical universe. Where constancies are hard to come by, as within human behaviour, the entitlement of any investigation to be called "scientific" begins to look correspondingly thin.[24]

Religious studies routinely undertaken within the field and framework of various branches of humanitarian sciences – anthropology, sociology, biology, history or archaeology – strive to explain everything in terms of matter because science cannot do without measurement and rational explanation. Because of this, the study of spiritual traditions in academic circles has remained largely on the level of amassing a great deal of detailed observations about the external aspects of various spiritual paths and – at least in Russian studies on Shamanism – recording the

---

Tibetan Buddhism but even reading a text containing an exposition of the teachings requires a transmission of Tib. lung. This literally means 'handle' but is most often translated into English as 'scriptural authorisation'. This transmission enables a student to realise the real meaning of the text and not just the words.

23 Tsultrim Allione, Women of Wisdom (New York, Ithaca: Snow Lion, 2000), p. 128. For a clarification on this point, see ch. XII.

24 Simon Blackburn, The World's Biggest Ideas: 10 Science, *New Scientist*, 17-23 September 2005, p. 41.

inner experiences of their practitioners. This information was (and is) measured and interpreted on the basis of materialistic concepts and theories inherent in sciences and humanities. What is the result? Very often it is misunderstanding, sometimes grave. However, I am not against scientific methods. Quite the opposite; such methods present a good and indispensable tool in certain fields of study and for certain tasks but they in no way represent a unique method for knowing the world and humankind – just one among many. As Simon Blackburn summarizes:

> It is a powerful force for good, but beware: it's not the answer to everything.[25]

Here I have tried to combine both the scholarly and the spiritual, experiential approach in order to arrive at a more complete picture of my subject.

This is particularly necessary for the study of Siberian Shamanism as several factors have hindered research in the past, rendering many scholarly works superficial and inaccurate as far as their conclusions and interpretations are concerned. Firstly, it is not easy to gain the trust of a Bɵ, particularly for Russians. The Buryats and other 'national minority' groups are naturally wary of Russians as they have been invaders and persecutors over a long period of history so it is not easy to gain the deep trust and not merely a superficially polite relationship. Researchers coming from Siberian ethnic groups who have a better understanding of the culture and spiritual background of Siberian nations and foreign non-Russian scholars often had more luck in gaining the trust of the Bɵ and shamans.

Secondly, during the Soviet Era when religion *per se* was seen as a scourge but even more so the 'primitive' naturalistic traditions of Siberia, Bɵ and shamans naturally didn't trust some of the researchers who they viewed as Soviet scientist-spies studying them only to disprove the validity of their religion and power, to prove that they were a peculiar anachronism. These 'studies' would then be used in Communist atheist propaganda, so naturally the Bɵ and shamans either refused to collaborate, provided disinformation or spoke very vaguely and as a result, the material collected was inaccurate and open to misinterpretation. However, despite the pressure of being 'ideologically correct' and ever obligatory references to the Marxist-Leninist doctrine of dialectical materialism – the official ideology of the Communist Party of the Soviet Union – several scholars

---

25 Ibid.

managed to gather invaluable ethnographic data on the fading culture and spiritual traditions of Native Siberian peoples.

Another obstacle to the scientist is that the Bɵ vows forbid them to interrupt their invocations or perform them without a serious reason. Therefore someone who wanted to write them down had to be versed both in the culture and language of Buryats[26] as well as having a fast hand! Shamans and Bɵ often keep their teachings very secret and do not speak of them glibly. In general it is difficult to understand and very easy to misunderstand the real meaning of the words of the invocations and the rituals without having tangible experience in these kinds of practices or a practising mentor as a guide.

A further cause for misunderstanding is that researchers may be conditioned by their own hypotheses and therefore naturally blind to obvious facts or tend to misinterpret them to suit their own theories. Of course, there are still a number of reliable works with accurate observations but due to these difficulties, the interpretation of the material is often misguided.

My approach in researching this book, then, has been to consult living masters, great adepts and erudite scholars in their respective traditions so as to base my conclusions on authentic sources. I have been privileged to observe and participate in many rituals from all three traditions and have also drawn on my own personal experience of Yungdrung Bön, Buddhism and Bɵ Murgel. This has been augmented with delving into a wide range of literature in both English and Russian, and in some instances, in other languages, too, covering many disciplines from archaeology to zoogeology, so I have been able to weigh book knowledge against my own insights and corroborate this with those who are steeped in each tradition.

Drawing a line between shamanistic traditions and Yungdrung Bön

Some of the newly-emerged Bɵ who have surfaced during the recent revival of Bɵ Murgel in Buryatia seem to be influenced by Theosophical and New Age ideas and techniques. Their terminology is often borrowed and mixed. Such 'New Age Bɵ' preach that all religions have emerged from Shamanism and that their canons are really the same, merely

---

[26] Like the Buryatian Professor of the Imperial University of St. Petersburg Tsyben Zhamtsarano (Rus. Цыбен Жамцарано), for example, thanks to whom we have a large collection of the Bɵ Murgel invocations of pre-revolutionary times.

appearing under a different 'sauce'. They claim that the source of Buddha's teachings is Shamanism and that the triads of Shamanism,[27] Buddhism[28] and Christianity[29] are the same. These are some of the 'modern features' which are being developed in some eclectic streams of Bɵ Murgel revival today. The reasons for the emergence of the 'New Age Bɵ' are understandable, too. They represent an attempt to bridge and smooth over the atmosphere of disagreements, intolerance and open religious animosity which have plagued Buryatia for many centuries and brought a lot of sufferings to its people. However, this naive approach shows a lack of deep study and understanding as regards the views and practices of the three distinct religions Bɵ Murgel, Buddhism and Orthodox Christianity which are active on Buryatian soil today. It is also dangerous to cobble these together as this creates a mixture which, if consumed, will cause spiritual indigestion.

All spiritual systems have their precise principles. If those principles are broken or changed the particular fruit of a given path will not manifest and one may find oneself completely lost and without protection from the painful experiences of life and death. All religions change and adapt to the circumstances and times they find themselves in; however, if their core is tampered with, real damage can occur. Therefore such statements as 'all religions have emerged from Shamanism' can lead to serious misconceptions. Certain religious systems – many streams of Hinduism, for example – are close to the 'shamanistic' religions in many of their outer and inner aspects or related in some way but we should be careful not to make glib comparisons. Notwithstanding some parallels, Yungdrung Bön and Buddhism cannot be said to trace their origins to 'shamanistic' religions as their teachings come from the Buddhas' own experience of the path to enlightenment and, as enlightened beings, Buddhas are completely beyond the control of any gods or spirits. On the contrary, it is in fact because of the Buddhas' total realization that they are beyond all the gods and demons in all universes. This is a completely different standpoint from that of any 'shamanistic' or theistic religion or path.

Another very important point of difference between the two traditions is the final goal of the practice. The final result of Yungdrung Bön is

---

27 Huhe Münhe Tengeri and the Sky Gods; Mother-Earth and the Underworld.

28 *Dharmakaya*, *Sambhogakaya* and *Nirmanakaya*.

29 Father, Son and Holy Ghost.

freedom from further reincarnation,[30] from the suffering of *samsara*, going beyond dualistic vision to liberation in the Natural State[31] of one's own mind which is the base of everything and is the ultimate Buddha. A Bɵ-priest, on the other hand, can never become Huhe Münhe Tengeri – Eternal Blue Sky, which is the ultimate source of existence according to the Bɵ Murgel religion. The highest realization a Bɵ can attain is to become one of the long-living, sky-dwelling Tengeri gods in the high heaven which is within the domain of the Eternal Blue Sky. That means that final goal of Bɵ Murgel is never outside *samsara*. This is very, very far from the final realization of Yungdrung Bön.

As the Buddhas' teachings came into a certain cultural and religious environment in a certain time and place, some already existing notions, outward forms, methods and terminology were adopted to facilitate understanding – people cannot relate to something which is explained in terms and categories completely beyond their experience and alien to them. Thus some aspects of 'native' systems were used and transformed by the Buddhas to convey the view and the main purpose of their teachings; this is a pattern seen throughout the history of religion. Similarities between certain external aspects of Yungdrung Bön and Buddhism in general and those of 'shamanic' systems may, at first glance, lead us to presume that they are related on a deeper, spiritual level, too, but when we look deeply and carefully into their origins and views we discover that these traditions are fundamentally different in terms of their path and final goal. One of the purposes of this book is to clarify these kinds of differences.

---

30 Although, having attained full realization, a newly emerged Buddha sends countless myriads of emanations to countless worlds to lead sentient beings out of *samsara* because of his Bodhisattva vows, s/he is beyond suffering, karmic causes, birth and death.

31 Tib. gnas lugs.

CHAPTER I

Historical Backdrop to Bön and Bɵ

Part I
The Lands of Bön

1. Lands of Prehistoric Bön of Eurasia

From time immemorial very archaic traditions with a common cultural and religious core were spread all over the Eurasian continent, including Scandinavia and the British Isles. I refer to this as the Prehistoric Bön of Eurasia. As we know that a great variety of nations and racially diverse tribes practised these similar traditions, we can assume this cultural and religious phenomenon had a universal character. This exceedingly ancient religion's ancestral lands most probably lie in the circumpolar region of Eurasia.[1] From there they spread all over the Eurasian continent with waves of migrating tribes, nations and races, eventually reaching North and then South America as the influx of Asian migrants crossed Beringia, the Bering land bridge. Scholarly opinion remains divided on the subject of when exactly these waves of migration occurred. Ice sheets advanced and retreated several times during the Pleistocene period[2] with intervals of 40,000 and 100,000 years and the last Ice Age ended around thirteen thousand BC[3] Due to the resulting rise and fall in sea level, this bridge was raised and submerged several times during the Pleistocene, providing several windows when Eurasians could have first used this perfect route to the Americas. Some scholars put the beginning of this

---

1 We will deal with the Polar Theory in more detail in ch. XV.

2 The geological period from 1,800,000 to 11,550 BP. The end of the Pleistocene roughly corresponds to the end of the Palaeolithic period.

3 E. P. Borisenkov, V. M. Pyasetskii, *Tysyacheletnyaya letopis' neobychainykh yavlenii prirody* (Moskva, 1999). Cited in N. P. Guseva, *Slavyane i Ar'i: Put' Bogov i Slov* (Moskva: Fair Press, 2002), p.31.

migration anywhere between 70,000 and 11,000 years ago and many agree that there were major movements of people over this land mass between 14,500 and 12,000 years ago. These migrants brought the culture and religious strands of the Prehistoric Bön of Eurasia with them into the Americas, as can be clearly seen by the many matching spiritual traditions and ritual objects across many tribes of Native Americans of both the South and North. Some comparative studies have been published on this subject but much more needs to be done to establish and explain these similarities in a clear and precise way.[4] Indeed, while in Mexico in 2000 I myself saw ritual objects identical to the Tibetan Bönpo *namkha*[5] hanging in an ordinary office. Some Mexicans use these for protection from ghosts and to deflect curses sent by witches. This is just a small example illustrative of how strands of the Prehistoric Bön of Eurasia are, in some shape or form, still very much a part of Native American culture even now.

Some strands of the Prehistoric Bön of Eurasia also reached Sumatra, Java, Borneo and other islands of Polynesia as people migrated either overland when these islands were connected to China and the

---

4 For example, Chögyal Namkhai Norbu mentions direct parallels between the *kiva* ritual constructions and *chog* used in rituals of the Bönpo deity Zhang Zhung Meri (Tib. Zhang zhung Me ri). See Chögyal Namkhai Norbu, *The Origins of Tibetan Culture and Thought,* (Merigar, Arcidosso: Shang Shung Edizioni, 1995). A large comparative study of Navajo and Tibetan spiritual traditions was attempted by Peter Gold in 1994 (Peter Gold, *Navajo & Tibetan Sacred Wisdom: The Circle of the Spirit* [Rochester, Vermont: Inner Traditions, 1994]). Well illustrated and informative, this work highlights many parallels in both cultures although there are many inaccuracies regarding Tibetan pre-Buddhist culture, largely stemming from the author's referral to predominantly Buddhist sources. Consequently the real root and origins of those aspects of Tibetan culture which can be directly compared to those of the Navajo are often overlooked; they are in fact borrowings which Buddhists took and adapted from Bönpo traditions. Both the Navajo and the Tibetan traditions have common roots in the Prehistoric Bön of Eurasia, a connection worthy of further study.

5 Tib. nam mkha' –'space', 'sky'. Can refer to the physical sky or spiritual dimension while in Dzogchen texts it is sometimes used to designate one of the Three Spaces (Tib. mkha' klong dbyings gsum), qualities of the Natural State. In terms of ritual objects, *namkha* is a multi coloured thread-cross which comes in many shapes and forms depending on the specifications given in the text for the ritual where it is used. Can symbolize the mind and energy of the person for whom the ritual is performed or a dwelling place for the gods and demons. *Namkhas* are used in a wide variety of astrological and ransom rituals.

Asian mainland,[6] or later by sea. These ancient traditions also reached Bali and Sri Lanka where there are still some ritual objects similar to *namkha* as well as ritual traditions which can be traced to Bön.[7] More study is needed to elucidate this. It is probable that the Prehistoric Bön of Eurasia reached or could have reached more lands and been practised there in some form. However, due to its extreme antiquity, the lack of written sources, persecution and destruction brought about by the spread of new Monotheist religions, it is inevitable that today some lands have completely lost all traces of these spiritual traditions.

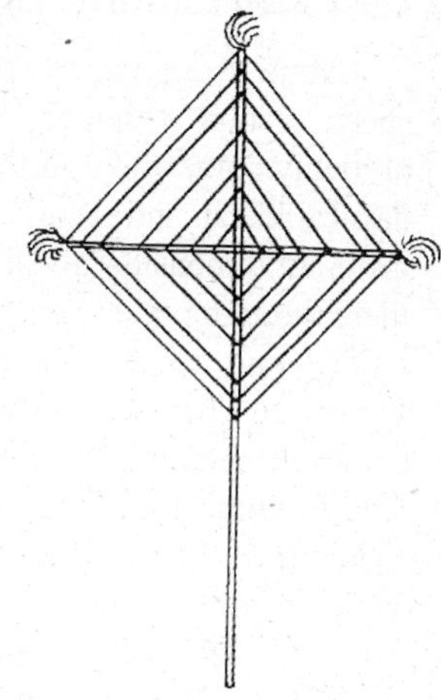

Fig. 1. Basic namkha *shape.*

2. Lands of Yungdrung Bön

Tagzig

Although the real origin of Yungdrung Bön lies beyond time, space and history, in terms of planet earth it began in Central Asia in the country of Tagzig which occupied a large territory covering the lands of the modern Central Asian states of Tajikistan, Kyrgyzstan, Kazakhstan, Uzbekistan, Turkmenistan and Iran. It is in Olmo Lungring,[8] the central region of this large country, in the southern royal palace of Barpo Sogyed[9] that the Buddha Mura Tahen,[10] known in Tibetan as Tonpa Shenrab Miwo, was born in 16,017 BC[11] and it was here that he turned the wheel of the teachings of Drungmu Gyer,[12] known in Tibetan as Yungdrung Bön.

---

6 Around 14,000 BP.

7 Gabriele Fahr-Becker (Ed.), *Arte dell'Estremo Oriente* (Köln: Konemann, 1999). For the discussion on the possible routes by which Prehistoric Bön of Eurasia may have spread see ch. XV.

8 Tib. 'Ol mo lung ring.

9 Tib. Bar po So brgyad.

10 Tib. dMu ra Ta hen.

11 This is the date according to traditional Bönpo chronology communicated by Yongdzin Lopön Tenzin Namdak. Chögyal Namkhai Norbu puts the date of his birth much later, at 1917 BC. See Namkhai Norbu, *Drung, Deu and Bön* (Dharmasala, LTWA, 1995), pp.156–158.

12 Tib. Drung mu Gyer.

The sacred land of Olmo Lungring

Olmo Lungring is the heartland of Tagzig and as such enjoys special status. Although its earthly location is to the northwest of Tibet probably somewhere in the Pamir or Tien Shan Mountains of modern-day Tajikistan and Kyrgyzstan, Bönpo scriptures say that it also lies in a different dimension invisible to the ordinary eye. One can only be born there through prayer and spiritual practice and while ordinary people can neither find it nor be born there, some Bönpo *yogi*[13] can reach it even within their physical body and some were able to go there once they had achieved an appropriate level of realization. Guide texts describing the way to Olmo Lungring still exist but no Bönpo masters have travelled there since the Chinese takeover of Tibet in the 1950's which resulted in the third persecution of Yungdrung Bön. Buddhists, too, know Olmo Lungring but give it the name Shambhala.[14]

Why did Buddha Tonpa Shenrab Miwo choose to be born in Olmo Lungring rather than any other place on earth? Yongdzin Lopön Tenzin Namdak, the most senior teacher of the Yungdrung Bön tradition alive today, gives the following reply:

---

13 Tib. rnal 'byor pa – an advanced practitioner of Tantra and/or Dzogchen possessing psychic powers and special realization.

14 The notion of Shambhala appeared with the spread of Kalachakra Tantra in India in 11th -12th c. AD. According to this Tantra, Shambhala is a spiritual country governed by the virtuous Wheel-Holding Universal Kings to whom Buddha Shakyamuni imparted the teachings of Kalachakra Tantra. It is said to lie to the north of India, therefore suggesting modern-day Tajikistan as the most likely geographical site. Like Olmo Lungring, Shambhala is located on this earth but on different plane so it cannot be seen by ordinary people. The various parallels and differences in the descriptions of Olmo Lungring and Shambhala can perhaps be studied at some later date, but the overall concept together with the geographical locations would support the view that these two names, in fact, refer to the same holy land. This is the view held by many Bönpo masters, both contemporary and of the past, including Yongdzin Lopön Tenzin Namdak and Shardza Tashi Gyaltsen (See Karmay, *Treasury*, p. 23; also ch. IV, *Bönpo cosmology and the cosmology of the Abhidharma of Vasubandhu*). Western Scholars have a range of views on the location of Olmo Lungring and the historical context in which Tonpa Shenrab Miwo appeared on this earth. For a critical apparaisal of Kuznetsov's views on this see ch. VI, *i) Erroneous equation of Zoroastrianism and Mithraism with Yungdrung Bön.*

The seven early Buddhas[15] were all born there and preached all their teachings there, so the sentient beings of that place were already qualified to be students; they were ready to receive teachings. That is one thing. Secondly, it is the only place suitable for a real Buddha to take birth. In other places, Buddhas can come and help sentient beings but not all kinds of activities can be done in all places; some things can only be done in Olmo Lungring so therefore [Lord Tonpa Shenrab] focussed on Olmo Lungring and was born there.[16] [...] Many of our doctrines are originate from there and were translated into many languages such as Tagzig[17] and Zhang Zhung, and finally into Tibetan. [...] This [Olmo Lungring] is a real human place and it exists on earth although it is not commonly visible because it is a paradise. If you go to Mount Kailash and Manasarovar and look to the northwest, the texts tell us how far it is. It isn't calculated in miles or kilometres but in days' walk. All the details are here but you still can't see it because the only beings who exist there are those qualified to receive great teachings; normal beings are not able or not allowed to be born there.[18]

---

15 Seven Buddhas of Bön which preceded Tonpa Shenrab Miwo. For more information see ch. III.

16 This tallies well with the biography of Buddha Shakyamuni and the parallel idea of Shambhala in Buddhism. Buddha Shakyamuni was born in India and during the course of his life he gave mainly Sutra level teachings there. The sole Tantric teaching Buddha Shakyamuni gave on earth was the Kalachakra Tantra which he imparted to the King of Shambhala in Shambhala. Dzogchen teachings were not taught by Buddha Shakyamuni during his lifetime at all. It was Garab Dorje, a miraculous emanation who appeared 500 years later in the country of Uddiyana, the modern-day Swat Valley in Pakistan, bordering on Zhang Zhung, who taught Buddhist Dzogchen. In contrast, Tonpa Shenrab Miwo gave teachings on all three levels: Sutra, Tantra and Dzogchen, as well as on numerous rituals of Causal Bön, all of which are recorded in the Bönpo *Kanjur*. According to Yungdrung Bön scriptures, in a previous life Buddha Shakymuni was a disciple of Tonpa Shenrab called Sangwa Dhüpa (Tib. gSang ba 'Dus pa). That is the reason why Bönpos do not consider the teachings of Indian Buddhism as something extraneous to Yungdrung Bön although they admit not having time to practise them as they are busy with their own tradition.

17 Tib. Mu sangs sTag gzig, the original language from which the teachings of Tonpa Shenrab Miwo were translated into 360 languages. This language in turn originated from the Tib. g.Yung drung Lha – 'the language of the Gods of Swastika from the dimension of the Sky'.

18 Yongdzin Lopön Tenzin Namdak Rinpoche, *The Nine Ways of Bön; A Compilation of Teachings in France, Volume I*, Transcribed and edited by Carol Ermakova and Dmitry Ermakov (Shenten Dargye Ling, Blou, 2006) *Bön of the Fruit*, p. 57.

Fig. 2. Holy Land of Olmo Lungring. Mural from Triten Norbutse Bönpo Monastery, Kathmandu.

Olmo Lungring has as its centre the sacred mountain Yungdrung Gutseg,[19] Pyramid of Nine Swastikas, from the base of which flow nine rivers which divide the central land into the islands where the Eight Great Palaces[20] are located. Tonpa Shenrab Miwo was born in the southern palace of Barpo Sogyed. Beyond that there are many secondary lands and holy places separated by rivers and waterways with the twelve great cities in the four cardinal and four intermediate directions. The entire country is enclosed within the Mukhyud Dalwai Gyatso[21] ocean which

---

19 Tib. g.Yung drung dGu brtsegs.

20 Tib. rGyal sa pho brang gling brgyad.

21 Tib. Mu khyud bDal ba'i rGya mtsho.

in turn is surrounded by an impenetrable snowy mountain range, Walso Kangri Rawa.[22] Thus the Holy Land is completely sealed from the outside world. As we have seen, only a person of outstanding spiritual virtue and realization can reach this hidden country in the physical body and the only physical way to enter is by the Arrow Way,[23] a tunnel in the outer mountain range created by Tonpa Shenrab Miwo himself as he shot an arrow through it when leaving Olmo Lungring in pursuit of the demon king Khyabpa Lagring.[24] The tunnel is very long and completely dark. Ferocious beings guard the entrance and it takes nine days to traverse it.

Olmo Lungrig is governed by the seven royal clans: Mushen, Ho, Shag, Po, Gya, To and Nyan.[25] Mushen is the chief clan among them and it is within this royal family that Tonpa Shenrab Miwo was born. In the Inner Region of the country the Divine Language of the Swastika[26] is spoken while in the other lands people speak eight Transformed Languages[27] derived from it.

The Zhang Zhung Confederation

To a large extent, Tibetan civilization was built upon the Bönpo culture and religion of the country of Zhang Zhung. Even Tibetan Buddhism itself is deeply influenced by both Prehistoric and Yungdrung Bön in its ritual and sometimes even in its doctrinal aspects. The study of Zhang Zhung civilization, culture and religion is therefore of paramount importance for those wishing to gain a deep understanding of Tibetan culture and for those seeking to preserve it.

Meaning of the name Zhang Zhung

The etymology of the name *zhang zhung* has been interpreted in several ways by scholars. The country was probably initially called Zhung, which translates into Tibetan as *khyung*,[28] horned eagle, and is the name of a class of very important and very ancient Bön sky-gods. The same type of divinity is also present in the Hindu pantheon and is related to the god Vishnu. This parallelism can be traced back to very archaic

---

22 Tib. dBal so Gangs ri'i Ra ba.

23 Tib. mDa' lam.

24 Tib. Khyab pa Lag ring.

25 Tib. dMu gshen, Hos, Shag, dPo, rGya, gTo, gNyan.

26 Tib. g.yung drung lha yi skad.

27 Tib. bsgyur ba'i skad.

28 Tib. khyung.

times before the sacred Hindu texts, the Vedas, were written down[29] and the Zhang Zhung and Aryan pantheons of gods were still within the same cultural and religious pool, namely, the Prehistoric Bön of Eurasia.

The meaning of the word *zhang* is not so clear. According to some scholars *zhang* means 'maternal uncle', an honorific title pointing to the supremacy of the Zhang Zhung confederation over lesser tribes and neighbours. This interpretation is further supported by the later stage of Zhang Zhung history when Tibetan kings began marrying princesses from Zhang Zhung.[30] According to another interpretation, *zhang* means 'sky', 'space' and as a synonym of the Zhang Zhung word *mu*[31] can be translated into Tibetan as *namkha.*[32] So the name *Zhang Zhung* can be translated as either Maternal Uncle Khyung or as Sky Khyung. This second interpretation underlines the paramount importance of the cult of the sky for the people of Zhang Zhung who indeed claim descent from the sky-gods.[33]

Geographical borders and the language of Zhang Zhung

Zhang Zhung was a very large country, or more correctly, it was a confederation of eighteen tribal states or kingdoms which covered the huge territory of the Tibetan plateau as well as some lands of western China to the east. It bordered Tagzig to the west. In the northwest Zhang Zhung bordered the large country of Thogar,[34] modern-day Chinese Turkestan, whose population was mainly made up of Indo-European Tokharians with some proto-Mongol peoples and, later, Kashgar. Towards the northeast Zhang Zhung bordered various establishments and states of proto-Mongol and Tyurkic peoples. In the southwest Zhang Zhung included Ladakh and bordered Uddiyana and Kashmir while in the south it included some territories of northern Nepal such as Dolpo and Mustang. Further towards the southeast Zhang Zhung encompassed some northern territories which are now under Bhutan, Sikkim and the Arunachal Pradesh State of India. In those days borders were not controlled in the same way as they are now; they were less well defined and highly porous, which often gave rise to armed conflicts between neighbouring tribes and

[29] I.e. before 4500 BC according to Bal Gangadhar Tilak, see ch. V.

[30] See Norbu, *Drung, Deu and Bön,* Introduction, p. xvi.

[31] Z-zng. mu, rmu, dmu.

[32] See Siegbert Hummel, *On Zhang-Zhung* (Dharamasala: LTWA, 2000) p. 82, n. 1.

[33] For other explanations on the meaning, see ch. XV.

[34] Tib. Tho gar.

Fig. 3. *Tagzig Pungso Chewa script (Tib. rTag gzigs kyi yi ge spungs so che ba).*

Fig. 4. *Tagzig Pungso Chungwa script (Tib. rTag gzigs kyi yi ge spungs so chung ba).*

states. Ruins of military outposts scattered throughout the Himalayas and Tibet provide physical traces of Zhang Zhung, as do rock carvings and inscriptions in places far beyond the borders of modern Tibet.

Living traces of the Zhang Zhung language are found in the later Tibetan dialects (notably those of Amdo and Kham), in languages of the neighbouring peoples such as Minyag, Lolo and Nakhi (Naxi) as well as in a number of Himalayan languages such as Bhotia, Hruso, Dafla, Toto, Dhimal and Kinnauri. For centuries many Tibetan Buddhist scholars and later those Western Tibetologists influenced by them, maintained that the Zhang Zhung language was artificially created by the Bönpos to give credibility to their 'fake' traditions which were, it was claimed, no more than plagiarized Buddhism. However, this false notion has been completely discredited following the discovery of authentic Zhang Zhung texts in the Dunhuang collection[35] in Chinese Turkestan, as well as that of several bilingual Tibetan-Zhang Zhung texts. Thanks to the work of great researchers of Bön such as Professor Namkhai Norbu, Yongdzin Lopön Tenzin Namdak, Siegbert Hummel and others, it is now clear that the Tibetan alphabet and scripts are modelled on those of Zhang Zhung and were not, as was previously maintained, created on the basis of Sanskrit by Thonmi Sambhota[36] on the orders of the Tibetan Buddhist king Srongtsen Gampo[37] in the seventh century AD. Although the seventh and eighth centuries AD did indeed see changes imposed on the Tibetan language, script and grammar, the aim of these modifications was to facilitate the spelling of Sanskrit terms and names into the newly translated Buddhist texts from India and as such these changes were merely incorporated

---

[35] See for example F.W. Thomas, 'The Źang Źung Language', *Asia major*, NS 13/1-2 (London, 1967), pp. 211–217.

[36] Tib. Thon mi Sam bho ta.

[37] Tib. Srong btsan sGam po.

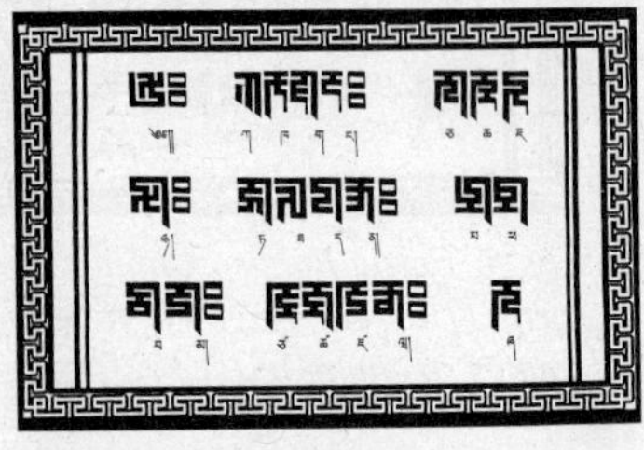

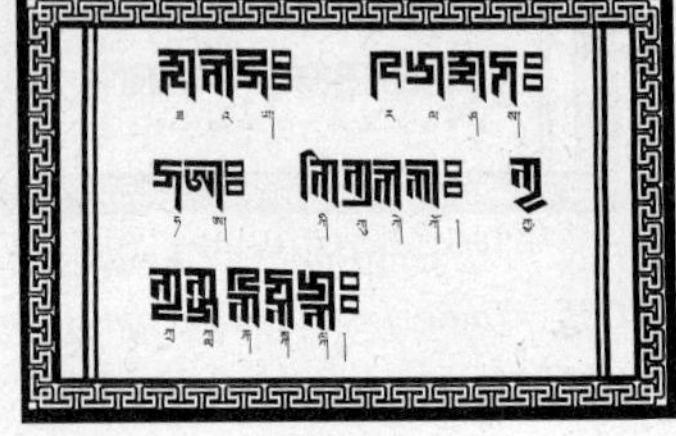

Fig. 5. Zhang Zhung Marchen script: Om Ma Tri Mu Ye Sa Le Du mantra, Triten Norbutse Monastery and alphabet.

Fig. 6. Zhang Zhung Marchung script.

into the already existing scripts and grammar which were based on the scripts and grammar of Zhang Zhung. The Zhang Zhung language had many writing systems with different scripts such as Dragyig,[38] Yiggen,[39] Mardrag,[40] Marchung[41] and Marchen[42] which developed from the Punyig[43] of Tagzig. The Tibetan Uchen[44] script developed from Marchung while the Druma[45] script developed from Marchen, both of which were used to write the dialects of Outer Zhang Zhung. The language of Zhang Zhung was the *lingua franca* of the Tibetan court well into the eighth century

---

38 Tib. drag yig.
39 Tib. yig rgan.
40 Tib. smar sbrag.
41 Tib. smar chung.
42 Tib. smar chen.
43 Tib. spung yig.
44 Tib. dbu chen.
45 Tib. 'bru ma.

AD.[46] This is evident from the fact that the Tibetan kings bore titles and names in the Zhang Zhung language. Objections may be raised on the grounds that legal documents pertaining to the Tibetan Empire of the eighth century AD were written entirely in Tibetan; however, this alone does not disprove the prominence of the Zhang Zhung language in early Tibet. Take, for example, nineteenth century Russia where the nobility and the educated spoke French while legal documents were written in Russian, the official language of the country.

Sacred geography of Zhang Zhung

Sacred Mountain

At the centre of the sacred geography of Zhang Zhung lies Mount Tise[47] or Kailash. An exceedingly holy site for many Himalayan peoples and several world religions, it is known under various names. Kailash is venerated by the Jains and Hindus of India and Kashmir, especially by Shivait tantric *yogis*, by Buddhists of all kinds both inside and outside Tibet, by the priests and followers of Prehistoric Bön traditions in Nepal and, of course, by Tibetan Bönpo following Prehistoric Bön, Yungdrung Bön and Bön Sarma,[48] New Bön. Spiritual practitioners from all these faiths consider it their religious duty to undertake a pilgrimage to Mount Kailash at least once in their lifetime as doing so is believed to be an extremely virtuous action which can purify eons of negative karma, bring spiritual purification and ensure a better rebirth in the next life.

Why does this mountain in a remote and empty region have such an elevated spiritual status? I believe it is because for all these diverse spiritual traditions Mount Kailash represents and symbolizes the World Mountain, the centre of the world where Sky meets Earth. To the Bönpo it is known as Rirab,[49] to Hindus and Buddhists it is Meru or Sumeru and to Jains it is Ashtapada. Each one of these spiritual traditions believes that very important and powerful deities reside on this mountain peak. For followers of Prehistoric Bön still practising in and around Tibet, Mount Tise is a residence of their gods and the source of their power. For followers of Yungdrung Bön in particular, Tise is the most important sacred geographical feature on the spiritual landscape of Tibet; it is

---

46 Oral information from Drubdra Khenpo Tsultrim Tenzin (Tib. sGrub grwa mKhan po Tshul khrims bsTan 'dzin). See also Karmay, *Treasury*, p.28 and Hummel, *On Zhang Zhung*, p. 8.

47 Tib. Ti se.

48 Tib. bon gsar ma.

49 Tib. Ri rab.

the soul mountain of Zhang Zhung,[50] Zhang Zhung Bönri,[51] the Bön Mountain of Zhang Zhung. It is the abode of an important meditation deity, a wrathful *yidam*[52] of Bönpo Tantra called Walchen Gekhöd[53] in his warrior-god form of Zhang Zhung Meri,[54] a wrathful Buddha-form taken by the Buddha of Bön Tonpa Shenrab Miwo in order to subdue and eliminate all inner and outer negativities and through which one can attain complete realization. A large number of important worldly gods who act as protectors of Yungdrung Bön, Zhang Zhung and Tibet also reside on Tise. For Shaivites and indeed for Hindus in general, Kailash is the residence of the god Shiva and his consort Parvati, also known as Uma, Gauri,Durga, Kali or Shakti. For the Jains Kailash is the seat of their founder-prophet Rishabanatha's spiritual realization. For Buddhists it is the residence of Chakrasamvara and Vajra Varahi, two important *yidam* deities of Buddhist Tantra, as well as of a number of *Dharmapala* (religious protector deities).

How is it this mountain, the centre of Zhang Zhung, can take precedence as one of the most sacred places for all these religions? I propose that the explanation lies in the fact that, no matter how different they are today, all these diverse traditions have their cultural roots in the Prehistoric Bön of Eurasia which was spread throughout Eurasia by migrating peoples. Some of the important migration routes to Nepal, India and Kashmir, especially for Aryans, must have passed through the territory of Zhang Zhung and many tribes of Nepal which still adhere to various forms of Prehistoric Bön today have actually migrated from this area at different points in time.[55] Even before Zhang Zhung became a multi-national state where people of various tribes and races mixed physically and culturally in some way similar to modern-day USA, diverse tribal groups and kingdoms must have gone through a long period of multi-cultural development in the very archaic epochs of prehistory.[56]

---

50 Tib. bLa ri Gangs dkar Ti se.

51 Tib. Zhang zhung Bon ri.

52 Tib. yid dam; a manifestation of Buddha in the form of the deity which is used as the primary means for obtaining realization. The Bönpo understanding of *yidam* is not limited to a tantric deity as it often is in Buddhism; the supreme *yidam* of Bön is the Natural State of Mind although even a text or prayer can be referred to as *yidam* if used as a primary practice. It is sometimes is translated into English as 'tutelary deity'.

53 Tib. dBal chen Ge khod.

54 Tib. Zhang zhung Me ri.

55 See ch. XV.

56 We will delve a little deeper into this fascinating subject in ch. XV.

Four Sacred Rivers

Mount Tise symbolizes the centre of our world and according to Bönpo texts the four great rivers flow in the four directions from the feet of the four surrounding mountains:[57]

- In eastern Zhang Zhung the River Tachog Khabab[58] flows east from the foot of Mount Tachogdzin[59] which has the shape of a standing horse;
- In northern Zhang Zhung the River Senge Khabab[60] flows north from the foot of the mountain Senge Gyingba[61] which has the shape of a standing lion;
- In western Zhang Zhung, in Khyunglung,[62] the River Langchen Khabab[63] flows west from the foot of the mountain Khyungchen Pung[64] which has the shape of a standing elephant;
- In southern Zhang Zhung the River Magya Khabab[65] flows south from the foot of the mountain Magya Dzejyi.[66]

These Four Sacred Rivers of Zhang Zhung correspond to the four major rivers of South Asia: Indus, Sultej, Brahmaputra and Karnali. Sutlej, Brahmaputra and Karnali are the main tributaries of the River Ganges or Ganga. According to Hindu scriptures, the divine River Ganga fell from the sky onto the summit of Mount Kailash where it was tamed by the god Shiva who, in order to prevent it from flooding the world, separated it into four smaller rivers and sent them flowing in the four cardinal directions so that the world would be properly irrigated.

This Hindu myth confirms the sacred geometry of Zhang Zhung as described in Bönpo texts and highlights its importance and spiritual influence over a huge region of Asia.

---

[57] After Namkhai Norbu & Ramon Prats, 'Ga‰s ti se'i dkar c'ag: A Bon-po Story of the Sacred Mountain Ti-se and the Blue Lake Ma-pa‰, Excerpts in English', Istituto Italiano per il Medio ed Estremo Oriente, Serie Orientale, Vol. LXI (Roma, 1989), p. 115.

[58] Tib. rTa mchog Kha 'bab.

[59] Tib. rTa mchog 'dzin.

[60] Tib. Seng ge Kha 'bab.

[61] Tib. Seng ge 'Gying ba.

[62] Tib. Khyung lung.

[63] Tib. gLang chen Kha 'bab.

[64] Tib. Khyung chen spungs.

[65] Tib. rMa bya Kha 'bab.

[66] Tib. rMa bya mDzes brjid.

Four Sacred Lakes

Mount Tise is surrounded by Four Sacred Lakes which are very important features of the sacred landscape of Zhang Zhung and of South Asia as a whole. According to Bönpo sources, the Four Sacred Lakes are said to be of celestial origin, formed from four cosmic eggs which appeared from empty space and burst by their own inner power:

- Lake Gurgyal Lhamo,[67] shaped like a round silver mirror, appeared at the foot of Mount Pöri Ngäden[68] from the white conch-shell cosmic egg. This lake is inhabited by the *Lu*[69] water-spirits who guard the masses of treasures hidden in their underwater world. It takes a day to circumambulate it on foot.
- Lake Mapang Yutsho[70] appeared from the blue turquoise cosmic egg.
  The wish-fulfilling tree of *Lha*,[71] *Lu* and humans grows inside the lake. Lake Mapang is the residence of two powerful *Lu*-goddesses,[72] Mapang Yuchugma[73] and Zichen,[74] who live in a great underwater palace, Yukhar Namkha Zitho,[75] made of precious turquoise and *zi*[76] stones and filled with the treasures of the *Lu*. The underwater dimension of the lake is filled with heaps of precious jewels, golden sand, crystals, corals and medicinal plants. On the surface the lake takes the shape of a turquoise *mandala*[77] and in the four cardinal and four intermediate directions it is surrounded by various treasures and holy places. It takes four full days to circumambulate it.
- Lake Langag Silmo[78] appeared from the golden cosmic egg. It is located to the left of Lake Mapang, on the right ledge of

---

67 Tib. Gur rgyal Lha mo.

68 Tib. sPo ri Nga ldan.

69 Tib. Klu.

70 Tib. Ma pang g.Yu mtsho (g.Yu mo).

71 Tib. lha, sky-gods.

72 Tib. klu mo.

73 Tib. Ma pang g.Yu phyug ma.

74 Tib. gZi chen.

75 Tib. g.Yu khar Nam mkha' gZi mtho.

76 Tib. gzi.

77 Tib. dkyil 'khor, a graphic two-dimensional representation of the sacred three-dimensional geography of the cosmos.

78 Tib. La ngag bSil mo.

Mount Tise between the mountains Tagri Trabo[79] and Dugri Nagpo.[80] The lake is full of the treasures of *Lu* and in its centre there is an island with many holy meditation places. It is in the shape of the four continents joined together and it takes eight days to circumambulate it on foot.

– Lake Gungchu Ngulmo[81] appeared from the iron cosmic egg. Mount Tsenden Marpo[82] lies to the east, Mount Lutsen Ngonpo[83] to the north, Mount Drongtse Nagpo[84] to the west and Mount Düdtsen Nagpo[85] to the south.[86]

There are many other important lakes in Zhang Zhung forming significant reservoirs of spiritual energy within its scared landscape. One is Lake Namtsho Chyugmo[87] (Tengri) at the foot of Mount Nyenchen Thanglha[88] and another is Lake Dangra Yutsho[89] at the foot of Mount Targo[90] in Changthang.[91]

Most major sacred lakes have dual status: they are perceived as living sentient beings while simultaneously serving as the residence of the eponymous *Lu* kings and queens who control large swathes of countryside even far beyond the borders of Zhang Zhung. This dual nature of the lakes' spiritual status no doubt shows the overlay of the religious ideas of Yungdrung Bön onto those of Prehistoric Bön; the more ancient layers of early Bön (according to which the lakes themselves were actually living beings) were fused with the ideas of incoming Yungdrung Bön in the collective culture of local nomad population descended from the ancient Zhang Zhung tribes.

Besides these two functions, the lakes also serve as the living space for other sentient beings such as aquatic animals, ordinary *Lu* and their

---

79 Tib. sTag ri Khra bo.
80 Tib. Dug ri Nag po.
81 Tib. Gung chu dNgul mo.
82 Tib. Tsan dan Mar po.
83 Tib. kLu btsan sNgon po.
84 Tib. 'Brong rtse Nag po.
85 Tib. bDud btsan Nag po.
86 This presentation is based on Norbu & Prats, *Ga‰s ti se'i*, pp.111–113.
87 Tib. gNam mtsho Phyug mo.
88 Tib. gNyan chen Thang lha.
89 Tib. Dang ra g.Yu mtsho.
90 Tib. rTa rgo.
91 Tib. Byang thang.

livestock of *Lu*-sheep,[92] *Lu*-horses[93] and *Lu*-yak.[94] Yongdzin Lopön Tenzin Namdak once told me that the water-sheep, water-horses, water-yaks and so on are not merely legendary, mythological animals; they are a reality of life for the local people and many nomads of Changthang have seen them. They look very much like normal 'earth' animals but their coats are a little blueish. They often mix with the nomads' herds and on occasion even interbreed with the earth-animals. Sometimes, however, when they return into the lake the earth-animals follow after them and drown causing the nomads to despair. Other inhabitants of the lakes include various fish and aquatic monsters, and dragons are frequent visitors.

Among all the sacred lakes of Zhang Zhung, Lake Mapang is the most important as far as multi-religious worship is concerned. For the priests of certain areas of Nepal who practise what can be recognized as strands of Prehistoric Bön, the lake is the residence of their ancestral gods and goddesses who enter them in mediumistic trance in order to heal, predict the future and exorcise negativities. *Dhami* and *dhangre* priests of the Humla region of Nepal in particular must complete at least three pilgrimages to Lake Mapang and Mount Kailash. Although they receive 'the calling' from the gods in the place where they live, to attain their full power they must travel to Lake Mapang where they undergo ritual purification through bathing in its waters, thereby receiving complete initiation and powers from the gods and goddesses residing in the lake before they can take up office as a priest.[95]

For followers of Yungdrung Bön, Lake Mapang is also known under its Zhang Zhung name Madrö Dangra[96] and symbolizes the primordial nature of the universe and the nature of mind. The lake is named after the King of *Lu*, Madrö, who resides in its depths. Tonpa Shenrab Miwo himself visited this lake and taught his doctrine of Yungdrung Bön to his disciples, Bönpo priests, humans and 100,000 *Lu* ruled by their queen Lumo Ödenma,[97] Black *Lu*-Queen of Light, who rides a blue water-ox, holds a black snake in her hands and wears a blue snake around her body.[98]

---

[92] Tib. klu lug.

[93] Tib. klu rta.

[94] Tib. klu g.yag.

[95] See Gelek Jinpa, Charles Ramble, Carroll Dunham, Thomas Kelly, *Sacred Landscape and Pilgrimage in Tibet: In Search of the Lost Kingdom* (New York, London: Abbeville Press Publishers, 2005), pp.42–44, 64, 97–112.

[96] Tib. Ma dros Dang ra.

[97] Tib. kLu mo 'Od ldan ma.

[98] Ibid., p.100.

This same lake is known under the Sanskrit name earlier Manasarovar to Hindus who believe it was created directly from the mind of the god Brahma. This legend is directly encapsulated within the name itself since *manas* means 'mind' and *sarovar* means 'lake'. Hindus also view Lake Manasarovar as *yoni*, the symbol of *Shakti*, the universal female energy and consort of Shiva while Mount Kailash is viewed as Shiva's *lingam* representing the universal male energy. For Hindus, then, the worship of the sacred lake Manasarovar goes as far back as the worship of Mount Kailash itself with circumambulation and the purifying of spiritual pollutions by ritual washing in its waters forming an integral part of pilgrimage to the holy mountain. Today, the lake's spiritual significance across South Asia is as great as ever, a status exemplified, for example, by the fact that some of Mahatma Gandhi's ashes were ceremonially scattered into its holy waters after his death in 1948.

Lake Manasarovar is holy for Jains, too, who traditionally undertake a long journey in order to purify themselves through bathing in its waters and recharge the powers of their spiritual realization.

Buddhists believe that Buddha Shakyamuni's mother, Queen Maya, was brought to the lake and purified by the gods before giving birth to her son. So Lake Mapang is revered by Buddhists, too.

Administrative divisions and Royal Dynasties of Zhang Zhung

As was said above, Zhang Zhung was a huge confederation with eighteen main tribal states or kingdoms at its heart. It was divided into the three large regions:

- Western Region;[99] the main kingdom of Zhang Zhung. This geographical area came to be called Ngari Korsum[100] after coming under the control of the descendants of the Tibetan royal line in the late ninth century.
- Middle Region;[101] this included Bu[102] and Tsang,[103] the area of modern Central Tibet. It is here that, at the time of Zhang Zhung supremacy, the ancient Tibetan Kingdom of Yarlung[104] gradually developed and gained power.

---

[99] Tib. stod.

[100] Tib. mNga' ris sKor gsum.

[101] Tib. bar.

[102] Tib. dBu.

[103] Tib. gTsang.

[104] Tib. Yar lungs/Yar klungs.

- Eastern Region;[105] this included modern-day Kham[106] and Amdo.[107]

The heartland of the Zhang Zhung confederation was also subdivided into three main regions: Outer,[108]Inner[109] and Middle.[110]. The Outer Region was further subdivided into Right,[111] Left[112] and Central:[113]

- The Right Outer Region had three areas: mountains Tagri Trabo[114] and Mengyiri[115] as its Inner Area; Lamo Gangra[116] and Phyiri[117] as its Middle Area; and Khandro Duling[118] and Tsairi[119] in the Outer Area;
- The Left Outer Region had three areas: Mount Tise (Kailash) and Lake Mapang Yutsho were in the Inner Area; Mount Targo and Lake Dangra Yutsho in the Middle Area; and Mount Thanglha[120] and Lake Namtsho Chyugmo as the Outer Area;

- The Central Outer Region had three areas: Mount Phugkhyung Chenpung[121] and Kyunglung Ngulkhar[122] (Silver Castle of Khyung Valley) as its Inner Area; Mount Lhari Gyangdo[123] and Gyalkhar Phanling[124] castle in its

---

105 Tib. smad.
106 Tib. Khams.
107 Tib A mdo.
108 Tib. sgo.
109 Tib. phug.
110 Tib. bar.
111 Tib. gyas sgo.
112 Tib. gyon sgo.
113 Tib. dbus sgo.
114 Tib. sTag ri Khra bo.
115 Tib. sMan gyi ri.
116 Tib. La mo Gangs ra.
117 Tib. Phyi'i ri.
118 Tib. mKha' 'gro 'Dus gling.
119 Tib. rTsa'i ri.
120 Tib. Thang lha.
121 Tib. Phug khyung Chen spungs.
122 Tib. Khyung lung dNgul mkhar.
123 Tib. Lha ri Gyang mdo.
124 Tib. rGyal khar Phan gling.

Fig. 7. Approximate territory covered by Zhang Zhung, Sumpa and early Tibet (U and Tsang). Approximate borders established with the help of Yongdzin Lopön Tenzin Namdak, Drubdra Khenpo Tsultrim Tenzin and Geshe Lungrig Nyima.

> Middle Area; and Sele Gyakar[125] county and the Khyungpo Tingdzong fortress[126] as its Outer Zone.[127]

Within this administrative structure, the kings of the royal dynasty of the central region, Zhang Zhung *per se*, had the function of emperor and the kings of other states were their vassals.

The early Zhang Zhung empire was located in the region around Mount Kailash and then grew to encompass a vast territory. It was already organized as a state at the time of Tonpa Shenrab Miwo, who visited it and taught Bönpo priests of Zhang Zhung and the neighbouring countries.[128] The king of Zhang Zhung in those days was Triwer Sergyi Gyaruchen,[129] the Holder of the Golden Horned Crown.[130] He was of divine origin and

[125] Tib She le rGya dkar.

[126] Tib. Khyung po gTing rdzong.

[127] Based mainly on Norbu & Prats, *Ga‰s ti se'i*, p. 125.

[128] These Bönpo were practitioners of Prehistoric Bön before they met Tonpa Shenrab.

[129] Tib. Khri wer La rje Gu lang gSer gyi Bya ru can.

[130] Tib. bya ru.

the first of a line of eighteen royal Holders of the Horned Crown. These kings ruled Zhang Zhung from their capitals located in different parts of Zhang Zhung. Triwer Sergyi Gyaruchen and the two subsequent kings[131] ruled from the Yulo Jonpa[132] Castle of Gyangri[133] in the Kailash region. They bore Horned Crowns of *khyung* feathers and crystal respectively. The next three kings[134] ruled from the country of Gyalwanye[135] in Kyunglung. They wore Horned Crowns of Jewelled Light, Iridescent Light and Conch-shell. The next two kings[136] ruled from the Pumarhring[137] country of Zhang Zhung. They were bearers of the Horned Crowns of Coral Light and Gem Light. The two kings who followed[138] ruled from the Tsina[139] district of Zhang Zhung. They had Horned Crowns of Iron and Blazing Light. Next came two kings[140] who ruled from the Tarog[141] district of Zhang Zhung. They wore Horned Crowns of the Light of the Sun and Moon Crystals. After them two kings[142] ruled from the Tago[143] district of Zhang Zhung. They were crowned with the Horned Crowns of Sparkling Light and Lapis-lazuli Light. After them came four kings[144] from the countries of Khakyor,[145] Khayug,[146] Ladag[147] and Ruthog[148] who wore Horned Crowns of *Gajang*[149] Light, Blue Lily Light, Meteorite Lightning

---

131 The other two being: Tib. Zhung Zhag Zil gnon and Tib. Hri do Gyer spungs.

132 Tib. g.Yu lo lJon pa.

133 Tib. rGyang ri.

134 They were: Tib. sLas khraGu ge, Tib. g.Yung yar Mu khod, Tib. Kyi la Gu ge.

135 Tib. rGyal ba mnyes.

136 They were: Tib. sPungs rgyung gyer, Tib. Nye lo Wer ya.

137 Tib. Pu mar hring.

138 They were: Tib. sTag rna gZi brjid, Tib. Dzwo dmar This spungs.

139 Tib. Tsi na.

140 They were: Tib. bDud 'dul dbal, Tib. Li wer gyer.

141 Tib. Ta rog.

142 They were: Tib. Shel rgyung Hri do, Tib. Lig mur Nam mkha'.

143 Tib. rTa sgo.

144 They were: Tib. Mu wer nor, Tib. Sad hri gyer, Tib. Nye lo Wer ya, Tib. Mu dmar Thog rgod.

145 Tib. Kha skyor.

146 Tib. Kha yug.

147 Tib. La dvags.

148 Tib. Ru thog.

149 Tib. Ga ljang.

Metal and *Ana*[150] Light.[151] The period of the eighteen royal Holders of the Horned Crown was the golden age of Zhang Zhung when practitioners of Prehistoric Bön converted to the Yungdrung Bön of Tonpa Shenrab Miwo and its light spread throughout Zhang Zhung and her neighbouring countries.

The Zhang Zhung Confederation later suffered a decline due to the strengthening of one of its vassals, namely the Tibetan Kingdom. The power of the Ligmincha[152] kings of the last Zhang Zhung royal dynasty had declined greatly. Many lands were annexed and, in the seventh century AD, when Srongtsen Gampo[153] ruled Tibet, Zhang Zhung became Tibet's vassal, a full reversal of the previous situation.

ཁ་ཆེན་པ་ཤང་ཡིག་ཞི་ར་ཙ།
ཐམས་ཅད་དབང་བསྒྱུར་
སྲིད་པའི་རྒྱལ་པོ།

Fig. 8. Seal of Ligmincha kings of Zhang Zhung. The inscription reads 'king of existence, master of all'. This seal was brought from Menri Monastery in Tibet by one of the monks fleeing persecution at the hands of the Chinese and is currently held in the new Menri Monastery in Dolanji, India.

The King of Tibet's sister, Semarkar,[154] was instrumental in this initial period of Zhang Zhung's downfall. Unhappily married to the King of Zhang Zhung, through symbolic messages and songs, she passed secret information to the Tibetans regarding the affairs and movements of Zhang Zhung's king, suggesting ways to conquer his country. As a result, Zhang Zhung lost vast territories to Tibet.[155] In the following century, the Tibetan King Trisong Deutsen[156] again used treachery against Zhang Zhung. He conducted a clever covert operation which was nothing short of a real spy drama. The Tibetan minister responsible for gathering intelligence advised Trisong Deutsen to exploit a weak point

---

[150] Tib. A na.

[151] Based on the list in Norbu & Prats, *Ga‰s ti se'i*, pp.127–128.

[152] Tib. Lig mir gya; this is a generic title.

[153] Tib. Srong btsan sGam po.

[154] Tib. Sad mar kar.

[155] See Norbu, *Drung, Deu and Bön*, pp.32–33; Hummel, *On Zhang-Zhung*, pp. 109–118.

[156] Tib. Khri srong lDe btsan.

in Ligmincha's family life. Ligmincha had three wives the youngest of whom, Nangza Dronleg,[157] was only eighteen. She had not yet borne the king a child and was discontented with her low position in the court hierarchy. Aware of her unhappy lot, this spymaster saw the chance to turn the situation to his advantage by convincing her to spy for the Tibetans. Trisong Deutsen approved the plan and so an extremely cunning and wicked spy, Nannam Legdrub,[158] was sent as an ambassador to recruit the young queen. Nannam Legdrub came to Zhang Zhung with a yak horn full of gold dust and deceitful words persuading the queen to help the Tibetans assassinate Ligmincha. In return he promised Trisong Deutsen would make her his first queen following a successful takeover of Zhang Zhung. He did not, however, keep his word. Through coded messages left in a secret mountain location, the young queen provided the Tibetans with Ligmincha's travel plans and route. Acting on this intelligence, a covert military operation was subsequently launched; Tibetan soldiers ambushed and brutally murdered the last Ligmincha king of Zhang Zhung and his bodyguards as they were travelling on government business to the vassal state of Sumpa.[159] With the king dead, a power vacuum ensued causing the Zhang Zhung state to collapse from within. Its people and territory were taken over by the Tibetans.[160] The kingdom of Zhang Zhung may have disappeared, but despite all subsequent efforts to eradicate it in favour of the Buddhist religion and culture newly arrived from India, the culture and religion of Zhang Zhung had deeply penetrated all levels of Tibetan society and survives there to this day.

India

Although Shenrab Miwo never went to India, he taught the Bön of Mantras[161] to Bönpos of Zahor, Kashmir and Gilgit who met him when he was visiting Zhang Zhung, so his teachings arrived in parts of India at a very early stage. The second and major wave of Yungdrung Bön reached India during the time of Shenrab Miwo's son and successor,

---

157 Tib. sNang bza' sGron legs.

158 Tib. sNan nam Legs grub.

159 Tib. Sum pa.

160 See John Myrdhin Reynolds, *The Oral tradition of Zhang-Zhung: An Introduction to the Bonpo Dzogchen Teachings of the Oral Tradition from Zhang-Zhung known as the Zhang-zhung snyan-rgyud* (Kathmandu: Vajra Publications, 2005), pp.119–128.

161 Tib. bon sngags.

Mucho Demdrug,[162] who, according to traditional Bönpo reckoning, descended to earth from the realm of the *Cha*[163] gods in 6016 BC. Mucho Demdrug initiated and oversaw a large translation project which was accomplished by the Six Great Translators, one of whom was Lhadag Nangdro[164] of India. A further stream of Yungdrung Bön reached India from Zhang Zhung through master Kakhyung Pungpa[165] at the time of the Indian king Seö Yungdrung[166] and later reached various parts of northern India through the translators Shenpo Lisha[167] of India, Shenpo Braba Meruchan[168] of Kashmir and Shenpo Ge Tene Logya[169] of Gilgit. In short, Yungdrung Bön was spread and practised all over the Himalayas and in India even in very ancient times. The cycles of Indian Bön are known in Tibet as *Gyagar Bönkor.*[170]

China

China is also prominent among the lands where Yungdrung Bön flourished. Yungdrung Bön reached China as early as the time of Tonpa Shenrab. It was brought there by the Chinese king known in Tibetan as Gya Kongtse Trulgyi Gyalpo[171] who was a direct disciple of Shenrab Miwo. He was particularly learned and was entrusted with the teachings of Bönpo astrology[172] belonging to Causal Bön.[173] It was Trulgyi Gyalpo who introduced the astrology of the five elements,[174] the twelve year cycle[175] and the cycles of nine *mewa*[176] and eight *parkha*[177] (*pakua* [八卦] in Chinese) from which further Chinese astrological and divination

---

162 Tib. Mu cho lDem drug.
163 Tib. phywa, phya.
164 Tib. lHa bdag sNangs dro.
165 Tib. Ka khyung sPungs pa.
166 Tib. gSas 'od g.Yung drung.
167 Tib. gShen po Li sha.
168 Tib. gShen po Bra ba Me ru can.
169 Tib. gShen po Ge lTe ne Lo rgya.
170 Tib. rgya gar bon skor.
171 Tib. rGya Kong rtse 'Phrul gyi rGyal po.
172 Tib. rtsis.
173 Tib. rgyu bon.
174 Tib. 'byung rtsis; nag rtsis.
175 Tib. lo mdzod bcu nyis.
176 Tib. sme ba dgu.
177 Tib. spar kha.

systems later developed. The Four Medical Texts[178] reached China through Chebu Trishe[179] and were disseminated there.

The next wave of Yungdrung Bön came to China at the time of the Six Great Translators, one of whom was Lethang Mangpo[180] of China. He translated many Yungdrung Bön texts into Chinese. The higher teachings, the Bön of Fruit, also reached China. Tantric Bön was brought by the Chinese Bönpo master Gyabön Zingwa Thuchen[181] and the Dzogchen teachings of *Zhang Zhung Nyen Gyud*[182] were brought to China by the master Gyabön Salwa Öchen[183] who was a student of Rasang Trineko,[184] a *kushen*[185] Bönpo teacher of the Tibetan king Tagri Nyenzig.[186]

In short, China became a land of Yungdrung Bön as early as the times of Shenrab Miwo and over the millennia all the levels of his teachings were preached there.

In early times, the Tagzig name *gyer*, which was translated into Tibetan as *bön*, was translated into Chinese as *tao*, a term already used by priests of Prehistoric Bön traditions practising in China. Over the centuries, methods and ideas from Yungdrung Bön penetrated many streams of Chinese Taoism, both Tao Chiao and Tao Chia.[187] This is clear not only from their philosophy of emptiness and rituals but in some cases also from their ritual dress; the T'ien-shih Tao School of the Heavenly Teachers is a prominent example. One of the most important books of Chinese culture is *I-Ching – The Book of Change* – and most systems of Chinese philosophy, astrology and divination spring directly or indirectly from it. It serves as a common base for both Taoism and Confucianism as the philosophies of both Lao Tzu and Confucius are born from the study and practice of the teachings and ideas contained in this book. In turn,

---

[178] Tib. rGyud bzhi.

[179] Tib. dPyad bu Khri shes.

[180] Tib. Legs tang rmang po.

[181] Tib. rGya bon Zing ba mThu chen.

[182] Tib. Zhang zhung snyan rgyud.

[183] Tib. rGya bon gSal ba 'Od chen.

[184] Tib. Ra sang Khri ne khod.

[185] Tib sku gshen, royal priest cum bodyguard.

[186] Tib. sTag ri gnyan zig.

[187] Tao Chiao – 'Taoist Sect' refers to Taoist streams which use rituals and magic such as T'ien-shih Tao, the School of the Heavenly Teachers, and those in pursuit of immortality, while Tao Chia, 'Taoist School', designates schools of philosophical Taoism based on the teachings of Lao Tzu and Chuang Tzu. For more information see Holmes Welch, *Taoism. The Parting of the Way* (Rev. ed. Boston: Beacon, 1966).

I-Ching is based on the system of eight *parkha* taught by Tonpa Shenrab Miwo. The belief that the source of Taoism lies to the west of China was upheld by many Taoist scholars, such as Ko Hsuan (3rd century AD), for example. These scholars acknowledged that the original source of their religion lies in the mountains of Kun'-lun where Hsiwang-mu, the Goddess-Mother of the West, dwells. With Kun'-lun being a borderland of Tagzig, it is clear that many of the early Taoist teachings correspond to Causal Bön. The great Bönpo scholar and master of the last century, Shardza Tashi Gyaltsen,[188] clearly says that the T'ien-shih Tao School is a kind of Bön and calls its hereditary chiefs 'Namgyi Bönpo',[189] Bönpo of Heaven.[190] Another sign of Yungdrung Bön's influence on China's culture and religion is the widespread use by both Taoists and Chinese Buddhists alike of the symbol of left-turning Bönpo swastika or *yungdrung.*[191]

Sumpa

There is considerable confusion about the exact status and location of the country of Sumpa as there are in fact at least two areas known under this name. The original country of Sumpa was situated in the north of Zhang Zhung in the Great Steppe and occupied a vast territory, as big as that of Zhang Zhung itself. The self-designation for Sumpa and its people was most probably 'Sumbe', the name still in use among the Buryats and Mongols, while the Chinese called this tribal establishment Syanbi (Xianbei).

Bönpo texts mention Sumpa as a vassal state of Zhang Zhung but in this context reference is probably being made to the lands where groups of nomadic Sumpa warriors settled within Zhang Zhung's borders and reached some kind of political agreement with the central administration rather than to the actual Sumbe Empire of the Great Steppe, which never came under Zhang Zhung's rulership.[192] There is debate among scholars as to the precise area of modern Tibet in which the Sumpa enclave was situated in the time of the Zhang Zhung confederation, although the most likely location is in the eastern Tibetan province of Kham,

---

188 Tib. Shar rdza bKra shis rGyal mtshan (1869–1935).

189 Tib. gNam gyi Bon po.

190 Samten G. Karmay, *The Treasury of Good Sayings* (Dehli: Motilal Banarsidass Publishers Private Limited, 1972), p.116.

191 Tib. g.yung drung. See discussion in ch. XV.

192 There is another intriguing possibility of the origin and location of Sumpa which we will look into in ch. XV.

in Khyungpo.[193] This Sumpa establishment in Khyungpo is known as Sumpa Langgi Gyimshö.[194]

Yungdrung Bön would have initially reached the country of Sumpa through one of the Six Great Translators, Hulu Paleg[195] of Sumpa. Later, during the reign of time of the Tibetan king Tagri Nyenzig, Dzogchen teachings arrived with the Bönpo Dzogchen master Sumpai Awadong.[196] At the time of the second persecution of Yungdrung Bön under KingTrisong Deutsen, Bönpo texts on divination and magic were brought to Sumpa by the master Sumpa Walgod.[197]

Tibet – Country of Bön

Early Tibet

Today Tibet is the principal country of Yungdrung Bön as it is here that this tradition has survived up until now. So much has already been written about Tibet in the West that I will limit this discussion to locations and events salient to the Bönpo aspect.

Fig. 9. Nyatri Tsenpo.

Yungdrung Bön was first preached in the lands which later became Tibet by Tonpa Shenrab Miwo himself when he visited the region briefly on his way to Kongpo[198] in pursuit of the demon Khyabpa Lagring.[199] The only teachings Shenrab Miwo gave the contemporary Bönpo of Tibet who were already following Prehistoric Bön was one part of Causal Bön, namely that dealing with divine invocations and exorcism. He ordered those Bönpo who came to him to stop offering any blood sacrifices they

[193] Tib. Khyung po.

[194] Tib. Sum pa glang gi gyim shod.

[195] Tib. Hu lu sPa legs.

[196] Tib. Sum pa'i Bon po A ba ldong. The last word in the name of this master suggests he was from the lDong tribe.

[197] Tib. Sum pa dBal rgod.

[198] Tib. Kong po.

[199] Tib. Khyab pa Lag ring.

may have previously practised under Prehistoric Bön traditions and taught them how to use *torma*[200] offering cakes, substitutes made from roasted barley flour and other ritual methods to satisfy the gods and spirits instead.

Fig. 10. Yumbu Lagang castle.

The country of Tibet as such began when Nyatri Tsenpo[201] (born 1136 BC[202]) descended from the celestial dimension of the gods[203] of *Cha* by way of the nine-runged Ladder of *Mu*[204] to alight on the top of Mount Lhari Gyangto[205] in Kongpo holding the *Mu*-cord.[206] Those who saw his miraculous descent were so amazed that they carried him on their shoulders to Yarlung Sogkha[207] and declared him their king.

Although Tibet was populated by various tribes before Nyatri Tsenpo and both Prehistoric Bön and Yungdrung Bön were practised by various kinds of Bönpo priests in that region, there was neither king nor central

---

[200] Tib gtor ma.

[201] Tib. gNya' khri bTsan po.

[202] Not all sources agree about this date. Some claim he appeared in 126 BC while others suggest 414 BC. Chögyal Namkhai Norbu suggests he may have been a contemporary of Buddha Shakyamuni and therfore appeared in 6th c. BC. See Namkhai Norbu, *The Necklace of Gzi: A Cultural History of Tibet*, Dharmasala: Narthang Publication, 1981), p.11. In this book I give the dates for the Tibetan kings according to the Bönpo chronology of (Tib.) *bsTan rtsis*, composed in 1842 by Menri Khenchen Nyima Tenzin (Tib. sMan ri mKhan chen Nyi ma bsTan 'dzin), the Abbot of Menri Monastery, and in *Introduction of Bon which opens the mind*, (Tib. *Bon gyi ngo sprod blo gsar sgo 'byed*) by Geshe Tenzin Dogtrag (Tib. dGe bShes bsTan 'zin 'Brug Grags) unless stated otherwise. Some of these dates were kindly extracted by Geshe Gelek Jinpa (Tib. dGe bshes dGe legs sByin pa).

[203] Tib. Lha gnam gyi steng.

[204] Tib. dmu skas.

[205] Tib. Lha ri Gyang to.

[206] Tib. dmu thag. A *Mu*-cord was attached to the top of the king's head and connected to the sky realm of the *Mu* gods. Although Nyatri Tsenpo's father was from the *Cha* race of gods, his mother was a *Mu* goddess.

[207] Tib. Yar lung Sog kha.

government. Nyatri Tsenpo built the royal castle of Yumbu Lagang[208] and established the Yarlung Tibetan royal dynasty.

It is in his time that Bön of Fruit was first disseminated in Tibet by his preceptor Mushen Namkha Dzogchen[209] who brought Tantric and Dzogchen teachings from Tagzig. Nyatri Tsenpo also had two *kushen*, royal bodyguard priests, who were adepts of *Sangngag*,[210] Bönpo Tantra. The new country was named Bönyul[211] (Bönkham),[212] the Land of Bön. Over the centuries the spelling was corrupted to Bodyul[213] which is still Tibet's self-designation today.

The governing power of this new kingdom of Bönyul rested on a triple foundation: the king, the Bönpo priest and the doctrine of Yungdrung Bön, and it was governed by the three principles: Bön, *Drung*[214] (historical narrative) and *Deu*[215] (the science of symbols, enigmas and secret language). These two triads ensured Tibet more than one thousand years of stability which were accompanied by spiritual and material development.

The territory occupied by the early Tibetan kingdom was limited to an area corresponding to modern-day Tibet's two central provinces, U and Tsang, and there was a succession of forty-two kings. Several of the early Tibetan kings, starting with Nyatri Tsenpo himself, were devout and powerful practitioners of Yungdrung Bön and his son, King Mutri Tsenpo[216] (born 1074 BC),[217] attained the highest spiritual realization and became a *rigdzin*[218] lineage-holder among the line of the early Bön *Mahasiddhas*.[219] In this period the lineages and teachings of Bönpo Tantra and Dzogchen were held by the powerful lay *yogis* and *yoginis*[220]

---

208 Tib. Yum bu bLa sgang.

209 Tib. dMu gshen Nam mkha' mDog can.

210 Tib. gSang sngags.

211 Tib. Bon yul.

212 Tib. Bon khams.

213 Tib. Bod yul.

214 Tib. sgrung.

215 Tib. lde'u.

216 Tib. Mu khri bTsan po.

217 Ibid. A traditional Bönpo date.

218 Tib. rig 'dzin.

219 Tib. Grub thob Chen po. *Mahasiddha* is a great religious practitioner who possesses supernatural psychic powers and the realization of the ultimate truth.

220 Tib. rnal 'byor.

(*pawo*[221] and *khandro*[222]). The kings supported them by offering land and erecting temples for worship and teaching. Kings venerated these early Bönpo *Mahasiddhas* who were granted three honours:[223]

Fig 11. Mutri Tsenpo

- As for the body, they were granted the honour of not cutting their hair, wearing a white silk turban decorated with vulture feather, wearing a robe of white lynx fur with a colour of leopard, tiger and caracal fur, wearing white shoes with laces of silver chains;
- As for the speech, they were granted the honour of always speaking before the king on all government business;
- As for the mind, they were freed from taxation.

Traditions of Bönpo Sutra were held in this period by monks who had several monasteries and were also supported by the kings and the government.

First persecution of Yungdrung Bön

However, not all the kings held Yungdrung Bön in such high esteem. Tibet's eighth king, Drigum Tsenpo[224] (born 710 BC),[225] initially followed in the footsteps of his forefathers but at the age of twenty-seven he grew hostile towards Bönpo priests; he grew weary of the limitations they posed to his absolute power. As we have seen, Tibet was governed by the triple power base of king, doctrine and priest meaning that Bönpo royal priests enjoyed the same privileges and power as the king himself and were in some ways even superior to him, representing as they did two out of the three sacred principles of governance. Hungry for absolute power, Drigum Tsenpo suppressed Fruitional Bön along with parts of

---

221 Tib. dpa' bo.

222 Tib. mkha' 'gro.

223 Karmay, *The Treasury*, p.44.

224 Tib. Gri gum bTsan po

225 According to traditional Bönpo *bsTan rtsis* chronology. Professor Namkhai Norbu gives 1st c. AD.

Causal Bön and banished most of the Bönpo priests and sages saying there was no room for both authorities in the country. In so doing, he ordered the first persecution of Bön in 683 BC. However, he nevertheless left some parts of Causal Bön intact and appointed two Bönpo priests to remain at the royal court as his *kushen* to continue performing rituals for prosperity[226] and long-life.[227] During this difficult period, banished Bönpo masters took the texts in their possession and hid them in various places inside and outside Tibet, including Sumpa, to be re-discovered in the future. It is in this period that Tibetan Bönpo monasteries were destroyed and most monastic lineages were cut except for the lineage of Muzi Salzang[228] of whom we will speak later.

Having destroyed most of Yungdrung Bön in Tibet, King Drigum and his courtiers indulged in all sorts of irregular behaviour and excesses. But after three years, in 680 BC, the king lost his mind and ordered his subject Longam Tadzi[229] to pit his army against his own in a kind of military game. Before the battle, a Yungdrung Bön protector sent Longam a dream instructing him how to slay King Drigum, which he did, and usurped the throne. All the seven previous kings, known as the Seven Divine *Tri*,[230] had not left their mortal remains on earth when they died but had ascended to the dimension of the *Mu* sky-gods by means of the *Mu*-cord and *Mu*-ladder; King Drigum, however, did leave a corpse behind as he had severed his own *Mu*-cord and *Mu*-ladder while wielding his sword over his head in the heat of the battle. All subsequent Tibetan kings have left corpses after their death.

First restoration of Yungdrung Bön

After thirteen years, Longam was killed and Tsenpo Pude Gungyal,[231] one of Drigum's sons, was enthroned in 667 BC. The new king invited the Bönpo *Mahasiddha* Tongyung Thuchen[232] and one hundred other Bönpo masters from Zhang Zhung. They brought with them many religious texts which were newly translated into Tibetan thereby re-establishing Yungdrung Bön and Tibet's triple governing principle. Another wave of new translations came with the Zhang Zhung *Mahasiddha* Nyachen

---

[226] Tib. g.yang.
[227] Tib. tshe.
[228] Tib. Mu zi gSal bzang.
[229] Tib. Lo ngam rTa rdzi.
[230] Tib. gNam gyi Khri bdun.
[231] Tib. bTsan po sPu lde Gung rgyal.
[232] Tib. sTong rgyung mThu chen.

Lishu Tagring[233] in 552 BC. He brought ten thousand Yungdrung Bön texts from Tagzig and the teachings of Yungdrung Bön spread far and wide in Tibet.

First signs of Indian Buddhism in Tibet

Tibet first came into contact with the Buddhism of India in the reign of King Lha Thotori[234] (born in 254 AD). Indian Buddhism was brought by the monks of Khotan[235] but as the king did not show much interest in the doctrine, at this time Buddhism didn't spread widely, although some people practised the *mantra* of Avalokiteshvara. It seems that Buddhism was then probably more or less forgotten until the reign of King Srongtsen Gampo (born 569 AD).

Srongtsen Gampo was a very ambitious king, a cunning and shrewd politician, and under his rule Tibet's power increased greatly. He established strong political ties with Zhang Zhung, China, Nepal and India through marrying princesses from these countries, and exercised a high degree of political leverage through intrigues and military operations. A large portion of Zhang Zhung was annexed, becoming a vassal of Tibet, while China, too, lost some borderlands to Tibet; Tibet was expanding in all directions, giving considerable cause for concern to all the neighbouring countries. Srongtsen Gampo invited Buddhist monks from India who brought Buddhist texts and images, and shrines were built to house them in Lhasa.[236] Although Srongtsen Gampo privately followed Buddhism, Yungdrung Bön was not suppressed and the majority of the population firmly adhered to it.

Introduction of Indian Buddhism as a state religion and the second persecution of Yungdrung Bön

The turning point in the history of Tibet and Yungdrung Bön came in the reign of the thirty-eighth king, Trisong Deutsen (born 718 AD).[237] This king brought Tibet to the peak of its power and turned it into a dominant empire feared by its neighbours. He conquered vast territories

---

[233] Tib. sNya chen Li shu sTag ring.

[234] Tib. Lha tho Tho ri sNan shal.

[235] Some sources maintain Buddhism came miraculously in the form of a golden *stupa* descending from the sky into the hands of the king.

[236] Tib. lHa sa.

[237] According to traditional Bönpo *bsTan rtsis* chronology. Professor Namkhai Norbu gives 742–797 AD as the dates for this king. See Norbu, *Drung, Deu and Bön, Introduction,* p. xvii.

on all sides including further gains from China; Tibetan military power was great at this time. Trisong Deutsen forcefully persuaded kings of large nations such as the king of Tagzig in the west, the king of Gesar Trom[238] and the Buddhist king of India in the south to bridge rivers thereby facilitating travel for Tibetan traders. The wealth of the Tibetan Empire was growing through war and trade. Trisong Deutsen had great political talent and was also a master of intrigue. Seeking to become absolute monarch, he staged a royal coup to overthrow the power and political influence of the Bönpo clergy who had strong and ancient ties with the kingdom of Zhang Zhung. He was advised by his ministers that the best strategy for winning this royalist revolution would be to supplant Yungdrung Bön with the foreign religion of Indian Buddhism. Trisong Deutsen himself felt very devoted to Buddhism and so he invited the abbot Shantarakshita from India and the tantric master Padmasambhava from Uddigana. The first Tibetan Buddhist monks were ordained and the first Buddhist monastery Samye[239] was built. Enjoying the king's royal patronage and the support of the pro-Buddhist party in his government, Buddhist clergy grew both in numbers and in political influence. For his part, Master Padmasambhava was not concerned with politics; he transmitted the teachings of his lineage, adapting it to the new cultural and religious environment by selecting talented students (many of whom had already received a complete education in the Yungdrung Bön tradition) and by adopting many original Bönpo methods into the framework of his Buddhist tradition. Abbot Shantirakshita,[240] however, and new, overzealous Buddhist converts were openly hostile to Yungdrung Bön and made the king and ministers very aware of their views. They did not accept that Yungdrung Bön could be the teaching of a Buddha, albeit a Buddha other than their own, and as such simply another form of the same timeless doctrine. Instead sectarian Buddhists levelled heavy accusations against Yungdrung Bön practitioners, falsely accusing them, for example, of performing blood sacrifices.

---

[238] Tib. Ge sar Phrom.

[239] Tib. bSam yas.

[240] Shantirakshita is often given the name 'Bodhisattva' and there is some degree of confusion as to whether he was, in fact, directly involved in the Buddhist political campaign which led to the persecution of Yungdrung Bön. According to Yongdzin Lopön Tenzin Namdak it was not Shantirakshita himself who rallied for the destruction of Yungdrung Bön but one of the Tibetan converts to Buddhism who was also called Bodhisattva.

Seeing that the time was right, in 749 AD[241] Trisong Deutsen embarked upon what was to become a second persecution of Yungdrung Bön, both politically and religiously. The king presented Bönpo masters with three options: convert to Buddhism, leave the four quarters of Tibet or 'drink white water' (commit suicide by drinking excessive amounts of water).[242] Thus it was that, despite being introduced by means contrary to the principles taught by its founder Lord Buddha Shakyamuni, Indian Buddhism, one of the streams of the universal teachings of the countless Buddhas, became the state religion of Tibet and immediately became embroiled in politics.[243]

The later chapters of Tibet's history were mainly written by the victors, i.e. by sectarian Buddhist clergy hostile to Yungdrung Bön so the tradition was demonised and portrayed as a backward 'shamanistic' religion little more than black magic which then plagiarized Indian Buddhist texts to survive and compete with the new Buddhist Schools emerging in Tibet. This false view of Yungdrung Bön together with the violent means by which Indian Buddhism was introduced to Tibet have soured relations between Bönpo and Buddhists for more than a thousand years, doing a great disservice to the Tibetan people and the Tibetan social structure as a whole; repercussions of the events of that time are felt in Tibetan society up to this day.

Early non-sectarian masters

Despite this general background of animosity, there were always masters who understood the real value of both religions as streams of

---

[241] According to traditional Bönpo *bsTan rtsis* chronology. Samten Karmay gives between 780–790 AD as the date for persecution. See Karmay, *The Treasury,* Introduction, p.xxxii.

[242] Ibid., p. 90.

[243] It should be pointed out that this was not the way in which Indian Buddhism generally came to other Asian countries. In neighbouring China, for example, Buddhism came in a peaceful way and there was no conflict with the already existing religious streams of Taoism. In fact, quite the opposite; during the initial stages there was a positive exchange between these religions as both take the concept of emptiness as their core teaching. Bearing in mind that, as we have shown, many core concepts and practices of Taoism are derived from Yungdrung Bön, we can legitimately say that to some extent this was in fact a meeting between Yungdrung Bön and Indian Buddhism. A similarly amicable exchange could have happened in Tibet but the introduction of Buddhism as a political tool to further consolidate the king's power rather than as a purely spiritual tradition meant that the meeting of Yungdrung Bön and Indian Buddhism in Tibet took a very different form.

the universal Buddhist doctrine and who, practising and holding lineages of both traditions, attained the highest levels of realization. This kind of understanding of the real nature of both religions is summarised in the saying of the great master and *terton*[244] Gyermi Nyiö.[245] When asked whether he was Bönpo or Buddhist he replied:

> 'When the sun shines on a golden mountain,
> The mountain and the gold are identical.
> If you take a dual view of things, you may fall into extremism'.[246]

Even during the persecutions period of the eighth century there were masters who practised and sought to preserve both traditions. One of the most prominent was Vairochana[247] of Pagor,[248] one of Guru Padmasambhava's twenty-five heart-disciples. Educated in Yungdrung Bön in the earlier part of his life, Vairochana later took Buddhist monastic ordination. He was charged with bringing some of the most important Buddhist Dzogchen texts from India and translating them into Tibetan; these are included in the collections of *Vairo Drabag*[249] and *Vairo Gyudbum*.[250] Despite being a Buddhist monk, Vairochana did not lose his interest in Yungdrung Bön but practised both Buddhism and Yungdrung Bön equally. His main Bönpo teacher was Drenpa Namkha[251] who temporarily converted to Buddhism in order to save some important Bönpo texts from destruction[252] and who was an instrumental figure in the development of Bön Sarma, New Bön.[253] Against the background of the destruction of Yungdrung Bön texts and the persecution of Bönpo practitioners, Vairochana translated a number of important Yungdrung Bön texts which had previously not been translated into Tibetan, thereby contributing to the future development of Yungdrung Bön in

---

244 Tib. gter ston, treasure-discoverer.

245 Tib. Gyer mi Nyi 'od.

246 Karmay, *The Treasury*, p. 157.

247 Tib. Bai ro tsa na.

248 Tib. Ba gor.

249 Tib. Bai ro 'dra 'bag.

250 Tib. Bai ro rgyud 'bum.

251 Tib. Dran pa Nam mkha'.

252 Drenpa Namkha was one of the most powerful Bönpo lamas of that time. Seeing that the tide of time had temporarily turned against Yungdrung Bön, he struck a deal with Trisong Deutsen: the King would allow him to copy and hide important Yungdrung Bön texts if he converted to Buddhism. See Karmay, *The Treasury*, p. 90–97.

253 See ch. III.

Tibet in more auspicious times. The Bönpo texts which he preserved and translated were *Tsewang Böyulma*,[254] texts of the Indian Bön cycle *Gyagar Bönkor* such as *Tsewang Gyagarma*[255] from the Sanskrit; *Thegrim*[256] from the language of Gilgit, and many texts from the language of Zhang Zhung, including the cycle of *Ka Drangngama.*[257] These were later hidden as *terma*[258] to be rediscovered in more propitious times once the persecution had passed. Due to the hostility of several Buddhist lamas and ministers at the court towards even the Buddhist version of Dzogchen, the work of translating both Buddhist and Bönpo texts on Dzogchen had to be carried out in secret so Vairochana was eventually forced into exile.

Fig. 12. Vairochana of Pagor.

At the end of his life Vairochana manifested the rainbow body,[259] the highest realization of Dzogchen, demonstrating his great knowledge and realization. This level of realization cannot be achieved if a practitioner engages in false teachings or activities contrary to his lineage and the instructions of his master. It is clear, therefore, that Vairochana could not have been at fault translating, practising and preserving Bönpo texts; his realization is proof that he didn't go against his main Buddhist master Guru Padmasambhava's instructions and wishes thus we can safely surmise that there was no conflict between his Bönpo and Buddhist spiritual heritage and practice. Were it otherwise, by working on Yungdrung Bön texts, he

[254] Tib. Tse dbang bod yul ma.

[255] Tib. Tshe bang rgya gar ma.

[256] Tib. theg rim.

[257] Tib. bKa' drang nga ma. See Karmay, *The Treasury*, p. 163.

[258] Tib. gter ma. This is often translated into English as 'hidden treasure' or 'textual treasure' and refers to religious texts of Yungdrung Bön and later of the 'ancient' Nyingma tradition of Tibetan Buddhism which were hidden in times of persecution so that they could be found and practised in the future.

[259] Tib. 'ja' lus. Rainbow body is the fruit of Dzogchen practice. When a realized practitioner of Dzogchen dies, his/her physical body dissolves into the essence of the elements and disappears from this plane of existence so the only remains which left are some hair and nails.

Fig. 13. Guru Padmasambhava.

would have broken *samaya*[260] with his root master and would therefore not have been able to manifest such a high realization. The only logical conclusion we can draw from this is that Guru Padmasambhava did not oppose the teachings of Yungdrung Bön on the spiritual level.

Further proof that Guru Padmasmbhava himself was not hostile to Yungdrung Bön and that he didn't aim to suppress it is found, among others, in a text called *The Dö for the King composed by the Master Padmasambhava.*[261] This is an offering ritual to Pehar,[262] the main worldly protector of Tibetan Buddhists and the main guardian of Samye monastery, where we read:

> When you reached Rakṣa temples, at the South and the North,
> You pledged
> never harm
> the Bonpo.[263]

This passage recalls one of the original pledges which Pehar gave to Guru Padmasambhava when the latter had just arrived in Samye from the land of the Uighurs and was walking around this monastic complex prior to taking up definitive residence there. So it is clear then that Guru Padmasmbhava was non-sectarian.

Events that prevented the complete destruction of Yungdrung Bön

Persecution forced Bönpo lamas into hiding or into exile in the Great Steppe, China, Nepal, Bhutan and other countries. They took with them

---

260 Tib. dam tshig. *Samaya* (Sans.) is the spiritual commitment given to the teachings and to one's spiritual guide which must be kept pure and unspoilt otherwise probelms arise for one's practice and realisation.

261 Tib. Slob dpon padma mdzad pa'i rgyal mdos. Samten G. Karmay, *The Arrow and the Spindle: Studies in History, Myths, Rituals and Beliefs in Tibet* (Kathmandu: Mandala Book Point, 1998), p. 354–358.

262 Tib. Pe har, dPe kar, Pe dkar, sPe dkar, dPe dkar, Be dkar, dPe ha ra, Pe ha ra.

263 Ibid. p.357.

Bönpo texts which they managed to copy, while other texts were hidden as *terma* in various places inside and outside Tibet. Despite these attempts, many were destroyed by the Buddhist dominated government. Some shrines and temples of Yungdrung Bön were destroyed while others were transformed into Buddhist places of worship. Several Bönpo priests used magic to retaliate against the new oppressive political regime. In one such incident, Pe Negu[264] caused the River Tsangpo[265] to flow backwards causing extensive flooding.[266] However, the persecution continued and Yungdrung Bön suffered greatly.

Paradoxically, it was the collapse of Yungdrung Bön's heartland, Zhang Zhung, at the hands of King Trisong Deutsen when he killed the last Ligmincha king which saved Yungdrung Bön from total annihilation. At the time of the Tibetan invasion, the king of Zhang Zhung's royal priest was the great *Mahasiddha* Gyerpung Nangzher Lödpo.[267] He was the lineage-holder of the Bönpo Dzogchen cycle *Zhang Zhang Nyen Gyud,* a very powerful tantric *yogi* who had realized the powers of his *yidam* Zhang Zhung Meri. When Tibetan military killed Ligmincha this sage was in mediation retreat on an island in Lake Darog.[268] The main queen of Ligmincha, Khyungdza Tshogyal,[269] requested an audience with him and asked Nangzher Lödpo to put a stop to the anti-Bönpo activities of the Tibetan government and punish Trisong Deutsen for killing Ligmincha and destroying Zhang Zhung. Seeing the disastrous consequences of Trisong Deutsen's actions for his country and religion, Nangzher Lödpo agreed. He returned to his meditation island and, with a quarter of an ounce of golden dust given to him by the queen, performed the destructive magic ritual of *Ngub*,[270] a kind of 'magic missile'.[271] After a week of practice he divided the gold empowered with destructive mantra into three parts and threw the 'magic missiles' into Tibet. The first landed on the slope of Mount Sogkhai Punpo[272] and hit seven deer: two were killed and five wounded. Since then the mountain has been known as Yarlung Shawareng,[273] the Stiff Deer of Yarlung. The second 'missile' hit

---

[264] Tib. sPe Ne gu.

[265] Tib. gTsang po.

[266] See Karmay, *The Treasury,* p. 92–93.

[267] Tib. Gyer spungs sNang bzher Lod po.

[268] Tib. Da rog mtsho.

[269] Tib. Khyung bza' mTsho rgyal.

[270] Tib. rNgub.

[271] Tib. dzwo.

[272] Tib. Sog kha'i sPun po.

[273] Tib. Yar lung Sha ba sreng.

Fig. 14. Nangzher Lödpo throwing dzwo *magic missile.*

the lake on the side of Mount Yarlha Shampo.[274] The lake evaporated and the resident *Lu* water-gods fled. Since then the lake has been known as Yarlung Tshokam,[275] the Dry Lake of Yarlung. The third 'missile' hit the royal castle of Chyiwa Tagtse[276] which caught fire, and Trisong Deutsen fell ill.

Nangzher Lödpo's power was known far beyond the borders of Zhang Zhung so the Tibetan king quickly realized where the 'magic missiles' were coming from and immediately sent a delegation of one hundred horsemen to Zhang Zhung with large quantities of gold dust and orders to placate the anger of Gyerpung Nangzher Lödpo and ask him to withdraw his magic. The emissaries finally found him on his island and, prostrating to him, asked for his mercy. Nangzher Lödpo agreed to cure the king to avoid further unrest; if Trisong Deutsen were to die, Tibet would collapse causing another power vacuum and further violence. However, the Bönpo priest put three conditions on the delegation:

1. A large golden shrine should be built at the expense of the Tibetan king to entomb the remains of the slain Ligmincha;
2. The people of the Gurub clan – to which he himself belonged – should be exempt from Tibetan government taxes and should have privileges at the Tibetan court in Yarlung Sogkha;[277]
3. None of the 360 types of Yungdrung Bön teachings practised and taught by Gyerpung Nangzher Lödpo should be suppressed in any way.

The envoys accepted these conditions and those events marked the beginning of the end of the second persecution of Yungdrung Bön in

[274] Tib. Yar lha Sham po is the residence of the protector-deity of the eponymous Tibetan royal dynasty.

[275] Tib. Yar lung mTsho skam.

[276] Tib. Byi ba sTag rtse.

[277] Tib. Yar lung Sog kha.

Tibet. Nangzher Lödpo performed the ritual of *Sangtikyi Ngag*[278] drawing threads of gold as thin as horse-tail hair from all the orifices and pores of Trisong Deutsen's body whereby he recovered.[279]

It was not only Nangzher Lödpo who applied magical pressure to the Tibetan King in order to stop the persecution. The principal guardian of Yungdrung Bön, Machog Sidpai Gyalmo,[280] appeared to Trisong Deutsen in a dream in the form of a terrifying naked woman with iron hair and ordered him to halt the persecution or lose his life. Furthermore, as the performance of many rituals of Causal Bön, including funerary rites, had been abruptly interrupted, the protector-deities of the Tibetan kingdom withdrew their services and the beings of the Eight Classes[281] sent drought, famine and infectious disease against humans and animals. Indeed, the king himself suffered ill health and the country's situation was grave. As the newly arrived Indian Buddhists were not equipped with methods for remedying the situation, Trisong Deutsen decided to recall the Bönpo lamas. He entreated the great Bönpo *yogini* Choza Bönmo[282] to find the Bönpo lamas in hiding or in exile and persuade them to return. He promised to end the persecution of Yungdrung Bön and allowed Drenpa Namkha to return to his original practice. Choza Bönmo brought many priests back from the northern frontier and the Takla Makan desert. On their advice, the black Bönpo *chörten*[283] and the Biharling Duse Khangtsig[284] Bönpo temple for subduing negativities were built in Samye. Long-life rituals were performed for the king and Tibet slowly began to prosper once more. The Bönpo were offered three districts of Tibet and dominion over several tribes. Thangpu[285] of Lhasa was designated as their worship place and Yarlung Sogkha as their dwelling place. The king said:

> 'As I have called you back, I ask you to bring out the textual treasures and practise Bön and Buddhism together.'[286]

---

[278] Tib. gSang this kyi ngag.

[279] For translation of the original historical text see Karmay, *The Treasury*, pp. 97–99 and Reynolds, *The Oral Tradition of Zhang-Zhung*, pp. 119–128.

[280] Tib. Ma mchog Srid pa'i rGyal mo.

[281] Tib. sde brgyad. See ch. V.

[282] Tib. Co za Bon mo.

[283] Tib. mchod rten.

[284] Tib. Bi har gling Du gsas Khang brtsigs.

[285] Tib. Thang phu.

[286] I.e. there should be religious tolerance in the kingdom. Karmay, *The Treasury*, p. 101.

Trisong Deutsen returned to the ancient tradition and reinstated the office of the *kushen* royal Bönpo priests. Despite the fact that most of the subsequent kings favoured Buddhism, the office of *kushen* was upheld by all the Tibetan kings until the end of the royal dynasty. Later on in life, Trisong Deutsen experienced a change of heart towards Yungdrung Bön and even sponsored new translations of Bönpo texts, such as *Lubum*,[287] from the language of Zhang Zhung into Tibetan. He also helped to preserve and conceal other important Bönpo texts and ritual objects; Bönpo texts were hidden in numerous locations all over the country, including within Samye monastery where they were placed inside the walls of Buddhist shrines and inside the huge Buddhist statues, an extremely clever strategy to ensure their preservation for 'the darkest place is right under the lamp', as the saying goes.

Bönpo sources differ as to the cause and date for Trisong Deutsen's death. Some say he died at the age of fifty-nine, i.e. in 777 AD[288] while others maintain he was poisoned by his wives at the age of thirty-six which would bring the date of his death even earlier, to 754 AD.[289]

The waning of the Tibetan monarchy and the demise of Tibetan independence

Trisong Deutsen was succeeded by one of his sons, Mune Tsenpo,[290] who was soon poisoned by his own mother. Muthug Tsenpo,[291] another of Trisong Deutsen's sons, was then enthroned. He respected Yungdrung Bön and later he and Shenpo Khyungpo Gyerdame[292] took many Bönpo texts, including medical texts and Tantras of Wạlphur,[293] from his father's treasury and hid them in Pagro,[294] Bhutan.

The next king was Darma Ralpachen,[295] one of Muthug Tsenpo's sons. He invited the Buddhist scholar Jinamitra from Kashmir and ordered the revision of the Buddhist translations made in the time of his

[287] Klu 'bum – *The Scripture of a Hundred Thousand Lu.*

[288] Samten Karmay gives 797 AD as the date of Trisong Deutsen's death. See Karmay, *The Treasury,* Introduction, p. xxxii.

[289] Provided we take 718 AD as his year of birth as found in Traditionsal Bönpo *bsTan rtsis* chronology.

[290] Tib. Mu ne bTsan po.

[291] Tib. Mu thug bTsan po.

[292] Tib. Khyung po Gyer zla med.

[293] Tib. dBal phur Nag po is the Bönpo Phurba.

[294] Tib. sPag ro phug gcal.

[295] Tib. Dar ma Ral ba can.

grandfather Trisong Deutsen. This king was a stern adherent of Hinayana Buddhism of the Vaibhashika[296] School so he forbade further translation of Buddhist Tantras. He was also fanatical about Indian culture and ordered all Tibetan traditional measures to be replaced with Indian ones. He venerated Buddhist monks with excessive zeal and ordered each monk to be given seven families over which he should act as lord and preceptor. In exchange they would provide the monk with anything he needed. Anyone criticizing or going against the Buddhist monks in any way risked severe punishment. Under these unnecessarily privileged and luxurious conditions, Buddhist monastic institutions grew extremely rich. As a result, not only did they depart from the word and spirit of Buddha Shakyamuni's doctrine but they also became corrupt, putting a huge strain on Tibet's people and economy. It was in Darma Ralpachen's reign that a Buddhist monk, Drankar Palgyi Yonten,[297] became a high-ranking minister and this king is accused of leaving the affairs of the state to such minister-monks.[298] It was against this background that a party of the royal court staged a *coup d'état*; they killed King Ralpachen and put his brother, Lang Darma[299] (born 901 AD),[300] on the throne. Despite his overzealous, almost obsessive devotion to Buddhism, King Ralpachen had retained the office of *kushen* Bönpo royal priests so the ancient tradition continued despite the switch in state religion and the king's personal religious preferences. The *kushen* and their relatives were protected from any physical harm by royal decree and their privileges and honours remained the same as in the old days.

Although it is generally believed that King Lang Darma favoured Yungdrung Bön, this notion stems from later Buddhist sources which are based not on history but rather are motivated by an anti-Bönpo political agenda. Studies carried out by Samten Karmay suggest that Lang Darma was in fact most probably a Buddhist put in power by lay ministers objecting to the growing influence Buddhist monks were exerting over the country and its economy. Indeed, there is little evidence to suggest he did much to significantly repair the damage Yungdrung Bön had suffered.

---

[296] Tib. sDe ba gZhi brag.

[297] Tib. Bran ka dPal gyi Yon tan.

[298] Karmay, *The Arrow and the Spindle.*

[299] Tib. gLang Dar ma. 'Lang' is a nickname heralding from his father, (Tib.) Se na legs, whose nickname was (Tib.) gLang mJing yon, 'the ox that has a crooked neck'. Lang Darma's real name was (Tib.) bTsan po Khri Dar ma, or (Tib.) 'Wu'i dun brtan. Karmay, *The Arrow and the Spindle,* pp. 15–29.

[300] According to the traditional Bönpo *bsTan rtsis* chronology. Samten Karmay gives 836–842 AD for Lang Darma's reign, Karmay, *The Treasury*, p.104.

Instead he became known for tough government reforms which saw the destruction of Buddhist monasteries and the defrocking of Buddhist monks (the monasteries of Yungdrung Bön having been destroyed and their monks disbanded previously, either in the times of Drigum Tsenpo or in the second persecution, or both). Buddhist scholars often present Lang Darma as a kind of devil incarnate who destroyed Buddhism but in reality his policies were not motivated by religious intolerance nor by a desire to persecute Indian Buddhism as such. Rather, they were economical and political countermeasures undertaken by the government to curb the excesses of the Buddhist monastic clergy and save the Tibetan economy, sucked thin by the monasteries, from collapsing. Buddhist lay practitioners, married Buddhist lamas and tantric *yogis* were not persecuted and were largely allowed to continue their life and practice as normal, hence we cannot speak here of a persecution of Indian Buddhism *per se* but rather of a dissolution of the monasteries in some way akin to that undertaken by King Henri VIII of England in 1535–1538. King Lang Darma was later assassinated by the Buddhist monk Lhalung Palgyi Dorje,[301] the abbot of Samye monastery, who, disguised, managed to steal close to the king on an official occasion and shoot him at point-blank range with a poisoned arrow from a bow hidden under his robes. He then fled. This murder caused the Tibetan Empire to collapse and fragmentize; the realm fell into a period of anarchy during which little is known about the developments in Yungdrung Bön or Buddhism.

The assassination of Lang Darma was a most unfortunate event in Tibetan history because with his death the triple principle: king, Bön and priest on which Tibetan society had initially been founded and had rested for almost two thousand years was shattered in one blow. That spelt the end of Tibetan unity and independence and gave ground for the continuous political and sectarian infighting which plagued Tibet until the Chinese People's Liberation Army took over in 1959 and all the conflicting parties and religious Schools were equally obliterated. Thus from Lang Darma's death up until now, Tibet has always been under the control of foreign powers – Mongols, Chinese, Manchu and British – either directly or indirectly.

Second restoration of Yungdrung Bön

Paradoxically, this dark time at the end of the Tibetan Empire was a period when the monastic lineage of Yungdrung Bön unexpectedly re-

---

[301] Tib. Lha lung dPal gyi rDor je.

emerged. One day, a Mongolian slave of the king of Menyag,[302] Sogpo Trelagchen,[303] was tending the king's horses in the mountains when he came upon the Dragkar Tsedu[304] cave. On entering it he saw a person dressed in monk's robes but with hair so long that it lay on the ground and his nails rolled in coils. The slave, filled with awe, first prostrated and then ventured to touch the sage, who remained motionless. The slave returned again and again to the cave and finally succeeded in waking the mysterious monk. He was in fact a Bönpo monk named Muzi Salzang, mentioned earlier, who had entered a special meditation of 'suspended animation' in 911 BC[305] at the time of the fierce internal struggle within Bönpo monastic community in order to preserve the *Dulwa*[306] or Rules of Monastic Discipline of Yungdrung Bön.[307] Muzi Salzang ordained the

---

302 Tib. Me nyag.

303 Tib. Sog po sPrel slag can.

304 Tib. Brag dkar rTse 'dus.

305 Per Kvaerne, A Chronological Table of the Bon Po The Bstan Rcis of Ni ma Bstan 'Jin, pp. 203–248, *Acta Orientalia*, XXXIII, p. 226.

306 Tib. 'dul ba, Sans. vinaya.

307 One might think this sounds like a fairy tale, some kind of 'sleeping beauty' but this kind of meditation result is relatively common among both Bönpo and Buddhist practitioners of Sutra. For example, a number of Chan' Buddhist monks entered a similar state at the end of their life. The latest example of similar kind of meditation hrecently came to light in Buryatia. In 1927 Hambo Lama Itigelov died while in meditation and was buried. Before his death he had told his students to come and check on him in a thirty year or so. So in 1955 Hambo Lama Barmaev together with some monks unearthed the body, which was still intact. They put it back as the Communist regime of the Soviet Union would not tolerate any display of Buddhist miracles. In 2002, 75 years after his death, the body of Hambo Lama Itigelov was unearthed once more and brought to the Gelugpa Monstery of Ivolginskiy Datsan called Hambyn Sume (Bur. Хамбын Сумэ). The body of the monk had no signs of decay and looked just as if he were alive. When it was examined by scientists two years later they were amazed to see that his skin was as that of a living person and his joints were fully flexible. Since 2002 the body of Hambo Lama Itigelov has attracted large numbers of people who, among other miracles, reported instances of spontaneous curing from diseases. The administration of Ivolginskiy Datsan is now bulding a special temple to house the body. This kind of realization at the end of one's spiritual path is not peculiar to Bönpo or Buddhists alone. In the town of Gubbio in the Umbria region of Italy there is a church where the body of a Catholic saint, Santo Ubaldo (1085–1160), is resting in a glass sarcophagus. Despite the fact that he died in 12th c. his face has a healthy complexion and it appears he is just sleeping. Santo Ubaldo is very highly venerated by the local population of Gubbio and many miracles are attributed to him, such as leaving a hand print in rock while saving the

slave, giving him the monastic name Tribar Tsultrim.[308] Tribar Tsultrim passed the lineage on and so the Bönpo monastic system revived and gradually spread[309]. As we have seen, King Lang Darma completely destroyed monastic Buddhism in Tibet and so the lineage of Buddhist Vinaya had been severed. However, in these dark times a Buddhist practitioner, Lhalung Paldo,[310] met a Bönpo monk called Nyotsun Arin[311] and requested to be brought into the presence of his abbot to ask for ordination. He gathered a group of seven Buddhists from the provinces of Tsang and U and they travelled together to see the abbot Lachen Gongpa Rabsal.[312] He ordained them saying:

> My spiritual lineage goes back to Bön and is the 'Order of the Individual Liberation.'[313] Follow this. As for (religious) practices, you should observe the customs and rules (of this order). I want you to take four signs in memory of my being (the officiating) abbot. Your doctrine will be very extensive. Whichever doctrines of an Enlightened One are spread, it is good.[314]

And so the Bönpo monastic lineage was introduced into Tibetan Buddhism. This is stated in both Bönpo and Buddhist texts.[315] The four signs which the Buddhists promised to observe were using blue for the three parts of their monastic robe and meditation mat. If it were not possible to make the entire robes from blue cloth, then at least the vest trimming should be blue. This can still be observed in the monastic robes of some of the older Buddhist monastic establishments. It also said that the Tibetan monks' custom of wearing a yellow hat started at this meeting.[316]

---

town from an earthquake and stopping a hostile army, as well as miraculous cures. Although both these instances of 'suspended animation' are similar to that of Muzi in their external aspect, there is a huge difference in the inner aspect as Muzi awakened from his absorption and came back to life in a physical sense. Not only that, he gave teachings, instructions and conferred the monastic initiation so that his spiritual lineage revived.

[308] Tib. Khri 'bar Tshul khrims.

[309] According to Samten Karmay this meeting occurred in 888 AD. See Karmay, *The Treasury,* p. 106, n 1.

[310] Tib. Lha lung dPal rdo.

[311] Tib. bNyos btsun A rin.

[312] Tib. bLa chen dGongs pa Rab gsal.

[313] I.e. similar to the Vinaya of Theravada in Buddhism.

[314] Karmay, *The Treasury,* p. 108.

[315] Ibid.

[316] Ibid., p 109.

Another important factor in the restoration of Yungdrung Bön was the discovery of *terma* texts. Although some teachings and lineages were not destroyed or concealed during the eighth century persecution, including very important ones such as the Dzogchen cycle of *Zhang Zhung Nyen Gyud* and Tantric cycle of *Zhang Zhung Meri* among the 360 texts practised by Gyerpung Nangzher Lödpo, the subduer of Trisong Deutsen, these teachings which were practised without interruption amounted to a mere drop in the ocean of Yungdrung Bön's scriptural wealth. It was in 913 AD that the rediscovery of the hidden textual treasures began and the first to come to light were the Tantras of Walphur Nagpo[317] and texts on magic. These were found by three Nepalese thieves who crossed into Tibet in search of gold and, after hunting high and low, finally came to Samye. There they found a sealed box and, thinking it contained gold, took it and ran away. However, when they opened the box later they only found three leather bags full of Bönpo texts. Undaunted, they carried this box with them until they ran out of food, by which time they had arrived a village in Tolung.[318] There they met a Bönpo, Tazhi Trulse,[319] and exchanged one volume from one of the bags for food. Tazhi Trulse practised the teachings in that volume and passed them on.

The Nepalese thieves then headed north and met three Tibetan Buddhists on their way to Samye in search of hidden Buddhist texts. The Nepalese told them they had already found textual treasure and would give it to them in exchange for a horse loaded with provisions. The Tibetans were suspicious and tried to pull out the texts out of the bags to check whether they were indeed Buddhist but their attempts were thwarted as each time they picked up a text it started emitting sparks. Taking this as a sign of authenticity, they agreed to the swop and took the texts with them. Later they stopped in a village in Latod[320] where they opened the bags but were dismayed to find that all were Bönpo. They then sold them to Zegur,[321] their host's nephew, who was himself a Bönpo. The bags contained a total of 340 texts mostly dealing with Walphur Nagpo. Zegur practised these teachings and passed them on, and so they spread.[322]

---

[317] Tib. dBal phur Nag po – Bönpo Phurba, one of the five main meditation deities of the gSas mkhar group of Bönpo Tantra.

[318] Tib. sTod lung.

[319] Tib. mTha' bzhi 'Phrul gsas.

[320] Tib. la stod.

[321] Tib. gZe gur.

[322] See Karmay, *The Treasury*, pp. 118–122.

Political turbulence meant that both Yungdrung Bön and Buddhism alike had lost a great number of texts and as this story illustrates, practitioners of both traditions found themselves in the same situation of trying to find the hidden texts and restore their traditions. When a Buddhist *terma* was discovered by a Bönpo *terton* treasure-finder he would give it to Buddhists, and vice versa. Several important *tertons* were both Bönpo and Buddhist. To a certain extent, then, the animosity between the two traditions gave way to cooperation, at least among some individuals.

Another dilemma was shared by the Bönpo and the Buddhists of the School of the Early Translations, Nyingmapa, as they later became known. Both these traditions found themselves in the same situation when their doctrines and authenticity were confronted by the new wave of Buddhism coming from India via the kingdom of Guge[323] in the west and spreading to central and eastern Tibet. Gradually the Kadampa,[324] Sakyapa,[325] Kagyudpa,[326] Jonangpa[327] and later the Gelugpa[328] schools of Tibetan Buddhism (collectively known as Sarmapa,[329] the New Schools) developed based on the new translations of Indian Buddhist texts by Rinchen Zangpo,[330] Marpa Lotsawa,[331] Ra Lotsawa[332] and others.

After the discovery of the first Bönpo *terma* in 913 AD many other *termas* were uncovered but it was not until about a hundred years later that Shenchen Luga[333] (996–1035 AD), from the Shen[334] clan descended from Tonpa Shenrab's son Kongtsha Wangden,[335] made his major discovery at Dritsham Thakar.[336] In 1017 he found a great number of Bönpo texts covering all levels of Yungdrung Bön teachings. Shenchen Luga had many disciples and the teachings spread far and wide. In particular, he entrusted disciples from other holy Bönpo clans with the task of maintaining and

323 Tib. Gu ge.
324 Tib. bKa' dams pa.
325 Tib. Sa skya pa.
326 Tib. bKa' brgyud pa.
327 Tib. Jo nang pa.
328 Tib. dGe lugs pa.
329 Tib. gSar ma pa.
330 Tib. Rin chen bZang po.
331 Tib. Mar pa Lo rtsa ba.
332 Tib. Rva Lo rtsa ba.
333 Tib. gShen chen Klu dga'.
334 Tib. gShen.
335 Tib. Kong tsha dBang ldan.
336 Tib. 'Bri mtshams mTha' dkar.

propagating the teachings. To Namkha Yungdrung from the Dru[337] clan he entrusted the teachings on cosmology[338] and metaphysics;[339] to Zhuye Legpo[340] of the Zhu[341] clan he entrusted Dzogchen teachings, and to Paton Palchog[342] from the Pa[343] clan he entrusted Tantric teachings. Two masters from the Meu[344] clan, Meu Lhari Nyenpo[345] and Meu Dampa,[346] met the lineage-holders of the Dru, Zhu and Pa and received teachings from them.

In 1072 lamas of the Dru clan established the monastery of Yeru Wensakha[347] which became a great centre for spiritual learning and practice until it was destroyed by flood in 1386. This family line came to an end when two reincarnations of the Panchen Lama[348] were recognized there, thus cutting the line of descent. Lamas of the Zhu clan established the monastery Kyikhar Rizhing[349] while those of the Meu family established the monastery of Zangri.[350] All these monasteries were situated in the Tsang province. This was a period when the unique form of Tibetan monasticism gradually took shape in both Bönpo and Buddhist religious communities, namely the study and practice of all levels of the teachings pertaining to Sutra, Tantra and Dzogchen as part of the monastic curriculum.[351] In particular, a very distinct approach to

---

337 Tib. Dru Nam mkha' g.Yung drung.
338 Tib. mDzod phug.
339 Tib. Gab pa.
340 Tib. Zhu yas Legs po.
341 Tib. Zhu.
342 Tib. sPa ston dPal mchog.
343 Tib. sPa.
344 Tib. rMe'u.
345 Tib. rMe'u Lha ri gNyen po.
346 Tib. rMe'u Dam pa.
347 Tib. gYas ru dBen sa kha.
348 Tib. Pan chen bLa ma, the second most important spiritual and political position in the Gelugpa School which has controlled the Buddhist central government of Tibet from 17th cent. The two Panchen Lamas born in the Dru family were the Second Panchen Lama (born 1663) and the Fifth Panchen Lama (1855–1881).
349 Tib. sKyid khar Ri zhing.
350 Tib. Zang ri.
351 In this period, Dzogchen teachings were included into the monastic curriculum of Yungdrung Bön and Nyingma monastic institutions alone as many scholars of the Sarmapa Schools fiercely rejected the validity of Dzogchen in numerous writings. However, Dzogchen entered the Karma Kargyud School at the time of the Third Karmapa Rangjyung Dorje (Tib. Rang 'byung rDo rje, 1284–

this unified spiritual training was developed in Yeru Wensakha where philosophic analysis, logic and debate were used to further the monks' understanding of Sutra, Tantra and Dzogchen.[352] A number of Bönpo Tantric *ngagpa*[353] communities were also active in many parts of Tibet led by lay Tantric *yogis*.

Among the many *tertons* who played a vital role in the restoration of both Yungdrung Bön and Buddhism, Bönzhig Yungdrung Lingpa,[354] known to the Buddhists as Dorje Lingpa[355] (1346–1405), deserves special mention. Considered a reincarnation of Vairochana of Pagor, he discovered many important hidden Tantric and Dzogchen texts of both traditions, among which are the Bönpo Tantric cycle of *Chyipung*,[356] the ritual cycle *Tsewang Böyulma* and the Dzogchen text *The Golden Needle of Great Perfection*[357] translated by Vairochana and hidden in Bhutan in the eighth century. As well as uncovering *termas* from both schools, Yungdrung Lingpa had a wide, non-sectarian attitude and taught both Buddhists and Bönpos. His idea became known as 'the oneness of Bön and Buddhism'[358] as is expressed in his song, *the Mystical Song of the Realization of the Oneness of the Bön Religion and [Tibetan] Buddhism.*[359] This open-minded attitude served as an inspiration for the nineteenth century masters of the non-sectarian Rime[360] movement in eastern Tibet such as Kongtrul Lodrö Thaye, Jamyang Khentse Wangpo, Choggyur Dechen Lingpa, Mipham Gyatso, Shardza Tashi Gyaltsen, Adzom Drugpa and Paltrul Rinpoche.[361]

The discovery of important Bönpo *termas* has continued up to this day and although most of the major teachings of Yungdrung Bön are

---

1339) and later many outstanding masters of all major Tibetan traditions practised and taught Dzogchen either openly or in secret.

[352] Tib. mdo sngags sems gsum.

[353] Tib. sNgags pa.

[354] Tib. Bon zhig gLing pa.

[355] Tib. rDo rje gLing pa. Karmay, *The Arrow and the Spindle*, vol II, pp.119–145.

[356] Tib. sPyi spungs.

[357] Tib. rDzogs chen gser thur, discovered in 1369 and written in 16 different scripts, including Indian, Chinese and Zhang Zhung.

[358] Tib. bon chos dbyer med.

[359] Tib. Ban bon gnyis med du rtogs pa'i 'gur.

[360] Tib. ris med.

[361] Tib. Kong sprul bLo gros mTha' yas; 'Jam byangs mKhyen brtse'i dBang po; mChog 'gyur bDe chen gLing pa; Mi pham rGya mtsho; Shar rdza bKhra shis rGyal mTshan; A Dzom 'Brug pa; dPal sprul Rin po che.

said to have been recovered, a number of textual treasures still remain concealed.[362]

Fig. 15. Nyame Sherab Gyaltsen.

Another very important Bönpo master of the late fourteenth century was Nyame Sherab Gyaltsen[363] (1346–1415). He was a contemporary of Tsongkhapa[364] (1357–1419), the founder of the Gelug Buddhist order, whom he met at the River Drichu[365] in Dome[366] where they allegedly exchanged four-line compliments.[367]

He was educated in Yeru Wensakha monastery and studied various spiritual disciplines with several Bönpo and Buddhist masters. He held a vast number of spiritual lineages and transmissions of Yungdrung Bön and was venerated by both Bönpo and Buddhists alike as Rabjampa,[368] a great scholar. After the destruction of Yeru Wensakha, in 1405 he founded the nearby monastery of Tashi Menri[369] which became the major centre of Bönpo studies in Tibet.

Although Yungdrung Bön made a full recovery in the spiritual sense it was practically excluded from Tibetan political life – a fate it shared with the Nyingmapa Buddhist order. Despite a number of disadvantages, this pariah position also had a positive side: Bönpo practitioners were able to direct most of their energies towards spiritual goals. As the position of *tulku*,[370] reincarnate lama, is not over-emphasized in Yungdrung Bön, this tradition escaped the corruption and politization which befell other Buddhist schools in Tibet. This does not mean there are no *tulkus* in Yungdrung Bön; there are, but there is no 'institution of *tulkus*' as such. Rather, through accomplishments in study and meditation, each

---

[362] Verbal communication from Yongdzin Lopön Tenzin Namdak.

[363] Tib. mNyam med Shes rab rGyal mtshan.

[364] Tib. Tsong kha pa.

[365] Tib. 'Bri chu.

[366] Tib. mDo smad.

[367] See Karmay, *The Treasury*, p. 141.

[368] Tib. Rab 'byams pa.

[369] Tib.bKra shis sMan ri.

[370] Tib. sPrul sku.

Fig. 16. Tashi Menri Monastery.

tulku must prove the authenticity of their recognized reincarnation and important positions within monastic or Tantric communities are not granted to them as a matter of course. At the other end of the spectrum we find the other Buddhist schools of Tibet where the *tulku* institution, pioneered by the Kagyudpa, quickly became corrupted, a tool to further political gains, increase power and ensure the continuity of accumulated material wealth within the tradition. Even though the Great Fifth Dalai Lama (1617–1682) was one of the most important Buddhist *tulkus* ever found, he himself was very critical about the real motives behind the *tulku* recognition process. This is clear from his own autobiography:

> Since there was a large Mongol army in the country and the Tibetan leaders were forced to yield much of their land to them, it became customary to recognize the sons of Mongol leaders as reincarnations. It was said that I, too, was one (even though I was not a Mongol) […] The official Tsha-ba bka'-bcu of dGa'-ldan pho-brang showed me statues and rosaries (that belonged to the Fourth Dalai Lama and other people), but I was unable to distinguish between them! When he left the room I heard him tell the people outside that I had successfully passed the test.[371]

[371] Karmay, *The Arrow and the Spindle*, p. 508.

From the thirteenth century Tibet was governed by Buddhocratic regimes headed by the supreme lamas of the Sakyapa and then Kagyudpa orders until, in 1548, Zhinzhag Tseten Dorje[372] established a new secular kingdom in Tsang which gradually came to control the whole of Central Tibet. Aspiring to reintroduce the institutions and governing methods of the royal period, the new dynasty sought a coalition with all the main contemporary religious-political powers – Sakyapa, Karma Kagyud and the emerging Gelugpa. All the schools supported the policy whose aim was to bring much-needed unification, peace and religious tolerance to Tibet. However, in 1577–1578, the Tumed Mongols, under the leadership of Altan Khaan, converted to Gelugpa. As Mongols were the major military and political power of the time, this changed the political balance and a bitter struggle for power ensued between the Gelugpa and the Karma Kagyud. In 1543 the Gelugpas found a reincarnation of the abbot of Drepung[373] monastery, Gedün Gyatso[374] (1475–1542), who was named Sonam Gyatso[375] (1543–88). He met Altan Khaan who granted him the title of Dalai Lama and he returned favour by proclaiming the Khaan a King of Religion. So it was that the institution of Dalai Lamas, as well as the military and political alliance of Gelugpa and Mongols, was established. Gedün Gyatso and Gedün Drubpa[376] (1391–1475), founder of Tashi Lhunpo[377] monastery, were posthumously 'recognized' as the Second and First Dalai Lamas respectively so Sonam Gyatso became the Third Dalai Lama. The new political and religious alliance of Gelugpa and Tumed Mongols began threatening the existence of the secular royal government in Central Tibet. After the death of the Third Dalai Lama, a great-grandson of Altan Khaan was recognized as the Fourth Dalai Lama and given the name Yonten Gyatso[378] (1589–1617) thereby increasing Mongol influence on Tibet's political situation. The Fourth Dalai Lama was later enthroned as Abbot of Drepung and when he met the King of Tsang he refused to bless him as a result of which the relationship between the Gelugpa School and the Tsang kingdom became quite tense. When the Fourth Dalai Lama died, the royal government forbade a search for his reincarnation. This, however, didn't solve the problem but instead led the Mongol army and Gelugpa monks to

---

[372] Tib. Zhing zhag Tshe brtan rDo rje.

[373] Tib. 'Bras spungs.

[374] Tib. dGe 'dun rGya mtsho.

[375] Tob. bSod nams rGya mtsho.

[376] Tib. dGe 'dun Grub pa.

[377] Tib. bKra shis Lhun po.

[378] Tib. Yon tan rGya mtsho.

launch a military campaign against the royal government. Meanwhile, Gelugpa leaders secretly selected three boys as candidates for the next reincarnation of Dalai Lama. Kunga Gyurme[379] from the Zahor[380] family was later chosen as the Fifth Dalai Lama and given the name Lobsang Gyatso.[381] The political situation was deteriorating as one of the leading Gelugpa politicians, Zhalngo,[382] formed an alliance with the Dzhungar Mongols from western Mongolia led by Gushri Khaan who through warfare subjugated the royalist forces among the Mongol tribes in the Kokonoor region. In 1641 Gushri Khaan defeated the Bönpo king of Beri in Kham, an ally of the royal family in Tsang, and after a long siege, in 1642 the king and his forces surrendered their fortress Samdrubtse[383] and lost their power. The new secular rule had lasted ninety-four years. The Fifth Dalai Lama was enthroned as King of Tibet by the Mongols and a new period of Gelugpa domination in religion and politics started which was to last until the Chinese invasion of 1959.

The Fifth Dalai Lama was a brilliant scholar and politician and, although he was put on the Tibetan throne by the Gelugpa party which he never failed to represent, he was broadminded and impartial as far as spiritual matters were concerned. And indeed, that is as it should have been; his father was friendly with Drugpa Kagyud[384] and his mother was connected with Jonangpa. In 1633 the Fifth Dalai Lama met a Nyingmapa master, Konchog Lhundrub,[385] a meeting which was to become a turning point in his life as regards spiritual practice. He was introduced to the secret aspect of Buddhist Tantra and Dzogchen which he practised clandestinely for the rest of his life. The Fifth Dalai Lama was favourably disposed towards Yungdrung Bön; in an edict he recognized it as one of the official Tibetan religious traditions and Yungdrung Bön's doctrinal position came to be accepted, to some degree at least. He also sought the counsel of Bönpo masters on several occasions. A shrine for Sidpai Gyalmo, the principal protectress of Yungdrung Bön, was set up in his residence at the Potala.[386] Despite this religious tolerance, political dissent was not tolerated and when Bönpos allied themselves with

---

[379] Tib. Kun dga' 'gyur med.

[380] Tib. Za hor.

[381] Tib. bLo bzang rGya mtsho.

[382] Tib. Zhal ngo.

[383] Tib. bSam 'grub rtse.

[384] Tib. 'Brug pa bKa' brgyud – one of the main sub-schools of the Kagyud order.

[385] Tib. dKon mchog Lhun grub.

[386] Verbal communication from Yongdzin Lopön Tenzin Namdak.

Karma Kagyud in Kham they were brutally punished and a number of Bönpo monasteries were destroyed by Gushri Khaan's army. The custom of sticking out one's tongue as a sign of respect towards high officials dates back to these times, although the original meaning of this was quite different; people stuck out their tongues to show the Mongol soldiers – who were effectively a Gelugpa army, a secular and religious police force – that their tongues were not black as it was believed that Bönpo and Nyingmapa practitioners' tongues turned black from reciting mantras.

Tibetan politics continued to swirl among intrigues, conspiracies and conflicts between major Buddhist political parties and their foreign enemies or friends, but the presence of Yungdrung Bön was quietly growing on Tibet's spiritual landscape. In the mid-nineteenth century, two more major Bönpo monasteries were built in the vicinity of Tashi Menri: Yungdrung Ling[387] and Kharna.[388] These three centres were major Bönpo monastic universities and by the beginning of the twentieth century there were around 360 Bönpo monasteries throughout Tibet, with the exception of the U province, the seat of the Gelugpa government. Many *ngagpa* centres where lay *yogis* and *yoginis* of Yungdrung Bön practised and transmitted the teachings of Tantra and Dzogchen were also dotted throughout the spiritual landscape of Tibet, especially in Amdo and even in Central Tibet, and some are still in existence today. Among them are: Shen Sergo Thramo,[389] a *ngagpa gompa*[390] which is a part of the Shentsang[391] complex, the seat of the Shen clan, located in modern-day Thonmon[392] county not far from Zhigatse,[393] which also includes Shen Triten Norbutse[394] monastery; Sergya Ngagmang[395] *ngagpa* community in the Kokonoor region; Böngya Ngagmang[396] *ngagpa* community in Rebkong,[397] Amdo.

In this period, an extraordinary Bönpo master, Shardza Tashi Gyaltsen (1859–1935), appeared. As a young boy he was ordained and

[387] Tib. g.Yung drung Ling.

[388] Tib. mKhar sna.

[389] Tib. gShen gser sgo khra mo.

[390] Tib. sgom pa – a word used to denote both meditation practice and the meditation centre or temple.

[391] Tib. gShen tshang

[392] Tib. mThon smon.

[393] Tib. gZhis ka rtse.

[394] Tib. gShen Khri brtan Nor bu rtse.

[395] Tib. Ser rgya sngags mang.

[396] Tib. Bon rgya sngags mang.

[397] Tib. Reb skong.

Fig. 17. Shen Sergo Thramo.

Fig. 18. Shen Triten Norbutse Monastery.

Fig. 19. Sergya Ngagmang.

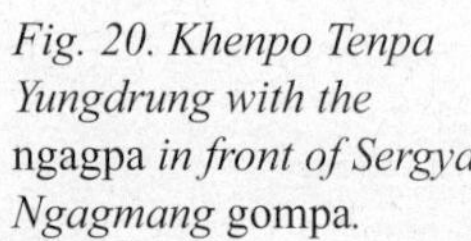

Fig. 20. Khenpo Tenpa Yungdrung with the ngagpa *in front of Sergya Ngagmang* gompa.

became a monk at the Dza Tengchen Gompa[398] in Kham and received teachings and initiations on all levels of Sutra, Tantra and Dzogchen from twenty-four masters. A great scholar and practitioner, he wrote many texts and commentaries elucidating the meaning of the teachings and methods of Yungdrung Bön. His students came from all religious backgrounds, not only Bönpo. He sponsored the reprinting of many books and built many temples and meditations places. At the age of seventy-six he manifested rainbow body, the highest realization of Dzogchen. Many of his students later manifested the same realization thereby showing the strength of his spiritual lineage, a lineage which today still flows in full strength both within and without Tibet.

Fig. 21. Shardza Tashi Gyaltsen as a Tantric yogi, statue from Shardza Ritrod.

The third persecution and restoration of Yungdrung Bön

With the Chinese invasion of 1950, the Tibetan Uprising of 1959 and the Cultural Revolution which followed, Yungdrung Bön shared the fate of all the spiritual traditions of Tibet and was persecuted for the third time. Monasteries, religious objects, relics and texts were destroyed and many practitioners were killed, although some managed to hide inside Tibet while others escaped over the Himalayas to India and Nepal. It is these refugee lamas and practitioners who undertook the task of restoring Yungdrung Bön yet again and bore the lamp of its teachings to the West.

Among the lamas who escaped from Tibet at that time was my teacher Yongdzin Lopön Tenzin Namdak[399] who played a paramount role in preserving? and restoring the Yungdrung Bön tradition in exile.

---

[398] Tib. rDza sTeng chen dGon pa.

[399] Tib. Yong 'dzin sLob dpon bsTan'dzin rNam dag Rin po che.

Born in 1926 in Khyungpo Karu,[400] Kham, he became a monk at Tengchen[401] monastery at the age of seven and later studied at Yungdrung Ling monastery and Tashi Menri monastery, where he also held the post of *Lopön* or Master of Studies. He also spent two prolonged periods in retreat. While fleeing Tibet in 1960 he was shot and captured but, after spending ten months in a Chinese concentration camp, managed to escape to Mustang, Nepal. Invited to Britain by Dr. David Snellgrove of SOAS, London University as a visiting scholar together with his teacher Lopön Sangye Tenzin[402] and Geshe Samten Karmay,[403] Yongdzin Lopön Tenzin Namdak remained in the UK until 1964 working on the publication of *The Nine Ways of Bon* by Oxford University Press. This book contains translated passages from the *Zijyid*,[404] the extensive biography of Buddha Tonpa Shenrab Miwo, and was the first scholarly study based on original Bönpo sources made in the West.

In 1964 Yongdzin Lopön Tenzin Namdak returned to India where he was engaged in the republishing important Bönpo texts including texts from the Bönpo Dzogchen cycle of *Zhang Zhung Nyen Gyud*. He also started looking into a way of establishing a Bönpo settlement in India. The situation of the Bönpo in exile was desperate; aid money given to the Tibetan Government in Exile was not reaching the Bönpo community as at that time Yungdrung Bön was not recognized as an official religious School of Tibet. As a result, many monks and even the thirty-second Abbot of Menri, Sherab Lodrö[405] (1935–1963), were forced to work as road workers in the hot climate and many, including the Abbot, perished. In 1967 Yongdzin Lopön Tenzin Namdak's fundraising efforts succeeded and a piece of undeveloped land was bought at Dolanji, Solan, Himachal Pradesh with money donated by the Catholic Relief Fund. The settlement was officially registered with the Indian Government that same year as the Tibetan Bönpo Foundation. Seventy Bönpo families were transferred to Dolanji from Manali and each was given a house and a plot of land. The Abbot of Yungdrung Ling Bönpo monastery came to Dolanji with a small group of monks and founded a new monastic community there. Religious texts on many subjects of Bönpo monastic curriculum were scarce and Lopön Tenzin Namdak was involved in the work of publishing a large number of Bönpo texts in New Delhi. When the thirty-third Abbot

---

400 Tib. Khyung po dKar ru.

401 Tib. sTeng chen.

402 Tib. sLob dpon Sangs rgyas bsTan 'dzin.

403 Tib. dGe bShes bSam gtan mKhar rme'u.

404 Tib. gZi brjid.

405 Tib. Shes rab bLo gros.

of Menri, Lopön Sangye Tenzin, died Lopön Tenzin Namdak became the main teacher of the Yungdrung Bön tradition in exile and in 1978 established the monastic college of Yungdrung Bön Shedrub Lobnyer Dude[406] in Dolanji which provided monks with a full religious education, leading them through the nine years of training to the Geshe degree.

Indeed, 1978 was a very important year for the Bönpo community in exile. The current Abbot of Menri, Jongdong Sangye Tenzin,[407] was enthroned and the Tibetan Government in Exile recognized him as the official head of the Yungdrung Bön religion of Tibet. The Dalai Lama and the Tibetan Government in Exile also recognized Yungdrung Bön as Tibet's fifth religious School with the right to have representatives on the Council of Religious affairs in Dharmasala. This was a very significant event in the modern history of Yungdrung Bön.

Fig. 22. Yongdzin Lopön Tenzin Namdak, Shenten Dargye Ling, 2007.

With the loss of their country and heavy repressions aimed at destroying their cultural heritage, many Tibetans inside and outside Tibet came to appreciate Bön – especially Yungdrung Bön – as a vital part of their national identity and religious and cultural roots. One such scholar is Professor Namkhai Norbu.[408] Like Yongdzin Lopön Tenzin Namdak, he fled Tibet and was invited to Europe as a visiting scholar, in this case by Prof. Giuseppe Tucci of the Istituto Italiano per il Medio ed Estremo Oriente, Rome. After four years as a research associate there, he moved to the Istituto Orientale of the University of Naples where he held the post of Professor of Tibetan and Mongolian Studies for thirty years. Thanks to his academic position and lively interest in Bönpo culture, Prof. Namkhai Norbu was able to access rare Bönpo texts held in Italian Universities and elsewhere and his years of unbiased study resulted in the publication of several books underlining the importance of Zhang Zhung's cultural Bönpo legacy and outlining its impact on the civilization, culture and

---

[406] Tib. gYung drung Bon bShad sgrub sLob nyer 'Dus sde.

[407] Tib. lJong ldong Sangs rgyas bStan 'dzin who is now known under the name Tib. sKyabs rjes Lung rtogs bsTan pa'i Nyi ma.

[408] Tib. Nam mkha'i Nor bu Rin po che.

religion of Tibet. In 1978 Prof. Namkhai Norbu visited Dolanji with a group of his students and since 1989 Yongdzin Lopön Tenzin Namdak has visited and taught at various branches of Chögyal Namkhai Norbu's Dzogchen Community throughout the world on his invitation.

In 1986 land was bought in Nepal for another monastery, and since 1987 Triten Norbutse has been Lopön Tenzin Namdak's main seat. It is now home to some 170 monks and a handful of nuns and, due to its reputation as a centre of excellence for education in Dialectic studies, Tantric and Dzogchen studies and meditation techniques, there is a constant flow of monks risking the perilous journey over the Himalayas to study under the guidance of the great masters in exile. It is hoped that when these students attain the Geshe[409] degree of proficiency in their study and meditation they will be able to return to Tibet and teach there, thus contributing to the revival of Yungdrung Bön within Tibet itself.

In 1988 H.H. the Dalai Lama visited the Tibetan Bönpo Foundation and was very pleased to observe the high standards of education as well as to see monks debating points of Sutra, Tantra and Dzogchen, a method unique to Yungdrung Bön. Subsequent envoys of Tibetan government found that both Dolanji's and Triten Norbutse's study programmes are among the best monastic education programs in the Himalayas and India. Yongdzin Lopön Tenzin Namdak has also been invited by the Dalai Lama to give presentations and teachings several times as part of the Kalachakra events.

Yungdrung Bön in the West

Since the invasion of Tibet by the Chinese, the teachings of Yungdrung Bön have been spreading in the West, too. There are now a number of authentic masters regularly teaching in Europe and North America and a few permanent retreat centres have been established, the latest of which is Shenten Dargye Ling in France, thanks to which Yungdrung Bön now enjoys the status of an officially recognized religion in France. It houses a complete Bönpo *Kanjur* and *Katen* and can provide a safe haven in Europe should Buddhism and Yungdrung Bön face peril amid political or civil unrest in Nepal.

Fig. 23. Khenpo Tenpa Yungdrung.

[409] Tib. dGe bshes –equivalent to Doctor of Religion and/or Philosphy.

There is also a growing volume of teachings and commentaries available in English and other European languages as well as increasing interest in academic institutions, notably the University of Oxford (UK), and the National Museum of Ethnology (Osaka, Japan).

As for Tibet itself, since the political situation eased slightly in the late 1980's, Yongdzin Lopön Tenzin Namdak, Kyabje Lungtok Tenpai Nyima and Khenpo Tenpa Yungdrung[410] have made several trips to encourage and support many projects furthering Bönpo revival in Tibet. Bön is now estimated to be the second most popular Buddhist School, along with Nyingma.

Part II
The Lands of Bө Murgel

Today Bө Murgel is practised in several countries, mainly parts of Mongolia and the former Soviet Union. In the People's Republic of Mongolia it is especially strong in the region of Lake Hubsuguul[411] although we find it in Chinese Inner Mongolia, too. In the Russian Federation, Bө Murgel mainly thrives in parts of Southern Siberia such as the Republic of Buryatia;[412] Ust'-Orda Buryat Autonomous Territory[413] in the Irkutsk region of the Russian Federation; Aga Buryat Autonomous Territory[414] in the Chita region of RF, and in the Republic of Tuva[415] to the southwest of Baikal. Bө Murgel still survives in the Kalmyk Republic[416] in southern Russia. It isn't a centralized religion and has many streams so a glance at the history of this region will help us better understand the development of this complex belief system.

Pre-history

People have lived around Lake Baikal from times immemorial, since at least 300,000 years ago. The people who lived in the area 15,000–

[410] Tib. mKhan po bsTan pa g.Yung drung.

[411] Bur. Хүбсүгүүл; Mong. Хувсгел-нуур.

[412] Rus. Республика Бурятия.

[413] Rus. Усть-Ордынский Бурятский Автономный Округ.

[414] Rus. Агинский Бурятский Автономный Округ.

[415] Rus. Республика Тува (Тыва).

[416] Rus. Республика Калмыкия.

8,000 years ago left behind them tools all but identical to those found in North American archaeological sites, indicating that in that distant period some ancestors of the Native American peoples migrated there over the Bering Straits from the Baikal region. We can assume, then, that some Native American tribes must have common cultural and genetic threads connecting them with the Tungus-Evenki, Yakut and Buryat peoples.

Bronze and Iron Age cultures

The Bronze and Iron Ages were important here as they saw the appearance, development and metamorphosis of several important cultures. Generally, archaeologists divide the thousand-year period of history in Southern Siberia and Central Asia from the second half of the second millennium BC to the second half of the first millennium BC into three large periods:

1. Epoch of developed bronze (16th-13th centuries BC)
2. Epoch of late bronze (13th-8th centuries BC)
3. Initial period of Scythians (8th-6th centuries BC)

This was a time when many ethnic cultures involved in animal husbandry and cultivation, such as the Andronovskaya,[417] Samusko-Okunevskaya[418] and Karasukskaya,[419] appeared on the great expanse of eastern Europe's steppes, in Kazakhstan as well as in western and southern Siberia, while a culture of hunter-gatherers, the Henteyskaya,[420] formed in the southern mountain regions of Transbaikalia.

Archaeological finds tell us that as early as the end of the third millennium BC there was a developed Kitoyskaya[421] culture in the Baikal region, followed by the Glazkovskaya[422] culture in the beginning of the second millennium BC.[423] The Glazkovskaya culture consisted of a group of related tribes speaking related languages who were probably the ancestors of the modern Tungus-Evenki, Even and Yukagir[424] peoples. This culture was spread around Baikal, along the River Angara, the upper

---

[417] Rus. Андроновская.

[418] Rus. Самусько-Окуневская.

[419] Rus. Карасукская.

[420] Rus. Хэнтэйская.

[421] Rus. Китойская.

[422] Rus. Глазковская.

[423] 1700–1200 BC.

[424] Rus. Эвенки-Тунгусы, Эвены, Юкагиры.

Lena and up to the source of the Yenisei in the west. Though ancient, this culture was quite similar to the contemporary cultures of peoples populating northern Manchuria, Mongolia and all the area to the south as far as Ordos and the Great Wall of China which gives us reason to believe that all the tribes living on this vast territory were related. The people of the Glazkovskaya culture were hunter-gatherers and fishers and we know that, as early as the times of the Shang-Yin dynasty[425] they engaged in indirect trade with China via middle-men tribes. Precious white and green jade discs, semi-discs, rings, furs and, possibly, slaves were sent from the Baikal region to China while bronze and tin arrived in return. It is interesting to note that an indispensable tool used by all Buryatian Bɵ and Utgan in rituals and magic is a round *toli*[426] mirror. *Toli* are made from either bronze or jade. There is archaeological evidence that these mirrors were already used in the Baikal region in the times of the Glazkovsakya culture.

The Glazkovskaya culture was followed by the Shiverskaya[427] culture which emerged in lands around Lake Baikal predominantly inhabited by Tungus people. This culture was contemporary with the Karasukskaya culture and although the 'melting-pot' process was similar, the ethnic and geographical backdrop was different. The new Shiverskaya culture differed from the previous Andronovskaya one in its fast development of metal crafts. It overlapped with a larger cultural phenomenon known as the Burial Slab Culture which extended over huge tracts of Asia, from Baikal in the north to the Gobi desert in the south, from the Hingan range in the east to Lake Hubsuguul in west Mongolia. In other words, the influence of this culture stretched 1,800km from west to east and 1500km from north to south covering an immense chunk of Central Asia. Archaeological remains of this culture have been found in areas very remote from one another, such as the foothills of Nang-Shang, the Angara region of Southern Siberia, and Olhon Island and the Barguzin valley in the Baikal region.

---

[425] 1766 (64) BC – 1066 (27) BC. See L. N. Gumilev, *Istoriya naroda Hunnu, Kniga I* (Moskva: Isdatel'stvo AST, 2002), p. 18 n. 4, and tr. Burton Watson, *Chunang Tzu*, *Basic Writings* (New York: Columbia University Press, 1996), Outline of Early Chinese History.

[426] Bur. толи.

[427] Rus. Шиверская.

Hunnu[428] period

Towards the end of the second and the beginning of the first millennium BC, a huge wave of migration from the northern side of the Yellow River in the north of China and the modern-day Amdo area of Tibet crossed the Gobi desert into Southern Siberia, including the Baikal region. These migrants were proto-Hunnu of Mongoloid and mixed Mongoloid-Europeoid racial types. According to Chinese historical tradition, Shun Wei, son of the last king of the Hsia (Xia) dynasty,[429] is considered to be the forefather of the Hunnu. After the fall of the Hsia, he took his family and some subjects to the northern steppe where his descendants mixed with peoples from the tribes of Hyang-yung and Hung-yui,[430] some of whom were of European type while others were already mixed with Mongoloids and were possibly some tribes of Zhun-Di nation,[431] This ethnogenesis resulted in the emergence of the Hu,[432]

---

[428] Often spelt Hsiung-nu or Xiongnu, based on the Chinese spelling and pronounciation. I keep 'Hunnu', as in Russian scholarly works (Rus. Хунну) because this is most probably their self-designation. That is clear from the fact that in Mongolian and Buryatian languages *hun* (Bur. хүн) means 'human being', 'person', 'man'. The Hunnu should not be confused with the Huns who later swept over western Europe and were one of the main forces behind the downfall of the western Roman Empire. Huns appeared as a result of metisazion in the southern steppe regions surrounding the Volga when the Hunnu migrated there after suffering a crushing defeat at the hands of the Syanbi in 155 AD. Many Hunnu were killed and only those able to travel on horseback managed to escape towards the west. As most of their womenfolk were lost, the Hunnu mixed with the local population when they settled thus giving rise to the Huns. (According to Gumilev, *Istoriya Hunnu,* II, pp. 325–398).

[429] Hsia (Xia) was said to be founded by a legendary hero Yu who was born in 2205 BC and was terminated in 1766 (64) BC as a result of the conquest by Shang-Yin. See Gumilev, *Istoriya Hunnu* I, p. 18 and Watson, *Chuang Tzu*.

[430] Another spelling is Xiang-yung and Xiung-yu.

[431] This is according to Gumilev, *Istoriya Hunnu* II, pp. 20–25.

[432] Later the collective name 'Hu' was used for the various nations living to the west of China including Iranian-speaking Sogdians. These Hu peoples were nomads and roamed a vast territory in theTarim Basin of Central Asia, western parts of the Gobi and Mongolian Altai in the north, with the part of them forming the famous state of Sogd or Sogdiana which bordered Persia in the west and modern-day Afghanistan in the south. These peoples were also known under the names Sogdoi and Yuezhi (according to Gumilev, *Istoriya Hunnu* 1, p.51, n 54; Gumilev, *Istoriya Hunnu* II, p. 330). More correctly, Yuezhi were the Indo-European Tokharians and probably some Indo-Iranian tribes who came into conflict with the Hunnu in 3rd-2nd c. BC. The Yuezhi lost

proto-Hunnu, who invaded Southern Siberia. They were able to cross the Gobi desert as climatic conditions changed, becoming more humid and cold, which in turn enabled vegetation to encroach, shrinking the size of the desert. These peoples gradually conquered Southern Siberia in around 1200 BC.[433] Although the proto-Hunnu subjugated the tribes living around Baikal, there was a period of intense ethnogenesis as the migrants mixed with the aboriginal population, exchanging cultural and religious beliefs and traditions. It was this exchange which later gave rise to the Hunnu nation as it is known in history. This rich multi-cultural environment with its many belief systems was also fertile ground in which the early developments of the Bɵ Murgel religion are rooted. Over the two thousand years from the end of the third millennium BC to the formation of the Hunnu Empire in the third century BC the beliefs and rituals of Bɵ Murgel gradually emerged and we can trace many elements of modern-day Bɵ Murgel to this period. One example is the jade and bronze mirrors produced by the Glazkovskaya Culture which still play such a vital role for the Bɵ and Utgan today.

One of the characteristics this new wave of (proto-Hunnu) migrants' culture was the erection of deer stones and *heregsur*[434] – large *kurgans* made of stone slabs which, as we have seen, overlapped with the Burial Slab Culture. Monuments of these two cultures are found in the same sites and radio-carbon dating shows they were laid at the same time. Russian and Buryatian scholars hold the view that initially the Burial Slab Culture was associated with the Mongoloid racial type while the Deer Stone Culture was associated with the European racial type. This might suggest that the proto-Hunnu who crossed the Gobi desert were primarily Europeoid. Be that it as it may, the process of metisation and ethnogenesis went on for around one thousand years and resulted in the formation of the Hunnu nation and their Empire governed by the Shanyui Emperors.

In the fourth century BC, the Hunnu formed a mighty state and by the third century BC the Baikal area and the whole of central Mongolia were firmly under their control. The Hunnu Empire was huge. Comprised of many nations of different racial and cultural origins, it stretched from Lake Baikal in the north to Amdo (Tibet) in the south with the Zhuns and Qiang-Tibetans around Lake Kokonoor also under its control. It extended from the Great Hingan range in the east to the lakes Issyk-Kul' and to

---

their lands to the Hunnu and went west overrunning Sogd around 150 BC. Later they built great they Kushana Empire.

433 This date is based on Gumilev, *Istoriya Hunnu* I.

434 Bur. хэрэгсур.

Balkhash in the west, and, spilling over the Great Wall of China, some of the Hunnu settled in conquered Chinese territories. The Hunnu era was another time of intense cultural and religious exchange in the Great Steppe and Southern Siberia, including the Baikal area which touched all the nations of the region.

Thanks to archaeological work in the area, we now have some material evidence about some of the traditions of that time. According to A.P. Okladinkov's interpretation based on his examination of archaeological material found around Baikal,[435] the cult of Sky and Earth was already present as early as the second millennium BC, emerging from a new understanding of the structure of universe and posthumous life. Okladnikov makes his suggestion on the basis of changes in funerary rites stemming from the concept of an underworld which the deceased reached by means of a river. Such changes may be connected to the transition from matriarchate to patriarchate. Be that as it may, the return of the spirits of the dead was now viewed as a negative event, bringing problems for those left on earth, whereas such visits had previously been considered a necessary link in the chain of life and death. In turn, Okladnikov argues, this led to the development of ritual offerings to appease and thank the spirits. This new understanding, he maintains, also gave rise to the dualistic system of Sky and Earth from which the solar cult developed with jade discs and rings symbolizing the sun. However, Gumilev holds a quite different view. He suggests that the 'shamanic' view together with techniques of ecstasy and possession were brought into Siberia by the proto-Hunnu.[436] I would suggest that, originating as they did in the Tibetan borderlands, what the proto-Hunnu brought with them to Siberia was in fact some kind of Prehistoric Bön. Then later, as the Hunnu themselves had prolonged contact with Zhang Zhung and Tibetan tribes when the Hunnu Empire first bordered and then controlled the lands around Lake Kokonoor inhabited by nomadic tribes of Tibetan stock such as the Qiang, and also because the Hunnu made incursions into Zhang Zhung and Tibet itself, they were then receptive to further Tibetan cultural and religious influence.[437]

Although the proto-Hunnu peoples and the Hunnu themselves undoubtedly influenced the aboriginal peoples of Southern Siberia and Transbaikalia, this was a two-way exchange, and the native population retained many of their traditions which were later adopted by the Hunnu.

---

[435] A. P. Okladnikov, *Neolit i bronzovyi vek Pribaikal'ya* Part III (Moskva-Leningrad, 1955).

[436] And semi-discs most probably symbolised the moon.

[437] See ch. XV.

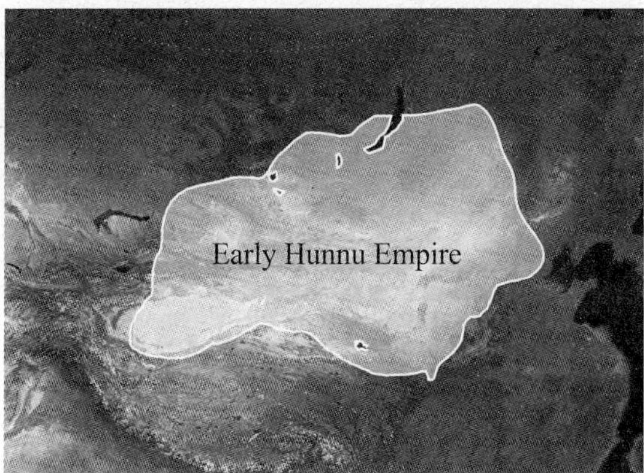

Fig. 24. Approximate area covered by the early Hunnu Empire in the third century BC.

Fig. 25. Approximate area covered by the Hunnu Empire at its maximum expansion 200 BC – 100 AD.

One example of this is the pre-Hunnu custom of human sacrifice. Slaves were taken in military expeditions, which were frequent due to the constant fighting between different tribes and clans, or were bought and it is these slaves who were used for human sacrifices. Some scholars interpret this tradition as a way of appeasing the ancestors, giving thanks and/or invoking the spirit of war. Whatever the original motive, this custom is also found later among the Hunnu showing that there was a continuity of culture in ancient Siberia.[438]

---

[438] Gumilev, *Istoriya Hunnu* I, p.46.

Further evidence of this can be found in the Hunnu burial sites south of Baikal. The sheer number of these sites shows that the Hunnu culture had a very strong presence in the area despite the fact that it was also populated by various Tungus tribes. However, the finds in these burial sites show many differences between the Hunnu culture of this area and that of the Hunnu further south; they point to a more or less settled way of life. This can most probably be put down to the influence of the Tungus. In those times this region south of Baikal was inhabited by the aboriginal population along with the Hunnu, but also by Chinese renegades, dissidents and exiles, and by the Syanbi tribe of Tabgach (Toba)[439] who moved there from the south in the first century BC. Like the Hunnu, the Tabgach were strongly influenced by the local Tungus culture and their men even took up the Tungus custom of wearing their hair in a long plait. The Tabgach spoke a variation of ancient proto-Mongolian dialect. All these tribes, however, were under the control of the Hunnu.

Chinese written sources – the main source of written information on the Hunnu – describe these people as 'savages', 'barbarians', 'wild' and so forth, but the Chinese perception of the Hunnu was far from objective; in general, the Chinese regarded only their own culture and customs as being elevated and advanced so to them, any other culture, even such advanced ones as those of India and Iran were 'barbaric'.[440] There are insufficient material artefacts remaining from the Hunnu era to form a precise understanding of their lifestyle, but even what little are available suggest they had a developed culture. The Hunnu were largely a nomadic people and their values and traditions differed from those of their more settled Chinese neighbours, but a difference in culture should not be mistaken for a lack of culture; the Hunnu had an efficient system of governing and a well-organized way of life with the army, society and all lands divided into two categories or wings: right and left,[441] the system which would lie at the foundation of succeeding Syanbi, Tyurkic and Mongol empires. The Hunnu also developed their own art styles and there is indirect evidence that they had their own writing system similar to the Indian script. According to the *History of the Three*

---

[439] Or T'o-pa.

[440] An illustrative example of this is the fact that the Chinese refered to the Indian Buddhist Guru Bodhidharma, founder of the Chan' school of Buddhism in China, as 'the Ginger-bearded Barbarian'.

[441] Gabdel'bar Faizrakhmanov, *Drevnie Tyurki v Sibiri i Tsentral'noi Asii,* Instityt istorii Akademii nauk Tartarstana, Panorama-Forum, 2000, №24 – Spetsial'nyi vypusk, Master Lain, Kasan', 2000.

Kingdoms,[442] the Chinese diplomat Kan' Tai reported upon his return from the mission to Funan' (early Cambodian state) in 245–250 AD that the people of Funan' had books written in a script similar to that of the Hunnu. We now know that a variant of the Indian script was used in Funan' and we also know that the Tokharians had a script similar to Sanskrit and that Aryans migrated to India from the Great Steppe. Even if there were no direct contact between Indians and Hunnu later, it is possible that they shared a common writing system back in the period of prehistory; material evidence of this would be scant at best due to the fragile nature of the mediums they would use for writing e.g. skin or bark would disintegrate very quickly. Hunnu had Indo-European substrata so there could have been a continuity of culture as well. Such a possibility is illustrated by the discovery of Tokharian culture in Takla Makan. If that was a case with Tokharians why couldn't it be the case with Hunnu? It seems the Chinese deliberately belittled Hunnu culture and censored the information about them in their records. Kan' Tai talks about the Hunnu script as if it were a well known fact that the Hunnu had a writing system.[443]

Syanbi period

The Hunnu's fortunes were waning and it was the Mongoloid Syanbi tribes, first mentioned in the Chinese historical records in 49 AD, who became the dominant force in the Great Steppe. The Syanbi were descended from the proto-Mongol tribes of Dunhu who were defeated by Hunnu Shanyui Mode in 209 BC. Those who survived escaped into the Syanbi (Xianbei) mountains in Manchuria from where they later emerged under the name of Syanbi. However, other scholars maintain that the Syanbi were one of the tribes of the larger Hunnu nation so in essence there was only a change in name from Hunnu to Syanbi as control over the whole Hunnu territory passed from one Hunnu tribe to another.

In the military campaign of 168–173 AD the leader of Syanbi Tanshihai (Tanshihuai) conquered Southern Siberia. Generally the Syanbi were active on the historical scene from the second century BC to the fourth century AD. Their various tribes created states in different parts of the Great Steppe, China, Tibetan Plateau and the Far East. The

---

[442] Here it refers to *Sānguó Zhì* (三國志) by Chen Shou (233–297), which is also translated as *Records of Three Kingdoms* and not to 14th c. *Romance of the Three Kingdoms, Sānguó Yǎnyì* (三國演義) by Luo Guanzhong.

[443] See D.G.E. Hall, *A history of South-East Asia*, (L., 1955) pp. 25–26, cited in Gumilev, *Istoriya Hunnu 1*, pp. 127–132.

Syanbi takeover of Southern Siberia marks the end of the early period in the history of the Baikal region as I see it and it is in this early period that the fundamental cultural and religious base of the Baikal region was formed.

Sumbe

The state of Sumbe[444] was founded by the Syanbi leader Tanshihai. It grew to control south Siberia, Mongolia, the Gobi, parts of northern China and, despite being constantly at war with its neighbours, lasted until the end of the third and beginning of the fourth centuries AD. There is good reason to suggest that this state is in fact what Tibetan sources refer to as Sumpa[445] and that various Syanbi establishments were active on the historical scene much earlier than this huge Sumbe Empire.

Fig. 26. Approximate territory controlled by Sumbe Uls.

---

[444] Bur. Сүмбэ улс. In Western historiography it is known as the Syanbi Khaganat.

[445] There were Sumpa establishments in Tibet which, as suggested above, were territories captured and settled by Syanbi tribes. We will deal with this and other hypotheses on the location and movements of Sumpa/Sumbe/Syanbi in ch. XV.

Post-Sumbe Syanbi states

Sumbe split into several independent territories or *Aimags* which soon became organized into the various Toba states (300–535 AD) governed by warlords of Tabgach[446] origin, with Toba Wei (Yuang Wei) (386–535 AD) being the most powerful state. Other states included Muyun(g) (Mu-jung),[447] governed by the Muyun(g)[448] royal clan of Syanbi, and Tuyuhun (Togon) (312–663 AD) near Lake Kokonoor ruled by descendants of the Muyun(g)s. A further contemporary state was that of Nirun Mongol[449] (402–555 AD) formed by the Zhu-Zhang (Jhou Jhan) leader Shelun. It controlled a vast territory from the Gobi in the south to Baikal in the north and from Harashar in the west to Korea in the east. The Zhu-Zhang had their own script and a comparatively high level of culture. Other important states of Syanbi were the four Yan kingdoms: Former Yang (337–370), Later Yan (384–407) and Southern Yan (398–410) led by the Murong royal clan.

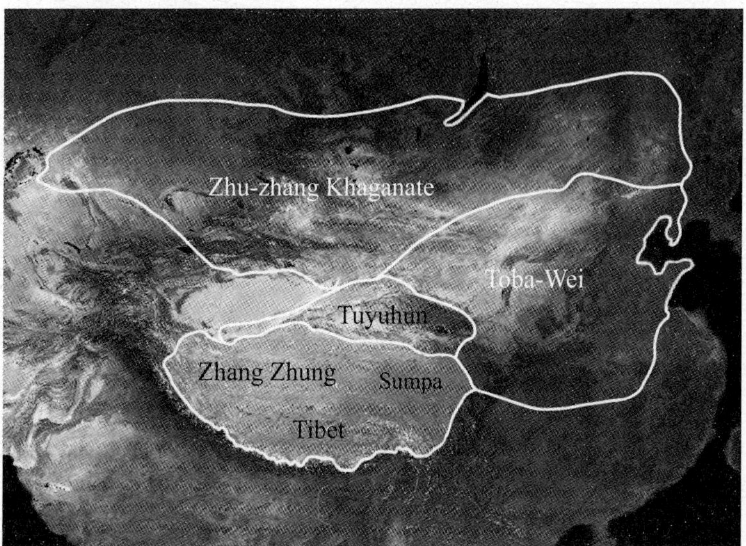

Fig. 27. Post-Syanbi proto-Mongol states.

---

[446] Tabgach was a large tribe of Syanbi.

[447] Bur. Баруун Муюн Аймак.

[448] Mongols and Buryats call this clan Muyun while Tibetan and Chinese sources have Muyung or Mu-jung.

[449] Bur. Нирун Монгол.

As the Hunnu before them, the Syanbi worshipped the Sky, sky-gods and the Earth and we can call this a kind of Bɵ Murgel or Prehistoric Bön. In Toba Wei however, Buddhism and Taoism were preferred. In 438 AD, Emperor Toba Dao instigated a persecution of both Buddhism and Bɵ Murgel under the influence of the Taoist priest Kou Tsyan'-tzu. In 444 AD worship of the Sky and of ancestral gods was prohibited and in 448 AD Toba Dao ordered the destruction of all Buddhist icons, statues and texts as well as the execution of all Buddhist monks regardless of age. The edict was delayed by Prince Toba Huang, thereby giving many monks time to escape and take some texts and relics to safety but the persecution lasted until 452 AD when Prince Toba Syun' became the new Emperor and annulled his grandfather's edict.

Tyurkic period

The Tyurkyut (Tyu-kyu),[450] who in the course of time became the Kök Tyurk (Blue Tyurks), formed as a nation in the Mongolian Altai mountain region in the fifth to sixth centuries AD. Interestingly, Tyurkyut legendary genealogy is similar to Mongolian legends telling of how they originated from a wolf. The legends have it that a she-wolf united with a nine-year-old boy, the only surviving member of a Hunnu (or Syanbi) clan completely wiped out by a rival tribe. The rulers of the Tyurkyut, Khagans (Khaans), were from the wolf-clan of A-Shina. According to Chinese historical records, Tai Wu of Wei attacked and defeated the descendants of Syanbi living in Ordos in 439 BC. Their leader, A-Shina (Great Wolf) fled with five hundred families to Nirun Mongol where they resettled in the foothills of the Mongolian Altai among the tribes of Tyu-

---

[450] Mong. Тюркут. Ancient Tyurks were ethnically very different from modern Turks of Turkey. Although the modern Turks speak a Tyurkic language, ethnically they represent a great mixture in which the proper Tyurkic component is extremely weak. Modern Turks largely descended from the Seljuk and Ottoman which belonged to the Oguz tribes of Central Asia. The Oguz were foreigners under Tyurk control and adopted the Tyurkic languge and name in the late medieval period. In principle, Oguz tribes were very similar to the earlier Kuls of the Hunnu period who were formed from all sorts of fragments of different tribes, military bands, Chinese defectors and escaped slaves. Although the Kuls were generally accepted by the Hunnu and spoke Hunnu language, they mixed between themselves but very rarely with the Hunnu who kept them at a distance. Although the Oguz were formed from different peoples in a different location and at a later historical period, their position within the social structure of hte Tyurkic Khaganats is analogous to that of the Kuls among the Hunnu.

kyu and where A-Shina was made leader of this new ethnic and military conglomerate subordinate to Zhu-zhang. The Tyurkyut were not only warriors but also skilful blacksmiths and crafters of military equipment.

Tureg

In 502 AD Tyurkyut's Tumen (Bumyn)-Khaan had such confidence in the power of this newly emerging nation that he provoked a war with their Zhu-zhang overlords by demanding Zhu-Zhang Khaan Anahuan's daughter's hand in marriage. Anahuan replied with an angry letter and so the war began. In 555 AD Mugan'-Khaan completely destroyed Zhu-Zhang and founded the state of Tureg[451] (555–745 AD).

The new empire rapidly expanded and by 590 AD already controlled a vast territory reaching the Caspian Sea, Amu-Darya, the Caucasus, the Aral Sea in the west and the Great Khingan range in the east. In the north it spread as far as Southern Siberia including Transbaikalia. Its subjects included the Sogd, the Bulgar and Khazar tribes inhabiting the area between the River Volga and the Sea of Azov in modern southern Russia. The Tyurkyut controlled the Silk Road, took taxes from China in silk and had diplomatic relations with many countries including Byzantium and Iran. In 603 AD, due to strife within its royal ranks, this empire split in two: Eastern and Western Khaganate. Kat-il Khaan of the Eastern Khaganate later surrendered to the Chinese Tang Empire and although the Western Tyurkyuts held out longer, by 630 AD they, too had fallen to Tang. Under Chinese control, the Tyurkyuts were forced to participate in military expeditions, including China's military operations in Korea and Tibet. The Tyurkyut had their own writing system and an advanced culture; they left numerous stone monuments with inscriptions throughout the Great Steppe and Southern Siberia, including the Baikal region.

In 689 AD the Tyurkyut revolted against Chinese rule and established the second Tyurkic Khaganate. Tyurks of this period were called Kök Tyurk – Blue Tyurks – because of their worship of Eternal Blue Sky and Tengeri sky-gods. They returned to the Great Steppe and, under the rule of Bilge Khaan and prince-general Kyul'-Tegin who were aided by the councillor Ton'yukuk, they fought off all their enemies and set about expanding their empire once more. The second Khaganate was smaller in size but nevertheless covered an enormous territory which again included Southern Siberia and Transbaikalia.

In both Khaganates the main religious practice was a form of Bө

---

[451] Bur. Турэг – 1st and 2nd Tyurkic Khaganates.

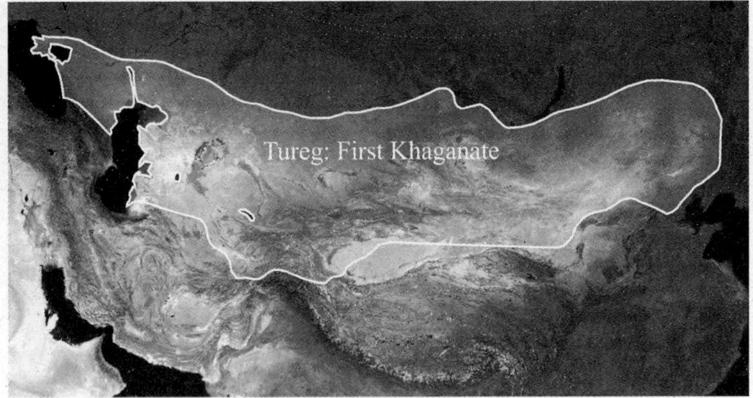

Fig. 28. Approximate territory covered by the First Tyurkic Khaganate.

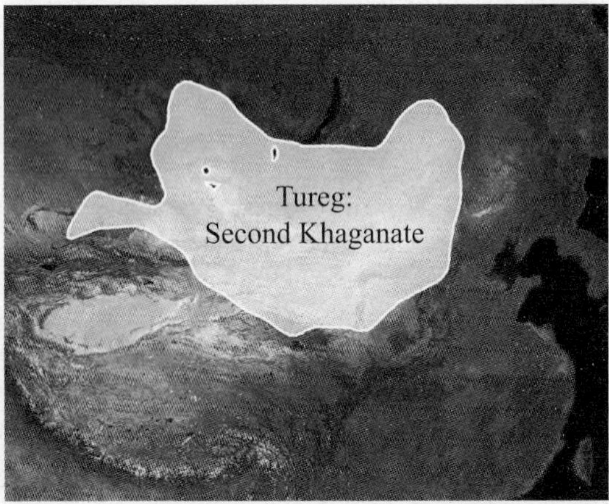

Fig. 29. Approximate territory covered by the Second Tyurkic Khaganate.

Murgel. The central cults were the worship of the Kök Tengeri, Eternal Blue Sky, and the sky-gods. Other cults were those of the ancestors, the sun, worship of holy mountains and mountain spirits, and there was also a priesthood of healer-magicians; all of these are characteristic of modern-day Bɵ Murgel. A relic which clearly shows the importance of the Sky is a marble head from a statue of prince Kyul'-Tegin recovered from the temple and memorial complex built after his death in Kosho-Tsaidam on the banks of the Orkhon, Mongolia. The head is adorned with an interesting headdress or crown with five cusps, and there is an eagle engraved just above the forehead. This is a clear indication of the importance of the cult of the Sky among Tyurks. It also shows the Kök Tyurks had a cult of the heavenly eagle comparable to that of the Tibetan *Khyung* and the Buryatian *Burged.*[452] The shape of the crown itself is reminiscent of the headdresses worn by the Bönpo deities depicted in the 'Berlin manuscript', an illustrated edition of *Zermig.*[453]

Hor

In 742 AD bickering among the Kök Tyurk royal family triggered civil war and the Uighurs under their dominance profited from this situation to rise against them. Although Uighurs spoke the same language as the Tyurks, they were ethnically different. The Uighur Khaan Peilo led the resistance and, joined by the Karluks, he finally won the war in 745 AD. Two years later, Peilo's successor Moyanchur Geleg Khaan ascended the throne of the new state of Hor (745–840 AD) built on the remains of the Tyurkic Empire. Events of this period are inscribed on the Stone Stella in Buryatia near River Selenga which flows into Baikal from Mongolia. The capital of the Hor state was Hara-Balgas (Karakorum) near the River Orkhon in Mongolia.

The Uighur Khaganate covered more or less the same territory as its predecessor but expanded further north to include the southern shore of Lake Baikal. The Uighurs, or Horpa[454] as they were known to Tibetans, led successful wars with Turgesh and Kyrgyz in the west, had an influence on Chinese politics and invaded Tibet in the south on several occasions. Some Horpas settled in Tibet in the Hor province. They must have been very fierce warriors and left a firm imprint in the memory of Tibetans because from that time on all subsequent waves of invading Mongoloid peoples were called Horpa.

At first the Uighur religion centred around the worship of the Sky and ancestral spirits and can be called a type of Bө Murgel. However, in the second half of the eighth century AD most Uighurs were converted to Manichaeism brought by missionaries from Sogdiana and Iran. It is

---

[452] Bur. бургэд. See ch. V.

[453] Tib. gZer mig, the medium version of the biography of Buddha Tonpa Shenrab Miwo. The manuscript held in Berlin's Staatsbibliothek Preussischer Kulturbesitz zu Berlin, Orientabteilung has many colour illustrations some of which were reprinted in Helmut Hoffman, *Quellen zur Geschichte der Tibetischen Bon-Religion*, (Akademie der Wissenschaften und der Litertur, Wiesenbaden: FranzSteiner Verlag, 1950) pp. 77, 83, 85, 88, 143; and in Per Kvaerne, *The Bon Religion of Tibet* (London: Serinda Publications, 1995), p.71.

[454] Tib. hor pa.

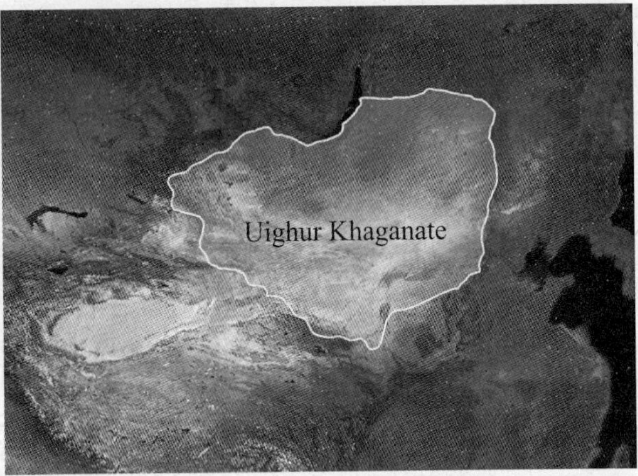

Fig. 30. Approximate territory covered by the Uighur Khaganate.

thought that Manicheans also created a Uighur writing system which was modelled on Sogdian writing and replaced the Tyurkic writing system.[455] Manicheans were extremely intolerant towards the old faith and towards any other religious system, a trait which alienated the Uighurs from their neighbours as religious tolerance was the overriding culture of the region. The Manicheans ordered the destruction of Uighur idols representing old ancestral gods thereby severing the nation's cultural and religious roots. There was a small number of Buddhist Uighurs, too. After the fall of the Uighur Khaganate, Manichaeism disappeared altogether whereas Buddhism enjoyed increasing popularity among the surviving Uighurs living around Takla Makan in the tenth century AD and beyond. They were all subsequently converted to Islam.

Kyrgyz Khaganate

Wars had weakened the Uighurs and the luck of the Hor state started to decline. In 755 AD the Tibetans began attacking Hor from the south and in the beginning of the ninth century they gradually lost their control over other peoples, too. The Uighurs most serious opponents were the

---

455 This is the most common view, although some Russian specialists in Tyurkic nations believe the Uighurs had a writing system based on previous writing systems of the Great Steppe. B. A. K. Muratov, K voprosu ob istorii vozniknoveniya tyurkskogo runicheskogo pis'ma, http://lib.userline.ru/samizdat/12798, accessed 22. 07.07).

Fig. 31. Approximate territory covered by the Kyrgyz Khaganate.

Yenisei Kyrgyz.[456] Under the leadership of warlord Ajo[457] they declared independence in 818 AD and threatened to destroy Hor altogether. In 840 AD the Kyrgyz sacked and destroyed Hara-Balgas (Karakorum) and dispersed the remaining Uighurs. One group fled to Dzungaria while others escaped to Manchuria in the Far East. The capital was moved to Kemzhiket on the River Yenisei in Southern Siberia.

The Kyrgyz took over most of the Uighur territory which included the River Selenga and the lands flanking Lake Baikal on the south. However, the remaining Uighurs later managed to re-establish their control over the lands bordering Tibet including Kucha, Kashgar, Khotan and the Turfan oasis in the Takla Makan desert.

The Kyrgyz Khaganate lasted several decades but from 928 AD it was gradually taken over by Mongoloid Hyadan'[458] (Kitai, Kithan, Kidan) peoples and by 1040 the Kyrgyz were reduced to their original lands in the Upper Yenisei.

---

[456] Yenisei Kyrgyz spoke Tyurkic but were a nation which came about as a result of the 'metisation' of Europeoids and Mongoloids with the prevalence of Europeoid characteristics.

[457] Interestingly, Ajo's mother was Tyurgesh and his wife was the daughter of a Tibetan general.

[458] Bur. Хядань.

Mongolian period

Liao

The Sacred History of Mongols, *Mongolyn Nuuts Tobchi*,[459] begins its narration in the tenth century AD but, as we seen, Mongoloid tribes were around much earlier than that. The first mention of Hyadan' in Chinese chronicles appears in the fourth century AD. Hyadan' were a branch of the Dunhu and had a common origin with other Mongol peoples such as Uhuan', Syanbi, Muyun(g), Toba and Zhu-zhang. Their original lands were in western regions of northern Manchuria in the basin of the River Nonni. From the fourth to the eighth centuries AD, the Hyadan' were engaged in continuous warfare with various Tyurkyut establishments and by the ninth century their own state of Baruun Muyun Aimag[460] was strong though small. The Hyadan' nation was made up of eight main clans governed by monarchs elected for a three-year period; it was, then, some form of a democracy with the institution of an 'elected monarchy' whose function and status did not differ drastically from those of modern-day presidents of the Western democratic system. In 907 AD Yelyui Ambagan refused to give up his office at the end of his and instead proclaimed himself emperor of Hyadan' Mongol Uls[461] or Liao. He started successful wars with this neighbours and conquered vast territories. When he died, his son, Yelyui Deguan, ascended the throne in 927 AD and it was at this time that the Yenisei Kyrgyz were pushed back to their original lands in the Yenisei basin. In 936 AD the Hyadan' annexed sixteen districts of northern China including Beijing and the conquered Chinese land became known as the Bezhin[462] region. In 946 AD the Hyadan' plunged deep into Chinese Sung territory and temporarily captured its capital, Kaifeng (Bian'). Liao's own capital, Dadin, was situated on the River Liaohe north of the Great Wall. From 966 to 973 AD, the Hyadan' were engaged in a bloody war with the

---

459 Mong. Монголын Нууц Тобчи. Translated into Buryatian as *Mongoloi Nyuusa Tobsho* by Ch. R. Namzhilovai and into Russian as *Sokrovennoe Skazanie Mongolov* by S. A. Kozin and published in one volume (Ulaan-Ude: Buryaadai nomoi kheblel, 1990), hereafter referred to as 'Kozin, *Sokrovennoe Skazanie*' when working from the Russian and 'Namzhilovai, *Mongoloi Nyuusa'* when working from the Buryatian. Unless otherwise stated, translations into English from Russian are my own, transaltions into English from Buryatian are my own with the aid of Utgan Vera Naguslaeva.

460 Bur. Баруун Муюн Аймак, the State of Western Muyun.

461 Bur. Хядань Монгол Улс.

462 Bur. Бэжин.

Tatars who they took under their control but never completely subjugated and they later fought an unsuccessful war with Korea. In the west and north the Hyadan' controlled Mongolia and lands south of Lake Baikal; in the east they ruled most of Manchuria, and in the north-east they had all the lands south of the River Amur which nowadays constitutes the border between Russian-controlled Siberia and Chinese territories.

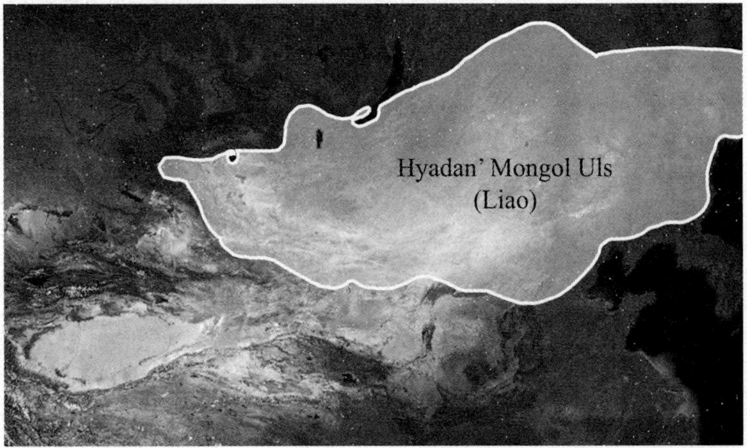

Fig. 32. Approximate territory covered by Hyadan' Mongol Uls.

Liao was at its height in the eleventh century. The Hyadan' developed an advanced culture in which sciences, arts and crafts, architecture and engineering, medicine and even sports flourished. As for religion, the early Hyadan' followed a kind of Bө Murgel with the cult of the Sky and worship of ancestral spirits predominant, but Hyadan' nobility of the Liao period disseminated Buddhism widely. Taoism and Confucianism also had some following. The Hyadan' had two writing systems: the 'large script' came into use around 920 AD and was modelled on Chinese characters, while the 'small script' created in about 925 AD by the Hyadan' scholar Diela was inspired by the Uighur alphabet. The two scripts were used in parallel. One of the best-known literary sources of Liao is *Liao Shi, The Chronicle of Liao*.

At the turn of the eleventh century Liao suffered a decline due to the strain of wars and internal conflict, and in 1125 it was overthrown by its vassals, the Manchu-speaking Jurchens who formed an alliance with the northern Chinese state of Sung. Some Hyadan' remained and were absorbed into the Jurchen state of Jin while another group of survivors, led by Prince Yelyui Dashi, fled westward to Central Asia where they encountered the Seljuks. In 1141 the Seljuk sultan Sanjar sent an army against the new arrivals but the Seljuks were defeated and the Hyadan' settled in Central Asia forming the small principality of Hara-Kitai or Si Liao.

Altan Tzin (Jin)

The Jurchen are first mentioned in Chinese sources in the seventh century AD and, according to the *History of Jurchen Jin Dynasty* by Yuan's Prime Minister Toktogan, their ancestors were Huji, descendants of the Dunhu. In the course of history these people changed their name many times. They were part of the ancient state of Sushen which formed around 2200 BC at the time of the Hsia Dynasty in China and dwelt in the basins of the Heilong and Wusuli rivers. After the period of the Warring States (474–221 BC) the tribe changed its name to Yilou. During the fourth to seventh centuries AD they became known as Huji and Mohe. At the times of Toba Wei (300–535 AD) Huji had seven tribes and in the times of Tang (618–690 AD) they split into two tribes, one of which, Sumuo, joined the Korean state of Kogurë. After Kogurë fell to Tang this tribe became independent and established the state of Bohai (698–936 AD). It seems that the people of Bohai were of mixed ethnic descent and included Tungus and proto-Mongol tribes. Bohai had a highly developed culture with architecture, music, an efficient governing system, its own script and five main cities. When Bohai was conquered by the Hyadan', the Jurchen were made to pay taxes to Liao. However, as Hyadan' strength weakened, the Jurchens rebelled and started an uprising in 1115 which led to Liao's collapse ten years later. That was the beginning of Altan

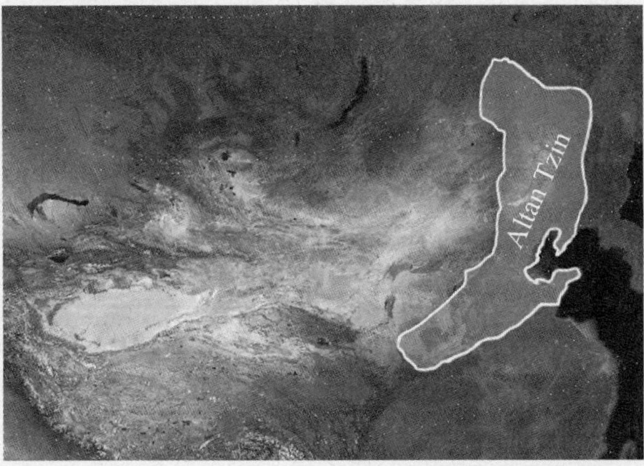

Fig. 33. Approximate territory covered by the Altan Tzin.

Tzin,[463] or Golden Jin. However, in 1126 the Jurchens turned against their northern Ṣung allies and conquered them, thereby expanding their territory deeper into China. They also took over Korë (Korea). Although Altan Tzin failed to gain direct control over Transbaikalia, the Mongols and other tribes there paid tributes to them and Jurchen vassal tribes (the Naimans, the Keraits and the Tatars) kept them in check. The Mongol tribes, however, gradually became stronger and stronger, finally taking most of Altan Tzin's territory under Chingis Khaan. Threatened by the Mongols, the Emperor of Tzin, Altan Khaan, moved his capital to Kaifeng. In 1215 Beijing fell to the Mongols but they failed to take Kaifeng. Nevertheless, Altan Tzin became marginalized and insignificant, finally disintegrating in 1234.

Initially Jurchen culture and religion were similar to the Tungus', a strand of Bө Murgel, but gradually they fell under Chinese cultural influence. They had their own script modelled on that of the Hyadan'.

Mongols

Strictly speaking, the Mongols could not, as yet, be called a nation; in fact, not even the word 'mongol' existed at this stage. Instead, the Mongols were loosely connected tribes who lived in the Baikal region and the steppes of Transbaikalia, the remaining fragments of nations previously populating the same lands in the times of the Hunnu and the Syanbi. This means that the Hunnu, and especially the later Syanbi, were their direct ancestors and indeed, in modern Mongolian and Buryatian the word for 'man' or 'human' is still *hun.* Under Tyurkic dominance, the previously developed culture of the Mongoloid tribes underwent a decline and the structure which had held them together was lost. From the tenth to the twelfth centuries the Mongols populated only a tiny fraction of the territory previously controlled by the Hunnu and Syanbi, and there was no peace in their lands. Tribes banded together forming fragile confederations, or Khaanates, which were engaged in constant armed conflicts with each other. Common causes for these conflicts included competition for natural resources, robberies, wife-stealing and various kinds of bloody vendettas. As was always the case in the Great Steppe, these tribes were of mixed origins, including Hunnu, Dunhu, Syanbi, Zhu-zhang, Tyurkyut, Kyrgyz and Bayirku (Bayegut). The Mongols and Tyurkyut share many common features such as parallels in their creation myths, common words and a similar Syanbi substrate all of which clearly suggest they were related.

---

[463] Mong. Алтан Цзин.

Mythological origins of the Mongols

According to Mongol mythology, the Mongols originated from the union of Burte-Chino[464] (Blue Wolf) and Gua-Maral[465] (Ginger Antelope). Burte-Chino came from the mythical area of Ergunu-Kun[466] in the forested Sayan Mountains in Bargujin Tokum,[467] now the Barguzin region of modern-day Buryatia lying to the west of Lake Baikal. His ancestors, probably a branch of the Syanbi, escaped there from the devastating destruction wreaked by a neighbouring tribe. Trapped in a deep valley, they were unable to find their way out until they came across a seam of iron ore in the mountainside and gradually melted it to form a tunnel out of the valley. Burte-Chino was miraculously born in that land by the decree of Huhe Münhe Tengeri, Eternal Blue Sky. After meeting his consort Gua-Maral, he left Bargujin Tokum and together they crossed Lake Baikal and established a nomadic camp along the upper reaches of the Onon River near Burkhan-Haldun[468] in the Hentei Mountains. A son, Batsagaan,[469] was born and it was from him that Chingis Khaan's Bordzhigin clan of the Hiad[470] tribe of Hamag Mongols descended.

Fig. 34. Barguzin Bald Mountains.

---

[464] Bur. Бүртэ-чино.

[465] Bur. Гуа-Марал.

[466] Bur. Эргүнү-Күн.

[467] Bur. Баргуджин Токум.

[468] Bur. Бурхан халдун уула. Burhan Haldun is a holy mountain where Eternal Blue Sky meets Mother Earth.

[469] Bur. Батцагаан.

[470] Bur. Хиад.

Ethnic map of Baikal and Transbaikalia prior to Chingis Khaan

During the late Tyurkic and early Mongol period, the largest Mongol tribes were Hamag Mongols, Kereit (Hereid), Merkit (Mergid), Naiman and Tataar[471] though there were many other smaller tribes. Hamag Mongols wandered the lands between the rivers Orkhon, Kerulen and Tuul; Kereits inhabited the area between the Hangai and Hentei Mountains; the Naiman lived between the Hangai and Altai ranges; the Tataars (Dada) lived in the Holon Buir area; the Merkit lived along the upper reaches of the River Selenge bordering the lands of the Forest Tribes, the ancestors of Buryats. The Forest Tribes inhabited the Baikal region and the forests of the eastern Sayan Mountains. There were roughly two dozen forest Tribes: Hori-Tumed, Barguud (Barga), Buryaad, Ehirit (Ikires), Bulagchin (Bulgat), Heremchin, Oin-Uryagnhai, Ursuud, Habhanas, Hanhas, Tuba, Shibir, Hesdin, Bayad, Tuhas,Tenlig, To'ols, Tas, Bayagid, Telenguud, Kestemi as well as Kuri, Harluut (Karluk) and Kyrgyz.[472] Some of those tribes were Mongol, others were of Tyurkic origin while the Kyrgyz were Indo-European. To the north side of Lake Baikal were Tungus tribes while Oirod[473] (Oirat) Mongols lived along the upper reaches of the Yenisei. Such was the ethnic map of Baikal and Transbaikalia prior to the advent of Chingis Khaan.

The formation of the Hamag Mongol Uls

Six or so generations before Chingis Khaan, the Jalairs massacred the Mongols in their homelands and few survived. One of them was Nachin-Baatar[474] who escaped the massacre because he was visiting his wife's relatives in Bargujin Tokum near Lake Baikal at the time. When he returned home he found his tribe slaughtered but, managing to recapture most of their horses, he led the remaining people to Bargujin and there they recovered. His son Haidu[475] later led a successful military expedition against the Jalairs, taking them under Mongol control and recapturing the ancestral lands. He gathered around himself what remained of the families of several Mongol tribes and they became known as Hamag

---

[471] Bur. Хамаг Монгол, Хэрэйд, Мергид, Найман, Татаар. Tataars here are different people from the Crimean Tatars.

[472] Bur. Хори-Түмэд, Барга, Буряад, Эхирит, Булгат, Хэрэмчин, Ойн Урянхай, Урсууд, Хабханас, Ханхас, Туба, Шибир, Хэсдин, Баяд, Тыхас, Тэнлиг, Төөлс, Тас, Баягид, Теленгуут, Кэстэми, Кури, Харлуут, Кыргыз.

[473] Bur. Ойрод.

[474] Bur. Начин баатар.

[475] Bur. Хайду.

Mongols. Haidu became the first Khaan of the Hamag Mongol Uls[476] confederation in the upper lands of the rivers Kerulen and Onon.

His grandson, Habul Khaan,[477] further increased Mongol territory and it was in his time that the Mongols became strong enough to draw the attention of the Jurchens in northern China. Habul Khaan was invited to meet the Golden Emperor, Altan Khaan of Jin. Although he managed to offend the Emperor with his wild and crude manners, the Jurchens decided to overlook this misdemeanour and let him go. Wary of growing Mongol influence in the Great Steppe, they ladened him with gifts and sent him back to Mongolia. However, no sooner had Habul left than the Emperor's advisers persuaded their ruler it had been unwise to let the Mongol go. Messengers were immediately dispatched to persuade Habul – who had only managed to travel around two miles – to return to the court. Habul at once suspected a trap and managed to escape, later killing Beijing's ambassadors to avenge the Jurchens' attempt to capture him.

From 1139–1147 the Jurchens fought the Mongols unsuccessfully and in 1148 Altan Khaan decided it would be more prudent to satisfy the Mongols with yearly gifts, which were, in fact, nothing short of a masked tax. Altan Khaan recognised Habul Khaan as Khaan of All Mongols, and as his vassal.

When Habul Khaan began ailing, the Mongols sent for a renowned Tataar Bө to cure him. However, the Bө's rituals and invocations didn't help and Habul Khaan died. On his way back home, the hapless Bө was ambushed and killed by Habul's relatives who suspected him of deliberately murdering the Khaan with magic. In revenge, the Bө's relatives took to arms and so a bloody conflict ensued. Ambagai,[478] who became Khaan upon his cousin Habul's death, decided to resolve the incident by giving his daughter in marriage to the Tataar tribe Airiud-Buiruud in a gesture of goodwill. As he was accompanying her to her new family, Tataars of the Juin tribe captured him and sent him to Altan Khaan in Beijing[479] where he and Habul Khaan's son were nailed to wooden donkeys. This was a fatal mistake for both the Tataars and the Jurchen; before his execution, Ambagai Khaan had managed to send a messenger

---

[476] Bur. Хамаг Монгол Улс.

[477] Bur. Хабул хаан.

[478] Bur. Амбагай.

[479] Strangely, *The Sacred History of the Mongols* (Namzhilovai, *Mongoloi Nyuusa*) says that Altan Khaan was Khaan of Hyadan' (Bur. Хитадай Алтан хаан). It would seem the Mongols didn't distinguish between previous the Hyadan' and the Jurchen who came after them. Russians call China 'Kitai', another variation of the name Hyadan'.

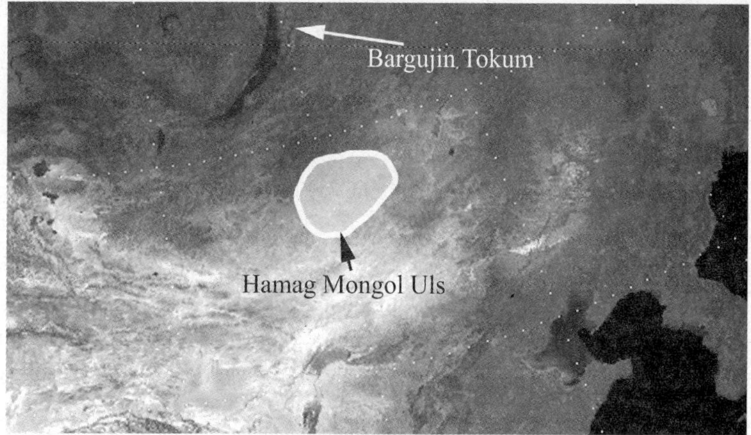

Fig. 35. Bargujin Tokum and Hamag Mongol Uls.

back home with a plea to his Taichuud[480] kinsmen not to abandon the vendetta 'until you lose all ten fingers', i.e. until they succeeded. This triggered a vendetta which was to drive Mongol military expansion for generations; the desire to avenge the dishonourable deaths of the Mongol royals was a powerful incentive behind the Mongol conquest of the Great Steppe and China which annihilated both Tataars and Jurchens alike and led to the creation of the Mongol superstate which, at its height, came to control most of Eurasia.

The birth of Chingis Khaan

Initial attempts to avenge the death of Ambagai proved unsuccessful, however. Ambagai's son Hutula[481] was elected Khaan and sent his brother, Hadaan,[482] against both Tataar tribes, but despite thirteen battles, victory eluded the Mongols and it was into this scenario of defeat and disintegration that Chingis Khaan was born. His future father, Yesuhei Baatar,[483] one of Habul Khaan's grandsons, met the newly-wed Chiledu[484] of the Mergid tribe returning home with his beautiful young wife Oelun.[485] Yesuhei was so taken with the girl that he rushed home and asked his two

---

480 Bur. Тайчууд.

481 Bur. Хутула.

482 Bur. Хадаан.

483 Bur. Есүхэй баатар.

484 Bur. Чилэду.

485 Bur. Оэлүн.

brothers to help him take her from Chiledu. When Chiledu's wife saw the men approaching she said:

> 'Don't you see what these people have in mind? It's clear from the expressions on their faces that they are going to kill you. But if you are alive and sane you will find a girl to marry in any nomads' carriage. As long as you are alive you will find a girl to marry. You must call her after me. Now kiss me and run for your life!'[486]

She took off her blouse and gave it to him. Seeing the wisdom of his wife's advice, Chiledu did as she said. And so Yesuhei and his brothers captured Oelun. She was from the Olhunoud[487] clan of the Hongirad[488] tribe from eastern Mongolia. Although Oelun was very distressed at first, she later came to love Yesuhei and in 1162[489] bore him a son, Chingis Khaan. Just as she was giving birth, her husband, Yesuhei Baatar, returned from one of the military expeditions against Tataars. Among the Tataars he had captured was a nobleman called Temuuzhin-uge[490] and Yesuhei called his first son Temuuzhin after the captive.[491] It is said that Temuuzhin was born clutching a large blood clot in his right fist and this was taken as a sign of unusual powers.

Overall, the Mongol military campaigns against the Tataars were unsuccessful in this period, culminating in a heavy defeat at the hands of joint Tataar and Jurchen forces near Lake Buir. Hutula Khaan was killed and Yesuhei became leader of the disintegrating Hamag Uls. In 1170 Yesuhei took Temuuzhin, who was just nine years old, on a trip to seek out a future wife for the boy. He found a beautiful girl called Burte[492] from the same tribe and clan as his own wife Oelun. The girl's father, Dei

---

486 Kozin, *Sokrovennoe Skazanie*, pp. 18–19.

487 Bur. Олхуноуд.

488 Bur. Хонгирад.

489 There is no unity among scholars about Chingis Khaan's year of birth. 1162, the year of the Black Horse, is accepted by the majority. Alternative dates are 1155 and 1167.

490 Bur. Тэмүүжин-үгэ.

491 This might seem strange but the Mongols had their own reasons; Chingis Khaan's birth at the moment his father returned with a noble captive was an omen. Naming the boy after the captive Tataar was a symbolic expression of Yesuhei's wish that his son Temuuzhin would take over the Tataars in the future. Moreover, by giving him the captive's name, the nobleman's power was transferred to Chingis Khaan.

492 Bur. Бүртэ.

Sesentei,[493] was a Bө and told Yesuhei about a prophetic dream he had had the night before:

> 'I had a dream last night. I dreamt that a white falcon grasping the sun and moon in his claws descended and landed on my hand. Then I was saying to people, "One can only see the sun and the moon with the physical eyes, but here comes this white falcon with the sun and the moon in his claws and descends on my hand. What does it predict?" No sooner had I started thinking this way than here you are Yesuhei, approaching with your son. How could it be that I saw such a dream? It must be that my dream was inspired by the *hulde*[494]-bearing protector of your Hiad clan.'[495]

This was the first prophetic dream foretelling Temuuzhin's fate as the future Khaan of all the Mongols and the Emperor of the largest empire the world has seen. It also clearly shows that Temuuzhin's Hiad clan was protected by the White Tengeri.[496]

Dei Sesentei agreed to a future marriage and asked Yesuhei to let Temuuzhin stay for a while with his family as a groom cum son-in-law. Yesuhei agreed and was returning home when he met some Tataars having a feast in the steppe. He was thirsty and asked for water. However, the Tataars recognised him and gave him slow-acting poison; he died upon returning home. After his death Chingis Khaan's mother Oelun became head of the Uls but mutiny followed. Ambagan Khaan's widows from the Taichuud clan started a quarrel with Oelun at the *tailgan*, Bө Murgel prayer festival, in the ancestral lands where the Mongols had gathered to give offerings to their *Zayaan*[497]-ancestors. Ambagan's widows insulted Oelun and denied her part of the ritual meal indicating that she and her children were about to be ostracized. Oelun boldly confronted her rivals but without success; the Taichuud clan left the nomadic camp taking the rest of the Mongols with them. Wielding her tribe's *tug*,[498] Oelun rode

---

[493] Bur. Дэй сэсэнтэй.

[494] Bur. Һүльдэ – is a complex Bө Murgel concept signifying prosperity, well-being, good luck etc. See ch. XIII for a detailed analysis.

[495] Kozin, *Sokrevennoe Skazanie*, p.20.

[496] See ch. IV.

[497] Bur. Заяан.

[498] Bur. туг. This kind of trident with a flag made of horse or yak tails is both a religious object and a military banner. It is a very important support for the protective deities among Mongols and Tibetan Bönpos alike, clear proof of the existence of cultural and religious connections between Mongol-Buryats and Tibetans in the remote past. See ch. IX, XIII.

after the people and although about half of them stopped, her speech fell on deaf ears and they left for good, abandoning Temuuzhin, his mother, brothers and sister. Temuuzhin's ten years of misery began. In those years he was constantly hunted by enemies of his father and his family, held in captivity and was near death several times.

Chingis Khaan as Bɵ-priest

In 1180s Chingis Khaan's luck started to turn, although this change began, paradoxically, with disaster. The Mergid attacked his family camp and stole his own wife, Burte, together with his late father's second wife in revenge for the kidnapping of Oelun by Yesuhei and his brothers. Temuuzhin himself fled to a holy mountain, Burkhan Haldun, and while he was in hiding there, he entered a trance in which he experienced a connection with Huhe Münhe Tengeri. Thus in spite of stalking him for a long time, the Mergid warriors circling the mountain were unable to find him; the holy place was protecting the future Chingis Khaan. When he came down from Burkhan Haldun Temuuzhin made offerings to it saying:

> 'Riding a cumbersome horse, following deer trails, resting in a shelter of willow twigs, I climbed Burkhan Haldun. My life which is similar to that of a swallow is protected by the shield of Burkhan Haldun. I experienced profound dread. So let us every morning worship the mountain and proffer the offerings! Let my descendants understand this!' So saying, Temuuzhin turned his face to the sun. Putting his belt around his neck as if it were a rosary, resting his *malgai*[499]-hat in the crook of his arm and baring his chest, he bowed nine times towards the sun and then sprinkled offerings and prayed.[500]

What we have here is in fact a classic Bɵ Murgel ritual pertaining to the worship of the Sky and the *Ezhen*[501]-Owners. Chingis Khaan wasn't

499 Bur. малгай – a Bɵ hat.

500 Namzhilovai, *Mongoloi Nyuusa,* p. 46–47.

501 Bur. эжэн, эжин, эзэн – a Buryatian word meaning 'Owner' or 'Lord of the place' and is equivalent to Tib. bdag po when used as a component word in such words as Tib. zhi bdag, sa bdag etc. *Ezhen* is a general name which can be applied to almost all the classes of various spiritual beings worshiped in Bɵ Murgel and inhabiting the Three Worlds from the Lord of the Underword Erlig Khaan to the highest Tengeri residing in the sky. On the earth's surface there are beings which 'own' and reside on the mountains and in the hills, islands, forests etc. and guard a varierty of geographical features. They are gods living in the space between heaven and earth or earth-dwelling gods of

only a secular and military leader – he was the supreme spiritual leader of the Mongol nation and his spiritual authority was higher than that of the supreme Bө. There is one interesting detail in the ritual sequence Temuuzhin performed: he put his belt around his neck as if it were a string of prayer beads. Was there a custom of putting a belt around the neck while praying or did Temuuzhin do this because he was in dire straits and didn't have with him one of a Bө's required ritual implements, namely a string of black prayer beads? There were no Buddhists among the Mongols of that time and although some Mongols, including part of Wan Khaan's Hereid tribe, were Nestorian Christians and could have used prayer beads, the Christian rosary has nothing in common with the prayer beads used by the Bө. Bө Murgel prayer beads are very large, number one hundred and eight beads and are made of black wood. The most plausible explanation of the presence of this ritual implement in the ritual attire of the Bө of that time is that it came from Tibetan Bön. Similar prayer beads, or *malas*, are used by Pachyu priests of Tamu (Gurung) in the Himalayas of Nepal who practise a remnant of Prehistoric Bön slightly influenced by Yungdrung Bön.[502]

Another insight into Mongol Bө Murgel religious customs of the time comes from an account of a dialogue between Temuuzhin and his childhood friend and *anda*,[503] blood-brother, Zhamuuha,[504] prince of the Zhadaran[505] tribe. Before the Mergid attack, Temuuzhin had made an alliance with his father's blood-brother the Hereid leader Wan Khaan To'oril[506] who provided ten thousand warriors, and after the Mergid attacked, his own *anda* Zhamuuha joined them with his *tumen*,[507] bringing the army to twenty thousand.[508]

Zhamuuha replied to Temuuzhin's request for help as follows:

'To my black *tug* that is seen from afar I have already sprinkled,
My drum made with the skin of a black bull I am already beating,
I am already sitting on my black horse wearing my *huyag*[509]-chain mail

---

different classes comparable to Tib. gnyan, btsan, klu and sa bdag. See ch. IV.

502 See ch. III.

503 Bur. анда.

504 Bur. Жамууха.

505 Bur. Жадаран.

506 Bur. Ван хаан Тоорил.

507 Bur. түмэн, a large military cavalry unit of 10,000 warriors.

508 According to other sources 40,000.

509 Bur. хуяг.

and raising my iron spear [...]
I have sprinkled to my tall *tug* which is seen from afar and am beating my roaring drum made of a black bull's skin...'[510]

The fact that this phrase is repeated twice underlies the importance of these ritual actions. Here we see a description of a Bɵ Murgel rite for consecrating the *tug* and invoking the tribe's protective deities into it. Judging from the colour of Zhamuuha's *tug*, drum skin and horse, we can conclude that the protectors of the Zhadaran tribe were Black Tengeri.[511] As we will see later,[512] other ritual objects described by Zahmuuha such as the drum, *huyag*-chain mail and iron spear are all used by the Mongol-Buryat Bɵ in a variety of offerings and magic rites. This clearly shows that the early Mongol Khaans were also the chief Bɵ of their clan. This doesn't mean they were perforce skilled in all Bɵ Murgel techniques and arts, but they did act as priests and even mediums, at least in times of war. From what Zhamuuha says it is clear that he is matching his image and attributes with those of the protective gods of his clan – black *tug*, black drum, black horse and so on. This suggests that at least some Mongol warrior leaders were possessed by their protective deities when in battle. Indeed, the whole army may have been fighting in a trance. If this were so, it could explain why the Mongols inspired such profound dread in their adversaries who, despite often having larger armies or a more advantageous position in battle, were simply unable to defend themselves. Such trance warriorship on a mass scale could only be possible if a nation were completely unified and in absolute accord with its protective deities. And this was exactly the task that Temuuzhin, future Chingis Khaan, was about to accomplish.

The rise of Chingis Khaan

Temuuzhin and his allies soundly defeated the hostile Mergid. Killing a large number of them, they took many slaves and destroyed their camps. Temuuzhin managed to retrieve his wife Burte and 'they lived happily ever after'.[513]

Temuuzhin's alliance with Wan Khaan lent weight and respectability to his position and after his victory over the Mergid, other tribes began

---

510 Namzhilovai, *Mongoloi Nyuusa,* p. 50.

511 See ch. IV.

512 See ch. VIII.

513 Althoug he was later to have many other wives, Burte was always loyal and provided Chingis Khaan with vital support and wise counsel.

to recognize him as a talented and charismatic leader. However, this 'triumvirate' didn't hold for long; after eighteen months the blood-brothers' ways split. Many tribes followed Temuuzhin, including a close relative of Zhamuuha, Horchi,[514] together with his people. He himself realized this was a disloyal act, but he was a Bө and was sent a prophetic dream by Huhe Münhe Tengeri:

> 'I shouldn't have come but Supreme Sky sent me a clear insight. And so I see a light ginger cow. She is circling around Zhamuuha and with her horns she scatters his wheeled yurts. She wants to batter Zhamuuha himself but one of her horns gets broken. And so she is digging the earth with her hooves and throwing it at him, bellowing and saying-repeating, "Give back my horn!" And now I see a brown bull dragging the main wheeled *gher*[515] along the main road, and following Temuuzhin. The bull is roaring-repeating, "Eternal Blue Sky and Earth have struck a deal! Temuuzhin is to be lord!" '[516]

Sure enough when the tribal chiefs met, Temuuzhin was elected as the supreme leader of Hamag Mongol Uls and given the title Chingis Khaan,[517] Ocean Khaan. For the first time the Mongols didn't look to China for recognition of their Khaan and gave him a purely Mongol title. This was the first step towards Mongol independence and their future dominion over China and most of Eurasia.

However, not all the Mongols supported Chingis Khaan. In 1201 Zhamuuha succeeded in gathering quite a large coalition of tribes who were dissatisfied with the new supreme Khaan and who proclaimed Zhamuuha as their Khaan instead. Civil war soon broke out but Chingis Khaan's enemies lost the first battle and the coalition collapsed.

Among Zhamuuha's allies were two Bө, Buirug Khaan[518] of the Naiman and Hutug Behi[519] of the Oirod, who had the capacity to control the weather. In the morning before the battle they performed a magic ritual, throwing stones into water to call up a tempest and turn it towards Chingis Khaan's army. At first they appeared to succeed: a powerful snowstorm blew up, but instead of wreaking havoc on Chingis Khaan,

---

[514] Bur. Хорчи.

[515] Bur. гэр – a Mongol yurt.

[516] Namzhilovai, *Mongoloi Nyuusa,* p. 56.

[517] Bur. Чингис хаан. Other versions are Bur. Тэнгис хаан (Tengis Khaan) and Bur. Далай хаан (Dalai Khaan).

[518] Bur. Буйруг хаан.

[519] Bur. Хутуг бэхи. The second part of his name, *Behi,* is a spritual title indicating that he was the supreme Bө of his tribe.

it turned against those who had summoned it and their army broke into a run. The warriors were crying out, 'We have aroused the wrath of the Tengeri sky-gods!'[520] Many fell into abysses while those who survived suffered severe frostbite to their hands and feet.

The use of magic in warfare was quite a widespread phenomenon in the Great Steppe and had been practised by the Yueban' and Tyurks before the Mongols. N.Y. Bichurin[521] reports that Yueban' magicians were able to cause blizzards and storms and had indeed halted the advancing Zhu-Zhang army by sending a snowstorm in which so many soldiers were frostbitten that the Zhu-Zhang had to turn back.[522] The magic used by Hutug Behi and Buirug Khaan was, in fact, identical to that used by the Tyurkyut. Tyurkyut wizards had the capacity to cause storms by reciting spells onto a stone taken from the stomach of a cow, a wild boar or a horse.[523]

Chingis Khaan's alliance with Wan Khaan of the Hereid lasted longer but it, too, proved unstable. Together they waged war on the Tataars and completely destroyed them, butchering every male taller than a cartwheel; the first part of the vendetta for Ambagai Khaan and other Mongol nobles was accomplished. However, in 1203 Zhamuuha managed to turn Wan Khaan against Chingis Khaan. He falsely accused Chingis Khaan of forging an alliance with Naiman tribes behind Wan Khaan's back. Although Wan Khaan himself was nonplussed, under pressure from his sons, he reluctantly conceded. As the two armies were readying themselves for battle, Wan Khaan asked Zhamuuha to be his commander but the latter turned traitor and, betraying the people he himself had

---

520 Bur. Бидэндэ тэнгэриин уур хилэн хүрэбэ.

521 N. Ya. Bichurin (Iakinf), *Sobranie o narodakh, obitavshikh v Srednei Azii v drevnie vremena,* vol II (Moskva-Leningrad, 1950–53), p. 260.

522 Another example of Tyurkic military magic is Firdousi's description of the Tyurkyut magicians' magic attack against the Persian army at the battle near Herat in modern-day Afghanistan. The night before the battle they sent a bad dream to the Persian general Bahram Chubin in which the Tyurkyut turned into a lion, his own army was destroyed and he himself was praying for mercy as he walked on the road without his horse. The general, however, wasn't easily alarmed and despite this ill omen, ordered his army into battle undetered. The Tyurkyut used magic to scare the Persians. By throwing fire into the sky they conjured up a black cloud which shot arrows at the Persian army. Bahram shouted to his people that it was merely a magical trick and that in reality there were no arrows, so the ploy failed. Firdousi, *Le Livre des Rois*, Ed. J.Mohl, VI. (Paris, 1868), pp. 60, 614, 622.

523 S. I. Malov, *Shamanskii Kamen' «yada» u Tyurkov Zapadnogo Kitaya,* SE, №1, 1947.

stirred up against Chingis Khaan, he secretly sent a messenger to Chingis Khaan with their tactical plan of attack. Wan Khaan lost the battle and his older son was wounded by an arrow in his cheek. Chingis Khaan's army also bore heavy losses – a 'Pirr's victory' – but some of Wan Khaan's vassals subsequently changed sides and joined Chingis Khaan.

After the battle Chingis Khaan sought peace with the Hereid but, against their father's wishes, Wan Khaan's sons prevented this. A chain of treacheries plagued the Hereid ruling elite and their allies, and Zhamuuha was forced to flee, subsequently allying himself with the Naimans. Wan Khaan's army was soon destroyed by Chingis Khaan and his lands and people were incorporated into the growing Mongol state. Wan Khaan managed to escape and led a miserable existence roaming the steppe but one day, unable to stave off his thirst any longer, he went down to the river to drink and was captured by a Naiman military patrol. He began to explain that he was Wan Khaan but they didn't believe him and so, taking him for a bandit, killed him on the spot. When Queen Gurbesu,[524] mother of Tayan Khaan[525] of the Naiman, learned of this she demanded Wan Khaan's head be brought to her, saying:

> 'Wan Khaan was from an ancient royal clan. Bring his head here and if it's really his then we must make offerings to it.' [...] The head was put on a white felt blanket and, folding their hands, everyone began praying and offerings were made. Daughters-in-law sang and the lute was played. Then all of a sudden the head started laughing. 'Why are you laughing?' Tayan Khaan cried, and ordered the head to be crushed underfoot.[526]

It seems that here we have another example of an ancient Bө Murgel rite but in this case it backfired. Mongol-Buryats believe that the head is the container for a person's *hulde*, good fortune, and for its *erdeni*[527] aspect in particular. Wan Khaan was from a powerful royal clan and through making offerings to his head, Gurbesu was seeking to neutralize the negative circumstances of his death, bring his *hulde* into her clan and maybe even persuade him to become their protective spirit. However, these aims were not realized because her arrogant son destroyed the head, taking its laughing as a bad omen, which it may well have been; the Naimans were later conquered by Chingis Khaan in 1204 and Queen

---

[524] Bur. Гурбэсү.

[525] Bur. Таян хаан.

[526] Kozin, *Sokrevennoe Skazanie*, p. 82.

[527] Bur. эрдэни – detailed analysis in ch. XIII.

Gurbesu was captured and forced to become his concubine. Mongols also captured the Uighur scribe Tatatunga who later adapted the Uighur script to Mongolian language.[528]

In 1205 the remaining groups of Mergid and Naiman were defeated and came under Mongol control. Zhamuuha was betrayed by his own men and brought to Chingis Khaan, who immediately ordered the execution of those disloyal servants and offered Zhamuuha his friendship. Zhamuuha replied:

> 'Please, *anda*-brother, hurry to see me off! In this way you will calm your heart. If possible, my friend, please kill me without shedding my blood. I give you a sacred oath that as long as my raised bones are resting in the High Earth I will be a spirit-protector of your descendants forever. I give you this sacred promise. […] Please don't forget my words, remember and repeat them in the morning and in the evening. But now, please let me go.'[529]

Chingis Khaan accepted Zhamuuha's choice but there was one problem: divination wasn't in favour of Zhamuuha's execution. Zhamuuha had never directly attempted to kill his *anda* and had on many occasions warned Chingis Khaan about his enemies' plans even though he sided with them against the Khaan. However, Chingis Khaan found an incident for which Zhamuuha could be lawfully executed and decreed:

> 'Now you will neither accept my friendship nor do you wish your life to be spared. Well, in this case you are permitted to die without your blood being shed. […] Do not disturb his remains but instead, with honours bury them.' Then Zhamuuha was killed, his remains were buried and his bones raised.'[530]

Once again, this is an episode based on Bɵ Murgel customs and beliefs. Mongol-Buryats believe that those who die a violent death – especially nobility, warriors or Bɵ and Utgan – become powerful spirits and this same belief was behind Queen Gurbesu's command to worship Wan Khaan's head in the hope of persuading him – now a powerful spirit – to protect her clan. Here, although the situation is somewhat different,

---

[528] This script was used until the early twentieth century when it was replaced by the Cyrillic alphabet by the Communists with the intention of undermining traditional culture and religion, both Bɵ Murgel and Buddhism, as their texts were written in this script.

[529] Ibid. p. 99.

[530] Kozin, *Sokrevennoe Skazanie*, p. 100.

the underlying meaning is analogous. Seeing that there is no place for him in the current order among Mongols, Zhamuuha is volunteering to become a guardian-spirit of Chingis Khaan's clan. Furthermore, he asks to be killed without shedding blood, another ancient Mongol custom and belief: royal blood should not be shown to the High Sky. The texts do not give details of his execution, but it is probable that he was rolled into a thick carpet and suffocated. Zhamuuha also asks his *anda* to 'raise his bones'.[531] This is the kind of burial given to a Bө whereby the body is buried on a high sacred hill or mountain, or in a tree. The place where the bones are raised then becomes the new protector-spirit's main residence. Zhamuuha goes on to ask that his words be remembered and repeated in the morning and evening and this, in effect, is a request to be honoured with offerings while the oath he gave to Chingis Khaan and his ancestors is repeated as an invocation. This way of invoking protector-spirits is common among Mongol-Buryats and Tibetans alike. In fact, this account of Zhamuuha's execution finds direct parallels in Tibetan history and is very much comparable, for example, to the controversy surrounding Dorje Shugden,[532] the spirit of a high Buddhist lama who committed suicide (or was assassinated by the government), an adversary of the Fifth Dalai Lama who, after his violent death, became a very powerful guardian of the most orthodox wing of the Gelugpa School. As no such methods for becoming a protective spirit can be found within Indian Buddhism or Yungdrung Bön, we must conclude that such a notion could only have come from the Bө Murgel culture brought into Tibet by the Mongols, who were ardent supporters of the Gelugpa order, or from some remnants of a darker stream of the Prehistoric Bön of Tibet. In either case, it demonstrates a matching phenomenon which points to ancient connections between these two religious streams.

Ih Mongol Uls[533] *– The Great Mongol Empire*

Subjugation of the Forest Tribes

With the destruction of the remaining groups of Naiman and Mergid and the death of Zhamuuha, most of the steppe Mongol tribes were under Chingis Khaan's rulership. However, the Mongols had paid a high price for unification; approximately half had been killed and some tribes had been completely wiped out. In May 1206 the remaining Mongols

---

[531] Bur. яhа бариха – literally: 'to lift up the bones'. See ch. XIII, Part II.

[532] Tib. rDor rje Shugs ldan.

[533] Bur. Их Монгол Улс.

gathered for the Grand Huryltai[534] and *tailgan* on the banks of the River Onon. After the ritual consecration of his white *tug,* Chingis Khaan was proclaimed the Supreme Khaan of the newly formed state, the Great Mongol Empire. The ceremony and ritual offerings were led by the powerful Bɵ Teb-Tenger.[535] On this occasion Chingis Khaan reorganized his army and state according to the ancient principles of Hunnu and Syanbi and introduced new rules of subordination; the army was divided into right and left wings mirroring the heavenly orders of Tengeri sky-gods which we will look into in the next chapter.

Although Chingis Khaan was proclaimed Supreme Khaan of all the Mongols, the Forest Tribes of the Baikal region were not as yet officially under his control. As we have seen, the Forrest Tribes were a mixture of Mongol, Tyurkic and Indo-European peoples, the ancestors of modern-day Buryats. Their way of life was different from that of the steppe Mongols as they were not livestock herders but hunter-gatherers. Their houses were not the felt *gher* of their cousins from the steppe but conical *gher* (*chum*) covered with tree bark or deer skins reminiscent of Native American tepees. In 1207 Zuchi,[536] Chingis Khaan's oldest son, was given command over the right wing of the army and sent to conquer the Forest Tribes. With the exception of the Hori-Tumed, the Forest Tribes put up no resistance and gladly accepted Chingis Khaan's

Fig. 36. Hamag Mongol Uls and early Ih Mongol Uls.

---

534 Bur. хурылтай, хуралтай or хурултай.

535 Bur. Тэб-тэнгэр.

536 Bur. Зүчи.

dominion. It seems the Hori-Tumed (Hori-Buryaad)[537] were the biggest tribe in the region because a separate contingent was sent against them under the command of Borohul,[538] Chingis Khaan's adopted brother. This expedition was a disaster; Borohul was killed. Crazed with anger and indignation, Chingis Khaan wanted to go and avenge Borohul's death in person, but his advisors calmed him and Durbei Dogshin[539] was sent instead. He led his army along animal trails, widening them with axes as they went thus enabling them to attack suddenly from an unexpected direction. The unsuspecting Hori-Tumed were feasting with their queen, Daiduhul Sohor Hatan (nicknamed Targan Botohoi,[540] Fat Botohon). They were captured without a battle and their queen was made a sex slave; the subjugation of the Forest Tribes was completed.

Mutiny of the Supreme Bɵ and the amalgamation of secular and religious authority

Next Chingis Khaan had to turn his attention to a scenario familiar to many rulers before and after him; he had to prevent a threat from within the religious congregation which had instigated a movement to curb his powers and take a leading position within the state. This threat came from within Chingis Khaan's immediate circle. On his deathbed, Chingis Khaan's father Yesuhei Baatar had asked a man named Honhoton Menlig[541] to look after the young Temuuzhin and so to Chingis Khaan he was 'father-Menlig'. Menlig had seven sons of his own, all of whom were very strong and wild. The oldest, Huhechu,[542] was the most powerful Bɵ around and held the title Teb-Tenger, Most Heavenly One. His magical powers were formidable and, riding his grey horse, he could fly into the sky for counsel with the Tengeri sky-gods. While presiding over the ceremony of Chingis Khaan's coronation, he entered a trance and announced that the Tengeri blessed Chingis Khaan and affirmed his title. Subsequently he delivered prophecies to Chingis Khaan and was a man of considerable influence. Gradually he began to interfere in all areas of government business and his arrogance and influence grew every day. One day the seven Honhoton brothers beat Chingis Khaan's brother Hasar who fell to his knees before the Khaan bewailing his misfortune.

---

[537] Bur. Хори-буряад.

[538] Bur. Борохул.

[539] Bur. Дүрбэй-Догшин.

[540] Bur. Дайдухул сохор хатан, Тарган Ботохой.

[541] Bur. Хонхотон Мэнлиг.

[542] Bur. Хүхэчү.

However, his brother was ill-disposed and said, 'You are supposed to be invincible but now you've lost'. Upset, Hasar left in tears and for three days didn't come to see the Khaan. Teb-Tenger profited from these tensions within the royal camp and, coming before Chingis Khaan, delivered a fake prophecy: 'The eternal Tengeri have communicated their will to me. It appears you and Hasar will rule the state alternately. If you don't hurry now the future cannot be secured.' The great Khaan believed his false words, jumped on his horse without delay and rode out to arrest Hasar. However, their mother Oelun found out about this turn of events and went after her son. She arrived just in time. Having taken away Hasar's hat and belt and tied his sleeves, Chingis Khaan was interrogating his younger brother but the sudden arrival of their angry mother put him to shame. She returned Hasar's hat and belt to him and untied his sleeves. So angry was she that, crouching down, she undid her blouse and swung her naked breasts on her knees saying:

> 'Can you see these breasts which you sucked? Oh, you eaters of your mother's gut and killers of your brother![543] What has Hasar done to you? In the past Temuuzhin used to empty one of my full breasts while Hachiun[544] and Otchigin[545] together couldn't empty even one. But Hasar soothed me and pleased me by emptying both my breasts. That is why Temuuzhin became wise and Hasar became strong and a skilled archer. Is it because Hasar crushed our enemies that you hate him?' Chingis Khaan managed to calm their mother and said, 'I am afraid of my mother's wrath and I am ashamed. We shall leave!'[546]

This incident is significant in that it illustrates another important Bө Murgel custom of the Mongol-Buryats which is also found among Tibetans. Wearing a belt and a hat was considered to be very tightly connected with one's energy, good luck and protection.[547] No-one would dream of setting out on a journey or of embarking on anything of importance without wearing both hat and belt. When Oelun saw Hasar's belt and hat in Chingis Khaan's hands she immediately understood the gravity of the situation and this explains her powerful emotional response.

The royal family, then, was in discord and Teb-Tenger's influence

---

[543] While still boys Temuuzhin and Hasar had shot dead their half-brother Begter (Bur. Бэгтэр) to stop him from bullying them.

[544] Bur. Хачиун.

[545] Bur. Отчигин.

[546] Kozin, *Sokrovennoe Skazanie*, p. 100.

[547] For adetailed analysis see ch. XIII.

was growing rapidly, so much so that subjects of Chingis Khaan's vassals were coming to Teb-Tenger in droves. Even Chingis Khaan's own subjects started thinking of moving to Teb-Tenger's camp and it would appear he was wielding magic as well as weaving intrigues to further his position. Chingis Khaan remained inert, fearing the Bo's magic and at a loss. However, events finally forced his hand.

Among those who had allied themselves with Teb-Tenger were many people under the command of Chingis Khaan's younger brother Otchigin. Otchigin sent an envoy to Teb-Tenger demanding their return but Teb-Tenger mocked the envoy and, taking away his horse, put the saddle on the messenger's own back and sent him away saying, 'Now you look like an envoy fit for your lord!' Otchigin's wrath was aroused and, deeply offended, the very next day he went in person to demand his men back saying, 'You ridiculed my envoy and sent him back on foot. Now I demand my subjects back!' But the seven Honhoton brothers surrounded him and retorted, 'Why do you think you have the right to send us your envoy?' Seeing the situation was growing dangerous, Otchigin retracted saying, 'I am guilty, I made a mistake.' In turn the brothers replied, 'If you are guilty then apologize on your knees!' and so he was made to kneel before Teb-Tenger and left humiliated without his people. Early the next morning Otchigin went to Chingis Khaan who was still in bed with his wife Burte. Crying bitterly, he told his sorry tale and before Chingis Khaan could say anything, Burte sat up in the bed covering her chest with the end of the blanket and, crying, said:

> 'What is it these Honhoton are doing! Just the other day they beat Hasar and now this. How dare they force Otchigin to his knees? What kind of civil order is this? If it goes on like this they'll do away with your brothers who are like larch and pine trees. When your body falls like a dry tree, who will they set to rule over your kingdom which by that time will be like scattered hemp plants? When your body collapses like a pillar who will they allow to rule your kingdom which by that time will be like a flock of birds? Will these people who are able to do away with even your brothers, who are like larch and pine trees, let me somehow raise my three or four little babies? What are they doing, these Honhoton? And how can you quietly bear such treatment of your brothers?' These words hit the mark. Chingis Khaan said to Otchigin, 'When Teb-Tenger comes I allow you to do with him as you wish.'[548]

Then Otchigin stood up and went away. He commanded three of his strongest men to be ready. Soon Menlig arrived with his seven sons.

---

[548] Kozin, *Sokrevennoe Skazanie*, p. 100.

They came in and Teb-Tenger immediately sat in the place of honour but Otchigin grabbed him by his gown and said, 'Yesterday you made me pray for forgiveness. Let's see how we fare now!' He started dragging him towards the exit. Teb-Tenger also grabbed Otchigin by the gown and a brawl ensued in the course of which Teb-Tenger's hat fell on the floor in front of the hearth. Menlig carefully picked it up, kissed and put it safely under his armpit for Mongols consider it bad luck to lose one's hat but here it even fell in front of the rival's hearth. At this point Chingis Khaan called out, 'Hey, you two, go and fight outside!' Otchigin dragged Teb-Tenger outside where his strongmen were waiting. They took the Bɵ, broke his spine and threw his corpse on the edge of the camp.

Coming back into the yurt, Otchigin said, 'Teb-Tenger made me pray for forgiveness but he himself doesn't want to take up my offer see how we fare today. He's pretending to lie down. It turns out he isn't a real friend after all!' Menlig understood at once what had happened, started to weep and said, 'Mother Earth doesn't have as many stones, the sea and the rivers don't have as many streams as I have done friendly favours for you!' Hearing these words the six remaining brothers surrounded the hearth blocking Chingis Khaan's way and started closing in on him. Shouting, 'Give way, disperse!' he pushed his way outside where he was immediately surrounded by his bodyguards. He saw Teb-Tenger's corpse and ordered a grey yurt to be brought from the back yard and put over the dead body. Some of the guards were ordered to close the smoke hole and lock the yurt door and stand there on guard while the rest of the camp packed and moved on. These actions clearly show that Chingis Khaan was afraid of the Bɵ even when he was dead. At dawn on the third day a miracle happened: the smoke hole opened by itself and Teb-Tenger's corpse flew into the sky. Divination was immediately done and revealed this was because of his magic powers. Chingis Khaan, however, declared, 'Teb-Tenger aggressively used his hands and feet against my brothers. He spread unfounded rumours between them. That is why the Tengeri sky-gods grew angry with him and on the orders of Eternal Blue Sky they took not only his soul but also his body!' Not only does this confound the results of the divination, it also runs contrary to Mongol ideas about the powers of a Bɵ and as such was surely dictated by political considerations. Under different circumstances such an event would be seen as an indisputable manifestation of the deceased Bɵ's incredible powers, that he had been taken to the Sky to dwell there with the Tengeri forever.[549] Far from being a punishment as Chingis Khaan suggested,

---

[549] See ch. XIII, Part II.

this is in fact an incredible privilege. If a Bө were to be punished by the gods, he would be imprisoned in the Underworld after his death, not in the Sky. Judging from some of Teb-Tenger's attributes, the fact that he was said to ride a grey horse into the sky and because Chingis Khaan ordered a grey yurt to be put over his corpse, it is clear that Teb-Tenger was neither a white nor a black Bө but could worship both Black and White Tengeri.[550]

Religious and social reform under Chingis Khaan

The threat of mutiny was crushed and after the death of Teb-Tenger Chingis Khaan faced no opposition from other Bө; after all, despite all Teb-Tenger's magical powers, it was Chingis Khaan whom Eternal Blue Sky had allowed to be the victor. In the eyes of the Mongols this could mean only one thing: Chingis Khaan was beyond doubt the Son of Heaven and Earth and thus more powerful than the most powerful Bө. Chingis Khaan promoted the Elder Usun[551] to the rank of *behi* saying:

> 'According to our Mongol law it is customary to hold the rank of *behi* as high as that of *noyon*[552] […] So, let Usun bear the title of *behi*. When the ceremony is performed he should wear a white fur coat, ride a white horse and then be seated on the throne. Let him deliver the predictions about the auspicious years and days (astrological conjunctions).'[553]

From Usun's attributes, it is clear that he was a White Bө. This passage also suggests that Bө Murgel already contained clear knowledge of astrology which must have been independent from Buddhist astrology as Buddhism had not yet arrived in Mongolia; such astrological knowledge most probably derived from Bönpo texts and oral traditions brought to the Great Steppe by Zhang Zhung and Tibetan Bönpo masters in early times, such as during the first and second persecutions.[554]

The events of the initial period of the Great Mongol Empire had a profound impact on the practices and rituals of the Bө Murgel religion. As a military leader, Chingis Khaan unified several Mongol tribes under his *tug* but this could not have been achieved without the spiritual traditions of all the Mongol tribes involved undergoing an intense process of

---

550 For details on various types of Bө see ch. VIII.

551 Bur. Усун.

552 Bur. ноён, a high-ranking feudal lord acting as a governor.

553 Kozin, *Sokrovennoe Skazanie*, p. 109.

554 See ch. XV.

Fig. 37. Chingis Khaan in his royal gher *with* tugs *and two wings of the army.*

integration and exchange as they adapted to the new social and political reality. In fact, Chingis Khaan actually had two *tugs*, one black and one white. At official ceremonies Chingis Khaan would be seated facing south flanked by the two wings of his army which, as we have seen, were divided to mirror the heavenly order. At his right, then, was the white *tug,* the *tug* for those tribes, including his own, whose protective deities were White Tengeri and it represented the right wing of his army. At his left there was the black *tug* for those tribes whose protective deities were Black Tengeri and it represented the left wing of his army. Chingis Khaan's central position indicated that he was beyond partiality and had indeed been promoted to the position of Supreme Khaan of Mongols by the will of Eternal Blue Sky and Mother Earth. Therefore no-one, not even the supreme Bɵ, had higher authority in either political or spiritual matters. The custom of facing south dates back to ancient times as Mongols have traditionally always turned towards the south to sprinkle offerings to the sun.[555]

---

[555] See ch. XV.

Under the unifying leadership of Chingis Khaan, the Bө Murgel cults of the various Mongol tribes were also revised, reformed and integrated. It is in this period that the ranks and hierarchy of the various deities and spirits forming the Bө Murgel pantheon were formalised, and this religious reform was accepted by all Mongol tribes of the day. The structure of Mongol society became an earthly reflection of the heavenly order of the gods and spirits. No matter how violent his methods may seem, Chingis Khaan's intention was to bring about universal harmony, to do away with violence and unrest – an aim he certainly achieved among Mongols. In an incredibly short time, a violent and fragmented society based on suspicion and fear where no-one could trust even their own relatives and friends, where constant robberies and bloodshed were an everyday reality, was transformed into a harmonious social structure. Foreign visitors to Mongolia described Mongols as kind to one another, there was reportedly no crime among them and they treated one another as brothers and sisters. Nevertheless, it was a medieval society with all that entailed, including institutionalized slavery, and the Mongols were extremely violent to any nation showing resistance, but within their own society a great transformation was brought about by the actions and policies of Chingis Khaan.

The majority of the Mongols of that time were devout practitioners of Bө Murgel (Shazhan) but some Mongol tribes, such as the Mergid and the Naiman had been Nestorian Christians for generations even before the tribes unified. Despite the fact that Chingis Khaan himself firmly followed Bө Murgel traditions and that the structure of Mongol society as a whole was inspired by the heavenly order of Tengeri, the leader was extremely tolerant towards other faiths, seeing them simply as other forms of worshipping Eternal Blue Sky. Thanks to this view, the Mongols of Chingis Khaan's day neither attempted to convert others nor did they persecute or seek to destroy other faiths. At the great Khaan's court one could meet Christians of various confessions, Taoists, Buddhists, Muslims and followers of other faiths. However, after Chingis Khaan's death this enlightened attitude gradually changed as the Mongol princes fell under the spell of foreign religious missionaries. This change did not augur well for the religion of their ancestors; from the seventeenth to nineteenth centuries Bө Murgel was severely persecuted in its own lands by Buddhists and Christians, and then by Communists in the twentieth century.

Further expansion of the Mongol Empire

With the internal unity of the Mongols secured, Chingis Khaan now had the strength he needed to pursue a more challenging vendetta against the Altan Tzin, and this developed into the rapid expansion of the Mongol Empire far beyond Mongol ancestral lands.

In the early thirteenth century, China was divided into three states, only one of which, Southern Sung, was ruled by ethnic Chinese. Northern China was under the rule of Jurchen emperors of Altan Tzin and modern-day Inner Mongolia was under the control of the Tanguut,[556] a nation of Tibetan origin. The campaign against China started with military expeditions against Altan Tzin and the Tanguut Hsi-Hsia (Xi-Xia) kingdom in 1211. In fact, the Tanguuts had come under Mongol attack several times from 1205–1209 because they were giving refuge to the remaining bands of Hereid and Naiman warriors. But in 1211 the Mongols penetrated enemy territory as far as Beijing. Several Jin cities were under siege prompting Altan Khaan to send a diplomatic mission with gifts and tributes of gold, silver, silks and even a princess. Chingis Khaan lifted the siege of Beijing and other cities, and the Mongol army withdrew for the time being, their horses staggering under the weight of the extensive tributes. That same year the Mongols came to Hsi-Hsia again but the Tanguuts gave no resistance. Their king, Ilahu Burkhan,[557] swore an oath of loyalty to Chingis Khaan and supplied the Mongols with a great number of highly prized white camels. The peace didn't last, however. Altan Khaan foolishly blocked Mongol ambassadors on a diplomatic mission to Southern Sung, Chingis Khaan's fury was aroused and the Mongols came once more to the walls of Beijing. Altan Khaan abandoned the city and retreated to Kaifeng. Beijing was taken and sacked and all its inhabitants killed.

In 1218 the kingdom of Hara-Kitai, the remains of the once all-powerful Hyadan', was conquered and, in response to the massacre of his commercial and diplomatic mission sent to Urgench, capital of Khorezm state, Chingis Khaan invaded Central Asia. The Mongol army invaded Khorezm and occupied eastern Turkestan and Persia. Bukhara and Samarkand were taken and then in 1221 Urgench fell to the Mongols. The Shah of Khorezm, Muhhamad, fled as far as the Caspian Sea where he died in hiding on an island. His son Jalal-ad-Din was a great warrior and with the remains of his army he fought many battles against the Mongols before finally managing to escape to India.

---

[556] Bur. Тангуут.

[557] Bur. Илаху Бурхан.

In 1221, Mongol armies under the command of Zeby[558] and Subedei[559] were sent on a prolonged reconnaissance raid westwards. They invaded Persian Azerbaijan and Georgia, then went on to fight and defeat Lezgin, Cherkes, Alan and Kýpchak forces, eventually reaching Russia where they heavily defeated the confederation of Russian kings at the Battle of Kalka on 31 May, 1222. On this occasion the Mongols didn't venture deep into Russia but turned towards Crimea where they destroyed the Genovese port of Soldaya. They then attacked the Bulgars living along the River Kama and, crossing the Volga and then the Urals, they conquered Tyurk-Kangly and returned to Mongolia through Tarbagatai. The Mongol army had covered a distance of eight thousand kilometres and gathered invaluable strategical information which was used by Subedei twenty years later when he was sent by Chingis Khaan's sons to conquer Europe.

In the autumn of 1225 Chingis Khaan returned to Mongolia and rested on the banks of River Tuula. He was then fifty-eight years old. However, he didn't rest for long. The following year he started a military campaign against the Tanguut to punish them for an earlier betrayal; in 1219 the Tanguut had reneged on their promise of assistance and, refusing to supply a military contingent for the war against the Shah of Khorezm, had insulted Chingis Khaan saying, 'If you're not strong enough then you shouldn't go!' Although angered to the quick, Chingis Khaan postponed the punitive expedition, vowing to destroy the Tanguut when the time was right. Now the time had come. At the beginning of the expedition Chingis Khaan was severely injured when he fell from his horse while out hunting.

Fig. 38. Chingis Khaan.

The Mongol military leaders held a council and decided to postpone the expedition and until Chingis Khaan recovered. They reasoned that, being a settled nation, the Tanguut would be in the same land the next year. Chingis Khaan, however, didn't accept the council's recommendations and said, 'The Tanguut may think we retreated because we are cowards. We should send an ambassador to them and wait here till he comes back

---

558 Bur. Зэбы.

559 Bur. Сүбээдэй.

to think over their reply.' So an ultimatum was sent to Tanguut. On hearing the ultimatum, the King of Tanguut, Ilahu Burkhan, retorted, 'I didn't say those offending words!' But his military commander Asha-Hambu[560] interjected, 'It is I who said those offending words. Now if you Mongols wish to fight then you must know I possess great wealth. Come to my camp in Alashai and we shall fight there!' These reckless words of an arrogant man sealed the fate of the Tanguut nation. Chingis Khaan quickly moved on Alashai, destroyed the army of Asha-Hambu and killed most of the Tanguut. Those who managed to survive the slaughter were taken into slavery. Ilahu Burkhan came to beg forgiveness with a magnificent array of rich offerings but it was too late; the offerings were accepted but Chingis Khaan ordered the king's execution. '*Burkhan*' means 'god' in Mongolian so in order not to offend the gods, Ilahu Burkhan was renamed Shudarga,[561] the Honest (not without sarcasm), and only then killed.

Meanwhile Chingis Khaan's health was deteriorating. He died on 18 August 1227 and his body was brought to Burkhan Haldun and buried in a secret spot according to his wishes. No monument or any other memorable sign was erected at his grave. The cult of the ritual worship of Chingis Khaan was subsequently introduced by Hubilai Khaan and is still alive in Ordos. In Buryatian Bө Murgel, Chingis Khaan is worshipped as *Ongon*[562] Tolitoi Burkhan[563] and has his residences at Barhan Uula,[564] Mount Shalsaana in Hezhenge,[565] Dushe Hada,[566] Uula[567] on Olhon Island and Mount Komushka in Ulaan-Ude[568] where he is known as Bayaan Baatar Khaan.[569]

Chingis Khaan made an impressive impact on all aspects of the Mongol nation. He was at once tough and soft, violent and kind, just and biased, truthful and cunning; he loved wisdom discourses and hunting – an invincible paradox which his adversaries were at a loss to decipher. The debate still continues as to whether he was fundamentally good or bad; none of these notions apply. He was a quintessential reflection of

---

[560] Bur. Аша хамбу.

[561] Bur. шударга.

[562] Bur. онгон, an ancestral protective deity and/or its support; see ch. IV.

[563] Bur. Толитой бурхан.

[564] Bur. Бархан уула.

[565] Bur. Шалсаана, Хэжэнгэ.

[566] Bur. Дүшэ хада.

[567] Bur. Уула.

[568] Bur. Комушка, Улаан-Удэ.

[569] Bur. Баяан Баатар хаан.

that time, space and nation. Chingis Khaan introduced law and order into a lawless society; he initiated an education system and presided over the creation of a writing system for the Mongol language; he consolidated the multiplicity of Bө Murgel traditions and didn't shy away from seeking the advice of men of wisdom pertaining to other spiritual traditions, such as Taoist Chang Chung and the Hyadan' scholar and astrologer Yelyui Chutsai.

Mongols and Bө Murgel after Chingis Khaan

After Chingis Khaan's death, the Mongols continued their expansion and during the rest of the thirteenth century ventured as far as Austria in the west, Morocco in the southwest, Java in the south and Japan in the east. Later this huge empire fragmented and many independent and semi-independent kingdoms and Mongol royal dynasties emerged within the vast conquered territories. Mongol royalty directly governed China, India and great swathes of Central Asia as well as controlling Tibet, Russia and many other countries and territories directly or indirectly. In terms of culture, military strategies and political methods, the Mongols' influence was considerable throughout Eurasia and beyond. Flexible and adaptive, the Mongols were gradually absorbed into the populations of the countries they conquered in the same way as the earlier Hunnu, Tyurkyut and Kök Tyurks had been, contributing to the genetic diversity of those nations.

Let us leave the Mongols in their vast empire for now and turn our attention to Buryatia, to chart the development of the Buryats after the Forest Tribes were conquered.

The peoples and history of Buryatia and the development of Buryatian Bө Murgel

One of the Buryats' ancestors we have not discussed so far are the Gooligan' or Kurykan,[570] sometimes called the Kurumchinskaya Culture. Although we don't know their precise racial type, they are generally considered to be of Tyurkic stock, that is to say, they appeared as a result of the mixing of proto-Mongol and Indo-European peoples which had been going on in Southern Siberia for thousands of years. The Gooligan' lived around Lake Baikal in the fifth to ninth centuries AD when the Great Steppe was dominated by the Tyurkyut Khaganates. The Gooligan' had a wide range of skills. Fierce warriors, they could muster an army

---

570 Rus. Гулигань/Курыкан.

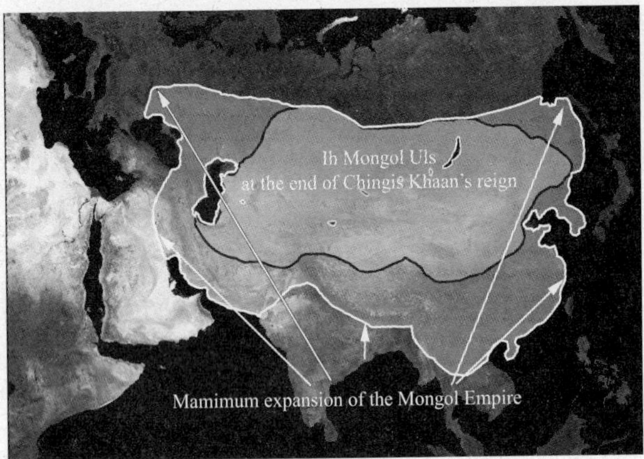

Fig. 39. Maximum expansion of Ih Mongol Uls.

of five thousand horsemen and were skilful hunters although they also kept domestic animals, including camels, and tilled the earth. They were superb craftsmen and their ironsmiths produced iron of 99.43% purity. Their culture was quite developed and they used the old Orkhon-Yenisei Tyurkic runes, very similar to the North European runes,[571] for writing their language. These people lived around the lower reaches of the River Selenga as well as in the Barguzin Valley, Tunka, the valley of the River Angara up to modern-day Balagansk, and along the upper reaches of the River Lena. The Gooligan' are considered common ancestors of both Buryats and Yakuts although both these nations have many other additional ancestral lines, too. The Yakut used to live around Lake Baikal until the last of them finally left the Tunka region of modern Buryatia in 1763, pushed out by the Hongodor[572] Buryatian tribe.[573]

---

[571] As we now know, over the centuries many tribes and nations from the Great Steppe and Lake Baikal migrated westward and settled in various parts of Europe bringing their culture with them, runes included. There is reason to suggest that a branch of the Gooligan' travelled as far as Ireland and became the Hoolihan/Hooligan clan. The name then became a synonym for a violent mobster, 'hooligan', after Patrick Hooligan murdered a London policeman in 1898. The first use of the name in this context is attributed to the Russian columnist I.V. Shklovskii who published an article on English current affairs in the *Russian Wealth* (Rus. Русское Богатсво) newspaper the same year. See Joan Neuberger, *Hooliganism: Crime, Culture, and Power in St. Petersburg, 1900–1914*, (Berkley-Los Angeles-London: University of California Press, 1993), Chapter I.

[572] Bur. Хонгоодор.

[573] A. N. Okladnikov, *Istoriya i kul'tura Buryatii* (Ulaan-Ude: Buryatskoe

To summarize, the main peoples who contributed to the formation of Buryatian nation, culture and religion are: Tungus (later Evenki), Hunnu, Syanbi, Tabgach (Toba), Uighur (Hor), Tyurkyut (Tyu-kyu), Gooligan', Bayirku (Bayegoot), Yakut, Orochi, Hori-Tumed, Barguud (Barga), Buryaad, Ehirit (Ikires), Bulagchin (Bulgat), Heremchin, Oin-Uryanhai, Ursuud, Habhanas, Hanhas, Tuba, Shibir, Hesdin, Bayad, Tuhas,Tenlig, To'ols, Tas, Bayagid, Telenguud, Kestemi, Kuri, Harluut (Karluk), Yenisei Kyrgyz, Oirod (Oirat) and many other smaller nations.

Main Buryatian tribes and clans

With the conquest of the Forest Tribes, the Baikal region became a part of the extremely well-organized Mongol Empire and so the Buryats, too, organized themselves into four main tribes with many clans within each tribe. The four main tribes are: Bulgat,[574] Ehirit, Horëodoi (Hori)[575] and Hongodor. Each of the many tribal clans has its own Bө Murgel traditions.

The Ehirit lived along the upper straits of the River Zulhe (Lena)[576] and on the northern shore of Baikal and the Olhon[577] Island. The Bulgat lived along the River Angara and its tributaries the Kuda, Ida, Udi (Ushakovka), Erhu (Irkut) and Hooti (Kitoi).[578] The Hongodor lived along the left bank of the Angara and at the mouth of the rivers Irkut, Bulen (Belaya)[579]and Kitoi. The Horëodoi (Hori) mostly lived along the upper straits of the River Uda and its tributaries.

In the seventeenth century there was a wave of migration of Halh[580] and Dzungar[581] Mongol clans from Mongolia, some of which had left the Baikal region for central Mongolia in the past. Halh Mongol clans who came were: Atagan, Hatagan, Horchi, Hahar, Tsongol, Tugchin, Uzon, Urat, Sratuul, Horlos, Dzhalair, Mingan and Hachitun.[582] They settled mainly in the area surrounding the Selenga and its tributaries.

---

knizhnoe izdatel'stvo, 1976), pp. 8, 22–32.

[574] Bur. Булгат.

[575] Bur. Хорёодой (Хори/Хорь).

[576] Bur. Зүлхэ (Rus. Лена).

[577] Bur. Ойхон (Rus. Ольхон).

[578] Bur. Куда, Ида, Уда, Эди (Rus. Ушаковка), Эрху (Rus. Иркут), Хути (Rus. Китой).

[579] Bur. Бүлэн (Rus. Белая).

[580] Bur. Халх.

[581] Bur. Зунгар.

[582] Bur. Атаган, Хатаган, Хорчи, Чахар, Цонгол, Тугчин, Узон, Урат, Сартуул, Хорлос, Джалаир, Минган, Хачиун.

The Dzungar Mongol clans who came over were divided into Zungar and Barungar,[583] right and left, and were the Sharanut, Haranut, Boronut, Segenuut, Huheut and Hureut.[584] They settled on the borderlands of the Bulgat and Ehirit. Today, both the Halh and Dzungar clans are small.

Some other clans not belonging to any particular major tribe are: Ashagabad,[585] ethnically close to the Halh; the Hurduud,[586] a powerful Bө clan who migrated to Buryatia from Hara-Darhat[587] in Mongolia; Khaan-Kyrgyz,[588] descendants of the Yenisei Kyrgyz; the Turgut and Burut,[589] descendants of the Tyurkyut; the Sratuul,[590] descendants of Persian slaves captured by the Mongols in Chingis Khaan's times; the Tanguut, people of Tibeto-Burmese stock, descendants of slaves taken in the conquest of the Hsi-Hsia kingdom, now almost extinct. There are many more small clans but we shall not go into further minute details here.

The conquest of Buryatia

From the times of Chingis Khaan up until the second half of the seventeenth century the Baikal region and the Buryats living there were under the yoke of the various central Mongolian Khaanates to whom they paid *yasak*[591] taxes in precious furs.

In 1580, however, the Russian conquest of Siberia had also begun, with a military campaign led by the Don Cossack Ataman,[592] Ermak (Yermak). He had initially been hired by a merchant family, the Stroganovs, to protect their business interests in the Ural Mountains from the attacks

Fig. 40. Ermak.

---

[583] Bur. Зунгар, Барунгар.

[584] Bur. Шаранут, Харанут, Боронут, Сэгэнүүт, Хүхэут, Хүрэнут.

[585] Bur. Ашабагад.

[586] Bur. Хурдууд.

[587] Mong. Хара-Дархат.

[588] Bur. Хаан-Кыргыз.

[589] Bur. Тургут, Бурут.

[590] Bur. Сартуул.

[591] Rus. ясак – from the Turkic and Mongol word meaning 'tax'.

[592] Rus. атаман – Cossack military leader.

of the Muslim Tatar Khaan Kuchum of the Siberian Khaanate with its capital city of Kashlyk (Sibir', Isker). Although nominally a vassal of the Russian Empire, in 1573 Khaan Kuchum made a raid on the Russian city of Perm providing the Cossacks with an excuse to venture east of the Urals.

In September 1581, together with 540 Cossacks and 300 people supplied by the Stroganovs, Ermak went after Khaan Kuchum. This was the first step in the long history of the Russian conquest of Siberia. Khaan Kuchum was eventually defeated in 1598 and so the first period of Russia's colonisation of Siberia began.

In the late 1620's the Russians built several *ostrog*[593] fortresses in key strategic locations to the west and north of Buryatia such as Yeniseiskiy Ostrog, Kransoyarskiy Ostrog and Yakutskiy Ostrog. These served as military bases for the invasion of Buryatia. Initially Russian Cossacks conducted covert reconnaissance missions in cahoots with Evenki hunters. In 1626 Ataman Perfilyev tried to reach Buryatia but didn't succeed. In 1627 he again set out but met Evenki tribes and, having taken *yasak* from them, turned back without reaching Buryatia. Rumours of great quantities of silver to be found in Buryatia started to circulate among the Russians and these, together with the already common knowledge of the large amounts of precious furs there, spurred the Cossacks on to enter Buryatia for the first time in 1628 under the command of Sotnik[594] Beketov who took the first *yasak* tax from the Buryats. The following year, 1629, saw the first military confrontation between Russian Cossacks and Buryats, near the mouth of the River Oka. In 1631 the Bratskiy Ostrog was built and in 1634 fifty or so Cossacks were deployed there but the Buryats, under the command of Kutugur and Kodogun, attacked them, killing them all. Having looted the gun-powder, bullets and so on, they destroyed the *ostrog*. In 1641 the Buryatian Chepuguev Ulus was devastated by a Russian military group led by Vlasyev and later the same year Verholenskiy Ostrog was built, with Nizhneudinskiy Ostrog following it in 1648. Although the Buryats put up constant resistance, Russian military power and logistic support were superior and so by the 1650's a network of *ostrogs* had been established and these became the base for the further conquest of Buryatia. In 1644 there was a Buryat uprising led by Bului, Bura and Chohora but it was swiftly suppressed and in 1649 the Balagat Buryats revolted. In 1658 many Buryatian clans moved to Mongolia to escape Russian expansion and the repressions of

---

593 Rus. острог – a fortified settlement surrounded by high wooden walls built from sharp-pointed logs.

594 Rus. сотник – a lieutenant of Cossack troups who commanded 100 warriors.

the governor Ivan Pohabov whom Buryats called Bagaba-Khaan. The corruption, bad management and repressions characteristic of his term in office reduced the amount of *yasak* trickling into the Imperial Treasury's coffers, and finally he was recalled to Russia as even the Cossacks complained about his conduct. In 1660 there was another exodus of Buryatian clans to Mongolia and the Balagat Steppe was deserted. There were further uprisings in 1669 and 1696 in which Buryats and Cossacks joined forces to revolt against the corrupt Russian administration.

The Mongols, too, were keeping a wary eye on the Russians. Having already lost a large chunk of Inner Mongolia to the Manchu state of Qing in the 1630's, the Dzungar Khaanate of Central Mongolia became concerned about the Russians making inroads into their backyard. They also saw Buryatian taxes growing thin as the Cossacks claimed *yasak* for the Russian Imperial Treasury. In 1668 Taisha Seigun attacked Balaganskiy, Verholenskiy and Ilimskiy Ostrogs. The following year Taisha Gygan again attacked Cossack *ostrogs* in Buryatia and it was only because Buryats from Angara stood against him that he was repelled. In 1682 Mongols attacked both Russians and Buryats. In 1687 the Mongol Khaan Ochiroi Sain attacked the towns of Selenginsk and Verhne-Udinsk (modern Ulaan-Ude, capital of the Republic of Buryatia) but was defeated. At the same time a constant struggle was raging between the Oirat and Manchu in Outer Mongolia and so Buryat clans who had earlier escaped to Mongolia started to return to Buryatia and began a military struggle against both Russians and Mongols. In 1688 the Mongols suffered several defeats in Buryatia at the hands of Fyodor Golovin. In 1689 the Russian Empire and Chinese (Manchu) Qing signed the Treaty of Nerchinsk which established the border running through the River Gorbitsa, Stanovoy Ridge and the River Argun, thus placing Transbaikalia and the Baikal regions under Russian control.

Life in Buryatia, and indeed throughout Siberia, was pretty grim. The native population found itself squeezed between the Russian, Mongol and Manchu Empires as they fought for control over the region, swallowing their lands and precious natural resources, plundering and killing. They were suffocated by the *yasak* and *yasyr*,[595] two ugly practices of legitimized robbery on an institutional level. The *yasak* was a kind of tax paid in prized furs or sometimes in domestic animals. Both Russians and Mongols used brute military force, intrigues, blackmail, threats and murders to extort this tax from the local Buryat, Evenki, Yakut and others. The Russian *yasak* consisted of two to six polar fox furs per

---

[595] Rus. ясырь from the Tatar word meaing 'prisoner', 'slave'.

person plus 'voluntary' presents for the Tsar, Russian Orthodox clergy and military commanders. *Yasyr* was the practice of taking hostages if a tribe, clan or family didn't contribute enough *yasak* or didn't have anything to give when the taxman called. Hostages had to be bought back by their relatives but if they were too late or if the captors took a fancy to the hostages, they were simply kept as permanent slaves, as was often the case with female hostages. The Russian market for native female sexual slaves was insatiable and they were sold and resold many times like animals.

Another cause of misery was the arrival of Russian Orthodox Christianity as the Orthodox priests in Buryatia practised forceful conversion. Although the Treaty of Nerchinsk included provision against this, it was overlooked on the ground. Natives who had been forcefully christened were given Russian names and taken as serfs by the clergy or became monastery peasants forced to pay the *obrok*[596] tax to the monasteries. They could even be sold like any other slave. The Russian state and the Russian Orthodox Church in Siberia ranked among the major slave traders of the seventeenth and eighteenth centuries. In 1733 an attempt to abolish the practice of forceful conversion to Christianity failed and it was only in 1744 that it was finally stopped, about a hundred years after its introduction. Needless to say, this practice dealt a serious blow to the Buryatian Bө Murgel religion. To the Orthodox Church leaders, Bө Murgel was a teaching of Satan and the Bө and Utgan were Satan's priests. Together with the Russian administration, the Orthodox clergy jumped at any excuse to undermine the native religious leaders' power and influence in Buryatian society, so Bө and Utgan were persecuted, physically assaulted and many were killed. As an active protagonist of a combined crusade and slave trade, the Russian Orthodox Church committed deadly sins in Siberia and greatly damaged the lives, cultures and religions of many Siberian nations, damage which is still felt by many today.

Although the Treaty of Nerchinsk established the border between Qing and Russia, it was not a very clear document and some clans still moved between Buryatia and Mongolia. Between 1665 and 1684, the Dzungar and Halh Mongol clans mentioned above migrated within the Buryatian territories. In 1691 the Halh Mongols fell under Qing and both the Russians and Manchu saw the necessity of imposing tougher regulations on cross-border movements and of taking cross-border trade under control. As a result, the Burinskiy and Kyahtinskiy Tractates were

---

[596] Rus. оброк.

signed in August and October of 1727 respectively, *de facto* closing the border and forbidding free movement without official permits. The Uryanghai[597] people were left on the Mongol side of the border. 1764–66 saw the establishment of the Buryatian Cossack military army. From 1782–83 there were three Russian Governor-Generals in Siberia in Tobolsk, Kolyvansk and Irkutsk and in 1796 the whole of Siberia was divided into two *guberniya*-provinces, Tobolskaya and Irkutskaya with Buryatia falling within the Irkutskaya Guberniya. In the eighteenth century the new phenomenon of monetary *yasak* was introduced, whereby government taxes could be paid in money.

The arrival of Buddhism in Buryatia

In the late seventeenth and early eighteenth centuries, Mongol and Tibetan Buddhist lamas started making inroads into Buryatia and gradually converting the population. They were mainly adherents of the Gelugpa School. The first two *datsans*,[598] Tsongolskiy Datsan and Gusino'ozerskyi Datsan,[599] were built in 1741 and altogether eleven Buddhist religious buildings and 150 monks were officially registered that year. While the Russian authorities were hostile to Bɵ Murgel with its loose structure and close associations with national Buryatian identity and resistance, they welcomed the incoming Lamaism,[600] seeing it as a potential political tool with which they could control the Buryats. Lamaism was a foreign religion, well organized with a clear hierarchical structure and no nationalist sentiment, so it suited the Russian government very well. The policy of forceful conversion into Orthodox Christianity was proving rather ineffective as even converted Buryats secretly continued worshipping the Tengeri and ancestral spirits. The Russian government hoped that Lamaism would succeed where Orthodox Christianity had failed and indeed, they were not so mistaken. Under the patronage of the Russian administration, Lamaism grew rapidly with newly arrived Buddhist lamas and overzealous converts taking a very hostile stance against Bɵ Murgel, its priests, priestesses and ordinary worshippers. They used their political clout, intrigues and destructive Buddhist Tantric

---

597 Bur. Урянгхай, Саха-Урянгхай, peoples who once lived along the shores of Baikal but then migrated to the southwest.

598 Bur. дацан, temple or a monastery.

599 Rus. Цонгольский Дацан, Гусиноозерский Дацан.

600 A term used to designate Tibetan and Mongolian forms of Buddhism with the accent on monasticism and the religious and secular authority of the Buddhist lamas. In the case of Buryatian Lamaism we are talking about the Gelugpa Buddhist order adapted to the political realities of the Russian Empire.

magic in their campaign to persecute and eradicate the native Bө Murgel religion, a scenario reminiscent of the persecution of Yungdrung Bön in eighth century Tibet. Sacred Bө Murgel power places were attacked and destroyed by Lamaists accompanied by the Russian police, and Bө and Utgan were beaten and killed. Practitioners of Bө found themselves caught between two fires: Lamaists pushing from the south and Orthodox priests pushing from the north. Add to this the generally hostile attitude of the Russian government and it is clear that these were indeed hard times for the Bө. By 1774 there were already ten large and six small *datsans* and 617 Buddhist monks. By 1882 the number of monks had jumped to 2,600 and in 1842 there were 5,545 monks.

In 1741 the Russian government installed the Tibetan Gelugpa lama Agvan Puntsuk[601] as the abbot of Tsongolskiy Datsan and in 1764 they officially approved the position of the Bandido Hambo Lama, the head of the independent Buryatian Buddhist Church under Russian patronage. The first Hambo Lama was lama Damba Dorzhi Zayaev,[602] awarded this title along with a government medal for his participation in the work on *Ulozhenie*,[603] the first legal document regulating Lamaist clergy. In the best political traditions of Tibetan Buddhism, Lamaists proclaimed Catherine the Great of Russia as a reincarnation of White Tara, Sagaan Dara Ehe[604] and other symptoms of 'political illness' followed. For example, although the position of Bandido Hambo Lama was initially attached to the Tsongolskiy Datsan, in 1783 a struggle flared up between the two Hambo Lamas of the main *datsans* (reminiscent of the epoch of the Fifth Dalai Lama of Tibet) with the candidate from Gusino'ozerskyi Datsan winning in 1809. A full collection of the Buddhist cannon of Gandzhur and *Dandzhur*[605] was bought in Tibet for twelve thousand domestic animals and so the Buryatian Lamaist Church was equipped with all the necessary materials. In the eighteenth and nineteenth centuries the Gelugpa Buddhist clergy gained considerable political influence in Buryatia as they allied themselves with Noyons and Taishas, administrative and political leaders of Buryatian tribes and clans. Seeing the usefulness of the Lamaist order in maintaining their regime in Buryatia, the Russian Tsarist government absolved monasteries from the *yasak* and even granted them lands. Each Buddhist monk received a piece of land, the size of which depended on their spiritual rank. Thus Hambo

---

[601] Bur. Агван Пунцук.

[602] Bur. Дамба Доржи Заяев.

[603] Rus. «Уложение».

[604] Bur. Сагаан Дара Эхэ.

[605] Bur. Ганджур, Данджур.

Lama was given 500 *desyatinas*;[606] *shiretui*[607] abbots received 200 each; each lama[608] received 60; each *bandi*-novice 30; and each *huvarak*[609]-novice 15. Needless to say, neither Bɵ nor Utgan were given any land from the government as they were not seen as useful to the authorities. Not only were *datsans* freed from the *yasak*, they were even allowed to keep offerings given to them by lay practitioners, as a result of which they grew rich and gradually corrupt. In 1853 Buryatian Buddhist monks were obliged to swear an oath to the Russian Tsar and although it was decided to reduce the number of 'official' lamas to five hundred, this was not put into practice. It was at this time, too, that the persecution of Bɵ and Utgan was forbidden by the Russian government.

Despite these measures, by the second half of the nineteenth century Bɵ Murgel had been practically destroyed by the Lamaists and Russians in Transbaikalia, with the exception of the Kudarinskaya Steppe.[610] Lamaism did not succeed to gain dominance in Tunka or the Alaraskaya Steppe[611] where Bɵ Murgel remained prevalent. Buryats living on the northern shore of Lake Baikal also retained their Bɵ Murgel faith. Many who had apparently converted to Christianity returned to Bɵ Murgel when the practice of forceful conversion was banned. In other regions of Buryatia both Bɵ Murgel and Lamaism were present and in many regions people followed both religions simultaneously. For example, despite the spread of Buddhism in Barguzin Bɵ Murgel remained very strong there. Often a person's decision to seek the help of the Bɵ or the lama was not based on their own religious convictions but simply on how they perceived the respective priest's psychic abilities; this is still the case with many lay people today. The majority of the local population didn't really grasp the fundamentals of Buddhist doctrine and, perceiving it through the prism of their previous Bɵ Murgel culture, saw it as just one of the new spiritual powers in the land. To a certain extent, this is true for Orthodox Christianity, too. Buryats are very practical, down to earth people and ordinary folks have no interest in theology or metaphysics

---

606 Rus. десятина. An old Russian imperial land measure. One *desyatina* corresponds to 1.45672 hectars.

607 Bur. ширэтуй.

608 Bur. лама. In Buryatia any monk is called 'lama'. This is different from the Tibetan system where in both Yungdrung Bön and Buddhist traditions alike, 'lama' (Tib. bla ma) means spiritual teacher of a high level of realization and may refer to a lay person, monk or nun.

609 Bur. баньди, хуварак – different ranks of novice monks.

610 Rus. Кударинская степь.

611 Rus. Аларская степь.

whatsoever; they judge a religion on the basis of its effectiveness in getting desired results on this plane of existence. Even now many Buryats do not understand the fundamental difference between Buddha and God, for example, and aren't really interested to find out; they simply relate to Buddha as a kind of benevolent god who is helpful in this life and after death. In times of need a citizen of Ulaan-Ude may well pop into the Orthodox Church to light a candle in front of a saint's image, visit the local Bѳ or Utgan and call at a *datsan* to make an offering and ask the lama to perform some *puja.*[612] This kind of attitude among the population was exacerbating the already very tense relationship between Bѳ, Utgan and Buryatian lamas who were competing with each other over the souls of ordinary Buryats.

The modern era

In the nineteenth century the Russian colonial government looked for ways to make Buryats more settled and less nomadic. As we have seen, the first step was closing the border with Mongolia. Subsequently the authorities reorganized the administrative structure of the Buryats not according to their tribal status but according to the territory where they lived, so they were redefined as Kudarintsy, Alartsy, Tunkintsy, Selenegintsy, Barguzintsy, Irkutsk Buryats, Olhontsy, Verholentsy[613] and so on. This new social order pushed Buryats living on the same territory closer to each other and that gave rise to differences in territorial cultures and customs. As a result, Buryats of the same tribe or clan who found themselves living in different administrative regions developed variations in their customs and Bѳ Murgel traditions as they were influenced by the traditions of their new neighbours and separated from their kinsfolk. This process was accelerated as a more settled way of life took hold, encouraged by government policies such as the introduction of agriculture which started in the 1790's.

Another important force in Siberia as a whole at this time, and in Buryatia in particular, was the process of capitalist development. In 1808 the government published a decree on the opening of shops and stores in Buryatia and this gradually transformed the local economy which until then had largely been based on barter deals. The major factor of economic development was the construction of the Siberian Railway between 1892–1905 which was to become the largest railway

[612] A Sanskrit word for a wide variety of offering rituals.

[613] Rus. Кударинцы, Аларцы, Тункинцы, Селенгинцы, Баргузинцы, Иркутские Буряты, Ольхонцы, Верхоленцы.

of that time, stretching from Chelyabinsk in the west and Vladivostok in the east. The railway meant fast growth for the coal and gold-mining industries as well as for the non-ferrous metal industry. Gold, rare metals and minerals, coal and furs were exported while agricultural machinery was imported from the USA, Britain and Germany.

The beginning of the twentieth century was marked by profound social changes and the degeneration of the Tsarist governing system throughout the Russian Empire, including Buryatia. From 1901–1904 the Buryatian peasants and labourers rioted, and during the 1905 Revolution Buryatian and Russian labourers captured stretches of the Siberian Railway barricading it for some time. But once the Moscow uprising in December 1905 had been brutally quashed, the central government sent two punitive military expeditions, one from Central Russia under the command of general Meller-Zakomelskiy and another from Manchuria under the command of general Rannenkampf. The city of Chita, the centre of the uprising in Buryatia, was taken without a fight in January 1906 and many were executed by firing squads or hung. In 1911 there were further uprisings, this time in the gold mines on the River Lena. During World War I Buryatian Cossacks fought on the south-western and Caucasian fronts where many were indoctrinated by the Bolsheviks. At the same time several Bolsheviks, who later became prominent figures in Lenin's Communist government, were banished to Buryatia. Among them were Frunze, Kuibyshev, Molotov, Stalin and others. Lenin himself spent time under guard in Siberia on the River Lena, hence his pseudonym. In 1916 Buryats were mobilised as labourers on the home front. The Bourgeois-Democratic Revolution came in February 1917 and the October Socialist Revolution followed. Civil war ensued and the whole of the Russian Empire disintegrated with various parties and individuals fighting for control. The Declaration of the Independence of Siberia was proclaimed in July 1918 and this led to the formation of the Government of Siberia which lasted for just six months until Admiral Kolchak established his dictatorship. At the same time Ataman Semenov had established himself in Chita. At a meeting of the Mongolian and Buryatian Noyons and governors of the regions of Mongolia and Buryatia at Dauria Station in February 1919, an announcement was made proclaiming the establishment of Great Mongolia based on the traditions of Chingis Khaan. It was envisioned as a federal monarchy under the leadership of a Buddhist lama, Neise Gegen Mendebayar[614], and was to include Inner and Outer Mongolia, Barga and Buryatia. Ataman Semenov

---

614 Bur. Нэйсэ Гэгэн Мэндэбаяр.

was given the title of *Wan*, Governor, and offered a white hat as the sign of his control over east Siberia. This Pan-Mongolian project, however, was never realized. Outer Mongolia lost its autonomy and surrendered to the Chinese and so Semenov became the sole military governor of east Siberia. In 1921 Semenov's army was pushed out of Chita by the Red Army of the Far-Eastern Republic loyal to Lenin and Buryatia was partitioned into two Buryatian Autonomous Regions. The first Mongol-Buryat Autonomous Region of the Far-Eastern Republic was formed in 1921 and then in 1922 the Mongol-Buryat Autonomy was created within the Russian Federation. In 1923 these two were unified into the Mongol-Buryat ASSR[615] within the RSFSR.[616]

Under the Communist regime Bɵ Murgel, Buddhism and Orthodox Christianity were persecuted with the repression reaching its height in 1937 when all the Buddhist *datsans* were destroyed. Lamas, Bɵ, Utgan and many ordinary Buryats were executed en masse and the Mongol-Buryat ASSR was partitioned with the districts of Ust-Orda and Aga stripped of autonomy and falling under the direct control of the RSFSR. In 1958 the Mongol-Buryat ASSR was reorganized into the Buryat ASSR and in 1992, after perestroika, it became the Republic of Buryatia. The central Russian government is currently looking into ways of completely dissolving the Buryatian Republic into the Russian Federation in keeping with its policy of enlarging the regions. Should this happen, it may well deal a blow to recent efforts to preserve and revitalise Buryatian culture.

Fig. 41. Head of Lenin, Ulaan-Ude, blackened bronze, 7 tonnes, 13.5 meters high.

As was said above, the Bɵ and Utgan were severely persecuted by the Communists but as Bɵ Murgel can be practised without elaborate ritual dress or ritual instruments, some Bɵ and Utgan have survived and preserved their lineages and traditions. When, in 1989, the policy

---

[615] Mongol-Buryat Autonomous Soviet Socialist Republic.

[616] Russian Soviet Federative Socialist Republic, the biggest administrative body of the Soviet Union.

of religious liberalisation was introduced as part of perestroika, these traditions gradually resurfaced and a Bө Murgel revival began. Today many sacred sites have been restored and many Bө and Utgan are practising all over Buryatia, public *tailgan* prayer festivals are held regularly according to the tradition and are very popular.

Conclusion

From this brief outline of how the peoples who practise Bön and Bө Murgel migrated, mingled and finally emerged as we know them today, we can see that they have many ancestral strands in common and had many opportunities to share their cultures, traditions and belief systems. It is no surprise, then, that modern-day Bön and Buryatian Bө Murgel show so many similar features, some of which we will explore together in the coming chapters.

CHAPTER II

Sacred Geography of Lake Baikal

Baikal as a geographical and geological feature

The main geographical and spiritual feature of the environment in which Buryatian Bɵ Murgel developed over the centuries and still thrives today is the sacred lake Baikal, possibly the world's most fascinating freshwater lake. Baikal is a huge crescent-shaped lake almost 650km in length, which spans the Buryatian Republic and the Irkutsk region of the Russian Federation. At 1,673m deep, it is the world's deepest lake, the greatest depression on the land surface of the globe. The lake bed is covered with an extremely deep layer of sediment which reaches 7km in some places. Although its surface area is larger than the territory of Belgium, it is only the seventh largest lake in the world in this respect (3,400km^2). Nevertheless, thanks to its great depth, Baikal still contains the world's largest volume of freshwater, greater than the waters of the five Great Lakes of North America put together and accounting for one fifth of the planet's resources of surface freshwater. It was formed between 20 and 25 – or possibly even 50 – million years ago, and this makes it by far the oldest lake on earth; most other lakes are less than 20,000 years old, although Lake Tanganyika – still a youngster in comparison with Baikal – is about two million years old.

Lake Baikal is home to 1,550 species or sub-species of animals and 1,085 plant species, of which over a thousand are endemic.[1] According to traditional Buryatian reckoning, there are 365 tributaries flowing into Baikal, some running underground, and this corresponds to the 365 of days of a solar year. But there is only one outlet: the Angara River. Because of the Angara's enormous force, a chain of hydroelectric stations was built along its shores in Soviet times.

---

1 John Massey Stewart, 'Baikal's hidden depths', *NewScientist*, 23 June 1990.

Bө believe that Lake Baikal is connected with Lake Hubsuguul in Mongolia via an underground river and indeed, with all the world's waters by means of underground water-veins. Scientists, although reluctant to accept these claims, have verified that certain types of flora and fauna are indeed identical in Baikal and Hubsuguul, and unique to these two lakes. In fact, Baikal's waters are extremely pure, and although the lake was polluted to a certain extent by paper mills and fishing boats under the Communist regime, this was only a temporary, minute event in the life of such an ancient lake. Since the arrival of perestroika the mills have been closed.

This colossal lake, itself at almost 460m above sea level, is flanked on all sides by several impressive mountain ranges: the Eastern Sayan[2] (rising to 3,492m) in the west; the Hamar-Daban[3] and Ulan-Burgasy[4] ranges in the south; the Barguzin[5] range in the east; and the Primorskiy[6] and Baikalskiy[7] ranges in the north. The bare Barguzin Mountains can have snowfall even in summer. All of these mountain chains are rich in power places associated with powerful local gods as well as in healing springs called *arshan.*[8]

The surrounding landscape, and indeed most of Buryatia, is dominated by pine forest with the inclusion of other trees such as birch, aspen, ash and mountain ash. This pine forest is known as *shibir'*[9] in Buryatian from which the Russian word *Sibir'*[10] is obviously derived. In the West this type of forest is known as *taiga*,[11] a Tungus word.

The people living around Lake Baikal are mainly engaged in forestry, agriculture, fishing, hunting and tourism.

Baikal as a spiritual feature

There is a Bө Murgel myth which tells of how Lake Baikal was formed:

---

2 Rus. Восточный Саян.

3 Rus. Хамар-Дабан.

4 Rus. Улан-Бургасы.

5 Rus. Баргузин.

6 Rus. Приморский.

7 Rus. Байкальский.

8 Bur. Аршан.

9 Bur. Шибирь.

10 Rus. Сибирь.

11 Rus. тайга.

In times long gone, the common ancestors of Buryats and Mongols dwelt in the holy land of Bargujin Tokum. Lake Baikal was as yet unformed. In its place there was a fire-breathing volcano, Bai-gal, the seat of the heavenly smithy Dabaan Zholo'o Tengeri.[12] The lord of the mountain was Bahar-Hara Khaan.[13] From the foot of this mighty volcano sprang the source of the great river Angar-Baigal Muren[14] (now the Upper Angara and Bargujin). Because of the sacred will of Eternal Blue Sky, a terrible cataclysm struck and Bai-gal was sucked deep under the earth leaving a gaping canyon which the waters of the river Angar-Baigal Muren rushed to fill.

This vast lake was given the name Baigal. The only part of the adjacent hills which survived formed the peninsular known as Halyuud Hada or Helmyn Hushuun which Russians call 'Holy Nose.'[15] This is a place for worship sacred to followers of Bө Murgel. Buryats believe that Eternal Blue Sky has mastery over the whole area around Lake Baikal and that the lake itself is a reflection of Eternal Blue Sky on earth, a connection has been honoured in ritual customs since time immemorial; the ancient ancestor of Buryats and Mongols, Burte-Chino, sprinkled the milk of a hundred white mares into Baikal's waters when he prayed to Eternal Blue Sky.

This aura of sacredness and purity is reflected in a range of taboos stretching back to archaic times. These taboos must be strictly adhered to, firstly as a sign of respect for the lake and the land, but secondly so as not to draw anger and retribution from the gods who protect it. It is forbidden to pollute the lake or the land in any way; no-one is allowed to throw rubbish into the water or leave litter on the earth or on the ice in winter time; sharp objects such as nails and knives must not be left lying around, and in the past women were banned from walking on the shore or taking water from the lake and the springs during menstruation, nor were they allowed to cook for religious festivals and the Utgan were not allowed to worship.[16]

---

12 Bur. Дабаан-Жоло Тэнгэри. B. D. Bazarov, *Tainstva i praktika shamanizma* (Ulaan-Ude, Buryaad Unen, 1999), p. 131.

13 Bur. Бахар-Хара хаан or Бахар-Хара ноён.

14 Bur. Ангар-Байгал Мүрен.

15 Bur. Халюуд хада, Хэлмын хушуун. The second name actually means 'sharp tip of the sword'; Rus. Святой Нос.

16 This set of rules is not always adhered to nowadays by the common people of the region.

However, Baikal is not only sacred to the Buryats; many earlier peoples revered this mighty lake, too. The Tungus-Evenki called it Lamu (Lama), the ancient Tyurkyut knew it as Tengis, the Mongols called it Tengis-Dalai and for the Chinese it was Baihai.[17] Baikal is venerated across the border in Mongolia. The Russians who conquered Siberia were also struck by the lake's beauty and power, and those who settled there came to revere it, even singing its praises in the such songs as the Russian ballad *Glorious sea, the Sacred Baikal.*[18] But Baikal is venerated even in much more distant lands. Some Bө and Utgan told me that Australian aboriginal priests know about Baikal and pray to it, so I was told by some. Australian aboriginal culture goes back 40,000 years or more, so it is a very archaic culture and as we have seen, Baikal is a very ancient lake. Nowadays, when there is much communication and exchange between different streams of ancient native traditions, many subtle connections such as this one come to light.

There are many tales illustrating Baikal's holy qualities, and here is one I heard near Kooltushnaya[19] in the summer of 1993:

> A man was swimming in Baikal when, paralysed by strong cramps, he started to drown. As he was fighting for his life, he desperately prayed to the lake to save him. Suddenly a huge wave swelled up and pushed the half-unconscious man ashore. When he regained his senses he was lying safely on the shore of the lake. Emotions overwhelmed him. Not knowing how to express his gratitude to the lake, he took off his expensive water-resistant watch and, with words of thanks, offered it to Baikal by flinging it far away into the lake's waters. To his great amazement the watch was brought right back to his feet by the very next wave.

This story is an illustration of the virtuous and uncorrupted nature of the lake, its role as benefactor and protector, and its intimate connection with the local people. It also illustrates how Lake Baikal is anthropomorphized. In fact, Baikal has dual status. The lake itself is considered by the Buryats to be a living being but at the same time it

---

[17] All these names, with the exception of the Chinese, which is just a phonetic transcription, mean 'ocean' or 'sea'. 'Tengis' is a variation of 'Chingis', the title given to Temuuzhin when he assumed leadership of the Mongol Empire.

[18] Rus. *«Славное море Священный Байкал».*

[19] Rus. Култушная. One of the villages on the southeastern shore of the lake.

also provides the residence for the chief divinity of Baikal who is known under seventy names, the most usual being Bahar-Hara Khaan (the name of the lord of the Bai-gal volcano). Bahar-Hara Khaan is male and has a female consort and a son. Interestingly, we find that the same dual status attributed to the sacred lakes of Tibet such as Mapang Yutsho, Namtsho and Dangra. As was said before, these lakes are considered to be the personifications of the actual goddesses themselves while simultaneously being the residences or palaces of the goddesses they represent. The lakes manifest as the anthropomorphic goddesses who, paired with their consort mountains, control the regions around the lakes, the weather and climate, the growth of plants and animals, and the wealth and well-being of people.[20] All this is also true for Baikal except that he is male and he doesn't have a mountain as his consort.

As well as being the residence of these powerful beings, Baikal is also inhabited by many *Lusuut* who are governed by the *Lusuut-Khaan*[21] and some spirits of deceased Bɵ. In the past, some Bɵ had the capacity to remain underwater for considerable lengths of time and could hide under water or spend the night there. Such Bɵ sometimes became water-spirits after their death.

The lake's islands are also home to many spiritual entities. The largest and most important island is Olhon which roughly mimics the shape of the lake. Olhon is the residence of a very powerful *Ezhen*, Oihon Baabai,[22] his wife Sarma Hatan,[23] his son the eagle Hotoi Burged[24] or Shubuun Noyon,[25] and the ten main divinities of his retinue. Oihon Baabai's main residence is a magical cave in the sacred cliff,[26] a much venerated power place and his son Hotoi Burged is said to have his residence on the summit of Mount Zhima,[27] the highest point on Olhon. This group of deities is very important for the eastern Buryats in general

---

20 See John Vincent Bellezza, *Divine Dyads*: *Ancient Civilization in Tibet* (Dharamasala, LTWA, 1997).

21 Bur. лусуут or лусуун corresponds to Tib. klu and Sans. naga, while Bur. Лусуут (Лусуун)-хаан correponds to Tib. Klu'i rgyal po and Sans. Nagaraja.

22 Bur. Ойхон баабай or Ута Сагаан ноён – one of Hormusta Tengeri's sons. He has many other names: Oihon Buural, Khaan Hoto Baabai, Khaan Hoota Baabai (Bur. Ойхон Буурал, Хаан Хото баабай, Хаан Хута баабай).

23 Bur. Сарма хатан.

24 Bur. Хотой Бүргэд or Bur. Гарууди (*Garuudi*), a Buddhist name.

25 Bur. Шубуун Ноён.

26 Bur. һумэ шулуун.

27 Bur. Жима.

and for the Hori-Buryats[28] in particular and is expressed in the cult of the Thirteen Northern Lords, Aryn Arban Gurban Tengeri.[29] Another important spiritual entity of Olhon is the spirit of the supreme Bө of the Ehirit clan, Uta Sagaan Baabai,[30] who is buried there. There are many reasons, then, why Olhon is a significant power place for followers of Bө Murgel and a popular pilgrimage destination.

The island of Olhon also influences the weather of the region. One of the area's three main winds rises from it. Sarma, Oihon Baabai's wife, creates and rides this wind and so it bears her name. It is a wind which comes suddenly and is quite violent, blowing from the northwest towards the east. It is very dangerous to be out on the lake when the Sarma wind blows up as it can easily capsize a fisherman's boat or even bigger ships.

The second wind which blows across Baikal is called Kultuk as it is created and controlled by Khaan Kultuk.[31] It blows from the south towards the north.

The third wind is called Barguzin because it comes from the Barguzin region. It is created and controlled by the mighty *Ezhen* Barhan Uula who resides on top of Mount Baraghan[32] (also known as Barhan Uula) in the bare Barguzin range.[33] This wind blows from the south towards the northwest.

In an attempt to assimilate these indigenous deities into the Lamaist pantheon, Buryatian Buddhists associated the Lord of Olhon, Khaan Hoto Baabai, and his consort Sarma Hatan with the Tibetan Buddhist deities Begdze[34] and Rigbi Lhamo.[35]

---

28 The Hori or Horёodoi tribe traces its origins from Olhon.

29 Bur. Арын Арбан Гурбан Тенгери.

30 Bur. Ута Сагаан баабай.

31 Bur. Хаан Култук.

32 Bur. Барагхан.

33 Rus. Баргузинские гольцы.

34 Tib. Beg tse. Also known as Tib. lCam sring.

35 Tib. Rig bi Lha mo also known as Tib. gDong dMar ma. These are a couple of protective deities linked to the Buddhist Tantric cycle of Hayagrīva (Tib. rTa mgrin).

Conclusion

This brief account of Lake Baikal's physical and spiritual properties shows us that it is indeed a magnificent lake, both on the material and metaphysical level. Small wonder, then, that it is the jewel in crown of Bɵ Murgel's rich spiritual geography.

Fig. 1. Lake Baikal.

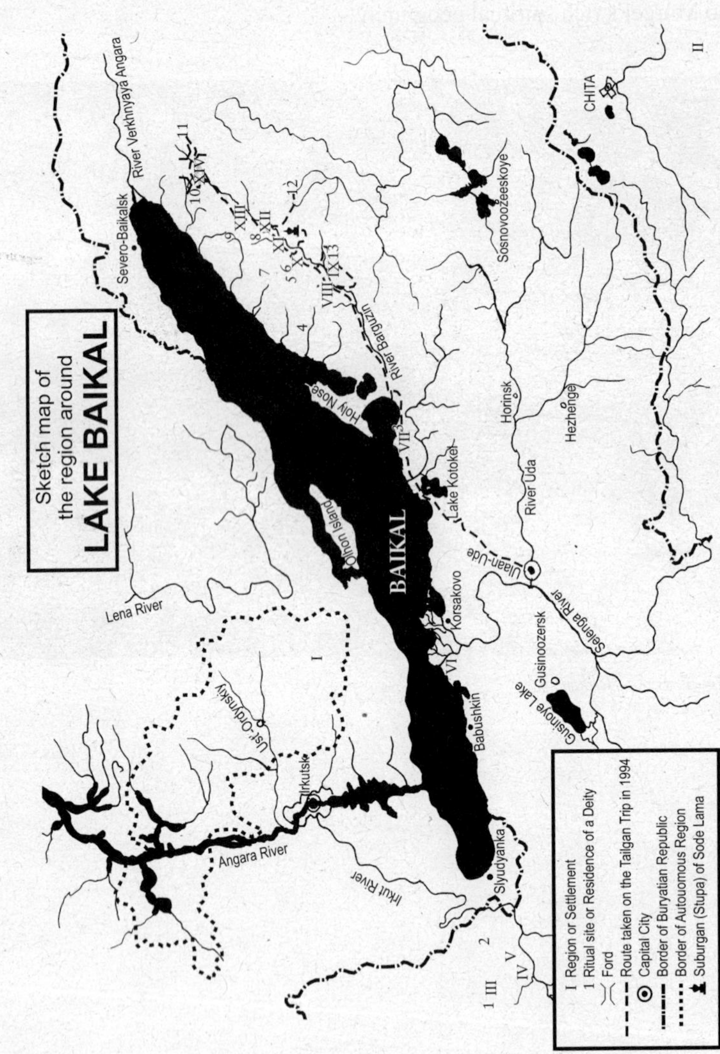

Fig. 2. Map of Buryatia showing Bө Murgel ritual sites and power places I visited.

Key to the sketch map of the region around Lake Baikal

I – Ust'-Ordynskiy Buryatian Autonomous Region
II – Aginskiy Buryatian Autonomous Region
III – Village of Arshan
IV – Village of Zhemchug
V – Village of Tunka
VI – Village of Istomino
VII – Village of Maximikha
VIII – Village of Barguzin
IX – Village of Suvo
X – Village of Borokhan
XI – Village of Kurumkan
XII – Village of Sakhuli
XIII – Village of Alla
XIV – Village of Ulyunkhan

1 – Residence of Hoimariy Tebi
2 – Residence of Buha Noyon Baabai
3 – Site of the ritual for inviting Lusuut-Khaan
4 – Residence of Mahagal Darhan
5 – Old *suburgans* (*stupas*)
6 – Healing springs
7 – Residence of De'ede Baabai
8 – Site of the *tailgan* near Village of Shamanka
9 – Site of purification of the healing springs near the village of Alla
10 – Site of purification of the healing springs
11 – Residence of Bulon Tumer
12 – Shiizga Bө cemetery
13 – Site of the *tailgan* near Buha Shulun sacred stone

CHAPTER III

Different Types of Bön

Clarifying the term 'bön'

Before the appearance of Tonpa Shenrab Miwo, the Buddha of Yungdrung Bön, many types of Bön were already being practised. Tonpa Shenrab is a Central Asian Buddha and, like other great teachers of other religious traditions, he taught in a particular place at a particular time so his teachings came through the cultural prism of his day. To distinguish his path to enlightenment from the existent religious traditions, his teachings became known as Yungdrung Bön, Eternal Bön. The methods practised before him by the prehistoric Bönpo were extremely diverse and were designed to appease, pacify and harness spiritual entities and energies to turn them towards benefiting the practitioner and his/her community. Streams of Prehistoric Bön were practised in Tagzig, Zhang Zhung, Tibet, China, Altai, throughout Siberia and even in Europe. If we glance at the methods and ritual objects of many Native American traditions we can see that these peoples, too, must have been connected to the Prehistoric Bön of Eurasia. Here we shall concentrate on those strands of Bön which were alive in Zhang Zhung and Tibet before and in the times of Shenrab Miwo.

When Indian Buddhism was brought to Tibet in the eighth century AD, confusion arose regarding the various types of Bön as the name 'bön' was applied to three distinct religious traditions of Tibet and used to denote a vast array of archaic magical and religious traditions. '*Bön*' generally means 'religious practice'. The term '*chö*'[1] was used for various ritual traditions, and the two terms often overlapped; *Lha Chö*[2] and *Lha Bön*,[3] for example, are synonymous. With the introduction of Tibetan Buddhism, the term '*chö*' came to almost exclusively mean 'Buddhist

1 Tib. chos, 'custom'.

2 Tib. lha chos.

3 Tib. lha bon.

doctrine', hence Buddhists were called '*Chöpa*[4]' to distinguish them from Bönpo. The Zhang Zhung word for '*bön*' is '*gyer*'[5] and in Zhang Zhung as well as in Tibet either term was used as a general name for a spiritual tradition. In its use, the term '*bön*' is similar to the Sanskrit word '*dharma*' which has a broad semantic field, including 'religious law' (or teaching). Different traditions of India, such as Hinduism, Jainism and Buddhism, all use the word '*dharma*' to designate their own doctrines, the truths of their spiritual teachings, and so these three traditions are all referred to as Dharmic Religions of India despite the fundamental differences in their views. The teachings of Hinduism, then, are called Hindu-Dharma, the teachings of the prophet Mahavira are called Jain-Dharma, and the teachings of Buddha Shakyamuni are called Buddha-Dharma. The word '*bön*' was used in exactly the same broad way in Tibet before the introduction of Indian Buddhism and precisely because it was applied to all the contemporary spiritual traditions of Tibet, incoming Indian Buddhists mistakenly perceived these diverse traditions themselves as being one and the same; an entirely erroneous view. This led to considerable confusion and problems; unfortunately, even today ignorance persists regarding the real nature of Prehistoric and Yungdrung Bön resulting in sectarianism and other obstacles for the Tibetan community as well as for Westerners who study Yungdrung Bön and Tibetan Buddhism. No-one even slightly familiar with Hinduism, Jainism and Buddhism, for example, would say they are the same religions just because they use the same word – '*dharma*' – to designate their religious doctrines; it is obvious that their doctrines are quite different. The same is true for the pre-Buddhist spiritual traditions of Tibet; although '*bön*' is part of their names, the teachings and the views of these diverse traditions differ greatly. In this chapter we will study these differences in order to dispel popular misconceptions regarding Bön.

Three types of Bön in Zhang Zhung and Tibet

1. Prehistoric Bön of Tibet and the coming of Tonpa Shenrab

Prehistoric Bön is called Dömai Bön[6] in Tibetan[7] and this, too, is a

---

4 Tib. chos pa.

5 Tib. gyer.

6 Tib. gdod ma'i bon.

7 Sometimes referred to as popular or folk religion in the works of Western scholars. In Tibetan it is also called *Lha Chö* and its practitioners, who

general name covering many ancient ritual traditions of Zhang Zhung and Tibet. Modern scholars label all these ritual traditions 'shamanic' regardless of whether they used ecstatic trance techniques (considered by many scholars as the shaman's main method), and therefore I find this blanket categorization unsatisfactory.

The ancient Bönpo ritual text *Sidpa Chyidö*[8] contains a list of the Bönpo traditions whose practitioners opposed the followers of Tonpa Shenrab's Yungdrung Bön. They are: Dön Bön, Düd Bön, Dur Bön, Srid Bön and Tsen Bön.[9] According to Yongdzin Lopön Tenzin Namdak, some of the Prehistoric (i.e. pre-Tonpa Shenrab) Bönpo traditions practised blood sacrifices and it is obvious from their names that each tradition was adept at appeasing a particular class of beings or resolving a particular circumstance. So Dön Bön dealt with provocations of negative energy;[10] Düd Bön had rituals to appease the class of *Düd*; Srid Bön contained practices to ensure the continuation of generations; Dur Bön was connected with death rituals, and Tsen Bön was related to the *Tsen* class.

Shenrab Miwo's teachings on the Bön of Cause, the four lower vehicles of Yungdrung Bön, also contain practices with similar aims. This is neither a surprise not a contradiction; Tonpa Shenrab was perfectly aware of the relative benefits such rituals can bring. However, in some Prehistoric Bönpo traditions the means of obtaining these temporal benefits, such as animal sacrifices, were unjustifiable, and although the followers were unaware of the consequences of their actions, the negative karma resulting from such practices is considerable. The Buddha of Bön changed these methods and instructed his followers how to use substitute offering cakes along with figures of dough and clay to replace the actual victims, and libations of barley wine to substitute blood. Thus those who practise the techniques of the four Lower Vehicles can still make peace with other beings thereby gaining worldly benefits without harming others or accumulating negative karma. The Causal Bön taught by Tonpa

---

are often mediums, are called *lhapa/lhama* (Tib. lha pa/ lha ma) or *pawo/nyenjomo* (Tib. dpa' bo/bsnyen jo mo (male/female). See ch. XIV.

8 Tib. Srid pa spyi mdos. An ancient ritual tradition dating back to the time of the Tibetan king Mutri Tsenpo (born in 1074 BC according to traditional *bsTan rtsis* Bönpo chronology) and written down by Lama Rasang Trinneko (Tib. bLa ma Ra sangs Khrin ne khod), a royal Shenpo of Tagri Nyenzig (sTag ri gnyan zigs) in 5th-6th c. AD (approximate dating by Yongdzin Lopön Tenzin Namdak).

9 Tib. gdon bon, bdud bon, 'dur bon, srid bon, btsan bön.

10 Tib. gdon. It is said in *Zijyid* that there are 60,000 types of Dön.

Shenrab includes a rich variety of such transformed methods, many of which betray very archaic origins. As these practices were touched and transformed by the Buddha, they became more than mere tools to harness the energies of this worldly life; they became stepping stones on the path which gradually leads those of lower capacity to Buddhahood.

The exact origins and evolution of these archaic traditions of Prehistoric Bön are shrouded in the mists of time. They were mostly oral traditions, now largely extinct in modern-day Tibet. However, looking into traditions which have survived in Tibet, Bhutan, Nepal and Siberia enables us to reconstruct a general outline of how the belief systems of Prehistoric Bön could have emerged. The most common way a spiritual tradition arises is when the beings (a being) of a particular class (classes)[11] select a human[12] endowed with particular body-energy-mind characteristics and teach him/her how to worship them, offering in exchange knowledge, spiritual realization of some kind and magical powers as well as protection and other benefits for the clan, larger community, nation or country. Those methods (and powers) are passed on to a successor who is found with the help of these same being(s), and so the lineage is established.[13]

In the case of the transformed traditions of the Bön of Cause, the situation is different; it is reversed. It is not the teacher Shenrab Miwo who is controlled by various supernatural beings but quite the opposite; these beings swore an oath to protect Yungdrung Bön, its practitioners and humans in general. Through the powers of their realization, Tonpa Shenrab and Shenpos[14] of Yungdrung Bön were able to conquer and subdue many powerful and arrogant supernatural beings.[15] Not only were they conquered and transformed into religious protectors, but they were also given teachings on how to end their own suffering and attain Buddhahood so in fact they were transformed into practitioners and followers of Yungdrung Bön. This was possible because, among other

---

[11] See ch. V.

[12] I.e. a future Bönpo, Bɵ, shaman or a prophet.

[13] This is true for most tribal traditions and indeed for the main world religions as well, with the exception of Yungdrung Bön, the Philosophical Taoism of Lao Tzu and Indian Buddhism. In these three traditions the revelation comes not from a god or spirit but from the innate nature of their prophets.

[14] Tib. gShen po, a follower of Tonpa Shenrab. This name has been used by practitioners of Yungdrung Bön since ancient times to distinguish themselves from other kinds of Bönpo priests.

[15] Other Buddhas of later times such as Shakyamuni and Padmasambhava did just the same.

profound truths, Tonpa Shenrab Miwo's Yungdrung Bön revealed that every sentient being, even an evil spirit or demon, has the same quality Buddha-nature. This Buddha-nature is the most subtle and indestructible base of every being's mind from the beginningless beginning.[16] It can never be corrupted or deluded in anyway and can be fully realized through practising correctly the methods of enlightenment revealed by a Buddha. How long this takes depends on each individual's karma, but once a being has come into contact with a Buddha's teachings, realization will manifest sooner or later.

2. Yungdrung Bön

One thousand and two Buddhas of Bön

The spiritual tradition of the Central Asian Buddha Tonpa Shenrab Miwo is usually called Yungdrung Bön[17] (Swastika Bön) but is sometimes referred to as Nyingma Bön[18] (Old Bön). Yungdrung Bön is variously translated into English as Eternal Bön, Eternal Light, and the Teaching of Unchangeable Swastika. Although we say it was taught by Tonpa Shenrab, Yungdrung Bön's origins lie beyond space and time and, therefore, beyond history.

Fig. 1. Tonpa Shenrab as king.

---

[16] According to the Yungdrung Bön doctrine the phenomenal world and the beings circulating in it are without beginning. However, there is an end. This end is the realization of Buddhahood, the fundamental incorruptible Buddha-nature beyond dualistic vision. This nature is neither permanent nor impermanent as these categories are born from dualistic reasoning and cannot describe something wholly beyond dualism.

[17] Tib. g.yung drung bon. Sometimes translated into English as Eternal Bön, because *yungdrung* (Sans. *swastika*) means indestructible and unborn i.e. eternal. '*Yungdrung*' has more or less the same meaning as '*vajra*' used in the Indian Buddhist tradition, especially in Vajrayana. Yungdrung Bön could also be called Central-Asian Buddhism because Buddha Tonpa Shenrab Miwo was born in Central Asia. For a discussion on the symbolism of the swastika, see ch. XV.

[18] Tib. rnying ma bon.

While in general there are countless Buddhas in countless realms in all the three times (past, present and future), it is said that in the present great time cycle[19] one thousand and two Buddhas will come to our planet earth. Some have already made their appearance and given teachings while others will manifest in the future. Tonpa Shenrab Miwo was not the first Buddha in this great time cycle but was preceded by seven Buddhas, all of whom propagated Yungdrung Bön and, according to traditional Bönpo chronology,[20] appeared in various epochs:

1. In the initial period of this time cycle, when the average human lifespan was 100,000 years, Buddha Tonpa Nangwa Rangjung Thugje[21]appeared;
2. In the second period, when the average human lifespan was 80,000 years, Buddha Tonpa Khorwa Kundren[22] appeared;
3. When the average human lifespan decreased to 60,000 years, Buddha Tonpa Kunshe Nyonmong Dugseg[23]appeared;
4. In the third period, when the average human lifespan was 40,000 years, Buddha Tonpa Legpar Tsame Thugje[24] appeared;
5. When the average lifespan decreased to 20,000 years Buddha Tonpa Tamche Kyenzig[25] appeared;
6. When the lifespan was 10,000 years Buddha Tonpa Trigyal Khugpa[26]appeared;
7. When the average lifespan shrank to 1,000 years Buddha Tonpa Togyal Yekhyen[27]appeared;
8. When the average human lifespan had decreased to 100 years, Buddha Tonpa Shenrab Miwo appeared.

---

[19] Tib. bskal bzang.
[20] *bsTan rtsis* of Menri Khenchen Nyima Tenzin.
[21] Tib. sTon pa sNang ba Rang byung Thugs rje.
[22] Tib. sTon pa 'Khor ba Kun 'dren.
[23] Tib. sTon pa Kun shes Nyon mongs Dug sreg.
[24] Tib. sTon pa Legs par Tshad med Thugs rje.
[25] Tib. sTon pa Thams chad mKhyen gzigs.
[26] Tib. sTon pa Khri gyal Khug pa.
[27] Tib. sTon pa gTo rgyal Ye mkhyen.

Fig. 2. Chimey Tsugphü and Sangwa Dhüpa.

Fig. 3. Buddha Shakyamuni. Statue below the stupa of Swayabhunath, Kathmandu.

The seventh Buddha, Tonpa Togyal Yekhyen, was one of Shenrab Miwo's brothers. There were three brothers – Dagpa,[28] Salwa[29] and Shepa[30] – who all attained enlightenment in the dimension of Sidpa Yesang.[31] The oldest brother, Dagpa (Purity), incarnated as Tonpa Togyal Yekhyen. The middle brother, Salwa (Clarity), was also known under the name Chimey Tsugphü[32] when he taught the teachings of Dzogchen and Tantra to his disciple, the sage Sangwa Dhüpa[33] in the heavenly realm of Sidpa Yesang.

---

[28] Tib. Dag pa.

[29] Tib. gSal ba.

[30] Tib. Shes pa.

[31] Tib. Srid pa Ye sangs.

[32] Tib. 'Chi med gTsug phud.

[33] Tib. Sang ba 'Dus pa.

Salwa incarnated on our planet earth in the country of Tagzig in the age when human lifespan had decreased to a hundred years and became known as Tonpa Shenrab Miwo. He is the source of Yungdrung Bön in its modern form. Sage Sangwa Dhüpa incarnated later in the same large time period of the present great cycle in India and is known under the name Buddha Shakyamuni. He is the source of the Buddha-Dharma teachings of India.

The youngest brother, Shepa (Knowledge) will be the future Buddha Tonpa Thangma Medron[34] who will appear when the average human lifespan is just ten years. In the present large cosmic cycle there will be twenty full cycles of complete decrease and increase of human lifespan and that is the epoch in which one thousand and two Buddhas will appear.[35]

The Buddha and teachings of the current cycle

The history of Yungdrung Bön in its present form starts with the birth of Tonpa Shenrab Miwo in 16,017 BC.[36] Shenrab Miwo had already realized complete Buddhahood in the heavenly realm of Sidpa Yesang but out of compassion he decided to incarnate among humans in order to save them and other beings from the suffering of *samsara.*[37] He took birth in the Barpo Sogyad palace situated south of the central mountain Yungdrung Gutseg in the country of Olmo Lungring, the inner spiritual region of Tagzig in Central Asia. He was born into the royal clan of Mushen which descended from the *Mu* sky-gods. His father was the king Mibön Lhabön Gyalbön Thökar[38] and his mother was the queen Michyi Lhachyi Yochyi Gyalzhedma.[39] According to traditional Bönpo accounts, his life is measured in *Shen* years[40] where one *Shen* year is equivalent to one hundred human years. In the course of his 81 years of on earth,

---

[34] Tib. sTon pa Thang ma Me sgron.

[35] For more detailed information on these Buddhas see Kvaerne, *A Chronological Table*, pp. 203–248.

[36] According to Yongdzin Lopön Tenzin Namdak. Chögyal Namkhai Norbu puts the date of his birth much later in 1917 BC. See Norbu, *Drung, Deu and Bön*, pp. 156–158. For a more detailed discussion, see ch.XV.

[37] Tib. 'khor ba, Cycle of Transmigration.

[38] Tib. Mi bon lHa bon rGyal bon Thod dkar.

[39] Tib. Mi phyi Lha phyi Yo phyi rGyal bzhed ma.

[40] Tib. gshen lo.

Tonpa Shenrab performed Twelve Great Deeds[41] of a Buddha before manifesting *Parinirvana*[42] in 7818 BC. The Twelve Deeds are:

1. Taking birth
2. Spreading the teachings of Yungdrung Bön
3. Subduing and converting beings
4. Rescuing beings from the lower realms
5. Marrying
6. Manifesting progeny
7. Vanquishing the Demon Prince
8. Victory over demons
9. Renouncing the world
10. Entering into solitude
11. Gaining liberation
12. Attaining the final realization[43]

While on this earth, Shenrab Miwo taught many different classes of beings, giving teachings suited to their various capacities. He taught beings how to calm their immediate sufferings and obtain provisional benefits through the methods of Causal Bön as well as showing the way to ultimate realization through the methods of Sutra, Tantra and Dzogchen (Fruitional Bön).

The Yungdrung Bön doctrines of Tonpa Shenrab Miwo will last for a cycle of thirty thousand years which is divided into three periods of ten thousand years each:

1. Teachings of the Body[44]
2. Teachings of the Speech[45]
3. Teachings of the Mind[46]

Every three hundred and thirty-three years and four months the average human life-span decreases by one year, and by the end of the

---

[41] Tib. mdzad pa bcu gnyis.

[42] Tib. mya ngan las 'das pa. Attainment of final Buddhahood.

[43] See Richard Gard and Sangye Tanbar, *The Twelve Deeds: A Brief Life Story of Tonpa Shenrab, the Founder of the Bön Religion*, (New Delhi: LTWA, 1995); and John Reynolds, *Yungdrung Bön: The Eternal Tradition*, (San Diego: Tibetan Translation Project, 1994).

[44] Tib. sku yi bstan pa.

[45] Tib. gsung gi bstan pa.

[46] Tib. thugs kyi bstan pa.

cycle it will decrease to just ten years. Humans will also decrease in size and will be just one cubit tall. It is at this time that the next Buddha of Yungdrung Bön, Tonpa Thangma Medron, will appear. He will be much taller than other humans and so people will be intrigued. The future Buddha will explain that he has refrained all negative actions and that is why he is so different from them. People will be inspired to start following him and the new cycle of Yungdrung Bön will begin; with the growth of virtue, human lifespan will begin to increase again.[47]

Tonpa Shenrab Miwo, whose original name in the language of Tagzig is Mura Tahen,[48] didn't appear in a cultural vacuum. Having entered this world in a particular time and place, he worked with the circumstances, religion and culture of the countries he visited in the course of his life. He adopted and adapted some aspects of the old religions, transforming them in the light of his teachings, incorporating them into the path to attaining complete Buddhahood for the sake of oneself and others. He discarded some parts of the ancient traditions which ran counteractive to this intent and reshaped other parts which were beneficial on a relative level. These provisional practices are now found in Causal Bön. Yungdrung Bön was brought from Olmo Lungring to Zhang Zhung and then Tibet in several waves, although initially it was Tonpa Shenrab himself who propagated them. While he gave more advanced teachings to the Bönpo of Zhang Zhung, to Tibetan Bönpo he only taught some rituals from the Bön of Cause. The fact that Tonpa Shenrab taught people called 'bönpo' makes it clear that there were already different streams of Prehistoric Bön in Zhang Zhung and Tibet before him; what he was teaching these Bönpo was termed Yungdrung Bön and was radically different from the Prehistoric Bön traditions they had previously followed.

Tonpa Shenrab taught in his native Musang Tagzig language which derived from the Yungdrung Lha language of the Eternal Gods. The same original language also gave rise to another 360 languages, 164 of which were spoken in Olmo Lungring. It is said in *Dragjyang*[49] that Yungdrung Bön was translated into 360 languages out of the 1000 existing in the world.[50] The teachings started to be systematized, translated and disseminated in many countries under the supervision of his son

---

47 This presentation is based on the oral teachings of Yongdzin Lopön Tenzin Namdak on *Zijyid.* See Namdak, *Nine Ways I*, *Bön of Fruit* pp. 55–56.

48 Tib. dMu ra ta hen.

49 Tib. bsGrags byang.

50 Karmay, *The Treasury,* p.17. Tib. 'Dzam bu gling can be interpreted variously as the whole earth or as Eurasia alone. See ch. IV.

and spiritual successor Mucho Demdrug soon after Tonpa Shenrab's *Parinirvana*:

> The 'Original Words'[51] were delivered by the Teacher, and the three profound forms of Propagation of Bon doctrine,[52] which developed in 'Ol-mo'i-gling after the death of the Teacher, were taken by the Six Great Translators to their own countries as soon as they had become proficient in the three wisdoms under Mu-cho in Ol-mo'i-gling. They made translations of them and made them known.[53]

Nine Ways of Bön

In the classification system known as the Bön of the Nine Ways[54] the entire corpus of Yungdrung Bön doctrines are gathered into two main groups: the Bön of Cause and the Bön of Fruit. The Bön of Cause is tailored for students of lesser capacity as it leads them gradually. The Four Ways of Cause[55] are:

1. Chashen Thegpa *The Way of the Shen of the Cha*: methods of divination, astrology, rituals and medicine [diagnosis and therapies];[56]
2. Nangshen Thegpa, *The Way of the Shen of the Visual World*, has four sections:

---

[51] I.e. Tib. bKa' 'gyur.

[52] Tib. bsGrags pa skor gsum which was spread in the Three Worlds (hence the name 'Triple Propagation') of the gods, humans and *Lu* (*Nagas*) by the Shenpo of the Gods Tib. Yongs su Dag pa, the Shenpo of the Humans Tib. Mi lus bSam legs, and the Shenpo of the *Lu* Tib. Ye shes sNying po. There are three divisions in the Triple Propagation Cycle which contain Secret Mantra and Dzogchen teachings.

[53] Karmay, *The Treasury,* pp. 15–16.

[54] Tib. Theg pa rim dgu'i bon. There are three versions of the Nine Ways according to the Southern, Northern and Central Treasures; this is according to the Southern Treasures (Tib. Lho gter lugs).

[55] Tib. rgyu'i theg pa bzhi:
1. Tib. Phya gshen theg pa.
2. Tib. sNang gshen theg pa:
- Tib. Chab nag;
- Tib. Chab dkar;
- Tib. 'Phan yul;
- Tib. dPon gsas.
3. Tib. 'Phrul gshen theg pa.
4. Tib. Srid gshen theg pa.

[56] Tib. mo, rtsis, gto, dpyad, sman.

- Chabnag, *Black Waters*: invocation of gods and exorcism rites;
- Chabkar, *White Waters*: ransom and suppression rites;
- Penyul, *Land of Phen*: ransom rituals of 'equal exchange';
- Pönse, *The Lordly Guide*: ritual practices for the various classes of gods and spirits.

3. Trulshen Thegpa, *The Way of the Shen of Magical Power*: fierce destruction rites to liberate the mind-streams of wicked beings and demons;
4. Sridshen Thegpa, *The Way of the Shen of Existence*: funerary rites.

The Bön of Fruit[57] contains more advanced teachings. The Five Ways of Fruit are:

5. Genyen Thegpa, *The Way of the Virtuous Lay Practitioners*: rules of conduct for the lay;
6. Drangsong Thegpa, *The Way of the Ascetics*: rules of monastic discipline;
7. Akar Thegpa, *The Way of the White A*: tantric teachings;
8. Yeshen Thegpa, *The Way of the Primordial Shen*: higher Tantric teachings;
9. Lame Thegpa, *The Supreme Way*: Dzogchen teachings.

The Central Treasures[58] give another list of the Nine Ways of Nangpa Shenrabpa,[59] followers of Tonpa Shenrab Miwo, which is also divided into Causal and Fruitional Bön albeit differently. According to this system, the Four Ways of Cause are:

1. Lhami Zhenten Thegpa,[60] *The way of Gods and Men*: contains the concept of the Ten Virtues and practices for obtaining worldly benefits and a higher rebirth within the god, human or demi-god realms;

---

[57] Tib. 'Bras bu'i theg pa lnga:
   5. Tib. dGe bsnyen theg pa;
   6. Tib. Drang srong theg pa;
   7. Tib. A dkar theg pa;
   8. Tib. Ye gshen theg pa;
   9. Tib. bLa med theg pa.

[58] Tib. Tib. dBus gter lugs.

[59] Tib. Nang pa gshen rab pa.

[60] Tib. Lha mi gzhan rten theg pa.

2. Rangtog Shenrab Thegpa,[61] *The Way of Shenrab Followers Who Understand by Themselves*: based on the view of Dagmepa[62] – 'lack of inherently existing self'. This Way is similar to Buddhist Theravada systems resting on the understanding of the Twelve Links of Interdependent Origination;
3. Thugje Sempai Thegpa,[63] *The Way of Compassionate Bodhisattvas*: based on the view of Semtsempa,[64] similar to the Chittamatra view of Mahayana Sutras;
4. Yungdrung Sempai Tromekyi Thegpa,[65] *The Way of the Bodhisattvas without Conceptual Elaborations*: based on the view of Tongnyi Togpai Sherab,[66] similar to Madhyamaka view of Mahayana Sutras.

The Five Ways of Fruit are:

5. Jawa Tsangcho Yebönkyi Thegpa,[67] *The Way of Primordial Bön of Pure Conduct and Ritual Activity*: based on the view Togpai Tawa.[68] This is the first of the Outer Tantras.[69] All levels of Tantra have Samaya Being,[70] Wisdom Being[71] and Non-dual Being.[72] Here the Wisdom Being is considered to be as a king, much more powerful than a practitioner. This level of Bönpo Tantra can be very loosely compared to Kriya Tantra of Indian Buddhism although there is a very big difference in the basic views of Buddhist and Bönpo Tantra. Any Bönpo or Buddhist Tantra rests on the fundamental principle of the Three Contemplations[73] which are: Contemplation of Emptiness,[74] Contemplation of Compassion[75] and Contemplation

---

[61] Tib. Rang rtogs gshen rab theg pa.
[62] Tib. bdag med pa.
[63] Tib. Thug rje sems dpa'i theg pa.
[64] Tib. sems tsham pa.
[65] Tib. g.Yung drung sems dpa'i spros med kyi theg pa.
[66] Tib. stong nyid rtogs pa'i shes rab.
[67] Tib. Bya ba gtshang spyod ye bon kyi theg pa.
[68] Tib. rtogs pa'i lta ba.
[69] Tib. phyi rgyud.
[70] Tib. dam tsig sems dpa'.
[71] Tib. ye shes sems dpa'.
[72] Tib. gnyis med las kyi sems dpa'.
[73] Tib. ting 'dzin rnam gsum.
[74] Tib. de bzhin nyid kyi ting nge 'dzin.
[75] Tib. kun tu snang ba'i ting nge 'dzin.

of Cause.[76] While the names are the same the meaning behind the First Contemplation in Yungdrung Bön Tantras and most Buddhist Tantras of Sarma[77] and Nyingma School, except for Anuyoga of the Nyingma system, is very different. The base of all Bönpo Tantras, which is designated as the Contemplation of Emptiness within the system of the Three Contemplations, is always Dzogchen – the Nature of Mind. Buddhist Tantras, on the other hand, with the exception of Anuyoga Tantras of Nyingma, mainly understand the Contemplation of Emptiness according to the Madhyamaka view of emptiness. This is especially true for all the Tantras of Sarma Schools, including Anuttarayoga Tantras, because, originally the Sarma Schools did not have Dzogchen teachings. Consequently, the cause of the *yidams* of the majority of Buddhist Tantras, except Anuyoga, is totally different from Bönpo Tantras. If the cause is different, the result is different, too. So the levels of all Buddhist Tantras, with the exception of Anuyoga, cannot be compared to the Bönpo Tantras in essence but in their outer characteristics only.

6. Nampa Kunden Ngönshegyi Thegpa,[78] *The Way of Clear Knowledge of All the Aspects*: here the Wisdom Being is considered as the practitioner's powerful friend. As regards external similarities, this level can be said to correspond very loosely to Charya of the Nyingmapa system.
7. Ngokye Thugje Ropa'i Thegpa,[79] *The Way of Manifest Compassion through Visualization of Generation Stage*: this is the first of the Inner Tantras.[80] Here the Wisdom Being is considered to be at the same level as the practitioner as it does not come from anywhere beyond the practitioner's own Natural State of Mind. Outer Tantras have no real Generation Stage[81] as it is understood in the Inner Tantras as the path of visualizing in order of stages. Consequently they don't have the Perfection Stage[82] as it is understood in the Inner Tantras as the path of perfection in order of stages: this is Kyerim and Dzogrim according to this level, with the emphasis on the Generation Stage. Based on outer similarities, Tantras of this level can be very loosely

---

[76] Tib. rgyu'i ting nge dzin.

[77] Tib. gsar ma, the New Schools.

[78] Tib. rNam pa kun ldan gyi theg pa.

[79] Tib. dNgos bskyed thugs rje rol pa'i theg pa.

[80] Tib. nang rgyud.

[81] Tib. bskyed rim.

[82] Tib. rdzogs rim.

compared with Mahayoga of Nyingma and Anuttarayoga of Sarma Schools.

8 Shintu Donden Kundzgogkyi Thegpa,[83] *Vehicle of Complete Meaning and Perfection*: this is the highest class of Bönpo Tantras. Here the Wisdom Being and Samaya Being appear spontaneously at the same time and are non-dual. Here, the emphasis is on the Completion Stage. This class of Tantra can be loosely compared to the Nyingma system of Anuyoga.

9. Dzogpa Chenpo Kyepar Yangtsewai Thegpa,[84] *The Unsurpassed Way of the Great Perfection*: this Way contains Dzogchen teachings.[85]

Gozhi Dzönga

A further classification of Yungdrung Bön is called Gozhi Dzönga,[86] *The Four Portals and the Treasury as Fifth* which contains:

1. Chabkar Dragpo Ngagkyi Bön, *The Bön of White Waters of Wrathful Mantras*: esoteric and higher Tantric practices;
2. Chabnag Sidpa Gyudkyi Bön, *The Bön of Black Waters of Tantra of Existence*: narratives; healing, ransom, funeral and magical rites;
3. Penyul, *The Bön of the Hundred Thousand Sutra from the Land of Pen*: rules of monastic discipline and philosophical teachings;
4. Ponse Mengag Lunggyi Bön, *The Lordly Guide of the Pith Instructions and Oral Teachings*: Dzogchen teachings;
5. Tsangtho Thogchyi Gyugdzökyi Bön, *The Highest and All-Embracing Treasury of Bön*: the essential aspects of all the Four Portals.

As we can clearly see from the contents listed above, and contrary to the misinformed claims of certain scholars, Yungdrung Bön is a complete

---

83 Tib. Shin tu don ldan kun rdzogs kyi theg pa.

84 Tib. rDzogs pa chen po kyad par yang rtse ba'i theg pa.

85 After Lopön Tenzin Namdak Rinpoche, *Namkha Truldzö: the Commentary on the Precious Oral transmission of the Great Perfection which is called the Treasury of Space, Shenten Dargye Ling, 23 July – 11 August 2006*, Trscr.&ed. Carol Ermakova and Dmitry Ermakov, (Blou: Shenten Dargye Ling, 2006), Week I , pp. 71–74; Week II, pp. 2–30.

86 Tib. sgo bzhi mdzod lnga:

6. Tib. Chab dkar drag po sngags kyi bon
7. Tib. Chab nag srid pa rgyud kyi bon
8. Tib. 'Phan
9. Tib. dPon gsas man ngag lung gyi bon
10. Tib. gTsang mtho thog spyi rgyug mdzod kyi bon

path to full enlightenment which lacks nothing. In no way, then, can it be labelled 'shamanic'. For a tradition to be 'shamanic' it needs the figure of a shaman but no such figure can be found in any of the ways or divisions of Yungdrung Bön. If Yungdrung Bön were 'shamanic' that would imply that by following its teachings on magic and its methods of manipulating energy, practitioners would merely be able to receive temporary results within the *samsaric* cycle of death and rebirth which a shaman can never go beyond and would not be able to attain the fully awakened state of a Buddha. A glance at the teachings and methods of Yungdrung Bön and the biographies of the great many Bönpo practitioners who manifested the highest realizations by following the teachings of Buddha Tonpa Shenrab Miwo should be enough to dispel such misconceptions. Unfortunately, the anachronistic stereotype of Bön as ultimately 'shamanistic' is still strong among Tibetans and Westerners alike even though these ideas originated during the persecution of Yungdrung Bön in the eighth century AD and rumours were spread with a view to further undermining Yungdrung Bön in favour of Buddhism. Clinging to this outdated and distorted stereotype arises from misinformation, ignorance and prejudice; I hope that the materials contained in this book will provide the reader with more information and facilitate a clearer understanding of the fundamental differences between the various types of Bön.

3. New Bön

The third type of Bön is Bön Sarma[87] or New Bön. This is a syncretic tradition combining elements of Yungdrung Bön and Indian Buddha-Dharma which was created by Drenpa Namkha and Vairochana in the seventh-eighth century AD. This stream of Bön has quite a large following in Eastern Tibet even now. It differs from Yungdrung Bön not so much along doctrinal lines, as Bön Sarma recognizes all the texts of the Yungdrung Bön *Kanjur* and *Katen,* but rather in terms of practice lineage and rituals, and in that it focuses on Drenpa Namkha and Guru Padmasambhava as its central refuge figures.[88]

Three Drenpa Namkhas and Guru Padmasambhava

Here we must make a brief excursion into the story of Drenpa Namkha and Guru Padmasambhava in order to clarify the confusion surrounding this issue. According to Yungdrung Bön sources there were

---

87 Tib. bon gsar ma.

88 Oral communication from Yongdzin Lopön Tenzin Namdak.

three different Drenpa Namkhas throughout history, all of whom were great *Mahasiddhas* and scholars.

i) The first Drenpa Namkha

The first Drenpa Namkha's life is shrouded in the mists of time. We know little about him except that at the time of his realization he transformed into a ball of rainbow light which disappeared into the sky through the rock ceiling of his cave leaving a passage in it. This cave still exists in Tibet.

ii) The second Drenpa Namkha

The second Drenpa Namkha was one of the most prominent *Shenpo* of Zhang Zhung. Born in 914 BC[89] in Khyunglung Ngulkhar as the Prince of Zhang Zhung, he renounced his princedom and went to practise in the wilderness, eventually becoming a great *Mahasiddha*. He held a great number of lineages and spread the teachings far and wide, including in Tibet, and many of the commentaries and teachings still used by Bönpo today can be traced back to him. Due to the power of his practice he had an extraordinary life-span and also figures as a contemporary of the eighth Tibetan king, Drigum Tsenpo, who lived in the seventh century BC. During this time Drenpa Namkha is accredited with saving religious texts, and indeed the Yungdrung Bön tradition in general, from the destruction ordered by Drigum Tsenpo.

This second Drenpa Namkha had two sons, the twins Tsewang Rigdzin[90] and Pema Thongdröl,[91] who were born in 888 BC. Their mother, Drenpa Namkha's consort, was Öden Barma,[92] a lady from the Brahmin caste of Uddiana. Both twins grew up to become *Mahasiddhas*, attained the extraordinary longevity and gained liberation. According to *Tsewang Nyengyud*[93] and *Rigdzin Dhüpa*,[94] Pema Thöngdrol, the second twin, is in fact Padmasambhava.[95]

---

[89] According to the traditional Bönpo *bsrTan rtsis* chronology.

[90] Tib. Tshe bang Rig 'dzin.

[91] Tib. Pad ma mThong grol.

[92] Tib. 'Od ldan 'Bar ma.

[93] Tib. Tshe dbang sNyan brgyud.

[94] Tib. Rig 'dzin 'Dus pa.

[95] See, for example, Jean-Luc Achard, *Tsewang Nyengyü № 1: Bönzhik Yungdrung Lingpa, La Transmission Orale de Tsewang Rigizin* (Courdimanche-sur-Essonne: Khyung-mkhar, 1997). However, Yongdzin Lopön Tenzin Namdak is unsure whether Pema Thöngdrol and the Guru Rinpoche who came to Tibet

Fig. 4. Zhang Zhung Drenpa Namkha.

Fig. 5. Tsewang Rigdzin.

Following a disagreement between Drenpa Namkha and Öden Barma over the corpse of a Brahmin, Tramze Kyewa Dünpa,[96] to be used in a particular Tantric rite, the twins were separated. Tsewang Rigdzin stayed with Drenpa Namkha in Zhang Zhung receiving teachings and practising while Pema Thöngdrol was taken by his mother to her native country, Uddiana, which bordered Zhang Zhung to the southwest and is generally thought to be the modern-day Swat Valley in Pakistan. While travelling through Uddiana, Öden Barma's clairvoyance revealed there was another Brahmin corpse suitable for her practice some way away. Setting her son Pema Thöngdrol down on one of the gigantic lotuses which were floating in the shallow waters near the shore of Lake Danakosha, she set off to fetch the Brahmin's corpse. However, it took her longer then she had expected and by the time she got back to the lake the sun had already set, the lotus flowers had closed their petals for the night and she was unable to find her son sleeping inside one of them. In despair she tore off the

---

in 8th c. AD are one and the same person due to the large time gap between them and also to the events surrounding the introduction of Indian Buddhism to Tibet and persecution of Yungdrung Bön. Chögyal Namkhai Norbu is also of the opinion that there were many successive incarnations of Guru Rinpoche and not just one Padmasambhava who lived for such an extraordinary length of time.

96 Tib. Bram za Kye ba bDun pa, a Brahmin who led a perfect religious life for seven consecutive lifetimes. The corpse of such a person is used in some Tantric rites to obtain certain psychic powers.

stalks of several plants. One of these flowers was carried by the current to the other shore of the lake and at sunrise opened up to reveal Pema Thöngdrol sitting in the centre, to the great surprise of King Indrabodhi who was walking nearby with his wife. This happened in 876 BC when Pema Thöngdrol was twelve years old, and that is the beginning of his story as the Lotus-Born Padmasambhava.

On seeing the boy, the King and Queen remembered an earlier prophecy foretelling the appearance of a miraculous child who was to become a very great and powerful prince. The royal couple was childless so they adopted the boy and made him a prince. However, as the boy grew up he wanted to leave the palace to continue his spiritual practice. One day he climbed up and sat on the palace roof. Children were playing down below. Pema Thöngdrol threw a pebble at one of the boys which, due to their previous karmic connection, hit him on the head and killed him. Although this appears to be a crime, in reality Pema Thöngdrol, already possessed of great spiritual powers, liberated the boy from his negative karma. However, this was not readily apparent to others. The dead boy was a government minister's son and his distraught parents demanded that Pema Thöngdrol be punished in accordance with the kingdom's laws. They stirred up the townsfolk and soon the palace was surrounded by demonstrating crowds calling for the law to be applied equally to everyone. The King called the council and it was decided that, in order to avoid a revolution, Pema Thöngdrol should be executed, the lawful punishment for murderers. Although deeply distressed, the King and Queen had to comply, but the Queen was allowed to choose the method of execution. She opted for the method of drowning in the lake, thinking it would be less painful than the other alternatives of being burnt alive or killed by the bite of a poisonous snake. So Pema Thöngdrol was thrown into the lake. However, he didn't drown. Instead he appeared sitting in meditation on a floating lotus. The mob wasn't satisfied, denouncing it as a trick conjured by the royal guards to save the boy. Pema Thöngdrol was then thrown into a place seething with poisonous snakes but he came out of the jungle riding one of them. The crowd still didn't abate and demanded he should be burnt. So a huge pile of wood was gathered, Pema Thöngdrol was seated on top and the pyre was lit. The wood blazed violently but when it had burnt out everyone saw Pema Thöngdrol sitting in the ashes in meditation completely unscathed.

Soon afterwards Öden Barma returned and met her son. She told him that now she had overcome all the obstacles of emotions through practice and gained *siddhi* so she wanted to reunite with his father, Drenpa Namkha, in Zhang Zhung. She said that due to the unfavourable situation in the royal household it would be better if Pema Thöngdrol returned with her to Zhang Zhung for the time being in order to receive more teachings and instructions from his father. The boy agreed and they set off to his native land. On the way Öden Barma pointed to a certain rock and told the boy that there was an important *terma* treasure text inside which he should open one day. Mother and son returned to Zhang Zhung where they met Drenpa Namkha. Öden Barma remained with the boy's father and Pema Thöngdrol stayed for a while, too, receiving teachings and instructions. When his education was completed he went back to Uddiana as it was his destiny to spread the teachings there. On the way he opened the textual treasure his mother had pointed out. It was *Kabje*,[97] a Tantric cycle of Eight Yidams.[98] Pema Thöngdrol practised this cycle in many places in Uddiana and attained great realization. That is the story of Bönpo Guru Padmasambhava.

His twin brother Tsewang Rigdzin practised in Zhang Zhung and attained the supreme realization of Dzogchen, the Great Transference of Phowa Chenpo.[99] He didn't manifest death at all but rather his physical body dissolved into the essence of the elements meaning that, while being a fully realized Buddha, he remains active on this level of being even now in order to help beings by whatever means is necessary.[100]

iii) Drenpa Namkha of Tibet

The third Drenpa Namkha was a native Tibetan active in the eighth century AD during the persecution of Yungdrung Bön under Trisong Deutsen. He was an incarnation of the previous (second) Drenpa Namkha of Zhang Zhung. It is this third Drenpa Namkha who was forced to temporarily convert to Indian Buddhism and became one of the twenty-five main students of Guru Padmasambhava in order to save Yungdrung Bön from total annihilation.

During that time, Drenpa Namkha, together with Vairochana of Pagor, another of Guru Rinpoche's principle students, composed a body of rituals which combined the characteristics of Yungdrung Bön and

---

97 Tib. sKab brgyad.

98 There is a Tantric cycle with the same name in the Nyingma tradition. Yongdzin Lopön Tenzin Namdak says that although the name is the same he is unsure whether the content is the same or not.

99 Tib. 'Pho ba Chen po.

100 See Yongdzin Lopön Tenzin Namdak Rinpoche, *Teachings on Zhang Zhung Nyen Gyud and Namkha Truldzö, Vimoutiers, 24 August – 11 September 2004,* Trscr.&ed. Carol Ermakova and Dmitry Ermakov (Blou:Shenten Dargye Ling, 2006), NT, pp. 2–18.

Indian Buddhism; it is on these texts that Bön Sarma is based. When Drenpa Namkha was later permitted to return openly to his Yungdrung Bön faith, he continued to teach and comment on pure Yungdrung Bön. Among his students at that time were Vairochana of Pagor, the Bönpo *yogini* Chöza Bönmo[101] and King Trisong Deutsen himself, who after his hostility towards Yungdrung Bön underwent a change of heart later on in life, began not only learning and practising Yungdrung Bön but also became actively involved in preserving it from further destruction.

Fig. 6. Drenpa Namkha of Tibet.

Bön Sarma, Tibetan Buddhism and Yungdrung Bön

Some scholars do not take the Bön Sarma tradition very seriously and dismiss it as merely a mixture of Bön and Buddhism. However, this is rather a poor argument as, strictly speaking, all Schools of Tibetan Buddhism are, to a greater or lesser extent, a peculiar blend of Indian Buddhism and various types of Bön. This reasoning is not specifically Bönpo but is an understanding coming from Tibetan Buddhists themselves:

> Thu'u-bkvan Chos-kyi nyi-ma, a great eighteenth century dGe-lugs-pa master, noted after completing his celebrated work on Tibetan Buddhist and Bönpo doctrines: 'Bön is so mingled with Buddhism and Buddhism with Bön that my analytic eye fails to see the difference between them.'[102]

Starting with Guru Padmasambhava, who brought a great number of adjusted Bönpo methods into his tradition, which later became known as Nyingma, lamas of the Sarma Schools of Tibetan Buddhism, including the most recent Gelugpa School, have imported a great body of Bönpo methods and adapted them to their own traditions. Consequently what

[101] Tib. Co za Bon mo.

[102] Karmay, *The Arrow and the Spindle*, p.533.

is known now as Tibetan Buddhism is also in fact a mixture of Indian Buddhism and Bön.

As for Yungdrung Bön, while it didn't completely escape the influence of Indian Buddhism in some of its outer aspects, such as the later Bönpo scholars' use of new grammar and spelling rules introduced after the Tibetan writing system was adjusted to accommodate translations of Indian Buddhist texts from Sanskrit in the seventh-eighth centuries AD, its main doctrinal textual base remained largely intact. Over time Yungdrung Bön mingled with Bön Sarma in some areas, but there have always been a great number of Bönpo practitioners and educational establishments which preserve and follow the Yungdrung Bön tradition in its pure form.

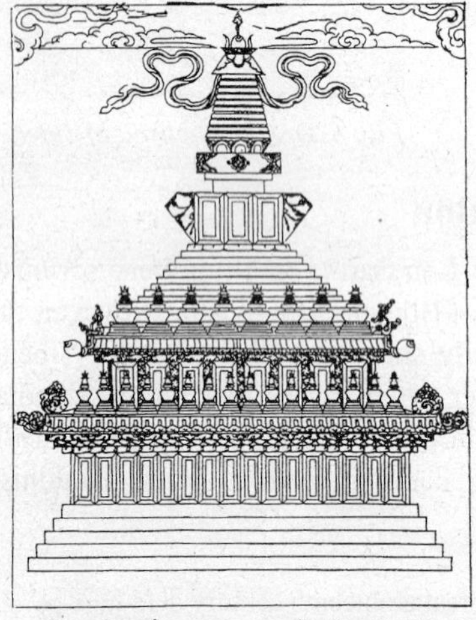

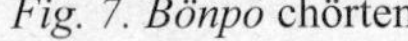

Fig. 7. Bönpo chörten.

Fig. 8. Newari Buddhist Stupa, Tahiti, Kathmandu, 2008.

Signs of this mutual penetration can also be seen in the religious art and architecture of both traditions. Most Tibetan Buddhist art forms – from *thangka*-painting to monastic buildings themselves – are based on or heavily influenced by Yungdrung Bön's canons and proportions for religious art and architecture. This becomes clear if we compare samples of Buddhist religious art from India with those from Tibet; the proportions, drawing techniques and general art forms of Indian Buddhist iconography and architecture, including *stupas* and temples, are entirely different from those of Tibet.

When some artists began painting for both Buddhists and Bönpo some details such as ritual implements and hand gestures permeated from one tradition to the other resulting in some mixed *thangka* standards. On several occasions Yongdzin Lopön Tenzin Namdak, who is from a highly acclaimed family of Bönpo artists and is himself an accomplished painter, pointed out discrepancies in Bönpo *thangkas* where the painters had mixed up Bönpo and Buddhist iconographical details. A pertinent example here would be the very common depiction of the Bönpo master Nyame Sherab Gyaltsen with his hands left over right. Bönpo texts clearly state that his hands should be right over left, but artists influenced by representations of Tsongkhapa routinely mix them up. Similarly, Sidpai Gyalmo's mule is often painted with an eye on her rump, whereas this is in fact a feature of the Buddhist protectress Palden Lhamo's[103] mule. The same is true for Buddhist art. Nevertheless, knowledgeable masters such as Yongdzin Rinpoche still preserve the pure standards of Bönpo religious art.

Some people allege that Bönpo plagiarized Buddhist deities, pointing out that some hold a *dorje*[104] (Sans. *vajra*) or implements decorated with one. In fact, this is conclusion is quite mistaken: the nine-pointed *dorje* is a genuine ritual object of Yungdrung Bön which came to Tibet from the Zhang Zhung Bönpo culture. Traditionally, it represents the Nine Ways of Bön. This nine-pointed *dorje* was adopted by the Nyingma from Yungdrung Bön in the eighth century AD as the Hindu and Indian Buddhist *vajras* are always five-pointed. It is this more recent type of *dorje* which is found among the ritual implements of the Sarma Schools of Tibetan Buddhism.

Fig. 9. Bönpo Mahasiddha *Shari Uchen (Tib. Sha ri dBu chen) wearing the nine-pointed* dorje *crown.*

All religions evolve and change to some extent in the course of time under the pressure of fluctuating cultural, social and political situations, and Yungdrung Bön is no exception. One such change occurred in how the lineages are preserved. Most of the early lineage-holders of Bönpo

[103] Tib. dPal ldan lHa mo.

[104] Tib. rdo rje.

Tantra and Dzogchen were *yogis* while during the Bönpo revival after the second persecution, many Tantra and Dzogchen lineages gradually passed into monastic establishments meaning that today it is largely high monk-lamas of Bönpo monasteries who continue to preserve and transmit those teachings in our times. This became the general situation in Tibet when both Bönpo and Buddhist monasteries alike developed into universal centres of education where all levels of Sutra, Tantra and Dzogchen teachings were studied and preserved. There were masters from both backgrounds who practised Yungdrung Bön and Buddhism simultaneously and so there were different degrees of mutual penetration maintained by these practitioners and their students in their practice, but as far as Yungdrung Bön is concerned, its doctrinal purity was rigorously guarded according to precepts handed down the lineages from ancient times. Contrary to the hostile anti-Bönpo attitude of some sectarian Buddhist scholars who accuse the Bönpo of plagiarizing major Buddhist texts and turning them into Bönpo doctrines, Yungdrung Bön is in fact based on the original authentic doctrines taught by the Central Asian Buddha Tonpa Shenrab Miwoche, collected and preserved in the Bönpo *Kanjur*, and in the *Katen*, the commentaries by subsequent realized Yungdrung Bön masters. This more open-minded understanding is gaining more and more ground among modern scholars as it is supported by new works in areas of textual analysis and history as well as by emerging archaeological research in Tibet and elsewhere.

Mixed Bön traditions of the Himalayas and Tibetan borderlands

Having looked at how Yungdrung Bön influenced Buddhism and vice versa we shall now turn back to see how Prehistoric Bön interfaced with Yungdrung Bön in some areas to form what can be called a fourth type of Bön. This fourth type of Bön doesn't fall within any general name. Rather, it is the variety of peculiar belief system which arose when local Prehistoric Bön traditions met Yungdrung Bön. This kind of Bön is still very much alive among the Nakhi (Naxi)/Dongba and Moso people of Yunnan. In the course of conversation Yongdzin Lopön Tenzin Namdak told me that while in Tibet he encountered one Bönpo who had recently returned from travelling in the Nakhi land. From him he learnt that Nakhi 'shamans' (called *Dongba*) frequently recite one of Yungdrung Bön's main mantras, *Om Ma Tri Mu Ye Sa Le Du*,[105] and use some

105 This is one of the Three Essential Mantras of Yungdrung Bön.

other methods of Yungdrung Bön but also perform animal sacrifices to the gods. They are renowned for their formidable and practical magic powers.[106] This example is particularly interesting for us here because it shows the process of integration; some aspects of Yungdrung Bön were adopted by a native Prehistoric Bön culture but the old traditions were not completely supplanted. In other places, such as Tibet, Yungdrung Bön almost completely replaced earlier Bönpo traditions, although there was inevitably a certain amount of borrowing and transformation. When Yungdrung Bön was initially introduced into Zhang Zhung and Tibet, there were surely many practitioners who tried to combine the two ways so the situation would have been quite similar to that of the Nakhi priests today. According to Yongdzin Lopön Tenzin Namdak, it took a long time before the people of Zhang Zhung and Tibet were converted to Yungdrung Bön. Although this process was almost completed by the eighth century AD, when Indian Buddhism first entered the scene, there were still some followers of Prehistoric Bön practising blood sacrifices and this was the cue for some Buddhists to accuse the Yungdrung Bön *Shenpo* of doing the same.

Other tribes and peoples still practising a mix of Prehistoric Bön and Yungdrung Bön can be found in the Himalayas in Nepal and Arunachal Pradesh State of India and include peoples such as the Tamang, Tamu (Gurung), Thakali, Sherpa, Yolmo, Khas, Magar, Dafla and many others. Many of these tribes have related languages or cultural and religious customs, or both. They have similar classes of priests who wear similar ritual dress and use similar techniques.

Tamu Priests

The belief systems of peoples such as the Nakhi and Tamu provide us with a living example of the kind of mixed Bön traditions most likely practised in Tibet in and before the seventh-eighth centuries, and the comparison is all the more valid as these peoples most probably migrated to their current locations from or via Tibet. The Tamu (Gurung) are of particular interest here as they have three classes of priests – Pachyu (Pajyu), Klehpre (Ghyabre) and Bön Lama – which reflect the three consecutive stages of development in their native tradition and clearly show different phases in the amalgamation of Prehistoric Bön, Yungdrung Bön and even Buddhism.

---

[106] Oral communication from Yongdzin Lopön Tenzin Namdak, Waldzell, Austria, 2000.

i) Pachyu

Pachyu, with their feathered headdresses and tiger-skin waistbands, represent the most archaic layer of the Tamu religion. Among their ritual items we find a half-drum, quivers with porcupine quills for warding off evil spirits, a *mala* of one hundred and eight beads and a hornbill beak symbolizing control over the spirits. Pachyu open and end Tamu funerary rites, recite *ngo* spells and tell *pe* mythical stories which contain references to some places and concepts of ancient Tibet. Pachyu, then, can be described as more or less 'pure' priests of Prehistoric Bön.

ii) Klehpre

Klehpre priests look completely different. They wear a long black gown with long sleeves ornamented with yellow and white stripes, and *rignga*,[107] five-petalled crowns decorated with images of the Five Buddhas of Bön.[108] They carry a stick topped with a metal or wooden bird which is the receptacle for their protective deity and magic power. Like the Pachyu, Klehpre priests also recite spells and myths but the content of their recitations is different. The Klehpres' specialized role in death ritual is to drive away evil spirits and demons and protect the living. Their original name in the ancient Tamu language was Poinbo or Paimu, probably a corruption of 'bönpo', and their doctrine is recorded in Nepali in a text known as *Kyerlo*. This book contains a mixture of local folk myths with Tibetan pre-Buddhist motives incorporated into them as well as references to the Buddha of Bön. From some elements in their invocations and rituals it is clear that the Klehpre were also influenced by Nyingma Buddhism at a later stage. We can safely say, then, that Klehpre are priests of a peculiar tradition of mixed Prehistoric Bön, Yungdrung Bön and Tibetan Nyingma Buddhism.

iii) Bön Lama

Bön Lama are similar to Klehpre in their appearance and function, although they are almost extinct now. Like the Klehpre, they wear a five-petalled crown with images of the Five Buddhas of Bön and a dark blue gown with stripes girded with a colourful waistband. They recite spells and tell myths while their specialization is averting hailstorms and protecting crops and livestock. They use some Buddhist ritual instruments

---

107 Tib. rigs lnga.

108 Tib. sku lnga.

such as *drilbu*[109] upright bell indicating that they were exposed to some kind of Buddhism at some stage.

All three types of Tamu priests know nothing of Yungdrung Bön doctrines and continue to perform blood sacrifices to the gods, as was common in some streams of Prehistoric Bön. Nevertheless, the content of some myths and some parts of the ritual attire of Klehpre and Bön Lama reveal they had contact with Yungdrung Bön at some point in the past. However, although the predecessors of modern Klehpre and Bön Lama must have met with the teachings of the Central Asian Buddha, if they learnt anything from its doctrines such knowledge was not passed on. It is only secondary, external aspects present in their traditions that provide clues to a meeting of the two (or more) traditions; no actual characteristics of Yungdrung Bön are present in their practice at all. In this case, then, we can say the Yungdrung Bön component in the Tamu native religion suffered degradation, especially as all three types of Tamu priest perform blood sacrifices, a practice shunned by *Shenpos* of Yungdrung Bön.[110]

Dhami priests of Humla

Another Mixed Bön tradition is found among the Nyinba people of Humla district of Nepal close to Tibetan Border, the territory which was ones controlled by Zhang Zhung. Many of these people trace their ancestry back to Zhang Zhung and Zhang Zhung clan names such as Khyunpo and Druwa are still common there. Many families have ancient Bönpo texts as heirlooms, although they are unable to distinguish them from Buddhist manuscripts, and the Bönpo flat *shang*-bell is used in some rituals. The Humla priests are called *dhangre* and *dhami* and receive their powers from the gods residing in Lake Manasarovar and Mount Kailash. *Dhami* are mediums channelled by

Fig. 10. Dhami priest.

[109] Tib. dril bu.

[110] See Gurung, *Bön in Himalaya*, pp. 218–246.

the god while *dhangre* are 'interpreters' – a model reminiscent of some traditions found among Tibetan *lhapa* and Buryatian Bɵ and Utgan alike. Geshe Gelek Jinpa holds that the god Gang Karpo who possesses *dhami* Pema from Topa is in fact the *Yullha* of this holy Bönpo mountain, known to them as Gang-Tise. A further connection is the white attire worn by the *dhami*, in particular the white woollen hat which forms part of the turban and seems to correspond almost exactly with the description of Bönpo priestly headdresses.[111]

Yongdzin Lopön Tenzin Namdak gave two examples of mixed Bön traditions still practised in Nepal:

> Our shaman neighbour calls himself a Bönpo and he knows some *yidam* names, such as Shenlha Ökar, but he still sacrifices goats and chickens and leaves them in the fields. However, he never offers blood to Shenlha Ökar. If you ask him where Shenlha Ökar lives, he points and says, 'Up there, in the highest point.' That is Mount Everest. Primitive Bön is practised in the Himalayan Gorge, too. They know many names [of Yungdrung Bön deities].
> Yungdrung Bön spread gradually right up through to the reign of the thirty-seventh king [of Tibet], and Primitive Bön became weaker, although it wasn't persecuted.[112]

Fig. 11. Ima Jhakri priest of Yakha Dewan Rai ethnic group, Nepal. A namkha thread-cross as used in Bön can be seen in the foreground.

A famous example of how Yungdrung Bön and Prehistoric Bön became confused in the minds of Tibetan people is the story of Milarepa[113]

---

[111] Kelly, Jinpa, Ramble, Dunham, *Sacred Landscapes*, pp. 54–65.

[112] Extract from teachings given by Yongdzin Lopön Tenzin Namdak, Pfauenhof, Germany, October, 2005.

[113] Tib. Mi la ras pa.

and Naro Bönchung.[114] According to Yongdzin Lopön Tenzin Namdak, the contest took place in Nepal and Naro Bönchung, although a Bönpo of sorts, was clearly not a practitioner of Yungdrung Bön; he is not found among any lineages in any level of Yungdrung Bön, nor is there any mention of him in any Yungdrung Bön texts:

> Milarepa lived on a mountain quite close to Kathmandu, and on the peak he met Naro Bönchung. His name means he was a high practitioner among shamans, so he was able to show magic. He had a competition with Milarepa to decide [who was the strongest magician]. There are many stories about this contest, but they are Nepali stories; they are not recorded in our texts. So Milarepa [who was also from a Bönpo family][115] was powerful. The other one, Naro Bönchung, was not so powerful. He was a kind of Bönpo of the Tamang or Gurung people.[116] So in Nepal there were many stories and people heard them over and over again and followed what they heard not what was written in the texts. This makes a mess for common people [who couldn't read and check the stories against the texts]. Some lamas always say that their own tradition is best and the rest are useless, and this distorts real, precise history and sullies it [...]. That always happens; people try to convert each other, mutually, even now.[117]

Fig. 12. Maili Lama, Tamang Bombo, Nepal.

---

[114] Tib. sNa ro Bon chung.

[115] Milarepa was born into the Bönpo *Khyung* clan. His father was Tib. Mi la Grub pa (Shes rab rGyal mtshan). His original name was Tib. Mi la Thos pa dGa' ba. He received the transmission of Causal Bön from the Bönpo master Tib. Gyer ston Khro gsas, in particular the text on hail-procurement Tib. *Thog smad dgu 'grol* which he practised on the request of his Buddhist lama Tib. Mar pa Chos kyi Blo gros even after his conversion to Buddhism. (See Karmay, *The Treasury*, pp. 13, 152–53.) There is every reason to believe that in fact the contest between Milarepa and Naro Bönchung happened while Milarepa was still a Bönpo.

[116] This was also verified by Martino Nicoletti who told me that many Tamang priests claim their lineage from Naro Bönchung. Discussion in Kathmandu on 28.12.2007.

[117] Extract from teachings given by Yongdzin Lopön Tenzin Namdak, Pfauenhof, Germany, October, 2005.

As for the well-known Tibetan version of this contest, it is evidently an adaptation. The events are taken out of context, out of their original location in Nepal and set in the Mount Kailash region of Zhang Zhung, the heartland of the Yungdrung Bön tradition. Thus the defeat of Naro Bönchung, who is portrayed as a great master of Yungdrung Bön (which he wasn't), becomes all the more humiliating. This story with all its embellishments, which was used for centuries in Tibetan Buddhist circles to demonstrate Buddhism's moral and magical superiority over Yungdrung Bön, is actually nothing short of misinformed gossip.

Erroneous classifications of Bön

The above presentation on how various types of Bön are classified according to authentic Bönpo systems would not be complete without mentioning in contrast the artificial and falsified classifications created by sectarian or ill-informed scholars. One such system speaks of Revealed Bön,[118] Derived Bön[119] and Transformed Bön.[120] According to this interpretation, Revealed Bön is said to be revealed by Tonpa Shenrab, who is described as a man with donkey's ears, a kind of medium-healer possessed by gods and spirits; Derived Bön is said to be derived from the false theories of heretics; and Transformed Bön is said to have been created by evil spirits who wanted to destroy Buddhism and includes texts plagiarized from it. This classification, however, has nothing to do with history nor with actual types of Tibetan Bön; rather, it is based on ignorance, baseless rumours and the prejudice of those who created it.

Another non-Bönpo classification of Bön divides all Bönpo traditions into Black Bön[121] and White Bön.[122] In this case Black Bön stands for Prehistoric Bön and White Bön stands for a Bön said to have plagiarized Buddhist texts. This kind of classification was probably prompted by the Yungdrung Bön cycles of *Chabkar* and *Chabnag* mentioned above; the names were taken out of context and misinterpreted to suit the contemporary Buddhist political agenda. It is possible that the traditions and practitioners of Tibet's Prehistoric Bön were divided into 'white' and 'black' because we find this classification in Buryatian Bө Murgel. Be that as it may, the meaning of 'white' and 'black' in such a context would have had nothing in common with the meaning lent them by Buddhist

---

118 Tib. rdol bon.
119 Tib. 'khyar bon.
120 Tib. bsgyur bon.
121 Tib. nag bon.
122 Tib. dkar bon.

scholars. These false classifications of Bön have been repeated so many times in Tibetan Buddhist texts that they are now accepted by many whereas in fact they create nothing but confusion and harm, serving only to fortify ignorance. In the light of current research on Bön carried out by western scholars, Bönpo and Buddhist lamas, such notions can clearly be exposed as wholly unfounded.[123]

Bө Murgel as a Mixed Bön tradition

The belief systems of the Nakhi, Tamu and other peoples from the Himalayan borderlands provide an interesting model which can, to some extent, be applied to Buryatian Bө Murgel. As an eclectic religion, Bө Murgel has incorporated various elements of Prehistoric Bön which were practised in the Baikal region by peoples from a wide range of cultures. It is also likely that it was influenced by Yungdrung Bön at some later stage. Bө Murgel, being true to its principle of syncretism, subsequently absorbed some methods and deities from the Tibetan Gelugpa School of Buddhism when the latter was introduced to Buryatia in the seventeenth century. Buddhist influence on Bө Murgel is especially evident in eastern areas of Buryatia where one can readily see how the Bө or Utgan use Buddhist ritual objects such as the *drilbu*-bell or prayer-wheel, invoke certain Buddhist protectors such as Dorje Legpa[124] and Mahakala, and even recite some Buddhist texts in rituals which are essentially Bө Murgel and involve animal sacrifice. In some areas of eastern Buryatia, Gelugpa lamas participate in mixed Bө Murgel/Buddhist rituals which involve animal sacrifices. In the same areas there are mixed Lama-Bө priests.[125]

We can see, then, that the way some aspects of Yungdrung Bön and Buddhism were assimilated into Bө Murgel is parallel to the way in which Yungdrung Bön teachings were mingled with prehistoric animistic traditions in the religion of the Nakhi of Yunnan and the Tamu of Nepal.

A similar process can be observed with regard to Buddhism in Nepal where Vajrayana Buddhists perform animal sacrifices in some of their rites. In his well-written and informative article, Bruce McCoy Owens demonstrates the vital role such rituals play in Newari Vajrayana Buddhism in the Kathmandu Valley where blood sacrifices are offered

---

123 See for example Norbu, *Drung, Deu and Bön*, pp. 38–45.

124 Tib. rDor rje Legs pa.

125 For a detailed analysis of mixed Bө Murgel-Buddhist rites in eastern Buryatia see ch. XII, part I.

to at least four *Bodhisattvas*.[126] In particular, blood sacrifice is connected to the worship of the *Bodhisattva* Bungadya in Patan, who is also known as Karunamaya or Rato Matsyendranath and is believed to be a manifestation of Padmapani Lokeshwar who in turn is an emanation of Avalokiteshvara, the embodiment of compassion. In this case, the rite is presided over by *vajracharya* and *panju* Buddhist priests and involves the mandatory killing[127] of thirty-three animals such as goats, sheep and buffaloes in the course of the annual chariot festival which carries Bungadya through the town and is attended by great crowds, including Hindus and Tibetans. Still more animals are killed if the chariot breaks during the festival, as well as when the chariot is rebuilt every five years and every twelfth year when the procession starts outside Patan city in the village of Bungamati. Bruce McCoy Owens suggests that:

> The structural factors that motivate the sacrifices offered by contemporary Buddhist Newars were undoubtedly present in India when Buddhism was in its ascendancy, and adherents of Buddhism then were likely to have responded to them in a manner similar to their contemporary Newar counterparts.[128] [...] The human population is scrupulous about avoiding the displeasure of powerful deities who favour blood as a means of propitiation. There is no reason to doubt that Buddhists of India were in a similar milieu, surrounded by deities who were worshipped prior to the coming of Buddha, and who continued to demand propitiation in spite of the Buddha's teachings [...]. Buddhism has never evolved in a spiritual or cosmological void.[129]

Thus the pattern of reverting to or integrating with certain deep-rooted cultural and religious aspects present before the introduction of Yungdrung Bön which resulted in the appearance of various traditions of Mixed Bön is not peculiar to Bön alone but has its direct parallel in Mahayana Buddhism. Indeed, this kind of phenomenon can be traced in many places in regard to many different religious traditions such as Christianity, for example, which adopted many aspects of Mithraism into its ritual side; however, we cannot go into more details here.

---

[126] Bruce McCoy Owens, 'Blood and Bodhisattvas: Sacrifice among the Newar Buddhists of Nepal', *Anthropology of Tibet and the Himalaya*, Ed. Charles Ramble & Martin Brauen (Kathmandu: Vajra Publications, 2008), pp. 258–269.

[127] These Buddhist priests do not kill animals themselves but bless the ritual implements used for killing.

[128] Ibid. p. 258.

[129] Ibid. p. 265.

End of baseless rumour

The information presented in this chapter shows that many of the misconceptions about Yungdrung Bön still being bandied about today are in fact just that: misconceptions. When Indian Buddha-Dharma arrived in Tibet in the eighth century it was against a backdrop of political change and the new religion became a tool to push the people towards the new political agenda. Members of the sectarian Buddhist party in the Tibetan government, which included Indian Buddhists, were seeking an excuse to launch a persecution against Yungdrung Bön and concentrate power in the hands of the state, not share it with influential Bönpo priests. We also know that, although most of the Tibetan population had already adopted Yungdrung Bön, the shift from one belief system to another is a gradual process and our brief look at the cultures of the Nakhi, Tamu and Buryatian Bɵ Murgel has given us some insight as to how that shift may take place. In other words, when Indian Buddhists came to Tibet they would have found a whole range of traditions all going under the name 'bön'. Motivated by their political agenda, they naturally didn't care to investigate thoroughly enough to distinguish between them. They must have observed rituals performed by Bönpo priests professing to the sort of mixture similar to the religions of Nakhi and Tamu or certain Nepali sects of Vajrayana Buddhism and that gave them grounds for falsely accusing the *Shenpos* of Yungdrung Bön of engaging in blood sacrifices; they chose to ignore the fact that Tonpa Shenrab Miwo himself had replaced animal sacrifices with substitute offering cakes and alcohol. Similarly, to promote the superiority of any new religion it is necessary to downgrade the old one, and in this case, this was achieved by denying the existence of higher teachings in Yungdrung Bön, accusing the *Shenpos* of copying Indian Buddhist texts and dubbing Yungdrung Bön as a purely 'shamanic' tradition.

Some rumours which arise when facts are manipulated can be very persistent, especially if they play to the ruling class's need to maintain its grip on power, and this is a case in point. Tales of fraudulent, bloodthirsty Bönpos have been endlessly repeated throughout the centuries up until now causing sectarianism, animosity and fighting among Tibetans. For all its ills, our time has some positive aspects such as reasonably free scholarship, better availability of information covering all aspects of knowledge, easier and faster travel and communication. These modern developments have a direct impact on comparative studies in many fields and, in particular, make it possible to gain a deeper and clearer understanding of the parallel processes underlying the way ancient traditions – for which written accounts are sparse at best – may have developed. It is also easier to root out dis- or misinformation contained in the written sources which are available. Humans of the past had basically the same shortcomings as we do today and one of them is a tactic employed by many governments and religious dignitaries worldwide, namely, demonizing a previous spiritual, cultural or social pattern by rewriting history in favour of the newly arrived doctrine. That is the case with Yungdrung Bön. It is my hope that the mispresentation of Yungdrung Bön as a 'shamanic' religion and the harmful, specious rumours and totally unfounded allegations regarding the practice of blood sacrifices will be completely extinguished by the power of the truth derived from unbiased study and reflection.

Setting aside sectarian tensions

The origins of the hostilities between Buddhists and Bönpo in Tibet date back to eighth century politics and power struggles about 1200 years ago, so it is about time to lay these tensions to rest. The cause lies in political manoeuvres, misunderstandings and the institutionalization of religion not on the spiritual level, so it is extremely detrimental to the spiritual development of both Buddhist and Bönpo practitioners to remain entrenched in this outdated conflict and maintain such tensions today. This is all the more true for Western students and practitioners of Buddhism and Yungdrung Bön whose primary goal is to learn and apply the spiritual methods of these traditions in everyday modern life for the benefit of others and themselves; negativities created in this murky period of Tibetan medieval politics should not be allowed to poison minds and practice with prejudice and suspicion. While Yungdrung Bön and Buddhism have different historical and cultural roots and differing methods, their primary origin and goals are the same. If that is understood through study and practice, sectarian conflict has no place. Fortunately, an ever-growing number of Tibetans are coming to understand the indispensible value Bönpo culture and Bönpo spiritual traditions hold for modern Tibetan society so there is hope that the dark echoes of the eighth century will stop reverberating within people's minds. History, of course, remains, but if it is used as a means to understand and rectify the mistakes of the past then it is no bad thing.

CHAPTER IV

Cosmology

Part I
Cosmological Model of Buryatian Bө Murgel

General structure of the universe

For Buryatian Bө Murgel, the cosmos, *Zambi Tubi*,[1] is an immeasurable sphere represented by a circle which contains the Three Worlds (the Upper World, the Middle World and the Underworld) stacked one on top of the other. Each of these three worlds encompasses the four directions: Front (south), Behind (north), Right (west) and Left (east). All the realms are held together either by means of the Cosmic Mountain, Sumber[2] or by the Sacred Tree Serge[3] which serves as the *axis mundi*[4] and penetrates all three worlds from the bottom to the top.[5] In rituals Serge is represented by specially dedicated trees or wooden posts, also called *tuurge*,[6] while the Cosmic Mountain Sumber is represented by an *obo'o*,[7] a specially sanctified cairn of stones constructed in a holy power place.

All the worlds exist in the triple time category of past-present-future and an experienced Bө can travel in the three worlds as well as the three times to retrieve information and perform magical actions. Therefore such a Bө must be well versed in the structure of space-time and its

---

1 Bur. Замби тү̄би.

2 Bur. Сүмбэр corresponds to Sumeru or Meru, the cosmic mountain of Hindus and then Buddhists.

3 Bur. Сэргэ – a cosmic world tree or the tethering-post of the Great Spirit to which Tengeri tie their sky-horses.

4 In Buryatian the axis is called *gol* (Bur. гол). Humans also have *gol*, a vertical energy-channel which runs in the centre of the body. In Sanskrit it is called Avadhuti and in Tibetan Tsawuma (Tib. rtsa dbu ma).

5 Depending on each tribe's tradition.

6 Bur. Түүргэ.

7 Bur. обоо.

inhabitants, the living beings of different classes and races, both material and non-material.

Bө Murgel creation myth

Before we can study the structure and inhabitants of the Three Worlds in more detail we should look into the Bө Murgel creation myth in order to gain some understanding of the origin of these different realms and their relationship to each other. Frankly speaking, we cannot find a single, comprehensive genesis story in Bө Murgel; there are many different fragments of different myths scattered in people's memories and in written sources, many of which are lacking the very beginning of the creation story. They tell us about the creation of human beings but the process of the creation of the Tengeri, the Sky-Dwellers, is omitted. I was searching for a complete version for years and found it only in September 2003 thanks to Dorjo Doogarov who kindly translated the myth from the Kudarinskiy dialect of the Irkutsk region for me. Looking into this and other versions enables us to better understand the mechanics of the creation process as it was seen by the ancient Buryats. We shall start by examining the condensed version of the Kudarinskiy myth as this contains the initial stage of creation, and then continue with two versions from the works of M.N. Hangalov. By combining these we should be able to gain a more or less complete picture and the sequence of events in the creation process according to Bө Murgel will gradually unfold.

> Before the beginning of time, before the Tengeri Sky-Dwellers were born, there was only Eternal Blue Sky, pure potentiality. There was no light, no sun, no moon, no air, nothing; emptiness. In this darkness and emptiness there suddenly was born the unique Ehe Yehe Burkhan,[8] the Great Mother Goddess, blazing with light. She was most powerful and there was no-one equal to her. In this total darkness she was very lonely. She went upwards yet there was nothing but immeasurable and boundless space. She went downwards yet there was nothing but the deepest depth. She experienced all she could in that primordial space and realized she was the only manifest being therein. A great sadness came over her but this then gave way to a raging wrath and Ehe Yehe Burkhan proclaimed, 'I shall put a limit to this limitless space! I shall create a beginning for this beginningless time! I have mighty powers and extraordinary potency! Everything

8 Bur. Эхэ Ехэ Бурхан.

there is lies within my power, everything is in my hands! There is nothing which I cannot do! All being is in my thoughts!' And so she charged into the darkness and roamed throughout it trying to span its depths. Then she decided to create Heaven and Earth. For that purpose she formed a duck which dived into the deepest depth of the primordial ocean and when it came up again it had some earth in its beak. Ehe Yehe Burkhan was overjoyed and shaped the Earth's surface out of it. But in the darkness this Earth started floating away. To prevent the Earth from doing so, Ehe Yehe Burkhan caught a wonderful four-legged turtle and set the Earth on its back. Thus it is said that the world is supported by the four legs of the turtle. Ehe Yehe Burkhan pressed her palm on the Earth's surface and the imprints of the lines on her palm became water courses, rivers and streams which flowed into the boundless ocean. Soon all the Earth was covered by flowering plants and trees, and it was very beautiful indeed. Very happy to see all this beauty, Ehe Yehe Burkhan went to sleep on a certain mountain. But then she thought, Such beauty all around yet there is no-one to use it or comprehend it! No sooner had this thought arisen in her mind than there appeared myriads of birds, animals and fish which spread all over the Earth. They were all very happy living and playing with each other. Then the Great Mother Goddess created Sun and Moon to mark the difference between day and night and provide the animals with warmth and light. Ehe Yehe Burkhan saw that they lived in pairs and produced offspring and the desire arose in her mind to have children of her own, and so she gave birth to a daughter, Ehe Sagaan Burkhan.[9] Ehe Sagaan Burkhan gave birth to two daughters, Manzan Gurma To'odei[10] and Mais Hara To'odei.[11] Manzan Gurma To'odei became the Grandmother of the White Tengeri Sky-Dwellers and Mais Hara To'odei became the Grandmother of the Black Tengeri Sky-Dwellers. Manzan Gurma To'odei had Nine White Sons and Nine White Daughters.[12]

Her sons were:

1. Shudarga Esege Malaan Baabai;[13]

---

9 Bur. Эхэ Сагаан Бурхан.

10 Bur. Манзан Гурма Төөдэй.

11 Bur. Маис Хара Төөдэй.

12 Retelling is mine.

13 'Shudarga' means 'skilful', 'talented', 'swift' and is a pre-name.

2. Shudarga Segeen Huhe Tengeri;
3. Shulma Burged Tengeri;[14]
4. Shulma Khaan Guzhir Tengeri;
5. Shudarga Naran Gerel Tengeri – Sun Light Tengeri;
6. Shudarga Abarga Sagaan Tenegri – Champion Tengeri;
7. Shudarga Udei Mungen Tengeri – […] Silver Tengeri;
8. Sholmo Hulman Sagaan Tengeri;
9. Sholmo Buuma Sagaan Tengeri.[15]

Her daughters were:

1. Guuli Shara Khatan or Buden Iren Sahala Sagaan Khatan – Proud Multicoloured White As Moustache;
2. Sagaadai Sagaan Khatan – Whiter Than White;
3. Hormoi Sagaan Khatan;
4. Gagar Basagaanin Holshorto Sagaan Duurei;
5. Gagar Basagaanin Untei Durtei Abagai – Sister Who Likes Expensive Things;
6. Gagar Basagaanin Ermog Sagaan Go'ohon Duuhei;
7. Dornoi Sagaan Abagai – White Beauty From The East;
8. Nalma Go'ohon Duuhei;
9. Erbed Duurei Abagai.[16]

---

14 'Shulma' means 'tough', 'wrathful', 'swift'. Burged is Buryatian for Tib. Khyung, Sans. Garuda, a horned eagle. Shulma also may mean 'demon'. Here it is used in a positive sense.

15 Bur. 1. Шударга Эсэгэ Малаан Баабай;
2. Шударга Сэгээн Хухэ Тэнгэри;
3. Шулма Бургэд Тэнгери;
4. Шулма Хаан Гужир Тэнгэри;
5. Шударга Наран Гэрэл Тэнгэри;
6. Шударга Абарга Сагаан Тэнгэри;
7. Шударга Удэй Мунгэн Тэнгэри;
8. Шолмо Хулман Сагаан Тэнгэри;
9. Шолмо Буума Сагаан Тэнгэри.

16 Bur. 1. Гуули Шара Хатан, Будэн Ирэн Сахала Сагаан Хатан;
2. Сагаадай Сагаан Хатан;
3. Хормой Сагаан Хатан;
4. Гагар басааганин Хольшорто Сагаан Дуурэй;
5. Гагар басааганин Унтэй Дуртэй Абагай;
6. Гагар басааганин Ермог Сагаан Гоохон Дуухэй;
7. Дорной Сагаан Абагай;
8. Налма Гоохон Дуухэй;
9. Эрбэд Дуурэй Абагай.

Mais Hara To'odei had Thirteen Sons and Seven Pretty Daughters. Her sons were:

1. Asarangui Hara Tengeri;
2. Atai Ulaan Tengeri – Red Flaming Tengeri;
3. Guzhir Bo'oma Tengeri;
4. Bulin Shuhan Tengeri – Blood Clot Tengeri;
5. Hara Darhan Tengeri – Blacksmith Tengeri;
6. Hara Sohor Tengeri – So Dark Can't See Anything Tengeri;
7. Buren Hara Tengeri – Black Grey Tengeri;
8. Haranhui Hara Tengeri – Dark Black Tengeri;
9. Bɵ Hara Tengeri – Black Bɵ Tengeri;
10. Helin Hara Tengeri – Black Tongue Tengeri;
11. Galzuu Hara Tengeri – Wildly Black Tengeri;
12. Balai Hara Tengeri – Just A Little Bit Black Tengeri;
13. Hazhagar Tengeri – There Can Be No Darker Tengeri.[17]

Her daughters were:

1. Han Dagnuuri Go'ohon;
2. Han Sharuuhai Abagai;
3. Han Shuuhai Abagai;
4. Han Dalsha Go'ohon;
5. Han Dalabshata Dangina;
6. Han Shubuuhai Dangina – Bird Dakini;
7. Shara So'ohor Abagai – Completely Yellow (Very Beautiful) Sister.[18]

---

[17] Bur. 1. Асарангуй Хара Тэнгэри;
2. Атай Улаан Тэнгэри;
3. Гужир Боома Тэнгэри;
4. Булин Шуһан Тэнгэри;
5. Хара Дархан Тэнгэри;
6. Хара Сохор Тэнгэри;
7. Бурэн Хара Тэнгэри;
8. Харанхуй Хара Тэнгэри;
9. Бөө Хара Тэнгэри;
10. Хэлин Хара Тэнгэри;
11. Галзуу Хара Тэнгэри;
12. Балай Хара Тэнгэри;
13. Хажагар Хара Тэнгэри.

[18] Bur. 1. Хан Дагнуури гоохон;
2. Хан Шаруухай Абагай;
3. Хан Шуухай Абагай;
4. Хан Далша гоохон;

This, then, deals with the initial stages of creation, the forming of the world and the coming of the Tengeri. There are many versions of how human beings were created by the Tengeri and these narrations, known as the 'new history', mostly fall into two main categories concerning relations among the Tengeri themselves. Stories belonging to the first category state that White and Black Tengeri were distinct from the outset and each descended from their own Grandmother, while stories in the second category maintain that all Tengeri were in the same camp until a quarrel broke out between them at a later stage.

Firstly let us look into the first category. Below are two stories from different sources which illustrate the later stage, namely the creation of human beings, how Bɵ Murgel was transmitted to them and how the vicious conflict flared up between White and Black Tengeri:

> Story 1:
> In the beginning there were no people but only Sky-Dwelling Tengeri, White Western and Black Eastern. The White Western Tengeri created people and animals which lived happily at first not knowing illness, miseries or sufferings. However, after some time the people aroused the anger of the Black Eastern Tengeri who sent diseases causing people and animals to fall ill and perish in great numbers. Concerned, the White Western Tengeri called a council first on Pleiades and then on the Moon in order to decide how best to help them. They agreed to send a white-headed Eagle to transmit the knowledge of Bɵ Murgel to the people and establish lineages of Bɵ who, through ritual actions and magic, could act as the regents of Tengeri on Earth protecting people and animals. The Tengeri commanded the Eagle to give such knowledge to the first person he encountered on Earth. Thus spreading his mighty wings he swooped down from the sky. The first human he met was a woman who had fled from her husband and was sleeping under a tree. The Eagle entered into sexual union with the woman at that spot; knowledge was magically transmitted and she became pregnant with a son. She returned to her husband and, thanks to the power of the Eagle's magic, they began living together in peace. The Black Eastern Tengeri, however, were unhappy with this turn of events and

---

5. Хан Далабшата дангина;
6. Хан Шубуухай дангина;
7. Шара Соохор абагай.

sent an evil spirit who, taking the guise of a beautiful woman, entered the happy family as a second wife. She insisted the man should banish his first wife but the Eagle saw this, snatched up the evil spirit and threw her far away over the sea. Husband and wife once again began living happily together. The woman gave birth to a baby boy. He was the Eagle's son and became the first Bө.[19]

Story 2:
Once upon a time when the leader of the White Tengeri was Hormusta[20] and the leader of the Black Tengeri was Atai Ulaan, a power struggle broke out between them. Atai Ulaan sent twelve magical missiles into the realm of the White Tengeri which struck the goddess of the sun, Naran Go'ohon,[21] causing her to fall sick. The sun's light grew dim and the world was in danger of being destroyed should Naran Go'ohon die. However, she was saved by the son of Hormusta Tengeri. Following the advice of Manzan Gurme To'odei, the Grandmother of the White Sky-Dwellers, he brought a white lark with magical writings to the goddess of the sun who, upon touching this magical bird, regained her radiant good health. Following Atai Ulaan's assault and unbeknown to the other, the same idea arose spontaneously in the minds of both Hormusta Tengeri and Atai Ulaan; each independently paid a visit to Sege'en Sebdeg Tengeri[22] who dwelt in the neutral territory. Thus it was that the two leaders met there. Each set about persuading Sebdeg to join their camp as Sege'en Sebdeg was indeed a very powerful magician. He was the forefather of Bө, the father of the White-Headed Eagle Burged sent to Earth to transmit the knowledge of Bө Murgel to humans, and so each side desperately needed to win his support to be sure of victory over the other. Stirred by their desire to persuade Sege'en Sebdeg to take their side, Hormusta and Atai

---

19 Based on the variation of the myth found in M. N. Hangalov, *Sobranie sochinenii*, Vol.I, (Ulaan-Ude: Buryatskoe knizhnoe izdatel'stvo, 1958) p.364.

20 Bur. Хормуста. There are very many variations of this name in different dialects. Here are some of them: Bur. Хюрмаста, Хюрмас, Тюрмас, Тюрмэс, Хирмас, Хирмус, Хёрмос etc.

21 Bur. Наран Гоохон.

22 Bur. Сэгээн Сэбдэг Тэнгэри also known as Golto Sagaan Burkhan Tengeri (Bur. Голто Сагаан Бурхан Тэнгэри).

Ulaan fell to fighting. Initially Atai Ulaan had the upper hand but Hormusta's son Buhe Beligte,[23] seeing that his father was in grave danger, quickly sped to Manzan Gurme To'odei and reported the happenings to her. The wise Grandmother told him that the souls of Atai Ulaan were hidden in the big toe of his right foot. The son hastened back to the battle to save his father and struck Atai Ulaan's right big toe with a spear. Atai's souls were left without support and ran away, enabling Hormusta to kill him easily.[24]

These stories encapsulate the first group of myths according to which the White and Black Tengeri are initially separate and distinct, a fight breaks out between them and it is the White Tengeri who are the protectors of people and animals. Now we will look at a couple of tales from the second category of the 'new history' which suggest that the split between the Tengeri came at a later stage.

Narrative 1:
In the dimension of the Sky there lived one hundred good White Tengeri and all were the patrons of people. But it happened that one day the oldest of the gods, Asarangi Tengeri,[25] passed away. In the aftermath, quarrelling broke out between Khaan Tyurmes[26] and Atai Ulaan. The former attracted fifty-four Tengeri to his side and the latter forty-three and so the Tengeri separated, fifty-five going to the western sector of the sky and forty-four going to the eastern zone. The Forty-Four Eastern Tengeri became hostile to the people because the Fifty-Five Western Tengeri took them under their care.[27]

Narrative 2:
All the Tengeri dwelt in one camp until later a quarrel broke between them and they split into two warring camps: Fifty-Five

---

[23] Bur. Бухэ Бэлигтэ.

[24] This story comes from the Buryatian epics of Abai Geser and this narration is based on a version found in *Abai Geser*, tr. Komment, A. Ulanov (Ulaan-Ude, 1960).

[25] Bur. Асаранги Тэнгэри. He seems to be the same as Asarangui Hara Tengeri mentioned earlier in the creation myth.

[26] Bur. Хаан Тюрмэс – another name for Hormusta Tengeri.

[27] Based on the version found in M. N. Hangalov & D. A. Clements, *Obshchestvennye okhoty u severnykh buryat,* 1920.

Western White Tengeri headed by their chief Khaan Hyurmas (Hormusta) and Forty-Four Eastern Black Tengeri headed by their chief, Atai Ulaan Tengeri. The two camps communicate with each other through the special envoy Sege'en Sebdeg Tengeri, Wavering Sky-Dweller, who remained neutral.[28] He earned this nickname when he unwittingly became the cause of the split; it is said that Sege'en Sebdeg had a beautiful daughter, Sesek Nogon Abhai[29] (Fire Flower Girl), and the Tengeri fell out with each other over her as both sides wanted to have her with them.[30]

Narrative 3:
The son of the Western Hormusta, Boho Muya,[31] and Boho Te'eli,[32] the son of the Eastern Tengeri Hashkhir Bogdo[33] discovered the technique of metal working together.[34] Later, however, Boho Muya took the smithy away from Boho Te'eli and so their friendship was shattered. Furthermore, Boho Muya helped sway Sege'en Sebdeg, the Neutral Sky-Dweller, to ally himself with the Western Tengeri. It is for these two reasons that the Western and Eastern Tengeri are in conflict.[35]

It is interesting to note that there is also another story which says that later the Western and Eastern Tengeri once again made peace and even became kinsmen through the marriage of Teme Nogon,[36] the daughter of one of the Western Tengeri, to the Eastern Guzhir Bomo Tengeri.[37]

---

28 However in the modern classification he is listed among the White Tengeri which may mean that he nevertheless took the side of the White Tenger*i* at some point.

29 Bur. Сэсэк Ногон Абхай.

30 Hangalov, *Sobranie* I.

31 Bur. Бохо Муя.

32 Bur. Бохо Тээли.

33 Bur. Хашкир Богдо Тэнгэри.

34 Although in this version it would appear that the Tengeri are already classified as Western and Eastern, they are obviously on friendly terms with one another as the children of prominent leaders are playing together.

35 D. S. Doogarov, *Istoricheskie korni belogo shamanstva na materiale obryadovogo fol'klora Buryat* (Moskva: 'Nauka', 1991), p. 252.

36 Bur. Тэмэ Ногон – probably an alternative name for Sesek Nogon Abhai, daughter of Sege'en Sebdeg Tengeri.

37 Bur. Гужир Бомо Тэнгэри.

Above we have examples from two different streams of stories narrating the events of the 'new history'. Story 1, a story belonging to the first category, fits well with the top part of the initial creation stages as told in the Kudarinskiy myth as although both White and Black Tengeri can ultimately be traced to the same source – the Great Mother Goddess Ehe Yehe Burkhan who sprang spontaneously from the pure potentiality of Eternal Blue Sky – they nevertheless have different female ancestors up the line and represent Positive and Negative respectively.

Narratives 1, 2 and 3 are stories of the second category and do not fit with the version of earlier events found in the Kudarinskiy myth as they state that all the Tengeri were initially White and benevolent and only split into two warring camps at some later stage due to the leadership struggle between Khaan Tyurmes (Hormusta) and Atai Ulaan. This version of events has Asarangi Tengeri as the Lord of all the White Tengeri before the split into White and Black. This contradicts the information we have in the Kudarinskiy myth where Asarangui Hara Tengeri is the first son of Mais Hara To'odei and is thus a Black Tengeri.

We cannot say that the first strand of narratives is correct while the second is wrong. However, as I have been unable to locate an initial phase of the myth which would fit the second strand, I shall use a combination of the Kudarinskiy myth and the stories of the first category as a blueprint for this research as this provides us with a complete and coherent storyline.

The Three Worlds and their inhabitants

As was said above, the Three Worlds are connected by means of a Cosmic Mountain or World Tree. Inhabitants of the Upper World are superior to those of the Middle World but the hierarchy of the beings in the Three Worlds is a complex one. While some deities residing in the Middle World are superior to those from the Underworld, that cannot be said of all Middle World inhabitants such as humans, animals and some classes of spirits: the Lord of the Underworld has power over the latter's destiny, over their life and death. Therefore, the Middle World is a kind of conglomerate of influences coming from the Upper World and the Underworld. Each of the worlds is further subdivided into three spheres which are the living spaces for its inhabitants and these are positioned in hierarchical order, so those of higher stature and power live in the upper level. I shall follow this schematic in the presentation below. However, this is not a universal pattern, either. According to other versions the Upper World consists of nine spheres where Tengeri reside, while the Middle World has one level and the Underworld seven.

As I have drawn upon a variety of sources both oral and written, the names of the Tengeri do not necessarily tally with those found in the Kudarinskiy myth. Moreover, here we have a 'modern' picture which includes Tengeri and other deities who came into being at later stages in the creation process.

Now let us look briefly into the structure of each of the Three Worlds.

The Upper World

The Upper World, or Deede Zambi,[38] is the dimension of Eternal Blue Sky, Huhe Münhe Tengeri. As we have seen, Eternal Blue Sky is the ever-alive generating principle from which everything arose. It is a universal, spontaneous creator and destroyer. Although in some traditions he also has an anthropomorphic appearance, usually he is symbolized by the cloudless blue sky and is held as the superior abstract power beyond time and space, unaffected by anything happening in the Three Worlds, the great maintainer of order in the universe. His other epithet is E'e Hairan,[39] the Merciful One. According to one of my sources, E'e Hairan is not identical to Huhe Münhe Tengeri but is superior, so E'e Hairan is the cosmic creative principle while Huhe Münhe Tengeri represents the creative spiritual Sky of our planet earth.

The Upper World is inhabited by Tengeri, Sky-dwelling Gods. On the upper level we find Altan Naran,[40] the Tengeri of the Sun; Alma Hara,[41] Tengeri of the Moon; and Khaan Tengeriin Odo Mushed,[42] the Star-Tengeri.

On the middle level dwell the Nine Tengeri Progenitors:[43] Ubgen Tengeri and his sons Esege Malaan Tengeri, Khaan Sogto Tengeri, Khaan

---

38 Bur. Дээдэ замби.

39 Bur. Ээ Хайран.

40 Bur. Алтан наран, Наран эхэ, Наяан Туяа Татаhан.

41 Bur. Алма hара, hара эсэгэ, Эсэгэ Туяа Татаhан. In Bө Murgel the Sun is considered to be female while the Moon is male. In terms of energy this can be compared with the undesrtanding found in Bönpo and Buddhist Tantric teachings where solar energy is considered to be female while lunar energy is male. In this undersrtanding the female energy harbours the active aspect of wisdom while male energy harbours the passive aspect of method.

42 Bur. Хаан Тэнгэриин Одо Мүшэд are the gods of the Star Constellations and planets such as Bur. Долоон убгэд (Dolon Ubged, lit. 'Seven Elders') – the Plough; Bur. Огторхойн хүтэл (Ogtorhoin Hutel) - Pleiades; Bur. Ухаа Солбон Тэнгэри (Uhaa Solbon Tengeri) – Venus; and so on.

43 Bur. Гарбал Тэнгэриин.

Shargai Noyon; Algan Sagaan Tengeri and his sons Khaan Hormusta Tengeri,[44] Atai Ulaan Tengeri, Bөluur Sagaan Tengeri, Golto Sagaan Tengeri.[45]

On the lower level of the Sky dwell Fifty-Five White Western (literally Right-Standing)[46] Tengeri with their head Khaan Hormusta Tengeri and Forty-Four Black Eastern (literally Left-Standing)[47] Tengeri headed by Atai Ulaan Tengeri.[48] As we have seen above, these two parties are locked in eternal conflict with one another.[49]

Tengeri appear mounted on horses, they have various weapons and attributes and carry spears with banners.

White Tengeri

White Tengeri reside in the west of the Sky and their Lord is Hormusta Tengeri. Most traditions say there are Fifty-Five White Tengeri although this varies from one sub-tradition to another; one of the alternatives has thirty-three White Tengeri, for example. Western White Tengeri are associated with the light part of the twenty-four hour cycle and represent the principle of goodness and virtue.[50] They are benefactors of humans and animals, protecting and supporting the virtuous, punishing and destroying the evil. They are said to be the 'smiths of human souls' and give guidance to White Bө,[51] White Bө-smiths and to righteous people in general. White Tengeri are called to assist in healing, prosperity, weather, protection, and wedding magic as well as in a huge variety of other magical and even administrative actions. Traditionally, pure White Bө

---

[44] As we have seen, Hormusta goes by many names and is sometimes called Hormusta-Burkhan. Burkhan means god, sometimes it also used to distinguish a particular class of gods or even the shrine erected as a support of the god(s).

[45] Bur.Үбгэн Тэнгэри, Эсэгэ Малаан Тэнгэри, Хаан Согто Тэнгэри, Хаан Шаргай Тэнгэри, Альган Сагаан Тэнгэри, Хаан Хормуста Тэнгэри, Атай Улаан Тэнгэри, Бөөлүүр Сагаан Тэнгэри, Голто Сагаан Тэнгэри.

[46] Bur. Баруунай.

[47] Bur. Зүүнэй.

[48] Although Khaan Hormusta and Atai Ulaan are included among the Tengeri of the lower level, in their capacity as leaders of the White and Black Tengeri and members of the lineage of progenitors they belong to the middle level of the Sky according to the structure of heavenly hierarchy.

[49] For a list and short description of their functions see Appendix.

[50] For discussion on why White Tengeri, associated with the light part of the 24-hour cycle, should reside in the west see ch. VI.

[51] Bur. сагаани бөө.

prayed only to the White Tengeri and White *Haats*[52] or directly to Eternal Blue Sky, Huhe Münhe Tengeri, and did not invoke other local gods or spirits of the dead as other types of Bө and shamans do. Nowadays it is difficult to find a pure White Bө; the practice of the modern Bө is an eclectic one and all the Bө I have met make offerings to the local gods and spirits in one form or another.

The visible sky has a special door to the Sky of the White Tengeri called Tengeriin Uden.[53] The Tengeri open this magical door from time to time and look upon the earth to see what is happening there, to see how people and other beings are faring. If there are misfortunes such as epidemics, famines, wars killing many people and animals then they take measures to halt this. When the door opens' a wonderfully brilliant white light shines from there and the whole earth begins to shine with it, too. This only happens for a short time, however. If someone should be lucky enough to see the door open they can ask anything from the Tengeri[54] and their wish will be granted.[55]

Black Tengeri

Black Tengeri reside in the east of the Sky. Generally there are Forty-Four Eastern Tengeri headed by their chief Atai Ulaan Tengeri although, as we have noted, there are some minor variations in different streams of Bө Murgel. Black Tengeri are associated with the dark part of the twenty-four hour cycle and generally represent the principle of evil, destruction and punishment. While many of the Black Tengeri are Owners of diseases and cause epidemics, famines, misfortunes and wars, some have a more benign function and are the patrons of hunting, edible plants, certain crafts and healing. Black Tengeri give guidance and support to Black Bө, Black Bө-smiths and black sorcerers,[56] and some of them also support *uligershen*-bards.[57] Black sorcerers engaged in black magic and unwholesome deeds invoke Black Tengeri and evil spirits when they want to curse somebody or wipe out a particular family.

---

52 Bur. Хаадууд, see below.

53 Bur. Тэнгэриин уудэн.

54 Of course, one cannot put some evil request to the White Tengeri as their nature is goodness.

55 Hangalov, *Sobranie* I, p.419.

56 I use the name 'black sorcerer' instead of 'black Bө' to avoid confusion. Black sorcerers always have evil intentions, are guided and inspired by the Black Tengeri or possessed by bad spirits. For more on this topic see ch. VIII.

57 Bur. үльгэршэн.

One Utgan whom I met on the *tailgan* pilgrimage was very afraid of such rituals. She explained that black sorcerers invoke beings which devour the souls of their enemies and this continues from generation to generation until the whole family completely dies out.[58] One of the important functions of any kind of authentic Bɵ therefore is to fight and destroy black sorcerers.

However, despite this negative alliance, Black Tengeri aren't universally viewed as evil. Some Bɵ, especially from eastern areas, maintain that Black Tengeri are manifestations of the natural destructive force of the universe which is not necessarily negative but has a 'purifying' function and guards law and order; a kind of police force. Black Tengeri punish those who commit acts of sacrilege, break taboo or go against the order of Eternal Blue Sky. While they can cause diseases, epidemics and wars they also have the power to prevent them when addressed in the right way through appropriate rituals and as such Black Tengeri are also associated with healing. Nevertheless, whatever view one takes, in one way or another their activities lie predominantly in the sphere of the 'negative' events in the life of the universe.

Other classifications of Tengeri

So far we have painted the position and functions of White and Black Tengeri in broad brush strokes. However, as we have said, this is not a hard and fast model, and different streams of Bɵ Murgel contain many variations. For instance, the division of Tengeri into White and Black is mostly found in the western areas of Buryatia while in eastern Buryatia[59] this distinction is blurred, and among some tribes it does not exist at all. Some clans of the Horëodoi tribe mainly worship Forty-Four Eastern Tengeri and Thirteen Northern Aryn Arban Gurban Tengeri[60] of the Olhon area and consider Hormusta Tengeri head of all Tengeri.[61] Traditions also vary as to the total number of the Tengeri in the upper sphere; there can be 77, 99, 275,[62] 1,000, 10,000 – or countless. These numbers refer to

---

58 There is also a Buddhist version of such a curse, a kind of 'lama's curse'. On this see ch. XIV.

59 Also on the northern shore of Lake Baikal in the Irkutsk region.

60 Bur. Арын Арбан Гурбан Тэнгэри.

61 According to the tradition of Borkhoev Boris Buzhgeevich (Bur. Борхоев Борис Бужгеевич), a Bɵ from the Irkutsk region, as related to me by Dorjo Doogarov.

62 The Sky and its inhabitants are divided into the four directions:
South – 99 Multicoloured Tengeri headed by Esege Malaan (Father Wise Sky-

the main, well-known groups of Tengeri who enter into direct contact with humans via Bө and Utgan. Their direct impact on human life is recognized by all Buryat clans but the rituals invoking and worshipping them differ from tribe to tribe. Moreover, each tribe, clan and even each family has its own patron Tengeri or group of Tengeri which explains why the same Tengeri can be known under a variety of names and epithets. Add to this the many Tengeri worshiped primarily by one particular tribe or clan, and the result is a huge variety of classifications. Despite these many attempts at classifying Tengeri, one certainly cannot say that the real number of Tengeri is known to humans and, as there are very many Tengeri, 'countless' is an equally correct definition.

The Middle World

The Middle World, Te'eli Zambi,[63] is inhabited by various deities and spirits, the most important of whom is the goddess Etugen,[64] the *Ezhen* of all the earth[65] with her retinue of seventy-seven lesser earth-goddesses, Etugen Ehe.[66] She gives form to everything which exists on earth. Another important *Ezhen* who dwells in this world is Sagaan Ebugen,[67] the White Elder who is the Owner of Earth-Water and is sometimes said to be an emanation of Esege Malaan Tengeri.

---

dweller) and his wife Ehe Yuuren To'odei; West – 55 White Tengeri headed by Zayaan Sagaan Tengeri (Creator White Sky-dweller, another name for Hormusta Tengeri) with his wife Zaarlik; North – 77 Clear Tengeri headed by Huhedey Mergen (the divinity of thunder and lightening, conqueror of bad spirits) and his wife Hultay Khatan; East – 44 Red-flaming Tengeri headed by Ata Ulaan Tengeri. Curiously, the directions aren't mentioned in their usual circular order but form a kind of cross going from front to back, then west to east. Instead of White and Black Tengeri we find here White and Red-flaming Tengeri but their functions and the names of their Lords are the same as those of White and Black. In this case the name 'red-flaming' has probably been given to the Left-standing (Eastern) Tengeri after their chief Atai Ulaan Tengeri whose name means 'Red-flaming Sky Atai'.

63 Bur. Тээли Замби.

64 Bur. Этугэн. In some traditions she is called Ulgen Ehe (Bur. Ульгэн эхэ) or Ulgen Delehe (Bur. Ульгэн дэлэхэ) and – apart from the epithet *ehe* meaning 'mother' – this name is identical to that of the Altai god of virtue. In the Altai tradition he is male and is associated with the sky and with the creation of mankind and all the good things on earth.

65 Bur. Дэлхэй дайдын эжэн.

66 Bur. Этугэн эхэ.

67 Bur. Сагаан Эбугэн.

The upper level of this world is where the sons of Tengeri called *Haat* or *Hahii*[68] reside. They were commanded to descend[69] to earth by their parents and are the lords of ninety sacred mountains. The fifty White Western *Haats*[70] are headed by Khaan Shargai Noyon[71] and Buha Noyon Baabai, a bull-baron, the ancestor of the Bulgat tribe, while the forty Black Eastern *Haats*[72] are led by Khaan Doshkhon Noyon.[73] Then there are also the Thirteen Northern Kings, the Aryn Arban Gurban Tengeri mentioned above whose lord, the *Ezhen*-owner of Olhon, Uta Sagaan Noyon Baabai, is the youngest son of Hormusta Tengeri. There are also thirteen Asarangi Tengeri who are connected with the Eastern *Haats* but seem to have among them some of the Tengeri from the Thirteen Northern Kings. To this upper level also belong Bayan Hangai Khaan,[74] *Ezhen* of the *taiga* and Lord-Owner of all plant and animal kingdoms, as well as other high gods and progenitors of various clans such as Tarilan Ere'en Buha, Dayan De'erkhi Khaan, Bogdo Burin Khaan and Khaan Hentei Noyon.[75]

Various helpers and servants of the above-mentioned gods reside on the second level of this world. They are owners of the peaks; ancient clan leaders; great *Zayaan*-ancestors and leaders of various tribes and clans; some divinities sent by the Tengeri; and high rank *Ongons*.[76] One of these *Zayaans*, Eastern Som Sagaan Noyon,[77] nicknamed Bydek,[78] serves as the messenger between the Eastern and Western *Haats*, and between the Eastern *Haats* and the Lords of the Underworld. He flies through the air in a horseless carriage.

Local guardian-deities and various spirits live on the lower level of this world. They are lords of particular places; patrons of various crafts; leaders of clans; *Ongon*-ancestors; spirit-patrons of clans (some being

---

68 Bur. Хаhии.

69 They are also called Buumal (Bur. Буумал), literally 'lowered from above'.

70 Bur. Баруунi Табин Хаhии.

71 He is simultaneously one of the Nine Progenitor Tengeri.

72 Bur. Зууни Душен Хаhии.

73 Bur. Хан Дошхон ноён.

74 Bur. Баян Хангай хаан.

75 Bur. Тарилан Эрээн Буха, Даян Дээрхи хаан, Богдо Бурин хаан, Хаан Хэнтэй ноён.

76 Bur. Онгон are high-ranking ancestral spirits, spirits of Bө, Utgan, Khaans, heroes etc.

77 Bur. Сом Сагаан ноён.

78 Bur. Быдэк from Bur. быхэ – 'to run'.

spirits of deceased Bө); lords of the soil; lords of the hearth; lords of progeny; lords of diseases and so forth.

The Middle World is also the place where human beings and animals live. They are subject to diverse sufferings and live the earthly life in order to develop virtuous qualities which will help them ascend into the higher worlds. In case they fail and accumulate sins instead, they fall into the Underworld, into the hands of Erlig Khaan[79] and his retinue who will punish them and decide their further destiny.

Totems and protective deities of the four major Buryatian tribes

Each Buryatian tribe, clan and family has its specific protective deities and spirits who belong mainly to the Upper and Middle Worlds. Here we will briefly look into the totems, protective deities and spirits of the main Buryatian tribes.

i) Totems

The main totems of the four main tribes are as follows:
Ehirit – Eren Gutaar,[80] Speckled Eel-pout;
Bulgat – Hoh Buha,[81] Grey-bluish Bull;
Hongodor – Hun Shubuun,[82] Female Swan;
Horёodoi – Hun Shubuun, Female Swan.

Additional totemic attributes, *zalaa*[83] cap-bands, show that in Chingis Khaan's time these tribes were among the Forest Tribes. These cap-bands are strips of wild animal fur[84] sewn onto the hats of the Bө or other important members of the tribe. The Bulgat have polar fox and squirrel

---

[79] Bur. Эрлиг-хаан, Эрлен-хаан depending on the pronunciation in the given dialect. Erlig Khaan can generally be compared with Ahriman (Angro-Mainyu) of ancient Iranian religions, with the Indian god of hell Yama and with the Tibetan Shinje (Tib. gshin rje). Shinje is the Lord of Death and can mean the King of Hell or, more generally, a class of beings who cause death and are associated with hell. Erlig Khaan is also listed among the 13 Asarangi Tengeri.

[80] Bur. Эреэн гутаар.

[81] Bur. Хөх-Буха.

[82] Bur. Хун шубуун.

[83] Bur. Зала.

[84] Bur. хээриин табан хушуутан.

cap-bands;[85] Ehirit have ermin cap-bands,[86] Hongodor have Siberian polecat cap-bands[87] and Horëodoi have roe deer or elk cap-bands.[88]

ii) Protective deities and spirits

Tribe	**Patron Tengeri**	**Zayaans**	**Ongons**
Ehirit	Huhe Mungen Tengeri[i]	Azharai Buhe; Uha Shara; Uta Sagaan Noyon (Lord of Olhon Island); Zulhein Ezhen (Lord of Lena River); Hongoldoin Ezhen[ii] (Lord of Mount Verkholenskaya)[iii]	Uete Hunerege, Yamaani Ezhen (Lord of the goat), Hadain Ongon[iv] etc.
Bulgat	Bulurgui Sagaan Tengeri[v]	Ulgein Ezhen Buha Noyon Baabai (Lord of Ulgein in Tunka); Sharbatyn Ezhen Shargai Noyon Baabai (Lord of Mount Sharbaty); Irhuuye Ezhen Emneg Sagaan Noyon (Lord of River Irkut)[vi]	Holongoto Ubgen Tunhei Mandahai (Lord of the Ermine); Zyaasha Ubgen Zaarlik Tehei (patron of happiness and progeny); Sezhin Bara (patron of hunt)[vii] etc.
Hongodor	Urag Sagaan Tengeri[viii]	Angarain Amani Ezhen Ama Sagaan Noyon (Lord of the source of River Angara); Turain Ezhen Tulba Sagaan Noyon (Lord of Irkutsk City); Hereni Ezhen Heremshi Sagaan Noyon (Lord of Mount Kyren); Uuragi Ezhen Ulaan Zalaa Mergen Degei (Lord of River Uurag)[ix]	Hetei (Bulagsha) Ongon; Saitani Ongon Burkhad; Anda Tumurshi (Anda Bara)[x] etc.
Horëodoi (Hori)	Sahilgan Sagaan Tengeri[xi]	Aryn Arban Gurban Noyod [Tengeri] (Thirteen Northern Lords); Sarbali Sagaan Noyon (Lord of Hudan in Horinsk administrative division);[xii] Orboli Sagaan Noyon (Lord of Sohondo Hill near Nerchinsk town);[xiii] Helgo Muriin Ezhen Hilar Sagaan Noyon[xiv]	Burte Ongon (Horton Zaarin Bɵ); Hesete Ongon (Bɵ-leader of the Galzuud[xv] clan from Barguzin, killed on Mount Barhan Uula[xvi] by invaders); Underi Ezhen (spirit of Bɵ-leader of Shalsaana[xvii] ulus, Lord of Shalsaana)[xviii] etc.

85 Bur. булган зала, хэрмэн зала.

86 Bur. саган үен зала.

87 Bur. һолонгото зала.

88 Bur. улаан зала гуран.

Notes to the Table:

i. *Bur. Хухэ Мунгэн Тэнгэри.*
ii. *Bur. Ажарай Бухэ, Уха Шара, Ута Сагаан Ноён, Зулхэйн эжен, Хонголдойн эжэн.*
iii. *Rus. Верхоленская гора.*
iv. *Bur. Уетэ Хунэргэ, Ямаани эжэн, Хадайн онгон.*
v. *Bur. Булургый Сагаан Тэнгэри.*
vi. *Bur. Улгэйн эжэн Буха Ноён Баабай, Шарабатын эжэн Шаргай Ноён Баабай, Ирхүүе эжэн Эмнэг Сагаан Ноён.*
vii. *Bur. Һолонгото үбгэн Тунхэй Мандахай, Заяаша үбгэн Заарлик Тэхэй, Сэжин Бара.*
viii. *Bur. Ураг Сагаан Тэнгэри.*
ix. *Bur. Ангарайн амани эжэн Ама Сагаан Ноён, Турайн эжэн Тулба Сагаан Ноён, Хэрэрни эжэн Хэрэмши Сагаан Ноён, Уураги эжэн Улаан зала Мэргэн Дэгэй.*
x. *Bur. Хэтэтй (Булагша) онгон, Сайтани Бурхад онгон, Анда Тумурши (Анда Бара).*
xi. *Bur. Сахилган Сагаан Тэнэгэри.*
xii. *Rus. Худан, Хоринск.*
xiii. *Rus. Сохондо сопка, Нерчинск.*
xiv. *Bur. Арын Арбан Гурбан ноёд (тэнгэри), Срабали Сагаан ноён, Орболи Сагаан ноён, Хелго муриин эжэн Хилар Сагаан ноён.*
xv. *Bur. Галзууд, a clan of the Horёodoi (Hori) tribe famous for its Bө-smiths who master the element of fire.*
xvi. *Bur. Бархан Уула.*
xvii. *Bur. Шалсаана улус.*
xviii. *Bur. Бүртэ онгон (Хортон Заарин бөө), Хэсэтэ онгон, Үндэри эжэн.*

The Underworld

The Underworld, Do'odo Zambi,[89] is under the dominion of Erlig Khaan and Uhaan Lusuut Khaan who reign in the Underearth and Underwater respectively. Descriptions of the Underworld differ; according to one model it is comprised of three spheres or levels while another model speaks of seven levels. However, I will not go into details here; suffice to say, it is a highly hierarchical world.

The domain of Uhaan Lusuut Khaan is the kingdom of the Underwater and is inhabited by various kinds of water-spirits, many of whom possess formidable magic powers including the capacity to send or heal diseases. As such they are invoked by Bө and Utgan[90] in certain healing rituals.

Certain kinds of spirits of the dead spend their post-mortem 'life' in Erlig Khaan's realm awaiting the circumstances to be reborn in the

[89] Bur. Доодо Замби.

[90] More precisely, Black Bө and Utgan or Bө and Utgan who can work on two sides. See ch. VIII.

Middle World once more; how long they remain there depends on their actions while they were alive in the Middle World.[91] In ancient times the realm of Erlig Khaan was not perceived as a hell but later, probably due to Buddhist influence, this perception changed and nowadays many Buryats think of it as a kind of hell where the spirits of the dead go if they performed unwholesome deeds while they were humans.

Traditionally, this realm is described as a highly bureaucratic one. The way it functions is very similar to a totalitarian state. Erlig Khaan has a huge number of assistants – scribes, judges, wardens and messengers – who help him keep records of the actions and thoughts, good and bad, of humans and other beings currently alive in the Middle World incarnated in bodies of flesh and blood. These records are contained in the Table of Fate and used to judge beings when they descend into the Underworld after their death in the Middle World; it is on the basis of these records that their fate is decided. The soul of the deceased may be imprisoned or tortured in the Underworld, made to dissolve into water or earth, or be reincarnated as a bird, an animal or a plant. In the case of a better destiny, one can become a human again or become a spirit-protector of a clan, a mountain, an area etc. Bө who made no mistakes in their career are not judged by Erlig Khaan as they are the protégées of the Tengeri so it is the latter who decide their posthumous destination. In some cases a very outstanding Bө or Utgan may ascend to the Sky and become a Tengeri. Interestingly, those who want to have a position in the bureaucratic apparatus in the Middle World pray to Erlig Khaan for help.

Despite being low, dark places, both sections of the Underworld are accountable to the Tengeri and both Uhaan Lusuut Khaan and Erlig Khaan follow the will of Eternal Blue Sky. Therefore, everything in the Three Worlds lies within the sphere of Huhe Münhe Tengeri's power.

Conclusion

To sum up Buryatian Bө Murgel's complex cosmological model, we can say that essentially Eternal Blue Sky is the generator of the Three Worlds and all beings living within them. It is only Huhe Münhe Tengeri who is eternal as, although the Tengeri have unfathomably long lifespans, they perish nevertheless. This is clear from the myths narrated above where we read that Tengeri can die of old age or even be killed. Other beings have varied lifespans and circulate within the Three Worlds in a

---

[91] This is only one view of the afterlife and isn't shared equally by all Bө and Utgan. See ch. XIII.

number of ways, but all the inhabitants of the Three Worlds and the Three Worlds themselves will ultimately dissolve back into Eternal Blue Sky at the end of this cycle.

Part II
Bönpo Cosmological Model

Creation of the universe from primeval eggs

In the cosmology of Yungdrung Bön[92] we find a great variety of creation myths known as *mang*[93] which narrate the origins and history of the universe. Among these are many variations of the *Myth of the Origin of Existence*[94] which describe in detail how the universe and all beings inhabiting it came into being. Here is a brief summary of this process according to the *Srid pa'i mdzod phug* and the sage Drenpa Namkha's commentary on it:

> At the beginning there was empty space, Namkha Togden Chosumje;[95] nothingness. However, it contained the five causes nonetheless. Trigyal Khugpa,[96] the forefather of *Ye*,[97] the positive dimension of light and virtue, drew those causes unto himself and released the sound 'ha' from which arose winds which, taking the form of a swiftly-spinning light wheel, started moving in the emptiness. From the rotation of the wheel there arose heat and thus the element of fire was formed. Through the contrast of the coolness of the winds and the fire's heat there arose a condensation which became dew, the water element. This in turn was churned by the winds causing particles of matter of the earth element to cluster onto it and be spread far and wide. Travelling in space, these particles condensed and attached to one another forming the earth and the mountains. From the essence of the created elements

---

92 Tib. mdzod phugs.

93 Tib. smrang.

94 Tib. srid pa'i grol phug.

95 Tib. Nam mkha' sTong ldan Phyod sum rje. He is the same as Tib. Kun tu bZang po.

96 Tib. Khri rgyal khug pa. His other names in Yungdrung Bön are Tib. mNgon rdzogs rgyal po and Tib. gShen lha 'Od dkar.

97 Tib. ye.

there appeared two cosmic eggs: the cubic egg of light and the pyramidal egg of darkness.

The egg of light hatched by the power of its own energy. From the rays of light blazing upwards were born 360 *Thorse*[98] deities of light who spread throughout space. From the light rays shining downwards were born 10,000 *Dase*[99] with 100,000 horses. From the heart of the egg there emerged a man of white light with seven turquoise plaits, Sidpa Sangpo Bumtri,[100] the emanation of Trigyal Khugpa. He became the King of the World of Existence[101] and the father of the *Lha*[102]-gods of the sky.

Meanwhile Kalpa Mebum Nagpo,[103] the forefather of *Ngam*,[104] the negative dimension of darkness, ignorance and evil, caused the egg of darkness to burst in the realm of darkness. From the black light which spread upwards darkness, ignorance and pollution were produced. The black rays which shone downwards produced mental torpor, madness and pollution of various kinds. From the heart of the egg there appeared a man of black light with three big plaits, Munpa Zerden Nagpo.[105] He became the King of the World of Non-existence[106] and the father of the *Düd*[107]-demons of the sky.

And this is how the ancestors of gods and humans appeared:

The dew and rain produced from the water element became oceans. Wind blew across their waters and a bubble appeared on their surface sheathing an egg of blue light within it. The egg burst by its own inherent power and a turquoise blue woman with her hair in seven plaits emerged from it. Sangpo Bumtri, the King of Existence, named her Chucham Gyalmo.[108] From their

98 Tib. 'thor gsas.
99 Tib. mda' gsas.
100 Tib. Srid pa Sangs po 'bum khri.
101 Tib. yod khams srid pa'i rgyal po.
102 Tib. lha.
103 Tib. bsKal pa Med 'bum nag po.
104 Tib. ngam.
105 Tib. Mun pa Zer ldan Nag po.
106 Tib. med khams stong pa'i rgyal po.
107 Tib. bdud.
108 Tib. Chu lcam rGyal mo.

union were born Nine Brothers[109] and Nine Sisters.[110]Through the force of their wish each of the Nine Brothers caused a female partner to appear and each of the Nine Sisters caused a male partner to appear thus the eighteen ancestral couples formed from which the various races of gods and humans descended. Sangpo Bumtri and Chucham Gyalmo also produced a myriad of wild animals and birds.

As for how the ancestors of demons and bad spirits appeared:

> Munpa Zerden, the King of Non-existence, created a consort Tongzham Nagmo,[111] Queen of Darkness, out of his own shadow. They coupled and Eight Brothers and Eight Sisters were born to them. The Eight Brothers created eight female consorts while the Eight Sisters created eight male consorts and thus sixteen ancestral couples of demons[112] were formed.

According to another version of the creation myth:[113]

> First there was nothingness and all was empty. Within this emptiness a life principle gradually began to form and within this there formed a Light and a Ray, Light being father and Ray, mother. Within these two, darkness and obscurity also manifested. Within the darkness and obscurity a breath of gentle wind appeared, within that wind there appeared a frost and within that frost, dew. Then from the union of frost and dew there arose a mirror-like lake. The upper layer of the lake rolled into itself and became an egg[114] from which two eagles emerged, black and white, called 'Luminous Appearance'[115] and 'Dark

---

[109] Tib. srid pa pho dgu.

[110] Tib. srid pa mo dgu. For a full list see Norbu, *Drung, Deu and Bön*, pp. 166–167.

[111] Tib. sTong zhams Nag mo.

[112] This presentation is based on Norbu, *Drung, Deu and Bön,* pp. 163–167, and Karmay, *The Arrow and the Spindle*, pp. 126–132.

[113] In Karmay, *The Arrow and the Spindle,* pp. 264–267.

[114] According to still another model, the five elements fused into a Cosmic Egg which further developed into 18 Cosmic Eggs from which beings and nations developed. See Norbu, *Necklace of gZi*, p. 2–3.

[115] Tib. sNang-ba 'Od ldan.

Ray'.[116] They united and produced three eggs, one white, one black and one multicoloured. From the white egg there appeared the divinities of light while from the black egg there appeared the divinities of darkness. The multicoloured egg turned into a strange being with neither sense organs nor limbs but then these took shape and he manifested as the King of Existence, Sidpa Sangpo Bumtri, who is also known as the King of Primeval Wish,[117] a procreator wisdom-god, a personification of the positive creative principle. Through the power of his aspiration or wish there came about the lineages of the *Cha*, *Mu*, *Tsug* and *Nyen*[118] gods who, mixing with each other, gave rise to the royal lineages of various countries and humans of various tribes, as well as to non-human beings, animals and so on.

Dualism of Light and Darkness: the polar forces of Ye and Ngam

According to Bön there are two polar forces which struggle over the control of the universe. They are the orders or worlds of *Ye* and *Ngam*. *Ye* stands for existence, positive,[119] light[120] while *Ngam* stands for non-existence,[121] negative,[122] darkness.[123] *Lha* are the beings of *Ye* while *Düd* are the beings of *Ngam*.

The world order of *Ye* has four[124] or thirteen[125] skies or levels according to different sources. Each of the skies has heavenly cities ruled by various kings of the *Lha*-gods. The highest sky is that of Trigyal Khugpa and is ruled by the king Chaje Yala Daldrug,[126] the ancestor of Tibetan kings. In this heaven the gods study special doctrines of Bön.

---

[116] Tib. Mun pa Zer ldan. These two are the same as the principal beings which emerged from the eggs in the version above.

[117] Tib. Srid pa Ye smon rGyal po.

[118] Tib. Phyva, dMu (rMu), gTsug, gNyan.

[119] Tib. yod khams.

[120] Tib. snang.

[121] Here, non-existence has a negative connotation as this side of energy and the beings powered by it bring about annihilation and the destruction of the positive aspect of the universe.

[122] Tib. med khams.

[123] Tib. mun.

[124] See Karmay, *The Arrow and the Spindle,* p. 131.

[125] See Norbu, *Drung, Deu and Bön*, p. 261, n. 30.

[126] Tib. Phyva rje Ya bla bDal drug.

The world order of *Ngam* is located to the north of *Ye* and has the same number of skies as are found in *Ye*. Its cities are populated by *Düd*-demons and ruled by *Düd* kings.

Armies of *Lha* and *Düd* are locked in an eternal struggle which affects all levels of the universe, and especially human beings who descended from the *Lha* but were also contaminated by the *Düd*. The *Düd* always seek to overthrow the virtuous order of the *Lha* and cause trouble in the realm their offspring, humans. It is, therefore, of utmost importance to humankind that the *Lha* win those battles as otherwise we would be wiped out by all manner of negativities unleashed by the *Düd*. It is for this reason that some traditions of Prehistoric Bön such as Lha Bön and a fair portion of the rites belonging to the Four Casual Ways of Yungdrung Bön are aimed at invoking the *Lha* and strengthening their energy.

However, *Lha* and *Düd* are not completely distinct and separate as they belong to the same level of existence and emerged from the same source: empty space. As we will see later, they can occasionally intermarry and produce seed of mixed descent.

According to Yungdrung Bön, the dualistic nature of the universe is reflected in human beings, too, on both the inner and outer level. Internally, each person has positive and negative aspects of their personality or mind called *Lhanchig Kyepai Lhadang Düd*,[127] or *Lhadre*,[128] literally 'the god and demon which are born together with oneself'. When a person enters the dualistic vision of *samsara*, these are the dualistic principles in the mindstream which are constantly at war. Consequently, they are the source of suffering and of all the dualistic tendencies of good and evil present in the mind of a person until they are purified by applying a Buddha's teachings. Outwardly, an individual's life is influenced by the external energies of *Lhadre* which manifest as actual non-human gods and spirits. This is the base from which the need arises for the countless variety of rituals in Casual Bön which aim to appease and pacify various beings and energies. Although these methods bring very tangible results, they are of temporary value; it is the higher teachings of Yungdrung Bön that enable someone to wholly pacify internal dualistic tendencies thereby bringing them to the fruit of complete Buddhahood.

In the context of cosmic dualism, the *Lha* and *Düd* of Tibetan Bön correspond to the White and Black Tengeri of Bɵ Murgel and are in fact merely different names for the same phenomena. We will compare these two pairs of orders shortly.

---

[127] Tib. lhan cig skyes pa'i lha dang bdud.

[128] Tib. lha 'dre.

The structure of our universe

The triple world system

The triple world structure is often is spoken of as one of the main attributes of 'shamanic' faiths but this definition is clearly far from satisfactory and falls apart on closer examination. A triple world view is common to many faiths which are not normally considered 'shamanic'. The Vedic tradition has Three Worlds, the cosmology of Indian Buddhism has Three Worlds, Zoroastrianism and Judaism have Three Worlds, and even later religions such as Christianity and Islam have the Three Worlds of paradise, earth and hell. Probably the majority of religions and spiritual paths have the triple world structure in their cosmological models. That, however, doesn't make them 'shamanic'. A spiritual tradition can only be considered 'shamanic' when the figure of the shaman is inherent within it. Bön, therefore, cannot be labelled 'shamanic' merely because it shares the triple world structure; instead it would be better to consider this structure as a common feature of the spiritual perception of the world.

In the Bön understanding, the Three Worlds[129] are the Sky World,[130] the World of Earth[131] and the World of Waters.[132] The Sky World is inhabited by *Lha* and *Düd*; the World of the Earth is inhabited by *Nyen* (gods and spirits of the intermediate space), humans and animals; and the World of the Waters is inhabited by *Lu* (water-spirits or water-gods). This is a very general description of the inhabitants of the Three Worlds. In fact, the countless variety of living beings is classified into Six Realms of Rebirth[133] with most of the powerful non-human gods and spirits who control the energies of our world listed in the category of Thirty-Three Races of Gods and Spirits[134] which will be discussed later.

The Three Worlds are held together by the Cosmic Mountain, Rirab[135] or Meru, in the same way as in the cosmology of Bɵ Murgel. It is eighty thousand *paktse*[136] high and eight thousand *paktse* wide. On the

---

[129] Tib. srid gsum. Lit. Three Existences.

[130] Tib. gnam.

[131] Tib. bar generally means 'intermediate' or 'in between', i.e. Middle World.

[132] Tib. 'og.

[133] Tib. rigs drug. Often translated into English as the Six Destinies of Rebirth, Six Realms or Six Lokas.

[134] Tib. g.yen khams sum cu so sum. See ch. V.

[135] Tib. ri rab.

[136] Tib. dpag tsad. This is the largest traditional measure in Tibet. It is built up as follows: one *sortsig* (Tib. sor tsigs) is the distance from the tip of the thumb to the knuckle, 24 of these (Tib. sor tsigs nyer bzhi) is one *trigang* (Tib. khri

top of Rirab grows the wish-fulfilling tree, Pagsam Jonshing,[137] on which perches the *Khyung*, the king of birds. The tree's roots are at the base of Mount Meru and between them is the abode of the *Lu,* the water-gods. The trunk of the tree grows inside the mountain through treasure palaces but it has no branches or leaves at this point. That is the domain of the *Lhamin*,[138] jealous demi-gods. They are jealous because when the tree comes out at the top there are branches, leaves, flowers and fruit which fulfil all the desires of the *Lha* gods. The beings of the Six Destinies of Rebirth live around the mountain with the higher gods dwelling above it and some hells lying below the mountain and the continents.[139]

The Cosmic Mountain is surrounded by seven golden square mountain ranges separated by seven seas. These mountain ranges function as border fences between the worlds of the gods, humans and water-gods. Beyond the mountain rings are four continents in an ocean, each flanked by two small islands. The main islands are populated by various human races while the satellite islands are the living space for diverse beings including animals and demons. In the semi-circular Eastern Continent humans are born from heat;[140] in the square Northern Continent humans are born miraculously;[141] in the circular Western Continent humans are egg-born;[142] in the triangular Southern Continent, our world, humans are born from the womb.[143] They differ from each other in terms of lifespan, appearance, size and other characteristics. The Southern Continent is the land of evolutionary action and is the best suited to spiritual practice. Beyond the continents and islands there is only ocean with the outermost border formed from a fence-like mountain range of volcanic iron which heats up the water causing it to evaporate, thereby preventing it from

---

gang) i.e. ~45cm; 4 *trigang* make one *dom* (Tib. 'dom) which is the distance from the tips of the fingers on one hand to the tips of the fingers on the other hand when a large man stretches out his arms, i.e. roughly around ~180cm; 500 *dom* make one *jangdra* (Tib. rjyang grags) which is around ~900 meters; 8 *jangdra* make one *paktse* which is around 7200 meters. So Rirab is around 576,000km high and ~57,600km wide.

[137] Tib. dpag bsam ljon shing.

[138] Tib. lha min.

[139] There are no fixed arrangements for the dwelling places of various beings as there are so many different types and classes. The classification into the Six Destinies of Rebirth is rather schematic and very general.

[140] Tib. drod skyes.

[141] Tib. rdzus skyes.

[142] Tib. sgong skyes.

[143] Tib. mngal skyes.

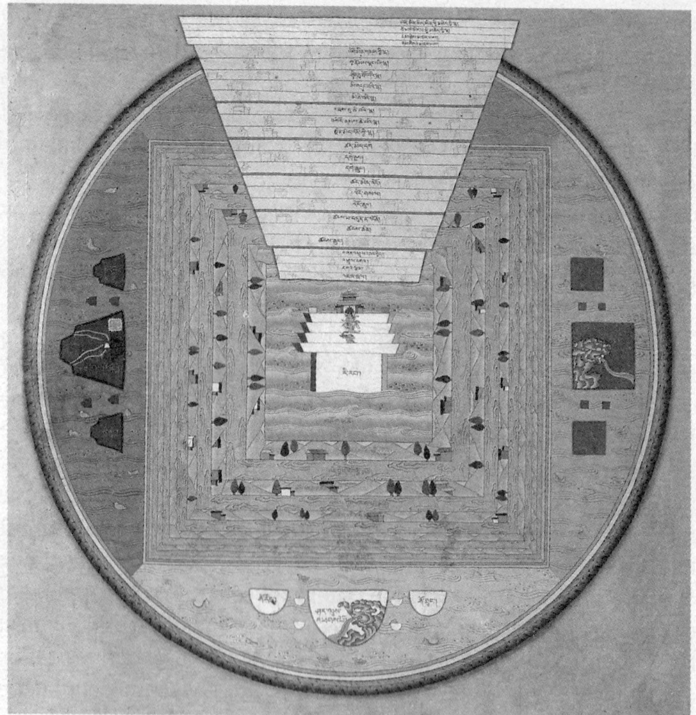

Fig. 1. Our Universe, mural from Triten Norbutse Bönpo Monastery, Kathmandu.

overflowing beyond the rim. The various God Realms are located on the top of and above the World Mountain in the form of an upturned truncated pyramid.

Beings of the Six Realms of Rebirth[144] *according to Yungdrung Bön*

Here we will give a brief overview of the beings inhabiting our universe. According to this classification, they are divided into six major groups: hell-dwellers, hungry ghosts, animals, humans, demi-gods and gods.[145] These beings dwell in six corresponding realms, but none are beyond suffering or beyond *samsara*. *Samsara* is classified into two

---

[144] Tib. 'gro ba rigs drub.

[145] Tib. dmyal ba; yi dwags; byol song; mi; lha ma yin; lha.

Fig. 2. The God Realms on the top of the World Mountain, mural from Triten Norbutse Bönpo Monastery, Kathmandu. In the centre there are palaces of the Thirty-Three Gods; in the inner upper left corner there is a triangular palace with a precious wish-fulfilling jewel where Buddhas give their teachings; in the inner upper right corner is the cave of Sangwa Dhüpa, the Holder of Secrets who, according Yungdrung Bön, was a student of Tonpa Shenrab and was later born in India as Buddha Shakyamuni; in the inner bottom right corner is the wish-fulfilling tree with Khyung perching on it; in the inner bottom left corner there is the Udumbara flower which blossoms when a Buddha is born; in the four cardinal directions there are Four Great Kings.

categories, container and content,[146] whereby the realms are the container and the myriads of sentient beings form the content. Both the container and the content are the product of beings' own karma so everything is ultimately created by the beings themselves.

Another way of classifying the beings and their realms is found in the higher teachings of Fruitional Bön. Here, there are three broad

[146] Tib. phyi snod; nang bcud.

realms and all the Six Realms of Rebirth fall under one of the following three classifications: Realm of Desire, Realm of Form, and Formless Realm.[147] According to this system, all the realms below those of the gods belong to the Realm of Desire, and within the God Realms we find realms belonging to all of these Three Realms.

1. Hell Realms

There are eighteen Hell Realms comprised of eight hot hells and eight cold hells plus a temporary hell and a peripheral hell. In the hot hells, temperatures are extremely high and the hell-dwellers suffer all kinds of burning while in the cold hells beings are subject to extreme cold and freezing. In the temporary hell beings are scorched one day and frozen the next whereas in the peripheral hell beings suffer from extreme cold in their upper body and extreme heat in their lower body. Lifespans in the different Hell Realms vary, but they are always very, very long. The main cause for birth there is hateful anger while the antidote is generating loving-kindness towards all sentient beings coupled with higher meditation practices which can liberate anger into the wisdom of emptiness.[148]

2. Hungry Ghost Realm

The hungry ghosts experience acute hunger in three different forms:

- Some perceive food as fire, weapons, poison, something dirty or unpleasant. Consequently they find no suitable food and cannot eat. Tormented by great hunger, they constantly roam around in search of food.
- Some recognize food as being edible but their body is structured in such a way that they are unable to eat. Their head is the size of a pepper corn, their neck is as thin as a blade of grass, their arms and legs are emaciated but their belly is gigantic so even if they manage to squeeze a tiny amount of food past their narrow neck it goes unnoticed in their vast stomach, and so they go on wandering around tormented by incessant hunger.
- The third type of hungry ghosts can see food as food and they can eat it, but as soon as it reaches their stomach it turns into fire or poison causing them to suffer tremendously.

---

[147] Tib. 'dod khams; gzugs khams; gzugs med khams.

[148] Tib. stong nyid ye shes.

The main causes for birth in the Hungry Ghost Realm are attachment and greed. The antidote is to develop generosity and practise higher meditation techniques through which greed and attachment are liberated into discriminating wisdom.[149]

While most of the Hell and Hungry Ghost Realms do not have a particular physical location, some are said to be under Mount Rirab or tucked inside its lower crevasses.

3. Animal Realm

Generally, there are three Animal Realms:

- *Undersea and Underground Animal Realm.* Creatures of this realm live underground or in the waters of the World Ocean which surrounds the World Mountain, continents and islands. They are generally soft, damp animals such as molluscs, crocodiles, fish, frog, snails, slugs and so on. Some are so big that they can wrap themselves around the World Mountain while others are so small that they cannot be seen at all. They are all plagued by fear and are driven to harm each other in various ways; the larger ones kill or chase the smaller ones while even the tiny animals can inflict unbearable suffering as parasites feeding off the bigger ones.
- *Animals which live in the great dark place between the continents.* These animals never see the sun or moon and cannot even see their own bodies. They are very dull and live out their days in misery.
- *Animals which live in the world together with humans.* These are the myriad animals, birds, fish and insects we see around us. They experience various sufferings such as being hunted by other animals and humans, slaughtered by butchers, going hungry for many days, disease and so forth.

The main cause for such a birth is ignorance and sloth. The main antidote is developing wisdom and meditating in accordance with the techniques of the higher teachings through which ignorance is liberated into mirror-like wisdom.[150]

---

[149] Tib. sor rtogs ye shes.

[150] Tib. me long ye shes.

4. Human Realm

We have already described the humans of the four main continents but in general there are twelve types of humans found in our universe. Other humans are grouped into four types:

- Miyamchi[151] (literally 'is it human or what?'). Some parts of their bodies appear human but others seem to come from animals or other strange beings. They can change their appearance and have other strange capacities making them not unlike the aliens in *Star Wars* or *Star Trek*. They live in the sub-continents which flank the four main continents.
- Humans also live on the seventh mountain range encircling Mount Rirab. There are seven families in each village, seven people in each family and so on, meaning that everything there is in multiples of seven.
- Then there are humans who live around a special tree. Their entire livelihood depends on the tree; they eat its fruit, drink its sap and wear clothes made from its leaves.
- The fourth group of humans live in a gigantic flower.

Out of all human beings, those living in the Southern Continent of *Dzambuling*,[152] the world we presently find ourselves in, are said to have the maximum opportunity to develop both the good and bad aspects of their lives. This is also considered the best realm for practising Buddhas' teachings as karma ripens faster here enabling us to more readily observe and understand the law of cause and effect. All human realms are marked by four fundamental sufferings: suffering of birth, suffering of sickness, suffering of old age and suffering of death. There are also four main fears: fear of meeting enemies or obstacles, fear of being separated from loved ones, fear of not having means for survival (for those who are poor) and fear of losing wealth (for those who are rich).

The main cause for being born in the Human Realms is jealousy and actions motivated by it. The main antidote is openness and meditative practices of the higher teachings through which jealousy is liberated into the wisdom of equanimity.[153]

---

[151] Tib. mi 'am ci.

[152] Tib. 'Dzam bu gling.

[153] Tib. mnyam nyid ye shes

5. Demi-god Realm

Demi-gods are the powerful gods and spirits dwelling in many locations of our universe below the peak of the World Mountain. In Yungdrung Bön we find two main systems classifying demi-gods, namely the Thirty-Three Races of Gods and Spirits mentioned above and the Eight Classes of Gods and Spirits[154] which we will deal with in more detail in the next chapter.

The main suffering of the Demi-god Realm is the misery of fighting. These beings are in perpetual conflict with each other, with the beings of the God Realms above and with the humans below. There is neither rest nor peace of mind as they are always plotting, scheming and sending disturbances to others although they can never gain victory over the gods, who have superior powers and virtues.

The main cause for being born as a demi-god is pride and arrogance while the main antidote is peacefulness coupled with the meditative practices of the higher teachings through which pride and arrogance are liberated into all-accomplishing wisdom.[155]

6. God Realms

There are actually very many God Realms situated on different levels of the Triple World.

i. Six God Realms of the Realm of Desire

The six lower God Realms[156] are still on the level of the Realm of Desire and the gods still experience attachment and desire for sensory objects.

- The first of these God Realms is the Realm of the Four Great Kings[157] who dwell in the four cardinal directions of the World Mountain.
- The second is the Realm of the Thirty-Three Gods[158] situated on the summit of Rirab. It consists of thirty-three cities with thirty-three principal gods living in each. The chief of this realm is Gyajyin Karpo.[159]

---

[154] Tib. lha srin sde brgyad, lha sri sde brgyad.

[155] Tib. bya grub ye shes.

[156] Tib. 'dod lha rigs drug.

[157] Tib. rGyal chen ris bzhi.

[158] Tib. sum bcu rtsha gsum lha gnas.

[159] Tib. brGya sbyin dKar po is the equivalent of the Hindu god Indra.

The splendour of these realms stirs the jealousy of the demi-gods bound to the realms below and they wage never-ending, helpless war against the gods. These two lower God Realms, then, are still on the earthly plane and are not free from conflict.

- Higher up are the four God Realms which are free from conflict: Free of Conflict; Joyful; Enjoying the Manifestations; Mastery Over the Manifestations.[160] These realms are located in space above the World Mountain and are very peaceful.

The cause for being born in these Six God Realms is the accumulation of virtue.

ii. Seventeen God Realms of the Realm of Form

Above are the seventeen God Realms of the Form Realm[161] and birth here is dependent on attaining progressively higher levels of *Zhine*[162] (the meditation of calm-abiding), *Lhagtong*[163] (the meditation of insight) and *Samten*[164] (meditative concentration). Gods who dwell here possess beautiful bodies of light, hence the name 'Realm of Form'.

The seventeen God Realms of this level are divided into five groups: four groups of three and one group of five. Birth in the one of the first four groups of three depends on which of the four levels of *Zhine* one has attained.

- The three realms of the first group are *Tsangpa* creator-gods, *Tsangpa* priests and Great *Tsangpa*[165] corresponding to the three degrees of the first level of *Zhine*.
- The three realms of the second group are Small Light, Measureless Light and Clear Light[166] corresponding to the three degrees of the second level of *Zhine*.

---

[160] Tib. 'Thab bral; Tib. dGa' ldan; Tib. 'Phrul dga'; Tib. gZhan 'phrul dbang byed.

[161] Tib. gZugs khams gnas rigs bcu bdun.

[162] Tib. zhi gnas.

[163] Tib. lhag mthong.

[164] Tib. bsam gtan/ Sans. dhyana

[165] Tib. Tshangs ris. Tsangpa gods are equivalent to the Hindu god Brahma; Tib. Tshangs pa'i mdun na 'don; Tib. Tshangs chen.

[166] Tib. 'Od chung; Tib. Tshad med 'od; Tib. 'Od gsal.

- The three realms of the third group are Small Virtue, Measureless Virtue and Complete Virtue[167] corresponding to the three degrees of the third level of *Zhine*.
- The three realms of the fourth group are Cloudless, Meritorious Birth and Great Result[168] corresponding to the three degrees of the fourth level of *Zhine*.
- The first four realms of the fifth group correspond to the progressively higher levels of concentration which combine *Zhine* with the special realization of emptiness-wisdom or self-less-ness. They are Not Greater, No Turmoil, Far-Reaching Vision and Vision of Richness.[169]

The fifth and highest realm among this last group of the Seventeen God Realms of Form is Ogmin,[170] Unsurpassable. This is the realm where *Yungdrung Sempas*[171] take birth after achieving the tenth *bhumi*,[172] the highest stage of practice prior to gaining full enlightenment. According to Bönpo Sutra teachings, complete Buddhahood cannot be accomplished on earth or any other realm of *samsara* in any body of the Desire Realm so to attain total realization one must first attain a light body of Ogmin. Ogmin, then, is a very high heaven where Yungdrung Sempas practise before becoming complete Buddhas of Sutra.

iii. Four Dimensions of the Gods of the Formless Realm

Then follow four categories of gods residing in the Formless Realm. Birth here results from achieving one of the Four Meditative Absorptions of the Formless Realm[173] which are deviations from the correct meditation path taught by the Buddhas:

- Meditative Absorption of Infinite Space;
- Meditative Absorption of Infinite Consciousness;
- Meditative Absorption of Nothingness;

---

[167] Tib. dGe chung; Tib. Tshad med dge; Tib. dGe rgyas.

[168] Tib. sPrin med; Tib. bSod nams skyes; Tib. 'Bras bu che.

[169] Tib. Mi che ba; Tib. Mi gdung ba; Tib. Gya nom snang ba; Tib. Shin tu mthong ba.

[170] Tib. 'Og min.

[171] Tib. g.yung drung sems dpa, equivalent to Sanskrit Bodhisattva.

[172] Tib. sa, lit. 'earth' but here referring to the progressive stages of the spiritual path of advanced Sutra practitioners.

[173] Tib. gZugs med snyoms 'jug bzhi.

– Meditative Absorption of Neither existence nor Non-existence.[174]

These gods have no shape or form, and their dimensions are without location or shape. Lifespans in these God Realms are extremely long, with some even lasting for a whole cycle of creation and destruction.[175]

Although birth in a specific God Realm is determined by the level of meditative practice attained, the general cause for being born as a god is laziness or indolence. This is not normal laziness but a kind of equilibrium of all the five negative emotional states which lead to birth in the other realms. Through meditative concentration these emotions can be suppressed for some time (in the case of gods, for a very, very long time) but not completely liberated. Consequently when the cause for birth as a god is exhausted, gods must suffer the painful deterioration of their external world and their bodies, and fall down to the lower realms. This constitutes the main suffering of the God Realm. No god is eternal; even the gods of the Formless Realm finally fade and fall. In some God Realms this process is very prolonged and painful as a falling god clearly sees where s/he is going to be born and which sufferings s/he must undergo. Moreover, relatives and friends abandon the falling god in fear of being defiled by ugliness and unpleasant odours radiating from them. So the dying god wanders alone in terrible sadness moving lower and lower until the vision of the God Realms completely disappears and the new realm of rebirth is reached.

Birth in the God Realms can be averted by generating great compassion and applying the practices of the higher teachings by which laziness is transformed into self-originated wisdom.[176]

Two main modes of circulation in samsara

No being in *samsara* stays in the same realm forever; instead, all beings constantly migrate from one life to another, from one realm to another and from one form to another, propelled by actions, or karma,

---

[174] Tib. Nam mkha' mtha' yas kyi skye mched; Tib. rNam shes mtha' yas kyi skye mched; Tib. Ci yang med pa'i skye mched;Tib. 'Du shes med min gyi skye mched.

[175] The complete cosmic cycle consists of four stages or periods: the Period of Formation (Tib. chags pa'i bskal pa); the Period of Abiding (Tib. gnas pa'i bskal pa); the Period of Destruction (Tib. 'jig pa'i bskal pa; and the Period of Nothingness (Tib. stong pa'i bskal pa).

[176] Tib. rang 'byung ye shes.

Fig. 3. The Wheel of Existence (Tib. srid pa'i 'khor lo). Mural from Triten Norbutse Bönpo Monastery, Kathmandu. Symbology of the this mural as follows: In the centre in the red circle there is the Cow of Samsara with the body of a cow and heads of cock, pig and snake and a snake's tail. The cock head represents desire, the pig head represents ignorance and the snake head represents hateful anger. These are the Three Poisons, the primary emotions which cause birth in the Six Realms. The next circle depicts the Six Realms with the hot and cold Hells at the bottom, the Hungry Ghost Realm adjacent on the right and the Animal Realm on the left. These are the Three Lower Realms. In the upper semicircle there is the Human Realm on the right, the Demi-god Realm on the left and the God Realm in the centre. Each of the realms has a guide Buddha emanated by Tonpa Shenrab Miwo at his enlightenment in order to guide the beings of the Six Realms to liberation. The third circle represents the twelve links of the Chain of Interdependent Origination, the mechanism which turns the wheel of samṣara. The twelve links are represented as follows with the wheel rotating clockwise from right to left: at the top right there is a blind old woman, symbol of Ignorance; below that there is a potter, symbol of karmic traces or predispositions; monkeys on a tree, symbol of consciousness grasping at objects; a sumptuously-laden table, symbol of name-and-form; the Six Fields of Senses is represented by a human head (probably because most of our sense organs are concentrated in the head); the path to enlightenment shown by the Buddha Tonpa Shenrab Miwo; contact of senses with the sense objects symbolized by a snake crawling through a hollow bamboo cane; water evaporating from a red-hot stone, symbol of sensation; a man unable to find the door of a house, symbol of craving; Gyagya (Tib. rgya bya) birds drinking water, symbol of grasping; existence illustrated by a man and woman in sexual union; a monk casting an image, symbol of birth; old age and death illustrated by an old man contemplating a corpse.

Beyond the Wheel of Existence are numerous ritual implements and items of clothing of a Bönpo monk or a Tantric yogi symbolizing the path to enlightenment shown by the Buddha Tonpa Shenrab Miwo.

stored from beginningless beginning and accumulated anew as they traverse the paths of *samsara*. There are two main ways in which this circulation proceeds.

The first one is comparable to a wheel turning on the road. In this case, a being may have accumulated, say, a hundred causes for being a human but it is impossible to be born as a hundred humans simultaneously. Instead this being takes one hundred successive rebirths as a human. The circumstances and fortunes of this being during these hundred lives will not be the same, but the rebirth will always be in the Human Realm; the wheel will never leave the road.

The second mode of circulation is similar to a waterwheel. In this case a being is born in the God Realm then falls to the Demi-god Realm and so on until reaching the lowest Hell, like water falling from one bucket of a waterwheel into the one below. According to Yungdrung Bön, the only way to escape the unimaginable sufferings and miseries of this cyclical existence in *samsara* is to follow the spiritual path mapped out by the Buddhas which enables one to completely rid oneself of all causes for re-birth in any of the Six Realms and achieve Buddhahood.[177]

The Multiverse

In both Bön and Buddhist texts alike, it is generally said that our universe is flat. However, as everything appears to sentient beings through the ripening of their karma, there is in fact no such thing as a fixed shape or a fixed universal perception; we can see different forms. At one time the universe is explained as being flat but the Yungdrung Bön texts also say that in some cases the form of the universe is seen as very long and narrow, or round like a ball, or completely square, or semicircular, or as very tall and narrow. Nothing is fixed as everything appears according to karmic cause and everything is projected by sentient beings. Nevertheless, in Yungdrung Bön the standard model of our universe is that it is flat with the World Mountain in the centre surrounded by the mountain ranges, the ocean with twelve islands and then the outer rim. That is known as one *tsangjung*,[178] or our universe.[179]

---

[177] The presenation on the beings of the Six Realms is given here according to Yungdrung Bön and based on the teachings of Yongzin Lopön Tenzin Namdak, Khenpo Tenpa Yungdrung and Geshe Gelek Jinpa. The Tibetan Buddhist model is very similar although there the causes for birth in the Human Realm and Demi-God Realm are reversed, jealousy for birth as a demi-god and pride for birth as a human. We will not go into details of further differences here.

[178] Tib. tsang rgyung.

[179] The relation between Bonpo cosmology and the cosmology of Buddhist

Our universe, however, is only a miniscule segment in the system of the Three Thousandfold Universe, which is in fact filled with similar universes. Each universe is flat and has a World Mountain in the centre surrounded by the four islands each with two small island companions. Each universe has beings similar to those of the Six Realms of our universe, and each universe has a Buddha who manifests an emanation in each of the Six Realms, all of whom teach simultaneously. One thousand of such universes are piled up one on top of another in twenty-five layers like biscuits in a packet or like beads on a thread. Our universe is in the centre with twelve universes above and twelve universes below. Forty strings of twenty-five universes are arranged around it like pillars thus making one thousand universes. Around them is a fence, and that is counted as the first thousand.

This thousand is counted as one unit and there are again one thousand of them arranged in the same manner, surrounded by a fence. That is the second thousand.[180]

This thousand is again taken as one unit and one thousand of them are arranged in a similar manner with a fence outside. That is *tongsum*,[181] the Three-Thousandfold Universe which consists of one thousand million universes.

This *tongsum* is multiplied one thousand times to make *kopa dangpo*.[182] *Kopa dangpo* in turn is multiplied one thousand times making *kopa barma*.[183] *Kopa barma* is multiplied one thousand times forming *kopa thama*.[184] This is the *dulzhing*[185] of Tonpa Shenrab throughout which his teachings are spread. No matter how many sentient beings are contained in the universes of this *dulzhing*, he can reach them all with his compassion.

Furthermore, in the ten directions[186] there are ten universe complexes similar to the *dulzhing* of Tonpa Shenrab. Each of them has its own Buddha who reaches all the beings within his *dulzhing*. Thus we have a group of ten universe complexes, including Tonpa Shenrab's *dulzhing*,

---

Abhidharma will be dealt with below.

[180] I.e. 1,000,000 universes.

[181] Tib. stong gsum.

[182] Tib. bkod pa dang po consists of 10^{11} universes.

[183] Tib. bkod pa bar ma consists of 10^{14} universes.

[184] Tib. bkod pa tha ma consists of 10^{17} universes.

[185] Tib. gdul zhing.

[186] I.e.the four cardinal directions, the four intermediate directions, above and below.

and this forms a multiverse called *muchu dangpo.*[187] This in turn is taken as one and multiplied one thousand times and that is *muchu barma.*[188] *Muchu barma* is multiplied by one thousand to make *muchu thama.*[189]

This is then again multiplied one thousand times forming *dogdal dangpo*,[190] which is multiplied a further one thousand times becoming *dogdal barma*[191] which is again multiplied one thousand times to make one *dogdal thama.*[192] It is said that even a Buddha loses count beyond this; there is no limit to the number of universes and sentient beings within them.[193]

Bönpo cosmology and cosmological models in quantum physics

This view of the cosmos may seem too archaic, too mythological to some but if we keep an open mind we can see it has a number of parallels with cosmological models in modern physics, and in quantum physics in particular.

The most obvious one is between the manifestation of the universe from the primeval eggs in the *Myth of the Origin of Existence* and the Big Bang Theory. Though using different language and terminology, these two ways of describing the beginning of our universe are uncannily alike: both postulate that the universe came into being through an eruption, an explosion from within a nothingness which nevertheless contained very subtle causes responsible for its own manifestation.

The next parallel lies in the Bönpo theory that the perception of the universe is determined by sentient beings and the Anthropic Principle, a revolutionary and unorthodox philosophical reasoning in quantum physics and cosmology first suggested by Brandon Carter in 1974 which has been developed ever since. In fact, the Anthropic Principle isn't just one principle but a number of principles (over thirty anthropic principles have been formulated so far) which stem from the main idea of cosmic 'fine-tuning' which postulates that if any of the many physical parameters had been very slightly different, there would be no-one to observe the universe. In their own ways both these theories are saying

[187] Tib. mu khud dang po consists of 10^{18} universes.

[188] Tib. mu khud bar ma consists of 10^{21} universes.

[189] Tib. mu khud tha ma consists of 10^{24} universes.

[190] Tib. dog bdal dang po consists of 10^{27} universes.

[191] Tib. dog bdal bar ma constists of 10^{30} universes.

[192] Tib. dog bdal tha ma consists of 10^{33} universes.

[193] Based on teachings and explanations by Yongdzin Lopön Tenzin Namdak, Khenpo Tenpa Yungdrung and Geshe Gelek Jinpa given 1995–2006.

that observed/universe and observer/sentient beings are fine-tuned to each other so that the parameters of the perceived universe are precisely set to enable sentient beings to perceive it and exist in it: without a perceiver there is no sense of a universe being as it appears. There is a difference, of course, between these two theories. There seems to be no clear explanation of 'why' in the Anthropic Principle: why should the universe be fine-tuned to the existence of life? Yungdrung Bön clearly explains that the parameters of a universe perceived by various types of sentient beings depend on their karma which in turn determines their karmic vision, their perception of the universe.

Another striking match between modern physics and cosmology and the cosmology of Yungdrung Bön is the idea of the multiverse. Many physicists and cosmologists have recently come to the idea that our universe is just one among many:

> According to this 'multiverse' idea, there are many different universes, with myriad possible laws of nature [...] According to the multiverse view, it is unlikely that ours is the only universe complex enough to support sentient beings. Martin Rees of the University of Cambridge goes further and believes there may be an archipelago of 'islands' in the multiverse, havens for life dotted in the vast sea of uninhabitable universes [...] Each island in the multiverse is actually a collection of hospitable universes, all with slightly different physical constants just like geographical coordinates on a terrestrial island. If Rees is right and we can show that our universe is part of the largest island in the multiverse, it would lend weight to the Anthropic Principle which asserts that our universe must be among the most common habitable universes and in no way special.[194]

The idea of the multiverse and the language used to describe it are in fact not so removed from the idea and language of Bönpo cosmology. Many Bönpo scholars agree that the description of the universe given in Bönpo texts should not be taken too literally, that it is a symbolical way of describing the very complex reality of the cosmos. According to the Bönpo cosmological model, the environments in which beings dwell, their appearance and lifespan vary greatly depending on which level of our universe they are born into.

For example, the lifespan of a Hungry Ghost is five hundred years, their day is equivalent to a human month while the lifespan of a god from the Heaven of the Thirty-Three is one thousand years, their day being

---

[194] 'My other univesre is a Porsche', *NewScientist*, 7 October 2006, pp. 38–39.

equal to one hundred human years. Gods in the upper levels of existence and beings of the lower hells have incredibly long lifespans, some of which may be equal to a whole cosmic cycle of creation and destruction. Even among humans lifespan, appearance and the environments in which they live differ greatly according to which of the four continents they are born on. Humans of *Lupagpo*,[195] the Continent of Majestic Body in the east, for instance, are eight cubits tall (according to the measures on our own continent of *Dzambuling* in the south) and live two hundred and fifty years; humans of the Western Continent *Benlangcho*[196] are twice as high as those of the Continent of Majestic Body and live five hundred years; humans of *Draminyen*,[197] the Continent of Unpleasant Sound in the north, are twice the size of humans in *Benlangcho* and live one thousand years. If we accept that the Bönpo model of our universe should not be interpreted too literally we can understand that it describes various kinds of humanoids in our universe not just those on our planet Earth. The continents can be taken as a metaphor for other inhabitable planets supporting humanoid life throughout our own galaxy in our plane of existence while the model of the Six Destines of Rebirth or the Six Realms describes the conditions and life-forms in other dimensions of our galaxy or in the multiverse as a whole.

This picture is very much comparable with the cosmological model of the multiverse as it is beginning to be understood in the avant-garde of quantum physics, particularly by the String Theory:

> […] which holds that all matter is composed of energy vibrating in 10 dimensions of space-time. String theory is the most popular attempt to reconcile quantum mechanics and general relativity, yet it doesn't describe one universe. It describes 10^{500} universes, each with different physical properties.[198]

According to Yungdrung Bön cosmology, it is normally impossible for beings from different realms to see each other directly or travel from one realm to another. Only higher gods, *Siddhas* and Buddhas endowed with clairvoyance and magical powers can do so. That oddly enough finds its analogy in modern physics, too. While physicists do not subscribe to the notion of magical powers, they admit that alternative or parallel dimensions cannot be observed directly:

---

[195] Tib. lus 'phags po.

[196] Tib. ban glang spyod.

[197] Tib. sgra mi shyan.

[198] Ibid., p. 39.

> Although we cannot observe alternative universes through telescopes, theorists can explore them on paper or in computer models and see whether galaxies would still form and stars would still shine.[199]

That wraps up our short diversion into the realm of quantum physics putting ancient cosmological ideas into a modern perspective and showing that, despite their antiquity, they do hold a significant amount of information and insights into the realities and mechanics of the cosmos which are just beginning to be understood by today's science.

Bönpo cosmology and the cosmology of the Abhidharma of Vasubandhu

Some Buddhist and Western scholars hold the view that Bönpo cosmology was copied from the Buddhist cosmological model in *Abhidharmakośakārikā* by the Indian Buddhist master Vasubandhu. However, from the Bönpo point of view it was quite the opposite; Bönpo would assert that their cosmology is the original one. They point out that Vasubandhu's system has a number of specific features which find no parallel in the general Indian cosmological model on which other Buddhist cosmological systems are based. It is precisely these features that are inherent in the Bönpo cosmology.

According to traditional Bönpo reckoning, Yungdrung Bön was spread in northern India, Kashmir and Gilgit long before the appearance of the Indian Buddha Shakyamuni, whose historical dates are far from clearly established although it is generally accepted that he appeared in India anywhere between 1000 and 500 BC. According to the traditional Bönpo account, it is Tonpa Shenrab Miwo, the Buddha of Bön himself, who taught the Bön of Mantras[200] to Bönpos of Zahor, Kashmir and Gilgit while passing through the mountains of Zhang Zhung on his way to Kongpo in pursuit of the demon Khyabpa Lagring who had stolen his horses.[201] After Tonpa Shenrab passed away, in the time of his son Mucho Demdrug there were the Six Great Translators among whom we find Lhadag Nangdro of India. The next generation of translators were mainly

---

[199] Ibid., pp. 38–39.

[200] Tib. bon ngags.

[201] See Karmay, *The Treausry*, Introduction, p. xix. Actually, according to Karmay Shenrab Miwo met those Bönpos on the frontier of Zahor. However, here I follow the version I was told by Yongdzin Lopön Tenzin Namdak who maintains they came to see Tonpa Shenrab in Zhang Zhung near Mt. Kailash.

from Tagzig and they transmitted the teachings to Shenpo Lisha of India, Shenpo Braba Meruchan of Kashmir, Shenpo Ge Tene Logya of Gilgit and others. Even if we do not accept traditional Bönpo chronology stating that Shenrab Miwo was born in 16,017 BC and lived 82 *Shen* years each equal to 100 human years but instead take a date suggested by Chögyal Namkhai Norbu, 1917 BC,[202] it still brings us to 1839 BC as the date of Shenrab Miwo's *Parinirvana*, assuming he had the lifespan of a normal human. Even if we further detract the 300 years said to be the period in which the initial expansion of Yungdrung Bön took place and when the Six Great Translators were active, this brings us to 1539 BC, which is still between 1000 or 500 years before the birth of Shakyamuni Buddha so, in any case, the Bön of India predates Shakyamuni's Buddhism. There are a number of texts from the Bön of India which were translated into Tibetan from Sanskrit by Vairochana of Pagor in the eighth century AD. Even in the reign of Trisong Deutsen in the eighth century AD there was a Bönpo of India in Tibet by the name Drenpa Yeshe[203] who concealed the textual treasure of *Samye Kakholma.*[204]

There is also much later evidence that elements of the Bön of India were incorporated into Indian Buddhism. We can clearly see that some elements of Bönpo astrology have found their way into the late Buddhist Tantric system of Kalachakra with its *mewa* and *parkha* systems which are definitely of Bönpo origin. Original Bönpo astrological systems[205] were spread to Zhang Zhung and Tibet either by Tonpa Shenrab himself who visited the region and taught local Bönpos some systems of Casual Bön, or through the Great Translator Trithog Patsa[206] of Zhang Zhung at the time of Tonpa Shenrab's son Mucho Demdrug and by the later Bönpo *Mahasiddha* Shari Uchen[207] of Tibet. Bönpo astrological systems of *parkha*, *mewa* and the twelve year animal cycle arrived to China through Gya Kongtse Trulgyi Gyalpo, a direct disciple of Tonpa Shenrab Miwo, and then at the time of Mucho Demdrug it was the Great Translator Letang Mangpo of China who brought the next wave of Yungdrung Bön to China. Similarly, Bönpo astrological texts must have reached India, Kashmir and other countries of the Trans-Himalayas via other great Bönpo translators coming from these respective regions.[208]

---

[202] See Norbu, *Drung, Deu and Bön*, pp. 156–158.

[203] Tib. Dran pa Ye shes.

[204] Tib. bSam yas ka khol ma. See Karmay, *The Treausry*, p. 122.

[205] Tib. rtsis.

[206] Tib. Khri thog sPa tsha.

[207] Tib. Sha ri dBu chen.

[208] See Karmay, *The Treasury*, pp. 16–18.

Kalachakra Tantra appeared in India in the eleventh century AD from the mystical kingdom of Shambhala which several Bönpo scholars, including Shardza Tashi Gyaltsen and Yongdzin Lopön Tenzin Namdak, associate with Olmo Lungring, Tonpa Shenrab Miwo's native land. According to Yungdrung Bön it is Tonpa Shenrab Miwo who originally taught Bönpo Kalachakra Tantra, *The Powerful Wheel of Time*,[209] in Olmo Lungring at the temple of Sekhang Barab Yongdul.[210] The root text of this Tantra is in 1,100 chapters and was entrusted to Serthub Ösung,[211] a Bönpo of the *Sadag*[212] earth-gods.[213] According to Yongdzin Lopön Tenzin Namdak only some parts of this system – dealing mainly with astrology and belonging to the Lower Tantra – have survived until now within Yungdrung Bön while the main corpus of the Tantra is lost. Buddha Shakyamuni taught Kalachakra Tantra in Shambhala in 880 BC according to Bönpo traditional chronology.[214]

From what has been said above we can clearly understand that Yungdrung Bön teachings and culture had been present in northern India from very early times and therefore it is natural that they would have profoundly influenced ancient Indian culture and religious. So in fact the culture in which the Indian Buddha Shakyamuni appeared had a genuine Bönpo substrate. Bearing in mind that Buddha Shakyamuni is considered an incarnation of the sage Sangwa Dhüpa who in turn was a student of Chimey Tsugphü, a manifestation of Tonpa Shenrab Miwo, it is not surprising that Yungdrung Bön and Indian Buddhism have some parallels even though Buddhists would generally refute this.

As for master Vasubandhu, he was born in the kingdom of Gandhara in Purushapura, modern day Peshawar in Pakistan, to a Hindu family. That region was open to various cultural and religious streams and is best known for blending Indian and Hellenistic influences creating a unique form of Buddhist art. Being close to Persia, Uddiyana and Kashmir, this region must consequently have been a melting pot of cultures for hundreds of years. That was the cultural environment in which Vasubandhu

---

209 Tib. dBang ldan dus kyi 'khorlo'i rgyud.

210 Tib. gSas khang ba rab yongs 'dul – The Temple of the All-Subduing Supreme Dome.

211 Tib. gSer thub 'Od srung.

212 Tib. Sa bdag.

213 This is taken from Shardza Rinpoche's *Legs bshad mdzod* p.39, Tibetan text. Thanks go to Jean-Luc Achard for kindly extracting this information and providing me with it.

214 Yongdzin Lopön Tenzin Namdak is unsure whether the two systems are related or not.

lived his early years and that, no doubt, had a profound impact on his personality and further development. He became a Hinayana Buddhist of the Vaibhashika School and travelled to Kashmir where he gathered teachings from various masters, thought them over and wrote them down in the form of *Abhidharmakosha*. Vasubandhu later converted to the Mahayana School of Yogachara founded by his brother Asanga after the latter had spent some years in the forest meditating and having visionary encounters with Maitreya, the Buddha of the future.

The fact that *Abhidharmakosha* is based on the teachings Vasubandhu gathered in Kashmir is crucial for our understanding of the similarities between his cosmological system and that found in Yungdrung Bön. As we have already said, Yungdrung Bön had been spread in Kashmir since the time of the Six Great Translators, i.e. it had been around for a very, very long time. Some of its aspects and even certain practices penetrated various spiritual streams of north India such as Kashmiri Shaivism where we find certain practices mirroring Dzogchen in outer appearance but with a widely differing doctrinal base and view. The existence of these practices in Kashmiri Shaivism was interpreted by some scholars inimical to Dzogchen as proof that Dzogchen isn't a Buddhist system at all[215] but is in fact a kind of Hinduism. Unfortunately this kind of reasoning is blind to the fact that Yungdrung Bön, of which Dzogchen is the highest path, had been established in Kashmir for thousands of years whereas Shiva is a relatively modern god; Shiva is not among the old Vedic gods brought by the Aryans but rather the cult of Shiva appeared in India after the Aryan conquest. If we use traditional Bönpo chronology to verify this, then the epoch of the Six Great Translators can be dated roughly as follows:

16017 BC – Birth of Tonpa Shenrab Miwo;
7817 BC – *Parinirvana* of Tonpa Shenrab Miwo;
6017 BC – The cycle of the Doctrine of the Body[216] ends;
6016 BC – Mucho Demdrug descends from the realm of *Cha* and the Doctrine of Speech[217] begins;
6016–5716 BC – Period of the Six Great Translators.[218]

---

[215] I.e. is not a teaching of any Buddha, rather than just not of the Indian Buddha Shakyamuni who actually never taught Dzogchen.

[216] Tib. sku bstan.

[217] Tib. gsung bstan.

[218] According to Geshe Tenzin Drugdrag, *Bon gyi ngo sprod blo gsar sgo 'byed*, kindly extracted by Geshe Gelek Jinpa.

Aryan migration to India took place between 2000–1500 BC. So here we can see things in perspective and no matter which set of dates we take for the Six Great Translators – 6016–5716 BC or 1839–1539 BC – this clearly shows that Yungdrung Bön was present in north India either much earlier than the appearance of the Vedic people there or, at least, arrived contemporaneously from Tagzig, the Central Asian region in which Tonpa Sherab was born. There should therefore be no doubt that practice methods in Kashmiri Shaivism which seem similar to those of Dzogchen are due to influences coming from Yungdrung Bön.

Part III
Common Aspects of the Cosmologies of Bɵ Murgel and Bön

The beginnings of the universe

The original creation myths of the Prehistoric Bön of Tibet did not survive intact and independently so for our analysis we must rely on the creation myths found in Yungdrung Bön texts which have been preserved and which have cultural substrata coming from Prehistoric Bön. Despite external cultural similarities, Yungdrung Bön's myths are based on a different view and understanding of the fundamental nature of the universe and, consequently, the process of its manifestation. Nevertheless, by comparing the external details and framework of these creation myths with those of Bɵ Murgel, we can gain a better understanding of many aspects of the Prehistoric Bön of Tibet and Eurasia.

Despite the great number of creation myths in both traditions making it difficult for us to come to a unified, detailed account of the creation process in both Bön and Bɵ Murgel alike, the mechanics of how the universe and the beings within it actually emerged from this primordial potentiality also broadly follow the same lines: empty space manifests the original god- and demon-ancestors who in their turn generate further subordinate gods, demons and other beings.[219]

---

[219] Although the details of how this actually happened differ in most stories, among the Buryats of the Irkutsk region we find a creation myth which narrates how the world manifested from an egg laid by a duck and this loosely reminds us of the primeval eggs in Bönpo mythology.

The primary source of our polarized universe is considered in a similar way in both Bɵ Murgel and Bön. That source is an empty space imbued with the creative potential or causes for the polar forces of the universe to manifest. In Bɵ Murgel it is called Huhe Münhe Tengeri while in Yungdrung Bön it is Namkha Togden Chosumje. Both names evoke the idea of primordial space or sky, both represent the abstract idea of emptiness imbued with the creative power, and both are often spoken of as a deity. However, the understanding of the real nature of this empty space and the deities which represent it differs fundamentally between Yungdrung Bön and Bɵ Murgel.[220]

A more detailed comparison of the initial stages of the creation stories from both traditions reveals some close parallels. In the Bönpo creation story we have learnt that ten thousand *Dase* deities went downwards at the very beginning of the formation of the world and became the deities who sustain heroism in men. This group probably corresponds to the Ten Thousand Primordial *Burkhans*[221] of Bɵ Murgel who appeared immediately after the universe manifest and went downwards towards Earth to create the conditions for life. In an ancient Bɵ Murgel invocation it is said:

> The earth's atmosphere was not yet formed,
> There was a great heat.
> But 10,000 *Burkhans* already existed.
> [...]
> Our most archaic source
> Are 10.000 *Burkhans*,
> Original source of our history
> Related to the beginning of life itself.[222]

It is clear from the quotation that, like the ten thousand *Dase,* these ten thousand (*tumen*) Tengeri have existed from the very beginning of the universe. Moreover, their relation to men is also similar.

---

[220] See ch. VIII.

[221] Bur. Арбан түмэн бурхад.

[222] Bur. ...Агаар дэлхэйн үгы байхада,
Аяма ехэ халуунай байхада,
Арбан түмэн бурхад байгаа юм.
...Анхан узуур гарбалнай –
Арбан түмэн бурхаднай,
Түүхэ узуур гарбалнай
Түрүүн сагаhaа эхитэй.

We find another reference to the ten thousand Tengeri in the opening of the Kudarinskiy creation myth. It describes the world at its initial stages.

When the High Sky
Was as a light haze,
When the wide ocean of this world
Was just a small puddle
The heavenly *tumen* of the Tengeri Gods
Were not yet born,
The myriad of Space Gods
Were not yet found.[223]

These were the circumstances in which Ehe Yehe Burkhan was born. Despite the fundamental differences in the nature of these two deities – Ehe Yehe Burkhan is a worldly goddess whereas Trigyal Khugpa of the Bönpo myth is, according to Yungdrung Bön tradition, a Sambhogakaya[224] Buddha – and although they are described as beings of opposite sexes, there is nonetheless a certain similarity in the way they are said to have caused the world to come about. While neither of them can be called a creator because neither is the primordial source – Emptiness or Eternal Blue Sky – both represent the active, manifest aspects of this source and both appeared spontaneously and seemingly without a cause. Therefore we can call them progenitors but not creators. In both traditions it is through their creative activity in this primordial space that the world with all its realms and beings came about.

The structure of the universe

Comparing the cosmological models of Bön and Bө Murgel we can see that on the blandest level both contain the identical triple division of the Three Worlds with the *axis mundi* being either a World Mountain or a World Tree or, as we have seen in Bönpo model above, a combination

---

[223] Bur. ...Ундэр дуулим тэнгэри
Манан уняар байхадан,
Ургэн улгэн дэлхэйн
Уhан шалбааг байхадан,
Тэнгэриин тумэн бурхадай
Турөө яагаа удыдэн,
Огторгойн олон бурхадай
Олдоо яагаа удыдэн…

[224] Tib. longs pyod rdzogs pa'i sku – Body of Perfect Enjoyment.

of the two. Interestingly, this way of combining the World Tree and the World Mountain is also found in Bɵ Murgel as *obo'o* cairns symbolizing the World Mountain are often topped with saplings or wooden posts or have them as their central axis. Moreover, the general description of the beings inhabiting the Three Worlds in both models also corresponds.[225] However, if we dig a little deeper we can find more subtle – and therefore more significant – similarities.

In Bön there are several classifications of the Three Worlds. Among them is a model called Sasum,[226] the three levels of the world, where we find the following three dimensions: Tenggi Lha[227] (Upper Sky-Dimension of the Gods); Bargyi Mi[228] (Intermediate Dimension of the Humans); and Öggi Lu[229] (Underworld of the *Lu*). Before we look at the striking resonance between Tengeri and *teng*,[230] let us first focus on the concept of Sasum.

'Sasum' literally means 'three earths', a concept with archaic overtones. In Bɵ Murgel the dimensions of the Sky, Earth and Underworld are perceived as different 'earths' or 'grounds' which are pinned one above the other on the central axis of the World Tree or the World Mountain. Thus the Tengeri above have the 'Sky-earth' on which they ride their horses, where they have their homes, where there are trees and where grasses grow. The level of the 'Sky-earth', then, is similar to our 'Earth-earth' (the Middle Earth) in appearance, it is merely of much better quality and imbued with magical properties which 'Earth-earth' doesn't share. The same principle is true for the realm of Erlig Khaan; the 'Underworld-earth' is also the 'ground' on which his dungeons are built, where his scribes have their offices and on which underworld beings ride or walk. Again it is of a different quality to the Middle Earth but the principle of there being the earth is the same. So the name Sasum, Three Earths, clearly demonstrates an analogous concept and betrays a

---

225 The description of beings inhabiting the triple world of generally corresponds with the Bɵ Murgel model. A detailed description of the Bönpo model follows in the next chapter.

226 Tib. sa gsum – lit. 'Three Earths'. Tibetan *sa* in this case also denotes a dimension or level.

227 Tib. steng gi lha.

228 Tib. bar gyi mi.

229 Tib. 'og gi klu.

230 *Teng* means 'sky' or 'space' and often forms part of the name for geographical features on the territories of the former Zhang Zhung Empire, especially in north-west Tibet, Changthang. An example of this is the Tengtsho/Tengri (Namtsho) lake.

very archaic origin. This is supported by the numerous Bönpo myths, stories and anecdotes about the realms of the *Lha* which describe them as being similar in appearance to the Earth but of much better quality and endowed with superior magical properties. Similarly, as the reader will recall from Chapter I, the *Lu* water spirits of Bön also live in a realm similar to our Middle Earth with kingdoms, palaces, subjects and even water-sheep and water-horses.

Despite the fact that the basic triple world structure is identical, the Yungdrung Bön model is much more elaborate than that of Bѳ Murgel. In addition to the basic system of the Three Worlds, equally present in both Prehistoric and Yungdrung Bön, the latter also contains the larger vision of our universe in the context of a greater cosmic order or multiverse which, no doubt, is related to Yungdrung Bön alone.

Of course, there are still a number of differences between these two modes of creation and cosmological models, but they are neither fundamental nor structural. The basic matrix of the creation process and the structure of the universe remains roughly the same. If we put aside differences in names and some secondary details, we see before us two structures which match so closely that we can safely say we are dealing with two traditions with a common origin. It would seem that at some point, Bѳ Murgel and Bön met or that they derived from the same ancient source-religion(s), which I call here the Prehistoric Bön of Eurasia.

Primordial Males and Primordial Females

There is another very important and direct parallel found in the creation myths of Bön and Bѳ Murgel in the guise of the progenitors. We have already noted the similarities between Trigyal Khugpa and Ehe Yehe Burkhan, and these parallels continue. The Nine Brothers and Nine Sisters, the children of Sangpo Bumtri, and the Eight Brothers and Eight Sisters, the children of Munpa Zerden of Bön, can be directly compared to the Nine White Sons and Nine White Daughters of Manzan Gurma To'odei and the Thirteen Black Sons and Seven Black Daughters of Mais Hara To'odei in Bѳ Murgel. In each tradition, both the parents and their children represent the original groups of sky-gods and sky-demons with exactly the same functions and characteristics. In Bön they are given the generic names *Lha* and *Düd* while in Bѳ Murgel they are called White and Black Tengeri. The similarities are striking, the differences minor; the number of *Düd* brothers and sisters is eight each whereas the Black Tengeri are thirteen brothers and seven sisters; Sangpo Bumtri and Munpa Zerden have consorts and their children are born through intercourse while Manzan Gurma To'odei and Mais Hara To'odei do not have consorts and their children are born to them in a miraculous way, in the same way as they themselves were born. These differences are not fundamental, however, but rather secondary, and in no way gainsay the common origin of these myths.

Let us take a closer look at the roles of these primordial males and females. In many Bɵ Murgel offering and initiation rituals the *Yuhenguud*[231] are invariably present. These are a group of attendants serving the chief Bɵ made up of nine youths clad in white and, in some cases, accompanied by another group of nine maidens also dressed in white.[232] These assistants perform various ritual actions including, on some occasions, riding white horses. The antiquity of this custom is testified to by the fact that the same tradition is found among other Siberian peoples such as the Yakuts who lived around Lake Baikal in ages past; if we go back far enough, Buryats and Yakuts have common ancestral lines in the peoples of the very distant past[233] suggesting that the role of The Nine must herald from an extremely archaic layer of Bɵ Murgel. This is further supported by the existence of a matching analogous concept of Nine Primordial Males[234] and Nine Primordial Females,[235] the children of Sangpo Bumtri. This group belongs to the cultural matrix of Prehistoric Bön which survives as a relict within the new religious mythology of Yungdrung Bön, and hints very strongly at contact between Bɵ Murgel and Bön in very ancient times, probably even in prehistory.[236] The symbolic significance of the groups of the *Yuhenguud* Nine Youths and Nine Maidens in the initiation rituals of modern day Bɵ Murgel isn't explained clearly; it appears to have been lost in the mists of time due to centuries of persecution, remaining a relict custom without explanation. However, if we reconnect it with the events and personages of the Bɵ Murgel creation myth we can say with a high degree of certainty that the *Yuhenguud* represent the Nine Sons and Nine Daughters of Manzan Gurma To'odei and so their presence in the initiation rite is entirely appropriate as they are the ancestors of the White Tengeri and of human beings. Indeed, many archaic cultures believed that re-enacting the

---

[231] Bur. Юhэнгууд – The Nine Youths.

[232] See ch. VII.

[233] See ch. I and ch. II.

[234] Tib. srid pa pho dgu.

[235] Tib. srid pa mo dgu.

[236] We will see in ch. XV that there is clear textual evidence that Yungdrung Bön reached lands populated by proto-Mongol peoples in 683 BC according to traditional Bönpo chronology or in 1st c. AD according to Chögyal Namkhai Norbu.

original procreation story, or any other significant story, be it religious or even historical, recharges the world's existence and ensures its continuity. By symbolically playing out the original sequence of events the energy of that situation together with the qualities and powers of its personages is invoked anew and passed on to the next generation. In essence, almost any codified ritual is based on this principle.[237] It seems, then, that the traditional initiation of a new Bɵ was in a way a re-enactment of the original pro-creation story in the dimension of the Middle World where Bɵ-father took on the symbolic role of the god/goddess progenitor surrounded by the Nine White Brothers and Nine White Sisters, the Tengeri from whom humans descended, to assist the spiritual birth of the new initiate. This is a phenomenon similar to the Bönpo *Cham*[238] dance, a colourful ceremony portraying important mythological or religious stories. The dances, which are still immensely popular both in Tibet as well as in the wider Bönpo community and have also found their way into Buddhist festivals, are performed by practitioners wearing sacred masks and attire to represent deities or cultural heroes. They empower the performers and benefit the spectators. In the case of Bɵ Murgel, as time passed and it absorbed strands and influences from other traditions, the mythological aspect became blurred by other ideas and eventually disappeared leaving only the outer aspect intact in many rituals. This is, in fact, quite a common phenomenon among old religions.

The sacredness of number nine in cosmological models

The study of the Nine Primordial Males and Nine Primordial Females brings us to another link between Bön and Bɵ Murgel which cannot be left unnoticed. It is the sacredness of the number nine in both traditions. Precisely why this number has been given such importance is not so clear but I tend to think that it, too, is derived from the fact that creation models in both religions have groups of extremely important deities in sets of nine.

A fundamental element found in the cosmological models of both traditions also features the number nine. Serge, the sacred World Tree of Bɵ Murgel, has nine branches while Yungdrung Gutseg, the sacred mountain of Yungdrung Bön in the holy country of Olmo Lungring, also has nine steps or layers. In each case, this nine-tiered king-pin of the world is closely linked to the way the teachings of the respective

[237] C.f. the retelling of the birth of Jesus Christ in nativity plays.

[238] Tib. 'cham.

traditions are grouped together. In the case of Buryatian Bө Murgel this is reflected in the initiation system of the Nine Stages while the nine steps of Yungdrung Gutseg symbolize the Nine Ways of Bön. As the World Tree and World Mountain are interchangeable and often combined two-in-one, it is clear that these two nine-pointed symbols of the *axis mundi* and the respective systems of organizing the teachings derived from them share the same archaic prototype, even though the content of each set of Nine Ways or Stages may be very different in the two religions.[239]

Another very clear example of the connection between the sacredness of the number nine and parallels in the cosmological systems of Bө Murgel and Bön is a ritual object called *jangbu.*[240] These are used in the Causal Bön ransom rituals and although there are many variations of this object, they all are all made by following the same general principle of winding threads around a stick and are similar in function to *namkha.*

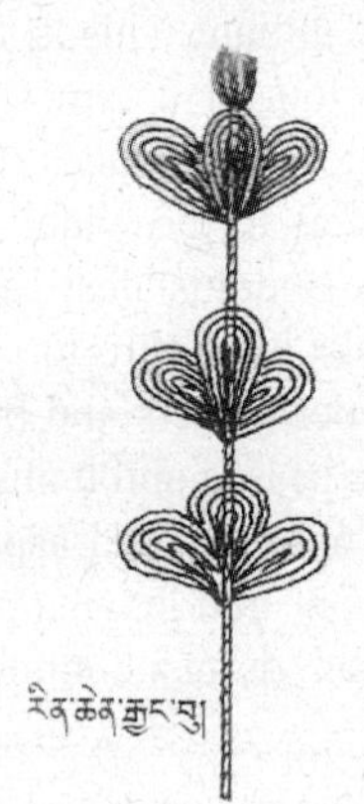

Fig. 4. Rinchen Jangbu.

Rinchen Jangbu is made by looping multicoloured wool around a wooden stick to form nine 'leaves' which represent the nine leaves of the Tree of Bön.[241] As such, *jangbu* directly correspond to the nine-branched Serge of Bө Murgel so we can understand that this object represents the same ancient concept of the World Tree and is, in fact, a remnant of Prehistoric Bön culture within the transformed methods of Causal Bön.

---

[239] The Nine Ways of Bön ultimately lead to full enlightment and the attainment of Buddhahood while even a fully initiated Bө cannot go beyond life/rebirth in the Three Worlds.

[240] Tib. rgyang bu.

[241] Oral communication from Yongdzin Lopön Tenzin Namdak, September 2007.

CHAPTER V

Classes of Gods and Spirits

In this chapter we will go a little deeper into the subject of the various classes of gods and spirits already studied to some extent in the preceding chapter. Here we will focus on the beings who command the vital energies of the elements, who wield power over many aspects of the world we live in and who, often unbeknown to us, can affect our natural environment, wild animals, crops and livestock. Depending on humans' attitude and behaviour, these beings can either hinder or help, and that is precisely why we find so many rituals dealing with them suited to a range of situations, actions and needs. The underlying aim of all these rituals in all kinds of Bön and in Bɵ Murgel is to ensure a harmonious relationship between these powerful entities and the human race, a very important task of Bönpos and Bɵ alike.

Thirty-Three Races of Gods and Spirits

Yungdrung Bön is a tradition with a wealth of knowledge on this subject. The gods and spirits which control the energies of our world generally belong to the Demi-God class of the Six Realms but there are many sub-classes and categories. One of the most elaborate and ancient classifications of these gods and spirits recognizes thirty-three races of gods and spirits who inhabit the Three Worlds and which are divided into three major groups:

– Thirteen Classes of the Upper Space[1] which include such beings as:
Wal – very powerful and wrathful entities; *Yog*; *Trin*;
Nyer; *Ö*; *Tsam*; *Mu* – very ancient beings who can either provide assistance or cause serious problems; *Sid* – controllers of existence, with tremendous powers over many aspects of the universe; *Kö* – gods who control many important cosmic energies; *Cha* – extremely ancient gods who command the

---

[1] Tib. yar g.yen gnyan bcu sum.

energies of well-being and prosperity and are invoked in numerous rituals of divination, long-life, prosperity, astrology, medicine and healing; *Tsen* – easily irritated wrathful rock-dwelling spirits of red complexion; *Düd* – very powerful sky-dwelling demons of black complexion who bring destruction, pollution and death; *Nyenpo Lha* – very high and clean divinities.[2] Some kinds of *Lha* belong to the God Realms while others are still counted among the demi-gods. Many of these gods are extremely ancient and as their names are often of Zhang Zhung origin, this obscures the meaning making it difficult to establish their characteristics clearly.

– The Nine Classes of the Intermediate Space[3] to which belong:
Da – moon gods; *Nyi* – sun gods; *Kar* – star gods; *Trin* – gods dwelling in the clouds; *Zha* – rainbow gods; *Dal* – gods of mist and fog; *Zer* – gods of light rays; *Lo* – controllers of the year, gods of the twelve-year astrological cycle with human bodies and animal heads; *Dzi* – air gods.[4]

– The Eleven Classes of the Earth[5] including:
Lu – water spirits; *Nyen* – tree spirits, *Gyal* – 'the kings', a relatively young class of very malicious spirits. Many recent *Gyalpo* are spirits of spiritual practitioners, often monks, who went astray in their practice, or of men and women who were killed; *Men* – lake goddesses; *Zed* – thunder-spirits; *Sin* – 'vampire' spirits who steal the life-force of the living; *Dre* – spirits of pollution who bring misfortune and chaos; *Si* – spirits of cemeteries connected with ancestors, kind of 'shadows of death' who often disturb children and pregnant women;[6] *Gyur* – ghosts; *Shinje* – lords of death or spirits causing death; and *Chüd*.[7]

Yongdzin Lopön Tenzin Namdak says that now it is difficult even for native Tibetan Bönpo scholars to understand the ranks and functions of these ancient Bönpo deities precisely:

---

2 Tib. dbal, yogs, khrin, gnyer, 'o, 'thsams, dmu, srid, skos, phywa, btsan, bdud, gnyen po lha.

3 Tib. bar g.yen gtod po dgu.

4 Tib. zla, nyi, skar, sprin, 'ja', dal, zer, lo, rdzi.

5 Tib. sa g.yen che ba bcu gcig.

6 Perhaps cot syndrome may be caused by these entities.

7 Tib. klu, gnyan, rgyal, sman, gzed, srin, 'dre, sri, byur, gshin rje, chud.

> There are so many different types of *Lha*. Some of them are Wisdom *Lha*[8] while others are sentient beings in *samsara*. […] The *Cha* may be a small proportion of *Lha* but *Mu*, *Düd* and *Tsen* are demi-gods.[9]

In the medium version of Shenrab Miwo's biography, *Zermig*,[10] belonging to the Bönpo *Kanjur* we find an episode where Bönpo priests come to give praise to the newly born Buddha Shenrab Miwo. In fact, these Bönpos were non-human, the priests of the non-human beings belonging to the two higher groups of the Thirty-Three Races of Gods and Spirits.[11] The sages' names refer to the class of beings to which they belonged e.g. Walbön Rompo[12] – Bönpo of *Wal*; Yogbön Togyal[13] – Bönpo of *Yog*; Trinbön Chasang[14] – Bönpo of *Cha* and so on.[15] The fact that these beings came to visit Tonpa Shenrab just after his birth demonstrates that this classification of the Thirty-Three Races of Gods and Spirits is extremely ancient and predates Tonpa Shenrab Miwo.

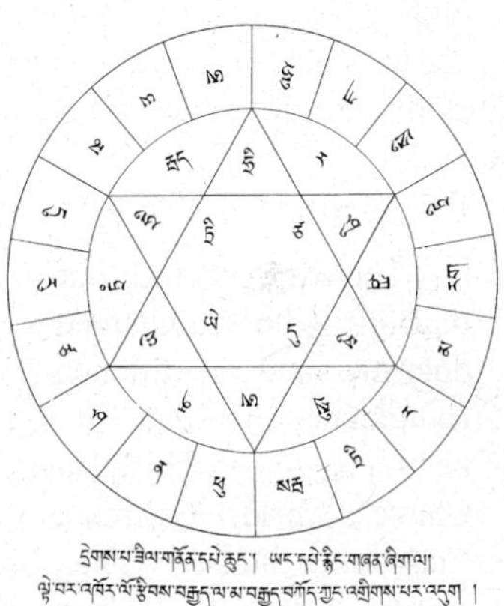

Fig. 1. Diagram of the Dregpa *spirits of the Universe.*

---

[8] Tib. ye shes lha.

[9] Excerpt from the transcript of an interview in Triten Norbutse Monastery, Kathmandu, April 2004.

[10] Tib. gZer mig.

[11] This is according to Bönpo lamas. Professor Namkhai Norbu's interpretation is that they were human Bönpo each of whom belonged to a ritual tradition related to a particular class of spirits. (See Norbu, *Drung, Deu and Bön*, p. 147.) Here I follow the traditional Bönpo version. For a full list of the Bönpo sages of the Thirty-Three Races of Gods and Spirits see Samten G. Karmay, 'Myths and Rituals' in *Bon: The Magic Word. The Indigenous Religion of Tibet*, Ed. Samten G. Karmay and Jeff Watt (Rubin Museum of Art, New York in association with Philip Wilson Publishers, London, 2007), pp. 151–154.

[12] Tib. dBal bon Rom po.

[13] Tib. Yogs bon gTo rgyal.

[14] Tib. Khrin bon Phywa sangs.

[15] For a translation of the passage and full list of the Bönpo sages see Norbu, *Drung, Deu and Bon*, p. 147.

Eight Classes of Gods and Spirits

This is another way of classifying powerful non-human beings which is found both in Yungdrung Bön and later in Tibetan Buddhism. There are several versions of this list but the most usual is: *Lha*, *Nojin*, *Mamo*, *Düd*, *Tsen*, *Gyalpo*, *Shinje* and *Lu.*[16] With the exception of *Nojin* and *Mamo*, all the classes or races of spirits on this list are also present in the classification just dealt with. *Nojin* are wealth gods and comprise eight main gods with Dzambala[17] as their leader. *Mamo* are fierce female spirits who cause wars, epidemics and famines. Many of Yungdrung Bön's worldly protectors belong to the Eight Classes.

Protectors of Yungdrung Bön

There is a special group of deities in Yungdrung Bön called Protectors of Bön[18] who are charged with the very specific task of guarding its doctrines and practitioners. There are two types of guardians: Fully Enlightened Guardians[19] who are Buddha-forms, and Worldly Guardians[20] belonging to the Thirty-Three Races of Gods and Spirits or the Eight Classes. Worldly Guardians were subdued and put under oath to guard Yungdrung Bön by Tonpa Shenrab Miwo and later by other realized *Shenpo*. Here is an account of how Tonpa Shenrab Miwo subdued the gods of Zhang Zhung and Tibet:

> Rage seized the gods (lha rigs) of Zhang Zhung under their leader Ti se, the ma rigs of Bod under Thang lha, 999,000 srid pa'i sman, and the twelve brtan ma, guardians of the world. However, Shenrab subdued them all, and to confirm their submission for all time they offered him the secret syllables enclosing the essence of their power (srog snying yig 'bru sa bon). In this way they became guardians of the teachings of rGyal ba gShen rab, they drank the consecrated water (dam bstag snying po dam chu kha ra btung) and bore the symbol of the Bon teachings, the swastika (g.yung drung) on their heads. From then on they were called dam can ye shes spyan ldan, 'those who have taken the vow and who possess the eye of transcendental consciousness.[21]

---

[16] Tib. lha srin sde brgyad: lha, gnod sbyin, ma mo, bdud, btsen, rgyal po, gshin rje, klu. Other version is lha, klu, btsan, bdud, ma mo, gshin rje, srin po, gza'.

[17] Tib. 'Dza bha lha; 'Dzam bha la.

[18] Tib. bon skyong/bon srung ma.

[19] Tib. 'jig rten las 'das pa'i srung ma.

[20] Tib. 'jig rten pa'i srung ma.

[21] Giuseppe Tucci, Tr. Geoffrey Samuel, *The Religions of Tibet* (London and Henley: Routledge&Keagan Paul, 1980), p. 240.

The four main Bönpo Protectors are *Ma*, *Düd*, *Tsen* and *Gyal*. The first two are Enlightened Guardians while the second two are Worldly Guardians.[22]

Sidpai Gyalmo

The principal Guardian of all the teachings of Yungdrung Bön is Machog Sidpai Gyalmo, the Excellent Mother, Queen of Existence. She is a wrathful manifestation of the Loving Goddess of Wisdom known as Sherab Jamma[23] in Tibetan and Satrig Ersang[24] in the language of Zhang Zhung – a manifestation of the wisdom of all the Buddhas.

Sidpai Gyalmo emanated many forms for different circumstances and needs. She is most commonly depicted riding either a red or black mule[25] and has three heads, six arms and four legs. Her retinues are made up of her own emanations and include: the Six Disciples for the six times of the day-night cycle (black for the late evening, blue for midnight, white for pre-dawn, yellow for sunrise, red for midday and brown for the afternoon)[26]; Nele Gyalmo[27] for the Four Seasons and four

---

22 The following descriptions of the Guardians are according to instructions given to me by Yongdzin Lopön Tenzin Namdak, Khenpo Tenpa Yungdrung and Geshe Gelek Jinpa in the course of over ten years. In particular, Yongdzin Rinpoche and Khenpo Tenpa Yungdrung have, on my request, rendered into English a number of such texts which were edited by my wife and I while we were staying in Triten Norbutse Bönpo Monastery in Kathmandu in 1996. The texts in question are: *Srid rgyal dre'u nag mo'i* (*The Sang Offering to Black Mule Sidgyal which is called The Heap of Jewels*); *Mi bdud zhal gzigs bzhugs* (*Midüd Who Manifests Visibly*); *Brag btsan bskang skul* (*The Rite of Propitiation to Satisfy Dragtsen [Apse]); rGyal po shel khrab kyi gtor bskang bzhugs* (*The Offering of Torma to Satisfy Gyalpo Sheltrap*). Other texts which served as a reference in this section are: *sNyan rgyud bka' srung srog bdag rgyal po nyi pang sad bka'bsgo* (*The Propitiation Rite of Sogdag Gyalpo Nyipangse, The King of the Owners of Life-Force, who is the Principal Guardian of the Precepts of the Oral Transmission of Zhang Zhung*); *rGyal po nyi pang sad dang sman mo gnyis kyi bskul ba* (*Prayer to Nyipangse and the Goddess Menmo*); and *The Wealth Practice of Dzamgon* all translated by John Myrdhin Reynolds.

23 Tib. Shes rab Byams ma.

24 Tib. Sa trig Er sangs.

25 Tib. Srid rgyal Drel dmar and Tib. Srid rgyal Dre'u Nag monpo.

26 Tib. Srod la Nag mo, Nam gung sNgon mo, Tho rangs dKar mo, Nyi shar Ser mo, Nyin 'phyed dMar mo, Phe 'phyed sMug mo.

27 Tib. Ne las rGyal mo.

elements (yellow, green, red and blue); Nine Zema[28] and Nine Djemo[29] with various animal heads. Besides this common form of Sidpai Gyalmo there is also a form with a hundred heads and a thousand arms as well as manifestations which ride bear and other animals steeds.

The secret emanation of Sidpai Gyalmo is Yeshe Walmo,[30] the special guardian of Tantra and Dzogchen teachings. Yeshe Walmo appears as a dancing wrathful *Walmo dakini*[31] trampling a malevolent spirit under her feet. She wears a crown of five skulls which represents dominion over the Five Poisonous Emotions and is dressed in a mantle of peacock feathers and a tiger-skin skirt. Human and elephant skins hang from her shoulders, representing the liberation of anger, pride and ignorance. In her right hand she holds a flaming sword of wisdom which cuts off karmic traces, obstacles and demons. In her left hand she holds a vase of long-life brimming with medicine.

Fig. 2. Black Mule Sidpai Gyalmo.

Fig. 3. Yeshe Walmo.

[28] Tib. gZe ma dgu.

[29] Tib. Gyad mo dgu.

[30] Tib. Ye shes dBal mo.

[31] Tib. mkha' 'gro.

Midüd Jampa Trakgo

Fig. 4. Midüd Jampa Trakgo.

The second Enlightened Guardian is Midüd Jampa Trakgo,[32] an emanation of the *yidam* Walse Ngampa.[33] His main manifestation has one head, two hands and two legs. He is blue and dressed in black robes. He wields an axe for destroying the enemies of Bön in his right hand and a spear with a black pennant in his left. He rides a ferocious otter amid a thunderous cloud of hail. There are many emanations of Midüd in the realms of *Sinpo*, *Mu*, *Shinje*, *Düd*, *Dza*, *Cha* and *Tsen*. He is surrounded by a retinue of countless *Düd* and *Tsen* spirits.

Apse

The first of the main Worldly Protectors is Apse Gyalwa,[34] a powerful *Tsen* from their *Se*[35] clan. His residence is in the Red Castle of the North-East and he is King of *Dragtsen*,[36] rock-dwelling *Tsen*. He is a red man as tall as a spear with red hair which stands on end. He is dressed in a red cloak although sometimes appears wearing a helmet and armour. His steed is a red horse with a white forelock. In his right hand he holds a spear with a red pennant and a lasso of the *Tsen*, and with this left hand he sends a rock owl against the enemies of Yungdrung Bön. He is a *Sogdag*,[37] the Owner of Life-Force, and is surrounded by a hundred thousand groups of slayers.

Some Tibetan Buddhist texts claim that in the eighth century AD Apse was subjugated by Guru Rinpoche who gave him the name of Dorje Legpa and converted him into a *Dharmapala* guardian of the Nyingma School. However, according to other Buddhist and Bönpo sources, this

---

32 Tib. Mi bdud 'Jam pa khrag mgo.

33 Tib. dBal gsas rNgam pa.

34 Tib. A bse rGyal ba.

35 Tib. bse.

36 Tib. brag btsan.

37 Tib. srog bdag.

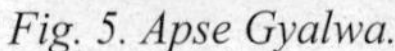

Fig. 5. Apse Gyalwa.

Fig 6. Dorje Legpa.

is incorrect. Dorje Legpa's appearance bears no resemblance to Apse and he belongs to the *Nyen* class while Apse is *Tsen*. Dorje Legpa's father is said to be Mudüd Karpo, i.e. a *Mu* demon, while his mother is Düddza Migkar;[38] i.e. half *Düd* and half *Dza*. This is completely different from the lineage of Apse whose father is *Tsen*, also called Apse Gyalwa, and whose mother is Sasin Mamo (Marmo),[39] half *Sinpo*, half *Mamo*. The dwelling place of Dorje Legpa is said to be in the bat-bone castle on Mount Malaya in the west while Apse resides in the red castle of the northeast.[40] It is very clear, then, that we are dealing with two unrelated deities.

Gyalpo Sheltrab

The second main Worldly Protector of Bön is Gyalpo Sheltrabchen,[41] a king of *Gyalpo* spirits. He is white and his appearance is that of a warrior-king. He wears crystal armour with a helmet and holds a spear with a white pennant in his left hand. His right hand is outstretched and shows the *mudra*[42] of control over negativities. He rides a beautifully

---

38 Tib. dMu bdud dKar po; bDud gza' Mig dkar.

39 Tib. Sra srin Ma mo (dMar mo).

40 For information on Dorje Legpa see Réne de Nebesky-Wojkowitz, *Oracles and Demons of Tibet: The Cult and Iconography of the Tibetan Protective Deities* (New Delhi: Paljor Publications,1998), pp. 154–159.

41 Tib. rGyal po Shel khrab can.

42 Tib. phyag rgya; a symbolic gesture used in Tantra for communication, empowering offerings and magical actions.

Fig. 7. Gyalpo Sheltrab.

Fig. 8. Menmo.

decorated white horse. He has a consort, Lumo Ökarma,[43] the White Light Lady of *Lu*, who is a powerful female protector in her own right.

Nyipangse and Menmo

Two other very important and ancient Zhang Zhung Guardians are Nyipangse[44] and Menmo.[45] They are the Guardians of the Dzogchen cycle of *Zhang Zhung Nyen Gyud*. We shall study Nyipangse in detail in the next chapter so I shall not describe him here. Menmo is his consort,[46] the Queen of all *Menmo* lake-goddesses. She has a peaceful, smiling countenance and white complexion. Riding a white yak, she holds a vase of nectar and a mirror. Both deities were subjugated in the seventh century AD by the great Zhang Zhung *yogi* Gurub Nangzher Lödpo when they swore an oath to protect the teachings and practitioners of *Zhang Zhung Nyen Gyud* cycle; Gurub Nangzher Lödpo was the sole knowledge-holder of the cycle at that time.

---

43 Tib. Klu mo 'Od dkar ma.

44 Tib. Nyi pang sad.

45 Tib. sMan mo. Her full name is gNam phyi Gung rgyal.

46 In Western scholarly works Menmo is often said to be just a companion of Nyipangse. However, according to Khenpo Tenpa Yungdrung she is his consort. (Oral communication, Triten Norbutse Monastery, Kathmandu, 16.01.08).

Fig. 9. Dzamgon.

Fig. 10. Dragpa Senge.

Dzamgon

Dzamgon or Blue Dzambala is an important protector of Yungdrung Bön. He is a *Nordag*,[47] Owner of Wealth. The Bönpo calendar indicates special days on which he is to be propitiated. His body is dark blue and he has the appearance of a Tibetan warrior-king. He wears a leather helmet and chain-mail covered with a leather garment. He rides a dark blue or brown horse. In his right hand he brandishes a sword and in his left he holds a mongoose which spits out precious jewels. He is the leader of the *Nojin* class and is surrounded by them, in particular by the Eight Great Wealth Gods[48] and the Eight Great *Lamlha*,[49] Protectors of the Road.

Dragpa Senge

Some Protectors were subdued and put on oath relatively recently. One such is Dragpa Senge.[50] He is said to be the spirit of the Tenth Shamarpa[51] Chödrag Gyatso[52] (1742–1792).

---

47 Tib. nor bdag.

48 Tib. Nor lha chen po brgyad.

49 Tib. Lam lha chen po brgyad – the deities which protect travellers and aid in commerce.

50 Tib. Grags pa Seng ge.

51 Tib. Zhva dmar pa, lit. 'red hat bearer'. It is a title for one of the four most important lamas of the Karma Kagyud order of Tibetan Buddhism. He is one of the four regents responsible for finding, looking after and educating the reincarnation of Karmapa, the head of Karma Kagyud.

52 Tib. Chos grags rGya mtsho.

This Shamarpa conspired with the Nepalese Royal family against the Tibetan government and triggered the invasion of Gorkha warriors into Tibet in 1792. The campaign was unsuccessful; the Tenth Shamarpa's property was all confiscated and he himself was forced to flee to Nepal, where he died. The Tibetan government dismantled the institution of Shamarpa and forbade the recognition of any future incarnations. After his death Chödrag Gyatso became a very powerful and malignant *Gyalpo* spirit causing trouble in Tibet. However, Sherab Gongyal[53] (1784–1835), the abbot of Menri monastery, then the main seat of Bönpo monastic education, summoned this spirit and placed him under oath to become a Protector of Bön. It is said that Sherab Gongyal was able to subdue this spirit because they had a karmic connection going back to the times of Shenrab Miwo. In those days Shamarpa was the son of a demon and the abbot of Menri was a disciple of Shenrab Miwo called Yungdrung Tsugshen Gyalwa[54] who looked after the demon boy because he had been born to one of Tonpa Shenrab's wives through trickery and deceit. The demon boy, known as Shenchung Gowo,[55] became very learned because of his contact with Tonpa Shenrab's student, later taking ten incarnations as Shamarpa Lama. Yungdrung Tsugshen Gyalwa was later reborn as the abbot of Menri Shenrab Gongyal and because of their previous connection as teacher and student he was able to subdue the spirit of the Tenth Shamarpa and put him under oath. Dragpa Senge appears as a Buddhist monk riding a horse, holding a banner of victory and a wish-fulfilling jewel.

There are many more Bönpo protectors of various magnitude and power. Each teaching cycle, religious monument, holy place and many Bönpo centres both lay and monastic have their own Protectors. There are special protectors[56] who were entrusted with guarding various *terma*-treasures concealed during times of persecutions to be rediscovered in more auspicious circumstances. The *terton*-discoverers are often a reincarnation of the master who hid the treasures and when a text is to be recovered, these Guardians often appear in a dream or vision to instruct them how to find it. Furthermore, before a *terma* is opened the *terton* often has to make extensive offerings to its Guardians so that they allow him or her to take it out of its hiding place. Once a *terma* is found, its transmission is connected with its Guardians and the practitioners of that

---

[53] Tib. Shes rab dGongs rgyal.

[54] Tib. g.Yung drung gTsug gshen rGyal ba.

[55] Tib. gShen chung Go bo.

[56] Tib. gter bdag.

lineage propitiate them regularly. Special protectors are also connected with the holy clans and families of Yungdrung Bön through which transmission of teachings runs from generation to generation.

Gods and spirits in Bө Murgel

The main categories of non-human beings were dealt with in general terms in the previous chapter. In fact, Buryatian Bө Murgel doesn't systemize the beings of the Three Worlds in the same detail as Yungdrung Bön. Nevertheless, we can find many parallels between the beings of all Three Worlds in both traditions. Some Tengeri correspond to some of the gods of the Thirteen Classes of the Upper Space as well as to certain beings from the Nine Classes of the Intermediate Space. Naran Ehe and Hara Esege, Tengeri of sun and moon, match *Nyi* and *Da* while the star-Tengeri Khaan Tengeriin Odo Mushed are comparable with *Kar*, for example.

Gods and spirits which Bө Murgel places in the Middle and Underworld correspond to beings from the Eleven Classes of the Earth and the Eight Classes. *Haats*, certain *Ezhen* and *Zayaan* are analogous to *Nyen, Gyal* and *Men* while *Lusuut*, Erlig Khaan and his messengers correspond to *Lu* and *Shinje*. The various groups of *Noyod*[57] king-spirits are directly comparable to *Gyal* or *Gyalpo* in particular while the female killer-spirits *Mu Shubuun*[58] are the equivalent of *Senmo*[59] (female *Gyalpo* spirits) and even resemble them in some aspects of their appearance.[60] Some categories of *Ada*[61] (spirits who disturb or kill newborn babies and cause miscarriages) are comparable to *Si* while *Dahabari*[62] (violent spirits of sexually frustrated women) can be loosely compared to *Mamo*. We will deal with these and other kinds of spirits in Bө Murgel in the context of the soul in Chapter XIII.

Sky-dwelling gods in Bön and Bө Murgel

However, the most remarkable and far-reaching analogies are found when we take a look at the sky-dwelling gods of Bön and Bө Murgel. These striking similarities are reflected in many aspects surrounding how

---

57 Bur. ноёд.

58 Bur. му шубуун, lit. 'bad bird'.

59 Tib. sren mo.

60 *Senmo* are often depicted as naked women with bird heads.

61 Bur. ада.

62 Bur. дахабари.

they came into being, their attributes and their role in the universe. As we hinted at earlier (in Chapter IV), there is even a semantic connection. The reader will recall the Tibetan word *teng* in the composite word *Tenggi Lha,* the Upper Sky-Dimension of the Gods, from our discussion on the Three Worlds of Bön cosmology. This obviously calls to mind the White Tengeri of Bɵ Murgel. While in Tibetan *teng* literally means 'above' it is also a word for the sky and is synonymous with *kha.*[63] Thus *teng* and *tengeri/tenger* are not only etymologically related but also express the same concept; a dimension of the sky as a living environment for the sky-gods, Tengeri/*Lha*. That leaves us in no doubt that the Tengeri sky-dwelling gods of Bɵ Murgel and the sky-dwelling *Lha* of Bön must be the same kind of beings and gives us yet another strong point to argue that both Bɵ Murgel and Prehistoric Bön were essentially the same religion in the very remote past.

As for their role in the universe, as we have seen in the chapter above, the cosmologies of both Bɵ Murgel and Bön rest on an understanding of the polar forces which fight for the dominance and control of the Universe. While their names and certain secondary aspects differ, the beings representing these polar forces share many common features and fundamental characteristics. In both religions we find these celestial gods and demons living in opposite directions of the sky. In the Bönpo model we find *Lha* living in the realm of *Ye* in the south of the sky while *Düd* inhabit the realm of *Ngam* located in the north of the sky. The White Tengeri live in the west of the sky while Black Tengeri dwell in the east, although according to some traditions some of the Black Tengeri are said to dwell in the north. What is important to establish here is that both *Lha* and *Düd* and White and Black Tengeri live in opposite directions of the sky and so represent the polarity of light and darkness.

Eternal conflict: Lha versus Düd and White Tengeri versus Black Tengeri

In Bön the *Lha* and *Düd* find themselves in constant war while in Buryatian Bɵ Murgel it is the orders of White and Black Tengeri which represent the same principle of the cosmic struggle of opposite energies.

Both *Lha* and White Tengeri are virtuous gods who, having created human beings and animals, protect them by various means, teach them rites for propitiating the gods, rites for purification and so on. *Düd* and the Black Tengeri, meanwhile, act in quite the opposite manner, creating diseases and negativities which constantly threaten the lives of humans

63 Tib. mkha'.

and animals and consequently they are associated with negativities and death.

In both Bɵ Murgel and Bön the stories of the war between the opposite orders have many parallels. There is the character who acts as mediator between the warring camps: the Neutral Sky-Dweller Sege'en Sebdeg Tengeri and Köje Drangkar[64] respectively. In each case, the gods and demons communicated through them before the start of the initial conflict and they both position themselves in the neutral territory of the sky, the border between the realms of gods and demons

In both belief systems, despite being opposing forces, the sky-gods and sky-demons are not completely separate and may even intermarry from time to time. The mythology of both traditions includes practically identical stories relating how, after a long war between the gods and demons a period of temporary peaceful co-existence dawns, a kind of pact of non-aggression sealed by a mixed marriage. In Bɵ Murgel it is the marriage of Teme Nogon, daughter of a White Tengeri, to Black Guzhir Bomo Tengeri. In Bön it is the marriage of a *Düd*-maiden, Yumen,[65] to one of the *Lha*, as explained in the myth of Gekhöd:[66]

> After living for some time among the *Lha* and giving birth to numerous offspring of mixed descent (Gekhöd being one of them), Yumen runs back to the *Düd,* no longer able to bear the company of the *Lha*. This triggers a new round of escalations in the perpetual conflict in the course of which Gekhöd unwittingly slays his own mother. Contamination from this action of matricide greatly defiles the realms of gods and men which are threatened by destruction but through the skilful actions of a tiny god, Kuji Mangke,[67] this misdeed and its consequences are purified so all the gods and men are spared calamity.[68] From those times the tradition of purification rites of Gekhöd began which contain *Tsen*[69] and *Sang* [70] rituals.

---

64 Tib. sKos rje Drang dkar. See Karmay, *The Arrow and the Spindle*, pp. 142–143.

65 Tib. dYu sman.

66 Tib. Ge khod.

67 Tib. Ku byi Mang ke.

68 For the full story see Karmay, *The Arrow and the Spindle*, p.143–144; 389–482, and Norbu, *Drung, Deu and Bön*, pp. 117–119.

69 Tib. Ge khod lo phrom e'i dmar tshan and Tib. Ge khod bsang ba'i dkar tshan.

70 Tib. Ge khod mnol bsang.

I haven't come across the end of the twin Buryatian myth so we can only guess at what happened between Teme Nogon and Guzhir Tengeri.

Nevertheless, both stories demonstrate a high degree of similarity in the initial phase except for minor details: in the Bönpo version we have a demoness married to a god while the Bɵ Murgel version tells of a goddess married to a demon. This, however, is not so important. What is important is that in both cases the intermarriage of gods and demons is a political event and acts as a seal on the pact of non-aggression. In my view we have here two variations based on a common cultural matrix. In general, Tibetan mythology is much better preserved than its Bɵ Murgel equivalent. Despite three major waves of persecution Yungdrung Bön is still very much flourishing. Buryatian mythology, in contrast, has suffered greatly over more than three hundred years due to the attrition of continuous persecution and attempts by Buddhists, Orthodox Christians and Communists to wholly eradicate the Bɵ Murgel culture to which it is closely tied. As a result of this hostile environment we often have just fragments of the stories surviving in many variations and this makes it difficult to see a coherent picture.

Drala and Tengeri

Drala are ancient sky-dwelling gods, a kind of *Lha*. Below is a short explanation of *Drala* provided by Yongdzin Lopön Tenzin Namdak:

> There are four races of *Drala*, and there are hundreds, thousands of them. No-one knows exactly what they look like. Some are foot soldiers, some are mounted. There are four classes: *Thugkar*, *Drala*, *Werma*, *Shungon*[71] each with many ranks. *Thugkar* is the highest, much higher, and they dominate space. They are a kind of demi-god; they belong to that race.[72]

As we have seen, the demi-gods are a very broad category including not only the *Drala* but also many other gods with quite different appearances and characteristics. Many of these various races of positive sky-gods are also known under the generic name *Lha* as in Bön the name *Lha* has two meanings: it can refer to a particular class of sky-gods called *Lha* or to all the positive sky-gods including the four classes of *Drala*. As

---

[71] Tib. thug kar, sgra bla, wer ma, shugs mgon. In some systems they are categorized as Drala, Werma, Changseng (Tib. cang seng) and Shungon.

[72] From a conversation in Triten Norbutse Bönpo Monastery, Kathmandu, Nepal, April 2004.

we have just established, the *Lha* sky-gods and White Tengeri are parallel names for the same type of beings and, as the categories of *Lha* and *Drala* overlap, the comparison between *Lha* and Tengeri holds for the *Drala*, too. Their general appearance is basically the same. White Tengeri appear mounted on white horses, they have various weapons and attributes and carry spears with flags. Below is an account of the Buddhist spokesman Shakyaprabha's experience of the flight of his soul. This happened during a contest commissioned by King Trisong Deutsen in the eighth century AD to test the magical powers of Bönpos and Buddhists. Shakyaprabha was killed and then revived by Bönpo *yogis* and we can see clearly from his description that the gods (*Lha*) he saw resemble White Tengeri:

> The King has asked Śākya: 'Where have you been? What have you seen?' (Śākya replied) 'I had the feeling I was being chased. I fell asleep. In my dream I was carried away by a man with dark complexion on a black horse. We reached the top of a pass. Before us, I saw a very welcoming land. There, a white man with white complexion told me: "Your time to be here has not yet come". There were a great many men with white complexion on white horses holding banners and spears. They said they were gods; they told me to go back. Then I woke up.'[73]

In their function and appearance, White Tengeri appear very similar to the *Thugkar* gods of the *Drala* class who are also called *Yesid Lha Karpo,*[74] the White *Lha* of Primordial Existence. The *Thugkar* are said to number 360 while there are generally said to be 55 White Tengeri. However, as there are many other numbers associated with both groups, this difference is not fundamental. The *Zijyid* tells us there are 90,000 *Thugkar*, that their army is 9,900 warriors strong and that their leaders are the Nine *Thugkar* Sons and the Father, making Ten, and the Seven Celestial Sisters and the Mother, making Eight.[75] Similarly, Bɵ Murgel sources mention One Thousand White Tengeri, Ten Thousand *Burkhans*[76] and so on, and, as the Bɵ and Utgan I know point out, these numbers are not fixed; when we speak of fifty-five or a thousand White Tengeri this refers to the number of main Tengeri.

---

[73] Karmay, *The Arrow and the Spindle*, p. 317–318.

[74] Tib. ye srid lha dkar po.

[75] Norbu, *Drung,Deu and Bon* pp. 51–54.

[76] Bur. бурхан is a synonym of Tengeri but nowadays simple people use it for any divinity whether heavenly or not. Some recent publications claim that *Burkhans* are a lower-ranking and less powerful class of gods than Tengeri but the Bɵ and Utgan I know say this is a misguided opinion.

If we compare classes of *Drala* other than *Thugkar* with the White Tengeri, although they correspond in function they may not necessarily correspond in appearance and characteristics. A closer comparison stands if we use the model of four groups of Tengeri dwelling in the four cardinal direction of the sky. According to this description, these four groups of Tengeri differ in appearance, colour and characteristics. There are ninety-nine multicoloured Tengeri in the south, seventy-seven clean Tengeri in the north, fifty-five white Tengeri in the west and forty-four red-flaming Tengeri in the east. These are very general descriptions showing that the Tengeri in fact take on many and varied forms, so it is likely that further research would uncover even closer parallels between *Drala* and these Tengeri.

Another group of Tengeri with counterparts in Bön dwell in different parts of the body. These Tengeri can be compared to the Bönpo concept of the Five Personal Deities,[77] five *Drala* deities which also dwell in different parts of the body.[78] In particular there is a Tengeri found on the crown of the head who guards the channel Bɵ and Utgan use when leaving their body in magical flight. This Tengeri's function is to open, close and protect this channel from intruders. A direct counterpart is the Bön Tsalam Tsangkha[79] or Tsadag[80] deities who guard and keep the trance-channel of Tibetan *lhapa*-mediums clean.[81] The trance channel runs down from the top of the head through the middle of the chest and to the ring fingers on both hands.[82]

The ancient spelling of the word '*drala*' reveals another parallel. The original Bönpo spelling is *sgra bla* where '*dra*' means 'sound' and '*la*' can be translated as 'soul' giving us a possible translation 'Soul of Sound'.[83] From this name it is obvious that these deities are connected to and should be invoked through sound. Sound is vibration, an aspect of energy which is linked to:

---

77 Tib. 'go ba'i lha lnga. Alternatively known as the Five Deities of the Head.

78 See Norbu, *Drung, Deu and Bon,* pp. 66–68.

79 Tib. rtsa lam gtsang mkha.

80 Tib. rtsa bdag.

81 See Bellezza, *Divine Dyads,* pp. 62–65.

82 In Yungdrung Bön the most common meditation posture, the '*mudra* of equipoise', is with the thumbs pressing on the ring fingers just where they join the palm. This is done to close this channel and to prevent disturbances during meditation.

83 The concepts of *la* and *soul* are discussed in ch.XIII. An alternative Bönpo spelling is Tib. sgra lha, which read as 'sound god' and conveys the same idea.

- *cha*, the positive energy of a person which serves as a base for prosperity and well-being and finds its parallel in the Buryatian term *hulde*;[84]
- *wangthang*,[85] Ascendance-Capacity, a kind of energy which allows one to excel in any field of activity;
- *lungta*,[86] the Wind Horse, a type of energy connected above all to a person's good luck and ability to accomplish things quickly.

According to Professor Namkhai Norbu, sound is considered to be the most important medium between a person and his/her *la.* The name *Drala*, 'Soul of the Sound', can be interpreted in two ways simultaneously. One meaning, 'the deity who protects a person's soul', points to the *Drala*'s function as protectors of humankind. The other, 'the soul which can be invoked through sound', is plausible because *Drala*, like all sentient beings, naturally have *la* or 'soul' even though they are non-material beings who live in the dimension of the energy of light, and this soul can be invoked through sound. Both these meanings are in complete accordance with the functions of the White Tengeri, too. Although the name 'tengeri' means 'sky-dweller', the function of White Tengeri is to protect virtue and to protect humans. Moreover, sound is absolutely indispensable for Bɵ Murgel rituals; White Tengeri are invoked through prayers and special rhythmical sound codes or drum beats which create the sound-energy communication bridge between a Bɵ and the Tengeri he is calling.

Black Tengeri and Düd

Although we have found several similarities between the White Tengeri and the *Drala*, no matter which model we use to describe or categorize Tengeri, the Forty-Four Black or Eastern Tengeri cannot be likened to *Drala* as their activity lies prevalently in the sphere of destruction. However, as we established above, Black or Eastern Tengeri do bear a striking resemblance to the *Düd* sky-demons of Bön and so can be directly compared to them. To further substantiate this understanding, here is a description of their Lord, Atai Ulaan Tengeri, Great Red-Flaming Tengeri, from Bɵ invocations:

---

84 Bur. hүльдэ.

85 Tib. dbang thang.

86 Tib. klung rta, rlung rta.

Holding in his hands the Owner of bad luck and misery,
Squeezing in his palms black sorcerers,
He is the Red-Flaming Evil Spirit Sky-Dweller.[87]

This quotation clearly depicts the lord of the Forty-Four Black Tengeri as a very powerful evil sky demon, although we may think that he is red. Here is another quotation showing that disease-creating spirits came down to earth clinging onto Atai Ulaan and his retinue of Black Tengeri:

...Came down holding onto the cheeks of the Great Black Tengeri,
Came down holding onto the buttocks of the Great Twilight Tengeri,
Came raging down from the Fiery-Red Tengeri,
Came down beating the flames from the Flaming-Red Tengeri,
Disseminating diseases,
Compelling towards crime,
Ensnaring in black magic,
Sticking like midges,
Swarming like a mass of mosquitoes,
Polluting and repulsive...
[names of the bad spirits who cause diseases][88]
[...]
So [after giving the offering]
We don't want to know or hear
Either your names or your nicknames.[89]

There is no doubt, then, that Atai Ulaan is in fact an evil sky-demon who controls diseases and misfortunes, and this fits well with the description of *Düd* both in function and appearance.

Mystical eagles in Bön and Bɵ Murgel

Tengeri and other deities may also take the form of an eagle or other bird of prey. The Bönpo *Khyung* and Bɵ Murgel Hotoi Burged are magical birds very similar both in appearance and actions. *Khyung* is a horned eagle, a heavenly divinity of which there are two broad categories: one is a class of worldly gods while the other is Wisdom *Khyung* – an emanation of Tonpa Shenrab and a *yidam* or Buddha-form.

---

[87] Bazarov, *Tainstva*, p. 87.

[88] Names removed for 'security' purposes. While Bɵ should and do know these spirits it's not necessary for the general public.

[89] Bazarov, *Tainstva*, p. 88.

Fig. 11. Wisdom Khyung.

Fig. 12. Worldly Khyung (Garuda)
Newari wood-carving, Bhaktapur.

The worldly *Khyung* lives on the summit of the World Mountain, Rirab, in the Upper Sphere of Existence and is said to possess great magical powers, be able to fly anywhere in the universe and have great knowledge. One of the original Bönpo clans bears its name and is said to have descended from *Khyung*. In the far distant past, there was enmity between *Khyung* and *Lu* and this destabilized the universe. However, through the power of his realization, Tonpa Shenrab was able to end the conflict and restore harmony in the world. Today we can still find a Yungdrung Bön rite for reconciling *Khyung* and *Chusin*[90] (*Makaru*), a mythical water-monster.[91]

Among the Bönpo *Drala* deities we find many in the form of *Khyung* or other types of eagles and hawks. One is the forefather of the armies of the *Drala* of Primordial Knowledge,[92] Khyungnag Yu'i Ralpachen,[93] Black Khyung with a Turquoise Mane. He is said to dwell in the world of non-being while watching from the world of being. He is the Lord of all Existence, *Drala* of both Being and Non-Being.[94] He emanated armies

---

90 Tib. chu sring.

91 See Lopön Tenzin Namdak/Karin Gungal, *Der heilende Garuda: Ein Stück Bön-Tradition* (Dietikon, Schweiz: Garuda Verlag, 1998), pp. 19–34.

92 Tib. ye mkhyen sgra bla.

93 Tib. Khyung nag g.Yu'i Ral pa can.

94 Tib. yod med gnyis kyi sgra bla.

of *Drala* among whom we find Khyungnag Shazan,[95] Black Carnivorous Khyung, and Ludul Khyungchen,[96] Great Khyung Subduer of the *Lu.*[97]

On the border of darkness and light[98] dwells the *Drala* of Light and Darkness[99] Khading Sergyi Chyanmigchen,[100] Golden-Eyed Eagle. He dwells in the world of darkness but watches through the lamp of Light and encompasses both Darkness and Light. On the border between *Ye* and *Ngam*[101] dwells the *Drala* of *Ye* and *Ngam*[102] Gyathra Chagkyi Chuderchen,[103] Hawk with an Iron Beak. He dwells in the world of *Ngam* while watching from the world of *Ye*.

These *Drala* are positioned in the area of equanimity, in neutral territory, unsoiled by the extremes of the universe's polar forces and this reminds us of the position of Sege'en Sebdeg Tengeri. As we have seen, he possesses the highest knowledge of magic and wizardry, controls the Main Entrance Gate and it is his son, White-Headed Eagle Khaan Burged,[104] who was sent to earth to transmit the knowledge of Bɵ Murgel to Buryats. Like his father, he dwells in the neutral territory between the lands of White and Black Tengeri but is counted among the White Tengeri. There are, then, certain parallels here. In particular Khaan Burged can be directly compared with Khading Sergyi Chyanmigchen as both straddle the borders of polar forces. Some Bɵ hold the view that because the knowledge of Bɵ Murgel was transmitted by a neutral Tengeri who did not take sides, the Bɵ, too, should remain impartial and aim their actions at restoring equilibrium in any given situation.

The mystical eagle is accorded a place of honour in Bɵ Murgel. Myths accredit him with bringing fire from the sky to earth and, most

---

95 Tib. Khyung nag Sha zan.

96 Tib. Klu 'dul Khyung chen.

97 See Norbu, *Drung Deu and* Bön, p. 54 and Adriano Clemente, *The Sgra Bla, Gods of the Ancestors of Gshen-rab Mi-bo*, (Merigar, Arcidosso: Shang Shung Edizioni, 1995), pp. 10-12.

98 Tib. mun snang gi so mtshams.

99 Tib. snang mun gi sgra bla.

100 Tib. mKha' lding gSer gyi sPyan mig can.

101 Tib. ye ngam gyi so mtshams.

102 Tib. ye ngam gyi sgra bla.

103 Tib. Bya khra lCags kyi mChu sder can.

104 He is known under the following names: Bur. Хаан бургэд (Khaan Burged), Хаан Гарууди (Khaan Garudi), Хотой Бургэд (Hotoi Burged). I use the first name in order to avoid confusion with Khaan Hoto Baabai's son who bears the same name. The name Khaan Garuudi is clearly the result of later Buddhist influence.

importantly, the Tengeri sent him to teach Bɵ Murgel to Buryats and he fathered the first Buryatian Bɵ priest. Among the many Bɵ deities appearing in the form of an eagle, of particular interest to us here are the central deities of the ancient cult of the Lord of Olhon, Khaan Hoto Baabai and his son Hotoi Burged. Both names include the word *hoto/hotoi* which came into Buryatian from the Yakut language where *hotoi* means 'eagle'. In fact, in the name 'Hotoi Burged' both parts have the same meaning: 'eagle', first in Yakut and then in Buryatian. According to the Bɵ of the Hori tribe, Khaan Hoto Baabai and his son take the form of huge eagles with iron wings, steel beaks and golden letters of wisdom-knowledge are inscribed on their metal chests. They are friendly with the *Lusuut* water-spirits of Lake Baikal, some of which also form part of their retinues. This reminds us of the reconciliation of *Khyung* and *Chusin* brought about by Tonpa Shenrab and indeed, is quite an interesting parallel as, in the majority of archaic cultures, the eagle is the snake's arch-enemy; these two eagle-snake alliances therefore do stand out. This similarity is underlined by the fact that both Buryatian Hotoi Burged and Tibetan *Khyung* are associated with the energy of fire. The form and attributes of the *Drala* above are very similar to those of Khaan Hoto Baabai and Hotoi Burged.

Although nowadays they are considered to be the local *Ezhen* of Olhon, Khaan Hoto Baabai and Hotoi Burged may well represent original archaic deities fully comparable with Tibetan *Khyung*. This is supported not only by the similarities discussed above, but also by their very names. As the Yakuts lived on the northern shore of Baikal and Olhon Island before Buryats, we can assume that the cult of Hotoi Eagle was practised before the arrival of Buryats there and this Owner may well have played a more important role than merely lord of an island. There is some confusion about the status of these two *Ezhens*, their origins and functions, and it is likely that later the Buryats, who had their own Eagle cult, superimposed their version over the preceding local cult. Khaan Hotoi Baabai is sometimes considered to be a son of Hormusta Tengeri and is also known under names which do not feature the word 'eagle'.[105] A further twist is that Sege'en Sebdeg's son, like Khaan Hotoi Baabai's son, is also called Hotoi Burged (Khaan Burged). In my understanding these two deities are one and the same but were split somehow later and became associated with different parents. Be that as it may, what is significant here is that all the Bɵ Murgel and Bönpo eagle-deities discussed in this section resemble one another closely in

---

[105] See in the description in ch. I.

their appearance, attributes, dwelling place and functions and, I would suggest, could ultimately be traced to similar origins.

The concept of Owners in Bön

The belief in Owners or Lords is a key concept found in both Bön and Bɵ Murgel. In both traditions, the title 'Owner' or 'Lord' does not refer to a particular class of spirits or gods but denotes instead their function and position in the hierarchy of beings controlling the universe. This concept is of paramount importance for understanding the principle behind any kind of offering ritual and many types of healing and divination in Prehistoric Bön, Bɵ Murgel and Yungdrung Bön, particularly the Causal Vehicles. Both Bɵ Murgel and Bön hold that the external world is dominated and controlled by various kinds of non-human beings who have power over its various aspects and energies. If humans upset or irritate these beings in any way, they are capable of causing many problems and misfortunes for an individual and for humanity as a whole. Here is an explanation of this point by Yongdzin Lopön Tenzin Namdak:

> Generally we can only see the earth [and not the non-material beings which in habit it], but spiritually [the world] is in fact controlled by Earth Gods. We say the earth is formed as a turtle and that the earth-gods look like turtles, but their appearance is not so important because they are spirits which are not usually visible to humans. They are a different race but they are very powerful Owners of the earth. The biggest is the Owner of the Universe and the smallest is an earth-god the size of a finger, yet it is still an Owner. Whenever we do anything rough [to the earth] that damages them even though we can't see them. As a result they challenge us. If somebody always has problems, they are coming from these earth-gods. Why? Because they take a kind of revenge on whoever destroys them. […] We don't know because we don't see them, and therefore we don't care about them or trust that they exist, but these earth-gods themselves are alive and own their property like a country, so if we take things [from the soil] they think we are robbing them or taking things by force and consequently they take revenge on us.[106]

However, we must once again draw a distinction here between Prehistoric Bön and Yungdrung Bön as the concept of Owners differs in Prehistoric Bön and different levels of Yungdrung Bön. In some archaic

---

[106] Namdak, *Nine Ways* I, *Bön of Cause*, pp. 21–22.

animistic belief systems water, fire, earth, trees etc. are themselves worshipped as actual deities while other systems worship the invisible beings dwelling within the elements. According to the level of Causal Bön, there are powerful Owners of Earth, Water, Fire and so on who control the energies of these respective elements. According to the level of Bönpo Tantra, the elements do not actually exist but are empty form which manifests as a divinity, a tantric *yidam* which can be peaceful, wrathful, joyful and so forth. According to the Dzogchen level, while the existence of these beings is acknowledged, they are considered as neither friends nor enemies; because everything is encompassed by the same fundamental nature, gods and demons cannot harm an advanced Dzogchen practitioner in the same way as fire cannot burn fire and water cannot drown water.

The teachings of Causal Bön contain very precise explanations about these powerful Owners as many astrological and healing rituals are designed to repay them for offences and distress caused by humans, either knowingly or unknowingly. These beings are worldly beings and as such are similar to humans in that they are controlled by their emotions; when they are irritated or offended they retaliate with diseases and disasters but if they are befriended they may become powerful helpers and allies, so it is important to court their friendship.

Owners in the Kabtse diagram

Now let us look into the description of these Owners or Lords and what they control. This is mainly explained in the First Way of Bön, *Chashen Thegpa*, particularly in the sections on Astrology and Ritual. The main Owners of the universe are the *Sadag* earth-gods who are symbolically depicted on an astrological diagram called *Kabtse.*[107] This astrological chart is used to calculate important astrological conjunctions when the human energy system is particularly susceptible to the energy of these and other non-human beings, thereby magnifying the disturbances or benefits they can cause.

The Owner of the universe is represented as a great turtle with concentric circles on the back of his shell. The inner circle has nine coloured squares with the numbers one to nine and represents the Nine *Mewa*[108] Owners, nine powerful *Sadag*, and their relation to the Five Elements. The next circle has eight *parkha* diagrams arranged in the four

[107] Tib. gab rtse.

[108] Tib. sme ba dgu

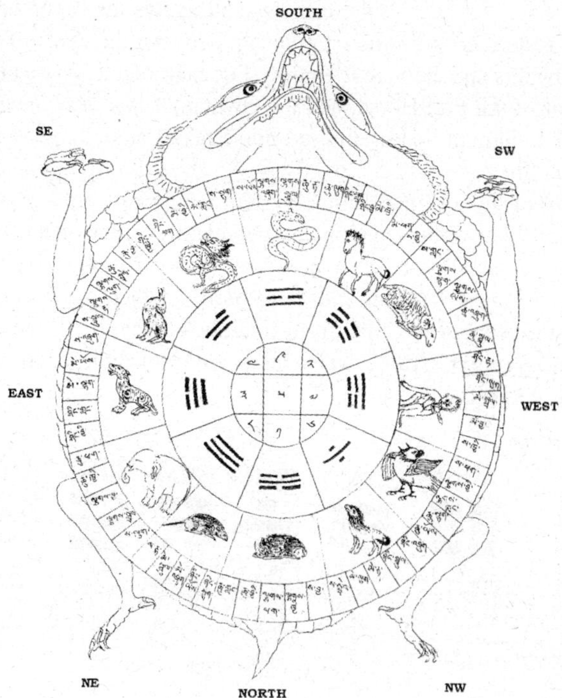

Fig. 13. Bönpo Kabtse *diagram.*

cardinal and four intermediate directions which represent Eight *Parkha* Earth Gods,[109] each of which also has a helper and destroyer.

The next circle represents Twelve *Lo*[110] or Year Owners of the twelve year cycle: Mouse, Elephant, Tiger, Rabbit, Dragon, Snake, Horse, Sheep, Monkey, *Khyung*-eagle, Dog and Boar.[111] This system is explained in the cycle *Lodzö Chunyi*,[112] *The Treasure of the Years*. In fact, each year has not just one Owner but many. There is a king, queen, servants, messengers etc. who look like humans apart from their head which is in keeping with the respective animal of the year they own.

---

[109] Tib. sPar kha brgyad kyi sa bdag.

[110] Tib. lo.

[111] In Tibetan Buddhist astrology, the twelve animals are the same with the exceptions of the Elephant which is replaced with an Ox, and the Khyung which is replaced with a Bird.

[112] Tib. Lo mdzod bcu nyis.

The outer circle on the turtle's shell shows the Sixty-Year Cycle[113] which is derived from the relationship between the cycle of the Twelve Year Owners and the Five Elements. For example, if we are talking about the year of the Fire Horse then the Owners of that year have red bodies similar to human bodies and red horse heads as red corresponds to the element fire.

Out of this original Bönpo system taught by Tonpa Shenrab Miwo many astrological, divination and geomantic systems later developed in China, the Far East and elsewhere in Asia. Some of the most well-known are the Chinese *I Ching* and *Feng Shui*[114] which are based on Bönpo teachings brought to China from Central Asia by the Chinese King Gya Kongtse Trulgyi Gyalpo who was a direct disciple of Tonpa Shenrab Miwo.

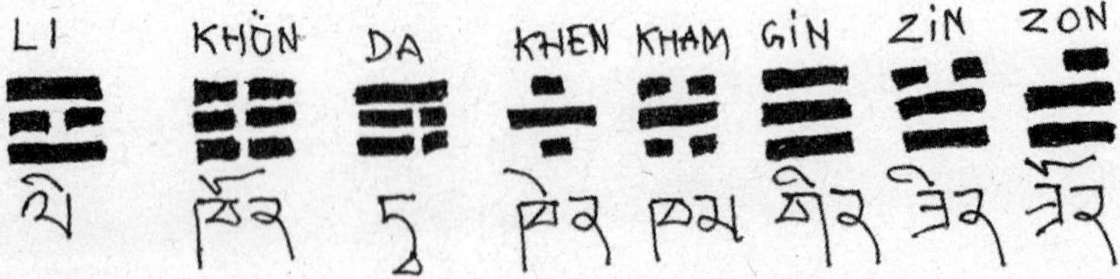

Fig. 14. Eight parkha *of the Bönpo astrological system.*

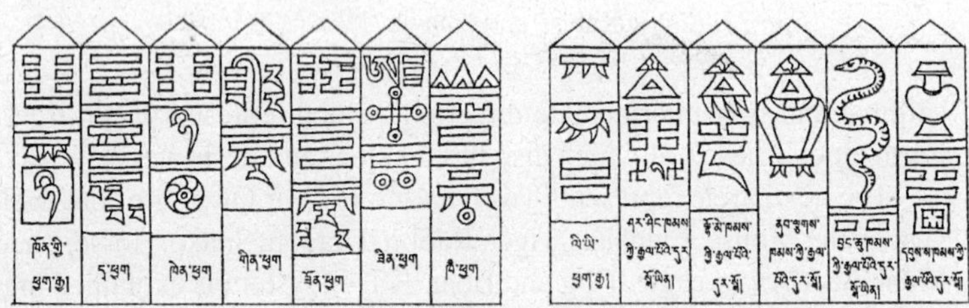

Fig. 15. Eight Parkha, *Four Directions and the Centre.*

Owners of the Four Directions and the Centre

The Owners of the Four Directions and the Centre are as follows:

The Guardians of the east are a red tiger and a glinting-blue raven;
The Guardian of the south is a dragon with a red crest;
The Guardian of the north is a tortoise with a yellow shell;

---

113 Tib. lo rgan drug cu.

114 Tib. sa chog.

The Guardian of the west is a red bird with red feathers;
The Guardians of the centre are the *Tenma*[115] Earth Goddess
who holds a precious vessel,
and the Earth God Tsangtsang Khorwa[116] who holds a golden wheel.[117]

Owners of the Elements

An important group of Owners are the Four Great Owners of the Elements[118] which are:

- *Lu* – Water Owners who are generally depicted with the upper body of a human, a snake decoration on the head and the lower body of a snake or a fish tail.
  Any activity involving water affects these beings so it is important to perform appropriate rituals before undertaking any irrigation works or any major works to do with water in order to ask their permission and inform them. Activities such as polluting and damming waterways cause the *Lu* to suffer bitterly and so they exact revenge on humans by sending diseases, especially skin and eye diseases and certain types of cancers.
- *Nyen* – Tree Owners who look similar to humans and wear white head-dresses.
  As forests, trees and bushes are their living space, any activity such as forest clearing or cutting trees disturbs them. Once disturbed these *Nyen* retaliate with various diseases which include some kinds of cancers.

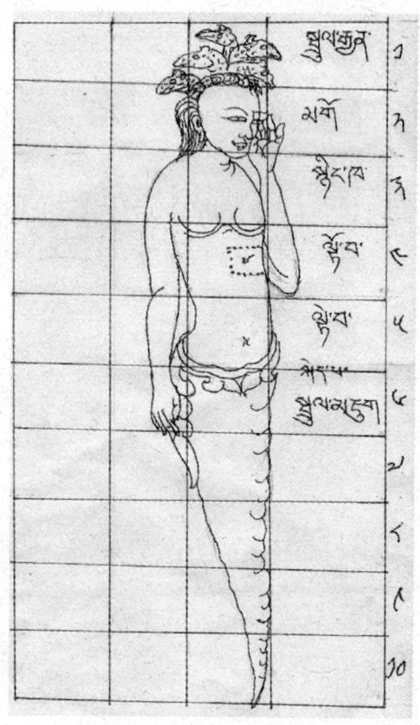

Fig. 16. Thogche *earth god.*

[115] Tib. rten ma.
[116] Tib. gtsang gtsang 'khor ba.
[117] Namdak, *Nine Ways* I, *Bön of Fruit*, p. 146.
[118] Tib. gnyan chen sde bzhi.

- *Tod*[119] – Rock Owners who crawl and look like tortoises. Rocks are their natural living space so when humans undertake activities such as quarrying, these beings' environment is affected causing them distress and suffering. They, too, retaliate with diseases.
- *Sadag* – Earth Owners who can be of various shapes and forms.

  Any activity involving earth such as digging, flooding the ground, mining or building houses causes problems for these beings. In particular, there is a class of *Sadag* called *Thogche*[120] which perceive the area of ground where they dwell as their own body and consequently when this ground is used or damaged in any way they experience this as though their own body were being scraped, bitten or cut into pieces. Therefore, before undertaking any activity to do with the earth, it is necessary to perform special rituals in order not to disturb them.

Fig. 17. Machen Pomra.

Yullha/Yulsa[121] *and Zhidag*[122]

These two kinds of Owners are very important as they are the beings who control geographical features. The difference between *Yullha* and *Zhidag* lies not in the class of beings they belong to but rather in the size of the territory a god or spirit rules. *Yullha* are the Owners of the Country and other lesser gods controlling specific locations are subordinate to them. *Yullha* are often powerful mountain gods such as Machen Pomra[123] and Yarlha Shampo,[124] protectors of the early Tibetan Bönpo kingdom and its royal dynasty. Some

[119] Tib. stod.
[120] Tib. lto phye.
[121] Tib. yul lha, yul sa.
[122] Tib. gzhi bdag.
[123] Tib. rMa chen spom ra.
[124] Tib. Yar lung gi Yar lha Sham po.

sources say *Zhidag* belong primarily to the classes of *Lu*, *Nyen*, *Tod* and *Sadag*, although they are not restricted to these beings alone.

The concept of Owners in Buryatian Bө Murgel

In Buryatian Bө Murgel we find exactly the same concept of Owners or Lords, the only difference being that the various types of Owners are not as precisely classified as they are in Bön. The Bө call these Owners or Lords '*Ezhen'*, which is a very general name; any kind of spirit or god can be called *Ezhen* if they have the function of *Ezhen* i.e. if they own or control certain aspects or energies of the universe. That would make Huhe Münhe Tengeri, Eternal Blue Sky, who controls everything in the universe, the supreme *Ezhen*. In practice, however, the name *Ezhen* is most often applied to the powerful beings dominating the energies and geographical features of the Middle World. For example, besides the normal roads used by humans there are also rarely used or long abandoned roads which serve as the transport arteries of the local *Ezhen*. In one of my journeys in Tunka I stumbled upon such a road:

> While in Tunka we visited several Bө. Our friends had some personal problems, so they were asking the Bө to resolve them. After one such visit, we stayed overnight in a place called Arshan. 'Arshan' means healing spring in Buryatian, and people come there from all over the Republic, attracted by the healing properties of the waters there. We went for a long walk the next morning. All the trees near the springs were festooned with multicoloured ribbons which people leave there as offerings to the local gods. We wandered further and soon got lost in the forest. I sat on the boulder and prayed to be shown the way. Suddenly I was very confident and we took a path which was barely visible. As we walked through the forest, we became aware of the invisible presence of some power. After a while I started to 'see' it as very tall old woman wearing traditional Buryatian dress. Later I was told that she was one of the three *Hoymariy Tebi* – Hoymariy Grandmothers,[125] the local *Ezhen* or Owners of the land and protectresses of Bө Murgel. Without any difficulties we shortly found ourselves on the edge of the forest. Everybody was relieved – sometimes it can be very serious if you are lost in *taiga*, it may take many days, sometimes weeks to find the way.[126]

---

[125] Bur. Хоймарий тээбии.

[126] A passage from my unpublished diary, *The Way of the Wind*.

Fig. 18. End of the spirit-path. Behind are the holy peaks of Sayan Mountains. Tunka, 1993.

Fig. 19. Sagaan Ebugen, the White Elder.

The two most powerful *Ezhen* in the Middle World are the goddess Etugen, *Ezhen* of all Earth, and Sagaan Ebugen, *Ezhen* of Earth-Water. These two control the dimension of our planet earth. According to Bönpo reckoning these two would probably be classified as Lords of the *Sadag* earth-gods.

Khaan Shargai Noyon and Buha Noyon Baabai, the leaders of fifty Western White Haats, and Khaan Doshkhon Noyon, the leader of forty Eastern Black *Haats* can be said to be Buryatian equivalents of Tibetan *Yullha* as they reside on important mountains and command the Sayan mountain range as well as all the land around Lake Baikal, and are the protectors of the Buryatian nation. Another important *Ezhen* comparable to the *Yullha* is Bahar Hara Khaan, god of Lake Baikal.

Bayan Hangai Khaan, *Ezhen* of the *taiga* and Owner of all the plants and animals, is comparable to the kings of *Nyen* and also acts as *Sogdag*, the Owner of Life-Force. This, again, is a general term and can be applied to any kind of god or spirit who has the capacity to master the *sog*,[127] life-force known in Buryatian as *amin.*[128] '*Sogdag*' is an equivalent term for Buryatian '*Zayaan*', a general term denoting a god or spirit who can control the fate or destiny of living creatures. In some cases *Zayaan* is used as a synonym for *Ezhen*. For the Owner(s) of Fire, for example, both titles are used. The Owners of Fire and Hearth, Gal Zayaashi[129] and Gol Zayaashi,[130] are directly comparable in their function to Bönpo *Melha*[131] and *Thablha*[132] although they differ in appearance. There are many other such 'pairs' but we cannot list them all here.

---

[127] Tib. srog.

[128] Bur. амин or Bur. амь.

[129] Bur. Гал заяаши.

[130] Bur. Гол заяаши.

[131] Tib. me lha.

[132] Tib. thab lha.

CHAPTER VI

Gods of the Prehistoric Bön of Eurasia in the Religions of Ancient Central Asia

When I began writing down my observations on parallel aspects of Bө Murgel and Bön in 1988 I had an inkling that Hormusta Tengeri of Bө Murgel and Nyipangse of Bön may, in fact, be the same god known under different names. As I was researching this, I accidentally stumbled upon an interesting discovery, an important god called Hormuzd Yazad (Yazata) of the Zoroastrian pantheon, who I believe to be the same as Hormusta Tengeri. Let's take a look at the similarities between these sky-gods to see if there are any grounds on which we can claim they are identical.

Hormusta and Nyipangse

Hormusta

We met Hormusta in Chapter III so the reader will remember he is a sky-god who resides right on the top of Sumber World Mountain in the vast expanse of the Sky. He is one of the sons of Algan Sagaan Tengeri and the leader of the Fifty-Five (Thirty-Three) White Tengeri. In some Hori Buryat traditions he is considered the leader of all Tengeri. He has many names. In Buryatia and Mongolia he is known as Hormusta Tengeri, Khaan Hormuzda, Hürmasta Tengeri, Khaan Tyurmas Tengeri, Tyurmes Tengeri, Hirmus Tengeri and Khaan Hërmos Tengeri; in Tuva as Kurbustu; and in Altai as Kurbustan Aakai. A long-living, white sky-god endowed with formidable magical powers, he appears as a white warrior clad in a white cloak with ninety-nine buttons. Three layers of impenetrable armour protect his body and his white hat is as bright as a star. He carries a spear with a white pennant, a silver quiver with magical arrows, and a yellow bow in a silver bow case as well as a lasso with thirteen knots and a whip with eighty-eight knots. His steed is a white horse the size of a mountain and he rides in the midst of the White Tengeri

Fig. 1. Hormusta Tengeri.

and their messengers. He is the leader of Tengeri, their children and grandchildren the *Haats, Ezhens* and *Zayaans* of the Middle World. He is the protector of all living creatures, the patron of White Bө and White Bө-smiths, watching over virtue and punishing evil. He also controls the weather and sends good rains which make grasses grow. He represents the positive aspect of the universal energy.

Nyipangse

Nyipangse is one of Yungdrung Bön's ancient protectors and, in particular, he is the main protector of the Dzogchen cycle of *Zhang Zhung Nyen Gyud.* He is an ancient sky-god of Zhang Zhung. In the language of Zhang Zhung his name means 'sun god' with *nyi* being an abbreviation of the Zhang Zhung word *nyi ri*[1] and *se*[2] being equivalent to Tibetan *lha.*

---

1 Z-zng. nyi ri.
2 Z-zng. sad.

Fig. 2. Werro Nyipangse.

Like Hormusta, Nyipangse is known by many names, two of the principal ones being Dapangse[3] ('moon god') and Zhapangse[4] ('rainbow god'). All these names underline Nyipangse's classification as a sky-god. However, Nyipangse isn't merely a sky-god. According to the *Zhang Zhung Nyen Gyud*, he is the chief among the sky-gods of Zhang Zhung and resides in the southwestern part of the sky on the summit of Mount Meru, the World Mountain. It was his position as chief of the sky-gods that made him the ideal candidate for principal guardian of this Bönpo Dzogchen cycle and all of the three-hundred and sixty types of Bön practised by the Bönpo *Mahasiddha* Gyerpung Nangzher Lödpo who subdued him and put him under oath in the eighth century AD. Nyipangse mainly appears as a man as white as a conch shell, as tall as a spear, dressed in white silk robes and wearing a white turban. A tiger-sword in a leopard skin scabbard hangs at his waist and in his hand he holds a spear with a triangular white silk pennant. He rides a white stallion with a red harness and is surrounded by a retinue of one thousand gods.

The magnitude of Nyipangse's power is clear from his invocations[5] which give the different appellations by which he is known in the Four Directions of the earth and the Centre:

– Shelgying Karpo Nyipangse[6] – Powerful White Crystal Sun-God in the Centre (Zhang Zhung Confederation);

---

3 Tib. Zla pang sad.

4 Tib. gZha' pang sad.

5 See translations of the two main invocations of Nyipangse: *sNyan rgyud bka' srung srog bdag rgyal po nyi pang sad* and *rGya lpo nyi pang sad dang sman mognyis kyi bskul ba* in Kvaerne, *The Bon Religion,* pp. 109–111; and Reynolds, *The Oral Tradition,* pp. 360–365.

6 Tib. Shel 'gying dKar po Nyi pang sad.

- Sogdag Sidpa Gyalpo[7] – Owner of the Life-Force (and) King of Existence in the North (country of Phrom (Throm)[8]);
- Shelgying Karpo[9] – Powerful White-Shining Crystal in the West (country of Tagzig);
  - Tsangpa Dunggi Thortsugchen[10] – Brahma with White Conch Shell topknot in the South (country of India);
  - Gyalpo Dapangse[11] – King Moon-God in the East (country of China);
  - Kyahrang Chenpo[12] – Great Kyahrang in the Centre (country of Tibet).

Nyipangse has eight further manifestations called the Five Kinds of Great Kings[13] who also demonstrate his control over the Four Directions and the Centre:

Nyipangse and Dapangse;
Zhapangse and Werro Gyalpo;[14]
Namkha Gyalpo,[15] Yacho Gyalpo,[16] Gyalpo Chenpo Tsugphüchen;[17]
Gyachen Nyipangse[18] and his retinue.

Among these, the name 'Namkha Gyalpo' translates as 'the King of Space/Sky', which further emphasizes his nature as a sky-god.

---

7 Tib. Srog bdag Srid pa'i rGyal po.
8 Tib. Phrom/Khrom; for a discussion on location and identity of this country see below.
9 Tib. Shel 'gying dKar po.
10 Tib. Tshangs pa Dung gi Thor tshug can.
11 Tib. rGyal po Zla pang sad.
12 Tib. sKya hrang (trang) Chen po.
13 Tib. rgyal po chen po sde lnga – five classes of the great kings.
14 Tib. Wer ro rGyal po; *werro* is a Zhang Zhung word meaning 'king' so here we have a combined Zhang Zhung-Tibetan name where 'king' is doubled in a similar way to the name of the Buryatian Eagle-Tengeri Hotoi Burged discussed in the previous chapter.
15 Tib. Nam mkha' rGyal po.
16 Tib. Yo co rGyal po.
17 Tib. rGyal po Chen po gTsug phud can.
18 Tib. rGya chen Nyi pang sad.

Parallels between Nyipangse and Hormusta

If we compare these two gods of Buryatian Bө Murgel and Tibetan Bön, their descriptions match on many counts. They both have a peaceful countenance, both are warriors clad in white with white headdresses, both hold spears with white pennants and both ride on white horses thronged by their retinue of vassal gods. They both reside in the dimension of the Sky on the top of the World Mountain (Sumber/Meru). Moreover, they both have the same function, namely, as king of the sky-gods they protect virtue and virtuous practitioners (White Bө/Shenpos).

As Hormusta and Nyipangse resemble one another so closely not only in terms of their appearance but also in terms of their function and position, it is highly likely that we are dealing with the same deity known by different names to the Buryatian Bө and the Tibetan Bönpo.

Parallels with Indra

There are direct references which show that both Hormusta and Nyipangse are, in fact, the same as the Indian god Indra. In the opening of the Mongolian version of the epic tale *Gesar* we read:

> Kormuzda, father of gods, ruler over the high heavens and guardian of the earth, came down from the great mountain of Sumeru and knelt at the feet of the Buddha, paying homage and requesting the Buddha's Blessing.[19]

In the Tibetan Buddhist version of this great epic, it is the god Indra who bows at the Buddha's feet. Here, in this Mongolian version, we see Hormusta in the place of Indra, even though this, too, is a Buddhist version of *Gesar*, a later adaptation from the Tibetan, and not the original Buryatian *Geser* epic, which most probably predates the Tibetan Buddhist one.[20] Why is this? We can only deduce that Hormusta's functions as leader of the virtuous sky-gods are identical to those of Indra.[21]

---

[19] Adapted by Zara Wallace, *Gesar! The Wondrous Adventures of King Gesar (Mongolian version),* (Berkeley: Dharma Publishing, 1991), p.3.

[20] It is not possible to compare the Buryatian Geser epic with the Tibetan version here in detail but there are valid reasons to suggest that the Buryatian version may be older than the Tibetan as it mentions the original Tengeri sky-gods of the Bө pantheon and a number of other cultural references pointing to its authenticity rather than being just a mere copy of the Tibetan Buddhist version. This theory is briefly explored below.

[21] Although some scholars maintain that the association of Hormusta with Indra

If Hormusta can be equated with Indra, then so, too, can Nyipangse. In the text describing how Nyipangse was subdued by Gyerpung Nangzher Lödpo using a 'magical missile'[22] and swore to protect Yungdrung Bön and the lineage of *Zhang Zhung Nyen Gyud,* he is addressed as Wangchengyi Gyalpo[23] (King of Supreme Power), a title which corresponds to the Sanskrit name Mahendraraja, one of Indra's appellations.[24] Another common name for Indra in Tibet is Gyagyin.[25]

We can see, then, that not only are Hormusta and Nyipangse likely to be one and the same deity because of their similarities, but also because they have both been interchanged with Indra.

Nyipangse and Pehar

It is also interesting to note that Nyipangse is sometimes compared with Pehar, one of the main protectors of Tibetan Buddhism. Réne de Nebesky-Wojkowitz, for instance, brings up some parallels between the two deities in his *Oracles and Demons of Tibet.*[26] Although these deities have both been propitiated in the same geographical region and have common cultural attributes, they are not, in my opinion, directly related. I shall demonstrate this below.

Fig. 3. Gyalpo Pehar.

Common characteristics

The reason for suggesting Nyipangse and Pehar might be the same deity stems from the fact that there are several appellations which are used for both of them (Tsangpa Karpo, Tsangpa Karpo Dunggi Thortsugchen, and Shelgying Karpo) and the manifestations bearing these names are outwardly very similar. More weight is added to this theory as, according to

---

is due to much later Buddhist influence I believe the connection goes back to prehistory. This will be demonstrated below.

22 Tib. btswo.

23 Tib. dBang chen gyi rGyal po.

24 Reynolds, *The Oral Tradition*, p.357.

25 Tib. brGya sbyin.

26 Nebesky-Wojkowitz, *Oracles and Demons*, pp. 94–133, 145–153.

Nebesky-Wojkowitz, Pehar was known to the Bönpo of Zhang Zhung as the Bön protector Tsanggi Khule Laggu.[27]

Differences

Despite these outer similarities, Nyipangse and Pehar belong to different classes of gods: Nyipangse is *Lha* while Pehar is *Gyalpo*. What is more, the histories of these two gods are completely different. According to Yongdzin Lopön Tenzin Namdak the epithet *gyalpo*, found in several names by which Nyipangse is known in various countries, does not signify that he belongs to the *Gyalpo* class, as Nebesky-Wojkowitz thought, but is simply an honorific title. Nyipangse's designation is undoubtedly *Lha*, a sky-god, as is clear from the Zhang Zhung word *se*, an integral part of many of his names, which translates into Tibetan as *lha*.

Reconstruction of the history and origins of Pehar

The story of how Pehar became a protector of Tibetan Buddhism is very complex with several versions giving different and sometimes contradictory accounts. The reason for these discrepancies is, I believe, that some Buddhist masters endeavoured to connect Pehar to India, the holy source of their religion; with the advent of Indian Buddhism in Tibet there was a strong movement in Tibet to relate many aspects of their native culture and religion to India, which was perceived as sacred and superior, denigrating their own history in the process. Such accounts claim that Pehar was initially a god of Zahor in Bengal and went from there to Tibet when Indian Buddhism was introduced.

Another version of Pehar's history, which in my opinion is the original one, says that before coming to Tibet he was a protective god of Uighur[28] tribes in the country of Hor. At that time Pehar's seat was in the temple of an undefined religious community[29] at Bhata Hor (Barda Hor)[30] where he was known as Pholha Namtheb Karpo,[31] Namthib Karpo[32] or Namlha Karpo.[33] *Pholha*[34] means 'male ancestral god', *namtheb/namthib*

---

[27] Tib. gTsang gi Khu le Lag dgu. Ibid., p. 97.

[28] Tib. Yu gur. Yugur actually seem to be a distinct ethnic group now, see Chinese Nationalities (China Nationality Photography and Art Press, Bejing, 1989).

[29] Tib. sgom rwa, lit. 'meditation school'.

[30] Tib. Bar mda' Hor.

[31] Tib. Pho lha gNam theb dKar po.

[32] Tib. gNam thib dKar po.

[33] Tib. gNam lha dKar po.

[34] Tib. pho lha.

karpo means 'white clouded sky' and *namlha karpo* means 'white sky-god'. These names must be Tibetan translations of Pehar's original name, which we can assume was in Uighur or some other Tyurkic or proto-Mongol language. The Tibetan translation nevertheless seems to have retained a part of the original name in the original language: *theb* or *thib*. We can say with a high degree of certainty that in the seventh and the first half of the eighth centuries AD the Uighur religion was a stream of Prehistoric Bön, a kind of Bө Murgel involving the worship of Eternal Blue Sky and Tengeri sky-gods. If we assume that Pehar was a deity of the Uighur pantheon, from this perspective the name *namtheb* or 'white clouded sky' makes no sense; the Sky was worshiped as clear and blue, the pristine ancestor of all and so a cloudy sky, even if white, has no religious significance in Bө Murgel.

The suggestion that the component *-theb* is a non-Tibetan element in the translation of Pehar's name is further strengthened by the many other variants of the name Namtheb Karpo where *theb* is replaced by similar-sounding words with divergent meanings: Tib. *gNam rde'u dKar po, gNam sde dKar po, gNam thel dKar po, gNam the dKar po, gNam the'u dKar po*. The last two variations (Tib. *the*, *the'u*) refer to a class of spirits called *Theurang*,[35] an ancient class of pre-Buddhist gods of Tibet. Some *Theurang* appear as monopods, others have snake-tails instead of legs. They are said to have inhabited the earth before humans did and as such, are certainly not sky-gods. This probably gave grounds for another version of Pehar's history which refers to him as a *Theurang*. However, in my opinion all these names simply demonstrate attempts to 'Tibetanize' the component *theb* and give this part of Pehar's original name some meaning in Tibetan. If we look at modern Buryatian and Mongolian languages which trace back to proto-Mongol and later Tyurkic languages such as were spoken by the Uighurs, *teb*[36] is a prefix indicating the superlative, often meaning 'supreme' or 'best' when used in combination with other words. A pertinent example here is Chingis Khaan's rival, the supreme Bө Teb Tengeri. If we take Tibetan *theb* as a phonetic transcription of proto-Mongol/Tyurkic *teb* then we can translate Pehar's name back into Buryatian, which retains older forms of the Mongolian language than modern Mongolian itself. Thus *pholha* becomes either *zayaan tengeri*[37] or *ongon tengeri*;[38] *namtheb* becomes

---

35 Tib. the'u rang.

36 Bur. тэб.

37 Bur. Заяаан тэнгэри.

38 Bur. Онгон тэнгэри.

teb tengeri[39] and *karpo* becomes *sagaan.*[40] So Pehar's original name was probably close to Buryatian Zayaan Sagaan Teb-Tengeri (Divine Ancestor White Supreme Tengeri) or Ongon Sagaan Teb-Tengeri (White Ongon SupremeTengeri). However, it is more likely that we are dealing here with variations of the two names: Zayaan/Ongon Teb-Tengeri (Divine Ancestor Supreme Tengeri), and Sagaan Tengeri (White Tengeri). This may lead us to conclude that the original Uighur deity known in Tibet as Pehar was some kind of White Tengeri. Indeed, Zayaan Sagaan Tengeri is one of Hormusta Tengeri's many appellations, so it is very tempting to say that Pehar is Hormusta Tengeri, and, by association, the same as Nyipangse.

However, there are several inconsistencies which demonstrate that this is not the case and that Pehar cannot be equated with either Nyipangse or Hormusta as he is in fact not a sky-dwelling god. Firstly, if we translate *pholha* as *ongon* it indicates that Pehar is not a Tengeri because *Ongons* are not sky-gods but ancestral protector-sprits of the Middle World, often spirits of powerful Bɵ, Utgan or *khaans*.

Furthermore, Pehar is said to have had a fixed residence at the Uighur Bhata Hor meditation temple. This is not a characteristic of sky-dwelling Tengeri but of some types of *Ongons* or *Haats,* children of the Tengeri who descended to earth to reside in some geographic area or feature and become its Lord-Owners acting as protectors of that locality and the tribes living there, just like Tibetan *Yullha*. Similarly *Tengeriin Buudal*[41] (literally 'Lowered by the Tengeri') who are spirits of outstanding *khaans*, Bɵ, *Noyons* and *khatans*[42] who were sent by the Tengeri to rule and teach religion usually have one or more fixed residences or 'palaces'. *Haats*, *Tengeriin Buudal* and *Ongon* are also sometimes called Tengeri, so this adds to the confusion.

The suggestion that Pehar is not a Tengeri sky-god but rather a *Haat*, *Ongon* or *Tengeriin Buudal* is further strengthened by his genealogy. Although it is as inconsistent as his general history given in Tibetan sources, the most common motif is that of Pehar's father being some kind of *Lha* and his mother being either a *Lumo*[43] water-goddess, a *Menmo* lake-goddess or a *Gyalmo*[44] spirit. In Bɵ Murgel terms, all these equate

---

[39] Bur. Тэб тэнгэри.

[40] Bur. саган.

[41] Bur. Тэнгэриин буудал.

[42] Bur. хатан – princess or queen.

[43] Tib. klu mo.

[44] Tib. rgyal mo.

with the female spirits of the Middle World. From this it is clear that Pehar cannot be a Tengeri but is a *Haat*, *Ongon* or *Tengeriin Buudal*.

Further clues as to which class of beings Pehar may belong to are found in the story of how he came to Tibet. There are many versions of this but the most credible one is contained in the introduction to the *Narthang*[45] edition of the Buddhist *Kanjur*. Here it states that the Tibetan army destroyed the temple of Bhata Hor and took the medium-priest, support and ritual objects associated with the cult of Pehar to Tibet. Pehar followed his support and came to Tibet.[46] This rules out the possibility that Pehar is a *Haat* as *Haats* are the highest deities in the hierarchy of Middle World gods and spirits. They often have more than one dwelling place and would not simply follow the ritual objects dedicated to them. Another text narrating a concurring version of Pehar's origin gives us a direct clue to his original status among the Hor people.[47] In this version it is Guru Padmasambhava himself who orders Pehar to move to Samye from the land of Bhata Hor and he finishes his order with the following words:

> 'And now you, the *pho lha*, we must go!'[48]

As we have seen, the Tibetan *Pholha* male ancestral deities correspond to the Mongol-Buryat *Ongons*. From this text we can firmly establish that Pehar was the chief *Ongon* ancestral spirit of Hor.

This claim is supported by one of the original ritual objects brought to Tibet from the Uighur/Tyurkic cult of Pehar. The object in question is an ancient leather mask known as Sebag,[49] or Sebag Mugpo,[50] the Purple-Brown Leather Mask. This shows the face of an extremely wrathful god and is reputedly imbued with awesome magic. This artifact helps us further clarify the original nature of the Pehar cult among the Tyurkic Uighurs as it provides a link with the living Bө Murgel tradition. Leather masks like that of Pehar are common ritual objects in Buryatian and Mongolian Bө Murgel where they are used as one type of *ongon*-support, a representation, support and dwelling for the powerful *Ongon* ancestral

---

45 Tib. sNar thang.

46 Nebesky-Wojkowitz, *Oracles and Demons,* pp.102–103.

47 'The *mdos* for the King composed by the Master Padmasambhava'. See translation in Karmay, *The Arrow and the Spindle*, p. 354–358.

48 Ibid., p. 356.

49 Tib. bse 'bag.

50 Tib. bse 'bag smug po.

protector-spirits.[51] They are used by Bɵ and Utgan in ritual trance dances when *Ongon* are invoked to enter and possess them, empowering the Bɵ or Utgan wearing them to give prophecies and cure diseases. These masks can only be used by the initiated as they are very intimately connected with the god or spirit they represent and can be extremely dangerous if ordinary people come in direct physical contact with them; the god or spirit whom the mask represents may interpret this as an act of defilement and punish the transgressor with disease or death. This would explain why the original mask of Pehar was kept locked in a wooden chest in the Protectors' House, Tsiumar Gönkhang[52] in Samye monastery apart from the masks of other protective deities which hang openly on the walls. It also explains why only very few of the highest dignitaries of the Tibetan government and Gelugpa hierarchy were allowed to see it, and only on rare occasions.[53] It is also interesting to note that despite the great importance given to the institution of the Tibetan State Oracle, which serves as the mouthpiece of Dorje Dragden,[54] an emanation of Pehar, who is asked for prophecies and advice on important aspects of the government and religious affairs, the original mask of Pehar brought by Tibetan soldiers from Bhata Hor is never used in rites involving the Oracle.

The Sebag provides us with another important clue to further clarify the identity of Pehar. The mask depicts Pehar as an extremely wrathful deity and, according to some sources, was made with coagulated blood instead of glue. It is also said that on some occasions when the mask was taken out of the chest it became as though alive, with its eyes rolling angrily and drops of blood becoming visible on its surface. This reminds us of the Bɵ Murgel tradition of 'enlivening' a Bɵ's ritual attire through placing a sacrificed animal's windpipe and bronchi on the ritual objects and costume then invoking the *Ongon* spirits to come and reside there.[55] Be that as it may, the mere fact that Pehar had a mask serving as his support reveals his identity; in Bɵ Murgel, such masks are never made for White Tengeri nor do the White Tengeri ever accept blood

---

51 *Ongon*-supports can be figures as well as masks often made from the fur or wood. Offerings of food and drink are put in front of them and also smeared onto them to satisfy them and make them do the bidding of a Bɵ, Utgan or household members. Often butter or other substances are smeared on the mouth of the *ongon*.

52 Tib. Tsi'u dmar mGon khang.

53 Nebesky-Wojkowitz, *Oracles and Demons*, p. 103–104.

54 Tib. rDo rje Drag ldan.

55 See ch. VIII.

sacrifices.[56] This confirms that Pehar cannot be a White Tengeri sky-god but an *Ongon*, a lesser god or spirit of the Middle World,[57] probably belonging to the rank of *Khaan* or *Noyon*. As many spirits within the *Khaan* and *Noyon* subsets of *Ongon*s are directly comparable to the Tibetan class of *Gyalpo* spirits, this also tallies with Pehar's designation as a *Gyalpo*, his most common designation found in Tibetan sources. It is very probable that Pehar's mask was a support for a composite group *Ongon* of which Pehar was the chief deity, akin to the Hutkhe Ongon[58] group of the Buryatian Bɵ Murgel, for example, which includes forty-nine spirits and has a single support. The pre-Tibetan Pehar of Bata Hor was probably the leader of a group of spirits, and this would explain his multiple manifestations belonging to different classes of gods and spirits; they would originally have been different spirits controlled by Pehar but when the cult was transferred to Tibet they were explained according to Tibetan Buddhist culture and became 'emanations' of Pehar rather than his subordinates. This suggestion is substantiated by the fact that Dorje Dragden, who possesses the Tibetan State Oracle, is variously described either as Pehar's emanation or as a companion who came with him from the Hor country. The fact that Dorje Dragden in turn is referred to as Five Gyalpo Spirits[59] further strengthens this line of reasoning.

Origins of the word 'pehar'

Analyzing the name *pehar* itself supports the view that we are looking at a powerful spirit of the Middle World and not a sky-god. As with everything else surrounding this mysterious protector, there are many theories about the origin of his name. Some scholars suggest it is derived from the Sanskrit word *vihara* meaning 'monastery', which seems logical bearing in mind Pehar's original residence in the temple of an undefined religious School at Bhata Hor.[60] However, this was located in Uighur territory and it is quite improbable that Uighurs would use

---

56 Although five accept bloodless animal sacrifice on occasion.

57 There are varoius categories of *Ongon* many of which mainly reside in the upper levels of the Middle World while others serve as messengers between the Upper and the Middle Worlds.

58 Bur. Хүтхэ онгон.

59 Tib. rgyal po sku lnga.

60 This meditation school following an unidentified religion could have been a branch of Bɵ Murgel, a kind of Bön or even some kind of Buddhist school as Buddhism was practised by some of the Uighurs, Tyurks and the Tokharians before them.

a Sanskrit name for their god. Linguistically it makes more sense to interpret the meaning of *pehar* either along the lines of Tyurkic and proto-Mongol languages, or along the lines of Tokharian or Iranian languages as Iranian influence spread to the region from the west, superimposed on the earlier Tokharian culture which had made its mark on both Tyurks and Uighurs.

If we go along the Iranian lines in search of the original meaning of the word *pehar*, there are two options suggested by Bleiçhsteiner:[61]

- Persian *paihar* (middle-Persian *pabhar*, Sogdian *patkr'g*, Avestan *paitikara*) meaning 'picture' or 'idol';
- Persian *paikar* (middle-Persian *patkar*, Avestan *paitikara*) meaning 'war' or 'fight'.

The first, *paihar*, seems too simplistic whereas the second, *paikar*, correctly describes Pehar's nature as a wrathful warrior-god or spirit. This may indicate that Pehar was propitiated not only by the proto-Mongols and Tyurkic peoples but by the earlier Iranian nations of the Great Steppe as well.

If we follow the Tyurkic trail, as the name *pehar* is often spelt as *pe ha ra* in Tibetan, the second part '*ha ra*' can be interpreted as the Tyurkic *kara* and Mongol-Buryat *hara* both meaning 'black'. Both Tibetan spellings, *pehar* and *pehara,* find a counterpart in the Buryatian pantheon of deities: Bahar-Hara, Black Bahar, the Lord of Lake Baikal. As we have seen, Bahar-Hara Khaan was initially Lord of the heavenly smithy on the top of the Baigal fire-mountain before it sank under the earth and Lake Baikal was formed. As such, he was Lord Blacksmith. If we analyze this name we find that *bahar* has no meaning in either modern Buryatian or modern Mongolian which suggests it is either a very ancient name or is of foreign origin.[62] *Hara* means 'black' and *khaan* is an appellation equivalent to Tibetan *gyalpo*, 'king'.

How does this relate to Pehar? A glance at the history of the Uighurs can clarify this. Long before the Uighurs formed their own state and came to control the large area stretching from the Tarim Basin to the southern banks of Lake Baikal in the eighth century AD, they were known under other names and were under the dominance of Hunnu,

[61] Mentioned in Nebesky-Wojkowitz, *Oracles and Demons*, p. 107.

[62] Curiously, *bahar* means 'spring' in Iranian and is a common female name but this meaning cannot be related to the status of Bahar-Hara Khaan so there is probably no connection between these two names.

Syanbi, Zhu-Zhang and the Tyurkic Khaganates. These ancestors of Hor Uighurs roamed the expanse of Southern Siberia, Altai, Transbaikalia and the southern shores of Lake Baikal itself, sharing the same general culture and religion as the other Tyurko-Mongol nations of the Great Steppe. They were known in Tibet as Hor, a name most probably coming from the Baikal region where the Hori/Horëodoi tribe of Buryats still lives today. These Buryats continue to worship Bahar-Hara Khaan.[63] There is, then, a high probability that Hor Uighurs had a cult of Bahar-Hara in his earlier form as a Blacksmith god, as Lord of Baikal, or both. Consequently Bahar-Hara Khaan might be the original name of Gyalpo Pehar which came to be spelt in Tibet as *pehar*, *pehara* or *bihara* with the latter spelling invented to fit myths created by later Buddhist lamas attempting to give this new cult more credibility by connecting it to India. There are many such myths but the main thrust is that this god was originally a Buddhist protective deity in India, hence the component of his name *vihara* meaning 'Buddhist monastery', 'Buddhist retreat centre'.

In the Horling[64] episode of the *Gesar* epic, we find *Horlha*,[65] the main protector-gods of Hor, who are still propitiated by contemporary Hortsho[66] people of Mongol Persian descent in eastern Tibet.[67] These three *Horlha* are said to be sky-dwelling Namthel Karpo (one of the names by which Pehar is known), Barthel Trawo[68] of the Intermediate Space and Sathel Nagpo[69] of the Earth. These deities were also worshiped by Jang[70] tribes of the Tibetan borderlands. The Tibetans associated these foreign deities with the *Theurang* class but the Tyurks, Hor/Uighur and later Mongols surely did not perceive them as such. We can be sure of this because this classification is not present in Buryatian Bɵ Murgel which we can take as a living reflection of the Prehistoric Bön most probably practised by their predecessors. *Horlha* are often associated with Pehar, so this triad of Hor gods can help us further clarify the process by which Pehar was adapted into the pantheon of Tibetan Buddhism's protective deities.

---

63 It is interesting to note that many Buddhist Hori families have Pehar as their main protector. (Oral communication from Dorjo Doogarov.)

64 Tib. Hor gling.

65 Tib. Hor lha.

66 Tib. Hor tsho so dgu, Thirty-Nine Hor Tribes.

67 Karmay, *The Arrow and the Spindle*, II, pp.199–202.

68 Tib. Bar thel Khra bo.

69 Tib. Sa thel Nag po.

70 Tib. lJang.

We have already established above that the name Namthel Karpo is a variant of Namtheb Karpo which we translated back into Buryatian as Zayaan Sagaan Teb-Tengeri, a name which in turn is very close to Zayaan Sagaan Tengeri, one of the appellations under which Hormusta Tengeri is known. However, we have rejected the possibility that Pehar is Hormusta on the grounds that they are different classes of gods and have come to the conclusion that Pehar could have been a figure belonging to a larger group of protective deities. This triad of Hor gods gives further weight to this theory. We cannot be sure exactly which category of Bѳ Murgel deities Namthel (Namtheb) Karpo could belong in this version, but we have two possibilities: Namthel Karpo can either be associated with Hormusta Tengeri, in which case he is different from the other two and cannot be a part of the same group as he would be an equivalent of Tibetan *Lha* and thus a sky-god, not a spirit; or he is a deity of the same group of spirits as the other two, which is more likely, and supports our theory that he cannot be linked to Hormusta Tengeri. The *Horlha* have a goat totem and a second set of names whereby Namthel Karpo is called Rakar,[71] White Goat, and the other two spirit-protectors are Ratra,[72] Variegated Goat, and Ranag,[73] Black Goat. As Hormusta Tengeri has no particular association with a white goat, we can be fairly sure that Namthel Karpo of Hor is not Hormusta Tengeri. If *hara* in the name *pehara* corresponds to the Mongol-Buryat *hara* and Tyurkic *kara* (black) then our candidate for Pehar in this group is Sathel Nagpo, which translates as 'Black Theurang of the Earth' or Ranag, Black Goat. If this is the case then we can say that Sathel Nagpo is a form of Bahar-Hara Khaan, the Lord of Baikal worshipped by Hori Buryats. The fact that these three deities are associated with different coloured goats suggests that originally such goats were sacrificed during special rituals dedicated to them, akin to Bѳ Murgel *tailgans*.[74] For example, Bѳ-smiths of the Shoho'olok clan in the Tunka region of Buryatia believe the transmission of their craft and powers traces back to Darhan Sagaan Tengeri[75] to whom a

---

[71] Tib. Ra dkar.

[72] Tib. Ra khra.

[73] Tib. Ra nag.

[74] For a comparative study of offering rituals see ch. XII.

[75] Bur. Драхан Сагаан Тэнгэри. There is no contradiction here. Although Hormusta Tengeri, like the majority of White Western Tengeri, does not accept animal sacrifice in any form, five patrons of the crafts do accept these bloodless sacrifices. So in this case Namthel Karpo can be loosely compared to Darhan Sagaan Tengeri, not Hormusta Tengeri.

light-coloured billy goat is offered through the *seter*[76] suffocation ritual.[77]

An earlier reference to this triad of gods of three different colours is found in the *Chronicle of the Fifth Dalai Lama* which says that in the land of the Uighurs there were three *Dregyal*[78] (royal demons), white, yellow and black, one of whom was brought to Tibet and became known as Pehar. Nebesky-Wojkowitz cites an oral tradition according to which it is Dorje Dragden who is in fact Namthel Karpo of the Uighurs and that both he and Pehar had their seat at Bhata Hor before they were brought to Tibet.[79] This is interesting on two counts: firstly it strengthens the theory that Pehar is one of a group of protective deities, and secondly that Pehar cannot be associated with Namthel Karpo.

Furthermore, as all three *Horlha* spirits are said to be brothers belonging to the same class and were *Polha* ancestral deities of Hortsho peoples, we can conclude that, as we suggested above, they are indeed a group of ancestral spirits directly comparable to Mongol-Buryat *Ongons*. If Sathel Nagpo is Bahar-Hara Khaan then the whole group could originally have been similar, in principle, to *Ongon-darhad*,[80] the ancestral spirits and patrons of the Bө-smiths.[81] This is consistent with the theory put forward above that Pehar was originally one of a group of ancestral protector-spirits whose cult included a common *ongon*-support, such as the Sebag mask. When the Hor Uighurs were defeated by the Tibetans and the cult of these spirit-protectors was transferred to Tibet, in the process of incorporating this cult into the Tibetan Buddhist pantheon all three deities became known under the common name Pehar.

Integration into the Buddhist pantheon

From all the arguments presented above we can clearly see that Nyipangse and Pehar, despite the similarity of some of their manifestations and appellations, are not the same deity but two distinct gods both propitiated in the country of Hor (Tyurkic Khaganate, Uighur Khaganate) with Nyipangse or Hormusta Tengeri being a peaceful sky-dwelling god of the Upper World, the leader of White Tengeri sky-gods, and Pehar being

76 Bur. сэтэр.

77 G. R. Galdanova, *Dolamaiskie verovaniya buryat* (Novosibirsk: Nauka, 1987), p. 88.

78 Tib. 'dre rgyal.

79 Nebesky-Wojkowitz, *Oracles and Demons*, p. 98.

80 Bur. Онгон-дархад.

81 See ch. VII and VIII.

a wrathful protector-god of some Uighur tribes comparable to the *Ongon* and *Zayaan* protector-gods and spirits of Buryatian Bɵ Murgel. Later attempts to associate Pehar with Tsangpa (Indian Brahma) and Gyagyin (Indian Indra) have to be put down to Buddhist lamas' efforts to integrate Pehar into the pantheon of the newly-arrived Indian Buddhism. These attempts actually run contradictory to Pehar's real nature; the Tyurkic Uighurs worshipped him as a wrathful warrior-god of the Middle World.

Stan Royal Mumford sheds light on how non-Buddhist gods were and still are integrated into the Buddhist pantheon in his *Himalayan Dialogue: Tibetan Lamas and Gurung Shamans in Nepal*. Here he is privy to the ideology behind Buddhist attempts to convince the Tibetan farmers of Thang-jet in Nepal to give up blood sacrifices to the goddess Devi Than, an emanation of the wrathful Hindu goddess Durga:

> But couldn't Devi be tamed just as Padmasambhava had tamed such goddesses in Tibet? I put the question to Tashi Drolma, one of the nuns who lives in the Gompa on the hill above Thang-jet village. She pointed out that the compromised laity in this case is poor tenant farmers who carry on the old habits even after their Gurung landlord has moved to Kathmandu. Beyond this social reality they honestly fear the goddess. The only way to break their custom would be to convince them that Devi Than is 'in fact' a manifestation not of the goddess Durga, but rather of the Tibetan goddess dPal-ldan Lhamo, who was tamed by Guru Rinpoche (Padmasambhava) in Tibet. Then they would have confidence that Lama Dawa's incantations (*sngags*) could control her.[82]

Similar methods were used in Tibet when native and foreign deities, such as Pehar, were absorbed into the Buddhist pantheon of *Dharmapala* protectors as Indian Buddhism was adapted to Tibetan culture. This explains why there are so many contradictory accounts of Pehar's history and origin; they can be seen as the efforts of several unrelated lamas to associate him with 'acceptable' deities of Indian origin. This process confused and obscured Pehar's original history and iconography (if there was any).

Location of the country of Phrom/Throm

Having established that Nyipangse and Pehar are two different deities, let us return to our investigation into Hormusta Tengeri and Nyipangse.

---

[82] Stan Royal Mumford, *Himalayan Dialogue: Tibetan lamas and Gurung Shamans in Nepal* (Madison: The University of Wisconsin Press, 1989), p. 82.

The theory that they are in fact one and the same god is strengthened by the information contained in the invocation mentioned above which says Nyipangse was propitiated in the country of Phrom or Throm as Sogdag Sidpa Gyalpo who in turn corresponds to Hormusta Tengeri. There is much debate among scholars about the identity of this country with some suggesting Phrom/Throm is the name by which the Roman Empire was known in Tibet. This may seem plausible as the names sound similar and one of the Dunhuang[83] documents[84] refers to it as being in the west. However, this doesn't correspond with directions given in the invocations of Nyipangse where Phrom is said to be located in the north. To the north of Zhang Zhung and Tibet we find Takla Makan with the civilizations of the Tarim Basin and Turfan. From the third millennia BC[85] until some time in the seventh century AD these were home to the Indo-European proto-Tokharians, Di, Dingling, and later Tokharians, known to Tibetans as Thogar and to Chinese as Yuezhi.[86] The Indo-European Tokharians are also said to have controlled a portion of northwestern areas of modern Tibet at some point. The study of burial grounds in the Hami Oasis in Turfan and archaeological data from the Tarim Basin, Takla Makan,[87] suggest these Indo-European and Indo-Iranian people were mixing with the proto-Mongol and later Tyurkic tribes in modern day Xinjiang for

---

83 Dunhuang is an ancient oasis town which was situated northwest of Tibet in Takla Makan, modern-day Chinese Turkestan and lay on the famous Silk Road. It was founded by Emperor Wudi of the Han dynasty in 111 BC and served as an outpost for the Chinese garrison which was facilitating Chinese control over the trade routes. For several hundred years after the collapse of the Han empire (206 BC-220 AD) the town changed hands many times. In 781 AD, during the Tang dynasty (618–906 AD), Dunhuang was captured by the Tibetans. Chinese control was restored in 848 AD. Later it fell under control the Western Xia kingdom (990–1227 AD) and then the Mongol Yuan dynasty (1271–1368). When trade routes shifted, it was abandoned and fell into oblivion, to be rediscovered in the beginning of 20th century. It is famous for its cave art and the large library preserved by the sands which contained, among other texts, ancient Tibetan Bönpo and Buddhist books, many of which were unknown to modern scholars and practitioners.

84 The document in question is *PT* 958, f1a-1b (Macdonald et Imaeda, 1978: Pl. 241–42). See Karmay, *The Arrow and the Spindle*, p. 482.

85 J. P. Mallory and Victor H. Mair, *The Tarim Mummies: Ancient China and the Mystery of the Earliest Peoples from the West* (London: Thames & Hudson, 2000).

86 Although Yuezhi probably refers to a larger Indo-Iranian group of tribes. At any rate they are Tokharians of the later stage.

87 Ibid.

thousands of years starting from the beginning of the second millennium BC.[88] The conclusion of this prolonged process of ethnogenesis came when the Uighurs,[89] who were a tribal union of Tyurkic/proto-Mongol peoples known in Tibet as Hor, took control over the area in the eighth century AD and gradually absorbed the remnants of the already-mixed Indo-European, Indo-Iranian and proto-Mongol population.

Other cultures which controlled the lands north of Tibet were the early proto-Mongol states of Hunnu, Syanbi, Tabgach (Toba), Tuyuhun/Tu-yü-hun (Togon)[90] and later Trugu[91] – Tyurkic Khaganates. The ancient cultural centres of the Turfan Oasis were Kashgar, Kucha, Harashar, Turfan, Yarkand and Hotan, the main hubs of the great trade artery between east and west known as the Silk Road. Phrom/Throm may refer to the Turfan area or another part of the Takla Makan region at the time when it was controlled by the Tyurkyut and later Kök Tyurk Khaganates in the fifth-eighth centuries AD.

The Tyurkic Khaganates were not states in the modern sense but were tribal confederation governed by Khaans (Khagans) dependent on the institution of military democracy and the council of tribe elders. As both Khaganates spanned vast conquered territories, they ruled over a great diversity of nations who had previously been organized into their own tribal unions or states. In many cases, the conquered peoples were allowed to retain the structures of their tribal unions or states within the framework of the Khaganates, so long as they provided troops, paid taxes and remained loyal to their Tyurkic overlords. The country of Phrom may well have been one of the Syanbi tribal unions which became sandwiched between Tibet and the Tyurks and then later, the Uighurs.

---

[88] Li Shuicheng, A Discussion of Sino-Western Cultural Contact and Exchange in the Second Millennium BC Based on Recent Archaeological Discoveries, *Sino-Platonic Papers*, 97 (December 1999), Department of East Asian Languages and Civilizations, University of Pennsylvania.

[89] Uighur refers to the tribal union of twelve Tiele tribes which was formed in 7th c. AD. In the course of earlier history these people were known under different names such as Gaoche, Chidi – 'Red Di' (according to Gumilev, *Istoriya Hunnu 1*, p. 339) and their ancestors lived in Southern Siberia along the River Lena and the southern bank of Lake Baikal. For a long time they were under Hunnu control and mixed with them to some extent. The name Hor by which they are known in Tibet is most probably just the name of one of the tribes of the Uighur tribal union. This tribe must have had common ancestors with the eastern Buryatian tribe Hor'/Hori/Horëodoi which still lives in the Baikal region today.

[90] State of the Tuyuhun is known as Togon in Russian scholarly works.

[91] Tib. Tru gu. Yongdzin Lopön Tenzin Namdak gives Tib. Tu ru khe.

Further evidence to support this can be gleaned from the geographical models contained in the Tibetan version of *Gesar* where Phrom, Gesar Phrom, Gesar Ling[92] or simply Ling,[93] Gesar's native country, is invariably said to be located to the north or northeast of Tibet, with the sole exception of the Dunhuang manuscript mentioned above. According to the standard Tibetan geographic model known as the Four Kingdoms of the Borderlands,[94] Tibet is in the centre, the kingdom of Trugu (Tyurkic Khaganates) is in the north, Tagzig (Iranian speaking countries) is in the west, India is in the south and China is in the east.[95] According to a thirteenth century AD historical text, *Dewu Chöjung*,[96] at the time when Tibet did not yet have a strong central government but was formed of twelve principalities, it was attacked from the north by the army of (Phrom) Gesar.[97] Following the geography of the *Gesar* epic itself, if Gesar's native country is taken as the centre, the country of Hor is to the north, Yar-khams (Yarkand) is to the west and China to the east.[98]

So according to this arrangement, Phrom must have been situated somewhere between Yarkand and various Chinese and Syanbi-Chinese states along the northern border of Tibet.

The word *phrom* or *khrom* is a Tibetan spelling of a foreign name which may have entered Tibetan from the language of Zhang Zhung as, if such a country existed before the seventh century AD, it would have bordered Zhang Zhung on the north. However, as it is a foreign word, it is very difficult to determine exactly which state or tribal entity from the large region north of Tibet it refers to. This difficulty is exacerbated by the fact that Tibetan names for foreign countries and peoples often sound completely different from their self designation; Mongolia, for example, is called Sogpo[99] in Tibetan. Nevertheless, when we bring all this data together it gives us very strong grounds to suggest that Phrom/Throm refers to a small principality or tribal state located in the enclave somewhere between the northern border of Tibet and the southern border of the Tyurkic Khaganates and later Hor (Uighur Khaganate).

---

92 Tib. Ge sar Gling.

93 Tib. Gling.

94 Tib. mtha' bzhi rgyal khab.

95 See Karmay, *The Arrow and the Spindle*, p. 481, Fig.I.

96 Tib. lDe'u chos 'byung.

97 Ibid., p. 482–3.

98 This is according to *lHa gling* and *bDud 'dul* sets. Ibid., pp. 483–4, Fig. IV–V.

99 Tib. Sog po.

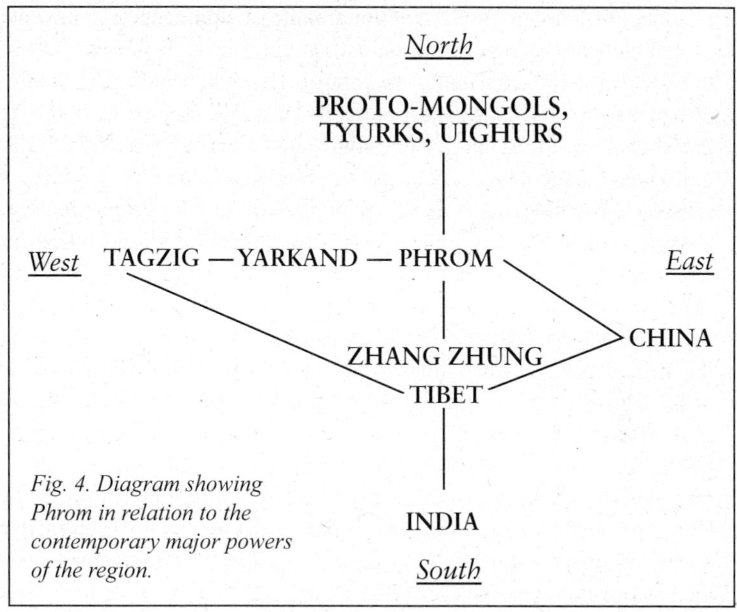

Fig. 4. Diagram showing Phrom in relation to the contemporary major powers of the region.

The most likely candidate for Phrom is the state of Tuyuhun (Togon), a union of tribes related to Syanbi some of which were known to Tibetans as Azha.[100] Tuyuhun bordered Zhang Zhung and then Tibet in the northeast. The centre of this establishment was in the region between Lake Kokonoor and Mt. Bailan[101] (Mt. Bayankala) near the source of the Yellow River. Tuyuhun controlled fluctuating territories from the end of the third century AD. At the high point of its expansion in the fifth century AD Tuyuhun led successful military expeditions in all directions conquering territories in northern Tibet, Toba Wei, Western Qin, and the Tarim Basin where they occupied Khotan. On this latter expedition Tuyuhun pushed as far as Kabul and Gandhara in modern day Afghanistan and Pakistan although it did not retain these territories. The

[100] Tib. 'A zha; probably a much older tribe than the Tuyuhun because some texts mention that some Bönpos arrived from the country of Azha as early as the reign of the 8th Tibetan king Drigum Tsenpo. According to traditional Bönpo chronology, then, we should put them in 7th c. BC or, according to Chögyal Namkhai Norbu, 1st c. AD. The Azha are also mentioned in relation to the Tibetan king Tagri Nyenzig who lived in 5th- 6th c. AD. So it seems that either the Tuyuhun conquered the Azha or that the Azha joined their tribal union for other reasons.

[101] Chin. 白兰山.

conquest of Khotan gave Tuyuhun a strategic and economic advantage as a large portion of the Silk Road running through the city-states of the Tarim Basin came under its control. However, located as it was in one of the most volatile and politically unstable regions of Inner Asia, Tuyuhun's territories and fortunes fluctuated constantly. In 635 AD Tang, motivated by the desire to control the Silk Road, invaded Tuyuhun and crossed the whole of its lands in pursuit of Tuyuhun *khagan* Fuyun, chasing him to Khotan where he was finally captured and killed. As a result many Tuyuhun territories went under Tang administration. Under the leadership of *khagan* Nohopo, Tuyuhun managed to hold onto the Kokonoor region (Qinghai) until it was invaded and its lands annexed by the armies of the Tibetan king Srongtsen Gampo in 663AD. These lands became incorporated into the Amdo province of Tibet. Tuyuhun state ceased to exist and the Tuyuhun tribal union was split. Some Tuyuhun tribes, known to Tibetans as Azha, remained on their lands which were now within Tibet while another part, led by Nohopo, went under Tang Chinese rulership and was used as border guards moved between garrisons on Tang's western borders.[102] A central motif in the *Gesar* epic is that of the warrior-hero leading constant military sallies to conquer his people's enemies in all four directions and the state of Tuyuhun would have been in just such a position, surrounded by aggressive neighbours on all sides (Zhang Zhung and then Tibet to the south, various Chinese states to the east, mixed Syanbi-Chinese states and then Tyurks to the north and west). It was a military arena for many centuries so the changing fortunes and volatile situation of this disputed region tally well with the events of the *Gesar* epic.

The *Gesar* epic is an important part of Mongol-Buryat, Tibetan and Tu mythology. Tu is a minority nation of modern China. Its self designation is Monguor or Tsagaan Mongghol (White Mongols) and these people live in the eastern Tibetan province of Amdo as well as the Qinghai and Gansu provinces of modern China. Tu are a mix of Tyurkic, Mongol and Tibetan tribes. Their main language is Monguor, related to Mongol, although some speak Wutunhua, which is derived from a conglomeration of Mongol, Tibetan and Chinese. Some scholars believe that Tu are descendants of the Tuyuhun branch of Syanbi.[103] After 670

---

[102] Gabriella Molè, 'The Tu-yü-hun from the Northern Wei to the Time of the Five Dynasties', *Serie Orientale* 41, pp. XV-XIX.

[103] Feng Lide and Kevin Stuart, 'Interethnic Cultural Contact on the Inner Asian Frontier: The Gangou People of Minhe County, Qinghai', *Sino Platonic-Papers* 33, 1992; 'Monguor/Tu sometimes are identified as Shirongol by some

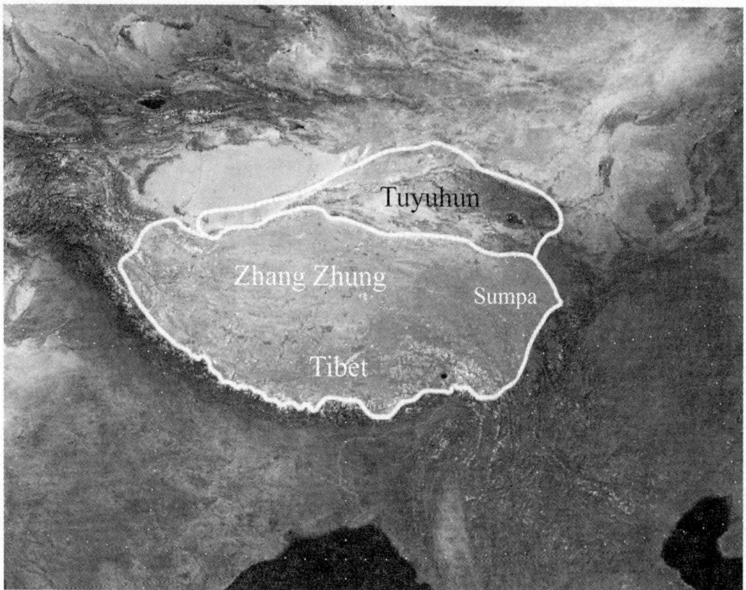

Fig. 5. Approximate territory covered by Tuyuhun at its maximum expansion.

AD they are mainly referred to in Chinese sources as Tuhun' (T'u-hun) and remained on the region's political arena as scattered military groups until at least 1042 when they are known to have provided horses to the Tanguuts.[104] As modern Tu call themselves Tsagaan Mongghol we can deduce that their protective gods were White Western Tengeri under the leadership of Hormusta Tengeri. According to the Mongol-Buryat *Geser* epic, Hormusta Tengeri is the hero Geser's father, another hint that Gesar's home country of Phrom was most probably the Tuyuhun state.

Now let's return to our theory that Hormusta and Nyipangse are different names for the same deity and see how it is supported by this new hypothesis on the location of Phrom. As the religion and culture of Hunnu, Syanbi, Tuyuhun, Tyurkic Khaganates and the state of Hor had continuity and was a kind of Bɵ Murgel, a stream of Prehistoric Bön, it would have been centered on the worship of Eternal Blue Sky and Tengeri sky-gods, and we know that Hormusta Tengeri is the head of

---

scholars but this a mistake': Mongolian languages, (2007) in *Encyclopædia Britannica.* Accessed from Encyclopædia Britannica Online <http://www.britannica.com/eb/article-9109789> accessed 22.04.07.

104 Molè, 'The Tu-yü-hun', pp. XXI–XXV.

the White Tengeri in some branches of this religion. Located in the same geographic and cultural environment, Phrom would have shared cultural and religious elements with the Hunnu, Syanbi, Tuyuhun, Tyurks and Uighurs, and according to his invocation, Nyipangse was worshipped there under the name Sogdag Sidpa Gyalpo. We can safely assume, then, that the name Sogdag Sidpa Gyalpo of Tibetan Bönpo sources refers in fact to Hormusta Tengeri.

Note on the origin of the Gesar epic and the name 'gesar'

Identifying Phrom as Tuyuhun (Togon), or indeed another similar Syanbi tribal state in the same region, gives us a new perspective on the origins of the personage Gesar himself. This hero was modelled on one or several exceptionally brave warrior-kings of one of the Syanbi tribal unions, most probably Tuyuhun, who fought enemies on all sides. From the end of the third millennium BC until well into the Middle Ages, the Lake Kokonoor region was a cradle of intense ethnogenesis involving many different tribes, nations and races. One of the ethnic and cultural substrata present in the region was proto-Indo-Iranian, represented by the early Di, Dinglin and then the Yuezhi-Tokharians. Some legends and myths of the proto-Indo-Aryans and later Iranians remained alive within the new population of Syanbi origin who moved into the area. These myths and legends could have been retained either as result of earlier contacts and mixing which had taken place in the region of Southern Siberia, or absorbed from the Indo-Iranian peoples living in the region around the Tarim Basin.

In this light the name *gesar*, which scholars often assume to be a corruption of Roman *caesar*, should be decoded along completely different cultural lines; we can reinterpret it according to the theory presented above that Phrom was located in the north and bearing in mind the view that the sky-gods Hormusta and Nyipangse are one and the same.

From the second millennium BC, Takla Makan, which bordered Zhang Zhung and later Tibet in the north, was populated by the Indo-European Tokharians and their culture was connected with the Iranian world in the west, with proto-Mongols and Tyurks in the north, with China in the east and with Zhang Zhung and Tibet in the south. Information gained from archaeological digs and the study of texts of other cultures which mention the Tokharians tell of a highly developed culture, both in the material and spiritual sense. According to Yongdzin Lopön Tenzin

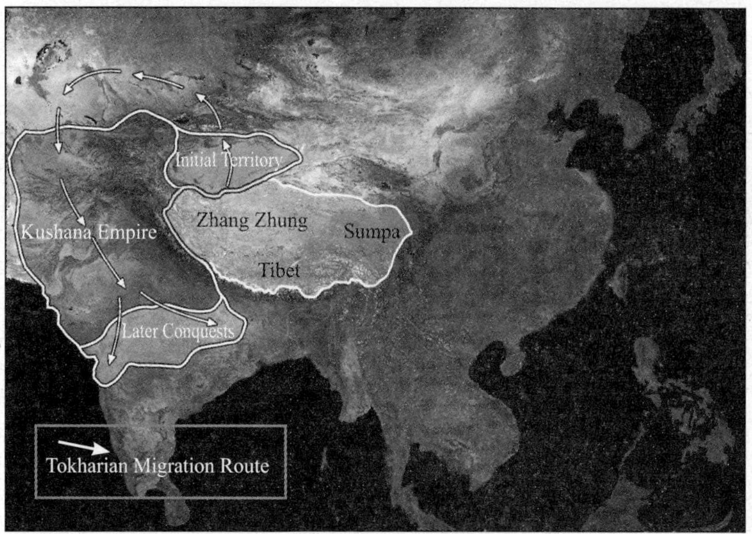

Fig. 6. Tokharians and Kushana Empire.

Namdak, Bönpo sources say that the Thogar, as the Tokharians were known in Zhang Zhung and Tibet, were once a very powerful nation controlling a vast territory including a considerable part of India, and were major political players.[105] This is a clear reference to Tokharistan, the Great Kushana Empire. Located on the Silk Road and being of Indo-European type, their culture was surely generally Indo-Iranian. There is also clear evidence that the Tokharians swapped cultural concepts with other tribes, including those of proto-Mongol origin, so they served as a conduit of ideas going both west to east and east to west. This is confirmed by archaeological digs and frescoes from the Kizil (Qizil) caves which depict Tokharians and peoples of other ethnic and racial groups engaged in cultural, commercial and religious exchange.

There was, then, a strong Indo-Iranian culture whose influence was spread by caravans travelling along the Silk Road between the major cultural hubs of the Takla Makan and Chinese outposts in the same region where Phrom was located, and we can infer that the culture of Phrom must

---

[105] That is also confirmed by the *Brahmana Vyasa* in the *Gandavyuha* section of *Avatamsaka Sutra* which lists Thogar among the sixteen large regions surrounding the Land of Jambu i.e. India. Jamgön Kongtrul Lodrö Tayé, *Myriad Worlds: Buddhist Cosmology in Abhidharma, Kālacakra and Dzog-chen* (Ithaca, New York: Snowlion Publications, 1995), p.111.

have been exposed to and absorbed at least some parts of Tokharian and Iranian ideas as did the Syanbi, Tyurks and later Uighurs. Another point of contact allowing for mutual influence between the Iranians, the proto-Mongols and later the Tyurks was the common borders and changing fortunes of war as the same territories and peoples were intermittently controlled by Iranian, proto-Mongol and Tyurkic states. Proto-Mongols and then Tyurkic nobility often intermarried with the nobles of various Iranian peoples. This, then, is the cultural perspective from which we should look for the origin of the name *gesar*. As *gesar/geser* has no semantic value in either Tibetan or Mongol-Buryat, we can propose that its etymology lies in the languages and culture of the Aryan proto-Indo-Iranian and later Iranian peoples.

According to the Mongol-Buryat version of the epic, Geser is the son of Hormusta Tengeri while according to the Tibetan version he is the son of Tsangpa or Gyagyin whom we have already identified as Nyipangse. Nyipangse and Hormusta Tengeri can be further equated with the Indian god Indra and, as we shall see shortly, are the same as Hormuzd Yazad, so we are dealing with a large cultural and religious phenomenon which has its roots in prehistory when proto-Indo-Iranian and proto-Mongol peoples lived side by side in the vast expanse of the Great Steppe. So can we find a cultural or mythological thread which can connect Gesar to one of these cultures? In Iranian mythology we find a warrior-saint Keresaspa/Kershasp/Gershasp, son of Thrita, a brave slayer of demons and dragons who displayed exceptional heroism in his life and is now said to be sleeping under the protection of Farrokh Farvardin Yazad and 99,999 Fravashi protector-deities. He will wake at the end of time to defeat the forces of evil at the great battle between good and evil. The myth of Keresaspa has many parallels with the epic of Gesar, the most prominent being the episode where Gesar defeats the Twelve-Headed Giant. There are several references to Keresaspa in *Avesta* and *Vendidad (Vi-daevo-dat)*, the holy books of Zoroastrianism. In *Avesta*, *Hom Yasht*, *Yasna 9*,[106] for example, Zarathushtra[107] is questioning Haoma, the god of the magic beverage, about the sages who preceded him in making this potent spiritual medicine. As Haoma lists the names, the third in line is Thrita, father of Keresaspa. It is clear from the text that Thrita

---

[106] The HomYasht, Yasna 9, lines 10–11 <http://www.avesta.org/yasna/y9to11s.htm> accessed 26.04.07.

[107] I have adopted the spelling used by modern Zoroastrians, taken from *Traditional Zoroastrianism: Tenets of the Religion* <http://tenets.zoroastrianism.com/> accessed 27.04.07.

preceded Zarathushtra and indeed, lived a long time before him. In the Vedic pantheon of the Indo-Aryans we find a god and his spiritual beverage, known as Soma, which are identical to the Iranian Haoma. The presence of these two matching gods/beverages tells us that the cult of Haoma/Soma was practised before the proto-Indo-Iranians of the Great Steppe split and the two diverging nations migrated towards Iran and India. Precisely when this migration happened is not clear, but scholars generally put it some time before two thousand BC when the proto-Indo-Iranian language began diverging resulting in the formation of two sacred Aryan languages, Sanskrit and Avestan, in which the Aryan *Vedas* and *Avesta* holy scriptures are written. While it is usually held that the *Vedas* were written down in Sanskrit around 2500 BC, Bal Gangadhar Tilak, a brilliant Indian Brahmin (*brāhmana*) scholar of the turn of the nineteenth century, puts the date at around 4500 BC.[108] He bases his calculations on astronomical information relating to the position of the Orion constellation, known in the *Vedas* as Mriga. By analyzing the position of the Pleiades constellation (Vedic Krittik), he further demonstrates that the date of 2500 BC relates not to the time when the *Vedas* were written but rather to the time when the *Brahmanas*, the commentaries on *Vedas*, were written. As Gathic Avestan is close to the Vedic Sanskrit of the *Brahmanas*, the *Avesta* should also be dated around the same time. If we accept Tilak's dates, we can push the date for the split of the proto-Indo-Iranians back to at least 4500 BC, not around 2500 BC because the passages regarding pre-Zoroastrian personages in Avesta are undoubtedly taken from the prehistoric Indo-Iranian traditions as these same personages and gods are also present in *Rigveda*.[109] As we have seen, the myth of Keresaspa arose before this split, so it would seem its origins lie in a remote period of prehistory. We cannot establish with certainty when and how exactly some of the motifs of this myth may have become a part of the culture of the proto-Mongol peoples but the material presented so far allows us to propose that this could have been

---

[108] B. G. Tilak, *Arkticheskaya Rodina v Vedakh* (Moskva: Fair-Press, 2002), pp.17–26. This is a Russian translation of Lokamanya Bal Gangadhar Tilak, *The Arctic Home in the Vedas: Being also a new key to the interpretation of many Vedic texts and Legends*, (Gaikar Wada, Poona City: Tilak Bros., 1956).

[109] Thrita appears in Russian magical tales as Ivan Tretiy (Rus. Иван Третий) which clearly suggests that this cultural hero is of extreme antiquity and belongs to the period when proto-Slavic and proto-Indo-Iranian languges either had not yet divided or when proto-Slavs and proto-Indo-Iranians lived in close proximity and shared similar cultural lore.

as early as the end of the third or beginning of the second millennium BC during the formation of the Hunnu nation when proto-Mongol tribes were mixing with the proto-Indo-Iranians in the regions of the Gansu Corridor, Lake Kokonoor and later in south Siberia. There are also many other reasons to suggest that proto-Mongols could have had shared common cultural roots with proto-Indo-Europeans even before or soon after the Last Glacial Maximum (20,000–18,000 BP).[110]

Gesar as Keresaspa

So is the *Gesar* epic of the Mongol-Buryats a transformed and enlarged version of the myth of Keresaspa/Gershasp? I think this is clearly the case. In some shape or form and not necessarily under the name *Geser*, this legend could have been part of the lore of the proto-Mongol and Tyurkic tribes for millennia. The key points of this theory are as follows:

i) As the proto-Mongols and Indo-Iranians lived side by side, mixed and had common religious ideas it is highly likely they would have a common mythical hero. Keresaspa/Kershasp/Gershasp, besides being a very archaic legendary hero of the proto-Indo-Iranians, was and still is a personal name in many Iranian languages. It is not difficult to see how *keresaspa* came to be spelt in Mongol-Buryatian as *geser* and in Tibetan as *gesar*.

ii) A khaan of Tuyuhun or another Syanbi tribal state could easily have come to have Geser/Gesar as a second name or a nickname. He could have been given this name, for example, by his mother if she were one of the princesses of Iranian descent married to a Syanbi khaan. Or, if the *Geser* epic in some form was already a part of his people's folklore, he could have been named after the hero at birth. Alternatively, as the real khaan's brave deeds began to gain fame, he could have simply been nicknamed Geser or this name attributed to him later as the real personage mingled with the legendary hero.

iii) Whatever the case may be, it seems that the *Geser* epic in its modern form started taking shape among the proto-Mongol and Tyurkic tribes as a result of the amalgamation

110 Dealt with in more detail later in this chapter and in ch. XV.

of the personage of Keresaspa/Gershasp from Iranian myths and an exceptionally brave khaan (or several khaans) from one of the Syanbi tribal states – most probably Tuyuhun – which was protecting its independence against the powerful enemies surrounding it in the four directions some time between the third and seventh centuries AD. When some tribes of the Tuyuhun tribal union, known to Tibetans as Azha, were defeated in the seventh century and annexed into the Amdo region of the Tibetan Empire, this myth was transferred into Tibetan folklore. Later still, some time after the eighth century AD, a Buddhist version emerged which incorporated the figure of Guru Padmasambhava along with some teachings and deities of Buddhism and was used as one of the skillful means by which Buddhist lamas spread Buddhism in Tibet.

iv) The fact that *Gesar* was not originally a Tibetan epic and did not, as some Buddhist scholars maintain, originate in the eleventh-thirteenth centuries is further corroborated by a statement in the thirteenth century Tibetan text *Dewu Chöjung* mentioned above. Here it says that the army of Gesar attacked Tibet from the north at the time when Tibet didn't yet have a strong central government. This means that (Phrom) Gesar already existed in the period when Tibet was still a vassal state of the Zhang Zhung confederation.

v) This is also in agreement with the fact that Nyipangse, a pre-Buddhist Bönpo protector deity of Zhang Zhung identical to Hormusta Tengeri, was worshipped in Gesar's country of Phrom under the name Sogdag Sidpa Gyalpo before Indian Buddhism was introduced into Tibet.

Xwrmzt (Hurmazta) and Hormusta Tengeri

Scholars have noted for some time now that Iranian Ahura Mazda and Tyurko-Mongol Hormusta correspond in some way. The position these two deities hold as leaders of the gods on the white side of the universal energy opposing the forces of evil on the black side within the dualistic view of the universe has led some scholars to conclude that the Mongol-Buryat cult of Hormusta Tengeri is explained by Zoroastrian influences coming into Mongol-Buryat culture via the Sogdians and later through the Manichean Uighurs. While this sounds plausible at first glance and I do not dispute that there is a connection between the two gods, I believe the correspondence between Ahura Mazda and Hormusta is not a result of Zoroastrian influence on the Tyurks and Mongols but that it goes back to a much earlier period of pre-Zoroastrian religious traditions. I believe we can trace it to the proto-Indo-Iranian tribes of the Great Steppe of Eurasia who populated southern Ukraine, southern Russia, the southern Urals, Central Asia and Southern Siberia as early as five thousand BC and who are associated with such archaeological cultures as Yamna (Pit Grave), Afanasyevskaya and Andronovskaya,[111] already mentioned in Chapter I. However, if we accept Tilak's Arctic Home Theory for the location of the Aryan ancestral land of Airyane Vaejo in the circumpolar region of modern day Russia, we can push the date for this connection back to the period between the last two glacial periods.[112]

The name 'Ahura Mazda' comes from the Avestan language but many variations are found in other Iranian languages and dialects. In Old Iranian it is Auramazdāh, its eastern-Iranian Sogdian form is Xwrmzt, probably pronounced Hurmazta,[113] and this form is closest to the Mongol-Buryat form Hyurmasta, one of the common spellings for Hormusta. In Middle and New Iranian we find many other spellings and pronunciations for 'Ahura Mazda', the most common being Aramazd, Hormazd, Hormizd, Hormuzd, Ohrmazd, Ormazd etc. The form used in *Avesta*, Zoroastrianism's original holy scripture, is Ahura Mazda and this is generally used nowadays in the West. However, it is not clear how this name was actually pronounced in the languages of contemporary Iranian tribes other than Zarathushtra's own. To complicate matters, western and eastern Iranian languages are said to have been mutually incomprehensible and as remote as German and French, for example. In the first *Fragard* section of *Vendidad*, paragraph four, we read:

> The second of the good lands and countries which I, Ahura Mazda, created, was the plain which the Sughdhas inhabit.[114]

---

[111] That is if we follow the Kurgan hypothesis and the Two Wave theory of the Aryan migration or the Sogdian Model proposed by Johanna Nichols. Further reading: J. P. Mallory, Yamna Culture, *Encyclopedia of Indo-European Culture*, Fitzroy Dearborn, 1997; Johanna Nichols, *The Epicentre of the Linguistic Spread*, Roger Blench and Matthew Spriggs (eds.), Archaeology and Language I: 122–148, (London: Routledge, 1997); Johanna Nichols, *The Eurasian Spread Zone and the Indo-European Dispersal*, Roger Blench and Matthew Spriggs (eds.), Archaeology and Language, II (London: Routledge, 1997).

[112] See ch. XV.

[113] Or Ahurmazta. Vowels were not represented in Sogdian script. <http://fas.harvard.edu/~iranian/Sogdian/index.html> accessed 08.06.07.

[114] Tr. James Darmesteter (From *Sacred Books of the East*, American Edition,

Here, the land of Sughdh (Sogd, Sogdiana) is one of the sixteen major lands of the Iranian Aryan tribes created by Ahura Mazda. There can be no doubt, then, that the Sogdians are a very ancient people, as is their language. Many modern scholars associate the country of the Sughdhas with historic Sogd (Sogdiana). The first historical record of the existence of such a country is dated the sixth century BC. It is the inscription of Emperor Darius I (522–486 BC) at Bihistun (Bisitun).[115] However, this date does not reflect the real antiquity of the Sughudh people and does not necessarily refer to their original land described in *Vendidad*; it is simply a record stating the date when Sogd came under the control of the Achaemenid Persian Empire. There are various views on the dating of *Vendidad* itself but many scholars agree that it contains very old material, some of which describes pre-Zoroastrian customs and so it is possible that the Sughdhas and their old language, *Old Sogdian,[116] could have already existed in the days when the *Gathas* of *Avesta* were written. Consequently, the Sogdian spelling 'Xwrmzt' (Hurmazta) could be as old as or even older than Avestan 'Ahura Mazda'. This implies that the Mongol-Buryatian cult of Hormusta (Hyurmasta) may in fact have been a cult practised by their proto-Mongol ancestors for a very, very long time and not merely brought to Baikal in the fifth-eighth centuries AD by the Manichean Uighurs.

Proto-Indo-Iranian Pantheon

To substantiate this claim we shall dig deeper and look into the common gods of the Vedic Indo-Aryans and pre-Zoroastrian Iranians. These gods came from the same source, proto-Indo-Iranian religion and we shall trace their transition into the Zoroastrian pantheon and compare them with Huhe Münhe Tengeri and Hormusta Tengeri of the Bɵ Murgel pantheon.

Below is a table showing corresponding pre-Zoroastrian and Vedic gods: [117]

1898.), online version <http://www.avesta.org/vendidad/vd1sbe.htm> accessed 22.05.07.

[115] Matteo Compareti, 'Sogdiana: Iranian culture in Central Asia', *The Iranian*, July 24, 2001<http://www.iranian.com/History/2001/July/Sogdiana/> accessed 22.05.07

[116] Khodadad Rezakhani, *The Iranian Language Family*, <http://www.iranologie.com/history/ilf.html> accessed 27.05.07. The * is used to denote a language or deity which most probably existed but for which there is as yet no historical proof.

[117] Based on the table in Dr Oric Basirov, *Old Iranian Religion & Zoroastrian*

Proto-Indo-Iranian Pantheon	
Iranian pre-Zoroastrian gods	Indo-Aryan Vedic gods
Ahura Vouruna (Apam Napat)	Asura Varuna (Apam Napat)
Ahura Mithra	Asura Mitra
Ahura Mazda	Asura Medha
Daeva Inder	Deva (Daiva) Indra
Verethraona (Verethraghna)	Vetrahan (Vritrahan)
Aryaman	Aryaman
Baga	Bhaga

This table demonstrates the direct correspondence between the main gods of pre-Zoroastrian Iranians and of the Indo-Aryans. These gods personify various aspects and energies of the universe. As some of them have very wide functions and share common, overlapping characteristics, the boundaries between these deities are often blurred. Let us look briefly into the common characteristics these pairs of gods exhibit.

Ahura/ Asura[118]

Meaning 'lord', designates a group of sky-gods who guard and uphold the universal law of righteousness (Asha/Rita).

Vouruna/Varuna

The king of the universe and personification of the infinite sky. As Apam Napat he is god of water-fire. Ancient Aryans believed that fire was born from water so Apam Napat is also one of the titles of the Vedic god of fire, Agni, who in turn is associated with Varuna. Vedic Varuna is the chief god, the leader of the Aditya sky-gods of sunlight.

Mithra/Mitra

God of sunlight. Iranian Mithra is the chief god. Both Mithra and Varuna are guardians of oaths and covenants and are very closely connected. In fact, Vedic Varuna and Mitra are spoken of as a Davandva

---

Reforms, *Paper 3*, 3rd November1998, <http://www.cais-soas.com/CAIS/Religions/iranian/Zarathushtrian/Oric.Basirov/zoroastrian_reforms.htm> accessed 22.05.07.

118 Iranian name on the left, Indo-Aryan on the right as shown in the table.

pair and are often invoked as Mitravaruna. [119] In pre-Zoroastrian Iran, Vouruna in his form of Apam Napat is twinned with Mithra.

Mazda/Medha

The god of wisdom, literally 'Wise Lord'.

Inder/ Indra

Leader of the Daevas/Devas ('heavenly ones'), warrior sky-gods who battle evil spirits. Verethraona/Vetrahan is a form of Indra as the dragon-slayer and is the god of victory.

Aryaman

God of friendship, one of the Aditya gods in the *Vedas*.

Baga/Bhaga

God of wealth. Iranian Baga was later associated with Vouruna (Apam Napat). In later Hinduism Bhaga became the god of marriage but also came to be used as a general term for 'god'.[120]

As the cultures and religions of Iranian and Indian Aryans were diverging and developing in their unique ways, the same gods became reinterpreted and appeared in a different light in later Zoroastrianism and Hinduism. Perhaps the most significant shift came in the interpretation of Ahuras/Asuras and Daevas/Devas. In the original proto-Indo-Iranian religion these gods were on the same side with the names Ahura/Asura and Daeva/Deva more akin to titles rather than denoting different classes of gods. An example of this is the fact that Vedic Varuna and Mitra are spoken of as both Asuras and Devas. However in later Hinduism, Devas became the virtuous gods while Asuras were relegated to the lower rank of jealous, evil demi-gods, with both groups locked in eternal strife. The interpretation in Zoroastrianism is diametrically opposed. Here the Ahuras retained their stature of virtuous gods while the Daevas became the agent-spirits of evil.[121]

---

[119] For example, *Rigveda*, Book 1, Hymn CXXXVI, st. 1; Book 1, Hymn CLII, st. 1; Book 1, Hymn CLIII, st. 1 etc. *Rigveda* tr. Griffith, <http://www.hinduwebsite.com/sacredscripts/rigintro.asp> accessed 29.05.07.

[120] Parallel use of this word is found in Slavic religions where it became *bog* (Rus. бог).

[121] Subhash Kak suggests that originally the gods of Indo-Iranian Aryans had

Transition of Ahura Mazda and the chief Yazatas from the proto-Indo-Iranian pantheon to Zoroastrianism

Having briefly described the ancient proto-Indo-Iranian pantheon and its transition into the distinct pantheons of Hinduism and Zoroastrianism, let us take a closer look at the process which brought Ahura Mazda to the forefront of the new Iranian religion created by Zarathushtra Spitama.

There is no doubt that Ahura Mazda, 'the Wise Lord', was one of the main gods of the pre-Zoroastrian Iranians. According to F.B.J. Kuiper, pre-Zoroastrian Ahura Mazda is the same as Vedic Asura Varuna.[122] In *Rigveda* Varuna is also called Asura Medhira,[123] 'Wise Lord', a direct parallel to Iranian Ahura Mazda. The archaic Iranian formula 'Miθra Ahura bərəzanta' ('Mithra and Ahura, the exalted ones') where 'Ahura' stands for 'Ahura Mazda', is an Iranian equivalent of the Vedic Mitravaruna. Another archaic twinned form similar to Mitravaruna is found in western Iran: *Miçā-Ahura (*Mithra-Ahura).[124] However, the proto-Indo-Iranian form of the name of Asura Varuna/Ahura Mazda cannot be established with certainty.[125] The *Avesta* mentions many kings and heroes who predate Zarathushtra so it is clear that Ahura Mazda was worshipped by the ancient Iranians as the god-creator long before the advent of this prophet. Zarathushtra, however, reinterpreted Ahura Mazda as the unique, uncreated god-creator thus elevating him to a completely new status.[126] It is a common view among modern scholars that the other Yazata (Yazad)[127] gods of the Iranian pre-Zoroastrian religion were incorporated into the pantheon of Zarathushtra's new religion in the form of Amesha Spentas and Yazatas who, in the Zoroastrian context, are said

---

tripartite division corresponding to the general model of the Three Worlds: Devas of the heavens, Asuras of the lower atmosphere and Daevas of the earth, and that this was later abandoned in both Zoroastrianism and Hinduism in favour of the dualistic system. Subhash Kak, *The Vedic Religion in Ancient Iran and Zarathushtra*, <http://subhashkak.voiceofdharma.com/articles/zoro.htm> accessed 23.05.07.

[122] F.B.J. Kuiper, 'Ahura', *Encyclopaedia Iranica* 1, pp. 682–683 (New York: Routledge & Kegan Paul, 1983).

[123] *Rigveda*, Book 1, Hymn 25, st. 20.

[124] Here * is used to denote gods of the proto-Indo-Iranian pantheon.

[125] Kuiper, 'Ahura', *Encyclopaedia Iranica* 1.

[126] Mary Boyce, 'Ahura Mazda', *Encyclopaedia Iranica* 1 (New York: Routledge & Kegan Paul, 1983), pp. 684–687; Mary Boyce, *History of Zoroastrianism, Vol. I, The early period* (Leiden: Brill, 1975); Mary Boyce, *History of Zoroastrianism, Vol. I, Under the Achamenians* (Leiden: Brill, 1975).

[127] Middle Iranian name.

to be emanated aspects of Ahura Mazda. The question is, then, are the Yazatas essentially the same as Ahura Mazda or are they his creations? If they are his creations, distinct beings, then Yazatas are highly evolved spiritual beings endowed with free will[128] who obey Ahura Mazda's laws because they freely choose to do so. This suggestion leads to a theological minefield and is best left to Zoroastrian theologians to debate, but according to Ervad (Dr.) Hoshang J. Bhadha[129] and an article by Cyrus R. R. Cooper,[130] Amesha Spentas and Yazatas are Ahura Mazda's creations while he himself is the first of them known under the name Hormuzd (Hormazd) Yazad. There are seven Amesha Spentas and they are the chief Yazatas of Zoroastrianism:

1. Ahura Mazda/Hormuzd[131]
2. Vohu Manu/Bahman
3. Asha Vahishta/Ardebehest
4. Kshathra Vairya/Sheherevar
5. Spenta Armaiti/Aspendamard
6. Haurvatat/Khordad
7. Ameratat /Amardad

---

[128] It is generally accepted that monotheism and the concept of free will were first introduced by Zarathushtra. All later monotheistic religions developed from the base of this original Zoroastrian model. Zoroastrian monotheism, however, has a much broader view of the world as it paradoxically incorporates the concept of cosmic dualism and is tolerates other religions, perceiving their chief-gods as manifestations of Ahura Mazda. Because of this view Zoroastrians do not seek to convert peoples of other faiths believing instead that they are already worshiping Ahura Mazda merely in a different form. The liberation of the Jews from captivity in Babylon and permission to return to their land and rebuild the Holy House (Bet HaMikdash), the Temple of Solomon in Jerusalem given by the Cyrus the Great in 536 BC is based on this Zoroastrian concept. Unfortunately, this non-sectarian attitude was not amongst many other aspects of Zoroastrianism imported into Judaism, Christianity and Islam. The lack of this vital ingredient in later monotheistic religions has often made their ideologies intolerant towards other religious systems, even those which proclaim monotheism. This intolerance has resulted in thousands of years of religious extremism and warfare which, unfortunately, still continue today.

[129] Ervad (Dr.) Hoshang J. Bhadha, *Ameshaspands – The Bountiful Immortals*, <http://www.britannica.com/eb/article-9109789> accessed 17.04.07.

[130] Cyrus R. R. Cooper, *Yazads and Ameshaspands*, <http://www.britannica.com/eb/article-9109789> accessed 17.04.07.

[131] I give the Avestan name followed by the Middle Iranian name.

In the Vedic pantheon we find a group of gods which most probably had their direct equivalent in the pre-Zoroastrian religion of Iran. *Rigveda* lists seven Aditya gods[132] of whom Varuna is the chief:

1. Varuna
2. Mitra
3. Aryaman
4. Bhaga
5. Daksha
6. Ansa
7. Surya or Savitr

These two groups of gods have much in common as they are all deities associated with the star constellations of the astrological calendar. The first four of the Vedic Adityas have counterparts in the pre-Zoroastrian pantheon, as we saw in the table above, and are also present in the Zoroastrian pantheon of Yazatas in one form or another. Varuna, the chief among the Adityas, is identical to Ahura Mazda[133] and has retained the leading position in the group of Amesha Spentas. While Zoroastrianism gives the Amesha Spentas a unique reinterpretation, the group is, no doubt, based on the earlier proto-Indo-Iranian model.

Yazatas and Tengeri

If we put aside the Zoroastrian reinterpretation of the nature of their relation to Ahura Mazda, the description of the ancient Yazata gods found in the Zoroastrian pantheon provides plentiful information about their original nature. There are thirty-three main Yazads headed by Hormuzd Yazad. Each is associated with one of the thirty-three constellations or star systems and controls a certain function of nature. *Yasht* prayer rituals dedicated to each of them are performed on particular days according to Zoroastrian astrology. These main Yazads are also called Fravashi or Guardian Gods. Thirty of them were later associated with the days of

[132] In later Hinduism they were expanded to twelve and associated with the twelve months. Zoroastrian theologicians such as M.N. Dhalla (in his *History of Zoroastrianism* (New York, London, Toronto: Oxford University Press, 1938), also published on < http://www.avesta.org/dhalla/dhalla1.htm#chap7> accessed 08.06.07) deny that there is a connection but such objections come from the position of the interpretation of these deities rather than a common structure of the group in the proto-Indo-Iranian religion.

[133] According to Kuiper.

the Zoroastrian Fasli calendar. Beyond these thirty-three main Yazads are many more secondary ones who cannot be precisely counted or categorized. Let us look briefly into the characteristics of some of the thirty-three Yazads.

The seven Amesha Spentas, principle Yazads are:

- Hormuzd – the supreme leader of all Yazads; protector of humanity;
- Bahman – bestows good mind, kindness and mercy; protector of cattle;
- Ardebehest – bestower of heat, light and lightning;
- Sheherevar – controls silver, gold and bronze; gives wealth and acts as protector;
- Aspendamard – controls earth, rain and bestows fertility;
- Khordad – controls sky, water and is giver of knowledge;
- Amardad – controls cattle and cultivation of crops.

Others include (not in order):

- Mohor – controls moon and growth of vegetation;
- Teshtar Tir – controls rain, planets and stars; gives longevity and good eyesight;
- Farrokh Farvardin – guardian of the immortal body of the hero Kershasp (Kersaspa/Keresaspa/Gershasp), the slayer of the evil dragon;
- Din – gives forgiveness; cures all diseases and miseries; helps unhappy women; protects from harassment and fright;
- Jamyad – controls 2,244 sacred mountains of the earth which help protect humanity. [134]

We cannot go into more detail here but this brief description of the functions of some of the thirty-three main Yazads resembles the White Tengeri of Bө Murgel; they, too, figure as the protectors of humanity and virtue and each controls certain aspects of nature, for example:

- Udaa Münhe Tengeri – creator of the element water and Uhan Haats;
- Huhe Manhan Tengeri – patron of human souls and those of domesticated animals;

---

[134] For the full list of the Thirty-Three Yazads see <http://tenets.zoroastrianism.com/yaz33.html> accessed 17.04.07.

- Ishkhii Bayaan Tengeri – controls *bayaan*[135]-well-being; patron of wealth and well-being;
- Uhaa Solbon Tengeri – creator of horses; lord of planet Venus;
- Mender Zalaa Tengeri – controls hail and meteorites; punishes evil-doers;
- Altan Tengeri – controls mineral riches and all the gold mines on earth
- Khaan Buudal Tengeri – controls birth and the Tengeri's actions on earth.[136]

A further correlation between the White Tengeri of Bө Murgel and the Iranian Yazads is their celestial origin. The Yazads are associated with star systems and the Tengeri gather for council in the various star constellations. Even their numbers match. Although the most common figure for the number of White Tengeri under the leadership of Hormusta Tengeri is fifty-five, different traditions of Buryatian Bө Murgel vary on this point and thirty-three is also a relatively common number. In spite of not being a major classification of the White Tengeri in modern Buryatian Bө Murgel, thirty-three was most probably the original one with more deities being added to the original group as it developed over time.

There are also thirty-three Devas in *Rigveda,* some of whom are found in the Zoroastrian pantheon, so this suggests that the thirty-three main Yazads in Zoroastrianism were also modelled on the earlier pre-Zoroastrian group of deities in the same way as the Amesha Spentas were. This in turn suggests that the thirty-three original White Tengeri of Bө Murgel are parallel to the thirty-three Yazata gods of the proto-Iranian pantheon and not to the transformed Zoroastrian pantheon. Interestingly, a synonym for *deva* in Sanskrit is *divaukas* – 'one who lives in the sky', a god or planet,[137] 'sky-dweller', which exact matches the semantic field covered by Mongol-Buryat *tengeri.* This further supports linking the thirty-three Devas of *Rigveda*, the thirty-three White Tengeri of Bө Murgel and the thirty-three Yazatas of the proto-Iranian pantheon. In later Hinduism the original thirty-three Devas are expanded to 330 million, in Zoroastrianism the final number of Yazads is said to be infinite while in Bө Murgel the original thirty-three White Tengeri became expanded to fifty-

---

[135] Bur. баяан.

[136] Not in order. For the full list see Appendix.

[137] According to Sanskrit Heritage Dictionary, on-line at <http://sanskrit.inria.fr/DICO/32.html#diva> accessed 28.10.07.

five, 1000, 10,000 or countless. As these religious traditions developed, the numbers changed and no longer correspond, suggesting that at this later stage these traditions evolved independently without influencing each other.

Fig. 7. Varuna.

However, perhaps the most striking support for the theory that the Bɵ Murgel pantheon of White Tengeri is directly related to the proto-Indo-Iranian one comes from the similarities between Huhe Münhe Tengeri and Hormusta Tengeri of Bɵ Murgel and the main Vedic gods, particularly Varuna. The White Tengeri are referred to in full as Baruunai Sagaan Tengeri. In Buryatian '*baruunai*' means 'right-standing', 'western' and comes from '*baruun*'[138] meaning 'right' or 'west'. One of Vedic Varuna's many functions was the Guardian of the West and so the Sanskrit word for 'west' is '*varuni*'.[139] It is not difficult to see how *varuni* transits to *baruun* and their semantic concordance is no mere coincidence. There is no doubt that both words come from the same word: *varuna*. Varuna of the Vedas is also the Guardian of *rita*, righteous cosmic order, justice and morality and all Indo-Aryan and Indo-European peoples associate this righteousness with the right side. This connection can be traced back to the times when the proto-Indo-Iranians were migrating southwards before they split into Iranians and Indo-Aryans; as the Guardian of the West, Varuna was always to the right as they travelled south, so his function as Guardian of *rita* also became linked with this right side, an association which is still alive in the majority of Indo-Iranian and Indo-European languages and cultures today.

The Mongol-Buryat word *baruun* meaning 'right' and 'west' must have come from the same period; Mongol-Buryats have the Front

---

138 Bur. баруун.

139 Guseva, *Slavyane*, p.127; G. Dumézil, *Verkhovnye bogi indoevropeitsev* (Moskva, 1986) (orig. pub. as George Dumézil, *Les dieux indo-européens*, publié aux Presses universitaires de France, 1952).

in the south, Right in the west, Back in the north and Left in the east corresponding to this ancient direction of migration which was not peculiar to the proto-Indo-Iranians alone.

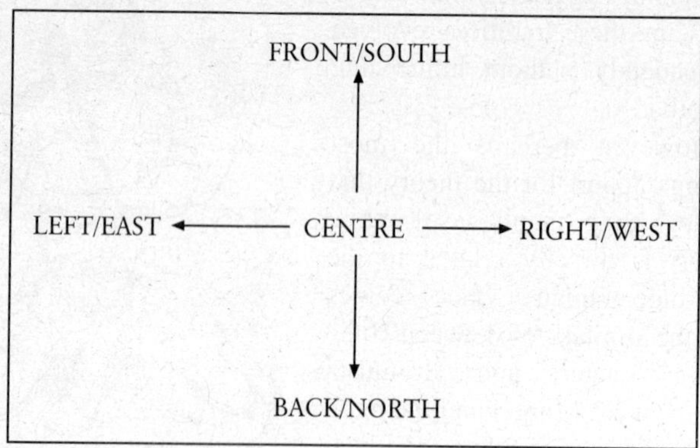

Fig. 8. Four Directions of Mongol-Buryats.

Furthermore, Mongol-Buryats also associate west and the right side with virtue; their virtuous sky-gods who protect the righteous cosmic order, justice and morality – namely Baruunai Sagaan Tengeri or Western (Right-standing) White Tengeri and their leader Hormusta Tengeri – are positioned in the right western sector of the sky.[140] These sorts of parallels between two cultures do not arise as a result of brief exposure to one another; rather, they are signs of prolonged contact, common cultural values and common history.

When could such prolonged interaction have taken place? Mongols had no direct or extended exposure to Vedic Indo-Aryan culture or to the Sanskrit language, and only came into direct contact with India as late as the fourteenth century. Although late Hunnu and Syanbi did interface with the Kushana Empire, Tokharistan and Sogd whose main religions were Shaivism, Zoroastrianism and Buddhism, the old Vedic gods did not play a prominent role in these religions so it is very unlikely that these contacts could explain such complex cultural parallels. Later Tyurkic tribes had first-hand exposure to India but only in the eleventh century AD when Seljuk Turks, an offshoot of the Oguz Tyurkic tribe, came to occupy a part of India but they had already forsaken their original faith

---

[140] The division of the state and army into central, right and left wings was an original Hunnu model which most probably corresponded to the position of the patron sky-gods. This structure was used later by the Syanbi, Tyurkyut and Mongols, clearly showing the continuity of culture in the Great Steppe.

and converted to Sunni Islam in Central Asia prior to that.[141] Neither did the early proto-Mongol Hunnu have direct contact with Indian culture. This suggests, then, that the matching ideas in Vedic culture and Bɵ Murgel must have their roots in prehistory. To further substantiate this theory, let's take a closer look at the qualities of Varuna and other proto-Indo-Iranian and Vedic gods to compare them with the Tengeri of Bɵ Murgel.

Proto-Indo-Iranian gods, Vedic gods and the Tengeri

Pre-Vedic *Varuna, and later Vedic Varuna of *Rigveda,* is the supreme god, All-Encompassing Sky. He created and supports sky and earth; he is the king of the universe, king of gods and men. He controls heavenly waters, dispenses rains and also commands the rivers and oceans.[142] As the Guardian of *rita,* one of his main functions is to ensure that the virtuous world order is maintained; this is a very ancient role of proto-Indo-Iranian *Varuna. *Mitra, the proto-Indo-Iranians' god of sunlight and virtue, is also concerned with maintaining virtuous world order, *rita*, and shares a number of other parallel functions with *Varuna. As we have seen, in *Rigveda* these two gods are twinned and are invoked as Mitravaruna.

In Bɵ Murgel, Huhe Münhe Tengeri or Eternal Blue Sky plays a strikingly similar role. He is the creator of all things, of sky and earth, the maintainer of the universal order of virtue. He is eternal space and time, ancestor of the sun, moon, planets, stars and other universal energies which are personified as Tengeri. Together with the Baruunai Sagaan Tengeri he is the creator and protector of humanity. Huhe Münhe Tengeri, Eternal Blue Sky, shares the same characteristics as and is fully comparable with All-Encompassing Sky i.e. Pre-Vedic *Varuna, Vedic Varuna and Mitravaruna in particular, who in turn is the same as *Mithra-Ahura and Ahura Mazda, as was demonstrated above. So Kuiper's theory of the identity of pre-Zoroastrian Ahura Mazda is thus confirmed from a new angle: Huhe Münhe Tengeri is the same as the chief Ahura/Asura of proto-Indo-Iranians. Indeed, he may even originally have been called *Baruun[143] by the prehistoric proto-Mongols, as suggested by the title and position of Baruunai Sagaan Tengeri.

---

141 'Seljuq', Encyclopædia Britannica. 2007. Encyclopædia Britannica Online. <http://www.britannica.com/eb/article-9066688> accessed 25.05.07.

142 In later Hinduism this became his main function.

143 Here I have adopted the use of * for a reconstructed name.

This suggestion is further strengthened by the existence of a god with a similar name among the Yakuts (Saha) who lived around Lake Baikal in the past and share a common genetic and cultural component with western Buryats which goes back to the Gooligan' (Kurykan) tribes who lived in the Baikal region in the fifth to ninth centuries AD. As a nation, the Yakuts went through a long period of ethnogenesis which can be traced back as least early as the second millennium BC. The modern Yakuts' main god-creator is Urun Aiyy Toyon[144] and is most probably the proto-Indo-Iranian deity Ahura *Varuna. Indeed, Yakut mythology and terminology surrounding their cult of Aiyy sky-gods resonates with Indo-Iranian culture, and with Indo-Aryan Vedic culture in particular. Moreover, the Yakut language also has a number of parallels with Sanskrit. This Indo-Aryan connection has been further verified through immuno-genetical studies. Recent research has shown that 29.1% of Yakuts have HLA-AI antigen, an antigen normally only found in European people. In Yakuts this European component is found in conjunction with another antigen, HLA-BI7.[145] The same combination is found among western Buryats but the percentage of the population displaying it there is lower. This same antigen combination is also found among the Hindu population of India. This clearly suggests that Indo-Iranians were among the ancient ancestors of Yakuts and western Buryats.[146] This in turn suggests that long ago the ancestors of modern Hindus (proto-Indo-Iranian Aryans) had prolonged contact with the ancestors of modern western Buryats (proto-Mongols) which resulted in genetic, cultural and religious exchange and explains the common cult of *Varuna/Urun/*Baruun. Indeed, this god must have been a universal godhead in the prehistoric religion of Eurasia as Slavic tribes of eastern Europe (the ancestors of modern Russians, Byelorussians and Ukrainians) worshipped him as Perun and he was the chief deity of their pantheon.

---

144 Yakut. Урун Айыы Тойон.

145 V.V. Ferfelova, 'Participation of Indo-European tribes in ethnogeny of the Mongoloid population of Siberia: analysis of the HLA antigen distribution in Mongoloids of Siberia', *The American Journal of Human Genetics* Vol. 47, pp. 294–301, 1990 cited in: Brigitte Pakendorf, Victor Wiebe, Larissa A. Tarskaia, Victor A. Spitsyn, Himla Soodyall, Alexander Rodewald, Mark Stoneking, 'Mitochondrial DNA Evidence for Admixed Origins of Central Siberian Populations', *American Journal of Physical Anthropology* № 120, 2003, pp. 211–224; and *Proiskhozhdenie yakutov* [*Происхождение якутов*], <http://www.kyrgyz.ru/?page=83> accessed 03.05.07.

146 Interestingly, the main Bө Murgel cult of western Buryats is the worship of Baruunai Sagaan Tengeri, their children and grandchildren, the Baruunai Haduud.

The original proto-Mongol name (possibly *Baruun) may have dropped out of use among the ancestors of western Buryats if it became taboo to pronounce the godhead's name, as indeed was the case among some Indo-Iranians (and still is among the Jews).[147] Consequently he would be addressed by one of his epithets, Sky (Tengeri), Eternal Blue Sky, which gradually became his main name while the ancestors of the Yakuts retained the original name, which they pronounced as 'Urun'. All this clearly demonstrates that D.S. Doogarov's suggestion regarding the nature of the religion practised by the Yakuts' and Buryats' Gooligan' (Kurykan) ancestors is correct:

> The ancient religion of the Kurykans – the cult of the tribal god Aia – which we have generally labelled as White Shamanism, was inherited by their descendants – Buryats and Yakuts. Ultimately, this cult has Indo-Iranian and, broadly speaking, common European origins.[148]

An Ancient Greek connection

Proto-Indo-Iranian *Varuna, Yakut Urun and proto-Mongol *Baruun find their direct equivalent in the pantheon of ancient Greeks in Uranus (Ouranos)[149]. Uranus is the Sky and the name itself literally means 'sky'. In Greek mythology, Uranus is husband (and son) of Gaia (Earth). Both of them belong to the Primeval Gods (*Protogenoi*)[150] born at the beginning of the universe. Uranus is the first ruler of the universe. Uranus-Sky came every night to copulate with Gaia-Earth and their union gave rise to the next generation of gods and goddesses – the Titans. Their younger son, Titan Cronos,[151] overthrew Uranus and ruled over the universe in the Golden Age. He in turn was overthrown by his son, Zeus, who became the next ruler of the universe and leader of the third generation of gods – the Twelve Olympians (*Dodekatheon*).[152]

Uranus, Gaia and other Primeval Gods of Greek mythology are clearly gods of the animistic religion of proto-Indo-Europeans as they are barely anthropomorphic and represent natural phenomena. For example,

---

[147] F. B. J. Kuiper, 'The Bliss of Aša, *Indo-Iranian Journal* 8, p.109, 1964–65.

[148] Doogarov, *Istoricheskie korni,* pp. 3–19.

[149] Greek. Οὐρανός.

[150] Greek. Πρωτογενοι.

[151] Greek. Κρόνος.

[152] Greek. Δωδεκάθεον.

the goddess Nix[153] is the night, the goddess Hemera[154] is the day, the god Khronos[155] is time and so on. Most of these ancient gods, though present in mythology, did not have offering rituals dedicated to them, which suggests that they were relicts dating back to a time long before the era of the ancient Greeks; they are most probably gods of distant Greek ancestors who worshipped them before they came to Greece. Cronos deposed Uranus by castrating him with a flint sickle.[156] This detail clearly suggests that the cults of Uranus and Gaia belong to the Stone Age and are thus directly comparable to the cults of Eternal Blue Sky and Etugen-Earth in Bө Murgel. Uranus is clearly the same as the proto-Indo-Iranian *Varuna as, when unifying with Gaia, Uranus is associated with the night sky, one of the aspects of *Varuna, the All-Encompassing Sky. So Uranus can be equated with *Baruun, later known as Huhe Münhe Tengeri. Clear evidence supporting this is the fact that the proto-Mongol Hunnu cult of Heaven and Earth included an idol personifying the Cosmos, directly comparable to Uranus of ancient Greek mythology and proto-Indo-Iranian *Varuna and Vedic Varuna.[157]

We have seen that *Varuna, *Baruun (Huhe Münhe Tengeri), Urun, Uranus and Perun resemble one another very closely, so closely in fact that we can surmise they are one god whose name was modified as time went by. This unmistakably points to the existence of an international religion and culture shared by the diverse ethnic and racial groups of Eurasia in prehistory. The pantheons of the proto-Europeans, proto-Indo-Iranians and proto-Mongols have a common source in this ancient religion, the Prehistoric Bön of Eurasia.

Hormusta Tengeri and the proto-Indo-Iranian gods

We can also draw many parallels between Hormusta Tengeri, the gods of the Vedic pantheon and pre-Zoroastrian Ahura Mazda (Xwrmzt – Hurmazta). In our comparison of Hormusta and Nyipangse, we demonstrated that both these gods are equivalent to Vedic Indra. Hormusta Tengeri is also comparable to Varuna, Mitra and, in particular, he is directly comparable to another twinned divine form from *Rigveda*, Indravaruna.[158]

---

153 Greek. Νύξ.

154 Greek. Ημερα.

155 Greek. Χρόνος.

156 The reign and castration of Uranus, Quote: Hesiod, Theogony 126, <http://www.theoi.com/Protogenos/Ouranos.html> accessed 19.06.07.

157 Gumilev, *Istoriya Hunnu* 1, pp. 132.

158 E.g. *Rigveda* tr. Griffith, Book 1, Hymn XVII, st. 1.

Fig. 9. Indra.

As the Lord of the thirty-three Western Tengeri, Hormusta is Indra's counterpart. However, he is positioned in the western sector of the sky, a position designated for Vedic Varuna. Varuna and Hormusta correspond in several ways. In some traditions of Bɵ Murgel in both Buryatia and Mongolia, Hormusta Tengeri is actually equated with Huhe Münhe Tengeri so the comparisons drawn between Varuna and Huhe Münhe Tengeri are also valid for Hormusta Tengeri. In the same way as Vedic Varuna, Hormusta is the protector of virtue, the leader of the Baruunai Sagaan Tengeri and creator of humanity. Among his attributes he has a lasso for catching evil-doers, an attribute he shares with Varuna, but his appearance is identical with that of Mithra as described in the *Mihr Yasht* (Hymn to Mithra) of *Khorda Avesta*, a text obviously based on the pre-Zoroastrian cult of Mithra:

> The warrior of the white horse, of the sharp spear, the long spear, the quick arrows; foreseeing and clever.[159]

In the Sassanid period (226–651 AD), Ahura Mazda himself is often depicted as a bearded warrior-king wearing a crown and riding a horse[160] and in his *The Histories*[161] Herodotus (484–425 BC) describes a much earlier custom of dedicating a chariot drawn by white horses as a support for Ahura Mazda.[162] This custom was surely a continuation of the pre-

---

[159] Mihr Yahst XXVI, st.102. Tr. Darmesteter <http://www.avesta.org/ka/yt10sbe.htm> accessed 28.05.07.

[160] See, for example, the relief from Naqsh-i Rustam, <http://www.hp.uab.edu/image_archive/ugp/> accessed 04.05.07.

[161] Robin A. H. Waterfield, *Herodotus: The Histories* (translation; introduction and notes by C. Dewald), 1.189, 7.40, (London: Oxford University Press (Oxford World's Classics), 1998).

[162] A somewhat similar tradition whereby living horses are dedicated to the Tengeri is also found in Buryatian Bɵ Murgel and other native Siberian traditions. See ch. XII.

Zoroastrian cult of Ahura Mazda, in his Mithra aspect, because in *Mihr Yasht* Mithra rides in an identical carriage:

> With his arms lifted up towards Immortality, Mithra, the lord of wide pastures, drives forward from the shining Garo-nmana, in a beautiful chariot that drives on, ever-swift, adorned with all sorts of ornaments, and made of gold.
> Four stallions draw that chariot, all of the same white colour, living on heavenly food and undying.[163]

Another way in which Hormusta resembles Iranian Mithra is in his function as the leader of the virtuous warrior-gods who aids warriors in battle and destroys evil:

> To whom the chiefs of nations offer up sacrifices, as they go to the field, against havocking hosts, against enemies coming in battle array, in the strife of conflicting nations;[164]
> Whom the horsemen worship on the back of their horses, begging swiftness for their teams, health for their own bodies, and that they may watch with full success those who hate them, smite down their foes, and destroy at one stroke their adversaries, their enemies, and those who hate them.[165]

Iranian Mithra rides in the midst of other Yazata gods in the same way as Hormusta Tenegri is surrounded by other White Tengeri.[166]

Hormusta Tengeri is also the lord of the sky-waters and a rain-giver, functions parallel to Vedic Varuna and Iranian Mithra ('thanks to whom water [rain] falls and plants grow')[167] while his power to send thunder and lightning are parallel to Vedic Indra and Mitra. In the ancient Buryatian ritual song Hormusta's function as a rain-giver is expressed in the following way:

> When Hormusta Tengeri wakes up the rains will probably return.
> When the hot sun rises the grasses will probably start growing abundantly.[168]

---

[163] Mihr Yahst XXXI, st.124–125, Tr. Darmesteter.

[164] Ibid. II, st.8.

[165] Ibid. III, st.11.

[166] Ibid. st.80, st .126, 127.

[167] Mihr Yasht XV, st. 61, John R. Hinnels, *Iran, iv. Myths and Legends*, <http://www.iranica.com/newsite/articles/v13f3/v13f3003.html> accessed 28.05.07. Darmesteter (ibid.) gives '…making the waters run and the plants grow up.'

[168] 'Хурмастал тэнгэриин тэлэрэмсээр Харинал бэзэ даа бороониинь.

In some traditions of Bɵ Murgel, Hormusta Tengeri is also considered controller of the earthly waters and the *Lusuut Khaans*, the Lords of the *Lusuut* water-spirits (Sanskrit *Nagarajas* and *Nagas*). In Noyohon[169] in southern Buryatia, for example, he is worshipped as the lord of the mountain Hormusta Khaan and is said to have once descended there in the distant past. At the base of the mountain there are two springs where *Lusuut Khaans* are said to dwell. Lusuudyn Tahilga,[170] the offering rite for the water-spirits, is performed on the summit of this mountain and is preceded by the invocation to Hormusta Tengeri. Each time this ritual is performed it invariably results in rainfall.[171] This function of Hormusta as the lord of the earthly waters directly matches Varuna.

As was noted above, in the pre-Vedic and early Vedic period the boundaries between different gods were not clearly defined as they personified cosmic forces beyond human comprehension and so some of them are often called by the same names or considered to be the same entities. In this light, direct parallels between Hormusta Tengeri, Mitravaruna and Indravaruna point to the prehistoric origins of this deity of the proto-Mongols.

From this and the other material presented above we can conclude that the name Hormusta (Hyurmasta) must have derived from its Sughdha (*Old Sogdian) equivalent Xwrmzt (Hurmazta) which refers to pre-Zoroastrian Yazata Ahura Mazda of Iran and not to the later Zoroastrian Ahura Mazda. Hormusta Tengeri cannot be compared to Zoroastrian Ahura Mazda because he doesn't fit into the new interpretation given to Ahura Mazda by Zarathushtra and, also, because there are no other Tengeri in the pantheon of Bɵ Murgel who have similar names or can be directly compared to the Zoroastrian group of Amesha Spentas. If Hormusta is to be compared to any deity of the Zoroastrian pantheon, it has to be Mithra, but the names do not match and Mithra himself is a pre-Zoroastrian god. It is clear, then, that Hormusta Tengeri is comparable to the pre-Zoroastrian supreme god Miθra Ahura bərəzanta/*Mithra-Ahura

---

С пробуждением Хормуста-тэнгри, должно быть, вернется (пора) дождей.

Халуун наранай мандалсаар Халюурнал бэзэ даа ногоониинь.

С восходом горячего солнца, должно быть, (начнут) переливаться травы.' (Ашабагад 1999. 20 мая). Б.С. Дугаров, *Этнос и культура. Культ горы Хормуста в Бурятии*, B. S. Doogarov, *Etnos i kul'tura. Kul't goryi Khormusta v Buryatii* <http://studlib.ru/article/a-1040.html> accessed 02.05.07.

169 Bur. Ноёхон.

170 Bur. лусуудын тахилга.

171 Ibid.

who, as suggested by Kuiper, is Vedic Mitravaruna. This also makes sense in the light of our discovery that Hormusta and Nyipangse are one and the same. As was said above, Nyipangse is associated with the sun and in this aspect is directly comparable to the *Mithra aspect of pre-Zoroastrian Ahura Mazda. This is also concurrent with the view of R.C. Zaehner who says that pre-Zoroastrian Ahura Mazda was associated, among other things, with the sun or sunlight:

> In the Seven Chapters, on the other hand, he is especially associated both with the sun and the fire as well as with daylight in general, and again he appears in the west[172], surmounting the great inscription at Bīsitūn[173], as a human head rising out of the sun-disc with the sun's rays stretching forth on either side. Further, his name survives in Khotanese as *urmayzd* and in Sangglechi as *ormōzd*, and in both languages the word means sun.
>
> It seems then probable that the original Ahura Mazdāh must have had solar connexions, but so complex is the nature of primitive deities that we are practically always wrong in assigning to them only one natural association, for pre-Zoroastrian Ahura was more evidently still connected with the concept of Truth or cosmic order as well as with the waters than he was with the light or the sun.[174]

In the light of this understanding, then, the two other principal aspects of Nyipangse are expressions of his complex nature. Thus Dapangse ('moon-god') can be interpreted as representing the night sky and therefore comparable to *Vouruna[175] while Zhapangse ('rainbow-god') could be interpreted as a combined form like *Mithra-*Vouruna as both sun and moon produce rainbows[176] and are generally perceived as auspicious, miraculous divine expressions. So pre-Zoroastrian Ahura Mazda/Xwrmzt = Hormusta Tengeri = Nyipangse and they are, in fact,

---

[172] Direction of Varuna.

[173] The inscription of the Emperor Darius I (522–486 BC) at Bihistun (Bisitun) mentioned above.

[174] R.C. Zaehner, *The Dawn and Twilight of Zoroastrianism*, (London: Weidenfeld and Nicolson, 1961), p. 75.

[175] This spelling indicates that here we are talking specifically about the pre-Zoroastrian Iranian form of *Varuna.

[176] Rainbows are usually associated with the sun but they can form from moonlight, too, not just as the circular rainbow around the moon but as a proper arc rainbow as well. I and the other islanders observed one such moon-rainbow from Holy Island off Arran in Scotland on the night of the full moon in September 1996.

the same compound deity, *Mithra-*Vouruna. Baruunai Sagaan Tengeri, then, are generally comparable to the rest of the thirty-three Yazata gods of pre-Zoroastrian Iran and the thirty-three gods of Indo-Aryan *Rigveda*.

Agni and the role of fire

A look at the god Agni strengthens this argument. In *Rigveda* Varuna is often identified with Agni, the god of Fire. Indra, who is twinned with Varuna as Indravaruna, also appears in a very close group of three gods: Agni, Indra (Vayu)[177] and Surya,[178] and is sometimes twinned with Agni as Indraagni.[179] Agni is so crucial to pre-Vedic, Vedic and later Hindu culture that his functions and characteristics have remained unchanged to this day; he is the divine personification of fire in all its functions. In his function as fire in the hearth, Agni is called Garhapatya (Fire of the Lord of the House); as the sacrificial fire into which offerings to the gods are burnt in the *yajna* rituals he is called Ahavaniya (Sacrificial), Dakshina (Offered), Abhimani (Demanding everything for himself); and as the receptor of blood sacrifices he is known as Kravyad (Blood-eating).[180]

Fig. 10. Agni.

Fire is an indispensable element of any offering ritual in the Vedic and later Hindu religions so Agni is the great deliverer, bringing the offerings to the gods. Pre-Zoroastrian Iranians also had a cult of fire where fire was personified as Atar. Sacrificial fire was an indispensable component in ritual *yasna* sacrifices in pre-Zoroastrian Iran, and the roots of this fire cult stem from earlier proto-Indo-Iranian

[177] Vayu is the god of Wind element and the Vedas depict him as either identical with Indra or as his constant companion who rides the sky with him in the same heavenly chariot. Indravayu appears, for example, in *Rigveda* tr. Griffith, Book 1, Hymn CXXXV, st. 5.

[178] Guseva, *Slavyane*, pp.127–134.

[179] E.g. *Rigveda* tr. Griffith, Book 1, Hymn XXI, st. 2.

[180] Guseva, *Slavyane*, p.132.

culture.[181] In Buryatian Bɵ Murgel the fire cult has exactly the same characteristics as in pre-Vedic and Vedic culture and the culture of pre-Zoroastrian Iran. All Bɵ Murgel rituals invariably start with an offering to the Lords of Fire, who are of celestial origin.[182] Then, as in Indo-Iranian culture, all offerings are burnt, as here, too, fire is said to be the means of delivering offerings to the Tengeri and other gods and spirits. It is a taboo to throw or burn rubbish in fire because if fire is defiled in this way it will send bad luck and diseases. According to Bɵ Murgel fire was given to the people by the sky-dwelling White Tengeri headed by Hormusta Tengeri and thus has heavenly origins. These parallel aspects of the Buryatian Bɵ Murgel fire cult emerged from prehistory and cannot be said to have equivalents in later Zoroastrianism as some scholars believe. Clear proof of this comes from the custom of fire-burials common to pre-Vedic, Vedic, Hindu and Bɵ Murgel traditions, while Zoroastrianism prohibits burning corpses as this would pollute the 'pure fire':

> Burial/burning of corpses are both considered wrong actions in the Vendidad. In an earlier Fargad (chapter), Mazda says that they were actions dreamed up by the evil one and taught to humanity to mislead them to pollute the earth and the Fire.[183]

In Zoroastrianism, fire was reinterpreted as an untainted substance which must be kept ritually pure. This differs from the earlier Indo-Iranian perception of fire as the universal purifier which cannot be defiled by the impurity of death, hence the Vedic and later Hindu custom of burning corpses as an offering to Agni. Sky burial, which is another common custom in Bɵ Murgel, is not particularly limited to the Zoroastrians either as Indian Jains use the same method. It seems that sky or air burial[184] was one of several ways corpses were disposed of not only among the various Aryan tribes but also among non-Aryans as well, as sky burials[185] are practised by Tibetans who surely inherited it from the Zhang Zhung Bönpo culture which preceded them.

A further difference in the way modern Zoroastrians and followers of Bɵ Murgel relate to fire is the Bɵ Murgel custom of using fire as the receptacle and deliverer of blood sacrifices. This differs from modern

---

[181] M. Boyce, 'Ātaš', *Encyclopaedia Iranica*, 1–5, New York, 2002.

[182] For the fire cult in Bɵ Murgel see ch. XII.

[183] *The Zoroastrian Dakhma-nashini mode of disposal of the dead*, <http://tenets.zoroastrianism.com/dakhma33.html> accessed 26.05.07.

[184] Dakhma-Nashini or Tower of Silence.

[185] Tib bya gtor; lit. 'strewn by the birds'.

Hinduism, too, where blood sacrifices have largely been abandoned, but is directly comparable to fire sacrifices in the proto-Indo-Iranian, Vedic and pre-Zoroastrian religions. The ancient pre-Zoroastrian ritual *Atash Zohr*, offering the fat of a sacrificial animal into a bonfire, practised by pre-Zoroastrian Iranian priests and the Brahmins of India alike, originated at least as early as the third millennium BC and found its way into Zoroastrianism. However, it is not directly comparable to blood sacrifices in Bɵ Murgel.[186] In *Mihr Yasht*, on the other hand, we find direct reference to animal sacrifices in Zoroastrianism where Zarathushtra Spitama is instructed by Ahura Mazda to make animal sacrifices to Mithra. This tradition, again, is no doubt of pre-Zoroastrian origin, as is the cult of Mithra itself:

> Offer up a sacrifice unto Mithra, O Spitama! And order thy pupils to do the same.
> Let the worshipper of Mazda sacrifice unto thee with small cattle, with black cattle,[187] with flying birds, gliding forward on wings.[188]

In modern Bɵ Murgel, Hormusta and his Baruunai Sagaan Tengeri are not offered blood sacrifices although five of the White Tengeri accept bloodless animal sacrifices through *seter* suffocation. This type of sacrifice was also practised in the Russian pre-Christian religion.[189]

A further analogous aspect of Buryatian Bɵ Murgel and the proto-Indo-Iranian religions is where these rituals were conducted. Bɵ Murgel doesn't have temples and its rituals are conducted at sacred spots in the natural setting of the *taiga*, steppe or mountains. Bɵ Murgel has no icons or statues to represent the Tengeri.[190] These characteristics are directly parallel to the religion of the proto-Indo-Iranian who built no temples and made no images of their gods.

Zurvanism

Further evidence that the cult of Hormusta Tengeri arose in deep prehistory when the proto-Indo-Iranians, proto-Indo-Europeans and

---

[186] M. Boyce, 'Ātaš-zōhr and Āzohrδδ, *Journal of the Royal Asiatic Society*, 1966, pp. 100–110.

[187] It is strange that black cattle offered here to Mithra who is the white god. This might be because it is based on the list of offerings to *Mithra-*Vouruna with black cattle originally offered to *Vouruna.

[188] Mihr Yasht XXX st. 119. Tr. Darmesteter.

[189] Guseva, *Slavyane*, p.194.

[190] Although there are *ongon*-supports for the ancestral and other kind s of lower spirits, this is a separate cult.

proto-Mongols lived side by side either in the Great Steppe or in the circumpolar regions of the Arctic[191] and shared a common culture and polytheistic religion – Prehistoric Bön of Eurasia – comes from the later Iranian religion known in the West as Zurvanism where Hormuzd (Ohrmazd) is not a supreme god-creator but one of the twin sons of the god Zurvan (Zervan), Infinite Time-Space. Although this view is branded as heresy by many orthodox Zoroastrian scholars and the god Zurvan-Time does not appear in the function of the supreme god-creator in early Zoroastrian texts,[192] an ideological base to support it is found in the *Avesta* itself where, in *Yasna 30,* we read:

> 3. Now the two primal Spirits, who reveal themselves in vision as Twins, are the Better and the Bad, in thought and word and action. And between these two the wise ones chose aright, the foolish not so.
> 4. And when these twain Spirits came together in the beginning, they created Life and Not-Life, and that at the last Worst Existence shall be to the followers of the Lie, but the Best Existence to him that follows Right.
> 5. Of these twain Spirits he that followed the Lie chose doing the worst things; the holiest Spirit chose Right, he that clothes him with the massy heavens as a garment. So likewise they that are fain to please Ahura Mazda by dutiful actions.[193]

In this model Hormuzd represents the positive principle of the universal energy while his twin brother Ahriman represents the negative aspect of the universal force. While chronologically Zurvanism, as an organized religion, appeared much later than Zoroastrianism,[194] there is good reason to suggest that its doctrine of twin brother gods predates Zoroastrianism and is rooted in the religious streams of proto-Indo-Iranian peoples which remained sidelined by official Zoroastrianism in Iran but did not completely die out. This can be deduced from Kuiper's theory of the origin of Ahura Mazda as the proto-Indo-Iranian nameless

---

[191] See ch. XV.

[192] For the translation and analysis of the passages of *Avesta* and *Vendidad* mentioning Zurvan see R.C Zaehner, *Zurvan: A Zoroastrian Dilemma* (London: Oxford University Press (The Clarendon Press, Oxford), 1955), p. 275.

[193] Tr. Darmesteter <http://www.avesta.org/yasna/y28to34b.htm> accessed 08.06.07.

[194] Zurvanism is first mentioned in Greek sources in the writings of Aristotle's disciple Eudemus of Rhodes (370–300 BC).

compound deity equivalent to later Vedic Mitravaruna where *Mitra represents the light and *Vouruna represents darkness. These traditions had more chance of surviving on the outskirts of the Persian Empire and beyond its borders among the descendants of the ancient Indo-Iranian tribes which did not migrate to Iran itself but remained in the Great Steppe and later became historical nations such as Sughdhas (and later historical Sogdians), Scythians, Indo-Scythians and Yuezhi. These archaic Aryan beliefs, of which there were many variations, were common to all proto-Indo-Iranians before they split with one part migrating to Persia and other invading India and, resurfacing later, mingled with Zoroastrianism resulting in the formation of Zurvanism.[195] Indirect evidence of this is found among the east Iranian Sogdians, for example, for whom Zrw (Azrua), i.e. Zurvan, was the supreme god which Sogdian Buddhists later considered to be the same as the Indian god Brahma.[196]

In this case, identifying Zurvan with Brahma does not constitute an attempt to bridge two unrelated deities of different religious backgrounds which was common practice among the Tibetan Buddhists, but is genuine as both Sogdian and Indo-Aryan cultures have the same cultural and religious roots.

Fig. 11. Brahma.

Further evidence pointing to the identical nature of the Iranian Yazatas and White Tengeri is the fact that Sogdian Buddhists later identified Xwrmzt (Hurmazta) as the Indian god Indra,[197] the king of the Thirty-Three Gods. Xwrmzt's association with Indra can be explained as coming from much earlier historical epoch than the time of the spread of

[195] Old religious and cultural practices are very resilient and can continue to be practised alongside the official new religion for thousands of years, as was the case with the pre-Christian religion of Russia. It remained very much alive among the peasants up to the 1917 Communist revolution and still survives in some from in some regions, especially in the north, even now, practised alongside the Christian Orthodox religion introduced in 8th c. AD.

[196] Zaehner, *Zurvan,* p. 22.

[197] Ibid.

Buddhism in Sogd. An Indo-Aryan tribe, the Mitanni/Maitanni, invaded northern Mesopotamia in the seventeenth century BC where, imposing their rulership over the native Hurri/Hanigalbat tribes, they set up a great state (~1500 BC ~1270 BC) with its capital Washshukanni in modern-day Syria. The text of their treaty with another major power of the region – Indo-European Hittites – contains invocations to the Indo-Aryan gods Mitra, Varuna, and Indra[198] so specifically Indo-Aryan religious traditions were already actively present in Mesopotamia in the middle of the second millennium BC. Similar processes of 're-mixing' the diverging pantheons of Indo-Aryans and Iranians were probably taking place in other geographical zones to the east and southeast.

Similarities in the mythology, ritual practices and some identical gods among the Indo-Aryan, Iranian, Tyurkic and Mongol-Buryat peoples are, in my opinion, rooted in the very remote past. Possible time periods include:

- the last interglacial period or some time before 4500 BC as suggested by Tilak;
- at the time of the Andronovo culture of the third to second millennia BC;
- during the period of the formation of the Hunnu nation in the second millennium BC when proto-Mongols mixed with Indo-Iranians in the region of modern-day Amdo, Lake Kokonoor and Takla Makan;
- in Southern Siberia where proto-Hunnu arrived after crossing the Gobi Desert.

These are the possible timeframes which we should look at to support the theory that Hormuzd Yazad of the Indo-Iranians and Hormusta Tengeri of the proto-Mongols are, in fact, the same deity.

Cosmology and pantheon of the Prehistoric Bön of Eurasia

Having established that Sogdian Zrw (Iranian Zurvan), Infinite Time-Space, the mystic creative invisible spiritual force, can be identified as Indian Brahma and also with Huhe Mṳnhe Tengeri/Kök-Tenger of Mongol/Tyurkic nations, we can then reconstruct a picture

---

[198] P. Thieme, 'The "Aryan Gods" of the Mitanni Treaties', *Journal of the American Oriental Society* 80, 1960, pp. 301–317.

of the perception of the universe and principles behind a hypothetical ancient common pantheon of the proto-Indo-Iranians, proto-Mongols and mixed tribes of Zhang Zhung.[199] This pantheon is headed by the invisible creative power identified with the spiritual sky or spiritual time-space, distinct from the ordinary, physical sky or physical space-time. This abstract spiritual principle generates two opposite orders of white and black sky-gods representing the polar aspects of the universe:

- Ahuras/Devas and demons (represented by Vritra and his manifestations Namuchi, Shushna, Shambhara, Vala, Pirpu, Kuyava etc.) of Indo-Aryan Vedas;
- Yazatas and Druj of pre-Zoroastrian Iranians;
- Lha and Düd (Dre) of Tibetan Bön;
- White and Black Tengeri of Bө Murgel;
- Ahuras and Daevas of the Avestan Zoroastrian religion;
- Devas and Asuras of later Hinduism.

The positive sky-gods create existence and human beings, act as their protectors, teachers and spiritual leaders while the negative sky-gods or sky-demons create all sort of negativities and seek to destroy humanity, the creation of the positive gods. At the end of the cosmic cycle the final battle between the forces of good and evil led by the sky-gods will determine which order takes the upper hand in the next universe. This is a general blueprint of the cosmic order and mythology common to proto-Indo-Iranian, proto-Mongol and ancient Tibetan spiritual traditions which have their roots in the Prehistoric Bön of Eurasia.

Yungdrung Bön and Zoroastrianism

It is against the backdrop of this prehistoric culture that the Yungdrung Bön teachings of Tonpa Shenrab Miwo and the later teachings of Zarathushtra should be compared. Although both traditions emerged within proto-(Indo)-Iranian and Iranian society and include ancient substrata of Prehistoric Bön culture as exemplified by their dualistic cosmology of opposite forces of light and darkness, the fundamental doctrines and divine pantheons of Zoroastrianism and Yungdrung Bön are not directly comparable.

---

[199] On the ethnic composition of Zhang Zhung confederation see ch. XV.

Erroneous equation of Zoroastrianism and Mithraism with Yungdrung Bön

Some scholars maintain that Yungdrung Bön either derives from or was heavily influenced by Zoroastrianism. The idea that Yungdrung Bön is a kind of Zoroastrianism or Mazdaism seems to have been pioneered by the Russian scholar B.I. Kuznetsov in the Soviet era of the mid-twentieth century when he attempted to compare Zoroastrian and Bönpo prophets, texts, historical records and pantheons. Unfortunately, his translations and interpretations of Tibetan material are misleading as he was heavily influenced by the ideas of L.N. Gumilev on the subject and together they wrote an article entitled *Bon (Ancient Tibetan Religion)* in which they drew untenable parallels between Bön and Mithraism, the geography of Olmo Lungring and Persia.[200] Despite its short-comings, their work did nevertheless play an important role in bringing this little-known religion to the awareness of many in the Soviet Union, including myself. Both scholars felt passionate about Bön which they understood as a down-to-earth shamanistic religion of the masses as opposed to the artificial, otherworldly Buddhism of the aristocracy. Perhaps this view was shaped by the necessity to present any historical and religious studies through the prism of the Dialectic Materialism of Marxism-Leninism – the only ideology of the USSR. Be that as it may, both scholars failed to distinguish between the various types of Bön so the view they present differs little from that of sectarian Buddhist sources. Moreover, as they had no access to Bönpo lamas, they could not verify their ideas so continued to misinterpret the doctrines of Yungdrung Bön following their own theories which did not, in fact, correspond to the actual tenets of the teachings. As a result, Kuznetsov in particular took a wrong turning in his research which led him to mistaken conclusions regarding the nature of Bön's relationship with Zoroastrianism. Citing passages from an Old-Russian literary work *A Word about the Twelve Dreams of Shahiash*;[201] *Zermig* (the medium version of the biography of Tonpa Shenrab); *History of Buddhism* by Taranatha; and *Septuagint*, the Koine Greek version of the Old Testament, he tried to fit the figure of

---

[200] [L. N. Gumilev, B. I. Kusnetsov, Bon (Drevnyaya Tibetskaya Religiya), *Doklady otdelenii i komissii Geograficheskogo obshchestva SSSR. Etnografiya.* 15 (1970).] Л.Н. Гумилев, Б. И. Кузнецов Бон (Древняя Тибетская Религия), Доклады отделений и комиссий Географического общества СССР. Этнография. 1970. Вып. 15- Ленинград, pp. 72–90, <http://marsexx.narod.ru/lit/gumilev.html#362> accessed 24.06.07.

[201] *Слово о двенадцати снах Шахиаши.*

Shenrab Miwo into the historical context of the Persian Empire, decoding 'Mura' – the first part of Tonpa Shenrab's original Tagzig name 'Mura Tahen' – as Persian 'Mithra' or 'Mitridat' and suggesting that Tonpa Shenrab was in fact a priest-minister of that name at the court of the Persian king Cyrus the Great (590–530 BC).[202] This argument obviously doesn't stand as the evidence presented to support the claim is plainly incorrect from historical, mythological and linguistic points of view.[203] The Tagzig name Mura Tahen cannot be associated with Mithra because the first part, which is *dMu ra* in Tibetan transliteration, refers to the Mushen clan which is descended from the *Mu* sky gods. The second part, *ta hen*, means 'great man'. So the whole name means 'great man of the *Mu*-clan'.[204] *Mu* sky-gods cannot be compared with Mithra because they are not associated with the sun or sun light. Paradoxically, Kuznetsov himself admitted the very fundamental lack of correspondence between the doctrines of Yungdrung Bön and Zoroastrianism in comparing two texts, Zoroastrian *Zaradushtnama,* a thirteenth century biography of Zarathushtra, and *Zermig*, a Yungdrung Bön biography of Shenrab Miwo. In his *Bön and Mazdaism,* Kuznetsov writes:

> The main discrepancy between the books lies in the fact that Zarathushtra preaches monotheism while Shenrab preaches polytheism. This clearly demonstrates that the Tibetan book is more archaic.[205]

The author patently contradicts his own theory here by admitting that *Zermig* is based on more archaic traditions, a conclusion I completely agree with, but for entirely different reasons. Furthermore, as the teachings of Yungdrung Bön are the doctrine of a Buddha, they show the path of liberation from circulating in cycles of death and birth, and have nothing to do with the polytheistic belief in multiple worldly gods who have ultimate control over human destiny but are still bound within the cycle of *samsara*.

---

202 B. I. Kusnetsov, 'Yavlyaetsya li Shenrab – osnovatel' religii bon – istoricheskoi lichnost'yu?', *Vostokovedcheskie issledovanniya v Buryatii,* Novosibirsk 1981, pp. 92–95.

203 For a critical appraisal of Kuznetsov's hypothesis from a geographical and historical perspective according to Bönpo sources, see Dan Martin, 'Olmo Lungring: A Holy Place Here and Beyond' in *Bon: The Magic Word*, Ed. Karmay and Watt, pp. 99–123.

204 According to oral explanations by Yongdzin Lopön Tenzin Namdak.

205 B. I. Kusnetsov, *Bon i Mazdaizm* (St-Petersburg: Evrasiya, 2001), p.130. Translation mine.

Moreover, as the concept of cosmic duality, light and dark, is prevalent among so many ancient cultures of Eurasia, this cannot stand alone as a base for comparing Yungdrung Bön and Zoroastrianism.

Deities of Yungdrung Bön and Zoroastrianism

A further point of contention is that, so far, no satisfactory correspondence has been established between the deities of Yungdrung Bön and those of Zoroastrianism. As Samten Karmay rightly stated:

> Even if Khri-rgyal Khug-pa corresponds to Ahura Mazda, it is rather difficult to see how other Bon deities, Sangs-Po 'Bum-khri, for example, correspond to any of the other gods in Zoroastrianism. This religion itself has gone through tremendous change. The number of gods and demons and their functions are almost totally different from those in Bon.[206]

How, then, does this relate to our discovery that Nyipangse and Hormuzd are one and the same deity? The connection between these two sky-gods clearly comes from the layer of Prehistoric Bön common to the Indo-Iranian Aryans and to the peoples of Zhang Zhung who had an Aryan component in their culture.[207] Nyipangse is not an original Yungdrung Bön deity but a god of the Prehistoric Bönpo pantheon of Zhang Zhung later incorporated into Yungdrung Bön's pantheon of protective gods. As Hormuzd Yazad was originally a pre-Zoroastrian deity later incorporated into the Zoroastrian pantheon, we can clearly see that the connection between Tibetan Bön and the ancient Iranian religions is pre-Zoroastrian. From this perspective, the correlating concepts of cosmic duality common to Yungdrung Bön and Zoroastrianism have to be explained in terms of both traditions' shared cultural roots in the Prehistoric Bön of Eurasia and not by any spurious direct influence of one on the other. So Trigyal Khugpa and Sangpo Bumtri of the Yungdrung Bön creation myth do not correspond to Zoroastrian Ahura Mazda but are deities specific to Yungdrung Bön.

However, Namkha Togden Chosumje is nevertheless loosely comparable to Huhe Münhe Tengeri/Kök Tenger (as was already noted in Chapter IV), and Huhe Münhe Tengeri in turn is analogous with pre-Zoroastrian *Mithra-*Vouruna and Zurvan (or however this deity was known in proto-Iranian religion). In terms of their external characteristics

---

[206] Karmay, *The Arrow and the Spindle*, p. 131.

[207] This will be discussed in ch. XV.

and cultural background, the pair Sangpo Bumtri and Münpa Zerden Nagpo appears somewhat similar to pre-Zoroastrian prototypes of Hormuzd Yazad of the white side and Ahriman of the black side. As, according to Sogdian Buddhists, Zurvan is identical to Indian Brahma, Namkha Togden Chosumje should also be comparable to Brahma, but it is Tibetan Tsangpa who is normally associated with Brahma. Why, then, do we have two archaic Tibetan deities who can both generally be compared to Brahma? I believe it is because they represent two superimposed levels of Bönpo culture: Prehistoric Bön and Yungdrung Bön. Tsangpa/ Nyipangse[208] is related to the cosmology of Prehistoric Bön while Namkha Togden Chosumje is related to the cosmology of Yungdrung Bön alone which, although explained through the earlier cultural frame of Prehistoric Bön, is radically different from it. Despite some similarities with earlier Bön, the cosmology of Yungdrung Bön is different in that its main deities such as Namkha Togden Chosumje, Trigyal Khugpa and Sangpo Bumtri are not the ordinary worldly gods of Prehistoric Bön but are sublime Buddha-forms beyond dualism. Here we can observe once again how Tonpa Shenrab Miwo imbued the old cultural matrix with new revolutionary meaning thus making his new doctrine more easily understood by the people of his place and time. In the cosmology of Yungdrung Bön the figure of the primary god-creator is replaced by the abstract concept of Namkha Togden Chosumje who represents the basic ground, the primordial Buddha-nature beyond any dualistic characteristics such as space and time, dark and light, good and bad. He is the same as Kuntu Zangpo and symbolizes the primordial ground, the nature of mind of any living being from which the illusory apparitions of the phenomenal world arise and are grasped as real by ordinary beings, leading them to transmigrate in *samsara*. This is *Bönku*[209] (*Dharmakaya*). The figure of the secondary creator (Hormuzd/ Hormusta of Prehistoric Bön) is replaced by two deities, Trigyal Khugpa and Sangpo Bumtri. The latter, although he appears to be a progenitor of the white side and is the King of Phenomenal Existence, is in fact also a non-dual Buddha-form representing the enlightened principle on the level of the energy of the universe. This is *Dzogku*[210] (*Sambhogakaya*). The external demon (Ahriman, Black Tengeri) is replaced by Münpa Zerden Nagpo who represents all negative tendencies and obscurations

---

[208] In Tibetan sources Tsangpa and Gyagyin, parallel to Indian Brahma and Indra, are often interchangeable.

[209] Tib. bon nyid dbyings kyi sku – Body of the Ultimate Nature of Phenomena.

[210] Tib. longs pyod rdzogs pa'i sku – Body of Perfect Enjoyment.

of the mind which are opposite to the realization of Buddha-nature and cause countless sufferings to all beings circulating in *samsara*. This is Lhanchig Kyepai Düd[211] – 'the demon born together with oneself'. Tonpa Shenrab Miwo himself represents the principle of enlightenment manifest on the level of physical reality, the only level of reality perceivable by the majority of ordinary sentient beings, in order to lead those beings back to their original undefiled and non-dual Buddha-nature. This is *Trulku*[212] (*Nirmanakaya*).

Can this cosmology be compared to the cosmology of Zoroastrianism? – Absolutely not.

While Zoroastrianism has Prehistoric Bön as its cultural background in the same way as Yungdrung Bön does, Zarathushtra's reinterpretation of this background culture takes a very different direction. In Zoroastrianism the passive, abstract primary god-creator is replaced by the active, personified god, the all-good Ahura Mazda who is elevated from the rank of a Yazata sky-god to a position of absolute authority as the uncreated god-creator who fashioned all existence, set the rules by which his creation should function and gave the moral and spiritual codex for humanity to follow. In this context, the figure of evil, Ahriman, becomes a theological problem: why is Ahriman, later the Devil, there at all? If Ahura Mazda, later God, is the almighty, omniscient god-creator, how can Ahriman/Devil be able to plot against him and obstruct his work? Zarathushtra's doctrine balances this point with the concept of free will given to all creations by Ahura Mazda but it doesn't give a complete reply to these questions, leaving a chink through which doubts can enter. Countless generations of Zoroastrians and later monotheistic religious scholars have struggled to answer these questions. It is this weak point in the theology of Zoroastrianism which probably prompted certain Zoroastrian scholars to re-examine the doctrines of pre-Zoroastrian Iranian religion still surviving among some parts of the population and reintroduce the ancient figure of Zurvan the god-creator back into mainstream Zoroastrianism. The status of Ahura Mazda and Ahriman were subsequently re-evaluated, returning to the position they occupied in pre-Zoroastrian religion. This resulted in the appearance

---

[211] Tib. lhan cig skyes pa'i bdud.

[212] Tib. cir yang sprul pa'i sku – Body of Manifold Multipurpose Emanation. (English translation of the terms Bönku, Dzogku and Trulku are given according to *The Seven Mirrors of Dzogchen,* Lachen Drenpa Namkha, tr. Khenpo Tenpa Yungdrung, ed. Carol Ermakova and Dmitry Ermakov, limited private edition, 2006.)

of Zurvanism which re-combined the doctrine of Zarathushtra with the ancient cosmologic model. Some aspects of Zurvanist cosmology appear similar to the cosmology of Yungdrung Bön but this again is due to this pre-Zoroastrian element stemming from Prehistoric Bön and not from the doctrine of Zarathushtra as such.

Chronology of Shenrab Miwo and Zarathushtra

To complete this brief survey let us have a quick glance at the chronology of the prophets of Yungdrung Bön and Zoroastrianism. Both Tonpa Shenrab Miwo and Zarathushtra appeared in far-distant antiquity and had to use the culture of the day in their unique ways to convey the new revolutionary spiritual ideas of their teachings. For each of the teachers there are at least two sets of different dates: traditional dates, not accepted by modern scholars; and dates suggested by modern scholars, not accepted by religious scholars of these traditions. Traditionally, Tonpa Shenrab Miwo is said to have been born in a very remote epoch, in 16,017 BC and Zarathushtra in around 6200 BC.[213] Modern scholars give much later dates for both teachers: 1917 B.C. for Shenrab Miwo[214] and 628 BC[215] or between ~1600–800 BC[216] for Zarathushtra. According to both sets of dates Zarathushtra and the Buddha of Bön are not contemporaries, with the latter being dated considerably earlier in both versions. From this chronological data it is clear that Yungdrung Bön could not possibly have been influenced by Zoroastrianism; any similarities in their cosmologies have to be put down to their common cultural background in the Prehistoric Bön of Eurasia.

---

[213] According to the dating of Achaemenian period based on the calculations of the Plato's school which put Zarathushtra's birth 5000 years before the Trojan War. (Dr. Oric Basirov, Zoroaster's Time & Place, Paper I, 20 October, 1998, <http://www.caissoas.com/CAIS/Religions/iranian/Zarathushtrian/Oric.Basirov/zoroaster_time_and_place.htm> accessed 24.04.07.

[214] Norbu, *Drung, Deu and Bön*, pp.156–158.

[215] 'Zoroaster'. Encyclopædia Britannica. 2007. Encyclopædia Britannica Online. 24 Apr. 2007 <http://www.britannica.com/eb/article-8135>.

[216] Dr. Oric Basirov, Zoroaster's Time & Place, Paper I - 20 October 1998, <http://www.caissoas.com/CAIS/Religions/iranian/Zarathushtrian/Oric.Basirov/zoroaster_time_and_place.htm> accessed 24.04.07.

CHAPTER VII

Transmission and Initiation in Buryatian Bɵ Murgel

Utkha: the spiritual lineages of the Bɵ and Utgan

Utkha[1] is a Bɵ or Utgan's spiritual root and origin and is absolutely fundamental to any Bɵ Murgel priest or priestess. It is a kind of magical spiritual energy, an empowerment given to the first Bɵ of a clan lineage and then transmitted within that clan from one Bɵ to another. The same principle of transmission is found in Yungdrung Bön and Tibetan Buddhism, although the origin and nature of the spiritual power and knowledge conveyed are very different. Nevertheless, we can still say that *utkha* can be called a spiritual lineage and a Bɵ/Utgan who has *utkha* can be called a lineage-holder.

The first *utkha* was received by the first Bɵ on earth, Mergen Hara, also called Buhumei.[2] He was the son of the first Utgan who was from the clan Shosho'olok[3] and was initiated and taught by the White-Headed Eagle. The White-Headed Eagle was the son of Sege'en Sebdeg Tengeri, who were both initiated and taught by their Spiritual Father (*Naizha*)[4] Bɵluur Sagaan Garbal Tengeri[5] – Bɵ White Ancestor Tengeri. One of the legends telling how the knowledge of Bɵ Murgel came to earth goes like this:

---

1 Bur. утха.

2 Bur. Мэргэн-Хара or Bur. Бохоли-Харя, also called Bur. Бухүмэй a complete Bɵ.

3 Bur. Шошоолок. Although another version maintains she was Hamnigan Ezhi (Bur. Хамниган эжи), obviously Hamnigan or Tungus. Hamnigan can refer to horseback Tungus or to tribes appearing as the result of Buryats mixing with Evenki plus other small tribes and clans.

4 Bur. найжа.

5 Bur. Бөөлүүр Сагаан гарбал тенгери.

To help people overcome the diseases unleashed by the Black Tengeri, the White Tengeri sent an Eagle down to earth. When he came down from the Sky he saw a woman sleeping under a tree and entered into sexual union with her so her spiritual vision was opened and she became able to 'see' the spirits and the gods. The Eagle taught her various techniques of Bɵ Murgel and in this way she received *utkha* from the Eagle and became the first Utgan. She bore him a son who became the first Bɵ, and so it was that *utkha* was passed on.

The word '*utkha*' is derived from the Tyurkic root '*ut*'[6] meaning 'fire' or 'hearth' and Bɵ Murgel myths tell that the White-Headed Eagle who taught the first Utgan and fathered her son also brought fire to earth. '*Utkha*', then, might be translated as 'spark of spiritual fire'. As the root '*ut*' also forms the first part of the word '*utgan*', a priestess of Bɵ Murgel, and because the doctrine of Bɵ Murgel was initially taught to an Utgan, we may conclude that the ancient Utgan priestesses were the initial holders of *utkha*, knowledge of Bɵ Murgel, and presided over rites involving fire. This role has changed over time as the Matriarchate gave way to Patriarchate and in modern Bɵ Murgel it is only specially initiated Utgan who are allowed to invoke *Zayaans* of Fire from the Sky and lead rituals devoted to them.[7] The first Utgan handed her knowledge on to her son so we can assume that passing *utkha* from female to male was a normal state of affairs in the early history of Bɵ Murgel. This, however, also changed as the religion developed, with male Bɵ lineages becoming more dominant and transmission from mother to son becoming undesirable, as we shall see below.

Different types of utkha

1. *Haluunai utkha*[8] – passed through the father's lineage.
2. *Hariin utkha*[9] – passed through the mother's lineage. Generally this *utkha* is very delicate to handle so usually the appearance of an Utgan wasn't especially welcomed. This is because of the belief that the *Ongon*-ancestors don't want to be 'transferred'[10] to another clan when the girl with *utkha* is married; it takes considerable effort

---

6 Bur. ут.

7 Bazarov, *Tainstva*, p. 94.

8 Bur. Халуунай утха – 'hot *utkha*'.

9 Bur. Хариин утха, from Bur. хари (*hari*) meaning 'other', 'stranger'.

10 Bur. Онгон шанар.

to convince them to go, so extensive offerings and invocations are performed. Even then a Bɵ has to be very careful in initiating someone with *Hariin utkha* and, on occasion, may even refuse to teach at all.[11]

3. *Tengeriin Darhan utkha*[12] – divine *utkha* of smiths which is further subdivided into:
   i. *Sagaan Darhan utkha*[13] – *utkha* of white smiths.
   ii. *Hara Darhan utkha*[14] – *utkha* of black smiths.
4. *Nerye'er utkha*[15] – *utkha* of those chosen by the Sky. This *utkha* is initiated when, by the will of the Tengeri, someone is struck by a ball of lightning. If the person survives unscathed, s/he becomes a very powerful Bɵ/Utgan.[16] Understandably, this happens very rarely; usually 'lightning transmission' results in either death or severe health problems. In this case, the Bɵ of the village or clan call a gathering to choose one of the deceased's descendants to be initiated. In some traditions this type of *utkha* cannot be passed on.
5. *Buudal utkha*[17] – *utkha* descended from the Sky. This *utkha* falls to a person who finds sacred meteorites, *zada shuulun*,[18] or other magical objects which have dropped from the sky such as magical Tengeri *toli* or even Sky-scriptures which descend from the Sky right onto a

---

11 Ibid., p. 23.

12 Bur. Тенгериин Дархан утха.

13 Bur. Сагаан Дархан утха.

14 Bur. Хара Дархан утха.

15 Bur. Нэрьеэр утха.

16 While listening to the Moscow radio station Kuranty (Rus. Куранты) I heard a somewhat unexpected confirmation of the special characteristics a person surviving a bolt of lightning may have. Under the rubric "Society" Kuranty reported that in the Russian town of Lipetsk a man called Dmitry Butakov staged a show; in the presence of journalists he drank a glass of acetone, washed it down with a glass of Tassol (a liquid used in Russia to cool radiators) and a glass of Pepsi. He finished off his toxic meal with a sweet bread bun. Dmitry Butakov didn't suffer any toxic effects whatsoever, he merely entered a happy mood. That is all. He said he got the capacity to eat poisonous substances without any health risk after he was struck down by lightning some years ago. He discovered his new ability by chance after eating poisonous mushrooms and suffering no ill effects. Source: Rubric Society, Radio Kuranty, Moscow, 89.90FM, 26th November 2003, 7.25pm. The same man drank a glass of apple juice with cyanide which did him no harm. Radio Kuranty, Moscow, 89.90FM, 11th February, 2004, 5.30pm.

17 Bur. Буудал утха.

18 Bur. Зада шуулун.

person's hands. This type of *utkha* also remains with a person for the length of his/her lifetime and is not transmitted.

6. *Zayaanai utkha*[19] – an *utkha* received from the *Zayaan*. A Bɵ or Utgan with this *utkha* did not take initiation and has a limited range of functions.

Furthermore, there are two general subdivisions of *utkha* which apply to all the above kinds: *sagaanai utkha*[20] and *haryn utkha*[21] – black and white *utkha*. This classification indicates whether the *utkha* was initially given by a White or Black Tengeri or *Haat*. By and large it was more important in the past than it is today:[22] it has been smoothed over in the last two hundred years and consequently there are Bɵ and Utgan who hold both *utkha* simultaneously. Such priests are called *Hoër te'eshe yabadaltai*,[23] 'Can worship on two sides', and are sometimes nicknamed *Tolmoosho*,[24] 'The Interpreter', because they are said to be able to mediate between and interpret from the languages of the White and Black Tengeri and spirits.[25]

In the past, reincarnations of particularly powerful and gifted Bɵ of the Zaarin[26] rank were found by means of the Bɵ-clan mark *tamga.*[27] This technique involved branding the clan symbol onto a certain part of the famous Bɵ's corpse during the funeral ceremony using a specially fashioned red-hot iron stamp. This stamp was often made in the shape of a swastika.[28] Later a child could be born bearing the *tamga* mark in the same special place and found by a knowledgeable Bɵ. This was a big event in the clan and one of the ways the continuation of a Bɵ lineage was maintained.

The *utkha* lineage of a Bɵ-clan can sometimes be cut, for example if a Bɵ dies or is killed without having children. If the Bɵ had no sons but only daughters, it was considered that the *utkha* passed into another clan when the Bɵ's daughter married but was completely lost as it could manifest in the next generation.

---

19 Bur. Заянай утха.

20 Bur. Сагаанай утха.

21 Bur. Харын утха.

22 There is some disagreement on this point; see discussion next chapter.

23 Bur. Хоёр тээшээ ябадалтай.

24 Bur. Толмоошо.

25 Here, 'languages' may be taken either symbolically or literally.

26 Bur. Заарин.

27 Bur. хании тамга – 'seal of the *Haats*'.

28 Bur. хас тамга – lit. 'jade stamp'.

The holy families of Yungdrung Bön and Tibetan Buddhism

Let's take a closer look at how spiritual power is transmitted in the Bönpo model. Among the lineages of Yungdrung Bön we find very ancient transmissions running through the six holy families of Mushen, Dru, Zhu, Pa, Meu and Khyung. All these lineages are of celestial origins and are connected with emanations of enlightened beings. Mushen,[29] for example, is the lineage of Tonpa Shenrab, the Buddha of Yungdrung Bön and this family lineage came to Tibet through the line of Shenrab Miwo's son, Kongtsa Yungdrung Wangden. Shenrab Miwo is the eighth person in this lineage which started with the great ancestor[30] Mugyal Chugpo[31] who descended to earth from the heavenly realm of the *Mu* in order to rule the human race. The lineage-holders preceding Shenrab Miwo all possessed great magical powers which enabled them to travel in many different dimensions of the universe and to receive various ritual items and weapons from the many races of *Drala* sky-gods. With the coming of Tonpa Shenrab, those sky-gods and protectors of the Mushen clan also became guardians of his doctrine, Yungdrung Bön. In the course of many thousands of years, numerous great masters and *yogis* were born into this lineage which is still alive today.

This is also true for all the family lineages with the exception of the *Dru* lineage which was terminated in the nineteenth century when its last descendant was 'recognized' as the Fifth Panchen Lama by the Gelugpas, a clever political ploy aimed at bringing the Bönpo of this lineage under Gelugpa control; the last holder of the Dru lineage became a monk and had no children. The Dru clan's great ancestor was Drusha Namse Chitol[32] and this lineage arrived in Tibet from the country of Thogar (Tokharistan).

The Zhu clan's great ancestor was Mugpodeng[33] and it came from western Tibet.

The Pa clan's great ancestor was Chagkyi Gyarucan[34] a descendant of Sangpo Bumtri and Chucham Gyalmo. He came down to Zhang Zhung from the place of the Gods of Clear Light.

---

29 Also known as Tib. Mi rje Srid pa.

30 Tib. Myes chen.

31 Tib. dMu rgyal Phyug po also known as dMu phyug sKye rabs or dMu phyug sKyer gzhon.

32 Tib. Bru sha gNam gsas sPyi brtol.

33 Tib. sMug po ldang.

34 Tib. lCag kyi Bya ru can.

Fig. 1. Yongdzin Lopön Tenzin Namdak, Khenpo Tenpa Yungdrung and Shentsang family, Tibet, 2007.

The Meu clan also traces its lineage to Sangpo Bumtri and Chucham Gyalmo. One of their descendants came down from the realm the Gods of the Clear Light, was born into Yigtsangchen[35] family and later had two sons Ma[36] and Meu, the latter becoming the great ancestor of the Meu clan.

The ancestry of the Khyung clan leads to Kuntu Zangpo's emanation Rignang Ögyi Gyalpo[37] who in turn emanated the three miraculous *Khyung* birds and sent them down to Khayug[38] in Zhang Zhung. These *Khyung* birds laid four eggs from which appeared four miraculous boys: Khyungkar Thoglabar, Khyungser Lhakhyung, Khyungpag Tramo and Mukhyunggyan.[39] They displayed many miracles and upheld the teachings of Yungdrung Bön in Zhang Zhung and later Tibet. Various Khyung lineages evolved from them.[40]

---

35 Tib. Yig tshang can.

36 Tib. rMa.

37 Tib. Rig snang 'Od gyi rGyal po.

38 Tib. Kha yug.

39 Tib. Khyung dkar Thog la 'bar, Khyung ser lHa Khyung, Khyung 'phags Khra mo, Mu khyung rgyan.

40 See Karmay, *The Treasury*, pp. 3–14.

Over the centuries, all these clans produced a great number of *yogis* and scholars through whom the teachings of Yungdrung Bön were spread and upheld.

The transmission of Yungdrung Bön runs within these six holy families or clans in strict succession from father to son or uncle to nephew[41] and, while all of these families are followers of Yungdrung Bön, they each have distinct customs and particular teachings. They played an especially important role in preserving tantric teachings and practices; each family had its own *yidam* which was practised from generation to generation in an uninterrupted line, so the lineage-holders of these families had formidable tantric powers. A great number of realized masters have been born into each family, introduced countless human and non-human beings to the teachings of the Central Asian Buddha, performed miraculous actions to benefit beings in numberless ways and established many centres of study and practice, both lay and monastic.

Tibetan Buddhism, too, has similar pathways for transmitting spiritual power, particularly in the Khön[42] lineage of the Sakyapa School. According to Bönpo sources,[43] Palden Sakyapa[44] is an alternative name for Sadru,[45] one of the two main branches of the Bönpo *Dru* family whose descendants converted to Buddhism in the time of Guru Padmasambhava (eighth century AD) so its transmission method follows the general Bönpo model.

---

41 Ibid., Introduction, p. xxxv.

42 Tib. khon. According to the Buddhist version history of the Khön tribe begins in the heavens of Clear Light of the Form Realm from whence the celestial beings descended to earth and took residence in Tibet. They were called Lharig and followed Yungdrung Bön. According to traditional Sakya history, this happened ten generations prior to the arrival of Guru Padmasambhava. The celestial Lharig gradually mixed with the local beings and eight generations later there a conflict erupted within the tribe and that is how it got its name, Khön, which means 'dispute' or 'strife'. In 750 AD some Khön became students of Guru Rinpoche and in particular received a Vajrakilaya transmission which they still hold today. (According to *A Brief Overview of the Lam Dre, By His Holiness Sakya Trizin* <http://www.simhas.org/sakya.html> and <http://www.geocities.com/Athens/Ithaca/4886/lamdre.htm>)

43 Karmay, *The Treasury,* p. 6.

44 Tib. dPal ldan Sa skya pa.

45 Tib. Sa bru.

Common features of family lineages

Transmission in Yungdrung Bön is not limited to the family lineages of these six holy clans. Many lineages are based solely on the principle of a spiritual link or kinship rather than a genealogical one and have been held by monastic and lay communities for centuries. However, here we are predominately interested in the former mode of transmission because it reveals archaic origins which are culturally and spiritually akin to those of Buryatian Bɵ Murgel, thereby giving us a link to the prehistoric environment in which both traditions began to evolve. While the contents of the knowledge transmitted within Yungdrung Bön and Bɵ Murgel can be partially compared when we look into certain aspects of the Four Ways of Cause of Yungdrung Bön, there can be no comparison between Bɵ Murgel and the higher teachings of Yungdrung Bön's Five Ways of Fruit. Nevertheless, the mechanics of transmission follow similar principles:

1. Both modes of transmission originate in supernatural dimensions;
2. Both modes are transmitted genetically by way of the family line;
3. While female members of the family are respected, transmission predominantly runs through the male lineage, usually from father to son;
4. In both modes a lineage is considered interrupted when there is no male offspring;
5. In both traditions a lineage-holder must know the line of preceding masters clearly along with the details of their lives and deeds;
6. In both modes a lineage, while being an integral part of the whole tradition and fully embodying its general doctrine and methods, nevertheless maintains its own special teachings and methods;
7. It is indispensable for both traditions that the transmission lineage runs uninterrupted so that the teachings it contains can be practised correctly and be preserved for further generations;
8. Both systems are protected by special guardians of the lineage who ensure right succession and transmission;
9. In both modes importance is given to the sacred ritual items which serve as supports for the protective deities.

While points five to nine can be applied to spiritual lineages in general, points one to four are peculiar to transmission modes based on the family line and genetic transmission, to which most of the *utkha* lineages of Bɵ Murgel and Bönpo lineages of the six clans belong. This very ancient custom is a common feature of spiritual traditions which developed in prehistoric times so these parallels point to Bɵ Murgel and Bön's common cultural background, now covered by the mists of time. As Buryatian Bɵ Murgel is very much alive, comparing its archaic aspects with those of Yungdrung Bön can give us a glimpse into the remote times and circumstances in which Tonpa Shenrab Miwo manifested and therefore help us better understand the cultural and spiritual environment in which he gave his teachings many thousands of years ago.

Ongon Daralga – the 'pressure of the Ongon-spirits' or 'shamanic disease'

Before we can look into how a Bɵ or Utgan is initiated, we first have to understand a fundamental prerequisite for all Bɵ Murgel priests and priestesses: *Ongon Daralga*[46] or 'pressure of the *Ongon*-spirits'. The *Ongon Daralga* is a calling to become a Bɵ or Utgan sent by the *Ongon*-spirits of the clan, spirits of the great Bɵ/Utgan of the past, Tengeri and other gods and spirits. This calling can manifest in various forms and under diverse circumstances but it is always the overture to a very difficult and painful period in which the *Ongons* are 'putting pressure' on the Bɵ-to-be who undergoes a process of tremendous inner transformation. Depending on individual circumstances, this metamorphosis can take up to several years. It is a period when the future Bɵ or Utgan's ordinary concepts and perceptions are all broken and destroyed. S/he undergoes a 'virtual death' and is then 'reborn', transformed into a spiritual being with a new experiential vision and perception of the universe and all its beings, accompanied by certain special knowledge and powers reserved for a Bɵ or Utgan. The calling may come in the dream-state or the waking state and each Bɵ or Utgan experiences it differently; each one has his or her own story. In Soviet times people usually received the calling quite late in life, often just before retirement, but it can come any time after puberty and now, with the post-perestroika policy of religious liberalization, more and more young people are being 'called'. Practitioners and priests of Bɵ Murgel were viciously persecuted under the Communist regime

---

46 Bur. Онгон даралга. *Daralga* literally means 'to press down', 'to put pressure on'.

and it seems that the spirits and gods didn't want to put people's lives in danger by calling them into service, so there were very few Bɵ and Utgan enlisted to practise in secret in Soviet times.

Sometimes the future Bɵ or Utgan may be as young as five when their spiritual education begins. The spirits of the ancestor-Bɵ take his/her soul from the body and bring it into the presence of the Sky Tengeri or to the palaces of the *Haats* where, for many years, it is taught the secrets of this difficult profession.[47] Such a chosen child may not be visibly different from other children and does everything in the normal way, although they often appear thoughtful, have visions of the Tengeri and spirits, see special dreams, may be able to foresee the future and such like. In the past the culmination of this pre-initiation process often came during puberty and in the majority of cases manifested by the age of twenty as the *Ongon Daralga*. At this time the soul returns to the body and begins to mould it to suit the activity of a Bɵ/Utgan. This is a very painful process. The calling is always sudden and pushes a neophyte into a very stressful condition: the world is crumbling, one hears voices giving orders and instructions day and night, one cannot sleep and becomes nervous and withdrawn, often seeking solitude and maybe wandering in remote places. Fits similar to epilepsy are not uncommon, or one may experience comatose-like states, a kind of paralysis, or be struck down by a serious disease which cannot be cured by ordinary means but only through a special ritual, then by surrendering to the pressure and taking up office as a Bɵ or Utgan. Trying to ease the 'pressure of the *Ongons*' may lead some to become addicted to alcohol. People tormented by the calling often ran away to the mountains or forest where they fell into a violent trance, shouting loudly, rolling on the earth, leaping and performing incredible feats. If local people noticed, they would send a horseman to watch over the neophyte from a distance to be sure they didn't harm themselves.

Visions experienced in this period vary considerably. One may often see and feel one's body being cut into pieces and then remade anew; being cooked in a big pot; being put into a metal cradle, sucking milk from a goddess' breast and then being re-forged on an anvil with a sledge-hammer in the smithy of the Tengeri. Sometimes when this cutting and re-forging takes place the chosen person's experiences are so intense that s/he lies in a kind of coma for days on end. Their face turns blue, their heartbeat almost stops and their eyes roll uncontrollably. In this period

---

[47] This is the only instance when a person doesn't die when their soul is separated from the body for a long time see ch. XIII.

no-one is allowed to touch the body. Experienced Bө, Utgans and people of the clan or village gather round and pray that the neophyte may return safely – and with magical powers.

Although the symptoms of *Ongon Daralga* may seem similar to those triggered by an ordinary physical or mental disease, their cause is completely different and it falls to an experienced Bө to determine that the person in question is not simply ill or mentally unstable as those with impaired sense organs, limbs or mental faculties cannot become a Bө or Utgan; the Tengeri and spirits will not accept their offerings but will be displeased instead. Even once initiated, if a Bө has some kind of accident and becomes an invalid, he must pass his *hayag*[48] onto his successor or relative and can no longer sprinkle to the gods and spirits as his energy is no longer whole. Once an experienced Bө has entered the trance state and confirmed that the person showing symptoms of *Ongon Daralga* really has the calling, special rituals are performed to ease the chosen one's suffering and prepare him/her for the initiation process.

One of these rituals is the *Ugaalga*[49] or body washing ritual. Not everyone who receives the calling becomes a professional Bө or Utgan but all must take part in this special washing ritual. Some of those called then take no further initiations and remain as helpers to an initiated Bө. During the *Ugaalga* certain deities are invoked and a number of stones of various colours taken from creeks or a riverbed are heated and put in sacred spring water so that it boils and is sanctified. Bunches of reeds or twigs are dipped in the water and used to slap the acolyte on the back or all over. S/he is then fumigated and purified.[50] The 'disease' is cured and in many cases the neophyte can decide whether to take on further initiations or not, although often they may have no choice but to take up office as a Bө or Utgan.

Who can become a Bө or Utgan?

There are two main categories of Bө: initiated and uninitiated An uninitiated Bө is called Sagaasha.[51] He is someone who has the *utkha* spark and who has gone through *Ongon Daralga* but has not taken further

48 Bur. хаяаг, the right to perform ritual services, the right to the office of a Bө.

49 Bur. угаалга. For a detailed description of this ritual see ch. XI.

50 Some scholars translate this as 'baptism' which is clearly inappropriate as the word 'baptism' has strong Christian connotations and the *ugaalga* ritual itself is very different from the Christian baptism in all but the use of water.

51 Bur. Сагааша.

initiations. As such, he is considered a Bɵ-apprentice and is not a fully fledged Bɵ. Bɵ-apprentices help initiated Bɵ perform various rituals and simultaneously learn the meaning of the invocations as well as the techniques of healing and so on. For various reasons, many of these apprentices never take initiations or take just one, two or three, remaining on that stage for life. Uninitiated or not fully initiated Bɵ are quite numerous and can be found in almost every village. They are allowed to sprinkle to the gods and spirits with tea, milk or alcohol, depending on their status, and take part in *tailgans*, helping the initiated Bɵ. They can pray for themselves and their relatives. They have some psychic powers, sometimes very considerable, and can be much respected but they don't cross the boundary of their rights and functions, which are limited in comparison with those of a fully initiated Bɵ. If they do overstep this boundary they will be punished by the protective divinities, spirits and Bɵ of the clan, Erlig Khaan and other gods. A Sagaasha Bɵ cannot lead a *tailgan* if a 'Bɵ-in-the-law' is present as they have to take a subordinate position to them. Neither do they have the final say in matters such as where to do the ritual, what substances to offer or which technique to use; they don't have spiritual or secular authority.

As for an initiated Bɵ or Utgan, the candidate must be someone who has *utkha*, who was chosen by the *Ongon*-spirits and Tengeri through *Ongon Daralga* and who studied seriously and earnestly through being around and helping his or her Bɵ-father for many years.[52] S/he should have a good character and virtuous qualities, as verified by the Bɵ-father, as well as magical abilities, the capacity to learn, devotion, sharp memory, clear mind, good mental abilities and be physically unimpaired.[53]

Before a neophyte can be initiated their candidature is discussed at the *hurultai*[54] of Bɵ and elders of the tribe, region, village and clan. They examine the candidate and look closely at their qualities. In days gone

---

52 Bɵ-father is a spiritual master who teaches the neophyte and takes full responsibility for him/her. As already mentioned he is called *Naizha.*

53 This taboo is mirrored in the Hebrew Bible, suggesting it was a wide-spread rule among many prehistoric religions of Eurasia and beyond. In Leviticus 21; 17–21we read: 'For generations to come, none of your descendants who has defect may come near to offer the food of his God [...] no man who is blind or lame, disfigured or deformed, no man with crippled foot or hand, or who is hunch-backed or dwarfed, or who has any eye defect, or who has festering or running sores or damaged testicles. No descendant of Aaron the priest who has any defect is to come near to present the offerings made to the Lord by fire'. The Holy Bible, the New International Version (London, Sidney Auckland: Hodder&Stoughton, 1990).

54 Bur. хурултай is an assembly or congress.

by the selection process had to be very rigorous because Bɵ had a huge impact on Buryatian society; their presence and know-how was required not only for healing and divination but in all the important aspects of life such as birth, marriage, death, hunting, war, government, matters of law, education and, of course, religious festivals. In the past the number of Bɵ was limited to one per three hundred tribe or a clan members. The administrative positions in the tribe such as head of the clan,[55] bailiff[56] and chairman[57] of the *hurultai*-assembly were also held by high-ranking initiated Bɵ.

Only an experienced Bɵ who has received seven initiations or more has the right to initiate the neophytes. Moreover, a Bɵ cannot initiate more than nine Bɵ and nine Utgan, eighteen spiritual sons and daughters altogether. This is a very strict rule; if broken it brings grave consequences upon the offender such as losing all his magical powers, the termination of his lineage, and maybe even death.

New Age shamans

It is natural for humans to long to understand the mysteries of the universe and our place in it, to yearn to find harmony and balance with our natural environment and unlock the secrets of the spirit, and that is why the colourful, powerful and mysterious world of shamanic experiences and actions is so attractive to many people, especially in a world ever more detached from nature's rhythms. This has given rise to a plethora of so-called 'contemporary' or New Age 'shamans so plentiful in the West nowadays.[58] However, there is a huge difference between a shaman – the priest – and a shaman*ist*, a follower of any kind of shamanic faith. For the majority of people it is quite impossible to become a shaman just because they want to be in tune with the unseen forces of nature; having some psychic insights and the desire to develop them and become a shaman is not enough. As we have seen, the process of becoming a shamanic priest or priestess is far from easy and the extent to which Buryats fear the 'pressure of the *Ongons*' was and is very great; there have been several cases when the family members of someone struck by the calling tied them up and left them to die in an abandoned dwelling such was their

---

55 Bur. гулваа.

56 Bur. шуленга.

57 Bur. тайшаа.

58 Unfortunately some pseudo-shamans of this kind can be found even in the East.

dread of them.[59] People didn't take the calling lightly, it wasn't welcome and in no way solicited; it was simply a matter of fate. No-one would volunteer to become a shaman if they realized the amount of suffering, pain and, sometimes, unbearable challenges which one has to go through on this path. On top of that one has to go through many years of rigorous study and practice (a minimum of fifteen years in the case of Buryatian Bө Murgel) before one can reach full potential. So from this perspective, New Age courses offering a 'shaman' diploma after one, two or three years of occasional workshops with dubious teachers look extremely paltry.

Nonetheless, people are increasingly disillusioned with the large institutionalized religions and are looking for more mystical paths to meet their spiritual needs. This has created a market for the New Age and the result is a kind of spiritual consumerism. There are many New Age Schools, workshops and institutes where anyone can study to become a 'shaman' if they so wish – and if they are ready to pay the fees. There are even some publications which claim that anyone who has read a book on any kind of shamanic faith has a cause to become a shaman. These sorts of books offer 'secret' shamanic techniques to anyone who cares to use them and encourage people to become shamans. However, such phenomena should be treated with care; no authentic Bө, Utgan or any other responsible Siberian shaman would say or write such things or reveal the secret methods of their lineage. By following concocted New Age 'Shamanism', both the New Age gurus themselves and their students will surely go astray.

Lastly, shamans have a precise function in society so there is no place and no need for a large crowd of them. There is no way shamans can or should be mass produced. By learning about shamanic cosmology, views and techniques one may gain a better understanding of the basic principles of this rich belief system and become a *shamanist* but not a *shaman*.

This holds true for all the native ritual traditions of Siberia falling within the spectrum of shamanism. However, many other native traditions of other places and cultures now go by the name 'shamanism', although the majority of them seem to have a strict criteria for candidates for the office of 'shaman', it may be that some hold a different view on the subject of how and why someone can become a shaman; I am not familiar enough with such traditions to comment. Nevertheless, the

---

59 Such is the story of Baraanag Toodei (Bur. Бараанаг тѳѳдэй) who became *Zayaan* after her death.

true definition of 'shamanism' is inextricably linked with the Siberian traditions so the qualities and characteristics needed to become a shaman should be understood and evaluated on the basis of the native religions of Siberia.

Stages of initiation and corresponding ritual objects of the Bө

When the Bө Murgel traditions were still very much intact there were many different stages or phases of initiation. In the nineteenth century these traditions started to weaken and many Bө began taking just a limited number of initiations. With the troubles brought by the Socialist Revolution and subsequent persecution, Bө Murgel suffered serious damage. It was no longer possible to perform the rituals for higher stages of initiation openly so there were very few who continued practising. The religious liberalization of perestroika in the 1990's resulted in a revival of Bө Murgel which brought with it the revival of the ancient initiation system. In Buryatian Bө Murgel this original system is highly complex and is divided into nine stages. In the Mongolian Bө religion, the initiation system of twelve stages is used and an exceptional initiation rite of the thirteenth stage is very occasionally performed for a truly outstanding Bө who is then given the title Gege'en Zaarin[60] where *gege'en* means 'enlightened'.[61] This kind of Bө appears very rarely. It is difficult to be completely sure how these systems correspond as opinion differs among the Bө themselves. Suffice to say that these systems are parallel and are based on different structures; the Buryatian one is not somehow incomplete because it has fewer stages. While the initiation system of Buryatian Bө Murgel is structured according to the nine branches of the World Tree and the nine spheres of the universe,[62] the Mongolian system is based on the twelve antlers of the Sacred Deer. Some Buryatian Bө speak of a thirteenth level of initiation which is probably parallel to Mongolian Gege'en Zaarin and this demonstrates that both initiation systems were used in Buryatia in the past.

---

60 Bur. Гэгээн заарин.

61 This material was kindly made available to me by Dorjo Doogarov BA, Oriental Faculty, Department of Archaeology and Ethnography of Central Asia, Buryatian State University, Ulaan-Ude, and comes from the notes he was taking while studying in Mongolia in 2001.

62 The Three Worlds each have a further three spheres within them as was explained in ch. IV.

The initiation process of Buryatian Bɵ Murgel is known as *shanar*[63] and through it an uninitiated Bɵ is transformed into a 'Bɵ-in-the-law'. However, it takes many years to traverse all nine or thirteen stages. Many tribal and local traditions evolved around the initiation rituals and some stages do not precisely correspond to the names commonly associated with them. Modern Bɵ see the initiation process from different points of view; while it is very important for some, others give more weight to the actual knowledge and power of a given Bɵ or Utgan rather than to their title or the level of initiation they are supposed to have reached.

First initiation

Here is a brief summary of a first-level initiation rite based on the account by M.N. Hangalov recorded in the Irkutsk region:

> Once the date for the initiation has been established, a purification rite is performed from three to nine times. The Bɵ-father and his nine spiritual sons, *Yuhenguud*, go to three springs where they sprinkle with milk and vodka and take water to bring to the site of the ritual. They also bring some young birch trees from the forest which they dig up together with the roots. The water is boiled, *arsa*[64] and juniper are sprinkled in it to purify it and some hair from a billy goat's ear is added. The billy goat is then sacrificed and some drops of its blood are spilled into the water. Then divination is performed on a sheep's shoulder blade and alcohol is offered to the ancestor spirits. The Bɵ-father dips a bunch of birch twigs into the water and touches the back of the initiate. One after another, the nine spiritual sons do the same while the Bɵ-father utters the words of instruction: 'When the poor need you, don't ask too much from them but take what they give. Think of the poor and ask the Tengeri to protect them from bad spirits and evil forces. When the rich call you, don't ask too much for your services, either. Should the rich and the poor seek your help at the same time, go first to the poor and then to the rich.'[65] The initiate swears to abide by these rules; all pray and

---

[63] Bur. шанар.

[64] Bur. арса, herbal incense.

[65] B.E. Petri gives two other variations of the Bɵ oath by the Bɵ Badya Malakshinov from Alarskaya Steppe and Bɵ Stepanov from Kuda region: *'To the poor client I will travel on foot, to the middle class client I will ride on the bull, to the rich client I will ride on the horse'*, and *'I won't ask for anything*

offer *serzhim* to the protective deities.[66]

Soon after the purification rituals have been completed, the main initiation is performed but first the Bө-father and his nine spiritual sons remain closed in a yurt for a nine-day fast, drinking only tea and eating only boiled flour.

Before the initiation ritual the Bө-father and his spiritual sons go to the forest and, after making offerings, dig up several large birch trees which they bring to the site of the ritual. On the morning of the initiation the ritual begins by erecting the birches.

The first birch is erected in the *gher* of the initiate. It is dug in with its roots in the far south-western corner of the yurt in the space just before the hearth where a bit of earth floor is left.[67] The top of the birch is pushed through the smoke hole.[68] This birch is the pathway to the Sky and is called *Udeshi Burkhan*[69] after the god who opens the *Tengeriin Uden*, the Door of the Sky.

The remaining birches are erected around the *gher* and are connected to the central birch within by red and blue ribbons or threads symbolizing the 'rainbow'[70] path by which Bө travel the universe. The birches surrounding the *gher* are decorated with various ritual items such as ribbons, bells and animal skins, and serve different functions: some of them represent *Serge*, others are used as a support for offerings.

Once all the trees are erected, the initiate, together with the Bө-father's nine spiritual sons *Yuhenguud*, sanctifies the Bө-to-be's ritual implements and call the *Ongon*-spirits to dwell on them. Then with a long ritual offering, the Tengeri, *Haats* and other *Zayaans* are asked to initiate the new Bө and assist him in his work. At this point the initiate should climb the birch tree in his *gher* holding a sword and come out of the smoke hole where he

---

but take what is given. If the distance is long I will ride the bull, if the distance is short I will travel on foot'. B. E. Petri, *Stepeni posvyashcheniya mongolo-buryatskogo shamana*, Isdatel'stvo NII Biologii-Geografii, Vol 2, ed. 4, 1926, pp. 2, 27.

66 This is a version of the 'body-washing' ritual which is a must for all Bө. Some perform it at least once a year while others have to do it every month at the time of the new moon.

67 The rest of the floor is covered with wood or felt.

68 Bur. өрхө.

69 Bur. Удэши-бурхан.

70 Bur. һолонго.

should call the Tengeri and other *Zayaans*. While he is doing this, those remaining inside the *gher* are constantly purifying themselves with smoke. Then the initiate descends back into the *gher*, is put on a white felt mattress and carried out of the *gher* by four spiritual sons of the Bɵ-father.

The initiate is taken to the *Serge*-birches where a billy goat is sacrificed and the initiate's head, ears and eyes are smeared with its blood. The body-washing rite is then repeated.[71]

After that, nine other animals are sacrificed and while the meat is being cooked, the ritual of the Ascent to the Sky is performed. The Bɵ-father climbs the *Serge*-birch and makes nine notches on its top. He then descends and is seated on the carpet beneath. The initiate is the next to climb the *Serge*, and after him all other Bɵ present do so, entering the trance state. In some traditions the initiate is carried around the nine birches on the white felt carpet, climbs each of them and becomes ecstatic. He also makes nine notches on the top of each tree, symbolizing the nine (or ninety-nine) Bɵ-Skies. After this a feast commences.[72]

Nine initiations

According to M.N. Hangalov and some other sources, subsequent initiations followed a basically similar structure with some variations in the ritual objects and attributes of the initiated Bɵ. However, this is not a universal understanding and so here I shall outline all nine initiations based on a compilation of oral and written sources from different traditions.[73]

---

[71] Cf the Jewish ritual for consecrating priests described in ch. XI.

[72] Based on Hangalov, *Sobranie,* Vol.1, pp. 374–384.

[73] The names and some attributes pertaining to the different stages of initiation can differ in different areas and among various tribes as each region, tribe and clan has their own tradition. The following presentation is a general scheme compiled from both oral and written sources. Oral sources include the Bɵ and Utgan listed in the Acknowledgements. Written sources are: Hangalov; Galdanova; Bazarov; *Huhe Münhe Tengeri: sbornik shamanskikh prizyvanii I*, [*Anthology of Shamanic Invocations],* (Ulaan-Ude: Respublikanskaya tipografiya, 1996); T. M. Mikhailov, *Buryatskii shamanism: istoriya, struktura i sotsial'nyie funktsii,* (Novosibirsk: Nauka, 1987); V. Hagdaev, *Shamanism i mirovye religii,* [monograph], <http://baikal.irkutsk.ru/php/statya.php?razdel=shamanizm&nomer=4.txt> accessed10.06.07. Mikhailov gives the titles for the Nine Stages in a different order and their functions also differ slightly (pp. 99–101.): 1. Shanartai Bɵ, from the word *shanar*, 'initiated Bɵ'; 2. Yedoto

First initiation

This is the very beginning of a Bɵ's path. A Bɵ who has received this initiation is accepted as a beginner with the right to sprinkle to the *Ongon*-spirits of his clan with milk and tea only. He is called either Yabagan Bɵ,[74] 'pedestrian Bɵ', as his means of magical travel are very limited, or Huurai Bɵ,[75] 'dry Bɵ' because he cannot sprinkle with alcohol. As his ritual objects and attributes he has a special ritual hat with a front band made of the fur of his clan's totemic animal; a birch *hor'bo*-cane[76] with notches showing how many Bɵ ancestors he had in the nine generations before him; a silk belt; a knife; and a flint-stone. Between the first and the second initiation there must be a gap of no less than three years.

Second initiation

This initiation brings more power and gives a Bɵ wider rights. After this initiation he is called Noitolkhon Bɵ,[77] 'a Bɵ who has been made wet', because the initiation includes a body-washing rite with water from three holy springs.[78] Another name for a Bɵ at this level is Duhaalgyn Bɵ[79] from the word '*duhaalga*'[80] 'to sprinkle', literally 'to drip' as he can now sprinkle with *tarasoon*[81] and melted butter not just tea or milk. After this initiation a Bɵ can invoke and pray to the local deities of his valley, those pertaining to the cult of fire and the *Ongon*-spirits of his clan. He

---

(Zhodoto) Bɵ – 'Bɵ with silver fir bark', i.e. one who received silver fir bark for performing the ceremonies; 3. Shere'ete Bɵ – 'Bɵ who has an altar' i.e. the right to initiate others into the next Bɵ stage; 4. Noitolhon Bɵ – 'Bɵ who has taken ritual of body-washing'; 5. Hor'bito Bɵ – 'Bɵ with canes'; 6. Orgoito Bɵ – 'Bɵ who has an iron crown with antlers'; 7. Hesete Bɵ – 'Bɵ who has one or more drums'; 8. Duuren Bɵ – 'complete Bɵ', i.e. one who has all necessary attributes as the result of several initiations; 9. Zaarin Bɵ – 'great Bɵ', one who has gone through the nine initiations. A detailed eye-witness account of the initiation process can also be found in ch. XIII.

74 Bur. Ябаган бөө.

75 Bur. Хуурай бөө.

76 Bur. хорьбо; can be made of different materials and have different attributes on them. See next chapter.

77 Bur. Нойтолhон бөө.

78 Some say nine. The water is boiled with red-hot stones taken from a river near the initiate's birth place and a small amount of goat's blood is added.

79 Bur. Дуhаалгын бөө.

80 Bur. духаалга.

81 Bur. тарасун, Buryatian milk-vodka.

receives a second birch cane which is longer than the previous one. After three years he can take the third initiation.

Third initiation

A Bө with the third initiation is called Hayalgyn Bө,[82] 'one who can sprinkle upwards' because now he can invoke and make offerings to some of the *Haat* and *Ezhen* divinities. In the course of this third initiation a billy goat is ritually sacrificed to Manzhilai Zayaan,[83] son of Hormusta Tengeri. He is a special *Ongon*-benefactor of the Bө because he is the divinity who goes back and forth between the Sky and the Earth and through whom the Tengeri are connected with the deities of the Middle World. He also aids the Bө in delivering offerings to the Sky. Therefore a Bө at this stage is also called Manzhilaitkhan Bө.[84] He has the right to perform offering rituals entailing the sacrifice of a white ram and receives his share at any *tailgan*. There should be a minimum one-year gap before the next initiation can be taken.

Fourth initiation

A Bө at this stage is called Zhodo'otoi Bө,[85] 'Bө who has silver fir tree bark' because he is given bark and three special birch tapers decorated with multi-coloured ribbons to hold it with. The smoke of the bark is used to purify the Bө and the offerings before and in the course of the ritual. The initiate also receives a *toli*-mirror and a whip[86] adorned with multi-coloured ribbons symbolizing the Bө's power over the people because at this stage a Bө receives the right to be a judge, ensuring that taboos are not broken and that the people under his jurisdiction adhere to the rules of moral conduct. He can mediate in disputes and punish those guilty of misconduct. In the course of the initiation the Bө is purified with water from nine springs and takes *tangarig*,[87] a special Bө oath, at a sacred place in the presence of his Bө-father and the elders of his clan and tribe. Among other things the oath includes promises to help all people regardless of their social status or wealth; not to ask the rich or the poor for anything in return for the services he provides but to take

82 Bur. Хаялгын бөө.

83 Bur. Манжилай заяан.

84 Bur. Манжилайтhан бөө.

85 Bur. Жодоотой (Ёдоотой) бөө.

86 Bur. ташуур/мина.

87 Bur. тангариг.

only what they give themselves; to protect the old, poor and weak; not to frighten people or speak badly about them; not to make public the secret knowledge and techniques.[88] Having taken the oath and widened his functions, a Bө of this stage is also called Yohotoi Bө,[89] 'Bө-in-the-law'. He can offer sacrifices with a white ram to the *Haats*, *Ezhen* and all the *Zayaan* he knows. There is a minimum one-year gap before the fifth initiation can be taken.

Fifth initiation

At this stage the Bө receives a *hese*[90]-drum or 'deer-drum' with a drum stick[91] and is called Hesete Bө,[92] 'a Bө who has *hese*'. Now he can use his deer-drum to fly wherever he needs in the universe performing various magical tasks such as returning the soul and communicating directly with various deities and spirits. In fact there are three kinds of *hese* at this level: one made of deer skin, another from goat skin and yet another from a bull's hide. At this stage a Bө meets his 'sky-consort', a spiritual female being from the dimension of the Sky who helps him in his work. He can also invoke certain Tengeri but he can only reach the three lower levels of the Sky. A Hesete Bө has the capacity to lick red-hot iron for the purposes of purification, healing and as proof of his power. He can make offerings involving the sacrifice of a ram or a goat. There should be a minimum one-year gap before the sixth initiation can be taken.

Sixth initiation

At this stage the Bө receives a metal horse-headed cane with nine rings and *hol'bogo*,[93] various metal objects, and is therefore called Hor'botoi Bө,[94] 'a Bө who has a cane'. By using this *hor'bө*-cane he can

---

88 So those who claim to reveal the 'secret' techniques to the public are either charlatans or renegade Bө (or shamans) who seek fame and money. Doing so they go against their sacred oath, a very serious offence against the Tengeri and lesser gods and spirits which is severely punished. Sometimes these renegade Bө turn into black sorcerers. This will be discussed in the next chapter.

89 Bur. Ёнотой бөө.

90 Bur. хэсэ.

91 Bur. дохюур. The *hese* and the drum stick are sanctified by the Bө-father who invites the *Ongon* to dwell on the objects.

92 Bur. Хэсэтэ бөө.

93 Bur. хольбого, a kind of little bell.

94 Bur. Хорьботой бөө.

immediately enter into the state of *ongo*[95] and let himself be possessed by the *Ongon*. At this stage the Bɵ is also given a *shere'e*[96]-altar and has the right to lead large offering rituals like *tailgan* which include the sacrifices of a horse and a bull, and can offer nine animals simultaneously. Moreover, he can sanctify ritual and religious objects by inviting the *Ongon*-spirits to actually descend and dwell on them. There should be a three-year gap before the next initiation.

Seventh initiation

This is quite a large initiation. Before this initiation the Bɵ has to undergo an extensive purification with smoke from silver fir bark. He comes out of the smoke hole of his *gher* by climbing the Udeshi Burkhan birch tree, 'god-protector of the gate to the Sky'. Sticking out of the smoke hole, this tree connects the hearth with the Sky. Then the Bɵ is put on a white felt carpet outside and purified either with water from sacred springs mixed with a little blood from a ginger horse or sometimes with blood alone. Then nine bottles of *arkhi*[97] are poured over his head. In the course of the initiation ritual the initiate receives a *maihabshi*,[98] a horned crown made from the top part of a deer's head taken together with the antlers, or made of metal with imitation iron antlers. A Bɵ at this stage is called Maihabshitai Bɵ[99] after the crown. Besides the crown he also receives five animal skins, a special cloak or *orgoi*[100] with metal objects sewn onto it and three *hese*-drums with *toibor*[101] drum sticks. Now he can invoke all the Tengeri, sprinkle from the sacrificial bowl with an eagle's feather and initiate Bɵ beginners. Because he has *orgoi* and can invoke all the Tengeri he is also called Tengeriin Orgoito Bɵ.[102] The next initiation can only be taken after three years.

---

95 Bur. онго; the trance state of an advanced Bɵ or Utgan when s/he is possessed by the *Ongon*.

96 Bur. шэрээ.

97 Bur. архи, a kind of vodka.

98 Bur. майхабши.

99 Bur. Майхабшитай бөө.

100 Bur. оргой.

101 Bur. тойбор is a kind of drums stick to which attached nine coloured ribbons.

102 Bur. Тенгериин Оргойто бөө.

Eighth initiation

At this stage the Bɵ receives his second metal horse-headed cane to which, among other metal objects, is attached a small metal ladder as a symbol of his ability to travel to the Sky. Actually, the cane is more than a symbol. It is quickened by inviting the *Ongon* to dwell in it and therefore it becomes a steed on which the Bɵ travels to the Upper World. He also receives a *malgai*[103]-hat made out of bear fur with the symbol of the sun on the front band. The Bɵ now has several canes and drums and all the other necessary implements, he knows all the canons, doctrines and rituals of Bɵ Murgel very well, he can invoke all the deities of the Three Worlds and can control the weather. Consequently he is called Duuren Bɵ[104] or Tengeriin Orgoito Buheli Bɵ,[105] 'complete Bɵ'. After a year he can take the final initiation.

Ninth initiation

Before the last initiation can be taken the Bɵ has to obtain permission to enter this stage from all the Lord-Owners of the upper level of the Middle World and from the Tengeri by performing an extensive prayer festival. In the course of the initiation he receives a human-headed metal cane which becomes an *ongon* and can perform magical actions by itself. He also receives three large *hese*-drums made out of deer-, goat- and bull-skin. Now he has extraordinary power and an impressive array of ritual objects among which there are nine drums and nine *toli*-mirrors. He is called Zaarin Bɵ, supreme Bɵ. He has realized the higher truth of Bɵ Murgel and is the messenger of the Tengeri. In the past Zaarin could do incredible things such as flying in the air or cutting their head off and then putting it back without leaving a trace. They also had extraordinary clairvoyance and clairaudience and were formidably powerful.

The whole process of arriving at the ninth stage takes a very minimum of fifteen years. The stages, attributes and titles given are not rigid so they do not always correspond exactly in different streams of the tradition. As was said above, this full initiation system practically stopped in Soviet times but it is now being revived and there is a movement to restore it to its former glory not just in form but also with the corresponding powers. The stages of the initiation are once again being followed and the ritual attributes are being re-made.

---

[103] Bur. малгай.

[104] Bur. Дуурен бɵɵ.

[105] Bur. Тенгериин Оргойто бүхэли бɵɵ.

Initiation among Utgan

The Utgan have their own stages of initiation, also nine in number, with similar titles and attributes. The order in which the titles go can vary but the highest title equivalent to Zaarin is Duuriskha.[106]

Here is a condensed account of how an Utgan from the Hongo'odor clan of Tunka was initiated in the nineties. The ritual took place in the mountains of Tunka and was performed by the Bɵ of her clan:

> A white goat was sacrificed to the gods and everyone prayed around a bonfire. The initiate entered a trance state. To determine whether the deities had accepted her and also to check the depth of her absorption into the trance, the Bɵ put two pebbles, one white and one black,[107] into the fire, leaving them there until they were red-hot. He then gave them to the Utgan to put into her mouth and suck until they cooled down. She was able to do so, and when the Bɵ examined her mouth later he found no burns. This was a sign that she had indeed been accepted and was now qualified to be an Utgan.[108]

This same Utgan told me that, according to one of the local traditions in Tunka, a Bɵ or Utgan achieves full power only after going through the Nine Circles of Suffering. The Nine Circles of Suffering is a kind of 'natural' initiation and refers to the sufferings and difficulties, sometimes extraordinary, which a Bɵ or Utgan encounters and overcomes in the course of his/her life and spiritual career. By going through these Nine Circles, a Bɵ or Utgan is purified and develops real compassion towards people because they have personally experienced sufferings 'on their own hide'[109] and so can understand the human condition very well. This means they are really ready for the work of helping fellow human beings.

---

[106] Bur. Дуурисха. The lower titles are Bur. Хэсэтэ, Хонхото, Жодоото etc.

[107] White and black pebbles probably signify control over the forces of good and bad and, also, mastery of both black and white techniques within Bɵ Murgel.

[108] This element has a parallel in Tibetan Bön. There is an ancient practice in Bön called Tib. gtar tshan len pa. In this practice a Bönpo takes and holds in his hand red-hot metal or stone to demonstrate his power. (According to Yongdzin Lopön Tenzin Namdak).

[109] A Russian expression.

Significance of the number nine

We mentioned the number nine in the context of cosmology, and it plays an important role in the initiation process of Buryatian Bө Murgel, too. According to some sources the nine initiation stages are connected with the nine branches of the sacred *Serge* World Tree. Although there is information attributing this system to the great Bө Ergil Buga[110] who lived at the turn of the BC/AD millennia, it could be a much older system connected with the Bönpo culture coming from ancient Prehistoric Bön traditions in Central Asia. As we have seen in Chapter IV on cosmology, the nine branches of the sacred *Serge* tree correspond to some extent to the nine-storied pyramidal mountain of Yungdrung Gutseg, the sacred mountain which represents the Nine Ways or Progressive Stages of Bön and find an even closer parallel in the nine-leaved *jangbu*. Moreover, the nine initiations of Bө Murgel and the Nine Ways of Yungdrung Bön both have the same function of leading a follower to the highest realization of the respective tradition, although the spiritual fruits of Bө Murgel and Yungdrung Bön are completely different. Nonetheless, the ancient source, the foundation of this nine-branched arrangement, is the culture (but not the spiritual teachings) of the Prehistoric Bön of Eurasia.

The twelve-branched Mongolian initiation system reflecting the sacred deer's antlers points to the presence within Mongol-Buryat Bө Murgel of the ancient lineages and teachings pertaining to the Bön of the Deer.[111]

Summary

We can see that the complex and well-structured initiation process in Buryatian Bө Murgel shows that this is a clear and coherent system which, although very ancient, is in no way 'primitive'; on the contrary, it demonstrates quite a high degree of sophistication which cannot be dubbed inferior to the ritual systems of so-called 'advanced' religions and is in some ways more complex. It is also clear that in order to become a bona fide Bө or Utgan an individual has to possess and nurture many special qualities which include wisdom, compassion, selflessness, an egalitarian approach and so on,[112] qualities which are a prerequisite for

---

[110] Bur. Эргил Буга, *buga* means 'deer' in Buryatian. This is a reference to the Deer Cult within Buryatian Bө Murgel. See ch. X.

[111] See ch. X.

[112] This, of course, applies to White Bө and Utgan and the Black Bө and Utgan of the first type. See next chapter.

priests and spiritual leaders in the majority of modern world religions. The use of animal sacrifices in Bɵ Murgel's initiation and offering rites is a complex issue arising from their world view. We will deal with it in detail in Chapter XII. No matter what one's attitude towards this phenomenon is, the universal positive human qualities which Bɵ and Utgan must possess in order to fulfil their spiritual work remain nonetheless.

CHAPTER VIII

Different Types of Bɵ, their Functions and Ritual Gear

Different ways of classifying White and Black Bɵ

The division of Bɵ into white, Sagaani Bɵ, and black, Haryn Bɵ is a very controversial issue as modern Bɵ are themselves not unified on this matter and scholars, too, after more than a hundred years of study, have come to different conclusions.

Many different shamanic traditions of Siberia divide their priests into black and white. It is generally held that white shamans propitiate the light deities of the sky and travel to the Upper World in their trance while black shamans invoke spirits of the dead and travel downwards to the Underworld in their trance states. In practice, many shamans combine these two functions, especially in Altai, and so cannot be defined strictly as 'black' or 'white'.

As a syncretic tradition, Buryatian Bɵ Murgel has amalgamated and elaborated many different streams of spiritual traditions over the centuries. There is not, in fact, a unified, standardized system of practice among the Buryatian Bɵ which could be classified as an organized religious system; although the general principles of practice are common to Bɵ from all the Buryatian tribes and clans, there are nevertheless significant differences in many aspects of the belief system, ranging from the pantheon of deities invoked by Bɵ of different areas and tribes, through their mythology up to the techniques used when conducting rituals. The explanation for this lies in the large genetic and ethnic variations among the inhabitants of different areas of Buryatia emerging from the intense processes of ethnogenesis which continued for thousands of years. Buryats are exogamic and marriage between relatives is prohibited for seven generations to avoid in-breeding, or 'stagnation of the blood'. Consequently Buryats took wives, mixed with neighbouring tribes and even intermarried with non-Buryatian peoples such as Hamnigan-Evenki, Yakut, Orochi etc. who not only revitalized genetic stock but also brought their protective deities and ritual customs with them.

This explains one interpretation of the term 'Black Bө'. As we saw in the preceding chapter, the *utkha* spark which comes through the mother's line is called *harriin utkha* and '*hari'* is the Buryat for 'stranger'. Some Bө maintain that this notion of 'stranger' goes back to the days when wives and mothers were strangers to their husband's clan, coming with their unfamiliar customs and ancestral deities. Later, in their zeal to denigrate the native traditions and elevate their own, Buddhist and Christian missionaries could easily have corrupted the word *hari*, 'stranger', to *hara*,[1] 'black', leading to misinterpretation and confusion with the passing of the years.

Another interpretation is connected to the division of the sky-dwelling Tengeri into White Western Tengeri and Black Eastern Tengeri. According to this interpretation, the Bө who propitiate the White Tengeri are called White Bө while the Bө who propitiate the Black Tengeri are called Black Bө. As White and Black Tengeri have different positions in the Sky and different functions, so, too, do the White and Black Bө (and also the White and Black Bө-smiths). Consequently they use different techniques and ritual apparel. This understanding is prevalent among the western Buryats; eastern Buryatian tribes such as the Hori-Buryats, don't clearly divide the Tengeri into Western and Eastern, good and evil, so there is almost no notion of White and Black Bө.[2] Instead Hori-Buryats have loosely retained the concept of dividing the pantheon of gods and spirits into the Upper Level populated by Sky-dwelling Tengeri and the Lower Level populated by earthly spirits. Black and White Bө, if they are talked about at all, are therefore understood more in this context. An explanation may lie in traces of Tyurkic Bө traditions coming from tribes such as the Gooligan', for example, as a similar classification is found among the *kams*[3] of Altai.

White Bө

White Bө receive their *utkha* from the White Western Tengeri so their practice consists of propitiating these Tengeri and their children, the Western *Haats,* as well as benign *Zayaans* and ancestral spirits. The task of a White Bө or Utgan is to attract the blessings and white magical powers of these benefactors to protect the community, increase

---

1 Bur. хара.

2 This is also generally true for the Buryats of Barguzin. Actually, among the Buryats of Transbaikalia the Eastern Tengeri are often perceived as positive, bringing benefit to animals and people.

3 *Kam* is a type of priest in the native tradition of Altai.

prosperity and preserve well-being. White Bө pray for good weather, a bountiful harvest, guidance and help in healing, healthy children and a long life as well as exorcising evil spirits. In the past they did not pray to the Black Tengeri in any way, nor did they make offerings to them, and this is still true for some Bө today. Traditionally White Bө wore white clothes, had attributes made from white metal and rode white horses. Some sources suggest that White Bө didn't have many ritual items or metal ornaments on their ritual dress, didn't use a *hese*-drum and didn't fall into trance while invoking the Tengeri; in other words, they were not what we would call 'shamans' but rather priests of a cult of positive, white sky deities. In fact, it is likely that there were many different kinds of White Bө reflecting the diversity of local traditions; while some didn't enter the trance state, others did. These different priests would have used different techniques, had distinct lineages and, possibly, even belonged to different religions with the same cultural base in a way similar to, say, Judaism and Christianity which are both culturally rooted in the Old Testament.

Black Bө

Black Bө have their *utkha* from the Black Eastern Tengeri and their practice consists of propitiating the Black Tengeri, their children the Eastern *Haats,* Black *Zayaans* and ancestral spirits. Black Bө can be divided into two categories:

i) The first category of Black Bө don't usually use their powers against people but protect them, acting as a sort of mediator between humans and the potentially negative forces of the universe. By performing offering rituals to the Black Tengeri, Black *Haats* and *Zayaans* they appease them and ask them not to send people or animals illnesses or misfortunes but become their protectors and patrons instead, to revoke the curses and to cure the diseases they had sent earlier. These Black Bө travel to the Underworld to bring back the souls of the sick from the prisons of Erlig Khaan and, even if they are provoked or deeply offended by someone, would not turn their powers against them to curse or kill them through black magic. They play the role of protectors and are very powerful healers and magicians bringing benefits to their community.
ii) The second type of Black Bө or Utgan also worship the Black Tengeri, Black *Haats* and *Zayaans* but bring people only evil. They are feared for 'eating' people's souls, killing with magical arrows

and other feats of black magic. When performing rituals they paint half or the whole of their face black, while some smear their faces or ritual items with blood. Malevolent forces possess them so they play the role of conductors and tools through which evil, punitive and destructive activities are actualized on earth. This type of Black Bɵ or Utgan actually comprises the first category of black sorcerers as their activity is exclusively evil-oriented.

Black sorcerers

The second type of black sorcerer is called Elbeshen[4] because they specialize in casting *elbe*,[5] the evil eye. Such black sorcerers cannot be called Bɵ or Utgan; they are connected with all kinds of lower-ranking malevolent spirits and have their own lineages. Transmission of black sorcery often runs through the family line. In some cases their knowledge is written down with blood instead of ink. They often try to spoil *tailgans* or other prayer festivals conducted by Bɵ and constantly cast curses on people, even on their own relatives if they cross them. Petty black sorcerers have become a real problem in Buryatia in recent years. In the spiritual vacuum of the Soviet times when followers of any religion were persecuted, lineages were interrupted and knowledge lost, but, as the Russian saying goes, 'the bad deed doesn't take much wisdom' so those with some psychic abilities used them to become black sorcerers wreaking considerable harm.

One of the very important tasks of both White Bɵ and Black Bɵ of the first category is to find and neutralize or destroy black sorcerers.

Universal Bɵ

Besides the clearly-defined White and Black Bɵ there is another category which we can call 'Universal Bɵ', a Bɵ or Utgan who has a dual *utkha*-spark from both White and Black Tengeri. These Hoёr Te'eshe Yabadaltai Bɵ are able to perform rites for both White and Black sides and can mediate between them, hence their name, which literally means 'able to travel to both sides'. They are also known as Tolmo'osho, 'The Interpreter'.

---

4 Bur. эльбэшэн.

5 Bur. эльбэ.

Bө-smiths

Another special category of Bө is the Bө-smiths. Bө-smiths, called Bө-Darhan[6] or Darhan Utkhatai Bө,[7] are held in highest respect among the Bө because of their special magical *utkha* from the Tengeri which gives them particular powers and extraordinary abilities – *shezhe abatai bagaa.*[8] An accomplished Bө-Darhan can perform miracles such as flying in the air, escaping from any closed space (even from the dungeon of Erlig Khaan), sitting unscathed in the midst of fire and becoming invisible, but they are also especially adept at healing difficult-to-cure diseases such as cancer and destroying bad spirits. Bө-smiths have a special range of magical techniques related to the fire element. They are also particularly skilled and gifted with metals from which many of the Bө's ritual attributes are made. In the past, working metal was an indispensable skill, highly prized in times of peace and war alike.

As we saw in the previous chapter, there are White and Black Bө-smiths. White Bө-smiths trace their *utkha* to the White Tengeri, more specifically to Dabaan Zholo'o Tengeri[9] whose son, Bozhintoi,[10] sent his nine sons and a daughter to the Middle World to teach people the art of metalworking.[11]

Black Bө-smiths trace their *utkha* to the Black Tengeri, specifically to Hara Mahagal Darhan Tengeri[12] with his seven sons who were sent to earth to teach people the skills of working black metals and the magic of healing thirteen difficult-to-cure diseases and other serious diseases. Hara Mahagal Darhan Tengeri (Mahakala) comes from the Buddhist pantheon and was integrated into Bө Murgel's pantheon some time after the seventeenth century. As Buddhism was successfully implanted among the eastern Buryat tribes such as the Hori, whose Black Bө-smiths received their *utkha* from the Black Tengeri, Mahakala was certainly superimposed by Gelugpa lamas onto another Black Tengeri, the original patron of Black Bө-smiths; the incoming lamas sought to take Bө Murgel under control by appropriating their gods and including them into the Lamaist pantheon as *Dharmapala* protectors. So Mahakala somehow

---

6 Bur. бөө дархан.

7 Bur. Дархан утхатай бөө, a Bө with the smith's *utkha*.

8 Bur. шэжэ абатай багаа.

9 Bur. Дабаан жолоо тенгери. He is also called Darhan Sagaan Tengeri already mentioned in ch. VI.

10 Bur. Божинтой.

11 Other sources say that Bozhintoi was a son of Hormusta Tengeri.

12 Bur. Хара Махагал Дархан Тэнгэри.

slipped back into Bɵ Murgel's pantheon and became fused with the original Hara Darhan Tengeri. In some eastern regions of Buryatia today there are mixed Bɵ and Buddhist traditions where Bɵ and lamas take part in the same *tailgan.*[13]

Both White and Black Bɵ-smiths have special protective abilities and can save people from the onslaught of dangerous spirits and black magic. They often 'borrow permission' from each other and can perform both Black and White Bɵ-smith's rites.[14] Both White and Black Bɵ-smiths have their own traditions, pantheons and even their own initiation stages and ranks with special Bɵ-Darhan initiations performed after and in addition to the common ones at each stage of the general initiation process. They have their own binding ritual obligations such as making offerings to the smith-ancestors on the ninth, nineteenth and twenty-ninth day of the lunar calendar, and the yearly[15] 'body-washing ritual'.[16] Both White and Black Bɵ-smiths have additional ritual items and details of ritual dress such as miniature hammer, tongs, anvil etc. The White Bɵ-smiths have a special short brown-red apron and wear a white belt. Then they have *dalabshi*,[17] a shoulder-piece with tassels symbolizing the wings of the Eagle who brought fire to the earth, and *he'ete hebeneg*,[18] a special cloak with pictures of eagles, stars and mountains decorated with nine *hol'bogo* (metal tassels) and nine silver bells. Black Bɵ-smiths have the same additional items but of different colour. Their *elgebshe*[19] breast-piece is black and they wear a red belt over it; their *dalabshi* and *hebeneg*-cloak has *hol'bogo*, bells and decorations of black metal.

Ooselshen-clairvoyants and Uligershen-bards

There are two further important types of spiritual practitioners in Bɵ Murgel who aren't Bɵ *per se* but play a significant role in Buryatian society nevertheless. They are *Ooselshen*[20]-clairvoyants and *Uligershen*[21]-bards.

Ooselshen may be a former Bɵ or Utgan who had to stop practising due to a physical injury or some other reason, or may be someone with the

13 This will be dealt with in more detail in ch. XII.

14 Bur. хоёр талын харгы

15 Or sometimes monthly.

16 We will look into this rite in detail in ch. XI.

17 Bur. далабши.

18 Bur. хээтэ хэбэнэг.

19 Bur. эльгэбшэ.

20 Bur. үзэлшэн.

21 Bur. үльгэршэн.

utkha-spark who didn't take full initiation but has clairvoyant abilities. *Ooselshen* don't have the right to perform rituals to the gods but they can deliver prophecies and predictions through clairvoyance, mediumistic trance or various kinds of divination techniques.

Uligershen are bards who know *uliger*,[22] the huge corpus of myths surrounding the pantheon of Bɵ Murgel, and related epic stories such as *Abai Geser*. These are sung at celebrations and on important occasions so Bɵ-lore is kept alive among the people and the young are taught the tenets of their faith and culture. *Uligershen* are directly comparable to Tibetan *drungkhen*[23] bards.

Costume

The persecutions of the Soviet era meant that until very recently modern Bɵ didn't have many ritual implements such as elaborate cloaks or antlered crowns. I remember once in 1994 a German friend went with me to a kind of shamanic seminar or meeting on the outskirts of Ulaan-Ude. He was excitedly expecting to see people in strange costumes with big drums etc., but when we arrived he looked around, bewildered, and asked me:

> 'But where are the shamans?'
> 'You're surrounded by them,' I said. 'All these people are shamans.'
> 'But hang on,' he argued, 'They look just like ordinary people from the street, nothing special. No special dress – nothing.'
> 'Well,' I said, 'That's how they are. You can't pick them out from the crowd on the street. You have to feel them.'

In Soviet times the Bɵ Murgel tradition was preserved in secret without its external attributes. This was all the easier as no special temples are needed as a place of worship; instead, rituals are performed in the natural setting of the mountains, forests and lakes or just at home, so once the Bɵ and Utgan shed their ritual dresses, it was easier for them to hide than for the Buddhists. Nevertheless, many were rounded up and sent to the *gulags* or killed. Their ritual costumes, crowns and implements were either destroyed by the Communists or taken into the collections of ethnographic museums and can now be seen in museums

---

22 Bur. үльгэр.

23 Tib. sgrung mkhan.

all around the Russian Federation. Some of these ritual objects have retained their spiritual power. I heard of an incident which happened to a museum worker in Soviet times who donned an *orgoi* ritual dress as a joke. A week later he was dead, struck down by a sudden and unknown disease. This can be explained by the fact that *orgoi* is connected to the beings a Bɵ invokes and some of these beings actually dwell on the dress. If an uninitiated is foolish enough to put this kind of dress on, s/he will certainly be 'taken away' by these beings.

We have already touched upon some of a Bɵ's ritual equipment, but now let's look at the full range of clothes used by Buryatian Bɵ. The complete costume is called *amitai.*[24] This name is etymologically connected to *amin* which means 'vitality', 'energy of breathing', so *amitai* means 'made alive'. That is literally so because the various components and the whole dress are purified, sanctified and made alive through special rites often involving animal sacrifice[25] during which the windpipe and bronchi of an animal are separated and put on some items of *amitai*. The *Ongon*-spirits are invited to actually dwell on the dress and their spiritual power is invoked into it. Each Bɵ or Utgan has their own personal *amitai* made especially for them which cannot be used by another Bɵ because of the personal protective deities and spirits dwelling on it. Each *amitai* has a special *Ongon*-spirit(s) connected to it who acts as its protector and Owner,[26] protects the Bɵ or Utgan to whom this *amitai* belongs and aids him or her in the performance of magical tasks. The full *amitai* consists of:

1. *Maihabshi* horned crown;
2. *Malgai* hat;
3. *Orgoi*-cloak with *hol'bogo* and other metal items;
4. *Dalabshi* 'winged' shoulder-piece;
5. *Elgebshi* short apron;
6. *Hebeneg* overcoat.

1. Maihabshi

The *maihabshi* horned crown can be of two types. The first are made from the whole top part of a deer's skull complete with antlers.

---

24 Bur. амитай. For a picture of a Bɵ in full ritual attire see ch. X.

25 Bur. Амитайн ээндэ.

26 Bur. Амитайн эжэн.

The second are made from two strips of iron crossed and bent to form a semi-sphere and attached to a metal ring which goes round the head. Imitation iron antlers are attached to the sides and a metal four-link chain with rings with *hol'bogo* is attached to the back. A metal spoon and awl or other similar objects are fixed to the end of the chain together with metal figures of animals, birds and fish. Multicoloured ribbons and the skins of small animals such as squirrel, ermine, mink, sable or hare can also be attached.

2. Malgai

The *malgai* is worn either by itself or under the *maihabshi* horned crown. It can be made of different materials and have various items attached to it depending on the Bɵ's rank. For high-ranking Bɵ the front-band is often made of bear skin.

3. Orgoi

A White Bɵ's *orgoi*-cloak is white while Black Bɵ have a blue *orgoi*. It is a cloak or gown made of silk or a kind of paper-cloth. Various small metal items such as bells, small figures of a human, horse, birds, snakes, and a miniature sword, hammer and tongs are sewn onto it. *Orgoi* can also be decorated with pictures and long strings with metal images of spirits, bells, feathers, coloured ribbons and other items. All of these aid the process of connecting with the beings invoked by a Bɵ or Utgan and help in his/her travels in the different dimensions of the universe as well as inducing magical powers and clairvoyant abilities. In addition to increasing his spiritual power, the Bɵ's *orgoi*-cloak also acts as protective armour when magical actions are performed.

To these main components of *amitai* can be added other items.

Hooyag

Hooyag[27] – a kind of coat of mail made out of iron or lead plates connected by metal rings. It can be worn over the *orgoi* or instead of it. This item is probably a remnant of those times when Bɵ were also military leaders. The original *hooyag* was given by the Tengeri.

---

[27] Bur. хуяг.

Head band

A head band with black tassels which cover the eyes and upper part of the face to separate the spiritual visions of a Bɵ from the physical reality around him.[28]

Mask

In certain cases a Bɵ or Utgan could also wear a leather, wooden, brass or iron mask of his/her chief *Ongon*-spirit(s). The function of such a mask is to induce possession by the *Ongon*-spirits especially when asking for predictions through oracular trance or when strong magic is required to accomplish a difficult task.

Ritual Objects

To be fully equipped for the needs of their profession, Bɵ Murgel priests and priestesses have many ritual objects[29] all of which have precise functions and uses. They include:

1. *Toli*-mirror;
2. *Hese*-drum and *toibor*, *dohyuur* drumsticks;
3. *Hor'bo*-canes;
4. Sword;
5. *Ho'orto*[30]-dagger;
6. *Hootaga*[31]-knife;
7. *Minaa* whip[32];
8. Bow and arrow;
9. *Zhada*[33]-spear;
10. *Zhodo'o*,[34] bark of the silver fir tree;

---

[28] Also used by Gelugpa Buddhists in Buryatia and Mongolia in their *Chöd* tradition and also for walking in the winter to protect the eyes from the light reflecting from the snow. A head band with black tassels is also used in Tibet and the Dölpo region of Nepal, one of the regions of the ancient Zhang Zhung Empire where Bön was a state religion.

[29] Bur. бөөгэй тоног.

[30] Bur. хоорто.

[31] Bur. хутага.

[32] Bur. минаа or Bur. ташуур.

[33] Bur. жада.

[34] Bur. жодоо/ёдоо.

11. *Huur*,[35] a mouth harp;
12. *Zeli*,[36] a special rope;
13. *Shere'e*-altar;
14. *Ongon* images;
15. *Hahyuusan*[37] amulets;
16. *Bө-hete*,[38] a flint stone;
17. *Shanginuur*[39]-bell;
18. *San hengereg*[40] cymbals;
19. Prayer beads;
20. Tobacco pouch and pipe.

1. Toli-mirror

Nowadays these are made of brass although in ancient times jade was used. Some types of *toli* have engravings on them. Bө can have up to nine mirrors of different sizes which are used for divination, healing and, in certain cases, as a protective armour, a kind of shield. Each *toli* is related to a different sphere of existence within the Three Worlds, a particular dimension of various classes of beings, or a different task. The mirrors must be sanctified by a special ritual before they can be used and are often handed down from one Bө in the line to another.[41]

---

[35] Bur. хуур.

[36] Bur. зэли.

[37] Bur. Хахюусан.

[38] Bur. бөө-хэтэ.

[39] Bur. шангинуур.

[40] Bur. сан хэнгэрэг.

[41] In Ancient Russia we also find a similar object called *zertsalo* (Rus. зерцало), a central round smooth metal mirror-plate in the protective gear of a *vityaz'* (Rus. вйтязь) – noble knight. *Zertsalo* is an old word for 'mirror' *zerkalo* (Rus. зеркало) in modern Russian. It is obvious that in olden times *zertsalo* served the same function as Tibetan *melong* and Buryatian *toli* because warriorship in those days was inextricably tied to protective magic and clairvoyance of many sorts. This can be seen from Russian folk tales. In the past *zertsalo* must have been used as a support, container and disseminator of the light energy, as a symbol of mind or soul, and represented the warrior-magician's life-force and protective energy. It is identical, then, in function to the *melong* mirrors of various non-human beings who serve as the Protectors of Bön who often wear their *melong* on their heart over their armor. The 'heart syllable' (symbol of the deity's life-force) is often shining in the mirror.

2. *Hese-drum and toibor, dohyuur drumsticks.*

Hese is a half-drum with a cross-handle on the inside. It is often decorated with pictures and a metal *ongon*-figure is attached to the cross-handle while multicoloured ribbons or fur are affixed to the outer rim. The drumsticks are also connected with *Ongons*. Like the *toli,* the *hese*-drum symbolizes the universe and a fully-fledged Zaarin Bɵ has nine *hese* of various sizes made out of deer-, goat- and bull-skins.

Each *hese*, also called *hengereg*,[42] has to be sanctified and animated through a special ritual before it can be used for practice. In the past, it was common for the whole village or family to be involved in making a *hese* for the Bɵ. They would go to the *taiga*, find a suitable tree and fell it, then find a suitable animal for the drum skin and finally assemble the *hese*. Then the old Bɵ would perform a ritual of quickening the drum to call the *Ongon*-spirit(s) to reside in it. A Bɵ's *hese* is very closely connected with his power and life-force, so if it breaks the Bɵ may fall ill or even die. When a Bɵ dies, his relatives make a slit in the drum skin and break the frame, thus enabling the Bɵ to use it in his posthumous life in the Otherworld. In Tibet, the closest equivalent of *hese* is a Bönpo drum called *chyednga*[43] or 'half-drum'. Like a *hese*, it has only one side but it is mounted on a stick while *hese* is held by a cross-handle inside.

Fig. 1. Utgan Nadezhda Stepanova with Hese-*drum, Barguzin, 1994.*

The *hese*-drum has many functions:

i) Firstly, it is used for calling the Tengeri and the spirits through special rhythmic codes known to the Bɵ. Combined with exclamations such as: *'So'ok!', 'Buugyt!', 'A-hure!', 'Do'om'*[44] etc. these codes ensure that communication with the deities and spirits flows securely and in the right way, that the offerings are delivered it the correct manner and that the Bɵ's magical command to his helper-spirits is fulfilled

---

42 Bur. хэнгэрэг.

43 Tib. phyed rnga.

44 Bur. Сөөк! Буугыт! А-хурэ! Доом!

precisely. It is like knowing someone's name and mobile phone number so that we can call them wherever they are to have a conversation or ask them to do us a favour.

ii) Secondly, *hese* is one of the Bɵ or Utgan's steeds used to travel to and in the different dimensions within the Three Worlds.

iii) Thirdly, *hese* is the receptacle of some *Ongon*-spirits who aid Bɵ and Utgan in their work.

iv) And lastly, *hese* can be used as a shield against magical attacks.

3. Hor'bo-canes

These canes come in different shapes and sizes and may be made of wood or metal. As the knob is often fashioned after the head of a horse, human or snake they are called *moriin*, *hun* and *mogoi*:[45] horse-, human- and snake-cane. *Hor'bo* is yet another type of steed which Bɵ use to travel in the universe. They are also a symbol of power, so a fully initiated Bɵ can have many *hor'bo*. Generally, wooden *hor'bo* are given to lower-ranking Bɵ and are made of birch, carved with a number of notches and decorated with coloured ribbons. Higher-ranking Bɵ have metal *hor'bo* with indwelling *Ongons*, some of which are so strong that they can jump and fly by themselves when their Bɵ performs rituals.

4. Sword

In the past a sword was among the Bɵ's ritual objects and it served various purposes. Firstly, it portrayed the Bɵ as a Spiritual Warrior who fights against negative forces to protect his fellow human beings and animals from illness or attacks provoked by evil spirits and black sorcerers. As the Bɵ mediates between the different worlds in order to bring harmony, it was also used in various magical rites. The sword points to the Bɵ's function of judge, too, a position held by many Bɵ until recent times.[46] A Bɵ-in the law would solve disputes between families and clans over hunting grounds as well as deciding all sorts of criminal cases. And finally the Bɵ's sword was simply used in time of war when Bɵ took on the function of military leaders.

---

[45] Bur. морийн, хүн, могой.

[46] It is interesting to note that in many cultures a sword is associated with justice.

5. *Ho'orto-dagger*

This is used for healing rituals, cutting off curses and so forth.

6. *Hootaga-knife*

This is used in various ways, similar to the dagger.

7. *Whip*

The whip is the symbol of a Bө's power over the people and could quite literally be used for punishing (whipping) offenders of tribal law. It is made of the skin of eelpout and coloured ribbons together with small metal charms such as *hol'bogo*, a sword or a hammer attached to the handle. Like most other ritual objects, it is animated.

8. *Bow and arrow*

These symbolize the Bө's abilities to ensure good luck in hunts and military expeditions but the Bө can use them to shoot and kill malevolent spirits. Arrows act as a support for *hulde*[47] and are used in the soul recalling rites of some tribes. An arrow may be shot to send a request to the Sky, to speed benefits or curses to the place towards which it was shot, or to make an 'arrow way', opening the way for a journey or some kind of enterprise.

9. *Zhada-spear*

This spear is a weapon used in magic, hunt and war and, most importantly, it is used for making *tug*,[48] the magical banner which acts as a support for the *hulde* of a clan, tribe and nation's protective deities.[49]

10. *Zhodo'o*

Zhodo'o is bark of the silver fir tree and symbolizes the Bө's magical abilities. Its smoke is used for fumigation.

---

47 See ch. XIII.

48 Bur. туг.

49 See ch. XIII.

11. Huur-mouth harp

This is an instrument used for calling beings to the offering and the sound it makes can be used to induce trance and as a means of travel in the Three Worlds. It can also be played as an offering of music.

12. Zeli-rope

The *zeli* rope is made of horsehair and hung with buckets and pendants. It can be used to secure the sanctified space, to establish a protective boundary when tied around a yurt or another space or object. It also can be used as a lasso to bind bad spirits.

13. Shere'e-altar

A Bɵ altar is in fact a kind of small cabinet used to put ritual objects in and on.

14. Ongon images

These figures or images are made of various materials and represent *Ongon*-spirits. They may also be masks of particularly powerful *Ongon*-spirits which are worn by Bɵ and Utgan when they go into the *ongo* trance state.

15. Hahyuusan amulets

These are protective, lucky talismans which the Bɵ and Utgan make for others.

16. Bɵ-hete flint stone

This flint stone symbolizes control over the element of fire. It is used to light the sacrificial fire and in modern times it is also used to light a pipe.

17. Shanginuur-bell

Nowadays Bɵ use *drilbu,* an upright Buddhist bell, a recent item which was adopted by Bɵ Murgel in the late seventeenth century. Some of the Utgan I know use *shang,*[50] a flat Bönpo bell. It is not entirely clear what type of bell was used in the past.

---

[50] Tib. gshang.

18. San hengereg-cymbals

These are two small brass cymbals also of Bönpo or Buddhist origin.

19. Prayer beads

Prayer beads, too, may be a late addition coming from Buddhism although they may well be more ancient, dating back to the times when early Bө Murgel traditions came into contact with Bön. Bө prayer beads have 108 large beads made of black wood. The Bө mainly use them for divination.

20. Tobacco pouch and pipe

These were also obviously added in recent times. They are given as an offering or smoked in some rituals to offer the smoke to those local *Ezhen* who like it.

CHAPTER IX

Cult of the Sky

Spiritual essence of the Sky

While both Yungdrung Bön and Bө Murgel have comparable cults surrounding their sky-gods, the spiritual meaning with which the sky itself is imbued is not the same. In the higher vehicles of Yungdrung Bön, the sky is one of the symbols for the Natural State of Mind,[1] the enlightened non-dual nature of all sentient beings, base of all manifestations, good and bad, inner and outer, intimately present from the beginningless beginning in each and every being endowed with a mind. This Natural State is both the peak and the base of all the Nine Ways of Yungdrung Bön and can be realized through following the Swastika Bön teachings of Tonpa Shenrab Miwo, especially those of Dzogchen, the teachings on Great Perfection. Here the sky is only a symbol, not the state itself.

In Bө Murgel, on the other hand, Eternal Blue Sky is perceived in a dualistic way as the eternal, live, generating spiritual principle, the Source of All to which one must pray and by whose laws one must abide in order to achieve spiritual and worldly goals. One can never realize the state of Eternal Blue Sky oneself. The Sky is always an external generator and receptacle while beings are always its product and content. Similar views were probably held by many traditions of the Prehistoric Bön of Eurasia and this view is fundamentally different from the symbolism of the sky in Yungdrung Bön.

Mu-cord, Mu-ladder and the rainbow-bridge

Rainbows are an auspicious sign and symbol in many belief systems, and Yungdrung Bön and Bө Murgel are no exception. In the Yungdrung Bön tradition a rainbow rope and a rainbow ladder form a link between the heavens and the earth. These two specific items, *muthag* and *muke*, Cord of *Mu* and Ladder of *Mu*, are made of a five-coloured rainbow

---

[1] Tib. sems nyid.

of the five elements and take their name from *Mu*, a class of ancient sky-gods. They are particularly associated with the royal dynasties of celestial origin. It was by means of these two celestial rainbow attributes that Mugyal Chugpo, the founder of the *Mushen* royal clan of Olmo Lungring into which the Buddha of Yungdrung Bön Shenrab Miwoche was born, descended from the dimension of the *Mu* sky-gods. The early kings of Tibet, known as the Seven *Tri* of the Sky, were also endowed with the *Mu*-cord and *Mu*-ladder. It is said that the *muthag* was attached to the top of the kings' head and at the end of their lives they used it to ascend to the sky realm of the *Mu* thus no mortal remains were left on earth. At the time of death their bodies dissolved into rainbow light from the feet up to the head, to the *muthag*, which then rolled up to the sky transporting the king to the pure abode of the *Lha*. As we saw in Chapter I, this direct connection to the sky realm of *Mu* ended with the eighth King of Tibet, Drigum Tsenpo, in the sixth century BC when he foolishly severed his own *muthag* cord.

However, the *muthag* rainbow cord is not reserved for royalty alone. In Tibetan Bönpo culture it is not only associated with the early kings but is a general attribute symbolizing, among other things, humanity's connection with the sky-gods from whom we are descended.

In Buryatian Bɵ Murgel we find something similar to *muthag*. One of the ways the Bɵ journey into the dimension of the Sky is by means of a rainbow,[2] a kind of 'rainbow bridge' by which a Bɵ or Utgan travels upwards either in trance or while dreaming. In the past some powerful Bɵ and Utgan also had the capacity to fly in their physical body, a feat which was observed by all who happened to be around.[3]

The rainbow *Mu*-ladder by which the first king of Tibet, Nyatri Tsenpo, came down from the dimension of the *Mu* gods also finds its counterpart in Buryatian Bɵ Murgel culture. The legends of some Buryatian clans tell of how they arrived to the area of Lake Baikal by means of a rainbow ladder:

> [They] descended by means of a rainbow-ladder connecting the outer and inner worlds to the water, deep as the sky, vast as the sky, venerated as the Sky.[4]

---

2 Bur. нолонго.

3 See the excerpt of my diary in ch. XIV.

4 'An Interview with Shaman Valentin Hagdaev', *Ot Dushi/От Души* [web magazine] <http://dusha.spb.ru/Newspaper/newspaper5.htm> accessed 20.01.05.

This directly mirrors the way the founders of Bönpo royal clans descended to earth. This analogous motif in Tibetan and Buryatian myths provides us with a valuable clue about the common origin, culture and religion of these two nations and demonstrates yet again that they most probably met in the remote past and have developed from a common set of cultural and spiritual values and practices.

Sacred bodies of water as the mirrors of the Sky

Another very important parallel apparent from the quotation above is the qualities attributed to Baikal's waters: *'deep as the sky, vast as the sky'*. That immediately reminds us of Namtsho (Tengri), the Sky Lake in Changthang, the heartland of Zhang Zhung in northwest Tibet, which we discussed in Chapter I. According to local Changthang tradition recorded by John Bellezza this lake, which perfectly takes on the colour of the sky above, is said to be the counterpart of the Nam[5] (Tibetan equivalent of Huhe Münhe Tengeri). This is expressed in its epithet 'the Mirror of the Sky.[6]

Fig. 1. Lake Namtsho Chyugmo and Nyenchen Thanglha mountain range.

---

5 Tib. gnam.

6 Bellezza, *Divine Dyads*, p. 96. Tib. gnam gyi me long.

It is obvious then that both the inhabitants of Changthang and the ancient Buryats shared the same perception and attitude towards sacred bodies of water which they saw as reflections of the Sky on earth. The Buryatian myth of origin which narrates how Burte Chino, the ancient forefather of the Mongol-Buryats, sprinkled the milk of one hundred white mares into Baikal while praying to Eternal Blue Sky, worshipping Baikal as his reflection on earth, is another clear reference to this perception.

There is an interesting clue which suggests this understanding may have been quite widespread among many nations of the Great Steppe and the Qinghai-Tibetan Plateau. In the Hungarian language, '*tenger*' means 'ocean', 'sea', 'deep' while '*tengeri*' stands for 'maritime'. Now, the Hungarian people have a Hunnu thread in their genetic pool, language and culture and, as the reader will recall from Chapter I, the Hunnu formed as a nation in the regions of southern Siberia and northern Mongolia which includes the Baikal region. They had prolonged contact with Zhang Zhung and Tibetan tribes over many centuries if not millennia. When their vast empire eventually collapsed, a group of Hunnu survivors went west of the Urals and then moved to the southern shores and delta of the Volga River in eastern Europe around 155 AD where, in the course of time, they mixed with Finno-Ugric tribes and other peoples. The result of this ethnogenesis was the formation of the new nation of Huns as they were known to Europeans in the early centuries AD. After European Huns ceased to exist in the fifth century AD, mixed tribes still remained. One of these was called Hunugur[7] and later became a part of the Hungarian nation. Here we can see the genetic, cultural and linguistic thread brought by the Hunnu from Baikal to Europe. In the long process of time the primary meaning of '*tenger*' and '*tengeri*' – 'sky', 'sky-dweller' – was forgotten but the secondary meaning related to the reflection of the sky in water remained in the language. This provides us with an indirect clue implying that the cult of Eternal Blue Sky and the link between heavenly and earthly waters was a common religious perception spread over the vast territory of Eurasia.

Another strand in the sky-water connection is the proto-Indo-Iranian god *Varuna and Huhe Münhe Tengeri spoken of before. Varuna is the all-encompassing sky, lord of heavenly and earthly waters, and from this we can assume that for the proto-Indo-Iranians, earthly waters were seen as reflections of divine, celestial ones. In other words, proto-Indo-Iranians also perceived sky and water as being inextricably intertwined and recognized that regulating earthly water is a function of the sky. In a

---

7 See Gumilev, *Istoriya Hunnu,* 2, p. 345.

similar way, for the followers of Bɵ Murgel, Eternal Blue Sky commands everything, and in particular, Hormusta, who can be counted as an emanation of Huhe Münhe Tengeri, is master of earthly waters.

The cult of the Drala sky-gods before and in the time of Shenrab Miwo

The lineage of the royal clan of Olmo Lungring, into which Shenrab Miwo was born, traced its origins to the *Mu* sky-gods, a connection clearly shown in Tonpa Shenrab's original name in the language of Olmo Lungring: Mura Tahen, the Great Man of the *Mu*. Mura Tahen didn't renounce his family lineage or the religious and cultural traditions pertaining to it but transformed them in the light of his Yungdrung Bön doctrine and used them for the benefit of beings. The Weapons of the *Drala* are a pertinent example. In the fifth chapter of *Zijyid*, *The Scripture of the Young Prince's Playful Sports*[8] we find a brief text, *Drala Gosang*,[9] *The Sang for the Weapons of the Drala*, which clearly illustrates an ancient tradition of invoking the *Drala* sky-gods used in this incidence by the young Shenrab Miwo to protect his friends from a magic assault. The text also narrates the lineage of the seven male ancestors preceding Shenrab Miwo who travelled to different dimensions of the universe to receive magical weapons and protective armour from *Yeje*, *Yewang Kö*, *Yesid Cha*, *Yekhyen Drala*,[10] *Werma*, *Changseng*, *Thugkar* and *Shungön* – the *Drala* deities of upper space. The text reiterates that the ancient spiritual tradition of Olmo Lungring which preceded Shenrab Miwo was connected with various benign deities of the sky as the founder of the royal dynasty, Mugyal Chugpo, descended from the dimension of the *Mu* sky-gods. The cult of *Drala*, which includes propitiation rites for various celestial deities, is generally known in Tibet as *Lha Bön*, the Bön of sky-gods. These sorts of practices and rituals were reshaped by Tonpa Shenrab in the light of his doctrine and are found in *Nangshen Thegpa*,

---

[8] Tib. gzi brjid is the extended biography of Shenrab Miwo. The text in question is found in the fifth chapter *rGyal bu gzhon nu rol brtsed kyi mdo*. Here I follow oral explanations given by Geshe Gelek Jinpa on 20.11.07 in Shenten Dargye Ling, France. He read from Kun grol Lha sras edition of *bKa' 'jyur* published in China, 1999. The text appears in Vol. XV kha: 53–57 and was summarized in English by Adriano Clemente in the booklet *The Sgra Bla, Gods of the Ancestors of Gshen-rab Mi-bo*, (Merigar, Arcidosso: Shang Shung Edizioni, 1995).

[9] Tib. sGra bla go bsang.

[10] Tib. ye rje, ye dbang skos, ye srid phywa, ye mkhyen sgra bla.

The Way of the Shen of the Visual World, the second Way of Cause of the Nine Ways of Bön.[11]

The story narrated in *The Scripture of the Young Prince's Playful Sports* shows how the Yungdrung Bön version of the rite propitiating the *Drala* arose and also tells us that the rite itself is much older, as it was practised by Tonpa Shenrab's ancestors for generations. Here is a summary of the story:

> One day the young prince Shenrab Miwo was enjoying a picnic with his playmates in one of Nagtsal Netogling[12] near the royal palace of Barpo Sogyed when the group came under an assault of black magic. Suddenly, horrible and terrifying sounds shattered the serenity, a tornado of black winds swirled upon them spewing stones, and a flaming magic missile (*dzöwal*[13]) fell from the sky amidst lightning and hail. A black light appeared in the sky and a terrifying black man with three staring eyes, a topknot and wrathful demeanour riding a horned black wind dragon with flaming wings colour of burnt conch emerged from it. He hurled nine bolts of black lightening metal charged with the Nine Impurities at the young prince but Shenrab Miwo showed *digdzub*[14] *mudra* and so the impurities fell down as *düdtsi*[15] blessing liquid which transformed into the Nine Weapons and Armour of *Drala*:[16]

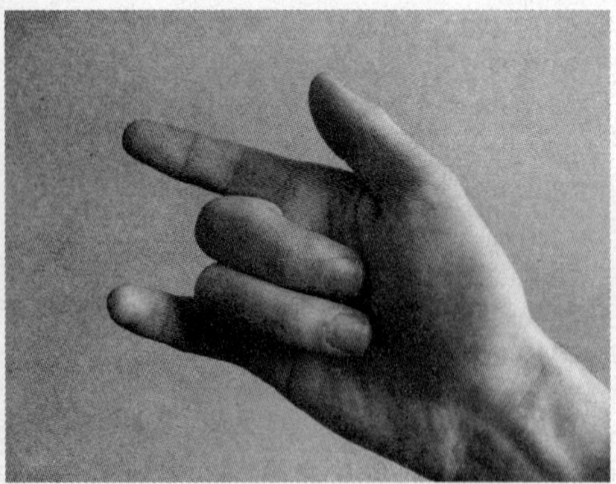

Fig. 2. Digdzub mudra.

1. The black hat of widowhood became the helmet of *Drala*;
2. The black gown of impurity became the body armour of *Drala*;

---

[11] See Snellgrove, *Nine Ways*, pp. 41–97 and Namdak, *Nine Ways I*, p. 49.

[12] Tib. Nags tsal ne tog gling.

[13] Tib. dzwo dbal.

[14] Tib. sdig mdzub.

[15] Tib bdud rtsi.

[16] Tib. sGra bla'i go mtshon sna dgu.

3. Thc murderous sword became the sword of *Drala*;
4. The horn of filth became the white bow of *Drala*;
5. The arrow of pollution became the arrow of *Drala*;
6. The spear of illegitimate birth became the spear of *Drala*;
7. The lake of incest became the shield of *Drala*;
8. The rope of misfortune became the lasso of *Drala*;
9. The axe of bad omens became the hook of *Drala*.

Then Tonpa Shenrab placed the weapons on the altar, and, performing the *Sang*[17] ritual fumigation, purified them. Proclaiming himself to be a Bönpo lineage-holder[18] of his royal clan, the prince sang the invocation to the six types[19] of *Drala* protector-gods of his male ancestral lineage.[20] He reminded the gods of the accords they had made with his ancestors, invited them to come to the offerings,[21] honour their pledges and manifest their activities. Then Shenrab Miwo performed a consecration rite for the nine weapons and armour by invoking the *Drala* to descend and charge the weapons and armour with their magic powers, to help and protect those who propitiate them. With the *Drala* armies actually manifest in front of him, the young prince narrated the deeds of the illustrious ancestors of his lineage, declaring his ownership of the weapons and armour as he himself was a member of this lineage. He states that these nine weapons and armour act as the supports[22] for the sixth group of *Drala* in particular, the Nine *Drama* Brothers:[23]

1. Drama Chagkyi Gyaruchen who wears the iron *gyaru* horn crown helmet;
2. Drama Lethrom Yangshamchen who dons blue armour;
3. Drama Walgyi Ngarsochen who carries the sharp, flaming sword;

---

[17] Tib bsang. A detailed analysis of purification rituals follows in ch. XI.

[18] Tib. srid pa rgyud kyi bon po – Bönpo of the lineage of existence.

[19] Most of these *Drala* were already discussed in ch.V, section *Drala and Tengeri, Mysitcal Eagles in Bön and BW Murgel.* For the full list see Clemente, *The Sgra Bla*, pp. 10–14.

[20] Tib. pha mes kyi rgyud gsas.

[21] The content of the offerings in this sort of rite will be discussed in detail in ch. XII.

[22] Tib rten.

[23] Tib. Dra ma mChed dgu.

4. Drama Zhunkar Tsatsachen who holds the bow which shoots by itself;
5. Drama Walgyi Daphüchen who possesses the arrow which hits the mark by itself;
6. Drama Meyi Wadangchen who holds the spear which strikes by itself;
7. Drama Lunggi Sholshamchen who has the shield which rotates by itself;
8. Drama Loggi Myuryogchen who carries the lasso which catches by itself;
9. Drama Trulgyi Shazungchen who has the hook which hooks by itself. [24]

The Nine Drama Brothers, the leaders of the nine hundred and ninety thousand troupes of horse-riding *Drala* warrior-gods of the sky, are reminded by Shenrab Miwo that they have been charged with the duty of protection and represent the power of his clan. He states that though young he is the new holder of the noble lineage of *Mu* and so these weapons and armour of *Drala* should act as the support of the prosperity[25] of his clan today just as they did in the past. Then he dons the armour, takes up the weapons and plays eighty-one martial art games with the *Drala* in the place called Düdtsi Awainethang.[26]

We can see, then, that Tonpa Shenrab obtains the weapons and armour of the *Drala* by transforming the weapons charged with the Nine Impurities hurled at him by the *Düd*. This is very different from the way in which the Nine Weapons and Armour of the *Drala* were received by his predecessors, as it is clear from the prince's discourse in *The Scripture of the Young Prince's Playful Sports* that his ancestors received them directly from the sky-gods. While keeping true to the external form of the tradition of his clan, he nevertheless takes it to a higher level. If we look closely into the circumstances described in the story it is clear from the context that, although Shenrab Miwo was

---

24 Tib. Dra ma lCags kyi Bya ru can; Dra ma Le phroms Yang gsham can; Dra ma dBal gyi Ngar so can; Dra ma Zhun dkar Tsha tsha can; Dra ma dBal gyi mDa' phud can; Dra ma Me yi Bad a can; Dra ma rLung gi Shol gsham can; Dra ma gLog gi Myur mgyogs can; Dra ma 'Phrul gyi Sha zung can.

25 Tib. g.yang rten.

26 Tib. bDud rtsi A ba'i ne thang. Here I follow oral explanations given by Geshe Gelek Jinpa on 20.11.07 in Shenten Dargye Ling, France.

attacked by an awesome *Düd*, he could not in fact be harmed as there is no magic which can harm a Buddha. Here we have a paradox: if he cannot be harmed by black magic and has the power to transform its negatively-charged agents into positive weapons and armour, why then does Shenrab Miwo bother to continue with his ancestors' ritual and go on to invoke the gods, perform the traditional ritual stages and then play martial art games with the *Drala*? There are, I believe, two reasons. Firstly, by making the charge to the *Drala*: '*just as in the past when you were honoured and propitiated in order to gain your protection, so in the same way now you should help and protect those who proffer offerings to you*,' it is clear that Shenrab Miwo makes a pact with the *Drala* for the benefit of future followers of his Yungdrung Bön tradition, particularly for the *Shenpos* of the *Nangshen Thegpa* vehicle who directly engage in practices related to the *Drala* sky-gods. The ritual tradition of his clan is thus transformed and made available to all qualified students of Yungdrung Bön rather than being reserved for his own royal family. Secondly, this story shows the cultural and religious background of the time, the concepts and ideas of Prehistoric Bön which Shenrab Miwo skilfully used to deliver his Yungdrung Bön doctrines. The symbolic value of this story is great because it lucidly demonstrates the way in which selected traditions of Prehistoric Bön were transformed by the Central Asian Buddha and included in the four vehicles of the Causal Bön within his tradition. When possible, he left the external forms intact and imbued them with revolutionary new meaning thus facilitating easier transition and understanding.

Nine Weapons and Armour of the Drala and the Bɵ's ritual apparel

The story and the ritual actions connected with the *Drala* sky-gods narrated in *The Scripture of the Young Prince's Playful Sports* find striking parallels in Buryatian Bɵ Murgel both in terms of concept and actual ritual implements. The way young Shenrab Miwo deals with the *Düd* sky-demon's magical onslaught is very similar to the way a White Bɵ would proceed were he to repel an attack of black magic. If we substitute White Tengeri for the *Drala*, especially the Nine *Drama* Brothers, and a Black Tengeri for the *Düd* demon, we have a classic situation when a White Bɵ, engaged by a Black Tengeri as a result of the evil invocations of a Black Bɵ of the second type or an *elbeshen* black sorcerer, invokes his White Tengeri to assist him in magical combat. Moreover, the Nine Weapons and Armour of *Drala* requested by Shenrab Miwo are very much comparable with – indeed, almost identical to – the ritual dress and objects used by the Bɵ:

1. The *gyaru* horned crown helmet directly corresponds to the *maihabshi*-horned crown of Bɵ. The *gyaru* was also worn by the Ligmincha kings of Zhang Zhung and their Kushen Bönpo priests as well as other important Bönpo Masters. Although the *gyaru* has *khyung* horns while the Bɵ crown has deer antlers, both the Heavenly Deer and *khyung*-bird represent the dimension of the Sky. There is, however, an even closer match in a crown worn by practitioners of the Bön of the Deer;[27]

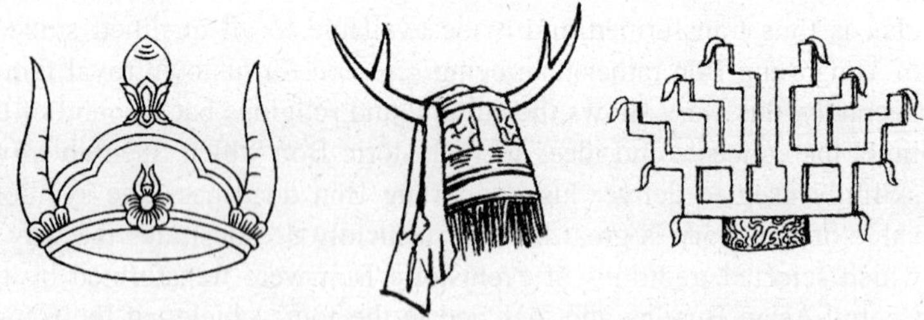

Fig. 3. Horned crowns: gyaru, maihabshi *and deer-crown of the practitioners of the Bön of the Deer.*

2. The protective armour is comparable with the *amitai*, *orgoi*, and, especially, the ritual *hooyag*-coat of mail of the Bɵ;[28]
3. The sword is comparable with the sword of the Bɵ;
4. The bow is comparable with the bow of the Bɵ;
5. The arrow is comparable with the arrow of the Bɵ;
6. The shield can be compared with the *toli*-mirror and *hese*-drum of the Bɵ;
7. The lasso can be compared with *zeli*-rope of the Bɵ;

---

27 See ch. X.

28 At the end of the text *Ge khod lo phrom e'i dmar tshan* on Red *Tsen* devoted to Gekhöd we find the following appellation to the deity:
'May he strengthen my spirit.
May he dress me in a solid coat of mail.
May he provide me with sharp weapons!'
See Karmay, *The Arrow and the Spindle,* p. 400.

8. The hook can be compared with *hor 'bo*, especially, *holbogoto hor 'bo*[29] of the Bɵ; both are symbols of power as well as tools for hooking;
9. The spear can be compared with the *zhada*-spear of the Bɵ. Spears with pennants are also used as a support in rituals for the mountain deities in Bɵ Murgel. This kind of spear is called *tug* in Buryatian and Tibetan alike and has exactly the same function.

Young Tonpa Shenrab uses the Nine Weapons of *Drala* as a support for his invocation and as a receptacle for the *Drala's* powers which enter and remain in them. As we have seen, the same principle applies to the Bɵ's ritual apparel; *Ongon*-spirits actually reside on a Bɵ's ritual dress, in his *hese*, *hor 'bo* and other ritual objects. Both Bönpo and Bɵ Murgel ritual costume and implements have to be quickened by invoking the gods and spirits and transferring their spiritual power, although the methods used for this differ fundamentally: while in Bɵ Murgel blood sacrifice is often used to animate the *amitai*, Tonpa Shenrab offers substitutes instead.

A further parallel lies in their celestial origin. These ritual supports were given to the ancestors of Shenrab Miwo and to the White Bɵ by benign sky-gods and either transmitted within the lineage or faithfully remade according to the original archetype. Some of the ritual implements of Bɵ such as *toli*, flint stones or a special kind of scriptures which bring healing are still being given or 'lowered from the Sky' by the Tengeri to selected Bɵ and Utgan even in modern times. One such text was given to an Utgan who performed miraculous cures in Buryatia simply by touching her patients' head with the celestial text. We know of this because as she became widely known in Buryatia, the Communists inevitably learnt of her activities and even summoned her to Moscow to heal Leonid Brezhnev, the then head of the Communist Party.

The fifth Weapon of the *Drala* is an arrow, and as we have seen, the Buryatian Bɵ are also equipped with arrows which they shoot to 'make a way' before going on a journey or hunt, to open the way for *hulde*-prosperity to enter a dwelling, or to prevent *hulde* from leaving the household or village when a deceased Bɵ is taken to the burial site.[30] A similar incident is found in Tonpa Shenrab's biography. When pursuing

29 Bur. хольбогото хорьбо.
30 Hangalov, *Sobranie,* I, pp. 385–392.

the demon Khyabpa Langrig of Kongpo,[31] the Buddha of Yungdrung Bön shot an arrow through the impenetrable mountain range surrounding Olmo Lungring creating the 'arrow way' tunnel to Zhang Zhung. This again underlines the similarities between a Bө's implements and the weapons of *Drala* stemming from a larger, common cultural concept.

There is another passage in the *Sang for the Weapons of the Drala* which resonates with Bө Murgel. The passage in question describes how the smoke of the *Sang* purification offering transforms into the rainbow clouds in the sky from which the armies of *Drala* appear before Shenrab Miwo.[32] I observed a strikingly similar phenomenon in the Barguzin area of Buryatia where I was travelling with a group of Bө and Utgan in the summer of 1994. The event in question happened at the *tailgan* performed near the village of Shamanka[33] which is linked to Sode Lama[34] who practised both Bө Murgel and Buddhism. Here is a passage from my diary:

> Then at last the ram was laid out on the altar along with offerings and butter lamps made from half potatoes. The ritual began. After a little while, a cloud in the shape of a dragon appeared in the sky. It moved to the spot where we had sprinkled and dissolved into the blue sky directly above us. After the ram was eaten, its bones and skin were placed on the fire, followed by the shirt and shawl.[35] I was sitting a little to one side of the fire, next to Vera Naguslaeva. She suddenly exclaimed, 'Look! Look! The shirt has flown up!' And indeed, you could clearly see how the smoke rose up from the fire in the shape of the shirt, and without changing form it rose right up into the sky. Simultaneously, a cloud in the same form appeared out of empty space and then quickly dissolved. Then something very unusual began to happen. From an absolutely clear sky, clouds of all possible shapes and sizes began appearing just above us, circular rainbows manifested and some drops of rain fell. The clouds were appearing and disappearing very quickly in the blue sky. Everyone was overwhelmed by a sense of great happiness. People were crying, looking into the sky in ecstasy and praying, raising their arms. No-one had seen anything like it before […] This phenomenon carried

[31] Tib. Kong po.

[32] Clemente, *The Sgra Bla,* p.15.

[33] Rus. Шаманка is Russian for a female shaman.

[34] Bur. Соодой Лама (Rus.Цыден Содоев). Sode Lama (1846–1916) was a remarkable figure in the Barguzin area. He combined the practices of both Buddhism and Bө Murgel in an apparently harmonious way and at the end of his life his body shrank. See ch. XIV.

[35] For the analysis of this custom see ch. XII.

on for quite a while, maybe an hour, and people soon calmed down and began to watch more peacefully. Everyone agreed that it was a miracle and that it was extraordinary good luck to be present and witness it.
[…]
Finally we decided to leave, and at that moment the clouds stopped appearing, but a long milk-white cloud spread eastwards from the site of the ritual, as if someone had poured milk into water. The Bө and Utgan said it was the offerings of milk and vodka which had transformed and taken that shape to show once again that the ritual had been accepted and that the *tailgan* should be performed every year at that sacred spot.[36]

Shamanka, Barguzin,14.06.94.

Fig. 4. Tailgan at Shamanka.

Despite the fact that the ritual described in the *Sang for the Weapons of the Drala* was performed by Shenrab Miwo many thousands of years before the *tailgan* I observed, the former, paradoxically, is a transformation of the latter; the *tailgan* is evidently based on an archaic version practised within the streams of Prehistoric Bön before the appearance of Shenrab Miwo on earth and has survived until now within the Buryatian Bө Murgel tradition. Despite the similarities between both rites we must note the difference in the contents of offerings – blood sacrifice does not form a part of any offerings of Yungdrung Bön of Shenrab Miwo while

[36] From my unpublished diary, *Tailgan Trip.*

in Bɵ Murgel it finds its place within the complete range of offerings while performing *tailgans* with the function of appeasing certain Tengeri and local gods.

Conclusion

Having examined the Cults of the Sky in Bɵ Murgel and Bön from several points of view, we can conclude that they must have their roots in the Prehistoric Bön of Eurasia. In particular, it would seem that some lineages of Buryatian White Bɵ and Tibetan Bönpo of the Lha Bön have a common source. This clearly demonstrates that Buryatian Bɵ Murgel is indeed a very ancient tradition and was not newly created in the times of Chingis Khaan in the thirteenth century as some scholars suggest. Therefore, cross-examining living traditions of Buryatian Bɵ Murgel and different kinds of Bön traditions of Tibet, some alive and some extinct, can yield a better understanding of the aspects of both cultures which are not, as yet, well understood.

CHAPTER X

Heavenly Deer

Tracing the ancient Deer Cult in the Prehistoric Bön of Eurasia

Traces of the cult of the Heavenly Deer are clearly noticeable throughout Eurasia, especially in Siberia, Central Asia, Tibet, Russia, Lapland, Karelia and Britain, and the Mystical Deer is also one of the spirit-guides of North and Central America medicine men.[1] Archaeologists have uncovered many carvings and ornaments depicting Deer or various aspects of its worship throughout these regions, and a Horn Dance is performed even today in rural Oxfordshire in England, although its real meaning has been lost.[2] The ancient Scythians and Hunnu revered the Deer very much; many small Deer sculptures have been found in the their *kurgans*[3] throughout Southern Siberia, and one of the most famous is currently on display in the Golden Warehouse of the Hermitage State Museum in St. Petersburg. It is made of gold and is a truly beautiful piece of art.

---

1 I am not sufficiently well-versed in Native American traditions to comment on possible relationships here, but I am sure many could be found.

2 The Horn Dance is performed by twelve Deermen at Abbots Bromley on the first Monday after the Sunday nearest to 4th September. This is undoubtedly a very ancient tradition which goes down in time for thousands of years. The deer antlers used for the dance are those of reindeer, unknown in the wild in the British Isles since the times of the Norman Conquest. Nowadays the antlers are stored on the top floor of the local church and one pair has been carbon dated as 900 years old. I passed through this village in 1996 while on a fundraising walk from London to Scotland in aid of Tibetan children's charities.

3 There are a great many *kurgan* burial mounds in southern Siberia, some of them so large that they can house up to 10 lorries. I visited one of these huge ones while on an archaeological expedition in Khakassia's Askiz (Rus. Аскиз) region in the summer of 1987.

Fig. 1. Sacred Deer Scythian golden shield emblem from the State Hermitage Museum, St. Petersburg.

It is, however, not merely art. Images of the Deer were sacred to the Scythians and Hunnu and were used in religious ceremonies. Archaeologists have discovered over six hundred sites with Deer Stones spread all over the Eurasian Steppe, with the highest concentrations found in Mongolia, Southern Siberia, modern-day Xinjiang and Amdo. The culture responsible for them is known as the Deer Stones Culture and has been dated second to first millennium BC. Peoples of this culture erected memorial stelas with many carvings, including images of the Heavenly Deer, warriors tattooed with images of the Deer, weapons, clothing and various tools. Most of the standing stones are oriented in the four cardinal directions and have three horizontal sections. The upper part symbolizes the dimension of the Sky and is carved with circles, and sometimes faces, representing the Sun, Moon and the Sky-dwelling gods. The central band stands for the Intermediate Space between the Sky and the Earth and is carved with images of Sacred Deer flying towards the Sky, their heads bent backwards so that their highly stylized antlers touch their backs. Deer images are oriented eastwards and upwards, clearly showing that they are flying towards the dimension of the Sky. Indeed, there are many clues which suggest that the Deer was associated with the Sun in prehistoric times.[4] Here, however, the Deer is clearly able to fly between the Middle and the Upper Worlds acting as a messenger between man and gods. The lower band of the Deer Stones represents the Earth and is engraved with images of weapons, tools and, sometimes, human figures.[5]

---

4 For Deer within the context of the Sun Cult see below.

5 My interpretation. Archaeologists often interpret the three levels of the Deer Stones as representing the Three Worlds with the upper band representing the Upper World, the middle band representing the Middle World and the lower band representing the Underworld of the dead.

Fig. 2. Scythian warrior riding a horse decorated with imitation deer horns. An Indo-Scythian stone palette from Sirkap, New Delhi Museum.

Fig. 3. Bronze Deer broach dated around 6 AD. Yenhor village, Dzhidinskiy district, Buryatian Republic. Found by Dorjo Doogarov on top of a kurgan *in July 1998.*

The Pazyryk[6] culture of the Altai also venerated the Deer, as can be seen by the Deer Stones in that region. Peoples of this nomadic culture were Indo-Iranian Scythians or Yuezhi tribes and one of their traditions was to attach imitation metal antlers to their horses' heads to make them look like deer, a custom which they brought with them as far as Afghanistan and India when they established the Indo-Scythian kingdom there in 80 BC–20 AD.

One of the best known examples of Deer Stones in Buryatia is the Ivolginskiy Deer Stone. Originally located 23km southwest of Ulaan-Ude, it is now in a museum in Irkutsk. It is made out of pink Transbaikalian granite measuring 3.5m in length with 2.9 meters above ground, 90cm in width and 20cm thick.[7] Another famous Deer Stone, called Altan-Serge,[8] is on the territory of the Gusino'ozerskiy Datsan having been moved from a nearby burial site when the *datsan* was constructed. Although badly damaged at the time of the religious repressions of the Stalinist era, it was restored during the religious liberalization of perestroika. Archaeologists date this stone at around 2,500 BC. What is more, other archaeological finds demonstrate the presence of the Deer Cult in Buryatia well into the first millennium AD; numerous broaches in the form of the Heavenly

6 Rus. Пазырык.

7 See Okladnikov, *Istoriya*, pp. 343–360.

8 Bur. Алтан-сэргэ.

Deer belonging to this period have been unearthed in burial mounds. These broaches are in keeping with the style and imagery as found on Deer Stones all over the Great Steppe.

White Deer

Among the cults of the Deer, the White Deer takes a special place. In Chinese myths[9] it appears as a messenger of the Heavenly Emperor and we find echoes of this cult in the native Shinto religion of Japan. There, the Sun Goddess Amaterasu Omikami (天照大神) which in some instances appears as a White Deer carrying the solar disc which rests on the crown of the tree fixed to the saddle on her back.[10] Fortune-telling paper slips – *omikuji* (御神籤) – are attached to the branches of the tree. Echoes of this image are found in Siberian mythology, for example, among the Tungus-Evenki, where the Lord of the Upper World is a solar deity in the form of a doe or female moose.[11] The *omikuji* paper slips tied to the tree (which most probably symbolizes the World Tree) also find their counterpart in Siberia and in the Baikal region in particular where Buryats tie coloured ribbons called *zalaa*[12] to trees and bushes around holy power places such as healing springs, rocks and woods as well as in the vicinity of other sacred objects such as a shrine to a powerful lama or local deity.[13]

Fig. 4. Visitors knotting omikuji *paper slips to shrub branches in Kasuga-taisha Shrine, Nara, Japan.*

We can surmise, then, that this tradition and the ancient religion which later became part of Shinto was brought to the Japanese

---

[9] Yuan' Ke: *Mify Drevnego Kitaya* [*Myths of Ancient China*]Tr. from Chinese by E. I. Lubo-Lesnichennko, E. V. Puzitskogo & V. F. Sorokina (Moskva: Nauka, 1987), p. 241.

[10] This form of Amaterasu was depicted by Kano Eino Genroku in 1691. Bhikku Satori Bhante, *Shintoismo* (Milano: Rizzoli Editore, 1982), pp. 11; 54–55.

[11] Boris Rybakov, *Yazychestvo drevnikh slavyan* (Moskva: Sofiya, Gelios), pp 58–59.

[12] Bur. Залаа.

[13] See ch. XIII.

islands from Siberia by the Ainu people who lived along the Amur River, in Kamchatka, the Kuril Islands (and some of whom still live on Sakhalin Island) in the prehistoric Jomon period (14,000–400 BC). The Ainu language is related to some extent to that of the Nivkh[14] who live around the estuary of the River Amur and Sakhalin Island. Genetic studies demonstrate that the Ainu are closely related to Siberian Nivkh and Koryak nations of northeast Siberia.[15] Interestingly, on the paternal side 87.5% of Ainu belong to Y-haplogroup D which is found mainly in Japan, Sumatra and is particularly prevalent in Tibet[16] where, as we will see below, the Bön of the Deer formed a significant part of Prehistoric Bön traditions.

Fig. 5. Ainu people at the beginning of the last century.

Furthermore, in Shinto there is a method of divination using a deer's shoulder blade, and in *semmë* – the edicts of the Japanese Emperors – the appearance of a white deer is greeted as an auspicious omen.[17] The

---

[14] 'Paleo-Siberian languages', Encyclopædia Britannica(2007) <http://www.britannica.com/eb/article-9109797> accessed 03.11.07.

[15] Tajima Atsushi; Hayami Masanori; Tokunaga Katsushi; Juji Takeo; Matsuo Masafumi; Marzuki Sangkot; Omoto Keiichi; Horai Satoshi; 'Genetic origins of the Ainu inferred from combined DNA analyses of maternal and paternal lineages', *Journal of human genetics*, 2004, vol. 49, n°4, pp. 187–193.

[16] <http://www.scs.uiuc.edu/~mcdonald/WorldHaplogroupsMaps.pdf> accessed 03.10.07.

[17] *Norito Semmyo*, tr, research & commentary by L. M. Ermakova (Moskva: Nauka, 1991), p.39.

Decree on granting drinks and gifts at the festival of Niiname deals with bestowing drinks and gifts on the harvest festival Niiname in recognition of the coincidental appearance of auspicious signs such as rainfall on the solstice day and:

> […] from the land of Iё there was brought to Us a deer with the white signs [on the body] and so We thought that it is for joy and happiness. We decided then that it is a special co-incidence when the three benefits appear simultaneously and took it with respect and submission. And so We wish to share the joy of the celebration of these surprising, wonderful and glorious white omens with all our subjects […][18]

This edict was written in the first part of the eighth century AD and, as the quotation shows, the appearance of a deer with white signs on it was clearly considered very auspicious. Deer, especially white deer, are sacred animals in Shintoism because of their association with some *Kami* (神).[19] The Deer God, Amenokaku-no-Kami (天迦久神), was sent as a messenger from the sun goddess Amaterasu to Takemikatsuchi-no-Okami (武甕槌大神), the highly venerated God of Thunder, Peace and Military Bravery and later protector of the influential Fujiwara clan (藤原氏). The two main shrines dedicated to Takemikatsuchi-no-Okami are: Kashima-jingu Shrine (鹿島神宮) in Kashima-city established in the seventh century BC; and Kasuga-taisha Shrine (春日大社) in Nara established in 768 AD to which the god is said to have arrived riding a sacred white deer and surrounded by many other deer carrying a great number of spirits. That is why both shrines have herds of deer living on their sacred grounds.[20]

Fig. 6. Deer among the stone lanterns with a relief of the sacred deer, Kasuga-taisha Shrine in Nara.

---

[18] Ibid. pp. 182–183, Semmё № 46; translation. mine.

[19] A wide term designating beings of the spiritual dimension. It is applied to both gods and spirits.

[20] Ermakova, *Semmyo,* p.16; and online photo gallery <http://p-www.iwate-pu.ac.

All this, no doubt, points to the existence of a Deer Cult in Japan since prehistory, probably originally brought from Siberia by the Ainu. This theory is clearly supported by the fact that white and spotted reindeer are venerated among many Siberian nations.

For the Tungus-Evenki of Siberia, for example, some of whom still live in the Baikal area, white and spotted reindeer are revered animals capable of driving away evil spirits. The hair from the dewlap and base of the tail is considered holy and even if the reindeer is killed, the hairs from this region are carefully wrapped in birch bark and kept as a sacred object.[21] In ancient times Tungus shamans used white and spotted deer or reindeer in healing rituals. The breath of a hallowed deer was believed to have powerful healing properties and so the shaman would bring his deer to breathe onto a sick person in the process of the healing rite.[22] White and spotted reindeer are not ridden nor are they are used as beasts of burden. They are left unmarked, never branded or caught by lasso. Instead these Tungus hallowed animals carry their owner's protective amulets and when he dies they bear his body to its burial place where, in the course of the burial ceremony, they are slaughtered in the belief that they will then follow their owner into the Other-World.[23]

Deer Cult in Russia

In Russia, remnants of the Deer Cult survived in many regions until the turn of the twentieth century when peasant girls still used to wear horned headdresses. In Kaluzhskaya Guberniya,[24] for example, brides wearing the *kichka*[25] headdresses with two huge horns made out of tough sack-cloth which reached up to 70–80cm in length were not allowed into church by the Orthodox priests.[26] This is one of the many clear examples of the strength and extreme tenacity of the Deer Cult which has survived tens of thousands of years and is still alive even now. Another example is the ancient deer sacrifices which were often still performed on the

---

jp/~acro-ito/Japan_pics/Japan_IKS/imageidx.html> accessed 03.11.07.

21 I. A Khudyakov, *Kratkoe opisanie Verkhoyanskogo okruga* (Leningrad, 1967), p. 109.

22 A. P. Okladnikov, *Istoricheskie rasskazy i legendy nizhnei Leny* (Anthology of Museum of anthropology and ethnography, XI, 1949), p. 84.

23 V. A. Tugolukov Polevye materialy, Archives of the Institute of Ethnography, 1970.

24 Rus. Калужская губерния.

25 Rus. кичка.

26 See Rybakov, *Yazychestvo*, p.77.

same day as and parallel to Orthodox Christian celebrations as late as the turn of the twentieth century. In many regions of Russia there was a widespread belief that two wild deer would come every year to a local church on the day of a particular celebration. One of them was caught and sacrificed while the other was left free. According to one version of the story, peasants once caught and killed both deer, after which the deer stopped coming and people began to sacrifice a bull instead.[27]

In the north of Russia deer antlers were traditionally mounted on the crest of the roof at the front of the house, a remnant of a very ancient cult. This part of the roof is commonly called 'little horse' in Russian[28] and is often decorated with a carved wooden horse head. The older image of a deer or antlers was later replaced by a horse when horses became the predominant means of transport.[29] Although there is wide-ranging debate among scholars about if and when deer were tamed or domesticated, if we look into the art and customs of peoples of very diverse ethnicities and wide geographical distribution we find the same principle of deer images being merged with and then replaced by the horse. Even though some scholars maintain that there is not enough hard archaeological evidence to support this conclusion (deer were often ridden bareback and no saddles have been found) it is apparent that deer were tamed and used first. The Pazyryk custom mentioned above of affixing imitation antlers to horses clearly demonstrates that deer were tamed and ridden before horses. This argument is further strengthened if we look at the oldest teased carpet in the world (found, incidentally, in Pazyryk) where figures of grazing deer are depicted on the inside, in the centre, while figures of horsemen are on the outside, a configuration giving greater importance and antiquity to the deer images.[30] Similar motives are observed in the

---

[27] Ibid., p. 53–54.

[28] Rus. конёк.

[29] There is an ongoing debate as to when the horse was domesticated and became the main means of transport. Some scholars suggest various dates between 5th/4th millennia BC. See, for example, <http://www.equiworld.net/uk/horsecare/evolution/domestication.htm> <http://www.imh.org/imh/kyhpl1b.html#xtocid2243616> DNA studies suggest that horses were domesticated in many places in the same epoch and not just in one particular civilization hub. See <http://www.pnas.org/cgi/reprint/152330099v1.pdf>

[30] See Tamara Talbot Rice, 'Skify: Stroiteli stepnykh piramid' [*Scythians: builders of steppe pyramids]* Тамара Т. Райс, *Скифы: Строители степных пирамид*, <http://www.kirsoft.com.ru/freedom/KSNews_545.htm> accessed 19.02.07.

ornaments on the Russian *ubrus*-towels[31] where images of the deer are gradually sidelined and replaced by images of horses and horsemen.[32] In the far distant past individually tamed deer were also used as hunting decoys, beasts of burden as well as for riding. They were later herded for milk and meat. These uses of reindeer can still be observed among the Siberian Evenki, Yakut and Chukchi nations and the Dukha/Tsaatan deer herders around Lake Hubsuguul in Mongolia as well as in Lapland.[33]

Traditionally, the deer motive often decorates various items of clothing as well as being a common emblem on the ritual *ubrus*-towels. *Ubrus* are often embroidered with two deer flanking a central female figure wearing an antler headdress. This reminds us of the Deer Goddess considered by many northern and Siberian peoples as the supreme deity of the universe which is reflected in the horned headdresses of Russian peasant girls.

Deer Goddess in Tungus and Nganasan cosmology

One such Deer Goddess is the Lady Owner of the Universe, Bugady Enintyn, of the Tungus-Evenki people. Queen of people and animals, she controls everything in the universe. Another example comes from the oral tradition of another Siberian people, the Nganasan.[34] This story tells of a shaman's initiation journey during which he meets two deer-women, Lady-Governors of the World:

> Two guides, a mouse and an ermine, took him onto a high, round mountain. He saw a hole and entering it, found himself in a *chum*[35] filled with light. The walls of the *chum* were covered with mirrors and in the middle there was what seemed to be a fire. There were two naked women. Their bodies were covered

---

[31] Rus. Убрус; a ritual object used in the Russian pre-Christian religion. These towels were used for offering bread and salt to a deity or important person as sign of respect. In this use they can be compared to Tibetan *khata* (Tib. kha btags) and Buryatian *hadag* (Bur. Хадаг). *Ubrus* were also tied onto sacred trees. This is similar to the Buryatian custom of tying *zalaa*-ribbons mentioned above. See ch. XIII.

[32] Rybakov, *Yazychestvo*, p. 79.

[33] I am sure that the folklore of the Laps is rich in tales of the mystical heavenly deer but unfortunately I have not had time to investigate this yet.

[34] Or Tavgi Samoyed

[35] *Chum* is a dwelling typical of many Siberian nations, the Siberian equivalent of a Native American tipi. It is constructed from wooden poles, deer hides or tree bark.

> with fur and on their heads they had deer antlers. He went to what he thought was the fire but it was the sun's light falling through the opening at the top of the *chum*. One woman gave birth to two fawns; one was to become the sacrificial animal for the Dolgan and Evenki, the other for the Samoyed. The second woman also gave birth to two fawns which were to become helpers and food for humans and ancestors of wild and domesticated deer.[36]

Beside the Nganasan story, virtually identical myths are found in the lore of such Siberian nations as Evenki, Dolgan, Nivkh and others. B. A. Rybakov suggests that the deer mentioned in this myth are in fact reindeer as only reindeer doe have antlers and this leads us to surmise that the origin of these myths and the Cult of the Deer are extremely ancient as reindeer were hunted as early as the Palaeolithic.[37]

Fig. 7. Evenki Chum. *Ethnographic museum, Ulaan-Ude.*

Heavenly origins

There is no doubt that ancient people believed in the celestial origins of the Deer. The scene in the extract of the Nganasan shaman's soul

---

[36] A. A. Popov, Tavgiitsy. Materialy po etnografii avamskikh i vedeevskikh samoedov, *Trudy Instituta Antropologii i Etnografii*, 1, 5, (Moskva i Leningrad, 1936) p. 84. Retelling is mine.

[37] Rybakov, *Yazychestvo,* pp. 59–60.

journey related above is set on top of a high mountain filled with light, clearly indicating the celestial dimension, while myths from the folk culture of northern Russia and other northern peoples show they believed that deer fawns, *olen'tsy*,[38] are born in the dimension of the sky among the stars and at certain times fall onto the earth like rain from special clouds and then disperse in the forests.[39] Indeed, there is now a great body of archaeological material unequivocally showing that long ago the Heavenly Deer was revered by very diverse ethnic groups and nations. As well as the images of deer flying skywards on the Deer Stones mentioned above, other artefacts from the Scythians and Caucasian Kobansk culture depict deer surrounded by birds in flight or even positioned above flying birds.[40] This belief in the Heavenly Deer is further supported by the fact that the constellation Ursus Major (the Plough or Big Dipper) was known to many Eurasian nations as The Deer while the Polar Star was called the Deer Star. Later the deer was changed into the bear in some nations.[41]

Deer Cult in Bө Murgel and Prehistoric Bön of Tibet

By examining traditions rooted in the ancient Cult of the Deer which was spread across Eurasia and beyond, we can recognize many features which have found their way into Buryatian Bө Murgel, and indeed, into Yungdrung Bön. Comparing notes in this way allows us to trace the origins of some ritual objects and customs, and provides us with some dates for when certain features of Bө Murgel may have appeared.

We have seen that many cultures have traditions connected to deer antlers and indeed, the ancient Buryats had a cult of worshipping them. According to G.R. Galdanova,[42] when a deer had been killed, the head and antlers were then severed, placed on white felt near the hearth and the ritual of Praying to the Deer Horns[43] was performed with everyone in the dwelling touching the deer head to receive a blessing.[44] A deer head was considered an *erdeni* or magical holy object able to bestow *hulde*. This custom helps us to understand why even today Bө wear ritual *maihabshi* crowns with deer horns. These crowns have practical applications but are

---

38 Rus. Оленьцы.

39 Ibid., pp. 54–55.

40 Ibid., pp. 72–73.

41 Ibid., p. 52–57.

42 Galdanova, *Dolamaistkie*, p. 39.

43 Bur. бугын эбэртэ мургэхэ.

44 Bur. адисаабаха.

also a symbol, showing that the Bɵ has internalised the power of the Sky and, having magical capacities equal to those of heavenly beings, has the ability to invoke and bestow *hulde*, and to travel in the Three Worlds in the fastest possible way (i.e. like a heavenly deer). It also gives us a clue as to when the tradition of wearing such crowns may have appeared, namely some time in the Upper Palaeolithic (40,000–11,000 BC) when reindeer were becoming important for humans. A further clue to the timing is the remarkable dancing figure of the Sorcerer wearing a headdress of deer antlers and bear's paws over its hands. Discovered in the French Pyrenees in the cave of Trois Frêres, this fascinating rock painting has been dated at roughly 13,000–14,000 BC.[45] Some make out a beak in the painting, giving this image a bird feature as well as deer and bear elements. Most of these features figure in the ritual dress of Siberian shamans, including the Bɵ, and symbolize the Bɵ/shaman's magic powers, mastery over diverse energies on different levels of the universe, and his ability to travel throughout the Three Worlds. Parallels between the Bɵ's ritual apparel and the image of the Sorcerer from the Trois Frêres cave demonstrate the extreme antiquity of Bɵ Murgel.

Fig. 8. The Sorcerer from the Trois Frêres.

Bɵ Murgel's direct connection with the ancient Cult of the Deer is further supported by the twelve-step initiation system found in Central Mongolia. Pictures of deer are also commonly featured on Bɵ *hese*-drums in both Mongolia and Buryatia where they act as an aid for swift travel in the universe, reminding us of the Deer's heavenly origins and ability to fly.

Galloping on the Deer

The names of some ancient Buryat deities also point to roots in the Cult of the Deer. We have seen that the Deer Goddess held a prominent place in the pantheon of many northern peoples, including the Tungus-Evenki, and she was also venerated by the Buryats. In ancient times the

---

45 André Leroi-Gourhan, Brigitte et Gilles Delluc, *Prehistoire de l'art occidental*, (Paris : Citadelle & Mazenod, 1965), pp. 308–309; and <http://donsmaps.com/cavepaintings3.html>.

Lady Owner of the Earth was called Buga Hatan[46] where '*buga*' is one of the Buryat words for 'deer'. The Owner of the *taiga*, Bayan Hangai, often appears riding a deer and indeed, two epithets for the Tengeri in general include deer elements. One is Haliutan[47] meaning 'secret' or 'concealed' from *haliun*[48] meaning 'deer', while the other is Buga Unsan,[49] Galloping on the Deer. These epithets match the characteristics of some *Kami* of Japanese Shinto mentioned above who are of celestial nature and also either appear as or ride on sacred deer. Moreover, these epithets give us three very important clues. Firstly, they show the importance given to the deer and give us reason to connect the ancient layers of Bɵ Murgel with the ancient Cult of the Deer. Secondly, they show that in ancient times deer, especially white deer, were considered heavenly creatures[50] as they were associated with the sky-dwelling Tengeri. Thirdly, they tell us that a form of the cult of the Tengeri similar to the present one could have existed as early as before 5,600 BC in the period before the domestication of the horse[51] when deer were the fastest means of transport available, hence the appellation 'Galloping on the Deer'.

An archaeological site on Oleniy Ostrov[52] ('Deer Island') in Lake Onega[53] in the northwest of Russia has also yielded some interesting clues. Dated 5000 BC and belonging to the Mesolithic period, one of its secrets is the grave of a priest in full ritual dress complete with ritual objects, two of which are of particular interest for us here: a hat with a female moose or deer head and sticks carved with moose or deer-headed handles[54] (moose, reindeer and deer are all of the same family and are used interchangeably as symbols).[55] These are most probably the predecessors of the Buryatian Bɵ's ritual attributes and as such the priest was likely to have been practising some form of Prehistoric Bön.

---

46 Bur. Буга хатан.

47 Bur. Халиутан.

48 Bur. халиун.

49 Bur. Буга унсан.

50 Bur. буумал ан.

51 See 'New evidence of early horse domestication' <http://www.eurekalert.org/pub_releases/2006–10/gsoa-neo102306.php>; <http://www.geosociety.org/news/pr/06–49.htm> accessed 22.10.06.

52 Rus. Олений остров.

53 Rus. Онега/Онежское озеро.

54 Rybakov interprets these artefacts as something attached to the shaman's headdress, but if we look at the living Bɵ Murgel tradition, it is clear that these huge sticks were in fact a kind of *hor'bo*-cane.

55 Rybakov, *Yazychestvo*, p. 60–62.

The headdress corresponds to the Bɵ's *maihabshi* horned crown while the moose-headed sticks correspond to the Bɵ's *hor'bo*-canes with the difference that the latter are now carved with either a horse or a human head. Similar large canes have been found on another 'Deer Island' in the Barents Sea, in the Shigirskyi peat bog in the Ural Mountains, and in the ancient settlement of Shvyantoye near Palanga, Lithuania.[56] The purpose of these walking sticks is to aid the Bɵ as he journeys through the Three Worlds and that is why some are decorated with horse heads; the horse was the fastest means of travel until very recent times and supplanted the deer so this seems to be another instance where the deer emblem is replaced by the horse. The moose or deer-headed sticks in the grave of the Oleniy Ostrov priest most probably served the same purpose as those of the Bɵ, so this connection provides us not only with further evidence of the antiquity of the Deer Cult but also further underlines its connection to Bɵ Murgel, the Prehistoric Bön of Eurasia and later Yungdrung Bön.

Transformation into the sacred Deer in Russian folktales and shamanic lore

The analysis of the archaeological, ethnographical and anthropological data presented above reveals that the Cult of the Deer was among the most archaic streams of Prehistoric Bön and was widespread all over Eurasia and the Americas. Folktales are another source of information. In his book, *The Historical Roots of the Magical Tale,* F. Y. Propp[57] demonstrates that magical folktales contain reflections of archaic rituals and beliefs which have been preserved and encoded within, even if sometimes slightly deformed. The following quotation emphasizes once more the deer's symbolic value of being fleet of foot, but also goes on to point to a more literal interpretation of the deer motif:

> On the basis of linguistic materials, M.Y. Marr has shown that the most ancient animal steed of Europe was the deer. These materials were later confirmed by archaeological digs. Folktales also preserved the deer. 'After walking about a mile he turned into a fast-legged deer and harried along as an arrow flies when shot from the bow; he ran and ran then, growing weary, turned from a deer into a hare; gave a start again from all hare's swiftness. He ran and ran but worn were his legs and so turn did he from a hare into a little golden-headed bird; again he flew

---

[56] Ibid.

[57] F. Ya. Propp, *Istoricheskie Korni Volshebnoi Skazki*, (Leningrad: Izdatel'stvo Leningradskogo Universiteta, 1986.

> even faster, he flew and flew and in one and a half days he managed to reach that kingdom where Maria the Princess was dwelling.' (A.F. 259)[58] 'Characteristically a deer is tripled with the more ancient bird and hare.[59] With the appearance of the horse the totemic tradition of transformation finishes and another one begins: an animal is ridden.'[60]

Here we see a pattern of transformation; the hero physically transforms into a deer which in turn changes into other animals to give him a new lease of life for his journey. This suggests another function of the deer crowns worn by priests of Prehistoric Bön and still very much a part of both Buryatian Bɵ and Tibetan Bönpo practising the Cult of the Deer, namely that in very archaic times these ritual headdresses could have been used as an aid for actually transforming into the Heavenly Deer. This hypothesis is supported by the Nganasan shamanic tradition of Siberia:

> The old shaman was lying on the floor with his head towards the *tundra.*[61] He was already journeying to the Underworld. His breathing was heavy and his head shaking in the same way as that of a running reindeer. The shaman always imitates the reindeer when travelling to the Underworld.[62]

In our Russian folktale the hero turns from man to deer to hare to bird, and the Bɵ's ritual dress and attributes also combine deer elements with those of an eagle. These could have come into Bɵ Murgel at different stages in the tradition's development and then become fused in the ritual costume, as with the Trois Frêres priest, or could have been used simultaneously to aid metamorphosis into one or other of these sacred animals as need dictated, as in the folktale.

Deer drums and magical flight

We have already seen that Buryatian Bɵ wear *maihabshi* horned crowns bearing antlers and it is no coincidence that these are very similar

---

58 A. N. Afanasyev, *Narodnye russkie skazki*, vol 1–3, ed. V. Ya. Propp (Moscow, 1957), p. 259.

59 Bird and a deer here are interconnected and serve as fast means of travel on the earth and in the air.

60 Propp, *Istoricheskie Korni,* p. 203, translation is mine.

61 The low vegetation of dwarf trees and shrubs in north Siberia.

62 B. O. Dolgikh, *Mifologicheskie skazki i istoricheskie predaniya Nganasan* (Moskva: Nauka, 1976).

Fig. 9. Bө and Bönpo priests wearing deer-crowns.

to those worn by practitioners of the Bön of the Deer in Zhang Zhung and Tibet in the past. This again suggests that both traditions are rooted in the Cult of the Deer, a universal cult of the Prehistoric Bön of Eurasia. Practitioners of the Bön of the Deer are credited with the magical power to fly through the air and, until recently, Buryatian Bө also had this capacity. The two steeds most frequently used by the Bө for 'flying' are the Deer and the Wolf, while the Rainbow already discussed in the previous chapter is another common vehicle. An experienced Bө can also travel through the air by sitting on his *hese*-drum, as is the case with Bönpo following the Bön of the Deer. The Bө's ritual *hese*-drum is made from deer skin, decorated with images of the deer and an alternative name for it is 'deer', *Heltegy Yehe He'er Hese.*[63]

In the past a powerful Bө's drum could actually turn into a deer when he was using it for flight. In Buryatian Bө Murgel the magical 'flight' itself is of two types. Firstly there is the 'flight of the soul', the Bө's ability to traverse the universe in a trance or in a dream. In this case the term 'flight' is metaphorical because the Bө's physical body remains on earth either beside the ritual fire or in bed. The second type of magical 'flight' is actual physical flight in the air. It seems that modern Bө have lost the capacity

[63] Bur. Хэлтэгы ехэ хээр хэсэ.

for this kind of flight and use only the techniques of 'flight of the soul'. However, in either case, the deer drum plays a vital role.

A parallel concept is found in Nepal among Tamu (Gurung) Ghyabre priests whose ritual drums are also made from deer skin.[64] Tamu consider themselves to be of Tibetan descent, having migrated from Tibet a very long time ago. Their tradition, then, must represent one of the branches of Prehistoric Bön. The identical motifs in the ritual apparel of both Ghyabre and Bɵ priests once again demonstrate the vast area, both geographically and ethnically, over which some form of the Bön of the Deer played a key role in people's belief systems, both today and in days gone by.

Fig. 10. White Deer deity. Trance drawing by the author, 1992.

The Heavenly Deer as a living deity

The mystical Deer is not a forgotten deity. Even nowadays he appears at sacred places when a *tailgan* or a sprinkling offering are performed. One such incidence occurred during the *tailgan* held in the summer of 1994 near the village of Kurumkan in Barguzin:

> Then Doogar Ochirov and I went to one side, some way away, and I 'saw' a White Stag on the highest mountain. Doogar Ochirov went to get some milk and we did *serzhim*. The Stag came very close. He drank the milk when Doogar Ochirov sprinkled. My sensations were very strong – a shiver and the sensation of a strong inflow of energy and joy.
>
> Near Kurumkan, Barguzin, 12.06.94.[65]

---

64 Mumford, *Himalayan Dialogue.*

65 From my unpublished diary *Tailgan Trip*, June 1994.

The Bön of the Deer from the system of the Twelve Lores

One of the ways of organizing the teachings pertaining to the Bön of Cause in Yungdrung Bön is the Twelve Lores.[66] The Twelve Lores are as follows:[67]

1. The Bön of the Protective Deities[68] which contains rites for invoking the *Thugkar* and *Drala*.
2. The Bön of Prosperity and Glory[69] which contains rites of prosperity.
3. The Lore of Ransom Rites[70] which contains rituals to ward off negativities through offering effigies to beings causing disturbance.
4. The Shen of Existence who performs the Funerary Rites[71] which contains funerary rites; rites to protect the deceased and the living from negativities; rites to guide the deceased to a better rebirth; rites of the ransoms of the *la* etc.
5. The Lore of Exorcism and Purification[72] which contains the *Sel*[73] rites among which are found *Sang* and *Tsentrü*[74] which we will study in detail in the next chapter.
6. The Lore of Release from Curses[75] which contains various rites to repel curses sent by beings of the Eight Classes.
7. The Lore of Healing and Therapies[76] which contains teachings on Tibetan medicine: herbal and mineral medicines, diagnostics, moxibustion, acupuncture, the concept of three humours, types of diseases, mantra healing etc.
8. The Lore of the Astrologer who controls the Order of Existence[77] which contains the various astrological methods.

---

66 Tib. shes pa bcu gnyis.

67 Very detailed information on the Twelve Lores is found in Norbu, *Drung, Deu and Bön*, pp. 35–50.

68 Tib. shes lha bon.

69 Tib. g.yang shes phywa bon.

70 Tib. 'gro shes glud gtong.

71 Tib. 'dur shes srid gshen.

72 Tib. gtsang shes sel 'debs.

73 Tib. sel.

74 Tib. tshan khrus.

75 Tib. 'grol shes gtad byad.

76 Tib. phan shes sman dpyad.

77 Tib. skos shes rtsis mkhan.

9. The Lore of the *To* Rites of the Proclamations[78] which contains the cosmic myths of the origin of the universe; rites for the continuation of human generations; rites for the removal of *Dre* and *Si* spirits; *To* rites to dispel astrological disturbances and those created by the Eight Classes.
10. The Lore of the Rites of the Deer and the Knowledge of Flight[79] which contains the *Dö*[80] ransom rites.
11. The Lore of *Juthig*[81] Divination which contains the divination methods using cords.[82]
12. The Bön of Magical Power and Destructive Rites[83] which contains various magical techniques related to the wrathful activities of subduing and destruction.[84]

Most of these Lores contain ritual traditions which were adapted to Yungdrung Bön from Prehistoric Bön, transformed by Tonpa Shenrab to lead beings to Buddhahood in a gradual way. The tenth lore, the Lore of the Deer and the Knowledge of Flight, is of special interest here, based as it is on very archaic traditions pertaining to the Cult of the Deer within the Prehistoric Bön of Eurasia, which also find their parallels in Bɵ Murgel. One of the major differences is that the earlier practice of blood sacrifice is replaced by various symbols and effigy offerings. From the *mang* of the *Rite of the Deer with Branched Antlers*[85] which details this practice's origin, we can see that it is Shenrab Miwo himself together with two

---

78 Tib. smrang shes gto dgu.

79 Tib. lding shes sha ba.

80 Tib. mdos.

81 Tib. 'phur shes ju thig.

82 We will deal with *Juthig* divination in detail in ch. XIV.

83 Tib. sgrol shes 'phrul bon.

84 For a slightly different spelling and interpretation see Norbu, *The necklace of gZi*, pp. 18–19. In the same book (p. 15) Namkhai Norbu lists another classification of early Yungdrung Bön: Lha bon sGo bzhi (The Four Doors of Heavenly Bön): Phya gshen; sNang gshen; 'Phrul gshen and Srid gshen; bShos kyi Lha bon (Divine Bön of Dorma); Grong gi 'Dur bon (Bön which overcomes Evil Spirits in the Villages); and Yang dag pa'i Sems bon (Bön of the Pure Nature of the Mind) i.e. Dzogchen.

85 Tib. sha ba ru gyas.

other *Shenbön*[86] who instigated this particular rite, although its cultural background is indisputably rooted in prehistoric traditions.[87]

What are the particular characteristics of the Yungdrung Bön version of the Rites of the Deer? Here we find nine categories of *Dö* ransom rites designed to repel curses sent by gods and spirits and to protect a person from misfortunes, punishments and diseases all of which focus around an elaborate ritual structure (the *dö*) with the deer figure at the centre. Another significant object among the offerings of this rite from the Bön of the Deer is a tree, also found in Bɵ Murgel rites,[88] which again betrays their common cultural roots. The deer figurine is made out clay or barley flour mixed with precious substances and, according to Prof. Namkhai Norbu's detailed analysis of the *Rite of the Deer with Branched Antlers*, it is the size of a three-year-old ram and is painted in many colours.[89] Ritual arrows, spindles, effigies, figures of various birds and animals, precious silks, *serchem*, incense and other items are gathered around the central deer figure. Before the ritual begins the deer is invoked into the figure and shown the way with butter lamps.[90] This is a very interesting detail. Although the text doesn't specify what kind of deer is invoked, it is clear from the context that some kind of Deer-god is called to enter the effigy to invigorate it with the energy and power necessary for the rite to be successful. The deer figure here is not merely an effigy but is a receptacle prepared for the Deer-god. Thus the deer figure is central to the arrangement of the *dö* and is quickened with the presence of the Deer-god. It is then dispatched to the dimensions of the classes of non-human beings whom it is designed to appease and pacify, thereby convincing them to withdraw their curses and magic. The function of the deer figure, which now serves as the support for the Deer-god, is that of an ambassador and negotiator. In the text of this rite the deer actually speaks to the gods and spirits whom he is sent to appease. Although the cultural base of this rite is that of Prehistoric Bön, the text is filled with the religious ideas and concepts of Yungdrung Bön such as Four Kinds of

---

86 Tib. gshen bon – followers of the Bön of Tonpa Shenrab Miwo i.e. Yungdrung Bön. Like *Shenpo*, this name was used to distinguish them from other contemporary types of Bönpo.

87 Norbu, *Drung, Deu and Bön*, pp. 175–183.

88 *Serge* or *tuurge*, symbol of the World Tree.

89 Ibid., pp. 176–183.

90 Tib. snang gsal sgron me.

Birth,[91] Five Aggregates,[92] Eight Consciousnesses[93] and so on which the deer uses in his speech. Because in the past the *Shenpos* who practised the Rites of the Deer were able to cause the effigy to actually fly in the sky, and because some kind of Deer-god is invoked into the effigy before the ritual, these rites encapsulate the general culture of the Deer Cult of Eurasia and, in particular, the religious ideas of the peoples of the Deer Stones Culture with their stelas engraved with deer flying skywards. The Yungdrung Bön rite retains echoes of the deer's celestial origin, its service as a messenger between gods and men, and its connection with flight. Similar practices were probably used in many parts of Central Asia with some versions involving animal sacrifices. We can deduce this on the basis of the contents of the offerings dispatched with the deer figure in the Yungdrung Bön *Rite of the Deer with Branched Antlers*; while this transformed version of the rite uses mainly[94] substitute figurines in place of animals and birds, in the Prehistoric Bön traditions the animals and birds would have been actually sacrificed to the gods and spirits. After Yungdrung Bön was introduced into Zhang Zhung and Tibet both the old and new versions of these rites existed side by side for a long time, a cause of confusion and misrepresentation among the proponents of newly arrived Indian Buddhism.

As was said above, the early *Shenpos* who practised the Yungdrung Bön version of the Deer Rites and the Buryatian Bө of the past could fly in the air astride their drums and it is no mere coincidence that this Lore on the Bön of the Deer also includes the Knowledge of Flight in its title. On the basis of the information already presented in this chapter we can reconstruct the magic technique most likely used by both *Shenpos* and the Bө for their flight on the drums; the magic powers of the Heavenly Deer would have been invoked into the drum in the same way as they are invoked into the deer figure in the *Rite of the Deer with Branched Antlers*. Such an authenticated drum then became a receptacle of the Deer-god who acted as the 'jet-engine' of this magic vehicle. Although the prehistoric traditions of the Bön of the Deer have vanished in Tibet leaving no written sources, they clearly serve as the cultural background to the rituals of Causal Bön, as demonstrated above. By comparing data

---

91 Tib. skyes gnas bzhi.

92 Tib. phung po lnga.

93 Tib. rnam shes thogs brgyad.

94 Cooked meat and animal bones are also among the offerings. This is, however, is different from a sacrifice. For a detailed analysis of how the offerings of Prehistoric and Yungdrung Bön differ, see ch. XII.

from the *Rite of the Deer with Branched Antlers* and techniques found in Bө Murgel – which represents a surviving branch of the Prehistoric Bön of Eurasia – we can say without doubt that the same technique would have been used by the Tibetan practitioners of the Prehistoric Bön of the Deer.

There is another rite in Yungdrung Bön which focuses on a deer figurine. This is one of the soul retrieval rituals in which a dough effigy in the form of the clan's 'soul emblem'[95] is used. The 'emblem of the clan's soul' is an ancient Tibetan custom which will be dealt with in more detail in Chapter XIV but suffice to say here that each ancient clan had a totemic animal which represented the clan's collective soul. The deer was associated with the Dong[96] clan, other animals with other clans. In the soul retrieval rites of Yungdrung Bön, a figurine of a human with the head of the clan's soul totem is made, but if a person doesn't know their clan emblem, a deer head is used. This preference for the deer over other animals shows the importance given to it in very archaic ritual practices and mythology.

Conclusion

We have seen that the Cult of the Deer was an extremely widespread and important strand running through Prehistoric Bön which influenced the spiritual traditions and customs of many peoples in Eurasia and the Americas. However, the close parallels between the living tradition of Bө Murgel and the Bön of the Deer now adapted into Yungdrung Bön are particularly striking, not only in terms of their external ritual objects, but more significantly in terms of their inner application and use. As Tonpa Shenrab is a Buddha of Central Asia, the prehistoric traditions which serve as the background for the Yungdrung Bön rites of the Deer would have been present in the general region of Inner Asia rather than being specifically Tibetan. These prehistoric traditions of the Bön of the Deer have survived to this day within Bө Murgel and it is by cross-examining Yungdrung Bön versions of the Rites of the Deer and Bө Murgel that we can arrive at a deeper understanding of the general culture and magical techniques of the Prehistoric Bön of Eurasia.

---

95 Tib. bla rtags.

96 Tib. gDong/lDong. On this see Karmay, *The Arrow and the Spindle*, pp. 327–328.

CHAPTER XI

Purification Rituals

Concepts of purity and pollution and the need for purification rites

If we turn our attention again to the parallel concepts of *Ye* and *Ngam* to which *Lha*/*Düd* and White/Black Tengeri belong, both pairs struggling for dominance over the universe, it becomes clear that in both Bön and Bɵ Murgel the origin of such notions as purity and impurity lies in the binary nature of our world, and it is this which gives rise to the need for purification rituals. This concept also lies at the heart of the practical ways of exorcism.

How did impurity and pollution, such fundamental factors in the cosmos, come into being? In Bön, impurity is associated with the ocean of poison in *Ngam* which spills over into the realm of humankind and sometimes even into that of gods causing chaos, diseases and much suffering. It can be said, then, that when negative circumstances occur they are due to pollution from *Ngam.*[1] Some physical substances, too, are said to have arisen from the poison of *Ngam* and these include rhododendron, sulphur and black aconite along with some other types of trees, shrubs and plants. Other Bönpo myths say that pollution arose from the mixing of good and evil, from the mingling of the principles of gods and demons at the beginning of the world resulting in the appearance of a lustreless grey egg which burst spawning all manner of diseases, bad spirits, impurities and negativities.[2] Whatever the origin, purification rites need to be performed in order to eliminate these negativities.

In Bɵ Murgel impurity comes from evil and dirty objects which appeared on earth because of the wars between White and Black Tengeri in the dimension of the Sky. In times of fierce battles in the Upper World of the Sky, the injured Tengeri shed blood which drips onto the Middle

---

1 See Karmay, *The Arrow and the Spindle*, p.142.

2 See Snellgrove, *Nine Ways*, p. 71.

World in the form of 'blood rain', toxic rain.[3] This is too strong a pollution to be cleansed so people simply abandon the places on which it fell. An example of this can be found in the Buryatian version of the *Geser* epic. As we have seen, this includes a description of the war between the White and Black Tengeri and narrates how it was won by the White Tengeri when Hormusta Tengeri managed to slay Atai Ulaan Tengeri with the help of his son Buhe Beligte, the future Geser. Hormusta then tore Atai's body to pieces and threw it from the Sky. Where the bits of the body fell to the ground they transformed into various types of poisons and toxic vapours which gave rise to diseases and evils. Consequently, the whole earth was affected by pollution and sufferings.[4] Later Buhe Beligte incarnated on earth as Geser to clean it from contamination and restore balance.

From this initial impurity many specific negativities and defilements arose and it is these which are the target of purification rites. According to Yungdrung Bön, this principle of pollution is encapsulated in the main impurities of ignorance, attachment, jealousy, anger and pride, and it is these negative emotions, known as the Five Poisons,[5] which then in turn give rise to other types of impurities and evil circumstances such as the murder of relatives, vapours arising from their blood, incest, widowhood, illegitimate children, leprosy, impure fumes from cremated corpses which were not ritually purified, adultery, defilement of the hearth and so on.[6] There are many objects, too, which can cause contamination if

---

3 Bur. шуһан дуһаа. We can observe similar phenomena today. An example of this is the red rain which fell on the Southern Indian state of Kerala for two months in July/August 2001. The scientific community is divided as to the cause of this phenomenon but some believe the red colour to be caused by microscopic alien life forms; could this be the blood of the sky-gods? The local Hindu population would say so and treated this as an extremely inauspicious event, throwing away much of the contaminated water. See, for example, Amelia Gentleman and Robin McKie, 'Red rain could prove that aliens have landed', *The Observer*, Sunday March 5, 2006 <http://observer.guardian.co.uk/science/2006/mar/05/spaceexploration.theobserver> accessed 26.01.08.

4 According to some versions Hormusta and Atai Ulaan were brothers so here we have an instance of killing a blood relative which creates strong spitirual pollution. See below.

5 Tib. dug lnga.

6 See Norbu, *Drung, Deu and Bön*, pp. 107–109. Karmay (*The Arrow and the Spindle,* pp. 384–385) gives the following list of the nine impurities (Tib. mi gtsang rdzas cha sna dgu) from *Zijyid*:
– Homicide/fratricide (Tib. dme);

one comes into contact with them, including: certain type of foods such as horse meat;[7] sexual intercourse with a woman-murderer;[8] wearing the clothes of a murderer or a sick person; touching corpses with bare hands; wearing contaminated or dirty objects and so on. Such contact defiles the protective deities of the person who then becomes prey for all sorts of demonic influences bringing unhappiness, disease and even death.

How do these defilements affect beings throughout the triple world system? There is a clear explanation in *Zijyid*:

> If defilement touches the gods of the Pure Abode,
> the domains of the Lords of the Soil are defiled.
> The vapours of their defilement
> strikes upon the company of human beings,
> and in this world region poverty, disease, famine, disturbances,
> unhappiness and suffering of all kinds arise.[9]

From this quotation we can clearly see the interdependence of all phenomena. As all the worlds are connected, should pollution arise in one of them it reflects in other worlds, too. In fact, purification rites have to purify several dimensions at once.

In Buryatian Bɵ Murgel we do not find such a precise classification or theory regarding poisons as we do in Bön; the notion of impurities is expressed more in terms of taboos. For example, tradition has it that

---

– The birth of a child just after the death of its father (Tib. mug);
– Incest (Tib. nal);
– Filthiness (Tib. btsog);
– Imprecations (Tib. Than);
– Inauspicious signs (Tib. ltas ngan);
– Possession by the (Tib. byur) spirit;
– Impurity due to the death of a spouse (Tib. yug);
– Pollution of the hearth (Tib. thab mkhon).

7 There are several reasons for not eating horse meat some of which seem contradictory: the horse represents the *Lungta* force (see ch. V and XIII) of an individual so eating it is considered to weaken one's *Lungta*; the horse is an animal which is ridden by man so in some way it is considered 'impure' (See Karmay, *The Arrow and the Spindle*, p. 391). According to Yongdzin Lopön Tenzin Namdak horse, donkey and *kyang* (Tibetan wild ass) meat and the meat of hares, rabbits, marmots and other rodents is considered impure because their upper teeth look like those of humans.

8 The Tibetan idea here is that a woman's calling is to give and sustain life so they musn't kill because it goes against their fundamental nature and the natural order of things (See Karmay, *The Arrow and the Spindle*, p. 392).

9 Snellgrove, *Nine Ways*, pp. 47–49.

a widow cannot remarry; menstruating women aren't allowed to attend religious rites or cook for the *tailgan*; it is forbidden to contaminate the hearth in any way, even by stirring the embers with a sharp object as this may injure the god of fire who will retaliate; the dead are traditionally wrapped in white felt so as not to contaminate the earth; one shouldn't wear the clothes of the sick nor touch impure objects or animals. If they had to kill relatives, people of their own clan or tribe or even foreigners of high rank such as ambassadors, Buryats and Mongols of the past tried to do so without shedding blood as it was considered inauspicious and improper to show the blood of one's kin or of noble people to the Sky.[10] The idea here again is that beings of the Upper World can be contaminated by defilements in another part of the universe.

There are also specific taboos for Bɵ. Some are not permitted to touch a pig or eat pork, for example. Some Bɵ should avoid certain situations such as funerals and weddings. Bɵ/Utgan cannot lead rituals or even do the simple *serzhim* for a year or so following the death of their father or mother as they are considered contaminated by the perceived impurity of the death of such a close relative. Indeed, it is not enough to merely abstain from religious activities for a year; purification rituals must also be done. If a Bɵ becomes afflicted with pollution they can lose their powers, fall unconscious, start bleeding from the nose and mouth and can even die if the purification rite of 'body-washing' is not performed. Before a *tailgan* Bɵ are sometimes commanded by the gods or spirits to send away certain people who are defiled or are of evil disposition so that they do not pollute the sacred places and religious activities:

> In the morning we drove to the site of the next ritual. The local people were inert and slow to understand. The guide waiting for us was drunk, and he didn't know the way very well. We forbade him to get out of the bus and eventually sent him back to the village and banned him from attending the *tailgan* as the local gods became angry as soon as he set foot outside the bus.
>
> Near village of Bayangol, Barguzin, 19.06.94.[11]

---

[10] The victims were killed by being rolled into a carpet and suffocated or by having their heels tied to the back of their head and their spine broken etc. Under the orders of Subedei-Baatar and Dzhebe-Noyon, Russian sovereign Mstislav of Galich and other Russian noblemen were bound and put under the wooden platform of a *gher* where Mongols then danced thus squashing them to death without shedding their blood. This took place after the battle of Kalka in 1222 which was disastrous for the Russians and although the Russians considered such killing savage and brutal, for the Mongols it was a 'respectful' way of killing high guests.

[11] A passage from my unpublished diary, *Tailgan Trip*.

Purification rites play an indispensable role in both Bön and Bɵ Murgel, purifying the participants and the offerings themselves from possible contamination prior to any offering ritual. However, purification rituals are not only performed as part of larger rituals but stand in their own right as a vital part of ritual lore in both traditions.

The importance of purification rituals, then, springs from the dualistic vision of the universe shared by both Bön and Bɵ Murgel; notions of good and bad, black and white, pure and impure are inextricably linked with their cosmological view and mythology, a concept which inevitably gives rise to the need for purification processes – if a person, group or protective deity is somehow tainted, they must be returned to the pristine condition. Similarly, only pure, clean things may be offered to the gods. This need is addressed through the purification rituals which we find in both Bön and Bɵ Murgel.

The highest teachings of Yungdrung Bön, Dzogchen, go beyond this dualistic vision. According to Dzogchen, everything, animate and inanimate, manifests from the great primordially pure Nature of Mind and is therefore inherently pure; there is ultimately nothing to purify if one can remain within this sphere of all-encompassing perfection. It is fitting, then, that in Yungdrung Bön the purification rites are found within the body of *Sel* rites of exorcism which pertain to *The Way of the Shen of the Visual World,*[12] the second Way of the Four Ways of Cause, the second rung on the ladder of the Nine Ways.

There are two main methods of purification in Bön, one using water and the other using smoke. The first is known as *Tsentrü*, purification by lustral sprinkling with specially prepared liquids, while the second is *Sang*, purification by fumigation with the smoke of aromatic plants. Besides these two types of purification, *The Way of the Shen of the Visual World* contains many other *Sel* rites which are used to exorcise various unfavorable conditions but which we shall not deal with here.[13]

Smoke and water are also the main vehicles of purification in Bɵ Murgel. Here, too, the smoke from aromatic herbs with special properties is used in purification rites[14] while others, using various water-based liquids, are generally labelled 'body-washing' rites which we touched

---

12 Tib. snang gshen theg pa.

13 For information on *Sel* rites see Norbu, *Drung, Deu and Bön,* pp. 103–107.

14 This is all but identical to the Native American concept of 'smudging', and even many of the herbs used are the same. This is no surprise; Native American culture is related to Prehistoric Bön and Bɵ Murgel as the former was brought to the Americas with the peoples migrating over the Bering Straits.

upon in our discussion on Initiation Rites. In both traditions, water and fire purification rites often follow one after another in varying order to ensure complete purification; a person can become polluted in many ways, some of which may go unnoticed.

Lustral sprinkling rituals

In both Bön and Bө Murgel the water used in these sprinkling rituals is collected from particular springs or other sources, mixed with other sanctified ingredients and consecrated before it can be used. The Tibetan version of this kind of purification preserved in Yungdrung Bön, *Tsentrü* (also known as *Tsen*[15] or *Trü*[16]), is of two types: White *Tsen*[17] and Red *Tsen.*[18] While the *mang* or mythical origin of both types of *Tsen* is tied up with Walchen Gekhöd, the Yungdrung Bön *yidam* appearing in the guise of the Lord of the *Wal*[19] sky deities, Red *Tsen*, like *Sang*, is specifically used to purify[20] 'impurities' of the *me*[21] type which arise from active, deliberate wrongdoing such as killing close kin or members of one's own clan, whereas White *Tsen* mainly purifies[22] 'contaminations' or 'pollutions' of the *nöl*[23] type which are more 'passive' – wearing contaminated clothes or inadvertently coming into contact with the impurity of murder, for example. However, in practice there is no strict rule.

White Tsen

There are two main versions of White *Tsen* and although the basic principle is the same, the source of the waters used as well as the other ingredients differs, as do the myths relating the origin of the practices. According to the first version, it was the Mother of Nectar, Namchi Gungyal,[24] who instigated the ingredients for both White *Tsen* and *Sang*

---

[15] Tib. tshan.

[16] Tib. khrus.

[17] Tib. dkar tshan.

[18] Tib. dmar tshan.

[19] Tib. dbal is often translated as 'piercing' or 'flaming' but according to Yongdzin Lopön Tenzin Namdak it means 'wrathful', 'ferocious'. (From an interview in Shenten Dargye Ling, France, 01.0.07.)

[20] Tib. bsang ba.

[21] Tib. dme.

[22] Tib. dag pa.

[23] Tib. mnol.

[24] Tib. g̱Nam phyi Gung rgyal.

as described in the ritual texts of the Gekhöd cycle.[25] Namchi Gungyal resides in the Milky Way and in the great Namtsho Lake in Changthang, Zhang Zhung's heartland in northwestern Tibet. Seeing earthly beings suffering from all sorts of pollution, she spat a mouthful of nectar onto the earth and her spittle became the components necessary for the *Tsentrü* and *Sang* purification rites. The components for White *Tsen* are:

- camphor – medicine of snows;
- cuttlefish bones – medicines of the waters;
- saffron – medicine of the meadows;
- white calcite – medicine of stones;
- brown bitumen – medicine of rocks;
- brown musk – medicine of the forests;
- intestinal concretions – medicine from elephant;
- snow from Mount Tise and water from Lake Mapang.

All these were mixed and poured into a silver ladle. The right wing of a white snow-cock,[26] the medicine bird of the gods, became the 'tongue' for sprinkling White *Tsen*.[27]

According to the second version,[28] the ingredients self-appeared naturally as the world was formed from empty space. The substances used here are:

- nine types of lustral water[29] from the river to the east of the world mountain and waters of the other three rivers in the other cardinal direction plus water of the river flowing from the four intermediate directions which became the substances;
- nine types of water from snow[30] and slate[31] which became the ingredients;
- milk of a white sheep, brown *dri* (female yak) and various medicines which became the protective substances;

---

25 For the translation of the myths see Norbu, *Drung, Deu and Bön*, pp. 109–110 and Karmay, *The Arrow and the Spindle*, pp. 144–145; 400–405.

26 Tib. gong mo.

27 See Norbu, *Drung, Deu and Bön*, pp. 113–115, and Karmay, *The Arrow and the Spindle*, pp. 400–402.

28 From the text *Lha'i rgyal po nam mkha' bcu'i tshan* from the ritual cycle of *Zhi khro'i sgrub skor*.

29 Tib. tshan dgu.

30 Tib. gangs tshan.

31 Tib. g.ya' tshan.

- a conch shell, golden ladle and five vases of precious metals which became the containers;
- the right wing of a snow-cock, wool from the head of a white sheep and hairs from the tail of a divine white *dri* which became the 'tongue' for sprinkling.[32]

In either case, water and snow-melt are taken from hallowed places, mixed with substances charged with medicinal properties and kept in a precious vessel. During the ritual, this lustral water is then flicked or sprinkled by means of feathers, wool or hairs from a divine bird or animal. Nowadays, White *Tsen* rituals follow the same basic formula.

Firstly the sacred liquid is prepared by blending the various precious medicines, minerals and incenses in a mixture of different types of clean water and milk in a special container, either a ritual metal vase or a conch shell. The practitioner then chants a liturgy while an assistant, holding the ladle with the lustral mixture, uses a sprig of juniper held in his right hand to sprinkle it over the spaces, people or objects to be purified.

Below is an essential version of White *Tsen* or *Trü* which is done in conjunction with an equally simple version of *Sang* to purify the

Fig. 1. Bönpo monk performing Trü *in the course of a ceremony marking the anniversary of Nyamme Sherab Gyaltsen. Left:* Lhatrü (*Tib. lha khrus*)*; purification of the gods. Right:* Trü; *purification of the site , altar, ritual implements and participants. Triten Norbutse Monastery, February, 2008.*

---

32 For the translation see Norbu, *Drung, Deu and Bön*, pp. 115–116.

offering objects, participants and the environment at the very outset of any offering ritual:

> Om!
> When the snow mountain of faults of the excellent body of
> Trogyal Chenpo,[33]
> The Great King of Wrathful Deities, is completely conquered,
> The offerings are meticulously arranged
> And through the lustral sprinkling of this pure and clean water
> All the obscurations, defilements and karmic traces are cleansed,
> May all the *Lha*-deities of the Upper World be cleansed,
> May all the *Lu*-spirits of the Lower World be cleansed,
> May all the *Nyen*-spirits in the Middle World be cleansed,
> May all the seats and thrones be cleansed,
> May all the clothing be cleansed,
> May all the objects and environment be cleansed![34]

Red Tsen

The ritual of Red *Tsen* arose out of the need to purify Gekhöd from the pollution of matricide. It was performed by the deity Kuji Mangke after he succeeded in waking Gekhöd from a deep sleep into which he had fallen out of distress upon learning that he had inadvertently slain his own mother. To purify Gekhöd from the pollution of this murder, Kuji Mangke took a ladle made from the horn of a wild yak and poured into it thirteen types of blood which purify contaminations:

- blood of a horse;
- blood of a crystal goat;
- blood of a rhinoceros;
- blood of a cemetery pig;
- blood of a brown ox;
- blood of a white vulture;
- blood of a female yak;
- blood of a snow leopard;
- blood and bile of the two kinds of bear;
- blood of the two types of wild deer;
- blood of a blue falcon.

---

[33] Tib. Khro rgyal chen po.

[34] Rendered into English by Khenpo Tenpa Yungdrung in Triten Norbutse Bönpo Monastery, Kathmandu, Nepal, March 2004.

Gekhöd's hands were washed in this mixture of thirteen types of blood and so the negativities of matricide were purified. Then Red *Tsen* was sprinkled over all the god-worlds so everything was purified and cleansed from pollution.[35]

In the text we find precise instructions on which type of blood should be used to lustrate each particular misdeed or broken precept;[36] for example, if one engaged in sexual intercourse with a murderess, one has to perform the purification rite with the blood of the snow leopard whereas if one has worn contaminated clothes of another person one has to use the blood of the cemetery pig.[37]

No animal is actually sacrificed for the ritual, but certain bloods have curative and purifying properties, as is clearly explained in Tibetan medicinal texts.[38] For Red *Tsen,* blood is sourced indirectly, either bought from a hunter who has already killed an animal for a completely different purpose, taken from an animal which died of a 'clean' disease,[39] or a small amount of blood is extracted from a living beast such as a yak, for example, in the manner similar to that of the Masai people of Africa.[40] The best is the 'clean' blood of a female animal which has just given birth. Blood can be acquired when it is available, then dried and stored to be applied when needed. However, this form of *Tsen* is much less commonly practised than White *Tsen* rituals.

A Red *Tsen* ritual follows the same matrix as White *Tsen*: first the mixture of water, various medicines and animal blood is prepared, then,

---

35 For the translation see Norbu, *Drung, Deu and Bön*, pp. 117–120 and Karmay, *The Arrow and the Spindle*, pp. 397–400.

36 For the list see Karmay, *The Arrow and the Spindle*, p.391.

37 See Norbu, *Drung, Deu and Bön*, pp. 119–120.

38 Ibid., pp. 122-124.

39 Non-contagious disease.

40 A small vein is opened and some blood is extracted. The vein is then carefully closed. This doesn't pose any danger to the animal and can, in fact, even bring benefit because it has the same function as blood-letting treatment. Indeed, Charles Ramble told me there is a blood-drinking festival in Southern Mustang, where the men let blood from live yaks in spring.
There is an episode in the *Gesar* epic where a blacksmith is sent by Gesar to fetch an eagle's blood and other substances for magical purposes. The blacksmith manages to lure an eagle into his trap. The cornered eagle strikes his beak against his captor's staff so hard that blood comes out of it and is collected into a stag's horn by the blacksmith, who soon releases the bird. (See Wallace, *Gesar!* pp. 47–65) Although the Tibetan version of Gesar in its present form is a Buddhist epic, it is nevertheless deeply rooted in Bönpo culture.

while the practitioner chants the liturgy, an assistant uses a sprig of juniper held in his right hand to sprinkle the lustral solution from a ladle in his left hand over the spaces, people or objects to be purified.

'Body-washing' rites in Bo Murgel

In Bɵ Murgel we find similar rituals used for purification and healing. Their names vary from place to place and depending on the particular purpose they are used for, but like the Bönpo *Tsen* rituals, there are two types, with and without the use of blood.

Uhan Tarim

When this rite is used for general healing and purification it is called *Uhan Tarim*,[41] 'purification by water' whereas when a similar ritual is performed as a preliminary part of a Bɵ or Utgan's initiation, it is called *Ugaalga*, 'body-washing'. In the western region of Tunka, the term *Ugaalga* is generally applied to all kinds of water purification.

The source of the water is important, so once the Bɵ has determined, through divination, the cause of the disease or contamination to be purified, he or his assistants then visit nine sacred *arshan* springs to collect hallowed water. They sprinkle offerings of milk and vodka to the *Lusuut*-owners of each spring thereby obtaining their permission to take and use the water. Next the water is boiled. There are two methods for this; it can either be simply heated over a fire, or as we saw in the description of initiation rites, heated by means of red-hot stones. In this case, nine stones are taken from a river near the birthplace of the person to be purified, or from the shores of Lake Baikal. The boiling water is purified by adding potent herbs 'god's grass',[42] *sagaan dali*[43] and juniper. The presiding Bɵ then chants an invocation of the deities while holding a specially prepared bunch of nine birch twigs, reeds or a mix of pine, larch, *sagaan dali*, cedar, birch, Siberian fir and a kind of willow. Dipping the bunch into the sanctified waters, he sprinkles it over the bare back of the person who requested the rite, sometimes touching the body or even hitting it slightly. After that the patient is fumigated with smoke from juniper or *zhodo'o* and further offerings such as vodka or other substances are sprinkled to the Tengeri and ancestral spirits.

---

[41] Bur. уһан тарим.

[42] Rus. богородская трава , Lat. *Thymus serpylum*.

[43] Bur. сагаан дали, Lat. *Rhododendron adamsii*.

Ugaalga

Ugaalga follows the same basic structure as *Uhan Tarim,* the main difference lies in its purpose as it is mainly performed during initiation ceremonies. There is a version of this rite which involves animal sacrifice, so fresh blood is sometimes added to the lustral waters. In this case the water is prepared in the same way as above and then some hairs from the ears of a billy-goat, horse or other animal (depending on the type of initiation) are added. The animal is then sacrificed and some fresh blood is poured into the mixture. The presiding Bө then purifies the initiate in the same way as above. *Ugaalga* is also performed each time a Bө becomes defiled through coming into contact with contaminating agents or situations.

Another version of this rite is performed specifically to purify and protect a new-born baby. Such rites are known as *Uhaan Budlyaa*,[44] 'washing by water'. The lustral solution is made in the same way as for *Uhan Tarim* and the baby is placed in the centre of eight white stones symbolizing a protective circle and one black stone symbolizing the closed gates through which no malevolent spirit can enter. With a bunch of twigs, the Bө or Utgan sprinkles the sanctified water over the baby, protection spells are uttered and a special silk protection cord with nine knots is tied around the baby's neck. Water is poured onto the roof of the *gher*-dwelling and the bunch of twigs is fixed above the entrance. The rite is repeated at regular intervals until the child reaches the age of fifteen. Such rites may be performed for adults suffering from certain diseases. In some cases the patient is actually whipped with the bunch of twigs moistened in the sacred liquid. Such rituals are called *Habalga*,[45] 'whipping'.

Fumigation rituals

Sang

The term *Sang* is derived from the verb *bsang ba*, 'to purify', and is also connected to the word *sangs pa*, 'to illuminate'.[46] The function of this rite is to purify defilements and recharge the weakened energy of an individual, group of people, their protective gods and other beings which may have been affected by the same polluting agents. It is a very archaic

44 Bur. уhан будляа.

45 Bur. hабалга.

46 Karmay, *The Arrow and the Spindle*, p. 382.

Bönpo purification ritual, and there are two broad categories. The first is *Sang* itself, a rite of purification through fumigation with the smoke of certain herbal and mineral substances. It can be done equally in one's house, in a holy place or any place which needs purification, but the ritual should be completed before noon as positive energy is on the rise from dawn to noon.

Fig. 2. Sang *as a part of the preliminary purification stage of the consecration of Drenpa Namkha statue in the hills near Sankhu, Kathmandu Valley, 04.04.2004.*

The second, called *Sangchö*[47] or '*Sang* offering', is a very popular ritual combining purification and offering. Guru Padmasambhava imported and adapted the Bön *Sangchö* rites into the Tibetan version of Buddhism in the eighth century AD. While the general principle of the ritual remained the same, the *mang* myth of origin and other Bönpo characteristics were removed and replaced with Buddhist concepts and deities. This Buddhist version became very popular and is now practised in all Schools of Tibetan Buddhism. *Sangchö* has undergone many transformations in the course of time giving rise to many different interpretations and variations of the Buddhist ritual; we shall not go into details here but shall study the original Bönpo *Sangchö* ritual in the next chapter.

---

[47] Tib. bsang mchod.

Fig. 3. Sang *offering during* Lhagyal *(Tib. lha rgyal) ceremony. Triten Norbutse Monastery, Kathmandu, 2008.*

In Yungdrung Bön, *Sang* rites are often preceded by a short *Dugchyug*[48] rite, a brief preliminary ritual during which impurities are burnt and thereby removed. Substances symbolizing impurities which came from *Ngam*, the negative dimension of the universe, such as sulphur, rhododendron leaves and so on, are burnt in a ladle or other receptacle. The burning impurities are taken into all the parts of the building or space where *Sang* is to be performed, after which the person performing the rite walks clockwise[49] around the site and, once they have completed a full circle, throws the burning impurities away from it. In this way impurities are prevented from entering the site where *Sang* is to be performed and have no power to hinder the purification process.[50]

With the impurities disposed of, *Sang* itself is performed. Specially prepared substances such as mugwort, juniper and cypress branches as well as various mineral substances, all of which were generated by the Mother of Nectar, Namchi Gungyal's spittle, are gathered and burnt to produce dense smoke.

As the fragrant smoke spreads through the area to be purified, a ritual text is recited. Some such texts are very essential and simple, others are far more elaborate. Below is an example of a simple *Sang* text:

---

[48] Tib. dug phyug.

[49] Usually the direction of ritual movement in Bön is anticlockwise, spiralling the positive energy inwards, but because here we are dealing with throwing out impurities, the direction is reversed.

[50] Oral explanation by Yongdzin Lopön Tenzin Namdak in Triten Norbutse Bönpo Monastery, Kathmandu, Nepal, 1996.

Om!
When the manifestation of the excellent body of Trogyal Chenpo,
The Great King of Wrathful Deities,
Gathers the essence of plants in the forests on the top of the King of Mountains,
The offerings are meticulously arranged,
By the offering of this fragrant incense
May all the *Lha*-deities of the Upper World be purified,
May all the *Lu*-spirits of the Lower World be purified,
May all the *Nyen*-spirits in the Middle World be purified,
May all the seats and thrones be purified,
May all the clothing be purified,
May all the objects and environment be cleansed![51]

More elaborate texts, such as those found in the purification rites dedicated to Gekhöd, may have several parts: the *mang*-exposition of the origin of the *Sang* rite, purification, confession of the misdeeds or carelessness which resulted in impurity, and repentance.[52]

Aryuud haha[53]

In Buryatian Bө Murgel we find a ritual custom parallel to Tibetan *Sang*, although it is in no way as elaborate as its Bönpo counterpart. It is called *Aryuud haha*, 'purification'. Buryats believe that fumigation destroys curses; impurities and pollutions, bad thoughts, evil intentions, the causes of many diseases and more, so this rite aids healing. The plants the Bө use for the ritual are either *zhodo'o* or *arsa*. The ritual may vary slightly depending on where and why it is performed, but the general pattern is outlined below.

Firstly, *zhodo'o* or *arsa* is placed in a burner and lit so it begins to smoulder, producing aromatic smoke. Holding it in the right hand, the Bө or Utgan firstly performs self-purification by passing the smoking substance three times in a circular clockwise movement firstly around their head, then around their upper torso, around their armpits (first left then right), around their hands (left then right), around their waist, then around their lower torso, around their knees and under each foot (left then right). Finally the brazier is lifted to heart level and rotated clockwise

---

[51] Rendered into English by Khenpo Tenpa Yungdrung in Triten Norbutse Bönpo Monastery, Kathmandu, Nepal, March 2004.

[52] For examples see Karmay, *The Arrow and the Spindle*, pp. 403–405 and Norbu, *Drung, Deu and Bön*, pp. 109–110.

[53] Bur. арюуд хаха.

three times in front of the chest, after which some smoke is inhaled to purify the inner energy dimension.

Having thus purified himself, the Bө generally then goes on to repeat the same sequence of movements around the person who requested the purification, although he may change the sequence according to the needs of the patient. While performing this purification the Bө or Utgan exclaims '*Shere'eg!*',[54] 'Purification in progress!', several times.[55]

If a large group of people needs to be purified, this ritual is modified according to circumstances. People come one after another to the Bө or Utgan and inhale some smoke of the *zhodo'o*-bark. They then proceed to the braziers which are set on the ground so that people can step over them one by one. Men and women form segregated, parallel lines and step over separate sets of braziers. I observed this way of purification by fumigation in the Barguzin area of Buryatia in 1994. It was a preliminary purification stage before the large *tailgan.*[56]

Aryuud haha is an indispensable part of all Bө Murgel rituals and is always done at the beginning of each one. It is not only people who are purified by fumigation but also the site of the ritual, ritual objects, altar, clothes etc. in just the same way as described in the *Sang* text above. Furthermore, before accepting any gifts Bө pass the money or other offerings given for their ritual services over smouldering *arsa*. Indeed, this custom of fumigation permeates almost all aspects of life in Buryatia as, for example, anything newly bought or newly received as a gift is passed through hallowed smoke. Nowadays, in the general decline of traditional values, this custom is observed less strictly, but in the past it was a must. In medieval Mongol-Buryat society purification by fumigation played a very important role. Foreign ambassadors and merchants bearing gifts had to pass between two ritual fires before they could be admitted into the presence of the Khaan. Refusal to do so cost the Russian sovereign Mikhail of Chernigov his life in 1246 because it was considered he was harbouring evil intentions against Batu Khaan.[57] Indeed, the preliminary purification through fumigation performed prior to any Bө Murgel ritual is based on the same assumption; the Bө and individual participants are purified to remove any impurities and improper motivations which they may harbour lest they offend and pollute the Tengeri and *Ongon*

---

54 Bur. Шэрээг!

55 This is the version according to Utgan V. G. Naguslaeva.

56 See next chapter for details.

57 N. Ts. Munkuev, *Kitaiskii istochnik o pervykh mongol'skikh khanakh* (Moskva: Nauka, 1965), 1965, p. 104.

ancestral spirits. Should that happen, at best the rite will not be fruitful, at worst the Bɵ and other participants may be punished by diseases, adverse circumstances, accidents and misfortunes. It is of utmost importance, then, that this purification should be performed meticulously. Often Bɵ purify themselves at the end of a ritual or healing session, too, so as to cleanse any negativities they may have picked up from their patients.

> Bɵ Doogar Ochirov began to fall ill. We went to the *arshan* and I purified him, fumigating him with fragrant *arsa*. As I was doing so, I 'saw' a dim silhouette of a young woman go out of him. I described what she looked like and asked him about it. He said it was a woman he had just treated and he had begun to feel ill straight afterwards.
>
> *Tailgan* for Mahagal Darhan[58] near Kurumkan,
> Barguzin, 18.07.94[59]

Comparative study of purification rituals

Even by merely reading a presentation on purification rites in Bön and Bɵ Murgel it becomes obvious that we are dealing with analogous rituals stemming from the same understanding of what impurity is and the subsequent need for purification. In both traditions, while lustral sprinkling and fumigation can stand as rituals in their own right, sanctified water and smoke are also used as a means of preliminary purification for the participants, altar and offering substances at the beginning of any other ritual. In Bön, White *Tsen* is done first, followed by *Sang*. For this purpose, non-elaborate versions are used which are very much comparable to the forms used in Bɵ Murgel. In *Uhan Tarim* we find the same sequence of purification methods: water purification is followed by fumigation.

Medieval Mongols also followed the same order. In his *History of Mongols*, P. Carpini gives an account of how the impurity a close relative's death is purified: members of the clan had to pass between two fires while two Utgan were sprinkling sanctified water over them.[60]

---

[58] I.e. Mahakala blacksmith.

[59] A quote from my unpublished diary, *Tailgan Trip*.

[60] Plano Carpini, *Istoriya Mongolov* (St. Petersburg: A. S. Suvorina, 1911) [orig. Giovanni da Pian del Carpini, *Historia Mongalorum quos nos Tartaros appellamus* or 'History of the Mongols, which we call Tartars'], p.62. This loosely is reminds us of the pre-Zoroastrian Iranian rituals connected with Mithra where the accused had to prove their innocence by passing through fire unscathed. M. Boyce, *On Mithra, Lord of Fire*, Monumentum H. S. Nyberg I, *Acta Iranica* 4, pp. 70–72, 1975.

In modern Bɵ Murgel fumigation is the main method of preliminary purification.

Sang and Aryuud haha

These two rituals are strikingly similar in terms of their scope, the plants used and the philosophy necessitating them. While Bönpo *Sang* has an elaborate mythological base and structure, Buryatian *Aryuud haha,* at least nowadays, does not seem to be directly associated with mythology, is far less elaborate and has a free structure. In my opinion, all this points toward it being an older form of fumigation ritual, probably closer to any number of such rites practised within the auspices of the Prehistoric Bön of Eurasia. The version of *Sang* found in Yungdrung Bön's *Way of the Shen of the Visual World* is, then, a later adaptation of fumigation rituals similar to *Aryuud haha* found in the Prehistoric streams of Bön in Central Asia, Zhang Zhung and Tibet in the times before Tonpa Shenrab Miwo.

The direction of ritual movement

However, despite all their similarity, *Sang* and *Aryuud haha* have a point of difference, namely, the direction of ritual movement which brings purification. In the Bönpo version this direction is anticlockwise while in Bɵ Murgel it is clockwise. Presently, the clockwise direction in Bɵ Murgel rituals is tied to the daily movement of the sun from our earthly standpoint. However, there is a major inconsistency between this and one of the most important symbols of Bɵ Murgel, the swastika. The swastika of Bɵ Murgel turns in the same way as its Bön counterpart, namely, anticlockwise. Why should this be?

There are two plausible explanations:

i) The original direction of ritual movement in Bɵ Murgel may have been anticlockwise, hence the use of the swastika turning anticlockwise, but switched to clockwise due to external influences, such as interfacing with Buddhist sources, or due to some internal factors which made it more logical to relate the direction of ritual movement to the movement of the sun, while the ancient swastika symbol remained intact;

ii) The original direction of ritual movement may have been clockwise with the swastika turning anticlockwise a sign of Bön influence, most probably Yungdrung Bön, at some point in the past.

Be that as it may, the question of why the Bönpo swastika turns anticlockwise remains a mystery. There is plenty of archaeological evidence showing that since the far distant past this type of swastika was very common in Eurasia as a whole, and in the Baikal region and Mongolia in particular. We will look into what lies behind this important symbol in Chapter XV.

Tsentrü and Uhan Tarim

Here again a cross-examination of *Tsentrü* and *Uhan Tarim* (*Ugaalga*) lustral sprinkling rituals leaves no doubt that they are reflections of the same ritual custom. As with the fumigation rituals, the reasons for performing such purification and the ways it is done are very much comparable in both traditions. There is also a very close correspondence between the two subtypes of the rite as in both cases one uses animal blood while the other does not. Again, as is the case with the fumigation rituals, the Bönpo version has an elaborate mythological base while this is not found to the same extent in its Bө Murgel counterpart. The latter is also less complex. The 'white' versions in both traditions have a number of parallels in the ingredients of the consecrated mixture – water from nine sacred water sources and so on, although milk is not usually used in these Bө Murgel rites. Nevertheless, I have no doubt that both Red and White *Tsen* are transformed versions of the archaic rites of Prehistoric Bön which were widespread throughout Eurasia from very ancient times.

Sacred spittle

In Bө Murgel there is another purification method which uses vodka as a lustral agent. In these simple rituals, the Bө or Utgan invokes the Tengeri and spirits to assist him or her in the healing session and sprinkles to them with vodka from a bottle brought by the patient, asking them to transform the vodka into *arshan* (sacred water) with healing properties. The Bө or Utgan then sips a mouthful of vodka and, without swallowing it, spits it like a spray over the parts of the patient's body affected by disease or by the evil eye.

This is a very effective method of purification (and therefore of healing) but, of course, its effectiveness depends on Bө or Utgan's power. A few years back my wife broke out in a very strange rash: her belly button was full of tiny bright red spots which itched terribly. One spray of sanctified vodka, and the rash rapidly vanished. The fact that vodka is used here instead of a water-based mixture is of little importance because vodka, like water, is clear and is transformed into *arshan*, consecrated healing water, through the action of the gods. What is of particular significance here is the way in which the Bɵ applies the purifying liquid: he spits it. This strongly reminds us of the way in which Namchi Gungyal delivered the substances for *Sang* and *Tsentrü*: the Mother of Nectar spat a mouthful of ambrosia on earth. This striking similarity cannot be mere coincidence, but I have as yet been unable to trace any mythological explanation for this technique in Bɵ Murgel.[61]

Blood as a purifying agent

We have seen that both Bɵ Murgel and Bön have 'red' versions of the washing rites. However, there is one very significant difference: no animal is killed especially for Red *Tsen* while some versions of *Ugaalga* require animal sacrifice. Other than that we have two parallel versions of the same ritual custom which evolved from the same root.

This is supported by Ancient Greek mythology. In the myth of *Argonauts* we find a custom of purifying pollution resulting from the murder of a blood relative which exactly corresponds to the Red *Tsen* purification of Gekhöd except that here animal sacrifice is involved:

> Sorceress Kírkē [Κίρκη] purified Medea [Μήδεια] and Jason from the pollution of murder (of Medea's brother, Apsyrtus [Ἄψυρτος], in the temple). She made a sacrifice to Zeus,[62] who purifies pollution resulting from murder, and, pouring the sacrificial blood over the hands of Jason, she prayed to the Erinyes [Ερινύες], [63] asking them not to pursue him and not to unleash their terrible wrath. Kírkē purified Medea from the terrible evil deed, too. Through the brilliant glow in Medea's eyes Kírkē realized that she was from the clan of Helios[64] to which she herself belonged.[65]

Here the details of purification perfectly match the way Gekhöd was cleansed in the Yungdrung Bön version: blood is poured over the hands of the defiled in order to effect purification. Consequently, we can

---

[61] Spittle is used for healing in many traditions, for example, Jesus Christ's healing of the blind man, John 9: 6–7.

[62] Zeus is equivalent to Vedic Dyaus Pita, Sky Father, father of Agni and Indra. *Rigveda,* tr. Ralph T.H. Griffith, Book 4, Hymn XVII, st. 4.

[63] Erinies are terrifying female goddesses of retribution.

[64] Helios is a Sun-god and is equivalent to Vedic Surya.

[65] Compiled on the base of N. A. Kun, *Legendy i mify Drevnei Gretsii* (Kaliningrad: Kaliningradskoe knizhnoe isdatel'stvo/yantarnyi skaz, 2000), pp. 279–280.

conclude that ancient Greeks had the same knowledge about the cleansing properties of animal blood.

An analogous concept of the purifying properties of blood is found in the Judaeo-Christian tradition. A clear example is found in the instructions Moses received on how to consecrate priests.

> This is what you are to do to consecrate them, so that they may serve me as priest: Take a young bull and two rams without defects. [...] Take the other ram, and Aaron and his sons shall lay their hands on its head. Slaughter it, take some of its blood and put it on the lobes of the right ears or Aaron and his sons, on the thumbs of their right hands and on the big toes of their right feet. Then sprinkle blood against the altar on all sides. And take some of the blood on the altar and some of the anointing oil and sprinkle it on Aaron and his garments and on his sons and on their garments. Then he and his sons and their garments will be consecrated.[66]

This passage from the Hebrew Bible is uncannily reminiscent of *Ugaalga* purification rituals carried out during the initiation of a Bɵ or Utgan, when blood from a ritually slaughtered animal is also daubed on the initiates head, ears and eyes as well as being added to the water-based lustral solution which is sprinkled all over the body and ritual implements. Blood is also used to purify sins:

> If the anointed priest sins, bringing guilt on the people, he must bring to the Lord a young bull without defects as a sin offering for the sin he has committed. He is to present the bull at the entrance to the Tent of Meeting before the Lord. He is to lay his hand on its head and slaughter it before the Lord. Then the anointed priest shall take some of the bull's blood and carry it into the Tent of Meeting. He is to dip his finger into the blood and sprinkle some of it seven times before the Lord, in front of the curtain of the sanctuary. The priest shall then put some of the blood on the horns of the altar of fragrant incense which is before the Lord in the Tent of Meeting. The rest of the bull's blood he shall pour out at the base of the altar of burnt offering at the entrance to the Tent of Meeting.[67]

Further evidence of blood's nature as a potent cleansing agent is found in the New Testament, too. In one of John's visions, an elder informs him that the great multitude he sees before him from every nation, tribe,

---

[66] Exodus 29: 1; 19–21 from *The Holy Bible,* NIV.

[67] Ibid., Leviticus 4: 3–7.

people and language who are clad in white robes before the throne of the Lamb (i.e. Jesus Christ):

> ...are they who have come out of the great tribulation; they have washed their robes and made them white in the blood of the Lamb.[68]

This, then, must be exceedingly archaic knowledge which spawned a practice observed by very different ethnic and racial groups throughout Eurasia and beyond. Thanks to the enlightened intervention of Tonpa Shenrab, the use of animal sacrifice was abolished in the Red *Tsen* rites of Yungdrung Bön which can be seen as a further development of this practice pertaining to Prehistoric Bön. Red *Tsen* is a benign form of this important purification ritual. This comparison highlights the absence of animal sacrifices in Yungdrung Bön; indeed, Yungdrung Bön is a religion which was instrumental and successful in eliminating such customs among many nations and in many lands.

Intermediate link: purification technique from the Lurol[69] festival of Rebkong

The *Lurol* offering festival and the *lhapa* who lead it will be dealt with in more detail in subsequent chapters but here we will examine the particular purification technique used in *Lurol* to glean further insights into the stages purification rituals may have developed through from Prehistoric Bön to Yungdrung Bön.

Here is how this ritual, known as *Khamar*,[70] unfurls. At a certain stage of the *Lurol*, twelve young men are purified by the *lhapa* through a fumigation rite, at the end of which he ties a white silk *khatag* offering scarf to their hair. This signifies that the men have become as pure as gods. Then two stones, one white and one black, are heated in a bonfire. The white stone symbolizes the white sky-gods while the black one stands for the black sky-gods. Once scalding hot, the stones are put to a bucket containing a mixture of water, alcohol, radish leaves, and essential oil of *zarma*.[71] The twelve youths then steam the lower parts of their faces in the vapour rising from the bucket. The metal spikes with which their mouths are to be pierced are also purified through fumigation and then with this vapour. This ritual is believed to have the power to cleanse not

---

[68] Ibid., Revelation 7: 14. Lamb here refers to Jesus Christ.

[69] Tib. glu rol.

[70] Tib. kha dmar.

[71] Tib. zar ma, Lat. *Linum sativum*: a type of flax or linseed.

only of the participants' pollutions but also those of family members not present at the ritual.[72]

This ritual matches the Buryatian *Uhan Tarim* not only in what is done, but also in the order of purification sequence: fumigation appears before the water purification. Furthermore, hot stones are put into sanctified water in the same way as in *Uhan Tarim* and even their symbology is identical with Buryatian Bɵ Murgel's concept of White and Black Sky-dwelling Tengeri. There are minor differences regarding the substances added to the water and purifying steam is inhaled rather than sprinkled with the help of the bunch of twigs. These, however, are secondary details.

In addition to water purification, at the end of *Lurol* a body-piercing is performed which is in fact a substitute for earlier animal sacrifices and also has a direct parallel in Bɵ Murgel. When they need to purify some strong impurity (such as breaking their initiation vows, drinking excessive amounts of alcohol, having sexual intercourse with an unsuitable woman or on a day when it is taboo, or being polluted by impurities such as touching a pig) before an important offering ritual, some Bɵ pierce their body until some drops of blood come out. This method is considered to have very strong purifying properties and is used as a way of atonement for transgressions against sky-dwelling gods in Tibetan *Lhachö*[73] and Buryatian Bɵ Murgel traditions alike.

This purification technique from Rebkong is interesting in that it stands somewhere between Bɵ Murgel's *Uhan Tarim* and Yungdrung Bön's Red *Tsen* rites. While there is no actual animal sacrifice in the *Lurol*, at the end of the ritual blood is nevertheless spilt as a means of purification and offering to the gods.

One of the reasons why this purification technique from Rebkong and Buryatian *Uhan Tarim* correspond so closely might be gleaned from a glance at the history of this region. Rebkong is stretched along the Guchu River in Amdo. Before the eighth century AD it was under the dominion of proto-Mongol tribal empires of the Hunnu and Syanbi and later it was the territory of the tribal state Tuyuhun (Togon) of whom Azha were a part. In the beginning of the eighth century Rebkong became an arena for fierce fighting between the armies of the rapidly

---

72 Sadako Nagano, 'Sacrifice and Lhapa in the glu rol Festival of Rebs-kong', *Senri Ethnological Reports 15, New Horizons in Bon Studies*, edited by Samten G. Karmay, Yasuhiko Nagano, (National Museum of Ethnology, Osaka, 2001), pp. 567–649.

73 Tib. lha chos, 'ritual custom of the gods', the religion of *lhapa/lhamo*.

expanding Tibetan Empire and the Chinese Tang Empire but as the result of a peace treaty in 710 AD, it was awarded to Tibet. Tibetan military garrisons were built and the Tibetan population increased, mainly thanks to the military personnel and their families from central Tibet. The proto-Mongols were gradually assimilated. Later, Amdo was repeatedly invaded by various Hor peoples. Although Tibetans generally use the name Horpa to refer to Uighurs, in reality it is a general name for various Mongoloid nomadic tribes and loose confederations which constantly attacked Tibet over the course of several centuries. The name Hor is most probably derived from the ancient Mongol-Buryat tribe of Hor'/Hori/Horëodoi. We can see, then, that proto-Mongol and later Mongol-Buryat culture was continuously present in Rebkong from very ancient times.[74] At present Horpa constitute 11% percent and Azha (Tuyuhun) 0.17% of the population of Rebkong[75] but their culture and religion must have had a strong impact on the general culture of that area in the past. This may partly explain why this *Lhachö* purification technique in *Lurol* is so similar in its details to the Buryatian *Uhan Tarim.* However, it does not explain *Khamar's* direct correspondence with the *Tsen* rites of Causal Bön; Yungdrung Bön vastly predates these interactions and originated in a different geographical location. The most plausible conclusion is that all three rituals from the three traditions – Yungdrung Bön, *Lhachö* and Bɵ Murgel – developed from a common cultural and religious background in Prehistoric Bön.

Conclusion

From the above discussion it becomes clear that Bön and Bɵ Murgel share analogous concepts of purity and pollution on which their fumigation and lustral sprinkling rituals are based as well as the rituals themselves. As these withstand close scrutiny, they no doubt developed from the same original archaic matrix, a matrix which comes from the very ancient ritual traditions and culture of the Prehistoric Bön of Eurasia. In the case of these particular purification rites, this hypothesis is supported by the two parallel rites purifying the impurity of murder found in the ancient Greek myth of Argonauts and the Bönpo myth of Gekhöd, and also by the wider understanding of blood as a purifier found in Judaism and Christianity. In general, the ritual forms found in Bɵ Murgel are less elaborate than their

---

[74] Various points of intersection of the Zhang Zhung/Tibetan – proto-Mongol, Tyurkic and Mongol-Buryat cultures will be studied in ch. XV.

[75] According to Nagano, 'Sacrifice and Lhapa', pp. 567–649.

Bön counterparts, and a further significant difference is that some of the Bɵ Murgel purification rites require animal sacrifice. While this tallies with the ancient Greek and Jewish views, it is not compatible with those of Yungdrung Bön where animal sacrifice is never used. From this we understand that the Bɵ Murgel rites represent more archaic forms than those found in Yungdrung Bön and that the Yungdrung Bön purification rites represent transformed rituals based on traditions of Prehistoric Bön which are similar to those found in Bɵ Murgel.

A short study of the purification technique used by the *lhapa* of Rebkong further strengthens this argument and provides us with an example of the intermediate form which has elements of both prehistoric techniques represented here by the rites of Buryatian Bɵ Murgel and the transformed techniques of Yungdrung Bön.[76]

---

[76] This will be even more evident when we study this ritual from a different angle in the next chapter.

CHAPTER XII

Offering Rituals

Part I
Ritual Offerings in Buryatian Bө Murgel

The nine main cults of Bө Murgel

Before looking into the various aspects of ritual offerings in Bө Murgel we must first take a quick glance at its main cults. In some traditions of modern Bө Murgel, worship works its way up from bottom to top according to the belief that one has to reach the higher echelons by passing through the many levels of subordinate spirits and gods one after another in order to 'open the way' for the offerings to arrive at the highest level, Eternal Blue Sky; you can't just walk straight in and talk to the boss![1] Whether this was the case in ancient times is not clear as according

[1] It is clear from historical works that the cult of Eternal Blue Sky was the core cult in the religion of the ancient Mongols before and in the times of Chingis Khaan and that he himself had a direct relationship with the Sky. In 13th c. Bө Murgel underwent certain transformations due to the process of unifying the Mongolian tribes. Chingis Khaan spelt out set rules for almost every aspect of life and this also had a strong impact on religion. Life in Mongol society at that time was meticulously ordered by means of a precise and clever hierarchical system with many different levels of control and command which was unequalled in terms of efficiency. This could well have changed the order in which offerings were made in Bө Murgel, to reflect the ways in which society worked: one couldn't approach the *khaan* directly with a request or complaint, one had to go through the various subordinates first. In many religions, offerings are made from 'top to bottom' as this is a natural way of showing respect to the more holy and powerful beings first. That should have been the case with Bө Murgel, too, in pre-Chingis Khaan times. However, we cannot prove this point on the basis of written sources because no Mongol written sources are available predating Chingis Khaan. Oral traditions cannot clarify this point either as many were probably altered in 13th c. as a result of general reforms in all the aspects of life. If there had been any information which could have shed light on this peculiar order it

to other traditions, especially in western Buryatia, the gods and spirits are addressed from top to bottom. In either case, offerings are always made to Fire first. The main cults, from bottom to top, are:

1. The cult of Fire and Hearth as sources of happiness and life-energy, giving nourishment, off-spring, happiness, wealth and clairvoyance. This cult is associated with the *Ezhen* deities of fire Gal Zayaashi Sahyaadai Noyon together with his consort Sakhala Hatan,[2] and the *Ezhen* of the hearth, Gol Zayaashi. Even today the cult of the hearth is very strong among Buryats and is observed by Bɵ Murgel followers and Buddhists alike. Women regularly make offerings to the hearth and no-one would ever contemplate burning any sort of rubbish in the fireplace; fire is considered pure and sacred so putting dirty substances in it would contaminate and offend it, destroying the prosperity and luck of the offender.
2. The cult of the five spirits *Mongol Burkhan* or *Ail Ubged Hamgad.*[3] These are patrons of animal husbandry, hunting, childbirth, prosperity and a career in state institutions.
3. The cult of the Great Ancestral *Ongon*-spirits who are patrons and protectors of a given tribe, clan or family.
4. The cult of the *Ezhen*-Lords of the mountains, valleys, streams and lakes who must be propitiated in order to live happily in or pass without problems through an area under their control.
5. The cult of the *Zayaan*s who are the patrons of a clan, tribe or an area. *Zayaan* can be founders of certain Bɵ Murgel traditions, spirits of *noyons*, great knights, great Bɵ, all those who performed miracles, lived a heroic life or died a heroic death. They protect people and animals from dangers and evils as well as granting happiness and health.
6. The cult of the *Haats* (*Hahii*), the sons and grandsons of Tengeri who descended from the Sky to reside on the mountain tops. They became protectors of people and animals, transmitters

---

might have been destroyed during the persecutions Bɵ Murgel suffered at the hands of Buddhists, Christians and then Communists in the space of almost 300 years.

2 Bur. Сахяадай Ноён, Сахала хатан. Other names for Gal Zayaashi are Otgalakhaan (Bur. Отгалахаан) and Ut/Od (Bur. Ут; Од).

3 Bur. Монгол-Бурхан, Айл-Убгэд Хамгад.

of various crafts and skills such as hunting, fishing, animal husbandry and metal working.

7. The cult of Mother Earth, the goddess Etugen (or Ulgen). This is ever-present among all tribes, clans and social groups of the Buryatian nation. She is worshiped as the source of material wealth, well-being and happiness.
8. The cult of the Tengeri sky-gods who control the destiny of living beings and various natural phenomena, maintain order in the universe and have power over the spirits and beings in the Three Worlds. They are invoked to help in a great variety of tasks and magical actions. This cult is absolutely indispensable in the life of all the tribes and clans.
9. The cult of Eternal Blue Sky. This can be called the central pillar of Bɵ Murgel because Huhe Münhe Tengeri is the most potent spiritual power, the source of everything, the eternal source of vital energy who gives beings their soul and life. He holds sway over all beings in the universe; everything happens because he wills it.

Alongside these nine main cults there is one other important cult which must be mentioned here as, although technically within the main structure, it nevertheless stands in its own right. It is the Cult of the Elements.[4] The elements are the divinities' living space and as such are sacred. As we have already seen, one of these elements, fire, is given a special place of its own. Fire is the great purifier, used before any ritual to cleanse ritual objects and participants. It purifies bad intentions and destroys curses. The energy of fire is also the main vehicle for contact with the gods and spirits so during *tailgans* alcohol and other offering substances are sprinkled over a bonfire[5] which delivers the offerings to them. Life in Buryatian society is permeated by the cult of the elements which finds expression in respect towards them as well as in various taboos such as not burning rubbish, not polluting streams and lakes, not cutting trees around holy places or in woods dedicated to a deity, not digging earth near holy shrines and not littering the land. Although during the period of Communist control these principles were undermined

---

4 Depending on the tradition there are either four elements: earth, fire, water and wind, or five: earth, fire, water, wood and metal. The five elements scheme corresponds to the ancient Bönpo astrological system.

5 Note that it is forbidden to sprinkle milk directly into fire because it causes a smell which disturbs gods and spirits.

among some parts of the population, they are now coming back via the educational work done by the Bɵ and Utgan at mass ritual gatherings, through private advice and through the media. The importance given to the Cult of the Elements can be understood from the fact that, in the past, polluting them was punishable by death.

Offering rituals in Buryatian Bɵ Murgel

Buryatian Bɵ Murgel has a rich variety of offering rituals which can be performed for different purposes and addressed to different groups of gods and spirits. Some rituals are compulsory while others are optional; some are regular, connected with the yearly lunar or solar cycles, while others can be done as and when needed. However, they can all be subdivided into collective or public rituals, and personal ones performed for a family or an individual.

Individual and family rituals

There are a great number of prayers and rituals for the family or an individual. They are performed for various purposes such as:

1. Requesting protection;
2. Thanksgiving;[6]
3. Asking permission for certain activities;
4. Healing and prevention of illness;
5. Requesting help in crafts, house work, business etc.;
6. Birth, marriage and death rituals.

Prayers and rituals for these purposes are done when needed. Rituals which are done regularly according to the seasons include:

1. Worship of the five *Mongol Burkhan* who protect each Mongol-Buryat family. They are asked to increase well-being, protect domestic animals, ensure continuation of the family line and wealth, and help in men's activities such as administrative tasks, military service and good luck in general;
2. Worship of ancestors;
3. Worship of water-spirits;
4. Worship of the spirits of the *taiga*;

---

6 Not the American one! These rituals are basically a form of saying thank you when petitions have been fulfilled.

5. Consecration of the hearth. In the past this was done twice a year, in autumn and winter, when the nomadic families moved with the seasons.

Each clan has its own rules and then each individual Bө and Utgan has their own, so the variety of personal ritual obligations is extensive.

Collective and public offering rituals

Collective rituals are called *tailgan*, *tahilgan*[7] and *sasali*[8] and are addressed to the Tengeri, *Haats* and *Ezhen*-Lords or Owners to request good luck in the new season or year, prosperity and happiness for families, good harvest, abundant herds and wild game. The gods are also asked to send away bad luck and ill omens, remove unhappiness and so on. These collective prayer festivals are held at clan, village or district level, with each clan or district having its own special forms of *tailgan* performed regularly according to local custom. They are held throughout spring and summer through to the end of autumn, but the severity of the Siberian winter prohibits holding large outdoor public ceremonies in later months.

However, even in the winter the *Ublei Tailgan*,[9] Winter *Tailgan* is performed in some places. Much less elaborate, it is dedicated primarily to the worship of ancestral spirits, *Noyon* spirit-governors and patron Bө-smiths. Some *tailgans* are very elaborate and draw large crowds of people while others have a more local character.

Among the most popular *tailgans* is the Big Summer *Tailgan*, *Ehe Tailgan*,[10] in July which is accompanied by public festivities and sports such as archery, horseracing and wrestling. Other popular *tailgans* include: *Habarai Tailgan*[11] in April dedicated to clipping horses' manes and tails; *Haan Hahii Tengeriin Tailgan*[12] in September dedicated to the Tengeri sky-gods and the Thirteen Northern Kings; *Zerlig Tailgan*[13] in October dedicated to the five *Hangai*[14]-Owners of the *taiga*; *Uhan Hahii*

---

7 Bur. тахилган is a kind of *tailgan*.

8 Bur. сасали.

9 Bur. Үблэй тайлган.

10 Bur. Эхэ тайлган or Тахил тайлган.

11 Bur. Хабарай тайлган.

12 Bur. Хаан Хаһии тенгериин тайлган.

13 Bur. Зерлиг тайлган.

14 Bur. Хангай.

Tahil[15] dedicated to the water-spirits and owners of the underwater rocks, and *Oboo Tahil Tailgan*[16] dedicated to the local *Buural*[17] Owner-spirits. The list can go on and on. There are also many more private *tailgans* to family and clan deities or to local gods, such as *Darhan Tahil*[18] which is celebrated by clans holding the *utkha* of smiths. Some *tailgans* are led by the local elders together with invited Bө or Utgan while others can only be performed by the Bө or Utgan themselves.

Sasali prayer festivals are often performed on the occasion of some important undertaking such as starting a new business or going on a long journey, hunt or fishing trip. They can also be held before political events or because of some bad happenings. Although *sasali* is a ritual in its own right, it also forms part of a *tailgan* and is done at the beginning as a preparation for the main part. The main difference between *tailgan*/*tahilgan* and *sasali* is that the latter is a collective prayer festival without blood sacrifice and consists of sprinkling offerings of tea, milk and alcohol. *Tailgans*, on the other hand, always include an animal sacrifice of some kind.

Animal sacrifices

It is important to understand that animal sacrifices are not an indispensable part of each and every ritual and are offered to a limited number of gods on particular occasions only. Only five out of the Fifty-Five White Tengeri and four out of the Forty-Four Black Tengeri accept animal sacrifices.

Blood sacrifices can take many forms depending on the way the animal is sacrificed, in which direction it is turned, on which platform or support it is laid, which animal is used, how many and of what colour, which parts are offered and so on. All these details are kept in the memory of the Bө and Utgan and are very important because if an offering is not performed in the right way and with the right content, the gods to whom the offering is addressed may be angered and punish the giver and his or her people. There is also the so-called 'bloodless' animal sacrifice, *seter*. Basically, this involves suffocating the animal which is then offered to the five White Tengeri, patrons of crafts, while the four Black Tengeri are offered true blood sacrifices.[19]

---

15 Bur. Υhан хаhии тахил.

16 Bur. Обоо тахил тайлган.

17 Bur. Буурал.

18 Bur. Дархан тахил.

19 For a more detailed discussion on blood sacrifices, see below, Part III.

Tailgan

General structure and stages of tailgan

1. Preparation stage:

a) Purification of the Bө, Utgan and other participants. This is done by fumigation and is carried out at a location other than the sacred site;
b) Travelling to the site in a special order;
c) Ritual circumambulation of the site (in some locations);
d) Preliminary sprinkling and some preliminary offerings to ask permission to go ahead with the ritual and proclaim the reason for calling the gods and spirits. The *To'oerih*[20] divination method is often used here and involves throwing a drinking bowl in a special way to determine whether the ritual will be accepted or not;
e) Slaughtering an animal. Sometimes this is done nearby and not at the site itself.

2. Main stage:

a) Purification of the offerings by means of fumigation;
b) The offering itself;
c) Verifying the gods have accepted the offering by throwing *To'oerih*;
d) Ritual exchange of drinks amongst the participants;
e) Feasting;
f) Burning the skin and bones with special gifts to the *Ezhen*-owners;
g) Concluding offerings and prayers.

3. Final stage:

a) Clearing the site;
b) Departing from the site in reverse order.

This is a very general structure based on the *tailgans* I observed. As there are many different types of *tailgans*, they naturally differ in some aspects.

---

20 Bur. Тооэрих. See below.

Eye-witness accounts

In 1994 I travelled in the Barguzin area of Buryatia with a group of Bɵ and Utgan and participated in several *tailgans* they led. Here are some excerpts from my diaries to illustrate the presentation above:

> After a short banquet, we began preparing for the *tailgan*. All the men had to be equipped with a hat and a belt. Before leaving the house, everyone inhaled smoke from some Siberian fir bark and then fumigated their feet by stepping through the smoke from some dried goat's dung (*kizyak*),[21] 'god's grass' and *arsa* which was smouldering on a plate on the doorstep. Then we left, remembering who came behind whom, as we should return from the ritual site in reverse order. We got into the cars and set off. Only men drove to that spot, which turned out to be very powerful. There were nine *Ezhen*-Lords of that place.
>
> First of all the Bɵ circumambulated the spot which was situated in a field not far from the mountain slope and constituted a small hill of boulders where pines grew. During Soviet times people had prayed with their backs to the mountains so that the rocks shut them off from the village, but as we circumambulated sun-wise, we saw that this had been wrong and so we carried out the *tailgan* with our faces turned towards the mountains and our backs to the village. As we walked round, we touched the outermost pine tree with our right hands. Doogar Ochirov, Bɵ from Kurumkan,[22] went in front. He was followed by some local men, then came Sodnom Gomboev, Bɵ from the Aginskaya Steppe, then two more men, and behind them, myself. In front of us was a huge mountain range with snow-covered peaks, and I 'saw' the Lord-Owner (*Ezhen*)[23] of those places (for the second time; the first time had been as we drove past in the bus). He looked like a huge 'grandfather'[24] (sage) rising above the mountains with a long white beard, wearing a multicoloured *del*, a traditional Buryatian gown. The main colour was light blue. His arms were outspread and in one hand he held a long staff.
>
> After circumambulating, we remained in the appropriate place and performed *serzhim*, after which we went back to where the rest of the group was waiting. They had already killed and were boiling a ram.

---

21 Rus. кизяк, borrowed from Tyurkic languages.

22 Rus. Курумкан.

23 Rus. хозяин, khozyain.

24 Bur. дайдын үбгэд (Daidyn Ubged); Rus. дедушки (dedushki) Both 'grandfathers' and 'grandmothers' (Bur. Төөдэйнүүд/To'odaynuud, Rus. Бабушки/babushki) are the spirits who control the area or a particular place. They are the spirits of deceased Bɵ and Utgan who took their residence in the environment.

Fig. 1. Kurumkan village in Barguzin near which this tailgan *was held.*

Fig. 2. Bө circumambulate the sacred place before the beginning of the tailgan.

While it was boiling, many people came and asked me questions. [...] Later the whole group went over to the sacred spot. We made a circumambulation and then the parts of the ram were spread out in a special way, first the head and then all the other parts of the body as if the animal were lying on the ground. The skin was laid out next to it and also some sweets, biscuits, butter etc. Then we performed a purification rite with tea, milk and vodka and prepared for the ritual. Doogar Ochirov stood at the head and led. He sprinkled with milk. Behind him stood people from different clans, also with milk, and behind them, people with *tarasoon* milk vodka. Behind them came people with ordinary vodka, and finally, people with tea. Everyone held a saucer or small dish in their right hand and the bottle in their left. Someone scattered *salamat*[25] (double sour cream mixed with butter and flour). Cigarettes were also among the offerings and these were snapped and put on the altar alongside biscuits and coins. The coins were placed with the eagle uppermost. Cigarettes were offered because it is considered that some of the local 'grandmothers' and 'grandfathers' smoke. [...]

Fig. 3. Beginning of the tailgan: *communal* serzhim.

Then the ritual began. Doogar Ochirov pronounced the invocation and requests and once he had sprinkled, the others did, too, calling, 'So'ok! So'ok! So'ok!'[26] Once the general requests had been made, the

[25] Bur. саламат.

[26] The exclamation 'So'ok!' (spelt Bur. сөөк) is most commonly used to call the gods and spirits to the offering in the Bɵ Murgel rituals. In my opinion this exclamation is related to Tibetan exclamation 'So!' (spelt Tib. bswo) which is used for exactly the same purpose. At the beginning of the Bönpo invocations the calling 'So!' is often repeated twice or thrice just as in Bɵ Murgel. In Yungdrung Bön 'So!' symbolizes the Body, Speech and Mind of

moment came for each person to sprinkle and pray for the solution of his personal problems, for his relatives etc. Then, on Doogar Ochirov's command, everyone threw their saucer in front of them. If the saucer landed the right way up, that meant that the request had been heard and everything would be successful. If someone's saucer landed upside down, they again made their request together with the Bө, and so on until each saucer had landed correctly.[27] When each person's prayers had been accepted, drinks were exchanged in the following manner: two people approached one another and offered their milk or vodka in turn. First one offered his drink from his own saucer and the second drank, raising his hat, and then the other way round.

Before the ritual the weather had been very hot with virtually no clouds, but in answer to the invocations, during the ritual a gusty wind got up and clouds gathered. Immediately after the prayers had been said, a light rain fell, growing stronger and stronger until towards evening it became a downpour. This meant that the prayers had been accepted favourably.

After the ceremony of offering drinks to one another, we began to eat the ram. Meat is taken from different parts of the animal, but everyone should take some from the right shoulder.[28] All this time, some people were sprinkling into the bonfire. Once all the meat had been eaten, all the bones were put in the fire and the skin placed on top. Nearby was another small bonfire where the intestines, bladder and other inedible organs were burnt. While the ram was burning, Doogar Ochirov recited words requesting that the offering be accepted. Afterwards people drank the rest of the vodka etc., collected their empty bottles and burnt all rubbish which could be burnt. The rest we took back with us and went to the cars in reverse order, so that the person who had been first was now last. The same applied to the cars. We returned to Kurumkan and after a short banquet drove on to Ulyunhen.[29] Ulyunhen used to be a Tungus-Evenki region, but now mainly Buryats live there. Under a thin layer of topsoil, the earth is permanently frozen.

On the evening of the same day, we arrived in Ulyunhen. There was such a heavy downpour that the road had been washed away and water had

---

all the Buddhas but if it had been used in Prehistoric Bön it could have had another meaning, now lost. So Buryatian 'So'ok!' might be either an archaic form of 'So!' with a slightly different pronunciation or it might have came into Bө Murgel as the result of contact with Yungdrung Bön at some point in the past. We will look into possible temporal crossroads when Bө Murgel could have interfaced with Yungrung Bön in ch. XV.

27 This is *To'oerih* mentioned above.

28 Note that the right shoulder blade of a sheep or a ram is also used for divination among Mongols and Tibetans, especially in Amdo.

29 Rus. Улюнхэн.

> appeared in the parched river beds. Just before we arrived at Ulyunhen itself, the mayor and several old men came to meet us. People were very happy because it was raining for the first time in several weeks. Everyone was feeling joyful and elated.
>
> Kurumkan – Ulyunhen, Barguzin, 12.06.94.

In this instance, the onset of rain after a drought was a sign that the *tailgan* had been completed successfully. There can be many other signs, often connected with birds or animals, indicating that the gods have accepted the offerings, and they may manifest simultaneously in several places a great distance from each other:

> While I was wandering outside, beyond the house gates, I had been watching two strange birds soaring one behind the other, circling a tree. The driver who had taken us to Shiizgha the day before came over to me and I asked him what birds they were. They were really unusual, a little like magpies but with pinky-red bodies and beige feathers on their wing tips and tail. But their size and cries were like those of a magpie. The driver was very surprised, saying it was the first time he'd seen such birds, although he had lived all his life in those parts. Soon there were more birds and they circled round the house in a small flock for a while before flying away.
>
> On the same day in London, my wife Carol was woken up in the morning by a bird flying around inside the room. It was an unusual bird with the same pinky-red and beige colourings as the ones we'd seen here in Barguzin, though smaller than a magpie. She was very surprised to find this bird inside as the window was only open a crack. It flew around the room a few times and then flew back out through the same tiny crack.
>
> Kurumkan, the morning after the *tailgan* near Shamanka and ritual in Shiizgha, 16.07.94.

On another occasion, both Bө and Utgan participated in the *tailgan* and the content of the offerings was somewhat different:

> At ten o'clock, the rest of our group arrived. We fumigated ourselves in the mayor's house and took a young silver birch tree with us for the ritual. A long convoy of cars set off from the village to the place for the *tailgan*.
>
> We made a stop at one sacred spot along the way and then drove on to the site of the main ritual. It was very picturesque, with fields on one side and a gentle wooded slope on the other. Mountains surrounded us on all sides. At this site we performed the 'ritual of the shirt and shawl'. The ritual goes as follows:

Sometime before the ritual, a Bɵ or Utgan has a dream or hears a voice telling him or her what colour the shirt and shawl should be. Alternatively, the colour may be known already from many years' practice. In this case, Vera Naguslayeva had a dream and was shown a white shawl with green embroidery. So three of us (Doogar Ochirov, Nadezhda Stepanova and myself) went into the wood where my two companions found two trees associated with the male and female gods governing that place. Doogar Ochirov put the shirt against one tree trunk, bowed his head to it and prayed. Then he took a step back, and the shirt remained in place against the tree, signifying that the gift had been accepted. Then we placed coins there, too. Nadezhda Stepanova took the shawl and placed it against the trunk of the 'female' tree and it, too, was accepted. We returned to the main group where preparations were being made for the ritual. [...]

This time, both men and women took part in the ritual. The men stood in the front row holding saucers and bottles while the women half knelt, half sat behind them, leaning on one knee with their hands folded in prayer. The Utgan stood with the men, flanking them on the right. They sprinkled milk and *salamat*. Nadezhda Stepanova stood to the left in front of everyone with her *hese*-drum. Behind her came Doogar Ochirov, and then everyone else. From the side the scene looked very much like warriors ready for battle.

The ritual began. Immediately after the sprinkling, an eagle again appeared and made a low loop in the sky. It passed directly overhead a few times, then a strong wind got up and a few drops of rain fell. People

Fig. 4. Bɵ D.D. Doogarov and Utgan N.A. Stepanova instruct villagers before commencing the tailgan.

> cried out and looked to the sky; it was a very auspicious sign. Everyone was glad, exchanging drinks and wishes of success and happiness.
> When all the meat had been eaten, two bonfires were lit and the bones of the ram and the sheep were burnt separately. The skins were laid on top. Everyone gathered round. First, Doogar Ochirov, holding the light blue shirt, said that the local gods had accepted it and, with words of prayer, laid it on the fire where the ram's bones were burning. Next, Nadezhda Stepanova showed the shawl and, with words of prayer, placed it on the fire where the sheep's bones were burning. With that, the ritual was over.'
>
> In *taiga* near the village of Ulyunhen, Barguzin,13.06.94.

Here is another passage which illustrates some other types of offerings. This is from the *tailgan* near the village Shamanka:

> One of the old men brought a white shawl embroidered with a rabbit and a squirrel. It was an offering to the Lord of the Taiga with the request that there might be more animals in the forests.
> Doogar Ochirov, his uncle and myself went again to the tree where we had performed the ritual with the shirt to Dede Baabai and offered a pouch with tobacco and a pipe which we hung on a branch after a short and sincere prayer.
>
> Near Shamanka, Barguzin, 14.06.94.

These excerpts illustrate once again the importance of fire in the *tailgan*[30] and show how it is used in the two ways mentioned above: firstly, as a purifier and secondly as a vehicle to deliver the offerings to the gods.

Mixed Bө Murgel-Buddhist tailgans

After Buddhism was introduced to Buryatia in the seventeenth century, Bө Murgel and Buddhism mingled and merged to some extent in some areas, especially in east Buryatia. The deities and concepts of both religions became strangely superimposed on one another in a peculiar amalgamation, and a type of mixed Lama-Bө priests appeared. Here is an example of an invocation by a Lama-Bө uttered on Mount Shalsaana in the Hezhenge region in 1999 at the beginning of a mixed Bө-Buddhist ritual:

---

[30] Although a few special *tailgan* are performed without fire.

Fig. 5. Bө D.D. Doogarov shows the shirt to people before offering it into fire.

Fig. 6. Utgan N.A. Stepanova offering the shawl into fire.

Fig. 7. People relaxing at the end of tailgan.

Fig. 8. Tailgan *at Shamanka.*

'Limitless space, All-embracing *Shunyata*[31]
The Sphere of Wisdom, Eternal Blue Sky – Huhe Münhe Tengeri,
Primordially pure and self-liberated,
Primordial Mind, my Father – A!'[32]

The author of this invocation identifies the Buddhist concept of *Shunyata* – Emptiness – with Eternal Blue Sky of Bɵ Murgel. It is, in fact, an artificial comparison made with the intention of creating a syncretic religious system by unifying two totally unrelated concepts. As we saw in Chapter IX, Eternal Blue Sky of Bɵ Murgel cannot be compared with the Emptiness concept of Sutra, Tantra or the Natural State of Dzogchen because one cannot realize Eternal Blue Sky as one's own state, as one's own Nature of Mind; one can only pray to Huhe Münhe Tengeri as the external divine generating principle for blessings and powers.

Below is a description of a mixed Bɵ-smith-Buddhist *tailgan* observed by Dorjo B. Doogarov in the village of Kul'kison[33] in July 1999 in which deities and ritual elements of both religions are mixed:[34]

The chief deity propitiated at this *tailgan* was Darhan Hara Mahagala Damzhan Garva Nagba,[35] Blacksmith Mahakala Oath-bound Protector Garwa Nagpo.[36] This compound entity is the peculiar overlay of three unrelated deities: Blacksmith Tengeri Hara Darhan of Bɵ Murgel; Mahakala,[37] one of the main Buddhist *Dharmapala* protectors of Indian origin; and Blacksmith Garwa Nagpo, another Buddhist protector said to

---

[31] Tib. stong pa nyid, is used to designate one of the major Buddhist concepts, namely the lack of inherent existence in any manifest phenomena.

[32] D. B. Doogarov, 'Sinkretizm Buddizma i Shamanizma v Buryatii na sovremennom etape/Nasledie Drevnikh i Traditsionnikh Kul'tur Severnoi i Tsentral'noi Azii,' *Materialy 40-i regiol'noi Studentcheskoi konferentsii, Tom II*. Novosibirsk, 1–6 February, 2000.

[33] Bur. Кулькисон.

[34] Ibid.

[35] Bur. Дархан Хара Махагала Дамжан Гарва Нагба.

[36] Tib. Dam can mGar ba Nag po.

[37] Mahakala – 'the great black one' – is one of the names of Shiva. Later this form of Shiva was absorbed into Tantric Buddhism where it was re-interpreted as an emanation of Avalokiteshvara (Tib. sPyan ras gzigs dBang phyug) or Chakrasamvara (Tib. 'Khor lo bDe mchog) and declared to be a Buddha-form. In Tibet Mahakala (Tib. Nag po Chen po, mGon po Nag po, mGon po phyag) became one of the main *Dharmapala*-protectors of all Schools of Tibetan Buddhism.

be an emanation of or one of the gods in the retinue of another Buddhist oath-bound protector Dorje Legpa. This syncretic 'New Age' Tengeri is worshipped on the ninth, nineteenth and twenty-ninth days of the lunar calendar, the special days of *darhan*-smiths. Once a year this amalgamated deity is offered a large *tailgan* in which Gelugpa lamas participate. For these occasions a *thangka* of Damzhan Garva Nagba is brought into the smithy and offerings are placed in front of it. The offerings consist of offerings nine lamps, a special smoke offering from a mix of larch needles, Siberian fir bark, *arsa*, powder of the dried blood of a billy goat, black sulphur 'nagbo zhugzhur',[38] milk products and meat, and a *torma*. Throughout the ritual, the fire in the forge is kept burning. Outside the smithy an offering table is prepared with a black ram or a billy goat's head and breast, three nine-tiered pastries, milk dishes, tea, milk, *arkhi*-vodka and silver coins. In front of the table three one and a half to two meter tall silver birch branches are stuck into the earth as *serge*-supports for the deity.

At the beginning of the *tailgan* Dorje Legpa is invoked and evil forces are expelled according to the structure of the rituals of Buddhist Tantra. Then *serzhim* made of vodka mixed with tea and coloured by a powdery mix of saffron, dried goat's blood and spices is offered together with a *torma*.

While chanting Dorje Legpa's mantra, a lama and a *darhan*-smith sprinkle *arkhi* into the smithy fire and offer it to the anvil and smith's tools. After this, invocations according to Bө Murgel are made to Damzhan, to the patron of the White Bө-smiths Darhan Sagaan Tengeri, to the patrons of the Black Bө-smiths: Daban Zholo Tengeri,[39] Haranhy Tengeri,[40] Hara Sohor Tengeri,[41] Burenhy Tengeri,[42] Buren Sohor Tengeri,[43] and to the smith-ancestors. A black ram or billy goat is sacrificed and then offered by burning it according to the *shere'e* method. This

---

38 Bur. нагбо жугжур.

39 Bur. Дабан Жоло (Холо) Тенгери. According to other sources this is actually the name of the heavenly smithy of the blacksmith god Bahar-Hara Khaan (Noyon) who is presently the Lord of Lake Baikal.

40 Bur. Харанхы Тэнгэри.

41 Bur. Хара Соохор Тэнгэри.

42 Bur. Буренхы Тэнгэри.

43 Bur. Бурен Сохоор Тэнгэри.

> technique involves constructing a nine-levelled support from crisscrossing logs to resemble an altar. The offerings are laid out on top, and then the whole construction is set alight. *Arkhi* and sets of male clothes are also offered and burnt. After this, the *Dalalga*[44] ritual for calling happiness is performed. Then a smith takes an iron rod, heats it up in the forge until it becomes red-hot and puts it on the anvil. At this point the Bө, lama and then all the men who participated in the *tailgan* hammer it into pieces. This symbolizes the destruction of all negativities and is the concluding stage of the *tailgan*.

This mixed *tailgan* represents a crude fusion of the elements of the Buddhist cult of *Dharmapala*-protectors and the Bө Murgel cult of the Darhan Tengeri, patrons of Bө-smiths, and presents a clear example of dual-faith in eastern Buryatia. While it helps maintain community cohesion, this ritual contains contradictions to the core beliefs and practices of both religions: animal sacrifices are against the Buddhist doctrine while propitiating Buddhist gods before the Tengeri and inviting a lama to lead the ceremony is against Bө Murgel principles. This mixed *tailgan* is also a living illustration clearly revealing the analogous processes which must have gone on in Tibet and Zhang Zhung when Yungdrung Bön was introduced to the practitioners of Prehistoric Bön there. As we noted in Chapter III, one outcome of the arrival of this new religion was the appearance of mixed Bön traditions in some areas, some of which survive to this day among the Himalayan tribes of Nepal and the Nakhi of Yunnan. The *tailgan* described above is directly comparable with these as it, too, represents a mixed tradition. If we imagine for a moment that some other religion arrived in eastern Buryatia and its priests, who knew nothing of Buddhism nor Bө Murgel, came to witness this *tailgan* in Kul'kison village, what sort of conclusion would they arrive at regarding Buddhism? They would conclude that the practice of animal sacrifices forms an integral part of Buddhist tradition! This exactly mirrors the situation in Tibet in the seventh and eighth centuries AD; Buddhists observed Mixed Bön traditions and on that basis made specious accusations that animal sacrifices form an integral part of Yungdrung Bön.[45]

---

[44] Bur. далалга, ritual to call happiness. See next chapter.

[45] See ch. III.

Part II
Lurol Festival in Rebkong

Introduction to Rebkong public offering rituals of the lhapa[46]

In the previous chapter we looked into the *Khamar* purification technique used by the *lhapa* of Rebkong, Amdo, in their *Lurol* festival and came to the conclusion that it represents a development stage somewhere in between the methods of Bɵ Murgel and Yungdrung Bön. It is logical, then, to look at this ritual in greater detail here and to compare it with the *tailgans* of Buryatian Bɵ Murgel before moving on to compare the offering rituals of Bɵ Murgel with those of Yungdrung Bön.

In Rebkong, the *lhapa* celebrate their two main offering festivals around the summer and winter solstices according to the *Hortsi*[47] solar calendar. The winter New Year offering rituals are much smaller, attended only by the *lhapa*, local elders and assisting men who perform fumigation, offerings, invocations and praises to the gods. This is also an occasion when the *lhapa* go into trance. It is an important festival which can be compared with the Bɵ Murgel Winter Tailgan, *Ublei Tailgan.*

The summer solstice festival of *Lurol*, on the other hand, is a big event attended not only by the *lhapa* and elders but by the general population, too, including women and children who make up a crowd of spectators while young men and women actually take part in some of the ritual activities. Neither Bönpo nor Buddhist monks participate in the festival in any way. The festival spans ten days, from the fifteenth to the twenty-fifth days of the sixth solar month. Its timing and size make it quite comparable with the Buryats' Big Summer Tailgan, *Ehe Tailgan.*

The materials I have at my disposal do not allow me to gain a precise understanding of the detailed structure of *Lurol*, so I will concentrate in similarities of technique.

Meaning and purpose of Lurol

The etymology of the name *lurol* gives us a good idea about the purpose and function of the festival. Tib. *glu* (*ri glu*) means 'song for the mountain gods' while Tib. *rol* means 'playing musical instruments to

---

46 All information about the *Lurol* festival in this section is based on Nagano, Sacrifice and Lhapa.

47 Tib. hor rstis.

entertain' (Tib. *rtsed mo*). *Lurol*, then, is a festival for entertaining and pleasing the gods. This is supported by another interpretation of the name: 'the play between gods and men'. This suggests establishing positive communication between humans and deities. Another alternative meaning is Tib. *klu rol,* 'play with the *Lu*'. All these possible interpretations convey the idea of good relations and enjoyment among gods and men, so in its purpose *Lurol* is very much comparable to the Buryatian *tailgans* which, as we have seen, are big offering festivals aimed at restoring the harmony between humans and various classes of gods and spirits, including the *Lusuut* water-spirits.

The following quote from Sadako Nagano's 'Sacrifice and Lhapa in the Glu rol Festival of Reb-skong' summarizing the purpose of *Lurol* can equally be applied to Buryatian *tailgans*:

> The villagers believe that the powers, conceived as the source of health, life, fertility, wealth, come from [a] different world (the Other World) from their own. How then, can such power of the gods be available to the impotent villagers? Only when the powers of gods are introduced into the human world by providing a bridge, or channel of communication between this World and Other World, the villagers' wishes can come true. In this sense, the glu rol festival functions as a religious means to provide that bridge or communication channel. [...] Villagers believe […] that 'go ba'i lha[48] and the Eight Classes will usually display their positive attributes as long as humans continue to make offerings to them.[49]

The Myth of Origin and historical background of Lurөl of Sogri[50]

According to legend, the *Lurol* festival was initiated by the Tibetan military as a celebration of victory over the Chinese in 710 AD. On the first day they propitiated and entertained the gods;[51] on the second day they propitiated and entertained the *Lu*;[52] and on the third day they fêted the warriors.[53] So we can see that from the outset *Lurol* was an offering

48 I.e. Five deities of the Individual. They are said to be connected to each person from birth and also reside in various locations throughout the physical body. See discussion on *Drala,* ch. IX; ch XIII.

49 Ibid. pp. 589–590.

50 Tib. Sog ri.

51 Tib. lha rtsed.

52 Tib. klu rtsed.

53 Tib. dmag rtsed.

ritual addressed to beings of all of the Three Worlds: the Upper World, the Lower World and the Middle World, and was most certainly based on existing Bönpo rituals and concepts of the time.

Although *Lurol* and the *lhapa* who preside over it undoubtedly represent an offshoot of Prehistoric Bön, nowadays they are generally absorbed into the framework of Tibetan Buddhism. Currently *Lurol* is performed by the people of Sachyil[54] village connected to the Buddhist Rongwo[55] monastery. The monastery, founded in the tenth century AD originally belonged to the Sakyapa Tibetan Buddhist School but was converted into Gelugpa in the fifteenth century.

The Lurol festival and Buryatian tailgans

Preliminary stage

Preparations for *Lurol* start on the first day of the sixth solar month of the *Hortsi* calendar. On this day the people of Sachyil village climb the holy mountain Amye Gyakhyung[56] together with people from other villages and fix poles topped with an arrow or spears near the *latse*[57]on the summit.

Some *tailgans* have a similar preliminary stage when the Bɵ and village elders go to the place where the *tailgan* is to be held and perform preliminary purification and offerings. Sometimes, as was said in the section on *tailgan* above, this stage is performed at a location other than the actual site of *tailgan*, a holy place nearby to which ordinary people are not allowed before the Bɵ and elders have completed the preliminary rites.

The shrine and the gods

The sacred space for the festival is a courtyard resembling an open-air theatre. A simple *latse* support with a long post topped with arrows and spears is set up in the centre. There is a brazier for burning *sang* offerings on the lower level of the *latse*. The right side of the courtyard is reserved for female spectators who are not allowed into the inner shrine, which is a small temple housing the images of the guardian gods propitiated in this festival.

---

[54] Tib. Sa dkyil.

[55] Tib. Rong po dgon pa.

[56] Tib. A myes Bya Khyung.

[57] Tib. bla rtsas, a receptacle or support for the *la* of the local guardian god. For a detailed exploration of *la* and corresponding concepts see ch. XIII.

The main god worshipped in this festival is Amnye Machen Pomra,[58] the most important mountain god of Amdo and east Tibet in general, who resides in the eponymous mountain range. Originally a Bönpo protective deity, he is widely worshipped by Buddhists as well. He appears as a white warrior-king riding a horse and flanked by other gods. The god of Taglung[59] (who resides in the eponymous holy mountain) and a red war-god Dradul Wangchug[60] are to his right, while the *Yullha,* a red Lonpo[61]-Minister and Lonpo Shanpa Tsitung[62] (a dependant of Lonpo) are to his left. All the gods are male. *Lu* water-spirits are also among the deities propitiated in the course of the *Lurol* but their images are not present in the shrine; instead, they are worshipped near the stream. Other deities not represented in the shrine but honoured with offerings are the Upper White Gods,[63] the Upper Black Gods[64] and the Eight Classes: *Lha*, *Düd*, *Tsen*, *Mamo*, *Shinje*, *Sinpo, Lu* and *Dza.*

The altar for a Buryatian *tailgan* is usually far less elaborate. While Bө do not normally use pictures to represent their gods, the *ongon*-supports which serve as representations and receptacles for the spirits come in all shapes and sizes and can be made of a wide range of materials. Other important places of worship are reminiscent of *latse.* These are the *obo'o*-cairns which represent the World Mountain and are often topped with a pole or tree symbolizing the World Tree.

The types of gods propitiated at *tailgans* are very much comparable to the gods worshipped at *Lurol*. The main focus of worship in both *Lurol* and *tailgan* are the powerful protectors of the country and geographical features, known in Tibetan as *Yullha* and *Zhidag* and in Buryatian as *Haat*, *Ezhen* and *Burkhan*. These powerful spiritual entities are the actual owners of the country or area so the people who live on the land must be on good terms with them if they wish to have a prosperous and happy life. Therefore, while other gods are propitiated as well, it is these Owners who are given primary importance on such occasions as they are closer to humans than the gods of, say, the Sky. Looking from this angle we can compare Machen Pomra with such deities of the Buryatian pantheon as

58 Tib. Am myes rMa chen sPom ra.
59 Tib. sTag lung.
60 Tib. dGra 'dul dBang phyug.
61 Tib. blon po.
62 Tib. bLon po Shan pa Tsi tung.
63 Tib. dkar phyogs pa'i lha.
64 Tib. nag phyogs pa'i lha.

Shargai Noyon Baabai and Bukha Noyon Baabai,[65] not so much in terms of appearance or genealogy but in their status and function.[66] In both traditions, these Owners reside on a particular mountain or mountain range but are worshipped far beyond their residence as protectors of the whole country and all the tribes living there.

Other gods honoured at *Lurol* also seem identical to those worshipped in Bө Murgel. The Upper White Gods and the Upper Black Gods are certainly equivalent to the White and Black Tengeri, while the *Lu* correspond to *Lusuut* water-spirits. Indeed, although not classified as such, the various beings of the Eight Classes are also known to Bө and Utgan;[67] verifying these correlations is a research topic it itself so we cannot go into more detail here.

Lhachukha[68] *rite*

As was said above the festival begins on the fifteenth day of the sixth solar month and goes on until the twenty-fifth day of the same month. At the beginning of the celebrations gods are invited to descend from the dimension of the Sky to the offering altar. They are shown the way by streams of smoke rising up from the *sang* fumigation. Then *karsang*,[69] a mixture of *sang* and roasted barley flour, is offered. The offering rituals and celebrations then continue for several days.

The central event of *Lurol*, however, is the *Lhachuka* bathing ritual. It is performed around 6 pm on the twentieth day. The *lhapa* carry sacred *thangkas* depicting the gods from the shrine to the nearby stream which flows to Guchu, Rebkong's main river. The *thangkas* are transported in special sacred palanquins to which willow branches are attached. Willow is considered a female tree[70] and is also associated with the *Lu* so these branches seem to act as both decorations and offerings for the *Lu*.[71] Once

---

65 See ch. IV.

66 According Yongdzin Lopön Tenzin Namdak, in Yungdrung Bön texts Machen Pomra is often said to be an emanation of Shenlha Ökar. (Oral communication, Shenten Dargye Ling, September 2007.) In this case he is comparable to Buryatian *Haats* only in function and basic external characteristics as, though he appears as a worldy god, his origin goes back to the *Sambhogakaya* Buddha-form.

67 For a short comparison see ch. V.

68 Tib. lha chu kha.

69 Tib. dkar bsangs.

70 Tib. mo shing.

71 The offerings to the *Lu* are compared below in Part III of this chapter.

at the stream, the *lhapa* first perform a white *karsang* smoke offering to the *Lu*, then bathe the palanquins and themselves. Subsequently anyone with eye or skin problems bathes to heal themselves from these diseases, considered as punishments sent by the *Lu* in retaliation for transgressions against them. This first part of the *Lhachuka* ritual is basically a ceremony of purification through fumigation and ablution.

Afterwards, the palanquins bearing the supports of the gods are carried into the village and brought to all the houses. The people of each household tie white *khatag* scarves onto them and offer money, food and alcohol. In each house the *lhapa* perform divination to establish the next year's fortune. If the outcome is negative, the householders make more and greater offerings and the divination is repeated until a favourable result is obtained. Each time more and more money and alcohol are offered until the gods are satisfied and the divination is auspicious.

This part of the *Lhachuka* consisting of offerings to the divine images and divination for each household is very much comparable to what happens at a *tailgan*. From my eye-witness accounts of *tailgans* given above, we see that the general offering rite is often followed by personal offerings or prayers when each participant offers alcohol, money etc. to the gods and prays for their relatives. After this session of individual prayer comes *To'oerih* divination. Just as in the *Lhachukha* rite in Rebkong, if the omen portends misfortune then the offering or prayer is repeated as many times as necessary with the aid of the Bɵ until a positive divination is obtained. The only difference between the Bɵ Murgel rite and that of the *Lurol* is that in *Lhachukha* the *lhapa* come into each household while in Buryatia the same ritual activity is carried out at the *tailgan* site not in the village.

Conclusion of the festival

At the conclusion of the festival a village elder reads out praises to the gods and implores them to show mercy to the villagers. A dance of gratitude is then performed. A senior *lhapa*, after using a black horn for divination, enters a trance which culminates in a dance during which predictions are uttered.[72]

Young lads carry the palanquins to a bonfire at a crossroads, jump over it and then bear the sacred litters to the shrine where the images of the gods remain until the next occasion.

---

[72] Tib. lha rtsed pa.

Willow sticks with *luta*[73] flags are thrown into the bonfire. Then a red brush made of yak wool is shaken over the men's heads to dispel negative energies. Everyone then sprinkles *chang* upwards and shouts, 'Lha Gyal!', 'May the gods win!' Finally, the *lhapa* distribute the remaining fruit and meat to the men, thus bringing the festival to a conclusion.

This stage of *Lurol* is also analogous with the concluding phase of a Buryatian *tailgan*. As in *Lurol,* praises to the gods are uttered at the end of *tailgan* by either the Bө, Utgan or by the village elder. Moreover, the manner in which alcohol is sprinkled to the gods is the same, as is the distribution of food among all the participants at the end. Some large Buryatian *tailgans* may be rounded off with sporting competitions such as horse racing, archery contests and wrestling competitions.

Offerings

The *Lurol* festival is rich in different offerings and offering techniques, each appropriate for different gods and situations. However, a general distinction can be drawn between White Offerings[74] and Red Offerings.[75]

White Offerings consist of *tsampa*[76] roasted barley flour, flowers, fruits, yoghurt, and a 'cold liquid offering' of water. These items are mainly presented to the Upper White Gods, Machen Pomra and the *Lu.* Red Offerings consist of meat, raw heart and 'hot liquid offerings' such as *chang* (barley-wine) and other types of alcohol. These items are presented to the Upper Black Gods. When these offerings are burnt together with *sang* they are called *karsang*, White *Sang,* and *marsang*, Red *Sang,* respectively.

Both white and red *tormas* are also offered which, generally speaking, belong to the White and Red Offerings although there is also a special *torma* of the Eight Classes.[77] The *tormas* are arranged on the upper row of the altar near the images of the gods until the red *torma* is burnt during the *Khamar* ritual on the last day of the festival. In the past the red *torma* was coloured using animal blood but nowadays that has been replaced by red dye. However, as we saw in the previous chapter, one of the elements of *Khamar* is an offering of blood through ritual wounding and a similar

[73] Tib. klu rta, lit. *Lu*-horse, small flags or paper squares depicting the *Lu.*

[74] Tib. dkar mchod.

[75] Tib. dmar mchod.

[76] Tib. rtsam pa.

[77] Tib. sde brgyad kyi gtor ma.

ritual, called *Gyabla khamar tabpa*,[78] is performed on the last day of the festival. In the course of this second rite, the skin on the men's backs is pierced with metal spikes which are then shaken off. If a spike comes out with a little blood it portends good fortune in the future. This offering is also used to purify pollution caused by the death of a relative.

There is another, more extreme, blood offering.[79] If someone has serious problems or wishes to be assured of good luck and good health in the coming year, they may ask an experienced elder to make a cut with a knife on their head while they themselves offer a white *khatag*. Blood streams over the offerer's face as they receive blessings from the senior *lhapa.* The offerer then scatters white yoghurt and paper *lungta*. Then he burns a *luta* and throws it away, after which he performs a dance.

Animals are also sacrificed during the festival and their meat cooked and offered to the gods. On the last day of *Lurol* meat is distributed to all participants who eat it on the spot. Strangely enough, four imitation goats are also offered to the gods and burnt at the end of the festival which may indicate that it was influenced by the methods of Yungdrung Bön or Tibetan Buddhism at some stage. There is no doubt that this festival went through various stages of development which were interpolated over each other in a bizarre manner. Other important offering items are white *khatag* scarves, *lungta*[80] and *luta* flags.

The offering substances and techniques of *Lurol* are very much comparable with those used in *tailgans*. Although Buryatian Bɵ do not classify the offerings into 'white' and 'red', all the components of White and Red Offerings are nevertheless present: milk, sour cream, butter, *salamat*, sweets etc. are parallel to the White Offering while alcohol, meat and blood match the Red Offering in *Lurol*. Animal sacrifice is used in both rituals, suggesting the same perception and understanding behind performing ritual sacrifice, based on ideology and culture traceable to Prehistoric Bön. Another very important point of similarity is that in both rituals fire is paramount as an agent for delivering offerings to the gods. In both cases, fire acts as purifier, transformer and as a 'delivery vehicle'.

---

[78] Tib. rgyab la kha dmar rtab pa.

[79] Tib. khrag mchod, dmar mchod.

[80] Flags symbolizing a person's good luck and fortune as well as his or her Five Personal Deities. See ch. XIII.

Conclusion

To conclude we can say with certainty that *Lurol* of Rebkong and the *tailgan* of Buryatian Bө Murgel display a high degree of similarity in their purpose, the pantheon of deities addressed and the ritual and offering techniques used. We can therefore surmise that they have common roots in the Prehistoric Bön of Eurasia. Furthermore, the very close parallel techniques and concepts of both *Lhachö* of Rebkong and Buryatian Bө Murgel traditions such as *Khamar*, and *Uhan Tarim* and *Ugaalga* respectively, White and Black Tengeri and Upper White and Black Gods etc. certainly point towards close and possibly prolonged contact between the Tibetans inhabiting Rebkong and Mongoloid tribes at some point in the past. As was said in the previous chapter, Mongoloid Tuyuhun/Azha people were already living in Rebkong before it came under Tibetan control in the early eighth century AD and a small number of them are still living there even now together with a number of descendants of later Hor Mongols. If we look into the earlier history we can see that proto-Mongol Hunnu conquered the Qiang proto-Tibetans who lived in the upper regions of the Yellow River around lakes Kokonoor, Orin-noor and Jarin-noor bordering onto Amdo as early as the third century AD when Amdo was the Eastern Part[81] of the Zhang Zhung Empire, a large confederation of eighteen tribes. Mutual cultural exchange, then, must have been going on in that area for a long time and this may partly explain these close similarities in the rituals of Buryatian Bө and Rebkong *lhapa*. The main point, however, is that Mongols, or in this case proto-Mongols, and peoples who inhabited what is now generally known as Tibet interacted from the dawn of history, as we will see later in Chapter XV. That means that the religious and cultural ideas of Prehistoric Bön – and possibly even of Yungdrung Bön – were travelling back and forth between Tibet, Mongolia and Siberia from times immemorial, and it is these ideas and practices that we find in many spiritual traditions of Inner Asia and the Far East even today.

---

[81] Tib. smad which also encompassed Kham and western regions of modern China. See, for example, Norbu & Prats, *Ga‰s ti se'i dkar c'ag.*

Part III
Comparative Study of the Offering Techniques in Yungdrung Bön and Buryatian Bɵ Murgel

Ideological base for the Four Offering Rituals in Yungdrung Bön

Four Guests[82] *and offering substances suitable for them*

In Yungdrung Bön and later Tibetan Buddhism we find four types of offering ritual practices which follow the same basic pattern and serve the same purpose. They are known as the Four Generous Actions:[83] *Sangchö*, *Chutor*, *Surchö* and *Chöd*.[84] The first three belong to *Drangsong Thegpa*, *the Way of the Solitary Ascetics*, the Sixth Way of the Nine Ways of Bön and the Second Way of the higher teachings of Fruitional Bön, which roughly corresponds to the Sutra level. They are based on similar and less elaborate rituals found in Causal Bön. The fourth ritual, the practice of *Chöd*, belongs to *Yeshen Thegpa*, *the Way of Primordial Shen*, the Eighth Way, where we find the teachings of high Tantra. Despite the fact that the Four Generous Actions are practised by followers of more than one Way, the Four Guests are always invited and unlimited offerings, both actual and mental, are presented to them. Moreover, all these practices are based on and aimed at developing compassion and generosity. For each of the Four Guests, items particularly suited and designed to satisfy them are visualized (and if possible, physically present). A practitioner should offer things of best quality without being mean or holding anything back, and without harbouring thoughts of how they might profit from the ritual. In short, the intention should be to benefit beings and the offerings should be unconditional and as vast as the sky.

First group

The first group are the High Guests.[85] These are the objects of refuge, namely the Three Jewels:[86]

---

[82] Tib. mgron po bzhi.

[83] Tib. byin pa rnam bzhi.

[84] Tib. bsang mchod; chu gtor; gsur mchod; gcod.

[85] Tib. sri zhu'i mgron.

[86] Tib. sangs rgyas, bon, gshen rab.

- Buddha (*Sangye*) – which includes all the Buddhas and in particular the Four Heroic Buddhas[87] who are: Lhamo, Lhachen, Sidpa and Tonpa;[88]
- Teachings of Yungdrung Bön;
- *Sangha* or the *Yungdrung Sempas*,[89] the Swastikasattvas, beings on a very advanced stage of realization.[90]

And the Three Roots:

- Lama;
- *Yidam*;
- *Khandro*.[91]

Offerings suitable for the High Guests are flowers, water, butter lamps or candles, incense and *torma*-cakes. This is an external or outer offering of sense objects. The inner offering consists of drinkable liquids and (or) alcohol, meat and bones which represent the complete purification Three Poisonous Emotions:[92] desire, anger and ignorance,[93] and their transformation into wisdom.

The fundamental principle behind making offerings to the Buddhas, who are the most elevated among the Four Guests, is to accumulate merits. Offerings to the Buddhas are made for the benefit of the practitioner, to develop generosity and devotion. Buddhas, being fully realized beings, are not some sort of gods who need to be propitiated in exchange for some benefit or blessing or who like receiving gifts and praises. Nor are they beings whose wrath must be placated should they be defiled or disturbed in some way; Buddhas are completely beyond all that. They need neither offerings nor praises. They derive no satisfaction from praises nor can they be upset, angry or defiled by any action in any way as they are beyond *samsara*. Instead, making offerings to them is a skilful means which increases the practitioner's stock of merits and positive karma.

---

87 Tib. bder gshegs gtso bzhi. They are all emanations of Tonpa Shenrab Miwo (Interview with Yongdzin Lopön Tenzin Namdak, Shenten Dargye Ling, France, 01.08.07).

88 Tib. Lha mo (Sa khrig Er sang), Lha chen (Shen lha 'Od dkar), Srid pa (Sangs po 'Bum khri), and sTon pa (gShen rab Mi bo).

89 Tib. g.yung drung sems pa.

90 Also known as *Bodhisattvas* in Buddhism.

91 Tib. bla ma, yid dam, mkha' 'gro.

92 Tib. dug gsum.

93 Tib. 'dod chags, zhe sdang, gti mug.

Fig. 9. Refuge tree of Yungdrung Bön.

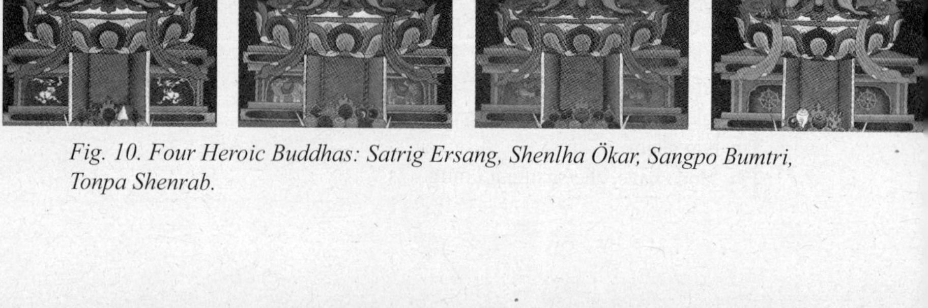

Fig. 10. Four Heroic Buddhas: Satrig Ersang, Shenlha Ökar, Sangpo Bumtri, Tonpa Shenrab.

Second group

The second group is the Guests with Virtuous Qualities[94] comprising the Guardians of the Teachings.[95] As we saw in Chapter V, there are two types of Guardians: fully enlightened Guardians such as Sidpai Gyalmo, and worldly and clean Guardians[96] who are cosmic and celestial beings such as gods of the stars, sun or moon. While meat and alcohol are offered to the Enlightened Guardians, Clean Guardians should be offered only pleasant things such as the Three Sweet Things,[97] the Three White Things,[98] *torma*, flowers and perfumes.

Third group

The third group consists of the powerful beings of the Eight Classes and those to whom we owe karmic debts.[99] They are offered medicines to ease their sufferings and anything they need to satisfy their desires in full and repay karmic debts.

Fourth group

The fourth group are the Guests of Compassion,[100] or in other words, all the beings of the Six Realms of *samsara*. They are also offered various things according to their liking and needs.

Time and support substance for the offerings

Each of the four practices is normally carried out at a particular time, although there may be exceptions. According to Yungdrung Bön, *Sangchö* is usually offered in the early morning (except for specific practices for the Guardians which are done both in the morning and the evening). The support is a fire where aromatic *sang* and other offerings are burnt. *Chutor* is done in the late morning or at noon and the support for visualization is water. *Surchö* is done at dusk and the support is the smoke of burnt food. *Chöd* is done at night before going to bed and in this case the support is one's own body. However, it is merely by visualization that the body is

---

94 Tib. yon tan gyi mgron.

95 Tib. bka' skyong.

96 Tib. 'jig rten pa'i gtsang rigs lha.

97 Tib. mngar gsum: sugar, molasses, honey.

98 Tib. dkar gsum: yoghurt, butter and milk.

99 Tib. lan chags kyi mgron.

100 Tib. snying rje'i mgon.

transformed into offerings according to the beings' needs; the physical body still remains intact after this ritual. The purpose of *Chöd* is not to destroy the body, which is considered a vehicle for realization, but to cut off the practitioner's attachment to it as otherwise this hinders the process of liberation from *samsara.*

In the teachings of Sutra and Tàntra we can find stories of Buddhas, *Bodhisattvas* or *Mahasiddhas* who, out of compassion, actually fed their bodies or parts of them to hungry wild beasts or evil spirits. There are several stories in *Zijyid*, the large biography of Tonpa Shenrab, which tell of his deeds before he became a Buddha. For example, one of them narrates an episode from one of his lifetimes as a *yogi* living in seclusion:

> One winter's day a pack of wolves was stalking a deer which collapsed in exhaustion in front of the *yogi*'s dwelling. The wolves were howling and circling nearby but sensing the presence of a human they didn't come close to slaughter their prey. The *yogi* clearly saw that both the deer and the wolves were suffering, the deer from fear and exhaustion, the wolves from hunger. He also saw clearly that he would have to die some day and be reborn again. He concluded that the time had come for him to actually give up his own body in order to benefit others and with this in mind, he went out of his retreat-hut, walked towards the wolves, undressed and lay down so that they could come and eat his body. He even cut himself and bled to make it easier for them. In this way he saved the deer, satisfied the hungry wolves and for himself realized ultimate generosity.

Another story relates how the future Tonpa Shenrab was a prince in a kingdom afflicted by famine.

> As a prince he lived in the royal palace completely cut off from the reality of life in the rest of the kingdom where people were dying from starvation. When he became aware of the real situation, he gradually gave away all his possessions and food, thereby managing to save many people. However, when he had given everything away another starving family arrived and he had nothing to give them to still their hunger. Seeing this, he gave up his own body so that they could eat and live.[101]

---

[101] Based on teachings given by Yongdzin Lopön Tenzin Namdak given in Paris, 16–17 October 2004.

There are many similar stories in both Yungdrung Bön and Tibetan Buddhist literature which demonstrate acts of ultimate generosity. However, these kinds of actions are quite beyond the capacity of most practitioners as they require exceptional realization. In order to increase capacity for generosity, the four methods of *Sangchö*, *Chutor*, *Surchö* and *Chöd* are used to train the mind as well as to actually benefit myriads of invisible beings.

According to Yongdzin Lopön Tenzin Namdak, only around two percent of all beings are visible to us; the rest of the beings inhabiting the universe we live in are invisible. These four practices, then, are very much beneficial as the gifts presented can be received by invisible beings thanks to mental visualization aided by the support of the physical substances offered. The following excerpt from the teachings of Yongdzin Lopön Tenzin Namdak further clarifies the benefits of performing the Four Offerings, in particular, *Sur* practice for the recently deceased:

> When a person dies, they are disconnected from the body and realize that they are dead, but it is not exactly the same for each being; each being has different circumstances. Some beings stay around [their] corpse for a few days, others see and look back at their corpse but see it as a different form; someone sees his body lying in the bed and tries to get up or ask somebody else [to help him up] but no-one replies or helps because other beings don't see or know anything. That makes this [deceased] person very sad because nobody helps him, nobody replies, nothing. So then he starts to think about what happened, to look back over the circumstances, and then he realizes that he is dead. Then he goes round to see his property, friends or relatives, but nobody sees him, no-one answers or replies. Maybe he comes to someone in a dream. When this happens, it is an experience related to the dreamer's spirit or consciousness [not his physical body]; this dead man has no connection with his material body and the person who is alive is sleeping so at that time his spirit or consciousness is alone [and not tied tightly to the physical body]. Even so, the dreamer's activities and feelings are just as if he were awake; it seems as if he is awake but his body is lying in bed. So meanwhile these two spirits meet together and the live person sees the dead one and they are talking together. Many people push [such spirits] away and think they are having bad dreams with many dead people. But that is the worst thing [you can do, it is] like pushing away a person who comes to your door and not replying. The feeling is exactly the same, [the deceased feels] just as if he were alive. So you have to be careful about this and try to be sympathetic and help. Therefore traditionally we have the practice of the *Sur* offering, the Water Offering, *Sang* Offering or *Chöd* Offering. We try to help sentient beings who don't visibly receive anything from the live person

> […] But it is very important to visualize. Visualization is the activity of the mind, so beings who have lost their connection with the material body can see [what you visualize]. If you are sympathetic or have good thoughts and compassion, they can receive something; it helps.[102]

Sur and its parallel in Buryatian Bɵ Murgel

The ritual of *Surchö* is of Bönpo origin but was adapted to Buddhist lore as Indian Buddhism spread in Tibet and is now practised in all Schools of Tibetan Buddhism as well. In *Sur*, smoke from burnt food is used as a support and offerings are delivered to the Four Guests accompanied by visualization and *mantra* recitation. *Sur* can be White or Red depending on the content of the offerings. The offering substance used in White *Sur*[103] is made out of *tsampa* mixed with butter and other milk products such as cheese or yoghurt, and sugar or biscuits can also be added. All these ingredients are mashed together and made into a sort of greasy powder which is then burnt in a bonfire making dense, pungent smoke. In Red *Sur*[104] one offers meat, blood, bones and such like. For a very simple *Sur* one can burn the first portion of freshly made food. The aim of this practice is to clear obstacles to one's practice and life through repaying karmic debts, to ask both the Enlightened and Worldly Guardians for assistance, and to harmonize one's energy with the environment. However, the fundamental base of this practice is compassion and the main purpose is training in generosity. According to Chögyal Namkhai Norbu, *Sur* is particularly good for satisfying the needs of all sorts of hungry ghosts[105] and as such is one of the powerful skilful means to put one's compassion in action and accumulate merits.

Sur finds its parallel in Bɵ Murgel. In Buryatia not only the Bɵ and Utgan but also ordinary people make an offering which is just like Tibetan *Surchö*. Taking the first portion of freshly prepared food, they burn it in a fire outside, offering it to the gods and spirits of the place. If we look into the *tailgan* offerings they resemble Red *Sur* in that the meat, blood, bones and fur of an animal are offered in a bonfire. The difference of course is that an animal is slaughtered especially for the occasion while for Red *Sur* one just buys some meat from a butcher or supermarket.

---

[102] Yongdzin Lopön Tenzin Namdak, *Teachings on Zhang Zhung Nyam Gyud: The Experiential Transmission of Zhang Zhung*, trscr. & ed. Carol and Dmitry Ermakovi, (France: Association Yungdrung Bön, 2005), p. 36–37.

[103] Tib. dkar gsur.

[104] Tib. dmar gsur.

[105] Especially Tib. dri za; Sans. Gandharva, the spirits which feed on smell.

Offerings to water-spirits

Types of water-spirits

Water-spirits are called *Lusuut* in Buryatian and their chiefs or kings are called *Lusuut-Khaan*. In Tibetan they are *Lu* although most western Dharma publications use the Sanskrit term, *Naga*. Nevertheless, all these names refer to the same class of beings. While Buryats consider them simply as water-spirits or water-gods without further elaboration, in the Yungdrung Bön tradition, *Lu* have been classified in a variety of ways. In fact, *Lu* is a very general name as different types of them belong to different classes among the beings inhabiting the Six Destinies of Rebirth or Six Realms. According to this classification the different types of *Lu* abide in the animal realm and the realm of demi-gods. This explanation can be found equally in Bön and Buddhist sources. As we saw in Chapter IV according to the ancient Bönpo system, our world is composed of the Three Worlds which are the World of Heavens inhabited by heavenly beings such as *Lha* and *Düd*, the World of the Earth inhabited by humans and animals, and the World of the *Lu*, the world of waters or underworld where *Lu* live. This cosmological model is basically the same as that of Buryatian Bɵ Murgel. Yet another way the *Lu* are classified is dependent on the direction from which the springs where *Lu* are considered to reside are flowing. *Lu* of the King cast[106] live in eastern springs, *Lu* of the Untouchable or lowest caste[107] live in northern springs, *Lu* of the Traders caste[108] live in western springs and *Lu* of the Servant or Peasant caste[109] live in southern springs.[110] Then there are also twenty-five different races of *Lu*.

There is another major class of *Lu* called *Lusin*[111] – *Lu*-demons. While both *Lu* and *Lusin* are water-spirits they are quite different. *Lu* are not evil by nature. Among the *Lu* there are some very virtuous beings and even followers of Yungdrung Bön including Yungdrung Sempas

---

[106] Tib. rgyal rigs klu.

[107] Tib. gdol rigs klu.

[108] Tib. rje rigs klu.

[109] Tib. dmangs rigs klu.

[110] This classification is from *Srid rgyal drag sngags gnad kyi dgongs thim, The Secret Text of the Primordial State (of the Goddess) which represents the Essential Points of the Fierce Mantra of Sidpa Gyalmo*, transmitted by Yongdzin Lopön Tenzin Namdak on several occasions and translated into English by John Myrdhin Reynolds. More information on *Lu* can be found in Nebesky-Wojkowitz, *Oracles and Demons,* p. 290.

[111] Tib. klu srin.

(*Bodhisattvas*) of the high stages who continue holding and practising teachings given to their ancestors by Tonpa Shenrab Miwo. Some *Lu*, when rightly approached, can become powerful allies and helpers. When *Lu* cause problems for humans it is an emotional response to the disturbances we cause them similar to the way humans respond to aggression. *Lusin* are different. They are evil by nature so they disturb humans and other beings all the time whether provoked or not. Powerful *Lusin* sometimes demand sacrifices in exchange for leaving humans alone for a certain period of time. When the period for which they received 'tax' has expired, they must be placated again. That is the reason behind animal and even human sacrifices to the river gods found in many ancient cultures.

The purpose of offering to the water-spirits

According to ancient Bönpo sources such as the *Collections of One Hundred Thousand White and Black Lu,*[112] the *Lu* inhabited this world prior to the appearance of the human race and that is why they and their subordinates *Sadag* (Lords of the Soil) and other classes of beings such as *Nyen* (tree-gods) are considered to be the true owners of the landscape in which humanity lives. In the course of its development the human race caused no little suffering to these beings, wittingly and unwittingly, by clearing forests, polluting and damming rivers, changing the landscape, extracting minerals, mining and quarrying, burning various substances which act as poison to non-human beings causing them illnesses, suffering and madness. These beings retaliate by sending diseases, epidemics, earthquakes, floods, fires, madness, quarrels and so forth against humans, their crops and livestock. Ritual offerings are made to the water-spirits to atone for human mistakes, repay our debts to them, purify and heal them, provide them with whatever they need, re-establish balance and harmony and turn them into friends and helpers who instead of harming humans will protect and benefit us. This attitude is the same in Bön and Bɵ Murgel.

Offering to the water-spirits in Yungdrung Bön

We shall take the ritual of *Lutor*,[113] *the Torma Offering to the Lu*[114] as an example of offerings to the water-spirits within the rich

[112] Tib. *Klu 'bum dkar nag khra gsum* discovered by Shenchen Luga (Tib. gShen chen klu dga).

[113] Tib. klu gtor.

[114] The name for this particular rite is: *Klu yi gtor ma nar ma btang ba'i cho*

Fig. 11. Naga water-spirits, Bhaktapur city, Nepal.

Fig. 12. Khenpo Tenpa Yungdrung performing Chutor offering.

lore of Yungdrung Bön. *Lutor* is a kind of *Chutor* or Water Torma offering.

While *Lutor* offerings are mainly directed to the *Lu,* the Four Guests discussed above are propitiated as well. In Yungdrung Bön one must be very careful in what one offers to the *Lu*. Things like meat, blood, alcohol and certain types of incenses containing animal ingredients are never offered as they are believed to offend and pollute the water-spirits, making them irritated and unhappy causing them to retaliate by unleashing problems on the hapless offender. Appropriate offerings for the *Lu* are the *chutor* water-*torma* which consists of nine plates or bowls (the central plate or bowl is raised on a kind of tripod) filled with the five kinds of water:

- water of generosity – running water from a pure stream;
- water from an ocean wave;
- water from a large river;
- water from a very pure, clear spring;
- water from very high snow mountains.

---

ga. Translated into English by John Myrdhin Reynolds, 1996, Vidyadhara Institute, San Diego. It is included as the part of the larger *Chutor* in the *Bonpo Monastic Rituals From The Menri Tradition: as performed by the monks of Triten Norbutse Monastery, Kathmandu, Nepal*, Tibetan Pronunciation and Interlinear Translation with Annotations by John Myrdhin Reynolds, (Dortmund: Bonpo Translation Project, 2005).

These waters are mixed with the Three White Things; the Three Sweet Things; the Five Grains: wheat, barley, rice, *solwa*,[115] pulses; the Five Medicines: *sle tre* (*Polygonum aubersti henry*), *kan tha ka ri*, *dgya mtsho lbu ba*, *bdang po lag pa*, *shu dag* (sweet flag/*Acorus calamus*); the Five Incenses: *dgya spos*, *spang spos*, *brag spos, tsan dan dkar po* (white sandalwood), *khu byug spos*; the Five Precious things: gold, silver, copper, turquoise, coral; the Three Fruits: *a ru* (yellow myrobalan /*Terminabli chebula*), *ba ru*, *skyu ru*; flower petals from plants without thorns; silk clothes; coloured wool, and so on.

The version of *Lutor* I am familiar with has seven sections:

1. *Refuge formula*: refuge is taken in Tonpa Shenrab, in the Teachings of Yungdrung Bön, Yungdrung Sempas and the Community of Practitioners.
2. *Subjugation and healing of the Lu*: with the help of visualization and *mudras* the practitioner, now transformed into the peaceful Buddha-form Shenlha Ökar, sends medicine to the *Lu* in order to heal their diseases, allay their sufferings and subjugate their noxious natures.
3. *Recitation of mantra*: to actualize the offerings and better establish contact with the *Lu*.
4. *Torma offering*: the water-*torma* is offered to the King of the *Lu* Murzang Werro[116] and his retinue of five casts and twenty-five races of *Lu* as well as the beings of the Six Realms. *Lu* and other beings are invited to refrain from negative actions and thoughts, and to generate thoughts of regret at having harmed others in the past. The wish is expressed that the *Lu* and all the beings of the Six Realms be happy, joyful and content, and finally attain the fruit of Buddhahood.
5. *Offering puja to the Lu*: here the offering substances described above are presented to the *Lu* both physically and through visualization. The wish is expressed that all karmic debts and hostilities be purified and the *Lu* are requested to prevent infectious disease, bring abundance, timely rain, long life and wealth to those who perform the ritual and their patrons. Then there is a prayer requesting *siddhi* from the *Lu*.

[115] Tib. sol ba.

[116] Murzang Werro is Zhang Zhung equivalent to Sanskrit Naga-raja and Buryatian Lusuut-Khaan.

6. *Praying for the Lu's forgiveness*: the practitioner confesses such actions as digging up the earth, breaking rocks, cutting down forests, damming water bodies, constructing irrigation channels, polluting the hearth and all other possible ways of polluting and defiling the environment which is the dimension in which these water-spirits live. The sufferings which befall the *Lu* as a result of these pollutions is described – they faint or go mad, thrash about, kill other beings and are, in short, very unhappy. The practitioner asks their forgiveness and through offering the water-*torma* these problems are purified, the *Lu*'s illnesses are cured and they become happy.
7. *Dismissing the Lu*: *mantra* is recited to ask the *Lu* to depart.

In the colophon it is said that this method was taught by Tonpa Shenrab Miwo himself who transmitted it to Takla Mebar,[117] then the further lineage is briefly narrated.

This ritual can be performed equally in the temple or at home in which case the water-*torma* is later poured into a nearby stream or any clean place, or somewhere *Lu* are known to reside. Often a *Lukhang*,[118] a small house or support, is built for them at such places.

Offerings to water-spirits in Bө Murgel

Offering to the Lusuut at the River Ulyun

Offerings to the water-spirits are called *Lusuudyn Tahilga* or *Uhan Tahil*.[119] As an example of the way in which offerings are made to the *Lusuut* in Bө Murgel, here is a passage from my diary of 1994:

> Having finished all our business at that place, we began making our way back to Ulyunhen. Before reaching the village, we stopped by a bridge over the River Ulyun to perform a ritual for the *Lusuut*, the water-spirits. This was a special place for them. We went down to the river and stood the small silver birch tree (which we had brought from the village) in the sand, right by the current. We tied ribbons to the branches, offered coins, biscuits and sweets and sprinkled in turn. Then one by one, almost following in each others' footsteps, we began to leave. On no account could anyone turn or look back. We got into the cars and drove off quickly to the village.
>
> On the river Ulyun near the village of Ulyunhen, Barguzin,13.06.94.

[117] Tib. sTag la Me-'bar, Flaming Tiger.

[118] Tib. klu khang.

[119] Bur. Уhан тахил.

For sprinkling we used milk and the Bɵ sprinkled *tarasoon* milk vodka. Villagers offered biscuits, coins and even cigarettes. It was forbidden to turn and look back because doing so we could easily receive a curse from the *Lusuut* who came out of the stream to feast on the offerings.

Offerings to Lusuut Khaan at Lake Baikal

In some contexts, the offerings presented to the water-spirits in Bɵ Murgel can differ widely from those traditionally found in Yungdrung Bön although normally there is considerable overlap in the offerings given to the *Lusuut* and those used in the Bönpo *Lutor.* One of the main differences is that the Bɵ sprinkle *tarasoon* milk vodka to the *Lusuut* whereas alcohol is never among the offerings to water-spirits in Yundgrung Bön. However, the type of vodka the Buryats offer to the *Lusuut* is made from milk, so maybe it can be categorized as a milk product rather than alcohol. Yungdrung Bön texts also stipulate quite firmly that no animal substances should be offered to the *Lu,* and this is true of the *Lhachukha* ritual in Rebkong and in Buddhist rituals, too. However, when offerings

Fig. 13. Preparing for the offering to the Lusuut on the River Ulyun.

Fig. 14. Offering of coins, sweets and cigarettes at the base of the birch dedicated to Lusuut. In the centre is a young birch tree sticking out from the sand on the river bank.

are made to the god of Lake Baikal, *omul*[120] fish are used. The fish are laid on a plate with their tails towards the lake. In days gone by a *tailgan* was performed regularly for Bahar-Hara Khaan, the Lord of the Baigal fire-mountain which went under water thus forming Lake Baikal and a red bull was sacrificed. This ritual ceased in the 1790's as the bull could only be accepted by fire drawn from the bottom of the lake and there were no Bɵ left mighty enough to call up this underwater fire.[121] The sacrificial bull was then replaced by nine sheep, but this tradition was halted when Communists overran Buryatia in the 1920's.[122] However, when a *tailgan* was performed on the shore of Baikal in 1994, a ram was among the offerings:

> The ritual was to invite Lusuut Khaan from one place to another. He had been residing at Korsakovo[123] on Lake Baikal and was the cause of the ground sinking there. The following day had been chosen because, according to Bɵ Murgel belief, it was the night when the Tengeri and spirits gather at the Holy Nose peninsular and decide the fate of people, spirits and animals and also any changes to the landscape, the course of rivers and other waterways, etc. From a technical point of view, the ritual was to go as follows: Bɵ 'Uncle' Sasha, who had stayed in Korsakovo, should perform a farewell ritual, sacrifice a ram and make other offerings. Not later than 8 a.m. a welcoming ritual should be performed here at Holy Nose, a ram should be offered to invite and welcome Lusuut Khaan to the new place. We sat for a long time bent over the map trying to find out the route Lusuut Khaan might take and where he would stop.
>
> In order to ensure that the next day's ritual would be accepted, before sunset we did *serzhim* on the lake shore. The place where Bɵ should 'give' had been previously determined. The intention of *serzhim* was to send requests to the god's council. That night one of the Bɵ would be 'called' to the meeting and given the answer and instructions on correct behaviour.
>
> Tourist base "Rovesnik" near the village of Maximiha,
> Lake Baikal, 19.07.94[124]

---

[120] Rus. омуль (Lat. *Coregonus autumnalis*), belongs to *Salmonidae* family.

[121] This concept of underwater fire reminds us of similar concepts in Indo-Iranian religions expressed in the deity Apam Napat. See ch. VI.

[122] Bazarov, *Tainstva* , p.137.

[123] Rus. Корсаково.

[124] From my unpublished diary *Tailgan Trip*.

This is how the last part of the ritual was performed:

> A young birch tree was planted on the sandy shore and an offering of *omul* fish was made to the god of Baikal. This type of *omul* lives only in Lake Baikal and is the main food for the Buryats living in the Baikal region. It is eaten in many forms – raw, fried, salted, smoked, boiled and even rotten in a special way! As an offering, it is placed on a plate with its tail towards Lake Baikal. All the Buryats of this region do it that way. As we pronounced the last words of dedication, the sun appeared over the peninsula of Holy Nose and the first rays slid over the water to the spot where we were. Everyone rejoiced.
> Headland Krestovyi[125] opposite Holy Nose (Helmyn Hushun), Lake Baikal, 20.07.94.[126]

Ritual items offered to the Lu in the Bönpo Rites of the Deer and offerings to Lusuut in Bɵ Murgel

From the accounts of the *Lusuut* offering rituals above it is clear that an indispensable item to present to the water-spirits is a young birch tree. We find something very similar in the Bön of the Rites of the Deer. In the *mang* origin myth of *The Rite of the Deer with Branched Antlers* the offerings to the Lord of the *Lu* are described as follows:

> So! So! Above the bird hovers,
> the yellow bird of the Lu hovers.
> In the middle the willow sways,
> the yellow willow of the Lu sways.
> On the earth the deer walks,
> the yellow-bellied deer of the Lu walks:
> with the bird and the willow that sways harmoniously
> we offer it as a gift to the Lord of the Lu.[127]

Here, too, a tree is offered, although it is not a birch but a willow. Tibetans consider both willows and birches as 'mother trees'[128] associated with the *Lu,* and as we have seen, willows are used in the *Lurol* festival of Rebkong. Indeed, in Bɵ Murgel not only birches can be used as a symbol of the World Tree and support for the spirits. One of the trees

---

[125] Rus. мыс Крестовый.
[126] Ibid.
[127] Norbu, *Drung, Deu and Bon*, p.179.
[128] Tib. mo shing.

Fig. 15. Utgans M.G. Danchinova and N.A. Stepanova praying to Baikal at the end of the tailgan at the Krestovyi headland facing Holy Nose (Helmyn Hushun) peninsula. A huge pan with the offerings of boiled ram can be seen in front. Behind the Utgan on the right women kneel in prayer.

used in ancient times was a red willow *huhai*[129] which was venerated by both Buryats and Mongols alike. Other trees were pine, fir and larch.[130] What is important is not so much the species of tree used in the ritual but its function: the tree connects the dimension of the earth where the deer stands with the dimension of the sky where the bird hovers and harmonizes the various levels of existence.[131] This is underlined by the refrain: '*[...] with the bird and willow which sways harmoniously we offer it as a gift to [...]*'.

> So! So! Above (*rtse la*) the bird hovers,
> the chough, the bird of the Düd hovers.
> In the middle (*bar na*), the willow sways,
> the black willow of the Düd sways.
> On the earth (*log na*) the deer walks (*khrol*),
> the black deer of the Düd walks:

---

[129] Bur. нунай.

[130] Doogarov, *Istoricheskie korni*, p.124.

[131] The tree also represents the material structure of the *dö* (mdos), a ritual object offered to the gods and spirit in ransom rites.

with the bird and the tree which sway harmoniously
we offer it as ransom to the Lord of the Düd.[132]

This stanza describes the ransom gifts offered to the *Düd*, demons of the sky, and later in the same text the same range of objects is presented to the Lords of *Mu*, *Tsen*, *Gyalpo* and *Lha.* The refrain is always repeated: '*[...] with the bird and willow which sways harmoniously we offer it [...] to [...]*'. A willow tree, then, is offered to several classes of beings and it is clear that it represents the World Tree which links all Three Worlds and as such is a symbol of harmony between the different dimensions. The World Tree supports the worlds of all the beings and is a vital element in their life so it is only fitting that it takes its place among the offerings of both Bɵ Murgel and Yungdrung Bön. This further reinforces the premise that both traditions share a common cultural background in the Prehistoric Bön of Eurasia.

Parallel ideas in the offerings to the Lusuut in Bɵ Murgel, the Lurol of Rebkong and Yungdrung Bön

In the *Lurol* festival of Rebkong, *Lu* are not propitiated together with other gods. Offerings to them, such as the *Lusang*[133] done during the *Lhachukha* rite and at the end of the festival, are performed at the stream near the village just as is the case with the offerings to *Lusuut* in Bɵ Murgel.

The *lhapa* and other participants leave the site of the *Lurol* festival in exactly the same way as the participants at a *Lusuut* offering ritual. The *lhapa* possessed by one of the gods uses a broom tipped with a sword to sweep wicked beings towards the crossroads. He then throws the willow twigs with attached *luta* flags onto a pile of burning straw and jumps on them. Sadako Nagano suggests that this is a kind of offering perhaps taken by the *Lu*.[134] The participants then depart and no-one is allowed to

---

[132] Ibid. p.178.

[133] Tib. klu bsang.

[134] Although this may seem like a rite of exorcism, the *luta* flags, which depict *Lu*, are also called *lutad* (Tib. klu gtad), a term for an offering object. Earlier in *Lurol* the same *luta* flags were used as a support and offering item for the *Lu* and willow twigs, which is the tree of the *Lu*, were attached to the palanquins of the gods. At the later stages *luta* were burnt in the fire in a way suggesting they were used as a kind of ransom. So this ritual is a peculiar cross between offering, exorcism and ransom.

look back.[135] The reason, as in Bɵ Murgel, is that no-one may see the *Lu* at that moment as instead of benefit they will send disturbances.

Another parallel motif, although not directly connected with the ritual activity, is found in a Yungdrung Bön story narrated in the eleventh chapter of *Zijyid*:

> Virtuous prince Kongtse[136] wished to build a temple in the middle of the lake. He enlisted the help of *Sinpo* and *Lu* spirits who agreed to aid him due to his previous karma with them but they laid one condition: no-one should know about the project and no-one should see them. Kongtse agreed. He only told his parents where he was going, ordering them not to reveal this to anyone, not even his wife, and he departed. Time was passing and passing and Kongtse's wife grew desperate to know why her husband was not returning. She didn't believe the stories told to her by her in-laws and put such pressure on them that they finally told her where Kongtse was. She immediately set off for that place. When she arrived on the shore of the lake she saw the *Sinpo* and *Lu* working on the building of the temple in the middle of it. They, too, saw her immediately and screamed at Kongtse, cursing him for breaking the promise, caused havoc on the building site and then departed. It was only later through the intervention of Tonpa Shenrab who manifested as Nampar Gyalwa[137] that the spirits were subdued and the temple finally built.[138]

Here we find the same motif of *Lu* and *Sinpo* spirits wishing to remain unseen by humans and causing grave problems when this taboo is broken. It seems, then, that the understanding of this particular character trait of water-spirits and other kinds of spirits was and is common knowledge among the practitioners of various kinds of Bön as well as Buryatian Bɵ Murgel, stemming most probably from the cultural base of Prehistoric Bön.

---

[135] Nagano, *Sacrifice and Lhapa.*

[136] Gya Kongtse Trulgyi Gyalpo, Chinese king and disciple of Tonpa Shenrab Miwo.

[137] Tib. rNam par rGyal ba.

[138] Based on the narration of Yongdzin Lopön Tenzin Namdak.

Sangchö

This is one of the most popular offering practices in Tibet. In some shape or form it is performed every morning in all Bönpo and Buddhist monasteries as well as by lay practitioners of both religions. Each monastery and household has a *sangkhang*,[139] a brazier for burning the *sang* offerings.

Principles underlying Sangchö

There are many types of *Sangchö* in Yungdrung Bön. Although they are addressed to all of the Four Guests in the same way as in *Surchö* and *Chutor,* the emphasis is often on propitiating the guardians of the teachings along with *Yullha/Yulsa* and *Zhidag*, the local Owners who often double up as worldly protectors as well. *Zhidag* are powerful gods and spirits who, though subordinate to *Yullha*, nevertheless have strong command over a particular location or geographical feature together with all the spirits, humans and animals who live there. Spirits usually listed under the category of *Zhidag* generally belong to the following classes: *Tod* rock-spirits, *Nyen* tree-spirits,[140] *Lu* water-spirits, and *Sadag* earth-spirits. Below is a quotation from *Zijyid*[141] where Tonpa Shenrab himself explains why the offerings to *Yullha* and *Zhidag* must be made regularly by all practitioners of Yungdrung Bön no matter what level of practice they are on according to the Nine Ways of Bön:

Fig. 16. Sangkhang *in Triten Norbutse, Kathmandu.*

[139] Tib. bsang khang.

[140] *Nyen* are not clearly defined. While tree-spirits are said to belong to this class, *Nyen* is often used as a generic name for the deities living in the intermediate space between earth and sky. Tree-spirits are often listed as the class of the *Nojin* wealth gods.

[141] From the section of *Yeshen Thegpa* where the teachings of the Higher Tantra are given.

Whichever *bon* way of the Nine Vehicles you practise,
if you fail to give milk-offerings and pure sacrificial cakes to the powerful lords of this world,
if you do not ask them (for a site for) your palace of the Blessed Ones,
these powerful lords, the lords of the soil, the serpents and the furies
are irascible, however much they may still protect the doctrine.
However gentle their disposition, their lineage is still that of the titans.
So these white offerings to lords of the soil, serpents and furies,
the ritual items of aromatic wood, sacrificial fire and sacred libations,
must be offered to the accompaniment of an exposition of the buddhas' truth.
You must give pleasure to the powerful ones of the phenomenal world,
and having made them happy, you can hold them to their former vows.
Ask them for a site for your worship and a place for you to stay,
hold them before witnesses to their oath to protect the doctrine.
Afterwards you can make them attend to whatever you want,
Thus happiness in phenomenal things depends on (the lords of) the soil.
Fertile fields and good harvests,
extent of royal power and spread of dominion,
although some half (of such effects) is ordained by previous actions,
the other half comes from the powerful lords of the soil.
If you do not know how to act methodically in this matter,
a root-cause of evil and harm springs from this.
So you must attend to the lords of the soil, the serpents and furies.[142]

In *Sangchö* the offerings are delivered mainly by fire and smoke from the burning *sang,* a powder or 'potpourri' made from the dried fragrant leaves of certain trees and bushes. The ingredients of *sang* can consist of *palü*,[143] mugwort, juniper, white sandalwood, cypress, pine, cedar, ash,

---

[142] Snellgrove, *Nine Ways*, pp. 197–199.

[143] Tib. ba lu, Lat. *Rhododendron anthopogon, Rhododendron adamsii. Palü* is the small fragrant bush which Western translators constantly render as dwarf rhododendron or fragrant rhododendron. Although *palü* is a distant relative of rhododendrons and has a Latin name of *Rhododendron adamsii*, it doesn't resemble them. In fact this translation is misleading as rhododendron leaves are poisonous and are considered among the dirty things such as sulphur which are burnt in the ritual for removing of negativities preceding *Sang*. In Buryatia *palü* is known as *sagaan dali* or 'white wing' and considered to be a remedy against 108 diseases and an aphrodisiac. It is valued very much especially in Tunka.

larch, birch, silver birch etc. One should not use poisonous plants such as rhododendron or any plants with thorns.[144]

All the beings propitiated in *Sangchö* have a direct or indirect impact on the dimension in which humans live so it is important to be 'good neighbours', not to offend them in any way but to maintain harmony. These beings control the external energies of the elements to which humans are connected through the environment but also through our body which is fashioned from the five elements and permeated by their energies. If we look at the human situation from this angle it becomes clear that our well-being fortune, health and longevity can be influenced by the beings who command the energies of these elements.

That is precisely the concept behind many Bɵ Murgel and Bönpo rituals; they work with external energies in order to effect changes in the external and internal conditions of human beings. Many kinds of healing rituals belonging to Prehistoric Bön and the Causal Vehicles of Yungdrung Bön are based on this principle, and so is *Sangchö*. When the energies of people are in harmony with the energies of the gods and spirits of the environment, everything goes well in both dimensions. Through making *Sangchö* offerings to non-human beings the practitioner satisfies their desires, their grudges against humanity are pacified and life runs smoothly.

In a similar way Bɵ and Utgan do fire offerings every day in order to protect the community from evil and increase its prosperity and well-being.

General structure of Sangchö[145]

There are many different versions of *Sangchö*. Some are very elaborate, compiled from several ritual texts, while others are very short, consisting of just a few lines. Often a practitioner has recourse to several sections of a *Sangchö* text, selecting short, medium or elaborate to suit different needs and situations; certain texts can be added or taken out according to circumstance.

Here is a *Sangchö* blueprint based on the practice compilation currently in use in Triten Norbutse Bönpo monastery in Kathmandu, Nepal and in Shenten Dargye Ling Bönpo centre in France:

---

[144] According to the instructions of Yongdzin Lopön Tenzin Namdak given in Triten Norbutse Bönpo Monastery, Kathmandu, Nepal, 1996.

[145] The information in this section is based on oral instructions by Yongdzin Lopön Tenzin Namdak, Khenpo Tenpa Yungdrung and Geshe Gelek Jinpa as well as tr. Reynolds, *Bonpo Monastic Rituals.*

Preliminary stages:

1. *Tru* Water Purification;[146]
2. *Sang* Purification through fumigation;[147]
3. Expelling the Obstructive Forces[148] and Securing the Boundary:[149] obstacle-creating spirits[150] and negative energies[151] are removed and destroyed through visualization and scattering white mustard seeds empowered with *mantra*. A protective circle[152] is established around the practice site and the practitioners so that nothing can be disturbed during the later stages of the ritual;
4. Generating *Bodhichitta*;[153]
5. Refuge;[154]
6. Confession:[155] misdeeds are confessed and purification is requested.

Main practice:

7. Generating the Fire Deities[156] and burning offerings in fire producing fragrant smoke, the main offering of *Sangchö*. The practitioner transforms into the peaceful Buddha-form Shenlha Ökar and sends the seed-syllables[157] of the elements onto the place of the fire offering which consequently transform into a palace of blazing light in the form of a *Yungdrung Koleg Chörten.*[158] Inside there is a blazing fire and a *mandala* at the centre of which are the Fire Deities.[159] These Fire Deities are not the same as the worldly Owners of fire. They are Buddha-forms and as such are empty manifestations of the primordial ground of being beyond duality. In the four cardinal directions

---

146 Tib. khrus gsol.

147 Tib. spos bsang.

148 Tib. bgegs bkrad.

149 Tib. mtshams bcad.

150 Tib. bgegs.

151 Tib. gdon.

152 Tib. srung 'khor.

153 Tib. mkhyen pa gsol. *Bodhichitta,* Tib. chang chub sems.

154 Tib. skyabs su 'gro ba.

155 Tib. sdig pa bshags pa.

156 Tib. me lha bskyed pa.

157 Tib. sa bon.

158 Tib. g.yung drung bkod legs mchod rten.

159 Tib. sku gsung thugs kyi me lha.

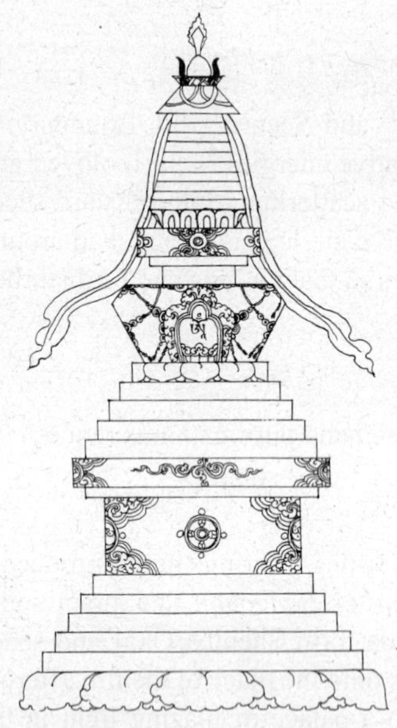

Fig. 17. Yungdrung Koleg Chorten.

there are the Deities of the Four Activities:[160] Pacifying,[161] Increasing,[162] Subduing[163] and Destroying,[164] while outside there are Protectors of Yungdrung Bön, wealth gods, beings of the Eight Classes and finally beings of the Six Realms of *samsara.* Rays of light emanate from the heart centres of the visualized deities to invite the actual Wisdom Beings to descend from the dimension of the Natural State and melt with visualization thus making it non-dual. Seed-syllables of the elements fire, wind and water are then sent from the heart of the practitioner, who remains as Shenlha Ökar. The syllables strike the offerings transforming them into measureless objects of enjoyment for all the senses and the mind in their outer aspect. In their inner aspect they become beautiful Offering Goddesses[165] and in their secret aspect they become vast offerings of primordial awareness which are offered to the Four Guests.[166]

Appendices

8. Subsequently there are three appendices.[167]
   First is *serchem* or Offering of the Golden Drink,[168] which is in fact a ritual in its own right. The Golden Drink is alcohol infused with gold pieces. An original Bönpo custom, *serchem* was later adopted by Tibetan Buddhists, although the Buddhist interpretation of the name

---

[160] Tib. 'phrin las bzhi.

[161] Tib. zhi ba'i lha.

[162] Tib. rgyas pa'i lha.

[163] Tib. dbang gi lha.

[164] Tib. drag po'i lha.

[165] Tib. mchod 'bul gyi lha mo.

[166] Up to now the text was *bSang gi dag gtsang sngon 'gro'i rim pa.*

[167] Tib. kha skong.

[168] Tib. gSer skyems mchod.

has departed from the original meaning and the offering itself has also changed. Buddhist lamas often explain *serchem* as an offering of sweet tea with butter named after the golden colour of this libation. In Bön we also find *yuchem*[169] or the Turquoise Drink, and in this case pieces of turquoise are steeped in the alcohol. Gold and turquoise are used because they were very highly valued in Tibet; gold is thought to prolong life while turquoise is the symbol of *la*.

Like *Sangchö*, *serchem* can be more or less elaborate. In this case it is quite long. First the *mantra* A Om Hung is recited three times, then extensive invocations are made, each stanza concluding with the offering and propitiating refrain:

a) Various peaceful and wrathful, male and female Buddha-forms and *Bodhisattvas* are invoked and offerings proffered to them;
b) The specific *yidam* deities of numerous meditation cycles are invoked and offerings are proffered to them;
c) Female Enlightened and Worldly Protectors are invoked and offerings proffered to them;
d) Male Enlightened and Worldly Protectors are invoked and offerings proffered to them;
e) Lesser Worldly Protectors and other non-human beings such as seventy two *Palgon*,[170] Eight Classes, thirteen *Gurlha*[171] ancestral gods, three hundred and sixty *Ma*[172] gods, ninety-nine hundred thousand *Menmo* goddesses, *Yullha*, *Zhidag* and guardians of the places of solitude are invoked, offerings proffered to them and their aid and friendship requested;
f) Offerings are made to the Four Guests with the prayer that all the beings of the Six Realms be satisfied and happy;
g) The final section deals with the action of showing strength towards the disturbing influences caused by the *Düd* from above, *Si* from below, *Tsen* from behind and *Mu* in front. The practitioner prays that these spirits may be pacified into the dimension of space, which in this case means the ground of being or the Natural State. If, however, the spirits do not want

---

[169] Tib. g.yu skyems.
[170] Tib. dpal mgon.
[171] Tib. 'gur lha.
[172] Tib. ma.

to be pacified then they are summoned into the support of the *mandala* of fire and liberated forcefully.

That concludes this appendix.

9. Entreating the Mind-Streams of the Tutelary Deities:[173] a historical recitation of the practice lineage through which a practitioner reasserts his or her connection to the lineage and ensures that the *yidams*, *dakinis* and guardians of Yungdrung Bön are propitiated correctly according to the tradition.
10. The Special Propitiation Rite:[174] various forms of *yidam* deities of the Four Activities are propitiated together with *dakinis*, *Walmo*[175] goddesses, Bönpo Protectors, all sorts of messengers and attendants, the Eight Classes and beings of the Six Realms. At the end ordinary and supreme *siddhi* are requested.

Offerings to the Protectors

11. Next comes the sequence of the *Sangchö* offerings to the Protectors of Yungdrung Bön starting with the Invocation of Yeshe Walmo, a form of Sidpai Gyalmo, the principal Guardian of Yungdrung Bön. Then follow propitiation and offering rites of other Bönpo Protectors.[176]

Offerings to Yullha and Zhidag

12. Offerings and Praises to the *Yullha* and *Zhidag* of the country wherever one has settled.[177]

Concluding prayers and dedication

13. Prayers of Aspiration[178] and Dedication[179] extracted from various Sutra texts.[180]

---

[173] Tib. thugs dam gyi rgyud bskul ba.

[174] Tib. khyad par bskang ba.

[175] Tib. dbal mo.

[176] We will deal with this kind of *Sangchö* in the section below.

[177] Tib. Rang nyid gar 'dug yul lha gzhi bdag gi sgrub mchod bstod pa bzhugs so.

[178] Tib. smon lam.

[179] Tib. bsngo ba.

[180] Tib. mDo gZer mig and Tib. Khri rje mdo mang gi mdo yan lag brgyad pa.

14. The Hundred Syllable Mantra:[181] recited in the language of Zhang Zhung.
15. Dedication of Merits to all sentient beings.

Sangchö for the Guardians[182]

Introduction

Sangchö rituals for the Guardians of the Precepts are also rituals in their own right as each of them can be performed as and when necessary. In Bönpo monasteries a special monk is traditionally charged with the task of making offerings to the Guardians morning and evening everyday in a specially dedicated shrine or house called Drubkhang.[183]

Lay practitioners of Tantra (and even Dzogchen) perform these practices on a regular basis. Although offering rituals to the Guardians also form part of the liturgy of all four main Buddhist traditions of Tibet, the principle behind these practices as well as their structure are, no doubt, of Bönpo origin. Such practices would have been incorporated into the Buddhism of India when it arrived in Tibet and underwent a period of adaptation to the cultural environment there. That cultural environment was permeated with many kinds of Bön. Indeed, most of the characteristics which distinguish Tibetan Buddhism from the Buddhism of India, Sri Lanka, Thailand, China and other Asian countries can be traced to Bön influence. The offering rituals to the Guardians are a good example of this.

General structure

When *Sangchö* for the Guardians is performed as a separate practice, preliminary purification of *Trü* and *Sang* are carried out first. The practitioner then recites prayers of Refuge and *Bodhichitta* before manifesting as a *yidam*. In some cases when the invocation of the chief Guardian Sidpai Gyalmo is done at the beginning, the transformation into a *yidam* can be omitted as she is simultaneously a Guardian and a

---

[181] Tib. yig brgya.

[182] Information in this section is based on oral instructions given to me by Yongdzin Lopön Tenzin Namdak, Khenpo Tenpa Yungdrung and Geshe Gelek Jinpa in the course of more than ten years as well as on the study and practice of the ritual texts which Yongdzin Rinpoche and Khenpo Tenpa Yungdrung rendered into English on my request in Triten Norbutse Bönpo Monastery in Kathmandu in 1996. For the list see ch. IV, n. 22.

[183] Tib. sgrub khang.

Fig. 18. Drubthon Yeshe Özer (Tib. sGrub thon Ye shes 'Od zer) doing Guardian practice in Drubkhang, *Triten Norbutse, Kathmandu, 2007.*

Fig. 19. Universal Guardian torma.

yidam. Then one recites the text of the offering accompanied by the drum, *shang*, cymbals, various wind instruments etc. depending on possibility. Invocations of the Guardians usually begin by praising the Guardian, describing his or her virtues and appearance, lineage, consort (if there is any), before reminding him or her of the vows taken in the presence of Buddha Shenrab Miwo or an early *Siddha* of Bön. The offerings are then proffered followed by the request not to forget the vows, to protect the teachings and the practitioners and, in particular, to fulfil the wishes of the one who is making the offering. A heart-*mantra* or a specific offering *mantra* of the Guardian is often recited at the end. Offerings of this kind vary greatly in both Yungdrung Bön and Tibetan Buddhism so this outline serves as a brief general introduction.

Principles behind the offering rites to the Guardians of Yungdrung Bön

What is the reason for performing these offering rituals to the Protectors of Yungdrung Bön and why are these kinds of practices done regularly by practitioners whose fundamental aim is the realization of Buddhahood, total liberation from *samsara*?

Fig. 20. Support structure for the chief Guardian Sidpai Gyalmo: torma, namkha *and* dadar.

There are several reasons why offerings to the Protectors form an integral part of the daily practice routine for Bönpo practitioners at different stages of the path. The Protectors are charged with the task of preserving the teachings, religious objects and relics, and ensuring that the teachings are practised correctly without becoming mixed or corrupted. The Protectors are also charged with the task of guarding practitioners because spiritual teachings are meant for practitioners, they live in practitioners, and without practitioners there is no continuation of the teachings. In a way, practitioners are like the treasure boxes which carry the living flame of Buddha's words and teachings in the darkness of *samsara*. As far as karma allows, the Guardians work to ensure that a practitioner has what they need to be able to live and practise, as well as watching over the correct spreading of the teachings. They look after practitioners as their kin, protecting them from mistakes, enemies, poverty, accidents, provocations of negative energies, malign spirits, diseases and other obstacles. Enlightened Protectors are Buddha-forms and some Worldly Protectors are advanced practitioners so by propitiating them one can receive the transfer of spiritual powers and grow closer to realizing the final goal, the state of Buddha. Another reason for making offerings to the Guardians is to atone for mistakes. As practitioners are not yet fully realized they may make mistakes in their practice or problems may arise within their community, or between master and student, and such actions, especially if serious, can displease the Protectors so it is very important to confess mistakes and make offerings not only to the Buddha-forms but also to the Guardians of the teachings who have direct responsibility for maintaining the purity of the teachings and tradition. If this is not done the protection provided by the Guardians may be withdrawn and they may send punishment instead Thus through making offerings to the Guardians a practitioner remains protected from inner and outer disturbances and continues on the correct way of the lineage she or he follows.

Offering substances

The offering substances for the Guardians were already briefly described at the beginning of Part III of this chapter. In addition, many Guardians have a special individual offering *torma* which should be made and offered with *Sangchö* when possible. If it is difficult to make an individual *torma* for each Guardian then a general round white *torma* and a triangular red *torma* can be offered. The red *torma* is for the Enlightened Guardians and Worldly Guardians from the Eight Classes and the white one is for the Clean Guardians such as Nyipangse and Menmo, for example. If circumstances are such that making a *torma* is inconvenient, they may be visualized in one's mind.

Indeed, this does not only apply to *tormas*; all the multitude of offering objects described in the text may be offered through visualization. Visualization is extremely important as, while the actual physical objects serve as a support, the real offering is delivered mentally for, as we have seen, this is how humans and non-humans (both non-material and those with some form of physical body dwelling in a dimension not usually visible to humans) may communicate. As an addition to the offering substances described in the beginning of Part III, blood, meat and other similar substances can be offered depending on whether the Guardian in question is an enlightened or a worldly one belonging to the Eight Classes. Some Guardians have preferences for specific offering items which are often described in the colophon with instructions or in the text recited during the ritual.

Fig. 21. Drubthon Tsultrim Namgyal (Tib. sGrub thon Tshul khrims rNam rgyal) making tormas in Triten Norbutse Monastery, Kathmandu, April 2004.

Sangchö for the Yullha and Zhidag

Offerings are made to *Yullha* and *Zhidag* to request wealth, health, prosperity, long-life, circumstances favourable for one's practice, success in commerce, protection on a journey, magical powers, to summon rain, stop hail, prevent epidemics of infectious disease from spreading, and to send away disturbances and provocations of various beings. There are many different texts of this kind of practice but the presentation below is based on a text used in Triten Norbutse Monastery[184] coupled with oral instructions Yongdzin Lopön Tenzin Namdak gave on a shorter text in 1996 when my wife and I stayed at his monastery in Nepal. At that time he took a short extract of just three verses from a larger text[185] and gave a thorough explanation on the mechanics, performance and idea behind this kind of practice.

Fig. 22. Zhidag *of* Sadag *class in Shardza Ritrod, East Tibet.*

Structure

Here we will follow the structure of the text used in the large *Sangchö* dealt with above:

1. Preliminaries: the offering objects and environment are purified with *Trü* and *Sang*, the practitioner takes refuge in the Three Jewels and Three Roots and generates *Bodhichitta*;
2. Self-Transformation: the practitioner transforms into the peaceful *yidam*, in this case Shenlha Ökar, and visualizes *Yullha*, *Zhidag* and *Lu* present in front of him- or herself;
3. Summoning the Spirits: the summoning *mantra* is recited once;
4. Generation of the Fire Deity: the practitioner transforms into a wrathful *yidam* and visualizes a Fire Deity in the form of a yellow *dakini* dancing in the fireplace in front;
5. As the offerings are put into the fire, a *mantra* is recited which empowers them to become whatever the *Yullha* and *Zhidag* desire. With the second part of the *mantra*, the spirits are charged with

---

[184] *Rang nyid gar 'dug yul lha gzhi bdag gi sgrub mchod bstod pa bzhugs so*. This text is also used within the frame of the large version of *Sangchö*. There are two slightly different versions of this text both of which have been translated into English by John Myrdhin Reynolds.

[185] Tib. Yul sa khol sgrud.

removing all obstructions and negativities. Personal wishes and requests may be inserted between these two *mantras*;

6. Main Offering:
   i) Summoning the Spirits: *Yullha* and *Zhidag* are praised and summoned to come to the offering.
   ii) Offering *per se*: a recitation describing actual and visualized offerings which in this case consist of:
      – Decorated torma
      – Yaks and sheep made of barley paste and visualized as alive
      – *Dadar*[186] arrows decorated with multicoloured ribbons and jewels as the supports of the sife-force
      – *Karsang*
      – First untouched samples of various kinds of alcohol
      – Serchem
      – Various grains
      – Three White Things
      – Three Sweet Things
      – Medicines
      – Fragrant leaves
      – Paper coins[187]
      – Multicoloured woollen threads.
   iii) The Charge to the Spirits: *Yullha*, *Zhidag* and *Lu* are requested to protect the practitioner and his/her associates against diseases, famines, weapons, disturbances, ghosts, hail, frost etc. They are asked to protect the human population and livestock, to bestow wealth and fame, protect on journeys, aid in commerce, avert accidents, destroy enemies and protect the teachings of Yungdrung Bön as well as fulfil all the practitioner's desires;
7. The *Torma* Offering: a *mantra* is recited and *torma* is offered to *Yullha*, *Zhidag* and *Lu*. This practice also has 'action *mantras*' for attracting wealth, bringing rain, averting the loss of property, repelling hail, taming evildoers, preventing plagues and protecting children from the provocations of *Si* spirits. These *mantras* are added to the main one and recited many times before the *torma* is dispatched.

The short version of this kind of practice I have at my disposal is much simpler in its structure. There are three verses. In the first verse

[186] Tib. mda' dar, is a ritual arrow used in offering, long-life, and prosperity rituals.

[187] Tib. dong tse.

Clean Gods of central Tibet, all the gods of Zhang Zhung and eastern Tibet are invoked as well as the Protectors of the Tibetan royal dynasty, all the Protectors of Existence, all the gods of all countries and all the *Yullha* and *Zhidag* of the country where one presently resides. In the second verse 360 *Tersung*[188](Protectors of *termas*) are invoked. In the third verse all the Owners of the Three Worlds, all the Worldly Owners of Existence, Country Owners, Owners of the places, mountains and earth where we presently reside, mountain gods, earth gods, *Nyen* tree-gods, and *Lu* are invoked. All three verses end with the same refrain:

> Please don't forget the promises you made in the early times!
> Come to my offerings and accept with delight everything I have arranged!
> Please complete whichever important actions I, the practitioner and follower of Tonpa Shenrab, ask of you![189]

Offerings

When this kind of practice is done in an elaborate way a special *mandala* is arranged with a bamboo *dadar*-arrow fixed in the centre. The principal *mantra* of this practice is written with cow's milk and white dye on a piece of sandalwood and then tied onto this *dadar*. Although there are some differences in how to decorate the *dadar*, generally offerings of multicoloured woollen threads, ribbons of five colours, a silver mirror, pieces of gold and silver, conch, turquoise, crystal rock and paper coins can be attached to it. The feathers used to top the *dadar* are either those of a vulture or a rock-dwelling owl.

A very tall tripod bearing an offering plate with the *torma* is set up above the *dadar*. The colour and shape of the *torma* depend on the aim of the ritual; it could be round or triangular, red when the offering is wrathful or white when the offering is peaceful.

The petals of the *mandala* are covered with flower petals of the appropriate colours, while *tsampa* figurines of many different animals such as yaks, sheep, goats, horses, deer, birds and insects, wild beasts such as wolves, bears and tigers are painted with butter and set around the *mandala* on a red offering platform. Other offerings include the Three White Things, the Three Sweet Things, first libations of *chang* and

---

188 Tib. gter srung.

189 Excerpt from *Yul sa khol sgrud.* Translated by Yongdzin Lopön Tenzin Namdak in 1996 in Triten Norbutse Monastery, Kathmandu and printed here with his permission.

different types of alcohol including *serchem*, *tsampa* mixed with butter, black-roasted barley grains and crack-roasted barley grains mixed in equal proportions.

Small bushes are planted around the *mandala*: *palü* in the east, juniper[190] in the north, birch[191] in the west and *nyareg*[192] in the south. These are the Trees of the Gods[193] which please them greatly. They, too, are decorated with paper coins and multicoloured woollen threads.

This is obviously quite an extensive and elaborate offering, so for a daily ritual whatever offerings one can get are arranged on the altar or offering platform and then burnt. Even if this kind of practice is performed with a minimum of material offerings, when intention and visualization are strong there will be benefit and success.

This kind of rite can be done on its own but is often added after the *Sangchö* for the Guardians, and it, too, is normally done in the early morning although may be performed morning and afternoon if there is an urgent matter to resolve.

Sangchö and Tailgan

Sangchö and the *tailgans* of Bө Murgel have much in common, especially when we look at the Yungdrung Bön rites for *Yulha* and *Zhidag*. In both traditions the site or shrine and participants must be purified before the main ritual can commence. Both traditions use fire and fire gods as the main means to convey the offerings. However, the traditions diverge in their understanding of the nature of these gods. While in Yungdrung Bön we have both worldly fire gods and Enlightened Fire Gods, Bө Murgel does not acknowledge the second category as there is no concept of Buddha. Be that as it may, the fire gods' practical function is the same in both traditions.

The offerings themselves are also very similar; white offerings, sweet offerings, aromatic herbs and shrubs, various foods and drinks are present, and libations of alcohol and other liquids are offered in a fire. The primary difference in the offerings is that animal sacrifice is often part of *tailgan* while animals are never killed specifically for any Yungdrung Bön ritual, even if meat and blood are used in some *Sangchö* rites for the Protectors.[194]

---

[190] Tib. shug pa.

[191] Tib. stag pa.

[192] Tib. nya breg, a kind of sage.

[193] Tib. lha shing.

[194] See below, discussion on blood sacrifices.

If we compare the deities invited for the *Sangchö* specifically dedicated to *Yullha* and *Zhidag* with those invited to *tailgan*, they differ only in name. However, the guest lists for other types of *Sangchö* are not the same, as the concept of the Four Guests is not present in Bɵ Murgel, although some Bɵ, especially from Mongolia, do invite various Buddhas to come to their ritual. This is not part of their original tradition but dates back to sometime after the seventeenth century when Gelugpa Buddhism had already established a firm foothold in Buryatia.[195]

Both rituals share a common purpose: to purify the universe, delight the gods and spirits and ask them to aid and abet the community. In the case of Yungdrung Bön the purpose goes deeper as the ritual also serves as a means, albeit indirect, to attain final realization.

All the points of similarity mentioned indicate that both rituals developed from a common archaic base, the Prehistoric Bön of Eurasia.

Method of Chöd

Aim of Chöd

Out of the Four Practices of Generosity, *Chöd* is the most complex but is considered the best type of offering one can make. Here the practitioner's body itself serves as the support for the visualization. Practising *Chöd* brings many benefits. Primarily, it severs attachment to the physical body and all the obstacles connected with it. These are classified as the Four Demons:[196] Demon of the Son of God which is basically attachment to relatives, friends, dear ones and so on; Demon of the Five Negative Emotions; Demon of one's body (i.e. attachment to it); Demon of the Lord of Death which is fear of death.[197]

---

[195] This date is, of course, different in Mongolia where Buddhism started to arrive as early as the time of Chingis Khaan and then continued to increase its hold under Khubilai Khaan (1216–1294) who converted into Sakyapa Buddhism but at this time Buddhism remained confined mostly to the nobility. Later Altan Khaan (1507–1582) bestowed the title of Dalai Lama (Mong. Далай лама) onto the abbot of Gelugpa Drepung monastery in 1578 thus establishing the line of Dalai Lamas. This became an important gateway to Mongolia for Gelugpa Buddhism which spread there widely in 17th c. and from where it entered Buryatia at the end of 17th c.

[196] Tib. bdud bzhi.

[197] Tib. Lha yu bu yi bdud, Nyon mongs pa'i bdud, Phung po'i bdud, 'Chi bdag gi bdud. This is according to Yungdrung Bön as explained by Khenpo Tenpa Yungdrung. According to the Buddhist *Chöd* system of Machig Labdron the Four Demons are: Tib. Thogs bcas kyi bdud – That Which Blocks the

It also cuts off all external disturbances bringing the practitioner *siddhi* and realization. It leads to the state beyond hope and fear, beyond the dualism of good and bad, pleasant and unpleasant. A powerful technique for developing generosity and compassion, especially towards harmful, malevolent spirits, *Chöd* helps the practitioner generate equanimity. It is also a skilful way of connecting those evil creatures with the cause for liberation from *samsara,* the teaching of Buddha. When a *chödpa*[198] has attained a certain level of realization she or he can cure various types of diseases which are otherwise are difficult to cure or incurable, in particular mental diseases such as schizophrenia or manic depression, and infectious diseases such as smallpox or BSE. An accomplished *chödpa* can even stop an epidemic of cholera or bubonic plague, such is his or her power over appearances.

History of Chöd[199]

The practice of *Chöd* belongs to the original core of Yungdrung Bön teachings. The oldest version of Bönpo *Chöd* belongs to the Tantric cycle of *Magyud*[200] or Mother Tantra. *Chöd* is contained in the text *Fearful Place Practice of the Mother Tantra*[201] and is part of the Six Yogas of this Tantra.

The lineage of this Tantra originated from the male and female primordial Buddhas and was disseminated among the *dakinis*. Their chief, Zangza Ringtsün,[202] is an emanation of Sherab Jamma, the Loving Lady of Wisdom, a wisdom aspect of all the Buddhas. Zangza Ringtsün passed

---

clarity of the senses and doesn't let the perceptions self-liberate; 2) Tib. Thogs med kyi bdud – That Which Doesn't Block following deceiving discursive thoughts; 3) Tib. dGa' drod – Puffed Up With Arrogance and Pride; 4) Tib. sNyems byed kyi bdud – Demon Of Ego. See, for example, Tr. Sarah Harding, *Machik's Complete Explanation, Clarifying the Meaning of Chöd,* (Ithaca, New York; Boulder, Colorado: Snow Lion Publications, 2003).

198 Tib. gcod pa, a practitioner of *Chöd.*

199 Information on the history of Bönpo *Chöd* presented here is according to the oral communications from Yongdzin Lopön Tenzin Namdak, Khenpo Tenpa Yungdrung and M. Alejandro Chaoul, 'Tracing the origins of chö (gcod) in the Bön tradition: a dialogic approach cutting through sectarian boundaries', MA thesis, (University of Virginia, 1999), which he kindly made available to me.

200 Tib. Ma rgyud.

201 Tib. Ma rgyud nyen sa lam khyer.

202 Tib. bZang za Ring btsun.

the lineage on to three masters: Yongsu Dagpa[203] from the realm of *Lha*; Yeshe Nyingpo[204] from the realm of *Lu*; and Milyu Samleg[205] who was a human. Milyu Samleg established a human lineage which ran without interruption through the line of early Bönpo *Siddhas* until it reached Sene Gawu,[206] a contemporary of the Tibetan king Drigum Tsenpo (710 BC).[207] Drigum Tsenpo launched the first persecution of Yungdrung Bön and so the texts were delivered by Sene Gawu to the *Jarama*,[208] the Six Mother *Dakinis,* who guarded them until the texts of the Inner Cycle,[209] *The Tantra of the Total Clarity of the Great Mother Jamma*[210] were rediscovered by the *terton* Trotshang Druglha[211] (956–1077 AD). The Secret Cycle[212] of *Magyud*, where we find *Chöd*, was rediscovered by Guru Nontse[213] in the eleventh century (born before 1027).[214] So in terms of the chronology of rediscovered

Fig. 23. Tsogkyi Dagmo (Tib. Tshogs kyi bDag mo), the red Chöd *Dakini of the* Magyud *cycle.*

---

[203] Tib. Yongs su Dag pa.

[204] Tib. Ye shes sNying po.

[205] Tib. Mi lus bSam legs.

[206] Tib. Sad ne Ga'u.

[207] According to *Bon gyi ngo-sprod blo-gsar sgo-'byed, Introduction to Bön which opens the mind* by Menri Khenchen Nyma Tenzin, Geshe Tenzin Doktrak. Information provided by Geshe Gelek Jinpa. According to Chögyal Namkhai Norbu Drigum Tsenpo lived in 1st c. AD. See Norbu, *Drung, Deu and Bön*, Introduction, p. xiv.

[208] Tib. Bya ra ma.

[209] Tib. nang skor.

[210] Tib. Kun gsal byams ma chen mo'i rgyud.

[211] Tib. rJe 'brug Chen po Khro tshang 'Brug lha.

[212] Tib. gsang skor.

[213] Tib. Gu ru rNon rtse.

[214] Chaoul, Tracing the origins.

Fig. 24. Guru Nontse. Mural from Merigar Gompa.

texts, this tradition of *Chöd* is the oldest in Yungdrung Bön.

The *Magyud* Tantra texts were written on both sides of long cotton scrolls and are interspersed with titles and passages in the Zhang Zhung Dragyig[215] script which is used alongside Tibetan Ume, a clear indication of the extreme antiquity of this Tantra. Zhonnu, a reincarnation of Trotshang Druglha's sister, requested them from Guru Nontse but had only managed to copy one side before the latter abruptly asked for them back.

Other types of *Chöd* appeared later and can be classified into four divisions:

1. Peaceful *Chöd.* [216] The principal texts[217] were transmitted to Marton Gyalleg[218] (born 1062) by the female Wisdom Deity Khandro Karmo Chyanchigma;[219]
2. Increasing *Chöd.*[220] The principal texts[221] were the precepts imparted by the early *Siddha* Tongyung Thuchen[222] to Shense Lhaje[223](born 1215);
3. Powerful *Chöd.*[224] The principal texts[225] were orally transmitted to *Tulku* Tronyen Gyaltsen[226] in 1386 These three types of *Chöd* belong to Yungdrung Bön proper;

---

[215] Tib. Zhang zhung drag yig.
[216] Tib. Zhi ba'i gcod.
[217] They were Tib. Du tri su'i zhi gcod.
[218] Tib. Mar ston rGyal legs.
[219] Tib. mKha' 'gro dkar mo sPyan gcig ma.
[220] Tib. rGyas pa'i gcod.
[221] They are Tib. Drung mu gcod chen.
[222] Tib. Stong rgyung mThu chen.
[223] Tib. dBang den gShen gsas Lha rje.
[224] Tib. dBang gi gcod.
[225] They are Tib. mKha' 'gro gsang gcod.
[226] Tib. Sprul sku Khro gnyan rGyal mtshan.

4. Wrathful *Chöd.*[227] This belongs to the later eclectic New Bön tradition. The texts of this type were discovered by a late *terton* [228] Nyagter Sangngag Lingpa[229] (born 1864) and his consort Khandro Dechen Wangmo.[230]

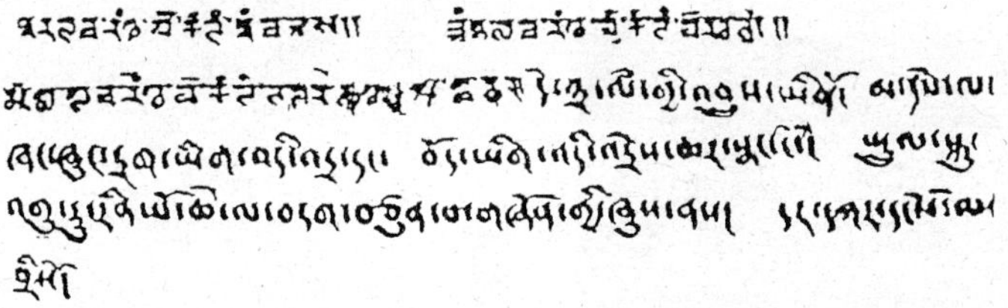

Fig. 25. A passage from Magyud in Zhang Zhung Dragyig and Tibetan Ume scripts.

The system of *Chöd* is also found in Tibetan Buddhism and the *yogini* Machig Labdrön[231] (1031–1129) is generally credited with its creation. However, before creating her own system she had learnt a version of *Chöd* from her Master Padampa Sangye.[232] Padampa Sangye was an Indian Buddhist *Mahasiddha* who roamed China and Tibet in the eleventh century and put together his own system of practice called *Zhigyed*[233] or *Pacification* into which he integrated some Bönpo traditions.

Padampa Sangye had verified contacts with native Bönpo lamas and received teachings from them. For example, it was he who introduced the

---

227 Tib. Drag po'i gcod.

228 Tib. gter ston – a treasure-discoverer. This term refers to the Masters who re-discovered *terma* (gter ma) or the teachings hidden by the early Masters at the times of persecution or for another reasons. Often the *terton* is a reincarnation of the Master who hid the teachings or one of his/her disciples. However, *terma* is not always refers to the teachings hidden in the rocks etc. Tib. sa gter but, also, to the revelations of the teachings stored in the *terton*'s own consciousness from previous lives are called mental treasures Tib. dgongs gter. There is also a kind of Oral Transmission which is given mystically by the early *Siddhas*, *Dakini* or Protectors to the *yogis* selected by them and is called Tib. snyan brgyud in Yungdrung Bön. In Tibetan Buddhism there is a similar mode of transmission received from the pure vision and it is called Tib.dag snang.

229 Tib. Nyag gter gSang sngags gLing pa.

230 Tib. mKha' 'gro bDe chen dBang mo.

231 Tib. Ma gcig Lab sgron ma.

232 Tib. Pha Dam pa Sangs rgyas.

233 Tib. Zhi byed.

Fig. 26. Padampa Sangye, clay tsa-tsa.

Fig. 27. Machig Labdrön.

Deutrul[234] Bönpo divination system into Buddhist Tantra.[235] He received this and other Bönpo teaching from his good friend Throtshang Druglha an important Bönpo *Mahasiddha* and *terton* who, as we have seen, discovered many *termas* including the texts of the Inner Cycle of *Magyud.*

There is no doubt that *Chöd* is an original Bönpo tradition native to Tibet as it is not found in the original core of Indian Buddhism. Padampa Sangye is considered a reincarnation of Guru Padmasambhava[236] so it is logical to assume that he continued his previous incarnation's work of adapting Indian Buddhism to Tibet's cultural and religious environment by integrating and applying some Bönpo teachings and principles within the Buddhist frame of practice. In the process of developing her *Chödyul*[237] system, Machig Labdrön must have drawn to some extent on already existing Bönpo *Chöd* traditions. Padampa Sangye's *Zhigyed*

---

[234] Tib. lde'u 'phrul.

[235] Norbu, *Drung, Deu and Bön*, p. 25.

[236] Alternatively, he was considered an incarnation of 8th c. AD Indian monk-scholar Kamalashila.

[237] Tib. gCod yul.

flowed organically into Machig Labdrön's *Chödyul* system in which she combined the teachings of Sutra, Tantra and Dzogchen and, also, *Dur* rites from the *Sidshen Thegpa* vehicle of Causal Bön[238] which serve the specific purpose of liberating the dead from the negativities of *Shed.*[239] Although Machig's system of *Chöd* started as an independent tradition, it became very popular and was later absorbed by all the Four Schools of Tibetan Buddhism.

Structure of Chöd

Despite the wide variety of *Chöd* teachings and practices in both Yungdrung Bön and Tibetan Buddhism, the general contents of these practices are more or less the same.

Preliminaries

As is usual for all Yungdrung Bön and Buddhist practices, one first goes through general preliminaries which include:

- Guruyoga;[240]
- Going for Refuge;
- Generating *Bodhichitta*;
- Offering of the Mandala.[241]

In *Chöd* we also have special preliminaries, the first of which is Performing the Wild Dance.[242] It has two purposes which are achieved simultaneously: subduing the external evil spirits of the place, and pulverizing one's own concept of ego and any false notions arising from it. Another part of the *Chöd* preliminaries is the Invocation to the *dakinis*, *yidams* and the Root Lama.[243] The order of the preliminaries varies depending on tradition.

---

[238] Also contained in the 4th Lore of the Twelve Lores briefly dealt with in the previous chapter.

[239] Tib. gshed. Generally *shed* means 'hindrance' but in the context of the *Shed Dur* (Tib. gshed 'dur), the Rites Which Vanquish the *Shed*, the meaning is more specific. See chapters XIII, XIV.

[240] Tib. bla ma'i rnal 'byor; the method unifying one's state with that of the Guru.

[241] Tib. man dal 'bul ba.

[242] Tib. bro brdung ba.

[243] Tib. rtsa ba'i bla ma. Root Lama (or Guru), the Master who really introduced one to one's own Natural State and made one to understand the real meaning of the teachings.

Main Practice

The main part of *Chöd* is the Offering of One's Own Body.[244] First the practitioner visualizes that their mind is expelled out of their physical body through the crown of the head into space where it immediately transforms into a wrathful *Khandro* or *Pawo*.[245] The physical body is left behind as a mere empty corpse. The wrathful deity holds a sharp curved knife or a sword.

Afterwards, the body is transformed according to the four different coloured offerings designed for various circumstances of time and place, although they may all be performed in one session. They are:

1. The White Offering;
2. The Variegated Offering;
3. The Red Offering;
4. The Black Offering.[246]

1. White Offering (morning)

The practitioner visualizes how the wrathful deity, which is their own mind, descends to the corpse and cuts off the top of its skull and the four limbs. The arms and legs form a platform[247] for the skull-cup[248] which grows large enough to hold the rest of the corpse, now dissected and put inside together with the blood. Rays of light stream from the deity's chest and, becoming fire under the skull-cup, cook the chopped body. This, together with syllables emanating from the deity, transforms it into nectar which satisfies all desires of all beings. The skull-cup and its contents increase beyond limits then offerings are made to the Four Guests who are satisfied. In this way all the aims of *Chöd* described above are achieved.

2. Variegated Offering (afternoon)

Here the adept visualizes their own body transforms into beautiful gardens, houses, clothes, farm animals, various riches, medicines and so forth which are then offered.

---

[244] Tib. lus sbyin.

[245] In this case female and male Buddha-forms.

[246] Tib. dkar 'gyed; khra 'gyed; dmar 'gyed; nag 'gyed.

[247] In some traditions the skull-cup is mounted on three smaller sculls set in a triangular base.

[248] Tib. ka pa la, thod pa.

3. Red Offering (evening)

The practitioner visualizes that the wrathful deity beheads and skins the corpse. Then their own body (now an empty shell) is chopped up and the flesh, bones and internal organs are piled onto the skin. This offering increases in size beyond any limits and is offered as a feast to the wild gods, ghosts and evil spirits of frightening places who like this kind of food.

4. Black Offering (night)

The practitioner imagines that all negativities, including illnesses, demons and bad actions, which they and all other sentient beings have accumulated from time immemorial, manifest as a huge black cloud. This cloud dissolves into heaps of corpses which are devoured by the demons whose bodies become black as coal.

Offering of the Supreme Gift

The coloured offerings are followed by the Offering of the Teaching[249] where the satisfied spirits and gods are given the possibility to enter the path of liberation, and the Offering of Protection[250] which is not ordinary protection but the Introduction into the Natural State of their own minds which, in reality, is the only protection from the sufferings of *samsara*.

Concluding Prayers and Dedication

The concluding part of the practice contains the Prayers of Dedication,[251] a wish that all beings and, especially those who create obstacles for others, come to realize final Buddhahood as soon as possible.[252] Lastly there is a general Dedication of Merits.[253]

Buddhist versions of *Chöd* follow the same general principle although individual sections can go in a slightly different order.

---

[249] Tib. bon sbyin.

[250] Tib. skyabs sbyin.

[251] Tib. bsngo smon.

[252] According to the Bönpo version I'm familiar with (*Yang zab nam mkha' mdzod chen las lus sbyin mkha' 'gro gad rgyang* by Shardza Tashi Gyaltsen), one must try to perform this practice while remaining in the Natural State from beginning to end but here is a special place when the contemplation of Dzogchen proper can be done.

[253] Tib. bsngo ba.

Developing the practice of Chöd

There are three aspects of practice in *Chöd*: outer, inner and secret. Outer *Chöd* is going to frightening places, playing instruments, singing and dancing. Inner *Chöd* is the quality of visualization (which should be very clear) and Secret *Chöd* is *Trekchö*,[254] remaining in the non-dual state, in the true nature of the mind.

One of the main aims of *Chöd* is to go beyond the limits of hope and fear, to overcome all dualistic notions, and one of the main ways this is achieved is by working with both the internal energies of emotions, feelings and sensations, and the external energies of the world in order to reintegrate them both into the single, unchangeable state, the Natural State of one's own mind. This principle explains many of the peculiarities of *Chöd.* Traditionally *chödpas* use the energy of sound (their own voice and ritual instruments) to make their practice more vivid, and perform the ritual in lonely, frightening places to stimulate strong emotions and feelings, especially fear, which are then released through the ritual into their own original condition.

This is a very powerful practice if done properly, but there are many cautionary tales about hapless practitioners who misunderstood the basic principles, became prey to their own fears and visualizations, and consequently became deranged. I was told the story of a Buryatian girl who studied *Chöd*:

> The girl violated her master's instructions and prematurely went to practise in a cemetery at night. While practising she had a vision of a huge mouth which started attacking her. Instead of recognizing this as merely an experience, a vision derived from practice and as such a manifestation of her own energy, she took it as an external appearance with inherent existence and became terrified. The mouth came closer and closer until it was on the point of devouring her. She broke into a run but the mouth flew after her wherever she ran. As she was fleeing she started taking off her clothes one by one and throwing them into the gaping mouth which immediately gobbled them up. But it still wouldn't leave her in peace and continued pursuing her until daybreak. Later people found her completely naked in the forest; she had become insane and never really recovered.[255]

---

[254] Tib. khregs chod, 'cutting off tensions', one of the two main modes of contemplation in Dzogchen.

[255] After the late Batodalai Doogarov.

To prevent such terrible mishaps, the *chödpa* must proceed in a gradual way to build the capacity of integration. *Chöd* is a very powerful and direct method but it is dangerous for those who don't follow it in the right way. Therefore, as is the case for all the teachings of Tantra and Dzogchen, it is indispensable to find and follow an accomplished Master. Indeed, it takes many years to master the practice as in general one firstly has to learn the principles of this offering, the visualization, chanting and how to play the ritual instruments very well, and then proceed to a long retreat. In the Mongolian *Chöd* tradition, for example, it takes four summers or twelve months to complete such a retreat.[256] In the first year the practitioner spends the three summer months wandering along lonely streams, practising beside them. Provisions are brought by an attendant who leaves them in prearranged places. The second year the three summer months are spent practising alone near a solitary tree in an isolated location. The third summer the *chödpa* spends three months in one or more abandoned haunted houses. Finally the practitioner is ready to spend the fourth summer practising in a cemetery.[257]

The technique of *Chöd* helps the practitioner to develop generosity and non-attachment simultaneously, so in a very condensed and simplified form it is practised from the very beginning of the spiritual path. In both Yungdrung Bön and the Nyingma School of Tibetan Buddhism it is included among the nine preliminary practices[258] which serve as a preparation for progressing to more advanced stages.

Chöd and the Siberian 'shamanic illness' or 'pressure of the spirits'

Over the years many scholars have persistently repeated the assertion that the practice of *Chöd* has its roots in shamanic traditions or that it is very much comparable to the phenomenon of 'shamanic illness' found in most Siberian spiritual traditions, including Bө Murgel. In this section

---

[256] Information on Mongolian *Chöd* is according to G. Purevsuren, the head of the Union of Mongolian Astrologists, the abbot of Nyingma Monastery Dechen Choenhorling (Mong. Дэчинчойнхорлин Хийд) in Ulaan-Baatar and the late Batodalai Doogarov.

[257] The Tibetan Buddhist *chödpa* Lama, Kianchak Rinpoche, whom I met in Paris in 1999 gave more or less the same outline. He cautioned those present from trying to use *Chöd* for healing others before all the required practices and retreats had been completed successfully and all the signs had appeared clearly so as to avoid creating grave problems for both the 'charlatan' *chödpa* and those s/he is trying to help.

[258] Tib. sngon 'gro.

I aim to dispel this misconception. Although at a glance some things do indeed seem similar from the outside, looking at superficial similarities alone is misleading and in fact *Chöd* has no common ground with shamanic views and practices in any of its aspects.

A Bɵ or a shaman undergoing the *Ongon Daralga* may have visions and sensations similar to those generated by a *chödpa* mentally offering his or her body but, in fact, the basis is completely different. A *chödpa* enters the practice voluntarily, motivated by the wish to achieve Buddhahood, and the visions they experience are deliberately evoked through special techniques which they have studied and practised; a *Chöd* practitioner uses their own mind and energy to create the vivid sensations and visions described in the text they are chanting and this will ultimately lead them to a non-dual state.

A Bɵ or a shaman, on the other hand, finds themselves in a completely different situation. Firstly, as we noted in Chapter VII, no Buryat would willingly seek to become a Bɵ or Utgan and secondly, the *Ongon Daralga* is beyond their control; the visions and sensations a Bɵ goes through while being transformed and while practising come automatically. Although the person called by the spirits often sees their body being chopped up, boiled in a cauldron and remade a new piece by piece, which may remind us of the visualizations used in the White and Red Offerings of *Chöd*, the fundamental principles are very different. These experiences have nothing in common with the created visualization used in *Chöd*. The spirits and gods are not called by the initiate or anyone else – they come by themselves because they have chosen this person and they do their ruthless work until the full metamorphosis into a Bɵ has taken place.[259] Throughout this process the 'chosen one' experiences great pain and distress, possibly even falling seriously ill, and it is not until the initial 'body-washing' ritual is performed and the person in question acknowledges their calling that the situation eases.

Thirdly, although the Bɵ or shaman is forced to submit to the 'pressure of the spirits', once their body has been purified and transformed the process is complete once and for all and there is no need to do it again. The gods or spirits may possess a Bɵ, depending on his or her status and working techniques, but that is something altogether different. A *chödpa,* on the other hand, is working to train their mind and so repeats this practice on a daily basis.

Moreover, once initiated, the Bɵ or Utgan will invoke spirits and gods, but would never use their own body as an offering; such a practice

[259] This is very similar to the process which a Tibetan oracle goes through.

is not a part of Bɵ Murgel or other Siberian shamanic traditions. Similarly, when there is a need to pacify malign spirits, to drive away illness or misfortune, the Bɵ would offer sprinkling, ransom or sacrifices to pay off debts and appease the spirits, or would simply engage them in magical fight, not offer their own body.

Some scholars argue that the use of the drum in *Chöd* betrays the shamanic origins of this practice. However, the *damaru*,[260] the ritual drum used in *Chöd*, is not found in Siberia at all and the symbolism behind it is completely different from that of the *hese*-drum. A *damaru* is a smallish hand-held drum with two sides which resound with a different tone and represents the dualities of female and male, solar and lunar energy, good and bad, pleasant and unpleasant etc. When a *chödpa* plays the *damaru* while performing the *sadhana*,[261] the two sides are struck simultaneously by two beaters attached to strings on the drum's frame. This represents the reintegration of all dualities into the unique Natural State of Mind.[262] Siberian drums, on the other hand, have only one side because one of their functions is to shield a Bɵ or shaman from evil adversaries when in magical battle.[263] As *damarus* are used by priests of many Himalayan tribes Yungdrung Bön probably adopted them from one of the streams of Prehistoric Bön in that region and it is likely they were peculiar to the Indo-Tibetan part of Asia.

Another ritual instrument used in *Chöd* is *kongling*,[264] a trumpet made out of human thigh bone. Some people tend to think that this is, too, somehow proves *Chöd*'s connection with some kind of shamanic practice. But once again, this instrument is not found in Bɵ Murgel or any other Siberian shamanic tradition. Indeed, Buryats in general have an

---

260 *Damaru* is a double-sided hand-held drum, often made of two skulls, used for *Chöd* and some other practices.

261 Tib. sgrub pa, tantric practice.

262 This is according to the oral instructions of some Bönpo and Buddhist masters. However, in the original Yungdrung Bön texts, playing *damaru*, *kongling* and any other musical instruments used in all other ritual practices is explained simply as a sound offering and no other symbolical meaning is mentioned. (Oral communication from Khenpo Tenpa Yungdrung, 17.01.08).

263 Some legends say that initially shamans used double-sided drums but they angered the gods by some inappropriate actions and so the gods halved their power and cut their drums in two halves. Whether this really happened or is simply a story invented later to somehow explain the decline of shamanic powers is of little relevance here as even double-sided Siberian drums cannot be compared with *damaru* because of the different construction.

264 Tib. kong gling.

*Fig. 28. Bönpo monk-*chödpa *playing* damaru *and* kongling.

abhorrence towards dead bodies and no-one would dream of disturbing a grave, chopping off a limb from a fresh corpse or picking up some dried bone to make an instrument. It would be considered a grave and terrifying act of desecration which, if committed, would disturb the spirit of the deceased causing it to transform it into a malevolent being who would wreak havoc on the culprit and the community as a whole. So strong is this taboo surrounding death that some Bɵ's vows prevent them participating in funerals lest they become polluted or problems arise in their practice. When a Bɵ's father or another close relative dies, the Bɵ or Utgan concerned isn't allowed to sprinkle to the gods for one year because s/he is considered contaminated by the impurity. Clearly, then, the *kongling* used in *Chöd* has nothing to do with shamanic practices or ritual of objects of Siberia. This applies to the tradition of performing *Chöd* in cemeteries, too, as no Buryat would wish to spend a night there,[265] neither do the Bɵ or shamans seek out such places for their practices. However, one thing which is the same for both Bɵ and *chödpa* is their fearlessness. For a Bɵ having fear would mean opening the door for his or her own death – s/he would be overcome by hostile spirits and murdered.

[265] Except for Buddhist *chödpa*, of course.

Finally, further proof that *Chöd* is in no way connected with any kind of 'shamanic' practice is that this technique is found within the Tantric cycles of the Fruitional Bön of the Eighth Way, *The Way of Primeval Shen, Yeshen Thegpa.* Both Bönpo and Buddhist *Chöd* teachings and practices are at the level of Higher Tantra[266] and as such are interwoven with tantric transformation techniques which are completely different from the techniques used by any type of Bө or shaman. This doesn't mean that Bө don't use transformation techniques in their practice; some do, but these techniques have nothing to do with transforming into a *yidam* or visualizing the universe as a *mandala* which is the case in Bönpo and Buddhist Tantra. Were *Chöd* a transformed method based on 'shamanic' tradition, we could expect to find it among the Four Ways of Cause of Yungdrung Bön where we find many methods adapted from Prehistoric Bön traditions, but that is not the case.

Our analysis has revealed that in fact *Chöd* and the Siberian 'shamanic illness' are unrelated phenomena. Their doctrinal foundations are different, as are all other significant aspects. *Chöd,* then, cannot be equated with any concepts of Buryatian Bө Murgel nor indeed with any Siberian shamanic traditions or any aspects of the Prehistoric Bön of Eurasia.

Tsokchö and Tailgan

General principles and structure of Tsokchö

Tsokchö[267] or 'accumulation of offering' is one of the main offering rituals of Bönpo and Buddhist Tantra. There are very many different varieties which can be extremely short, comprised of just a couple of mantras, or very elaborate with many sections. We cannot go into much detail here but below is a list of the main sections from the *Tsokchö* of the peaceful *yidam* Shenlha Ökar[268] as an example.

---

[266] But in both Yungdrung Bön and Tibetan Buddhism *Chöd* is also practised by Dzogchen practitioners as a secondary practice.

[267] Tib. tshogs mchod; Sans. ganapuja.

[268] *Dren pa chog drug las gshen lha 'od dkar gyi tshogs mchod*, translated by John Myrdhin Reynolds, *Offering to Shenlha Odkar from "The Six Sufficiencies" by Drenpa Namkha*, Bonpo Translation Project, Vidyadhara Publications, 2001. Yongdzin Lopön Tenzin Namkdak added the first three sections, taking them from the *Practice Text of the Flaming Red Garuda* (*dBal khyung dmar po'i sgrub gzhung*).

Preliminaries:

1. Securing of the boundaries;[269]
2. *Trü*;
3. *Sang*.

Four recitations:

1. Inviting the High Guests;[270]
2. Presenting the offerings;[271]
3. Hymn of praise to the *yidam*;[272]
4. Praise for the heart-mantra of the deity.[273]

Main part:

1. Invitation;
2. Rite of deliverance[274] when all negativities are slain and delivered into primordial awareness;
3. Offering;[275]
4. Confession;[276]
5. Deliverance;
6. Offering to the mouths of the Guests;[277]
7. Fulfilment of spiritual commitments[278] – offering to the lineage-masters;
8. Special fulfilment of spiritual commitments[279] – dissolving appearances into the Natural State and promising to keep Shenlha Ökar as one's *yidam*;
9. Requesting *siddhi*;[280]
10. Offering of leftovers[281] to the beings of the Eight Classes and Six Realms;

---

[269] Tib. phyi mtshams bcad.
[270] Tib. spyan drangs pa.
[271] Tib. mchod pa 'bul ba.
[272] Tib. sku bstod pa.
[273] Tib. A dkar snying po dngos bstod pa.
[274] Tib. bsgral ba.
[275] Tib. mchod pa.
[276] Tib. bshags pa.
[277] Tib. bstad pa.
[278] Tib. thugs dam bskang ba.
[279] Tib. khyad par bskang ba.
[280] Tib. dngos grub zhu ba.
[281] Tib. lhag ma bsngo ba.

11. Prayer of aspiration;[282]
12. Hymn of praise to the *yidam*;
13. Dispatching the *torma* for the guardians of the teachings;[283]
14. Dance which suppresses evil spirits;[284]
15. Prayer for good luck and fortune;[285]
16. Asking the Guests to depart;[286]
17. Completion stage.[287]

Tsokchö has many important functions. It is an effective means of accumulating merits through presenting offerings to the Four Guests; of removing obstacles or conflicts within the community of practitioners and between teacher and disciple; of purifying mistakes in practice and conduct; of obtaining spiritual wisdom; and of receiving blessings and *siddhi* from the enlightened beings. In addition to these main functions, *Tsokchö* can be used in particular situations, too. For example, it is always done at the end of significant spiritual events such as a personal or teaching retreat or a series of Dzogchen or Tantric empowerments to preserve accumulated merits and eliminate any negativities which otherwise may obstruct practice. It is done when practitioners meet or before they part for a long time to repair any previous problems which may have arisen between them, before a long or important journey to ensure guidance and protection, and in many other circumstances. In short, it would not be an exaggeration to say that *Tsokchö* is one of the most important Tantric rituals; it is invariably included in the *sadhana* practices of every Tantric *yidam* deity.

Although the example given above suggests that *Tsokchö* is a complex ritual, the essential principle is the visualization of countless offering objects and substances which are presented to the Four Guests, primarily to enlightened beings and protectors of the teachings. There are a great number of objects to satisfy the desires of the senses[288] and offerings symbolizing the transformation of negative mental states into wisdom[289] may be presented, but the main support for this visualization

---

[282] Tib. smon lam gdab pa.

[283] Tib. gtor ma gtang ba.

[284] Tib. bro brdung ba.

[285] Tib. bkra shis gsol ba.

[286] Tib. lha bskang ba.

[287] Tib. rdogs rim.

[288] Which include the offerings items described at the beginning of this section.

[289] Such as Five Nectars (Tib. bdud rtsi lnga): faeces, urine, blood, flesh and sperm

is food and drink. Empowered with *mantra* and visualization, these serve as the repository of the *siddhi* or spiritual powers, becoming a symbolic representation of the *siddhi* which are transferred to the practitioners when they share the food and drink in the final stages of the ritual meal.

While *Tsokchö* can be done by a single practitioner in retreat or in the course of their daily practice, it is largely a collective offering ritual which harmonizes the energies and minds of practitioners with those of the Buddhas, protectors and other beings. It is this aspect of *Tsokchö* which can be compared to Bɵ Murgel *tailgan* in form but not in spiritual essence. *Tsokchö* is undoubtedly a transformation of much earlier proto-Indo-Iranian and proto-Indo-European collective sacrificial offerings similar to the later *Yajna/Yasna* rituals of Indo-Aryans and Iranians, and also to ancient Slavic communal sacrificial rituals.[290] Indeed, something akin to these rituals, which incorporated a communal meal, would have been practised since time immemorial in many streams of Prehistoric Bön of Eurasia, including Bɵ Murgel. The aim of these rituals was to keep the connection with the gods and ancestral spirits intact so that they would bestow blessings, protection and prosperity on the community. These rituals were also a very important means of maintaining harmony between members of the tribe. When Tonpa Shenrab Miwo was later expounding his Yungdrung Bön teaching, he incorporated some elements of the structure of such tribal communal rites into the *Tsokchö* thereby facilitating understanding and practice. He abolished the custom of blood sacrifice, replacing it instead with symbolic offerings and visualization techniques. He also shifted the main focus from the worship of worldly gods and spirits to propitiating the Buddha-forms in order to gain the realization of Buddhahood. The new ritual form of *Tsokchö* came to be imbued with revolutionary new content and was fine-tuned as a skilful means for attaining the ultimate goal of his doctrine. A similar process happened later within Buddhist Tantra in India; the external foundations of *Ganapuja*, the Buddhist equivalent of *Tsokchö*, are derived from Hindu *puja* offering rituals while its inner content is in accordance with the Buddhist doctrine and has the same final goal as that of Yungdrung Bön – realization of final Buddhahood, the primordial ground of everything, the enlightened state of mind beyond duality.

---

which purify the five elements and five poisonous emotions. The Tantric feast (Tib. tshogs kyi 'khor lo (Sans. ganachakra) also includes offering of sexual union (Tib. sbyor ba). Such offerings can be done only by advanced Tantric practitioners who have a stable realization of emptiness and non-duality.

[290] See ch. VI.

Differences in the view and approach to ritual offerings in Bɵ Murgel and Yungdrung Bön

Offering rituals as an integral part of the Nine Ways

Although the offering rituals of *Lutor*, *Sangchö* and *Surchö* belong to *Drangsong Thegpa* of the Fruitional Bön, many aspects and ideas behind them have their roots in the teachings expounded in the Bön of Cause, especially in the First Way, *Chashen Thegpa*, in the sections on Divination, Astrology and Ritual. In the system of the Nine Ways, teachings of this level were presented such that they could be more easily understood and applied by the people of that time, whose culture and religion was Prehistoric Bön. Although the methods used in these practices seem very similar to those of Prehistoric Bön externally, internally they differ, coming as they do from Buddha Tonpa Shenrab Miwo. He taught these methods as a means of removing conflicts between various classes of gods, spirits and humans in order to bring harmony and happiness to the universe and send beings on their way to realization. They have been handed down through the lineages of *Shenpos* or Bönpo Lamas until today. The Nine Ways of Bön is a very logical and coherent gradual system where each new level is built upon the firm foundation of the preceding level. So the First Way, *Chashen Thegpa*, is the foundation level of Yungdrung Bön. A quotation from Yongdzin Lopön Tenzin Namdak elucidates this point:

> The Nine Ways were preached to introduce beings to religion, but not by force. We use these four methods[[291]] [of the First Way] and so people realize there is something invisible and powerful which exists, and that will help them practise. But the *Chashen Thegpa* is more than this; it is underpinned by quite a high attitude for developing one's mind and situation. Based on this, people use these for simple benefits and do many things for the nation or country.[292]

In higher vehicles of Tantra these kinds of practices and methods are given new impetus in the nine auxiliary actions[293] where they are reinterpreted again from the angle of the higher view.

---

[291] I.e. Divination, Astrology, Ritual and Medicine.

[292] Namdak *Nine Ways Vol. I, Bön of Cause,* p. 49.

[293] Tib. las kyi tha ma 'chong dgu ni. Snellgrove, *Nine Ways*, p. 189.

Pacts with the local gods and guardians

When the Buddha of Yungdrung Bön appeared on this earth, all his actions and teachings were for the benefit of all sentient beings. That is why all the practices of all the Nine Ways of Yungdrung Bön include taking refuge in the Three Jewels and a prayer for developing *Bodhichitta.* Sometimes, in order to tame aggressive spirits and prevent them from harming others and therefore clocking up negative karmic traces for themselves, the Buddha of Yungdrung Bön needed to take on a wrathful form and subdue them. This was often the case when dealing with powerful *Yulha* and *Zhidag,* so while performing offerings to different classes of beings Shenrab Miwo frequently manifested as a *yidam* such as Drugse Chempa,[294] Meri,[295] Wisdom Khyung, Walse Ngampa[296] or many others.

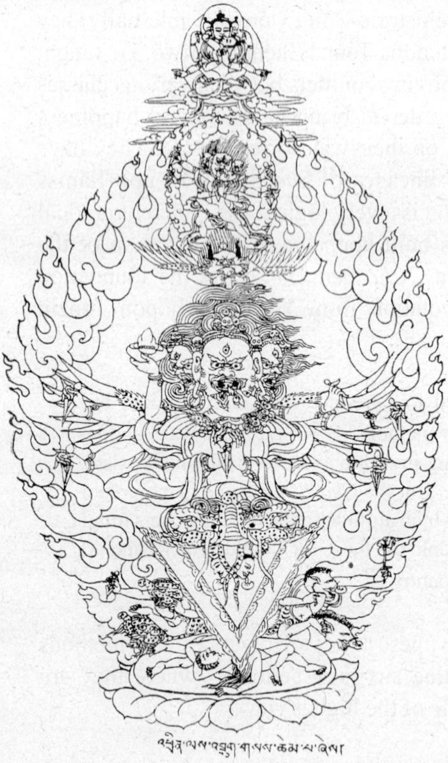

This method was taken up by the early *Siddhas* of Yungdrung Bön who, like their later Buddhist counterparts, subdued many ferocious local spirits and harnessed them as protectors of the Buddha's teachings. These acts are recalled in the texts of many offering rituals where the lineage of the *Shenpos* is recited and the power of Tonpa Shenrab is invoked as a witness to the pact they made with a particular being or class of beings. The beings and spirits are reminded of the oaths they swore to these masters, exhorted to keep them and help the practitioner who invokes them now. The practitioner him- or herself often transforms into a wrathful *yidam* when invoking and making

འཕྲིན་ལས་འབྲུག་གསས་ཆེམ་པ་ཞེས།

Fig. 29. Drugse Chempa.

[294] Tib. 'Brug gsas Chem pa, Bönpo Phurba.

[295] Tib. Me ri.

[296] Tib. dBal gsas rNgam pa.

offerings to the Guardians, but when Yeshe Walmo, who is both an Enlightened Guardian and *yidam* deity, is invoked first the transformation may be omitted. Very polite and elevated language is used to address the high Guardians of Yungdrung Bön but rough language is sometimes used when lesser gods and spirits are summoned and charged with actions. Here is an example of such an approach:

> (So) if you receive an order of everlasting Bön
> do not forget the oath you have sworn
> to come running like dogs when you are called,
> to hurry like servants if exhorted to action,
> to submit when conquered if your power is reduced and
> to vanish if you are dismissed
> and to do everything you are commanded!
> Subsequently, in the intermediate cycle of time,
> the great *shen* Sangwa Düpa,
> after having practised in nine caves (*dgu rgyud*)
> manifested in the wrathful aspect of the 'Subduer of Düd'
> and bound by oath the deities and demons of the nine dimensions,
> taking their vital essence in pledge.
> (So) do not forget the oath you have sworn
> to perform any action asked of you:
> you descend from those deities and demons,
> I belong to the lineage of that master,
> so do not violate the pact![297]

This is a fragment of the *mang* from a text belonging to the cycle of Zhang Zhung Meri, one of the Bönpo *yidams*. As we can see, the original circumstances of the pact between Sangwa Dhüpa and the gods and demons are narrated to remind their descendants to obey the pledge. Rough language is used because the gods and demons were subdued and their arrogance crushed by the power of sage Sangwa Dhüpa's realization; they could not be subdued by peaceful means. The gods and demons fell under his control, he captured their vital essence or life-force and their lives were in his hands, so they had to submit to him in order to survive. In exchange, they swore to help practitioners of Yungdrung Bön. The power of such an oath is so great that it is passed to subsequent generations of gods and demons who in turn must continue fulfilling the pledge of protecting and assisting practitioners belonging to the lineage of this master and followers of Yungdrung Bön in general.

---

[297] Norbu, *Drung, Deu and Bön*, p. 168.

There are also peaceful means of reminding the gods and demons of their promises. For that purpose the practitioner transforms into a peaceful Buddha-form such as Shenlha Ökar or Tonpa Shenrab himself as, for example in *Sangchö* studied above. If these offering rituals are performed from the viewpoint of higher Tantra, the practitioner must remain in the form of their *yidam*, maintaining the visualization and a feeling of 'divine pride'[298] throughout the ritual. One must also remain in the Natural State or maintain the understanding of the emptiness of all phenomena, not thinking that the protective gods and spirits are beings which exist. In all cases, although presenting offerings and gifts to the various beings to satisfy them, the practitioner is in no way begging or pleading with them but is in fact acting out of compassion.

When the Bɵ or Utgan make offerings to the gods and spirits, although there are many external similarities with Yungdrung Bön rituals, the underlying principles are quite different.

The Bɵ have no comparable methods of transformation and when they invoke different beings they do not usually change their form.[299] Neither do they visualize the forms of the beings they are invoking; they 'see' them directly because of the special qualities of their souls.[300] For the Bɵ and Utgan, these beings exist inherently and are as real as anything else they see. The concept of emptiness or the Natural State found in Yungdrung Bön and Tibetan Buddhism is not part of Bɵ Murgel doctrine or belief system. Rather, in Bɵ Murgel, emptiness is more like the emptiness of an empty room and all the worlds of the different beings are contained in this empty space. This emptiness, however, is made 'alive' by the virtue of the spiritual substance, the creative principle Huhe Münhe Tengeri, Eternal Blue Sky, but even so, the objects found in this empty space are real to a Bɵ or Utgan. Their visions during trance-journeys,

---

[298] According to Yungdrung Bön there are two main aspects of Tib. bskyed rim – Development Stage: Tib. gsal snang sgom pa – 'clarity' which is the clear perception of oneself as one's *yidam* and all the universe and its beings as the *yidam's* mandala; and Tib. nga rgyal sgom pa – 'divine pride' which is stable courage and certainty that in this Buddha-form of the *yidam* one now possesses all the qualities, wisdoms and powers of Enlightenment and is fully capable of benefiting beings through peaceful, increasing, subduing or wrathful actions. One must have no doubt in one's capacity to do that.

[299] It is difficult to generalize on this point as some Bɵ and Utgan naturally have a different form on the level of their mental body which is visible to the gods and spirits, but even if they deliberately assume a different form it is not comparable with the *yidam* of Tantra.

[300] Detailed discussion on the concept of soul is found in ch. XIII.

sacrifices, prayers and dreams are also considered real ones, existing inherently. The Bɵ-viewer's soul is shifting in space so that they actually enter the various 'super-real' worlds and can see and communicate with the various spiritual beings there. This, actually, is the main technique used by the Bɵ and Utgan. The so-called 'technique of ecstasy' whereby a shaman is possessed by spirits who talk through him/her is something altogether different and it, too, has its place in Bɵ Murgel. However, when the Bɵ and Utgan are moving in different dimensions they do so through the power of their own energy, though often aided by the Tengeri or spirits. According to Bɵ Murgel the souls of a person are substantial. Some of them are impermanent but others are almost eternal[301] so the ritual activities of the Bɵ and Utgan on one hand and the practitioners of Yungdrung Bön on the other, are based on quite different views.

As for the language of invocations in Bɵ Murgel, this depends on the particular Bɵ and Utgan. Lesser Bɵ, Utgan and ordinary people always put themselves in a submissive position and plead with the spirits to accept the offerings, not to disturb them but to bestow benefits instead. An accomplished and powerful Bɵ, however, has a great variety of techniques to use depending on the circumstances. The accomplished Bɵ or Utgan is always a poet who composes beautiful verses spontaneously whether invoking gods and spirits, casting a spell, performing a healing ceremony or proffering the offerings. They have complete control over their spirit-helpers, other spirits and sometimes even certain *Ezhen*-Owners. Depending on the status of the given spirit and the task they are to be charged with, the Bɵ or Utgan will speak to them kindly or roughly. If the spirit-helpers fail to fulfil their task the Bɵ may swear at them and even beat their *ongon*-support images. There were cases when powerful Bɵ swallowed or subdued the *Ezhen*-Owners of deadly diseases. Hangalov relates the story of Bɵ Bohon who tricked and subdued the *Ezhen*-Owner of the Siberian plague who came to his territory:

> Bɵ Bohon challenged the *Ezhen* of Siberian plague to a contest of magical powers, to which he agreed. Taking the Bɵ onto Mount Bohon, he laid out his rules. They were to jump into the River Ida and he who came to the opposite bank first would be the victor. Bɵ Bohon agreed. Then the Lord of Siberian plague immediately sprang into the river. However, instead of leaping after him, Bɵ Bohon flung his *shere'ehen*[302] onto the surface

[301] More on this see ch. VII.

[302] Bur. шэрээхэн, a little box-altar.

> of the river which was at once covered in thick ice. The *Ezhen* couldn't come out from under the ice and began begging the Bө tofree him. Bohon demanded that he never walk along the River Ida and that in the future no human or animal should die from his Siberian plague in that area. The *Ezhen* agreed, swore an oath and was then released by Bohon. From that time on Siberian plague has never appeared in that area.[303]

The actions of Bө Bohon in this story are quite comparable in their outer aspects to the actions of a Bönpo *Siddha*; a malevolent being is subdued and swears to no longer cause harm. Although a powerful Bө commands his spirit-helpers and certain *Ezhen* of the land, the Tengeri are beyond the bounds of his power. Indeed, the Tengeri sky-gods oversee the Bө's actions and effect punishment if their sacred oath is broken or serious mistakes are made.

Differences in the content of offerings

Among all the multitude of offerings described above, perhaps the most significant are the substitute images of animals used in Yungdrung Bön. Here lies the fundamental difference between Yungdrung Bön on one hand and the Prehistoric Bön of Eurasia and Bө Murgel on the other. As we have seen, animal sacrifice is often an integral part of Bө Murgel *tailgans* and other offering rituals in sacred places and was undoubtedly present in many streams of Prehistoric Bön. Indeed, the custom of blood sacrifices was spread all over the globe and is still practised to some extent on all the earth's inhabited continents. According to Yungdrung Bön, the practice of blood sacrifice was introduced to humanity by the *Sinpo* vampire-spirits in the dark mists of prehistory[304] and subsequently some lower-ranking gods and spirits[305] began demanding offerings of blood and life-force in return for allowing humans to live on their land, for providing favourable environmental conditions and for holding back diseases and epidemics.

---

[303] Hangalov, Sobranie I, p. 455.

[304] Oral information from Yongdzin Lopön Tenzin Namdak.

[305] According to the Six Realms classification, these entities belong to various Demi-god realms and lower levels. Higher gods do not normally accept blood sacrifice and even punish those who dare to make such offerings as the offered blood and the suffering of the slaughtered human or animal greatly defiles them.

When Bө perform offering rituals in sacred places for religious festivals or *tailgans*, a sheep, ram or other animal is often sacrificed and even when Bө are just sprinkling offerings of tea, milk and alcohol the gods sometimes take their offerings violently by themselves. Here is an example of such an event from my diary:

> A few hours later we were leaving Arshan[306] in the car. The weather was changing rapidly. Within minutes a powerful thunderstorm whipped up with torrential rain and sudden mighty gusts wind. Lightening crisscrossed the sky in all directions. We just made it to the place where we were staying when the storm became really dangerous, everything was shaking. Only later I realized that it was the very day the Bө and Utgan [...] were performing the ritual on the other side of the same mountains. Soon after they started the rituals, a thunderstorm began and while one of the local Bө was sprinkling with vodka to Buha Noyon, lightning came and struck nine sheep on the slope of the mountain. Buha Noyon is considered to be the protector of all Buryatian tribes and revered equally by all of them, but his residence is on the top of one of the mountains of Tunka which is in the Eastern Sayan range.
>
> Summer 1993, Tunka region.[307]

When Tonpa Shenrab appeared on earth some eighteen thousand years ago he transformed the way of Prehistoric Bön and taught how to use *torma* cakes, substitute figures of animals and people from dough or clay, along with other objects such as *namkha* and *dö* instead of real live victims. There are two reasons for this change: firstly, according to Yungdrung Bön, it is impossible to gain happiness at the expense of another's suffering – sooner or later retribution will come and one will pay dearly for one's ignorance and negative actions.

Secondly, offerings could not simply be abolished as many levels of Yungdrung Bön doctrine recognize the indispensable role of such practices on two counts: out of compassion to the beings to whom the offerings are made, and to benefit oneself and one's community. In this way the twofold benefit is fulfilled for oneself and others as, when other beings' wishes are satisfied and their sufferings allayed and purified, the practitioner gains the merits necessary to attain the fruit of Buddhahood. Moreover, the gifts, coupled with the pacts sworn by these beings, ensure that they act as friends and helpers for the practitioner and his community. In fact, in Yungdrung Bön the Eight Classes are often called

---

[306] Rus. Аршан.

[307] A passage from my unpublished diary, *Ways of the Wind.*

the Eight Classes of Helpers because of the oaths they have sworn to Shenrab Miwo. A Buddha's compassion is not limited to human beings as is the case with 'love' in many world religions; rather, as Buddha is beyond duality, true compassion encompasses all life-forms, visible and invisible, good or evil. The offering methods of Yungdrung Bön, then, are based on this principle of compassion to all beings and aim to better the condition of even the most wretched of them thanks to the skilful methods transmitted by the Buddha of Bön.

One of the fundamental concepts underlying this switch from sacrifice to substitute figurines is the understanding that normally these different classes of spirits and gods cannot take actual material offerings. If they could, practitioners would see the offerings disappear; normally they don't.[308] What is important is the intention, concentration and visualization – the work of mind; the recitation of an appropriate text and empowering *mantras* – the work of energy or the voice; and the *mudra* gestures, which are the work of the body. When these three aspects are present, the offerings are actualized for the guests. The physical offerings merely act as a support. Indeed, when it is impossible to obtain all the ingredients, they are simply drawn on a piece of wood or just visualized in one's mind. As we saw earlier, it is this mind to mind contact which enables invisible beings to benefit from a practitioner's offerings and which explains why a clay or dough figurine can replace a real animal sacrifice. This is the fundamental point where Yungdrung Bön diverges from Bө Murgel and Prehistoric Bön for whom offerings must be real, not merely visualized.

Fig. 30. Shingri[309] *stakes which serve as support for visualization in the offering rituals of Yungdrung Bön.*

---

[308] There are instances when material offerings do indeed disappear, as was the case with milk offered to the Hindu god Ganesh on 21.09. 95 and 21.08.06. This was a worldwide phenomenon; wherever devotees offered milk to his statues, it slowly disappeared as if he were really drinking it. See, for example, <http://www.milkmiracle.com/> accessed 03.05.07.

[309] Tib. shing ris.

Views on the practice of blood sacrifice

We have looked into the doctrines explaining why blood sacrifices were abolished by Tonpa Shenrab, so now let us turn to the archaic principles behind animal sacrifices to gain a better understanding of Bɵ Murgel's position. The Russian researcher of folklore V.Y. Propp sheds light on this in his book *The Historical Roots of the Magical Tale,* in which he examines a recurring archetype in Russian tales. The motif goes as follows:

> The hero of a tale encounters an eagle in difficulty, either wounded or ill. He is then instructed by the eagle or a third person to take it home and feed it until it recovers. Our hero feeds the eagle for a long time, giving it plenty of food. In some versions of the tale, seeing how much the eagle eats, the hero becomes desperate and thinks of killing it but then changes his mind. Finally, after two or three years the eagle gets better and flies with the hero to a magical realm where its sister and relatives live. There it tells them how kind the hero was and how he saved the eagle's life. The eagle's sister then offers the hero gold, silver and jewels in gratitude but he takes only a copper box with keys – a magical tool which grants all wishes.[310]

How is this story connected to the practice of animal sacrifice in Bɵ Murgel? According to Propp, all folktales are to some extent a transfigured reflection of archaic rites and customs common to the society where they originated. Despite being somewhat distorted and taken out of context, these customs are nevertheless quite recognizable, it is just a matter of sifting them out with the help of ethnographic materials from other nations which might have preserved them, too. This method helps to unlock some obscure passages of the tale and makes it possible to relate them to the context of the rituals performed in the past. To elucidate the meaning of this particular motif, Propp turns to the Siberian custom of feeding eagles for a special purpose:

> [The eagle] must be fed until it dies [...], then buried. Never and under no circumstances should one complain because of the expenses related to feeding the eagle: he will repay a hundredfold. People say that in the past the eagles sometimes used to arrive at a human dwelling for the winter. In those cases the householder might even feed half of his farm animals to the eagle. Before flying away in the spring the eagle would

[310] Propp, *Istoricheskie Korni*, pp. 167–8.

> thank the man by bowing several times. In those cases the householder would suddenly and unexpectedly become very rich.'[311]

This is just like the Russian folktale; a man feeds an eagle and then is rewarded for it. Propp argues that the passage quoted above is related to quite a late period and, basing his arguments on the materials collected by L. Y. Sternberg in the1920's-30's, points out that in ancient times the eagle was ultimately killed. This is clear if we glance at a custom of the Ainu, people of Siberian descent, who did just that. Before killing the eagle they would say the following prayer:

> 'Oh, precious divinity! Oh, you, the divine bird! I ask you to hearken to my words! You do not belong to this world because your home is where the creator and his golden eagles are […] When you come to him (your father), tell him: I lived for a long time with the Ainu who were like a father and mother to me and raised me.'[312]

On the base of these two passages and the recurrent theme from the Russian folktales narrated above, Propp concludes that the real meaning behind the feeding and then killing or setting free of an eagle is to appease the spirit-owner of the eagles who later takes on the role of a creator-god.

This sheds light on the attitude to the ritual killing of animals – any animal not just an eagle – in the cultures of prehistoric Eurasia. It seems that it was not considered as killing at all, but was seen rather as a way of sending an animal's soul as a messenger with gifts to its real home, the world of the spirits and the gods. It was believed that an animal actually benefited from being sent back in this way, and this is the belief on which the views of Bɵ Murgel are based. What is more, even the details of animal sacrifice in Bɵ Murgel mirror the descriptions found in Russian folktales and the Ainu custom. Before an animal is sacrificed, the Bɵ first feeds it with milk from a spoon (although it is not fed for a year or two) and prays that its soul will be transferred into the heavenly dimension. Then the animal is slaughtered.[313] This startling similarity points to a widespread custom common among such diverse ethnic groups as the

---

[311] This passage is quoted on ibid., pp. 167–168 and is taken from D. K. Zelenin, *Kul't ongonov v Sibiri* (Moscow, Leningrad, 1936), p. 183.

[312] Quoted in ibid. p.168 from L. Ya. Shternberg, *Pervobytnaya religiya v svete etnografii,* gl. 'Kul'tura u sibirskikh narodov', (Leningrad, 1938), p. 119.

[313] Normally, the Bɵ himself doesn't kill the animal. It is done by some other men who came to participate in the *tailgan.*

ancient proto-Indo-European ancestors of the Russians, Japanese Ainu and proto-Mongol ancestors of the Buryats.

Indo-Aryans also had similar views and parallel customs. In the *Laws of Manu* we read:

> 39. Svayambhu (the Self-existent) himself created animals for the sake of sacrifices; sacrifices (have been instituted) for the good of this whole (world); hence the slaughtering (of beasts) for sacrifices is not slaughtering (in the ordinary sense of the word).
> 40. Herbs, trees, cattle, birds, and (other) animals that have been destroyed for sacrifices, receive (being reborn) higher existences. […]
> 42. A twice-born man who, knowing the true meaning of the Veda, slays an animal for these purposes, causes both himself and the animal to enter a most blessed state.[314]

Here, too, the sacrificed animal is sent onto a higher plane while the offerer is also said to receive great benefits.

Both Indo-Iranians and ancient Slavs had large public sacrificial prayer rituals similar to Buryatian *tailgans* where, among other edible offerings, animals were sacrificed and offered to the gods; the first sample of each dish was burnt in the sacred fire. At the end of the ritual the participants ate the meat and remains of the offerings at a communal meal. Slavs believed that offering animals and then consuming their meat in a ritual meal was a magical action which would cause their herds to increase; indeed, eating meat without offering the first part to the gods and ancestral spirits was taboo.[315] The *Laws of Manu* contain similar ideas and injunctions:

> 22. Beasts and birds recommended (for consumption) may be slain by Brahmanas for sacrifices, and in order to feed those whom they are bound to maintain; for Agastya did this of old.
> 23. For in ancient (times) the sacrificial cakes were (made of the flesh) of eatable beasts and birds[[316]] at the sacrifices offered by Brahmanas and Kshatriyas. [...]
> 31. The consumption of meat (is befitting) for sacrifices,' that is declared to be a rule made by the gods; but to persist (in using it) on other (occasions) is said to be a proceeding worthy of Rakshasas.

---

[314] The laws of Manu, Manusmriti, V st. 39. *The Laws of Manu (Sacred Books of the East, Vol. 25)* tr. George Bühler, <http://www.sacred-texts.com/hin/manu/manu05.htm> accessed 03.05.07.

[315] Guseva, *Slavyane*, p.202–203.

[316] This also clearly states that originally *torma* were mad of animal parts

32. He who eats meat, when he honours the gods and manes,[317] commits no sin, whether he has bought it, or himself has killed (the animal), or has received it as a present from others.[318]

Here the punishments for not obeying the laws that govern ritual eating of meat are described:

33. A twice-born man who knows the law must not eat meat except in conformity with the law; for if he has eaten it unlawfully, he will, unable to save himself, be eaten after death by his (victims).
34. After death the guilt of one who slays deer for gain is not as (great) as that of him who eats meat for no (sacred) purpose.
35. But a man who, being duly engaged (to officiate or to dine at a sacred rite), refuses to eat meat, becomes after death an animal during twenty-one existences.
36. A Brahmana must never eat (the flesh of) animals unhallowed by Mantras; but, obedient to the primeval law, he may eat it, consecrated with Vedic texts.
37. If he has a strong desire (for meat) he may make an animal of clarified butter or one of flour, (and eat that); but let him never seek to destroy an animal without a (lawful) reason.[319]
38. As many hairs as the slain beast has, so often indeed will he who killed it without a (lawful) reason suffer a violent death in future births.
[...]
41. On offering the honey-mixture (to a guest), at a sacrifice and at the rites in honour of the manes, but on these occasions only, may an animal be slain; that (rule) Manu proclaimed.[320]

From all this it is clear that killing animals was not taken lightly and that animal sacrifice followed by communally eating sanctified meat was an extremely sacred act in many traditions of the Eurasian Great Steppe's international culture, i.e., of Prehistoric Bön. Reference to the sacrificial rites to honour horse manes (st.41) is further direct evidence of the interconnectedness of Aryan and proto-Mongol Bɵ Murgel traditions. This Aryan ritual is directly comparable to the large April *Habarai Tailgan* dedicated to the clipping of horses' manes and tails. It would seem that Bɵ Murgel had direct contact with proto-Indo-Aryan culture in the

---

[317] This is directly comparable to Buryatian *Habarai Tailgan*. See below.
[318] *Laws of Manu* tr. Bühler.
[319] This is clearly a an edible substitute comparable of the animal figures of dough used in Yungdrung Bön offering rituals but here the function differs.
[320] Ibid.

remote past and most likely arose from the same international q-religion and culture. However, I am not suggesting traditions found all over the Great Steppe were uniform; there must have been many differences and variations, but the basic, fundamental cultural and religious background was unmistakeably similar.

Blood sacrifices in the Hebrew Bible

The Hebrew Bible, an ancient literary source and the foundation of the modern monotheistic religions of our time, contains many extremely detailed instructions on the practice of blood sacrifice. The first instructions on how to carry out blood sacrifice are found in Genesis 15 when the god of the Hebrew Bible made a pact with Abraham; more highly detailed instructions, however, are concentrated in other early books such as Exodus and Leviticus where Moses receives details on the laws to be passed on to the priests, Aaron and his sons, and the Israelites in general. Many analogies are evident between these Biblical rituals and those of Buryatian Bɵ Murgel, and with *tailgan* in particular.

Among the various animal sacrifices made to the Lord, one of the most important is the burnt offering. This consists of a bull or other male animal without defect which is ritually slaughtered by the priest and burnt on a special altar in the Tabernacle. Before killing it, the priest lays hands on the animal's head, just as the Bɵ do. Although the significance of this is not spelt out to Moses, we can assume that it is some kind of blessing. Once the animal has been killed, its blood is sprinkled against the sides of the altar as purification. The animal is to be burnt in the following way:

> He is to skin the burnt offering and cut it into pieces. The sons of Aaron the priest are to put fire on the altar and arrange wood on the fire. Then Aaron's sons, the priests shall arrange the pieces, including the head and the fat, on the burning wood that is on the altar. He is to wash the inner parts and the legs with water, and the priest is to burn all of it on the altar. It is a burnt offering, an offering made by fire, an aroma pleasing to the Lord.[321]

Here the whole animal, once purified with water, is offered to the Lord; in other animal sacrifices, however, the meat is eaten:

> The sin offering is to be slaughtered before the Lord in the place where the burnt offering is to be slaughtered; it is most holy. The priest who

[321] *Holy Bible,* NIV, Lev. 1: 6–9.

> offers it shall eat it; it is to be eaten in a holy place, in the courtyard of the Tent of Meeting. Whatever touches any of the flesh will become holy, and if any of the blood is spattered on a garment you must wash it in a holy place. [...] Any male in the priest's family may eat it, it is most holy.[322]

The so-called fellowship offering resembles the *tailgan* as, in addition to an animal sacrifice, other items such as cakes, unleavened bread made with oil and wafers spread with oil are offered. Moreover, as in the *tailgan* and many other ancient communal sacrificial feasts, the meat is shared more widely and is eaten either immediately or before the third day after the sacrifice.[323]

However, it is not only blood sacrifices which are offered to the Lord. There is also a grain offering:

> The priest is to take a handful of fine flour and oil, together with all the incense on the grain offering, and burn the memorial portion on the altar as an aroma pleasing to the Lord. Aaron and his sons shall eat the rest of it [...] I have given it as their share of the offering made to me by fire. Like the sin offering and the guilt offering, it is most holy. Any male descendant of Aaron may eat it. It is his regular share of the offering made to the Lord by fire for the generations to come. Whatever touches it will become holy.[324]

The principle of this offering seems to be an exact parallel of Bönpo White *Sur* and its equivalent in Bө Murgel – the first portion of a mix of flour and oil/butter is burnt together with aromatic herbs as an aroma pleasing to the gods.

The Hebrew Bible contains further concepts regarding animal sacrifice similar to those of ancient peoples of the Great Steppe. The *Laws of Manu* clearly stipulate that certain animals are destined for sacrifice to the gods and this is mirrored by the following passages in Leviticus:

> Any Israelite or any alien living among them who eats any blood – I will set my face against that person who eats blood and will cut him off from his people. For the life of a creature is in the blood, and I have given it to you to make atonement for yourselves on the altar; it is the blood that makes atonement for one's life.[325]

---

322 Ibid., Lev. 6: 25–29.
323 Ibid., Lev. 12: 12–17.
324 Ibid., Lev. 6: 15–18.
325 Ibid., Lev. 17: 10–11.

And:

> Do not eat any of the fat of cattle, sheep or goats. The fat of an animal found dead or torn by wild animals may be used for any other purpose, but you must not eat it. Anyone who eats the fat of an animal from which an offering by fire may be made to the Lord must be cut off from his people.[326]

It seems, then, that the paramount motif behind blood sacrifices is to atone for transgressions committed – knowingly or unknowingly – against the Lord. He clearly instructs the Israelites on which types of animals are acceptable as repayment for which types of sins and lists the rewards they can expect if they follow his commands, and indeed, what will befall them should they fail to do so:

> If you follow my decrees and are careful to obey my commands, I will send you rain in its season, and the ground will yield its crops and the trees of the field their fruit. [...] I will grant peace in the land and you will lie down and no-one will make you afraid. I will remove savage beasts from the land and the sword will not pass through your country. You will pursue your enemies and they will fall by the sword before you. [...] I will look on you with favour and make you fruitful and increase your numbers and I will keep my covenant with you. [...] But if you will not listen to me and carry out all these commands, and if you reject my decrees and abhor my laws and fail to carry out all my commands and so violate my covenant, then I will do this to you: I will bring upon you sudden terror, wasting diseases and fever that will destroy your sight and drain away your life. [...] I will send wild animals against you, and they will rob you of your children, destroy your cattle and make you so few in number that your roads will be deserted. If in spite of these things, you do not accept my correction but continue to be hostile towards me, I myself will be hostile towards you and will afflict you for your sins seven times over. [...] But if they will confess their sins and the sins of their fathers [...] and pay for their sin [...] I will remember the covenant with their ancestors.[327]

Taken together with what was said above about other belief systems, all these passages suggest that the religious customs of the Israelites of the early Hebrew Bible are not so dissimilar from the general cultural matrix of the Prehistoric Bon of Eurasia, especially that of the

---

[326] Ibid., Lev. 7: 23–25.

[327] Ibid., Lev. 26: 3–45.

Great Steppe. The covenant between the Lord and the Israelites is in fact generally very similar to the pacts found between the gods and peoples of many ancient religions of Eurasia. In exchange for following laws given by a god – especially those connected with notions of purity – and making regular offerings, people are promised timely rain, abundant harvest, victory over enemies and so on. In the case of this pact, the benefits are purely on the plane of this world, nor is there any strong evidence that the 'soul' of the sacrificed animal goes heavenwards.

The covenants or pacts between the god (or gods)[328] of the Hebrew Bible and the Jewish prophets invariably include promise of land on the part of the god(s). For example in Genesis 15 we find the following:

> He also said to him, "I am the Lord, who brought you out of Ur of the Chaldeans to give you this land to take possession of it."
> But Abram said, "O Sovereign Lord, how can I know that I shall gain possession of it?"
> So the Lord said to him, "Bring me a heifer, a goat and a ram, each three years old, along with a dove and a young pigeon."
> Abram brought all this to him, cut them in two and arranged the halves opposite each other; the birds, however, he did not cut in half. [...] On that day the Lord made a covenant with Abraham and said, "To your descendants I give this land[...]."[329]

This strong connection with a particular parcel of land allows us to draw a parallel between the god(s) of the Hebrew Bible, *Yulsa/Yullha* of Bön and *Ezhen* of Bɵ Murgel. Below is an excerpt from the offering to *Yulsa* and *Zhidag* studied earlier in this chapter which in its essence contains a pact very similar to that found in the Leviticus passage quoted above:

> Moreover, by having satisfied all your desires,
> For us practitioners, together with our retinues,
> May all diseases, plagues, famines, weapons, disturbances,
> All hail and frost and arrows of lightning (that harm) our harvests,
> All damage to our animals, all ghostly apparitions and evil omens,
> be averted!
> May all human illnesses and cattle diseases not be sent against us!
> May whatever we think or desire be realized!
> Please befriend us and help us in terms of the white virtues,
> And bestow upon us the attainment of merit and wealth!

---

328 See below.

329 Ibid., Gen. 15:7–18.

May all hostile enemies and harmful obstacles be ground to dust!
And when we travel abroad, may you come to meet us and accompany us!
May obstructions and accidents not be sent against us!
May sickness and diseases amongst humans not be sent against us!
May loss and damage to our cattle not be sent against us!
When going into war, may you act as generals!
When going to the bazaar, may you act as merchant princes!
And when we stay in our own land, may you be like herdsmen for us!
May you hoist aloft the ensign of the Teachings in the sky!
May you realize whatever we wish for or think (with our minds)!
Please continuously guard the Teachings as their custodians!
And becoming our friends and helpers, support our backs with your hosts of magical powers,
And accomplish the realization of those deeds with which you are charged!
KI SWO CHE-O......! LHA GYAL-LO [Victory to the gods]![330]

The validity of a comparison between the Lord and *Yulsa* is supported by the growing body of evidence coming from both textual research and archaeology which suggests that Yahweh was in fact one of the gods in the wider pantheon of Semitic peoples of the Near East and may even originally have had a female counterpart:

> It seems almost certain that the God of the Jews evolved gradually from the Canaanite El, who was in all likelihood the 'God of Abraham' [...] If El was the high god of Abraham – Elohim, the prototype of Yahveh – Asherah was his wife, and there are archaeological indications that she was perceived as such before she was in effect 'divorced' in the context of emerging Judaism of the seventh century B.C.E.[331]

Excavations at the site of Ugarit in northern Syria which began in 1928 have yielded an unequalled collection of texts in four languages which clearly reveal the Ugarit/Canaanite pantheon headed by El Elyon (God Most High). The gods of this pantheon are collectively known as Elohim (the Sons of God). The god of the Hebrew Bible is referred to variously by these very same names and many researchers suggest that,

---

[330] *Rang nyid gar 'dug yul sa gzhi bdag gi sgrub mchod bstod pa bzhugs so*, tr. Reynolds, *Bonpo Monastic Rituals*.

[331] David Leeming, editor, *The Oxford Companion To World Mythology* (Oxford University Press, 2005), p. 118. Further reading: Israel Finkelstein and Neil Asher Silberman, *The Bible Unearthed: Archaeology's New Vision of Ancient Israel and the Origin of Its Sacred Texts* (New York: Free Press, 2001).

as Elohim is a plural form, the early Israelite religion has its roots in Henotheistic culture.[332] In Deuteronomy 32.8, there is clear reference to this Henotheistic pantheon:

> When the Most High (traditional rendering of Heb. Elyon) appointed the nations their inheritance, when he divided humankind, he fixed boundaries for the peoples according to the number of the gods; the Lord's own portion was his people, Jacob his allotted share.[333]

This short passage also further supports the idea that the Lord of the early Israelites was in fact one of many, and, like the other gods, was given a certain portion of mankind and the land. This is very similar to the concept of Lord-Owners found in both Bön and Bө Murgel, particularly the *Haats*, the sons of the Tengeri, who were sent to earth to govern certain territories and peoples living on them. The Lord of the early Israelites seems to have the same powers as the Owners, and his people must offer regular propitiation to remain in his favour and live peacefully on his land. In particular, he demanded blood sacrifice. A link to the culture and customs of the Great Steppe is provided by the ancient libraries of Ugarit; one of the four languages of the clay tablets (written between 1300 and 1200 BC) from the port of Ugarit is Hurrian,[334] a language of the Indo-Aryan Mittani kingdom.

While blood sacrifices to the Lord *per se* have stopped due to the destruction of the Temple in the 70 AD, prayers are offered by devote Jews that the Temple may be rebuilt and sacrifices recommence. A continuation of this ancient tradition of blood sacrifice from the Hebrew Bible is found in modern monotheism, too. While in Christianity the death of Jesus Christ, who is often referred to as the sacrificial Lamb, is seen as the ultimate sacrifice buying full atonement for the whole of humanity, in Islam actual animal sacrifice is performed as part of the Eid-al-Adha annual festival. At this time, each Muslim man and woman who has sufficient minimum yearly income is required to make Qurbani/ Udhiya – literally 'blood sacrifice' – to Allah, as Muhammad himself did. The origins of this festival lie in the story of Ibrahim and Ismail (Abraham and Isaac) found in the Hebrew Bible[335] and, like his forefathers, the

---

332 *Ugarit and the Bible*, <http://www.theology.edu/ugarbib.htm> accessed 14.11.07.

333 *The Holy Bible* NRSV (London: Darton.Langman+Todd, 2005). See also 1 Kings 22: 19–22.

334 The others being Ugarit, Sumerian and Akkadian.

335 Gen. 22: 1–18.

devout Muslim reaffirms his complete obedience to Allah and is purified. As the slaughtered animal represents a substitute for one's own child and thus carries the idea of a ransom, the offerer should ideally choose, feed and become acquainted with it. A domestic animal such as a goat or a sheep should be slaughtered for every man and woman, preferably by the benefactor himself, and a larger animal such as a camel can be slaughtered for up to seven people. The meat is divided into three parts: one is eaten by the offerer; one is shared among his friends and family; and the third is distributed among the poor.[336] Once again, there seems to be no mention of the fate of the sacrificed animal, it merely serves to buy the offerer reward and atonement.

From all the material above we can see three distinct views behind the custom of ritual blood sacrifice: firstly, killing a human or animal to a placate a blood thirsty god or spirit, who is thus temporarily pacified and allows the community live and use the land; secondly, to show complete submission, atone for sins and obtain the rewards; and thirdly, killing an animal in the belief that it is an act of liberation, of returning its soul to its real home with gifts to its heavenly creator(s) who is then petitioned to help the group who performed the sacrifice.

These are completely different viewpoints and belong to different types of prehistoric religions. The third one is more prevalent in Bө Murgel although the first view is also present as the base for sacrifices to the Owners of Diseases, some Black Tengeri and Black *Zayaans* to avert disasters and pay 'rent' on land.

Views on blood sacrifices as an integral part of religious Weltanschauung

In Buryatia the use of blood sacrifice is currently under debate. Some Bө and Utgan maintain that there is no difference between their sacrifice of an animal for the *tailgan* and Buddhists using meat bought from a butcher for their *Tsokchö* and Guardian-*pujas*. Let's examine this claim in the light of what Yungdrung Bön and Buddhism have to say on this matter.

The fundamental difference between these views and that of Bө Murgel lies paradoxically not in the question of whether it is right or wrong to kill animals for sacrifice but on a much deeper level of their

---

[336] 'What is Udhiya (Qurbani)?' <http://www.inter-islam.org/Actions/Qurbani.html> accessed 14.11.07.

doctrines; it goes back to the divergent views on how the universe came about. While in Bɵ Murgel, as in other poly- and monotheistic religions, the basic belief is that the universe and all living beings were created by one or more super-potent creator-gods, according to Yungdrung Bön and Buddhism the universe manifests as a result of sentient beings' collective karma. Sentient beings themselves are uncreated[337] and responsible for their own actions which in turn shape their destiny. According to many ancient religions, the god(s) created some animals specifically for sacrificial rituals necessary to maintain the continuity of the world – the movements of the sun and moon, rotation of the seasons, replenishing of livestock and so on. That is one reason why many ancient rituals of the Indo-Europeans and proto-Mongols included blood sacrifices in one form or another. As an almighty god-creator(s) finds no place in either Yungdrung Bön or later Buddhism, blood sacrifices become unacceptable because all living beings equally possess Buddha-nature:

> When beings follow delusion, believing in ghosts or divinities, they don't understand that the Nature of everything is Equanimity.
> Because they don't know the Equanimity-Nature, they can even take and offer the lives of other sentient beings to ghosts and gods. Yet the beings they are offering to are also among the *samsaric* beings.[338]

Nevertheless, as we have seen, the cravings of powerful spirits and demi-gods are still addressed through symbolic offering rituals and visualization.

When scrutinized from a Yungdrung Bön or Buddhist point of view, the arguments put forward by the Bɵ in defence of animal sacrifice do not hold water. Firstly, in Bɵ Murgel an animal is slaughtered specially for the occasion of satisfying the needs of gods and spirits while Bönpos and Buddhist alike just buy whatever meat is available; they do not kill one being to satisfy another. Killing animals for food is a normal practice in most human societies and no-one, so far, has succeeded in putting a stop to it. However, when accomplished Tantric *yogis* use meat for *Tsokchö* and for offerings to the Guardians and worldly beings, they do so in a way which uses this sad situation to actually benefit the

---

337 I.e. they are not created by any god but are themselves a product of their own karma.

338 Excerpt from the translation and commentary by Yongdzin Lopön Tenzin Namdak on the Bönpo Dzogchen cycle of *gSas mkhar g.yung drung ye khyabs lta ba'i rgyud ces bya ba bzhugs so*, Chapter VII. Triten Norbutse Monastery, Kathmandu, 27.01.08.

animal. An animal such as a cow, for example, has very little chance of entering the path to Enlightenment. It suffers life after life with no hope of release. But when the meat of a slaughtered animal is used by a *Shenpo* or a Buddhist Tantric practitioner for practice,[339] that animal becomes connected to the teachings of the Buddha and to the particular person performing the rite. This ensures that this animal's sufferings will come to an end. In his or her *Bodhichitta* prayers, the practitioner has vowed to achieve Buddhahood and liberate all sentient beings so as s/he advances towards that goal, they will meet the being whose meat was used for the *puja*, now under different circumstances and reincarnated, in successive lives and bestow teachings which will ultimately lead them to final liberation. Besides being a symbol of ignorance being transformed into wisdom, this is actually one of the main reasons why meat is used in Yungdrung Bön and Buddhist Tantric rituals.[340] In the case of Bɵ Murgel, the animal's soul or mind-principle is sent to serve some god or spirit who himself is circulating in the cycle of deaths and births. That is not liberation; it doesn't bring relief from the sufferings of *samsara* and, therefore, cannot justify the killing.

Secondly, if a Bɵ or Utgan wishes to appease some god or spirit by offering them an animal sacrifice, it is quite unnecessary to slaughter an animal specially for that purpose for, as we noted above, the gods and spirits are unable to consume actual blood and flesh. Instead, they are consumed by people after or in the course of the ritual. That is why practices using substitute figurines as taught by Tonpa Shenrab are a much more powerful method – there are no 'side-effects' of negative karma due to taking life yet the needs of other beings are amply satisfied.

There are other arguments against the use of animal sacrifice. Many priests of various religious backgrounds recognized blood sacrifice as a relict offering technique with heavy karmic consequences a very long time ago. For example, the book of *Ashvamedhaparva*[341] from the Hindu epic *Mahabharata* which is based on events in early Vedic India at the turn of the first millennium BC contains an interesting dialogue between a wandering *yogi* and a priest on the verge of sacrificing a goat:

---

[339] At the Sutra level in both Yungdrung Bön and Buddhism meat is not used for offerings and in many traditions the ordained and some lay people are strictly vegetarian.

[340] Based on the oral teachings of Chögyal Namkhai Norbu.

[341] Named after Ashvamedha, an ancient Vedic ritual which entails horse sacrifice.

> The *yogi* declared the sacrifice as an act of killing but the priest replied that the goat would benefit as a result of the ritual because everything it had would unify with nature. To this the *yogi* said that if the goat's essence would unify with nature, then its fellow goats [as part of nature] would receive the benefits and people should not kill the goats in order to worship god. The priest countered saying that every being is continually killing others when drinking, breathing, walking etc. as everything is filled with countless invisible sentient beings. That proves, he said, that it is impossible to live without killing others [therefore killing in sacrifice is not wrong].[342]

This passage indicates that from ancient times views on the subject of blood sacrifice differed among Indo-Aryans. To counter the last argument put forward by the priest from the point of view of Yungdrung Bön and Buddhism, we must say that while it is true that most sentient beings unwittingly kill others on a daily basis, this in no way justifies blood sacrifices; the main point which distinguishes positive and neutral actions from negative ones is the intention behind them. The mere fact that we unwittingly kill other beings does not create strong negativities because we have no intention of harming them and any slight defilements which result from this unintended killing can be easily purified through general confession and purification practices. Killing an animal with intent in order to gain benefit for oneself or the larger community by offering it to another being, on the other hand, does result in negative karma for two reasons: because it is a killing with intent; and because it is an act based on what followers of Yungdrung Bön and Buddhism would see as the wrong view, and holding wrong views is considered the heaviest negative action of the mind as it blocks the way to enlightenment.

In the case of Buryatian Bɵ Murgel, the custom of animal sacrifice also creates many problems and tensions between its followers and Buryatian Buddhists who generally view it as very harmful. As we have demonstrated, this technique is not absolutely essential, as the gods and spirits can be effectively appeased in other ways, so it would bring immense benefit if the actual blood sacrifices were replaced by more symbolic ones. Apart from bringing vast spiritual benefits, this would ease tensions with Buddhists who would lose one of the main arguments which they bring against Bɵ Murgel, and may even bring harmony into Buryatian society. Some forward-thinking Bɵ and Utgan share this opinion.

---

342 Guseva, *Slavyane*, p. 208.

Bloodless rituals of animal dedication

Symbolic offerings are not unknown to Buryatian Bө Murgel. In the distant past animals were sometimes offered with no loss of life. In such cases an animal was ritually dedicated to a particular god or spirit. Various animals, birds or fish could be used but each one was meticulously selected according to its species and colour, as each god or spirit has a preference for a certain kind of animal. The animal to be dedicated was The dedicated animal is first purified through sprinkling with sanctified water and fumigation, then alcohol was offered to the god or spirit to whom the animal was to be dedicated. After that the animal was decorated with coloured ribbons and set free.

For Uta Sagaan Noyon, the *Ezhen*-Owner of Olhon Island, for example, the dedicated animal was a pigeon decorated with white and blue ribbons while Uhan-Haat, the king of *Lusuut* water-spirits, accepts an eelpout as a dedicated animal. It seems that Tengeri were offered special horses festooned with ribbons. The dedicated animal could not be hunted and was left to wander freely and unharmed. Should someone kill or injure such an animal, they would be severely punished by the Tengeri or spirit to whom the animal was devoted. Unfortunately this technique is not used nowadays although M.N. Hangalov reports it was still in use at the beginning of the twentieth century.[343] It seems that it was somehow completely forgotten in the years of repressions which followed the Socialist Revolution of 1917. Nevertheless, this is a solidly authentic Bө Murgel custom which could be reinstated if there were understanding and goodwill on the part of the Bө and Utgan.

This custom of dedicating animals decorated with coloured ribbons to the gods is also found in the branch of Bө Murgel practised in Tuva, and in Tibetan Bön. In Tibet the main animals designated to the gods are horses and yaks although goats and sheep may sometimes be dedicated in a similar way. An animal set aside for the gods is bedecked with ribbons, freed from all labour and looked after until its natural death. It is not set free as in Buryatia to prevent it being killed in the wild.[344]

---

[343] Hangalov, *Sobranie I*, pp. 351–362.

[344] Animals are also sometimes freed from labour to extend someone's life (Tib. thse rta, tshe yag) but this is based on an entirely different principle, namely that by showing compassion one accumulates positive karmic traces which can then be dedicated for someone else's benefit. Similarly, an animal destined for slaughter can be bought and freed, and the merits of saving life dedicated to extend the life of a lama or someone else.

Some Bönpo *yogis* who attained a high degree of spiritual power used animals dedicated to the gods in a very practical way. One such was Lhundrub Muthur,[345] a Master of *Zhang Zhung Nyen Gyud* who lived in the tenth century. After devoting a white goat to the guardian Nyipangse and a white female yak to his companion the lake-goddess Menmo, Lhundrub Muthur asked them to look after his herds of goats, sheep and yak so he didn't need to employ the herdsmen.[346]

A similar way of dedicating animals is also found among the Yakut (Saha) people who now live to the north of Lake Baikal and share a common ancestor, the Gooligan', with Buryatian tribes. There is evidence that the Yakuts had a custom of dedicating horses to the sky-god Urun Aiyy. Selected horses were set aside and consecrated to this god and then young lads clad in white holding sticks stripped of bark (to make them white) chased them far away from the herd so that they could not come back.[347] Similar traditions are found among various Siberian nations indicating that this ritual custom was widespread in the area from very ancient times. Some scholars suggest this tradition stems from Zoroastrian influences which allegedly reached Siberia in the period of early Tyurkic states via Sogd. This idea is based on the assumption that Zoroastrians were opposed to the practice of animal sacrifice.[348] However, this argument appears invalid; as we saw in Chapter VI from our analysis of the passage from the *Mihr Yasht*, animal sacrifices were in fact practised in Zoroastrianism. Moreover, although white horses, or a carriage drawn by them, were dedicated to Mithra and

Fig. 31. A white goat dedicated to the gods, Tibet, 2007.

345 Tib. Lhun grub Mu thur.

346 Yongdzin Lopön Tenzin Namdak Rinpoche, *Teachings on Zhang Zhung Nyen Gyud and Namkha Truldzö, Vimoutiers, 24 August – 11 September 2004,* Trscr. &ed. Carol Ermakova and Dmitry Ermakov (Blou: Shenten Dargye Ling, 2006), (Experiential Transmission of Zhang Zhung, p. 53); oral communication from Yongdzin Rinpoche.

347 N. A. Alekseev, Kul't Aiyy – plemennykh bozhestv-pokrovitelei yakutov, *Etmograficheskii sbornik*, 5 (Ulaan-Ude: Buryatskoe knizhnoe isdatel'stvo, 1969), p. 146.

348 For example, Galdanova, *Dolamaistkie*, p. 86.

Ahura Mazda, this tradition is no doubt of pre-Zoroastrian origin. In this case, the horses and the carriage serve as a support for the god's presence in religious ceremonies. There is no other custom of animal dedication found in Zoroastrianism. In Bɵ Murgel, the assigned animals are set free, so the underlying concept is quite different.

If we compare Buryatian and Tibetan customs of dedicating animals to the gods, on the other hand, it becomes clear that they have a common origin. According to Yongdzin Lopön Tenzin Namdak, the Tibetan version is proper to Yungdrung Bön which may indicate that the analogous Bɵ Murgel custom is related to Yungdrung Bön rather than Prehistoric Bön. This gives us an important clue to argue that Yungdrung Bön found its way to Buryatia in some distant past and that some rites and customs of Bɵ Murgel may therefore be derived from or influenced by its teachings. Yungdrung Bön spread in all directions of Eurasia from Tagzig, which was probably situated somewhere in the Pamirs, so in Chapter XV we will suggest possible times and routes whereby Tonpa Shenrab's teachings could have reached Southern Siberia and, in particular the Lake Baikal region.

CHAPTER XIII

The Soul

The soul is a mysterious concept in any religious system. It is generally connected with the spiritual dimension, the afterlife, that which communicates with the gods. As it is not made of physical matter like the body, it can be somewhat elusive to conceptualize. However, in both Bön and Bɵ Murgel we find very similar ideas of what the soul is and how it affects a person's life. This understanding forms the vital foundations on which the lore of magic rests.

Part I
Soul and Related Concepts

The concepts of la, yi and sem, tse and sog[1] in Yungdrung Bön

Let's start with the concept of *la*. According to Yungdrung Bön *la* is the karmic traces of the individual[2] which have been accumulated in the course of countless lives. Metaphorically, *la* is symbolized by *lanay*,[3] the receptacles of the *la*, such as *la*-lakes, *la*-mountains,[4] *la*-animals or other objects and even persons.[5] The *la* and its receptacle are very tightly interlinked so when there is some problem with the latter it also manifests in the condition of the person who is connected with it and vice versa.[6]

---

1 Tib. bla, yid, sems, tshe, srog.

2 Also known as Tib. bag chags.

3 Tib. bla gnas.

4 Tib. bla mtsho, bla ri etc.

5 E.g. when a parent has a particularly strong attachment and affection towards one of the children in the family in Tibet they say that the *la* of this parent resides in the child. Oral communication from Khenpo Tenpa Yungdrung.

6 E.g. if the *la*-mountain of the king is damaged he may become seriously ill or die, or if the king is seriously ill or dies his *la*-mountain may be damaged by an earthquake or something similar.

This phenomenon is explained by the fact that through attachment to a particular place, object or person, a very strong connection is established between a person's *la* and that special place. Although *la* has an aspect of energy, it is not itself a kind of energy. It is said that if one's *la* has been lost or stolen, one experiences obstacles or poor health, bad luck and other negative circumstances. If life seems to be going well, one's *la* is said to be strong. According to Tibetan medical theory, *la* constantly moves and changes its location in the body following the thirty day lunar cycle, but this is in fact a kind of metaphor as karmic traces or *bagchag* are not something physical which can move around. Similarly, *la* cannot be 'lost' or 'stolen'. The real explanation for the apparent disappearance of *la* is that the results of positive karma have stopped manifesting for a period of time due to secondary causes. On the other hand, when a person is healthy and everything is going well that means *lungta* is strong. *Lungta* depends on *la* as we will see below. Again, the real meaning is connected with karma; in this case, positive karma has come to fruition.

La also acts as a support for *yi*, subtle wind,[7] a kind of energy which moves the mind, and for *sem* – mind itself. In the Dzogchen teachings we find a parable which illustrates the workings of *yi* and *sem*. In this parable *sem* is likened to a crippled man who is riding a blind horse which represents *yi*. Together they can move around, with the lame

---

7 *Yi* is the most subtle kind of *lung* (rlung) and is very tightly connected to the mind. *Lung* is a Tibetan name for the subtle energy which in Sanskrit is called *prana* and in Chinese *chi (qi)*. There are many different kinds of *lung* as it is a very general term denoting a wide range of energies or 'winds' inside the human body's energy system and in the outside world. There are primal winds which brought about the formation of the universe known in the language of Zhang Zhung as *tshan ting*, *nan ting* and *sprin ni* and in Sanskrit as *vāyu*. Then there are universal life-sustaining energies which are absorbed through breathing known in Sanskrit under the general name *prana* and in Chinese as *chi* (*qi*). Then there are five main winds within the human body which make it function: Tib. gyen rgyu rlung – ascending wind coursing in the central channel between throat and crown chakras; Tib. srog 'dzin gyi rlung – life-supporting wind which resides in the heart-chakra; Tib. me mnyam – equally abiding fire wind between the navel chakra and the stomach; Tib. khyab byed kyi rlung – all-pervading wind in the whole of the body; and Tib. thur sel rlung – descending wind in the secret chakra. (This is according to Geshe Gelek Jinpa, *Tummo: A Practice Manual by Shardza Tashi Gyaltsen*, Transcribed and edited by Carol and Dmitry Ermakovi, Shenten Dargye Ling: Association Yungdrung Bon, 2005. [Some medical texts and other traditions have slightly different explanation.]) In fact, there are countless other types of *lung,* both internal and external.

man guiding the horse's movement. *La* acts as food for the horse. In this way these three can function together. When the mind is stirred by the subtle wind, thoughts are produced and circulate through the subtle channels within the body. According to one theory, the principle of the famous *lungta* prayer flag practice is connected above all with *yi*, the subtle wind, and works through connecting *yi* to the external element of wind. In this case the word '*lungta*' and the horse depicted in the centre of the flags represent *yi* and the external element of wind, while the four animals in the corners symbolize the other four elements.[8] The *lungta* flags work together with visualization and *mantra* recitation so this practice transforms and harmonizes *yi* which in turn controls the movements of the mind. In general, the aspect of Tantric practice which uses the voice – i.e. *mantra* recitation – is aimed at transforming *yi* while specific visualizations are aimed at transforming *sem*. These two, *mantra* recitation and visualization, are applied simultaneously. The specific fruit of Tantra is the realization of the Illusory Body, *gyulu*,[9] at the end of a practitioner's life. When the physical body is left behind at the moment of death, the practitioner's transformed and purified *yi* and *sem* fuse together inseparably in the form of the *yidam* on which s/he meditated during his/her lifetime.

La also serves as support for *sog* and *tse* thus forming another triad. This triad is connected above all with the physical condition of the body. As long as *la* is in the body we can talk about *sog* and *tse*. *Sog*, Vital Principle or Essence, is a combination of the subtle wind and karmic traces. It is like a pillar which connects mind and body. *Tse*, Life, is the duration or length of *sog*; it is the duration for which this pillar fulfils its function. *Tse* and *sog* can be understood as different aspects of the same thing. They are very deeply interconnected but differ in their manifestation and function.

All sentient beings possess *la*, *yi* and *sem* whether they have taken a physical body or other form or find themselves in the intermediate state of *Bardo*[10] between death and the next life. All incarnate beings also have *la*, *tse* and *sog*. Buddhas, however, as totally realized beings, do not have *la* because all their karmic traces are completely purified; were it otherwise, they could not have achieved Buddhahood. Similarly, they do not have *tse* and *sog* because these two do not function without karmic traces.

---

8 According to another theory these are the Deities of *Lungta*. See Norbu, *Drung, Deu and Bon,* pp. 68–72.

9 Tib. sgyu lus.

10 Tib. bar do; lit. 'in between'. See below.

However, realized beings do have *yi* and *sem* in their purified form. The example of water is often used to explain the difference between the *sem* of sentient beings and that of a Buddha. In the case of an ordinary being's mind, water is full of dust particles (thoughts, emotions etc.) making it impossible to see through. An enlightened being's mind is likened to crystal clear water which is limpid and transparent without any traces of dirt. Another example for the *sem* of Buddha likens it to a piece of ice which has dissolved back into its original condition, water. Here, water symbolizes the Natural State of Mind. The mind of ordinary beings is like ice, hard as a stone, conditioned by its own appearances which seem real to it. Ice melting into water signifies a mind's return to its original condition: ice is always water. When ice has melted and turned back into water it is just the same water which had previously appeared as ice but is now once again in its original condition. There is, then, a continuation of *sem* after the attainment of Buddhahood but this *sem* is not the same as the reincarnating consciousness of an ordinary sentient being, *nampar shepa.*[11] Mind has dissolved into its own Nature.[12]

Yongdzin Lopön Tenzin Namdak further clarified this matter in a short reply to my question on how *la* and dream-body are connected:

> The dream body is naturally related to *la* by karmic cause. Generally dreams and dream views are all connected with karma. Sometimes we explain bad dreams as a sign that the *la* is lost. Such dreams don't always have the same meaning but sometimes they may show that the *la* is lost.
>
> The human body is formed from five elements and they all have energy. They are integrated with consciousness and consciousness is influenced by very subtle air (*yi*). Air (*yi*) and mind are combined together and can lift or push, wax or wane. And that is all according to karmic cause. There are general and private karmic causes and this depends very much on the individual.
>
> Karmic cause is connected with the energy of the elements which you are formed from. The five elements develop and sometimes disturb each other causing sickness and problems, and at that time energy is leaking and that is called losing *la*. If the elements help each other then everything goes well, it is good.[13]

---

[11] Tib. rnam par shes pa. *Sem* and *nampar shepa* or *namshe* are synonymous in the case of a sentient being but not in a Buddha.

[12] These examples are given according to Dzogchen teachings. This presentation is in accordance with explanations given by Khenpo Tenpa Yungdrung.

[13] Triten Norbutse Bönpo Monastery, Kathmandu, Nepal, April, 2004.

> Traditionally, we know about *la yi sem sum*[14] from dreams. In dreams, visions change and move and show *la yi sem sum*. We can see everything, but there is no substance, no inherent existence.[15]

The understanding of soul in Prehistoric Bön

There can be little doubt that the concepts of *la*, *tse* and *sog* existed in Prehistoric Bön. However, they would have been viewed somewhat differently as, before the coming of Buddha Shenrab Miwo, these archaic traditions would have lacked the understanding of the Nature of Mind. Any understanding of karma and reincarnation would also have been different. Siberian cultures, for example, believe that souls reincarnate on the physical plane of existence but in a very particular pattern. If one had been a man one could be born again as a man but not as any other species; deer return as deer, wolves as wolves and so on. This is the notion underlying the 'reincarnation' ritual for bears killed in a hunt which is also sometimes performed when a captured bear is ritually suffocated. Hunters often cry over the killed animal to appease its spirit or apologize, explaining that they just needed meat for survival and didn't mean to harm the soul. When hunting a bear Buryatian hunters often try to deflect any possible negative backlash by deceiving the spirit of the animal saying, 'Oh great father! Come out of your bear's den, but know it is not the Buryats who are killing you but Russians (or Evenki etc.)'. When the bear's meat is eaten the bones, skull, claws and skin are returned to the exact place where the bear was killed so that he can return again. Although this shows some kind of understanding of the cause-effect relationship it is not the same as the understanding of karma in Yungdrung Bön and Buddhism.

According to Professor Namkhai Norbu, in archaic Bön *la* was understood as a particular type of psychic energy and the only aspect of a person which interacts with the energies of the external world. As such, it had a protective function. *Tse* and *sog* were believed to be strictly tied to *la*, only being able to survive without it for a maximum of six months. Consequently, if *la* left the body one would die within six months.[16]

---

[14] Tib. bla yid sems gsum.

[15] Excerpt from the translation and commentary by Yongdzin Lopön Tenzin Namdak on the Bönpo Dzogchen cycle of *gSas mkhar g.yung drung ye khyabs lta ba'i rgyud ces bya ba bzhugs so*, Chapter VII. Triten Norbutse Monastery, Kathmandu, 27.01.08.

[16] Norbu, *Drung, Deu and Bön*, p. 246, n. 51.

La, wug and sog

However, there is another triad of which *la* forms a part and, in my opinion, it is this triad which comes from the very archaic layers of Prehistoric Bön because it finds an almost exact equivalent in Bө Murgel. The triad in question is *la, wug*[17] and *sog.*

We have already dealt with the two components *la* and *sog* from the point of view of Yungdrung Bön. However, in the framework of this second triad, *sog* retains the same meaning as explained above – Vital Principle – while *la* is understood slightly differently. Here, *la* is thought of as a support for all the psychological, intellectual and physical aspects of a human being and there is no talk of it being identical with karmic traces. As such, it dwells within the body, either in the heart or pervading all the body equally. In either case, it depends on *wug*, Respiratory Breath, to function and *wug* is inseparably tied with *tse*, Life. Should *wug* cease, *tse* will collapse and the person will die. *La*, however, can still remain temporarily in the corpse or be ejected. In this interpretation, then, it is considered that *la* and *sog* remain after death while *wug* ceases to exist.[18]

According to this more archaic view, *la* can indeed be abducted or damaged by the spirits and gods[19] or can jump out of the body[20] because of fright or severe pain. If this happens, the person falls ill and can die if a 'recalling of the *la*'[21] or 'ransoming of the *la*'[22] rite is not done or is not successful. Even after death it is necessary to protect the *la* of the deceased as it may be captured and enslaved by evil spirits[23] and so cut off from *yi* and *sẹm*, which in turn would prevent it entering the *Bardo*, the intermediate state leading to the next rebirth. Yungdrung Bön has a great variety of *Dur*[24] funerary rites aimed at easing the suffering of the dead and safeguarding the living from negativities which may result from death. These rites address all possible circumstances and modes of death, cutting off obstacles which may hinder the deceased in its passage to a better rebirth. Some serve to liberate the deceased's *la* from captivity and reunite it with *yi* and *sem*. We shall look into these rites in detail

---

17 Tib. dbugs.

18 According to Karmay, *The Arrow and the Spindle,* p. 311–314.

19 Tib. lha 'dre.

20 Tib. bla 'khyams pa.

21 Tib. bla bod.

22 Tib. bla bslu.

23 Tib. gshed ma 'dre.

24 Tib. 'dur.

in the following chapter. Here it is enough to say that these methods most probably have their roots in Prehistoric Bön and were adapted and transformed by Tonpa Shenrab. As we shall see later, there are certain parallels between these rites and those of Bө Murgel.

It is clear, then, that *la* comprises a vital and indispensable component of a human being's complex mind-energy-body system so, naturally, practitioners of various types of Bön throughout the millennia were seeking to obtain control over their *la* and the *la* of other beings. As we shall see, this has important implications in magic and healing; many of a magician's miraculous powers are derived from an unusual degree of control over his or her *la*.

Multiple souls in Bө Murgel

In Buryatian Bө Murgel we find a very similar concept of soul. Here, the soul is a kind of psychic energy and not what is considered to be a soul in theistic religions such as Hinduism, Judaism, Christianity and Islam. Moreover, according to Bө Murgel, humans possess at least three souls which have different functions and different destinies after death.

i. Hain hunehen[25] *or zayaashi*[26]

This appears at conception. It is sent from the Sky and stays with a person for the duration of their life. It has a protective function, taking care of the health, well-being, sanity and prosperity of its owner. It has the capacity to communicate with the Tengeri, *Haats* and other gods of high stature, petitioning them and asking favours for its owner. If a person lives well then their *zayaashi* is well-dressed, happy and rides a good horse. If a person's life isn't so good, their *zayaashi* is badly-dressed, sad and travels on foot. At death *zayaashi* withdraws to the Sky regardless of what actions one has committed while alive and continues living with the Tengeri. If *zayaashi* happens to leave a person and wander off it does not result in death but one will certainly have a miserable life. This first soul is tightly connected with a person's destiny so in Russian ethnographic works it was nick-named 'fate-soul'.[27] The word '*zayaashi*' is derived from the word '*zayaa*' meaning 'fate', 'destiny', 'lot'. The

---

25 Bur. һайн һүнэхэн – 'good soul'.

26 Bur. заяаши. *Zayaashi* can mean 'creator'. Some also call it *hulde/sulde* but if we look closely we can clearly see that *hulde* generally means something else and has a different function (see below).

27 Rus. душа-судьба.

name *zayaan,* a god or spirit who has the capacity to control the fate of humans, is derived from the same root.

As we can see, this soul is quite an independent entity. Although attached to a person, it has an autonomous and actually more refined and powerful existence than that of its owner due to the privilege of direct communication with the Tengeri. This soul is very much comparable with the Tibetan concept of the Five Personal Deities,[28] the Deities of *Lungta*[29] and, to some extent, resembles the Western notion of the guardian angel. Although the Five Personal Deities are actually five deities and the Deities of *Lungta* comprise four or five deities[30] with many attendants, their nature and functions are parallel to those of the *hain hunehen* soul and their multiple manifestations serve to highlight the multiple protective and nurturing tasks they fulfil. These deities stay with a person while they are alive, never leaving them but following them everywhere as a shadow, increasing well-being, health, good luck and prosperity. The Five Personal Deities in particular are very tightly connected with the physical body and reside in its various parts. They have power not only over the fortune, ascendance capacity and prosperity of the individual but also affect the energies of those functions in the outer world. The Deities of *Lungta*, on the other hand, are more connected with the elements from which a person is composed and also control the energies of the external elements. In reality the conditions of inner and outer energies are not separate but are always interconnected and influence each other. This is the basic principle behind many practices contained in Yungdrung Bön's Four Ways of Cause, and in Bɵ Murgel. Many rituals balance the internal energies of a person by acting on the external elements or even on other beings. Well-known examples here are offering medicines to the *Lu* water-spirits to appease them so that they withdraw curses from an ill person and turning prayer-wheels and hanging *lungta* prayer flags. If a person's elements are balanced and in harmony with the environmental energies then they are healthy, lucky and happy as they cannot receive negative influences from outside.

ii. Dunda Hunehen[31]

This is the soul *per se*. It is an 'astral double' of a living person and looks exactly like his/her body, so it can be short or tall, fat or thin

---

28 See Norbu, *Drung, Deu and Bön*, pp. 65–68.

29 Tib. klung rta'i lha, rlung rta'i lha. Ibid., pp. 70–72.

30 Depending on the interpretation.

31 Bur. дунда һүнэхэн, 'middle soul'.

depending on the physical constitution of its owner. It is the double of a living person on the emotional plane, too, so if a person is evil and mean, their soul is also evil and mean whereas if a person is generous and happy, their soul is likewise good-natured. *Dunda hunehen* is material but is very subtle. In fact, it is nicknamed 'shadow-soul'[32] because it follows a person everywhere and mimics the physical body. That is why in the past it was considered dangerous to step on a person's shadow – there was a risk of damaging this soul which is the core or vital soul. If *dunda hunehen* happens to wander away, be damaged or stolen, the person to whom it belongs is sure to fall ill or die. However, it can leave the body for short periods of time, for example during sleep. According to Bө Murgel, dreaming is explained by the *dunda hunehen* soul wandering away from the body and visiting different places while we are asleep,[33] then returning to the body with memories of these travels which manifest as dreams. This accounts for the period of 'blankness' when people sleep and have no dreams; it is the time when the soul travels away. Dreaming starts when it comes back to the body and unfolds its memories. That is why dreams can be grotesque or symbolic, lucid or unclear, frightening or happy and so on; it is all to do with this soul's experiences as well as its intelligence and memory. For instance, if someone's soul has a bad memory and is a little dull then that person will have confused, unclear dreams or may not remember their dreams at all.

Experienced Bө and Utgan have an incredible degree of control over their *dunda hunehen* soul and can consciously make it travel in all the dimensions of the Three Worlds, sometimes for very long periods of time during trance, without endangering it or causing it any harm. For ordinary people, however, the presence of this soul in the body is indispensable. If it wanders off or is stolen by malevolent spirits or gods, its owner will fall ill and, if the soul is not returned and reunited with the body in time, die. So when Bө or Utgan perform 'recalling of the soul' or 'ransoming the soul' rituals, it is mainly to return this *dunda hunehen* soul. Death occurs when this soul has irrevocably left the body either because of old age, accident or due to being stolen by evil beings or because of a black magic rite cutting it off from the body. It is this soul which reincarnates after death.

---

32 Bur. hүүдэр, 'shadow'.

33 We find the same explanation in Chuang Tzu, 'In sleep, men's spirits go visiting; in waking hours , their bodies hustle'. Tr. Watson, *Chuang Tzu,* p. 32. It seems the ancient Chinese, particularly Taoists, had the same explanation for the dreaming process.

Dunda hunehen, mind-body and dream-body

This type of soul closely resembles the mind-body[34] which experiences the dream state[35] as it is explained in both Yungdrung Bön and Tibetan Buddhism. The dream-body[36] is a form assumed by consciousness and *la* during sleep or in the sixth *Bardo,* the Bardo of Becoming. It is an exact double of a person, both physically and emotionally, although when we are awake, consciousness and *la* do not have a particular form but are found within the physical body:

> This form is only an imaginary form, like a dream; dreams are evidence as to what this [*Bardo*] will be like. Everyone has this experience. In our dreams we have eyes, ears – everything is perfect. We call these spiritual organs – they are not material but (exist) only according to our own experience.[37]

According to Yungdrung Bön dreaming is the process of revisiting of the karmic imprints kept in the *kunzhi nampar shepa*[38] – Basic Storing Consciousness. During the day consciousness is mainly fixed on the objects of the phenomenal world except for daydreaming or when flashbacks occur. During the night, consciousness sinks into the Basic Storing Consciousness and looks through the karmic traces kept there. This is how Yongdzin Lopön Tenzin Namdak explains dreaming and the process of collecting karmic traces:

> First of all, you have to think that our own mind is the creator. This creator created many different things, both virtuous as well as sinful, negative things; positive and negative, everything is created by our own consciousness. We often speak about negative actions, about sins, and say they leave karmic causes, but how do we make karmic causes? Where are they kept? What are they? Who knows about them? They are not merely a story, so we have to realize how we collect karmic causes, be they positive or negative. We have our consciousness, body and speech, but (the latter two) are only created temporarily according to time; the main thing is our mind; that is always there. We are always changing our body, just as we always change our clothes.

---

[34] Tib. yid lus.

[35] Tib. rmi lam.

[36] Tib. rmi lam gyi lus.

[37] Dru Gyalwa Yungdrung, *Gyalwa Chagtri Chapter II: Zab mo gnad kyi gdams pa dngos gzhi bzhugs so*, Teachings by Yongdzin Lopön Tenzin Namdak Rinpoche, trscr.&ed. Carol and Dmitry Ermakovi (Blou: Shenten Dargye Ling, 2007), pp. 51–52.

[38] Tib. kun gzhi rnam shes.

So how are karmic causes created? We have many different kinds of mind (consciousness). According to our texts, we have the mind, the senses and basic Alaya,[39] or Kunzhi[40] in Tibetan. We have mental consciousness, the senses and Ignorance.[41] We call mental consciousness 'Yidkyi Nampar Shepa'[42], we call Alaya 'Kunzhi' and we call Ignorance 'Dagdzin'.[43] These three are the main (types of consciousness).

Then there are the five senses:

– the sense of sight;
– the sense of hearing;
– the sense of smell;
– the sense of touch;
– the sense of taste.[44]

These are all like lights radiating out from the main mental consciousness which we can say is like a torch. The lights spread out and each is going on its way. Or we can say that the mental consciousness is like a householder or a landlord, or the father of a family. Ignorance is like the mother; these two are important in a family. We can say this is like the structure of a family. The Alaya is like the family treasure chest or treasure trove – everything is saved in there. Ignorance is very important, it is like the mother or wife, and the senses are like servants – that was in the early times, not nowadays; this is an early story! Forms, sounds, smells, tastes etc. and all objects are like property which is used. So the mental consciousness is in charge of all the senses and is very important.

How do the senses collect karmic causes? The mental consciousness sends the different senses to the objects and, for example, the eye sense sees a flower and collects the form of its petals and its colour while the olfactory sense takes its scent. In the same way, the sense of hearing collects sounds, the sense of touch collects sensations and the tongue collects tastes. Then once they have collected everything from the objects, the sense consciousnesses bring them back and they are immediately checked by the mental consciousness. How are they checked? They are checked to ascertain whether they are good or bad,

---

39 Alaya Vijnana is the Sanskrit equivalent of *Kunzhi Namshe*.

40 Tib. kun gzhi, in this case it refers to *Kunzhi Namshe*.

41 In this case it refers to Tib. nyon mong yid kyi rnam par shes pa – the fundamental ignorance which misinterprets reality in dualistic terms giving rise to the ideas of 'self' and 'other' and a mistaken believe in the inherent existence of subject and object.

42 Tib. yid kyi rnam par shes pa.

43 Tib. bdag 'dzin.

44 Tib. mig gi rnam par shes pa; rna'i rnam par shes pa; sna'i rnam par shes pa; lus kyi rna par shes pa; lce'i rnam par shes pa.

useful or useless; they are all judged by the mental consciousness. It doesn't matter what has been collected, whether it is something big or small, everything is collected and given to the mental consciousness, to the householder, and he puts it in the treasure house or Kunzhi. It doesn't matter what has been collected – everything is kept in the Alaya whether it is good or bad. Good things are called virtues, bad things are called sins, and many other things are simply neutral, neither good nor bad, but they are still kept in the Alaya. It is similar to writing on a blackboard. Everything is kept in the Alaya and nothing is wasted. Who keeps it? It is kept by Ignorance. Ignorance always checks and keeps whatever is in the Alaya very tidily, very well – like a wife does – so nothing is spoilt. This is like a family structure.[45]

The Kunzhi and karmic cause are not only a story, you see. You can see everything. When you go to sleep you will have dreams, so when you wake up slightly from deep sleep – you are not completely awake but your sleep is lighter – meanwhile your mental consciousness is looking around and sees the karmic traces inside the Kunzhi. These karmic traces are like treasure or like a supermarket – you go round and you can see many things. (In this example), the mental consciousness is like you and the karmic traces are like the goods in the supermarket; you can see so many things there, and those are the dreams. Thus dreams are evidence – whatever you see, you are not going deeply into your store consciousness, although sometimes people say they have very strange dreams of things they have never experienced and at that time they are going back a bit to things which happened long before and were saved. But this is very rare. Usually we see fresh things which we have collected in this life, things which are just in the doorway (of our store consciousness).[46]

So although the mind-body/dream-body closely resembles *dunda hunehen,* the process of ordinary dreaming in Yungdrung Bön is explained in a quite different way, as are the mechanics of prophetic dreams and dreams involving spirits. According to Yungdrung Bön teachings, the dream-body has the same quality as the mental form in the *Bardo*, and that is the reason why people may have dreams of the deceased. These states of the mind when dreaming and when in *Bardo* have a similar quality and this similarity allows beings to see each other almost as we do in the corporeal world. Prophetic dreams or dreams of clarity come as result of practice which purifies the obscurations of mind

---

45 Ibid., pp. 22–24.

46 Yongdzin Lopön Tenzin Namdak, *Bönchyod Gurim: Preliminary Practices for Zhang Zhung Nyen Gyud*, Trscr.&ed. Carol and Dmitry Ermakovi, 27th (Blou: Shenten Dargye Ling), pp. 24–25.

which imprison people's perception within the limitations of time and place. When gross mind becomes lighter and calmer, when karmic traces are greatly purified and when realization of the Natural State of Mind dawns, then all sorts of knowledge and clairvoyance manifest within a practitioner's experience. These manifest directly from the Natural State itself as it is all-encompassing and is the ultimate source of everything. This is the explanation given in the Higher Tantra and Dzogchen. Causal Bön, especially *Chashen Thegpa*, the First Vehicle, has many dream-methods which involve *mantra* recitation and other techniques linked with the *Drala* sky-gods and these are outwardly quite comparable with the techniques of Bɵ Murgel.[47]

iii. Mu Hunehen[48]

This is the third soul. It is very tightly connected to the physical body and never leaves it. According to some sources its main dwelling place is in the bones and skeleton. There are two views on the post-mortem fate of this soul: some maintain that after death it remains in the corpse and does not leave it while others say it is taken to the realm of Erlig Khaan or becomes a dangerous bad spirit. That is why it is called 'bad soul'.

iv. Amin

According to Bɵ Murgel, a human being is made up not only of the three souls described above but has two further vital components in his/her consciousness-energy system. While not souls as such, these phenomena are inextricably interwoven into this system. These components are *amin* and *hulde*. Some Russian scholarly works describe the triad of the souls as *hulde-amin-hunehen*. However, to me this appears to be unjustified because *amin* and *hulde* are not actually souls but rather aspects of energy connected to the three souls described above.

Amin means 'breath' and 'life'. In Russian scholarly works it is often translated as 'soul-breath'.[49] It is a life-sustaining energy possessed by all living organisms for the duration of their life. Although connected with breathing, it is not breathing itself. If all the parts of *amin* are stolen by a malevolent being then a person will die as death comes when *amin* exits the physical body and breathing thus ceases, *amin garaa.*[50] Sometimes

---

47 See next chapter.

48 Bur. му һүнэхэн – 'bad soul'.

49 Rus. душа-дыхание.

50 Bur. амин гараа.

it is said that after a person dies *amin* transforms into a whirlwind and dissolves. According to Bɵ Murgel, *amin*'s main location in the human body is in the blood, bronchi and windpipe.

We can see, then, that *amin* is not a type of consciousness but is rather a life-force or life-sustaining energy. As such, it cannot be called a 'soul'. It is connected with consciousness but is not consciousness itself.

In terms of its function, *amin* is very much comparable to two of the Bön life-sustaining energies discussed earlier, namely *wug* (Respiratory Breath), and *tse* (Life). Both *amin* and *wug* are connected with the breathing process, both serve as a support for the soul, both are indispensable for life and both dissolve at death. We have here two parallel concepts.

At first glance, *amin* also exhibits characteristics of some types of *lung* – literally 'wind' – because of its connection with movement and the breathing process. However, we cannot make a direct comparison here because, although *amin* is connected to physical breathing, it is primarily an internal energy. Yet if we look into rites to 'enliven' ritual attributes we see that animal sacrifice is often an integral part and the animal's bronchi and windpipe are placed onto the objects to be invigorated. This leads us to conclude that at least some aspects of *amin* can be transferred and thus a comparison with some kinds of *lung* nevertheless stands. *Amin* should be understood as a general, not a specialized, term for several kinds or manifestations of life-force and life-sustaining energies. Although Bɵ and Utgan have a certain tendency to categorize their knowledge base, as we have seen in many instances, they are in no way as complex in this as the Bönpos so their terminology tends to be more general; the specific aspects of energy or understanding are known by each Bɵ and Utgan experientially, supra-verbally, and not all aspects of a certain phenomena are given a name.

v. Hulde

This is a multifaceted term. It denotes a type(s) of energy which sustains glory, prosperity, well-being, good luck, continuation of generations, progeny, health, long-life, sanity, respect, honour, military victory, protection, straight life path etc. In Russian anthropological works it is dubbed 'soul-fate'. While *hulde* is necessary to enjoy a good life, if it happens to leave for whatever reason or be stolen, the person will not die, although they will experience a deterioration of good luck, health etc. and all the qualities described above may disappear altogether if *hulde* is not restored.

Hulde is not just a personal energy. It is much wider than that. Each person, clan, tribe and nation has their *hulde*. For a clan, tribe and nation, the implications of losing *hulde* are the same – fortune disappears and things start going wrong. Quarrels and disagreements break out leading to the deterioration of the clan's, tribe's or nation's wealth and successful development is hindered. In its wider sense, *hulde* is an external energy present in the universe which can be invoked and internalized through offering and praying to the protective deities of the clan, nation and tribe. For example, one can invoke *hulde* of children to have descent, *hulde* of domestic animals to obtain wealth, *hulde* of military luck to gain victory in battle and so on. Thus *hulde* is a principle and a force with many aspects. When it manifests as happiness and prosperity it is called *hesheg* or *hesheg hootag*,[51] *bayan hesheg* or *bayan*,[52] literally meaning 'happiness', 'blessing': the essence of happiness and prosperity.

Hulde must have a support to dwell in. In the case of an individual it may be said to be his or her body, so if *hulde* of children is summoned then it is invoked into the womb of a woman who wants to have a baby. However, there is also an external support for personal *hulde*, namely a specially dedicated arrow. Arrows can serve as a support for a whole family's *hulde*, too, whereas for larger units such as a clan, tribe or nation, the support is a *tug* or specially made spear with a kind of trident on top decorated with animal tails and other ornaments. *Tug* is more than a receptacle of *hulde* as it also acts as a support for the protective deities. The best example of *tug* as a receptacle for a whole nation's *hulde* is the *tug* of Chingis Khaan[53] which had nine white horse-tails. Each tail signified *hulde* of one of the main Mongol tribes unified under that great leader. To be more precise, Chingis Khaan's own *tug* was white but the Mongol Empire had two *tugs*, one white and one black. The white *tug* symbolized tribes whose protective deities were White Tengeri and also served as their support while the black one symbolized the tribes whose protective deities were Black Tengeri and served as their support. Should an arrow or *tug* break, it augurs ill and another support should immediately be made and *hulde* invoked anew.

Although in many Russian scholarly works *zayaashi*-soul and *hulde* are considered synonymous and are both referred to as 'soul-fate', there is a clear difference between them. *Hulde* is a universal energy of prosperity, good luck and well-being while *zayaashi* is a personal protective deity

---

51 Bur. хэшэг, хэшэг хутаг.

52 Bur. баян хэшэг, баян.

53 Mong. Тэнгэриин Цаган Тук, lit. 'Tug of White Tengeri Sky-dwellers'.

which has the function of 'managing' *hulde*. *Zayaashi* brings *hulde* to its owner from the Tengeri, guards and multiplies it. If a person has strong *zayaashi,* his/her *hulde* is abundant. If on the other hand their *zayaashi* is weak or has wandered away, their *hulde* is also weak or lost.

The more personal aspect of *hulde* which is possessed by each person is called *erdeni*, happiness/sacred blessing. It dwells in or above the head and is a kind of protective and illuminating energy, a kind of inner clarity which influences a person's actions, a source of intuition which helps them attain their goals. This is why it is considered inauspicious to step over someone's head when they are lying down or to put some unclean objects on it.[54]

Comparative concepts relating to the soul in Bɵ Murgel and Bön

The qualities of *hulde* described above give us strong grounds to compare it together with its aspects *hesheg*, *erdeni* and *hii moriin* with such Bönpo concepts as *cha*, *yang*,[55] *pal*,[56] *wangthang* and *lungta*.

Cha and hulde

Cha is a positive principle or force in the universe which serves as a base for all positive qualities and conditions to manifest in the life of a person – or indeed of any sentient being. If a person is rich, healthy and happy, that means that their *cha*-force is strong and in harmony with the universe; if a person is weak, poor, unhealthy and miserable then their *cha* is weak or has left them and is out of balance with the *cha* of the universe. *Yang* is the function or manifestation of *cha* which corresponds

---

[54] Similarly, because *erdeni* is connected with the head it is also connected with the hat which is worn on it and so one's hat shouldn't be given to another, put on the floor or dirty places, one shouldn't step on it, lose it or throw it away as this could bring all manner of misfortune. One shouldn't wear another person's hat. That is also true for other items of clothing. This taboo is especially strong for Bɵ and Utgan who aren't allowed to wear other people's clothes and must be careful not to allow others to step over them. If this taboo is broken, a Bɵ or Utgan can become polluted, fall seriously ill or lose his/her power. They may even break down, have a kind of seizure or start bleeding. If that should happen, a 'body-washing' ritual must be performed immediately to cleanse the pollution. See ch. XI.

[55] Tib. g.yang.

[56] Tib. dpal.

to the Buryatian concept of *hesheg,* a manifest aspect of *hulde*. Both *cha* and *yang* can be invoked or summoned through special rituals.

In divination methods *cha* is perceived in association with a person's destiny so consequently all aspects of human life depend on *cha* force, and all beings and situations have this force. There is *cha* of gods, of elements, of prosperity, of heroism, of longevity; *cha* of food, drink, and ornaments; *cha* of fame, of military victory and so on. All these aspects of *cha* force can be invoked. The similarities between the various types of *cha* and those of *hulde* are quite striking, and they can both be lost, stolen and invoked in an analogous way. This suggests that they are in fact the same force with the same functions.

We can see the importance given to the *cha* force in Yungdrung Bön through the fact that the First Way or Vehicle among its Nine Ways is called *Chashen Thegpa* or '*The Way of the Shen of the Cha*'. This Way is mainly connected to a particular group of *Drala* sky-dwelling deities and has four subdivisions: sortilege, astrological calculations, *To*-rituals and medicine, all of which deal with *cha* force in one way or another. In particular, there is a very ancient class of *Drala,* also called *Cha,* who maintain and control the *cha* of the universe as well as protecting and sustaining the *cha* force of an individual. The chief deity of this group is Khyilchen Phuwer Karpo[57] and he presides over several smaller groups, the main one comprising the Three Phuwer Brothers[58] and their Three Singmo Tsamin Sisters.[59] This group of *Cha Drala* is invoked in the great variety of rituals designed to summon and develop *cha* and *yang*[60] thereby increasing prosperity, fortune and longevity. The Phuwer Brothers and Sisters are offered alcohol, various precious things, cereals and other items and asked to bless the containers of the *cha* which can hold or be used as supports for this force.[61] For example, in one such ritual *cha* is invoked into a special vase[62] which is then buried under or near a house to attract prosperity to that place. Among these supports we find the Arrow of the *Cha*[63] which can be directly compared to the arrows used as support for *hulde* in Bө Murgel.

---

57 Tib. dKhyil chen Phu wer dKar po.

58 Tib. dKhyil chen Phu wer mChed gsum.

59 Tib. Sring mo Tsa min mched gsum.

60 Tib. phywa sgrub; g.yang sgrub.

61 See Norbu, *Drung, Deu and Bön*, pp. 72–73.

62 Tib. phywa g.yang gi bumpa.

63 Tib. phywa mda'.

The second group of deities controlling *cha* has already been dealt with in relation to the *zayaashi*-soul. This group comprises the Five Personal Deities and Deities of *Lungta*.

The third and final group is that of *Phuglha*,[64] the Deities of the Home who protect and nurture a family's *cha* and *yang*. A special support[65] similar to a *namkha* is made for the *Phuglha* who are then invited to dwell within the home. *Phuglha* all seem to be female. It is considered very important to make offerings and purification rituals for them because if they become polluted or offended or leave the home then misfortunes and miseries are sure to befall the family.

In general, then, the deities who control *cha* are the ancient sky-dwelling *Drala* who, as we have already established,[66] are of the same nature as White Tengeri. Their common function of controlling *cha/hulde* and bestowing it upon those who approach them in the right way further underlines this. Additional evidence for the identity of the *Drala*

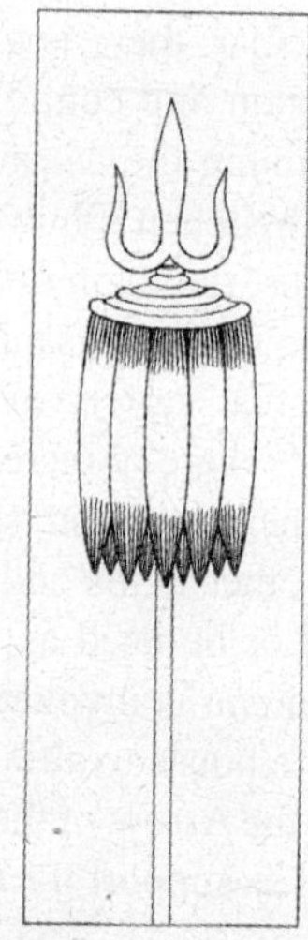

Fig.1. Left: Bönpo tugs *which serve as supports for the Protectors of Triten Norbutse Monastery held by young monks in the course of the Gutor (Tib. dgu gtor) ceremony. Kathmandu, February, 2008. Right: Mongol-Buryat* tug.

[64] Tib. phug lha or khyim lha, the Deities of the Family. On these deities see Norbu, *Drung, Deu and Bön*, pp. 73–75.

[65] Tib. phug lha'i rten.

[66] See Chapter V.

and Tengeri connected with *cha/hulde* is provided by *tug*. As explained earlier, *tug*[67] is a ritual support for *hulde* and there is in fact an identical word in Tibetan and Buryatian for an identical object with the same function and form. *Tugs* were used for the same purpose by the proto-Mongol, Tyurkic, Mongol, Zhang Zhung and Tibetan tribes from the times immemorial. The general form of *tug* is a specially dedicated spear or a kind of trident with yak-, horse- or other animal tails attached on top below the prongs. In Yungdrung Bön there are more complex types of *tug* but their main structure is always the same. Some of them are a kind of closed cylinder filled with yak's wool with a shaft running through the centre and topped with a trident. They are erected on the corners of the roofs of both Bönpo and Buddhist Tibetan temples and serve as supports for the protective deities.

Wind Horse

There is a deep and rich doctrinal base in Yungdrung Bön regarding *lungta* prayer-flags which reveals that the practice and concept of *lungta* force are interconnected with other aspects of a human being such as *yi*, *sog*, *lu*,[68] *wangthang*, *bagchag*, *la* as well as with external energies of the elements and beings who dominate them:

> How do *lungta* [flags] work? There are many different types of prayers according to many different cycles of teachings. There is a specific ritual or practice called *lungta*. It mainly contains prayers for improving, purifying and ensuring the good development of one's *sog*. *Sog* is life-force, *lu* is the body which is related to one's sickness [or good health] and so on. [...] Then there is *wangthang* [...] That is related with one's fortune, all one's wealth, property, prosperity – all these things. Then there is *lungta*, the 'wind-horse'. That is also kind of fortune. Then there is *la*. *La* is a very famous and popular word but its meaning is mostly unknown in Tibetan Buddhism. In the Bön tradition, *la* has many different levels of meaning. On the most subtle level it refers to karmic traces; it is very much connected with karma. So everything – whether we are successful and enjoy good fortune [or whether we do not] – depends on our karma; finally everything boils down to karma. It is not as though we can change negative karma into positive karma, but through certain practices and by creating certain circumstances we can make positive karma more visible, more effective than the negative karma. So when some negative karma is ready to

---

[67] Bur. тyr (ᠲᠤᠭ) and Tib. thug (ཐུག).

[68] Tib. lus; body.

ripen, there is a method to bring the positive karma to the forefront so that it ripens and brings good result and things go better and better. Generally everything completely depends on karma, so how can this method work? Karma has cause and secondary cause, and when we perform certain actions and merits they become a very strong secondary cause which brings you to the ripening of all your good karmas. That is the reason [...] The *lungta*, these prayer flags, and all these different kinds of rituals work in the same way. This is how the *la* is connected with this practice. [...]

There are *sog*, *lu*, *wangthang*, *lungta*, *la* – there are five things to develop. By 'develop' we mean, to turn them into a good way, into a positive way. Even if we don't develop then, we have all these (five), and if we just live (in a normal way), sometimes they are ruled by negative energies, negative circumstances, negative conditions, and then everything turns in a negative way. Then we can get disease, sickness, a short life and many different kinds of disturbances; all these things can happen. But if we try to bring (these five) into a more positive way, to influence them by positive things, good actions and good intention, then they all turn in a positive way and all good things ripen – all our good karmas ripen and give their result.[69]

So this is how *lungta* prayer-flags can help to develop the inner aspects and energies of a human. As far as the external energies and beings are concerned, it is important to be on good terms with one's neighbours and immediate environment. Since according to the Bönpo world view, the universe is populated by countless beings both visible and invisible if one wishes to have prosperity, happiness, good luck, good health and long life one must be on good terms with them, too. As we saw in Chapter V, each element, each moment of time and each place has its Owner god or spirit and as humans are born on this planet earth with physical bodies made of the five elements, on the subtle, invisible level, humans are naturally connected to the external elements, energies and beings who dominate them, whether we like, believe and accept it or not. Each element also has its ruling planet and so that connects humans to the entire cosmos. So the conjunction of the moment and place of birth creates a specific connection between each human, the elements, planets, stars and their Owners expressed in Bönpo astrology through the combination of the Twelve Year Cycle, *parkha* and *mewa* dealt with in Chapter IV. When we act in the ways which upset and irritate the beings controlling elements and planets and put ourselves out of harmony with

69 Excerpt from teachings given by Khenpo Tenpa Yungdrung in Shenten Dargye Ling, 22.07.2007 following the *tarchog* ceremony.

Fig. 2. Raising tarchog *(Tib. dar chog) pole with* lungta *flags in Triten Norbutse Monastery, February, 2008.*

Fig. 3. Yongdzin Lopön Tenzin Namdak, Pönlob Tsangpa Tenzin and Drubdra Khenpo Tsultrim Tenzin performing Lhagyal, *Triten Norbutse Monastery, 2008.*

the environment and the universe as a whole we naturally experience deterioration in prosperity, health, good luck and so on and can become depressed and seriously ill. In order to redress the offences, restore the harmony between the inner and outer elements, create a positive atmosphere and purify any pollution which may have been created on either the spiritual or physical level, the *lungta* ritual is performed in conjunction with and at the end of *Sangchö*, which was studied in the previous chapter, and followed by *Lhagyal*[70] prayer at the end of which the offering of *tsampa* flour is tossed in the air by each participant.

Lungta Prayer

A OM HUNG RAM DZA!
I pray: May my Life and Life-Force increase and grow strong!
I pray: May the health of my body be strong and increase!
I pray: May my Ascendance Capacity increase and grow strong!
I pray: May my Good Luck increase and grow strong!

---

70 Tib. lha rgyal.

I pray: May my La (Soul) and Glory increase and grow strong!
I pray: May the Tiger, Lion, Garuda and Dragon bring me Fortune and may it increase and grow strong!
I pray: May my Long-Life, Life-Force, body
Ascendance Capacity, Lungta, La and Glory
increase and grow strong!
If my Lungta, La and Glory had ebbed before may they now increase and grow strong!
RAK SHA RAK SHA YE SO HA![71]

Fig. 4. Sangchö *and consecration of the* lungta*, Shenten Dargye Ling, France, 2007*

Lhagyal Prayer

May the great compassion of the Buddha shine on us!
May the aspirations and prayers of the divinities be perfectly realized!
May the Teachings of Bön grow and spread!
May all sentient beings be happy
and may all their wishes be fulfilled!
May the hosts of negativities and unvirtuous actions wane!
May all *Sinpo* spirits and bad spells be suppressed!
May all miseries and sufferings
of all sentient beings in Samsara be cut!
May all obtain excellent and auspicious conditions!
So! So! Kyi! Kyi! So! So! Lha Gyal Lo![72]

---

[71] Translated by Geshe Samten Tsukphü and edited by Dmitry Ermakov, Shenten Dargye Ling, France, February 2006. Specific mantras are excluded.

[72] Ibid.

Lungta flags have a picture of a horse carrying a whish-fulfilling jewel on its back in the centre representing the *lungta* force and wind element. Pictures of the *khyung*, dragon, tiger and snow lion are drawn in the corners and symbolize the other four elements. On some flags the animals are not drawn but their names are written in the corners. All five animals also represent the Deities of *Lungta*. Inscriptions on *lungta* flags are prepared as follows:

> You write all the mantras and prayers on the flags and you make a wish – normally when you do this practice you say whatever you wish for but you also can write it on the flag. You have to write your name, your birth-year and everything, and then you put it as a *lungta* prayer flag in the wind. It is said that the wind reads, but it doesn't mean that the wind reads word by word; in this way, the mantric formulas are shaken by the wind and this creates a kind of good energy. We can say 'good energy'. That is how it develops. That purifies the external wind – when the external wind is purified, that naturally helps our internal wind element which is very much connected with the mind. We usually say that the subtle level of the mind rides on the subtle wind, subtle wind makes mind to move. So the subtle wind and the subtle mind are closely associated with each other. That is very much connected with the *bagchag*, the *la*. *La*, karmic traces, are all left within the mind; without mind there is no place to leave the *la*. [...]
> Then we also write other kinds of prayers and mantras and put them as a flag so when they flap that creates good energy in space, in the wind, and that helps the whole atmosphere, the whole area, and that person's mind. When we put such a prayer flag and do the ceremony, we also do *Sangchö*.[73]

In Bɵ Murgel find a concept and magical object related to *hulde* which is a matching equivalent of Bönpo *lungta* flags: it is *hii moriin* – the wind horse. *Hii moriin* is a subtle energy, a manifest aspect of *hulde* which raises a person's energy thereby bringing them success in whatever they do. This aspect is identical to the Bönpo concept of *wangthang* or Ascendance Capacity connected with the *lungta* force. Just as the word '*lungta*' refers to both the concept of 'wind-horse' and the prayer flag, so *hii moriin* energy has an eponymous physical support: a flag depicting a winged horse similar to Pegasus of the Ancient Greek myths. Just as a *lungta* prayer flags do, this flag acts through coming into contact with the wind so it is fixed either on a high pole inside the courtyard or on the peak of a mountain in one's locale. The function of

---

[73] Yungdrung, 22.07. 2007.

these flags is to sustain and increase a person's or a household's *hulde* i.e. *hesheg hootag* – to bring good luck, happiness, blessings, prosperity and so on. Thus the concepts of *hii moriin* and *lungta* coupled with the flags representing them are conceptually, semantically and physically all but identical. This suggests that both are rooted in the culture of Prehistoric Bön. However, in Yungdrung Bön *lungta* flags are based on a wholly different concept of the 'soul', making the *lungta* ritual not only a mere aid for worldly happiness but also a tool ultimately leading to the higher spiritual realization of Buddhahood. A further slight difference is that *hii moriin* flags make no reference to the other four elements, represented on *lungta* by the four animals drawn or written in the corners. The central picture also differs. While *hii moriin* flags feature a winged horse in the centre, *lungta* show a horse with a flaming wish-fulfilling jewel on its back.

The fact that the pictures on *hii moriin* differ from those on *lungta* clearly suggests that it is an original ancient Bɵ Murgel concept and ritual object rather than a later borrowing from Tibetan or Mongolian Buddhists, who make very wide use of *lungta* and who, in turn, borrowed them from Bön. Had *hii moriin* flags been borrowed from Buddhists at a later date, they would undoubtedly have retained the Tibetan design in full. We can be quite sure of this by looking at Buddhist ritual objects adopted by the Bɵ (mainly in eastern areas of Buryatia) such as *drilbu*-bell, *phurbu*-dagger and so on. In all these cases Bɵ simply use the original Buddhist objects without making any alterations. In fact, the Bɵ and Utgan have a very clear explanation of how the tradition of making and hanging *hii moriin* flags originated and developed. In the distant past when a male child was born or when a son was married, a ritual was performed to increase his *hii moriin* energy. In the course of this ritual, a horse was festooned with multi-coloured[74] *zalaa*-ribbons, symbolizing the union of Sky and Earth, and set free. This horse represented the boy's *hii moriin* energy racing between the Sky and the Earth. Later this ritual became

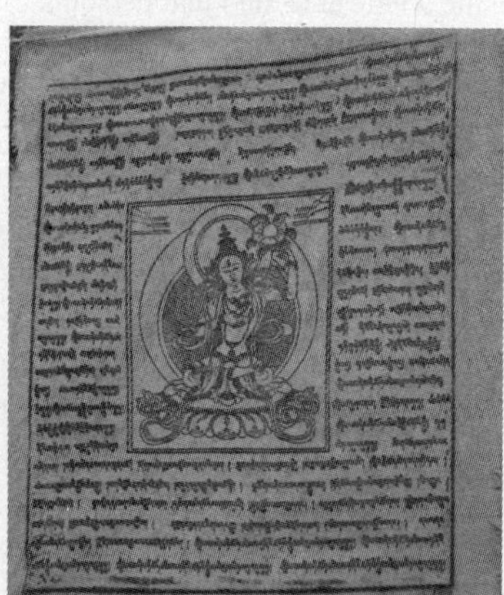

Fig. 5. Lungta *with the image of and prayers to Sherab Jamma.*

[74] With the exception of red colour.

Fig. 6. Bönpo lungta *and* hii moriin.

more symbolic and the dedicated horse was depicted on *hii moriin* flags as a winged horse with the wings symbolizing *zalaa*, originally tied on the horse. Each member of the family had a *hii moriin* flag raised for them to ensure good luck and increase the *bayan*.[75] This is perhaps the original tradition of Prehistoric Bön on which Tibetan Bönpo *lungta* flags are also based.

There is a Bönpo custom which uses *lungta* flags as a support for *yang* just as is done in Bɵ Murgel. For this purpose a special arrow called *Dagod*[76] is used. It is bigger than a normal arrow, topped with wooden imitation feathers and can be up to fifteen feet long. A special *lungta* flag bearing a printed section of text from the ritual to recall the *yang* is attached to it. At a certain time of year the villagers take these arrows and plant them into a *latse* cairn (equivalent to Buryatian *obo'o*) on a nearby mountain. This is accompanied by the *Sang* offering to *Yullha* (equivalent to the local *Ezhen*-owners) who are asked to look after the arrow, or in other words, to protect the *yang* of the family or person who planted it.[77] These are completely parallel customs and the fact that Tibetans use an arrow to attach the *lungta* while Buryats attach *hii moriin* to a pole or a tree in the mountains is of little importance. What is

---

75 Oral communieation from Bɵ B.D. Bazarov and Utgan V.G. Naguslaeva, 29.11.2007.

76 Tib. mda' rgod.

77 Karmay, *The Arrow and the Spindle*, p.152; pp. 426–431.

important is the reason behind these practices and the mechanics of how they work, and these match perfectly. Buryatian Buddhists, however, do not use *lungta* in this way so we can safely assume that the Buryatian concept of *hii moriin* and the flags themselves are a very ancient pre-Buddhist indigenous practice.

There is another fact which indirectly supports the antiquity of *hii moriin*. One of the offering items in the *tailgans* which I observed in Barguzin in 1994 was a little flag with a picture of a hare and rabbit brought by an old man. He tied it onto a tree so as to expose it to the wind. This kind of flag is used as an offering to Bayan Hangai, the Lord of the Taiga, to ask him for *hulde* of wild animals so that they fill the forests. That, no doubt, is a very ancient tradition based on the same principle as *hii moriin*.

Zalaa

Another very common custom reflecting a similar principle is the widespread practice of tying coloured ribbons, *zalaa*, on trees and bushes in holy power places such as healing springs, rocks and woods where the *tailgans* are held, and other revered sites such as the shrine to a powerful lama or a local deity:

> Close to the resort buildings, literally ten to fifteen paces away, there is *stupa* built and dedicated by Sode Lama. A little higher up the mountain side is a *burkhan* dedicated to him. It is a much revered place. All the trees around are festooned with *zalaa* ribbons, and on one someone had even hung a red hat trimmed with polar fox fur. The *burkhan* itself consists of a wooden box supported by four posts. Inside are a photograph of Sode Lama, images of Buddhist deities, offerings and butter lamps. Similar *burkhans* can be found at almost every *arshan* (spring), *stupa* and other sacred places.
>
> In the *taiga* near Borokhan, 17.07.94[78]

Sodnam Gomboev, a Bɵ from Aga who participated in the 1994 *tailgan* trip, told me that in the past during a *tailgan* or other offering ritual each person had to tie two ribbons on the branches of trees at the sacred site. One ribbon was blue or white symbolizing the sky, the other yellow for the earth so in this way the energies of the sky and earth were united and harmonized. Now any kind of cloth is used for this purpose. In my understanding this custom also serves the purpose of connecting

[78] A passage from my unpublished diary *Tailgan Trip*.

Fig. 7. Buryats tying zalaa *on a birch tree growing from a sacred stone at a power place in the course of the* tailgan *near Kurumkan, Barguzin, 1994.*

Fig. 8. Burkhan *of Sode Lama near Borokhan, Barguzin. The surrounding trees and poles are covered with* zalaa.

the individual energies of *hunehen* with the energies of the souls and life-forces of the deities of the power place. Hangalov notes that during initiation ceremonies, white and blue ribbons were tied on trees as an offering for white Bө, and yellow and red ribbons for black Bө.[79] This would suggest that at some time White Bө were associated with the sky while Black Bө were associated with the earth. Bө V. Hagdaev gives

---

[79] Hangalov, *Sobranie I*, pp. 374–384.

Fig. 9. Kolomenskoe stone, Moscow, 2003.

another explanation for the custom of tying ribbons in power spots.[80] He says that it derived from offerings to the wrathful *Ezhen* spirit-owners of power places. When Buryats were passing near such wrathful places they would tear a piece of material from their clothing and some hairs from the mane of their horses and tie them onto a nearby tree or *serge* as a payment for passing the spot. According to this interpretation, the ribbons were in fact a kind of ransom. All of the above interpretations are valid as in all cases the ribbons serve as offering to the gods and spirits of the holy place as well as a tangible means of reinforcing one's connection with them.

A direct equivalent to *zalaa* is found in Tibetan Bönpo culture. Here, five-coloured ribbons or woollen threads are attached to ritual objects, dedicated animals and in particular, to branches of trees dedicated as offerings to *Yullha* and *Zhidag*, as we saw in the discussion on *Sangchö*.

This custom of tying coloured ribbons onto trees and bushes in holy places isn't peculiar to Buryatia or Siberia. A striking example is right in the centre of Moscow. In the large Kolomenskoe park near the heart of the city there is small canyon with many bubbling springs of healing waters. People still revere the spot, coming to collect the waters and bathe there. Further up, high on the slope, a very particular boulder looms out of the earth. Its strange, smooth surface looks like interwoven plaits, somewhat like a giant bread plait and although it is not clear whether it has been

---

80 article<http://baikal.irkutsk.ru/php/statya.php?razdel=shamanism&nomer=4.txt> accessed spring 2004.

carved, it seems to have occurred naturally. According to legend, it fell from the sky in very ancient times and is believed to have healing properties.[81] Buryats would recognize this stone as *zada shuluun*[82] or *buudal*,[83] a holy object 'lowered from the sky' by the Tengeri. Believed to possess magical and holy properties they are venerated. People still come to the stone to ask for blessings, healing, good luck and prosperity, especially for newlyweds, and tie strips of material (ribbons from the wedding limousine, for example) to the trees and bushes around it as offerings; it looks just like some power place in Buryatia.

The same custom of tying ribbons has found its way to Japan, too. As we saw in Chapter X, Kano Eino Genroku's painting clearly shows many white ribbons decorating the Deer's antlers from which we can deduce that this practise extended to tree branches, too.

Hesheg and Yang aspects of Hulde and Cha

The high degree of similarity between *hesheg* and *yang* is clearly demonstrated by the identical concepts and rituals surrounding them in both Bön and Bө Murgel. For example, in both Tibet and Buryatia it is considered that some good domestic animals are blessed with *hesheg/yang* and should they be sold, stolen or die, they can take *hesheg/yang* away from the owner or the household. Thus when a man wants or needs to sell a good horse or other animal, he first pulls out some hairs from its mane, ears or tail and attaches them to the door of the enclosure where it was kept or woven into the *chagtaga*[84] rope; only then would the owner dare sell the animal. This action is a kind of sympathetic magic which prevents *hesheg/yang* from departing with the sold animal.[85]

---

81 Once while walking in the canyon I met an elderly local who was born, bred and lived all his life in the area of Kolomenskoe park. He remembered the times when it wasn't yet part of Moscow but in countryside with villages and *kolhoz*es (soviet collective farms). He told me this legend which he himself had heard from his primary school teacher who told it to his class while visiting the spot. That was around 1937 so his teacher must have been a very brave lady to tell such things to the children in those times.

82 Bur. зада шулуун.

83 Bur. буудал.

84 Bur. чагтага, a rope attached to *to'ono* smoke whole (Bur. тооно) Buryat and Mongol *gher*. For balancing the *gher* in bad weather a stone tied to it, otherwise it istied into a kind of knot resembling a sheep's stomach which is said to catch and keep in good luck and prosperity.

85 Galdanova, *Dolamaistkie*, pp. 118–135.

In Tibet this custom is most widespread in Amdo.[86] This is interesting because Amdowas have a dialect which is so distinct and has so many ancient words akin to the language of Zhang Zhung that Tibetans from other provinces cannot understand it and have to resort to a translator. It is highly probable, then, that like the language, the culture of Amdowas has preserved some archaic ideas dating back to the ancient times of Zhang Zhung. According to Yongdzin Lopön Tenzin Namdak this is because when Zhang Zhung was split up and defeated by the Tibetans in the eighth century AD, many Zhang Zhungpas fled to the area of Amdo where they settled and mixed with the local population.[87] Moreover, Amdo covers areas where proto-Hunnu mingled with the Indo-European Di in prehistory and which were later controlled by proto-Mongol tribes such as Hunnu, Syanbi and Tuyuhun who practised the Prehistoric Bön of Eurasia related to Mongol-Buryat Bɵ Murgel. Syanbi and Tuyuhun, known to Tibetans as Sumpa and Azha, were home to renowned Bönpo doctors invited to treat Tibetan royalty and to *Shenpos* of Yungdrung Bön such as Sumpai Awadong from the lineage of the *Zhang Zhung Nyen Gyud* Dzogchen. This link with Amdo points to the very ancient nature of beliefs surrounding the properties of *yang/hesheg*. Due to Amdo's historical connections, the 'Amdo factor' also points to a correlation between this concept and related magical rites within the frame of Bɵ Murgel, and the ancient Bönpo culture of the Zhang Zhung Empire which was contemporary with Tonpa Shenrab himself.

Another custom found in both Tibet and Buryatia is the practice of special rites to retain *yang/hesheg*.[88] These are commonly performed when an old family member or an animal possessing *yang/hesheg* dies, and also when a girl marries and leaves for the house of the groom. On such occasions there is a danger that the family's *yang/hesheg* may depart, so a special ritual is called for.[89] In Bɵ Murgel, the specific rite to retain *hesheg* after the death of an elderly person can take various forms such as shooting an arrow (symbolizing *hesheg*) towards the dwelling

---

86 Karmay, *The Arrow and the Spindle*, p. 149.

87 There is another view which is articulated by the German scholar Seigbert Hummel who suggests that northeast Tibet (Amdo) was the original land of the Zhang Zhung empire which expanded towards the northwest of Tibet in the times of King Drigum Tsenpo. See Hummel, *On Zhang Zhung*, pp. 69–85.

88 Tib. g.yang 'gugs; Bur. хэшэг хурылха.

89 See Galdanova, *Dolamaistskie*, p. 57;.Karmay, *The Arrow and the Spindle*, p.149; and Norbu, *Drung, Deu and Bön*, n. 11 (Notes to Chapter VII), p. 255.

where the deceased lived, or making an offering of milk products and asking *hesheg* to remain.

Tibetan and Buryat marriage rituals provide us with a further interesting parallel relating to *yang/hulde*. In Tibet a *palda*[90] arrow is given as a parting gift from the father (representing god Zom 'brang) to his marrying daughter (goddess Srid lcam' Prul mo che), or in some regions an arrow is attached to the bride's collar when she leaves her parental home to live with her future husband.[91] The meaning of this ritual arrow is not well understood in modern-day Tibet, but by comparing it with an analogous custom in Buryatia, I believe we can shed some light on it. In Buryatia the bride brought a quiver full of arrows into the house of her husband.[92] Here, the arrows are known to symbolize *hulde*. Due to the close similarity between the Tibetan and Buryatian customs and the twin understandings of *yang/hulde*, I believe we can safely assume that the underlying concept is the same and thus clarify the significance of the *palda* arrow in the Tibetan marriage ritual. Bearing in mind what was said above, this custom may seem somewhat contradictory at first; on one hand the relatives of the departing bride perform a rite to prevent *yang/hulde* from leaving their house with her, but on the other hand she is given an arrow(s) symbolizing *yang/hulde* to bring to the house of her husband. I believe this can be easily explained by examining which aspect of *yang/hulde* we are dealing with at each stage. The ritual of recalling *hulde/yang* is performed to prevent the family's *hulde/yang* from leaving the house where the bride's parents, brothers and sisters live, thereby preserving the family's integrity. The arrow(s) which the bride is given to take to her new home symbolizes her personal stock of *hulde/yang*, ensuring her continued good fortune in her new life in a different household.

From this brief comparison it is clear that the Buryatian term *hesheg* is identical to Tibetan *yang*. This underlines the complete correspondence between *hulde* and *cha* because *hesheg* is an aspect of *hulde* while *yang* is the equivalent aspect of *cha*. These parallel customs and concepts once more point to the common cultural and religious traditions lying at the base of both Bɵ Murgel and Bön. Moreover, we find the same kind of ritual (known as *prenji*) for recalling good fortune and good luck[93] still performed by Tamu priests in Nepal and other Himalayan

---

90 Tib. dpal mda'

91 Karmay, *The Arrow and the Spindle*, pp. 148–153.

92 Galdanova, *Dolamaistskie,* p. 49.

93 Nep. saha.

peoples such as Tamang, Thakali, Sherpa, Yolmo as well as many other peoples in Ladakh, Yunnan, Sikkim and Buthan.[94] This is clear evidence of Prehistoric Bön's wide dissemination among diverse ethnic groups throughout the vast territory of Asia over large stretches of time from prehistory up until now.

Hurylha, Dalalga and Tsokchö

In relation to *hulde* we should also mention *uurag.*[95] *Uurag* is a magical substance which brings good luck and virtue-prosperity (*hesheg* and *bayan*) and is requested by means of a *hurylha*[96] rite. It is the heavenly food of the Tengeri and is comparable with Tibetan *düdtsi*[97] and Sanskrit *amrita,* both of which denote food of sky-dwelling gods. When performing a *Hurylha*, offerings are first made to the gods and then the presiding Bө or Utgan holds a plate of various foodstuffs such as biscuits, milk products, sweets, meat etc and, rotating it clockwise, cries, '*A-hure! A-hure!*' In this way, *uurag* is invoked and descends into the food. This rite is often done as part of private rituals or even at bigger rituals such as *tailgans*. The consecrated food is then taken home and eaten by the all family members so in this way heavenly blessings are received. If the Bө or Utgan who led the ritual has real power, auspicious signs will subsequently appear and the family's prosperity and fortune will increase as requested during the rite.[98]

Hurylha also forms a part of a larger ritual called *Hesheg Dalalga*[99] – 'calling happiness' – which is often combined with offerings to the *Zayaan* of fire, Sahyadai Noyon or Galyn Tengeri:[100]

> For this ritual, a white cloth is spread on the offering table and laid out with various 'white offerings' of milk products including

---

[94] Gurung, *Bon in Himalaya*, p. 231.

[95] Bur. ураг.

[96] Bur. хурылха.

[97] Samten Karmay argues that *bdud rtsi* – lit. '*Düd's* crop' – is an antidote to the poison which grew in the land of the demons and is an indigenous Bönpo concept. When Buddhist texts were translated into Tibetan, the Sanskrit word *amrita* was translated as *düdtsi* but these two words are unrelated. Karmay, *The Arrow and the Spindle*, p. 145.

[98] According to Utgan Vera Naguslaeva.

[99] Bur. хэшэг далалга.

[100] Bur. Галын тэнгэри.

a bucket of *tarag*[101] together with the large quantity of *tarasoon* milk vodka, a bucket of Buryatian milk tea and cooked meat of a fat ram slaughtered for this occasion. Meat from the breast is carefully cut and after having been rotated thrice sunwise, is hung back on the first breast bone. After that another sizeable bucket lined with red silk is filled with melted butter, *airul* and *urma*[102] with cotton wool and feather-grass on top. A human figure made of the ram's breast fat is stood on the cotton wool and covered by various bones from the ram's carcass and colon. Finally the bucket is tightly closed with a white lamb skin and the brisket, prepared earlier, is placed on top. This bucket is a support for *hesheg*-happiness and *bayan* virtue-prosperity. Then outside the *gher* a triangular 'courtyard' is made from thin twigs with the 'door' turned towards the *hoimor*,[103] the 'venerated' northern part of the *gher*. This construction is put on top of the smouldering embers. Twigs are fixed at the three corners and pieces of the ram's fat and bundles of its wool are hung there. The Bɵ simultaneously invokes *hesheg and bayan* into the bucket and *uurag* into the offerings on the table. While calling *hesheg* Bɵ walks in the circular sun-wise motion exclaiming, '*A-hure! A-hure!*' The recipients unbutton their tops, take plates with the offerings and drinks from the altar and, holding them in their hands, also rotate them sunwise receiving the blessings. The Bɵ then comes to each member of the family and, starting with the householder, touches their chest with the bucket now full of blessings of prosperity and good luck, thereby transferring blessings to them saying: *'This is bayan-virtue of the Tengeri, Noyons and your ancestors (ug garbal);*[104] *this is the precious jewel; hesheg-blessing which will make you rich, prosperous and increase your offspring.'* The bucket is then given to the head of the household. Offerings are made to the *Ezhen* of fire after which the participants feast on the offerings until late into

---

[101] Bur. тараг, a kind of yoghurt made from a blend of sheep's, goat's and cow's milk to which camel and yak milk are sometimes added.

[102] Bur. айрул; урма. *Airul* is kind of cheese made of the by-product from the distillation of milk vodka. *Urma* is boiled milk skins.

[103] Bur. хоймор тала, the northern, upper part of the *gher* associated with the ancestral spirits. It is in this part of the *gher* that the *ehe ooheg* (Bur. эхэ ухэг) shelf is fixed on which the family's ritual objects and *ongon*-supports are kept.

[104] Bur. уг гарбал.

> the night. In the morning of the next day, the Bɵ performs a 'tin divination'[105] to establish whether the ritual went well or not. After this family members eat and drink the remains of the offerings and are instructed not to give anything to outsiders in the course of three days.[106]

Hurylha and *Dalalga* can be partly compared with *Tsokchö* and *Ganapuja* rites of Yungdrung Bön and Tibetan Buddhism which also involve offering foodstuffs to the Buddhas and other Guests, invoking blessings into them and then receiving these blessings by sharing a communal meal. However, unlike *Hurylha* and *Dalaga*, the main goal of *Tsokchö* is to purify the precepts and obtain spiritual attainments, although attainments of good luck and prosperity are always included nevertheless as they are part of 'ordinary' *siddhi.* Another difference is the source of the blessings. In the Yungdrung Bön and Tibetan Buddhist rituals it is primarily enlightened beings who are asked to bestow them as opposed to the sky-gods petitioned in *Hurylha* and *Dalalga*. However, the blessings and the magical powers of worldly gods who became protectors of Yungdrung Bön and Tibetan Buddhism are also invoked, and the basic technique of invoking blessings into food is the same in all the rites. Some kind of *Tsokchö* was surely practised in Tibet in very ancient times before the arrival of Tonpa Shenrab's Yungdrung Bön teachings in the same way as *Yajna* and *Puja* offerings were a part of traditional religious lore in India before the appearance of Buddha Shakyamuni. Both Buddhas transformed this practice and included it in the ritual side of their teachings. A similar principle of offering food to the gods and then invoking their blessing into it was behind the communal rituals of Indo-Iranians and Indo-Europeans and early Israelites, as was discussed in the Chapters VI and XII. We can say, then, that *Hurylha* and *Dalalga* represent one form of an ancient practice which was and still is performed over a vast territory by various religious and ethnic groups; sharing food is a fundamental part of human communal life, so it is only natural that it should also take its place in religious life, too.

---

105 See next chapter.

106 According to *Khronika Vandana Yumsunova* [Vandan Yumsumov, *Genin-Lubsan Tseden Dorzhi Tarbaev*] *Istoriya proiskhozhdeniya odinnadtsati rodov Horintsev,* 1875, in tr. N. Poppe, *Letopisi Horinskikh Buryat* (Trudy instituta Vostokovedeniya XXXIII, Moscow-Leningrad: AN USSR, 1940).

External receptacles of la/dunda hunehen

We have seen that many of a person's soul-energy aspects are connected with external objects and that well-being can be increased if the positive energies of *yang/hesheg/hulde* or the blessings of the gods are invoked into particular receptacles such as arrows, *tugs* or representations of the heavenly food. Now we shall return to the core concept of the *la* or *dunda hunehen* soul (which I shall refer to from now on as simply *hunehen* for easier reading) and look in more detail at the soul's receptacle or support, a concept common to both Bɵ Murgel and Tibetan Bön.

As was noted above, mountains and other objects which are considered inanimate in modern times can in fact be the containers of the *hunehen/la* according to both Bɵ Murgel and various types of Bön, as well as Tibetan Buddhism. Tibetans believe that holy mountains, *lari*, serve as the support for the *la* of the deities residing there and, in some cases, for the *la* of an individual being or beings. For example, the *la* of the famous protectors of west Tibet[107] Nyenchen Thanglha[108] and Targo Rinpoche[109] reside in the eponymous mountains which also serve as the deities' resident palaces. Their consorts' *la*-receptacles and residences lie in the lakes bearing the goddesses' names, Namtso and Dangra.[110] Another *la*-mountain is Lhari Tsenga[111] which lies one and a half day's journey to the southwest of Lhasa[112] and is considered to be the soul-mountain of the Tibetan Chögyals[113] or Buddhist Kings. A mountain or a sacred lake can serve as the *la*-receptacle not only for a god or a king but also for a whole nation. Tibetans widely believe that Lake Yardrogtsho[114] is the *la*-lake of their nation as a whole and that if it dries up for some reason the whole population of Tibet will die. Below is an extract from the teachings of Yondzin Lopön Tenzin Namdak which elucidates the function of *lanay*:

> *La* could be said to be karmic traces; *yi* is a kind of air or wind connected with consciousness and *sem* is mental consciousness. Movements

[107] Tib. byang thang.
[108] Tib. gNyan chen thang lha.
[109] Tib. rTa rgo rin po che.
[110] On this see Bellezza, *Divine Dyads*.
[111] Tib. lHa ri tse nga.
[112] Tib. Lha sa is a capital of Tibet.
[113] Tib. chos gyal.
[114] Tib. Yar 'brog mtsho.

between these three all depend on karmic traces and these karmic traces are called *la* or *bagchag*. However, *la* is not only *bagchag*. For example, if someone is very deeply attached to something precious such as gold or turquoise, money or a computer, then we can call that their *lanay*. Why? Due to the person's deep connection with this object, their *la* becomes connected with it and so it becomes a kind of support for the *la*, *lanay*. In the days of Zhang Zhung the kings were very much connected with Mount Kailash and it became the kings' *lari* or life-force mountain. Lakes can also be a *lanay*, the support for *la*.

In the past turquoise was expensive and very important, much more highly prized than gold, and that is why it is still used in some rituals to recall the *la*; turquoise acts as the *la*-support. In some villages they still maintain the ancient traditions and there they have a special person who does divination once a year to determine what each family's condition will be in the coming year. When a child is born they call the *amye*[115] who gives the initiation of the Five Buddhas and also gives the child a name. In the olden days, if the baby was a boy he would make an arrow very nicely and fix it to the central pillar of the family house. If the baby was a girl, he would make a little spindle and fix that to the central pillar. These both act as a support for the baby's *la*. The *amye* also does a long-life ritual for the baby using turquoise, and the stone is then tied around the baby's neck like a necklace. It is the same for both boys and girls. That is the *lanay*.[116]

In Buryatia, too, mountains and lakes serve as the residence and support for the life-force of *Ezhen* deities such as Oihon Buural (cave in the Hume Shuluun cliff, Olhon Island), Bahar Hara-Khaan (Lake Baikal), Barhan Uula/ Hazhar Sagaan Noyon[117] (Mount Baraghan Uula[118] in Barguzin), Buha-Noyon (Under Mundarga[119] in Tunka), De'ede Baabai (eponymous mountain in Barguzin) and others.[120]

However, many different inanimate objects can serve as the receptacles of the *la/hunehen,* including geographical features such as rocks, hillocks and trees, but also precious gems and so on. That is one reason why it is taboo to fell trees, dig up the earth, pitch tents or hunt

---

115 Tib. a mye.

116 Excerpt from the translation and commentary by Yongdzin Lopön Tenzin Namdak on the Bönpo Dzogchen cycle of *gSas mkhar g.yung drung ye khyabs lta ba'i rgyud ces bya ba bzhugs so*, Chapter VII. Triten Norbutse Monastery, Kathmandu, 27.01.08.

117 Bur. Хажар Сагаан ноён.

118 Bur. Барагхан Уула

119 Ундэр Мударга.

120 See map ch. II.

near the holy places in Buryatia; if this taboo is broken, the offender runs the risk of destroying the support of the soul or life-force of the powerful local gods, spirits or deceased Bө. Consequently, their wrath will be incurred and punishment will most surely follow in the form of disease, death or some other unfortunate occurrences.

There are many types of animals which can also serve as external containers for the *hunehen/la.*[121] For people of high standing (kings, priests or Bө), these can include wolves, tigers, lions, bears, deer, yaks, *uzyubr'*[122] as well as various birds such as eagles, hawks, geese and white cranes. Not only gods, royalty and powerful magicians can have external seats for their *hunehen/la*; according to Tibetan belief, common people also have them. In the case of ordinary individuals this seat can be in a horse, mule, sheep, ox or yak from one's own herd, or indeed another animate or inanimate object. Once someone knows which kind of animal or other object serves as their *la*-receptacle, they should refrain from destroying or killing them.[123] Similarly, the *hunehen*-souls of some Bө are said to reside in wild animals and birds. In the past powerful Bө and Utgan had also ability to manifest as various animals such as bears, *uzyubr'*, camels, wolves, birds, snakes, frogs and so forth according to the totem of their clan, while after death some actually transform into the respective animal. The *hunehen*-soul of both Bө and Utgan, as well as of ordinary people, can also take the form of a bee, bumblebee or wasp so Buryats don't kill these insects for fear of killing someone's soul. An accomplished Bө or Utgan has an impressive degree of control not only over their own soul but also over the souls of other beings; the spiritual founder of the Hurduud[124] Bө-clan, for example, arrived from Mongolia riding a bear with a tiger on a lead.

Bear transformation techniques in Bө Murgel and the pre-Taoist religion of China

Transforming their soul into a bear and then travelling in that guise performing magical actions was a favourite technique of powerful Bө and Utgan from certain tribes, particularly among Black Bө and Utgan. Several Buryatian myths trace the origin of the bear to a Black Bө.

---

[121] Tib. bla gnas kyi sems can.

[122] Rus. узюбрь, Lat. *Cervus Elaphus* – a species of deer found in Buryatia.

[123] See Nebesky-Wojkowitz, *Oracles and Demons*, pp. 481–482.

[124] Bur. Хурдууд.

A powerful Black Bɵ died and human sacrifices were made to him according to the custom. But *Burkhan* ordered him to transform into a bear and suck his paw in the winter time. And so it was that human sacrifices stopped.[125]

Once a great Black Bɵ transformed into a bear and went so far as to try to frighten *Burkhan*. His wrath aroused, *Burkhan*, forced him to remain as a bear forever.[126]

This predilection for a bear as animal-receptacle for the Bɵ's soul is of particular interest here because the technique of transforming into a bear for the purpose of performing magical actions is found in other traditions and cultures of Eurasia, too. This is clearly illustrated by legends concerning the ancient Chinese sage-kings whom the Chinese traditionally consider as both mythological and historical figures. One version of the legend about Great Yü (大禹) [127] who overcame the Great Flood is of particular interest:

Yü was an ancient pre-Taoist *Wu*-priest (巫) who was miraculously born from the body of his father Gun (鯀), killed on the orders of King Shun' (舜) for failing in his task to stop the flood. His corpse lay on the mountain slope for three years, and all the while Yü was inside the dead body of his father. After the three years had passed, Gun's corpse resurrected itself and became a brown bear. Cutting open his belly, he pulled out Yü, who immediately became a bear. In the course of his life Yü periodically changed his appearance; sometimes he was like a man, sometimes like a bear. He had the scraping walk of a bear which was imitated by the priests of ancient China a thousand years later who donned bearskins and growled to imitate him while performing rituals.
Yü is famous not only for stopping the Great Flood but also for opening the way for magical flight to the stars and the Plough constellation[128] in particular where he received instruction from

[125] Hangalov, *Sobranie II*, p. 210.

[126] Ibid., pp. 211–212.

[127] Born ca. 2205 BC according to tr. Watson, *Chuang Tzu,* Outline of Early Chinese History.

[128] In Buryatian Bɵ Murgel the Plough is known as a group of Seven Elders – Dolon Ubged (Bur. Долоон убгэд). In the past in every family someone had to sprinkle to the Seven Elders with milk because they can help or cause

> the spirits of heaven. There are still Taoist texts detailing the scheme of his magical steps in the sequence which leads to the dimension of the Sky, some of which most likely served as the base for some martial arts techniques. Yü had the capacity to communicate with and transform into various wild animals, and performed many other magical tasks.[129]

The story and activities of Yü are comparable with those of Buryatian Bɵ. Even if Yü wasn't an actual historical figure as Chinese tradition maintains, still he must represent a general or collective image of the ancient *Wu*-priests who were magicians, healers, clairvoyants, soothsayers and diviners as well as kings and military leaders, just like the ancient Bɵ. It is also worth noticing the phonetic similarity of the self-name '*Wu*' with 'Bɵ' and 'Bön'. This, coupled with the number of correspondences in magical techniques and functions among all three kinds of priests, makes is very likely that they represent different branches of the same religion and that these three names are, in fact, directly related to one another.[130]

Summary

We can see, then, that there are several analogous aspects in the understanding of the soul and related energies in Bɵ Murgel and Bön and that both traditions emphasize the importance of strengthening this aspect of an individual or unit by empowering a range of objects believed to support it. We have established that *dunda hunehen* and *la*, as it was understood in Prehistoric Bön, are identical concepts. The same is true for such notions as *amin* and *wug, hii moriin* and *lungta*. It is also clear that *zayaashi* or *hain hunehen* corresponds to such Bönpo ideas as the Five Personal Deities and the Deities of *Lungta*. Coupled with analogous aspects of *hulde* and *cha* such as *hesheg*/*yang,* this gives us further reason to argue that Bɵ Murgel and Tibetan Bön had a common source

---

harm depending on whether they are propitiated or not. This constellation is also very important in the Vedic Aryan religion where it is called Saptarishi – Seven Rishi (Seven Sages), sons of Brahma. This ancient cult is still alive within modern Hinduism despite the fact that this constellation is barely visible even from northern India.

[129] Ева Вонг, *Даосизм*, (Moskva: Fair-Press, 2001) [tr. Y. Bushueva from Eva Wong, *The Shambhala Guide to Taoism* (Boston & London: Shambhala, 1997).], pp.19–29.

[130] See ch. XV.

in the ancient layers of Eurasia's religious and cultural base, as well as supporting the view that, at some time and to a certain extent, Bɵ Murgel could have been influenced by Yungdrung Bön.

PART II
Post-Mortem Fate of the Soul

Post-mortem destiny in Bɵ Murgel

Here we will talk mainly about the post-mortem fate and properties of the *dunda hunehen* soul and the various forms it can take. As over the course of its long development Buryatian Bɵ Murgel has integrated the belief systems and pantheons of many diverse tribes, many customs and doctrines exist side by side, and this in turn has affected how the post-mortem fate of the soul is viewed so we find ancient views on the subject mingled with more recent ideas, perceptions and influences. Generally, for ordinary people – i.e. those with no special spiritual powers – the afterlife plays out either in the twilight world located on the same plane as our physical world but in a parallel dimension, or in the kingdom of Erlig Khaan situated under the earth.

Belief in reincarnation is also present in Bɵ Murgel and, as we noted above, appears to be of pre-Buddhist origin because the understanding of the mechanism of reincarnation differs from that of Buddhism. Although there is some concept of cause-result correlation, this doesn't fully match the concept of karma in Yungdrung Bön and Buddhism.[131] According to Bɵ Murgel, after death *hunehen* can reincarnate again on the physical plane as a human, bird, animal, fish or insect; it can become a wandering ghost or spirit, be it benevolent, malevolent or neutral; it can descend

---

131 Some of the modern Bɵ use the word 'karma' in the sense of 'destiny', 'fate' but this is not how it is understood in Yungdrung Bön or Buddhism. The basic point of difference lies precisely in the fact that karma cannot be completely equated with fate. While it is true that a person's fate or destiny is determined by their accumulated karma – i.e. by their thoughts, words and deeds of this and countless previous lifetimes – if the person in question is a practitioner, that destiny can be changed through practising the teachings. If karma were unchangeable there would be no way to become a Buddha, so the view of karma in Yungdrung Bön and Buddhism isn't fatalistic. However, if we take an ordinary person not involved in following these doctrines, it is true that they are completely controlled by karma. This is a very complicated matter which cannot be understand or interpreted easily. See next chapter.

to the Underworld where it can work for the 'bureaucratic machine' of this realm or end up imprisoned in one of Erlig Khaan's dungeons. The *hunehen*-soul of a strong Bө or Utgan can become a local protective *Zayaan* divinity for a clan, tribe, or area, residing in a particular place such as a hillock, wood, stream, lake, mountain, village or town. Alternatively it can be taken by the *Haats* or Tengeri into their dimension and live in their palaces on the mountain tops or in one of the Skies. These holy spirits have different names depending on their spiritual rank, burial place and residence. For example, *Buural Ubged*[132] are spirits controlling certain areas, spirits of high ranking *khaans*, military and tribe leaders and so on; *Hada Ezhed*[133] and *Hada Uulyn Ubged*[134] are spirits of deceased Bө residing on the mountain tops; *Daidyn Ubged*[135] and *Daidyn Hamgad*[136] are Elders and Women of the Soil; *To'odei Nuud*[137] are 'Grandmothers', powerful female ancestral spirits of the tribes and clans.

Fig. 10. Female Zayaan. *Trance drawing by the author, March, 1994.*

Animals are also said to have souls. There are two distinct customs among different tribes to ensure the reincarnation of a slaughtered or killed animal. As we saw in the context of bear-hunting, one is to bring the bones back to the place where the animal was killed and ask it to return and take again the form of this type of animal, an ancient practice relating to animals killed by hunters. The second custom is to break a piece of one of the slaughtered animal's ribs so as to liberate its soul from the body thereby enabling it to take rebirth. Both these traditions may stem from the belief that the soul – or at least, the *mu hunehen* soul – resides in the body.

---

132 Bur. буурал үбгэд.

133 Bur. хада эжэд.

134 Bur. хада уулын үбгэд.

135 Bur. дайдын үбгэд.

136 Bur. дайдын һамгад.

137 Bur. төөдэйнүүд.

'Newly' dead

According to Bɵ Murgel, when someone dies their *hunehen* wanders near the site of their death for three days and looks exactly as it did when alive. At first, the dead person (or more correctly his/her *hunehen*) doesn't understand that it is dead. The relatives and friends of the deceased soon arrive to welcome him or her to the realm of the dead and throw a big party. However, the 'newly' dead often doesn't believe them when they say he or she is one of them now, so to prove it they ask the newcomer to walk on the ash in the hearth; no traces are left on the ash so there can no longer be any doubt that the deceased's *hunehen* now belongs to the realm of the dead. After this three-day period has passed, the spirit of the deceased moves further and further from the place where they died until finally it finds the new location where it will spend its afterlife. This may take several weeks depending on the deceased's personal qualities and other circumstances. Some spirits always remain close to the place where they died out of attachment to property or relatives left behind and they can become ghosts and dangerous spirits harming people and livestock.

Gooideg[138] *and other dangerous spirits*

Many of the Bɵ Murgel beliefs surrounding the fate of souls after death link them to bad spirits. The *mu hunehen*, or so-called 'bad soul', is commonly thought to transform into a dangerous spirit which tries to kill other people, although some maintain it remains in the corpse. As for the *dunda hunehen*, in the Tunka region of Buryatia in particular, it is believed to become a *Boholdoi*[139]-spirit which can be benevolent or malevolent although they also believe that *Gooideg*[140] 'runner-spirits' manifest after a person dies, and these are always evil, trying to enter the houses of relatives, friends or local villagers to kill or seriously harm them. These spirits try to kill two or three people in a forty-nine day period after a death. Each person may have several *Gooideg* depending on how they died, their age, virtue and spiritual power and a truly virtuous person with highly-developed spiritual powers will not have manifestation of *Gooideg* upon death. However, this is rather rare. To

138 Bur. гүйдэг.

139 Bur. боохолдой.

140 There is also Gooideg Noyon (Bur. Гүйдэг ноён), Running Lord, also called Bydek. He is the scribe and messenger of Erlig Khaan and is the mediator between White Western *Haats* and Black Eastern *Haats*.

minimize the harm they cause, it is very important to swiftly determine the direction from which the *Gooideg*-spirits will come and perform an exorcism ritual, *Gooideg Garguulha*,[141] to send them to the Underworld and thus protect the living from their harmful influences.[142] *Gooideg* can be directly compared with the *Shed*-spirits in Tibetan Bön.

There are also other types of bad spirits which cause trouble to the living such as *Shudher*,[143] *Mu Shubuun*,[144] *Ada*,[145] *Anahai*,[146] *Dahobar*,[147] *Sholmos*[148] and so on.

Twilight World

Although nowadays the term *Boholdoi* has a negative connotation among Buryatian Buddhists, this wasn't the case before Buddhism arrived in the seventeenth century. Prior to that, *Boholdoi* were considered simply as the spirits of ordinary people who don't have enough spiritual power to rise up to the Sky or become a local divinity, aren't good enough craftspeople to be taken to the workshops in Erlig Khaan's Underworld but were spared the fate of souls stolen and imprisoned in the dark dungeons of that world. *Boholdoi* live on the same land as the living but in a kind of parallel dimension. They have more or less the same kind of existence filled with the same activities as the earthly plane. They eat, drink, go to parties, are happy or not so happy, rich or poor, good or bad. They feel pain, can be wounded and even killed. In many ways their world resembles the world of the living and they perceive and can utilize some parts of the landscape and even buildings pertaining to it but their perception of them is different. In their world there is no sun but some kind of dim light and at night they burn bluish fires making this a twilight world. *Boholdoi*-spirits mainly appears at night. The closest parallel to this world in western culture would be the Fairy realm of the Celts. This kind of spirit doesn't leave footprints nor do they break dry twigs when they walk. They are afraid of sharp objects such as thorns, needles, knives and swords which is why these are used in rituals of protection and exorcism.

---

141 Bur. Гүйдэг гаргуулха. See ch. XIV.

142 See T. A. Zabrueva & P.E. Marnuev, Gooideg zargoolkha – "obryad izgnaniya zlogo dukha", in *Materialy 40-i regional'noi Studentcheskoi konferentsii II.*

143 Bur. шүдхэр is an equivalent to Rus. чёрт (chyort).

144 Bur. му шубуун – lit. 'bad bird'.

145 Bur. ада.

146 Bur. анахай.

147 Bur. дахообар

148 Bur. шолмос.

Otherwise, they look just like humans and often behave as humans. The meeting point between this kind of spirit and the living are weddings and funerals when they come to look at their living relatives, meet the 'newly' dead, learn gossip and feast on the general offerings which are always present in one way or another at any public rituals, as well as offerings made specifically for them. Offerings for the dead include sprinkling alcohol with the ring finger of the right hand downwards towards the earth or touching a table surface with a finger dipped in alcohol.

Although ordinary folk can see spirits, especially the *Boholdoi*, on certain occasions, Bɵ and Utgan are professional 'seers' and can have contact with them at any time. Small children often have the ability to see spirits; dogs and horses also sense them and that is a reason why horses, for example are used in some rituals for recalling the soul.[149]

World of the Ancestors

Different sources give different locations for this dimension, setting it either in the south, in landscape features or holy places such as hillocks, mountains, or in a heaven. Unlike the Twilight World and the Underworld of Erlig Khaan, the World of the Ancestors is not open to the souls of ordinary people as only powerful, virtuous people such as Bɵ, Utgan, *khaans* and *noyons* can go there. The ancestors are different from *Boholdoi* spirits and because of their virtue they have the power to help their kin living on this earth, and so there are many rituals dedicated to them.

World of Erlig Khaan

The third post-mortem destination is the Underworld realm of Erlig Khaan with its prisons, dungeons and torture chambers. This becomes home to the 'bad' souls, *Gooideg* and, also, stolen *hunehen*-souls abducted by the messengers of Erlig Khaan. Despite its generally gloomy nature, this realm can only partly be termed a kind of hell as it is not only the souls of the non-righteous who go there, nor is everyone tortured. In ancient times this world was thought of merely as a place where souls went after death so originally there was most probably no association whatsoever with something like hell. The perception of this realm has changed with time so it is viewed differently in different areas and among Bɵ and Utgan of different tribes and traditions. One characteristic, however, is universal: its highly bureaucratic and totalitarian

---

149 See next chapter.

structure. The 'bureaucratic machine' of Erlig Khaan needs many scribes, so the souls of the educated are taken there to work, and the souls of good craftsmen also have designated areas where they continue their work.

Factors determining the post-mortem destiny of the hunehen

As we have seen, there are various possible afterlife destinations, and according to Bө Murgel the post-mortem fate of a person depends on several factors:

i. Will of the *Zayaans*;
ii. Type of death;
iii. Age at which death occurred;
iv. Social and spiritual status;
v. Personal qualities and actions performed while alive;
vi. How the death ritual was performed.

i. Will of the Zayaans

The *Zayaan* – Tengeri, *Haats* and ancestral spirits – meet regularly to decide the fate of the living and other business such as the fate of animals, various events, changes in landscape and so on. These gatherings, called *sooglan*,[150] are rather like court hearings dealing with legal matters and disputes. The *hunehen*-souls of the accused are summoned in time of sleep. Broadly speaking, there are two types of *sooglan*: white ones called by White Western *Haats* and black ones called by Black Eastern *Haats*, although mixed *sooglan* can also be held. Depending on the level of the meeting, they take place at various locations such as mountains, the steppe, holy sites or empty houses but the Tengeri meet for their *sooglans* on planets and constellations. The *hunehen* of the living are summoned to these *sooglans* and their fate is decided by the *Zayaan*. Spirits of living and deceased Bө and Utgan attend these meetings in the capacity of 'defence lawyers'. They try to protect the souls of people under their care, bringing up arguments in their favour and persuading the *Zayaans* not to punish the accused and not to cut their life, or they bargain for a more favourable afterlife. When a person is condemned to death by the *Zayaans* they also determine how they will die and give

---

[150] Bur. суглан.

orders to the lower spirits who arrange the necessary circumstances.[151] As we will see in the next section, the way a person dies influences their post-mortem fate. There are also four main permanent *sooglan* courts of appeal: *Sooglan* of Erlig Khaan, *Sooglan* of Oihon Buural (owner of Olhon Island, *Sooglan* of Saitani Burhad (positive Western gods) and *Sooglan* of the Western *Haats*. A person's *hunehen*-soul can wander from one to another following the hierarchy until final judgment is passed. Sometimes the *hunehen*-soul can win the case if a higher level of justice deems that the judgment or actions of some lower *Zayaans* was mistaken.

ii. Type of death

There are two main categories here: natural and unnatural. Natural death is death from old age; all other types of death are considered unnatural. Thus any death occurring before one has achieved a full measure of life (after fifty or sixty in the past) falls into the second category, even death by so-called 'natural causes' such as disease. According to Bɵ Murgel, a fatal illness is unnatural because any sickness is caused by the *hunehen* being damaged or stolen by evil spirits or messengers of Erlig Khaan. This in turn determines its post-mortem fate: if stolen, it stays in the place to which it was abducted, for example, in the realm of Erlig Khaan. Moreover, disease may ultimately be due to the person's non-virtuous actions, a punishment from the Tengeri, *Haats* or offended spirits who orchestrate this demise, cutting the *hunehen* off from the body and taking it away.

Then there is violent death from accident, drowning, murder and so forth. These are the worst types of death as the person who died in this way often becomes a dangerous spirit. The frustration and anger experienced when someone dies violently can lead them to try to cut off the life of others. One example is the *Dahobar* spirits, ferocious spirits of women who died in childbirth, from female diseases or from being abused by their husband or other family members. In the past there were several cases when young women received the calling to become an Utgan but were murdered by relatives. So great was the fear of witnessing the terrible feats which accompany the *Ongon Daralga*, they would tie these young women up and abandon them in a closed *gher* while the family moved to another place. After such a death, the spirit of the Utgan may start taking the lives of many. Here is a story to illustrate this:

---

151 Based on Hangalov, *Sobranie II*, pp. 134; 215–217 and various oral sources.

> There was a beautiful maiden with a sweet, melodious voice, a leader among the youngsters. When the time came, she was married to a man from the neighbouring village but soon afterwards was stricken by the *Ongon Daralga.* Wracked by violent fits, she began behaving very strangely. Fearing his son's new bride, her father-in-law fastened a wooden collar to her neck, bound her and left in an abandoned house. Many days went by, but her husband's brother was finally moved to free her. They fled from that place and on their way they came upon a wedding. There the girl began singing and dancing and her beauty was such that the groom fell in love with her and asked for her hand, ignoring the maid already betrothed to him. A terrible uproar ensued and the new lovers fled, only to commit suicide later. After her death the girl became a powerful spirit and began gathering companions for herself and her lover through making many young people of that area suddenly die or commit suicide. It is said her 'retinue' has reached three hundred and sixty-six spirits of young people.[152]

Another example of a malevolent spirit resulting from violent death is *Uhanai Boholdoi.*[153] These are spirits of people who drowned and became ill-willed water-spirits who drown others.

However, sometimes these negative circumstances surrounding death can prompt a soul to become a benign spirit who tries to protect other people from unnatural death and other dangers.

iii. Age at which death occurred

In the past it was believed that if a baby or a child dies, they don't go far away from the house where they were born but remain nearby and try to be reborn into the same family. The idea behind this is that child-death is mainly caused by the *hain hunehen* or *zayaashi*-soul of the child when it feels that s/he was not cared for properly or abused. In such cases the *zayaashi*-soul takes *dunda hunehen*-soul of the child to the Sky where it dwells with the Tengeri, waiting until the parents repent and enter a conducive condition of body and mind so it can be reborn into the family again. Consequently, children were buried not far from the house in the hope of their quick rebirth. If, however, the family does not repent or put

---

[152] *Sbornik shamanskikh prizyivanii I,* pp. 269–270. (Names omitted).

[153] Bur. уханай боохолдой.

the situation to rights, the *hunehen* of the child may be born into another family or become an *Ada*-spirit. There are two types of *Ada*, one positive and one malign. The malign ones are said to eat other infants' souls, a second cause of child-death. Their benign counterparts, however, protect babies.

Another type of malevolent spirit harms unborn babies and pregnant women. These are called *Anahai* and are described differently in various sources. Sometimes they are generally referred to as evil spirits, other sources say they have only one eye in the middle of their forehead while still others say they are the souls of wicked childless women who cause miscarriages and other harm to pregnant women.

If a person dies young there is a danger that their soul will become a dangerous spirit because they may look at the world of the living and feel envy and frustration at their missed opportunities. An example of such spirits is *Mu Shubuun*, the spirits of sexually frustrated girls and young women which dwell in the *taiga*.[154] These malevolent spirits take on the guise of beautiful women and seduce hunters or lonely travellers. Then, while engaging in intercourse, they transform into a bird with a hard red beak and kill them or eat, steal or damage their *hunehen*-soul. A story I heard from a Bө of Aga illustrates this:

> A hunter was travelling in the steppe. The sun was setting and dusk would soon fall. His thoughts turned to how he would spend the night when he saw a *gher* with light shining through the half-open doorway. He was surprised to see a *gher* in that unpopulated area but rode up to it nevertheless and looked inside. To his even greater surprise, he saw a very beautiful young woman sitting in front of a fire. Seeing him, she invited him in. So he unsaddled his horse and joined her inside. She wouldn't reply to his questions about where she was from but offered him food and drink. Once he had finished eating, she looked at him lovingly and kissed him. Then she took him to bed and they made love. She was very gentle, tender and loving. She told him that he now belonged to her. He was very happy and fell asleep. At dawn he woke up from cold and found himself lying on the bare earth, his clothes all undone and his horse running around nervously. There was no sign of the *gher*, no ash from the fire, and no girl. He felt frightened and uneasy. When he came home he fell ill and always dreamt of that girl calling to him. Soon he died.[155]

---

[154] They can also dwell in the steppe or empty spaces.

[155] The story was told to me by the Bө S.D. Gomboev from Aga on 13.06.94 near the village of Alla, Barguzin.

Not all the souls of those who die young become bad spirits. The *hunehen* of young people can also become benign spirits but they cannot find their way to the land of the ancestors and so remain wandering around on the earth.

If person has lived a full measure of life then they are likely to become a benign *Zayaan*-ancestor. However, if they were of bad character, a Black Bɵ or Utgan of the second type, or an *Elbeshen* black sorcerer, they may become a bad spirit. In times gone by it was believed that if a person lived to be more than eighty they could become a bad spirit. Living above this age was regarded as negative because Buryats thought that such old people live at the expense of the happiness and prosperity of their descendants, stealing their life-force, happiness and prosperity.[156] Should a person die at the age of eighty-one this was considered very inauspicious because it was believed this would create a cause for the termination of the family.[157]

In Tibetan culture we find a parallel concept. Tibetans consider that if a family member dies at a very old age this can cause the family's prosperity to dwindle. To prevent this, living relatives tried to bury the corpse of an elderly relative near the house or, if that was not possible, to perform a particular rite to recall prosperity.[158]

There are indications that in the distant past Buryats and many other Siberian nations did just the same as the skull and bones of the elderly were often buried under the threshold of the dwelling or left in the northern corner.[159]

iv. Social and spiritual status

The soul's post-mortem destiny can depend on the social, and especially spiritual, status of the deceased. In a purely mercenary way, a person of high rank or from a wealthy family has more chance of obtaining a better afterlife because more riches are spent on lavish death rituals, as a result of which the deceased will have more riches and power in the other world. However, a person's character also plays a role. If s/he was well-to-do but of bad character this can cause negative circumstances in the afterlife, including being imprisoned in Erlig Khaan's dungeon or becoming a powerful but malign spirit which harms people. Conversely,

---

[156] There was a tradition of taking old people to the *taiga* and leaving them there to die alone. That tradition has stopped long time ago.

[157] Galdanova, *Dolamaistskie*, p. 55.

[158] Norbu, *Drung, Deu and Bön*, n. 11, (Notes to Chapter VII), p. 255.

[159] Galdanova, *Dolamaistskie*, p. 50, 64.

if a person was from a poor family but of good heart they may still have a happy post-mortem existence despite a very modest burial rite; the power of their positive actions will draw the attention of the Tengeri and other *Zayaans*, who will help and take care of that person after death.

Of special importance is the spiritual stature of the deceased. A Bө, Utgan or village elder responsible for performing some offering rites may follow one of several destinies after death. They may become a local protective deity or the protective deity of a family, clan or tribe; they may move to the palaces of the *Haats* on the mountain peaks or even, in the case of a truly outstanding practitioner, go to dwell with the Tengeri in the dimension of the Sky. In the Tunka region of Buryatia there is a belief that the souls of ordinary people who lived a good life will be automatically taken by the Western White *Haats* after death to live in their palaces. In Tunka some also believe that the souls of good people go to the heaven of Hormusta Tengeri.[160]

According to other sources, the souls of White Bө and Utgan are taken to the palaces of the positive Western Saitani Burhad[161] gods near the Sadamtyn Sagaan lake[162] while Black Bө and Utgan are taken to work for Erlig Khaan or the Lord of the River Lena Azhirai Buhe Zulhein Noyon,[163] or to the Noyohi Sooglan[164] palaces of Khaan Hoto Baabai on Olhon Island.[165]

v. Personal qualities and actions performed while alive

Although a person's fate in the afterlife is affected by the circumstances at the time of death, the predominant factor determining whether *hunehen* becomes a good or a bad spirit is the person's character and personality while alive. Nevertheless, the attitude with which one dies can play a key role and people of a generally kind and honest disposition can turn into a malefic spirit as a result of the confusion and frustration they may experience in the process of death.

In ancient times there was a custom, *Gazya Gargaha*,[166] of punishing people who broke taboo or caused discord within the community. During

---

[160] Information gathered in the village of Zhemchug in 1993.

[161] Bur. Сайтани Бурхаад хи суглан.

[162] Bur. Садамтын саган.

[163] Bur. Ажирай Бухэ Зүлхэйн ноён.

[164] Bur. Ноёхи суглан.

[165] Hangalov, *Sobranie I*, pp. 385–392.

[166] Bur. газя гаргаха.

a special ritual, those who broke the tribal law were mutilated by, for example, breaking an arm and a leg, gauging out an eye or damaging or amputating some other parts of the body. The person was then left alone in the *taiga* to die. Souls of these people became bad spirits, some headless, some without hands and legs, some without eyes, and some with only half the body.[167]

A person's stock of merit also seems to influence reincarnation. As the *hunehen*-souls of people and animal souls can sometimes reincarnate in this world, how long they reside in the other worlds can vary. They may subsequently come back and take a body of flesh and blood; even very outstanding *Zaarin*-Bɵ who dwell with the Tengeri after death do take reincarnation on this earth from time to time in order to help people. However, while the majority of Bɵ and Utgan believe in reincarnation, opinions differ as to how this works in practice. According to some information people can also be reborn as animals and animals reborn as people, all depending on the amount of virtue or negativity accumulated.

vi. How the death ritual was performed

Buryats give a lot of importance to the death ritual and choosing the right burial site for their dead as they believe that the post-mortem existence is strongly influenced by these two factors. Everything should be done in a correct way to benefit the dead and protect the living. In the past a dead person was 'sent' to the other world with an array of objects such as fine clothes, jewellery, weapons, household items, sacrificed animals (especially horses) and, sometimes, even people. All these objects would accompany the deceased's soul to the other world and so relatives normally gave generously as, if the deceased were to become unhappy in the otherworld, they might come back as a bad spirit to haunt the family.

The burial site is also significant and should be bought from the Owners of the Land who will otherwise deny the deceased a place in the post-mortem existence and cause problems for the living. For that purpose special ritual requests and sacrifices to the local *Ezhen* are performed. Each tribe and clan had their own distinct burial sites which were normally on high sunny spots in the *taiga*. Surface burials were preferred, the corpse just lightly covered with a bit of earth due to the

---

[167] Hangalov, *Sobranie II*, pp. 124–128.

belief that should the dead be put into a deep hole, their soul would remain stuck there forever. Consequently burials were shallow and sometimes the corpses were simply left on the ground in the *taiga* in a specially designated place. Before burying the corpse it was covered in white felt as not to pollute the earth.[168]

Bɵ, Utgan and *Darhan*-smiths were buried apart from ordinary people in separate burial sites. There were many types of Bɵ burials. Sometimes the dead Bɵ, fully dressed in his *orgoi* and with all his ritual objects, was left on a wooden *aranga*[169] platform for sky burial in the woods; sometimes they were left sitting facing south in a purpose-built *gher*; sometimes they were cremated in a specially dedicated grove called *aiha.*[170] After the cremation the ashes and bones were put in a box and skilfully hidden high up in a tree trunk[171] so that no traces were visible.[172] The deceased Bɵ's ritual objects were hung on the surrounding trees.[173] Bɵ burial sites are very much revered and feared by the ordinary people and only Bɵ and Utgan can enter there to perform special offering rituals. Should an ordinary person even inadvertently disturb the peace of deceased Bɵ and Utgan, they will at best have a very frightening experience but could fall sick or even die. Should they be unlucky enough to cut down a Bɵ spirit's support tree, the consequences would most certainly be grave. The following story from my first trip to Buryatia is a good illustration:

---

[168] Some scholars believe that this custom points to Zoroastrian influences (Galdanova, *Dolamaistkie,* p.86) but there is nothing particularly Zoroastrian in it as this custom was common to many Indo-Iranian Aryan tribes. Its relict has survived to this day in modern Hinduism where a dead body is ritually cleansed and draped in a white cloth prior to cremation. The concept of ritual impurity of the family of the deceased is common to Vedic and pre-Zoroastrian Iranian religions, an attitude which has continued in later Zoroastrianism and Hinduism to this day (see for example Hindu Death Rituals and Beliefs, article, ed. Rishi <http://mailerindia.com/hindu/veda/index.php?death> accessed 08.06.07) where the family isn't allowed to visit others' homes, attend religious festivals and temples, or visit *swami*-priests. Some maintain this taboo for as long as one year, which is the same in Bɵ Murgel. In short, these sorts of similarities in the concept and attitudes towards the impurity of a dead body and death indicate direct and prolonged contact between the Buryats' proto-Mongol ancestors and the proto-Indo-Iranians in prehistory.

[169] Bur. аранга.

[170] Bur. айха.

[171] Bur. бөөгe нархан - 'the Bɵ-pine'.

[172] Bur. яна бариха, lit. 'to lift up the bones'.

[173] For details see Hangalov, *Sobranie I*, pp. 385–392.

While I was camping near the Ivolginskiy *Datsan* outside Ulaan-Ude in the summer of 1990 awaiting the *Maidari Huural*[174] ceremony, there was a mighty commotion one night. In the morning a couple of dishevelled and bewildered guys appeared near the tent where I was staying with my girlfriend. Like us, the lads were from St. Petersburg and had also come for *Maidari Huural*. They told us they had arrived when it was already dark and so they had hurriedly found some place and quickly pitched their tent. In the middle of the night they were woken by loud, weird and spine chilling noises as if someone were hitting large metal sheets. A herd of crazed cows then stampeded their tent with a loud mooing. The guys ran for their lives and managed to escape. In the morning locals told them that they had camped right on a Bө cemetery.

While travelling with the Bө in 1994 I visited a Bө burial ground which proved to be a remarkable place filled with awe-inspiring power and inhabited by masses of white cranes:

> The place we were travelling to is called Shiizgha.[175] It is a burial place for Bө and Utgan, and also a place where the 'little people'[176] live. It lies in a steppe region between two mountain ranges. The soil is mainly sand [...] We drove on a bit further and a beautiful vista opened before us. It was a hilly place scattered with trees twisted into queer forms, like something from a magical tale. Huge nests were everywhere among the branches and great white cranes rose up from them majestically. Some were already soaring high in the sky, their shrill cries resounding all around. More and more flocked around. The local people believe that they are the souls of dead Bө and Utgan,[177] and so this place is much feared and respected; only Bө and Utgan can come here. After swinging round in a semi-circle, we drove into the inner expanse of that country. Then we had to continue on foot. It was a very responsible

---

174 Bur. Майдари хуурал is the celebration dedicated to Maitrea, the Buddha of the Future.

175 Bur. Шиизга.

176 A kind of dwarf-spirits.

177 Interestingly, in Russia we find a belief that souls of warriors/soldiers killed in battle become white cranes. There is even a song of the Soviet era written in remembrance of those who died in World War IIwith the following line, *'It seems that the soldiers didn't fall into the damp soil years ago but have transformed into white cranes...'* This belief has no connection to Orthodox Christianity and must have come from Russia's pre-Christian religion.

moment in our journey; we couldn't afford to make any mistakes on that land. All actions must be precise and in agreement. The successful completion of future rituals, and also of life in general, depended on that. Bө Doogar Ochirov had been told that one should sprinkle with the left hand while circumambulating sunwise. We approached the centre of the burial place in single file. Doogar Ochirov went first, then myself, followed by the Utgans Nadezhda Stepanova, Vera Naguslaeva, Rosa Nadogoorova and a few others. When we reached the right place, we began to circumambulate. Doogar Ochirov sprinkled with milk, I sprinkled with milk vodka. At first there was a spooky feeling; the presence of a mighty power was almost physical. We made several circumambulations, sprinkling every few steps. Nadezhda Stepanova was beating the *hese*. In the centre of the circle there were offerings of sweets and *salamat*. The circumambulations over, we turned our faces South-West. Almost straight in front of us, a little to the right, a huge red-orange sun was sinking below the horizon. The orange glow reflecting on the tree trunks and the grass set us in a fairy-tale world. Our ears were ringing. Nadezhda Stepanova and Doogar Ochirov 'saw' many spirits of the Bө and gods, right in front of us. We began to sprinkle again, one after the other. Doogar Ochirov swapped bottles with me and began sprinkling with *tarasoon*; I simply stood holding the bottle of milk. Suddenly someone tugged at my trousers and I clearly heard a voice. 'Pour!', it commanded. I looked down and 'saw' a little man. He was almost as high as my knee, had a beard and was dressed very oddly in something a bit like a gown. I answered him by thought: 'Doogar Ochirov said not to sprinkle until he's finished sprinkling vodka.' The little man again tugged my trousers, twice, saying, 'Pour!' […] And just to make sure I didn't have any more doubts, he pulled my trouser leg a few more times. So from a small silver goblet, I quickly poured a few drops of milk just in front of me, after which the vision disappeared.

When everyone had done *serzhim*, we returned, trying to follow in each others' footsteps and as far as possible, not stepping on any dry branches or lumps of earth. Having walked round in a complicated loop, we arrived back at the cars where the other members of our group were waiting for us. As soon as we got back, they put on their hats and ent off in a slightly different direction to tie *zalaa* ribbons and place coins at trees. Throughout the whole ritual, hats and belts must be worn, and all buttons fastened. [178]

Bө cemetery, Shiizgha, 14.06.94.[179]

Black Bө or Utgan of the second type and *Elbeshen* black sorcerers who were known to steal and eat the souls of people were buried differently. When they were caught there was a kind of court hearing and, if it was proven that they were doing evil and killing people, then they were taken to the *taiga*. A ditch was found and a deep hole dug in it. Then the Black Bө or sorcerer(ess) was put into the hole alive, face down and covered with earth. After some time people returned and hammered an aspen stake into the grave so that the evil-doer's soul couldn't get out but must stay there forever. The stake wasn't hammered in straightaway for fear of killing the black sorcerer(ess) and letting his/her soul escape. If they died from suffocation under earth then the soul would remain in the hole and with the stake acting as a lock on top of it.[180]

---

[178] This taboo is called Bur. Үндэр тэнгэридэ орьёо жарыылхагүй – 'not to show the bare head to the Exalted High Sky'. This is a sign of respect for the gods and also a technique to protect one's energy by leaving no gaps through which negative influences can be received. Hat and belt are indispensable items of clothing when on pilgrimage to holy places. A similar attitude is found among Tibetans, yet another match between Bө Murgel and Bön culture. Furthermore, the custom of wearing hats/head coverings while performing religious ceremonies is present in a large variety of ancient spiritual traditions and religions such as Bön, Zoroastrianism, various Siberian shamanic and Native American traditions, Buddhism, Mithraism, Judaism, Christianity, Islam – in short, most known spiritual traditions. However, some traditions have lost the precise reason behind this custom while others (such as Christianity) adopted it from earlier religions (in this case Mithraism) as they integrated with the cultural and religious environment they found themselves in (in this case the Roman Empire). To find the real meaning of this custom, then, we have to go to the older religions, its source, such as Bө Murgel. Here and elsewhere, the religious headdress is inextricably connected with the particular type of energy and power which actually resides in it so as a receptacle of such power, the headdress originally served as a conduit connecting with the gods who gave the custom of wearing that particular type of headdress to the priests of a given religion.

[179] A passage from my unpublished diary, *Tailgan Trip*.

[180] Hangalov, *Sobranie I.*

The post-mortem fate as understood in Yungdrung Bön

According to Yungdrung Bön nothing is stable, permanent or final in *samsara* and so the cycle of life and death is explained through the teachings on the *Bardo* intermediate states. These are:

- *Bardo* of Natural Abiding[181] – what we call life;
- *Bardo* of Dream[182] – dream state;
- *Bardo* of *Samadhi* (Contemplation)[183] – state of meditation;
- *Bardo* of the Time of Death[184] – period starting at the beginning of a fatal disease[185] and ending in death;
- *Bardo* of Primordial Dharmakaya[186] – period of returning to the fundamental ground of being, the Nature of Mind;
- *Bardo* of the Clear Light of Emptiness[187] – threshold between *samsara* and *nirvana* where lights and rays appear from the Nature of Mind;
- *Bardo* of Taking Rebirth[188] – the intermediate state between life and death before taking rebirth in one of the Six Realms of *samsara*.

The post-mortem fate of any being, not only humans, depends on karma which pushes the spirit to reincarnate in the body of one of the beings of the Six Realms of *samsara* and one lives out that life until the next death when the process is repeated again until one day, due to meritorious karma and tireless practice, one gains the realization of a Buddha. In very simplistic terms, in the case of human beings, the post-mortem fate largely depends on our actions in this life. Generally, if one led a good and virtuous life then one's post-mortem destination is likely to be a happy one in one of the three Upper Realms as a god, demi-god or human. If one's acts were evil then one will have a miserable rebirth in one of the three Lower Realms as an animal, hungry-ghost or hell-dweller. Although this seems a simple model, it is actually quite complex. As was said in Chapter IV, birth in any of the Six Realms depends on the accumulation of causes related to negative emotions

---

[181] Tib. rang bzhin skyes gnas bar do.

[182] Tib. rmi lam bar do.

[183] Tib. ting 'dzin bsam gtan gyi bar do.

[184] Tib. 'chi kha'i bar do.

[185] Tib.chi kha'i nad.

[186] Tib. ka dag bon sku bar do.

[187] Tib. bon nyid 'od gsal gyi bar do.

[188] Tib. pha rol srid pa'i bar do. Generally, when the term *Bardo* is used it is predominantly for this last *Bardo* unless specified otherwise.

such as envy, greed, jealousy, hatred, anger, mental torpor and pride. These are collected by any given being throughout countless lives. All beings, and humans in particular have amassed many negative causes which manifest as obstacles and sufferings in life and also affect the post-mortem destiny. All humans are always conditioned by thoughts and emotions; one moment there is a bad intention and thoughts conditioned by a negative emotion, the next moment there may come good intentions arising from virtuous thoughts. In actual fact, then, there are almost no absolutely 'good' or one 'bad' people so we can only speak of people who are more positive than negative or *vice versa*. Humans, however, have an advantage over other beings of the Six Realms, namely, enough intelligence and the necessary circumstances to understand the causes of suffering brought by continuously wandering in *samsara*. This means that – at least theoretically – humans are able to enter the spiritual path laid out by the Buddhas through which one can go beyond dualism and suffering, and help others to do the same. So the after-death experiences and fate of ordinary people, be they good or bad, is entirely different from those of realized practitioners of Yungdrung Bön and other forms of Buddhism.

Death is the separation of the mind (or 'soul') from the physical body composed of the five elements. What dies is the physical body; mind cannot die because it is immaterial. As the elements dissolve into each other, an ordinary dying person experiences a series of overwhelming visions and sensations which they perceive as coming from outside. These experiences bring great suffering and fear. For example, when the earth element starts to melt into the water element one feels as though crushed by a heavy mountain. Coupled with attachment to friends, relatives, unfinished tasks, possessions and the whole situation of life in general, this makes them suffer greatly. It is very important to try to relax at this stage, to let go of grasping and emotions as strong negative emotions at this juncture are tremendously powerful and will push one towards an unfortunate rebirth. Violent death brings other dangers. Through inverse attachment and desire for revenge, the spirit of a murdered person, for example, may become a dangerous ghost harking back after its murderer(s) and turning against the living in general. Similar things may happen to the spirits of the victims of an accident.

The situation is quite different for an experienced practitioner who practised Buddha's teaching and trained his/her mind in the realization of the illusory nature of all phenomena. When the visions and experiences related to the separation of body and mind appear, such a practitioner knows the order and characteristics of this process and realizes that all these visions and sensations are not something external but are manifestations of his/her own mind. The power of such person's practice alleviates the sufferings of death. Whether one suffers at this stage or not depends, of course, on how much and how thoroughly one has practised during the lifetime and how strong one's meditative stability is. For example, Dzogchen practitioners of the highest capacity do not enter the death process at all. Extraordinary practitioners such as Tsewang Rigdzin or Guru Padmasambhava dissolve their physical body into the essence of the elements while still alive, manifesting the Rainbow Body which is immaterial. The process is invisible to others who continue seeing them as if they had a normal physical body. This highest realization is known as Phowa Chenpo,[189] the Great Transfer. Such masters can reappear and disappear at will and give teachings to students with the necessary qualification in any time and place. Other Dzogchen masters of high capacity enter the final meditation at the end of their life. This lasts approximately a week. In the process of this final meditation session the Dzogchenpa's body dissolves into the essence of the elements and only some hair and nails are left behind. Rainbow Body is the most active form of a Buddha and can directly help sentient beings who have devotion and karmic connection to this particular Buddha. Lesser practitioners of Dzogchen rely on *Phowa*[190] methods by which the consciousness is transferred thereby avoiding the sufferings of dying altogether and instantaneously arriving at the final realization of the Natural State of Mind thus becoming a fully realized Buddha. Many *Phowa* transference methods belong to different levels of Tantra, too. In the case of Higher Tantra, for example, a *yogi* transfers their mind into a form of the *yidam* deity, a Buddha-form they have familiarized themselves with all their life through meditation and dream yoga, and attains the realization of the Illusory Body. On lower levels of Tantra a practitioner's consciousness is transferred directly into the paradise of Ogmin, for example, where one can continue practising without obstacles until achieving final realization. In short, there are very many methods in Yungdrung Bön, and in Buddhism in general, which bypass the sufferings of dying and instantly deliver the practitioner's consciousness to one of various levels of spiritual realization.

All those who have to go through the process of dying finally arrive at the *Bardo* of Primordial *Dharmakaya*. Here, too, a practitioner's experiences differ greatly from those of ordinary beings. Ordinary people experience this period as a blackout, unconsciousness, which can

---

[189] Tib. 'pho ba chen po.

[190] Tib. 'pho ba.

last from just a few seconds to up to three days. Sutra teachings also generally view it as an unconscious state. For an advanced practitioner of Dzogchen or Higher Tantra, on the other hand, this period presents a chance to gain full liberation because they have trained all their life to recognize this state, the fundamental nature of their mind, through the practices of contemplation and dream yoga. Now, when their mind arrives at this *Bardo*, it remains inseparable from this primordial state and the practitioner gains liberation from *samsara*.

While an accomplished Bɵ or Utgan is also fully aware of his/her dreams, their awareness is fundamentally different from that of a Dzogchen or Tantric *yogi*. Dream practice in Dzogchen and Higher Tantra is based on the knowledge that the process of falling asleep – when the mind turns its grasping attention from external objects and situations to the *bagchag*, karmic traces stored in the *Kunzhi Namshe* or Basic Storing Consciousness –.is very similar to the process of dying. When we fall asleep, the mental consciousness roams through the random mixture of memories and tensions accumulated during countless lifetimes and stored in the *Kunzhi Namshe* and we see these karmic traces as dreams. In the case of dying, these visions are the visions of the *Bardo* of Taking Rebirth. But in both cases, before the internal visions appear to the mind, the mind dissolves for some time, no matter how short, into its base, the Nature of Mind which is also called the Nature of Phenomena.[191] Dzogchen and Higher Tantra have different methods of dream yoga. While in Dzogchen a practitioner tries not to lose but to maintain continuous awareness of the Natural State while sleeping and dreaming, Tantric *yogis* use dreams to train in transformation into the *yidams* in order to be able to manifest as a *yidam* when they die– the realization of Illusory Body. As the Bɵ and Utgan have neither knowledge nor understanding of the fundamental base of their mind, nor Tantric techniques of transformation, their dream practice consists only of many methods of dream manipulation to gain some specific magic results and does not allow them to liberate from *samsara*.[192] Consequently when they die they experience a period of unconsciousness in the *Bardo* of Primordial *Dharmakaya* in the same way as ordinary humans.

---

[191] Tib. bon nyid.

[192] Although some dream techniques of Bɵ Murgel in which a Bɵ or Utgan takes on a different form or guises might seem similar to some specific Tantric methods, they are in fact very different in that Tantric dream yoga is based on an entirely different view and uses an entirely different method of transformation, which we already discussed in ch. XII, section on *Chöd*.

After the *Bardo* of Primordial *Dharmakaya* one 'wakes up' in the *Bardo* of the Clear Light of Emptiness. This *Bardo* is said to have a general duration of three days and four nights. Here lights and rays start manifesting from the primordial ground. Advanced practitioners recognize these lights and rays as the display of their own Nature of Mind and thus gain liberation. Ordinary beings perceive and grasp the lights and rays as the external objects, follow after them so the lights and rays solidify and turn into the visions of the *Bardo* of Taking Rebirth. These *Bardos* pose many challenges and has many potential sufferings. Firstly, one may not realize that one is dead. This is especially true for people who died in an accident or in some other violent way. After a period of blackout in the *Bardo* of Primordial *Dharmakaya* the senses 'wake up' and continue to function. The power of attachment drags the deceased towards relatives, friends, enemies, places where one used to live and so forth. The mental body, the spirit of the dead person is immaterial, so it can go right through material objects and people and travel in an instant to any place just by 'thinking' of it. The deceased may try to talk to relatives and friends but they cannot hear him/her so they feel rejected and alone. The spirit can become very upset, frightened and confused seeing its former body burnt, buried or destroyed in another way. On top of that, although one has left the physical body behind, due to attachment and grasping one may still feel hot or cold, desire food, clothing and other objects and suffer greatly because one cannot get them. The *Surchö* rituals in Yungdrung Bön[193] alleviate these sufferings. Another danger at this time is presented by the *Shed* spirits who try to take possession of the deceased's *la* and enslave him/her. This kind of problem is cut off by the *Shedur*[194] rites performed in the first three days following a person's death, or as soon as possible if the death was violent. Through these rites the *la* of the deceased is reunited with *yi* and *sem*, and propelled towards the next rebirth while the relatives are liberated from the demonic appearances of *Shed*.

In the *Bardo* of Taking Rebirth, experiences of different beings vary considerably:

> The condition in the Bardo is just the same as this condition in dreams. We have feelings and (see) everything perfectly, but nothing is stable; things are always moving and no matter what comes into this being's thinking, he cannot stop it. [...]

---

[193] See ch. XII.

[194] *Shedur* will be studied in the next chapter.

> When these kinds of spirits are in the Bardo time, they are like flies or insects in summer – when flies see some meat, too many of them come and swarm around it. In a similar way, too many Bardo-beings swarm around when a couple is uniting. But it is not easy for the Bardo-beings to be connected with the couple; it is important to have a previous karmic cause with them. Otherwise, the Bardo-beings can see the couple but it is not easy to integrate with them. How they integrate depends on previous karmic cause, whether it was good, bad or neutral; there are many ways. If the Bardo-being was a practitioner or a religious person in their previous life, then (when a couple unites) they may see a flower garden or a beautiful place or a palace and so they go there and have a rest. But after they have rested, they are stuck there like an insect which has walked in some glue. That means they have united with this couple (conception), and are beginning to take the next life.
> (The experience of conception) very much depends on karmic cause. Even for normal beings which were not connected with good things, with religion or virtues or merits in their previous life, which were just ordinary, there are different capacities. Some are chased (in Bardo). They have enemies behind them and so they run away. In some cases they try to hide in a cave, and that is how they take birth in the Lower Realms. Once they have hidden, they can't move any more, just like an insect caught in glue. So that is another way.[195]

In the first part of this *Bardo* one's feelings and visions are more related to the form and circumstances of one's previous life. In the second part of this *Bardo* one's feelings and visions change and are related to the form and circumstances of the next life. For example, a human first sees him/herself as human and has visions and experiences related to human existence. If that human is to be reborn as a cat then in the second part of this *Bardo* their experiences and feelings change to that of a cat. In the same way a cat may initially feel like a cat but if it is to be reborn as a human, in the second part of this *Bardo* it begins to feel and see itself as a human. If a person was a practitioner or at least received some teachings, they will have visions of various peaceful and wrathful Buddha-forms. If they recognize them as self-manifestations of their own mind and not as external forms, then their mind is liberated into these visions and they become a *Sambhogakaya* Buddha. In order to help the mind of the deceased through the stages of this *Bardo* there are several purification methods in Yungdrung Bön such as *Zhitro,*[196] *Yoga of the Peaceful and Wrathful Deities*. This is given as an initiation and should be practised

---

[195] Namdak, *Yetri Thasel*, p. 13–14.

[196] Tib. zhi khro.

during the lifetime to enable one to recognize the manifestations of this *Bardo* when they appear and attain liberation at this stage. Alternatively this practice is done by living friends or other practitioners to purify the obscurations and defilements of the deceased's mind and enable them to be liberated or, at least, obtain a better rebirth.

For those who did not receive any teachings or initiations, these manifestations will appear as external, often frightening, emanations chasing one's spirit which cannot hide anywhere. One is blown like a helpless feather by the hurricanes of the karmic winds arising from one's previous actions. An experienced lama can help the troubled spirit even at this stage, leading them to liberation or a better rebirth by performing a *Phowa* practice or a *Jyangbui Choga*[197] ritual in the course of which the deceased's consciousness is summoned into a support and instructions regarding the *Bardo* are read, or by reading the *Bardo Thödrol*[198] text. The *Bardo* of Taking Rebirth is generally said to last forty-nine days, but this is an approximation. Indeed, some beings may skip this stage along with the two previous *Bardos*. This is true for realized practitioners who become a Buddha before or straight after dying, as well as for those who go straight to hell because they committed one or more of the Five Actions Without Interval:[199]

---

[197] Tib. byang bu'i cho ga.

[198] Tib. bar do thos grol; (lit. 'liberation through hearing in *Bardo*') texts containing methods and instructions to guide the consciousness through the *Bardo*. Although in the West the version of *Bar do Thos grol*, most commonly translated as *Tibetan Book of the Dead*, is a compilation of texts based on the discoveries made by Buddhist *terton* Karma Lingpa (Tib. Kar ma gling pa) who lived in 14th c., the origin of such texts is likely to belong to Yungdrung Bön. In *Zhang Zhung sNyan brGyud* cycle which was never hidden as *terma* and was written down by Gurub Nangzher Lödpo in 8th c. AD we already find several texts dealing with *Bardo* such as *Byang chub sems kyi gnas drug*, '*Khro lo bzhi sbrag* (tr. John Myrdhin Reynolds, *Selections from the Bonpo Book of the Dead* [San Diego and Copenhagen: Bonpo Translation Projetc, Vidyadhara Institute for Studies in Comparative Religion, 1997]) and *sGron ma Drug gi gDams pa* (translated by Giacomella Orofino, *Sacred Tibetan Teachings on Death and Liberation*, Prism-Unity, 1990, pp. 61–81). *Rin chen phreng ba* prayer for *Bardo* by the 11th-c. master Gurzhogpa (Tib. Gur zhogs pa), brother of Meu Gogdzö (Tib. rMe'u dGongs mdzod (1038–1096) compiler of *A khrid* Dzogchen cycle, as well as the Bönpo *Yul lugs zhi khro*, *Bru lugs zhi khro* and *Hor lugs zhi khro* cycles all predate the *Kar glind zhi khro* of Karma Lingpa which served as the base for the Buddhist *Bardo Thos grol*, a compilation by Rigdzin Nyima Dragpa (Tib. Rig 'dzin Nyi ma Grags pa, 1647–1710).

[199] Tib. mtsams med pa lnga.

- Killing a spiritual adviser or lama;
- Killing a student of a spiritual teacher;
- Killing one's father;
- Killing one's mother;
- Killing one's own child.

Those who committed these grave negative actions are instantly reborn in one of the eighteen hells when they die. Furthermore, the minds of some religious practitioners who were killed or disturbed while dying and thus became trapped in one of the negative emotional states may turn into a very dangerous spirit immediately after passing for a brief moment through the *Bardo* of Primordial *Dharmakaya*.

Conclusion

Both Yungdrung Bön and Bɵ Murgel recognize that the soul/mind/ consciousness lives on after the physical body perishes and both traditions see this as a time when the spirit is particularly vulnerable to negative forces. However, Yungdrung Bön also acknowledges death as a special time when one's practice can bear fruit and one 's consciousness can be liberated from the sufferings of this plane of existence for ever by realizing one's full potential as a Buddha. This is lacking in Bɵ Murgel. Be that as it may, the post-mortem fate of 'ordinary' people can be compared as the circumstances of death, how the death rituals and subsequent prayers are performed (which in turn depend at least to some extent on the wealth and generosity of the deceased's relatives), whether the death was violent or not and, of course, the deceased's own personal qualities all play a role in determining the spirit's conditions in the afterlife.

CHAPTER XIV

Healing and Magic

Part I
Theoretical Base

Understanding of the causes for illness and death in Bө Murgel

The Bө's healing techniques are based on an intimate knowledge of the causes underlying illness and death, many of which are related to the soul, so in order for us to understand healing and magic of Bө Murgel, we, too must know more about this fundamental basis. We have seen that, in the majority of cases, disease and death occur because spirits or gods prompt a malevolent attack as a result of which one or more souls departs or is damaged, weakening the person's energy field.

Damage and loss of the soul

A soul may jump out of the body because of sudden fright[1] or injury, caused for example by falling from a horse (or motorbike). In such cases, it is not only the soul which may leap out, but a part of the *amin* energy may also go with it. Parts of *amin* also can be stolen and this, too, results in various diseases. Some accidents or sudden, frightening incidents are deliberately caused by bad spirits trying to provoke the

---

[1] We find similar understanding in other cultures, too, in common turns of phrase such as: 'my heart leapt to my mouth', 'my heart sank' or in Russian 'my soul has run into my heels'. These describe what happens when we are very frightened, an example of the soul-energy being displaced by fear. This type of energy disorder is also well known in Chinese Qi-Gong traditions where it is said to damage kidneys, while another type of fright pushes the energy into the heart which can be sometimes fatal. Actually, in Qi-Gong the first type is linked to emotion of fear while second is caused by fright, sudden fear.

exit of soul, which they then seek to enslave, but others are caused by *Yabadal*[2] 'travellers', the name given to spirits, local *Ezhen* and *Zayaan* when they are on the move. As the dimension of the spirits overlaps with the human one, some features of the human landscape are also used by spirits, and roads are an example of this. Some road accidents are caused by passing *Yabadal*. *Yabadal* can be pedestrian, ride on various steeds or in carts, and their arrival is often announced by a sudden breeze or a gust of wind. Should someone be unlucky enough to be on the road at the exact time and place when a powerful *Yabadal* is also travelling by it, there will be an accident as the *Yabadal* will sweep aside any human in their way. Many accidents which happen seemingly for no reason, when for example the driver inexplicably loses control of the car are in fact due to crashing into a *Yabadal*. Similarly, everyone has probably had the experience of tripping over on an absolutely flat surface for no apparent reason and this is due to being in the way of a pedestrian *Yabadal*. The gravity of such accidents and resulting injuries depends on the power of the *Yabadal* encountered. Unlike malign spirits seeking to enslave the soul, *Yabadal* are not necessarily aggressive towards people, they simply possess superior speed and power so humans are thrown off their way reminiscent of an animal struck by a car. Nevertheless, there are, of course, aggressive *Yabadal* who push people aside deliberately or some accidents can happen because of the wrath of a local *Ezhen* who is displeased by a person or a group of people and so causes a crash.

There are also invisible roads used only by a certain class of spirits, and these, too, can have a detrimental effect if humans inadvertently intersect with them. An episode from the life of Bө Sodnom Gomboev – which he told me while resting between *tailgans* in summer 1994 – illustrates this:

> When I was very small we lived in a *gher* moving from one place to another in the steppe. Once we pitched our tent in a new place and that night I was woken up by strange metallic noises. I couldn't understand what was going on and looked around, puzzled. Then I saw many dwarves walking through the middle of the *gher* right through the hearth. Some of them were taking an interest in our metal pans and other kitchen utensils, poking around and making them clang. The spirits didn't seem to see me and the adults were sleeping like logs. Soon afterwards, my mother fell ill and was getting worse every day. Everyone was worried about her and sent for a Bө. I kept quiet about my night visions because I thought they'd laugh at me. After examining

[2] Bur. ябадал.

> my mother and the place, the Bɵ said her disease was because we'd put the *gher* right on a spirit-way and that we needed to move it at once. Only then did I speak about my visions [...] My mother recovered soon after we moved our *gher* to another place.[3]

It is very important not to put or build any kind of accommodation on spirit roads and especially their crossroads. Although there has been a certain interest in geomancy in recent decades, in our modern world too little importance is given to spiritual matters in general and to choosing construction sites in particular. In the West most constructors would just laugh out loud if you suggested a site was not suitable because it blocked a spirit-road and that a professional should be called to check it. In practice, however, people living in accommodation built on desecrated ground, on the dwellings or roads of spirits, on land negatively charged due to 'heavenly' contamination (blood or other impurities falling to earth as a result of wars between sky-dwelling beings etc.) suffer from various serious diseases just as if they were, say, living on a radioactive site. The importance of this aspect of the work of a Bɵ, Utgan or any other spiritual practitioner with similar capacity cannot be overestimated.

'Taxes' to the Lord-Owners

Epidemics of infectious diseases among people and animals often break out when certain ill-willed Tengeri, *Haats* or *Ezhen* are collecting *alban*[4]- 'taxes' from the population living on the land they considered their property. To exact these 'taxes', the spirits send infectious diseases such as small pox or Siberian plague so that the people are forced to make offerings to them through the Bɵ and Utgan to ensure they will not fall ill or, if already ill, to stand a better chance of recovery. Despite these offerings, the evil Lord-Owners take many souls of people and animals and enslave them. If the wrath of a malevolent *Ezhen* is especially strong they may wipe out the population of an entire region.

Techniques of soul-stealing

A soul can be stolen or harmed in many ways but it is often the messengers of Erlig Khaan who capture it. As these messengers are themselves essentially spirits of the dead, they are well suited to this purpose. Frightening and fierce, these messengers of death ride on black

---

3 A passage from my unpublished diary *Tailgan Trip*.

4 Bur. альбан.

horses[5] or in black carts, their sleeves are rolled up and their hands are smeared with blood. When sent to steal a soul they break into the victim's house at night, jump on their bed, cut a hole in their chest and, thrusting their hand through it, press the arteries so the person dies.

There are many techniques of soul-stealing which take place at night. While a person is asleep, his/her soul wanders off out of the body and that is when malign spirits can chase it and try to steal it. Alternatively, bad spirits creep close to the sleeping person and try to make them sneeze in their sleep. If they succeed then the victim's soul jumps out of the body and they give chase it. Dreams of being pursued by frightening men or women, vicious animals or some invisible, frightening presence most often appear because the soul is being chased. If the soul doesn't manage to hide or escape but is captured, then Erlig Khaan's messengers take it to the Underworld where it is kept in one of the prisons. Therefore, if someone sneezes in their sleep[6] it is an ill omen often pointing to provocation from negative forces. On other occasions the soul-stealers take on a variety of guises which are not necessarily ferocious; some can appear very pleasing and attractive so a soul is lured into following them but ends up imprisoned nevertheless.

To avoid imprisonment, the pursued soul must try to escape or hide. There are several possibilities. It can turn into various animals, birds or insects. It can escape if it manages to jump on the soul of its owner's horse as then it can easily gallop away from its predators. If the person is religious then they may have a good connection with the Tengeri, *Haats* and ancestral spirits so previous offerings may have opened a way to their abode. In this case the soul escapes there and the Tengeri and protective spirits of one's clan or tribe fend off the attack, after which the soul returns to the body and all goes well. Alternatively, the soul can flee to the *Zayaans* of fire who emit fire-sparks which destroy or frighten the malevolent spirits. Or the soul can hide in the fur of sacred animals

---

5 In Tibet there is a similar perception of the messengers of the Lord of Death: '*I had the feeling I was being chased. I fell asleep. In my dream I was carried away by a man with dark complexion on a black horse.*' *Karmay*, *The Arrow and the Spindle,* pp. 317–318.

6 It seems that many archaic cultures held similar views. The custom of saying 'Bless you!' when someone sneezes may well stem from the belief that the devil can enter at that moment or that one's soul could shoot out with the sneeze. In Russia yawning is also considered a dangerous moment when the devil can slip in and so the custom was to cross one's mouth after yawning. Although these customs are observed in Christian cultures, they are most probably of pre-Christian origin.

dedicated to the White Tengeri or *Haats*, in the kennel of a good dog, in wild animal tracks, or run to the house of a good neighbour or friend. If caught, the soul emits cries which can be heard by humans.[7]

Understanding of the causes for illness and death in Yungdrung Bön: the concept of karma and its implications

Understanding of the causes of illness and death in the Bön of Cause

In the Four Ways of Cause, the understanding of how provocations in the form of negative energy can be sent by spirits and gods reflects that found in both Bɵ Murgel and Prehistoric Bön in general because Causal Bön contains ritual methods and techniques stemming from Prehistoric Bön which were adapted and transformed by Tonpa Shenrab. While many techniques of the Bön of Cause seem similar to those of Prehistoric Bön and Bɵ Murgel at first glance, they are built upon a fundamentally different view; any ritual performed must be based on compassion and *Bodhichitta*, an aspiration to achieve Buddhahood for the sake of all beings. In Causal Bön we do not find rituals which save one being by harming or killing another because the concept of karma is a key principle of Tonpa Shenrab's teachings. Even though there are destructive rituals in Causal Bön, especially in the Third Way, *Trulshen Thegpa*, and the Fourth Way, *Sidshen Thegpa,* they are performed in a completely different way from those in Bɵ Murgel and Prehistoric Bön as they instead of merely destroying an evil being, they also ensure that destroyed being obtains a better rebirth and comes onto the path of Yungdrung Bön which ultimately leads to complete liberation from any sort of suffering.

A great number of methods in Causal Bön are aimed at bettering people's condition through working on secondary causes. Despite the fact that death, for example, is caused by one's karma, there are nevertheless 'natural' and 'unnatural' causes of it. Yungdrung Bön recognizes eighty-one causes for death, and as with Bɵ Murgel,[8] only one is natural: the consumption of the body and life-energy due to old age. The vast majority of causes are therefore 'unnatural'. Among these, twenty are due to provocations from other beings intervening in the human energy system and can be viewed as a killing of sorts; twenty are caused by

---

7 Based on oral sources and Hangalov, *Sobranie* I, pp. 395–400.

8 See previous chapter.

accidents; twenty by an imbalance of the elements; and twenty because of wounds from weapons.[9] If we look closely into these 'unnatural' causes it becomes clear that even such triggers as accidents, wounds from weapons and imbalance of the elements can be largely attributed to the spirits or gods acting as a secondary cause as they may trigger accidents, arguments and wars. Even many cases when the elements are out of balance can stem from contact with spirits and gods and, if not treated, can lead to death. The Ancient Chinese shared this view, as can be seen from the following passage from Chuang Tzu:

> Duke Huang was hunting in a marsh, with Kuan Chung as his carriage driver, when he saw a ghost. The duke grasped Kuan Chung's hand and said,
> 'Father Chung, what do you see?'
> 'I don't see anything', replied Kuan Chung.
> When the duke returned home, he fell into a stupor, grew ill, and for seven days didn't go out.
> A gentleman of Ch'i named Huang-tzu Kao-ao said,
> 'Your Grace, you are doing this injury to yourself! How could a ghost have the power to injure you! If the vital breath that is stored up in a man becomes dispersed and does not return, then he suffers deficiency. If it is ascends and fails to descend again, it causes him to be chronically irritable. If it descends and does not ascend again, it causes him to be chronically forgetful. And if it neither ascends nor descends, but gathers in the middle of the body in the region of the heart, then he becomes ill.'[10]

Ultimately, both 'natural' and 'unnatural' causes arise from one's karma. The divination, diagnostics, healing and other types of magic used to combat these negative influences not only relieve suffering, prolong life and increase prosperity but also provide patients with a better chance to correct their mistakes, become acquainted with the Buddha's teachings and enter the path of liberation either directly or indirectly.

Causes of disease according to Bum Zhi

> The Five Poison Consciousnesses develop from the root of ignorance and create 404 kinds of sickness. There are 404 corresponding methods of medical science.[11]

---

9 See Norbu, *Drung, Deu and Bön*, p. 89.

10 Tr. Watson, *Chuang Tzu*, p. 124.

11 Excerpt from the translation and commentary by Yongdzin Lopön Tenzin Namdak on the Bönpo Dzogchen cycle of *gSas mkhar g.yung drung ye*

Bum Zhi[12] are the Bönpo texts on medicine taught by the Buddha Tonpa Shenrab which he transmitted to his son, Chedbu Trishe,[13] and the Eight Sages of Medicine.[14] They have since come down a long line of transmission in Tagzig, Zhang Zhung, Tibet and elsewhere, and it is the knowledge contained in these texts which forms the basis of all Tibetan medicine, both Yungdrung Bön and Buddhist alike. As Buddhism developed in Tibet, these Bönpo texts were rewritten as the *Gyud Zhi*,[15] the Four Medical Tantras, and attributed to some Indian sages. However, it is clear that these later texts are borrowed from Bön because of the close similarities in structure, content, and particularly because many of the plant and animal medicinal ingredients mentioned are native to Zhang Zhung and Tibet alone. Moreover, many medical substances are in the language of Zhang Zhung.[16]

One of the main texts pertaining to the *Bum Zhi*, the *Multicoloured Myriad of Healing Methods*,[17] gives the following descriptions for the onset of disease:

> Chapter 8: The Primary Causes of Disease
> 1. Remote Causes: an explanation of ignorance and three mental poisons – desire, hatred and delusion.
> 2. Immediate Causes: an explanation of the three humours – wind, bile and phlegm.
>
> Chapter 9: The Secondary Causes of Disease
> 1. The Cause of Aggravation of Disease: an explanation of the impact on disease of the seasons, the function of sense organs and inappropriate actions of body, speech and mind.
> 2. The Covert Gathering and overt Arising of Secondary Causes: an explanation of how wrong diet etc. accumulates and leads to the manifestation of disease.

---

khyabs lta ba'i rgyud ces bya ba bzhugs so, Chapter VII. Triten Norbutse Monastery, Kathmandu, 27.01.08.

12 Tib. 'Bum bzhi.

13 Tib. dPyad bu Khri shes.

14 Tib. gSo rig 'dzin pa'i drang srong chen po brgyad.

15 Tib. rGyud bzhi.

16 After oral information from Yongdzin Lopön Tenzin Namdak, Khenpo Tenpa Yungdrung, and Chögyal Namkhai Norbu, *The Origins of Tibetan Culture and Thought* (Merigar: Shang Shung Edizione, 1995), pp. 13–14.

17 Tib. dpyad 'bum khra bo.

3. The Secondary Causes from which Disease actually Arises: an explanation of how disease arises from imbalance of the three humours.

Chapter 10: The Inception of Disease

1. How the Disease Comes In: an explanations of how the factors of time, provocation of negative energy, diet and behaviour cause hyperactivity, under-activity or disbalance of the various body components.
2. The Gateway through which Disease Enters: an explanation of how disease comes in and progresses through the skin, flesh, channels, bone and six inner organs.[18]

Understanding of the causes of illness and death in the Bön of Fruit

The Fruitional Vehicles of Yungdrung Bön take quite a different view on the matter of illness and death. The Yungdrung Bön *Mahasiddha* Drenpa Namkha elucidates this clearly:

> Future sentient beings of deluded mind! Although you accuse spirits, ghosts, animals and livestock of being portents of misfortune, birth and death are caused by your own karma. How sad to hold the wrong view![19]

It is not that illness and death are not caused by spirits and gods; rather, the spirits and gods are not the primary cause and can trigger only illness or death because of the negative karma accumulated by the person affected. In order to better understand this view, we must first take a look at the complex concept of karma, a cornerstone of both Yungdrung Bön and Buddhism.

---

[18] From *Curriculum Guide for Certificate in Amchi Duera-pa (Bum Zhi Tradition),* of the Himalayan Amchi Association, Kathmandu, Nepal, April 2004. This Curriculum was prepared for the Nepali government as part of a project to train young doctors in the medical tradition of Yungdrung Bön. My wife and I assisted in the translation of this presentation under the guidance of Khenpo Tenpa Yungdrung, Amchi Gegen and other Bönpo Geshes.

[19] Drenpa Namkha, *A Message of Provisional Meaning from the Assembly of Rigdzins,* tr. Khenpo Tenpa Yungdrung, Carol Ermakova, Dmitry Ermakov, awaiting publication.

The workings of karma

The law of karma – or *ledre*[20] in Tibetan – is the driving force for continuous rebirths in *samsara* and the true creator of the worlds in which sentient beings live. Each being's perceptions and life experiences derive from karma and are known collectively as 'karmic vision'. However, for ordinary beings and most practitioners, it is all but impossible to descry even their own karma, let alone that of other beings. Nevertheless, without a clear understanding of the workings of karma one cannot practise Yungdrung Bön or any other Buddhist tradition effectively as this is a kingpin of both Yungdrung Bön and Buddha Dharma.

So what is karma? In a nutshell, it is the law of cause and effect. Every action – be it positive, negative or neutral – produces a corresponding effect which will manifest either in this life or in lives to come, so there are generally three types of karma: positive, negative and neutral. Positive karma produces good fruit which ripens in a person's life as happy conditions such as a healthy, beautiful body, longevity, prosperity and success. Negative karma brings sufferings such as illness, misfortune, poverty, an unattractive appearance, disturbed mind, violence and so on. Neutral karma – actions such as just sitting doing nothing, not having particular thoughts, doing things automatically without any good or bad intention – brings similar situations in future lives. These three types of karma can be created through the activities of our body, speech and mind, so we speak of the karma of body, karma of speech and karma of mind. What makes karma so complex is that positive, negative and neutral karmas interact with each other in countless ways within a person's karmic pool, so the manifest result of a single karma/action is often modified by our other karmas. Any karma – good, bad or neutral – can be affected by the supportive, counteractive or destructive effect of our other karmas. Supportive karma further strengthens the results of an action, counteractive karma weakens the effect of an action while destructive karma annuls the result altogether.

Four stages of karma

The complexity of karma doesn't end here. Each individual karma goes through four stages of development: intention, entering into action, completing the action and satisfaction derived from that action. If an action is cut short at any of those stages, the fruit of that karma will not be completed.

---

[20] Tib. las 'bras.

Let's imagine for a moment that you want to kill someone. That is a thought, an intention and if you recognize it as a negative intention and correct it, you stop yourself before you actually enter into action, so no heavy karma is produced. You may suffer in your own mind thinking what a terrible person you are to entertain such thoughts and so on, but it will not produce a bad fruit in the future. If you plan to kill someone, take the knife and sneak up on them but then stop yourself before it is too late, although you have entered into a bad action, once again, you have caught yourself in time and so the karma will not be complete. If you are truly sorry and purify yourself, the result of your attempted negative action will be weakened and maybe completely purified. If, however, you not only plot the murder and initiate the plan but actually carry it out, there is still time to repent immediately. If you feel true remorse at your deadly deed and try to make amends, you may prevent the karma from fully ripening and so it is easier to purify it. Finally, if you plan the murder, enter into action, carry it out and are then satisfied with your work, that is like a seal; karma is then sealed and fruit is going to come back to you sooner or later. The same mechanism is true for good karma, too. For example, if you have a good intention but don't act and complete the action, or don't feel satisfaction from it, then benefits will be minimal.[21]

The force of karma is very powerful so, even if one only nurtures harmful intentions and malignant thoughts, continually wishing harm on others without entering into action, that will create a very negative karma of mind which can manifest in a variety of ways such as madness, poverty, serious diseases or – when a sufficient amount has been accumulated – can even become a cause for violent death For example, the Sutras speak of a beggar who lived near a king's palace and always wished that the king's head would be cut off. Early one morning as the king and his retinue were leaving the palace and the beggar was asleep in the road, the wheel of the royal chariot sliced off his head.

Collective karma

Apart from each individual's personal karma, there are other types of karma which affect the lives of all beings. These are the different types of so-called 'collective karma': karma of various realms and dimensions, universes, planets and so on; karma of species (in the case of the human species we have karma of the race, karma of the nation, karma of the tribe, karma of the family, karma of the city or village, karma of a party or group of people, karma of the trade) and so on. A person's individual karma

---

[21] Like the saying: 'The road to hell is paved with good intentions'.

determines they will be born in a certain family of a certain tribe, nation and race in a particular time and place and in turn all the general karmas of that situation affect the course of that person's life. For example, if one is born into a rich and virtuous family in beautiful surroundings in a time of peace and plenty, one has more potential for a relatively untroubled and enjoyable life than someone who is born into a poor family in a time of war or genocide. These wider circumstances are called secondary causes and although they act as a support for either good or bad karmic seeds to ripen and bear fruit, the main, primary cause always rests on the individual's personal karma. This means that external circumstances can change, a person who presently enjoys perfect circumstances can develop negative trends and end up badly while someone who has been deprived even of basic necessities may later become very lucky.

The impermanence of karma

One good thing about karma is that even the heaviest karmic traces can be completely purified or annihilated by applying the Buddhas' teachings. This is because all sentient beings – even the most heinous murderers, evil doers and hell-dwellers – have Buddha-nature which is immaterial, indestructible, incorruptible, non-dual and ever-present at all times and in all circumstances. In other words, all beings have the potential to become a Buddha. In fact, many higher Sutra teachings say that although they do not realize it, all beings are Buddhas; to gain realization one needs to meet the right teacher and apply the virtuous spiritual methods, then one will surely arrive at full Illumination either in an instant, a year, a life or many lifetimes. That, again, depends on one's karma.

We have established, then, that according to Yungdrung Bön and Buddhism in general, the principal cause of all kinds of diseases and sufferings lies in the accumulation of negative karma. Spirits, ghosts and gods are secondary causes which act upon this negative accumulation. As each sentient being has amassed infinite amounts of negative karma, they all circulate in *samsara* and experience infinite suffering according to the results of their deeds. In this situation, merely treating the external manifestations of a disease is like cutting some branches off a poisonous tree; it doesn't bring lasting relief because new branches or shoots always spring up again. From this point of view, simply curing a disease isn't enough; the being in question has not been liberated from *samsara* and so another problem or disease will come later, and death, too, will surely come for all. The only lasting relief from suffering and disease is the complete elimination and purification of karma itself, not just some of its results. That's why in one way or another all the practice methods in both Yungdrung Bön and Buddhism deal with purifying karma, and all of them are directed towards the attainment of final Buddhahood. This can be likened to cutting off the root of the poisonous tree which is ignorance of our real condition, of our primordial state which is pure from the beginningless beginning. Once this has been severed at the root, no more shoots (representing *samsara*) can grow.

According to this view, only Buddhas, *Mahasiddhas* and *Bodhisattvas* who have progressed to a high level can be said to be 'healthy' as they have sufficiently or completely purified the cause for rebirth in *samsara*.[22]

Healing and magic in the context of the gradual path of Yungdrung Bön

However, the view presented above doesn't mean that there is no place for healing rituals or divination in Yungdrung Bön; quite the opposite. The teachings of the Central Asian Buddha Tonpa Shenrab, unlike those of the Indian Buddha Shakyamuni, contain a wide range of techniques for healing, divination, exorcism, prognostication, weather magic and so on. As beings are endowed with different potentials, these methods are beneficial for bringing beings of lower capacity onto the path of liberation from *samsara* as well as for remedying particular problems of those already on the path. Yongdzin Lopön Tenzin Namdak describes this process very clearly:

> When our religion was first introduced, it was very difficult [...] Very few people knew meditation techniques so everything had to be explained. The people were nature worshippers, they worshipped rocks[23] etc. So the best way to introduce the Teachings was through medicine. If someone was sick, they were given medicine and some were cured and so they believed that if the Teachings could cure, then there must be something worth knowing.
> Medicine, however, can't cure everything, so then what is to be done? Then you ask divination. There are four methods of divination: divination as such, dreams, consulting an oracle or using a mirror. The mirror is the best way; letters or images come to the mirror. Divination tells us if something is disturbed by spirits or whatever, and then there are rituals and rites which can cure that. That is the second way.

[22] Based on teachings received over the years from Lopön Tenzin Namdak Rinpoche, Namkhai Norbu Rinpoche and many other Bönpo and Buddhist lamas.

[23] I.e. they were animists.

So most things can be cured with a combination of medicine and divination, but that is still not certain. Sometimes farmers were disturbed and their crops destroyed by hail or long drought and they would ask the priest if he could do something to summon rain or stop hail. In this way the Teachings became more widespread and people had more and more trust in what the priests were saying.

Fig. 1. Tapihritsa – 25th master of Zhang Zhung Nyen Gyud.

That is how our religion and culture started, and it is the source of Zhang Zhung civilization and also of Tibetan civilization. [...]

This country [Zhang Zhung] had a religion long before Tibet did, and that is the source of its civilization. The *Zhang Zhung Nyen Gyud* is the essence coming from that region. We are not sure when it started; we only know that the twenty-fifth master[24] lived in the seventh century (AD).

In particular there were practitioners of Dzogchen who lived in solitude by the snow mountains, opposite Mount Kailash and there are ruins of many solitary places in the valleys which practitioners had used long before. We know some of their biographies.

Quite often robbers would come from Kalog,[25] Mongol types, and

---

24 25th master is Tib. Ta pi hri tsa. He was active in 7th – 8th c. AD.

25 Tib. gar log. Yongdzin Lopön Tenzin Namdak identifies them as Mongoloid peoples coming from the area of Sogd. Western scholars generally consider Sogdians to be of Indo-Iranian stock and later Yuezhi (who lived in the Tarim Basin until 162 BC [Craig Benjamin, *The Yuezhi Migration and Sogdia*, <http://www.transoxiana.org/Eran/Articles/benjamin.html> accessed 09.06.07] when a large part of them was pushed out by the Hunnu) to be of Indo-European type. Yuezhi lived in the Tarim Basin since ancient times and the first reference to them in Chinese sources appears in 645 BC. This people are thought to be either the same as Tokharians or some Indo-European tribes, possibly some of the tribes which made up the earlier Pazyryk culture in Altai. But most probably they were of a mixed type or their confederation consisted of Indo-European tribes which were dominant and some proto-Mongol tribes which were vassals. Yuezhi swept through Sogdiana and Bactria and founded Tokharistan in Central Asia which later become Kushana Empire (1st- 3rd c. AD) and included northern India. In Khotan-Saka script the name of this people is given as *gara* which appears in Tibetan as *gar* which forms the part of two names Tib. tho gar and Tib. gar log. (*The Kingdom of the Da Yuezhi* 大月氏 *(the Kushan)*, <http://depts.washington.edu/silkroad/texts/hhshu/

Fig. 2. Master Namkha Nangwa Dogchen – tsakli *from the cycle of Rigdzin Dhüpa.*

they would rob horses and yaks in particular, but also people to use as slaves. They were always robbing men and women for slaves. There were few practitioners of Dzogchen among the people of Zhang Zhung but one Dzogchen master[26] was very sympathetic and he saw that there was too much suffering, so he wrote the four sentences of refuge on a bit of wood and gave it to people when they came and asked for protection. First of all he wrote a few copies and tied it to whoever had connection to him, and they were safe from the robbers, so more and more people heard about it and came and learned refuge. Then instead of writing the verses on wood and tying them to a necklace, the people learned [the verses of] refuge from him and it spread all over the country. So the Teachings spread

---

notes13.html> accessed 9.06.07; Liu, Xinru, *Migration and Settlement of the Yuezhi-Kushan. Interaction and Interdependence of Nomadic and Sedentary Societies,* Journal of World History, 12 (No. 2) 2001, p. 261–292) While Tib. tho gar no doubt refers to Tokharians, Tib. gar log is often taken to mean Karluk (Qarluq). However, this doesn't fit into the time-frame of Zhang Zhung as Karluk are the later Tyurkic peoples who came to prominence when they staged the successful rebellion against their Tyurkyut overlords together with some Uighur tribes in 745 AD and then established the Karluk Kaganate in 766 AD. The Karluk's origins are obscure but they seem to be a branch of the Tyurkyut who in turn trace their origins to one of the Hunnu or Syanbi tribes (Gumilev, *Drevnie Tyurki*, pp. 27–30, 87–94), hence they may in fact have been an ancient tribe although there is as yet no hard evidence to support this. Another possibility is that Tib. gar log actually refers to the Yuezhi whom Tibetans distinguished from the Tokharians and whose tribal union comprised some proto-Mongol tribes (maybe even ancestors of the historic Karluk) and it is these tribes who actually attacked the Zhang Zhung Confederation. This interpretation is in accord with the views of many Tyurkologists working in the Russian Federation and Turkey who believe that many nations of the Great Steppe such as the Scythians and Hunnu were in fact mixed tribal unions of Indo-Europeans, proto-Tyurks and proto-Mongols. (Faizrakhmanov, *Drevnie Tyurki*.) See ch. XV.

26 Tib. Nam mkha' sNang ba mDog chen. He later became the teacher to the first and second Tibetan kings Nyatri Tsenpo and Mutri Tsenpo.

in this country of Zhang Zhung and slowly developed and gradually masters were able to teach and people tried to make time to practise.[27]

The Lower Vehicles are for any kind of raw people, for those who are not trained. This is how to teach the mind.

First of all is *Chashen Thegpa.* You go and talk about health. Many beings have problems with health, and so then they try and use medicine. They can see that this works, that it helps; this is something visible. This is the Bönpo method of bringing beings into the religious way. You can help one, two, three, four... beings and then that spreads and develops; there is no need to send brochures everywhere. If one person is cured, they tell their family and everyone sees that they had some problem before and now it is gone, so then they tell other people and it spreads by word of mouth as many people realize it can be helpful. So that is the first stage, to cure beings with medicine.

But sometimes medicine doesn't work, and so the people think, 'What is wrong? Usually this medicine helps, but not now.' So then (the practitioners) ask divination, using an oracle or dreams or *Tra*, mirror-divination. They ask what is wrong and are told which ritual to do, which spirits are disturbing. Then they use the ritual and the people think: 'Ah, yes! Rituals can help!' And so the people realize that even if you do something invisible (i.e. not using tangible medicine), it can still help. So they know for themselves. This is a direct, personal method. This is the Bönpo way to bring people into religion; it is not just about collecting followers and things. Nowadays a lot of lamas go against this. Lamas or scholars try to have more followers but the background (motivation) is to gain reputation and property. These all go completely against this traditional method.

There is no need to kill or 'hurl' beings to tame their mind. For example, when the Chinese Communists came to Tibet it was very hard during the Cultural Revolution, so many were killed in concentration camps. The young generation can remember how cruel those times were, but they have no experience of how it was before. Yet still they are learning from some signs here or there and they are coming back (to the traditional religious ways) automatically. Even the Chinese officers who are specially trained Communists, who have to take an oath about how they act, who are not allowed to do anything except serve the government, for whom the government is like their own *yidam*, who can't keep any property and this enables them to work their way up the ranks and get a good position – even these people go and ask (practitioners) to

[27] Excerpt from *Evening Conference on Bön with Lopön Tenzin Namdak Rinpoche*, Paris, 19 May, 1998, unpublished transcript. Trscr. & ed. C. Ermakova and D. Ermakov. Published here with permission of Yongdzin Lopön Tenzin Namdak.

do something for them. They go in the evening when there is no-one around. So the government can't control the mind completely. That is our experience.

Then the Second Way is *Nangshen Thegpa*. People have to live in this world, they have to have food, and so they have to grow crops and herd animals. In Tibet we have two main types of people: nomads and farmers, and both depend on the earth, on crops and grass. A farmer has to have rain at the right time, and when the rain comes, he can work the earth and grow his crops. But then in the autumn, hail and frost are great dangers. If hail comes, the crops are completely flattened, right down to the earth. The farmers have worked very hard, but they get nothing. The crop is destroyed. The other hazard is frost. One night, if there are no clouds, the frost can come and the crops freeze. The grain is seriously damaged – it is small and shrinking. So frost is a great danger. And the farmers need rain at the right time as there is no irrigation. So they can ask (a practitioner) to bring rain. They can do this, there are methods for bringing rain and for stopping frost and hail. They use *dö*. A *dö* represents the whole of the universe and all kinds of things are arranged there, such as images of humans. There is no need to slaughter anyone as replicas such as statues or pictures are used. This is all written there in the Second Way. Then this *dö* is offered. First of all it is offered to Sidpai Gyalmo, then to all the high mountain gods and goddesses, to everyone. That is like a preparation. It makes them happy and then once they have received this, then when you need to, you can use them. It is like a kind of *bakshish* or bribe. You offer it to them and say: 'When I ask you to stop hail or send rain, please do so.' So in this Second Way, everything is arranged to benefit people's livelihood.

The Third Way is *Trulshen Thegpa*. Not everybody always thinks about how to help beings' living conditions. Sometimes beings are cruel to one another, they are not at ease when someone else is happy and so they do strange things, cause disturbances and fight. Such beings try to disturb practitioners of *Chashen Thegpa* in particular, to disrupt their work. So to counteract and destroy these disturbers, some practitioners practise Walse[28] and other *yidams*. But some of them don't practise *bodhichitta* beforehand, they only visualize themselves as the *yidam*. That is the wrong way. They have taken some instructions but they are like Western practitioners who think that reciting a mantra is just enough to stop their enemy or those who disturb them. There are two different things: one is to do this practice thinking about your own enemy, like the American man who always wanted to destroy the man who took his wife away. These people don't think very much, they just recite mantras and so on. They can have some result – they can stop disturbers and do something, they can summon an invisible enemy or some person's

[28] Tib. dBal dsas.

spirit, they can have some power and destroy or kill them so that maybe something happens to their enemy – but the right way is to do this for the doctrines, to help beings and meditators, because sometimes other beings are against them and don't like what they do. So you should do such practices to protect (practitioners and the doctrines), because then that will be good for all poor people so you must think that the only purpose of these practices is to guard Yungdrung Bön; this Way is part of Yungdrung Bön. This is a general summary (of this Way).

Once you have done this and killed the trouble-makers, killed is killed and nothing visible remains alive. You have been hurling, cutting, chopping, but what happens to their *namshe* [consciousness]? Where does their mind go? The practitioners of *Trulshen Thegpa* stop disturbances for general beings and for Yungdrung Bön; they do this, they have power. But they don't know or care about where the *namshe* goes. If you are like a butcher, only thinking of selling and getting profit, then that is a sinful action. So you need to think. You have destroyed your enemy but has his *namshe* disappeared or not? You must think about this. You must lead the enemy's spirit after you have killed him, otherwise if you just leave it you are like a butcher. So what can you do? This comes in the next Way, *Sidshen Thegpa*.

You need to make a figurine, summon the enemy's spirit and integrate it into the figurine, and then explain to it, saying: 'You disrupted the Teachings and therefore you were destroyed and I acted wrathfully. If you do many such things, you collect bad karmic causes, so now you have met with a powerful practitioner. I am Tonpa Shenrab and I will explain this to you and help you. Don't think bad things about the practitioner who destroyed you. Instead, you should think that he is very kind and has helped you stop doing sinful things. The *mandala* is arranged here with all the deities, so you can take a rest there, listen to the Teachings and look back towards your mind.' This is *Sidshen Thegpa.*

There is also *Phowa*, when the mind is finally integrated back into Nature. Someone asked me for a *Phowa* practice not long ago, and I said to him: 'What kind of *Phowa* do you want? *Phowa* means transference in Tibet, so what do you want to transfer? And what into?' The best *Phowa* is when the mind is liberated into the Natural State. That is teal *Phowa*, *Bönku Phowa.*[29] But if you are not able to do that, then you visualize that your consciousness goes from you to your *yidam*, so your spirit and your *yidam* are inseparable. That is *Longku Phowa.*[30] Or if people don't understand this but have devotion towards their lama, they can visualize their lama and integrate with him. Yet you can't integrate two minds into one person! So when you visualize your lama, it is with

---

[29] Tib. bon sku 'pho ba.

[30] Tib. longs sku 'pho ba.

> your own imagination, and you are integrating your mind with your visualization. That can be helpful. You feel a lot of devotion for your lama, you visualize him and then integrate with that, and it can help you to remember why you know your lama, what he taught you. He taught you the Teachings and so by visualizing him, you can remember the Teachings and practise with devotion. Your lama cannot lead you, but through your devotion you can remember your lama. You visualize him, recognize him and ask him to help you, and then you integrate your spirit with him. That means that your mind is integrated with your visualization; your lama doesn't go anywhere. Usually people think that they integrate with their lama but it is impossible for two minds to become one.
>
> That is how to practise *Sidshen Thegpa*. They summon (the *namshe*) into a picture, offer it food, tell it everything is as illusion, that it should have no attachments, that it should stop all attachments, that it should remember and realize whatever it practised previously. All this is in this text.
>
> It is important to have the context. Otherwise, if you take some quotations out of context, it looks like black magic. Most people who say that Bönpos practise black magic take little pieces out of context and then say: 'The Bönpo text says such and such. Bönpos are doing magic.' But that is out of context. If you take things out of context, you may not know what you get.[31]

Here, Yongdzin Lopön Tenzin Namdak emphasizes the role these methods of Causal Bön play in inspiring people and creating auspicious circumstances in which their understanding of the higher teachings can develop. The main point of *Thegpa Chenpo*[32] (*Mahayana*) is trying to help others as much as possible and the methods of the Four Ways of Cause provide an excellent means for accomplishing this. As Lama Böngya Geleg Lhundrub Gyatso[33] who currently lives in Tibet says:

> The various methods of the Four Ways of the Cause pacify all kinds of sufferings in the dimension of illusory existence; their practice results in the happiness and benefit to sentient beings. Through this power, they also establish and develop faith and devotion in the hearts of beings. [...] There are many ways in which the great princely action of all Bodhisattvas can benefit sentient beings at different levels. [...] Putting into practice the Four Ways of the Cause is therefore not only

---

31 Spontaneous teachings given by Yongdzin Lopön Tenzin Namdak during a private interview, Shenten Dargye Ling, France, 19.08.07.

32 Tib. theg pa chen po.

33 Tib. Bon rgya dGe legs Lhun grub rGya mtsho.

> free from fault, but it is also in accordance with the commitment to the teaching (dam tshig).[34]

The methods pertaining to the Bön of Cause are useful for practitioners of all levels:

> [On the path] obstacles may arise, caused by demons, evil spirits, human and non-human beings. In that case, it is really beneficial to utilize methods pertaining to the Way of Phyva gShen, the Way of sNang gShen, the Way of 'Phrul gShen and the Way of Srid gShen, since they can satisfy the desires and requests of those beings creating obstacles, thus not allowing them to be of any harm to one's way to realisation. Even at the level of rDzogs chen these methods can be useful.[35]

Part II
Divination, Diagnostics and Healing Techniques

Divination

Before any problem – be it a health problem, misfortune or weather abnormality – can be addressed, the cause must first be established and then an appropriate remedy found. Divination and diagnostics, then, are a fundamental part of any healing and always precede whatever treatment is to be undertaken. Both Bɵ Murgel and Bön have a wide range of clairvoyance and clairaudience techniques at their disposal for this.

Divination methods in Buryatian Bɵ Murgel

Looking through a bottle of vodka

A very common but relatively recent method used in the Tunka region of northwestern Buryatia today is to look through a bottle of vodka brought by the patient. The vodka must be of the highest quality and in an

---

34 Donatella Rossi, The Nine Ways of the Bonpo Tradition: an oral presentation by a contemporary Bonpo Lama, *Tibetan Studies*, Proceedings of the 6th Seminar of the International Association for Tibetan Studies [Fagernes, 1992], vol. II, ed. Per Kvaerne, pp. 676–681.

35 Ibid.

uncoloured glass bottle. The Bɵ or Utgan first looks through the closed bottle to gain a preliminary assessment of the patient's problems, then it is fumigated and opened. The lower ring of the seal is customarily broken and taken off as a symbolic sacrifice. The Bɵ or Utgan then recites a prayer, strikes three matches and drops them into the bottle. As they are extinguished, the matches leave trials of smoke in and above the vodka. The Bɵ or Utgan holds the bottle up to a source of light such as a window, the sky, the sun, a candle or an electric bulb and are able to see visions there. They may simultaneously hear a voice(s) explaining the visions. Once the source of the problem has been established and the remedy ascertained, *serzhem* sprinkling or some other more complex ritual is done to alleviate it. This method is similar to European magicians' technique of looking into a crystal ball.

Another method of clairvoyance is simply to gaze at a strong light source such as the sun, moon, a candle, an electric bulb or fire as these can also serve as a support for visions.

Toli-mirror

A very effective and probably the most ancient divination method in Bɵ Murgel is to use a *toli*, a metal mirror identical to the Tibetan *melong.*[36] *Toli* can be of different sizes and made from different combinations of metals, although most *toli* I have seen contain fair amounts of copper detectable by its yellowish-pink hues. A *toli* is often worn at the front or back as it also fulfils the function of a shield, reflecting negative energies and any bad thoughts the Bɵ's adversaries may harbour towards him. In the far distant past *toli* used to be made of jade.

To illustrate the way in which *toli* is used for diagnosis and healing in Bɵ Murgel, here is a passage describing my encounter with Bayir, a Bɵ from the village of Zhemchug in Tunka:

> On another occasion we visited a Bɵ who practises the art of healing with a mirror. It was quite late in the evening when we arrived at his place, so he didn't have much time as he isn't allowed to heal after midnight. First he treated my wife. He took a large brass mirror the size of a small saucer and cleaned it with some paste. Then he murmured spells over it and laid it on my wife's bare chest. After some time he took the mirror off and began describing and explaining what he saw in it. Then he showed it to my wife. To her amazement, she, too, saw pictures in it, as clear as etchings. [...] Then the Bɵ explained that the

---

[36] Tib. me long.

mirror has a head which is marked by a small dot engraved in the brass and to reflect the curse one needs to turn it upside down, which he immediately did. He went on to massage some pressure points in my wife's legs, and advised her to do a blood-letting to avoid future health complications.[37] Next it was my turn. He repeated the same procedure and then showed me the mirror. I could very clearly see a picture of kidneys. He explained that my kidney problems were due to magical pressure sent by a magician in the recent past, which I knew was true. He then turned the mirror upside down and made a pushing gesture. 'It's flown back', he said.

Summer 1993, village of Zhemchug, Tunka.[38]

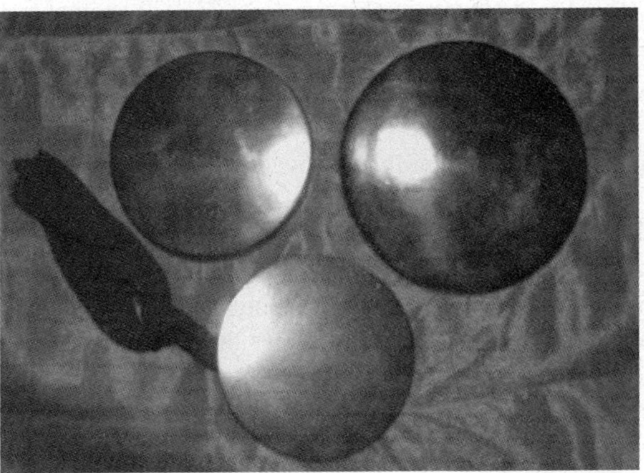

Fig. 3. Buryatian toli-*mirrors.*

Observing signs

Various unusual happenings are considered to be signs sent by Tengeri, *Haats* and *Zayaans* and are always carefully observed and interpreted. Signs such as an animal or a bird crossing one's path can have different meanings depending on the type of animal, from which side it appeared and the gender of the person whose way it crossed because the positive directions are opposite for men and women.

---

[37] Our friends were anxious to leave early the next morning and so unfortunately we were unable to carry out this procedure, and as Bɵ Bayir had foreseen, health complications did indeed arise several years later.

[38] From *The Ways of the Wind*, my unpublished diary of 1993.

Ram's shoulder blade

Divination on a ram's shoulder blade was common in the past. First an offering rite was performed with a ram's right shoulder blade which was burnt in a bonfire. At the end of the rite, the shoulder blade was taken out and examined. Predictions were ascertained from the pattern of the cracks appearing on it. This method is also used in Tibet, especially in the Amdo province still inhabited by the Mongoloid Azha (Tuyuhun) and Hor. It was also common to many other cultures of Eurasia.

Pebbles and coins

Another popular method is the range of divinations using pebbles and coins. These bear close resemblance to the *Mo*[39] divination techniques of Bön such as *Deutrul.*[40]

Tin divination

A cup is filled with milk and covered with soft sheep wool which is made into a shape resembling a bird's nest. This is held by the client. The Bɵ takes an iron ladle in which he puts some butter and 15–20g of tin which are then melted together over the fire. The Bɵ invokes the Tengeri and *Zayaans* after which he pours the molten tin into the cup covered by the nest of wool held by the client. When the tin falls to the bottom of the cup, it solidifies forming peculiar shapes which are then examined and interpreted by the Bɵ.[41]

Dreams and trance

Some powerful Bɵ simply know the cause of a problem or disease straightaway without seeming to apply any particular technique. They may have received information previously in a dream, which is often the case, or may be continually in trance communication with their deities through whom they receive information as soon as it is needed. Such Bɵ and Utgan often deliver prophecies revealing the causes behind certain events of the past, present and future whereas others act primarily as mediums for certain deities and spirits, often serving as a bridge between the living and their ancestors and gods who speak through them to give instructions on rituals or life in general, and to deliver prophecies. We will look into this more closely later in this chapter.

---

39 Tib. mo.

40 Tib. lde'u 'phrul.

41 *Khronika Vandana.*

Divination methods in Yungdrung Bön

In Yungdrung Bön, too, we find a vast array of divination methods called *Mo* which include most of the methods of prognostication used in Bɵ Murgel described above (except for the tin divination and method of looking through the vodka bottle which is truly Siberian stuff!) All the divination methods are divided into four major groups and belong to the First Way of Cause, *Chashen Thegpa*.

Mirror divination

Tra[42] or mirror divination is parallel to the Bɵ Murgel method of using *toli*. There are very many methods of *Tra* but nowadays it is rare to come across someone who really does this form of divination in a proper way because after the introduction of Indian Buddhism to Tibet in the seventh-eighth centuries AD, Yungdrung Bön was persecuted and many texts were destroyed. Moreover, many original Bönpo methods pertaining to the Way of Cause were extracted and modified by Buddhists after which the mother-texts were destroyed. Although the Buddhist versions retained the general working principles, the gods initially associated with these methods were substituted by other gods more concordant with the Buddhist pantheon. In the case of *Tra* it is the ancient *Drala* sky-gods who were originally propitiated by Bönpo diviners but Buddhists invoke some mountain gods or Gesar instead.

We have already established in previous chapters that some *Drala* and Tengeri sky-dwelling gods of Bön and Bɵ Murgel are parallel, so it is not surprising that the mirror divinations of these two traditions are connected with their respective sky-gods.

Juthig[43]

Juthig divination uses six cords and is an extremely complex form of divination, far more complex in the preparation of the materials, performing and interpreting the outcome than even the *I-Ching*. Below is an edited transcript of the demonstration and oral instructions on *Juthig* kindly given by Yondgzin Lopön Tenzin Namdak for this publication:[44]

> When the cords are tossed they form different knots which are interpreted with the help of a manual. The tossing can result in practically

---

42 Tib. pra.

43 Tib. ju thig.

44 Shenten Dargye Ling, France, 13/20.08.07.

Fig. 4. Model Juthig *cords tied into the 'crane knot' by Yongdzin Lopön Tenzin Namdak.*

innumerable combinations. There are 360 major types of knots which form 10,000 combinations. Depending on whether the cords twist to the right or left, upwards or downwards, the pattern of the ornaments on the small cords and other considerations, the combinations are innumerable. All the names for the knots and combinations are in the language of Zhang Zhung and have no meaning in Tibetan. The root text on *Juthig* is in *Kanjur* and in the Bönpo *Katen* alone there are 266 pages of explanations on this practice, contained in the *Zhang Zhung Juthig*[45] text written by master Kyangtrul.[46]

Preparing the cords is also extremely complicated and requires many ingredients such as white wool from a sheep and a yak. To make the cords two girls should spin the wool upwards in the morning and downwards in the afternoon. Five cords are one cubit long and are called *juthig* which simply means 'cord' in the language of Zhang Zhung. The sixth cord is called *mota*[47] – 'divination horse'. It is the length of the span between two hands when the arms are stretched out behind the back. Many tassels of yak hair hang from the ends of the cords and claws of the hawk, leopard, Tibetan bear and so on are attached to the end of the *mota* which is put on the altar. If the cords are not used very often, they are bound in a special way known as 'crane'. The short *juthig* are doubled over and the *mota* is first wrapped around the loop at the top, then down and up one leg, then down and up the other leg, then finally tucked in at the 'head' loop.

Preparation

Before divination can begin, an altar with an image of Phuwer, a *dadar*, *melong*, lamp, heaps of grains, *tsampa* mixed with butter, *serchem*, a bowl of milk and so on should be set up. A white felt mat is placed in front of the practitioner, and anything else needed for the rite is kept beside the diviner.

First the *Modar*[48] text is recited for purification and sending away disturbances. The meaning is roughly as follows: 'I am going to do

45 Tib. Zhang zhung ju thig.

46 Tib. sKyang sprul.

47 Tib. mo rta.

48 Tib. mo brdar.

Fig. 5. Yongdzin Lopön Tenzin Namdak demonstrates Juthig *technique, Shenten Dargye Ling, September, 2007.*

Juthig, please send away any disturbances.' Incense, *serchem* etc. are offered while reading and also all bad smells/poisons are sent away by a *Dugchyug* rite.[49] The person requesting the divination is seated on the diviner's left.

Throwing the Cords

The long *mota* cord is wrapped over diviner's shoulder from left to right.

The others are held by the index finger, thumb and little finger, looped over the middle fingers. The thumb is called *Khyung*, the index finger is the Tortoise and the little finger is the Cow. These animals represent the divinities which explain the divination and show what will come.

Holding all the *juthig* and the *mota* like this in the left hand, waft them over incense to purify them while reciting a mantra.

Then put the question.

Then with the index finger and thumb of the right hand (which represent a beak of a small bird), take two of the threads and tie a loop knot in them. Flick these knotted cords over, away from you, and take two more. When all the cords have been tied, hold the left end of the *mota* and the single remaining cord and toss them on the white felt mat in front of you.

Examining the signs

The cords are examined and the pattern of knots noted. In early times, each configuration was represented by a pebble or stick (of various shapes and colours), so the complete set of symbols was vast and diverse. Nowadays the names of the configurations are used, as each

---

49 See ch. X, *Sang and Aryuud haha fumigation rituals*.

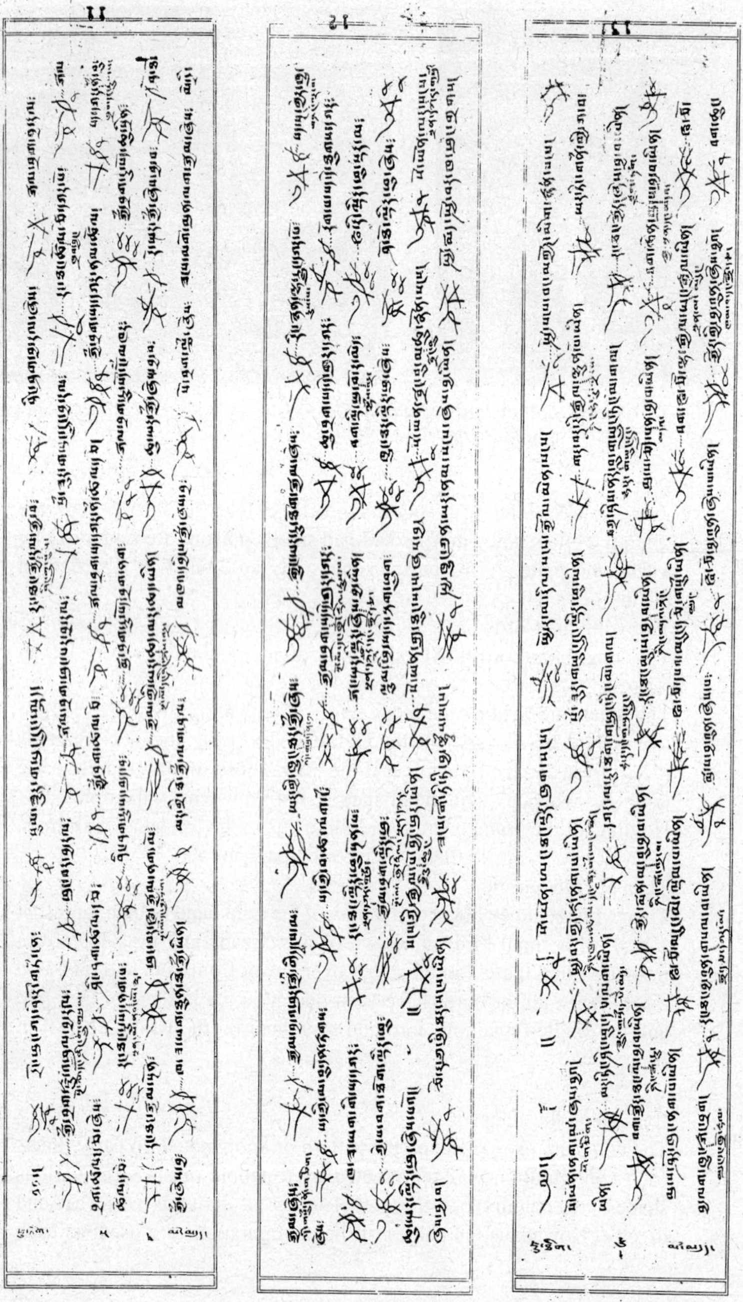

Fig. 6. Pages of Zhang Zhung Juthig *manual with the drawings of the knots.*

pattern has its own name – all in the language of Zhang Zhung. These are noted down as the procedure is repeated 13 times in all.

The range of configurations is virtually limitless, and the various patterns are grouped together, so an experienced *Juthig*-diviner can recognize the configuration family and then quickly ascertain the specific pattern.

The configurations are noted in a crossed table, with each of the thirteen throws addressing a particular aspect of the matter being put to divination.

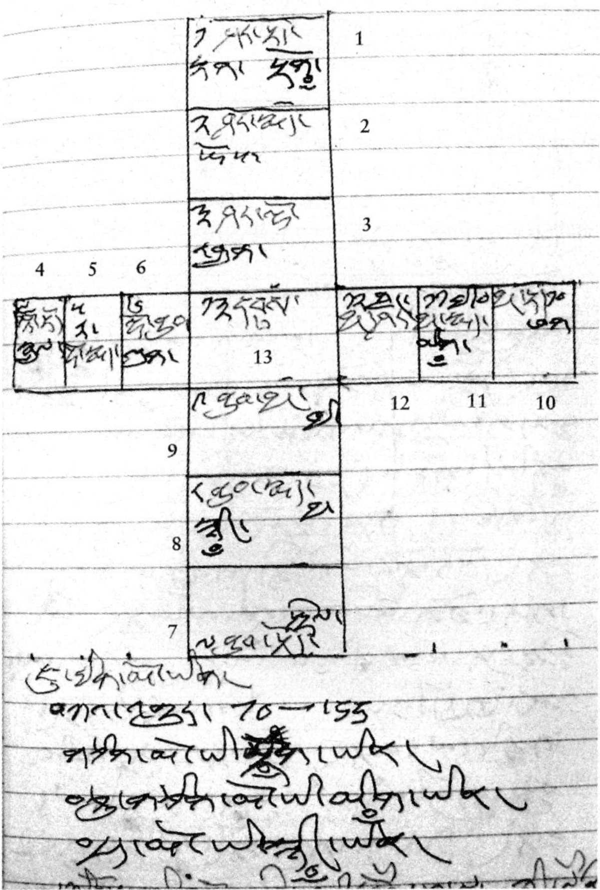

Fig. 7. Juthig *table drawn by Yongdzin Lopön Tenzin Namdak, Shenten Dargye Ling, September, 2007.*

Slot	Direction	*Lo* animal
1	Upper East	Tiger
2	Lower East	Hare
3	South East	Dragon
4	Upper South	Snake
5	Lower South	Horse
6	South West	Sheep
7	Upper West	Monkey
8	Lower West	Garuda
9	North West	Dog
10	Upper North	Pig
11	Lower North	Rat
12	North East	Elephant
13	Centre	-

Many different aspects are examined related to the *parkha*, *mewa*, and Twelve Animal signs to provide a very detailed reply to the central matter of the inquiry. Each different throw can be interpreted to shed light on the central issue from different angles:

Whether things look good or bad for the future	13
Whether the matter central to the divination will be good or bad	4, 6, 2
If you are sick, whether you will be cured or not	8
If you engage your enemies, whether you will win or lose	12
If you go to court, whether you will win or lose	5, 7
If you are engaged in battle, how strong your enemy is	4
Whether family conditions will be good or not	6
Whether activities involving your work/property will be successful	4
Regarding children	3
What the causes and conditions of sickness are	9
If something is lost, whether it will be found or not	2
Whether you will be disturbed by enemies or not	5
Whether a place is suitable for burying your ancestors or not[i]	2
To check past and future conditions	1, 2
General (prediction) about the past or present	1, 2
Prediction for the long-term future	12, 13

[i] *This was very important in early times in Zhang Zhung and Tibet, so it was essential to check. If ancestors were buried in an unsuitable place, it would be a cause for misfortunes for generations and generations to come. This was extremely important. It is a kind of geomancy called* Sabchyel *(Tib. sa dbyal), or what the Chinese would call* Fengshui.

The Juthig-Diviner

Nowadays *Juthig*-diviners are most common in Amdo, where they are known as *Amye.* Every year in the first month of Tibetan calendar they visit each household to make a prediction for the coming year. A special transmission is required to become *Amye*, and this is usually handed down from generation to generation within families. The *Amye* also has many other roles, such as giving a new name to a bride and performing a special initiation for new-born babies. This involves purifying the baby with water, giving him or her a name, putting butter on the head (*Sungjyug*[50]) and invoking the Five Deities of the Body.[51]

This form of divination has no counterpart in Bɵ Murgel. However, the pre-Columbian Inkas of South America used a 'writing' system based on tying knots in ropes. We also know that a similar writing system existed in prehistoric China:

> Let the people tie knots in ropes
> and use them instead of script.[52]

Lao Tzu, who lived at the turn of the seventh century BC,[53] gives this advice in the context of returning to the simplicity of ancient times and no doubt refers to the epoch before 7000 BC when the Jiahu Script[54] and the later hieroglyphic script had not yet been invented and the accumulation of 'knowledge'[55] this facilitated had not yet begun. The existence of analogous writing systems among the Inkas, prehistoric Chinese and *Juthig* divination in Zhang Zhung demonstrates that this sort of 'writing' was already in use among the Asian people at the times of the migration to the Americas over the Bering land bridge anywhere between 70,000 and 11,000 years ago,[56] dates which fit the traditional dates for Shenrab Miwo who is said to have been born in 16,017 BC. The reason why this

---

50 Tib. srung byug.

51 I.e. the Five Personal Deities (Tib. 'go ba'i lha lnga).

52 Lao Tzu, *Tao Te Ching*, *The Richard Wilhelm Edition*, (London: Penguin Arkana, 1989). p. 64, Te; 80.

53 Ibid., p. 1.

54 Paul Rincon, Earliest writing found in China, *BBC Science,* 17 April, 2003, <http://news.bbc.co.uk/2/hi/science/nature/2956925.stm> accessed 09.06.07.

55 In this context 'knowledge' is the opposite of wisdom and refers to the creation and passing on of artificial customs, cultural limitations and idea of 'progress' which Lao Tzu considered a great evil damaging man's connection to his original nature.

56 See ch. I.

system is found in South America and not in the North is because it came with the earlier wave of migrants who continued southwards until they arrived in Peru. It is reasonable to suggest, then, that the origins of Bönpo *Juthig* divination lie in remote antiquity before or in the time of the early migrations over the Bering land bridge and that it has very probably developed out of the 'rope writing' similar to that of the Inkas of Peru.

Dream divination

This is known as *milam*[57] or divination through observing dreams. Before going to sleep a practitioner performs specific visualization and recites *mantra* in order to have a dream which clearly shows a reply to a particular question.

This method can be generally compared with the methods used by the Bɵ. However, Bɵ do not use *mantras* as such but invoke the Tengeri or *Zayaans*.

Oracle[58]

In early times Bönpos practising of this type of divination would call *Drala* to possess them. Once the *Drala* entered the oracle, s/he was fully under the influence of that deity who used the medium as a mouthpiece to deliver prophecies. After the séance, the medium had no memory of what they were doing or saying while in trance. During the eighth and ninth centuries AD the use of this method declined among Bönpos and this ritual was taken over by Buddhists. However, as with *Tra*, Buddhists did not invoke the *Drala* but instead called their own protective deities.

'Talking doll'

Among the many Bönpo divination methods there is one which has a peculiar parallel in Bɵ Murgel. Below is a description of this Bönpo method given by Yongdzin Lopön Tenzin Namdak:

> This method is used particularly in medicine. All doctors are supposed to use it. They can check the pulse and the urine but there could still be very many doubts, so here another practice is included besides the four subdivisions of Divination. For this, you take a small piece of birch wood and make a kind of little doll, practise and recite mantras while doing visualization. You make nice clothes for the doll and keep

[57] Tib. rmi lam.

[58] Tib. lha bka'.

> it warm, keeping it just under your collar on your right so it can talk in your ear. You also keep some herbs by it and when you are ready, it can speak. Other people can't hear [it] but you can, and in the best case, you hear it speaking directly into your ear, telling you how to cure the patient and what to do. In the second best case you just suddenly remember what to do, and in the third case some symbols come [which prompt you to remember what to do]. In early times this was especially important for practitioners of medicine as they could clearly see the patients' problems and so they could then know very clearly what they should use to help. It is very necessary to practise all these. Now this is very rare, even Bönpo doctors find it difficult to access this text because there was one lama who used it a lot but the little doll talked too much and said too many things so he had to burn it.[59]

Here is a somewhat similar method found in Bө Murgel:[60]

> The [Buryatian] diviners have 'chatterbox spirits'. They run everywhere and gather all sorts of information for the diviners. They are always female and are frightened by loud voices. Day and night they whisper all sorts of gossip into the diviner's ear and sow discord with his neighbours. They see the past and present very well but are unreliable for seeing the future. They are called *Hobushi-ongon.*[61]

Diagnosis

Diagnosis in Bө Murgel

No matter what kind of prognostication a Bө is using, the aim is always to establish the cause of a problem or to foresee events. In general diagnosis is quite complex as Bө and Utgan look into different aspects of the patient's life including environment, relationships with family, neighbours and friends, work, habits, and diet. Special attention is given to the patient's family dynamics so the father's and mother's lineages are examined through clairvoyance and conversation. Disease or misfortune is often due to a curse put on the family in the past or may be a 'self-curse' arising from the negative actions of one's ancestors. Sometimes the ancestors themselves can directly cause the problem if they died a violent death or are not propitiated in the proper manner. All sorts of incidents in the patient's life are also examined, such as felling trees,

---

[59] Conversation with Yongdzin Lopön Tenzin Namdak, Shenten Dargye Ling, France, 06.05.06.

[60] Hangalov, *Sobranie* II, pp. 124–128.

[61] Bur. Хобуши-онгон.

polluting waters or causing other types of environmental damage because such actions bring retribution from the spirits who reside in and protect the environment. This retribution can come in the form of diseases, accidents, bad luck, one's soul being stolen and so on. The cause of a problem or illness often lies in the patient's energy being 'polluted' as a result of contact with impure substances such as: clothes or objects belonging to the sick or deceased; objects charged with negative energy; evil people; or *elbe*, the evil eye.

Once the Bɵ or Utgan has clearly established the cause of the problem by whatever means, they apply the appropriate method to relieve the patient.

Medical diagnosis in Yungdrung Bön

Yungdrung Bön has an extremely well-defined and effective core of medical doctrines contained in the *Chashen Thegpa*. An important part of this is diagnosis, and the skilled doctor has several methods, all of which should be applied in order to determine the cause(s) of disease and the appropriate treatment. As in Bɵ Murgel, the doctor spends time talking with the patient about their lifestyle, diet, family relationships, and also examines the patient's dreams.

Pulse diagnosis

This is a very special technique. The doctor places his or her fingers on the patient's wrist and 'listens' to the pulse. Different internal organs and 'humours' can be distinguished by varying the pressure and position of the fingers. This is such a precise method that an accomplished doctor can even diagnose a close family member of the patient. Some also use it as a means of divination to descry the future or the past. The *Bum Zhi* lists twelve sub-categories on pulse diagnostics:

1. Preliminary Questioning.
2. Instructions on Pre-examination Conduct and Diet.
3. Techniques of Pulse Diagnostics: including timing, the exact point, manner and pressure to be applied.
4. Checking the Natural Pulse.
5. Checking the Pulse according to the Four Seasons and Five Elements.
6. Checking the Seven Wonderful Pulses.
7. The Frequency of Pulsation.
8. Identifying the Disease through General and Specific Pulse observed during Diagnosis.

9. The System of Comprehensive Pulse Diagnosis using Three Fingers.
10. The Pulse of Death.
11. The Pulse showing the Provocation of Negative Energy.
12. The Pulse of the Soul (bla rtsa).[62]

Urine

A fresh sample of the patient's urine is examined for colour, smell, vapour, transparency and consistency. The doctor also stirs it and, by placing four sticks over the glass to form the nine places of *mewa*, can ascertain whether the patient is currently under attack from a malevolent spirit, and if so, of which kind.

Feeling (*kham*)[63]

This includes checking the patient's complexion, eyes, tongue, his or her manner and thinking as well asking how the problem started.[64]

Healing

In both Bө Murgel and Bön healing should be understood in the widest sense of the word, as both these traditions seek to treat the root cause of a problem as well as alleviate the symptoms. Consequently, the healer makes recourse to a great variety of techniques ranging from rituals to medicines.

Healing methods used by the Bө and Utgan

There are many different ways of healing in Bө Murgel. All Bө and Utgan use methods handed down to them through the lineages and adapted to their own practical experience. They also have their own unique methods which were taught to them personally by the Tengeri, protective deities and spirits of their line and which are, naturally, kept secret. We cannot go into all these here but shall briefly outline the basic principles behind most methods and describe the most popular ones.

---

62 Himalayan Amchi Association, *Curriculum Guide*.

63 Tib. khams.

64 Based on teachings of Namdak, *Nine Ways* I, p. 39 and my own experience as a patient of Tibetan doctors in London and Kathmandu.

Fig. 8. Utgan Vera Naguslaeva sprinkles to Tengeri, Zayaans *and* Ezhens *at the conclusion of the* tailgan *near Borokhan in Barguzin, 1994.*

- One of the most frequently used techniques is *duhaalga* (*hayalga*,[65] *serzhim*) sprinkling, offering alcohol and various other substances to the gods and spirits, who are asked for guidance in healing or to directly cure the patient. Sprinkling almost always precedes any other healing method applied.
- If the problem is localized in one particular part of the body, a common method is spitting.[66] The Bɵ or Utgan sprinkles the first part of a bottle of vodka to the gods and invokes curative qualities into it. They then take a large sip from the bottle and spit it out on the affected place. This method is very effective but, of course, it depends on the Bɵ's power.
- 'Mud pancakes' are sometimes used to cure tumours. The 'pancakes' are empowered with a spell and placed on the affected area. They are then left for some time. When they are taken off they are buried. The procedure is repeated as many times as needed.
- Some old Bɵ use their feet to cure the patient. After going into trance they hold their feet on red-hot metal or glowing embers for a while. Then they step out and put their feet on the affected part of the patient's body.

---

65 Bur. хаялга.

66 See ch. X.

- Others lick red-hot metal before a healing session to purify and charge themselves with the healing power of fire. This method is primarily used by Bɵ-smiths. An identical method is found in Bön[67] where it is known as Tartsen Lenpa.[68] It is a very archaic practice whereby a Bönpo holds or licks red-hot metal or stone to demonstrate his power.
- Another healing method of Bɵ Murgel is to use the organs of a freshly slaughtered animal. For example, if one has a kidney or liver problem then a sheep is ritually slaughtered and the animal's still warm kidneys or liver are put over the corresponding organ of the patient.
- Often various animal substances are used to treat the disturbances of a particular organ. For example, in the case of spleen diseases one is advised to eat boiled sheep blood. Bear's bile is considered a very powerful remedy against many diseases.
- Various herbs and herbal compounds are also used. Although Bɵ Murgel herbal remedies aren't as complex as Tibetan herbal compounds, they are effective nonetheless. Knowledge of local plants and their uses which had been gathered and preserved by the Bɵ and Utgan for countless generations was later absorbed into the Tibetan medical knowledge brought to Buryatia by Buddhists. The result is a powerful tradition of medicine based on the Tibetan model but with a distinct local flavour.[69]

---

[67] See ch. VII.

[68] Tib. gtar tshan len pa.

[69] This 'Buryatian' Tibetan medicine was brought to St. Petersburg by brothers Alexandr (Sultim) and Pyotr (Zhamsaran) Badmaev who led their lineage from Dobu Mergen (Bur. Добу Мэргэн) and so were, in fact, an off-shoot of the genealogical tree to which Chingis Khaan himself belonged. Alexandr Badmaev opened a herbal pharmacy and clinic in St. Petersburg in the 1860's. After his death in 1873, Pyotr Badmaev took over the practice and went on to become a personal physician of the Tsar. He was the first to translate *Gyud Zhi*, the Tibetan Buddhist medical tractate based on the earlier Bönpo *Bum Zhi* into Russian. Pyotr Badmaev was arrested, incarcerated and interrogated several times after the Socialist Revolution of 1917 but in his absence the clinic was run by his wife Elizaveta Badmaeva. Despite his death in 1920, the clinic continued to operate thanks to the efforts of his wife. It was closed in 1937 due to Stalinist repressions. However, some of the Badmaevs' medicinal knowledge and recipes were taken abroad by Pyotr's nephew and was kept alive in Poland. In the 1960s one of the descendants of the Badmaevs handed over the medical formulas to the Swiss pharmacist Carl Lutz who was keen to explore Tibetan medicine. Lutz ran rigorous testing on the medicines and

– In Buryatia there are many places with healing springs or *arshan* where the sick go in summer. Each spring is associated with a deity or a spirit and so they represent sacred sites. The Bө are asked to perform a ritual, some offerings such as *zalaa* ribbons are tied on the trees or placed nearby and then the patient begins the course of water therapy. Many springs are renowned for specific curative properties, e.g. for a particular organ or ailment:

> The mountain rose steeply. Soon we came to a sheer cliff with tall deciduous trees. The spot differed sharply from the surrounding pine forest. There were four healing springs there; for the heart, the stomach, the skin and the eyes. Bө Doogar Ochirov explained how one should drink from them. The water from each spring had its own special smell and taste. You shouldn't drink much from the heart *arshan*, but you can from the stomach *arshan*. The water from the skin *arshan* isn't usually so much drunk as rubbed on the skin for eczema and other skin disorders. Bayan Dalai said that he himself had cured severe outbreaks of eczema on his legs several times with that water. When you drink water from an *arshan*, you should concentrate on the sick organ; the energy contained in the water goes straight there. For example, if you drink from the heart *arshan*, you experience a wave of cold tingling energy going straight to your heart, and you don't feel it going into your stomach. The water seems to dissolve in your heart. The eye *arshan* has two outlets, one for the right and one for the left eye. You wash your eyes in the water, then drink it. As we sat by the skin *arshan*, noises came from downstream, as if some animal were there. Bayan Dalai said that sick animals often come to that spring to cure themselves and that it was probably a *kabarga*, a small Buryatian deer. Later, we found out who it really was. [...]
>
> Soon the forest resounded with the cries of the *soyka* bird. That bird is the friend of the wild beasts, the enemy of the hunter. If she notices a hunter in the forest, she starts to shout and fly after him until he leaves the woods. The *soyka* bird shouted a few more times, and suddenly,

---

in 1969 he founded Padma Inc. in Zurich which started to manufacture them in the form of tablets using modern production methods. In 1970 the Swiss Agency for therapeutic products licensed Padma Lax and in 1977, Padma 28 was licensed. So the power of the unique Tibeto-Buryatian medical system, albeit in new shape and form, continues to bring benefit in the West. (*Петр Александрович Бадмаев,* автор внук П.А. Бадмаева - писатель Борис Сергеевич Гусев, <http://ricolor.org/history/eng/medicina/badmaev/>; *PADMA Inc. History*, <http://www.padma.ch/en/company/history.shtml>; *ПАДМА 28*, <http://www.padma28.ru/de/produkte/padma28.php> accessed 21.11.07).

about twenty metres in front of us, a bear crossed the path. He came from the direction of the springs, so it was probably he who we had heard.

In the *taiga* near Borokhan, 17.07.94[70]

- Sometimes patients are told by the Bɵ or Utgan to go to the Buddhist *Datsan* or Russian Orthodox Church to make offerings there.
- Another widespread healing method is to send energy from the hands to the ailing organs and in general balance the patient's energy system in a way similar to the technique of non-contact massage practised by healers of many diverse traditions around the globe. Some types of evil eye are also removed in this way. The effectiveness of this method depends on the strength of the Bɵ or Utgan's personal energy and their protective deities.
- The water purification rites dealt with in Chapter XI constitute another very important healing technique. They effect cure through cleansing the impurities which pollute and poison a person's energy.
- In the case of an epidemic, elaborate offerings are proffered to the *Ezhen*-Owners of the disease. In fact, the offering rituals to the *Ezhen* of diseases are often performed regularly on certain dates established by local tradition and serve as a kind of preventative medicine; if the Lords of diseases are paid in advance, so to speak, they will not unleash an epidemic. In cases where the 'prophylactic' offerings and offering rituals done at the onset of an epidemic have failed to pacify the spread of the disease, a very powerful Bɵ or Utgan can try to subdue the *Ezhen* in question through magical powers or trickery. In such situations the technique will be improvised, tailored to deal with the particular evil *Ezhen* as illustrated by the story about Bɵ Bohon in the previous chapter. This kind of encounter may take the form of a prolonged magical battle. If the Bɵ succeeds, the epidemic will abate and people and animals start recovering. The earth and water from the locale where a Bɵ subdued a disease-holding *Ezhen* becomes imbued with healing properties which help to cure this kind of disease, so if the same kind of disease has struck in another area, someone is sent to bring water or stones from the sacred ground or river. These are put on the ill person's

70 A passage from my unpublished diary *Tailgan Trip*.

body who is healed due to the power of the pact between the Bɵ and *Ezhen*.[71] However, if the Bɵ fails, he, too, will fall sick and perish unless another more powerful Bɵ is called who succeeds in subduing the evil *Ezhen*.

No matter which method is used, at the end of the healing session patients are customarily told how to change their life in order to effect or sustain the cure, what to do and what not to do, how to change their attitude and habits. This is very important because without the patient's active participation, the cure may not last;[72] faith and meticulously following instructions given by the Bɵ or Utgan are necessary requirements for the success of any healing method.

Healing techniques in Yungdrung Bön

Yungdrung Bön has several volumes of medical treaties detailing precise methods for every eventuality. Bönpo *amchi*[73] doctors must study for many years alongside a qualified physician before being ready to practise themselves, but perhaps the most important factor is their motivation. As Yongdzin Lopön Tenzin Namdak says:

> First of all the practitioner or medicine man must think of all sentient beings and want to help release their sufferings and miseries. That means *Bodhichitta*, but this isn't usual *Bodhichitta*. […] The medicine man must only think about the patient in front of him, about how to release their suffering, how to cure them. […] They mustn't think about the fees or fame [they may obtain as a doctor]. Think of sentient beings with Compassion; you must have unlimited, Immeasurable Compassion.
>
> A practitioner of medicine must also take and practise Refuge in the Three Jewels and the Medicine Buddha Bendurya Wö Gyalpo[74] and his Eight Disciples and make Mandala Offerings to them. We have the Mandala of Medicine and the cycle of Tangka and these two are all the Deities of the Medicine Buddha Cycle. The ritual is explained here and so everything is complete – the Mandala, the Cycle and the Ritual. These three are very important for a medicine practitioner to have. [...] From the beginning, this practitioner must learn properly – it is very

---

[71] Hangalov, *Sobranie* I, p. 455.

[72] That is, of course, excluding cases of exorcism where patients often don't want to be treated.

[73] Tib. em chi.

[74] Tib. Be du rgya 'Od rGyal po.

> serious as otherwise you can kill beings! So it is very, very important to learn and then practise. It takes a long time and you must have prefect experience and motivation, and then you can practise Medicine.[75]

While resting on the view that ultimately all suffering, including sickness, arises from ignorance and the Three Poisons that develop from it, the medical system of Yungdrung Bön – like that of Tibetan Buddhism which is based on it – recognizes four or five physical causes of sicknesses:

- Fever;
- Cold;
- Phlegm (*peken*);[76]
- Bile (*tripa*);[77]
- A mix of these.

The medicine man's task is to rebalance these elements (or humours as they are often called), and he has several methods at his disposal. These are largely grouped into four categories:

- Medicine;
- Food and clothes;
- Activities and exercise;
- Advice and lifestyle.

It is clear that, like his Bɵ counterpart, the Bönpo doctor treats the patient as a whole and seeks to cure the root of the illness not merely alleviate the symptoms.

If herbal medicine is to be applied, the herbs must first be carefully gathered and prepared. Lopön Tenzin Namdak Rinpoche describes this very succinctly:

> There are several methods for making medicine. One is to collect herbs according to the text. Or another is to make powder, pills and extracts, liquids for drinking or lotions for massage, and we also extract essences and mix them with butter. You prepare all these and then when you need to, you can use them very carefully and without making any mistakes.[78]

---

75 Namdak, *Nine Ways, Bön of Cause*, p. 38.

76 Tib. bad kan.

77 Tib. mkhris pa.

78 Namdak, *Nine Ways, Bön of Cause*, p. 41.

There are further interventions a doctor can make such as blood-letting or moxibustion. There is also a highly-developed system called *ngag*,[79] the recitation of healing *mantras*, which contains specific *mantras* to cure many specific ailments. In cases when the disease is caused by the provocations of negative energy, *To* rituals must be used before the treatment, otherwise medicine may not work:

> [...] there are 360 different provocations created by disturbers, and there are 360 corresponding *To* rituals which can help to stop these temporarily and purify them.[80]

In cases of mental disturbance caused by provocations from demons, the patient may also be beaten with a consecrated bag full of *mantras* as a kind of exorcism.

Part III
Buryatian Bɵ and Tibetan Medium-Healers and Oracles

Buryatian mediums

As we have already pointed out, trance is not used by all Buryatian Bɵ; some always use it, some only sometimes while others never use it, depending on the lineage, tradition and techniques of each individual Bɵ and Utgan. We should also draw a clear distinction between two fundamentally different types of trance: the 'flight of the soul' where a Bɵ is in complete control, and mediumistic trance or possession where the situation is reversed and the Bɵ is completely controlled by the gods or spirits who possess him or her. Although these two may look similar from outside, they are in fact as far removed from each other as day and night. Techniques of the flight of the soul were dealt with in Chapter X so here we shall concentrate on mediumistic trance. Over the years I have observed this kind of trance on various occasions during my work

---

[79] Tib. sngags.

[80] Excerpt from the translation and commentary by Yongdzin Lopön Tenzin Namdak on the Bönpo Dzogchen cycle of *gSas mkhar g.yung drung ye khyabs lta ba'i rgyud ces bya ba bzhugs so*, Chapter VII. Triten Norbutse Monastery, Kathmandu, 27.01.08.

and encounters with Buryatian Bө, but this excerpt from my diary is probably the most complete example of it. It also clearly shows the first stage of a Bө-apprentice's initiation. Despite the fact that the candidate was not accepted by the Tengeri and *Ongon*, all the details are present so it is very useful for the purpose of our study here. I was intending to do a week-long closed retreat at Utgan Vera Naguslaeva's log cabin in the Kabanskiy[81] region on the shore of Lake Baikal:

> Friday, 05.09.2003
> I went to Istomino[82] where Vera Naguslaeva's allotment and log cabin are located. I travelled with three Buryatian lads, one of whom is Vera's nephew [...] Initially, Vera had wanted to come with us to introduce me to the local *Ezhen*-Owners but she was tired and in the end decided not to come.
> Our journey was smooth. On the road we stopped many times to sprinkle to the *Ezhen*-Owners, especially to the spirits of Hongor Zula[83] and his friend Don Cossack Ivan Timofeyevich,[84] both of whom control the pass beyond Ulaan-Ude on the road to Irkutsk [...]
> [...] When we came to the place I sprinkled near the *Burkhan* of the Owner Tolyuun Zhargal[85] located right on Vera's land. My offerings went not so well – I felt resistance, that the place wasn't favourably disposed towards me right now. I was very tired so decided to do *Tsokchö* and then go straight to bed. I was so tired that I even neglected to sprinkle to Gal Zayaashi, Owner of Fire, and Gol Zayaashi, Owner of the Hearth using the new electric stove I had brought with me from Ulaan-Ude. As a result the stove caught fire and burnt the next morning. This created a serious obstacle for my retreat and made everything very inconvenient as I had to use the woodstove to boil meat and sneak out to the shop, which was not my original plan.[...]
> I also made offerings to the local *Ezhen*-Owners Tolyuun Zhargal, Posol Noyon[86] and Solhatan.[87] Posol Noyon is the spirit of a murdered Russian ambassador and Solhatan is his wife. They are Lord-Owners of the town of Posolskoe[88] to the west of Istomino. I didn't 'see' them,

---

81 Rus. Кабанский район.

82 Rus. Истомино.

83 Bur. Хонгор Зула.

84 Rus. Донской казак Иван Тимофеевич.

85 Bur. Толюун Жаргал.

86 Bur. Посоол ноён from Rus. посол (posol) – ambassador. This is the spirit of Russian ambassador Yerofei Zabolotskiy (Rus. Ерофей Заболоцкий) who was murdered by the Mongols in this area and became an *Ezhen.*

87 Bur. Солхатан, wife of Posol Noyon.

88 Rus. Посольское.

just felt their presence, but Tolyuun Zhargal appeared several times as an old Buryatian man or a strange animal with the head of an old man. [...]
I had quite a few obstacles on that retreat and had to resort to divination to understand how to adjust to the circumstances. I had planned to do one particular practice which required certainty that I wouldn't be disturbed. Divination, however, indicated I would have three unexpected guests; it was clear that I wouldn't manage to do a strict retreat and somehow this knowledge brought relaxation.

10.09.2003, full moon: Arrival of the Utgan and Lama-Bө
On Wednesday morning I got up and started doing my morning practice, expecting someone to show up. I thought maybe the fishermen would turn up again and ask me to do *serzhem* or that Vera would arrive. But the morning passed and nobody came. I did Guru Yoga and had lunch. I started thinking that maybe nobody would show up and that my divination might be somewhat metaphorical, that it just meant it wasn't the right time for me to do the practice I had wanted to. I went out and lay on the bench. It was a warm day, blue sky and few mosquitoes. I was gazing at Lake Baikal, just relaxing and feeling happy. Then suddenly there were cars revving on the track leading to the gates. Moments later three cars drove in – so that's what the divination meant! It was Vera with a group of unfamiliar people. All were Buryats except for one tall Russian guy. As it turned out Vera had brought three Utgan , two female apprentices, a Lama-Bө, a Tatar guy from Moscow called Stas and another Buryatian guy. They had come to do a Bө initiation rite for Stas. The house was suddenly open and my retreat came to an abrupt end.
At first there was a bit of awkwardness in the air but soon everyone relaxed. The head of the group was Utgan Galina Dabaeva from Muhor Shibir'.[89] She was accompanied by her students, two Utgan and two female apprentices, as well as by a medium Lama-Bө called Zundy. They were all from Hezhenge in eastern Buryatia. Without wasting any time they quickly cut five big birch branches in the woods nearby and brought them to the house. The branches were stuck into the ground outside right next to the veranda window. A red thread was attached to these *Serge*-birches, slotted through the slit between the glass and the window frame, wrapped in a circle and left resting on the *shere'e*-altar. The improvised altar was quickly filled with offering bowls of biscuits, sweets and *arkhi*-vodka along with ritual objects such as *damaru*, *phurba*, a small prayer wheel, *vajra* and *drilbu*-bell as well as *arsa*-incense.[90]

89 Bur. Мухор Шибирь.

90 As was noted in the preceding chapters, in eastern Buryatia Bө Murgel is mixed with Buddhism.

The ritual consisted of the invocation of Nine Tengeri with their consorts and Thirteen Northern *Haats* according to the tradition of the Hori-Buryats. Utgan Galina Dabaeva and two of her helpers put on blue ritual gowns. Galina took her *hese*-drum, *toibor*-beater and *dogour*-mouth harp. She put on four *toli*-mirrors of different sizes and an *orgoi*-headdress with five tails made of coloured silk with *hol'bogo*-bells attached. She started to beat the drum and sing, invoking the Tengeri and Thirteen *Haats* while her helpers were intermittently slipping out to sprinkle offerings. Two other helpers were preparing *chai*, *pel'meni*[91] and slicing salami.

After Galina finished her invocations her place near the altar was taken by the two helpers in ritual dress. They didn't have *orgoi* and *hese* but were wearing large black prayer beads over their left shoulders. They recited a ritual text, most likely a short Buddhist sutra. Then the Tatar guy Stas was seated near the altar and the end of the red thread coming from the *serge*-birches was tied on the ring finger of his left hand. He was told to relax and let the *Ongon*-spirits enter into himself.

Simultaneously Lama-Bө Zundy fell into a deep trance. A mattress was immediately fetched from the adjoining room, put in front of the altar and the medium was sat on it. It was folded thrice to make a soft surface so that Zundy didn't hurt himself while falling or rolling around. He was fully in the trance. *Ongons* started entering him and talking through him. Each time a new *Ongon* entered or exited Zundy's body he made the medium burp and shake; his voice, facial expression and behaviour changed dramatically. Sometimes *Ongons* made him hobble around the veranda leaning heavily on a female apprentice and the wooden horse-headed *moriin hor'bo* walking stick decorated with metal *hol'bogo*. Each new spirit demanded offerings as soon as s/he arrived and so the medium was given a bowl of milk, *chai* and, sometimes, a lighted cigarette when the spirit wanted to smoke. I was sitting aside and observing. Sometimes Zundy was making gestures as if pulling some invisible strings towards himself or making hand movements similar to *mudras*. At times his body would shake with convulsions when an especially powerful or tough spirit arrived. Questions were put to the medium by those present, mainly by Utgan Galina Dabaeva, and answers were written down by her and one of her helpers.

Meanwhile the Tatar, Stas, wasn't succeeding in entering into trance at all. I 'saw' that the Tengeri and *Haats* didn't want to come for him. A blue, semi-wrathful Tengeri riding a deer appeared and was circling the air around the house but wasn't intending to help the poor guy. I felt that the *Haats* and *Ongons* wouldn't accept Stas and, frankly speaking, his motivation for taking the initiation was unclear. On top of that the red thread coming from the serge 'accidentally' got caught around a butter

---

91 Russian-style *pozy* or *momos*, rather like huge ravioli.

lamp and burnt, severing his link with the dimension of the Sky. Galina Dabaeva came to Stas. She pulled more thread through the slit and again ordered him to tie it around the ring finger of his left hand. Galina Dabaeva took her *hese* and performed the invocation again standing right behind Stas.

While all this was happening Zundy was intermittently entering and exiting the trance state. When he was coming out of trance he would throw his head and body backward and his face became totally absent and indifferent for some time. When he regained his senses fully, he didn't remember anything and others were telling him which spirits had possessed him and what they had said. His eyes were bloodshot. When he was in trance his eyes were closed even when he was walking.

Now he again suddenly entered the trance and I simultaneously 'saw' the White Elder Sagaan Ebugen approaching. I told the others about what I saw and also said that Sagaan Ebugen would enter Zundy now. Meanwhile the medium was occupied by another spirit who immediately retorted in a harsh voice, 'No, he won't!' However, after some time that spirit left and the White Elder entered Zundy. He told me (through Zundy's mouth) to come near and said that he had come from the Silver Mountain to reply to my questions.[92] I asked the Elder about my ancestors in the line of my maternal grandmother [her father was Hungarian]. Sagaan Ebugen replied that our ancestral land was in Barguzin which my ancestors left 3000 years ago before finally finding themselves in the west, which implied that my great grandfather was from the Hunnu line. While Sagaan Ebugen was replying through him, Zundy was walking around leaning on a horse-headed *hor'bo*. Then I asked what should be done in order to cure my liver problem. The medium took me by the left arm and told me to take a bowl with milk from the stool in front of him. He told me to drink it in three gulps. He said after a while there would be heat in my liver. True enough, after a short while I felt heat in my liver. Simultaneously my mouth opened uncontrollably and I emitted the sound 'A-a-a-ah'. At the same time I had a strong feeling of energy entering my liver. He spoke again and gave me a recipe for a medicine […] Later he […] said I could invoke him when I need help. Then Sagaan Ebugen departed.

Next came one of Vera Naguslaeva's *Ongon*-ancestors and started shouting at her. He threw the cup with tea given to him on the flour, was swearing, smoking and behaved roughly but, also, comically. He said something about Sode Lama.

Meanwhile the guy from Moscow wasn't having any success; the *Ongons* refused to enter him. Finally he was told to untie the thread and get out of the room. He was told by the Utgan that he wasn't ready and there was no calling for him, at least for now.

---

[92] That wasn't my first contact with this deity. He had first appeared to me near the Ivolginsky *Datsan* in July 1990 during my first visit to Buryatia.

Zundy continued drifting in and out of trance. This time mainly Vera's *Ongon*-ancestors were coming, and some of them were very ancient. One of them was dressed in a fur coat and fox *malahai*-hat decorated with a wolf tail. Last came someone claiming to be a *Chöd* lama dressed in red robes but I wasn't convinced; he could have been a *Gyalpo* spirit. Although Zundy, later suggested it was his previous incarnation, a great *Chöd* lama who had 500 disciples, he gave neither name nor time reference.

Zundy came out of trance but then abruptly went in again. He started jumping and moving as if he were a bull; Buha Noyon Baabai[93] had entered him. And, sure enough, half a minute later a young bullock ran into the courtyard and a bit later a herd of cows appeared walking along the road returning from the fields. Buha Noyon said there would be early snow this year and some other things.

Gradually the altar was dismantled. All the offerings were poured into one big bowl and offered outside. Meanwhile the *pel'meni* were ready and when we went back inside some people were already eating. At the same time Galina Dabaeva and her young Utgan helper went outside and pulled the birch branches out of the ground. The branches were broken and burnt in the stove together with the red thread which I gathered up. The altar was completely disassembled and we sat down to eat.

Later we drove to Lake Baikal to swim because that day was the beginning of the week when all the water in the Baikal region became healing waters.[94] We jumped in and then bottled some water to take with us. The water was burning cold and purifying. It cleansed all impurities. My body felt fresh and clean inside and out. After that everyone left and I was again on my own.

I did my practice and went to sleep. Before going to bed I felt it might be better for me to leave before Wednesday and so I did divination, which advised me to leave next morning otherwise there would be serious difficulties. At night various female Tengeri and spirits were coming down. A male spirit also came and told me his name. He asked me to ask Vera Naguslaeva to sprinkle for him. He seemed to have a Tatar surname. Next morning I left on the first mini-bus.

That same evening we were drinking tea in the kitchen of Vera's flat in Ulaan-Ude. Batashka, her grandson, was sitting on my lap when he suddenly closed his eyes tightly and started rolling his head from side to side like a bull in the same way as Zundy had done in trance when he was possessed by Buha Noyon. Despite the fact that Vera repeatedly told him to stop, he paid no attention whatsoever.[95]

---

93 Bull Noyon-Father, a highly-venerated deity in the form of a great bull.

94 The position of the Dolon Ubged (Vedic Seven Rishis) constellation in the sky made all water in the Baikal region sacred.

95 Extracted from the unpublished diary of my trip to Buryatia in September 2003.

Tibetan lhapa/pawo mediums and Buryatian Bɵ

Among the many types of mediums in Tibet, some of the most common are *lhapa* and *lhamo*[96] or *pawo* and *nyenjomo*[97] depending on the area.[98] Nowadays Tibetan mediums are mainly men who are generally possessed by male deities or spirits. Although there are some female mediums in Tibet, Nepal and India who are generally possessed by goddesses or female spirits, they usually have a lower standing. In Tibetan society *lhapa*/*pawo* fulfil two main tasks: they act as oracles and cure diseases. In the remote past, prior to the arrival of Yungdrung Bön in Zhang Zhung and Tibet, the *lhapa*/*pawo* must have carried out all the functions associated with Buryatian Bɵ and had different names according to their specializations.[99] Centuries of 'competition' from *Shenpos* and later Buddhist Tantrists reduced their importance and influence. Nevertheless, the *lhapa* tradition has remained particularly strong in Rebkong, Amdo and eastern Tibet in general, and is also practised in Changthang in western Tibet, the Chumbi Valley in Sikkim and in parts of Bhutan although even here this ancient type of medium has been strongly influenced by both Yungdrung Bön and Buddhism.

Unlike the Oracles of Yungdrung Bön who were tied exclusively to the *Drala* sky-gods, *lhapa* can be channelled by mountain gods, protective deities, *Yullha* and, in some cases, by the spirits of the dead. This, too, indicates that it is a pre-Yungdrung Bön tradition belonging to Prehistoric Bön and in Siberian terms *lhapa/pawo* can be said to combine the techniques of White and Black Bɵ.

Despite the huge Buddhist influence in some areas, the mode of initiation has more to do with the practice of Yungdrung Bön as the *bumpa*[100] and a handheld prayer wheel are used as supports for the

---

[96] Tib lha pa is male and Tib. lha mo is female.

[97] Tib. dpa bo is male and Tib. bsnyen jo mo is female.

[98] Other names used for higher Buddhist mediums are Tib.sku rten pa and Tib. lus khog.

[99] They were called by the generic name Bön, or Bönpo plus the class of deities a particular priest propitiated eg. Lhabön, Düdbön etc. as was explained in the ch. V.

[100] Tib. bum pa, a metal vase often made from gilded brass and decorated with precious gems. It is used in rites of initiation and empowerment as well as in a wide variety of Bönpo and Buddhist Tantric practices such as *Ganapuja*, meditation on the *yidam*, rites of purification, healing, long-life etc. In Yungdrung Bön the *bumpa* often serves as a support for the Tantric deities invoked and represents their *mandala*.

Bönkyong, Guardians of Bön.[101] These are the traces of adaptation of Prehistoric Bön traditions to the new cultural and religious environment at the time when Yungdrung Bön was introduced. Yungdrung Bön assimilated local deities and spirits into the practices contained in the Four Ways of Cause. Actually, these deities and spirits were subjugated and given vows by Tonpa Shenrab himself when he briefly visited Tibet.

A new *lhapa* usually appears in a family where a medium has already manifested, as is the case with Bɵ lineages. The new *lhapa* becomes possessed by the deities or spirits and manifests symptoms identical to the so-called 'shamanic illness' or 'pressure of the sprits' which normally come at the time of puberty, as was the case with Buryatian Bɵ and Utgan before the 1917 Socialist Revolution. In some areas the neophytes are then taught by an experienced *lhapa* or *lhamo* instead of a lama. This mode of transmission is concordant with that of Bɵ Murgel[102] and some other native Siberian traditions.

Nowadays the tradition has become heavily mixed with Tibetan Buddhism so it is most often a lama who establishes connection with the gods and opens the '*god's door*'[103] and '*god's word*'[104] for the *lhapa* whereas before the arrival of Yungdrung Bön and Buddhism they undoubtedly had their own original methods and rituals for this purpose. The *lhapa* is possessed by a god or spirit who enters into his body through the trance channels running from the ring fingers on both hands to the heart and then to the top of the head.

Fig. 9. Oracle lhaba *entering a trance as she is possessed by the mountain god Targo, Dingri area, October, 1998.*

This is the same channel as used by the Bɵ. Gods enter some *lhapa* by themselves while others have to beg them to come which also has a direct parallel in the techniques of Buryatian Bɵ. While possessed the *lhapa* performs various activities such as: delivering prophecies by means

---

[101] For *pawo* see Nebesky-Wojkowitz, *Oracles and Demons,* p. 425; Bellezza, *Divine Dyads*, pp. 62–65.

[102] See ch. VII.

[103] Tib. lha sgo 'byed.

[104] Tib. ngag sgo 'byed.

of looking into a mirror or uttering them; subduing and destroying bad spirits; performing healing and other types of magic including weather magic. The speech of a powerful *lhapa* is clear while a less powerful *lhapa* needs an 'interpreter'.[105] This, too, closely reflects the technique used by Lama-Bө Zundy and Utgan Galina Dabaeva which I observed in Buryatia, although in fact Zundy is somewhere in between as he sometimes spoke clearly when the higher gods were coming but when other spirits came his speech was mostly unintelligible and interpreted by the Utgan.

A widespread healing technique used by the *lhapa* is to suck the illness out of the patient using a *khata* offering scarf. The illness comes out as a black worm or black liquid which the *lhapa* spits out. A similar technique is also used by many native traditions in Siberia but is not so common among Buryatian Bө. I heard that some Bө use this technique, sucking out the disease either directly or through their *hor'bo*-cane, but I myself have never seen this done by modern-day Bө or Utgan.

Other techniques of *lhapa* include the use of a sword for divination, healing, exorcism and weather magic; the use of fire or red-hot metal for healing; spitting at patients; swearing and beating patients in order to drive away negativities, and so on. As we have seen, these are also common ritual objects and techniques of Buryatian Bө described above.

Another important function shared by *lhapa*, Bө, Bönpo and Buddhist *ngagpa* (Tantric *yogis*) alike is their ability and duty to control weather and all of them can and do perform rain-making or rain-repelling, repelling of hail and preventing of frost. In the case of the Bө, they are not only expected to bring rain but are also called to prevent such disasters as floods and earth falls into Lake Baikal. That was the main objective of the sequence of *tailgans* performed by the Bө and Utgan in 1994 in which I participated. Bө are also responsible for maintaining the environmental balance between humans and the animals of the lakes, rivers and forests. In the past they regulated fishing and hunting. Bө stand as the mediators between our level of being in the Middle World, the Upper World of heavens and the Underworld, a function also fulfilled by the *lhapa/pawo*, as is clear from the Lurol festival of Rebkong.[106]

There are very close similarities between many ritual garments and objects pertaining to *lhapa* and Bө. However, in many areas *lhapa* nowadays no longer use the full attire (as is the case with some modern Bө in Buryatia) either because they cannot afford it or because they don't

---

[105] Tib. lha pa bdag.

[106] See ch. XII.

give much importance to it and, also, because they have been side-lined by the Buddhist oracles, therefore we will not go into much detail here. Indeed, often the only pieces of ritual gear *lhapa* have while in trance are a *melong*-mirror and/or a *dadar*-arrow. Moreover, several ritual objects and items of the present-day costume of *lhapa* were borrowed from Buddhist Tantric attire and as such are not of interest for the purpose of our study here.

In short, there is no doubt that Bө Murgel and traditions of the *lhapa/pawo* are branches of the same ancient tree of Prehistoric Bön and still retain a striking number of common features despite thousands of years of separate development and adaptation in different geo-cultural environments.

Tibetan State Oracle and Buryatian Bө

Tibetan Buddhist Oracles

The State Oracle and other official oracles played an important role in Tibetan society before the Chinese Communist invasion. Oracles were consulted regularly in order to receive prophesies about important religious and state affairs. Even nowadays the Neychung[107] Oracle is regularly consulted by the Tibetan Government in Exile.

As we have already noted, Buddhists copied this method in its entirety from Yungdrung Bön texts belonging to *Chashen Thegpa*, the First Way of Cause, so it is fitting to examine it briefly in the context of our research here. As they did with many other methods taken from Bön, incoming Buddhists left the basic matrix of this practice intact but substituted their own protective deities for the original Bönpo ones. The deities invoked today are *Dharmapala*, various worldly spirits belonging to the Eight Classes of demi-gods, whereas the Bönpo would invoke sky-dwelling *Drala*.

The main priests possessed by the Buddhist *Dharmapala* protective deities are called *Chöje*[108] or religious master. Nowadays they are predominantly connected with the Gelugpa School which ran Tibet from the seventeenth century until the Chinese invasion of 1950 and which included the Oracles within the scheme of the government apparatus. The principal oracle-priest of Neychung is always a monk and is possessed by Dorje Dragden, either an emanation or a companion of the *Dharmapala*

---

[107] Tib. gNas chung.

[108] Tib. chos rje.

Pehar.[109] There are several stories surrounding how this spirit moved to Neychung Monastery, but it was in the mid-sixteenth century that he possessed a medium for the first time. In the seventeenth century, during the reign of the Fifth Dalai Lama, the Neychung Oracle was elevated to the role of State Oracle of Tibet because he foiled a Nepalese plot to kill the people of Lhasa by poisoning the city's wells. Since then the Neychung Oracle has always been connected with the Dalai Lamas and the Central Tibetan Government, playing a significant role in politics as well as in the affairs of the Gelugpa School such as the discovery of reincarnations (especially the Dalai Lamas), and predictions about external and internal dangers to the State and the School.

Two other important Buddhist Oracles were the Karmashar[110] in Lhasa where the medium was possessed by Pehar's companion Monbuputra,[111] and Gadong[112] Monastery where the deity was Shingyachen.[113] All these three main Oracles in fact belong to the class of *Gyalpo* spirits. There are a number of other Oracles in Tibet who do not play such prominent roles.

People destined to become receptacles of the *Dharmapala* are possessed and experience all the aspects of the 'shamanic illness' or *Ongon Daralga*. However, they differ from the Bɵ and Siberian shamans in general in that they normally do not live long; for some reason, they do not tolerate well the mediumistic trances with their wrathful spirits. A possible explanation is that, as Buddhists copied this technique from Bönpos, something may have been lost in transition.

Stages of the ritual trance of Tibetan Buddhist medium-priests and Buryatian Bɵ

The way a medium enters into trance and the ritualistic aspects of the séance also have many parallels with Buryatian Bɵ. We shall compare the following stages of Tibetan Oracle ritual trance given by Nebesky-Wojkowitz[114] with those of the Bɵ Murgel trance I witnessed in Buryatia.

---

[109] See ch. VI.

[110] Tib. sKar ma shar.

[111] Tib. Mon bu pu tra.

[112] Tib. dGa' gdong.

[113] Tib. Shing bya can.

[114] Nebesky-Wojkowitz, *Oracles and Demons of Tibet*, p.. 429–432.

Tibetan Buddhist Oracle	**Buryatian Bɵ**
Preparing the altar on which ceremonial dress, ritual objects and weapons are placed together with offerings of tea, *tormas*, milk, alcohol etc.	Preparing a less elaborate *shere'e* altar with ritual objects, instruments and offerings of biscuits, sweets, arkhi, butter lamps and so on.
The altar and the objects are consecrated by *mantras* and *mudras*	*Amin* life-force is invoked into *amitai* and *orgoi* ritual dress and *hese*-drum of a Bɵ
The medium is dressed in ritual dress and the *Dharmapala* who is to possess him is invoked. Vast amounts of incense are burnt and, in particular, blown into the medium's face to purify him as the ritual hat or helmet is lowered on his head, at which point the spirit enters the medium's body	The Bɵ, participants, altar etc are purified with *arsa* incense. The Bɵ may don the *maihabshi* horned crown and/or the masks of their *Ongon* when they are about to enter the trance-state
Tea, milk, beer etc. are offered to the *Dharmapala*, now possessing the body of the medium, who accepts and drinks them	Zundy was given tea, alcohol, cigarettes and so on as offerings to welcome entering spirits
The medium is given weapons such as a sword and spear (which in the original Bönpo version were the weapons of *Drala*) and he dances with them and makes various movements which show that the *Dharmapala* has taken a full control of the medium as well as his complete control over negative forces.[i]	The Bɵ exorcises the negative spirits from the site of the ritual with the help of his ritual weapons: sword, *ho'orto*-dagger, *hootaga*-knife, whip, and *zhada*-spear[ii]
Khatags and drinks are offered to the medium in trance and questions posed to the deity which possesses him	Drinks etc are offered to the Bɵ in trance and questions are put to the spirits possessing him
Often a possessed medium would ask for additional milk or beer and pour it into the hands of the surrounding people who drink it immediately as it is considered a powerful medicine	Lama-Bɵ Zundy possessed by Sagaan Ebugen, ordered me to drink water mixed with milk in order to help my health problem

While the *Dharmapala* speaks through the medium, attendants carefully write down the words which are later interpreted	As the spirits spoke through Lama-Bɵ Zundy, Utgan Galina Dabaeva and her helpers wrote down and interpreted what was said
After the prophecies are delivered the medium suddenly collapses and remembers nothing when he comes to his senses	Lama-Bɵ Zundy went completely blank when the spirits left him and could remember nothing of what had happened while he was in trance
[i] *This also reminds us of the young Tonpa Shenrab sporting with the Weapons of Drala. See ch. IX.* [ii] *See ch.VIII.*	

It is clear from this comparison that the essential meaning and function of each and every stage of the trance experienced by the Tibetan State Oracle exactly matches those of a Buryatian Bɵ-medium. This strongly suggests that the origins of the Bönpo, Bɵ Murgel and Buddhist versions of this archaic practice lie in Prehistoric Bön.

Ritual apparel of Tibetan State Oracles and Buryatian Bɵ

If we examine the details of ritual dress and ritual objects of Tibetan mediums who serve as the mouthpiece for important Oracles with those of Buryatian Bɵ, we will find further evidence of close cultural and religious affinity. This model is based primarily on the attire of the Neychung medium.

Headdress

The Tibetan medium of Neychung Oracle and those of other official Buddhist Oracles wear a variety of hats which reflect the attributes of the deity possessing them. In particular, mediums of Pehar, Tsiu Marpo[115] and Tsangpa Karpo wear weighty metal helmets. *Bumog*,[116] the helmet worn by the Neychung medium is particularly heavy and is said to weigh around sixty pounds. The helmet has two sets of decorations, one relatively modern, the other truly archaic. The modern decoration consists of five human skulls[117] – no doubt inspired by Buddhism[118] –

[115] Tib. Tsi'u dmar po is an important protective deity of Nyingma School.

[116] Tib.dbu rmog.

[117] Tib. khro bo rigs lnga.

[118] Five skulls are a common Tantric symbol often worn as a crown by wrathful

together with various ornaments made of precious metals and stones. The archaic part comprises bunches of long vulture tail-feathers, five upright standing triangular flags[119] and long broad ribbons of silk which hang from the back of the helmet.

If we concentrate on the details which form the archaic part of the helmet, they are clearly a copy of the helmets of some Bönpo *Drala* gods and therefore betray the ancient origin of this practice.[120] As a transformed version of the Helmet of the *Drala*, the helmet of Neychung is directly comparable to the iron *maihabshi*-crown of Buryatian Bө. The long silk ribbons hanging from the helmet of the Neychung medium are also present in the *maihabshi* and head part of the *orgoi* as worn by Utgan Galina Dabaeva for the initiation rite I witnessed in Buryatia in 2004. Although the long tassels hanging from the back of the *maihabshi* are often made of metal while the five ribbons on Galina's *orgoi* – like those on the Neychung helmet – were made out of silk, their function is the same: to extend the wearer's energy and power. A medium's headdress serves to induce the trance state, enhance the connection with the deities invoked and is donned last by both the Bө and Tibetan mediums alike. Other types of headdresses worn by Tibetan mediums are mostly various types of hats or turbans which are particular attributes of the deities who possess them. Some of these can be broadly compared to the *malgai*-hat of Buryatian Bө. In addition to a headdress, some Bө also wear a mask of the deity or spirit who possesses them.

Gown and body garments

The next part of Neychung's medium ritual dress is *gyalche*,[121] 'ritual dress of *Gyalpo*' and consists of several parts:

- *Shago*:[122] heavy, long-sleeved gown which is directly comparable to a Bө's *orgoi*.
- *Todle*:[123] a shoulder piece covering the shoulders, part of the breast and back to which white vulture feathers are attached

---

yidams and representing the transformation of the Five Poison Consciousnesses into the Five Wisdoms.

[119] Tib. rgyab lag.

[120] We compared the Nine Weapons and Armour of the *Drala* and the ritual implements of Buryatian Bө in ch. IX.

[121] Tib. rgyal chas.

[122] Tib. sha gos.

[123] Tib. stod le or Tib. stod g.yog.

directly comparable with *dalabshi* shoulder piece of the Bɵ which symbolizes the wings of the sacred eagle.

- *Pangkheb*:[124] an apron made of brocade comparable to the *hebeneg* overcoat of the Bɵ.
- *Japang*:[125] a kind of breast ornament comparable to the *elgebshi* breast-piece of the Bɵ.
- *Pawoche*:[126] armour worn by some oracles possessed by warrior gods in addition to the attire mentioned above which is directly comparable to the *hooyag* chainmail coat of the Bɵ.

The ritual dress for mediums of deities other than *Gyalpo* do not differ to any significant degree, although another kind of hat and different coloured main gown are worn.

All types of Tibetan mediums wear *thugkyi melong*,[127] the 'mirror of mind', at their heart level. This mirror is often engraved with the seed-syllable of the deity which possesses them. As we have already noted, the *melong* is equivalent to the Bɵ's *toli*-mirror.

Tibetan oracles wear different types of shoes made of felt or animal skins depending on their stature. These shoes are more or less the same shape as those traditionally worn by the Bɵ.

Ritual weapons

In addition to their ritual dress, Tibetan oracles also have ritual weapons such as swords, bows and arrows, knives, spears with the pennants, lassos, snares and so on, all of which find their counterparts in a Buryatian Bɵ's arsenal of ritual weapons examined in detail in Chapters VIII and IX.

Conclusion

From the comparative study above we can clearly see that the mediums of Tibetan Buddhist State Oracles and Buryatian Bɵ show a very close affinity with direct parallels not only in all aspects of their activities but even in the specific details of their ritual dress and implements. Bearing in mind that the phenomenon of Tibetan State Oracle, though Buddhist

---

[124] Tib. pang khebs.

[125] Tib. 'ja' pang.

[126] Tib. dba' bo chas.

[127] Tib. thugs kyi me long.

today, is actually a direct import from the First Way of Yungdrung Bön, what we are in fact comparing here is a somewhat modified original Yungdrung Bön oracle system of divination and its equivalent in Buryatian Bɵ Murgel, both of which developed from Prehistoric Bön. This is further strengthened by the fact that Tibetan *lhapa*/*pawo* medium-healers, and certain Nepali priests who are the living remnants of some streams of Prehistoric Bön, use very similar techniques and ritual items.

Part IV
Retrieving and Ransoming the Soul

In the previous chapter we examined *hunehen* and *la* in some detail and saw that *hunehen/la* is a vital component of all sentient beings, be they human or otherwise. Its capture or displacement for whatever reason bodes ill for the person affected, so in both Bɵ Murgel and all types of Bön it is considered of utmost importance to reunite the *hunehen*/*la* with its owner as soon as possible. Both traditions have many methods for achieving this goal.

In fact, there are two types of rituals which can be done: retrieving and ransoming. Retrieving is done when the *hunehen/la* has run away following a severe shock or accident, while ransoming is done when it has been abducted by gods or spirits. In this section we will compare the Bɵ Murgel ritual of *Hunehen Hurylha*[128] with the Bönpo *Lagug*[129] ritual. These are mostly based on the technique of retrieving the soul and can be further classified into two kinds: recalling the soul and summoning the soul. Recalling the soul is begging the soul to come back by offering it gifts, while summoning the soul is forcefully ordering it to return. These rituals often also involve the technique of ransoming, known as *Dolë*[130] in Buryatian and *Lüd*[131] in Tibetan. Both words have the same meaning, 'exchange' or 'ransom', and denote rituals which stand in their own right so we shall look into them in more detail in the section below.

---

[128] Bur. Хүнэхэн хурылха.

[129] Tib. bla 'gugs.

[130] Bur. долё.

[131] Tib. glud.

Rites for retrieving the soul

Hunehen Hurylha

In Bɵ Murgel we find various methods for retrieving *hunehen* but they are not as elaborate as those in Bön. Before any ritual can be done, it is very important to ascertain from which location *hunehen* exited the body. It can jump out from the top of the head, throat, heart, tummy button and so on. The place through which *hunehen* exited feels cold and empty, so Bɵ and Utgan establish where it will re-enter through their psychic abilities.

Perhaps the most straightforward way to return *hunehen* into its rightful location is simply to hit a particular spot on the body. However, this method can only be used in certain cases when *hunehen* is displaced within the body because of an accident. Another relatively simple remedy is to sprinkle to the Tengeri or spirits and ask them to talk to the patient's *hunehen* and persuade it to return. Consecrated vodka is then spat on the crown of the patient's head or onto the spot from which *hunehen* has left the body.

If, however, these methods prove unsuccessful, a *Hunehen Hurylha* ritual is performed. The Bɵ or Utgan sprinkles to the Tengeri and *Zayaans* asking them to come and help return the patient's *hunehen*. Then an arrow, which serves as support for life-force, *hulde* and *hunehen*, is put into a bucket together with the patient's favourite food (and toys when the ritual concerns children). If possible, Bɵ and patient go to the place where *hunehen* jumped out of the body as it is believed to stay nearby at first, moving further and further away as time passes. If that is not possible then the *Hunehen Hurylha* ritual is done at home, at the Bɵ's dwelling or at a *tailgan*. Ideally it should be performed at the same time of day as the incident which caused *hunehen* to exit because it returns to the place at the same time. *Hunehen* is invoked, offered food and other objects it likes and asked to enter the body. When *hunehen* does so, the patient will cry because *hunehen* is overjoyed to find its body again. This signifies that the ritual is successful. If, on the other hand, the ritual is not successful, it is repeated up to three times. If the ritual is still unsuccessful, the patient may eventually die,[132] depending on which kind of *hunehen* has been lost.[133]

---

[132] I.e. if *dunda hunehen* is stolen and not recovered the patient will die. See ch. XIII.

[133] Hangalov, *Sobranie* II, pp. 215–217.

Nowadays a simplified version of this ritual is often performed. Food is arranged on a plate, the officiate performing the rite comes out of the house and rotating the plate sunwise, exclaims, '*A-hure!*' several times. *Hunehen* is then invoked into the offerings, begged to accept, enjoy them and enter the body. Finally wishes for long-life and prosperity are uttered.[134]

When *hunehen* has been stolen, other techniques are called for. *Hunehen* can be abducted by gods, spirits and black magicians so depending on who stole it, there are two principal methods which can be used: buying it back through various ransoms, or retrieving it by force if those who stole it refuse to cooperate.

The first step, then, is to ascertain who stole the *hunehen* and where it is being kept. This can be accomplished either by various types of divination, by asking the gods and spirits for their assistance, or by the 'flight of the soul' technique when the Bɵ sends his own *hunehen* in search of the patient's lost *hunehen*. The Bɵ's *hunehen* travels through many dimensions, often on its steed which can be a rainbow, deer, wolf, bear or another spirit-animal depending on the Bɵ's clan and lineage. Some Black Bɵ and *Elbeshen* black sorcerers use the *hunehen* of other people as their steed. Having found the captured soul, the Bɵ enters into negotiations with the beings who stole it. He offers them various gifts (which should be prepared beforehand) in exchange for the patient's *hunehen*. Offerings may include items such as food, clothes, shoes, weapons and *dolë*, a human ransom figure in the form of the beneficiary of the rite which can be made of various materials such as cloth, fur, wood and so on. If the barter is successful, the Bɵ returns back with the patient's *hunehen* and s/he will recover from disease, misfortunes are reversed and happiness is restored. In some Bɵ Murgel traditions a horse is tied near the entrance of the *gher* or other dwelling where the ritual is taking place. The horse acts as a kind of indicator for establishing whether *hunehen* has returned or not as it starts shaking when *hunehen* enters the dwelling through the door.

If the captors refuse to accept the gifts and release the soul, the Bɵ has a last resort; he engages the thieves in a magical battle. This is very dangerous and in some cases may cost him his life. If the situation has gone this far, the Bɵ needs to use all his powers, magic skills and trickery. He invokes the Tengeri, spirit-protectors and may sometimes ask other friendly Bɵ or Utgan to help him in this dangerous business. And so the 'army' charges into battle, a 'battle of the souls' which will be won by

---

[134] According to Utgan Vera Naguslaeva.

the strongest. For the Bo and the patient, winning this battle is literally a matter of life and death.

Lalu[135] *and Lagug*

The Bönpo *Lagug* ritual is done to recall the soul when certain signs and symbols a person's *la* is missing. For example, if a person suddenly feels weak, if his/her face grows pale or looks somehow different or if certain inauspicious signs and symbols appear in dreams (such as walking in a cemetery, walking around naked, being taken away or called by the dead, being ridden by bad spirits or riding on certain animals in certain directions), these show that the person is losing the energy of the elements, losing *la*, vital energy and power. To remedy the situation, *Lagug*, *Lalu* or *Lüd* rituals must be performed as soon as possible. *Lagug* and *Lalu* are often done together one after the other. *Lalu* literally means 'buying *la* back'. It is a kind of ransom rite and usually comes first. *Lagug* means 'calling *la*' and usually comes second. Other sections such as prayers for longevity may be added to these rituals depending on the given text; there are many different texts as these kinds of rituals are found in each Bönpo Tantric cycle.

> Firstly the ransom is prepared. This usually consists of a human figurine made of *tsampa* dough which is to be offered as ransom in cases when *la* was stolen. A male effigy is made for a man, a female for a woman and a child effigy for a child. It must be beautifully dressed and decorated. Depending on the specifications in the given text, other items can be offered such as circular white *tormas* and triangular red ones,[136] *namkha*, *jangbu*, *changbu*[137] and so on.[138]
>
> *Lalu* is done in the following way:
>
> The demons who stole the *la* are then called to come using a special invocation originally pronounced by Tonpa Shenrab or one of the early *Siddhas* of Yungdrung Bön. The demons are

---

[135] Tib. bla bslu.

[136] Tib. dkar gtor zlum po, dmar gtor zur gsum.

[137] Tib. changs bu.

[138] For more details see Norbu, *Drung, Deu and Bön*, pp. 90–97 and Karmay, *The Arrow and the Spindle*, pp. 326–327.

offered various gifts such as a *lalüd*[139] effigy and so on. The demons are told that the effigy has all the best qualities and is much better than the real person. They are exhorted to accept it and release the patient's *la.* To further convince the demons they are told that if they do not, countless wrathful Buddha emanations will come and grind them into dust. At the end of *Lalu,* the effigy and other offerings are taken outside and left by the roadside, at a crossroads or taken in the 'enemy direction'.[140]

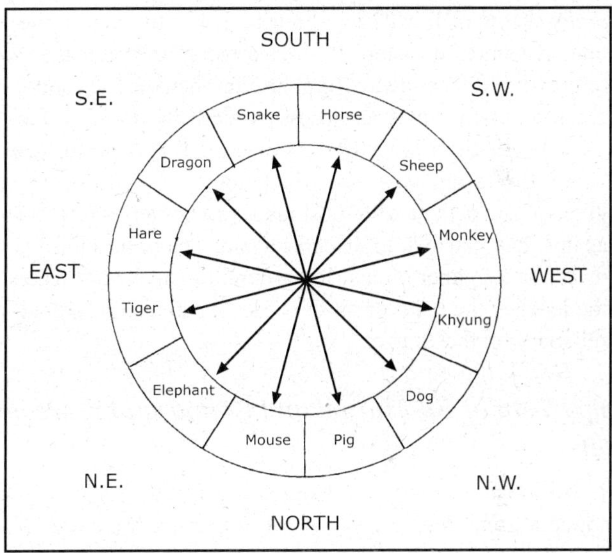

Fig. 10. Enemy direction diagram.

Lalu, the ritual to buy back *la*, is followed by *Lagug.* Here, a human figurine representing *la*[141] is made out of butter. It should have a human body and an animal head corresponding to the person's clan emblem which is known as the tribe's 'soul emblem'.[142] This tradition comes from very archaic times when there were only five main tribes in Tibet so any person must have belonged to one of them. Each tribe had its soul emblem:

---

[139] Tib. bla glud.

[140] The enemy direction is the direction opposite to the animal symbol of one's year of birth.

[141] Tib. bla gzugs.

[142] Tib. bla rtags.

sheep for *Ga*, goat for *Go*, deer for *Dong*, horse for *Dra* and yak for *Dru.*[143] If the patient's clan is not known, a deer head is used. The figurine holds the arrow of life[144] in its right hand and the turquoise of the *la*[145] in its left. It is put on a light plate and floated in a large, decorated tub filled with water mixed with medicine and flowers. The tub represents the lake of *la.*[146] An invocation is recited which is in fact a request to Tonpa Shenrab, a *Siddha* or a *yidam* to help in returning *la*. While this text is being recited, the water in the tub is stirred anticlockwise with a *dadar*-arrow of life. The *la*-figurine is left to float on the water until it comes to a stop. If it rests facing the altar then *la* has returned; if it faces away from the altar then the rite is performed again as many times as necessary until the figurine faces the altar.[147] Finally a long-life empowerment[148] is performed after which the turquoise of *la*, which serves as a *la*-receptacle, is given to the patient who must take care not to lose or damage it as this may cause *la* to disperse again. The *la* turquoise is worn on the body either on a string around the neck so it hangs over the level of the heart or on the head. It can also be stored in the reliquary on the altar.[149]

Comparison of Bө Murgel and Bönpo soul retrieving rituals

If we look into both Bө Murgel and Bönpo soul recalling rituals we notice a great degree of similarity or, even, sameness of structure, offering substances, techniques and concepts behind them. As the Bönpo version came to us through Yungdrung Bön, the doctrine behind

---

[143] Tib. sGa, sGo, gDong or lDong, 'Gru.

[144] Tib.tshe mda.

[145] Tib. bla g.yu.

[146] Tib. bla mtsho.

[147] Karmay, *The Arrow and the Spindle*, p. 334 reports an additional section, a game of dice between the patient and the demon of death. White and black dice are thrown on white and black boards. If white dice shows a higher number then *la* has definitely returned but if the black dice shows a higher number then the game is repeated up to three times. If black still wins then a rite is performed to *Shinje*, the Lord of Death.

[148] Tib. tshe dbang.

[149] Based on a conversation with Yongdzin Löpon Tenzin Namdak, Triten Norbutse Bönpo Monastery in Kathmandu, Nepal, 12.04.04.

it is that of Tonpa Shenrab so it is based on the intention of achieving final Buddhahood. Therefore, the deities invoked are Wisdom Gods,[150] peaceful and wrathful Buddha-forms. However, because this technique belongs to the Causal Ways of Yungdrung Bön where we find archaic methods adapted to Yungdrung Bön by Buddha Tonpa Shenrab Miwo, structurally it is almost identical to the Bɵ Murgel ritual which may, in fact, be an earlier 'non-adapted' form of the same rite. While the two main sections of the rite – buying the soul back and recalling the soul – may follow in opposite order, the sections themselves are all but identical in structure.

Many identical implements such as the arrow of life, bucket and tub, ransom human figurine and so on can be found in all sections of these rituals of both Bɵ Murgel and Yungdrung Bön. Indeed, not only are the objects themselves identical, they fulfil the same functions, and the concepts behind them are the same, too. The structure of 'recalling of the soul' rituals in both traditions follows the same pattern.

Let us first list the parallel aspects of the recalling sections:

1. The soul's absence is established through examining signs and through various kinds of clairvoyance;
2. An auspicious time and place for the ritual are determined;
3. Ritual objects (arrow, ransom figure etc.) and offerings (food/*tormas* etc.) are prepared and placed into the receptacle or support (bucket/tub and altar);
4. Deities are called for assistance. The difference is only in the status of the deities. While in Bɵ Murgel worldly gods (Tengeri and *Zayaans*) are called down, in Yungdrung Bön enlightened beings are invoked;
5. While invocations recalling the soul are recited, the officiating priest performs circular movements (with the plate of offerings/stirring the water) to spin the energy and draw the soul to the site of the ritual and, eventually, into the patient's body;
6. The effectiveness of the ritual is verified by observing signs and omens (crying of the patient, shaking of the horse/direction in which the *la* figurine faces, game of dice);
7. Invocations for the patient's long-life and prosperity are performed.

Rituals for 'buying back the soul' show identical structure, too:

1. Offerings are prepared (ransom figure, food/ransom figure, *torma*);
2. Spirits who stole the soul are summoned to the offerings;

[150] Tib. ye shes lha.

3. Gifts and ransoms are offered in exchange for the soul;
4. Spirits are urged to take the offerings and release the soul or face the consequences of magical actions of destruction;
5. Ransom is taken outside and left in some place away from the patient's home;
6. The effectiveness of the ritual is verified through observing signs;
7. Invocations for the patient's long-life and prosperity are performed.

There are other indications that these rites share common cultural and spiritual origin. Although the Bө Murgel rite doesn't use the emblem of the tribe in this particular ritual, its role in the Bönpo ritual points to a cultural phenomenon paralleled in Bө Murgel: each Buryatian tribe has an animal totem and the Bө' ritual *malgai* hat must be decorated with the fur of a specific animal.[151]

A further clue pointing to the common cultural and spiritual origin of these rites in both traditions is provided by the translation of the text from a Dunhuang manuscript summarized by Samten Karmay:

> The son of the god Gön-tshun-cha[152] from his Demoness wife provokes his maternal uncles' wrath and so they kill him through magic. Next day Gön-tshun-cha notices that his son lies motionless. The god asks his son why he is sad and promises him a castle, fields, domestic animals etc. if he rises. Seeing that his offer has no effect, the god calls his Bönpo priest to bring his son back to life. However, the Bönpo doesn't succeed.[153]

Here we see that as 'first aid' to resuscitate his son the god uses a method identical to the Buryatian rite of *Hunehen Hurylha*: he promises his dead son material gifts which he knows will please his soul and may beckon it back. The god doesn't try to pay a ransom to those who killed his son straight away but first tries to lure the soul back to his son's body with items which would normally excite his son's desire. Clearly, this kind of method was in use in Tibet in ancient times even though it doesn't seem to have been formalized into a ritual and doesn't seem to be used nowadays. This suggests that the soul retrieval rituals in both Bө Murgel and Yungdrung Bön have a common cultural and religious source in the Prehistoric Bön of Eurasia which predates Yungdrung Bön itself.

---

[151] See ch. IX.

[152] Tib. mGon mtshun phyva.

[153] Karmay, *The Arrow and the Spindle,* p. 316.

Buryatian and Tibetan ransom rituals Dolë and Lüd

Introduction

A very important method for healing and also for averting the evil eye, curses, epidemics and misfortunes of all kinds is a ransom rite. Although they may form a part of rituals to recall the soul, as we have seen above, ransom rituals also form a class of their own and both Bө Murgel and Bön have a rich variety to choose from. The Buryatian version is called *Dolë* while its Tibetan equivalent is *Lüd*. Both rites are based on the same principle of equal exchange and use human figurines known as *dolë*, *ngarlüd* or *ngarmi*,[154] although both cultures do have a practice whereby a living person is used as the ransom for another's soul. In Buryatian this is called *Hun Dolë*[155] and in Tibetan Buddhism it survived as *Lüdgong.*[156] Rituals using one human being in exchange for the life and well-being of another (or of a whole community) are very archaic indeed, as they are a form of human sacrifice with similar rites found in many ancient and prehistoric societies. Indeed such rituals are probably the base from which all other types of ransom rites developed; as more advanced religious forms appeared the live victim was substituted by an effigy of some kind.

In particular, all Tibetan ransom techniques, be they Bönpo or Buddhist, which use substitute figures and other gifts or substitutes instead of real people or animals (with the exception of Buddhist *Lüdgong* and *Chilüd* rituals which were clearly imported directly from a stream of Prehistoric Bön), come from Tonpa Shenrab's Yungdrung Bön. By recognizing the fact that all beings are equally important because they all have Buddha-nature, these teachings gave equal weight to the well-being and happiness of all beings large or small, high or low, important or unimportant, humans or animals, spirits or the gods etc. and thus came as a spiritual revolution. Tonpa Shenrab also taught the law of karma, which in practical terms can be summed up as: *Don't do to others what you don't want them to do to you.* So in the light of the doctrine of Yungdrung Bön, it became clear that the happiness of one being simply cannot be achieved at the expense of another's misery and sufferings but, on the contrary, is achieved by increasing others' well-being. Although this may seem quite straightforward, in practice it is rather difficult as some beings require the lives of others to stay alive, or are happy only when others harmed.

---

[154] Tib. ngar glud, ngar mi.

[155] Bur. хүн долё.

[156] Tib. glud 'gong.

Resolving this situation requires the omniscience and power of a Buddha and Tonpa Shenrab, a fully enlightened being, possessed such omniscience through which he saw the way to transform already existing techniques of offering rituals and, especially, ransom rites. Instead of live beings he taught his students how to offer substitutes which, empowered with meditation and *mantra*, became equally effective as offerings and ransoms to evil and haughty beings without causing any more suffering to anyone else. Not only do these methods not cause suffering, they also benefit the malevolent beings by creating a cause for them to enter the path leading to Buddhahood. That, indeed, is skilful means. Of course, wild animals still hunt for food, humans still make war and hunt for food or pleasure – that is the nature and gruesome reality of *samsara*. Nevertheless, Tonpa Shenrab's reformation means that at least spiritual practitioners are offered a real way to benefit others without contributing to further suffering, and that is an enormously precious gift of Yungdrung Bön to all humanity.

Buryatian Dolë rites

Like all ransom rites, *Dolë* are generally based on the concept of equal exchange: malevolent forces are offered a substitute and gifts in exchange for the patient's *hunehen*-soul and *amin* life-force. For the ritual to be successful it must be carried out in the proper way by a knowledgeable and powerful Bө or Utgan. There are various kinds of *Dolë* rites and White and Black Bө may use different techniques:

- A *dolë* figurine, large or small, is made in the form of a human being. Various materials can be used;
- An animal is ritually slaughtered and its soul is offered in exchange for the patient's soul and life-force;
- Both a *dolë* and an animal are offered.

The *dolë* figurine may either be offered as a straightforward payment, or alternatively, the spirit causing the problem may be lured into the it through trickery. Once there, it is trapped and the figurine can be buried far away from the patient's house. This second method is known as transferring a curse or a malign spirit into a substitute receptacle. However, this method does not work when the patient's soul has been captured, but only when a powerful entity has sent a curse or ordered a subordinate disease-creating spirit to enter the patient's body. The first method can be used both when the patient's soul has been stolen by malevolent spirits or by Black Tengeri, as well as in the latter case.

Hun Dolë

Some Black Bө may resort to *Hun Dolë,* in which the soul of another human is used as a ransom to buy back the patient's life. This rite is comprised of two stages: capturing the victim's soul, and offering it as a ransom. If the ritual is successful the patient will recover while the person whose soul was stolen and used as a ransom will fall ill and die. Naturally, nobody wants their soul to be captured and sold to evil forces, so the Black Bө's task of finding and catching a soul is far from easy. Villagers would often quickly guess what was afoot when a Black Bө or Utgan was invited to perform a healing ceremony in a sick person's house, especially if the patient was a rich one (one had to pay dearly for this kind of ritual) and people would use all possible forms of protection against the Black Bө's magic. For example, they would put a brush on the doorstep in the belief that the Black Bө's soul would see it as a bunch of needles or other sharp objects and be repelled. Or they would seal the entrance to their dwellings by sticking a knife into the doorstep or would attach a knife above the doorway, inside, with blade facing down, or attach it outside pointing out of the dwelling so that it would pierce the Black Bө's soul on entry. The fire in the house would be up and burning all night because it is very difficult to steal the soul of someone who is awake. Sometimes people grew so desperate and electrified by fear that they would try to capture and murder the Black Bө or the sick person who invited him. There are other counteractive measures which can be taken which we will discuss in the section on Destructive Magic below.

If the Black Bө manages to capture a soul, he either transfers it into the *dolë* figurine and then offers it to the evil forces, or drags it directly into the domain of the gods or spirits who hold the patient's soul. Then he strikes a deal with those beings, giving them the soul of the victim in exchange for the soul of his patient. If the patient's soul was abducted by the messengers of Erlig Khaan and kept in Erlig Hama,[157] one of the eighty-eight dungeons of the Under World, *Hun Dolë* is offered to Dombo Noyon,[158] Erlig Khaan's official, with the request to liberate the patient's soul and take instead the soul of an animal or another man or woman. There are other dungeons in the Underworld which are difficult for even a powerful Black Bө to reach, and if the soul was taken to Erlig Tama[159] there is no way to recover it and the patient will surely die as

---

157 Bur. Эрлиг-хама.

158 Bur. Домбо-ноён.

159 Bur. Эрлиг-тама.

this dungeon is under the direct control of Erlig Khaan himself.[160] If, however, the Bɵ is successful, he returns from his magical journey with his patient's soul and reunites it with his/her body, at which point his task is finished. The patient will recover but the person whose soul was stolen will ail and die unless an even more powerful Bɵ is invited and is able to retrieve their soul by some means.

Hun Dolë is, no doubt, a relict of human sacrifice rituals. In ages past the Black Bɵ's task of soul-stealing would have been much easier as another person, usually a slave, would simply have been captured[161] and sacrificed in exchange for the patient's soul. Human sacrifices often formed part of the burial rites for the rich and wealthy and for powerful Black Bɵ. There is Buryatian legend which tells of how human sacrifices were stopped:

> Long ago a particularly powerful Bɵ passed away, and human sacrifices were customarily offered to him. However, the Tengeri ordered the Bɵ to be transformed into a bear and suck his paw in the winter instead of accepting human sacrifices. That is how human sacrifices were stopped.[162]

There is another peculiar form of *Hun Dolë* which can, in some way, be compared to the actions of a *Bodhisattva*, although of course the fundamental point is missing: what makes a *Bodhisattva* a *Bodhisattva* is not only compassion but *bodhichitta*, the intention of attaining Buddhahood for the sake of all sentient beings. Nevertheless, in the past some Bɵ would actually agree to die on the patient's behalf if the patient's family promised them a special burial rite and that all the necessary attributes would be put in the grave alongside them for use in the afterlife. Such a Bɵ no longer saw the difference between life and the after-life and, neither afraid of nor attached to either, were able to act selflessly with the intention of benefiting others. There is a story I heard about one such Bɵ:

> A villager was on his deathbed and so his relatives sought out a Bɵ and begged him to retrieve the person's soul. Through his clairvoyance, the Bɵ saw that the person's life could only be saved by the *Hun Dolë* and so he agreed to die in the patient's place on condition that the family would perform all the necessary death

---

160 Hangalov, *Sobranie* I, pp. 454–455.

161 Or selected in cases when the sick was powerful and wealthy.

162 Hangalov, *Sobranie* I, p. 210.

rituals for him and put into the grave the objects he requested. The family eagerly agreed and so the Bө lay down and died, then and there. The patient began to recover at once and was soon in good health again. The family, however, neglected their promise and did nothing for the Bө; they didn't bury him at all but left his body to rot in his dwelling. From the afterlife the Bө saw this and decided to return to the land of the living. So he entered his body, which was by now half rotten, swarming with maggots, and walked to the village. Some of the local villagers saw him walking along and froze with fear. Halfway to the village the Bө said to himself, 'This body is really quite useless now. There is no way I can stay in it again.' And so he left for the afterlife once more. His body dropped where he left it.

Another example of this kind of voluntary[163] *Hun Dolë* comes from *The Sacred History of Mongols*:

> Ugedei Khaan himself led the military campaign to China in the Year of the Hare (1231 AD). [...] Ugedei immediately obliterated the Hyadan' (Khitan) army and, having broken it as if it were a bunch of dry twigs, he went over the Chabchiyal pass and sent military divisions in different directions to attack Hyadan' towns and cities. But suddenly Ugedei Khaan was struck by disease and his tongue was paralyzed. Worrying greatly, his courtiers called several Hyadan' Bө and ordered them to do divinations. The divinations showed that the disease was caused by the extreme wrath of disturbed spirits, *Ezhen*-Lords and *Lusuut Khaans* – Owners of Haydan' lands and waterways outraged by the enslaving of the people and usurping of their dwellings, raging at the destruction of the towns and villages within their domain. Divination was done once more, this time using the innards of animals, to ask the spirits whether they would be willing to accept a *zolig*[164]-ransom gold with silver, or livestock or various foods. But the reply came that on this condition they would not be pacified but would rage all the more strongly night and day. Once again, divination was done with animal innards, to determine whether the spirits would accept as ransom a relative of the ill; at that very moment, the Khaan opened his eyes and asked for water. He drank it and asked, 'What was the outcome?' The Bө then reported: 'The *Ezhen*-Owners of the Hyadan' lands and waterways are consumed by a mighty rage due to the enslaving of their people and their people's dwellings. Although we suggested offering them as a ransom anything

---

[163] Although he volunteered, in the light of Mongol customs of the time, Tolui didn't really have a choice.

[164] Bur. золиг.

they could desire, they agree to stop causing havoc only if given a *Hun Dolë* of your relative. If that is not given they threaten to whip up even more savage fury. So we report this to your Royal Highness.' When it had been reported thus to the Khaan, he enquired, 'Who from the princes is among us?' There was Tolui.[165] He said to the Khaan, 'Our father, may he be blissfully remembered, our monarch, Chingis Khaan, when he chose you, my elder brother and Khaan, he selected you carefully as if selecting a gelding, and checked you by touch as if feeling a ram. He personally appointed you to sit on the great throne of the supreme Khaan and placed the troubles of all our nation on your Highness's shoulders. As for me, I was ordered only to stay close to the Khaan, my elder brother, to wake him from sleep and remind him of things forgotten. If I were not to protect you now, who then would I rouse from sleep and remind of things forgotten? Let it be then that this very moment I shall stand for my brother and Khaan when, though he is as yet unharmed, all Mongols are already full of grief as orphans and the Chinese are celebrating. I broke the spine of a *taimen',*[166] I broke the spine of a sturgeon. I took victories in front of you, I fought when you didn't see, I am tall and handsome. So read your incantations, you Bɵ, and put the spell on water!' At these words the Bɵ, chanting magic formulas, put the spell on water. Prince Tolui drank it and, after sitting for a while, pronounced, 'I became drunk at once! Please, look after the orphans and wife Berudy'ye[167] of your little brother, my Khaan. Take care of them until I come to my senses. That is all I wanted to say. I am drunk!' Saying these words he went out. But it transpired thus that his death did not come about.[168]

This passage is very interesting as it clearly demonstrates the causes for the disease which struck Ugedei Khaan, the methods of divination by which they were determined and the cure. It is also interesting because the Bɵ who were called to resolve the problem were not Mongols but Hyadan'. That shows that, although the Hyadan' had been living in China for three hundred years prior to this episode, they still retained their original Bɵ Murgel religion which did not differ from that of the invading Mongols. Both the Hyadan' and Mongols descended from much earlier proto-Mongol nations of the Dunhu and Syanbi who in turn were related to the Hunnu in one way or another, but both the Hyadan' and the Mongols

---

165 Bur. Толуй.

166 Rus. таймень. *Hucho taimen* is a huge river fish which can be as long as 2.7 meters and weigh up to 100 kg. <http://fish-news.teia.org/taim_sig.htm> accessed 10.06.07.

167 Bur. Бэрүдые.

168 Kozin, *Sokrovennoe Skazanie,* §272, pp. 139–140. Translation mine.

underwent further processes of ethnogenesis in different geographic locations. This quotation demonstrates the remarkable continuation of Bө Murgel culture and religion in the Great Steppe among many proto-Mongol, Tyurkyut and later Mongol tribes.

Tibetan ransom rituals

Bönpo *Lüd* ransom rituals are based on the same principle of equal exchange[169] as Buryatian *Dolë* but they are far more complicated with precise specifications regarding the content, quantity and quality of the offerings. The three main types of *Lüd* are applied in particular cases depending on the circumstances, the status of the person to be ransomed, and the type of being responsible for the provocation. All these *Lüd* ransom rites originally belong to the *Chabnag* or Black Water, a general name for the Four Ways of Cause which is also used by higher vehicles of Tantra such as the seventh and eighth Ways (third and fourth Ways of the Fruit). These rites all fall under the three main categories: *Dö*,[170] which are the most elaborate, *Lüd* and *Ye*[171] but the *lüd* ransom itself is the main and most important element in all these rites. Each is further classified into three sub-categories: rites for men, women and children.[172]

Dö

Dö is the most important and complex of the three types of *Lüd*. It is used in cases of severe disturbance such as mortal peril, diseases and provocations of negative energy sent by the Thirty-Three Races of Gods and Spirits. There are 360 main types of *Dö* which include very complex and elaborate rituals as well as simple, short ones. However, the central offering item in all these rites is *dö*, an elaborate construction in the shape of a palace representing the universe and filled with numerous offering items and ransoms including *namkhas* (which can vary greatly in shape and form), *jangbu* and *lüd* effigies.[173]

Lüd

These can also be highly elaborate or much simpler, with various kinds of *Lüd* specially tailored to ransom different ranks of people and

---

[169] Tib. mnyam brje.

[170] Tib. glud.

[171] Tib. yas.

[172] Tib. pho glud, mo glud, chung glud.

[173] For detailed description of a *dö* see Norbu, *Drung, Deu and Bön*, p. 176.

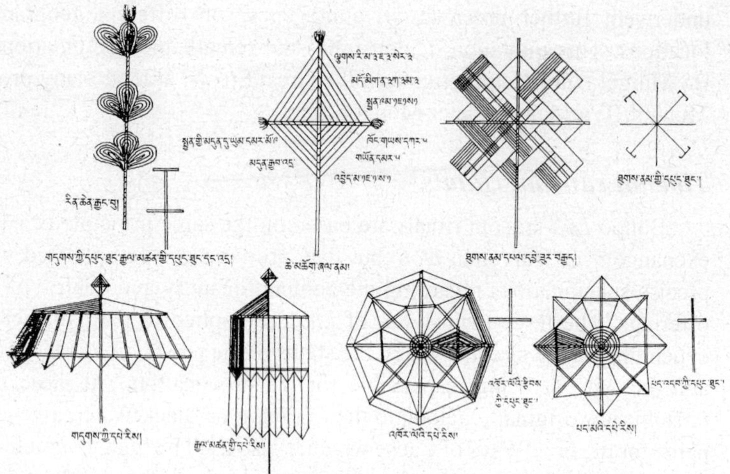

Fig. 11. Namkhas *of various shapes used in* Dö *and other similar rituals.*

animals from the king to the simple subject and domestic animals. *Lüd* counteract negativities sent by beings of the Eight Classes, lesser bad spirits and negative energies.[174] The names of the particular types of *Lüd* in this category reflect the status of the person or animal targeted, so we find *Ransom for the king*,[175] *Ransom for the lama*,[176] *Ransom for the horse*,[177] *Ransom for domestic animals*[178] and so on.

Ye

Ye, the last category of *Lüd* ransom rites, is a payment to the beings to whom a beneficiary of the rite owes karmic debts,[179] as a gift to rid the patient of disturbances created by other people who are jealous or harbouring bad intentions towards the beneficiary; as a fine to avert punishment by the authorities; as pay-off to evil spirits who cause harm, and so on.

One of the main ritual offerings in any of these rites is the *lüd* ransom itself. These, too, vary, depending on the type of ritual and the person for

[174] Tib. 'dre gdon.
[175] Tib. rgyal glud.
[176] Tib. bla glud.
[177] Tib. rta glud.
[178] Tib. phyugs glud.
[179] Tib. lan chags.

whom the ritual is performed. For instance, the *ngarlüd* effigy is a figurine in the shape of a human usually made of *tsampa* dough whereas the *ngarmi* human figurine is made with the addition of precious materials. A very simple effigy is *changbu*, made by squeezing *tsampa* dough in the fist (right for males, left for females) and making an impression of the thumb on the top of it thus leaving five dents which represent the enjoyment objects of the five senses.

Fig. 12. Changbu.

The *ngarlüd* and *ngarmi* are identical in their appearance and function to Buryatian *dolë*. Other types of *lüd* effigy can also be compared with the *dolë* of Bө Murgel, as, among other things, they may be represented by an animal.[180]

Tibetan rituals of human ransom and Hun Dolë

The Tibetan Buddhist *Lüdgong Gyalpo*[181] ritual, Ransom for the Demon-King,[182] bears very close resemblance to Buryatian *Hun Dolë*. Introduced by the Regent Sangye Gyatso[183] in the late seventeenth century, it is based on much earlier rituals. Here, humans were used as living ransom effigies, initially to increase the regent's health and power in the next year, then subsequently to ensure the well-being of the consecutive reincarnations of the Dalai Lama. In the course of this annual ceremony starting on the twenty-ninth day of the second Tibetan month, one or two men called *lüdgong*[184] took on the role of living *ngarlüd* and *kulüd*[185] ransoms. One was sent from Lhasa to Samye in the south in order to appease the *Dharmapala* Pehar while the other was dispatched to Phanpo[186] in the north. The *Lüdgong* were recruited from the low castes and were given money and goods in exchange for taking on this role. According to Samten Karmay, similar Buddhist ceremonies

---

[180] *'...a white lamb is offered in exchange for the spirit (thugs glud)'*, Karmay, *The Arrow and the Spindle*, p. 341.

[181] Tib. glud 'gong rgyal po.

[182] Ibid., p. 365.

[183] Tib. Sangs rgyas rGya mtsho.

[184] Tib. glud 'gong.

[185] Tib. sku glud – 'body ransom' for a person of high social standing.

[186] Tib. 'Phan po.

were performed in Gyalrong[187] and Mongolia prior to the Communist takeover.[188]

A similar, though less elaborate Buddhist ceremony also makes use of a human ransom. Known as *Chilüd*,[189] it is performed for the gravely ill or someone for whom divination predicted untimely death. In this case, a beggar or a man of low caste is found who is willing to act as a living *lüd* and given some payment. Dressed in the patient's clothes, he is seated next to the beneficiary of the rite and a lama performs the ritual to transfer the negative influences from the patient into a dough *lüd* and the living *lüd*. The living *lüd* is then given another effigy resembling the patient and the dough *lüd*. Holding them at his heart level, he leaves the patient's house and walks away in a direction established earlier through astrological calculations. Thus there is a triple ransom: the person dressed as the patient to resemble him or her, the effigy made in their image, and the dough *lüd*. To dispel any lingering negativities, all present at the ritual perform *Dogpa*[190] by clapping their hands. After the ritual the patient must put on new clothes and take a new name. The man who played the role of the living *lüd* can keep the patient's clothes but may never enter his home. This ritual is done in both Gelugpa and Nyingmapa Schools of Tibetan Buddhism.[191]

The existence of similar rituals in Tibet during the pre-Buddhist period is evident from Bönpo myths, but such rituals have nothing to do with Yungdrung Bön and belong squarely to Prehistoric Bön. The Buddhist *Lüdgong Gyalpo* ritual is modelled on those ancient Prehistoric Bön rituals which so closely match *Hun Dolë* of Buryatian Bɵ Murgel.

> The Prince Trishang[192] fell seriously ill. A diviner advised his parents to offer as a ransom for his life his servant who was of the same age, to exchange 'flesh for flesh'.[193] The Prince was against this decision, but his parents were insistent and so a ransom ritual was performed and the servant sacrificed at the hands of the priest. However, the Prince died in the instant the servant was killed. The servant's parents sought revenge; the king and queen committed suicide. The diviner was ashamed of

---

[187] Tib. rGyal rong.

[188] Ibid., p. 359.

[189] Tib. 'chi glud.

[190] Tib. zlog pa.

[191] Nebesky-Wojkowitz, *Oracles and Demons*, pp. 511–514.

[192] Tib. Khri shang.

[193] Tib. sha brjes.

> his advice and the priest repented for having performed the ritual killing. Tonpa Shenrab entered the scene and delivered teachings showing the right way.[194]

This clearly shows that the rituals exchanging life for life are rooted in the ancient Prehistoric Bön traditions which predate Tonpa Shenrab Miwo. These ancient Tibetan *Lüd* rites and the rite of *Hun Dolë* are based on the same principle, are directly comparable and, I would suggest, arose from the same ancient source of Prehistoric Bön. Tonpa Shenrab corrected these macabre practices and introduced rituals where effigies and symbolic figurines substitute the actual living victim. This figurine is made as good as the real person by means of *mantra* recitation and visualization.

Original Yungdrung Bön versions of *Lüd* never use a human or any other living being as a ransom. A clear illustration of the methods to avert death, including *Chilüd* as done in Yungdrung Bön, are found in the text by the Bönpo *Mahasiddha* Lishu Tagring[195] entitled *The Clear Lamp of the Signs of Death*[196] which comes from the *Dzogchen Yangtse Longchen*[197] cycle, the commentary on the *Dzogchen Dragpa Korsum.*[198] The first part of *The Clear Lamp of the Signs of Death* details numerous methods to establish whether one's life is in danger and if so, when one will die. This section is further subdivided into sections dealing with signs for others and signs for oneself. The methods in the second part were intended for *yogis* staying in a place of solitude with no access to either doctors or medicines. This part of the guide is very important for such practitioners; by checking their symptoms against this manual they can clearly determine whether any sickness will be fatal, how long they left to live and whether the sickness can be allayed by the unelaborated *Tö* and *Lüd* rituals described in the second part of the text. Here are a couple of examples of this kind of rituals as they are done in Yungdrung Bön:

> Take some white clay and make a ransom effigy one cubit in height. On a piece of silver birch, draw one cross for each year of your life and put this in the effigy's chest at the heart level. In the early morning, take this

[194] After Karmay, *The Arrow and the Spindle*, p. 370.

[195] Tib. Li shu sTag rings.

[196] Tib. 'Chi rtags gsal ba'i sgron ma.

[197] Tib. rDzogs chen yongs tse klong chen.

[198] Tib. rDzogs chen bsGrags pa skor gsum.

ransom and walk once around your dwelling clockwise and then send it to the east of where you live.[199]
[...] mill twenty different grains into flour and make an effigy. This time, the text doesn't mention the size, so a small one is enough. In the centre of its chest at the heart level, put bits of human, horse and dog bones. Then wrap the effigy up in your old clothes and on the night of the eleventh lunar day, as dusk falls, another person should send this to the south of where you live. They should take one hundred and ten steps in that direction, dig a hole and put the effigy inside. This person should say the name of the person for whom the ritual is being done, and try to make themselves cry [as though the beneficiary had died and were being buried]. They put the effigy there, close the hole and then come back.[200]

[...] make torma and ransom effigies. Mix (the dough) together with some of your hair, saliva etc. and wrap the effigy up (in your old clothes). Make one for each year of your life. Put these effigies together with a small red flag, hedgehog spines and figurines of a human, a horse and a dog and send them all to the roadside.[201]

At the end of the text there are instructions on how to perform a general ritual to avert ill omens, bad dreams, disease and so on:

There are many rituals, and there is one in particular which you can use in many cases, not only if the signs (of approaching death) come and you want to recover. I have told you many different methods and rituals, but they can all be summed up in one general, simple one.[202]

Pray to the Gurus, offer Ganapuja to the *dakinis* and give generous gifts with the body.[203]
Use this as a ransom to buy back from the evil spirits and gods.
Make an effigy with the flour of various grains and paint it with the tears, saliva and sweat of the person for whom the ransom ritual is being

---

[199] *Rainbow Tent Phowa 'Pho ba 'ja gur ma, Volume II: Instructions, Including The Clear Lamp of the Signs of Death, 'Chi rtags gsal ba'i sgron ma, by Lishu Tagring,* Teachings by Yongdzin Lopön Tenzin Namdak Rinpoche, Shenten Dargye Ling, 23–29 September, 2007, Trscr.&ed. Carol and Dmitry Ermakovi, (Blou: Shenten Dargye Ling), p. 41. This text was also translated by Giacomella Orofino, *Sacred Tibetan Teachings on Death and Liberation* (Dorset: Prism, 1990), pp. 85–100.

[200] Namdak, *Rainbow Tent Phowa*, p. 42.

[201] Ibid., p. 44.

[202] Ibid., p. 45.

[203] I.e. practise *Chöd.*

performed. Put some of his hair and fingernails on the effigy and dress it in his old clothes.

Around it, place various types of grains and precious things;[204] a stick with one cross drawn on it for each year of the beneficiary's life; Jangbu, Changbu[205] and Tebchö,[206] one of each for each year of the beneficiary's life.

Then say the verses to bless this ransom with mantras and mudras. Whether you use the extended version or the condensed one depends on whatever is convenient for you. Add the following four verses to the end of the mantra:

Take away, take away, all you powerful ones!
Whoever has desire, attachment and lust,
Whoever thinks eagerly, wants to own and grab –
All of you, take this ransom and be at peace!

Put various feathers on the effigy.

Then take this ransom to a great flowing river and throw it there.

The person for whom the ritual is being performed and the person performing it should remain in contemplation free of thoughts. Keep on in the contemplation of Nature without elaboration and practise the generosity of Chöd.

This is a very important method for reversing any of the signs indicating the approach of death. For example, if it is predicted that a person will die in one month and this ransom ritual is performed, his lifespan can be extended for at least three years. There is no doubt.[207]

---

[204] These don't need to be large jewels; shavings of precious or semi-precious stones will suffice.

[205] This is a simple dough effigy made by taking a lump of dough in the right hand for males, the left for females, and squeezing it with all the fingers of that hand as well as with the thumb of that hand above and the thumb of the other hand below forming five 'mountains' representing the five objects.

[206] These are small dough pieces made by taking a small lump of dough and pressing it between the thumb and forefinger of each hand.

[207] Ibid., pp. 52–53. This and other ransom rituals described in this text as well as the specific signs of death which they are designed to avert (not included here) are mirrored very closely, and in many places are identical, to those found in Buddhist *Bardo Thödrol*'s chapters *Natural Liberation through [Recognition of] the Visual Indications and Signs of Death* (*'Chi ltas mtshan ma rang grol*) and *Natural Liberation of Fear through the Ritual Deception of Death* (*'Chi bslu 'jigs pa rang grol*). (See First Complete Translation, *The Tibetan Book of the Dead* [English Title], The Great Liberation by Hearing in the Intermediate States [Tibetan Title], Composed by Padmasmbhava, revealed by terton Karma Lingpa, Translated by Gyurme Dorje, Edited by Graham Coleman

Such methods are considered very useful not only for practitioners of the Causal Bön but also for those following the Fruitional Ways, and even Dzogchen. In fact, the text containing the rituals described above is part of a Dzogchen cycle. While the primary practice of Dzogchen is concerned with the methods revealing and stabilizing the realization of the Nature of Mind, rituals of this kind, though secondary, can be very helpful nevertheless:

> This chapter is part of Yangtse Longchen, and Yangtse Longchen is a commentary of Dragpa Korsum. Dragpa Korsum is one of our biggest and most important (cycles of) Dzogchen Teachings, so this is a part of that. Generally, if any of these signs come, the best practice is to continuously practise Guru Yoga and the Natural State – that is the best (remedy) for all these signs; it is universal, it can cover any of them. But don't think that these small things are useless; that all depends on the individual. If someone is interested in doing these, they can help and you can recover. If you are an advanced practitioner of Dzogchen, maybe you don't need to do these, but as I said before, in fact these (instructions) are for Dzogchen practitioners as not all practitioners are on the same level. These methods are very important, they come up again and again in Bön and in the Nyingma tradition.[208]

Despite the wide dissemination of Tonpa Shenrab's Yungdrung Bön with its substitute ransoms, the old practices lingered in Tibetan society for centuries. For example, there is a story of how King Trisong Deutsen removed his maternal uncle in order to clear the way for the introduction of Indian Buddhism:

---

with Thubten Jinpa, (London: Penguin Books, 2006), pp. 155–195). Since the Bönpo text *'Chi rtags gsal ba'i sgron ma* quoted here is authored by Lishu Tagring who considerably predates Padmasambhava and was rediscovered by Zhodton Ngödrub Dragpa (Tib. bZhod ston dNgos grub Grags pa) in 1088 while Karma Lingpa, the discoverer of the texts forming the base of Buddhist *Bardo Thödrol* compilation lived in 14 c., it seems reasonably clear that the Bönpo text dealt with here is the original one. This conclusion is reinforced by the fact that rituals in the Buddhist version are more elaborate suggesting that specific Buddhist elements were added at a later date. The question remains open of when and how *'Chi rtags gsal ba'i sgron ma* was incorporated into the Buddhist tradition but it could have been adapted to Buddhism by Guru Padmasambhava himself in the same way as other Bönpo rituals such as *Sang*, *Lungta*, and *Surchö*.

[208] Ibid.

> While Trisong Deutsen was still a small boy, his uncle Mazhang[209] passed a law forbidding the practice of Buddhism. When Trisong Deutsen grew up, he became interested in bringing Indian Buddhism into Tibet but faced opposition from his uncle. The minister Go Trizang,[210] who was in favour of Buddhism, came up with a plan to remove Mazhang and the king, Trisong Deutsen, approved it. Go Trizang then ordered some diviners to disseminate a fake prophesy alleging that Trisong Deutsen would fall ill and face political problems unless a ransom ritual were performed. Alarmed by these ill-omens, the king's two main ministers – his uncle Mazhang and Go Trizang – volunteered to be the *kulüd* body-ransom for him. They were to remain in an underground tomb for a duration of three years[211] to avert the alleged danger to the King. However, as the two ministers were entering the tomb, Go Trizang sneaked out and locked Mazhang in the tomb forever and so he perished.[212]

This episode closely mirrors the Bө Murgel *Hun Dolë* rite performed on behalf of the Mongol Ugedei Khaan described above. Although the way of 'delivering' the ransom differs, the ransom itself is the same, namely, a close relative of the king who volunteers to take the burden. Although the Tibetan story may have been politically manipulated playing on Buddhist/Bönpo sectarian tensions, it is no doubt based on a contemporary ritual, which, because of its similarities to Bө Murgel *Hun Dolë* and bearing in mind Tonpa Shenrab's teachings, clearly belongs to Prehistoric Bön and not Yungdrung Bön. The Buddhist versions of *Lüdgong Gyalpo* and *Chilüd* also reflect traces of this Prehistoric Bön custom; although the low caste men who take on the role of *Lüdgong* are not killed, they are nevertheless used as living ransoms to appease worldly gods in order to ransom the lives of other human beings from a high class, in this case, high Buddhist lamas and government officials. Most of the men who took upon themselves the burden of *Lüdgong* died shortly after completing their journey.[213] This sort of practice clearly goes against the fundamental principles of both Yungdrung Bön and Buddhism. Bearing in mind the strength of Mongol influence on the political and

---

209 Tib. Ma zhang.

210 Tib. sGos Khri bzang.

211 Obviously they would have been provided with food.

212 After Karmay, *The Arrow and the Spindle*, pp. 369–370.

213 Nebesky-Wojkowitz, *Oracles and Demons*, pp. 510–511.

religious aspects of seventeenth-century Tibet and the Gelugpa School in particular (as it was the Mongols who initiated the institution of Dalai Lamas and brought the Gelugpas to power), it is entirely possible that the *Lüdgong Gyalpo* ritual arose not without the influence of the general culture of Mongolian Bɵ Murgel. Although many Mongols converted to Gelugpa Buddhism following the conversion of Altan Khaan, some aspects of Bɵ Murgel can still be clearly recognized in Mongol Gelugpa rituals even today. Since the close and intense interaction of two nations never, or very rarely, results in unilateral influence, it is reasonable to say that there was a cross-pollination of cultural, political and religious ideas and practices. Therefore, based on the analysis of Bɵ Murgel, Bönpo and Buddhist ransom rituals above we can suggest that *Lüdgong Gyalpo* is in fact a conglomerate of all three.

Part V
Exorcism of Negativities connected with Death

Both Buryatian and Tibetan cultures have similar ideas about the negative manifestations which can occur after a person's death. These spirits cause harm and endanger both the afterlife of the deceased themselves as well as the friends and relatives left behind, so Bɵ Murgel, Bön and also Tibetan Buddhism are equipped with rites to exorcise these dangerous entities. The evil spirits which are exorcised are called *Gooideg* in Buryatian and *Shed* in Tibetan. In fact, *Shed* is a general name for many kinds of malevolent spirits and it is *Shished*,[214] *Shidre*[215] and *Zadre*[216] who menace and torture the deceased.

The rite of exorcising Gooideg

The tradition of exorcising *Gooideg* 'runner-spirits' is especially prominent in Tunka, northwestern Buryatia, where the ritual *Gooideg Garguulha* is performed after a death in the family or village, especially if the death was caused by violence or an accident. In Chapter XIII we saw that Buryats of Tunka consider *Gooideg* spirits to be manifestations of the *Mu Hunehen* or 'bad soul' of the deceased. It is said that one dead person

[214] Tib. shi gshed.
[215] Tib. shi 'dre.
[216] Tib. za 'dre.

can manifest multiple *Gooideg* who run in the village and try to murder the relatives, friends or neighbours of the deceased. To some extent, this understanding of *Gooideg* can be compared with the Bönpo concept of *Lhanchig Kyedre*[217] or Innate Demon. This is a part of the deceased's own consciousness which appears to them after death in the guise of evil spirits who chase and torture them. The opposite of Innate Demon is *Lhanchig Kyelha*,[218] Innate God, which protects the deceased from the attacks of negative forces. According to Fruitional Ways of Yungdrung Bön, both the Innate Demon and Innate God are manifestations of one's own mind; which takes the upper hand depends on the person's stock of merits and, for a practitioner, the level of practice. In Prehistoric Bön, however, the evil spirits which torture the dead and endanger the living were perceived as entities independent from the soul of the deceased. Moreover, the understanding of *Gooideg* as being manifestations of the 'bad soul' isn't universal in Bө Murgel; in some traditions it is believed that the 'bad soul' remains in the skeleton after death so *Gooideg* are interpreted as the messengers of Erlig Khaan. It is possible, then, that the Tunka Buryats' interpretation which recognizes them as something internal, might have been influenced by Yungdrung Bön or Buddhism.

In Tunka, *Gooideg Garguulha* is performed as follows:

> On the day someone dies, relatives of the deceased consult a Bө and/or a lama to establish when and from which direction *Gooideg* spirits will appear and when to do the burial. The Bө then performs an exorcism ritual. First he makes a trap for the evil spirit by cutting a figure out of black cloth and adding a red cloth 'tongue'. The figure, which is 10–15cm tall and 5–6 cm wide, symbolizes the *Gooideg* and is fixed on a dry twig stuck into a raw potato or a lump of dough. After that the Bө prepares a *han*,[219] a plate of smouldering embers onto which sweets, clarified butter and *arsa* incense are put to produce smoke. The plate is set on a high place and fulfils two functions: firstly, the smoke rising from the burning food and incense serves as a bridge between Sky and earth; secondly, it is an offering directly parallel to Bönpo *Sur*. After purifying all the objects through fumigation, the Bө begins the ritual. Facing west, he sprinkles with milk, tea and vodka to the Western *Haats*, calling them all

---

[217] Tib. lhan cig skyes 'dre.

[218] Tib. lhan cig skyes lha.

[219] Bur. һан.

by name and starting from the highest ranks. Then he turns to the east and sprinkles to the Eastern *Haats* in the same manner. The *Haats* are requested to send the *Gooideg* to the Underworld realm of Erlig Khaan. The *Gooideg* 'doll' is then placed in the doorway which symbolizes the border between the realms of the dead and the living. The Bɵ walks around the house with the smouldering *han*-plate in one hand and a *hootaga*-knife in the other. Coming to the doorway, he stabs the *Gooideg* figure thrice, throws grain at it thrice and then spits at it thrice. It is then taken out of the house and burned.[220]

The rite of vanquishing the Shed

To protect both living and deceased from attacks by *Shished*, *Shidre*, *Zadre* and general negativities, sufferings and confusion connected with death Tonpa Shenrab Miwo taught the *Dur* funerary rites:

> There are so many rituals and prayers to put both the living and the deceased in the right way. These are called *Dur*. There are 360 types of *Dur* in four main groups and they correspond to the 360 causes of death. So there are many different methods to help both sides.
>
> The practitioner must be skilled in using these methods so as to help both the living and the deceased, and he must take compassion as his basic practice. This is very important for both the family who are alive and for the deceased; it is important for the living so their fortune [*yang*] does not wane, and it is important for the dead so they don't have too much suffering or misery. So it is this practitioner's job to help both parties. How can *Dur* help the deceased? The practitioner can try and purify the obscurations, miseries and sufferings connected with *samsara*.
>
> Such a practitioner and the followers of this [level] believe in *la yi sem sum*. The priest believes in and understands these, so he helps and purifies according to this understanding [...] There are several methods connected with these three. Originally this comes from *Sidshen Thegpa* but it is also used in High Tantra.[221]

---

[220] According to the description given by T. A. Zabrueva, P. E. Marnuev city of Ulaan-Ude East Siberian State Academy of Culture and Art.

[221] Excerpt from the translation and commentary by Yongdzin Lopön Tenzin Namdak on the Bönpo Dzogchen cycle of *gSas mkhar g.yung drung ye khyabs lta ba'i rgyud ces bya ba bzhugs so*, Chapter VII. Triten Norbutse Monastery, Kathmandu, 27.01.08.

The Bönpo ritual of *Shedur*, the rite of Vanquishing the *Shed*, is one of the many *Dur* funerary rituals belonging to *Sidshen Thegpa*, the Fourth Causal Vehicle of Yungdrung Bön. It was introduced to Tibet in the seventh century BC[222] to deal with the consequences of the death of King Drigum Tsenpo and has many parallels with *Gooideg Garguulha*. Here is a condensed summary of the ritual:

> The initial stage consists of preparing the ritual implements such as offering *torma* and a *drubkhung*[223] wrathful triangular receptacle used for destructive rites. A fireplace is prepared on a black base and a pan set on it. A triangle is drawn with blood inside the pan and three swords are placed there, blades upwards. Ritual weapons and implements used for this rite include knife, rope, sack, sickle, bow, axe, foreleg of a sheep, tail of a black yak, mustard seeds. Seven or twenty-one white pebbles, twenty-one black pebbles and a *phurba*-dagger are arranged. A *linga*-effigy representing *Shed* is then drawn in light blue, the head of which depends on the deceased's status, sex, age and the circumstances of their death and is that of a particular animal or bird. *Mantras* with the power to summon the actual *Shed* into this effigy are put on and around the drawing. It is then passed over fire and shaken in the air to purify it, then tied up with coloured threads. Other ritual objects needed for the rite include nine *jyangbu*[224] which in this case are made in the form of wooden tablets inscribed with *mantras* similar to those written on the *linga*. The deceased's name and a seed-syllable representing his/her life-force is drawn on card and some other small effigies are made out of dough.
>
> The rite begins by the practitioner assuming the form of a Wrathful Buddha[225] and invoking the guardians of the teachings. They then narrate a description of the ritual objects and the *linga*-effigy after which the *linga*, tablets and pebbles are put into the sack which is tied with a knot. An assistant then takes the sack in his right hand, the sickle in his left, and, with the thong wrapped around his left elbow and the axe over his left shoulder, he walks in an easterly direction and then beats the sack on the ground.

---

[222] According to traditional Bönpo chronology of Khenpo Nyima Tenzin.

[223] Tib. 'brub khung.

[224] Tib. byang bu, different from *jangbu* and *changbu*.

[225] The principal *yidam* of *Sidshen Thegpa* is Durse Mawo (Tib. 'Dur gsas rMa bo) but the rite presented here is based on another *yidam*.

At the same time the practitioner visualizes that messengers of the wrathful *yidam* into which he has transformed are helping to corner the *Shed* into the sack.

The assistant returns, opens the sack and pours out its contents inside the triangle formed by the swords. How the tablets land shows whether the *Shed* was caught or not. Tablets that fell correctly are put into the *drubkhung* but those which did not land correctly are put back into the sack together with the *linga* drawing and dough *lingas*. The assistant then goes out in the other three directions one by one and beats the sack to make the *Shed* enter. At the end of each trip the same procedure is repeated. If all the tablets have still not fallen in the right way then the sack is beaten in and around the house until it is established that the *Shed* has been caught.

The *Shed's* escape route is then blocked; holding ritual weapons, the men present surround the pan make striking gestures while the practitioner reads the text which closes exits in all directions.

Once the *Shed* has been captured it is liberated through killing.[226] The practitioner takes the knife and the sickle and the men take other weapons. The practitioner's visualization at this stage is determined by the cause of death. For example, if the person was murdered then he visualizes a rain of swords falling on the *Shed*. The men then place the weapons on the *drubkhung* and the practitioner stabs the *linga*-effigy with his *phurba*. The chopped up *linga* is displayed in the four directions and its limbs are offered to the wrathful deities. The mind of the *Shed* is simultaneously transferred and liberated into the dimension of the *yidam*-deity.[227]

The success of the ritual is determined through dreams. As a result of this ritual the *la* of the deceased is liberated from the *Shed's* captivity and unified with its *yid* and *sem* so that it can enter the *Bardo* and proceed on the way to the next rebirth. Yongdzin Lopön Tenzin Namdak likened this kind of ritual to saving a lost sheep from wolves and returning it into the pen. Once this ritual has been successfully accomplished, other practices for helping the deceased attain liberation or a better rebirth can be performed. This ritual not only helps the deceased but also the living who are freed from attacks by the *Shed* who often assume the guise of the

---

226 Tib. bsgral.

227 This presentation is based on Norbu, *Drung, Deu and Bön*, pp. 97–102.

dead relative or friend and come in dreams or visions to torture, deceive or try to kill those connected to the deceased.

Conclusion

Although *Shedur* is much more elaborate than *Gooideg Garguulha*, it is based on the same basic idea and employs similar techniques and ritual implements. In both cases protective deities are invoked to help capture the evil spirit(s) and force it into the effigy and how this is done using similar methods: the Bɵ walks around the house scaring the *Gooideg* into the effigy while in the Bönpo version the bag is beaten all around the house to suck the *Shed* into it. In both traditions, the effigy is then destroyed with a knife or *phurba.* While Bönpo use destructive *mantras*, Bɵ simply spit at the effigy. The main difference between these two rites is ideological as the Bönpo version is designed to bring benefit to all three parties: the dead, the living and the bad spirit(s). Although the *Shed* is killed at the end, this is no ordinary killing. What is destroyed is the wicked and malevolent nature of the spirit which drives it to torture others and suffer itself. Its 'consciousness principle' is not killed. Rather, the mind of this evil spirit is transferred and liberated into the dimension of the Buddha, i.e. into its own Natural State. *Gooideg Garguulha*, on the other hand, is primarily concerned with the well-being of the living. Here the *Gooideg* spirit is killed and transferred into the Underworld, hardly liberation from suffering. In the Bɵ Murgel version, then, there is only one party which benefits from this ritual – the living.

Despite these fundamental differences in view, both rituals no doubt arose from the culture of Prehistoric Bön with *Gooideg Garguulha* actually being one of the rites of Prehistoric Bön still practised today. Similar rituals of Prehistoric Bön were reshaped and given a new ideological base by Tonpa Shenrab Miwo when he was teaching his doctrine of Yungdrung Bön in the cultural environment of Prehistoric Bön. He took existing rituals of this kind and adjusted them in such a way that they became skilful means to bring benefit to countless sentient beings, good and evil, living and dead. Later, Guru Padmasambhava, seeing the great benefit of these methods and being non-sectarian, introduced them into his Buddhist tradition. Other Buddhist masters followed suite and so the *Dur* rites are now found among the rituals of all Schools of Tibetan Buddhism.

Part VI
Destructive Magic

Here we will look into the applications of magic in Buryatia and Tibet, in particular the techniques of destructive magic along with methods for countering magical assault, and compare them in order to see whether the ideas and methods used have a common background.

Magic powers of the Bɵ and Bönpo

Bɵ and Utgan come to possess magical powers which are demonstrated to inspire faith, heal, repel black magic, subjugate enemies, destroy black magicians and bring peace and harmony. These powers were much stronger in the past and have been diminishing in recent times due to the general characteristics of this time cycle when spirituality is in decline and materialism is on the rise. In the past Bɵ and Utgan could pierce their body with a scythe, sword or a knife and continue performing a ritual as if nothing had happened; they could cut their head off, put it on a tree stump or somewhere else and still continue doing household chores or even go to do some tasks in the *taiga*. While riding a horse, some Bɵ would cut their head off, put it behind them on the saddle as if it were a passenger and then put it back in place. Other great Black Bɵ and Utgan would slit open their belly, take out the intestines and wave them around. Then they would push the intestines back in place, and, stroking the cut with their thumb, would recite a spell after which the cut completely disappeared leaving no scar. Other powerful Bɵ and Utgan could slice each other in two halves from head to groin with a sword. Each half of the body would jump around on one leg and then reunite as if nothing had happened. Some Bɵ and Utgan could grow frightening fangs, others could transform into and ride wild animals and birds. Others were able to ride or fly in the air in a cart without horses or any other beast of burden. Some could make a bridge of ice on a river or lake in summertime, they could not be poisoned, drowned or burned in fire, or they could control weather. When some Bɵ wanted to drink *tarasoon* milk vodka or any other alcohol, and none was available, they would stick their knife into a tree or a wall, take it out and alcohol would gush from the ensuing slit. Bɵ and Utgan of the past had strong clairvoyance, clairaudience and telekinetic abilities. Even just before the 1917 Revolution their magic powers were still very strong.[228] Here is a story told by Duuriskha Utgan Vera Naguslaeva:

> Vera Naguslaeva told a story about her grandmother, who is also Doogar Ochirov's grandmother, and was a very powerful Utgan. She was born in this place. Vera Naguslaeva and Doogar Ochirov are from the Galzuud clan of Bɵ-smiths. Their clan is 'in the law', in other words, they have the right to use silver fir bark for purification during rituals and are under the protection of special guardians. They also have a special connection with fire energy. During *tailgan*, their grandmother would fly in the air, and once she even flew to the top of a pine tree. It wasn't such a long time ago, at the beginning of the twentieth century. Vera told us how, when her grandmother was young, she used to like to dance the *yohar*,[229] a traditional Buryatian dance with a strong circular movement. Her grandmother always used to go at night to dance the *yohar*, right at the very place where our car had broken down. She used to take her friend with her and they would dance around the fire all night and leave before dawn. A lot of people took part. One night they stayed longer than usual. The first rays of sunlight appeared and grandmother's friend saw with horror that they were dancing the *yohar* with skeletons! She fell down in a faint and nearly died of fear. Grandmother brought her round, but never took her dancing again.
> Barguzin, on the way to the Bɵ cemetery in Shiizga, 14.06.94[230]

Such powers of Bɵ and Utgan as flying in the sky and riding a cart without horses are probably the result of employing spirits as a coach although they may arise from another type of technique as not all the Bɵ and Utgan's psychic powers can be explained just by the fact of harnessing protective deities or spirits. Such feats as sitting in the centre of fire without being burnt even slightly or remaining under water for many hours are surely signs of command over the elements and point to a different system of psychosomatic training similar to the techniques of *Qi-gong* or various types of *yoga.* The Bɵ and Utgan use a vast array of personalized visualization and mind-control techniques.

Prehistoric Bönpo of Zhang Zhung and Tibet possessed similar powers but there are no 'pure' traditions of Prehistoric Bön left in Tibet itself as the traditions of *lhapa* and *pawo* who were practising Prehistoric Bön mixed with Yungdrung Bön and then Buddhism, and their magical

---

[228] This is based on the oral communications from Bɵ and Utgan I met and Hangalov, *Sobranie* II, pp. 179–182.

[229] Bur. ёхар.

[230] Passage from my unpublished diary *Tailgan Trip*, 1994.

Fig. 13. Dhami *licks the red-hot metal strip.*

powers also diminished. Several traditions pertaining to Prehistoric Bön are still practised by the Himalayan tribes in Nepal, Bhutan and the Arunachal Pradesh state of India. *Dhami* priest of Humla district in Nepal, for example, demonstrate the depth of their trance-state by licking red-hot iron before the oracular or healing séance.

Early masters of Yungdrung Bön also had miraculous abilities, the signs of their realization. Some of by the realized *Shenpos* from the Tantric lineage of Chyipung[231] manifested many signs. For example, Mushen Nangwai Dogchen was venerated by the gods and demons who offered him food. He caused flowers to fall like rain from the sky. The Tibetan Bönpo King Mutri Tsenpo manifested many miraculous abilities such as flying in the sky, sitting on the surface of water, spitting fire, transforming into a dragon, an eagle or a lion and roaming in space. Hara Chipar[232] of Mon[233] made demons serve him, could make rivers flow upstream, rode on wild animals, and could make his adversaries roll on the ground just by fixing his gaze on them. His consort Tagver Liver[234] overpowered *Lu* water-spirits, *Sadag* earth-spirits and *Tod* rock-spirits; she could transform into anything and lived for 360 years after which she disappeared without leaving physical remains behind. Sene Gawu[235] could cure leprosy, turn away armies and floods, and emit flames from his body. Temi Teke[236] made armies of the four countries numbering 16,000 warriors faint when they tried to arrest him. He threw his hat into the air which became an eagle and chased away the enemies. He extinguished raging flames with his spittle. He

---

[231] Tib. sPye spungs rgyud.

[232] Tib. Ha ra Ci par.

[233] Tib. Mon, the old name for Bhutan.

[234] Tib. sTag ver Li ver.

[235] Tib. Sad ne Ga'u.

[236] Tib. Thad mi Thad ke

lived 277 years and at the end of his life he disappeared into the sky riding a turquoise dragon.[237]

There are countless Yungdrung Bön *yogis* who manifested similar incredible signs of realization.

Although some of the powers of Bө and *Shenpo*s show external similarities, their source is completely different. The magical powers of the Bө and Utgan come from the Tengeri and *Ongon*-spirits while *Shenpos* draw their powers from the inner realization of their own Buddha-nature. A realized Bönpo *yogi* can control both gods and spirits and can even make the most powerful worldly gods serve them as illustrated by the example of Gyerpung Nangzher Lödpo who subdued powerful gods Nyipangse and Menmo.[238] They are never under the dominion of any gods or spirits. However, this cannot be said of the Bө and Utgan. While they can control very powerful spirits, both beneficial and malevolent, they cannot and would not dream of even trying to command sky-dwelling Tengeri to whom they are always subordinate. Therefore, the scope of their magic powers always lies within the worldly sphere and is never superior to that of the high gods.

Magic combat: black magic assault and countermeasures

Magic powers can be used to bring benefit or to cause harm so in both Bө Murgel and Bön there are many techniques which protect from curses or destructive magic, and allay negative influences and the black sorcerers who send them. Often the same technique can be used to either harm or protect, just as conventional weapons can be used in defensive or offensive ways.

Magical action targeting soul-receptacles

To illustrate the practical applications of offensive and defensive magic related to the external receptacles of *hunehen*, let's look at two Buryatian stories:

> It so happened that a wealthy man fell gravely ill and called for the Black Bө Hahool to perform the rituals which would cure him. However, unbeknown to the householder, one of the rich man's neighbours was secretly eavesdropping and learned that

[237] Based on Karmay, *The Treasury*, pp. 44–47.

[238] See ch. XII.

they had decided to steal his *hunehen*-soul and exchange it for that of the rich man as *Hun Dolë*. No sooner had he heard this than he swiftly set off to the *taiga* and did the *Doohahoo* rite – he felled a small pine tree saying: 'I am felling the Bө Hahool.' Then he took the tree with him and went home where he poured some water into a wooden tub and started to whirl the water in it with the top of that pine tree saying: 'I am whirling the water with the Bө Hahool. May his head spin so that he forgets his *utkha*-origin, grows bewildered and mad.' In this manner he was whirling the water in the tub till the dawn of the next day. That night the Bө Hahool was performing the *Hun Dolë* rite to steal that neighbour's *hunehen*-soul and give it in exchange for the soul of the rich man. But the Bө's head was spinning and he couldn't do anything. His Black *Zayaan* deities wouldn't come no matter how much he invoked them. The next morning the Bө Hahool went home and died soon after. His rich patient also died.[239]

A very long time ago there was an orphan. He was brought up by three powerful lamas who taught him the secrets of a lama's knowledge. But as time went by, one of those lamas grew jealous of the orphan's achievements. Consumed by envy he performed a magic ritual against the orphan and the older lama, the orphan's principal teacher. However, signs appeared to the older lama so he discovered about his jealous colleague's evil deed. He instructed the orphan to go to the Sea of Baikal and find on its shore three birch trees growing together. The lama-teacher told his pupil to break the middle birch and bring it to him. These three birches contained the *hunehen*-souls of the three lamas and the middle one was the receptacle for the *hunehen* of the jealous one. The orphan did as his master bid him and brought him the broken birch. Taking it, the old lama started reciting the text of a ritual and *mantras* and by this means he slayed the renegade lama.[240]

These two stories from Bө Murgel and Buddhist backgrounds respectively both show the technique of averting an evil-doer's black magic and destruction by acting directly on the *hunehen*-receptacle, which in these cases is a tree. While in the first story a neighbour has taken just

---

239 Hangalov, *Sobranie* II, pp. 208–209.

240 Ibid.

any pine and invoked the Black Bө's *hunehen* into it, in the second the birch was known to be the receptacle. The difference in the species of tree used as a support is of no significance. From these examples we can clearly see how knowledge of the principle of the *hunehen*-receptacle was used here as defensive magic by the followers of Bө Murgel and Buryatian Buddhism alike. If used with mal intent and under different circumstances, the same techniques would qualify as black magic.

We find a similar mechanism behind some forms of destructive magic in Tibetan Bön and Tibetan Buddhism. A clear example of this sort of magic is the historical episode of the seventh-eighth centuries AD, narrated in Chapter I, when the Zhang Zhung Bönpo *Mahasiddha* Gyerpung Nangzher Lödpo hurled magic 'missiles' from Zhang Zhung into Tibet to subjugate the Tibetan King Trisong Deutsen and put a stop to the Tibetan government's policy of persecution and destruction towards Yungdrung Bön. Let us closely examine the targets of this magic 'missile' attack. The first missile was thrown into Tibet at sunrise and hit the lake at the foot of the Yarlha Shampo mountain, the residence of the Tibetan King's eponymous *Yullha* protective deity. The lake dried up and the *Lu* water-spirits, who controlled the prosperity of Tibetan kingdom, fled. As the lake and Yarlha Shampo mountain itself were the *la*-lake and *la*-mountain of King Trisong Deutsen and his royal clan,[241] the missile in fact hit the very heart of the external energy-system supporting the king personally and the Tibetan kingdom in general. The second missile arrived at midnight. It killed and paralyzed several deer – *la*-animals of the king – on the slope of mount Sogkha Phungpo. The third missile arrived early the next morning and hit the ancient royal castle, Chingwai Thagse, which burst into flames. The castle probably contained some sort of support for the ancestral cult so it, too, was a direct hit and Trisong Deutsen became terminally ill.

Another example of this sort of magic is found in one of the episodes from the *Gesar* epic where Gesar is fighting against the king of Satham.[242] Gesar had to kill the seven white bears which were the seats of the king's *la*, and only then could he defeat his opponent. On another occasion when Gesar was fighting against the kingdoms of Horser, Horkar and Hornag[243] we find mention of the *la*-fish[244] which was a *la*-receptacle for these three countries.[245]

---

[241] Reynolds, *The Oral Tradition from Zhang Zhung*, Notes, p. 477.

[242] Tib. Sa tham.

[243] Tib. hor ser, hor dkar, hor nag.

[244] Tib. bla nya.

[245] Nebesky-Wojkowitz, *Oracles and Demons*, p. 482.

From these episodes we can see the importance given by both Buryats and Tibetans to capturing or destroying an adversary's soul-receptacle. This was an indispensable action if one wanted to dominate or destroy one's enemies.

Offensive and counter magic in Buryatia

The following passage from my 1994 diary illustrates one of the techniques the black sorcerers, in this case a black witch, can use to spoil *tailgan* or other activities the Bө and Utgan carry out for the benefit of the community:

> I started to feel sick, and climbed a slope on the other side of the path. Soon Vera Naguslaeva joined me. We decided not to go down, but to watch the ritual from above. Everything went as usual, except that no signs appeared. We were sure that the Bө of Tunka had carried out their ritual on time because a large cloud in the shape of a bull's head appeared from that direction.[246] After a while, we noticed something unpleasant. The young woman who had been talking to Bө Doogar Ochirov before the ritual was walking behind the crowd of praying people. She stopped, lifted her skirt above her knees and shook it. That is what black witches do to send a curse. What's more, she hadn't covered her head – another bad omen. The people praying couldn't see her, but to us, she was clearly visible. We understood that we had been deliberately guided to our seat in order to see and neutralise her action. The ritual ended, still without any signs. We climbed down and told Doogar Ochirov about the woman and that we should leave that place immediately. When we were in the bus, the woman came and asked Vera to heal her again. Vera told her that we had seen everything, and she wasn't going to heal her any more. You should have seen the look with which she answered those words! She was from a family of black magicians, as one of the local old women told us later.
>
> Near the village of Bayangol, Barguzin,19.06.94.[247]

In Tibet we find a technique of black witchcraft used by the women which closely mirrors the one described above. It is called *Bume Mözor*,[248]

---

246 They were performing an offering ritual to Buha Noyon who appears as a huge bull so the appearance of the cloud shaped as a bull-head from the direction of Tunka was interpreted as the sign that their ritual was successful.

247 A passage from my unpublished diary, *Tailgan Trip*.

248 Tib. bud med dmod zor. Nebesky-Wojkowitz, *Oracles and Demons*, p. 356, 483.

'the cursing *zor*[249] of women'. The women caste a curse while shaking their apron, the hem of their dress or their hair. When pronouncing curses, lamas shake their hat in the air.[250] This suggests a common theme which most probably has its roots in Prehistoric Bön.

Black Bɵ and Utgan of the second type present a real danger to other types of Bɵ and ordinary people. They have many techniques of offensive black magic, one of the grimmest being 'soul-eating'. For this they use two principal methods which have many variations. For example, a Black Bɵ or Utgan of the second type makes a *hor 'bo*-stick and smears one half of it with coal or blood. They also paint the left side of their face black. Then, upturning a cooking pan inside their *gher* dwelling, the Black Bɵ invokes the Black Tengeri and Black *Zayaans* asking them to attack the victim's family and 'eat' his soul and those of his wife and children, or harm them in another way.[251]

Another method employed by Black Bɵ and Utgan of the second type is to attack and 'eat' the victims' souls themselves. In this case the Black Bɵ enters the trance state of the 'flight of the soul' at night. His soul then flies in the astral plane in search of the souls of the victims which are wandering in the dream state. When the soul of Black Bɵ sees the souls he wants to 'eat', he pounces on them as a falcon attacks a pigeon. His soul then devours the souls of his victims and flies away. When the victims wake up they feel unwell and soon die. The Black Bɵ absorbs the *amin* life-force and *hunehen* souls of the victims into his own becoming evermore powerful.

Other techniques of black magic used by the Black Bɵ and Utgan include various kinds of visualizations and sympathetic magic. One such method is to visualize the victim clearly and then shoot that target with an arrow and so the person dies. This technique is directly parallel to the *Dazor*[252] or 'arrow *zor*' used in *phurba* rites. To do *Dazor* one prepares an arrow from poisonous wood with a tip resembling a *phurba*-dagger. The tip of the arrow is then dipped into a mixture of blood, *gugul*[253] incense and fat. This arrow and a bow are placed in front of a *torma* and at the end of the ritual the arrow is shot in the direction of the enemy while destructive *mantras* are recited.[254] This technique, no doubt, has its origins in Prehistoric Bön.

---

[249] Tib. zor; magical weapon, receptacle of destructive magic.

[250] Ibid., p. 483.

[251] Hangalov, *Sobranie* I, p. 373.

[252] Tib. mda' zor.

[253] Tib. gu gul.

[254] Nebesky-Wojkowitz, *Oracles and Demons*, p. 355.

In the Hubsuguul[255] region of Mongolia if someone wants to curse a Bɵ they visit Mount Ulaan Uul[256] which is sacred to all Mongol Bɵ. There they performs a ritual worshipping the *Ezhen*-Owner of the mountain, bathe in a particular red spring there and then recite a curse.[257]

Another very dangerous technique is called *zya.*[258] It can be used by various types of Bɵ and Utgan for a variety of reasons and shall be dealt with separately below.

As was said in Chapter VIII, *Elbeshen* black sorcerers and Black Bɵ and Utgan of the second type have their own lineages and traditions. Some of these traditions are written down in special books and in some cases blood is added to the ink. Blood, sometimes human blood, is also used as an ink for certain destructive spells and rituals. It is interesting to note that in many Tibetan rituals of destructive magic both Bönpo and Buddhist, different types of blood are also used as ink for writing destructive spells.[259] This suggests that the use of destructive spells written in blood originated in some streams of Prehistoric Bön of Eurasia as similar techniques are found in some so-called 'pagan' traditions of Europe as well.

White Bɵ and Utgan and Black Bɵ and Utgan of the first type have many methods for neutralizing and destroying the Black Bɵ and Utgan of the second type and *Elbeshen* black sorcerers. They can be destroyed in a magical fight or a Bɵ can send his protective deities and spirits to destroy a sorcerer. One technique used in the past to protect a Bɵ and their clan from physical or magic attack was very simple. The Bɵ would prick his ring finger and sprinkle some drops of his own blood in the direction of the enemy while invoking Eastern Yuhen Shuhan Tengeriin[260] (Nine Bloody Tengeri), whose function is to destroy all living things, and asking them to kill the enemy.[261] Other methods are based on sympathetic magic. To give an example, one technique was for a Bɵ or Utgan to obtain a piece of a black sorcerer's clothing and burn it at midnight on the full moon with an appropriate spell and ritual.

---

[255] Bur. Хүбсүгүүл аймаг.

[256] Bur. Улаан уул.

[257] From the field-notes of D.B. Doogarov.

[258] Bur. зя.

[259] Nebesky-Wojkowitz, *Oracles and Demons*, pp. 483–509.

[260] Bur. Юhэн шуhан тэнгэриин. № 3–11 Among the Eastern Black Tengeri.

[261] Bazarov, *Tainstva*, pp. 119–120.

Destructive magic of Bө-smiths

Bө-smiths have special magical abilities so their destructive magic, especially that of Black Bө-smiths, is the most powerful among all the Bө. A Black Bө-smith had several related methods at his disposal to destroy an enemy. For example, saying, 'Die, shrivel!', he would tie a red-hot iron rod symbolizing his enemy's life-force into an iron knot, after which the victim would die; there is no remedy. Or if someone should steal something from the Bө-smith he would make an iron figurine, made it red-hot in the smithy and then beat it with the hammer breaking its hands and legs off. After this the thief would ail and finally die.[262]

If a violent argument should break out between a Bө and a Bө-smith, the latter would most likely win:

> Black Bө-smith Horshigoldo[263] and Bө Hende[264] had an argument which ended in a fight. On coming home the Bө-smith invoked the Black *Zayaans*. Then he set about making a human figure from the bark which he dressed. He also made a horse figure from bark, fashioned a bridle and saddle for it and saddled it. Setting the human effigy on the horse effigy, he performed the *Amilha*[265] enlivening ritual to invoke Bө Hende's *amin* life-force and soul into it. Thus the human figure became Bө Hende riding the horse figurine representing his *hii moriin*, the Wind Horse energy of life and good luck. The Bө-smith then took the figurines to his smithy. Stoking the fire in the forge, he once again invoked his Black *Zayaans*, and, standing the human and horse effigy on the anvil, crushed them with his hammer and threw them away. After that Bө Hende died.[266]

Bө-smiths use the same methods to destroy an evil spirit or a curse and may sometimes simply use a red-hot iron rod in place of the figurine.

Tantric rites of destruction in Yungdrung Bön and Buddhism include similar methods of smashing an enemy or malign spirit with a hammer. It is likely they represent transformed techniques of Prehistoric Bön.

---

[262] Galdanova, *Dolamaistkie*, p. 90.

[263] Bur. Хоршиголдо.

[264] Bur. Хэндэ.

[265] Bur. Амилха.

[266] Based on Hangalov, *Sobranie* II, pp. 130–131.

Magical combat in the form of animals

Buryatian Bө sometimes use their magical abilities not only for fighting black sorcerers but also to fight between themselves for command of territory, to show off their magical powers or when their jealousy is aroused. In the past, animals such as bears or wild bulls were often used for these combats. The Bө would either transform into the animal themselves or would send magical apparitions in the form of wild animals or monsters. In both cases, the outcome of such a duel was that the Bө who lost fell seriously ill or died.

Similar competitions also took place earlier in Tibet. For example, it is said that a fourteenth-century Bönpo lama, Shen Nyima Gyaltsen,[267] founder of Triten Norbutse Bönpo monastery in Tsang, was challenged by Nyingmapa Rongdzö Ngagpa.[268] Using magic, Rongdzö Ngagpa emanated a horse, making it gallop in the fields. In response, Shen Nyima Gyaltsen emanated a magical yak which attacked the horse and killed it. In fact, nobody was killed as these animals were the masters' magic creations, not real living beings.[269]

Another analogous magic technique is found in Tibet is the *Sumpa Langzor*,[270] 'the bull-*zor* of the Sumpa country'. It consists of modelling a bull figurine from dough, charging it with magic and then sending it to kill the adversary. Strong magicians could make the effigy actually transform into a wild bull. This technique is said to have been brought to Tibet from the Sumpa country.[271] As was already said in Chapter I, Sumpa corresponds to the Sumbe Empire, also known as Syanbi Khaganate, a nomadic state of proto-Mongol peoples which bordered the Zhang Zhung Confederation and to whom later Buryats are related through culture, religion and genetics. So *Sumpa Langzor* must be one of the techniques of Bө Murgel imported to Tibet from Sumbe.

The technique of transforming into an animal or an insect in order to injure or kill the opponent is found also among sorcerers in Nepal:

> Fleeing the Chinese crackdown following the 1959 Tibetan Uprising, a group of Tibetan refugees crossed into Nepal. Among

---

[267] Tib. gShen Nyi ma rGyal mthsan.

[268] Tib. Rong dzo sNgags pa.

[269] Narrated by Yongdzin Lopön Tendzin Namdak, Shenten Dargye Ling, France, 2006.

[270] Tib. Sum pa glang zor.

[271] Tibetans also believe that yaks and bulls were introduced from Sumpa. Ibid. p. 358.

them was a Bönpo master and practitioner of Walchen Gekhöd, Amchi Sherab.[272] They came across a vegetable field and, being very hungry after their long trek, stopped to pick a small handful to eat. Some locals who were passing warned them that the field belonged to a black witch with renowned magical powers. Undaunted, Amchi Sherab went ahead, saying he was not afraid of black magic. However, some time later while he was eating with many people in the village, a large bee appeared and started flying around aggressively, closing in on him. The locals he was with agitatedly shouted, 'It's the witch! Watch out!' But Amchi Sherab took some mustard seeds from his pocket, blew the Gekhöd *mantra* on them and hurled them at the bee, which at once disappeared. The next morning the villagers saw the witch hobbling around with a large black eye.[273]

Bө – Buddhist rivalry

It is not only black sorcerers and Bө who use destructive magic in Buryatia; there is also a Buddhist version, a kind of 'lama's curse' performed by Gelugpa lamas seeking to destroy a Bө or Utgan and wipe out their lineage. The Buryats call it *Zhaadkha*,[274] the Buryatian pronunciation of the Tibetan word *byad kha* (pronounced *cheka*). This type of curse relies on the power of destructive *mantra* which unleashes the power of non-human beings against the victim-target. The effects of such a rite persist for a long time and may strike several generations[275] and the mechanism seems to be almost identical to black sorcerers' techniques as it uses non-human beings as a vehicle to deliver the magical blow. The principle behind the *Cheka* rites most probably comes from Prehistoric Bön. It was adapted to certain destructive rituals of Bönpo Tantra by Tonpa Shenrab where, based on compassion, it is used to suppress and destroy evil-doers in order to forcefully liberate them from their wretched existence and deliver them to the realization of Buddha-nature. Later on these techniques were incorporated into Tibetan Buddhist Tantra. In essence, then, the Buryatian *Zhaadkha* 'lama's curse' which Buddhists use against Bө is, ironically, based on the techniques of Prehistoric Bön of which Bө Murgel is a branch. Although *Cheka* magic

---

272 Tib. Em chi Shes rab.

273 Narrated by Yongdzin Lopön Tendzin Namdak, Triten Norbutse Bönpo Monastery, Kathmandu, 1996.

274 Bur. жаадха.

275 Norbu, *Drung, Deu and Bön*, p. 125.

is very severe, Yungdrung Bön has a series of rites for averting it. These are known as *Chedrol*[276] and if performed correctly by an experienced lama, can completely annul the effects of a *Cheka* curse so the victim is freed from its harmful influence. I haven't met anyone in Buryatia who could explain the exact mechanism of the local version, *Zhaadkha*, so I can only speculate that it might be some kind of Tantric rite of destruction tied to Yamantaka[277] practice or a kind of *puja* ritual which directs the wrath of the *Dharmapalas* onto a particular Bɵ or Utgan.

In some areas of Buryatia there are strong tensions between Gelugpa lamas and the Bɵ. When Gelugpa Buddhism arrived in Buryatia it naturally met with resistance from the Bɵ and the people, so Gelugpa lamas put considerable effort into converting Buryats to Buddhism[278] but they were only partially successful. Even now, more than three hundred years later, large areas of Buryatia adhere to Bɵ Murgel alone while in others people happily go to both the lamas and the Bɵ depending on their needs and who has more magical power in that particular area. This situation leads to competition, jealousy and fighting, both magical and even physical. The main outward point of friction seems to focus around the debate on the practice of animal sacrifices. However, it is more complicated than that; there are other powerful political and doctrinal reasons behind this centuries-old conflict. People who live in areas where both Bɵ Murgel and Lamaism are maintaining a sturdy presence sometimes become victims to their attempts to comply with both competing parties simultaneously out of fear of magic reprisal:

When we arrived there first time, Bɵ Doogar Ochirov took me to the house of the one-eyed child's brother, who told me this sad story:

---

[276] Tib. byad 'grol.

[277] Sans. Yamantaka – Destroyer of Yama (Yama is god of death) or Terminator of Death, the main *yidam* of the Gelugpa School in Buryatia.

[278] Aided by the Russian government of *tsaritsa* Catherine the Great which recognized Buddhism as one of the legitimate religions of the Russian Empire. For this reason Buddhist lamas of Buryatia maintain that Catherine was an emanation of White Tara, which certainly did not fit her profile. She was moved, however, rather by political considerations – it is much easier to control a nation which is in turn controlled by an established religious-political institution such as the Lamaist church. Bɵ Murgel, on other hand, was decentralized and also connected with the nationalist sentiment and resistance.

Fig. 11. Brother of the one-eyed child.

At the beginning of the twentieth century, a child with only one eye in the centre of its forehead was born to a family in Kurumkan.[279] The parents were very frightened and didn't know what to do. The father went to a lama for advice. The lama said the boy was an incarnation of the demon and to throw him out of the house into the frost. It was winter and extremely cold. The father returned home even more afraid than ever, and did as the lama had said. Three days passed, but still the child's cries could be heard from the backyard. The father, caught between strong parental feelings and the fear instilled in him by the lama, went again to the Buddhist *datsan*. The lama said it was a demonic child and should be beaten to death with a cart axle, which the father did. The child died this time. After that, the family suffered many misfortunes. Later, when one of the family members met Sode Lama and asked him about it, he replied that the baby had been an incarnation of a high Bɵ, but unfortunately the Powers had not allowed him to live out his life on earth and he had left for another dimension. In order to escape the guilt lying on the whole family, they should invite him back. The brother told me the invitation had been unsuccessful.

His father had acted in such a way partly because in those parts people are very afraid of the lama's curse, called *Zhaadkha*. Once a lama curses someone, they fall ill, die and the whole family line may die out. I heard many stories about *Zhaadkha.* […]

---

[279] Interestingly, we find a one-eyed man in Chingis Khaan's ancestral lineage. Before they moved to the Burkhan Haldun (Bur. Бурхан халдун) area in Mongolia, Chingis Khaan's ancestors' homeland was Bargujin Tokum, the modern-day Barguzin region of Buryatia where Kurumkan viallge is now located. The man in question is Duva Sohor (Bur. Дува сохор), son of Borzhigidai Mergen (Bur. Боржигидай мэргэн) and is 11th in the line from the ancestor Burte Chino. With his only eye Duva Sohor could see very far ahead, up to a distance of three days' journey on horseback. This is recorded in the *Innermost Story of the Mongols* in Kozin, *Sokrovennoe Skazanie,* p.12, §4–§6. The fact that we find Duva Sohor in the Mongol royal lineage which has its roots in Barguzin suggests that individuals with this kind of physical appearance and magical abilities may reappear among the Barguzin Buryats from time to time, and that it might be also somehow recorded and passed on a genetic level.

> The lamas from one local monastery had the capacity to burn houses and whole villages and they used it against some houses of the Bɵ. It looked as if two fiery hands stretched out of the monastery in the direction of the village and when they reached the houses of the disobedient, they burst into flames.
>
> Village of Kurumkan, Barguzin,12.06.94.[280]

Buryatian Zya, Magar Zyā and Bönpo Ted destructive magic

Zya

Buryatian *Zya* and Bönpo *Ted*[281] are rituals of destructive magic which show some underlying similarities in terms of technique. *Zya* is a very dangerous black magic object which causes grave problems for those against whom it is used. To make a *zya*, the black sorcerer or Black Bɵ draws an upside down human figure on a piece of cloth and puts a spell on it to attracts a dangerous spirit (often a wandering ghost of the dead) to enter it. One or several *zya* are then secretly hidden in or around the *gher* of the family to which the black magician wants to cause harm. *Zya* cause sufferings, misfortunes, diseases and death to strike as many people within the family as the number of *zya* objects hidden in or under their dwelling. *Zya* pollute all the activities of the family and, should the people try to avert misfortunes by invoking and making offerings to their *Ongon*-ancestors, *Zayaans* or Tengeri, the *Zya* defiles the gods and protective spirits by appearing in the guise of a dead woman on the roof of the *gher* in the course of the ritual. The gods and protective spirits then leave the family which becomes easy prey for all sorts of evil spirits. *Zya* belies its presence through crackling noises, ghostly cries and flashes similar to a shooting star. If a family suspects someone has hidden *zya* in their dwelling, divination is performed and, if it indicates that such a curse might be present, a Bɵ is immediately called to find and neutralize it. Upon his arrival the Bɵ is given two *hor'bo*-sticks made by the family. He invokes and sprinkles to the Tengeri and *Zayaan* Ganza[282] asking them to help him to find *zya*. The Bɵ then runs around inside and outside the *gher* trying to locate where the objects are hidden. When he indicates a place where *zya* might be, the family members try to find it. If *zya* is not found soon after the Bɵ has indicated the spot, it moves by itself and

---

[280] A passage from mu unpublished diary, *Tailgan Trip*.

[281] Tib. gtad.

[282] Bur. Ганза.

hides in another place. Once found, *zya* are immediately burnt. After that the evil entity which resided in the effigy returns to the Black Bө who made it and annoys him by its presence so he is forced to make another *zya* receptacle and hide it in someone else's dwelling. If the drawing on the *zya* fades over time, no-one can find it but the Black Bө who hid it. In this case he is paid a ransom and invited to neutralize it. If he is unable to find *zya*, the Black Bө makes forty *dolë* effigies which he puts in many locations in and outside the *gher*. These effigies neutralize the power of the *zya*.[283]

Presently, a similar form of black magic is causing many problems in Buryatia. In the spiritual vacuum left after seventy years of Communist rule and the increasing materialism of the post-perestroika years, a brand of petty black sorcerers appear who, although they have neither lineage nor great power, manage to cause sufferings to many people nevertheless. Such evil-doers use a new form of magic which is a mix of the Buryatian *zya* technique and the techniques of black sympathetic magic brought to Siberia by Russians using a doll made of beeswax or paraffin. A doll or a number of dolls, one for each member of the family, is pierced by needles or pins in the places where harm is intended and then hidden upside down in the house of those to be cursed, often inserted behind the door- or window lintel. Appallingly, this kind of magic is sometimes done indiscriminately while new blocks of flats or houses are still under construction making it very difficult to find these dolls as they might be embedded in concrete, and destroy them.

Zyā

The malevolent spirits which enter the *zya* effigy seem to have a direct counterpart in the spiritual tradition of the Magar peoples of Nepal who are ethnically related to Tibetans. The Magar of northern Nepal believe in evil female spirits called *Zyā* and the Magar priests make a pact with them and propitiate them at the end of each ritual to prevent them causing harm.[284] There are three man types of *Zyā* spirits: the Nine Sisters from which all evil witches descended; spirits causing accidents and diseases such as the *Sarazyā* which make people fall from cliffs, the *Rāzyā* which attack newborn infants (equivalent to Buryatian *Ada*) and the *Aulazyā* which cause malaria; and wandering spirits of dead women comparable

---

[283] Based on Hangalov, *Sobranie* I, pp. 335–336; and other sources.

[284] Anne de Sales, *Je Suis Né De Vos Jeux De Tambours ; La religion chamanique des Magar du Nord*, (Paris: Société d'Ethnologie, 1991), pp. 142–147.

to Buryatian *Dahobar*. While Magar evil witches do use effigy figurines in their magic,[285] it is not clear at this stage whether they can be directly compared to Buryatian *Zya* magic. However, the ghosts and evil spirits entering *Zya* effigy are definitely female and their harmful actions are comparable to *Zyā* spirits of Magars. These parallels would suggest that the pantheons of malign spirits and even the transmission of some black magic techniques shared by Buryats and Magar have a common source in Prehistoric Bön.

Ted

Ted is a Prehistoric Bön technique which was adapted to the action rituals of Bönpo Tantra by Tonpa Shenrab. It was later incorporated into the Buddhist Tantra of the Nyingmapa School. In many ways *Ted* mirrors Buryatian *Zya* although a different object is used as the receptacle of the curse. Here, the main receptacle is a yak horn filled with diverse impure substances and objects empowered by destructive *mantras*. The horn is then sealed and a ritual to charge it with destructive power is performed. At dawn or dusk a magician tries to conceal the *ted* under the main pillar of the enemy's house or bury it near a corner. After this the magician must sever all contacts with the family. This magic can strike several generations of the family with misfortunes, accidents, loss of property and prestige, and ultimately death. If ill omens and misfortunes start to befall, a family may suspect they are caused by *ted.* A divination is done to verify this, and if the family's fears are confirmed, further divination is performed to establish the exact location of the concealed *ted*. Once the object is found, it is thrown into a river or burnt to destroy its power. If the horn is not found then lamas are invited. They make several *lüd* effigies and *tormas* which are buried under the foundation of the house and are designed to counteract the malevolent influence emanating from the *ted*.[286] This ritual is called *Tedrul*.[287] Different versions of *Tedrul* and *Chedrol*, which averts the effects of *Cheka* (mentioned above), are found on many levels of Yungdrung Bön from the Causal Bön to the High Tantra of the Bön of the Fruit.[288]

It is clear from the description above that the structure of *ted* magic matches that of *zya*. In both cases the objects are charged with destructive

---

[285] Telephone conversation with Anne de Sales, May 2007.

[286] Nebesky-Wojkowitz, *Oracles and Demons*, pp. 483–486.

[287] Tib. gtad rul.

[288] Oral communication from Yongdzin Lopön Tenzin Namdak, Shenten Dargye Ling, France, 11.08.07.

magic intended to harm the enemy and his family, they are hidden in, under or around the dwelling and if not quickly found and destroyed very serious damage and even death will follow. The counteractive measures to destroy the curse are also very similar. The bewitched object must be found as soon as possible and destroyed by throwing into a river or fire. If it cannot be found, *dolë* or *lüd* effigies are hidden in or under the dwelling to neutralize the evil curse. The degree of similarity between *zya* and *ted* rituals is such that we can safely conclude that the principle on which both the curses and the magic to counter them is rooted in the techniques of Prehistoric Bön.

Offering rituals and magic related to the gods of the Underworld in the Prehistoric Bön of Eurasia

To demonstrate the close parallels between the archaic techniques of magic used in Asia and Europe let us compare a Bө Murgel ritual dedicated to the scribes of Erlig Khaan and a ritual to the goddess Hecate[289] described in the ancient Greek myth of *Argonautica*.[290]

The Bө Murgel offering ritual to the scribes of Erlig Khaan[291] is performed when young lads are called to serve in the army. Erlig Khaan and his scribes are asked to protect them from injury or death.[292] The ritual is done on a dark, moonless night and involves offering a sacrificial black ram and vodka into fire. Although some sources suggest it is a relatively recent ritual it is, no doubt, based on ancient traditions.

Hecate is an ancient goddess worshiped in Asia Minor in the region of Anatolia in modern-day Turkey and the Caucasus by peoples such as the Colchis (their ethnicity is not clear) who occupied the territory of modern-day Georgia and parts of Turkey and formed their kingdom there around the thirteenth century BC.[293] She was later incorporated into the Greek pantheon where she is said to be a daughter of the Titan Perses[294]

---

289 Greek. Εκάτη.

290 Greek. Ἀργοναυτικά.

291 Bur. Эрлег хаанай бэшээшэ нүүдтэ or Bur. бэшээшэдтэ (Beshe'edte).

292 It is also done before children go to school for the first time. It is believed that Erlig Khaan's scribes help in matters to do with the government and bureaucratic institutions and that they are the spirits of educated people. In the past a child had to leave home to be educated far away from his parents' and required protection from diseases, injury and death.

293 David Braund, *Georgia in Antiquity: A History of Colchis and Transcaucasian Iberia 550 BC-AD 562.* (Oxford: Clarendon Press, 1994).

294 Greek. Περσίς.

and star-goddess Asteria. Like many ancient gods and goddesses, Hecate originally had many roles but they gradually narrowed and she became the goddess of magic, witchcraft and the night, goddess of graveyards and crossroads, companion and minister of Hades the god of the Underworld and the Realm of the Dead and his wife Persephone.[295] Hecate has many forms but often appears as a frightening woman with three heads, one of a mare, a black bitch and a pole cat, or as three women standing back to back. She may appear holding torches, a knife, a rope, a key and a pomegranate (fruit of the World of the Dead), surrounded by snakes, ghosts and monsters. She accepts sacrifices of black dogs or black sheep and was often propitiated before a journey was embarked upon, either by land or sea. Hecate features in the great Greek epic poem *Argonautica* written in the third century BC by Apollonius Rhodius, a librarian at the Great Library of Alexandria in Egypt, on the basis of ancient Greek myths and legends. The poem describes the epic journey of the crew of the ship *Argo* under command of the hero Jason to recover the Golden Fleece from the Kingdom of Colchis (Qulha, Kolkha, Kilkhi) in the Caucasus. Book III of *Argonautica* contains a detailed description of the offering ritual to Hecate performed by Jason who learnt it from Medea, a powerful sorceress and Hecate priestess, daughter of Aeetes,[296] the King of Colchis. Medea falls in love with Jason and helps him to obtain the Golden Fleece thus betraying her father and family. In one episode Medea aids Jason with her witchcraft to defeat the magic army which grew from the dragon teeth sown in the field of Ares[297] near the palace of the King Aeetes. She told him to perform a sacrificial ritual to Hecate during the night before the battle:

> Night fell. Jason donned black clothes and went to the banks of the River Phasis. There in the dead of night, at midnight, he washed himself in its fast-flowing waters. Then near the water he dug a deep hole which he filled with firewood. Above it he sacrificed a black sheep, slitting its throat. He lit the wood and let the sheep's carcass burn. Pouring libations of honey into the blaze, he called Hecate to appear and help him. The sheep was burnt on ritual fire in the holocaust[298] manner. No sooner was

---

[295] Greek. Περσεφόνη.

[296] Greek. Αιήτης.

[297] Greek. Άρης, god of war

[298] Greek. Ὁλόκαυστον – an animal sacrifice which is completely incinerated in fire.

> the sacrifice complete than the earth opened up and great Hecate herself manifested with smoking torches in her hands. She was surrounded by fearsome monsters, fire-spitting dragons and the dogs of hell. The earth trembled under her feet. Consumed by fear, local nymphs screamed and shrieked as they tried to flee. Jason, though frightened, remembered Medea's words and returned to his ship *Argo* without turning or looking back.[299]

This ritual is remarkably similar to that of the offering to the scribes of Erlig Khaan (and, indeed, many other offering rituals of Bɵ Murgel). The purpose of both rituals is to propitiate the gods and spirits of the Underworld to obtain their magic protection and strength in military activities. Both rituals are performed on moonless nights and primarily addressed to the helpers of the principal gods of the Realm of the Dead (the scribes of Erlig Khaan or Hecate, Hades' minister). The content of the ritual offerings and the method of offering itself are virtually identical, small differences in the sex of the animals are of little importance. The libations of honey offered by Jason to Hecate were probably mead and thus a kind of alcoholic beverage comparable to the vodka offered to the scribes of Erlig Khaan. Jason is expressly prohibited to turn and look back once the offering is complete, a taboo we have seen in Bɵ Murgel offerings to *Lusuut* water-spirits and other rituals. Before the offering rite Jason had to wash in the waters of the River Phasis so we can suppose the ritual was addressed to both the Under earth and Underwater realms or, in Bɵ Murgel terms, to the retinues of Erlig Khaan and Han Hat. Moreover, as this ritual bathing was to be done at night, the River Phasis most probably symbolized one of the five rivers of Hades' Underworld which were governed by eponymous gods and goddesses: Styx, Acheron, Phlegethon, Lethe and Cocytus. The River Phasis most likely represents Styx or Acheron as Styx is the border between the Earth and the Underworld and Acheron is its tributary over which the spirits of the newly dead have to ferried by Charon.[300] This ritual nocturnal bathing was probably a symbolic way of obtaining protection from death and injury.

---

[299] Compiled from Apollonius Rhodius (b. ~ 270 BC), tr. R.C. Seaton (1912) with parallel Greek text, *The Argonautica*, Book III, lines 1191–1224, <http://www.sacred-texts.com/cla/argo/index.htm> accessed 18.06.07 and Kun, *Legendy i Mify*, pp. 274–276.

[300] Greek. Χάρων.

Another ritual from the cycle of myths about the Argonauts has is mirrored in the rituals and ideas of Bɵ Murgel. This ritual to prevent death and return youth to Jason's father Aeson was performed by Medea in their home in the city of Iolkos in Thessalia:

> At the time of the full moon, at midnight, Medea left the house barefoot, clad in a dark tunic. She went to the junction where three roads met, she turned about thrice and, raising her arms, shouted three times. Then she knelt down and whispered spells to the Night, Stars, Moon, Earth, Winds, Mountains and Rivers.[301] She invoked the gods of the forests and night and, above all, the great goddess Hecate to come and help her with the task. Hecate heard her pleas and manifested in front of Medea riding a chariot drawn by winged dragons. For nine days and nights Medea gathered magical herbs and roots from the sacred mountains, forests, riverbanks and on the seashore. Then she returned home and erected two altars: one for Hecate and one for the goddess of youth. She dug a pit in front of each altar and sacrificed two black sheep to Hecate and the gods of the Underworld Hades and Persephone. She poured libations of mead and honey as offering to them and begged them not to take the life of old Aeson. Then she ordered Aeson to be brought and hypnotized him so that he fell into a deep sleep. Laying Aeson on a carpet of magic herbs, she sprinkled him with water, sulphur and purified him with fire. The second portion of the herbs she boiled together with precious gems, an owl carcass, midnight dew, warm entrails of a werewolf, snake skins, the liver of a long-lived stag and the head of a nine-hundred-year-old raven in a copper cauldron. It became a magical potion which rose with a white froth. Medea took a dry olive twig and dipped it into the magic potion. The twig was immediately covered with green leaves and olive fruits. Everywhere the drops of this potion fell there sprang up grass and flowers. Medea then slit Aeson's throat and let out all his old blood. Then through the gaping wound in his neck she poured the magic potion into him. As soon as she finished the miracle happened – Aeson's grey hair and beard turned brown, all his wrinkles and other signs of old age vanished without a trace. He woke up looking as though he had just turned forty.[302]

---

[301] Ancient Greeks perceived them as the gods.

[302] Compiled from Ovid (43 BC-17 AD), *Metamorphoses*, Book 7, Tr. Sir Samuel

This very complex ritual combines:

- elements of the ransom of the soul through animal sacrifice parallel to *Dolë* of Bɵ Murgel;
- an offering ritual analogous to those addressed to Erlig Khaan, his messengers and scribes who are offered black ram, horse or bull in the dark of the night;[303]
- knowledge of healing herbs and mineral substances;
  sympathetic magic represented by the parts and internal organs of various animals (including mythical ones) believed to have long life and the ability to shape-shift.

As the Kingdom of Colchis was in existence as early as the thirteenth century BC, the details of the offering rituals to Hecate, Hades and Persephone may be as old, if not earlier. In any case this ritual tradition is of great antiquity and passed into Greek ritual lore later. The parallel aspects it shares with the rituals of present-day Buryatian Bɵ Murgel demonstrate once more that there was an international cultural with common religious traditions adhered to by many ethnically and racially diverse peoples spread across a vast area. Bɵ Murgel represents a living branch of this Prehistoric Bön of Eurasia which must have been of great antiquity.

Conclusion

We have found that the methods of healing and magic in Tibetan Bön and Buryatian Bɵ Murgel bear close resemblance indicative of a common cultural base suggesting multiple contacts between these two traditions at different points in time. The level at which the parallels appear is mostly related to the Prehistoric. Nevertheless, the similarities we have found in the healing and magic techniques are mainly linked to the external form of rituals and general culture and so are mostly related to the substrate of Prehistoric Bön running through them. These similarities are not, however, on the level of the traditions' underlying ideologies.

Garth, John Dryden, <http://classics.mit.edu/Ovid/metam.7.seventh.html> accessed 20.06.07 and Kun, *Legendy i Mify*, pp. 283–284.

[303] Hangalov, *Sobranie* I, p. 538.

CHAPTER XV

Spread of Bön in Eurasia

The ancient beginnings

The prehistory of Eurasia, including the development of religion on this continent, is the subject of an ongoing scholarly debate giving rise to many contradictory theories and ideas. So diverse are the opinions on this subject that the picture of the processes of migration and the growth of culture presented by the different theories can often be interpreted in diverse ways. These theories focus on almost all major aspects of human activity in this part of the world such as the evolution of language and writing, development and dating of religions and their founders, patterns of migration, the racial identity of the prehistoric tribes and nations, cross-cultural contacts and influences, to name but few. Here we will venture into and navigate through some areas of this very complex and often controversial terrain as the cultural and spiritual roots of both Buryatian Bө Murgel and Tibetan Bön can be traced to prehistoric Eurasia. However, rather than analyzing many different views and theories here, we shall refer to those sources which can help us gain a clearer insight into the possible origins and interactions of our two traditions.

B.G. Tilak's Arctic Home Theory and the Prehistoric Bön of Eurasia

We have already glanced at the Arctic Home Theory of Indian Brahmin and scholar, Lokamanya Bal Gangadhar Tilak (1856–1920) in previous chapters. As a Brahmin, Tilak studied *Vedas* and other Sanskrit texts all his life and had a unique insight into their meaning, but he was also well versed in modern science. This combination allowed Tilak to correlate the Vedic myths with scientific data for the first time. His research led him to formulate the Arctic Home or Northern Pole Theory expounded in his book *The Arctic Home in the Vedas* published in 1903. He analyzed many passages of *Rigveda* and *Avesta*, the two most important and ancient religious texts of the Indian and Iranian Aryans, and linked them to the scientific information on geology and astronomy available to him at that time. Through this research he was able to demonstrate that the original ancestral lands of the Aryans (Aryana Vaejo of *Avesta*) and, possibly, other ancient nations and races of Eurasia, were located in the circumpolar regions close to the Northern Pole. He also came to the conclusion that ancestors of the Aryans inhabited the circumpolar regions as early as sometime in the last interglacial period (ended 30.000[1] or 41,000–39,000 years ago[2]) and that references to the onslaught of the cold winter which Angra Manyu (Ahriman) sent to destroy Aryana Vaejo point to this period:

> I, Ahura Mazda created the first of the good regions, Aryana Vaejo, beautiful creation (according to Darmesteter, by the beautiful river Daitya,). Then Angra Manyu, the destroyer, counter-created the great serpent and winter (or snow), creation of the Daevas. There are ten months of winter and two months of summer.[3]

> There are ten winter months there, two summer months; and those are cold for the waters, cold for the earth, cold for the trees. Winter falls there, the worst of all plagues. [Hum 35: 'Ten are there the winter months, two the summer months, and even then [in summer] the waters are freezing, the earth is freezing, the plants are freezing; there is the centre of winter, there is the heart of winter, there winter rushes around, there (occur) most damages caused by storm.']⁴

> And Ahura Mazda spake unto Yima, saying: 'O fair Yima, son of Vivanghat! Upon the material world the evil winters are about to fall, that shall bring the fierce, deadly frost; upon the material world the evil winters are about to fall, that shall make snow-flakes fall thick, even an aredvi deep on the highest tops of mountains.'[5]

---

1 This dating is according to modern Russian sources B. G. Tilak, *Arkticheskaya Rodina v Vedakh* (Moscow: Fair-Press, 2002), p. 7.

2 S. Y Popov, Istoriya razvitiya rastitel'nogo pokrova v Evrope za poslednie 150,000 let <http://bio.1september.ru/articlef.php?ID=200003603> accessed 26.06.07; Guseva, *Slavyane*, p. 50.

3 *Vendidad*, *Fargard 1*, st 3.4, quoted in Tilak, *Arktichekaya Rodina*, p. 380; translation mine.

4 *Vendidad*, *Fargard 1*, st. 3., Tr. James Darmesteter, <http://www.avesta.org/vendidad/vd1sbe.htm> accessed 25.06.07.

5 *Fargard 2*, st. 22. Tr. Darmesteter <http://www.avesta.org/vendidad/vd2sbe.htm>

This sudden, intense cooling forced the Aryan ancestors to migrate south and they remained in more southern regions until the onset of the next interglacial period in around 13,000 BC when rapid global warming began.[6] The ice gradually melted and slid into the Arctic Ocean causing the deluge known as the Great Flood which destroyed people and culture. The Vedic tradition was damaged to some extent at this point but thanks to the *rishi* sages' remarkable memories, it was preserved in oral tradition. Once the flood subsided in northern regions of eastern Europe,[7] animals began migrating northwards and were followed by the Aryan ancestors and other peoples. Subarctic forests shifted some 300 km north of their current limits and large swathes of the circumpolar region gradually became covered by pine and deciduous forest and grasslands teeming with wild life. In the eighth millennium BC the general temperature in the circumpolar regions did not fall below 0°C[8] so it had all the necessary conditions for human habitation.

However, in the seventh millennium BC the cold returned once again and this prompted the Aryans and some other nations living in the north to migrate south again. By the fifth millennium BC Aryans were living in the Great Steppe where the *Vedas*, until then an oral tradition, were faithfully written down from memory by Aryan *Rishi* priests. These texts retain many direct references to the realities of the Aryans' life in the circumpolar region including the fixed position of the Polar Star directly overhead and the rotation of the stars around it without setting and rising for days; polar day and polar night; prolonged dawns which last 45–60 days; the sun rising from the south and so on.[9] All these phenomena were reflected in the rituals and beliefs of the ancient Aryans recorded in *Vedas*.

Vedic *Sattra* nocturnal offering rituals could span many nights in a row, in particular the *Shataratra*, which lasted a hundred nights. This ritual was a continuous offering of *soma* drink to the god Indra in order to aid him in his battle with the powers of darkness and it is this ritual which lent him the epithet Shatakratu – Lord of the Hundred Sacrifices.[10]

---

6 Borisenkov&Pyasetskii, *Tysyacheletnyaya letopis'*. Cited in Guseva, *Slavyane*, p. 31.

7 Rybakov, *Yazychestvo*, p.119. A similar scenario happened in the North Asia but here we are talking about Aryan ancestors who lived in the north of eastern Europe.

8 Ibid.

9 Tilak, *Arkticheskaya Rodina*, pp. 68–91.

10 Ibid., pp. 233–250.

According to Tilak, the *Shataratra* ritual was performed by the ancient Aryan priests throughout the polar night, a time of darkness which lasted 100 days and nights. At this time Indra was wrestling with the demon Vritra and the powers of darkness to bring back the dawn, light and sun. The Russian scholar of Hinduism N.R. Guseva went one step further and, using meteorological data from *The Sun Tables for the city of Murmansk*,[11] she calculated the exact longitude of the lands where ancient Aryans may have performed *Shataratra* ritual, namely, 82.6°. This longitude crosses Franz Josef Land, Severnaya Zemlya and Spitsbergen as well as many shallow shelves.[12] These islands and submerged shelves may have been attached to the mainland before the last glacial period when they could have been submerged under the weight of the ice cap then subsequently flooded when the next global thaw set in around 13,000 BC.

The Arctic as the cradle of humanity

Did peoples other than the Aryan ancestors live in the circumpolar regions? Tilak does not give a definitive reply to this questions but suggests 'there are serious reasons to believe that five races of people (*panca janah*), often mentioned in *Rigveda,* could have lived with the Aryans in their ancestral land.'[13]

Another scholar contemporary with Tilak also sought a reply to this question. In 1885, Professor of Systematic Theology William Fairfield Warren (1833–1929) published the results of his studies in comparative mythology married with contemporary scientific data in his book entitled *Paradise Found: the Cradle of the Human Race at the North Pole.*[14] In this book, Warren studied the descriptions of paradise and the gods' holy lands found in many ancient spiritual traditions. He discovered that the mythologies of diverse ancient civilizations far apart from one another such as the Egyptian, Jewish, Etruscan, Greek, Assyrian, Iranian, Indo-Aryan, Chinese, Japanese and Navajo invariably locate paradise or the land of the gods in the circumpolar regions around the North Pole. Through comparative analysis, Warren revealed that the descriptions of the mythical land in these cultures fall into the same matrix:

---

11 Sun tables for the city of Murmansk, murmanskii gidromettsentr.

12 Guseva, *Slavanye*, pp. 51–53.

13 Tilak, *Arkticheskaya Rodina*, pp: 461–462.

14 William F. Warren, S.T.D., LL.D., *Paradise Found: The Cradle of the Human Race at the North Pole. A Study of the Prehistoric World* (Boston: Houghton, Mifflin and Company,1885). I use the Russian translation of this edition (Fair Press, Moscow 2003).

- In the centre is a World Mountain, World Tree or World Pillar connecting the earthly paradise with the celestial paradise of the Polar Star.
- Four sacred rivers flow from the World Mountain in the four cardinal directions, and the whole land is surrounded by ocean.
- This holy island is the cradle of humanity and the place where religion was taught by the gods.

If we add the triple division of the Universe into Sky, Earth and Underworld we arrive at the universal blueprint on which the cosmological models of most spiritual traditions of the earth, and of Eurasia in particular, are based.

Linking the insights he had gained from his study of comparative mythology with contemporary scientific data and theories from a wide range of other disciplines such as geography, mathematical and astronomical geography, physiographic geology, prehistoric climatology, palaeobotanics, palaeozoology, palaeoanthropology and ethnography, Warren went on to prove his own theory that humanity originated in the Miocenic[15] continent of Arctida.

Although some scientific data used to support Warren's theory is now outdated and the Miocene is generally considered too early a period for the appearance of modern humans, the theory itself still stands. Modern science persistently pushes the age of humanity further into the past and there is as yet still no clear scientific evidence of the ultimate link in the chain between humans and apes.[16] Neither has the theory of an arctic continent disappeared; on the contrary, it is supported by some modern scientists. Two modern Western scholars, M.C. Boulter and S.B. Manum, have presented further evidence for the existence of this

---

[15] The Miocene is the geological time period between 23.03 to 5.33 million years ago.

[16] Until this chain link is found this theory still remains uncertain. Even if humans did evolve from apes, Africa is not the only place where this could have happened. It is generally believed in palaeoanthropology that hominids diverged from apes around 14 Ma thus leaving the possibility that modern humans developed much earlier and not necessarily in Africa. So the Arctic and the Tibet-Qinghai Plateau are suggested as alternative cradles of humanity. See, Gelek, The Tibetan Plateau – One of the Homes of Early Man, *Anthropology of Tibet and Himalaya*, pp. 73–79, Ed. Charles Ramble and Martin Brauen (Vajra Publications: Kathmandu, 2008).

ancient continent in their article *A lost continent in a temperate Arctic*[17] in which they argue that a microcontinent existed in the North Atlantic from 33 to 10 million years ago (Ma) at palaeolatitudes of some 8° to 10° beyond the Arctic Circle. This microcontinent was covered by *taiga*-like conifer forests and low-lying ferns and enjoyed a cool, moderate climate which barely altered for millions of years. The continent gradually disintegrated and formed a chain of archipelagos. The same researchers maintain that in the Quaternary, at around 2.3 Ma, forests existed as far north as beyond 82° latitude with estimated temperatures of 10C° in summer and –15C° to –17C° in winter.[18] The famous Soviet scholar and Arctic explorer, Arctic oceanographer Y.Y. Gakkel (1901–1965) and zoogeographer E.F. Gurjanova (1902–1981) both held the view that many of the Arctic archipelagos were connected in some way and that some of the arctic lands and mountain ridges now under water – such as the land surrounding the Novosibirskie and Vrangel islands which include the Lomonosov Ridge – were only submerged some 5000 years ago.[19] There is, then, considerable evidence suggesting there was indeed an Arctic continent or a series of connected archipelagos and it is highly possible that this Arctic landmass was in places connected by dry land to the mainland of North America and Eurasia, although the exact period cannot yet be established with certainty. If this is the case, the highest points of this sunken landmass remained as the Arctic archipelagos while the submerged parts became shallow shelves and underwater mountains.

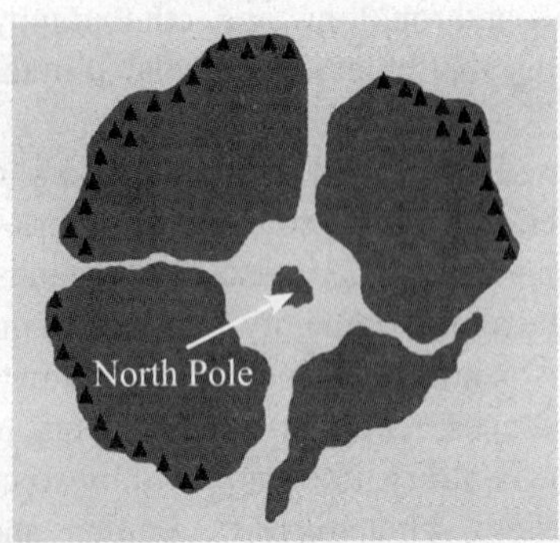

Fig. 1. Arctic continent according to Gerard Mercator.

In short, Warren's theory seems to be based on a firm foundation but there is as yet insufficient data to be able to prove or disprove it, although such data may become available in the future when global warming allows for precise scientific exploration in various fields of study in the

---

[17] M.C. Boulter, S.B. Manum, 'A lost continent in a temperate Arctic', *Endeavour* Vol.21 (3), pp. 105–108, CNRS,1997.

[18] Ibid.

[19] Ed. Gakkel & Govorukha, Morya i ostrova Severnogo Ledovitogo okeana, *Sovetskaya Arktika,* AN SSSR , Institut geografii (Moskva: Nauka, 1970).

circumpolar regions of the Arctic. If it is found to be correct, adjustments will have to be made nevertheless in keeping with the ever developing scientific knowledge in many disciplines.

Symbology of the swastika

Many scholars believe that in its earliest form the swastika is a solar symbol indicating the movement of the sun. However, the clockwise turning swastika most likely represents a general movement of sun, moon and stars.

Fig. 2. Clockwise swastika on Newari incense burner.

If we approach this question from the angle of Tilak's Arctic Home Theory, it becomes clear that it originated from observations made by ancient peoples in the circumpolar regions of the Arctic. These observations are recorded in the *Vedas*, *Mahabharata* and Indo-Aryan works on astronomy. In his book, Tilak cites passages from *Vanaparva*, the 'Forest Book' of *Mahabharata,* which clearly demonstrate this point:

> Sun and Moon circle Meru from left to right (paradakshinam)[20] every day, as do the stars.
> Day and night together equal a year for those who live there.[21]
> According to our astronomers, Mount Meru is considered to be the Northern Pole of the earth[22] [...] 'Gods dwelling on Meru see the sun after its single rise and at the midpoint of its full revolution which starts from Ari'[23] [...] One day of the gods coincides with the movement of the sun from the spring to the autumn equinox when the sun can be seen on the Northern Pole or Mount Meru while night is the return movement of the sun through the south from the autumn to the spring equinox.[24]

---

20 I.e. clockwise.

21 Tilak, *Arkticheskaya Rodina*, pp. 100–101, translation mine.

22 Ibid. p. 98.

23 Ibid. p. 98, A quote from Surya Siddhanta (XII, 67), translation mine. Ari is the 'sixth house' of the planets or the sky in ancient Indian astrology.

24 Ibid., p. 98.

This clearly refers to the polar day and night in Arctic circumpolar regions. During the months of the polar day when the sun is visible, it always circles the sky in clockwise motion while during the winter months of the polar night, the same is true for the moon and stars. Originally, then, the clockwise turning swastika symbolized the general direction of the movement of celestial bodies. As the sun, moon, stars and planets were perceived either as gods, their residences or both, this clockwise movement was in turn perceived as the divine law of movement of the universe, an understanding reflected in Vedic rituals as the main ritual direction.

However, the cosmological system of *Bhagavata Purana* described in the text *Shrimad Bhagavatam* also speaks of the anticlockwise movement of the sun riding in a single-wheeled chariot on Bhumandala[25] along the yearly orbit of the ecliptic, an observation supported by modern science.[26] Yungdrung Bön's cosmological and astrological systems possess the same knowledge.[27] If we follow the interpretation of the origin of the swastika as a solar symbol, then the swastika which turns anticlockwise should be connected to this orbit of the sun around the ecliptic plane.

Fig. 3. Anticlockwise yungdrung-*swastika on the back of a Bönpo monk's robe. Triten Norbutse Monastery, 2008.*

Examples of both kinds of swastika abound in Eurasia, the Americas and Northern Africa with the earliest examples belonging to the Palaeolithic and early Bronze Age. While observing the circular movement of the sun and stars is an easy task, observations related to the anticlockwise movement of the sun along the ecliptic orbit require a high degree of astronomical knowledge. Such knowledge would be in keeping with the highly advanced and sophisticated culture of the ancient

---

25 A multifaceted model representing several cosmic planes, in this case it represents the earth or ecliptic plane. For a wonderful graphic presentation see the video of Richard Thopmson, Sanskrit consultation Dr. Howward Resnick, *Mysteries of the Sacred Universe* released by the Bhaktivedanta Instituite on <http://video.google.com/videoplay?docid=-538297875584368796&q=mysteries+of%20+the+sacred+universe> accessed 01.07.07.

26 Ibid.

27 Oral information from Yongdzin Lopön Tenzin Namdak, Shenten Dargye Ling, France. 11.08.07.

Aryan people; not only did they know about this ecliptic orbit, they were also able to resolve the apparent contradiction of this knowledge with the visible clockwise movement of the sun.[28]

The Bönpo swastika – or *drungmu* in the language of Zhang Zhung and *yungdrung* in Tibetan – turns to the left and in Yungdrung Bön it represents the ultimate, indestructible Buddha-nature beyond time and space. On another level it represents the sacred ritual direction which leads to spiritual realization. Traditional Yungdrung Bön texts do not comment on the reason for this anticlockwise movement, *yekor*,[29] but we can suggest two possible explanations. Firstly, this anticlockwise direction of the Bönpo swastika may have been originally related to the sun's ecliptic orbit as was explained above, and in this case it would have represented the sacred direction of movement for some branches of the Prehistoric Bön of Eurasia dominant in the time and place when Tonpa Shenrab Miwo manifested. Like many other symbols, concepts and rituals of Prehistoric Bön, it would then have been infused with a new layer of meaning by this central Asian Buddha to reflect his revolutionary doctrine. The second possibility is that the anticlockwise rotation of the *yungdrung* arose in another way. If the clockwise swastika represents the normal movement of the universe and its development from the primordial source, it may also be interpreted as the symbol representing *samsara*. In this case, *yungdrung* with its anticlockwise rotation would symbolize the reversal of *samsara* and the return to the primordial source, Buddha-nature.

In Yungdrung Bön the swastika is rich in symbology. While its primary meaning is the unchangeable, indestructible state, the Nature of Mind or fundamental ground of all existence, the four arms and the centre also represent the four directions and the centre. The five sections are painted different colours representing the five purified elements and each section is also inscribed with one of the five heroic syllables, making this symbol a sort of *mandala* of the five Buddha-clans, a representation of the universe in its pure spiritual dimension.

---

[28] In *Shrimad Bhagavatam* this contradiction is resolved by explaining that the direction of this movement depends on the position from which this movement is observed. To illustrate this, the example of a potter's wheel is given. The wheel spins anticlockwise while the ants on it run around it clockwise. From the point of view of the ants they move clockwise while for an outside observer the potter wheel as a whole moves anticlockwise. Ibid.

[29] Tib. gyas skor.

Colour	Place	Direction	Syllable
White	Below	East	Yang
Green	Right	North	Ram
Red	Above	West	Kang
Blue	Left	South	Srung
Yellow	Centre	Centre	Om

Fig. 4. Yungdrung Bön swastika with five heroic syllables in Zhang Zhung Marchen script and key.

In the large *mandala* of 1000 Buddhas of Yungdrung Bön there are 200 *yungdrung*-swastikas, each one representing the five Buddhas of body, speech, mind, quality and activity manifested in the ten directions.

Has tamga,[30] the swastika of Mongol-Buryat Bɵ Murgel, also turns anticlockwise. Anticlockwise swastikas are very common motifs in the cave art and Deer Stones in Mongolia, Inner Mongolia and Amdo, generally dated second to first millennia BC. The British-Mongolian Rock Art Survey expedition of 2004 found one such swastika in a cave complex along the rivers Chuluut, Ider and Selenge (which flows into Lake Baikal in Buryatia) in Arkhanghai Aimag in Mongolia: 'Site 6 contained some interesting images, notably a swastika (which the Mongolians interpreted as four horses heads), and an image containing two humans holding hands.'[31] When I visited Buryatia in 2003, Dorjo Doogarov sketched a similar swastika which he had seen in some Mongolian research papers (shown below).

In Chapter XI we noted that this anticlockwise rotation apparently contradicts the clock-wise ritual movement in modern Bɵ Murgel. However, there are two possible explanations for this contradiction, but either way it is a relict of an extremely ancient culture. The first possibility

---

[30] Bur. хас тамга.

[31] *British-Mongolian Rock Art Survey 2004*, Universities of Newcastle, Edinburgh and Mongolia, Chuluut river basin Arkhangai aimag, Central Mongolia, July-August 2004, <http://64.233.183.104/search?q=cache:S4SC6CJAY8kJ:www.expeditions.ed.ac.uk/Reports%25202004/MongolianRockArtSurveyPrelReport2004.doc+Mongolian+swastika&hl=en&ct=clnk&cd=16&gl=uk&client=firefox-a> accessed 01.07.07.

is that *has tamga* is an extremely old symbol based on knowledge of the sun's ecliptic orbit which represents the sacred ritual direction in many streams of Prehistoric Bön of Eurasia but both the knowledge and the ritual direction were later inexplicably lost in Bɵ Murgel and the direction of rituals changed to follow the daily movement of the sun leaving only the symbol *has tamga* intact. This is a very probable explanation especially because *has tamga* literally means 'jade stamp',[32] a name which may have arisen in or before the time of the Jade Route (second millennium BC), a trade artery connecting the Glazkovskaya culture of Southern Siberia, which included Lake Baikal, and the Shang-Yin Empire in China via intermediary tribes. The Chinese imported precious discs, semi-discs, rings and mirrors made of white and green jade from Siberia.

The second explanation for Bɵ Murgel's anticlockwise swastika is that it came with Yungdrung Bön influence; as we shall see later in this chapter, there are several occasions when these two traditions could have interfaced.

Evidence of proto-Mongol north-south migration

The research by Tilak and Warren presented above suggests that circumpolar regions of Arctic were inhabited in remote prehistory by several human races. Is there evidence to suggest that the proto-Mongols also lived there and migrated south due to climate change in the same way as the Aryans did? We looked at some of the evidence supporting this in Chapter VI where we analyzed in detail the parallel gods in the pantheons of proto-Mongols, proto-Indo-Iranians and proto-Indo-Europeans. In particular we found that proto-Indo-Iranian *Varuna, Uranus of the Ancient Greeks, Perun of the ancient Russians, Yakut Urun, and proto-Mongol *Baruun refer to the same godhead. The fact that all these nations belonging to different races and language groups have the same godhead

Fig. 5. Horse-headed swastika from a Deer Stone in Mongolia, ~ second millenium BC.

[32] According to M. D. Zomonov, I. A. Manzhicheev, *A Short Dictionary of Buryatian Shamanism* (Ulaan Ude: Buryatskoe Izdatel'stvo, 1997).

along with comparable mythology, concepts and ritual techniques is indicative of prolonged contacts in antiquity. Coupled with the Mongol-Buryat world orientation (Fig. 6) and the common etymology of Sanskrit *varuni* and Buryatian *baruun* (both meaning 'west' and both linked to the position of *Varuna-*Baruun in the west), this gives us strong grounds to suggest that proto-Mongols and proto-Indo-Iranians were indeed neighbours in the circumpolar region of Eurasia and that climate changes forced them both to leave that area and migrate southwards.

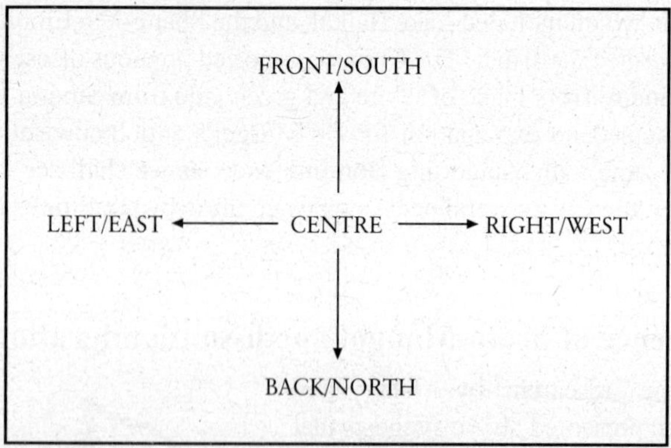

Fig. 6. Mongol-Buryat world orientation.

Further evidence pointing to the common cultural practices of proto-Indo Iranians and proto-Mongols is their knowledge of how to brew alcoholic beverage from milk products. Vedic *soma* (*haoma* in *Avesta*) was offered to the gods but also consumed by the populous. According to Vedic sources, it was of three kinds: *gavashir* – made with milk; *dadhyashir* – made with sour milk; and *yavashir* – made with barley.[33] Traditional alcoholic beverages of the Mongol-Buryats are made from milk so *gavashir* may correspond to *tarasoon* and *arkhi* (*airag*) milk-vodka while *dahyashir* may correspond to *koomys*, fermented mare's milk. Herodotus (fifth century BC) described the Scythian process of making *koomys* in his *Histories*:

> The plan they follow is to thrust tubes made of bone, not unlike our musical pipes, up the vulva of the mare, and then to blow into the tubes with their mouths, some milking while the others blow. They say that they do this because when the veins of the animal are full of air, the udder is forced down. The milk thus obtained is poured into

---

[33] Guseva, *Slavyane*, pp. 225–226.

deep wooden casks, about which the blind slaves are placed, and then the milk is stirred round. That which rises to the top is drawn off, and considered the best part; the under portion is of less account.[34]

Scythians were mainly of Indo-European origin and this description of churning milk in large wooden containers is reminiscent of the process of preparing *soma* in wooden caskets. The seventh mandala of *Rigveda* describes boiling milk as a stage in the preparation of *soma*,[35] and this could refer to a process similar to preparing *tarasoon* and *arkhi*.

Memory of life in the circumpolar region and the subsequent migration remained encoded in the ritual customs of Mongol-Buryats. According to information gathered by V. Rubruk, thirteenth-century Mongols worshipped the sun and fire by bowing and sprinkling in the direction of the south.[36] Moreover, Hangalov recorded a Buryatian song with the following words: *'from the south comes the glistening red-yellow sun.'*[37] This clearly points to the realities of the circumpolar region of Eurasia where the sun rises in the south. Buryats retained mixed ideas about the northern direction which is considered negative yet is also the direction where the land of the ancestors is located. This, too, is explained by the north-south migration due to the onslaught of the cold which brought death, hence the superimposed negative connotation attributed to the north. The positive connotation of the northern direction is the mythologized memory of the ancestral lands as a place of abundance and spiritual harmony where proto-Mongols lived before the onset of the cold.

Further evidence pointing to the cohabitation of many nations in the northern regions of Eurasia in prehistory comes from linguistic studies. Siegbert Hummel provides a very interesting linguistic observation in his book *On Zhang Zhung*.[38] He examines a number of linguistic parallels in such seemingly remote languages as Sumerian, Egyptian, Canarian, Etruscan, Basque, Greek, Latin, Mongolian, Zhang Zhung, Chinese, and Nakhi demonstrating that all these languages contain an [Ural-] Altaic substratum.[39] The common linguistic particles in all these

---

34 *The History of Herodotus, Book IV*, Tr. George Rawlinson, <http://classics.mit.edu/Herodotus/history.4.iv.html> accessed 02.07.07.

35 Guseva, *Slavyane*, p. 226.

36 V. Rubruk, *Puteshectvie v vostochnye strany* (St. Petersburg: Isdatel'stvo A. S. Suvorina, 1911), pp. 63–178.

37 Hangalov, *Sobranie* II, p. 350 (56–91).

38 Hummel, *On Zhang Zhung*, pp. 70–71.

39 He brings up the following parallels: Mongolian *tengri* = Sumerian *dingir*, both

diverse languages can be explained by the ancestors of all these diverse nations living side by side in the remote past in the northern regions of Eurasia before separating as they migrated south at different times. If we superimpose this suggestion on Tilak's Arctic Home Theory, the southern-most ancient peoples such as the Egyptians and Sumerians may have migrated far south at the end of the last interglacial and beginning of the last glacial periods and continued until they settled in North Africa and Mesopotamia. Other races and nations would have migrated south at the same time but returned to the northern and circumpolar regions when the last glacial period ended sometime after 13,000 BC.

The Golden Age of many religious and mythical traditions probably refers to these periods in prehistory when the ancestors of many ancient cultures and civilizations of Eurasia lived in the northern and circumpolar lands sharing many common aspects in their religions, mythologies, languages and ways of life. Southward and other subsequent migrations brought these cultural and religious traditions of Prehistoric Bön into different areas of the Eurasian continent and the Americas where they continued developing in their unique ways resulting in the formation of several quite distinct belief systems which mingled with each other giving rise to new religious and cultural phenomena.

Tonpa Shenrab Miwo and Yungdrung Bön in the context of prehistory

According to traditional Bönpo chronology, Buddha Mura Tahen – known in Tibet as Tonpa Shenrab Miwo – was born in 16,017 BC in the country of Olmo Lungring, the central region of the larger country of Tagzig. As we saw in Chapter I, Olmo Lunging is interpreted as both a physical and 'hidden' land in Yungdrung Bön. If that is so, this Buddha would have lived in the Last Glacial Maximum (LGM, 20,000–18,000 BP) somewhere in the steppe-tundra of Central Asia between 40° and 50° longitude. Human populations, although reduced, remained in this strip of Asia which crosses modern Turkmenistan, Uzbekistan, Kazakhstan, Kirgizstan and northern parts of the Tarim Basin. South of 40° there were deserts, north of 50° there was permafrost.[40] Although the Tibetan

meaning 'sky', 'god'; Mong. *ere* = Canarian *era* both meaning 'man', 'hero'; Zhang Zhung *zla* = Mong. *sara* = Canarian *sel* meaning 'moon'; Canarian *cuna* = Zhang Zhung *ku [-ra]* = Chinese *kou* = Nakhi *k'ö* all meaning 'dog' etc. Ibid.

40 Stephen Oppenheimer, *Ice Age Refuges*, <http://www.bradshawfoundation.

Plateau is below 40°, the climate there was different and the Plateau was populated even at the height of the LGM, which substantiates claims of the Zhang Zhung civilization's extreme antiquity. David Zhang and S.H. Li of the University of Hong Kong found handprints and footprints of at least six individuals optically dated as 20,000 years old 85km from Lhasa in rocks which were once mud, as well as a fireplace nearby with the remains of a primitive stove. This suggests there was a camp or even a settlement near Lhasa 18,000 BC. It also discredits the theory that Tibet was covered by a thick ice cap in this period and proves that at least some part of the Tibetan Plateau was ice-free.[41] Basing himself on the scientific data gathered between 1956 and 1993, Gelek, in his article *The Tibetan Plateau – One of the Homes of Early Man*,[42] argues that the Tibet-Qinghai Plateau itself could have become the cradle of hominids around 14 Ma. Returning to the LGM, the south, east, and southeast Asia may have been separated from Central and North Eurasia in this period but human populations remained in the centre and the north.[43]

These geographic realities of the LGM may be echoed in descriptions of Olmo Lungring and Tonpa Shenrab's journey to Zhang Zhung and Tibet. Can the ring of impenetrable mountains surrounding Olmo Lungring on all sides through which Tonpa Shenrab made an Arrow Way tunnel be interpreted as glaciation? Can the arid deserts which Tonpa Shenrab had to cross on his way to Zhang Zhung and Tibet be interpreted as the deserts covering Asia south of the 40°? Can Olmo Lungring refer to some unknown LGM refuge, a kind of 'oasis' somewhere to the northwest of Tibet where pre-LGM civilization survived? At present there is insufficient data to give a definitive yes or no to these questions; nevertheless, this general line of reasoning should not be ruled out.

The traditional date for Tonpa Shenrab's birth – 16,017 BC – is calculated on the basis of the traditional interpretation of the one *shen*-year[44] being equal to 100 human years. As it is said that Tonpa Shenrab Miwo lived 82 *shen*-years, his whole lifespan according to this reckoning is 8,200 years. This does not pose a problem from the spiritual point of view as extremely long lives are reported in a wide variety of religious

com/journey/corridor2.html>; <http://www.esd.ornl.gov/projects/qen/NEW_MAPS/eurasia1.gif>; <http://www.esd.ornl.gov/projects/qen/nerc EURASIA.html> accessed 03.07.07.

41 Philipp Ball, 'Humans dwelt in Ice-Age Tibet', *Nature*, 27 March 2002.

42 Gelek, *The Tibetan Plateau.*

43 Oppenheimer, *Ice Age Refuges.*

44 Tib. gshen lo.

sources. King Yima Kshaeta (Jamshed), for instance, who lived before and in the time of the Great Flood is said to have lived 1000 years[45] while the Hebrew Bible details the extraordinary lifespans of Adam's descendants prior to the Flood: Adam – 930 years; Seth – 912 years; Lamech – 777 years[46] and so on. However, such longevity is not accepted by modern science. This traditional dating for Tonpa Shenrab's birth can be interpreted in many ways, from a spiritual, scientific or combined point of view:

1. The traditional point of view accepts that his extraordinary lifespan is due to his spiritual stature as an omnipotent Buddha and is thus beyond the comprehension of the ordinary mind caught in dualistic perception and imprisoned within the dungeon of time-space.
2. Tonpa Shenrab's apparent longevity can be explained by the interpolation of several reincarnations of this Buddha. Some Buddhist lamas also use this method to explain Guru Padmasambhava's colossal lifespan of over a thousand years. Chögyal Namkhai Norbu, for example, explains Guru Padmasambhava's longevity in terms of the interpolation of the eight incarnations of the same master over this period of time. Similarly, Tonpa Shenrab Miwo manifested several forms and so performed many activities over an extraordinary length of time. This explanation might be acceptable to both spiritual practitioners and modern scholars alike.
3. Although Tonpa Shenrab, a real Central Asian Buddha, lived in this remote epoch of the LGM, his lifespan could have been exaggerated meaning that, while the date is correct, his lifespan is legendary.
4. Yet another dating for Tonpa Shenrab Miwo's life was suggested by Chögyal Namkhai Norbu in his book *Drung, Deu and Bön.*[47] He traces the date for Tonpa Shenrab's birth to 1917 BC and so according to this dating and using a lifespan of 82 human years, Tonpa Shenrab's *parinirvana*[48] should have occurred in 1835 BC. This would put his life

[45] *Vendidad*, *Fargard 2*, Tr. Darmesteter, <http://www.avesta.org/vendidad/vd2sbe.htm> accessed 25.06.07.

[46] NIV Bible, Gen. 5.

[47] Norbu, *Drung, Deu and Bön*, pp. 156–158.

[48] *Parinirvana* (Tib. mya ngan las 'das pa) is a Sanskrit word and means departure to *nirvana*, attainment of final Buddhahood.

and the development of Yungdrung Bön at the beginning of the second millennium BC contemporary with the Chinese Hsia (Xia) dynasty (2205–1766 BC).[49] This dating, however, is not accepted by Bönpo scholars I consulted[50] who consider it too late. From the point of view of modern science, too, this dating poses a problem because it is based on the lifespan of another early Yungdrung Bön *Siddha*, Lishu Tagring,[51] who in turn is recorded in traditional Bönpo sources as having lived over 2500 years.

5. In discussions on this matter, Khenpo Tenpa Yungdrung suggested another method of determining dates for Tonpa Shenrab. He maintains that, the date of Tonpa Shenrab's *parinirvana* (7817 BC) is certain and that it is this date which should be used as a historical reference.[52] He does not rule out calculating this Buddha's lifespan simply as 82 human years as opposed to 82 *shen* years. This dating might be more acceptable to modern scholars.

Our knowledge of the realities of time, space and the history (or rather prehistory) of ancient civilizations is very far from being clear. Rather, it is in a state of constant flux due to ongoing research in a wide gamut of fields which brings out new facts, challenging existing theories and timescales. A pertinent example is the prehistoric city which was accidentally discovered by Indian oceanographers conducting a survey of pollution in 2001. This remarkable find revealed the existence of a pre-Harappa civilization in the modern-day Indian state of Gujarat. Carbon dated at 7500 BC – roughly the same time as Tonpa Shenrab was on this earth – the city is five miles long and two miles wide, now flooded off the Bay of Cambay. It is thought to have been submerged at the end of the last glacial period when sea level rose as the ice cover melted.[53] The

---

49 Hsia Dynasty, *Encyclopædia Britannica*, Encyclopædia Britannica Online, <http://www.britannica.com/eb/article-9041275> accessed 04.07.07.

50 Yongdzin Lopön Tenzin Namdak, Khenpo Tenpa Yungdrung, Geshe Gelek Jinpa.

51 Tib. Khyung po sTag sgra Don gtsug Li shu sTag ring.

52 Interviews with Khenpo Tenpa Yungdrung from 2005 to 2007.

53 Pravasi Bharatiya Divas - Second Plenary Session with Minister of HRD, S&T and Ocean Development, January 10, 2003: Address by Shri Murli Manohar Joshi, Minister of HRD, S & T and Ocean Development, <http://www.ficci.com/media-room/speeches-presentations/2003/Jan/pbd-murli.htm>; BBC article, Saturday, 19 January, 2002, 06:33 GMT, Lost city "could rewrite

area where the city was located shows evidence of a developed human civilization going back to at least 14, 840 BC.[54] Some Hindu scholars believe that this city is mentioned in *Mahabharata*, but in any case, the discovery of this pre-Harappa city demonstrates that human beings were already capable of developing an advanced culture and civilization and this in turn means that we cannot simply discard the possibility that the ancient civilizations of Tagzig and Zhang Zhung existed or that the traditional dates for Tonpa Shenrab are correct, all the more so because in the period between 8000 BC and 5000 BC the climate in the Tibetan Plateau[55] and Central Asia was mild and suitable for human habitation. Unfortunately, Tibetan archaeology is still in its infancy but as it develops it may uncover solid proof of an advanced culture in the Tibetan Plateau in this period. If Tagzig and Zhang Zhung civilizations existed in the eighth millennium BC, they would of course differ from the civilization off the Bay of Cambay in that they, especially Zhang Zhung, would most probably be nomadic and thus leave much less archaeological material behind them. Myths and ancient religious texts are important sources of information which may help to locate the ancient kingdoms where Yungdrung Bön was the state religion but extraordinary talent and determination is required to relate these to historical and geographic realities. Here we should remember the case of Genrikh Shliman who found the ancient city of Troy basing his search on the information contained in Homer's *The Iliad* which had previously been considered a mere tale of the Ancient Greeks.

At present, therefore, we shall have to leave the question of the exact dating of Tonpa Shenrab Miwo open. However, one thing is sure: he lived in extreme antiquity, a religious reformer who appeared in the complex and sophisticated cultural environment of prehistoric Central Asia.

The spread of Prehistoric Bönpo culture in Eurasia

The most ancient surviving textual evidence of prehistoric culture is found in *Vedas* and *Avesta* which contain a wealth of information on

---

history",<http://news.bbc.co.uk/1/hi/world/south_asia/1768109.stm>; '9,500–Year-Old City Found Underwater Off India', <http://www.spiritofmaat.com/announce/oldcity.htm>; accessed 3.07.07.

54 Badrinaryan Badrinaryan, 'Gulf of Cambay Cradle of Ancient Civilization, Evidence from Microlithithic Tools', <http://www.grahamhancock.com/forum/BadrinaryanB1.php?p=6> accessed 03.07.07.

55 *Ancient Tibet,* Research Materials from The Yeshe De Project, (Berkeley: Dharma Publishing, 1986).

the religious practices of the Indo-Iranian Aryans. While the traditions of the *Vedas* and *Avesta* are better known and attributed to the Aryans because these peoples wrote them down and their texts survived, this doesn't mean that the religious traditions described in these texts were peculiar to them alone. We have already presented considerable evidence which demonstrates that many nations and races of prehistoric Eurasia shared a common international culture and religion, called here the Prehistoric Bön of Eurasia, the roots of which may go as far back as before the last glacial period to the Golden Age. Further scientific evidence supporting this timescale for an international culture comes from the field of genetics. Research published by Welsh geneticist Steve Jones shows a link between the Welsh, Irish, Scots, Basques, Native Americans and the Ket tribe of south Siberia, who presently live in the basin of the Yenisei River in the Krasnoyarsk region, through the male Y-chromosome.[56] This suggests that the predecessors of the aforementioned European, Siberian and American nations shared common ancestors in Eurasia as long as 40,000–50,000 years ago. It is well established that the Baikal region was an LGM refuge so when global warming began, people spread out from there with some going north as the ice retreated, eventually reaching the Americas. Others went west and became the first settlers of western Europe and the British Isles after the LGM. This genetic data generally supports Tilak's and Warren's theories about the existence of pre-LGM culture in Eurasia. Linguistic studies also support this. It has been proved that Ket, Yug, Pompokol and Arin languages from a Siberian linguistic group which is now almost extinct are related to Native American, Chinese, some Caucasian and possibly Basque tongues.[57] So the ancestors of these people could have been the *panca janah* – the five races of *Rigveda* who lived side by side with the Aryan ancestors and shared a common international culture and religion even before the LGM. This international culture became widely disseminated in Eurasia and the Americas, especially after the LGM, due to the high mobility which characterised ancient peoples.

One of the most intense arenas of ethnogenesis after the last glacial period was the Great Steppe. This huge expanse from the Carpathians in the west to the Ussuri river in the east, from the mixed forests of the eastern Europe and the Siberian *taiga* in the north to the Caucuses, Iran, Caspian and Yellow River in the south was roamed by tribes of various ethnicity and belonging to different racial types.

---

[56] Steve Jones, *Y: The Descent of Men* (London: Abacus, 2003), pp. 182–194.

[57] Ibid., pp. 183–184.

Since before the dawn of history, millions of people were moving from one side of the Great Steppe to another adjusting to the climatic and political changes. They met, mixed and created international tribal unions and multinational empires which, despite their mixed ethnicity, had a religion and social organisation spanning national differences. The renowned French comparative philologist Georges Dumézil (1898–1986) made a very fine definition of this international Eurasian culture:

> Marcel Granet, who liked impressive generalizations, said there was only one civilization from the Irish coast to the Manjurian coast. What he meant is that, from prehistoric times, there was no physical obstacle which could have obstructed interrupted or uninterrupted contact from one end of the whole North-Eurasian plane to the other, which itself is cut only by the easily surmountable chain of the Ural mountains.[58]

One early example of such mixed universal culture is the Late Neolithic Tazminskaya culture (beginning of the third millennium BC) in the basin of mid-Yenisei in Khakassia, Southern Siberia. Russian scholars believe that these people practised Tengrism,[59] in other words, Bө Murgel, a branch of Prehistoric Bön. L.R. Kyzlasov, one of the main experts on Tazminskaya culture, highlights its similarity to the culture of Mesopotamia of the fourth to third millennium BC :

> Some rocks and stellas have images of extremely ancient four-wheeled chariots, sometimes drawn by bulls. They are related to the sun cult and the thunder-god[60] [...] These sacral drawings remind us of the images from Mesopotamia of the fourth to third millennium BC. [61]

---

58 G. Dumézil, *Verkhovnye bogi indoevropeitzev* (Moscow, 1986), p. 136. Translation mine.

59 L. R. Kyzlasov, *Ocherki po istorii Sibiri i Tsentral'noi Azii* (Isdatel'stvo Krasnoyarskogo Universiteta, 1992), pp. 5–7, cited in Faizrakhmanov, *Drevnie Tyurki*, p. 26.

60 Rus. Громовик (Gromovik) which often refers to Perun or Swarog gods of pre-Christian religions of Russia.

61 L. R. Kyzlasov, *Drevnyaya i srednevekovaya istoriya Yuzhnoi Sibiri* (Khakasskoe otdelenie Krasnoyarknizhizdata, 1991), p.17 cited in B. A. Muratov, *K voprosu ob istorii vozniknoveniya tyurkskogo runicheskogo pis'ma* [Л.Р. Кызласов, *Древняя и средневековая история Южной Сибири*, p. 17, Хакасское отделение Красноярккнижиздата, 1991, cited in Б.А. Муратов, *К вопросу об истории возникновения тюркского рунического письма*] <http://lib.userline.ru/book_print.php?id=12798&page=1> accessed 06.07.07.

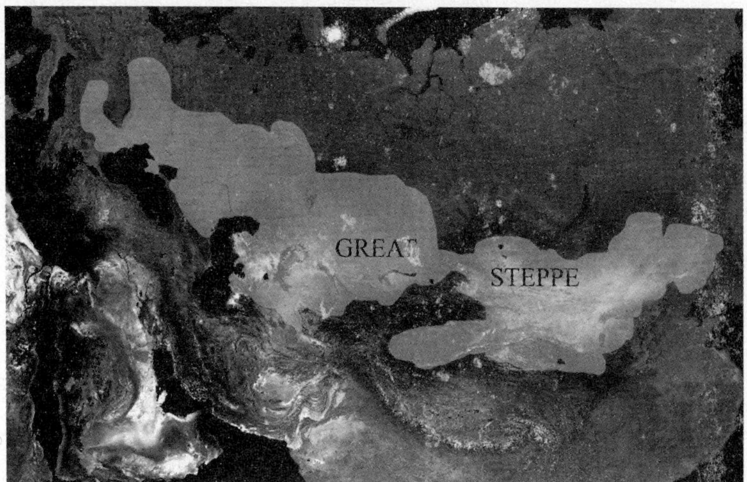

Fig. 7. Outline of the Great Steppe.

We have already seen that Sumerian, Mongol and Zhang Zhung languages have an Ural-Altaic substrate which, according to Hummel and other scholars, points to the Ural-Altaic language. The modern languages which contain these elements are now geographically very far apart, so these correspondences must be prehistoric. Indeed, if we accept Joseph Greenberg's[62] proposal of Eurasiatic-Amerind language families spoken by people who migrated to lands freed from ice as the climate warmed, we can put this phenomenon back to at least 13,000 BC. A variety of scripts were used to record these languages, although the runic script probably had the widest geographical range as it had been used since very early times by several nations in Southern Siberia, Mongolia, southeast Asia, Europe and Scandinavia. There are currently several theories regarding the origin of the runic script with some scholars suggesting it is related to Sumerian cuneiform. Runes were also used by the Etruscans.

The Bashkirian scholar B.A. Muratov demonstrated that the Tyurkic Orkhono-Yenisei runic script is extremely ancient and was probably used by the proto-Hunnu as early as the second millennium BC in what is now Chinese Turkestan.

---

62 J. H. Greenberg, *Indo-European and Its Closest Relatives: The Eurasiatic Language Family, Volume 2, Lexicon* (Stanford: Stanford University Press, 2002).

Fig. 8. Tyurkic runes used in the inscriptions on monument to Kyul' Tegin.

Fig. 9. 'Tengeri' in Tyurkic runes.

Based on his studies of Hunnu and later Tyurkic *tamga*-stamps, A.Y. Shifner (1817–1879) comes to the same conclusion. He maintains that these *tamgas* display all currently known runic symbols, both western (Scandinavian and European) and eastern (Siberian). These stamps are the only surviving examples of Hunnu runes because the leather and bark used for ordinary writing materials have disintegrated long ago.[63] As was noted in Chapter I, in the *History of the Three Kingdoms*, the Chinese diplomat Kan' Tai mentions the existence of the Hunnu script as a matter of fact. The spread of the runic script throughout such a vast area as Eurasia demonstrates once more that an international culture existed there from prehistoric times. Indeed, because of their great antiquity, these runic scripts, together with oral traditions and other ancient writing systems, would have ensured the continuation, dissemination and transmission of the knowledge, culture and religious ideas of the Prehistoric Bön of Eurasia through the ages.

Ancient and intimate connections between nations of the Great Steppe, Europe and Asia are also demonstrated through their religious symbols. Let us take the mythical griffin as an example. A griffin has the head and wings of an eagle or hawk and the body, paws and tail of a wolf or a lion. Griffins played an important role in the cultures of the Scythians, Etruscans and ancient Iranians as well as in Yungdrung Bön of Zhang Zhung where they are found in the *mandala* of Walphur Nagpo, Bönpo *Phurba*. In all these cultures griffins have protective functions, and all these cultures have links to the ancient culture of the Great Steppe,

---

[63] Muratov, *K voprosu* <http://lib.userline.ru/samizdat/12798> accessed 22.07.07.

Fig. 10. Griffin from the Walphur Nagpo mandala, *fragment of* tsakli *initiation card.*

Fig. 11. Roman Griffin.

either because they lived there, migrated from there or became recipients of this culture.

Coupled with the linguistic analysis and the existence of common or compatible writing systems, we cannot help but put all the evidence together and accept the existence of an international culture and religion in prehistoric and early historic Eurasia. The numerous parallels in the pantheons of gods, cosmologies, myths, magical techniques and cultural traits spanning the pre-Christian traditions of diverse peoples in Eurasia must be explained by their common roots in this prehistoric, international culture. How this culture disseminated was not dissimilar to the modern process of globalization, although the latter is mainly materialistic, more to do with the spread of political ideas, technology, goods and cultural traits connected with leisure. The diffusion of Prehistoric Bön was also very similar to the dissemination of many world religions such as Buddhism, for example, where Thai, Japanese and Tibetan Buddhism share a common nucleus but still differ greatly in many inner and outer aspects. While the core religious ideas of the Prehistoric Bön of Eurasia such as polytheism, creation myths, cosmology, magic and so on remained very similar, each nation created its own distinct form. Even monotheistic systems such as Judaism, for example, are traceable to this ancient religious core. Although Judaism, Christianity and Islam are labelled monotheistic they have a strongly pronounced polytheistic aspect – the hierarchy of angels, which is traced directly to pre-Zoroastrian Yazata gods adopted into Zoroastrianism from the polytheistic pantheon of proto-Indo-Iranians. The position of god in these monotheistic religions is in fact not so different from the position of the godhead of polytheistic system where the main godhead often acts through the lesser gods, represented in this case by the angels. Strictly speaking, then, these religions are in fact, henotheistic. Indeed, we could go as far as to say that the cult of saints in both Christianity and Islam is directly comparable to the worship of the *Zayaan*-spirits of powerful Bɵ and Utgan in Bɵ Murgel, and as such is based on a cultural matrix including previous customs pertaining to the Prehistoric Bön of Eurasia. In both Bɵ Murgel and modern so-called monotheistic religions, the spirits or souls of outstanding practitioners are prayed to for protection, beseeched to resolve various problems and used as the channels of communication between the living and the god. In short, many aspects of Prehistoric Bön of Eurasia survived in later organised religions and still play an important role in the spiritual life of millions of people today.

The spread of Prehistoric Bön in Siberia, Central and East Asia

Here we shall try to reconstruct possible routes along which the Prehistoric Bön of Eurasia may have spread and developed in Central and East Asia. We have already noted that Russian scholars consider the religion of Tazminskaya mixed culture in Khakassia to be Tengrism ~ Bɵ Murgel. Throughout this book we have drawn numerous direct parallels between Bɵ Murgel and the Prehistoric Bön of Tibet and have deduced that they represent branches of the same prehistoric religion. Looking at this connection through the prism of the current state of research in archaeology, linguistics and history, we can identify the general hubs, routes or arteries of communication and cultural exchange between Siberia and East Asia. There were several such routes in operation from prehistory well into the Middle Ages. One of the most important cultural hubs of the Prehistoric Bön of Asia was in modern-day Xinjiang, Chinese Turkistan. The earliest traces of humans in this region may date back to 500,000 years ago:

> Uighur archaeologist Dolkun Kamberi believes the Tarim Basin people existed as a tribe in the region from time-before-time; he has discovered a single piece of human skull in the mountains near there that dates back a half-million years. '*We can't say anything about its ethnic background*', Kamberi said of the skull fragment, '*But at least it gives us evidence that 500,000 years ago there were people there.*'[64]

---

[64] Ellen O'Brien, 'Mystery of the mummies' <http://www.fi.edu/inquirer/mummy.html > accessed 20.06.07.

Modern archaeological and DNA research into the Xinjiang mummies shows that Europoid people were the first to occupy the Tarim Basin starting from at least 2000 BC.[65] This people – known to the Bönpos of Zhang Zhung and Tibet as Thogar and to modern scholars as Tokharians – most probably migrated to the Tarim Basin from the west. They had a culture which was distinctly Indo-European and some aspects, such as tartan weaving and gold foil death masks, even have direct parallels in Celtic and Ancient Greek cultures. Indeed, contrary to claims of Chinese sources which portray them as primitive barbarians, theirs was an advanced culture. For instance, the level of culture in prehistoric Europe is demonstrated by the discovery of another mummy, the famous Ice Man found in the Italian Alps in 1991 which was dated at 3200 BC. Besides the bronze axe which the man carried before he died, researchers found astonishing evidence of very developed medical knowledge. The man was infested with whipworms and knew about his condition; he was treating himself with the fruits of the *Piptoporus Betulinus* fungi, known to modern medical science as a remedy against this condition, which he was carrying with him. He also had several 'tattoos' formed from incisions in the skin on which herbs had been burnt to provide a healing effect similar to moxibustion therapy. There were 15 groups of such marks on his back and legs, 80% of which correspond to acupuncture points known today, some of which are used to treat back pains and rheumatism, from which he most probably suffered. This sort of medical knowledge goes far beyond the basics. These findings suggest that acupuncture may have been known to the Europeans as early as 3200 BC and thus predates the earliest evidence of its existence in China (1000 BC) by at least 2200 years.[66] It is possible, then, that this art was brought to China by Indo-European migrants. Horse-riding and the invention of the chariot are also innovations brought to the regions of Takla Makan and northwest China from the west of Eurasia.

---

65 J. P. Mallory, V. H. Mair, *The Tarim Mummies: Ancient China and the Mystery of the Earliest Peoples from the West*, (London: Thames & Hudson, 2000); 'Genetic testing reveals awkward truth about Xinjiang's famous mummies', *Kaleej Times Online*, 19 April 2005, <http://www.khaleejtimes.com/DisplayArticle.asp?xfile=data/todaysfeatures/2005/April/todaysfeatures_April37.xml§ion=todaysfeatures> accessed 07.07. 07.

66 Linsey Dyer and Rick Effland, 'The Iceman: Medical Knowledge We Never Dreamed of 5,200 Years Ago' <http://www.mc.maricopa.edu/dept/d10/asb/anthro2003/legacy/iceman/iceman.html> accessed 07.07.07.

Between 1300[67] and 1000 BC, people of Europoid and Mongoloid racial types began living alongside one another in this region and formed mixed communities. This is clear from the appearance of burial sites where Indo-Europeans and Mongoloids are buried side by side, another indication that they shared a common religion. At the same time, the Karasukskaya culture emerged in Southern Siberia with similar characteristics. Gumilev considers these people to be proto-Hunnu, a mixed nation of Indo-Europeans and Mongoloids, migrants from northern China who crossed the Gobi around 1200 BC.[68] Gumilev suggests that the proto-Hunnu emerged from the mixing of Europoid Di and Dinling[69] with Mongoloids but they most probably appeared as the result of more than two Indo-European and Mongoloid peoples which certainly would have included Tokharians. Kan' Tai reports that Hunnu script is similar to that of Funan (ancient Cambodia) and India, so it was probably modelled on Tokharian script, of which there are two distinct versions. The exact ethnicity of the Dinling has not been established, but dating back to prehistoric rimes this Europoid nation lived in Southern Siberia as well as in the basin of the Yellow River. It is possible that they travelled backwards and forwards between Southern Siberia, the Tarim Basin and the Yellow River basin following the mountain ranges to avoid the deserts. It is clear, then, that there were channels of communication between Southern Siberia, the Tarim Basin and the Yellow River basin, and that Indo-Europeans who probably arrived from the west and other Europoids from the north began mixing with Mongoloids in the regions bordering Zhang Zhung to the north and northeast. At the same time, tribes of Tibetan stock such as the Qiang and Minyag (Tanguut) were also living in Qinghai and Amdo which was connected with the Tarim Basin by the Gansu (Hexi) Corridor. This huge region was a major cross-cultural hub which connected west and east, north and south, a major Asian melting pot where intense processes of ethnogenesis and cultural and religious exchange took place. And it is to and from this region that traditions of Prehistoric Bön travelled in all directions with migrating peoples and via the trade routes.

---

[67] According to Li Shuicheng, A Discussion of Sino-Western Cultural Contact and Exchange in the Second Millennium BC Based on Recent Archeological Discoveries, *Sino-Platonic Papers* № 97, (December 1999).

[68] Gumilev, *Istoriya Hunnu* I, p.36.

[69] Gumilev belives that Di and Dinling are two different Europoid peoples while other researchers believe they are the same. It is also possibility that Chinese referred to all Indo-Europeans to the west of its borders as Di.

Zhuns and Zhang Zhung

Another obscure though very ancient nation of this region which is important for our research is the Zhuns. Records state that the Chinese were at war with the Zhuns as early as the Hsia dynasty (2205–1766 BC). The Zhuns are said to have lived in the mountains to the north and northwest of Hsia which occupied modern Henan and the southwestern part of Shaanxi provinces of China at that time. It seems that the Zhuns were a very loose confederation of tribes and they are often referred to as Zhun-Di. We know that the Di were Europoids so the Zhun-Di were most probably an interracial tribal union of proto-Mongols and Indo-Europeans and/or Paleosiberian white peoples. Hsia waged constant wars against the Zhuns, pushing them towards the west, north and south. Following the expansion of the Chinese state of Shang-Yin, which opened the trade routes between China and Southern Siberia, the subsequent Chou (Zhou) continued battling the Zhuns with mixed results; they were overrun by them on occasions and were even ruled by them. Interestingly, the Chou dynasty itself emerged from a mixed Chinese-Zhun line. In 1797 BC, Chinese courtier Gun-lyu was exiled from Hsia and went to live with the western Zhuns together with a number of his followers. Descendants of these Chinese lived with the western Zhuns and mixed with them until in 1327 BC this mixed population was expelled by the Zhuns and returned to Shaanxi led by Shan-fu where they formed a new nation, eventually producing the Chou dynasty.[70]

Throughout history Chinese sources describe many sub-groups of Zhun-Di such as Guan'-Zhun, Shan-Zhun (Bei-Zhun), Chi-Di, Bai-Di, Gun'-Zhu, Di-Wan', Gin-Shui, Qi-Shui, Ikyui, Dali, Yuezhi (An'-din), Syuyang, Linhu, and Leufan'. Shan-Zhun or 'Mountain Zhuns' are said to have been an extremely ancient nation as they came into contact with Chinese even before the Yao dynasty which began in 2357 BC.[71] That means that both western Zhuns and Shan-Zhuns were contemporary with the Zhang Zhung Confederation. They were living in the huge territory between the Hami (Rami) oasis in Takla Makan and the Hingan mountains. N.Y. Bichurin acknowledges the confusion surrounding the Zhuns and the Hu, both names being applied to the wide variety of non-Chinese nations which either controlled parts of Chinese territory or bordered it on the north and west. He maintains that when the names

---

70 Gumilev, *Istoriya Hunnu* I, pp. 18–20.

71 According to Bichurin, *Sobranie svedenii* on-line <http://www.vostlit.info/Texts/Dokumenty/China/Bicurin/Sobr_sved_o_narodach/Tom_I/text11.htm> accessed 09.07.07.

'Zhun' and 'Hu' refer to the nations to the north of China they mainly indicate Mongoloid tribes, but when they refer to the nations to the west of China then Zhuns are Tanguut (Minyag) – a mix of Zhun and some Tibetan tribes – whereas Hu are the proto-Tyurkyuts and Indo-Iranians of the Tarim Basin. Furthermore, Bichurin describes the Zhun-yi and Guan'-yi who dwelled in Gansu as a mixture of proto-Mongols and Tanguut.[72] Gumilev suggests that we should consider the Zhun-Di to be the original nation with the Shan-Zhun as part of Zhun-Di later cut off from the main body after they lost the One Thousand Years War against the Chinese and mixed with proto-Mongol Dunhu in Inner Mongolia. In short, the ongoing scholarly debate about the precise ethnical and racial origin of the Zhuns[73] is far from over.

Bearing in mind that the Zhung-Di were contemporary with Zhang Zhung and bordered it from the southeast, east, northeast and north, we can legitimately ask: could the tribes forming the Zhang Zhung Confederation have been related to the Zhuns in some way? There are good grounds for assuming so. The arguments presented here is primarily focused on religion and culture, so adds a new angle from which we can suggest, at least culturally, that the Zhuns are related to the peoples who formed the Zhang Zhung Confederation on the Tibetan Plateau.

Since prehistoric times, the Yellow River basin was a hot point of civilization populated by diverse tribes of different national and racial types which included Europoid, Mongoloid, mixed Europoid-Mongoloid Zhun-Di, proto-Chinese, proto-Mongols and proto-Tyurks as well as some other tribes of unspecified ethnic and racial types. These diverse peoples interacted with each other in many ways: through intermarriage, political unions, armed conflicts, religious ceremonies and so on. Indeed, descriptions of the ancient Chinese Emperors bear little resemblance to modern Chinese features; they are often said to have an 'eagle's profile' and bushy beards, while some had ginger hair and blue eyes.[74]

Other contemporary hubs of similar ethnogenesis and cultural exchange were the Tarim Basin and modern-day Amdo (affiliated with Zhang Zhung from prehistoric times until it was annexed by the Tibetans in the seventh century AD). Ancient Chinese *Wu*, proto-

---

[72] Ibid.

[73] Gumilev, Dinlinskaya problema: Peresmotr gipotezy G. E. Grumm-Grzhmailo v svete novykh istoricheskikh i arkheologicheskikh materialov, Izvesstiya Vsesoyuznogo Geograficheskogo obshchestva SSSR No. 1, 1959; Gumilev, *Istoriya Hunnu* I, pp. 23–25.

[74] Ibid.

Mongol Bo Murgel and Zhang Zhung Bön represented related branches of the common international Prehistoric Bön religion practised among the many nations of this huge region of Asia. As we saw in Chapter I, Bönpo sources tell us that the knowledge of medicine and astrology, in particular the system of eight *parkha* (*pakua*) trigrams and nine *mewa*, was brought to China in antiquity by the students of Tonpa Shenrab himself. So the legendary Fu Hsi (2953–2838 BC),[75] the first *Wu*-priest king of China who is credited with the discovery of the *pakua* trigrams in China, may in fact correspond to Gya Kongtse Trulgyi Gyalpo of Bönpo sources.[76] Interestingly, the religion of the *Wu*-priests was reorganised and institutionalised at the time of the Chou dynasty and as we have seen, the Chou dynasty was founded by the mixed Chinese-Western Zhun people on their return to China following their 300 year long stay in unspecified western mountains. The institutionalization of *Wu* in Chou may well, then, be due to new cultural and religious influences brought by this mixed tribe from the Zhuns. This in turn may point to the existence of an institutionalised state religion among the Zhuns, which fits the profile of Zhang Zhung where Yungdrung Bön was the state religion and Bönpo priests had obligations to the kings and the state, precisely the characteristics the *Wu*-priests were granted in newly formed Chou where they were tied to the ruling dynasty. The practices of the *Wu*-priests of Chou are also directly comparable to those of the Bönpos of Zhang Zhung and Tibet in many aspects such as predictions through oracular trance, dream interpretation, divination, weather control, medicine and astrology found within the Causal Bön. It is these traditions which later developed into the Tao Chiao schools of Taoist ritualistic magic. The philosophical systems of Lao Tzu and Chuang Tzu or Tao Chia with their doctrine of emptiness also arose from the background of late Chou culture and display a number of characteristics common to Yungdrung Bön. Furthermore, the Chinese swastika turns anticlockwise, another reference to Bön.

Hsia Chinese describe the Zhuns as 'the western mountain dwellers' which matches the description of Zhang Zhung to the west of Hsia.

---

75 According to M. E. Ermakov, *Magiya Kitaya* (St. Petersburg: Azbuka-klassika, 2003) p. 35.

76 Modern scholars tend to identify Gya Kongtse Trulgyi Gyalpo with Confucius but he doesn't fit Confucius' profile. Gya Kongtse Trulgyi Gyalpo was a Chinese king while Confucius was an adviser to the kings. He isn't credited with bringing out a new system of astrology or divination but simply wrote commentaries based on already existing and extremely ancient texts such as *I-Ching*.

During the war between the Hsia and the Zhuns, the latter are said to have been pushed to the north, west and the south with the southern branch reaching modern-day Yunnan. It is perhaps no coincidence, then, that the modern Nakhi, who live in Yunnan on the border with ancient Zhang Zhung, practise a kind of Mixed Bön. What is more, as the Nakhi themselves, who originally inhabited the northeastern borderlands of Zhang Zhung,[77] probably came to this region later, they must have absorbed elements of local Zhun culture. The branch of Zhuns pushed north was cut off from the rest of the nation and mixed with the proto-Mongol Dunhu. They may well have gradually adopted the language of the Dunhu or spoken a pidgin and were therefore identified as Mongoloid on the basis of language rather than ethnicity – a common occurrence in the Great Steppe.[78] The Zhuns who were squeezed west must have returned to Zhang Zhung and the Takla Makan region. We saw in Chapter I that Zhang Zhung covered an enormous territory and was divided into three main regions: Western, Central and Eastern. The picture painted by Chinese historians of the geographical distribution of the Zhun-Di and their mixed ethnic composition leads us to suggest that the Zhuns were, in fact, an outflow of tribes from Eastern Zhang Zhung (*smad*). This fits the profile of the Zhang Zhung Confederation as a tribal state comprised of many ethnically and racially diverse nomadic tribes who nevertheless shared a common culture and who roamed the Tibetan Plateau and beyond, sometimes forming their own states on the outskirts of the Confederation. The example of the Qiang and Tanguuts (Minyag) partly demonstrates the high mobility and wide geographic distribution of Zhang Zhung tribes. While the heartland of these peoples was in Kokonoor, Gumilev demonstrates that the Fans of Shaanxi and Sichuan were in fact Tanguuts[79] while the Yang-t'ung tribe of Qiang was reported by Tang historians as living in Zhang Zhung territory in western Tibet in the seventh century AD.[80]

The suggestion that the Zhuns and Zhung-Di were some of the tribes of Eastern Zhang Zhung also finds support from linguistic research. Hummel underlines many close similarities between Zhang Zhung language, languages of Minyag and Hsi Hsia (Xi Xia) (branches of Tanguut), Qiang, Moso (Nakhi) and Lolo. Moreover, Zhang Zhung has

---

[77] Hummel, *On Zhang-zhung*, p. 69.

[78] A good example of this is the so-called Tyurkic people, classified as such on a merely linguistic basis.

[79] Gumilev, *Dinlinskaya problema*.

[80] *Ancient Tibet*, Yeshe De Project, p. 135.

some traces of archaic Chinese.[81] All these peoples match the geographical and ethnic parameters of the Zhuns and Zhun-Di, as was demonstrated above. Their languages were related to the dialects of Eastern Zhang Zhung but were also partially influenced by Chinese as they were in constant contact with the Chinese.

The name 'Zhun' is not necessarily the self-designation but rather is probably the name given by the Chinese to the tribes which bordered their lands on the west and north. This name could either reflect these people's self-designation or it may simply be a Chinese name unrelated to it. Curiously, the original name of Zhang Zhung was simply 'Zhung' which translates into Tibetan as *khyung*, a sacred horned eagle. According to Chögyal Namkhai Norbu, the second syllable, 'Zhang', was added later. He interprets it as a sign of respect on the part of Tibetans and takes it to mean 'maternal uncle' because many Tibetan kings married Zhang Zhung princesses.[82] However, in the light of the above discussion, it seems reasonable to suggest that *zhun* is a phonetic representation of *zhung* and refers to the border tribes of Eastern Zhang Zhung. If that is so then the word 'Zhang' may have yet another undiscovered meaning. If 'Shan-Zhun' and 'Zhang Zhung' refer to the same or related peoples then it is also possible that 'Zhang' may have the same or a similar semantic field as Tibetan and Chinese '*shang*'[83] meaning 'mountain' or 'high' whereby the full name – Zhang Zhung – may mean 'Mountain Eagle'. This is plausible because Zhang Zhung is located in a high mountain region and the *khyung*-eagle plays a very important part in both Prehistoric and Yungdrung Bön. If Zhang Zhung is called after the mythical eagle, this would suggest that the Zhang Zhung people are much more ancient than if the element 'zhang' had been added later by Tibetans. Furthermore, the importance of the mythological eagle, which does not feature prominently among Chinese mythological animals, in the culture of the Tibetan Plateau and the Asian part of the Great Steppe, even in the later period, can be put down the strong repercussions of the Zhuns, Zhun-Di and Shan-Zhuns being assimilated by the proto-Hunnu and Dunhu. We can find many examples showing the continuation of this cultural affinity through the millennia in the religions and customs of the peoples of the Tibetan Plateau, west and north China, the Great Steppe, and Siberia, many of which have been explored in this book.

---

81 Hummel, *On Zhang-zhung*, pp. 8–9, 69–70.

82 Norbu, *Drung, Deu and Bön*, Introduction, p. xvi.

83 Tib. shang; Chin. shang. See Hummel, *On Zhang-zhung*, p. 82, n. 1.

The significance of the sacred eagle in Zhang Zhung, Tibet and the Great Steppe is further emphasized by its presence in the royal apparel on special occasions. Here is the description of the Tibetan kings' dress for the New Year ceremony:

> On this occasion a costume was worn which recalls vividly the dress of the shamans. It was white, the hair of the head was rolled up and held together by silver bands, protected by a turban bearing the image of khyung.[84]

Indeed, this dress is directly comparable to the attire worn by White Bɵ who dressed in white and wore a white hat. The Khaans of the Tyurkyut and Mongols were also the supreme Bɵ and so dressed in the same way. This example of the headdress worn by Tibetan Kings is matched in the headdress of Kyul'-Tegin, the great *khagan* of the Tyurkyuts who lived in the beginning of the eighth century AD. The head of his memorial statue is topped with a five-pointed crown with the image of the eagle just above his forehead.[85] This demonstrates that the cult of the heavenly eagle akin to Zhung/*Khyung* was of paramount importance in the Tyurkyut religion. The tremendous continuity and tenacity of culture in the Great Steppe has already been demonstrated many times in this book so there is every reason to suppose that this cultural and religious symbol most probably comes from the Hunnu who were contemporary with the Zhang Zhung Confederation and whose proto-Hunnu ancestors included the Shan-Zhuns. This in turn again suggests that the Shan-Zhuns are, or are related to, the tribes of Eastern Zhang Zhung.

Initial spread of the various types of Bön to, from and around Zhang Zhung

Languages and multinational culture of Zhang Zhung

It might seem strange that we start this section with a short summary of the ongoing research on the language of Zhang Zhung but results in this field show to some extent the cultural and geographical spread of Bönpo culture and the peoples involved in this process. The exact provenance of the Zhang Zhung language is not firmly established and there is ongoing research and debate as to its origins. There are currently two predominant views. One relates Zhang Zhung primarily to the languages

---

[84] Tucci, *The Religions of Tibet*, p. 237.

[85] Gumilev, *Drevnie Tyurki*, p. 361 mentioned in ch. I.

of the western Himalayas, Bhotia languages of the Almora district of Uttarkhand, India, Nepal and the languages of the eastern Himalayas such as Hruso, Dafla, Toto and Dhimal with some scholars suggesting that Zhang Zhung was primarily an Indo-European language. The second view, presented by Hummel, holds that Zhang Zhung is related to the languages of the northeastern and southeastern borderlands such as Minyag, Qiang and Nakhi and has some parallels with archaic Chinese. This second view seems to suggest that the Zhang Zhung language was primarily of Tibetan origin with possible proto-Mongol traits. These two theories are not necessarily contradictory as Zhang Zhung culture emerged when nomadic peoples of different ethnic and racial types mixed. According to Hummel, there were eight major and twenty-four minor dialects of Zhang Zhung, some of which differed widely; they may even have been related languages rather than dialects. Furthermore, many different writing systems were used in Zhang Zhung, which is not surprising bearing in mind its mixed ethnic background.

Fig. 12. Zhang Zhung Lhabab Yige script (Tib. Zhang zhung lha bab yig ge).

Precisely when Zhang Zhung developed its scripts is not known, but it most definitely happened millennia before the introduction of Indian Buddhism in the seventh-eighth centuries AD. We can be sure of this because the Aryans and Indo-European Tokharians, who played a significant role in the early ethnogenesis in Zhang Zhung, had their writing systems in very early times. The Hunnu, who as we have seen most probably contained a Zhang Zhung substrate, had their own script, and the Chinese pilgrim Sung-yin reported in 518 AD that the Azha, who were very closely connected to Zhang Zhung and later Tibet from very early times, had their own script, a century before the Thonmi Sambhota allegedly created the Tibetan script modelled on the Gupta one used to write Sanskrit.[86]

---

[86] *Ancient Tibet*, Yeshe De Project, p. 136.

Zhang Zhung was comprised from a wide variety of culturally sophisticated ethnic groups and sub-groups. The Zhang Zhung Confederation could in some ways be compared to the EU as it was a huge multinational and multicultural union of smaller tribal states with common religion(s) and similar political organisation defined in this case by the geography of the Tibet-Qinghai Plateau. Central government was located in west Tibet, a Brussels of a sort, but important assemblies were also held in Eastern Zhang Zhung,[87] its Strasbourg. Like the EU, Zhang Zhung's political, religious and cultural influence spread far beyond its borders. These borders, though, were fluctuating and not clearly defined because of the nomadic nature of the Confederation's peoples and changing political realities as border tribes came in and out of Zhang Zhung's control. Yongdzin Lopön Tenzin Namdak describes life in ancient Zhang Zhung in the following way:

> The Tibetan civilization comes from the Zhang Zhung civilization. Zhang Zhung was one of the biggest kingdoms in early times, until it was destroyed by the Tibetan king Trisong Deutsen in the seventh century [...] Zhang Zhung existed in what is now the West and North of Tibet, and Tibet was only the central part. Throughout most of the country people were nomads although some people lived and farmed by the lakes. There were very special holy places beside the lakes and people grew good quality barley and turnips; those were the only crops. Other places were too cold for crops, they were only suitable for nomads. Even now grains are grown on the lakeshores and they are very special and large, so that's why they are called holy places. Elsewhere there were only nomads. So it is difficult for archaeologists and historians who want to prove something because, although it was a rich civilization, it is difficult to find out about it. In some parts of the kingdom there are remains similar to ruined castles which are still visible. In the past, very few scholars mentioned the names of those places and it is even hard to locate the castles. In the central kingdom there was a castle called 'White Syllable Castle', Khyunglung Ngulkar. There was a forest where even sandalwood trees grew. Now there is nothing, hardly even any grass; it's mainly dry now. From time to time you can see how the lakes dried up and the lake's age can be deduced by examining the shoreline. Most lakes don't contain drinking water – many are soda or salt – so it is difficult to find pure water. Sometimes

[87] The last Ligmincha king of Zhang Zhung was murdered by Tibetan special forces deep in Zhang Zhung territory while travelling to an assembly in the Sumpa region of Eastern Zhang Zhung in Kham.

> people make pilgrimages to the Northern plateau and follow animal tracks to find drinking water. Such a search might take days on foot or maybe on a yak or a horse. In early times the Northern plateau was very big but now Chinese trucks and lorries go everywhere so it's easy to travel and the plateau is not so big. Maybe it's got smaller! [...] In winter you can drive anywhere but in summer there is a lot of water – if there's too much water you get stuck in the mud.
>
> Most people lived in tents, not canvas ones, but ones made of yak hair. There are two types of yak hair, rough and smooth. The rough one is woven and of very good quality. It is used for the tents. In summer it is water- and heatproof and in winter it is cold-proof. It is really very good. The smooth part of the yak hair is made into blankets and is very warm. When the animals had grazed all the grass from around about, the nomads would move to the next place and leave only ash behind, nothing else. Therefore scholars can't find anything and many Western scholars say Zhang Zhung didn't exist and that it was made up by Bönpos when there was conflict with Buddhists in the seventh century. Maybe in the past it was easy to say that and people wrote books and said it was true. Now, however, the Chinese have come and the doors are open, so where are the books now? Who will buy them? What's the use?[88]
>
> The rest of the people who lived as farmers had very small houses made of stone and clay. This was the same in the kingdom of Zhang Zhung. Zhang Zhung means Garuda Valley, Khyung Lung in Tibetan. These places were huge towns. Namkhai Norbu Rinpoche made a film there, so now you need to hide the early books carefully in the bookcase, because the film shows there was a kingdom. These castles and ruins are comparable with those of Egypt or Mesopotamia, Babylon. It seems that in the past they forgot about them and thought they were hills. Now the buildings are in ruins or like caves and the homeless live there, but if you look, you can see it was a big, dried town.
>
> That is not the only castle – the North, West and East as well as parts of Western Nepal have ruined castles. It was a huge country, so many ruins and castles belong to Zhang Zhung and even now they are gradually discovering more.[89]

This description of the lifestyle of Zhang Zhung people is very similar to that of the peoples of Great Steppe to the north of it.

---

[88] An allusion to the recent studies made by the Tibetan, Chinese and Western scholars in the fields of archaeology, anthropology and linguistics etc. which clearly and scientifically demonstrated the existence of ancient Zhang Zhung, dispelling misconceptions of the past.

[89] Namdak, trscr. & ed. Ermakovi, *Evening Conference on Bön.*

Eastern and Western vectors along which Bönpo culture was distributed in Zhang Zhung

There seem to have been two major routes by which different strands of Bön travelled into the Tibetan Plateau and two major racial types which combined creating the Zhang Zhung Confederation and its international culture. The process of ethnogenesis and cultural exchange on the Tibetan Plateau was probably very similar to, and to some extent connected with, that of the neighbouring northern and northeastern regions of the Gansu corridor and the Tarim Basin. However, there were two major points or hubs of ethnogenesis in Zhang Zhung: one in west Tibet in Changthang, and one in east Tibet in Kham and Amdo.

Strands of Bön coming in and out of the Tibetan Plateau from this eastern hub certainly pertained to Prehistoric Bön. Strands of Bön coming into the Tibetan Plateau from the west were brought by Indo-European people, most probably Indo-Iranian Aryan tribes who passed through western Tibet on their way to India and southeast Iran. Some stayed and later mixed with the tribes coming from the east and this explains the layer of Sanskrit sounding words in the Zhang Zhung language. So the Arya Bönpo[90] priests of Zhang Zhung who wore the white turbans, a characteristic headdress of many Indo-Iranian peoples,

Fig. 13. Dhami *priests of Humla, Nepal wearing white robes and white turbans decorated with strands of white wool.*

90 Tib. ar ya bon po, a ya bon po.

were initially ethnic Aryans and it was only later that the word *arya* came to mean 'noble', the meaning transferred into Tibetan language. There were probably two different types of Arya Bönpo who brought with them Prehistoric and Yungdrung Bön respectively. This is concurrent with information from Yungdrung Bön sources which tell us that when Shenrab Miwo came to teach in Zhang Zhung, there were already Bönpo priests of Prehistoric Bön of various ethnicity, with some Bönpo priest travelling to see him from Zahor, Kashmir and Gilgit.[91] Whether the Aryans used the term 'bön' in eastern Europe, the Caucasus and the Great Steppe before they came to Zhang Zhung is unclear, but their priests were certainly called Arya Bönpo in Zhang Zhung and in the Himalayas in general. This justifies the use of the term Prehistoric Bön of Eurasia in this book from yet another angle. Arya Bönpo of Prehistoric Bön, for example *dhami* and *dhangre* priests of Nyinba in Humla, Nepal, can still be found practising in the villages in the Himalayas.[92]

Some strands of the Vedic tradition probably underwent a transformation in the area of Mount Kailash, the seat of Shiva, a new god not found in Vedas. The appearance of this new, very powerful mythical and religious strand connected with Shiva might have been a result of Vedic traditions integrating with the traditions of Prehistoric Bön coming into the same area from the east brought by the proto-Tibetan, proto-Mongol, proto-Tyurk, Indo-European and mixed peoples from Xinjiang and Amdo.

Since we find many dark skinned people in the Himalayan borderlands and in Tibet itself, it is not impossible that the Kailash region was also the home of some tribes of mixed proto-Dravidian/proto-Australoid type similar to the peoples of Harappa and Mohenjo Daro[93] whose culture and religion became one of the components of the melting pot. Parallels between Kashmiri Shaivism and Yungdrung Bön relating to some external aspects of Tantra and meditation techniques indicate that this new tradition was exposed to Yungdrung Bön as well as Prehistoric Bön, absorbing some of its techniques but not its views. It is no coincidence that Mount Kailash is the most important sacred place in later Hinduism.

---

[91] See ch. IV.

[92] Jinpa, Ramble,Dunham, Kelly, *Sacred Landscape,* p. 60.

[93] Ed. John Marshall, *Mohenjo-Daro and the Indus civilization: being an official account of archaeological excavations at Mohenjo-Daro carried out by the Government of India between the years 1922 and 1927*, Vol. I Asian Educational Services, Ne Delhi-Chennai, 2004, pp. 107–111.

Fig. 14. Shiva and his family in their dwelling on Mount Kailash.

Aryans had firsthand knowledge of the geography of Mount Kailash as the palace of Shiva and the source of the four major rivers of India and must have lived there for some time before most of them moved to India bringing the new Shaivit cult with them, which then evolved further in India. While not all Aryans passed through west Tibet on their way to India, some tribes definitely did. Some strands of Yungdrung Bön reached Zhang Zhung from Gilgit (Drusha) with the Dru tribe. However, as this tribe originated in the country of the Thogar/Tokharian (Yuezhi) inter-tribal union of Indo-Europeans, Qiang and proto-Mongols[94] who originally lived in the Tarim Basin, it is just possible that Yungdrung Bön was initially spread in the Tarim Basin independently of Zhang Zhung in an earlier epoch. The progenitor of the Dru, Özer Dangden,[95] who possessed the essence of all Buddhas of Yungdrung Bön, descended to the country of Thogar from the dimension of the Sky-gods where he was teaching and took the name Drusha Namse Chyitol.[96] The King of Thogar, Seve Salbar,[97] was so impressed by the appearance and teachings of Drusha Namse Chyitol that he offered him his kingdom. Descendants of Drusha are said to have later ruled Gilgit and western Tibet before part of the lineage spread into the central Tibetan province of Tsang.[98] Originally from the Tarim Basin, the Thogar later formed an empire (also known as Kushana, first to third centuries AD), which controlled large swathes of land which, at its peak, included Bactria, Tajikistan, Afghanistan, Pakistan and parts of northern India.

---

94 Some scholars suggest that Tibetan Gar (Tib. 'gar) clan might be related to Yuezhi. (*Ancient Tibet,* Yeshe De Project, p. 134.)

95 Tib. 'Od zer mDangs ldan.

96 Tib. Bru shag Nam gsas sPyi brtol.

97 Tib. Sad ve gSal bar.

98 Tib. gTsang. Karmay, *The Treasury*, pp. 6–8.

Southward spread of Prehistoric Bön along the borders of Zhang Zhung

When the mixed Zhun-Di and proto-Mongol tribes from Xinjiang, Amdo and western China were forced southwards by the Chinese Hsia this became another important route along which Prehistoric Bön was spread in the Himalayas on the borders of Zhang Zhung. The process of the movement and resettlement of this and subsequent waves of mixed tribes similar to them lasted many centuries. They continued moving south along the Himalayan foothills bypassing south-eastern and southern parts of the Tibetan Plateau and settling in different places along the way. Some of them came as far south as Arunachal Pradesh in India and Nepal where they became the ancestors of tribes of Mongoloid and mixed stock such as Tamang, Thakali and Tamu (Gurung). Modern researchers find parallels between the Tamu and the modern Tu of Qinghai and Amdo who are the descendants of the Tuyuhun and the Azha of the Kokonoor region before them, and the Qiang of Sichuan, also originally from the same region.[99] Yongdzin Lopön Tenzin Namdak believes that the original language of the Thakali, Thamu and Tamang could have been Seke,[100] a Zhang Zhung dialect.[101] This would all seem to support the suggestion that part of the Zhuns who were an outflow of the tribes of Eastern Zhang Zhung arrived in Nepal via this southward migration route, bringing the traditions of Prehistoric Bön with them.

Spread of Yungdrung Bön within Zhang Zhung and beyond

From the picture painted above we can see that Zhang Zhung had two polar centres or cultural hubs of Bön, one in the west and one in the east with the western hub being the initial point of entry of Yungdrung Bön, the teachings of the Buddha from Central Asia. As the Yungdrung Bön tradition gathered strength in the west its area expanded eastwards and it became the official state religion of the three regions of the Zhang Zhung Confederation. Yungdrung Bön gradually supplanted Prehistoric Bön although some tribes and individuals continued practising Prehistoric Bön or mixed Prehistoric and Yungdrung Bön forming minor but strong traditions which survive to this day on the borders of Tibet. Yungdrung Bön continued spreading from the region of Mount Kailash towards the

---

99 Gurung, *Bön in the Himalaya*, p. 239.

100 Tib. se skad.

101 Ibid., p. 237–238.

south, east and north. In the east it reached Amdo and western China, in the north it reached the Tarim Basin and was carried throughout the Great Steppe and further distributed in the Great Steppe by diverse nomadic tribes. In the south it reached Central Tibet, Mon (Bhutan) and Nepal.

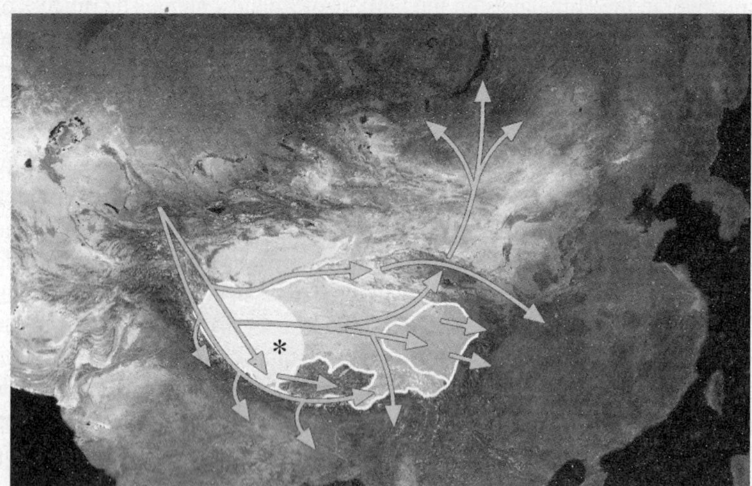

Fig. 15. Map of the initial spread of Prehistoric and Yungdrung Bön in and around Zhang Zhung from the Western Hub (*).

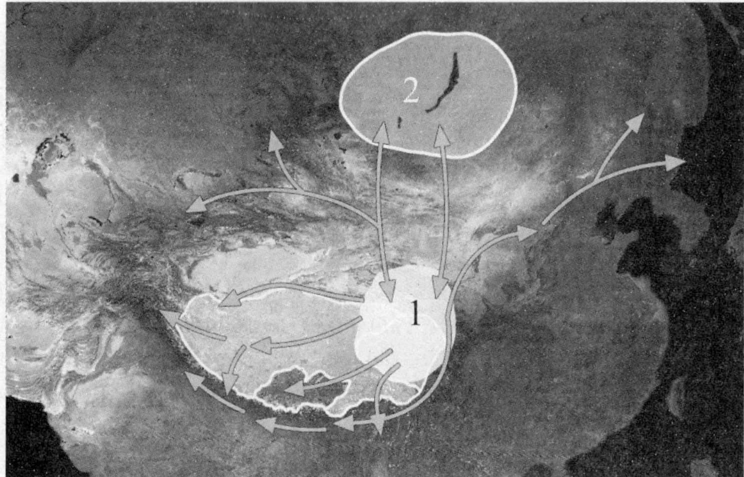

Fig. 16. Map of the initial spread of Prehistoric Bön in and around Zhang Zhung from the Eastern Hub. (1: Eastern Hub; 2: Baikal Region).

Spread of Bön from the Tibetan Plateau into the Great Steppe, Europe, Mongolia and Siberia

Hunnu

Traditions of Prehistoric Bön, Yungdrung Bön and Mixed Bön flowing from Zhang Zhung's eastern hub and the Kokonoor region went north and northeast into the Great Steppe and also penetrated western and southwestern China. It is difficult to understand to which extent pure Yungdrung Bön was present beyond the Tarim Basin and what percentage it represented in the Mixed Bön traditions which passed into the Great Steppe and reached Southern Siberia. Proto-Hunnu crossed the Gobi around 1200 BC bringing the first wave of Bön from Eastern Zhang Zhung with them. Subsequent great empires of the steppe, many of which included Southern Siberia, spread different strands of Bön in all directions. At the end of the first millennium BC and beginning of the first millennium AD this sort of 'Steppe Bön' began moving westwards into Central Asia, the Urals and eastern Europe, first with the Yuezhi, who were pushed west by the Hunnu, and then with the Hunnu themselves when their empire began disintegrating and split into four main branches.

The northern Hunnu were defeated by the Syanbi and pushed from their lands while one branch of the northern Hunnu known as the 'Indomitable Hunnu' migrated to south and west Siberia, the southern Urals, and the lower reaches of the Volga and Don.[102] In the Urals and Europe, the Hunnu conquered and mixed with the local tribes of various ethnic origins and became known as Huns. This new nation reached the height of its power under Atilla (434–543 AD),[103] known to the Mongols as Itil Khaan, and this tribal union of the Huns unified the tribes of Goths, Ostgots, Geruls, Gepids and so on. Led by the Huns, this tribal union repeatedly attacked the Western Roman Empire which eventually collapsed. The European Huns also disintegrated, breaking into several mixed tribes which in the Greek sources of the fifth to sixth centuries AD appear as Huno-Savirs, Huno-Utigurs, Huno-Kutigurs, and Hunugurs.[104] These tribes, especially the Hunugurs and Huno-Kutigurs, played an important role in the ethnogenesis which eventually gave rise to modern Hungarians and Bulgarians while the Huno-Savirs are one of the ancestral strands of modern Chuvash. The Hunnu's religion survived

---

[102] Faizrakhmanov, *Drevnie Tyurki*, p. 64.

[103] Ibid. p. 76.

[104] Gumilev, *Istoriya Hunnu* II, p. 345.

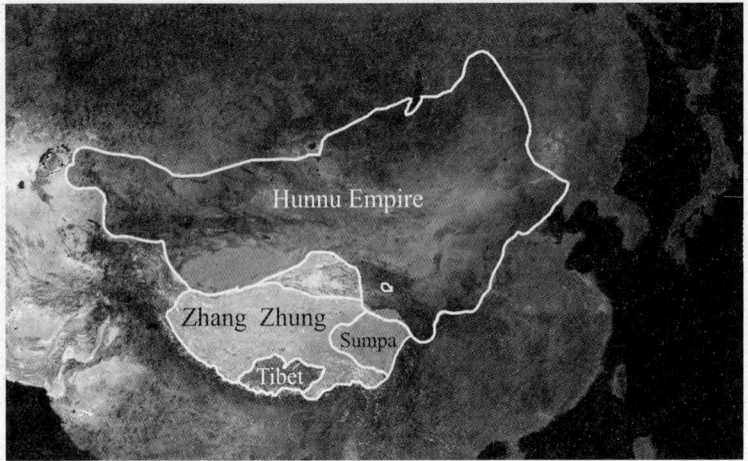

Fig. 17. The Zhang Zhung Confederation and the Hunnu Empire.

in eastern Europe within the Bulgarian Khaanates in the Danube and Volga regions until the ninth-tenth centuries AD when Christianity was adopted in Danubian Bulgaria and Islam in the Volga region. Several monuments with runic and Greek inscriptions are found in both regions. In particular, a marble column near Madar in Bulgaria describes the worship of Tangra (Tengeri) by Bulgarian Khaan Omurtag[105] providing irrefutable evidence that the Prehistoric Bön traditions of the Hunnu were continued in Europe.

Another group of the Indomitable Hunnu remained in western and Southern Siberia where they mixed with the local proto-Tyurkic tribes becoming the ancestors of the Tyurkyut.

The southern Hunnu moved to northern China in the period between 48–87 AD bringing their Bön traditions with them. They submitted to the Chinese with whom they mixed to a certain extent. In 304 AD they rose against the Chinese under the leadership of Lyu Yuan who was declared the Shanyui of Hunnu and took the title Wan, thus forming the mixed Hunnu-Chinese dynasty of Lyu-Han with its capital in Pinyang. Lyu-Han fought against the Syanbi state of Muyun(g) in the east and Jin in the south but lasted until 318 AD when it broke into two: Older Zhao and Younger Zhao. Younger Zhao took over Older Zhao in 329 AD and subsequently controlled the whole of northern China. However, in 350 AD Chinese traitor Zhang Min (Shi Min), adopted son of the Hunnu emperor Shi Hu,

---

[105] Veselin Beshevliev, *Prvoblgarski nadpisi* (Sofia: Isdatel'stvo ha BAN, 1979).

usurped power and ordered the extermination of the Hunnu dynasty and all Hunnu in the state. That was the end of this branch of Hunnu.

Two hundred thousand 'Weak Hunnu' moved to Tarbagatai and became known as Yueban'. They fell under the influence of Sogdian culture but their state survived until the fifth century AD when it was overrun by the Tele tribes.

Another branch of one hundred thousand Hunnu joined the Syanbi in 93 AD and took their name, so their culture continued within the frame of Syanbi.[106]

Sumpa and Syanbi, Azha and Tuyuhun

As we saw in Chapter I, the *Shenpos* from the country of Sumpa played an important role in the spread of Yungdrung Bön in the east of the Tibetan Plateau. Here we should take a closer look at Sumpa's connection with the Great Steppe and its role as a cultural mediator between Zhang Zhung and the nomadic empires of the Great Steppe. One of the first *Shenpos* of Sumpa was the translator Hulu Paleg who was active in the far distant time of Mucho Demdrug, the son and spiritual successor of Tonpa Shenrab. Sumpa is said to have been located in the modern-day Khyungpo district of the Kham province in eastern Tibet. Later, in the second century AD, Sumbe – a great nomadic empire of Syanbi, a confederation of proto-Mongol tribes – was formed in the

Fig. 18. Zhang Zhung, Sumpa and Sumbe.

---

106 This presentation is based on Gumilev, *Istoriya Hunnu* I&II; Fraizrakhmanov, *Drevnie Tyurki*, pp. 63–65.

Great Steppe and its influence stretched from the Ussuri to the Volga at the height of its expansion.[107]

So is there a connection between Sumpa of Zhang Zhung and Sumbe of the Great Steppe? In Chapter I, we looked at one possible explanation of the connection between Sumpa and Sumbe namely, that some tribes of historical Syanbi may have moved into the eastern lands of Zhang Zhung and formed a small state there which allied itself with Zhang Zhung. While this is highly plausible, it does not explain how Sumpa could have been located in Eastern Zhang Zhung in prehistory. However, bearing in mind the suggested connection between the Shan-Zhun and Zhang Zhung people, we can approach this from a new angle. According to the sources cited in this chapter, the Zhuns, Zhun-Di and Shan-Zhuns were involved in a process ethnogenesis which contributed to the formation of the Hunnu who, according to this scenario, would have carried a considerable gene pool and cultural inheritance from Eastern Zhang Zhung. The origins of the Syanbi are not very clear; some sources suggest they are branch of Dunhu while others maintain they were a tribe of Hunnu. We know that Shan-Zhuns lived and mixed with Dunhu in the north, so in either case we can suppose that the Syanbi ancestors originally lived in Eastern Zhang Zhung and the Kokonoor region and were in fact none other than Sumpa. Within the body of Shan-Zhun, some tribes of Sumpa migrated or were pushed by the Hsia Chinese to the north and northeast and mixed or allied themselves with the Dunhu and the proto-Hunnu thus remaining in the Great Steppe for many centuries before reappearing on the historical stage as the Syanbi state of Sumbe in the second century AD. This is a very plausible explanation as the history of the Great Steppe is full of examples of similar events related to other nations; well known nations and tribes seemed to disappear after dividing, with small bands remaining in ancestral lands while others migrated elsewhere or seemingly vanished altogether until coming back from obscurity hundreds or even thousands years later to dominate the historical arena and the original geographical area which had once been their home. A pertinent example is the Hunnu who returned to the Yellow River basin, Xinjiang and Amdo from the northern side of the Gobi and Southern Siberia. There are good reasons to suggest that this was the case with the Sumpa/Sumbe/Syanbi. If so, then it is possible that some doctrines of Yungdrung Bön could have already reached the Great Steppe at the time of the Hsia dynasty in the third to second millennia

[107] Fraizrakhmanov, *Drevnie Tyurki,* p. 63.

BC. This is also concordant with the spread of the Deer Stone culture[108] in Amdo, Mongolia and southern Siberia which features by many petroglyphs depicting carvings of anticlockwise turning swastika such as are associated with Bön in general and Yungdrung Bön in particular. Interestingly, the royal family of Sumbe/Syanbi was called Muyun(g) (Mu-jung).[109] Branches of this royal clan ruled not only Sumbe but also many post-Sumbe states such as Muyun(g) and Toba-Wei well into the sixth century AD as well as the Tuyuhun, of which the Azha were a part until the very end of the eighth century AD.[110] The name 'Muyun(g)' is very interesting because the first part shows linguistic affinity to Zhang Zhung, Tibetan, Qiang, Minyag and Nakhi languages where the word *mu* means 'sky' or 'man', depending on the spelling.[111] As we have seen, *Mu* is also the name of the class of ancient sky-gods from which the royal *Mu*-clan of Tonpa Shenrab as well as the royal lineages of Zhang Zhung and Tibet originated. Many important *Shenpos* were from these *Mu* lineages. Moreover, the Nakhi, who are thought by some scholars to be an offshoot of the Qiang, were ruled by the Mu family in the time of the early Ming dynasty (1206–1368).[112] The second part of the royal family's name, *yun(g)*, also appears to be related to the languages of the Tibetan Plateau and forms part of the word *yungdrung* – 'swastika'. This indicates that, very probably, the Muyun(g) royal family of Sumbe/Syanbi was originally from the Eastern Zhang Zhung region of Sumpa. They were Bönpo, maybe even followers of Yungdrung Bön or Mixed Bön, before they left for the Great Steppe and came back to dominate Xinjiang and Eastern Zhang Zhung once again after many centuries. It is possible that some part of Syanbi, albeit heavily mixed with Manchu and Chinese, still survives in Xinjiang and northwest China where they are known as Xibe. The Xibe are no doubt descendants of Shiwei, a branch of Hyadan' (Khitan) tribes. However, among the Shiwei there was a tribe known as Syanbi-Shiwei who lived in northeastern China in the seventh century AD.[113] This tribe was either pure Syanbi who allied themselves

---

[108] See chs. I & X.

[109] Originally a clan or a tribe of Syanbi, Muyun(g)s rose to the royal position. There was another prominent Syanbi royal clan which had the particle '*mu*' as a part of their name: Murong who ruled Former Yan, Later Yan and Southern Yan between 337 and 410 AD.

[110] Molè, 'The Tu-yü-hun', p.XIX.

[111] Hummel, *On Zhang Zhung*, p. 9.

[112] *The Naxi ethnic minority*, <http://www.china.org.cn/e-groups/shaoshu/shao-2-naxi.htm> accessed 13.07.07

[113] Лю Сюй, *Старая история Династии Тан, Шивэй*, in B.C. Таскин,

with Shiwei taking a double-barrelled name as a mark of loyalty (a common occurrence in the Great Steppe), or they were a mixed tribe of Syanbi and Shiwei. The Xibe are said to have had their own script until the beginning of the Qing dynasty (1644–1911) when they began adopting Manchu and Chinese. In 1947 some Xibe intellectuals revised the Manchu script which was used by Xibe at that time. They dropped some phonetic symbols and added letters from the Xibe alphabet and this Xibe script was used as an official language by the administration of their autonomous region.[114] It is possible, then, that Syanbi culture may have survived in some form into the twentieth century.

In contrast to the Sumpa, the Azha, a related and ancient tribe, probably stayed in Eastern Zhang Zhung and Kokonoor at least from the time of Drigum Tsenpo[115] (b. 710 BC). Sometime in the third century AD the Azha entered the Tuyuhun tribal union led by the branch of Muyun(g) clan of Sumbe/Syanbi. This coalition with the Syanbi is rational bearing in mind that the tribes were connected in the remote past and probably shared a common ancestry and religion. Later, in the seventh century AD, the Tuyuhun-Azha, then ruled by *khagan* Muyun(g) Nohopo, were overrun by the Tibetan army of Srongtsen Gampo which was taking over the territories of Eastern Zhang Zhung and its neighbours. The other part of Tuyuhun managed to hold up until the thirteenth century when they are last mentioned in Chinese chronicles as providing horses to the Tanguuts of Hsi Hsia.[116] The Azha were eventually assimilated into the Amdo region of the Tibetan Empire and produced many important government officials. We can safely assume, then, that the numerous correspondences between the rituals of *Lhachö* and other types of Bön in Amdo and Bө Murgel stem from the common culture and religious thread connecting the Muyun(g) of Sumpa/Sumbe/Syanbi, the Azha and the Mongol-Buryats through time and space.

Yungdrung Bön must have been strong in both Sumpa and Azha as throughout the ages many illustrious *Shenpos* such as Sumpa Mucha,[117]

Материалы по истории древних кочевых народов группы дунху, Москва, Наука, 1984. [Lyu Syui, *Staraya istoriya Dinastii Tan, Shiwei*; V.S. Taskin, *Materialy po istorii drevnikh kochevykh narodov gruppy dunkhu*]. Web version at <http://www.vostlit.by.ru/Texts/rus/ZsuTanSu/tz1.htm> accessed 13.07.07.

[114] *The Xibe ethnic minority*, <http://www.china.org.cn/e-groups/shaoshu/shao-2-xibe.htm> accessed 13.07.07.

[115] *Ancient Tibet*, Yeshe De Project, p. 156.

[116] Molè, 'The Tu-yü-hun', p. XXV.

[117] Tib. Sum pa Mu phya.

Sumpai Awadong[118] and Azha Lodrö Gyaltsen[119] and Azha Düdtsi Gyaltsen[120] have come from these tribes. In particular, during the reign of the Tibetan king Mulong Könpa Tashi[121], the Blind One (late fifth to early-mid sixth century AD),[122] Bönpo doctors were invited from Sumpa and Azha to treat the king's blindness. The success of the treatment was phenomenal. The king not only completely regained his sight but his eyes became so strong that he could even see antelopes on the Tagmori[123] mountain far away from his royal palace. So he became known as Tagri Nyenzig,[124] One who sees the Antelopes on the Tagri Mountain.

This king's royal *Kushen* priest was Lama Rasang Trinneko[125] from Zhang Zhung, a lineage-holder of the *Zhang Zhung Nyen Gyud* Dzogchen cycle. Rasang Trinneko had a disciple, Sumpai Bönpo Awadong, who returned to his country after receiving the Long Transmission.[126] Yongdzin Lopön Tenzin Namdak explains that Sumpai Awadong was of Mongol type and that Sumpa from which he came was part of or bordered some proto-Mongol state.[127] When he returned to his country he established the Dzogchen teachings there but no details are available regarding the following masters as the lineage continued outside Tibet.[128] As Mongolia *per se* had not yet come into existence, Sumpai Awadong must have been from Sumbe or one of the succeeding Syanbi states in Xinjiang and Amdo. Sumpai Awadong is also said to have transmitted the teachings of *Zhang Zhung Nyen Gyud* to a Chinese Bönpo called Gya Yi Bönpo Salwa Öchen[129] who spread them in China. Both Sumpai Awadong and Salwa Öchen dissolved their bodies into the essence of the elements and

---

118 Tib. Sum pa'i Bon po A ba ldong.

119 Tib. 'A zha bLo gros rGyal mtshan.

120 Tib. 'A zha bDud rsti rGyal mtshan.

121 Tib. dMu long dKon pa bKhra shis.

122 According to Yongdzin Lopön Tenzin Namdak and Khenpo Tenpa Yungdrung.

123 Tib. sTag mo ri.

124 Tib. sTag ri gNyan zigs, lTag ri gnyan gzigs.

125 Tib. bLa ma Ra sangs Khrin ne khod.

126 Tib. ring brgyud.

127 This no doubt refers to the Syanbi as the name 'mongol' was not used until 13th c. Tibetans, however, call the territories of the proto-Mongol and later Mongol peoples by the name 'sogpo'.

128 Interview in Waldzell, Austria, summer 2001.

129 Tib. rGya yi Bon po gSal ba 'Od chen.

obtained the Rainbow Body, the highest realization of Dzogchen, at the end of their lives.[130]

Could the ancient lineage of Bönpo Dzogchen have survived in Buryatia?

If the Zhang Zhung lineage of Bönpo Dzogchen was indeed carried to the proto-Mongol Syanbi in the reign of King Tagri Nyenzig, how long could this lineage have survived and could it have reached Mongolia and Buryatia at some point?

While travelling with the Bɵ and Utgan in Barguzin in northeast Buryatia in 1994 I accidentally stumbled upon information which suggests that Bönpo Dzogchen not only could have reached Buryatia but that the lineage might have survived there right into the beginning of the twentieth century. Here is the story of Sode Lama (1846–1916) who lived and practised in Barguzin:

Fig. 19. Sode Lama.

Sode Lama lived and practised in these parts shortly before the Revolution. He was from a strong Bɵ lineage, but became a Buddhist lama and combined both traditions in a harmonious way. He had two special students. One of them was very talented but died young; during a ritual in one of the villages he received a strong negative charge. Sode Lama was far away at the time, but he knew about the incident through his meditation and hurried back to help. However, he was too late. The second student was less talented and did not receive the lineage from Sode Lama. Sode Lama was able to communicate to all the local gods of the area and possessed unusual powers. People revered him greatly. Before he died, he asked to be shut in his *shalash*[131] and not disturbed for nine days. His remaining student, however, began to have doubts and the *shalash* was opened after only seven days. Inside was the body of Sode Lama which had shrunk to the size of a small baby. More detailed information remains to be collected, but the old people

---

[130] Karmay, *The Treasury*, p.54.

[131] Rus. шалаш - a shelter made from branches and twigs.

> say that Sode Lama's father and grandfather died in the same way without leaving a body. But they were not lamas. They were powerful Bɵ. Doogar Ochirov and Vera Naguslaeva are related to Sode Lama.
>
> Near the village of Sakhuly, 14.06.84[132]

Sode Lama's realization was so strong that extraordinary signs such as spontaneous rainbows appear in the places where he lived and practised when rituals are performed there. In the summer of 1994 I participated in a Bɵ Murgel *tailgan* in Barguzin near the village of Shamanka at a spot associated with him and I, too, observed many very unusual signs appearing in the sky.[133] This is just one story of a very remarkable lineage surviving within the auspices of Buryatian Bo Murgel, but until my visit in 1994, these events remained very much local knowledge. There is no reason to discredit the villagers' account as they are simple people who knew little of the intricacies of Buddhism and had surely never heard of Dzogchen. It is unlikely anyone in those parts knew of Tibetan Bön in those days. Therefore they would have had no reason to invent the stories to prove some doctrinal or sectarian point; the old people simply told me what happened and indeed, the facts described in this story remained very much local knowledge until 1994.

Nevertheless, this report of Sode Lama's death matches all the characteristic signs and manifestations when an adept of Dzogchen attains the Rainbow Body.[134] It is very difficult to explain these specific signs of Sode Lama's realization from the perspective of the practice lineage of the Gelugpa School to which he formally belonged. We can hypothesize that he could have practised the Dzogchen tradition of the Fifth Dalai Lama,[135] which was apparently present in Buryatia to some extent before the Communists took over as texts in Old Mongolian script pertaining to this tradition were found in the *Datsan* near Hezhenge village, in a different region of Buryatia, at the beginning of the nineteen nineties. However, there are apparently no accounts of any masters of this lineage taking Rainbow Body, even in Tibet. So it is highly unlikely that the signs of Sode Lama's realization can be explained by any possible contact with this Dzogchen tradition. The fact that Sode Lama was from a powerful Bɵ family and actually combined Buddhist and Bɵ Murgel ways apparently harmoniously in his practice suggests a

---

[132] A passage from my unpublished diary *Tailgan Trip*, 1994.

[133] See ch. IX.

[134] Tib. 'ja lus.

[135] However, I am not aware of any account of any maters of this lineage taking Rainbow Body.

different explanation. Moreover, as both his father and grandfather were not Buddhists but pure Bɵ and manifested an even higher realization by completely dissolving their bodies, we can deduce that the signs of his realization came through his Bɵ family lineage. This also would explain the ease with which Sode Lama combined his Bɵ lineage and Buddhist practice (Yungdrung Bön and Buddhism have the same goal although they come from the different Buddha lineages). The story of Sode Lama demonstrates that some traditions of Bɵ Murgel may have carried within them strands of Yungdrung Bön and even Bönpo Dzogchen lineage(s) which may be an offshoot of the *Zhang Zhung Nyen Gyud* lineage continuing from Sumpai Awadong. As was said in the chapters above, certain types of White Bɵ were never involved in the practice of blood sacrifices while some were not even involved in the propitiation of the lesser local deities. Instead, they were almost exclusively concerned with the dimension of the Sky and White Tengeri, whose king Hormusta Tengeri is identical with Nyipangse, the main protector of *Zhang Zhung Nyen Gyud* Dzogchen. The white dress of the White Bɵ closely resembled that of the Arya Bönpo of Zhang Zhung and Tibetan Bönpo kings, as we have seen above. The practices of this type of White Bɵ were never properly recorded nor were they understood by outsiders and nowadays this type of Bɵ has vanished from this world altogether meaning we can only speculate about what they really practised and what the origin of their transmission lineages was. In the light of the evidence presented here, however, we have very good reason to suggest that the *Zhang Zhung Nyen Gyud* Dzogchen lineage may have reached the Baikal region and survived there until the early twentieth century, probably as an oral transmission, within the Bɵ lineage which terminated with Sode Lama. If Bönpo Dzogchen did indeed reach Buryatia it would have stood better chances of survival there than in Central Mongolia as Gelugpa Buddhism – hostile to Bɵ – did not take hold in Buryatia until the beginning of the eighteenth century.

Spread of Tibetan Bön in the Great Steppe and Southern Siberia in the Tyurkic period

The culture and religion of the Tyurkic Khaganates was related to those of the earlier Hunnu and Syanbi. Although not much is known about Zhang Zhung's relations with the Tyurkyut and later Tyurks, Tibetans seem to have had contact with them as early as the reign of King Namri Tsenpo[136] in the mid sixth century AD. His son, Srongtsen Gampo, took

[136] Tib. gNam ri bTsan po.

over the Azha, a part of the Tuyuhun and his grandson, Gungsong,[137] married the Azha princess Mangmoje Trikar.[138] In the reign of Mangsong Tsenpo,[139] who was half Tibetan and half Azha, Tibetans forged a military alliance with the Western Tyurkic Khaganate against the Tang Chinese whom they fought for control over the Silk Road. This alliance continued into the reign of his son Dusong Tsenpo[140] who married a Tyurk princess, Gatun.[141] 'Gatun' is not a personal name but a Mongol-Tyurkic title *hatun* (*hatan*) which simply means 'princess' or 'queen'. Dusong married the Tibetan princess Triwang[142] into the Azha royal family and she had a son, Maga Togon Khagan,[143] by the Azha leader.[144]

The succeeding Tibetan king, Meagthom Tsenpo,[145] continued this alliance with the Tyurks, especially with the Tyurgesh tribes. This alliance was strengthened by the marriage of Tibetan princess Jewa Dronmalo[146] to Tyurgesh Sulo Khagan.[147] Meagthom also allied himself with Karluk (Qarluq) Tyurks.[148] The alliances with Karluk Tyurks, Shato Tyurks and White Tyurks continued into the reign of his son, Trisong Deutsen.[149]

It is clear, then, that Tibetans had prolonged contact with various Tyurkic states and tribes which surely resulted in cultural and religious exchange facilitated by similarities in culture, intermarriages and so on. Although Srongtsen Gampo was interested in Buddhism, it was not widely spread in Tibet during his reign, with Yungdrung Bön remaining Tibet's main religion until well into Trisong Deutsen's rulership. Military commanders and diplomats were all Bönpo. As the predominant religion of the Tyurkic Khaganates was a kind of Bө Murgel which included Zhang Zhung and Tibetan strands of Bön which reached the Great Steppe in the Hunnu and Syanbi periods, Tibetans and Tyurks must have had

---

137 Tib. Gung srong.

138 Tib. Mang mo rje Khri dkar. *Ancient Tibet*, Yeshe De Project, p. 215.

139 Tib. Mang srong bTsan po.

140 Tib. 'Dus srong bTsan po.

141 Tib. Ga tun.

142 Tib. Khri bangs.

143 Tib. Ma ga Tho gon Kha gan. Note the middle part of the name, 'Togon', is the alternative name by which Tuyuhun and Azha are known. It is this name that used in the Russian sources.

144 Ibid., p. 238.

145 Tib. Mes ag tshoms bTsan po.

146 Tib. Je ba Dron ma lod.

147 Ibid., p. 246.

148 Ibid., p. 249.

149 Ibid., p. 279.

many common aspects in their culture. This period is another 'window' in which some traditions of Yungdrung Bön probably reached the Great Steppe from Tibet and were perhaps even brought back from the Great Steppe into Tibet as the tribes conquered by Tibetans (such as the Azha and various branches of Sup'i/[150] Sumpa/Syanbi) had maintained Yungdrung Bön traditions since most ancient times.

Indeed, there is information which suggests a small group of Tibetans reached the Baikal region, possibly in the time of the Tibetan king Namri Tsenpo. Dunhuang records say that Namri Tsenpo caused his enemy's son to flee to the lands of the Tyurks.[151] Okladnikov reports that Buryats of the Bohan[152] village in the Irkutsk region say that the ancient irrigation channels, remains of which are found nearby, were built long ago by the people called Bot or Bod.[153] This name is identical to Tibet's self-designation, Bod.[154] I spoke about this with Yongdzin Lopön Tenzin Namdak who said it is quite possible that a military group led by some Tibetan Tsenpo – a title applied not only to the main king of Tibet but also to many lesser vassal kings and even leaders of armed bands – could have reached Lake Baikal either having lost their way in the Great Steppe or during a reconnaissance mission, and stayed there for whatever reason. These settlers would have continued practising their Bön religion which was passed on to subsequent generations and integrated with local traditions becoming a part of Bɵ Murgel.

Spread of Yungdrung Bön into the Great Steppe and Siberia from Tibet due to persecutions

During the two persecutions Yungdrung Bön suffered in Tibet for political reasons in the reigns of Drigum Tsenpo and Trisong Deutsen, many Bönpo masters were forced into exile. Some fled to the northeast bringing the teachings with them into Takla Makan, Amdo and further into the Great Steppe:

> The king summoned all the priests and said: 'Listen priests. It seems to me that in this country there is no room for both authority mine and yours. I shall have the "Four Ways of Divine Bön" and Ge-khod This-

[150] Ibid., pp. 215, 276.
[151] Ibid., p. 175.
[152] Bur. Бохан.
[153] Okladnikov, *Istoriya*, p. 24.
[154] Tib. bod.

'phen and gCo Gyim-bu Lan-tsha as my attendants. The rest of you must all leave the four corners of Tibet'[155]

Wild asses and buffaloes were loaded with all the Bönpo texts except the first two Ways of the Bön of Cause and the *Shenpos* headed to Zhang Zhung where they held council. It was decided they would hide the texts in various locations and then travel in the four directions beyond the borders. One group of *Shenpos* went to the northeast:

> Thus having hidden texts like treasures, the priests travelled down from Sum-pa glang-gi gyim-shod. On setting out they prayed: 'May we reach Sog-po sprel'u-slag gon-pa, 'Jang-mi mig-dgu, Hor and rTsha-mi shing-mi, etc., without interference.'[156]

The places mentioned in the passage above are located in Eastern Zhang Zhung and beyond in Takla Makan and northwest China, the gateways to the Great Steppe and the Great Steppe itself. Although the priests were not fully equipped with texts, they were very highly accomplished practitioners of Yungdrung Bön and carried numerous transmissions so it is highly likely that several traditions of Yungdrung Bön spread from them in the Great Steppe. Some may have survived for a long time while others would have become mixed into already existing streams of Prehistoric Bön creating Mixed Bön similar to such traditions as Dongba of modern Nakhi. According to traditional Bönpo chronology, this took place in 683 BC while Chögyal Namkhai Norbu puts it in the first century AD.

The second persecution followed in 749 AD, according to traditional dates, or between 780–790 AD according to Samten Karmay:[157]

> Thenceforward,[158] up to Khri-song lDe-btsan, during the reigns of thirty-seven kings, all Bön-priests were the object of their homage. But when in the course of these reigns an evil-minded king and his ministers wickedly caused the doctrines to decline, all the gShen-po, having hidden the Bön texts, departed, some to the 'Celestial Sphere', some to solitary places for meditation and others to Sog-po sprel-slag-can (Mongolia).[159]

---

[155] Karmay, *The Treasury,* p. 62.

[156] Ibid., p. 64.

[157] Ibid., Introduction, p. xxxii.

[158] I.e. after Yungdrung Bön was restored in the reign of Drigum Tsenpo's son Tsenpo Pude Gungyal.

[159] Ibid., p. 5. As was already said above, Mongolia as such did not yet exist but Sogpo refers to proto-Mongol tribes of the Great Steppe.

> Many priests, including Zhang-zhung Verstag, Khu-stod Bya-zhu-can, sTag-lo Bya-ru-can, and Sum-pa d Bal-rgod loaded wolves, tigers, and leopards with the texts of magic and prognostication and went to Mongolia, 'Jang, and China.[160]

This is very clear evidence that the teachings of Yungdrung Bön reached proto-Mongols of the Great Steppe from Tibet in the eighth century AD. Moreover, the passage quoted above specifies the Bön of Cause in particular. Judging from their names, the priests were from Zhang Zhung, with the exception of Sumpa Walgod who was probably Syanbi. This wave of Causal Bön must have reached Lake Baikal, the Altai and the Sayan mountains in Southern Siberia because at that time the eastern part of the Great Steppe was unified under the Hor (Uighur Khaganate) (745–840 AD). The traditions of Causal Bön stood a high chance of taking root and surviving there not only as oral transmissions but also as written texts; the Uighurs, like the nations preceding them in the Great Steppe, had a script meaning that texts could be translated and copied. As the teachings brought to Hor by the *Shenpos* belonged to the Bön of Cause, the methods they contained would resonate with some streams of the Prehistoric Bön and Mixed Bön already spread among the nomads of the Great Steppe in very early times. The subsequent steppe empires – Kyrgyz Khaganate (840–1040 AD) and Hyadan' Mongol Uls (Liao) (907–1125 AD) – which in turn controlled the northern shore of Lake Baikal, Transbaikalia, the Altai and the Sayans, both had writing. After the Hyadan' Mongol Uls collapsed and was taken over by the Jurchen state of Altan Tzin (Jin), culture in Transbaikalia suffered a sharp decline. Altan Tzin did not control Baikal or Transbaikalia directly so the region descended into chaos and anarchy becoming the arena for constant vicious inter-tribal and inter-clan warfare. The harsh reality of life in this period is described in the *Sacred History of the Mongols*. Due to fragmentation and degradation, some Bönpo streams would probably have ceased to exist in this period. The Hamag Mongol Uls formed by Haidu Khaan was too small to bring stability to the region which continued to be engulfed in violence. It was not until Chingis Khaan that stability came. Following the long civil war in which half the tribes living in the region were exterminated, Chingis Khaan unified those who came under his *tug* into the new nation called the Mongols and formed the Ih Mongol Uls – the Great Mongol Empire – which was to span most of Eurasia. Bɵ Murgel emerged as a systematized conglomerate of many traditions of Prehistoric, Mixed and Yungdrung Bön practised

---

160 Ibid., p. 93.

by many tribes forming the nucleus of this new empire and became its state religion. Its attitude towards other spiritual traditions was one of extreme tolerance as, from the point of view of Bɵ Murgel, the whole universe is under the control of Huhe Münhe Tengeri, Eternal Blue Sky, who acts and manifests in mysterious ways. Although Mongols would tolerate no disobedience from the nations they conquered and punished such crimes mercilessly, the Mongol Bɵ and state administration did not persecute followers of other faiths who could freely come and preach right in the heart of the empire, even to the emperor himself. Moreover, as Bɵ Murgel has no 'evangelizing' tendency either so the aureole of its spread remained confined to the territories originally occupied by Tyurkic and proto-Mongol tribes who were amalgamated into the nucleus of the Mongol Empire. Today Bɵ Murgel is still present in varying degrees over all the territories of Greater Mongolia (Buryatia in Russia, Mongolia *per se* and Inner Mongolia in China) as well as in Tuva which was under the control of the Uryanghai tribes.

There is not the slightest doubt that a substratum of Zhang Zhung and Tibetan Bön is present within Bɵ Murgel although it might not be obvious as most Bönpo terms were translated from Zhang Zhung and Tibetan into the languages of the tribes where the Bönpo lineages coming from the Tibetan Plateau originally spread. By the time they were retranslated into other languages or changed within the original languages the linguistic threads were mostly lost. The process of translating Bönpo terminology into the languages of the Great Steppe was very similar to the way in which the texts of Indian Buddhism were translated from Sanskrit into Tibetan; the vast majority of terms were translated by coining new terms on the basis of the recipient language. These new terms, though concordant with the meaning of the original, were completely different from the Sanskrit originals in sound and written form. For example, Sans. *vajra* = Tib. *dorje*; Sans. *vihara* = Tib. *gonpa* and so on. This happened again when Tibetan Buddhist texts were later translated into Mongolian; equivalent Mongolian words were found and linguistic borrowings were rare, thereby rendering the 'foreign' terms unrecognizable. For example, Tib. *dorje* = Mon. *ochir*; Tib. *gonpa* = Mon. *datsan* and so on. Without knowing both Sanskrit and Tibetan one would not be able to guess that Sans. *vajra* = Mong. *ochir* and Sans. *vihara* = Mong. *datsan*, for example. The various Bön teachings which had been coming into the Great Steppe from Zhang Zhung and Tibet since prehistory were translated and then further translated in a similar multitier process. As the original recipient languages changed, mixed with others or disappeared altogether, it is difficult to trace linguistic threads of Bön in the Great Steppe. Nevertheless, there are some very clear linguistic imprints which point to the common religious root of the Tyurkic, Mongol, Zhang Zhung and Tibetan religious streams. One such trace is the root *ten(g)* which means 'sky', 'upper space' in Tibetan, Tyurkic and Mongol languages: Tib. *teng*[161] = Mong.-Bur. *tenger*, *tengeri* = Altai. *tengeri*, *teneri* = Kumyk. *tengiri* = Yakut. *tangara* = Old Bulgar. *tangra* = Balkar-Karachai. *teiri* =Khakas. *tigir* = Tatar. *tenre* = Turk. *tanri*[162] and so on. This root is found, for example, in the names of lakes in Changthang, the heartland of Zhang Zhung which are important in Bönpo tradition, such as Namtsho/Tengtsho/[163]Tengri and Tengchyugtso.[164] The eighth and ninth Tibetan kings Drigum Tsenpo and his son Pude Gungyal, who lived in the seventh century BC, are known as the.[165] Although exact equivalents of Zhang Zhung and Tibetan words *bön* or *bönpo* are not necessarily found in all languages of Great Steppe nations, this doesn't mean that these nations didn't have Bön lineages in the past or have them at present under another name. For example, even in Zhang Zhung itself there were two synonymous words for Bön: *bön* and *gyer*, and the word *bön* has survived in the Mongol-Buryat dialects until this day as *bɵ*. On my request, Dorjo Doogarov presented an interesting reconstruction of the etymology of the Mongol-Buryat word *bɵ*:

> The Tibetan word *bön* correlates with Mongolian word *bɵɵn*[166] (Mong. бөөн), but in Old Mongolian script it is written as ᠪᠥᠭᠡᠭᠡᠨ (*bɵɵgegen*) and is made up of two words: *bɵɵ* and *gegen*. The word ᠪᠥᠭᠡ (bɵɵ) means 'shaman' and also consists of two syllables, ᠪᠥ and ᠭᠡ. The ending syllable ᠭᠡ (*ge*) is not pronounced in modern dialects and if we compare its use in other words, we discover that it might be read as the sound ŋ. For example, 'camel' – ᠲᠡᠮᠡᠭᠡ (*temege*) reads as *teme* (Mong. тэмэ) in Halha dialect, and as *temen* (Bur. Тэмэн) in Hori Mongolian dialect (classic modern Buryatian) which is older than Halha dialect. In this way we recover the ancient pronunciation of the word *bɵɵ* ᠪᠥᠭᠡ as *bɵɵn* i.e. *bön*. One of the meanings of the Tibetan word *bön* is 'to recite (mantras)'. The Tibetan verb *bonpa* (Tib. bon pa) 'invoking', 'to invoke' is directly comparable to Buryatian (Hori) and Halha ᠪᠥᠭᠡᠯᠡ

---

[161] Tib. steng.

[162] Tyurkic equivalents taken from R. N. Bezertinov, *Drevnetyurkskoe mirovozzrenie 'Tengrianstvo'*, Ministry for Science and Education of the Republic of Tatarstan (Kazan: Shkola, 2006), p. 37.

[163] Tib. sTeng mtsho.

[164] Tib. sTeng phyug mtsho.

[165] Tib. sTod kyi sTeng gnyis.

[166] With deep double *o* sound similar to English *oar*.

(bɵɵgegene), pronounced as *bɵɵgnɵ* (Mong. бөөгнө) in Halha dialect and *bɵɵlnɵ* (Bur. бөөлн) in Buryatian, meaning 'to say invocation', 'to adjure', 'to charm' and with ᠪᠥᠭᠡᠯ, an imperative from 'to say invocation'. So in my opinion, in ancient times the word ᠪᠥᠭᠡ (bɵɵ) also meant 'invocation' but in modern Mongolian and Buryatian languages it has come to mean only 'shaman'. It seems to have lost its ancient meaning.

The word ᠭᠡᠭᠡᠨ (*gegen*), the second part of ᠪᠥᠭᠡᠭᠡᠨ (*bɵɵgegen*) has several meanings:

– 'saint' or 'enlightened person';
– 'spiritual master' or 'teacher' comparable to Tibetan *gegen*;[167]
– 'to study' ('education').

The word ᠭᠡᠭᠡᠨ (*gegen*) also forms part of the word ᠭᠡᠭᠡᠷᠡᠬᠦ (*gegerhe*), 'to reach enlightenment'. So the reconstructed meaning of the word *bɵɵn* ᠪᠥᠭᠡᠭᠡᠨ (*boogegen*) is:

– 'teaching of mantra'
– 'teaching of enlightenment'
– 'to study mantra teachings'.[168]

The presentation above strongly suggests that Yungdrung Bön traditions were present at least to some extent in the body of archaic Bɵ Murgel. A possible scenario is that the Siberian shamanistic tradition tightly connected with the cults of sky, fire and ancestors presided over by Utgan priestesses was gradually replaced by male Bɵ priests when the proto-Mongol and proto-Tyurk societies transited from matriarchate to patriarchate. At some stage in prehistory Mixed and Yungdrung Bön streams from Zhang Zhung and later Tibet began entering the Great Steppe from the Tibetan Plateau and Xinjiang with the migration of the Zhuns who contributed considerably to the ethnogenesis of many proto-Mongol and Proto-Tyurk peoples. It is not clear whether these incoming Bönpo traditions could have caused the division of the Bɵ into white and black or whether this division was already there. In any case, it was primarily the White Bɵ, very similar in their appearance and functions to the Aryan Bönpos of Zhang Zhung, who absorbed streams of Mixed and Yungdrung Bön which were related mainly to the Bön of Cause but also could have included some lineages of Bönpo Tantra and Dzogchen.

---

[167] Tib. dge rgen.

[168] Edited extract from the presentation on the meaning of Buryatian words *tug* and *bɵ* by D.B. Doogarov BA, Oriental Faculty, Department of Archaeology and Ethnography of Central Asia, Buryatian State University, Ulaan-Ude.

Conclusion

We have seen, then, that there were several waves of Zhang Zhung and Tibetan Bön which reached the various peoples of the Great Steppe in different times. Zhang Zhung and Tibetan Bön survived in their pure form at least among some of these nations and mixed with the native traditions of Prehistoric Bön in the Great Steppe and Southern Siberia to varying degrees. This gave rise to many closely related spiritual traditions and religions of Tyurkic and Mongol tribes displaying a very high degree of affinity and similarity. In the nineteenth century they were labelled 'shamanic' after one particular type of Tungus-Evenki priests of Siberia. Although this term was also applicable to the practices of some Siberian priests other than the Tungus-Evenki *šaman*, it later resulted in the stereotyping of the Siberian spiritual traditions. The label 'shamanism' was further extended to include all native traditions the world over not falling into the category of so-called 'world religions'. This unfortunate and unjustified overgeneralization has distorted understanding and research in the fields of anthropology and religion for many decades blinding many scholars to the real common ground shared by the so-called 'primitive' or 'folk' religions (another quite unjustified term). Russian researchers coined a much more appropriate term for the common religion of the Tyurkic and Mongol peoples – Tengrism[169] – which doesn't seem to have taken root in Western academic circles. This term is not based on the name of one kind of tribal priest but instead reflects the supreme importance of Tengeri (Tengri, Tenger, Tenra etc.), the Spiritual Sky, as the common source of creative spiritual power which has been the main object of veneration for a very large number of the Tyurkic and Mongol peoples of the Eurasian Great Steppe and Siberia from at least the third millennium BC up until now. Tengrism is one of the most ancient 'world religions', older than Judaism, for example. Modern Tyurkic nations do not seem to have retained the original name for this religion as many were later converted to Christianity or Islam. The Mongol nations, however, retained the original name Bө (Bөөn) which must have had close equivalents in the Tyurkic languages. Misconceptions about the high level of the cultural and religious development of the nations of the Great Steppe and their ethnic composition arose because initially the information about the Great Steppe, taken primarily from Chinese sources, wasn't critically examined. The Chinese, who arrogantly believed themselves and their culture to be superior to all other nations, far or near, and for whom even

---

[169] Rus. Тэнгризм, Тэнгрианство; Tengrianstvo.

Indian civilization was barbarian, deliberately belittled and distorted the truth about the peoples of the Great Steppe out of a superiority complex and for political reasons. Although, up to now, Chinese sources have undoubtedly provided the bulk of information about the Great Steppe starting from prehistory, this information should be taken with a pinch of salt. Having said that, we must nevertheless thank Chinese historians for keeping track of history and blame for their lack of objectivity towards the 'barbarians' lies not necessarily with them but rather with the governments they worked for which demanded events to be presented in the way that suited their political goals and ambitions. Another difficulty which researchers of the Great Steppe have to overcome is the seeming disinterest of the many nations of the Great Steppe in writing down their own history, a problem also faced by scholars researching early Tibetan history and history of Zhang Zhung. This is the product of a culture focussed on the here and now. Although many of the nations of the Great Steppe had writing, being nomadic they were not keen on writing documents on stones (with the exception of the Orkhono-Yenisei Tyurkic stellas) but used fragile materials such as bark and leather which did not survive. The research of outstanding Russian explorers and scholars, such as Bichurin, Grumm-Grzhimailo, Kyzlasov, Gumilev and many others, forms a matrix against the background of which the picture of nomadic civilizations in the Great Steppe is becoming clearer and clearer.

Prehistoric Bön of Eurasia, a term I suggest for an even larger international and intercontinental religious phenomenon, includes Tengrism, Bɵ Murgel, Dömai Bön and many other related religious and spiritual traditions originating in remote prehistory and early history. This term reflects the direct correspondences between their magic techniques, mythology, pantheons, cosmology and religious symbols compared in this book. Although these ancient religions may be known today by names other than Bön, the use of the term here is justified for the following reasons:

- the original Zhang Zhung and Tibetan word *bön* doesn't a have restrictive meaning tied up to just a couple of magical techniques as is the case with 'shamanism'. On the contrary, it is a general term for the very diverse archaic spiritual traditions and religions of different ethnic and racial groups of Eurasia which nevertheless have a common cultural and religious background;
- many kinds of Bön came into Zhang Zhung and Tibet from elsewhere, brought by diverse ethnic and racial groups of

both Europe and Asia and therefore are not, strictly speaking, 'native';

- those Bön traditions which can be called 'native' may in reality be the continuation of extremely archaic spiritual streams brought to the Tibetan Plateau in the times when it was first colonized and may therefore also have come from elsewhere.

It is clear, then, that this ancient q-religion and culture formed the base for later belief systems and still constitutes a thread running through many modern societies.

Buryatian Bɵ Murgel is a living branch of this ancient religion which allows us to compare it with many aspects of traditions which did not survive or which only partially survived as little-understood elements in a wider belief system or which have remained in myths, legends and historical records. By holding up the living tradition of Buryatian Bɵ Murgel, we can gain a much clearer picture of the religion and culture of ancient civilizations, not only of the Great Steppe, but of Eurasia as a whole.

Studying Bɵ Murgel in relation to Tibetan Bön also provides us with an invaluable tool with which we can further clarify poorly-understood aspects in both traditions. By comparing the living practices of Bɵ Murgel with those of Yungdrung Bön, we gain a better understanding of the processes which led to the formation of the Mixed Bön traditions of many Himalayan border tribes. In particular, it enables us to draw a line between the three major types of Tibetan Bön, namely: Prehistoric (Dömai) Bön, Yungdrung Bön and Bön Sarma thereby eradicating confusion, one of the grounds for sectarian divide between followers of the two Buddhas Tonpa Shenrab and Shakyamuni.

Thatsen Mutsug Marro![170] May all be auspicious!

---

[170] Tib. tha tshan mu tsug smar ro.

Appendix

Buryatian Pantheon of Ninety-Nine Tengeri Sky-Dwellers

Here I list White and Black Tengeri with the names spelled in Latin script and a very short description of their functions. Those who read Russian can find more detailed information in Б.Д. Базаров, *Таинства и практика шаманизма,* pp. 113-121.

Fifty-Five White Tengeri (Right standing, Western)

1. Khaan Hormusta Tengeri – Lord of the White Tengeri.
2. Udaa Münhe Tengeri – creator of the element of water and Uhan Haats.
3. Sege'en Sebdeg Tengeri – 'Wavering Sky-dweller', 'Neutral Sky-dweller'. Has most powerful magic, father of the divine Eagle Burged who brought the knowledge of Bɵ Murgel to Earth.
4. Buudal Uhan Huhe Tengeri – creator and patron of all the healing *arshans.*
5. Homon Huhe Tengeri – spiritual father of Uta Sagaan Noёn of Olhon.
6. Dolon Ungete Huhe Tengeri – controls rain.
7. Huhe Manhan Tengeri – patron of human souls and those of domesticated animals.
8. Shara Hasar Tengeri – patron of the Sharyaat, Sharanut and Hangin clans.
9. Bɵluur Sagaan Tengeri – spiritual father of White Tengeri and an Elder.
10. Dabaan Zholo Tengeri (Darhan Sagaan Tengeri) – patriarch of heavenly White Darhan-smiths; father of Bozhintoi.
11. Odon Sagaan Tengeri – controls the gates to the realm of the White Tengeri.
12. Khaan Buudal Tengeri – controls birth and any actions of Tengeri on earth.
13. Oёor Sagaan Tengeri – tightly connected to Esege Malaan Tengeri; master of Amitai Noёn who controls all the ritual regalia of Bɵ.
14. Uurag Sagaan Tengeri – controls *uurag* (milk ambrosia); patron of the Hongodor clan; sends riches to earth.
15. Pison Sagaan Tengeri – patron of the Barguut clan.
16. Zada Sagaan Buudal Tengeri – gives *buudal utkha* to selected Bɵ; sends the heavenly power objects *zada shuluun*; controls rough weather.
17. Budurgu Sagaan Tengeri – patron of the Bulgat clan; father of Uhaa Solbon Tengeri, Buha Noёn Baabai and Sahyaadai Noёn.
18. Ishkhii Bayaan Tengeri – controls *bayaan*-well-being; patron of wealth and well-being.
19. Hurei Bayaan Tengeri – controls descent, child birth, family; gives children

20. Uhaa Solbon Tengeri – creator of horses; lord of planet Venus
21. Huhe Ehe Noën Tengeri (Great Axe Lord) – ancestor of the famous White Hurduud Bɵ clan.
22. Sahilgaan Sagaan Tengeri – patron of all Buryat-Mongols; rules over 77 *mongol-darhan* deities.
23. Hute Buumal Tengeri – patron of milk products.
24. Buumal Sagaan Tengeri – patron of the Bulut clan.
25. Mender Zalaa Tengeri – controls hail and meteorites; punishes evil-doers.
26. Hundari Sagaan Tengeri – patron of weddings and parties.
27. Gutaar Bayaan Tengeri – oversees *utkha* and punishes impostors.
28. Khaan Sagaan Tengeri – patron of Buryats; guide of the nomads and patron of travelers.
29. Noën Sagaan Tengeri – controls length of human life; patron of kings, ministers and other politicians.
30. Hun Sagaan Tengeri – controls *hulde* of people; controls conception (impregnation); controls the re-incarnation process of *Zaarin Bɵ.*
31. Gal Ulaan Tengeri – patron and ancestor of smiths and technology.
32. Manha Malaan Tengeri – patron of ascetics and saints; aids mental development.
33. Oir Münhe Tengeri – patron of fruits; repels insects.
34. Zayaan Buudal Tengeri – protector of people; protects from evil spirits; patron of protective amulets; controls good luck
35. Altan Tengeri – controls mineral riches and all the gold mines on earth.
36. Huhe Zalaa Tengeri – controls plants.
37. Hazhir Sagaan Tengeri – controls human energy; patron of healers and bone-setters.
38. No information was found.
39. Dun Sagaan Tengeri – controls wealth, treasurer of the White Tengeri.

40–43. Hultei Halhin Tengeri – Four Western Winds.

44–47. Durben Emershe Tengeri – Four Eastern Purifying Winds.

48. Oëdol Sagaan Tengeri – patron of clairvoyance; sends heavenly *toli*-mirrors.
49. Somol Huhe Tengeri – controls anomalous zones of earth and sky; defines places of residence for Bɵ in the Sky.
50. Ohiruu Sagaan Tengeri – provides Bɵ with information; provides communication between various Tengeri .
51. Amitai Sagaan Tengeri – gathers meetings and oversees *suglan*-courts of various levels.
52. Yashil Sagaan Tengeri – sends dreams to Bɵ; reveals the future.
53. No information was found.
54. Uran Sgaan Tengeri – controls certain types of *utkha*; patron of arts, astrology, bohemians, various elite groups.
55. Urhe Uuden Tengeri – 'press attaché' of HormustaTengeri.

Forty-Four Black Tengeri (Left standing, Eastern)

1. Atai Ulaan Tengeri – Lord of the Black Tengeri, tough and vicious; patron of horses and domestic animals.
2. Khaan Bomo Maha Tengeri – controls and sends 13 heavy diseases.

3–11. Yuhen Shuhan Tengeri – Nine Bloody Tengeri which destroy all life forms.

12–24. Asaranga Arban Gurban Tengeri – patrons of bөө-healers with black *utkha.*

25–33. Hozhiroi Dolon Tengeri include: Guzhir Gunger Tengeri – patron of the hunt and edible plants; Godli Ulaan Tengeri – gives *hulde* to farm animals; Zulhe Ulaan Tengeri – patron of warriors; Hara Mahagal Darhan Tengeri – ancestor and patron of black smiths; Bolinguud Tengeri – a group of five which act as patrons for some types of Bө, *ulgershen* etc.

34. Uhin Hara Tengeri – sends female diseases and venereal diseases.
35. Haraan Buudal Tengeri – patron of clairvoyance.
36. Helin Tengeri – great magician, can send bad influences and damage human energy system but can also avert curses from bad spirits; patron of Black Hurduud Bө clan.
37. Gug Hara Tengeri – controls various types of *utkha.*
38. Tad Hara Tengeri – patron of black *darhan*; patron of the Underworld, Tungus shamans and some other tribes.

39–41: Gurban Manan Tengeri – send mist, dew, humidity and dampness.

42–44: Gurban Boron Buudal Tengeri – patrons of strong rains, acid and 'blood' rains and blizzards.

Glossary of Buryatian, Tibetan and Sanskrit Terms and Concepts

Abai Geser: Bur. Абай Гэсэр; Mongol-Buryat version of the *Gesar* epic.

Ada: Bur. ада; type of spirit. Some types of Ada are said to either harm or protect infants.

Amin: Bur. амин or амь; life-force. Often translated in Russian scholarly works as 'soul-breath' (Rus. душа-дыхание); c.f. *sog.*

Amitai: Bur. амитай; the full costume of a Buryatian Bө/Utgan.

Anahai: Bur. анахай; a type of malevolent spirit.

Anda: Bur. анда; blood-brother.

Arkhi: Bur. архи; while in modern usage this is now a general name for vodka, *arkhi* originally referred to milk-vodka; see also *tarasoon.*

Arsa: Bur. арса; Lat. Juniperus pseudosabina; a kind of juniper used for herbal incense and purification rites.

Arshan: Bur. аршан; sacred spring with healing properties.

Aryuud haha: Bur. арюуд хаха; a fumigation ritual for purification.

Axis mundi. In Buryatian, this axis is known as ***gol***(Bur. гол). Humans also have *gol*, a vertical energy-channel running through the centre of the body. In Sanskrit this central channel is called Avadhuti and in Tibetan rtsa dbu ma.

Bagchag: Tib. bag chags; karmic traces.

Bardo Thödrol: Tib. bar do thos grol; (lit. 'liberation through hearing in *Bardo*'). These are texts containing methods and instructions to guide the consciousness through the *Bardo*. Although the version of *Bar do Thos grol* most readily available in the West (and most commonly translated as *Tibetan Book of the Dead*) is a compilation of texts based on the discoveries made by Buddhist *terton* Karma Lingpa (Tib. Kar ma gling pa) who lived in 14th c., the origin of such texts is likely to belong to Yungdrung Bön. The *Zhang Zhung sNyan brGyud,* a cycle which was never hidden as *terma* and was written down by Gurub Nangzher Lödpo in 8th c. AD, already includes several texts dealing with *Bardo* such as *Byang chub sems kyi gnas drug* and '*Khro lo bzhi sbrag* (tr. John Myrdhin Reynolds, *Selections from the Bonpo Book of the Dead* (San Diego and Copenhagen: Bonpo Translation Projetc, Vidyadhara Institute for Studies in Comparative Religion, 1997)).

Bardo: Tib. bar do; the intermediate state. Although there are in fact six or seven intermediate states, Bardo most commonly refers to the stage between death and the next birth.

Bhumi: Tib. sa; literally meaning 'earth', it is used in Bönpo and Buddhist works to refer to the progressive stages of the Sutra path.

Bɵ-pine: Bur. бɵɵге нархан – tree in which a Bɵ is 'buried'.

Bodhichitta: Tib. chang chub sems; the unbendable intention to attain Buddhahood for the benefit of all sentient beings. There are two types of *bodhichitta*: relative and absolute. Absolute *Bodhichitta* is the Natural State of Mind or final Buddhahood (according to Dzogchen). Relative *Bodhichitta* has two subdivisions: *bodhichitta* of intention and *bodhichitta* of application. The former is the generation of thoughts of love and compassion towards others and mental contemplation of ways to help other beings while the latter is actual activity which brings concrete benefit to others. Absolute *Bodhichita* encompasses Relative *Bodhichitta.*

Boholdoi: Bur. Боохолдой; spirits of the dead.

Burged: Bur. Бургэд; heavenly eagle. C.f. *khyung*.

Burkhan: Bur. Бурхан. *Burkhan* are a class of ancient gods which most sources maintain are synonymous with the Tengeri, although some information suggests they existed before the Tengeri. Nowadays this word is also used as a generic term applied to beings of elevated spiritual status including Huhe Münhe Tengeri, Hormusta Tengeri, Buddha, god, Christian saints and so on. Some recent publications claim *Burkhan* is a lower-ranking and less powerful class of gods than the Tengeri although the Bɵ and Utgan I have consulted hold this to be a misguided opinion.

Buudal: Bur. буудал; a spiritual being or a holy object lowered from the sky. C.f. *zada shuluun*.

Buural: Bur. буурал; local spirit-owners.

Bɵ Murgel: Bur. Бɵɵ Мүргэл; the native religion of Buryatia and Mongolia. Also known as Bɵ Shazhan (Bur. Бɵɵ Шажан).

Bɵ: Bur. бɵɵ; a priest of Bɵ Murgel.

Bɵ-Darhan or **Darhan Utkhatai Bɵ**: Bur. бɵɵ дархан/дархан утхатай бɵɵ; Bɵ-smiths. These are a powerful and respected group of Bɵ-smiths with special lineages, techniques, rituals and spiritual obligations.

Bɵ-hete: Bur. бɵɵ-хэтэ; Bɵ's flint-stone.

Cha: Tib. phy wa; very ancient Bönpo gods who command the energies of well-being and prosperity and are invoked in numerous rituals of divination, long-life, prosperity, astrology, medicine and healing. *Cha* also refers to the positive energy of a person, the energy which serves as a base for prosperity and well-being. C.f. the Buryatian term *hulde*.

Chöd: Tib. gcod; ritual practice of High Tantra whereby one visualizes offering one's body to Buddhas, wordly gods, spirits and beings of the Six Realms. The melodious chant is accompanied by a strong rhythmical beat on the *damaru* drum, the *shang* bell and the *gangling* thigh-bone trumpet.

Chödpa: Tib. gcod pa; a practitioner of *Chöd.*

Chörten: Tib. mchod rten; a monument symbolizing the mind of Buddha.

Chutor: Tib. chu gtor; water offering.

Chyednga: Tib. phyed rnga; a Bönpo half drum.

Da: Tib. zla; moon gods.

Dadar: Tib. mda' dar; a ritual arrow used in offering and long-life rituals.

Dahobar: Bur. дахообар; type of ferocious female spirit.

Dakini (Sanskrit) or Tibetan ***khandro*** (Tib. mkha' 'gro) literally means 'sky-goer' or 'space-traveller'. *Dakinis* are celestial female deities and may be worldly ('jig rten mkha' 'gro) or enlightened ('jig rten las 'as pa'i mkha' 'gro) which literally means '*dakini* beyond the world' and designates fully realized *dakinis* such as Satrig Ersang of the Bönpos and Tara of the Buddhists. There are many classes of worldly *dakinis* who either cause trouble for or assist humans depending on how humans relate to them. Both enlightened and worldly *dakinis* are found among the Guardians of Yungdrung Bön and Buddhism.

Dal: Tib. dal; gods of mist and fog.

Dalabshi: Bur. далабши; part of a Bө-smith's attire, a shoulder piece with tassels symbolizing eagles wings.

Damaru (Sanskrit); a double-sided hand-held drum, often made of two skulls, used by both Bönpos and Buddhists alike for *Chöd* and some other practices.

Dase: Tib. mda' gsas; 'arrow-gods' which appeared at the beginning of existence.

Datcha: Rus. дача; a simple Russian country house used mainly in summer.

Datsan: Bur. дацан; the Mongolian word for a Buddhist monastery, temple or monastic complex.

Deu: Tib. lde'u; the science of symbols, enigmas and secret languages.

Deutrul: Tib. lde'u 'phrul; a Bönpo divination system.

Dhami and **dhangre**: priests of the Humla region of Nepal.

Dharmapala: Tib. chos skyong; Buddhist religious protector-deity.

Dö: Tib. mdos; Yungdrung Bön ransom rites in which an elaborate offering structure of the same name is used. Such constructions may also include *namkha* of various shapes and forms.

Dogpa: Tib. zlog pa; a technique for sending away disturbances and provocations of negative energy.

Dre: Tib. 'dre; ghosts.

Drenpa Namkha: Tib. Dran pa Nam mkha'; there were three extremely powerful Bönpo *Mahasiddhas* called Drenpa Namkha. The latter two played a very important role in dissiminating and preserving Yungdrung Bön during the persecutions in the reigns of the two Tibetan kings, Drigum Tsenpo and Trisong Deutsen.

Drilbu: Tib. dril bu; upright bell used by Tibetan Buddhists.

Drung: Tib. sgrung; historical narrative.

Düd Bön: Tib. bdud bon; Bön of the Demons.

Düd: Tib. bdud; very powerful sky-dwelling demons. C.f. Black Tengeri.

Düdtsi: Tib. bdud rtsi; literally 'demon's crop', a spiritual substance charged with blessings. C.f. *uurag* and *amrita.*

Dulwa: Tib. 'dul ba, Sans. Vinaya; Rules of Monastic Discipline.

Dunda Hunehen: Bur. дунда һүнэхэн; 'middle soul'. Nicknamed 'shadow soul' by Russian scholars (Bur. һүүдэр – 'shadow').

Dunhuang: an ancient oasis town which was situated northwest of Tibet in Takla Makan, modern-day Chinese Turkestan, and lay on the famous Silk Road. It was founded by Emperor Wudi of the Han dynasty in 111 BC and served as an outpost for the Chinese garrison which was facilitating Chinese control over the trade routes. For several hundred years after the collapse of the Han Empire (206 BC-220 AD) the town changed hands many times. In 781 AD, during the Tang dynasty (618-906 AD), Dunhuang was captured by the Tibetans. Chinese control was restored in 848 AD. Later it fell under control the Western Xia kingdom (990-1227AD) and then the Mongol Yuan dynasty (1271-1368). When trade routes shifted, it was abandoned and fell into oblivion, to be rediscovered in the beginning of 20th century. It is famous for its cave art and the large library preserved by the sands which, among other texts, contained ancient Tibetan Bönpo and Buddhist books, many of which were previously unknown to modern scholars and practitioners.

Dur: Tib. 'dur; Bönpo funerary rites.

Dzi: Tib. rdzi; air gods.

Dzogchen: Tib. rdzogs chen; Great Perfection, the Nature of Mind. This term refers to both the state of liberation and the teachings which show the path to obtaining it. Dzogchen teachings, the pinnacle of all the teachings of Yungdrung Bön and Tibetan Buddhism, the highest level of meditation practice, are contained in the Ninth Way of Yungdrung Bön and the Ninth Vehicle of the Nyingma School of Tibetan Buddhism.

Ehe Tailgan: Bur. Эхэ тайлган or Тахил тайлган; Summer *Tailgan*.

Ehe Yehe Burkhan: Bur. Эхэ Ехэ Бурхан; the Great Mother Goddess.

Eight Classes of Gods and Spirits: Tib. lha srin sde brgyad, lha sri sde brgyad; powerful spiritual entities who can either harm or help in worldly and even spiritual matters depending on one's relationship to them. This classification is found in both Yungdrung Bön and Tibetan Buddhism.

Elbe: Bur. эльбэ: the evil eye.

Elbeshen: Bur. эльбэшэн; black sorcerer(ess).

Elgebshe: Bur. эльгэбшэ; Bө-smith's breastplate.

Erdeni: Bur. Эрдэни; a holy object able to bestow *hulde*. It also denotes the personal aspect of *hulde* – happiness or blessing.

Erlig Khaan: Bur. Эрлиг-хаан or Эрлен-хаан depending on the dialect; Lord of the Underworld. Erlig Khaan can be compared with Ahriman (Angro-Mainyu) of ancient Iranian religions, with the Indian god of hell Yama and with the Tibetan Shinje (Tib. gshin rje). Shinje is the Lord of Death and can mean the King of Hell or, more generally, a class of beings who cause death and are associated with hell. Erlig Khaan is also listed among the Thirteen Asarangi Tengeri.

Ezhen: Bur. эжэн (эжин, эзэн); a Buryatian word meaning 'Owner' or 'Lord of the place', equivalent to Tibetan *bdag po* when used as a component word in such words as Tib. zhi bdag, sa bdag etc. *Ezhen* is a general name which can be applied to almost all the classes of various spiritual beings worshiped in Bө Murgel and inhabiting the Three Worlds from the Lord of the Underworld, Erlig Khaan, to the highest Tengeri residing in the sky, thus they include gods living in the space between heaven and earth or earth-dwelling gods of different classes comparable to Tibetan *Nyen*, *Tsen*, *Lu, Tod, Sadag* and so on. On the earth's surface *Ezhen* 'own' mountains, hills, islands, forests and so on, residing in them and guarding a variety of geographical features..

Five Buddhas of Bön: Tib. sku lnga; principal Buddhas of the mandala of Peaceful Deities.

Deities of *Lungta*: Tib. klung rta'i lha; deities connected with a person's elements and *lungta* energy of good luck and prosperity.

Five Personal Deities: Tib. 'go ba'i lha lnga; protective deities dwelling in the physical body who appear at birth and stay with a person for life. They provide protection and look after the individual's well-being.

Five Poisons: Tib. dgu lnga; ignorance, attachment, jealousy, anger and pride.

Four Guests: Tib. mgron po bzhi; four groups of guests invited to partake of offerings in Yungdrung Bön rituals such as *Sangchö*, *Chutor*, *Surchö*, *Chöd* and *Tsokchö*. These guests include Buddhas, Protectors, the Eight Classes and beings of the Six Destinies of Rebirth.

Fully Enlightened Protectors or Guardians: Tib. 'jig rten las 'das pa'i srung ma; Wrathful Buddha forms which protect the integrity of the teachings and aid prctitioners on their path.

Gelugpa: Tib. dGe lugs pa; the youngest order of Tibetan Buddhism founded by Je Tsongkhapa.

Geser: Bur. Гэсэр; Tibetan/Mongol-Buryat epic narrating the activities of the hero Gesar/Geser. The Tibetan epic is Buddhist while the Mongol-Buryats have both a Bө Murgel and a Buddhist version.

Gher: Bur. гэр; Mongol-Buryat felt or wooden yurt.

Gooideg: Bur. гүйдэг; malevolent 'runner' spirits.

Gooideg Garguulha: Bur. Гүйдэг гаргуулха; rite to exorcise *Gooideg* spirits.

Great Transference or **Phowa Chenpo**: Tib. 'Pho ba Chen po; the highest level of Dzogchen realization.

Guru Padmasambhava alias Pema Thongdrol: Tib. Pad ma mThong grol; according to Yungdrung Bön, he is one of the Bönpo sage Drenpa Namkha's twin sons who was adopted by the Kings Indrabodhi of Uddiyana when he and his wife found the young boy floating in a lotus. Tibetan Buddhists considered him to have been born miraculously. Padmasambhava is said to have brought Indian Tantric Buddhism and the Dzogchen lineage of Garab Dorje to Tibet in the eighth century AD.

Guru Yoga: Tib. bla ma'i rnal 'byor; the method of unifying one's state with that of the Guru, a principal practice in Tantra and especially Dzogchen.

Gyal(po): Tib. rgyal (po); 'the kings', a relatively young class of very malicious spirits. C.f. *Noyod* and *Noyon.*

Gyulu: Tib. sgyu lus; Illusiory Body – the highest level of Tantric realization which is the union of subtle *prana* (Tib. yid) and mind (Tib. sems).

Haat: Bur. Хаадууд or Хании; children and grandchildren of Tengeri who descended to this earth to become Lord-Owners of the land in the Middle World. They reside on mountain peaks.

Hadag: Bur. хадаг; a white silk scarf. C.f. *khatag*.

Hahyuusan: Bur. хахюусан; protective amulets made by the Bɵ and Utgan for their clients.

Hain Hunehen: Bur. Һайн Һүнэхэн; 'good soul'. Also called *Zayaashi*.

Hariin Utkha: Bur. Хариин утха; transmission of the *utkha*-spark of Bɵ and Utgan's power and knowledge through the mother's line.

Haryn Utkha: Bur. Харын утха; transmission lineage of the Black Bɵ and Utgan.

Hayag: Bur. хаяаг; the right to perform ritual services, the right to the office of a Bɵ.

He'ete hebeneg: Bur. хээтэ хэбэнэг; a Bɵ-smith's cloak.

Heregsur: Bur. хэрэгсур; large burial *kurgans* made of stone slabs.

Hese: Bur. хэсэ; Bɵ/Utgan's drum; sometimes called *hengereg* (хэнгэрэг).

Hesheg, Hesheg Hootag: Bur. хэшэг, хэшэг хутаг; happiness, blessing – an aspect of the *hulde* energy of prosperity and well-being.

Hii moriin: Bur. хий мориин; Wind Horse, an energy of good luck and good fortune which allows one to be successful in whatever one undertakes. Also refers to the eponymous flag depicting a winged horse used in rituals to increase this energy. C.f. *lungta*.

Ho'orto: Bur. хоорто; Bɵ's dagger.

Hol'bogo: Bur. хольбого; a little bell tied to the Bɵ and Utgans' ritual dress and implements.

Hootaga: Bur. хутага; Bɵ's knife.

Hooyag: Bur. хуяг; a kind of coat of mail made of iron or lead plates connected by metal rings. Bɵ sometimes wear this over their *orgoi* or instead of it.

Hor'bo: Bur. hорьбо; a ritual cane which may be made of different materials and have different attributes on it. Different kinds of *hor'bo* are given to the Bɵ on different levels of initiation.

Hormusta: Bur. Хормуста, also known as Khaan Türmes, Khaan Hürmas etc.; leader of the White Western Tengeri or according to some versions, leader of all Tengeri.

Huhe Münhe Tengeri: Bur. Хүхэ Мүнхэ Тэнгэри; Eternal Blue Sky, the supreme creative principle in Bɵ Murgel.

Hulde: Bur. Һүльдэ; a complex Bɵ Murgel concept signifying prosperity, well-being, good luck and so forth.

Hunehen: Bur. Һүнэхэн; 'soul'.

Hunehen Hurylha: Bur. Хүнэхэн хурылха; the ritual of soul-retrieval in Bɵ Murgel.

Hurultai: Bur. Хурултай; an assembly or congress.

Hurylha: Bur. хурылха; ritual requesting the *uurag* substance of prosperity and good luck from the Tengeri.

Huur: Bur. хуур; mouth-harp.

Jonangpa: Tib. Jo nang pa; one of the Sarmapa Schools of Tibetan Buddhism.

Juthig: Tib. ju thig; very complex Bönpo method of divination using cords.

Kadampa:Tib. bKa' dams pa; a Sarmapa Buddhist School established by the Indian Guru Atisha.

Kagyudpa: Tib. bKa' brgyud pa; a Sarmapa School of Tibetan Buddhism established by Marpa Lotsawa which traces its lineage to the Indian *Mahasiddhas* Tilopa and Naropa.

Kalpa Medbum Nagpo: Tib. bsKal pa Med 'bum Nag po; a Bönpo mythological figure, the forefather of *Ngam,* the order of darkness and negativity.

Kam: Rus. кам; a type of priest in the native religion of Altai.

Kanjur: Tib. bka' 'jyur; compendium of the teachings given by the Buddha of Yungdrung Bön, Tonpa Shenrab Miwo.

Kar: Tib. skar; star-gods.

Karma: Tib. las; literally 'action', a cornerstone concept in the doctrine of cause and effect.

Karmic Debts: Tib. lan chags; debts owed by someone to other beings with which s/he interacted during one or more of their countless life-times.

Katen: Tib. bka' brten; compendium of great Yungdrung Bön masters' commentaries on the teachings contained in the *Kanjur*.

Khatag: Tib. kha btags; silk scarf traditionally given as an offering to show respect. C.f. *hadag*.

Khyung: Tib khyung; a mythological horned eagle. It is a very important deity in Bön. Khyung can be of two types: a Buddha-from or a worldly god. Garuda of the Hindu pantheon, which is related to the god Vishnu, is somewhat parallel to the worldly Khyung.

Kö: Tib. skos; gods who control many important cosmic energies.

Koldun: Rus. колдун, колдуны; a Russian wizard with abilities in healing, magic and clairvoyance. *Kolduns* may be white, black or both.

Kongling: Tib. kong gling; a trumpet made out of human thigh bone used in *Chöd.*

Kunzhi Namshe: Tib. kun gzhi'i rnam shes; basic consciousness or store consciousness, the type of consciousness which stores karmic traces.

Kurgan: a Scythian burial mound. There are a great many *kurgan* burial mounds in Southern Siberia, some of them so large that they can house up to 10 lorries.

Kushen: Tib sku gshen; Bönpo royal priest who fulfilled the function of spiritual teacher, adviser and perfomed rituals for protection of the king.

La: Tib. bla; a very complex Bönpo concept often translated into English as 'soul'. This translation might be somewhat acceptable if we speak of *la* in the context of Prehistoric Domai Bön but is wholly inadequate in the context of Yungdrung Bön as there we find nothing which resembles the Western notion of soul. Instead, *la* is explained in Yungdrung Bön as being roughly equivalent to *bagchag*, an individual's karmic traces.

Lagug: Tib. bla 'gugs; ritual to re-call the *la*.

Lalu: Tib. bla bslu; rite of buying the *la* back.

Lanay: Tib. bla gnas; *la*-receptacle.

Latse: Tib. bla rtsas; a receptacle or support for the *la* of the local guardian god.

Lha Bön: Tib. lha bon; Bön of the Deities.

Lha: Tib lha; gods. C.f. Tengeri. In Yungdrung Bön this can refer to Wisdom gods or worldly sky-gods. Wisdom gods are Buddhas whereas worldly sky-gods are powerful superhuman beings of which there are many types. The highest *Lha* are the sky-gods living on the very top of or above Mount Meru. Other types of *Lha* are celestial demi-gods of a positive nature known in Bön under the name of *Drala*.

Lhachö: Tib. lha chos; literally the 'ritual custom of the gods', this refers to the religious streams of Prehistoric Domai Bön still practised in some shape and form by the *lhapa/lhamo* and *pawo/nyenjomo* medium-healers of Tibet and the Tibetan borderlands.

Lhachukha: Tib. lha chu kha; a purification bathing ritual which forms part of the *Lurol* festival in Rebkong, Amdo.

Lhagtong: Tib. lhag mthong; insight-mediation.

Lhamo: Tib. lha mo; a female medium-healer.

Lhanchig Kyedre: Tib. lhan cig skyes 'dre; literally meaning Innate Demon, this refers to inner ignorance and negative tendencies of the mind which cause obstacles on one's path. Innate Demon also refers to the ignorance and dualistic grasping which manifests as soon as one enters the *Bardo* of the Clear Light of Emptiness.

Lhanchig Kyelha: Tib. lhan cig skyes lha; literally meaning Innate God, this refers to inner wisdom and positive tendencies of the mind which aid one on the path. Inner God also refers to the non-dual awareness of the Natural State of Mind which leads to full realization in the *Bardo* of the Clear Light of Emptiness.

Lhapa: Tib. lha pa; a male medium-healer.

Lo: Tib. lo; year, and by deference, the twelve Owners or controllers of the year which are gods of the twelve-year astrological cycle with a human body and the head of the animal of the year they govern.

Lu and **Lumo**: Tib. klu , klu mo; water-spirits and water-goddesses, usually referred to in the West by their Sanskrit name *Naga*. C.f. *Lusuut.*

Lukhang: Tib. klu khang; support structure for the *Lu* water-spirits.

Lungta: Tib. klung rta, rlung rta; literally Wind Horse. This is an energy of good luck and good fortune which allows one to be successful in whatever one undertakes. It also refers to the eponymous flag with a central image of a horse bearing a wish-fulfilling jewel and a *khyung*, tiger, dragon and snowlion in the four corners which symbolize either the deities of lungta or the five elements. C.f. *hii moriin*

Lusuudyn Tahilga or **Uhan Tahil**: Bur. лусуудын тахилга, Bur. уhан тахил; offering ritual to the water-spirits in Bө Murgel.

Lusuut, Lusuut-Khaan: Bur. лусут or лусун are water-spirits which correspond to Tib. klu and Sans. *Naga* while Bur. лусуут (лусун)-хаан is the king of water-spirits and corresponds to Sans. Nagaraja and Tib. klu'i rgyal po.

Lutor: Tib. klu-gtor; a *torma* offering to the *Lu*.

Magyud: Tib. Ma rgyud; the Mother Tantra of Yungdrung Bön.

Mahakala: Tib. mGon po phyag; 'one who is beyond time', one of the names of Shiva. Later this form of Shiva was absorbed into Tantric Buddhism where it was reinterpreted as an emanation of Avalokiteshvara or Chakrasamvara and declared a Buddha-form. In Tibet, Mahakala became one of the main wrathful *Dharmapala* protectors of all the Schools of Tibetan Buddhism. There are many forms and emanations of Mahakala which differ in the number of faces, hands and ritual implements they hold but they are all of extremely wrathful appearance. Mahakala has a consort called Mahakali.

Mahasiddha: Tib. grub thob chen po. a great religious practitioner who possesses supernatural psychic powers and the realization of the ultimate truth.

Maidari Huural: Bur. Майдари хуурал; the Maitrea festival celebrated in Mongolia and Buryatia.

Maihabshi: Bur. майхабши; a Bө's horned crown.

Mais Hara To'odei: Bur. Маис Хара Төөдэй; Grandmother of the Black Tengeri Sky-Dwellers.

Makaru: Tib. chu srin; a mythical sea monster somewhat similar to a crocodile.

Malgai: Bur. малгай; a Bө's hat made of bear fur.

Mamo: Tib. ma mo; a class of fierce and extremely powerful female spirits.

Mandala: Tib. dkyil 'khor; a graphic two-dimensional representation of the universe, or the dimension of an enlightened Buddha-form or a worldly god and its graphic two-dimensional representation.

Mang: Tib. smrang; myth of origin. A narration recited in the course of many Bönpo rituals belonging to the Causal Bön. It traces the lineage of a particular ritual tradition or a class of beings to its origin. Many *mang* also narrate the history and the process of how the universe and the beings inhabiting it were created.

Mantra: Tib. sngags; a sound formula possessing spiritual or magic power. There are many types of *mantras* with different functions which are tied to emanations of enlightened beings or worldly gods and spirits. *Mantras* are used in many oriental religions such as Yungdrung Bön, Zoroasantrism, Hinduism, Jainism, Buddhism and so on. Originally, *mantras* were probably a kind of prayer with a precise meaning and indeed, in Zoroastrianism 'manthra' means 'prayer'. While many *mantras* do encapsulate a meaning which can be understood intellectually, their main function lies on the level of energy. Many *mantras* are sentences in very archaic languages or the languages of superhuman beings and spirits, so the exact meaning cannot be clearly explained. Nevertheless, they possess a power and function which is independent of language. Many *mantras* must be employed together with visualization while others work purely through sound.

Manzan Gurma To'odei: Bur. Манзан Гурма Төөдэй; Grandmother of the White Tengeri Sky-Dwellers.

Melong: Tib. me long; a metal mirror used in divination, magic and Tantric rituals. In Dzogchen it is used as a symbol of the Natural State of Mind.

Men: Tib. sman; lake goddesses.

Mewa: Tib. sme ba; nine spaces of the *Kabtse* astrological diagram. Each mewa is governed by a specific *Sadag*.

Mina: Bur. минаа or Bur. ташуур; Bө's whip.

Mo: Tib. mo; divination. Yungdrung Bön contains a great number of divination methods many of which were copied and reinterpreted by Tibetan Buddhists.

Mu Hunehen: Bur. му hүнэхэн; 'bad soul'.

Mu shubuun: Bur. му шубуун, literally 'bad bird'. These are female killer-spirits which are the souls of sexually frustrated young women who died prematurely. They are somewhat equivalent to *Senmo.*

Mu: Tib. dmu; very ancient sky-dwelling beings, also one of the ancient royal clans of Tagzig, Zhang Zhung and Tibet.

Mudra (Sans.): Tib. phyag rgya; a symbolic gesture used for communication, transferring spiritual power, magic and empowering offerings. *Mudra* is a Sanskrit word which has several meanings. It can designate the hand gestures accompanying chanting and visualization made while performing offering rituals or Guru Yoga which are used to make the contact and offerings more concrete. Another meaning of *mudra* is 'symbol', found in such Sanskrit terms as *Mahamudra* – the Great Symbol – and in the name applied to highest realization in Tantra – *Karmamudra* – a name which also denotes the practice of sexual yoga in Buddhist Tantra. It is interesting to note that the Russian word *mudrost'* (Rus. мудрость) – 'wisdom' – is undoubtedly derived from this word.

Muke: Tib. dmu skas; the Ladder of *Mu* or *Mu*-ladder. A rainbow-light ladder connecting humans to the dimension of *Mu*-gods. Some exalted beings such as the first Tibetan king, Nyatri Tsenpo, descended to earth by means of this ladder.

Munpa Zerden Nagpo: Tib. Mun pa Zer ldan Nag po. The King of the World of Non-existence and the father of the *Düd*-demons of the sky which appeared at the beginning of the universe.

Muthag: Tib. dmu thag; the *Mu*-cord. A cord of rainbow-light connecting a person to the dimension of the *Mu*-gods. *Mu*-cords were attached to the top of the early Tibetan kings' heads and it is said that the kings did not die in an ordinary way by that their bodies dissolved into the rainbow-light of *muthag* which rolled back up into the dimension of the *Mu*.

Namkha Togden Chosumje: Tib. Nam mkha' sTong ldan Phyod sum rje; primordial ground of being, primordial Buddha-nature, an alternative name for Kuntu Zangpo.

Namkha: Tib. nam mkha'; a kind of thread-cross used in a variety of a rituals.

Nampar Shepa: Tib. rnam par shes pa; mental consciousness. *Sem* and *nampar shepa* or *namshe* are synonymous in the case of a sentient being but not in the case of a Buddha.

Nature of Mind, Natural State: Tib. sems nyid, gnas lugs; the enlightened non-dual nature of all sentient beings, base of all manifestations, good and bad, inner and outer, intimately present from the beginningless beginning in each and every being endowed with a mind; a tenet of the Dzogchen teachings.

Ngagpa: Tib. sngags pa; Tantric practitioner.

Ngam: Tib. ngam; the negative principle of universe, dimension of darkness, ignorance and evil.

Ngub: Tib. rngub; a kind of Bönpo magical missile.

Nine Impurities: Tib. mi gtsang rdzas cha sna dgu; these are defiling actions or circumstances which deeply pollute the spiritual dimension of both oneself and others, including that of the gods:
- Homicide/fratricide (Tib. dme);
- The birth of a child just after the death of its father (Tib. mug);
- Incest (Tib. nal);
- Filthiness (Tib. btsog);
- Imprecations (Tib. Than);
- Inauspicious signs (Tib. ltas ngan);
- Possession by (Tib. byur) spirits;
- Impurity due to the death of a spouse (Tib. yug);
- Pollution of the hearth (Tib. thab mkhon).

Nine Ways of Bön: Tib. Theg pa rim dgu'i bon ; a system of categorizing the teachings of Buddha Tonpa Shenrab Miwo. There are three versions of the Nine Ways according to the southern, northern and central systems.

Nojin: Tib. gnod sbyin; wealth gods.

Noyod: Bur. ноёд; king-spirits directly comparable to Tibetan *Gyal* or *Gyalpo*.

Noyon: Bur. ноён; a high-ranking feudal lord acting as a governor or a king-spirit directly comparable to Tibetan *Gyal* or *Gyalpo*.

Nyen: Tib. gnyan; tree spirits; spirits living in the intermediate space between the sky and the earth.

Nyi: Tib. nyi; sun gods.

Nyingma: Tib. rNying ma; rNying ma pa; the 'Ancient' School of Tibetan Buddhism established by Guru Padmasambhava and Shantirakshita in the eighth century AD.

Obo'o: Bur. обоо; a sanctified cairn representing the World Mountain.

Olmo Lungring: Tib. 'Ol mo lung ring; the central region of the much larger Central Asian country Tagzig where Tonpa Shenrab Miwo was born and from where his Yungdrung Bön doctrines spread in all directions. According to traditional Bönpo reckoning, Olmo Lungring, while being located on this earth, is a special dimension which cannot be reached by ordinary means but only when one gains a high level of spiritual realization. C.f. Shambhala.

Omul: Rus. омуль; a fish from the salmon family. One type of *omul* unique to Lake Baikal is used as an offering to the Lord of Baikal and also forms part of the Prebaikal Buryats' staple diet.

Ongo: Bur. онго; the trance state of an advanced Bɵ or Utgan when s/he is possessed by the *Ongon*.

Ongon: Bur. Онгон; a wide category of protective spirits of the Middle World closely connected with a practising Bɵ or a particular family, clan, or tribe. *Ongon* can often denote an ancestral protective deity and/or its support. *Ongon* supports can be a figure or mask, often made from fur or wood, to which offerings of food and drink are made. Butter is often smeared onto the support's mouth to satisfy the spirits and encourage them to carry out some specific action and fulfill the wishes of the household members or a Bɵ.

Ongon Daralga: Bur. Онгон даралга; 'pressure of the spirits' or so-called 'shamanic disease'. *Daralga* literally means 'to press down', 'to put pressure on'. This refers to the period of intense suffering during which the Tengeri and Ongon-spirits prepare a person to become a Bɵ or Utgan.

Ooselshen: Bur. үзэлшэн; clairvoyants.

Orgoi: Bur. оргой; a Bɵ/Utgan's ritual cloak.

Ostrog: Rus. острог; a fortified Cossack settlement surrounded by high wooden walls built from sharp-pointed logs. The Russian Cossacks and settlers, led by Ermak and successive *atamans*, built many of these as they entered and occupied Siberia and Buryatia.

Pal: Tib. dpal; 'glory' – an aspect of *cha*-energy which brings renown and success.

Palda: Tib. dpal mda'; a symbolic arrow, a support for *pal*-glory used in Tibetan marriage rituals.

Palu: Tib. sur dkar ba li; known in Buryatia as *sagaan dali* ('white wing'), a herb used in both Tibetan and traditional Buryat medicine as well as an ingredient in smoke offerings. Although *palu* belongs to the wider rhododendron family, it is neither poisonous nor similar to the rhododendron commonly planted in the West.

Parinirvana: Tib. mya ngan las 'das; attainment of final Buddhahood.

Parkha: Tib. spar kha; eight trigrams used in Bönpo (and later Tibetan Buddhist) astrology where they symbolize certain energies of the universe controlled by particular *Sadag* gods.

Phuglha: Tib. phug lha or khyim lha; the Deities of the Family.

Phurba: Tib. phur ba, phur bu; a ritual dagger used in both Yungdrung Bön and Buddhist Tantra. Phurba is also the name of a wrathful *yidam*.

Protectors of Bön: Tib. bon skyong, bon srung, bka' skyong; spiritual entities who are charged with the task of protecting Yungdrung Bön from both external dangers and corruption from within.

Puja: a Sanskrit term for a wide variety of offering rituals.

Rainbow Body: Tib. 'ja' lus. Rainbow body is the fruit of Dzogchen practice. When a realized practitioner of Dzogchen dies, his/her physical body dissolves into the essence of the elements and disappears from this plane of existence. The only remains left behind are some hair and nails.

Rigdzin: Tib. rig 'dzin; literally 'holder of awareness', a highly realized practitioner, lineage-holder or completely realized master of Yungdrung Bön or Tibetan Buddhism.

Rirab: Tib. ri rab; the World Mountain, equivalent to Mount Meru or Sumeru of the Hindus and Indian Budhists, and to Sumber of Bɵ Murgel.

Root Lama: Tib. rtsa ba'i bla ma; the Tantric or Dzogchen master who really introduced one to one's own Natural State and opened the real meaning of the teachings.

Sadag: Tib. Sa bdag; earth-gods.

Sadhana: Tib. sgrub pa; Tantric practice arranged according to the order of the stages.

Sagaasha: Bur. Сагааша; an uninitiated Bɵ.

Sakyapa: Tib. Sa skya pa; a Sarma School of Tibetan Buddhism where the transmission lineage is held by the male members of the Khön clan of a previously Bönpo family, an offshoot of Dru.

Salamat: Bur. саламат; a traditional Buryat delicacy made of double sour cream mixed with butter and flour.

Samaya (Sans.): Tib. dam tshig; a spiritual commitment given to the teachings and to one's spiritual guide which must be kept pure and unspoilt. If this commitment is broken, problems arise for one's practice and realization.

Samsara (Sans.): Tib. 'khor ba; Cycle of Transmigration. This refers to the way in which all sentient beings circulate in the various realms, continuously following from one life to another pushed by their karma to experience various sufferings. In the case of the human realm, the four main sufferings are birth, illness, old age and death and fundamental suffering of all *samsara* is impermanence. The only way out of *samsara* is to follow a Buddha's teachings which show the way to *nirvana*, (Tib. sde), Buddhahood beyond dualism and the afflictions of *samsara*. *Samsara* is not only the external realms and situations where the beings transmigrate but, most importantly, it denotes the deluded mind which follows and grasps dualistic vision.

Samten: Tib. bsam gtan; Sans. dhyana; meditative concentration.

San hengereg: Bur. сан хэнгэрэг; Bɵ's small cymbals.

Sang: Tib. bsang; rite of ritual fumigation or the substance used for smoke offerings.

Sangchö: Tib. bsang mchod; a fumigation ritual combining purification and offering.

Sarma Bön: Tib. Bön gsar ma. Also called New Bön, this is the syncretic tradition created by Drenpa Namkha and Vairochana in the seventh-eighth century AD combining elements of Yungdrung Bön and Indian Buddha-Dharma.

Sarmapa: Tib. gSar ma pa; the New Schools of Tibetan Buddhism based on the new wave of translations of Indian Buddhist texts by Rinchen Zangpo, Marpa Lotsawa, Ra Lotsawa and others.

Sasali: Bur. сасали; a collective prayer festival without blood sacrifice. These rituals consist of sprinkling offerings of tea, milk and alcohol. They are often performed on the occasion of some important undertaking such as starting a new business or going on a long journey, hunt or fishing trip. They can also be held before political events or because of some bad happenings. *Sasali* often forms an initial stage of *tailgan*.

Se'egen Sebdeg Tengeri: Bur. Сэгээн Сэбдэг Тэнгэри; also known as Golto Sagaan Burkhan Tengeri. He is the neutral, wavering Sky-Dweller, neither white nor black, who dwells in the neutral territory of the Sky. However, nowadays he is listed among the Western White Tengeri.

Seed syllable: Tib. sa bon; a symbolic letter representing a sacred sound. A seed syllable may be interpreted in one of two ways, depending on the stature of the deity it represents. In case of Bönpo Tantric *yidams* who are enlightened Buddha-forms, the seed syllable represents the cause from which the deity arises, i.e. the union of the Natural State and compassion. In the case of worldly gods belonging to the Eight Classes (many of which have vows to protect Yungdrung Bön), the seed syllable represents the essence of their life-force.

Sem: Tib. sems; mind.

Senmo: Tib. sren mo; female *Gyalpo* spirits.

Serge: Bur. сэргэ; the cosmic World Tree or the tethering-post of the Great Spirit to which Tengeri tie their sky-horses. During rituals it is represented by trees or posts. The *Serge* is said to have nine scared branches.

Serzhim: Bur. сержим, сэржэм; (c.f. *serchem,* Tib. g*ser skyems*). Ritually sprinkling a liquid such as tea, milk, Buryatian *arkhi* or Russian grain vodka as an offering to the gods and spirits. The drink is usually sprinkled into a fire, dripped on the ground or thrown up in the air. The proper Buryatian word for this is *duhaalga* or *hayalga* (Bur. дунаалга/хаялга) literally meaning 'dripping' or 'sprinkling' while the term *serzhim* is a borrowing from Buddhism originally stemming from Bön. In Bön, *serchem* refers to offering the 'golden liquid', alcohol infused with pieces of gold, as *ser* means gold.

Seter: Bur. сэтэр; bloodless animal sacrifice whereby an animal is suffocated and then offered.

Seven Divine *Tri* or the Seven *Tri* of the Sky: Tib. gNam gyi Khri bdun; first seven kings of Tibet.

Seven Early Buddhas: Seven Buddhas of Bön which preceded Tonpa Shenrab Miwo.

Shamanka: Rus. шаманка; a Russian word for a female shaman.

Shambhala: the notion of Shambhala appeared with the spread of Kalachakra Tantra in India in 11th –12th centuries AD. According to this Tantra, Shambhala is a spiritual country governed by the virtuous Wheel-Holding Universal Kings to whom Buddha Shakyamuni imparted the teachings of Kalachakra Tantra. It is said to lie to the north of India, suggesting modern-day Tajikistan as the most likely geographical site. Like Olmo Lungring, Shambhala is located on this earth but on a different plane meaning it cannot be seen by ordinary people. The various parallels and differences in the descriptions of Olmo Lungring and Shambhala would make an interesting study, but the overall concept of these two kingdoms together with their geographical locations would support the view that these two names in fact refer to the same holy land. C.f. Olmo Lungring.

Shanar: Bur. шанар; Bө Murgel initiation process.

Shang: Tib. gshang; Bönpo flat bell also used by some Buryatian Bө and Utgan.

Shanginuur: Bur. шангинуур; Bө's bell.

Shazan: Bur. Бөө шажан; generic word for 'religion'. There is no significant semantic difference between *murgel* and *shazhan* and they are similar in use to Tib. bon and Tib. chos. While the word *murgel* has remained closely tied to the Bө religion, *shazhan* is nowadays mostly used to designate the Buryatian adaptation of Tibetan Buddhism.

Shed: Tib. gshed; generally meaning 'hindrance', *shed* is also the name of the class of malevolent spirits which enslave the *la* of the deceased preventing it from going on to the next rebirth. These spirits also take on the deceased's appearance and torture family and friends through ghostly apparitions, misfortunes and frightening incidents. The large body of Bön rituals to exorcise these spirits is known under the name of *Shed Dur* (Tib. gshed 'dur), the *Rites which Vanquish the Shed.*

Shenbön: Tib. gShen bon; followers of the Bön of Tonpa Shenrab Miwo, i.e. practitioners of Yungdrung Bön. Like *Shenpo*, this name was used to distinguish such practitioners from other contemporary types of Bönpo.

Shenpo: Tib. gShen po; a follower of Tonpa Shenrab. This name has been used by practitioners of Yungdrung Bön since ancient times to distinguish themselves from other kinds of Bönpo priests.

Shere'e: Bur. шэрээ; an altar-chest of Buryatian Bө and Utgan.

Shere'ehen: Bur. шэрээхэн, a small *shere'e*-altar.

Shinje: Tib. gshin rje; lords of death, spirits causing death.

Sholmos: Bur. шолмос; a type of bad spirit.

Shudher: Bur. шүдхэр; an evil spirit, equivalent of Russian *chyort* (Rus. чёрт).

Shunyata (Sans.): Tib. stong nyid; one of the major concepts of Yungdrung Bön and Buddhism, namely the lack of inherent existence in any manifest phenomena.

Si: Tib. sri; spirits of cemeteries.

Sid: Tib. srid; controllers of existence.

Siddhi (Sans.): Tib. dngos grub; spiritual attainments. Ordinary *siddhi* are various kinds of magic or psychic powers together with wealth, prosperity, long-life etc. while the supreme *siddhi* is the realization of the state of Buddha.

Sidpa Sangpo Bumtri: Tib. Srid pa Sangs po 'Bum khri; a *Longku* (*Sambhogakaya*) form, one of the Four Heroic Buddhas of Yungdrung Bön.

Sin: Tib. srin; 'vampire' spirits.

Six Classes of Beings: Tib. 'gro ba rigs drub; six types of beings dwelling in the Six Realms of Rebirth.

Six Great Translators: dMu tsah Tra he of Tagzig, Khri thog sPa tsha of Zhang Zhung, Hu lu sPa legs of Sumpa, lHa bdag sNgags dro of India, Legs tang Mang po of China, gSer thog lCe 'byams of Phrom.

Six Holy Families of Yungdrung Bön: *Mu-shen*, *Dru*, *Zhu*, *Pa*, *Meu* and *Khyung*: Tib. dMu-gshen, Bru, Zhu, sPa, rMe'u, Khyung. The beings who dwell in the Six Realms are: hell-dwellers, hungry ghosts, animals, humans, demi-gods and gods (Tib. dmyal ba, yi dwags, byol song, mi, lha ma yin, lha).

Six Realms of Rebirth: Tib. rigs drug; often translated into English as the Six Destinies of Rebirth, Six Realms or Six Lokas, these are the places which make up *samsara* where mind-streams of sentient beings circulate in the beginnigless cycle of death and birth.

Sode Lama: Bur. Соодэ Лама; a Buryatian lama who lived in Barguzin at the turn of the nineteenth century. He apparently harmoniously combined ways of Buddhism and Bɵ Murgel, and and when he died his body shrank to the size of a baby – a sign which may indicate he was a Dzogchenpa.

Sog: Tib. srog: life-force; vital principle. C.f. *amin*.

Sogdag: Tib. srog bdag; Owner of Life-Force, a title applied to very powerful worldly gods who have control over the destiny of men and other creatures. C.f. *Zayaan*.

Sooglan: Bur. суглан; a gathering of the *Zayaan*.

Sumber: Bur. сүмбэр; the World Mountain in Bɵ Murgel which corresponds to *Sumeru* or *Meru*, the cosmic mountain of Hindus and later Buddhists.

Surchö: Tib. gsur mchod; offering of smoke and burnt food.

Swastika: Tib. g.yung drung, Bur. хас тамга; ancient powerful symbol of good luck and auspiciousness with many layers of meaning. Not to be confused with the Nazi German's *Hakenkreuz* which is formed from two 'S' letters, stylized and combined as runes.

Tagzig: Tib. sTag rzig, rTag gzigs; Tagzig was a very large country or confederation of states to the north-west of Zhang Zhung and Tibet. It spread over northern Central Asia and its centre was possibly located in modern-day Tajikistan and the Pamir mountain-range, but it also included territories in modern-day Kirgizstan, Turkmenistan, Uzbekistan, north-eastern Iran and perhaps some parts of northern Afghanistan. Tonpa Shenrab Miwo was born in the central region of Tagzig called Olmo Lungrig and Yungdrung Bön teachings spread from there in all directions.

Tahilgan: Bur. тахилган; a type of *tailgan*.

Taiga: Rus. тайга; a Tungus word denoting the forest of pine with some silver birch which covers vast stretches of Siberia.

Tailgan: Bur. тайлган; a communal sacrifice and celebration pertaining to Bɵ Murgel led by Bɵ, Utgan and elders. It is usually held at special power places at regular intervals.

Tamga: Bur. хаhии тамга; 'seal of the *Haats*', a Bɵ-clan mark.

Tangarig: Bur. тангариг; a sacred oath taken by Bɵ and Utgan.

Tarasoon: Bur. тарасун; Buryatian milk-vodka.

Tengeri: Bur. Тэнгэриин, literally 'Sky-dwellers'. These are long-living sky-gods who dwell in the dimension of Eternal Blue Sky.

Tengeriin uden: Bur. Тэнгэриин уудэн; the door to the realm of the Sky.

Terma: Tib. gter ma; scriptural treasures, hidden during times of persecution to be rediscovered in more auspicious times by *tertons*. However, *terma* does not only refer to texts or statues hidden in rocks etc. (Tib. sa gter); it can also denote mental treasures (Tib. dgongs gter), the revelations of the teachings stored in a *terton*'s own consciousness from previous lives. There is also a kind of Oral Transmission given mystically by the early *Siddhas*, *dakini* or Protectors to chosen *yogis* known in Yungdrung Bön as Tib. snyan brgyud. In Tibetan Buddhism there is a similar mode of transmission received from the pure vision called Tib.dag snang.

Terton: Tib. gter ton; a discoverer of religious treasure. This term refers to masters who rediscovered *terma*, teachings or sacred objects hidden by the early masters during times of persecution or for the sake of future generations. The *terton* is often a reincarnation of the master who originally hid the teachings or a re-incarnation of one of his/her disciples.

Thangka: Tib. thang ka; an iconographic painting, usually executed on canvass and framed in silk according to detailed instructions contained in religious texts.

Thorse: Tib. 'Thor gsas; Bönpo deities of light.

Three Jewels: Tib. rin chen gsum ; Buddha, Yungdrung Bön, Community of *Bodhisattvas* (Tib. sangs rgyas, bon , gshen rab), objects of refuge in the Sutra level of Yungdrung Bön.

Three Poisonous Emotions: Tib. dug gsum; desire, anger, ignorance: Tib. 'dod chags, zhe sdang, gtu mug.

Three Roots: Tib. rtsa ba gsum; *lama*, *yidam*, *khandro* (Tib. bla ma, yid dam, mkha' 'gro), objects of refuge in the Tantra and Dzogchen levels of Yungdrung Bön.

Three Sweet Things: Tib. mngar gsum; sugar, molasses, honey. These are included in many offerings.

Three White Things: Tib. dkar gsum; yoghurt, butter and milk. These are included in many offering rituals.

To lift up the bones: Bur. яна бариха, lit. 'to lift up the bones'. A method of sky burial used for Bө or war-lords of high nobility.

To'oerih: Bur. тооэрих; Bө Murgel divination technique whereby a bowl is tossed in a certain way. If it lands the right way up, that augurs well; if it lands upside down, further offerings and prayers are made and the bowl is thrown again. The process is repeated until the bowl lands the right way.

Tod: Tib. stod; a class of Rock-Owner spirits.

Toli: Bur. толи; a mirror made of jade or a mix of metals.

Tolmoosho: Bur. толмоошо; 'the interpreter', a Bө who holds both black and white *utkha*.

Tongsum: Tib. stong gsum; the Three Thousand-fold Universe, i.e. the universe we live in.

Tonpa Shenrab Miwoche: Tib. sTon pa gShen rab Mi bo che; the Buddha of Yungdrung Bön.

Torma: Tib. gtor ma; a sacrificial offering cake of which there are two major types: wrathful (red) and peaceful (white), although there are very many different shapes and forms.

Tra: Tib. pra; Bönpo mirror-divination.

Transmission: there are different levels of transmissions and empowerments in both Yungdrung Bön and Tibetan Buddhism but even reading a text containing an exposition of the teachings requires a transmission of Tib. rlung (literally 'handle') or 'scriptual authorisation' which will enable a student to realise the real meaning of the text and not just the words.

Trekchö: Tib. khreg chod; 'cutting off tensions', one of the two main modes of contemplation in Dzogchen.

Trigyal Khugpa: Tib. Khri rgyal Khug pa; forefather of *Ye*. In Yungdrung Bön he is also known as Tib. mNgon rdzogs rGyal po and Tib. gShen lha 'Od dkar.

Trin: Tib. sprin; gods dwelling in the clouds.

Tsampa: Tib. rtsam pa; roast barley flour, a staple Tibetan food also used to make many offering figurines and effigies.

Tse: Tib. tse; life, duration of life.

Tsen: Tib. btsan; wrathful rock-dwelling spirits of red complexion.

Tsentrü: Tib. tshan khrus; purification of spiritual pollution through lustral sprinkling. The water based mixture of various liquids, herbs and minerals believed to have purifying properties used for this can be of two types, 'white' or 'red'. The 'red' variety also includes the blood of certain animals.

Tsokchö: Tib. tshogs mchod; Sans. Ganapuja; ritual offering and symbolic meal designed to repair spiritual commitments and empower the practitioner with blessings and *siddhi*.

Tug: Bur. туг: Tib. thug; a trident or spear with a banner, cylindrical flag or round container made of horse or yak tails. It can be both a religious object and a military banner and is a very important support for the protective deities among Mongols and Tibetan Bönpos alike. A simpler version – a spear with a pennant – is commonly used as a support for mountain gods in both traditions.

Tulku: Tib. sprul sku; Dimension of *Nirmanakaya*, *Nirmanakaya* Buddha or a reincarnation of a high lama.

Tumen: Bur. түмэн; a Mongol cavalry unit of 10,000 warriors.

Tundra: the low vegetation of dwarf trees and shrubs found in north Siberia.

Twelve Lores: Tib. shes pa bcu gnyis; one way of classifying the Bön of Cause.

Ublei Tailgan: Bur. Үблэй тайлган; Winter *Tailgan*.

Ubrus: Rus. убрус; a ritual 'towel' in the Russian pre-Christian religion. Such 'towels' were used for offering bread and salt to a deity or important person as a sign of respect and as such can be compared to Tibetan *khatag* and Buryatian *hadag*, white silk scarves offered as a token of respect. *Khatag* *and hadag* are usually decorated with the Eight Auspicious Symbols, and *ubrus*, too, are embroidered with various religious and secular emblems. *Ubrus* were also tied to sacred trees in a way reminiscent of the Buryatian custom of tying *zalaa*-ribbons.

Ugaalga: Bur. угаалга; body-washing ritual.

Uhan Tarim: Bur. уһан тарим; a purification rite using water, also used for general healing purposes.

Uliger: Bur. үльгэр; myths and epics of Bө Murgel.

Uligershen: Bur. үльгэршэн; bards who sing the *uliger* myths and epics of Bө Murgel. C.f. Tibetan *drungkhen* bards (Tib. sgrung mkhan) who sing the *Gesar* epic.

Utgan: Bur. утган, удган, одёгон, одигон; a priestess of Bө Murgel.

Utkha: Bur. утха; a Bө or Utgan's spiritual root or spark.

Uurag: Bur. уураг; heavenly food of the Tenegeri akin to Tib *düdtsi* and Sans. *amrita*.

Uzyubr: Rus. узюбрь; a kind of deer living in Buryatia.

Vairochana of Pagor: Tib. Bai ro tsa na; a very gifted translator and practitioner from a Bönpo background who became one of the twenty-five heart-disciples of Guru Padmasambhava. While fully committed to his new faith he nevertheless did not forsake the faith of his ancestors which he helped to preserve from the persecution launched by King Trisong Deutsen who was advised by sectarian Buddhists. During the height of the persecution, Vairochana secretly translated many Yungdrung Bön texts on the subject of philosophy, Tantra and Dzogchen from the languages of Zhang Zhung, Gilgit, Drusha, Sanskrit and so on. Vairochana became a disciple of the Bönpo *Mahasiddha* Drenpa Namkha with whom he was engaged in saving Bönpo texts from destruction. Drenpa Namkha and Vairochana later created a syncretic tradition of New Bön (Tib. bon sar ma) which combined elements of Yungdrung Bön and the Buddha-Dharma of India.

Wal: Tib. dbal; powerful, wrathful gods.

Wangthang: Tib. dbang thang; Ascendance-Capacity, an energy tightly connected to *cha* and *lungta* forces.

Wisdom Gods: Tib. ye shes lha; Buddha-forms.

Worldly Guardians: Tib. 'jig rten pa'i srung ma; worldly gods and spirits who swore an oath to protect Yungdrung Bön.

Clean Guardians: Tib. 'jig rten pa'i gtsang rigs lha; high gods of stars and planets who swore an oath to protect Yungdrung Bön. These gods accept only 'clean' offerings which exclude blood, meat, bones and so on.

Wu: pre-Taoist priests of ancient China, in particular, priests of Chou.

Wug: Tib. dbugs; Respiratory Breath.

Yajna/Yasna: sacrificial rituals of proto-Indo-Iranians and their descendants the Zoroastrians and Hindus.

Yang: Tib. g.yang; literally 'prosperity', an aspect of *cha* energy.

Yasak: Rus. ясак; from the Mongol and Tyurkic word meaning 'tax'. The *yasak* was a system of taxation in the Great Steppe and Siberia whereby taxes are paid in precious furs.

Yaşyr: Rus. ясырь; from the Tatar word meaning 'prisoner', 'slave'. *Yasyr* was the practice of taking hostages if a tribe, clan or family failed to contribute sufficient *yasak* or had nothing to give the taxman when he called. Hostages then had to be bought back by their relatives. However, if the ransom money came too late or if the captors took a fancy to the hostages, they were simply kept as permanent slaves, as was often the case with female hostages.

Ye: Tib. ye; the positive dimension of light and virtue.

Yi: Tib. yid; subtle inner wind.

Yidam: Tib. yid dam; a manifestation of Buddha in the form of the deity which is used as the primary means for obtaining realization. The Bönpo understanding of *yidam* is not limited to a Tantric deity as is often the case in Buddhism, and the supreme *yidam* of Bön is the Natural State of Mind, although even a text or prayer can be referred to as *yidam* if used as a primary practice. *Yidam* is sometimes translated into English as 'tutelary deity'.

Yogi: Tib. rnal 'byor pa; an advanced practitioner of Tantra and/or Dzogchen possessing psychic powers and special realization.

Yogini: Tib. rnal 'byor ma; female *yogi*.

Yuhenguud: Bur. Юhэнгууд; 'The Nine', a group of youths clad in white who assist the presiding Bө in his ritual activities.

Yullha/Yulsa: Tib. yul lha, yul sa; powerful Lord-Owners of the counryside and mountain ranges.

Yungdrung Bön: Tib. g.yung drung bon. Sometimes translated into English as Eternal Bön because Yungdrung (Sans. *Swastika*) means indestructible and unborn, i.e. eternal. 'Yungdrung' covers more or less the same semantic field as '*vajra*' in the Indian Buddhist tradition, especially in Vajrayana. Yungdrung Bön could also be called Central-Asian Buddhism as it is the teachings taught by Tonpa Shenrab Miwo, the Buddha who was born in Central Asia.

Yungdrung Sempa: Tib. g.yung drung sems dpa; equivalent to Sanskrit *Bodhisattva*, also sometimes know as *Swastikasattva*. Yungdrung Sempa, literally 'one who possesses the mind of *yungdrung*', is a practitioner of Yungdrung Bön on the high level of realization who traverses the path to the Buddhahood by the means of the ten *bhumi* (Tib. sa) stages.

Zaarin: Bur. заарин; a Bө who has attained the highest level in Buryatian Bө Murgel's system of Nine Initiations.

Zada Shuluun: Bur. зада шулуун; a holy object lowered from the dimentsion of Sky. C.f. *buudal*.

Zalaa: Bur. залаа; multi-coloured ribbons tied to trees in power places or onto sacred objects; cap-band made of fur, usually of the tribe's totemic animal.

Zayaan: Bur. заяан; derived from the Buryatian word *zayaa* (заяаа) meaning 'fate', 'destiny', 'lot'. *Zayaan* is a general term denoting a god or spirit of the Upper World or Middle World with the capacity to control the fate/destiny of the living, therefore – like the term *Ezhen* – it is applied to various types of deities and spirits of different rank. In some cases, *zayaan* can mean 'creator'. It may be compared to the Tibetan term *sogdag* (Tib. srog bdag) which literally means 'the owner of the life-force of beings', i.e. someone who has power over the life and fate of other beings.

Zayaashi: Bur. заяаши; a type of soul, known in Russian scholarly works as 'fate-soul' (Rus. душа-судьба). Also means 'creator'. C.f. *hain hunehen*

Zeli: Bur. зэли; Bө's rope made of horse hair used for various ritual activities such as binding evil spirits.

Zer: Tib. zer; gods of light rays.

Zermig: Tib. gzer mig; the medium version of the biography of Buddha Tonpa Shenrab Miwo.

Zha: Tib. 'ja'; rainbow gods.

Zhada: Bur. жада; Bө's spear.

Zhang Zhung: Tib. zhang zhung; an ancient empire or tribal confederation with Yungdrung Bön as its state religion. Zhang Zhung covered a large chunk of the Tibet-Qinghai Plateau but was conquered and eventually completely overthrown by the rising Tibetan empire in the sixth-eighth centuries AD.

Zhidag: Tib. gzhi bdag; powerful Lord-Owners of the land.

Zhigyed: Tib. zhi byed; literally 'pacification' – a meditation system created by the Indian *Mahasiddha* Padamba Sangye during his stay in Tibet.

Zhine: Tib. zhi gnas; the meditation of calm-abiding.

Zhitro: Tib. zhi khro; 'cycle of peaceful and wrathful deities' – a Tantric meditation system to purify the sufferings of Bardo and gain total liberation.

Zhodo'o: Bur. жодоо/ёдоо; bark of the Siberian fir tree (Lat. Abies sibirica), used in fumigation rites.

Zi: Tib. gzi; stones with special geometric ornaments, probably a type of agate treated in a special way. Zi are connected with Zhang Zhung culture and are often found in the vicinity of Zhang Zhung sites.

Zijyid: Tib. gZi brjid; the large version of the biography of Tonpa Shenrab which contains detailed teachings on the Nine Ways of Bön.

Bibliography

Materials in English:

Achard, Jean-Luc. *The Dzogchen Tradition of Bön-Zhik Khyung-Nak* (Courdimanche-sur-Essonne: Khyung-mkhar, 1998).

Allen, Thomas B. 'The Silk Road's Lost World', *National Geographic*, March, 1996.

Allione, Tsultrim. *Women of Wisdom* (London, Boston, Melbourne & Henley: Routledge & Keagan Paul, 1984).

Ancient Tibet: Research Material from the Yeshe De Project (Berkeley: Dharma Publishing, 1986).

Bansal, B.L. *Bon, Its Encounter with Buddhism in Tibet* (Delhi: Eastern Book Linkers, 1994).

Bellezza, John Vincent. *Divine Dyads, Ancient Civilization in Tibet* (Dharmasala: LTWA, 1997).

Ed. Bercholz, Samuel and Sherab Chödzin Kohn, *Entering the Stream* (London: Rider Books, 1994).

Blackburn, Simon. 'The World's 10 Biggest Ideas'; 2: Science, *NewScientist,* 17 September 2005.

Ed. Blezer, Henk. 'Tibet, Past and Present', *Tibetan Studies I, PIATS: Tibetan Studies: proceedings of the Ninth Seminar of the International Association for Tibetan Studies, Leiden 2000* (Leiden-Boston-Köln: Brill 2002).

Blofeld, John. *I Ching; The Book of Change* (London: Penguin, Arkana, 1991).

Boyce, Mary. *History of Zoroastrianism, Vol. I, The early period* (Leiden: Brill, 1975).

Boyce. 'Ahura Mazda', *Encyclopaedia Iranica* 1: pp 684–687 (New York: Routledge & Kegan Paul, 1983).

Bracey, John /Liu Xing-Han, *Ba Gua: Hidden Knowledge in the Taoist Internal Martial Art.*

Bunce, Fredrick W. *An Encyclopaedia of Hindu Deities, Demi-Gods, Godlings, Demons and Heroes with special focus on Iconographic Attributes. Volume 1* (New Delhi: D.K. Printworld (P) Ltd., 2000).

Cech, Krystina. *The History, Teaching and Practice of Dialectics According to the Bon Tradition* (Solan, (H.P.): Hill Star Press, 1984).

Chaoul, M. Alejandro. 'Tracing the origins of chö (gcod) in the Bön tradition:

a dialogic approach cutting through sectarian boundaries', MA thesis, (University of Virginia, 1999).

Chenagtsang, Nida. *Mantra Healing in Tibetan Medicine*(Merigar: Shang Shung Edizioni).

Choden, Tashi and Lham Dorji, Dorji Penjore, Sonam Kinga, Karma Galay, Ugye Pelgen. Monograph 11: 'Wayo, Wayo – Voice from the Past, *The Centre for Bhutan Studies*, Thimphu, Bhutan, April, 2004.

Clemente, Adriano. *The Sgra Bla, Gods of the Ancestors of Gshen-Rab Mi-Bo* (Merigar: Shang Shung Edizioni, 1995).

Tr. Clemente, Adriano *Shense Lhaje, Visionary Encounters and Dzogchen Teachings from the Golden Advice* (Merigar: Shang Shung Edizioni, 1995).

Csorba, M. 'The Chinese Northern Frontier', *Antiquity* 70 (September):564, 1996.

Curriculum Guide for Certificate in Amchi Duera-pa (Bum Zhi Tradition) of the Himalayan Amchi Association, Kathmandu, Nepal , April 2004, prepared for the Government of Nepal.

Dakpa, Nyima. *Opening the Door to Bön,* (Ithaca, New York: Snow Lion, 2005).

Ermakov, Dmitry. *The Way of the Wind*, unpublished diary.

Ermakov, *Tailgan Trip*, unpublished diary.

Ermakova, Carol. 'From Shamanism to Socialism: Religion and Land-Use around Lake Baikal', MA dissertation (SSEES, University of London, 1994).

Ferfelova, V.V. 'Participation of Indo-European tribes in ethnogeny of the Mongoloid population of Siberia: analysis of the HLA antigen distribution in Mongoloids of Siberia', *The American Journal of Human Genetics* Vol. 47, 1990, pp. 294–301.

Fremantle, Francesca and Chögyam Trungpa. *The Tibetan Book of the Dead* (Boston and London: Shambhala, 1992).

Gold, Peter. *Navajo& Tibetan sacred Wisdom; The Circle of Spirit* (Rochester, Vermont: Inner Traditions, 1994).

Goldberg, Jay and Doya Nardin. *Mo: Tibetan Divination System*, text by Mipham (Ithaca, New York: Snow Lion, 1996).

Gurung, B.C. *Bon in Himalaya* (Kathmandu: Mrs. Uma Gurung, Tongi Sadan, Maharajgunj, 2003).

Gyaltsen, Shardza Tashi. Commentary by Lopon Tenzin Namdak, *Heart Drops of Dharmakaya: Dzogchen Practice of the Bön Tradition* (Ithaca: Snow Lion Publications, 1993).

_____. *Kusum Rangshar, Oral Teachings by Lopön Tenzin Namdak Rinpoche, Paris, April 1999,* Trnscr. & ed. Carol Ermakova and Dmitry Ermakov, Shenten Dargye Ling, Blou, 2006.

Hadingham, Evan. 'The Mummies of Xinjiang', *Discover,* April, 1994, pp 68-77.

Tr. & ed. Harding, Sarah. *Machik's Complete Explanation, Clarifying the Meaning of Chöd* (Ithaca, New York; Boulder, Colorado: Snow Lion Publications, 2003).

Holy Bible, New International Version (London, Sidney, Auckland: Hooder&Soughton, 1990).

Hummel, Seigbert. *On Zhang-Zhung*, (Dharmasala: LTWA, 2000).

Hyde-Chambers, Frederick and Audrey. *Tibetan Folk Tales* (Boston & London: Shambhala, 2001).

Jinpa, Gelek. *Tummo: A Practice Manual by Shardza Tashi Gyaltsen*, Trnscr. & ed. Carol and Dmitry Ermakovi, (Shenten Dargye Ling: Association Yungdrung Bon, 2005).

Jinpa, Gelek and Charles Ramble, Carroll Dunham, Thomas Kelly. *Sacred Landscape and Pilgrimage in Tibet: In Search of the Lost Kingdom*, (New York, London: Abbeville Press Publishers, 2005).

Karmay, Samten G. *The Treasury of Good Sayings* (Delhi: Motilal Banarsidass Publishers Private Limited, 1972).

_____. *The Arrow and the Spindle: Studies in History, Myths, Rituals and Beliefs in Tibet* (Kathmandu: Mandala Book Point, 1998).

_____. *The Arrow and the Spindle: Studies in History, Myths, Rituals and Beliefs in Tibet, Vol.II*, Mandala Book Point, Kantipath, Kathmandu, 2005

_____. *The Little Luminous Boy* (Bangkok: White Orchid Press, 1998).

Ed. Karmay, Samten G. and Yasuhiko Nagasano, 'New Horizons in Bon Studies', *Bon Studies 2, Senri Ethnological Reports 15, National Museum of Ethnology*, Osaka, 2000.

Ed. Karmay, Samten G. and Jeff Watt. *Bon: The Magic Word. The Indigenous Religion of Tibet* (Rubin Museum of Art, New York in association with Philip Wilson Publishers, London, 2007).

Kharitidi, Olga. *Entering the Circle*, (San Francisco: Harper, 1996).

Kind, Marietta. 'Mendrub: A Bonpo Ritual for the Benefit of all Living Beings and for the Empowerment of Medicine Performed in Tsho, Dolpo 1996', Am Ethnologischen Seminar der Universität Zürich Philosophische Fakultät I, Zürich, May 1999.

Kuiper, F. B. J. 'The Bliss of AÞa', *Indo-Iranian Journal* 8, 1964-65.

_____. 'Ahura' *Encyclopaedia Iranica* 1, pp 682–683 (New York: Routledge & Kegan Paul, 1983).

Kvaerne, Per. *The Bon Religion of Tibet* (London: Serinda Publications, 1995).

Kvaerne. 'Mongols and Khitans in a 14th Century Tibetan Bönpo Text', *Acta Orientale* XXXIV, Budapest, 1980, pp. 80-104.

Kvaerne. 'A Chronological Table of the Bon Po: The Bstan Rcis of Nima Bstan'Jin', *Acta Orientalia*, XXXIII, Apud Ejnar Munksgaard, Havinae, 1981, pp. 203-248.

Ed. Lopez, Donald S. Jr. *Religions of Tibet in Practice* (New Jersey: Princeton University Press, 1997).

Mair, Victor. 'Mummies of the Tarim Basin', *Archaeology*, March, 1995: pp 28-35. (See also *The Journal of Indo-European Studies*, vol 23, no. 3&4, articles by: Mair; E.J.W. Barber and I. Good; J.P. Mallory; Paolo Francalacci).

Mallory, J. P. and Victor H. Mair.*The Tarim Mummies: Ancient China and the Mystery of the Earliest Peoples from the West*, (London: Thames & Hudson, 2000).

Massey Stewart, John. 'Baikal's Hidden Depths', *NewScientist*, 23 June 1990.

Molè, Gabriella. 'The Tu-yü-hun from the Northern Wei to the Time of the Five Dynasties', *Serie Orientale Roma* 41. (Rome: Istituto Italiano per il Medio ed Estreme Oriente, 1970).

Mullin, Glenn. H. *The Selected Works of Dalai Lama I: Bridging the Sutras and Tantras* (Ithaca, New York: Snow Lion).

Mumford, Stan Royal. *Himalayan Dialogue: Tibetan lamas and Gurung Shamans in Nepal* (Madison: The University of Wisconsin Press, 1989).

'My other universe is a Porsche', *NewScientist*, 7 October 2006, pp. 38-41.

Ed. Nagano, Yasuhiko and Randy J. LaPolla. 'New Research on Zhangzhung and Related Himalayan Languages', *Bon Studies 3, Senri Ethnological Reports* 19, National Museum of Ethnology, Osaka, 2001.

Namdak, Yongdzin Lopön Tenzin Rinpoche. *Nyam-zhag Gom-pa'i Lag-len (lTaba spyi-gcod kyi mnyam-bzhag sgompa'i lag-len), Shambhala Centre, Paris, April 1997,* Trnscr. & ed. Carol Ermakova and Dmitry Ermakov (Blou, Shenten Dargye Ling, 2006).

____. *Nyamgyud, Morning, Volume I, Blanc, 3 – 15 June 2001,* Trnscr. & ed. Carol Ermakova and Dmitry Ermakov (Blou, Shenten Dargye Ling, 2006).

_____. *Nyamgyud, Morning, Volume II, Blanc, 17 – 29 June 2001,* Trnscr. & ed. Carol Ermakova and Dmitry Ermakov (Blou, Shenten Dargye Ling, 2006).

_____. *Gyalwa Chaktri, Afternoon, Volume I, Blanc, 3 – 15 June, 2001,* Trnscr. & ed. Carol Ermakova and Dmitry Ermakov (Blou, Shenten Dargye Ling, 2006).

_____. *Nyam Gyud, Chyaru, Afternoon, Volume II, Blanc 18 – 29 June, 2001,* Trnscr. & ed. Carol Ermakova and Dmitry Ermakov (Blou, Shenten Dargye Ling, 2006).

_____. *Teachings on Zhang Zhung Nyen Gyud and Namkha Truldzö, Vimoutiers, 24 August – 11 September 2004,*Trscr.&ed. Carol Ermakova and Dmitry Ermakov (Blou:Shenten Dargye Ling, 2006).

_____. *Dringpo Sorzhag, Chapter II: The Clothes, Pith Instructions of Zhang Zhung Nyen Gyud Masters, Blanc, 15th – 17th September 2002,* Trnscr. & ed. Carol Ermakova and Dmitry Ermakov (Blou, Shenten Dargye Ling, 2006).

_____. *Zhang Zhung Nyam Gyud, The Experiential Transmission of Zhang Zhung,Vimoutiers, 25 August – 14 September, 2003,* Trnscr. & ed. Carol Ermakova and Dmitry Ermakov (Blou, Shenten Dargye Ling, 2006).

_____. *Teachings on Zhang Zhung Nyen Gyud and Namkha Truldzö, Vimoutiers, 24 August – 11 September 2004,* Trnscr. & ed. Carol Ermakova and Dmitry Ermakov (Blou, Shenten Dargye Ling, 2006).

_____. *Chö: Commentary on Yang zab nam mkha' mdzod chen las lus sbyin mkha' 'gro gad rgyan of Shardza Tashi Gyaltsen, Teachings in Paris 16-17 October 2004*, Trnscr. & ed. Carol Ermakova and Dmitry Ermakov (Blou, Shenten Dargye Ling, 2006).

_____. *Teachings on Zhang Zhung Nyam Gyud: The Experiential Transmission of Zhang Zhung*, trnscr. & ed. Carol and Dmitry Ermakovi, (Vimoutiers, France: Association Yungdrung Bön, 2005).

_____. *The Four Wheels of Bön, Shenten Dargye Ling, 2 – 3 July 2005,* Trnscr. & ed. Carol Ermakova and Dmitry Ermakov (Blou, Shenten Dargye Ling, 2006).

_____. *Namkha Truldzö: the Commentary on the Precious Oral transmission of the Great perfection which is called the Treasury of Space, Shenten Dargye Ling, 2 – 21August 2005,* Trnscr. & ed. Carol Ermakova and Dmitry Ermakov (Blou, Shenten Dargye Ling, 2006).

_____. *Ngöndro Teachings, Shenten Dargye Ling, September 4 – 10, 2005,* Trnscr. & ed. Carol Ermakova and Dmitry Ermakov (Blou, Shenten Dargye Ling, 2006).

_____. *Namkha Truldzö: the Commentary on the Precious Oral transmission of the Great perfection which is called the Treasury of Space, Shenten Dargye Ling, 23 July – 11August 2006*, Trnscr. & ed. Carol Ermakova and Dmitry Ermakov (Blou, Shenten Dargye Ling, 2006).

_____. *Bönchyod Gurim; Ngöndro teachings from Zhang Zhung Nyen Gyud, Shenten Dargye Ling, 27th August – 1st September, 2006*, Trnscr. & ed. Carol Ermakova and Dmitry Ermakov (Blou, Shenten Dargye Ling, 2006).

_____. *The Nine Ways of Bön; A Compilation of teachings in France, Volume I*, Trnscr. & ed. Carol Ermakova and Dmitry Ermakov (Blou, Shenten Dargye Ling, 2006).

_____. *Rainbow Tent Phowa 'Pho ba 'ja gur ma, Volume II: Instructions, including the Clear Lamp of the Signs of Death, 'Chi rtags gsal ba'i sgron ma, by Lishu Tagring, Teachings by Yongdzin Lopön Tenzin Namdak*

Rinpoche, Shenten Dargye Ling, 23-29 September, 2007, Trscr. & ed. Carol and Dmitry Ermakovi (Blou, Shenten Dargye Ling, 2007).

Namdak, Lopön Tenzin. Trnscr. & ed. John Myrdhin Reynolds, *Bonpo Dzogchen Teachings*, (Kathmandu: Vajra Publications, 2006).

Namkha, Lachen Drenpa. *The Seven Mirrors of Dzogchen,* trans. Khenpo Tenpa Yungdrung, ed. Carol Ermakova and Dmitry Ermakov, limited private edition, 2006.

Namkha, Lachen Drenpa.*The Seven Mirrors of Dzogchen*, Commentaries by Lopön Tenzin Namdak Rinpoche and Khenpo Tenpa Yungdrung, trnscr. &ed. Carol Ermakova and Dmitry Ermakov (Blou: Shenten Dargye Ling, 2006).

Namkhai, Norbu. *The Necklace of gZi: A Cultural History of Tibet* (Dharmasala: Narthang Publication, 1989).

_____. *Drung, Deu and Bön* (Dharmasala: LTWA, 1995).

_____. *The Origins of Tibetan Culture and Thought* (Merigar: Shang Shung Edizioni, 1995).

_____. *Chöd,* (Arcidosso: Shang Shung Edizione, 1999).

Namkhai, Norbu & Ramon Prats, 'GA¥S TI SE'I DKAR C'AG: A Bon-po Story of the Sacred Mountain Ti-se and the Blue Lake Ma-pan', *Instituto Italiano per il Medio ed Estremo Oriente, Serie Orientale,* Vol. LXI, Roma, 1989.

Narain, Ak. 'The Tokharians: A History without Nation-State Boundaries', Rajiv Gandhi Memorial RGF-NERC-ICSSR Lectures, March 1999 (Shillong: North Eastern Hill University Publications, 2000).

de Nebesky-Wojkowitz, Réne. *Oracles and Demons of Tibet*: *the Cult and Iconography of the Tibetan Protective Deities* (New Delhi: Paljor Publications, 1998).

Neuberger, Joan. Hooliganism: Crime, Culture, and Power in St. Petersburg, 1900-1914 (Berkley-Los Angeles-London: University of California Press, 1993).

Nichols, Johanna. 'The Epicentre of the Linguistic Spread', *Archaeology and Language I*, ed. Roger Blench and Matthew Spriggs (London: Routledge, 1997), pp 122-148.

Nicoletti, Martino. *Shamanic Solitudes. Ecstasy, Madness and Spirit Possession in the Nepal Himalayas* (Kathmandu: Vajra Publications; & Bergamo: Ev-K2-CNR/Cinnabaris – Series of Oriental Studies, 2006).

Orofino, Giacomela. *Sacred Tibetan Teachings on Death and Liberation* (Dorset – Lindfield: Prism-Unity, 1990).

Pakendorf, Brigitte and Victor Wiebe, Larissa A. Tarskaia, Victor A. Spitsyn, Himla Soodyall, Alexander Rodewald, Mark Stoneking, 'Mitochondrial DNA Evidence for Admixed Origins of Central Siberian Populations', *American Journal of Physical Anthropology* № 120, 2003, pp. 211–224.

Ed. Ramble, Charles and Martin Brauen. *Anthropology of Tibet and the Himalaya* (Kathmandu: Vajra Publications, 2008).

Reid, Daniel. *The Complete Book of Chinese Health and Healing: Guarding the Three Treasures* (Boston: Shambhala, 1995).

Reynolds, John Myrdhin. *Self-Liberation through seeing with Naked Awareness* (Barrytown NY: Station Hill Press, 1989).

_____. *Yungdrung Bon – The Eternal Tradition*, Bonpo Translation Project, 1991.

_____. *Invocation of the Guardian Deity Nyipangtse and the Goddess Menmo*, Bonpo Translation Project.

_____. *The Golden Letters: The Three Statements of Garab Dorje, the First Teacher of Dzogchen* (Barrytown NY: Station Hill Press, 1991).

_____. *Selections from The Bonpo Book of the Dead* (SanDiego and Copenhagen: Bonpo Translation Project, 1997).

_____. *The History and Lineages of the Zhang-Zhung Nyan-Gyud* (San Diego and Amsterdam: Vidyadhara Publications, 2000).

_____. *Bonpo Monastic Rituals from the Menri Tradition: as performed by the monks of Triten Norbutse Monastery, Kathmandu, Nepal*, Tibetan Pronunciation and Interlinear Translation with Annotations by John Myrdhin, (Dortmund: Bonpo Translation Project, 2005).

_____. *The Oral tradition of Zhang-Zhung: An Introduction to the Bonpo Dzogchen Teachings of the Oral Tradition from Zhang-Zhung know as the Zhang-zhung snyan-rgyud* (Kathmandu: Vajra Publications, 2005).

Rossi, Donatella. 'The Nine Ways of the Bonpo tradition: an oral presentation by a contemporary Bonpo Lama', *Tibetan Studies, Proceedings of the 6th Seminar of the International Association for Tibetan Studies* [Fagernes, 1992], ed. Per Kvaerne, Olso, 1994, volume 2.

Rossi, 'Holy Mountains and Saint Immortals in the Bon Tradition: A Preliminary Survey of the History of Chang-cha-Dur', *Revista degli Studi Orientali* 2005 vol 78 no. 1-4 (University of Rome 'La Sapienza'), pp 413-420.

Semyonov, Yuri. *Conquest of Siberia: An Epic of Human Passions* (London: George Routledge & Sons LTD, 1944).

Shuicheng, Li. 'A Discussion of Sino-Western Cultural Contact and Exchange in the Second Millennium BC based on Recent Archaeological Discoveries', *Sino-Platonic Papers*, 97 (December 1999), Department of East Asian Languages and Civilizations, University of Pennsylvania.

Snellgrove, David. *The Nine Ways of Bön*, (London: Oxford University Press, 1967).

Sopa, Geshe Lhundub, and Roger Jackson, John Newman, *The Wheel of Time: The Kalachakra in Context* (Madison, Wisconsin: Deer Park Books, 1985).

Tayé, Jamgön Kongtrul Lodrö. *Myriad Worlds: Buddhist Cosmology in Abhidharama, Kālacakra and Dzog-chen*, Tr. &ed. the International Translation Committee of Kunkhyab Chöling founded by the V.V. Kalu Rinpoché (Ithaca, New York: Snow Lion Publications, 1995).

Tautscher, Gabrielle. *Himalayan Mountain Cults. Sailung, Kalingchok, Gosaikund. Territorial Rituals and Tamang Histories* (Kathmandu: Vajra Publications & Bergamo: Ev-K2-CNR/Cinnabaris – Series of Oriental Studies, 2007).

Tenga Rinpoche. *Transition & Liberation: explanations of meditation in the bardo* (Osterby: Khampa Buchverlag, 1996).

Thieme, P. The 'Aryan Gods' of the Mitanni Treaties, *Journal of the American Oriental Society* 80 1960, pp 301-317.

Thomas, F.W. 'The Źang Źung Language', *Asia major*, NS 13/1-2 (London, 1967).

Tucci, Giuseppe, Tr. Geoffrey Samuel. *The Religions of Tibet* (London and Henley: Routledge&Keagan Paul, 1980).

Tzu, Lao. *Tao Te Ching*: *The Richard Wilhelm Edition*, (London: Penguin, Arkana, 1989).

Ad. Wallace, Zara. *GESAR! The Epic Tale of Tibet's Great Warrior-King*, (Mongolian version), (Berkeley:Dharma Publishing, 1991).

Waters, Frank. *Book of the Hopi* (reprint edition, New York: Viking Press, 1985).

Tr. Watson, Burton. *Chuang Tzu, Basic Writings* (New York: Columbia University Press, 1996).

Welch, Holmes. *Taoism. The Parting of the Way* (Rev. ed. Boston: Beacon, 1966).

Ed. Yungdrung, Tenpa and Pre Kvaerne, Mushashi Tachikawa, Yasuhiko Nagano, *Bonpo Thangkas from Khyungpo, Bon Studies 10*, National Museum of Ethnology, Osaka, 2006.

Yungdrung, Dru Gyalwa. *Gyalwa Chagtri Chapter II: Zab mo gnad kyi gdams pa dngos gzhi bzhugs so*, Teachings by Yongdzin Lopön Tenzin Namdak Rinpoche, trnscr. & ed. Carol and Dmitry Ermakovi (Blou: Shenten Dargye Ling, 2007).

Zaehner, R.C. *The Dawn and Twilight of Zoroastrianism* (London: Weidenfeld and Nicolson, 1961).

_____. *Zurvan, a Zoroastrian Dilemma* (Oxford: Clarendon, 1955).

Materials in Russian and Buryatian:

Абаев, Н.В. *Чань Буддизм и культурно-психологическе традиции в средневековом Китае*, «Наука», Сибирское отделение, Новосибирск, 1989.

[Abaev, N. V. *Chan' Buddhism i kulturno-psikhologicheskie traditsii v srednevekovom Kitae,* (Novosibirsk: Nauka, 1989)].

Афанасьев, А.Н. *Народные русские сказки*, т. 1-3/ Подгот. Текста, предисл. и примеч. В.Я. Проппа, p. 259, Москва, 1957

[Afanasyev, A. N. *Narodnye russkie skazki*, vol 1-3, ed. V. Ya. Propp (Moscow, 1957)].

Afanasyev Народные Русские Сказки из сборника А.Н. Афанасьева, «Правда», Москва, 1982

[Collected by Afanasyev, *Narodnye Russkie Skazki iz sbornika A. N. Afanasyeva* (Moscow: Pravda, 1982)].

Алексеев, Н.А. *Культ Айыы –племенных божеств-покровителей якутов,* Этнографический сборник, Вып. 5, Бурятское книжное издательство, Улан-Удэ, 1969

[Alekseev, N. A. 'Kul't Aiyy – plemennykh bozhestv-pokrovitelei yakutov', *Etnograficheskii sbornik*, 5 (Ulaan-Ude: Buryatskoe knizhnoe isdatel'stvo, 1969)].

Балдаев, С.П. *Родословные предания и легенды бурят, часть первая,* Бурятское книжное издательство, Улан-Удэ, 1970

[Baldaev, S. P. *Rodoslovnye predaniya i legendy Buryat, Part One* (Ulaan-Ude: Buryatskoe knizhnoe izdatel'stvo, 1970)].

Банзаров, Д. *Черная вѣра или шаманство у монголовъ и другія статьи,* Типография Императорской Академии Наукъ, Санктпетербургъ, 1891

[Banzarov, D. *Chernaya vera ili shamanstvo и Mongolov и Drugiya stat'i (*Tipographiya Imperatorskoi Akademii Nauk', St. Petersburg, 1891)].

Базаров, Б.Д. *Таинства и практика шаманизма*, Буряад Үнэн, Улан Удэ, 1999

[Bazarov, B. D. *Tainstva i praktika shamanisma* (Ulaan-Ude, Buryaad Unen, 1999)].

Безертинов, Р.Н. *Древнетюркское мировоззрение «Тэнгрианство»*, Министерство образования и науки Республики Татарстан, Школа, Казань, 2006

[Bezertinov, R. N. *Drevnetyurkskoe mirovozzrenie 'Tengrianstvo'*, Ministry for Science and Education of the Republic of Tatarstan (Kazan: Shkola, 2006)].

(Иакинф) Бичурин, Н.Я. *Собрание сведений о народах, обитавших в Средней Азии в древние времена*, Т. 2, М.-Л., 1950-1953 [Bichurin (Iakinf), N. Ya. *Sobranie svedenii o narodakh, obitavshikh v Srednei Azii v drevnie vremena,* vol II (Moscow-Leningrad, 1950-53)].

Сборник, *Источниковедение и Историография Истории Буддизма: страны Центральной Азии*, (в особенности Д.И. Бураев, *К Истории Изучения Религии Бон*), «Наука», Новосибирск, 1986.

[Buraev, D. I. 'K Istorii Izucheniya Religii Bon' in the anthology: *Istochnikovedenie i Istoriografiya Istorii Buddizma: strany Tsentral'noi Azii* (Moscow: Nauka, 1986)].

Вонг, Е. *Даосизм*, Фаир-Пресс, Москва, 2001.

[tr. Bushueva Y. *Eva Vong, Daosizm* (Moscow: Fair-Press, 2001). Tr. into Russian from Eva Wong, *The Shambhala Guide to Taoism* (Boston & London: Shambhala, 1997)].

Бычков, А.А. *Энциклопедия Языческих Богов: мифы древних славян*, «Вече», Москва, 2001

[Bychkov, A. A. *Entsiklopediya Yazycheskihk Bogov: Mify drevnikh slavyan* (Moscow: Veche, 2001)].

Карпини, П. *История Монголов,* Издательство А.С. Суворина, Санкт-Петербург, 1911

[Carpini, P. *Istoriya Mongolov* (St. Petersburg: A. S. Suvorina, 1911). From the original: Giovanni da Pian del Carpini, *Historia Mongalorum quos nos Tartaros appellamus* or 'History of the Mongols, which we call Tartars'].

Чанышев, А.Н. *Курс Лекций по Древней и Средневековой Философии,* «Высшая Школа», Москва, 1991

[Chanyshev, A. N. *Kurs Lektsii Drevnei i Srednevekovoi Filosofii* (Moscow: Vysshaya Shkola, 1991)].

Долгих, Б.О. *Мифологические сказки и исторические предания нганасан*, Главная редакция восточной литературы издательства «Наука», Москва, 1976

[Dolgikh, B. O. *Mifologicheskie skazki i istoricheskie predaniya Nganasan* (Moscow: Nauka, 1976)].

Дугаров, Д.Б. г. Улаан-Удэ, Бурятский Государственный Университет, *Синкретизм Буддизма и Шаманизма в Бурятии на современном этапе/ Наследие Древних и Традиционных Культур Северной и Центральной Азии –Материалы 40-й региональной Студенческой конференции, Том II,* Новосибирск, 1-6 февраля 2000

[Doogarov, D. B. 'Sinkretizm Buddizma i Shamanizma v Buryatii na sovremennom etape/*Nasledie Drevnikh i Traditsionnykh Kultur Severnoi i Tsentral'noi Azii, Materialy 40-i regional'noi Studencheskoi konferentsii, Vol. II*. Novosibirsk, 1-6 February, 2000].

Дугаров, Д.С. *Исторические корни белого шаманства на материале обрядового фольклора Бурят*, Издательство «Наука», Москва, 1991

[Doogarov, D. C. *Istoricheskie korni belogo shamanstva na materiale obryadovogo folklora Buryat* (Moscow: Nauka, 1991)].

Дюмезиль, Ж. *Верховные боги индоевропейцев,* Москва, 1986

[Dumézil, G. *Verkhovnye bogi indoevropeitsev* (Moscow, 1986). Originally published as: George Dumézil, *Les dieux indo-européens*, publié aux Presses universitaires de France, 1952)].

Ермаков, М.Е. *Магия Китая*, Издательство «Азбука-классика», «Петербургское востоковедение», Санкт-Петрбург, 2003

[Ermakov, M. E. *Magiya Kitaya* (St. Petersburg: Azbuka-klassika, 2003)].

Ермакова, Л.М. перевод, исследование и комментарий, *Норито Сэммё*, «Наука» Главная редакция восточной литературы, Москва, 1991

[tr., research & commentary Ermakova, L. M. *Norito Semmyo* (Moscow: Nauka, 1991)].

Ред. Гаккель, Я. Я., Л. С. Говоруха, *Моря и острова Северного Ледовитого океана*, Советская Арктика, АН СССР. Институт географии, Наука, Москва, 1970

[Ed. Gakkel Ya. Ya & L. S. Govorukha, Morya i ostrova Severnogo Ledovitogo okeana, *Sovetskaya Arktika,* AN USSR , Institut geografii (Moscow: Nauka, 1970)].

Галданова, Г.Р. *Доламаисткие Верования Бурят,* Издательство «Наука» Сибирское Отделение, Новосибирск, 1987 [Galdanova, G. R. *Dolamaistkie verovaniya Buryat* (Novosibirsk: Nauka, Siberian Branch, 1987)].

Груссе, Р. *Чингисхан*, перевод с Французского Е.А Соколова, серия *Жизнь Замечательных Людей*, «Молодая Гвардия», Москва, 2002

[Grousset, Rene. *Conqueror of the World: The Life of Chingis-khan* tr. E. A Sokolova (Moscow: Molodaya Gvardiya, 2002)].

Гумилев, Л.Н.Динлинская проблема: Пересмотр гипотезы Г.Е. Грумм-Гржимайло в свете новых исторических и археологических материалов, Известия Всесоюзного Географического общества СССР. No 1, 1959

[Gumilev, L. N. 'Dinlinskaya problema: Peresmotr gipotezy G. E. Grumm-Grzhmailo v svete novykh istoricheskikh i arkheologicheskikh materialov', *Izvestiya Vsesoyuznogo Geograficheskogo obshchestva USSR* No. 1, 1959].

Гумилёв, Л.Н. *Древние Тюрки*, «Айрис Пресс», Москва, 2002

[Gumilev, L. N. *Drevnie Tyurki* (Moscow: Airis, 2002)].

_____. *Этногенез и Биосфера Земли*, «Азбука-классика», Санкт-Петербург, 2002

[_____. *Ethnogenez i Biosfera Zemli* (St. Petersburg: Azbuka, 2002)].

_____. *История Народа Хунну*, в двух книгах, Издательство «АСТ», Москва, 2002

[_____. *Istoriya naroda Hunnu, Vol I&II* (Moscow: Isdatel'stvo AST, 2002)].

Гумилев, Л.Н., Б. И. Кузнецов Бон (Древняя Тибетская Религия), Доклады отделений и комиссий Географического общества СССР. Этнография. 1970. Вып. 15- Ленинград, pp. 72-90

[Gumilev, L. N. and B. I. Kusnetsov, 'Bon (Drevnyaya Tibetskaya Religiya)',

Dokladyi otdelenii i komissii Geograficheskogo obshchestva SSSR. Etnografiya. 15 (1970)].

Гузеев, И.А. г. Владивосток, Дальневосточный Государсвенный Университет, *Ойкумена – расширение на Восток/ Наследие Древних и Традиционных Культур Северной и Центральной Азии –Материалы 40-й региональной Студенческой конференции, Том I,* Новосибирск, 1-6 февраля 2000

[Guzeev, I. A. (State University of the Far East, Vladivostok), 'Oikumena – rasshirenie na Vostok' in *Nasledie Drevnikh u Traditsionnykh Kultur Severnoi i Tsentral'noi Azii, Materialy 40-i regional'noi Studencheskoi konferentsii, Vol. I.* Novosibirsk, 1-6 February, 2000].

Гусева, Н.Р. *Славяне и Арьи: Путь Богов и Слов*, Фаир-Пресс, Москва, 2002

[Guseva, N. R. *Slavyanie i Ar'i: Put' Bogov i Slov* (Moscow: Fair-Press, 2002)].

Хангалов, М.Н. *Собрание сочинений*, *Том I*, Бурятское книжное издательство, Улан-Удэ, 1958

[Hangalov, M. N. *Sobranie Sochinenii* Vol. I (Ulaan-Ude: Buryatskoe knizhnoe izdatel'stvo, 1958)].

_____. *Собрание сочинений*, *Том II*, Бурятское книжное издательство, Улан-Удэ, 1958

[_____. *Sobranie Sochinenii* Vol. II (Ulaan-Ude: Buryatskoe knizhnoe izdatel'stvo, 1958)].

Хангалов, М.Н. Д.А. Клеменц, *Общественные охоты у Северных бурят,* 1920

[Hangalov, M. N. and D. A. Klements, Obshchestvennye okhoty u Severnykh Buryat (1920)].

Худяков, И.А. *Краткое описание Верхоянского округа*, Ленинград, 1967

[Khudyakov, I. A. *Kratkoe opisanie Verkhoyanskogo okryga* (Leningrad, 1967)].

Козин, С.А. перевод, *Сокровенное Сказание Монголов/Монголой Нюуса Тобшо*, Бурятское книжное издательство, Улан Удэ, 1990

[Tr. Kozin, S. A. *Sokrovennoe Skazanie Mongolov/Mongoloi Nyica Tobsho* (Ulaan-Ude: Buryatskoe knizhnoe isdatel'stvo, 1990)].

Кудрявцев, С.Ф. *история Бурят-Монгольского народа,* Издательство Академии Наук СССР, Москва/Ленинград, 1940

[Kudryavtsev, S. F. *Istoriya Buryat-Mongol'skogo naroda* (Moscow/Leningrad: Isdatel'stvo Akademii Nauk, 1940)].

Кун, Н.А. *Легенды и мифы Древней Греции*, ОГУП «Калининградское книжное издательство», ГИПП «Янтарный сказ», 2000

[Kun, N. A. *Legendy i mifi Drevnei Gretsii* (Kaliningrad: 'Kaliningradskoe knizhnoe isdatel'stvo' & 'Yantarnyi skaz', 2000)].

Кузнецов, Б.И. *Является ли Шенраб – основатель религии бон – исторической личностью?*, в сборнике «Востоковедные исследования в Бурятии», Новосибирск, 1981

[Kuznetsov, B. I. 'Yavlyaetsya li Shenrab – osnovatel' religii bon – istoricheskoi lichnost'yo?', *Vostokovednye issledovanniya v Buryatii,* Novosibirsk 1981, pp. 92-95].

_____. *Бон и Маздаизм*, «Евразия», Санкт-Петербург, 2001

[_____. *Bon i Mazdaizm* (St. Petersburg: Evrasiya, 2001)].

Данзан, Лубсан. *Алтан Тобчи («Золотое Сказание»),* Перевод с монгольского, введение, комментарии и приложения Н.П. Шастина, Издательство «Наука», Москва, 1973

[Lubsan Danzan, *Altan Tobchi "Zolotoe Skazanie",* tr., introduction, commentary and appendix by N. P. Shastina Moscow: Nauka, 1973)].

Малов, С.И. *Шаманский камень «яда» у Тюрков Западного Китая*, СЭ, №1, 1947

[Malov, S. I. 'Shamnskii kamen' "yada" u Tyurkov Zapadnogo Kitaya' in *SE* №1, 1947].

Дао-Дэ цзин, Ле-цзы, Гуань-цзы: Даосские каноны, перевод В.В. Малявин, «Астрель» и «Аст», Москва, 2001

[tr. Malyavin, V. V. *Dao-De tsin, Le-tsy, Guan'–tsy: Daosskie kanony* (Moscow: Ast/Astrel', 2002)].

Чжуан-Цзы: Даосские каноны, перевод В.В.Малявин, «Аст» и «Астрель», Москва, 2002

[tr. Malyavin, V. V. *Chzhuan-Tsy*: *Daosskie kanony* (Moscow: Ast/Astrel', 2002)].

Михайлов, Т.М. *Бурятский Шаманизм: история, структура и социальные функции*, Новосибирск, Издательство «Наука», 1987

[Mikhailov, T. M. *Buryatskii shamanism: istoriya, struktura i sotsial'nyie funktsii,* (Novosibirsk: Nauka, 1987)].

Мункуев, Н.Ц. *Китайский источник о первых монгольских ханах*, «Наука», Москва, 1965

[Munkuev, N. Ts. *Kitaiskii istochnik o pervykh mongol'skikh khanakh* (Moscow: Nauka, 1965)].

Чогьял Намкай Норбу, *Беседы в Петербурге*: *Ритрит 1992 года*, «Шанг-Шунг», Санкт-Петербург, 2002

[Namkhai, N. *Besedy v Peterburge* 1992 (St. Petersburg: Shang Shung, 2002)].

Окладников, А.П. *Исторические рассказы и легенды нижней Лены*, Сборник Музея антропологии и этнографии XI, 1949

[Okladnikov, A. P. *Istoricheskie rasskazy i legendy nizhnei Leny* (Anthology of Museum of anthropology and ethnography, XI, 1949)].

_____. *Неолит и бронзовый век Прибайкалья*, Ч.III, М-Л, 1955

[_____. *Neolit i bronsovyi vek* Part III (Moscow-Leningrad, 1955)].

_____. *История и культура Бурятии,* Бурятское книжное издательство, Улан-Удэ, 1976

[_____. *Istoriya i kul'tura Buryatii* (Ulaan-Ude: Buryatskoe knizhnoe izdatel'stvo, 1976)].

Петри, Б.Э. *Степени посвящения монголо-бурятского шамана, Том II,* Издательство Биологии-Географии НИИ, выпуск 4, 1926

[Petri, B. E. *Stepeni posvyashcheniya mongolo-buryatskogo shamana*, (Izdatel'stvo NII Biologii-Geografii, Vol 2, ed. 4, 1926)].

Попов, А. 'Тавгийцы'. Материалы по этнографии авамских и ведеевских самоедов, Труды Института Антропологии и Этнографии, I, 5, Москва и Ленинград, 1936

[Popov, A. A. 'Tavgiitsy'. *Materialy po etnografii avamskikh i vedeevskikh samoedov*, Trudy Instituta Antropologii i Etnografii, 1, 5, Moskva i Leningrad, 1936].

Пропп, В.Я. *Исторические Корни Волшебной Сказки*, Издательство Ленинградского Университета, Ленинград, 1986

[Propp, V. Ya. *Istoricheskie Korni Volshebnoi Skazki* (Leningrad: Isdatel'stvo Leningradskogo Universiteta, 1986)].

Рыбаков, Б. А. *Язычество Древних Славян*, «София» и «Гелиос», Москва, 2002

[Rybakov, B. A. *Yazychestvo drevnikh slavyan* (Moscow: Sofiya, Gelios)].

Сангиров, В.П. *«Илэтхэл Шастир» как источник по истории ойратов,* «Наука», Москва, 1990

[Sapgirov, V. P. *'Iletkhel Shastir' as a source of the history of the Oirats* (Moscow: Nauka, 1990)].

Шаргаев, М. *С Природой Наши Предки Были На Вы,* газета «Бурятия», 28 Февраля, 1992

[Shargaev, M. 'S prirodoi nashi predki byli ne vy', in the newspaper *Buryatia*, 28 February, 1992].

Тилак, Б.Г. *Арктическая Родина в Ведах*, Фаир-Пресс, Москва, 2002

[Tilak, B. G. *Arkticheskaya Rodina v Vedakh* (Moscow: Fair-Press, 2002) – B. G. Tilak, *Arkticheskaya Rodina v Vedakh* (Moscow: Fair-Press, 2002), This is a Russian translation of Lokamanya Bal Gangadhar Tilak, *The Arctic Home in the Vedas: Being also a new key to the interpretation of many Vedic texts and Legends* (Gaikar Wada, Poona City: Tilak Bros., 1956)].

Туголуков, В.А. *Полевые материалы*, Архив Института этнографии, 1970

[Tugolukov, V. A. Polevye materialy, Archives of the Institute of Ethnography, 1970].

Абай Гэсэр, Пер. Коммент. А. Уланов, Улан-Удэ, 1960

[tr. & comment., Ulanov, A. *Abai Geser*, Ulaan-Ude, 1960].

Юань Кэ, *Мифы Древнего Китая*, перевод с Китайского Е.И. Лубо-Лесниченко, Е.В. Пузицкий и В.Ф. Сорокин, издание 2-е исправленное и дополненное, Главная редакция восточной литературы, «Наука», 1987

[Yuan' Ke: *Mify Drevnego Kitaya* (*Myths of Ancient China*) Tr. from Chinese by E. I. Lubo-Lesnichennko, E. V. Puzitskii & V. F. Sorokin (Moscow: Nauka, 1987)].

Забруева, Т.А., П.Е. Марнуев, *Гуйдэг гаргуулха – «обряд изгнания злого духа»/ Наследие Древних и Традиционных Культур Северной и Центральной Азии –Материалы 40-й региональной Студенческой конференции, Том II,* Новосибирск, 1-6 февраля 2000

[Zabrueva, T. A. and P.E. Marnuev, 'Gooideg garguulkha – "obryad izgnaniya zlogo dukha"' *Nasledie Drevnikh u Traditsionnykh Kultur Severnoi i Tsentral'noi Azii, Materialy 40-i regional'noi Studencheskoi konferentsii, Vol. II*. Novosibirsk, 1-6 February, 2000].

Зомонов М.Д., Манжичеев И.А., *Краткий словарь Бурятского Шаманизма*, Бурятское книжное издательство, Улан-Удэ, 1997

[Zomonov, M. D. and I. A. Manzhicheev, *A Short Dictionary of Buryatian Shamanism* (Ulaan Ude: Buryatskoe knizhnoe isdatel'stvo, 1997)].

Сборник, *Дао: гармония мира*, «Эксмо», Москва и «Фолио» Харьков, 2002

[Anthology: Dao: Garmoniya mira (Moscow: Eksmo; Kharkov: Folio, 2002)].

В. Рубрук, *Путешествие в восточные страны,* pp. 63-178, Издательство А.С. Суворина, Санкт- Петербург, 1911.

[Rubruk, V. *Puteshectvie v vostochnye strany* (St. Petersburg: Isdatel'stvo a. S. Suvorina, 1911).

Хроника Вандана Юмсунова [Вандан Юмсунов (Гэнин-Лубсан Цэдэн Доржи Тарбаев) *История происхождения одиннадцати родов хоринцев*, 1875] in Пер. Н. Поппе, *Летописи хоринских бурят*, Труды института Востоковедения XXXIII. М-Л. АН СССР. 1940

[*Khronika Vandana Yumsunova* [Vandan Yumsumov, *Genin-Lubsan Tseden Dorzhi Tarbaev*] *Istoriya proiskhozhdeniya odinnadtsati rodov Horintsev,* 1875, in tr N. Poppe *Letopisi Horinskikh Buryat* (Trudy instituta Vostokovedeniya XXXIII, Moscow-Leningrad: AN USSR, 1940)].

Е.П. Борисенков, В.М. Пясецкий, *Тысячелетняя летопись необычайных явлений природы*, Москва, 1988. Cited in Н.Р. Гусева, *Славяне и Арьи: Путь Богов и Слов*, Фаир-Пресс, Москва, 2002, p.31

[Borisenkov, E. P. and V. M. Pyasetskii, *Tysyacheletnyaya letopis' neobychainykh yavlenii prirody* (Moskva, 1999) Cited in N. P. Guseva, *Slavyane i Ar'i: Put' Bogov i Slov* (Moscow: Fair Press, 2002)].

Габдельбар Файзрахманов, *Древние Тюрки в Сибири и Центральной Азии*, p. 71, Институт истории Академии наук Татарстана, Панорама-Форум, 2000, №24 – Специальный выпуск, Мастер Лайн, Казань, 2000

[Gabdel'bar Faizrakhmanov, 'Drevnie Tyurki v Sibiri i Tsentral'noi Asii,' Institut istorii Akademii nauk Tatarstana, Panorama-Forum, 2000, №24 – Spetsial'nyi vypusk, Master Lain, Kazan', 2000].

История Сибири с древнейших времен до наших дней, Издательство «Наука», Ленинградское отделение, Ленинград, 1968

[*Istoriya Sibiri s drevneishikh vremen do nashikh dnei* (Leningrad: Nauk, 1968)].

Историко-Культурный Атлас Бурятии, изд. «Дизайн. Информация. Картография», Москва, 2001

[*Istoriko-Kul'turnyi Atlas Buryatii* (Moscow: Dizain Informatsiya Kartografiya, 2001)].

Наследие Древних и Традиционных Культур Северной и Центральной Азии, материалы 40-й Региональной Студенческой Конференции, Новосибирск, 1-6 Февраля 2000г.

[*Nasledie Drevnikh Traditsionnykh Kul'tur Severnoi i Tsentral'noi Asii,* 40th Regional Student Conference, Novosibirsk, 1-6 Feb, 2006].

ХУХЭ МҮНХЭ ТЭНГЭРИ, сборник шаманских призываний, книга 1, АО «Республиканская типография», Улан-Удэ, 1996

[*Huhe Münhe Tengeri: sbornik shamanskikh prizyivanii, книга I*, *[Anthology of Shamanic Invocations],* (Ulaan-Ude: Respublikanskaya tipografiya, 1996)].

История Бурят-Монгольской АССР, Том I, Бурят-Монгольское книжное издательство, Улан-Удэ, 1954

[*Istoriya Buryat-Mongol'skoi ASSR* Vol. I (Ulaan-Ude: Mongolskoe knizhnoe izdatel'stvo, 1954)].

Materials in other languages:

Achard, J-L. *Tsewang Nyengü № 1: Bönzhik Yungdrung Lingpa, La Transmission Orale de Tsewang Rigdzin* (Khyung-mkhar, Courdimanche-sur-Essonne, 1997).

Tr. Achard, J-L. *Le Rire des Dakinis: La Pratique de Chö (gCod) d'apres la tradition du Yangzab Namkha Dzöchen*, Shardza Tashi Gyaltsen (Khyung-mkhar, Courdimanche-sur-Essone, 1999).

Бешевлиев, В. *Първобългарски надписи,* Издателство на БАН, София, 1979

[Beshevliev, V. *Prvoblgarski nadpisi* (Sofia: Isdatel'stvo na BAN, 1979)].

Bhikku Satori Bhante, *Shintoismo* (Milano: Rizzoli Editore, 1982).

Dall' "Essenza del Cuore" di Longchenpa, *La Practica del Chöd: La Fragorosa Risata della Dakini.*

Ed. Fahr-Becker, G. (Ed.), *Arte dell'Estremo Oriente* (Köln: Konemann, 1999).

Firdousi, *Le vivre des rois*, ed. J.Mohl, VI., Paris, 1868.

Ghesce Ciapu, *Le gioiose vicende di Kunga Legpa,* tr. Elio Guarisco – Cura di Leo Alfonso (Merigar: Shang Shung Edizioni, 1994).

Hoffman, H. *Quellen zur Geschichte der Tibetischen Bon-Religion*, (Akademie der Wissenschaften und der Litertur, Wiesenbaden: FranzSteiner Verlag, 1950).

Leroi-Gourhan, A. *Prehistorie de l'art occidental*, Paris, 1965.

Lung rtogs rGya mtsho, *'Bras rsthis bdeu don snying po mkha drub*, Bon Dialectic School, Menri Monastery, Dolanji, 2005.

Namdak, T./Gungal, K. *Der heilende Garuda: Ein Stück Bön-Tradition* (Dietikon, Schweiz: Garuda Verlag, 1998).

de Sales, A. *Je Suis Né de Vos Jeux de Tambours, La religion chamanique des Magar du nord,* (Paris: Société d'Ethnologie, 1991).

Internet resources:

http://www.ozemail.com.au/~zarathus/kayani33.html

http://tenets.zoroastrianism.com/deen33e.html

http://tenets.zoroastrianism.com

http://tenets.zoroastrianism.com/histar33.html

http://www.ozemail.com.au/~zarathus/deen33e.html

http://www.artarena.force9.co.uk/medes.html

http://www.pbs.org/wgbh/nova/transcripts/2502chinamum.html

http://sln.fi.edu/enquirer/mummy.html

http://203.147.210.170/

http://www.archaeology.ncs.ru

http://marlowe.wimsey.com/~rshand/streams/scripts/shambhala.html

http://www.yungdrung-bon.org

http://www.vajranatha.com

http://dusha.spb.ru/Newspaper/newspaper5.htm *(*An interview with Valentin Khagdaev *"Всё имеет свое божество" [everything has its divine aspect])* http://baikal.irkutsk.ru/php/statya.php?razdel=shamanism&nomer=4.txt (монография: В. Хагдаев, *«Шаманизм и мировые религии»* [monograph by Hagdaev 'Shamanism and world religions'])

http://www.ex.ac.uk/equinet/origins

http://www2.vet.upenn.edu/labs/equinebehavior/hvnwkshp/hv02/levine.htm

http://new.mypetstop.com/NR/exeres/F37A21C7-00E9-48ED-B5EB-7F9F9AEF3319%2C813F0A28-0246-4740-881A-A67DCAA8206C%2Cframeless.htm?Section=Relationship

http://www.spiritofmaat.com/announce/oldcity.htm

http://www.eurekalert.org/pub_releases/2006-10/gsoa-neo102306.php; http://www.geosociety.org/news/pr/06-49.htm (article: 'New evidence of early horse domestication')

http://www.equiworld.net/uk/horsecare/evolution/domestication.htm

http://www.imh.org/imh/kyhpl1b.html#xtocid2243616

http://www.pnas.org/cgi/reprint/152330099v1.pdf

http://www.kirsoft.com.ru/freedom/KSNews_545.htm

(Т. Райс, Скифы: Строители степных пирамид)

http://donsmaps.com/cavepaintings3.html

http://ricolor.org/history/eng/medicina/badmaev/

http://www.padma.ch/en/company/history.shtml

http://www.padma28.ru/de/produkte/padma28.php

http://gumilevica.kulichki.net/articles/Article89.htm

http://www.alexhistory.narod.ru/World/Hronology/Titles/Shahs_of_Persia.htm

http://www.avesta.org/yasna/y9to11s.htm

http://myfhology.narod.ru/heroes/k/kersaspa.html

http://www.hp.uab.edu/image_archive/ugp/ - Stone Relief, 6

http://www.cais-soas.com/CAIS/Religions/iranian/zarathushtrian/notion_dualism.htm#2 (Professor Dr. Jamsheed K. Choksy, The Notion of Dualism)

Encyclopædia Britannica Online: http://www.britannica.com/eb/article-9109789 (Encyclopædia Britannica 2007; mongolian languages)

http://www.cais-soas.com/CAIS/Religions/iranian/Zarathushtrian/angel.htm

http://www.cais-soas.com/CAIS/Religions/iranian/Zarathushtrian/avestan_geography.htm (Farrokh Jal Vajifdar, Research fellow of the Royal Asiatic Society CAIS at SOAS Lecture - 1998, 'Avestan Geography: some topographical aspects')

http://www.cais-soas.com/CAIS/Religions/iranian/Zarathushtrian/Oric.Basirov/zoroaster_time_and_place.htm (Dr. Oric Basirov, Zoroaster's Time & Place, Paper I - 20 October 1998) http://www.britannica.com/eb/article-8135 (Encyclopædia Britannica. 2007, 'Zoroaster')

http://tenets.zoroastrianism.com/dakhma33.html

http://subhashkak.voiceofdharma.com/articles/zoro.htm (article: Subhash Kak, 'The Vedic Religion in Ancient Iran and Zarathushtra')

http://www.cultureofiran.com/pre-zoroastrian.php

http://dusha.spb.ru/Newspaper/newspaper5.htm ('An Interview with Shaman Valentin Hagdaev', Ot Dushi/От Души [web magazine])

Index

General Index

Index of Deities

Names

Places

List of Illustrations and Maps

Chapter V

Chapter VI

Chapter XI

Chapter XII

Chapter XIII